THE GOOD OPERA GUIDE

Denis Forman

PHOENIX

To Moni

A PHOENIX PRESS PAPERBACK

First published in Great Britain
by Weidenfeld & Nicolson in 1994
Phoenix edition published in 1997
This paperback edition published in 2001
by Phoenix Press,
a division of The Orion Publishing Group Ltd,
Orion House, 5 Upper St Martin's Lane,
London WC2H 9EA

Second impression December 2003

A CIP catalogue record for this book is available from the British Library.

Printed and bound in Great Britain by
Clays Ltd, St Ives plc

ISBN 1 84212 470 6

THE GOOD OPERA GUIDE

Sir Denis Forman was a founder member of Granada television and for many years its Chief Executive and Chairman until his retirement in 1987. During that time he was personally responsible for many of Granada's major drama series including *The Jewel in the Crown*. Sir Denis was Deputy Chairman of the Royal Opera house for nine years.

Also by Denis Forman

The Good Wagner Opera Guide

My Life so Far

A Night at the Opera: An Irreverent Guide to the Plots, the Singers, the Composers, the Recordings (Ed. with Ian Jackman)

Persona Granada

John Grierson (with Gus Macdonald)

Contents

The Guide and how to use it

- The operas in this Guide are those that have passed the simple popularity test of having three or more versions listed in the *Gramophone* CD catalogue of December 1992. The temptation to let in some outstanding outsiders (*Peter Grimes*) and to chuck out some of the weaker qualifiers (*Lakmé*) has been resisted, with difficulty. Every one of the 83 operas is a guaranteed three-entry item.
- Proper names are used in the form that comes most naturally. Opera people tend to talk of *Meistersinger, The Flute, Lucia*, not *The Mastersingers, Zauberflöte* or *Lucy*. Every opera has its proper title in its own language at the head of each entry.
- The same principle spreads far and wide throughout the Guide. In some operas the names of some of the cast are anglicized, others are left in German, Italian or whatever. This may seem odd but it is done to fall in with common usage and anyway consistency is 'the hobgoblin of small minds'. In the cast list after the title on the first page the names are given in both languages except in those operas – 2 out of 83! – where the opera is in English anyway. Accents, umlauts, circumflexes and cedillas are commonly done away with unless they are needed as a guide to pronunciation. A good deal of dog-Italian occurs and even the English language is treated with scant respect.
- Throughout the guide Acts are Acts – I, II, III, IV and in extreme cases V. After Scene 1 (Sc 1) scenes are only newly numbered as scenes (Sc 2) where there is a change of scenery. This may seem arbitrary and sometimes goes against the book. But when you get at one end of the spectrum an early opera giving every aria a fresh scene number and at the other end 2 hours 40 minutes of continuous music in *Rhinegold* broken into only four scenes, you have to give the word 'scene' some sort of common meaning. Anyway that's it.
- The LOOK OUT FOR section which comes after the telling of the story in the opera section is designed for the armchair listener (or for the listener who sits at a table or lies on the floor, and why should all listeners' chairs have arms anyway?) in order to alert them to look out for the best bits, to give them some idea of what is going on simultaneously both in the music and on stage, and thereby take them an inch or two

nearer to the experience of actually being in the opera house. Timings are approximate and must be since they can vary greatly between different performances. The slowest *Tristan* in the records at Bayreuth played for THIRTY MINUTES longer than the most speedy.

- Stars are awarded at the whim of the author as follows:
  - * Worth looking out for
  - ** This is really good
  - *** Stunning. Brilliant

- At the end of the COMMENT in the opera section each opera is given a rating from alpha-plus to gamma. Author's whim again, and whereas no reader is likely to want to swap any of the gammas with the alphas, these ratings are susceptible to a wide range of disagreement. But what the hell. Everyone their own opera critic.
- The aim of the Guide is to avoid every technical term in music that can be described in plain English, but there are some basic truths which have to be tackled by anyone who wants to get a fix on certain musical forms (aria) or on basic musical structure (tonality). These are dealt with in a summary fashion in the *Words* list and more fully in the *Operatica* section. Would true musicologists please look the other way.
- The *Artists* section includes some sixty conductors and singers, again selected on whim, but with three criteria in mind:
  1. They must be world class.
  2. They must be household names. (At least in households that are opera-prone.)
  3. They must be well represented on disc.

THE OPERAS

Adriana Lecouvreur — Backstage tragedy

Cilea

The one about the star of stage and screen whose rival sends her a bouquet of poison gas violets. She sniffs it: snuffs it.

CAST

Adriana Lecouvreur, star of the Comédie-Française	Soprano
Michonnet, stage manager of the Comédie	Baritone
Prince of Bouillon, opera-going prince	Bass
Princess of Bouillon, his wife	Mezzo
Abbé of Chazeuil, his companion and social fixer	Tenor
Maurizio, Count of Saxony	Tenor
Actors, servants, etc.	

4 acts: running time 2 hrs 5 mins

STORY

Act I · Backstage in the Comédie-Française

We are waiting for curtain up on one of Racine's smash hits in Paris France 1730. Backstage it is all go: final touches to costume and make-up: a heavy demand for beauty spots etc.: distracted stage manager Michonnet urges everyone to hurry up: the Prince arrives plus his sidekick the Abbé seeking his good friend star actress Duclos: Duclos is not available. Rival star Adriana comes on spouting Racine like mad. Poncey pair offer her fatuous compliments. She says come off it I am a humble working actress and the only good guy here amongst you phoneys is Michonnet (M. is very chuffed). All go on stage.

The Prince asks why Duclos is not available: she is busy writing a letter says Michonnet: the Prince orders the creepy Abbé to get the letter using bribery or whatever. Exit the poncey pair. Michonnet is moonstruck by Adriana. There is some roundabout talk about marriage. Adriana has no idea what the hell Michonnet is going on about. I'm in love too! she says. Whizzo! My lover's in the front of house tonight. Michonnet (hopes dashed) exits: Maurizio (really the Count of Saxony) comes in. Big hellos. How's your career? asks Adriana. Have you been promoted Company Commander yet? My boss the Count of Saxony (ho ho) keeps promising but never delivers says he: bastard. I am seated in Box 3 let's meet after the show. Adriana gives him a posy of violets. Both exit.

The poncey pair come on. I got the letter says the Abbé. He reads:

'Meet me at 42 rue Rouge tonight.' Zut! says the Prince: 42 RR is the house I use for assignations with Duclos: double-crossing whore and Zut! again. The letter is addressed to Box 3 says the Abbé. It's that Maurizio says the Prince. What to do? Invite all the cast to a party at 42 RR says the Abbé give 'em a surprise. Ha ha and very good says the Prince go ahead. Send on the letter to Box 3: exits.

Actors rush off stage. All is chatter scandal and gossip: they say Duclos meets many lovers at 42 RR and also gives the key to the Princess who indulges in adulterous fancies there. 42 will be busy tonight for sure. Who will meet whom? Buzz buzz. Michonnet left alone watches Adriana on stage adoringly. He holds a property letter for Adriana's next scene.

Maurizio comes on. (The letter he received in Box 3 was not from Duclos but written by her on instructions from the Princess who demands an immediate meeting at 42 RR to discuss an urgent political crisis.) Maurizio writes a message on the property letter: 'Tonight's meeting is not on. I have to see a man about a dog': Adriana reads the message on stage. Shock and anger greatly improve her performance: she gets a standing ovation. Offstage she receives an invitation to a midnight party to meet the Count of Saxony (our Maurizio!). Aha thinks Adriana I'll get after that Duke to make my Maurizio a Company Commander.

Act II A room in maison 42 rue Rouge with French windows and garden beyond

The Princess awaits Maurizio with anxiety: will he come? He comes. There is an incomprehensible discussion. Maurizio is interested in politics not sex: the Princess in sex but not in politics. Have you gone off me or something? she asks. Well he says hum haw we shall always be good friends. Good friends! Pshaw! she says. She sees the violets. There must be another woman she says: who is she? They're for you he says.

A coach draws up. The Princess panics. Quick jump into the fridge says Maurizio. She jumps. (As he opens the fridge door he drops the violets.) The Prince plus the Abbé come in. Got you Maurizio! they cry. Where's the lady old boy? What lady? says Maurizio. Duclos they reply (a mistake, of course). I was going off her myself you can take her over old boy says the Prince. (Maurizio twigs the mistake.)

Enter Adriana: surprise all round. I thought you were seeing a man about a dog she says. So I came to meet the Count of Saxony to plead your cause. Go ahead for I am he! says Maurizio. Another surprise. Well fancy that she says I always thought you were officer material. The poncey pair plus Michonnet come on. Michonnet says he must go and seek Duclos.

She's here says the Abbé. Eh? What? says Michonnet. She's in that fridge there says the Abbé. Is she hell I'll soon see says Adriana (jealous).

No! says Maurizio it's not Duclos: I came here to talk politics. It's a serious matter. There is a person in the fridge true enough but it's not Duclos but a political contact. Do you believe me? I believe you says Adriana. We must keep the poncey pair away from the fridge says he. It would be politically disastrous if the person were exposed. You must release the occupant in the dark: and the person must not be seen even by you. OK says the trusting Adriana. Take this secret key says Maurizio. Exits.

Meanwhile Michonnet goes and opens the fridge but it's too dark to recognize the occupant. He closes the fridge. Now the Abbé proposes getting candles and opening the fridge. Adriana interposes, as instructed. The Abbé goes off to get the Prince: Michonnet stands guard. Adriana blows out the candles and opens the fridge and the Princess jumps out. What now? she says. Escape! says Adriana. All exits are blocked says the Princess. Here's a secret key says Adriana. Get out.

Who are you? asks the Princess. Mind your own business says Adriana. Do you know Maurizio? asks the Princess. By the way I love him. He's mine. Rubbish he's mine says Adriana. A big argument is terminated by the Prince and helpers appearing in the garden with torches etc. The Princess scarpers. The search party enters: Michonnet finds the Princess's specs on the floor. He hands them to Adriana.

Act III A large room in the Bouillon palace prepared as private theatre

The Abbé fusses around fixing furniture and sucking up to the Princess. The Princess is perplexed about the identity of the woman who rescued her the night before. The Prince and Princess receive their guests. Adriana arrives. The Princess thinks hello-oo didn't I hear that voice last night perhaps?

Let's get started says the tiresome Abbé. We must wait for Maurizio says the Prince. He's not coming says the Princess (watching Adriana like a stoat) because of the duel ... What duel? asks Adriana. The Abbé told me about this duel says the Princess. He saw Maurizio covered in blood ... Adriana passes out (Oho oho thinks the Princess) but revives as Maurizio is announced.

Are you wounded? asks the Prince. Not so the other fellow was totally outduelled says Maurizio [What the hell is this duel? Ed.]. Maurizio whispers thanks to the Princess for springing him from prison [Whazzat? First we've heard of prison? Ed.] and greets Adriana coolly (why?). He tells of a boring military exploit won by his bravery daring sagacity (load of bull: generally behaves quite out of character and confuses an already nearly incomprehensible plot).

The Prince announces the ballet: it is the Judgement of Paris (allegory, geddit?): the Princess and Adriana start to row: you were the woman last night says the Princess: proof these violets. You were the woman last night says Adriana: proof these specs. Certainly these look very like the wife's specs says the Prince.

Meanwhile the poor sods are struggling on with the ballet. Paris presents the prize to the Princess. She asks Adriana to do a party piece. Adriana delivers a chunk of drama concerning a guilty adulterous wife clearly aimed at the Princess. The Princess is as mad as hell. Adriana having avenged herself exits to a big ovation.

Act IV The drawing room in Adriana's home

Maurizio is apparently off the picture: Adriana pines for him: she has jacked in her acting career. She is sad and ill. Michonnet (still in love with Adriana) comes on a visit and writes a note to Maurizio 'You must come' while waiting: Adriana enters very low: Michonnet tries to comfort her. It's no good – Adriana remains suicidal.

A group of friendly actors arrive bringing birthday presies chockies etc. There is a lot of jokey gossip. Michonnet gives Adriana her own diamond necklace redeemed from the pawnbroker. It has cost him his life's savings. But seriously they all say you are a great star and must make a comeback. Yes OK says Adriana (smell of greasepaint or something).

A parcel arrives 'from Maurizio'. The guests exit into the dining room seeking bubbly: Adriana opens the parcel (actually from the jilted Princess): she looks in the box and sees the same old violets (soaked in phosgene): Maurizio is a beastly cruel cad she cries and chucks violets on to the fire (but not before one long last lethal sniff). She bombs out. Steady! says Michonnet I'm sure Maurizio will explain everything.

Hey presto! Maurizio arrives. Hugs and kisses. Why did you abandon me? asks Adriana. I was wrongly informed you were fixed up with another guy says he. [Weak: Ed.] What about that other woman? asks Adriana. She is a lying bitch and also a slagheap says he anyway how about marriage? Gosh! he must love me thinks Adriana. They clinch in mutual ecstasy: Adriana totters. Are you ill? he asks. It's these stinking flowers you sent me says she. I never sent you no flowers says he: he smells shoe box (phosgene): Adriana has convulsions: hallucinates.

Maurizio phones for a doctor. He calls Michonnet. Tries medication. It's no good Adriana is raving mad and declaims unsuitable lines from plays she has performed. She writhes in agony and carries on something terrible but in the tradition of all mad dying operatic heroines she enjoys a short burst of sanity to deliver a touching last aria. Expires.

MINUTES FROM START **LOOK OUT FOR**

Act I

The show-biz clatter of the opening scenes abates
only slightly when the poncey pair, the Prince and the
Abbé, start their backstage rounds. They send them-
4: *Dell' augei di Leda* selves up in a pastiche duet* with highflown senti- 4
ments, loads of classical references and
tongue-in-cheek music. We know where we are: in
the pretend never-never land actors inhabit when not
acting. Chatter continues.

Adriana's entry (impressive); she rejects the hype
of the poncey pair and sings sweetly and humbly
6: *Troppo signori, troppo* about her vocation as an actress.** Not a number to 6
stop the show, but fortunately the show does stop for
it. The feverish pace is halted to let her do her stuff.
So we learn the opera is going to be a little serious too.

Michonnet moves stealthily towards the topic of
13: *Adriana!* marriage with Adriana* (inconceivable of course). 13
His oblique approaches and her ripostes – she hasn't
the faintest idea what he's on about – are married skilfully to a tender melody flowing along in the strings –
which puts his case more persuasively than he could
do himself – poor sod.

This is Maurizio's first chance and he grabs it with
18: *La dolcissima effigie* both hands. A stirring tenor aria** with a big tune in a 18
style nearer to a Mario Lanza movie than Rossini but,
boy, does it go well. Develops into a duet with
Adriana in which the big tune surfaces again.

23: *Or dunque Abate* A quick-fire two-hander** leading to a racy en- 23
semble as the poncey pair get excited about the letter
from la Duclos. The actors' quartet sings against
rather than with the main melody which comes from
the pit. The whole scene is a little marvel of speed and
wit and the ensemble quite delicious.

The serious sentimental Michonnet watches from
the wings. He thrills to Adriana's performance. Two
27: *Ecco il monologo* great bursts of melody here,** the first from the or- 27
chestra and the second vocal when poor Michonnet
finds in her performance something to compensate
him for his disappointment.

Act II

The Princess's vigil: she describes (very accurately) what it's like to wait for a lover. She finishes strongly

2: *O vagabonda stella* in a noble melody*** (which we will hear again) ad- 2
dressed to the star of the East (for some reason or other).

15: *Ma, dunque è vero?* The duet Adriana/Maurizio:* she adjusts to his 15
new status but not easily: another helping of the warm sentiment of their earlier duet: different tune: lower voltage.

As Adriana prepares to release the mysterious woman the Princess's star melody wells up in the or-
27: *Ho capito* chestra* and lingers on beautifully calm and quite in- 27
appropriate as the two rivals grope about in the dark.

Act III

A refined sort of hornpipe sets the ballroom scene spinning. It crops up pretty often like a punctuation mark over the next ten minutes.

Adriana is introduced to the Princess who wonders uncertainly – is she isn't she the lady I groped with last night? – whilst Adriana's How Dos are set to the
6: *Commossa io sono* sweetest melody* with (regrettably) a whiff of 6
schmaltz about it – but only a smidgin.

The Prince asks Maurizio for an account of his re-
11: *Il russo Mencikoff* cent battle.* Which he won by dint of outstanding 11
courage, daring skill and by blowing up a houseful of Cossacks with a keg of gunpowder. An enjoyable tongue-in-cheek number.

The music of the ballet is joined by distant and rather magical voices: this is followed by some brassy military music that has a touch of the Finlandias, but then it falls away and although the double act (Paris judging away on stage and the Princess and Adriana face to face just off it) may work dramatically the music is disappointing.

The bizarre end to the act – a chunk of declaimed
23: *Giusto cielo!* *Phèdre** from Adriana (a second play-within-a-play, 23
hammering home the Princess/Adriana situation): it moves from something near to parlando (spoken: no accompaniment) to melodrame (spoken against dramatic musical accompaniment) and finally a moment of real singing. A stirring finish.

Act IV

The posse of actors who visit Adriana on her birthday
12: *Una volta c'era un principe* to persuade her back on the boards sing a neat little
stanza* about the Prince who is doing the rounds of 12

the pubs and clubs.

20: *No, non fu invano* Maurizio's proposal and duet with Adriana* is urgent and dramatic and OK but Cilea seems to have run out of big tunes or surely he would have given us one here. 20

Without making any big deal of it the death
33: *Respira* scene** is strangely effective. Adriana's shout 'Save 33
me! I don't want to die' strikes home with more power than the traditional leading ladies' deathbed arias of sweet resignation. Her last whispered vision as she is in the act of dying is spooky, and the earth trembles a little. Note the preemptive harp. On its second appearance it is punctually posthumous.

NOTES

Adriana Lecouvreur	Cilea's fourth
First night	Teatro Lirico, Milan, 6 November 1902
Reception	Terrific (Caruso as Maurizio)
Libretto	Colautti
Source	Play of the same name by Legouvé and Scribe

NEWS AND GOSSIP

Cilea had a success with his third opera *L'Arlesiana* and the publisher Sonzogno (by now as good a talent-spotter as his older rival Ricordi) commissioned *Adriana* with high hopes. It was a good bet. Adriana is a wonderful vehicle for an experienced actress/soprano who can be getting on a little but who can hold the stage and has enough voice to carry the part. A great actress who can sing will make a better fist of Adriana than a great singer who can't act. *Adriana* got off to a flying start and soon spread across the opera No. 1 circuit and has remained in the repertory ever since, but more as a standby and as a vehicle for a slightly fading star than as a popular piece in its own right. This is a mistake. See below.

COMMENT

Perhaps the most underrated opera in the book. Cilea is an inventive composer, can write a tune, orchestrate brilliantly and has great musicality and absolute certainty of touch. Just occasionally we skate along the frontiers of schmaltz, but never cross them. Because his music is so wonderfully easy and mellifluous – he is a sort of Rakhmaninov of the opera house – the super musical are a bit sniffy. Let them sniff.

Scribe's play is said to have an 'intricate' plot which usually means you can't follow it. In cutting the play and tidying it up for the opera, Colautti did a sloppy job. Maurizio's behaviour in Act II is strange. Why doesn't he tell Adriana of his true relationship with the Princess? He asks her for a carte blanche vote of confidence, which he gets. To ask her to believe the true story would have been less demanding. The silly business of neither rival recognizing the other in the dark does not help the plot. Maurizio's political problems (in danger of his life, the duel, prison) are totally incomprehensible. Again in Act III why is he cool to Adriana? There seems to be no motive for this nor for his desertion of Adriana after the party, except that he heard some gossip about her. Not good enough: neither Verdi nor Puccini would have tolerated this sort of thing.

On the credit side, Adriana herself is adorable, one of the great credibles amongst prima donnas, a part fit for Ellen Terry or Peggy Ashcroft (had they been able to sing). The backstage atmosphere is true to life, the ballroom act has its appropriate shock. And then, surprise, surprise, this light-hearted opera, so far almost a light opera, suddenly takes a downward twist into a tragedy with the simple and affecting last act. Despite the amazingly lethal violets, there is true verismo in Adriana's death scene. To see her struggling with hallucinations and with death itself is frightening – a million miles away from the melodrama of the deaths by stabbing in *Cav* and *Pag*, and the sweet pathos of Mimi, Butterfly and Violetta. But to return to the music, the great joy of *Adriana* lies in the score. Never before had anyone written page on page of witty one-liners floating on a sea of orchestral froth. There are lots of musical mottos and tags of identity which crop up from time to time, but there is no need for them to bother the listener at all. For those with a quick ear they have the advantage of alerting our subconscious to anticipate a person, an emotion (Hello again, Adriana!). But we are free to relax and enjoy the music as it comes without any struggle. Then there is the orchestration, as clear as spring water, for to hear *Adriana* after one of the other late Italians – *Gioconda*, *Cav* or *Chénier* – is like clearing the palate with a Rimsky-Korsakov sorbet after a big helping of brown stew from Brahms. A glorious orchestrator who can also, when called upon, write the big tune. Although melodic inspiration does not irrigate the whole system all the time, as it does with Puccini, there is enough to give satisfaction. Adriana's piece about acting, Maurizio's first act solo and duet with Adriana, the Princess singing to the star of the East, all of these are – if you measured arias as you do oysters – Colchester Number Ones, that is large, juicy and with the authentic native flavour, in this case, Italian. *Adriana*, we love you. An unexpected alpha.

Aida

Egyptian tragedy

Verdi

The one where the four-star Egyptian general loves a slave girl named Celestial Aida, where there is a Grand March and a terminal entombment for two.

CAST

The King of Egypt (unnamed)	Bass
Amneris, his daughter	Mezzo
Aida, one of Amneris' slave girls	Soprano
Amonasro, Aida's father	Baritone
Radames, an Egyptian general	Tenor
Ramfis, the High Priest	Bass
A messenger, a priestess	

4 acts: running time 2 hrs 33 mins

STORY

Act I Sc 1 The Royal Palace, Memphis

We are in Memphis not Tennessee but Ancient Egypt. News agencies report that despite their recent defeat the Ethiopians are on the march again. Radames, a two-star general, hopes to be C-in-C. The High Priest is enigmatic – he won't forecast promotion. Radames announces his (socially unacceptable) love for the slave girl Aida. But the King's daughter Amneris is quite crazy about Radames: she suspects something is going on between Radames and Aida. The King enters plus priests, guards, all sorts. He calls on a messenger to read the latest fax. Bad news: rapid advance of Ethiops under gallant General Amonasro (my Dad! exclaims Aida). The King nominates Radames C-in-C (no surprise): we hear pep talk, warlike songs etc. Aida (now alone) has a problem: either Dad wins and Radames is killed or vice versa.

Act I Sc 2 Interior of the temple of Vulcan, Memphis

In the temple there is prayer and ritual, so that Radames' leadership will be endorsed by deity Phtha (!). Sacred dance etc.: all impressive (no plot advancement).

Act II Sc 1 Amneris' suite in the palace

Amneris is dressing for her official engagements (triumphal pageant to celebrate the Ethiops being licked): chorus sings songs of praise for Radames: Moorish slaves dance. Amneris, dead jealous, tells Aida that Radames has been killed in action (a lie): Aida very upset. Aha says crafty Amneris: so you do love him – he's not dead at all. Good-o! says Aida thus annoying Amneris yet more: Amneris gives Aida a hard time for presuming love above her station: sorry I couldn't help myself says Aida. There is noise of the returning army without.

Act II Sc 2 Triumphal arch. City of Thebes

The royals take up their station for the big parade. Parade occurs: Ethiop prisoners are led on: Aida spies her Dad!: he says don't let on it's me they think I'm just a common soldier. He requests the King to show mercy on the prisoners: the priests say no: everyone else yes: big ding-dong. Radames says since their leader Amonasro is dead (ho ho) Ethiops are no longer a threat, I vote for releasing them. The King says OK but I will keep Aida's Dad as a hostage. What's more you can marry Amneris. Whoops of joy from all but the secret lovers Radames and Aida.

Act III Banks of the Nile. Another temple in view

Priests and priestesses sing anthems of joy for the forthcoming royal wedding. A boatload of VIPs sails in with Amneris and Radames aboard. Aida (alone) sings of her love for Radames and of nostalgia for her homeland. Her father Amonasro joins in with praises and love for their homeland. He suggests Aida prise out of Radames the Egyptians' secret battle plans: the Ethiops are ready to strike again (quick regrouping): Aida is first shocked then agrees to try: Amonasro jumps into the bushes.

Radames comes on: he proposes marriage after his next victory: he will persuade the King. What about Amneris? she says, powerful threat there: much better fly with me. Radames hums and haws but at last agrees. Our route must avoid the Egyptian army says she – which way will they go? By M11–A120 says he. Amonasro jumps out of the bushes: I'm the Ethiop King he cries I have now got decisive intelligence. My God says Radames Aida's shopped me and I've shopped my country. Amneris exits temple with ears aflap: I heard all she cries, you traitorous dog. Amonasro assaults Amneris: Radames interposes. Amonasro and Aida exit fast and Radames surrenders to the clergy.

Act IV Sc 1 Judgement Chamber. Also Radames' cell

Amneris is in psychological shock: she loves Radames but he is now a traitor. She sends for him: she says let's get top QC for your defence. I want no defence says he. I want to die now that Aida is dead (who told him that?). She is not dead says Amneris; her Dad is dead, Aida has gone missing. Good news says he. Give her up, boy, marry me and save your life says she. Nothing doing says he: my eternal love for Aida makes death preferable. O come on! says she. Not on your life says he. He is led off to the condemned cell. The charges are read by the priests: they are met by dumb insolence: Radames is convicted as a traitor.

Act IV Sc 2 Split screen (horizontally): temple of Vulcan above, tomb/vault below

Clergy close the tomb exit with a mighty stone. Radames' spirits are understandably low: suddenly he sees Aida: ghost? vision? No, it's the real Aida who has crept in to share death throes with her beloved Radames (simultaneous suttee). Priests and priestesses chant: Aida and Radames face up to death: they bid earth farewell: the repentant Amneris in the temple prays for Radames' soul. Slow curtain.

MINUTES FROM START — LOOK OUT FOR

Act I Sc 1

Dignified exchanges between Ramfis and Radames
(latter hopes to get the top job) lead to Radames'
7: *Celeste Aida* — famous opening aria** – If I'm C-in-C and we lick the 7
Ethiops, what a VE Day hero I'll be, and I'll make
Aida, my secret love, queen. A great tenor piece.

Guarded exchanges between the jealous Amneris
and the cautious Radames (very tuneful) lead to the
15: *Trema, o rea* — arrival of Aida and a magic trio*** (Amneris: Watch 15
it Aida I believe you're the one he fancies, Radames: I
hope to God she doesn't suspect, could be nasty,
Aida: My tears are not because I'm exiled, I carry a
torch for Radames). Aida takes the lead in a clear soprano line whilst the other two chunter on below. But
none of the three can hear what the other two are
saying.

17: *Alta cagion* — The first big razzmatazz ensemble** – trumpets, 17
chorus, soloists, great occasional stuff leading to a
20: *Su! del Nilo* — foot-tapping military march*** started off by the 20
King solus and spreading irresistibly to one and all.

Aida ponders the problem of her father leading one
24: *Ritorna vincitor!* army and her lover the other, in a free range arioso** 24
piece ending with a concise little prayer, delicate and
heartfelt.

Act I Sc 2

30: *Possente Fhthà* A wonderfully ingenious extended choral scene:** 30
first the slightly spooky priestesses addressing the
god Phtha in un-Verdian modal tones – harps twanging away below like crazy – then the sombre priests
make their pitch: next solos addressed from Ramfis
and Radames and suddenly the chorus swells into a
38: *La mano tua distendi* mighty song of war*** swaying and lurching towards 38
battle, only to die away again and end with echoes of
the opening spooky bit. Terrific!

Act II Sc 1

The act opens with one of the most beguiling scenes
0: *Chi mai fra gl'inni* in all opera:*** the slave girls sing hopefully of glory 0
for Radames – harps and little bursts of trumpet –
Amneris floats in with a passionate aside – how she
loves him, how much she longs for him to love her –
interrupted by a (mercifully short) rumbustious
Moorish dance. But the slaves' chorus and Amneris'
magic aside return again to haunt the ear.

The second half of the scene is taken up by the duet
6: *Fu la sorte* of confrontation between Amneris and Aida.** 6
Amneris cons Aida into admitting she loves
Radames: high dramatic stuff: then Aida asks for pity
12: *Pietà ti prenda* in a duet* first with a bassoon then with an absolutely 12
relentless Amneris who threatens death: the choral
march of Act I is heard outside: Amneris says Aida
will be humiliated in the triumphal bonanza about to
take place: Aida is left alone onstage to make her last
pathetic prayer to the gods for mercy.

Act II Sc 2

17: *Gloria all' Egitto* The great choral triumph of the Egyptians*** (and of 17
Verdi). The mighty opening stanza (all citizens) is
answered by the women only with a quieter section
which has an upward spiral at the end: then some vigorous counterpoint from the men and back into the
big tune once again. Followed by the grandest and
best-known march in the business. Nothing like it before or since.

The majestic scene rolls on: after the ballets** –

Verdi's Class I ballet music here – and Amonasro's
plea for mercy, look out especially for:

27: *Che veggo!* 1. The ensemble** which debates the matter of to 27
kill or not to kill the prisoners (in favour: Ramfis and
priests, against: slaves and prisoners, populace – big
majority): meanwhile Radames 'thinks' (Doesn't my
Aida look just lovely when she's sad), also Amneris
(He's eyeing her in a very disturbing fashion): two
threads in a mighty ensemble which ebbs and flows in
elegant counterpoint, but mainly flows.

29: *Gloria all' Egitto etc. (again)* 2. The final ensemble*** after the King has made 29
the unfortunate suggestion that Radames should
marry Amneris. The populace just love the idea and
bang on about the glory of Egypt once again, but Aida
is shattered while Amneris (the fool) thinks her
dreamboat has come in. Another sensational ensemble: a final race to the tape with a brief repeat of
the Grand March.

Act III

5: *Qui Radames* Aida's big solo* (nostalgia for the environs of Addis 5
Ababa): a bit reedy to start with (influenced by the
really queer opening prelude and chorus? Egyptian
plainsong?) and continuing as a bit of a stop–start
Willow-Songish affair, but flowering into moments
of great beauty.

21: *Pur ti riveggo* The duet** Radames/Aida which develops the 21
plot in Act III – lengthy, varied and exciting throughout. First he presses his case (matrimony and the
queen's crown) urged on by little snaps and stings
from the trumpets: she says Whoa! What about
Amneris, she's vicious: let's get out of the country: so
23: *Là … tra foreste* then a pause as they reflect** in suspended ani- 23
mation, ending on an insistent pedal: they decide to
27: *Sì, fuggiam* flee: then a breathless joyful let's-go-quick section.** 27
(But they don't go: the betrayal is followed by the
noisy turmoil of Radames' arrest.)

Act IV Sc 1

Amneris thinks aloud: frightens herself at the
thought of Radames' death: reflects on her great love
2: *Oh! che mai parlo?* for him in a sudden, sweet, lyrical burst of emotion** 2
(tune lies in the accompanying strings).

4: *Già i sacerdoti* The last great duet*** Amneris/Radames: it 4
opens rather formally dealing with the matter of

Radames' defence against the charge of treachery
(one stanza each) then drifts into an argument (he
won't defend himself) with a strong fresh impulse
livening up the scene as Amneris says: I won't let you
6: *Sì, all'amor* die: you must live and love me.** Impossible says he 6
9: *Chi ti salva* I love Aida. So go to hell;** now I hate you says she in 9
the final splendidly forceful ensemble: let me die,
says he.

Once more Amneris 'thinks', this time sadly.
11: *Ohimè! morir* Again a sustained tune of great beauty** in the lower 11
strings. Followed by the high drama (lots of heavy
drumming: sombre theme from prelude) of
14: *Spirto del nume* Radames' conviction to death by entombment.** 14
(Very good too.)

Act IV Sc 2

24: *Morir! sì pura* The last scene: the duet Radames/Aida:** he has 24
caused Aida's death: he regrets this: she sees a vision
of a rather friendly angel of death: the priests and
priestesses (offstagers) quietly chip in with their
spooky hymns to Phtha from Act II. Radames fails to
move the stone: gives up rather quickly and moves
30: *O terra, addio* into a series of lingering wistful goodbyes*** to life 30
fading slowly as Amneris (much mollified) joins in
with a quiet prayer. Not a dry eye in the house.

NOTES

Aida	Verdi's twenty-sixth opera
First night	Cairo Opera House, 24 December 1871
Reception	Very good. But some critics carped (see below)
Libretto	Ghislanzoni
Source	Very strange: one Mariette, an archaeologist on the staff of the Khedive of Egypt dreamt up the idea and sent a draft to Verdi's friend du Locle

NEWS AND GOSSIP

In spite of pressing invitations, Verdi was not interested in writing an opera to open the Cairo Opera House until du Locle passed him this odd piece from Mariette. Du Locle wrote to Verdi that if he didn't want to take it on 'then Wagner might do something really fine with it'. Maybe this stung Verdi into action, anyway he set to with his usual zeal. The opening night was fixed for early 1871 but the sets got stuck in Paris, which was having a little trouble, first with the Prussian army then with the Commune. Eventually it went on in Cairo on Christmas Eve 1871, but without Verdi (the first time he had missed a first night) who was busy working with the Scala company rehearsing their production of *Aida* which opened in February 1872. Both first nights went well but the notices were what are called mixed, which, being interpreted, means bad. The critics thought *Aida* old-fashioned, a sort of grand opera seria. Verdi, like most composers, was paranoid about critics ('stupid objections and even stupider praise'), but he needn't have worried – no one need ever worry about the critics, for it is the public that has the last word – and *Aida* immediately became a huge success and has stayed at the top ever since, probably lying fourth after Verdi's pop three, *Rig*, *Trov* and *Trav*.

COMMENT

Aida is the *enjoyable* opera. Nothing difficult, nothing boring, terrific spectacle, rousing choruses, lots of high-quality brass band music, pathos, passion and a basketful of good tunes. It has got everything, except flesh and blood characters. The Egyptian and Ethiop stereotypes are taken straight from the frieze in a Pharaoh's tomb and one half expects them to move like Wilson, Keppel and Betty. And yet the emotions the cardboard crew express are so human, so universal and set to such convincing music that we can believe there is some real humanity lying behind the puppet show. In this way, and in this way alone, *Aida* can be compared to Mozart's *Tito*. Uncompromisingly classical characters moving through history in a stately frolic but with hearts that beat, blood that is warm, sometimes hot, and passions as up to the minute as our own. *Aida*'s pomp and circumstance is unmatched in all opera (though *Carlos* comes close), the duets are dramatic as can be, the romanzas (Radames' 'Celeste Aida' and 'O patria mia') romantic in the extreme. But perhaps *Aida* sticks in the memory most of all not for the crash and bang of the big stuff but for the gentle moments, the wistful dying fall of Amneris' cry: 'Ah! vieni amor ...' and Aida's 'O terra addio'. Verdi at the zenith of his power: alpha-plus.

Andrea Chénier

Revolutionary tragedy

Giordano

The one where the butler leads a riotous mob into the Countess's drawing room, where there is a march past of named French Revolutionaries, and a court scene leading to tumbrils for two.

CAST

Andrea Chénier, poet, liberal sympathies	Tenor
Countess de Coigny, aristo	Mezzo
Maddalena, her daughter	Soprano
Bersi, Maddalena's maid	Mezzo
Carlo Gérard, revolutionary, butler then activist	Baritone
Incredibile, a spy for the revolutionaries	Tenor
Roucher, Chénier's friend	Baritone
Mathieu, rank-and-file revolutionary	Baritone
Madelon, blind old woman	Mezzo

Fléville (writer), the Abbé (poet), Dumas (Tribunal President), Fouquier-Tinville (Tribunal prosecutor), Schmidt (jailor), Major Domo, newsboy.

4 acts: running time 1 hr 55 mins

STORY

Act I A drawing room in the Chateau de Coigny

We are in the environs of Paris in 1786 and look out! – the French Revolution is going to happen. Servants set up the room for a party. Gérard talks shocking revolutionary stuff to a sofa. Old dad staggers in carrying another sofa. Gérard relieves him and says wait for it you upper classes – today you boss us tomorrow we boss you. Maddalena plus Bersi enter. Gérard gives her a silent wolf whistle: he fancies her. The Countess enters and fusses around. Guests Fléville and the Abbé arrive.

Fléville as MC introduces amateur theatricals with shepherdesses etc. Another guest performs on the Steinway. Chénier is unwilling to perform at all. Maddalena makes an obscure wager with friends to get him to say the word 'love'. He does so: big joke. Chénier nettled embarks on a lengthy dissertation on love including strong anti-clerical anti-aristo attack plus other liberal sentiments (guests are outraged): he finally tells Maddalena she alone is compassionate.

She runs out: the Countess diplomatically calls for an instant gavotte.

The gavotters are interrupted by a howling peasant mob led by butler Gérard (for it is he). Dad intercedes but Gérard strips off his uniform and chucks it at the Countess. Exit with mob. The Countess says let's get on with that gavotte (thinks O Lord and good butlers are so hard to find).

Act II Café Hottot, Paris

Three years later. The Revolution is going full swing. Mathieu dusts a bust of Marat. Chénier waits: Bersi turned hooker thinks MI5 man Incredibile is watching her so she makes it plain she's right in there relishing blood wine tumbrils etc. Incredibile is actually on the trail of Maddalena plus he makes notes on Chénier and Bersi.

Roucher arrives and says Chénier old boy things are hotting up they're after you. You are no longer considered politically correct here's a passport best scarper quick. Nuts says Chénier. Destiny instructs me to await a meeting with a mysterious woman and eternal love. What woman? says Roucher. This woman says Chénier: named 'Hope': he shows a letter. Roucher sniffs the letter. Smells like a tart's boudoir he says this woman is a cathouse whore. Jesus! says Chénier you're right. Gimme that passport. I'm off.

A parade of the Revolution's stars goes by: Gérard (rising in the charts) is one of them. He leaves the procession and gives verbal identikit of Maddalena to Incredibile says he must have her. I'll deliver her tonight says Incredibile. Bersi runs on and tells Chénier an important woman in distress is coming here to meet you. Incredibile observes. It's a trap says Roucher (it is: Incredibile will tell Gérard): I'll stay on guard.

Darkness falls. Maddalena disguised as a street prostitute arrives: Chénier recognizes her: I've always fancied you she says: I am falling have fallen for you he says in fact I will love you until death: me too until death she says [little do they know: Ed.].

Gérard arrives and grabs Maddalena. Get off says Chénier: he slashes at Gérard. Gérard draws: they fight: Gérard is badly wounded: Incredibile fetches squaddies: Gérard (decent chap at heart) says: Chénier old boy you're on the death list! Get away fast! Squaddies come pounding in and ask Gérard who done it? Dunno he says. Never seen him before [terribly decent: Ed.].

Act III The courtroom of the Revolutionary Tribunal

Mathieu appeals for funds for the party: he is a total flop. You have a go Gérard he says. Gérard does better: gold trinkets etc. are chucked in the kitty. Aged Madelon with many sons and grandsons already killed offers his last 15-year-old grandson (poor sod) to fight for liberty equality etc.

The crowd exits to booze in the street.

Incredibile tells Gérard Chénier has been arrested. And her? he asks. She'll hear about him on the Six o'Clock News says Incredibile then she'll be down to see him in a flash. He gives a short lecturette on the magnetic power of love. Get on write the charge sheet quick he tells Gérard, the court is waiting. Gérard is in a moral hang-up. He used to be a decent chap now he's manufacturing false charges: he was a pure idealist now a lecherous shit. (But he signs the charge sheet.)

Maddalena enters. I have arrested your lover Chénier says Gérard. I was potty about you when I was butler you were a nice young girl. I would like to have sex now. I will kill myself first says she: I won't let you says he advancing. OK you can have me if Chénier goes free says she (what a gutsy girl says he). Lemme tell you she says: our home has been burned down, Mummie has been murdered, I've wandered all over Paris ill and starving: an angel's voice from heaven said 'stick it old thing love will save you'.

Gérard (decent again) says I would save him but it's too late: the court has assembled. Go on! Save him! she says. I will do my best he replies. The courtroom fills. Many get the black cap.

Chénier is called. His defence speech is prolix but he maintains he is not a traitor not guilty. Evidence? says the President. The accusation is a lie I fudged it all says Gérard. OK says the Public Prosecutor you stand down I will make the same accusations. My God says Gérard I am a true son of the Revolution and I can't stand this mindless hatred distorting French justice. The crowd shouts shut up Gérard: to the guillotine with Chénier. Guilty says the President. Death. Chénier sees Maddalena across the courtroom: he waves: I will see you soon I swear says Maddalena.

Act IV St Lazare prison

Chénier writes one last poem. He reads it to Roucher. Maddalena enters having been granted a last meeting. She bribes the gaoler to substitute her for a young woman LeGray already booked for the tumbril. The gaoler accepts the deal. Chénier and Maddalena sing a mini-Liebestod. They climb into the tumbril and move off to death at dawn – together.

MINUTES FROM START

Act I

LOOK OUT FOR

It is not easy to pick the highlights of the opening scenes because with the best will in the world there aren't any – just a succession of highly agreeable chunks of mood music following each other in a mu-

sical switchback – first the subversive butler's address
to the sofa (fiery), Maddalena's entry (sweet), the
Countess's check-up on the party arrangements (tripping), the arrival of the guests (rousing), the divertissement (fairy music), the party pieces and jokes
(mickey-mousing), etc. But don't be put off, you'll
love it – but mildly.

19: *Un dì, all' azzurro* Chénier's manifesto* – a switchback in itself – 19
starts with a strenuous contest between Chénier and
the upper strings as he describes the beauties of
21: *Su dalla terra* nature. Then a really nice lyrical passage** when 21
some metaphorical person kisses him (he doesn't
know who), some high dramatics as he gets anti-
clerical and the final enjoyable soaring endpiece as he
23: *E dissi* turns a loving gaze on to Maddalena.** 23

24: *La notte il giorno* The rent-a-mob break in to the sort of chorus* 24
suitable for the lower classes, in unison. On the nose
but effective.

Act II

The act floats in over a sea of revolutionary music
(there is one good tune struggling to get out) and soon
2: *Temer? Perchè?* Bersi gives us her view of the Revolution.* She loves
it, starts in a fairly low key but soon drunk with blood
and wine she's right into the stormy revolutionary
stuff too (to a background of revolutionary songs
somewhat genteelly orchestrated for the salon rather
than the saloon bar).

Chénier's flight of fancy about Destiny, Love and a
5: *Credo a una possanza* Strange Woman* – pretty ornery to start with but 5
soon gets off the ground and reaches a passionate cli-
7: *Credi all'amor* max** when his inner voice tells him to believe in 7
love, then tails off to the accompaniment of a reprehensible solo violin.

11: *Viva Robespierre!* One of the most mixed-up ensembles in all opera.* 11
Chénier and Roucher do a spot of race reading as the
procession of big shots goes by: the fans yell out the
names of the stars: meanwhile Gérard gives Incredibile a verbal identikit description of Maddalena. An
ingenious attempt and quite exciting.

Now for the most substantial item in the opera so
18: *Ecco l'altare* far – the duet between Chénier and Maddalena** in 18
her role as a revolutionary hooker: a sweet recogni-
tion scene: some agitato stuff (this place is danger-

ous): Maddalena, solo, asks for Chénier's protection: a soft final plea: they discover they are in love and celebrate this situation with some tumultuous joint re-
24: *Ah! Ora soave* joicing.** Then BANG! and we are into the 24
histrionics of the Act end (and very effective too).

Act III

1: *Dumouriez traditore* The courtroom scene* opens with sonorous chords 1
(terror of the Revolution) and addresses by Mathieu and Gérard are all good solid stuff.

Suddenly Madelon's offer of the last male in the
6: *Son la vecchia Madelon* family*** strikes a chord of genuine pity and terror: 6
both the gesture itself and the tender music cast a spell – until we get to a patch of goo (when Gérard horns in). But it finishes in true pathetic style. Gérard's thoughts about revolution (and sex) hang
14: *La coscienza nei cuor* about a bit at the start but get airborne at last** when 14
he recalls his undergraduate idealism.

At the heart of the third act stands the Gérard/
20: *Se ancor di me* Maddalena duet* (well, scarcely a duet, more a turn 20
and turn about); Gérard tells her how he lusted after her when she was a young girl and he a butler – a mel-
24: *Io t'ho voluto* odious section** with the nearest thing to a really 24
memorable tune in the opera – the whole piece improved by the fact that for once we have tonal stability and don't flit about restlessly from key to key. Her reply is more patchy but again there is a good bit when
26: *Voce piena d'armonia* she hears the heavenly voice of Love* and the dra- 26
matic ending (a true duet) is quite a buster.

28: *Mamma Cadet!* The closing court scene* rests on the high drama of 28
the trial. The music is bombastic (deafening drumming) but does succeed in raising the tension.

31: *Sì, fui soldato* Chénier's oration* reaches a degree of nobility. 31
The rather too vocally verismo crowd tend to drown it.

Act IV

2: *Come un bel dì* We have a fine flight of fancy from Chénier** as he 2
faces death bravely, nobly and poetically in a flowing melodic piece of real beauty.

9: *Vicino a te s'acqueta* The final duet Chénier/Maddalena*** is on a 9
higher plane. It breaks through the critical barrier with its warm honesty, genuine passion and its cool salute to death at dawn. And musically it flows naturally and convincingly to its great climax. (Interest-

ing that opera composers often pop in a harp or two just *before* their prima donnas are due to pass through the heavenly gates.)

NOTES

Andrea Chénier	Giordano's fourth
First night	La Scala, Milan, 28 March 1896
Reception	Good
Libretto	Illica (of Puccinian fame)
Source	An Illica original, based on real events in the French Revolution

NEWS AND GOSSIP

Illica's libretto followed the current fashion for so-called 'verismo'. But *Chénier* is a million miles away from what we would call a drama-doc or a dramatic reconstruction. It is a romance peppered with real names and supposed real sounds of the Revolution and maybe in the right production it might catch some whiff of the true mood of the time. Illica wrote the libretto for a now forgotten composer Franchetti, a baron and an addict of fast cars (as was Puccini). He appears to have handed it over to Giordano without demur. Giordano was on Sonzogno's list of promising composers belonging to the Giovane Scuola or young lions of Italian Opera. None of them grew up to roar much. The artful Giordano married a wife who owned the hotel where Verdi stayed in Milan and thereby scraped an acquaintance with the Maestro who is alleged to have given him hot tips as to how to write a good opera. *Chénier* was the only success of the 1896 Scala season which was organized by Sonzogno who with typical publisher's spite excluded works of his great rival Ricordi. *Chénier* caught on and has stuck around in the rep. perhaps partly because it is a great favourite with tenors. Not too much heavy work early on, good applause points and their big moment coming in the last act when they can belt it out for all they are worth.

COMMENT

The story of *Chénier* makes a good yarn though Chénier as a character suffers from the nineteenth century's rather ridiculous image of a 'poet': aesthetic, impulsive, wildly idealistic – something like W. S. Gilbert's Bunthorne in *Patience*. The brutal sectarian politics of the Revolution come over well though the tribunal scene is a bit rent-a-mob. Gérard is a good character and Maddalena's plight can wring the withers of even the most hardened opera-goer. Unfortunately the score lacks the guts demanded by such a high-tension story. A great deal of it is film music – not in the sense of the Hollywood track that was put on sound films but something much superior, the sort of score Prokoviev composed for *Ivan the Terrible* or Carl Davis assembled for Stroheim's *Greed*. It is a restless score: from minute to minute it mickey-mouses not the action but the emotion. Giordano is also a tonal fidget and often seems incapable of staying in the same key for more than a few bars. Off he goes – from here to there, and then – not back to here (the home key) but whoring off after something exotic in the next apartment. It is an uncomfortable mode of life. There is a lot of high string stuff in unison and the vocal line too is often in unison with the leading orchestral part which is as tiresome as two people reading the same poem at the same time. It is all agreeable music, more than just competent, but devil a bit will stick in the ear for long. Yet when he steadies up and settles down to it there are some really effective and indeed touching items in *Chénier* – the Act II duet between Chénier and Maddalena, Gérard's assessment of his own character in Act III and above all in Act IV Chénier's pre-death solo and the final duet as the two lovers await the tumbrils.

Chénier does not purge the soul with pity and terror nor does it fill the mind with wonder and admiration, but it is always enjoyable, sometimes touching and never for a moment dull. More than you could say for a number of much more famous titles. A beta.

Angelica, Suor *see* Suor Angelica

Ariadne on Naxos (Ariadne auf Naxos)

Backstage comedy

Richard Strauss

The one where a troupe of comedians are instructed to do their act on stage at the same time as a classical tragedy, with confusing consequences.

CAST

The prologue:	**A Prima Donna**	Soprano
	A Tenor	a Tenor
	Zerbinetta, a song-and-dance artist	High Soprano
	A Composer	Mezzo
	A Music Director	Baritone
	A Ballet Master	Tenor
	A Major-Domo, a wig-maker, a footman, an official	
The opera:	**Ariadne** sung by the Prima Donna	Soprano
	Bacchus sung by the Tenor (above)	Tenor
	Zerbinetta	High Soprano
	A Naiad	High Soprano
	A Dryad	Contralto
	Echo	Soprano
	Four male members of a commedia dell'arte group	

1 act: running time 2 hrs

STORY

The prologue. Backstage in a rich man's private house where a theatrical event is about to take place

We are in Vienna in the time of Molière because the story began life in France (see NOTES) but seems to have drifted eastwards and settled in Strauss' home town.

The Music Director nails the official in charge of the evening's events and says Hey Major-Domo I've heard a terrible rumour that some clowns from the Talk of the Town are going to put on a show after my opera. That's right says the Major-Domo. Opera first, comedy second and fireworks at nine o'clock sharp. My God how can I break this to Johnny says the Music Director. Exits.

Enter Johnny the Composer. Get the first violins here for a final rehearsal Jim he says to a lackey. All fiddles are on duty in the governor's salon says the lackey rudely. The Composer thinks of a tune. He gets involved in a row between the Tenor and a member of the wardrobe department. Zerbinetta comes out of her dressing room and chats with a posse of backstage folk. Whossat? asks the Composer. A member of the comedy act coming on after your opera says the Music Director. Comedy act? After my show? Impossible says the Composer. He does his nut. Zerbinetta and the Prima Donna slag each other off.

It's all buzz and bumble backstage when the Major-Domo comes back and says last-minute change of plan chaps: my master says the comedy has got to be played on stage at the same time as the opera. Hubbub. Is the man crazy cries everyone. My master has such a high opinion of your professionalism says the Major-Domo that he is sure you will all manage splendidly. Also he says, the whole performance must be cut to finish in time for the fireworks. Also he doesn't like the Naxos set but thinks that a few comics on the stage will cheer it up no end.

This is hopeless says the Composer. My beautiful opera will be destroyed. I'm off. There's nothing to lose. There's five hundred quid to lose says the Ballet Master. Sit down young man and make the cuts. He sits him down at a table with the score. The singers get anxious about losing lines. The Ballet Master tells the tenor the Composer's cutting the soprano's part and tells the soprano that it's the tenor who is losing numbers.

Zerbinetta gets into the act and distracts the Composer who finds her very sexy. The two casts move towards stage positions, the opera folk very sniffy about the comics. The Composer gives a short oration about the holy art of music and we're off into the opera.

The Opera. A rocky scene with a cave on the island of Naxos

Three nymphs, a Naiad, a Dryad and a Triad (Echo) are hanging around the cliffs. Ariadne lies on the ground. How is she? asks the Naiad. Much as usual says the Dryad. Weeping a lot. Low pulse. Depression. Frequent fits. Asleep just now. (Just now says Echo.)

Ariadne wakes up. Where am I? Who am I? And what the hell anyway? she asks (crazy as a coot). Poor thing too say the comics from the wings. A sweet girl like her gone potty. What a shame. (A shame says Echo.) There was this guy called Theseus or maybe not I'm totally confused says Ariadne.

Ariadne! call the nymphs (-adne says Echo who is beginning to get on everyone's nerves) wake up, love, it's us, your friendly neighbourhood nymphs. Music sometimes does the trick says Harlequin from the wings. Let's try a song. He sings, quite nicely. She moves a little but not much.

You fancy her or something? says Zerbinetta to Harlequin. Yeah, I do he says.

But Ariadne is now awake and almost compos. Death, she says at some length, is beautiful. I want Death. A noble messenger will come and carry me off to Death. Only then will I be free and happy. [But also dead: Ed.] She definitely needs cheering up say the comics. They come out of the wings and caper around in a commedia dell'arte fashion but they sing in a twentieth-century style. Zerbinetta tells them they're not helping. Would they please leave her alone with Ariadne.

She then sings for eleven minutes thirty-seven seconds mainly for the purpose of showing off her voice for she has only a short message and one that could be said in five seconds, namely that men are all bastards but we can't live without them. Pretty good singing says Harlequin but it didn't do anything. He makes a pass at her. She resists. But not for long. Soon they are into a clinch. Zerbinetta lets fly a burst of coloratura and leads the troupe into a second song-and-dance number during which Zerbinetta and Harlequin slip off into the bushes.

Back in opera seria land the nymphs are all excited about the arrival of a young god who is lurking on his ship somewhere offstage. Then he appears on a rock but only the audience can see him so when he sings he is talking to himself not to the nymphs nor to Ariadne. It is Bacchus in person. So I got away from Circe he sings. Whew! that was a close one.

Ariadne wakes up. It's Theseus! she cries. No it isn't Theseus she cries again. It's a messenger. What a stunning young girl says Bacchus. Is that cave your place? Will you take me in? Who are you? What's going on? I'm not very strong in the head says Ariadne. I know who you are she says getting on to her favourite pitch you're Hermes the guy who will take me to the happy land. Not so you've got it wrong says Bacchus. I don't want you to die no how. Contrariwise. I'm jolly well going to die just the same says Ariadne breathing rather heavily.

At this point the sky comes down and surrounds Bacchus and Ariadne to the exclusion of all else. Has she died? Yes? No? Probably not, because Bacchus kisses her and she likes it. You're magic! she says. All my troubles have fallen away. I am full of godlike yeast and I love you says Bacchus and Hey Presto! the cave turns into a lovers' bower or maybe a king-size bed. Don't ever let me go says Ariadne. Never will says Bacchus. The nymphs nymph around singing happily and even Echo is now singing simultaneously, not even a bar behind everyone else.

MINUTES FROM START

LOOK OUT FOR

0

The short overture* runs through some of the best tunes in the show including the Composer's Ode to St Cecilia and what will become the big Bacchus/ Ariadne duet. It is quick, light and easy on the ear.

2: *Mein Herr Haushofmeister!*

The Music Director kicks up hell (in recitatif) to the Major-Domo (who talks). He gets nowhere. This novel idea of *Spiel/ Sing* at the same time comes off a treat.* 2

12: *Du, Venus' Sohn*

Backstage there are tantrums: Zerbinetta explodes in a strange form of recitatif accompanied by a piano. The Composer is reeling under the shock of finding out that his [her? see below: Ed.] opera is going to be debased by association with a burlesque show. So far the recitatif has had a clever but scrappy accompaniment. Now we have a set piece as the Composer's rage is interrupted by inspiration. And it is not a bad inspiration – a sweet song* to Venus but with gaps in 12
it through which he la-las his way adroitly.

26: *Sie hält ihn für den Todesgott*

Order, counter-order, disorder as the bad news about the simultaneous performance rolls in. There is a lot of talk backstage, not much of it practical. We have the impression we are listening to a play, with some of the lines sung and all of them pointed rather brilliantly. Out of all this chatter, and when he should be cutting the score, the Composer explains the vision of beauty he sees in the Ariadne story in a noble (but interrupted) short aria.* 26

30: *Ein Augenblick ist wenig*

Zerbinetta takes off the motley. She is not what she would seem to be on stage. Suddenly we have a love duet** of searing intensity between the Composer 30
and now romantic Zerbinetta. [It's beautiful but why isn't he cutting the show? Ed.]

35: *Sein wir wieder gut*

The Music Director who is desperately trying to get the show on has to listen to an ode to St Cecilia (we heard the tune in the overture) from the Composer. It is one of the high piercing flights of 35
song** that Strauss does so brilliantly (to a Rakhmaninov-style accompaniment). The Composer has decided he will try and make a go of it.

The Opera

After an inconsiderable overture and some introduct-

ory hellos telling us Ariadne is really sad, we come to a
5: *Ach, wir sind es eingewöhnet* beguiling trio* for a Naiad, a Dryad and an echo 5
chamber. But the echo chamber is alive and therefore
able to adjust her echo-time to suit Strauss's requirements. Always happy to write for three female voices,
he gives us a piece that is really nice in its quiet soothing way.

Ariadne is sad and is also a psychiatric case, prob-
7: *Wo war ich?* ably a manic depressive. She sings so beautifully** 7
that she wins the sympathy of the troupe of com-
edians who are observing her from the wings. The accompaniment is light but full of interest.
Adventurous solo instruments have a lot to say, especially a viola, not in the least reprehensible, also a
cello, a horn and a bassoon, as well as other
woodwinds.

Harlequin, a decent soul, tries to persuade Ariadne
to take an interest in the matter of staying alive. He
18: *Lieben, Hassen, Hoffen, Zagen* does this in three neat verses* set as a pastiche of 18
music of an earlier age (Mozart?) and Echo echoes on,
this time without words, only oo-ahs.

20: *Es gibt ein Reich* Ariadne is on about death again.* But this time she 20
has a vision of leaving her body behind and trekking
off, soul only, to the happy land with Hermes. It
would be hard to take more than a clinical interest in
the mental problems of this poor lady (we have known
her for only a few minutes) were it not for her song-
power, especially a superb closing burst of melody**
with which she looks forward to the afterlife. She is
assisted (unusually) by a harmonium. The aria so far
has been Strauss in his semi-classical mode, but in
this last surge he unleashes all his romantic fire power
and stuns us.

The good-hearted comedians come on doing a
26: *Die Dame gibt mit trübem Sinn* song-and-dance number** in hopes of cheering 26
Ariadne up. This catchy piece starts as if it were an
item in a college sing-song, moves through a phase of
barber's shop quartet and then settles down as a
Bavarian beer-garden number with a lilting oom-pah
accompaniment and a perky little figure repeated over
and over which lives on in the ear. Zerbinetta adds a
fancy descant. Nice one, Richard.

Zerbinetta's big set piece, a recitatif, aria, rondo, all on a big scale.

1. Recitatif. Allow me to help you Madam says
31: *Grossmächtige Prinzessin* Zerbinetta in a long recitatif,* all of it accompanied by 31
the piano with some of the more adventurous members of the orchestra joining in from time to time. One feels that Strauss is trying to show what can be done to bring alive old-style recitatif in twentieth-century musical language and the answer is quite a lot. But Strauss was evidently not convinced by the results for he never tried it again.

34: *Noch glaub ich dem* 2. Aria,** and a lovely one in two parts or maybe 34
two ariettas. Now Strauss is not trying to prove anything, just writing a good piece. Zerbinetta debates the pluses and minuses of lifelong love for one man.

36: *So war es mit Pagliazzo* 3. Gymnastics for high soprano.* Just see what I 36
can do. A sequence of strenuous coloratura fireworks (high E) – mighty spectacular and a hundred years earlier would have stunned any opera audience. But here they seem out of time, out of character and out of place. If Strauss had had the pianist play Chopin's Minute Waltz at this point it would have been just as relevant and a little shorter. A star only for brilliant perversity.

38: *Als ein Gott* 4. The Rondo* (three verses each starting with the 38
same first line). We are back to good sense and a good singable number. Zerbinetta has had satisfaction from a number of lovers. Look out especially for a nice solo cello towards the end and the final very high note once again.

44: *Eine Störrische zu trösten* Another knockabout number** but without the 44
verve of the first one until it breaks into fast waltz time. Look out for Zerbinetta's vocal cascade just before the romp begins, the rolling piano accompaniment and the really well-worked-up-to climax and die-away end. The plot of this little piece is mainly to do with Zerbinetta getting off with Harlequin whilst still giving the other three cause for hope.

The nymphs make a big fuss over the impending arrival of Bacchus. Echo all over the place. Ear-filling
50: *Ein schönes Wunder!* three-part singing** but the ear does get pretty full 50
rather quickly for it goes on in much the same way for some time.

54: *Circe, kansst du mich hören?* The arrival of Bacchus.* He has escaped from 54
Circe but seems bugged by his experience with her and can sing of little else. The nymphs sing a sort of Hymn of Welcome in two bursts, very agreeable.* They are enchanted by his song, but they enchant easy for Bacchus' opening bursts are quite the least sympathetic bit of all his music, shouting, as he does, like a sergeant major. But a great musical moment comes when Ariadne recognizes him for what he is, not Theseus, but a lusty young god of the best type, ideally suited to carry her off to her death. This is rather glorious.

The Ariadne/Bacchus duet.

61: *Du schönes Wesen!* 1. Bacchus sings to Ariadne,** much more 61
sweetly now but foolishly, for he thinks Ariadne is out to cast spells on him, as did Circe. Ariadne replies even more sweetly with a soft woodwind accompaniment. She is still totally confused.

2. Ariadne tells what it's like in the happy land
67: *Ich weiss, so ist es dort* beyond the grave.* A hint of the icicle chords that go 67
with the silver rose in *Rosenkavalier*. Bacchus replies in a stalwart fashion. He advises her strongly not to die. But she is dying.

71: *Ich sage dir* 3. They sing together.** (The tune was heard in 71
the overture.) Bacchus has fallen in love with Ariadne! [In ten minutes flat: Ed.] He kisses her. She shows glimmers of sanity. Are all her troubles behind her? Is she perhaps dead already and into the happy land with this nice chap? (Is he a magician?) No great bursts of musical joy. They sound passionate but tense and worried. Shades of the psychiatric ward still hang around.

4. Now true happiness breaks in. All worries melt away and they sing like prisoners who have escaped
73: *Gibt es kein Hinüber?* from darkness,*** and all of this over a strenuously 73
happy mainly string backing with runs on the piano and chords on the harp.

The nymphs say How Nice! to the tune of their hymn of welcome. Echo seems to have lost some of her echo power. Bacchus and Ariadne are thoroughly satisfied with each other, Zerbinetta chucks in a bromide about one lover being as good as the next, the orchestra heaves and lurches in a dreamy fashion towards the concluding chords (celeste, piano and harps) and the opera is over.

NOTES

Ariadne on Naxos	Richard Strauss' sixth opera
First night	
original version (I)	Hoftheater (Kleines Haus) Stuttgart, 25 October 1912
revised version (II)	Hofoper Vienna, 4 October 1916
Reception (I)	Mixed, which means bad
Reception (II)	Much better
Libretto	Hofmannsthal
Source	Original: the Opera section based on scraps of Greek mythology

NEWS AND GOSSIP

As Strauss and Hofmannsthal basked in the success of *Rosenkavalier* they looked at three possible new projects. One was a serious opera which became *Frau ohne Schatten*. One was to put incidental music and choruses to a Molière play for Max Reinhardt. This would be by way of a thank you for rescuing *Rosenkavalier*. The third was for a short funny, a serious treatment of the Ariadne myth invaded by a troupe of strolling players. As time went on the second and third got combined. At the end of the Molière play (it was *Le Bourgeois Gentilhomme)* the host figure would call for some in-house entertainment and the Ariadne project would be it. As they worked towards the finish they found that the pit in Reinhardt's Berlin theatre was too small even for Strauss' chamber orchestra (36 players, short commons for a man who was used to writing for three times that number). So they looked around and got Reinhardt to take his Berlin company to Stuttgart where a new theatre was being opened. The resident company was not pleased, neither was the first-night audience who became restive and then noisy. The critics did not dare to be anything but respectful, but the two pros Hofmannsthal and Strauss knew that they had got a turkey on their hands. For one thing it was much too long, for another no house would want to put on a show that needed both an acting company and an opera company, and for a third the audience clearly hated it. So they scrapped *Ariadne I* and four years later produced *Ariadne II* with no Molière play and a prologue instead, also several major changes to the opera section. This time, perhaps because there was a war on and nothing much else, it was a big success. *Ariadne* is played from time to time in most opera houses but it lies low in the Strauss popularity stakes.

COMMENT

When Hofmannsthal and Strauss first thought of putting two operas on the stage at the same time the idea must have seemed hilarious. And as they hatched the scheme they saw a wonderful chance to send up the ignorant snobs who sponsored the arts and to be wickedly satirical about the tantrums and vanities of their theatrical friends and acquaintances. What a scream it would be to have a Greek tragic heroine bumping into Frankie Howerd. In the cold light of day and certainly after the first night it can't have seemed such a good idea and eighty years later it still doesn't.

Clearly the second version was better than the first, but as drama the piece was past redemption. The new prologue has only one character of interest – the Composer – the others being no more than caricatures of backstage folk whose vanity is made the target for schoolboy humour. The opera itself is equally dim since there is no plot, only an arrival. Ariadne deserted by Theseus is in despair and waits only for Hermes the messenger of the gods to take her to Hades. But instead of Hermes, Bacchus arrives and falls in love with her and she with him. That's all folks, that is absolutely the entire plot of the serious bit of *Ariadne*. But wait, it's going to be farced up by the injection of the Crazy Gang dell'arte. Alas, this doesn't work either. There is no interaction between Ariadne and the pranksters whatsoever. They don't cheer her up. She hates them. Harlequin doesn't fall in love with her. Zerbinetta doesn't seduce Bacchus. Nothing happens. Nothing at all. We all have our off days and Hugo von Hofmannsthal made a real pig's ear of it this time.

The tragedy of it is that Strauss never wrote better music in all his life and to hear such wonderful numbers wasted on this crackpot piece is a real pain. The prologue has good stuff in it but only the Composer's part hits any high spots. His song to Venus, his duet with Zerbinetta and his final version of a mission statement for the Arts Council are full of true passion. He is indeed dedicated to his art and sings nicely too, although why on earth Strauss couldn't have made him a her if he wanted a mezzo voice in the part it's hard to understand. Even a couple of café chauvinists such as Richard and Hugo must surely have known that female composers did exist.

Musically the opera is wonderful. Ariadne longs for death with a mesmeric intensity: we feel that if she goes on much longer she will suffer death by singing, so much of her heart does she put into it. The great duet with Bacchus overwhelms us even before it overwhelms them. (Beecham, a great Strauss supporter in the days when he was not popular, always said that this section of *Ariadne* was the finest music he wrote.) Less moving but a great *tour de force* is Zerbinetta's firecracker piece. Both the Crazy Gang numbers come off with spirit and the waltz is a great goer though it does not alas get a single foot-tap out of Ariadne.

It is, to tell the truth, an enormous relief to have such a small orchestra. Strauss uses it quite brilliantly with lots of new sounds coming from the strings (who have a much better showing than in his big-band works). There is still a huge contribution from the woodwind, often acting as soloists, and there are new sounds for opera such as the cool clear accompaniment from the piano and the dusky tones of the harmonium. One wonders whether *Rosenkavalier* would perhaps have gone even better if the orchestra had been cut to *Ariadne*'s size. After all he had fired one of the noisiest salvos ever with *Elektra*. Perhaps he was beginning to realize how nice it was for the audience to hear the singers.

I would never advise anyone not to go to any opera but I would not encourage any but the very Strauss-prone to go to *Ariadne*. It's a piece that's much better heard than seen. What your imagination conjures up as you listen to the wonderful second half may not have anything to do with the story but believe me it can only be better than what goes on on the stage. A gamma.

Attila

Visigothic drama

Verdi

The one with lots of Goths and Vandals where the Christians with help from above lick the Druids hollow and which ends with the quickest death in all opera.

CAST

Attila, Führer of the Huns	Bass
Uldino, Attila's senior slave	Tenor
Ezio (Aetius), a Roman general	Baritone
Foresto, leader of the refugees from Aquileia	Tenor
Odabella, daughter of dead Lord of Aquileia, Foresto's fiancée	Soprano
Leone, Christian Bishop of Rome	Bass

3 acts, 1/2 intervals: running time 1 hr 50 mins

STORY

Prologue Sc 1 The main square of Aquileia, a city occupied and sacked by the Goths etc.

We are in the Dark Ages in the midst of Huns, Goths, Ostrogoths, Herulians, Visigoths and also Romans who are not doing so well just now. The Roman town of Aquileia is a smoking ruin and Huns etc. exult: Attila gloats. Uldino comes on with a platoon of Roman ATS now prisoners. Attila, the archetypal chauvinist amused at the bizarre sight of women warriors, says what can I do for you? Gimme your sword says platoon commander Odabella secretly hoping to stick it into him when appropriate: he gives it.

Ezio comes on, envoy for the Romans: he proposes a disgraceful secret deal: international affairs are very fluid he says: give me Italy – you have the rest of the world. No sir you are a treacherous dog says Attila. OK so now as envoy I tell you that Rome will fight to the death says Ezio.

Prologue Sc 2 Venice before it was built: with huts etc. on stilts

Amphibious hermits creep out of their huts to praise God. A stormy morning. Foresto leading a bunch of refugees from Aquileia arrives by boat and although distracted by the disappearance of his fiancée Odabella asks for planning permission to build a city (Venice to be) on this unpromising site. Everyone thinks it's a great idea. The sun comes out etc.

Act I Sc 1 Moonlight in a wood by Attila's camp near Rome

Odabella thinks about her old Dad who was slaughtered by Attila: she sees his face in the clouds but it turns into Foresto for real disguised as a Goth. It's a bad reunion. Foresto accuses Odabella of fraternization. Not so says she: my tactics are modelled on Old Testament Judith: I am here to kill my father's killer. Is that so? says Foresto, great news. Ecstatic embraces etc.

Act I Sc 2 Attila's tent

Attila tells Uldino of his bad dream – an elderly bearded person accosts him saying 'Get off Attila you can push humans around but not gods. Rome is off limits for you.' Attila recovers his bottle with difficulty and orders his troops to fall in and sing a chorus to Odin.

Act I Sc 3 A hill behind Attila's camp

A procession of juveniles in white ducks and nighties appears led by priests and an elderly bearded person (Bishop of Rome) singing hymns saying get off Attila you can push humans around etc. It's the man in my dream says Attila. Morale is very low, especially on seeing Saints Peter and Paul in the sky unchristianly warlike with flaming swords etc., barring the way to Rome. Attila keels over in psychological shock. The Huns etc. he think he's lost his marbles. Christians sing happily on.

Act II Sc 1 The Roman camp

Ezio is mad because the inexperienced youthful Emperor has decreed peace with Huns. Ezio is to report back to him forthwith. He thinks the Emperor fears his own army (mutinous) more than the Huns: he thinks Rome is going to dogs. Foresto brings an invite from Attila to a party: says why not attack the Huns when they're half smashed at the party? I'll arrange the signal. Good idea says Ezio.

Act II Sc 2 Attila's camp set up for feast

Attila receives guest Ezio and his retinue (not the party just a social call): there is a lot of singing but the Druids forbode: Attila says naff off you dreary sods – but a sudden whirlwind blows out the candles: all are daunted. Ezio again raises his world-sharing deal: Attila is still not interested. Foresto tells Odabella that Uldino will shortly offer Attila poisoned wine. The storm abates.

Attila is about to scoff the wine. Hold it says Odabella – it's deadly (she wants the satisfaction of murdering him personally herself). Who done this? cries Attila: I done it says Foresto (he put Uldino up to it). I'll kill you says Attila. O no please let me do it says Odabella (a trick). What a spunky little woman says Attila: yes sure you can and you can marry me as well. Odabella tells Foresto to get out while the going's good. Let's get after the Romans sings everyone.

Act III Sc 1 The wood as in Act I

Foresto (fool) really believes Odabella will marry Attila. Uldino tells him the bridal procession is under way. Ezio appears to say that everything is ready for action. Odabella scampers on in bridal disarray: I couldn't stand the thought of that Attila says she: Foresto honey I love you. It's a bit late says Foresto, you went off with big A. Big A. runs on in person in pursuit of his disappearing bride. Oho says he what have we here: plotting and scheming no doubt.

He is interrupted by loud noises of mayhem from his camp: the Romans are at it. Attila your number's up says Ezio: Attila you're a real nasty says Foresto: Attila you killed my father says Odabella and sticks a sword through him. He dies with unoperatic haste.

MINUTES FROM START

LOOK OUT FOR

Prologue Sc 1

6: *Viva il re*

The usual choral start: not immediately inspired, but two nice passages, the second* the better (things perk up when Attila addresses the troops). 6

9: *Allor' che i forti corrono*

Odabella has two belligerent solos* joined for a little duetting by Attila and later the chorus: a good vigorous melodic line: attractive. 9

17: *Tardo per gli anni*

The Ezio/Attila duet:* Ezio makes his proposition in four-square style: Attila's negative response is in the minor, a surprisingly mild reproof, the final confrontation is jaunty and confident on both sides. 17

Prologue Sc 2

24: *Qual notte!*

Some good weather (receding storm) and sunrise stuff from the orchestra and effective holy choruses (one lot off stage).* 24

Foresto's first outing: two solos, the first conven-

tional but sound, whingeing about Odabella being
35: *Cara patria* captured, the second* (the better) urging his fol- 35
lowers to make their home in the frightful swamp in which the scene is set.

Act I Sc 1

The opening scene is a musical delight: some unusual chromatics in the prelude: a light setting for Odabel-
0: *Liberamente or piangi* la's lovely romanza,** flutes and harp fluttering 0
around.

8: *Sì, quell' io son* The lengthy melodious affecting duet** between 8
Odabella and Foresto. He: you faithless woman; she: what on earth are you talking about? Then expla-
12: *Oh, t'inebria nell' amplesso* nations leading to a blissful rapid fire cabaletta.** 12
Bravo!

Act I Sc 2

16: *Mentre gonfiarsi l'anima* Attila's bad dream* – slow to start, overcome with 16
panic at the memory, recovering himself in a short oom-pah then defiant in a final (repeated) stanza in every way fit for a fighting general.

Act I Sc 3

Suddenly what is shaping up to be a pretty ornery military finale is interrupted by distant voices (Verdi very prone to employ offstagers) and a magic spell is
21: *Vieni, le menti visita* cast*** – the contrasting choruses – the old man of the 21
dream comes alive, the Christians singing sweetly, Attila's men quite foxed, Attila himself repeating over and over 'This thing is bigger than me'. Original, inspired and quite wonderful.

Act II Sc 1

Ezio has a nice solo deploring the fact that Rome is
2: *Dagli immortali vertici* not what it used to be.* 2

And again when he decides to disobey orders and
7: *È gettata la mia sorte* fight.* He sings this over twice to make sure we know 7
he means it.

Act II Sc 2

9: *Del ciel' l'immensa vôlta* A more-than-usually tuneful drinking chorus,* fol- 9
lowed by gloomy Druids, ominous priestesses, a
15: *Lo spirto de' monti* storm and into another most unusual pre-finale:*** 15
the chorus at first chuntering on sotto voce about the weather with Ezio saying to Attila how about a deal now? and Attila replying: Not on your life. Then Foresto to Odabella: All will be OK Attila's going to be poisoned. Odabella: Not if I can help it. Uldino:

Pretty scary job this poisoning. Then suddenly the most glorious salute to better weather by the
18: *L'orrenda, procella* chorus.*** 18

High dramatics as the non-poisoning takes place
21: *Oh, miei prodi!* and a vigorous final run** to the tape (Attila: I'm go- 21
ing to get married, Odabella: Hop it quick Foresto, Foresto: You double-crossing bitch, Ezio: I'll get you tomorrow Attila, Uldino: Who grassed on me?).

Act III

An agreeable but rather dim solo from Foresto is fol-
5: *Che più s'indugia?* lowed by an oom-pah appearance by Ezio* whilst we 5
have yet another soft offstage bridal chorus with Foresto and Ezio exclaiming above it.

8: *Te sol, quest' anima* A pretty harp-accompanied trio* (Odabella: I love 8
you, Foresto: I don't believe it, Ezio: let's get moving).

12: *Scellerati!* A good dramatic quartet** (Attila: You bastards, 12
Odabella: You killed my father, Foresto: I'm going to kill you, Ezio: You've got it coming to you) followed by a brief final chorus and the quickest death in all opera.

NOTES

Attila	Verdi's ninth opera
First night	Fenice Theatre, Venice, 17 March 1846
Reception	Verdi wrote that it was 'a fair enough success. The applause and the calls were too much for a poor sick man (see below). Perhaps it was not completely understood.... My friends would say that this is the best of my operas. The public question that. I say it is not inferior to any of the others.'
Libretto	Solera/Piave (see below)
Source	A German play by one Werner

NEWS AND GOSSIP

Verdi approached first Piave as his librettist (*Ernani*, *I Due Foscari*), but after working with him on two further operas and after the lapse of two years he seemed to get fed up with him and transferred the piece to Solera (*Nabucco*, *Lombardi*, *Giovanna d'Arco*). Solera had to go absent to Spain and so Verdi went back to Piave who finished the job. Solera didn't like the result one bit and wrote a bitchy letter to Verdi saying that Verdi was the only person who had managed to persuade him that he was not cut out to be a librettist.

The first night was billed for New Year's Eve 1845, but rehearsals got behind schedule and when Verdi became ill with a gippy tummy it was postponed. Never one for understatement, Verdi wrote that he finished it 'in an almost dying condition'. *Attila* quickly penetrated the opera houses of Europe and was much played until it was submerged by Verdi's top three (*Rig*, *Trov*, *Trav*). It disappeared from the repertory by the end of the century until it was resurrected by Giulini at Venice in 1951. Now quite popular again. See below.

COMMENT

When *Attila* was revived at Covent Garden in 1989 it brought the house down. Critics marvelled that such a fine work had been so long neglected. It was partly due to this 'discovery' that the plan to perform all of Verdi's operas at the Royal Opera House over three years was put in place. We have to admit that *Attila* is not in truth all that good a work. The plot is a pretty creaky old thing, Attila himself a simple military soul, a sort of sexually liberated Monty, Ezio hard to read, Foresto a fool and Odabella the sort of amazon found only in opera (Brünnhilde). Together their motivation ebbs and flows uncertainly. Why is Foresto so crazily suspicious? Is Ezio going to march on Rome or isn't he? And why on earth did Uldino allow himself to be persuaded to try to poison Attila? But if the story is weak the situations are strong and the Risorgimento element in Ezio's attempted deal, the founding of Venice and the victory of Christ over Odin (Christians 3 – Druids 0) must have given the piece a flying start. Most of the music is strong vigorous early Verdi, the best yet, choruses not too long and most of them (especially when offstage) are mighty effective. Odabella's romanza in Act I is quite lovely, the musical sunrise, storms etc. get reasonably near to nature, the Act I finale is pure magic and the Act II finale has an inspired and sustained flow of Verdi's top quality ideas. *Attila*, then, makes a rousing evening in the theatre, for if we have to put up with the Goths, Druids, Amazons, Christian maidens and other characters not too familiar in real life, the music we get in exchange from the young Verdi is good stuff – tuneful, forceful and altogether satisfactory. But only a beta.

Un Ballo in Maschera (A Masked Ball)

Historical tragedy

Verdi

The one where a gypsy tells the King that the next man he shakes hands with will murder him, so he shakes hands with his best friend who duly murders him.

CAST

Verdi/ Somma	*Auber/ Scribe (see NOTES)*	
Riccardo, Earl of Warwick, Governor of Boston	**Gustavus III,** King of Sweden	Tenor
Renato, a Creole, his secretary	**Anckarstroem**	Baritone
Amelia, Renato's wife	**Amelia**	Soprano
Ulrica, a gypsy	**Arvidson**	Contralto
Oscar, a page	**Oskar**	Soprano
Samuel, a conspirator	**Count Ribbing**	Bass
Tom, ditto	**Count Horn**	Bass
Silvano, a sailor	**Cristian**	Baritone
A judge, servants etc.		

3 acts: running time 2 hrs 10 mins

STORY

Act I Sc 1 A hall in the Governor's house

We are (surprise surprise – see NOTES) in Colonial Boston. Richard Earl of Warwick (Riccardo) holds his morning assembly: his page Oscar runs over the invitation list for a ball: he reaches the name 'Amelia'. Riccardo blushes, simpers, clearly smitten: Amelia's husband Renato enters: Riccardo fears he suspects but no: he tells of an assassination plot: Riccardo is relieved, says he is protected by the love of God and his subjects and therefore does not require security men.

The Chief Justice comes in: he wants to banish an illegal immigrant gypsy woman. Page Oscar stands up for human rights: he wants her to stay: I know says Riccardo let's dress up as fishermen and go to her cave and get first-hand evidence; what a lark. (Conspirators Sam 'n' Tom present in the crowd take note.)

Act I Sc 2 Ulrica's cave

We hear witchcraft stuff from Ulrica: Riccardo arrives: he is pretty sceptical: simpleton Silvano a sailor on the Royal Yacht asks Ulrica what's in store for me? Riches says she. Prankster Riccardo writes out a cheque and slips it into Silvano's pocket. God bugger me sideways says Silvano she was right.

Amelia arrives seeking a cure for her guilty love for Riccardo (all the others slink off). Ulrica says she must go to get a herb growing in the frightful spooky graveyard: Riccardo overhears and decides to meet her there: exit Amelia. Riccardo asks to have his fortune told: you will be killed by the first guy whose hand you shake says Ulrica: Renato enters and shakes hands: Ho ho ho laughs Riccardo he's my best friend what a joke [will opera folk never learn prophecies are always fulfilled: Ed.]. Sam 'n' Tom that ludicrous pair are lurking in the crowd and they at least believe it.

Act II A graveyard outside Boston

Amelia is herb-hunting in the scary graveyard place: she says her midnight prayers: she hallucinates but not seriously: but lo! It is Riccardo: he loves her: he says so: after an unconvincing attempt at the rebuff virtuous she admits she loves him: both are blissful but guilty. A stranger approaches: she pulls down her veil: it's Renato: he tells Riccardo there are some hit men down the road who plan to kill him: Riccardo is loth to leave Amelia: she threatens to unveil herself unless he runs for it: Riccardo asks Renato to give safe conduct to the anonymous veiled woman back to city limits.

Tom 'n' Sam and their gang arrive: they are disappointed to find no Riccardo only Renato: the villains demand that Amelia unveil: Renato draws his sword: Amelia to avert hostilities drops her veil: Sam 'n' Tom think it very funny that Renato has a secret assignation with his own wife: Renato goes through shock anger then decision – he'll get his revenge on his double-crossing boss. He makes a date with Sam 'n' Tom for next morning. All go home.

Act III Sc 1 Renato's study

Renato has strong views about adultery and tells Amelia she must die: she asks to see her son before her execution: she is shut in a cupboard to await his arrival. Sam 'n' Tom arrive: Renato says he would like to join their gang but he himself must be allowed to kill Riccardo. That is not acceptable: all three want to do it: they decide to draw lots: Amelia (escaped from the cupboard?) enters to say Oscar is at the door with an invitation from Riccardo to the ball: Amelia is forced to conduct a raffle: Renato wins the role of murderer. Oscar comes in: he goes on about the masked ball: perfect, think the plotters, it suits us very well, we'll go.

Act III Sc 2 Riccardo's study separated strangely enough from the ballroom by a curtain

Riccardo, a decent chap and honourable Governor, signs a document despatching Renato and Amelia to London. It is a big sacrifice. But now he feels comfortable. Oscar brings a note from Amelia saying look out they're going to slaughter you at the ball. Pah! says Riccardo I'm not chicken. A curtain is pulled and lo! the ballroom is full of fancy guests: the band is playing and all. No one has the faintest who anyone else is owing to the masks [unlikely but persistent opera convention: Ed.].

Renato bullies Oscar who grasses on Riccardo being gone on Amelia. He's the one with the pink ribbon he says. Riccardo has a tête-à-tête with Amelia: he tells her he has fixed air tickets for Renato and herself to London: they say tearful farewells: but boom! Renato springs on and stabs Riccardo. Shock horror: Renato is unmasked: the dying Riccardo asserts Amelia is pure as driven snow, and hands the London letter to Renato (struck with guilt) thus proving his nobility which is acknowledged by one and all as they sadly watch him expire.

MINUTES FROM START

LOOK OUT FOR

Act I Sc 1

Ballo starts strongly: a powerful prelude:* opening
mysteriously: a fuguetta: a sweeping melody: a coda.
(Echoes of the main tune run through the opening
scene.) A dawn chorus of chaps [officers, nobles?
How many of these in Boston in 1690?: Ed.]: a good
4: *Posa in pace* curtain-raiser.* Riccardo enters to a burst of pomp, 4
sees the name Amelia on the invitation list and moves
8: *La rivedrà nell'estasi* into his first tuneful cavatina,** repeating his lines 4
over a chorus of chuntering chaps. Very nice.

Oscar's cavatina in defence of Ulrica: finishes very
16: *Volta la terrea* strong.** 16

Riccardo goes mad: let's have a lark: let's visit
Ulrica's cave dressed as fishermen! And he bursts
20: *Dunque, signori, aspettovi* into a galop*** that leads to an ensemble that antici- 20
pates the wilder moments of Offenbach. Marvel-
lously cabaletted and truncated in a racing finish.

Act I Sc 2

37: *Consentimi, O Signore* — After a great deal of gypsy stuff – atmospheric,
spooky but not terrific – we get a sparky trio** (Ame- 37
lia: God send me enough bottle to cope with this love thing, Ulrica: Try my medicine and you will soon be OK, Riccardo: I'm going to tail you wherever you go).

40: *Di' tu se fedele* — Riccardo's canzone,* like a Gondoliers' barcarolle 40
rocking and swaying gently through smooth and rough water (he pretends he is a ship) mild as milk but easy on the ear.

46: *È scherzo od e follia* — The quintet*** of reaction to Ulrica's prophecy: 46
Riccardo laughs at her gloomy forecast, Ulrica points the finger at Sam and Tom who rumble on in the bass, Oscar panics about what may happen. The solo contributions come together and the whole thing begins to swing along in a most beguiling fashion.

48: *O figlio d'Inghilterra* — The finale** ends with a big Aida-like four-square 48
chorus (big drum and all) from which various soloists swing out in the liveliest manner and with many changes of speed, mood and rhythm, we reach a bang bang finish.

Act II

2: *Ecco l'orrido campo* — Amelia's vigil of penitence and terror: a long and
varied solo* ending in an impassioned prayer to the 2
Almighty to have mercy on her.

9: *Teco io sto* — The very fine duet*** between Riccardo and Ame- 9
lia: first, breathless excitement of this strange meeting then some tuneful debate about marital fidelity then the challenge 'Do you love me' and the answer 'I do', followed by a few moments of dreamy reflection, finally an orgy of ecstatic rejoicing with an almost Wagnerian climax on Amelia's repeat of the vital words I love you. Then it calms down emotionally a little but speeds up in tempo to the end. Ten minutes. Great.

19: *Ahimè! S'appressa alcun!* — Fast, breathless and urgent, the very effective
scene where Renato surprises the lovers* (Amelia 19
veiled and unrecognized); both urge Riccardo to push off before the dread conspirators get him – wonderful theatre music.

24: *Seguitemi* — And now for something entirely new: the mocking
chorus*** of Sam, Tom and others as Amelia reveals 24
herself to be Renato's wife: they continue to mock

under the duet of agony between Renato (betrayed) and Amelia (overwhelmed with shame) – an astonishing conjunction: diminuendo ending as all parties make to go back to the city. A *tour de force*.

Act III Sc 1

Amelia's plea to see her son before her husband kills
2: *Morrò, ma prima* her – affecting final high soprano stuff.* 2
9: *Eri bu che macchiavi* Renato's aria** in two halves: (1) I'm really disap- 9
pointed in you Riccardo – military backing, the trum-
11: *O dolcezze perdute!* pets punctuating with rat-ti-tats; (2) I'm sorry my 11
delicious Amelia turned out so badly – caressing flute
accompaniment.
16: *Dunque l'onta di tutti* A strange little trio* celebrating the palship of con- 16
spirators (Renato, Sam and Tom) to the accompaniment of harps. Followed by the intensely dramatic drawing of names leading to the final very lively quar-
19: *Il mio nome!* tet*** – Renato: It's me, hooray!, Amelia: They're 19
going to kill Riccardo, Tom and Sam: We are going to get even with him.
22: *Ah! di che fulgor* Another good ensemble, this time a quintet* 22
started off by the innocent Oscar hyping up the proposed ball in a debonair opening stanza, but soon joined by Renato (darkly planning the murder), Amelia (What a pity I drew the wrong name), Sam and Tom (Masked ball – perfect: just what we wanted) – all meeting in a pacey conclusion.

Act III Sc 2

26: *Ma se m'è forza perderti* Riccardo's aria of renunciation: noble and affecting:* 26
ends with his cry of joy at the thought of seeing Ame-
30: *Sì, rivederti* lia at the ball.** 30
The brass section gives the ballroom a big hello and we are into dance music that forms the background to almost the whole scene up to the death. The effect of the plotters plotting above this is weird, but Oscar's
33: *Saper vorreste* coy little aria* stops the ballroom band for a while. 33
But it starts again and even the fraught encounter between Riccardo and Amelia is played over a finicky little fiddle dance tune and only when they get going
38: *T'amo, sì t'amo* in a passionate duet** do they overwhelm it. But it 38
comes back *again*.

The last scene from the stabbing to the end is both original and mighty effective: dying Riccardo has a last aria: Amelia's virtue is unspotted and just look at

43: *O rimorsi dell'amor* this letter. Shock horror trio follows** – Oscar: Oh 43
my God how awful, Amelia: My love did neither of them any good, Renato: What a ghastly mistake I've made. A whispering chorus that supports Riccardo's dying utterances, then his last adieu and the final shout of grief from one and all.

NOTES

Un Ballo in Maschera	Verdi's twenty-third opera
First night	Teatro Apollo, Rome, 17 February 1859
Reception	Good, but it was hissed when opening in Milan in 1861
Libretto	Somma
Source	Scribe's libretto for an earlier opera by Auber

NEWS AND GOSSIP

Censorship! Censorship! It dogged Verdi's creative life and this time one can see that he was pushing it a bit. The script he picked up from Scribe was based on the story of the assassination of King Gustav III of Sweden at a court ball. In no way, said the Neapolitan censors. Verdi changed the king to duke (the *Rigoletto* trick), Sweden to Pomerania, but it was no good. At this point there was an assassination attempt on Napoleon III, which didn't help. The censors now wanted the royal (ducal) murder off-stage, Amelia to be the king's (duke's) sister not lover, and more. Verdi said he would write them another opera on another subject at another time, and took *Ballo* to Rome. Problems again. Everyone was apparently getting very jumpy about sticking a knife into a royal on stage in case (as with television today) people actually started doing it themselves (and remember, at that date there were plenty of stabbable royals around in Europe). So Verdi and Somma had a brainwave. America! And that is why the King of Sweden was shanghaied and carried off to Boston, Massachusetts and turned into a colonial governor. The result is ludicrous – especially to us Anglo-Saxons. The Earl of Warwick with a Creole chief of staff? Sam and Tom two cotton-pickin' negroes as the chief conspirators? Sam's father's 'castle' confiscated by the Governor? But restored to Sweden, as it is in most sensible productions today, *Ballo* is quite at home. After its big success in Rome, *Ballo* was put on by European houses as soon as they could get it into the schedule. Today, after the famous three (*Rig*, *Trov* and *Trav*), it is as often performed as any other of the popular Verdis.

COMMENT

Ballo has a pulse like a cannon. The plot surges along from disaster to disaster, mercifully with no ballets, no longueurs and no hanging about, no golden memories, no thoughts on the nature of love and only brief invocations to the Almighty. The story is clear, credible and compelling (at least when transferred from the American colonies back to Sweden). The characters are not so real as in *Traviata*, but as types they are real enough for us to feel and fear for them. Oscar, perhaps, is a stage conceit (perky young male impersonator pages are not often met in real life) and Sam and Tom are only risible because they aren't Swedish counts, but Riccardo is a genuine sort, one in a long line of public heroes whose duty conflicts with his love life, Amelia in unremitting panic is touching and Renato is a man who does what a man has to do. The drama of the story is matched by a quite splendid score which also drives the show along with calculated precision towards the final tragedy. There is not a single dud number and there is a great deal that is quite new to opera: Riccardo's dizzy lead off into the quasi-Offenbach ensemble, the Aida-like chorus in the finale to Act I, the abrupt changes of mood in the great duet between Riccardo and Amelia in Act II, the mocking chorus beneath the agony of Renato's recognition of his wife as Riccardo's lover and above all the macabre drama leading up to the assassination played over the perpetuum mobile of mincingly irrelevant dance music. *Ballo* is a rattling good yarn: and if it does not bring a tear to the eye and a wrench to the heart, as does *Traviata*, it continually delights and amazes us with the power and ingenuity of its score. Certainly an alpha.

The Barber of Seville

Knock-about comedy

(Il barbiere di Siviglia)

Rossini

The one where Figaro's here, Figaro's there and Figaro's helping Count Almaviva to abduct Rosina from her nasty old guardian Doctor Bartolo.

CAST

Figaro, a barber	Baritone
Count Almaviva ('Lindoro'), travelling nobleman	Tenor
Dr Bartolo, disagreeable elderly bachelor	Bass
Rosina, ward of Dr Bartolo	Mezzo (but see NOTES)
Don Basilio, a singing teacher	Bass
Berta, Rosina's governess	Soprano
Fiorello, the Count's servant (soon disappears)	Bass
Ambrogio, servant to the doctor	Bass

2 acts (first very long): running time 2 hrs 15 mins

STORY

Act I Sc 1 Outside Bartolo's house

We are in Seville Spain in the late eighteenth century. Count Almaviva has fallen for Rosina (although in true operatic style he has never met her, only gazed). He organizes a dawn serenade outside her house. The serenade is a flop – no Rosina, despite deafening hubbub as the musicians demand their payoff.

Figaro strolls in on his way to work or rather works which he tells us are multifarious. The Count explains that he is working incognito under alias of 'Lindoro' and enlists Figaro's help in his pursuit of Rosina. Know-all Figaro fills the Count in on details: the lecherous old Doctor Bartolo plans to marry his rich and beautiful ward Rosina.

From her balcony Rosina spots lurking 'Lindoro': she drops a letter from the balcony asking for his C.V. Bartolo observes this but when he goes to pick the letter up it has gone with the wind (Figaro nicked it). Figaro reads it to the Count who has a second try at serenading (this time without orchestral accompaniment). It is a success: Rosina asks for an encore and gets it. So what to do? In exchange for cash up front arch-plotter

Figaro devises a scheme for billeting 'Lindoro' on Bartolo as a drunken soldier: he departs to his barbering.

Act I Sc 2 Inside Bartolo's house

Rosina tells us she is going to get her man come what may. She writes a letter to him to give to Figaro. But Bartolo returns and dresses down Rosina and bad-mouths Figaro (who has hidden). Enter music man Basilio with news: Count Almaviva has been seen in town. The one who is said to fancy Rosina? asks Bartolo. The very same says Basilio. How can we get rid of him? asks Bartolo. Why blacken his character disgrace him says Basilio, and gives full set of instructions how to conduct this matter. No, says Bartolo I've got a better plan – I'll marry her at once and that will settle it. He goes off to draft the marriage contract.

Figaro comes out of hiding: he tells Rosina of Bartolo's nefarious plan, also that 'Lindoro' – the man she fancied from the balcony – loves her. She gives Figaro the letter for 'Lindoro'. Bartolo comes in: with accurate amateur sleuthing he deduces she has been writing a letter. Rosina prevaricates: Bartolo gives her burst of male chauvinism; he says he will lock her up.

Berta admits a drunk cavalryman (it's the Count/'Lindoro'). Bartolo, terrified, tries to throw him out. Rosina comes in: 'Lindoro' insinuates to her that he is the chap she saw under the balcony (thrills for Rosina): slips her a letter. Bartolo claims he has exemption from billeting. He snatches the letter from Rosina (for which she has substituted a laundry list). The Count and Bartolo get physical.

Figaro arrives and says the shindy is so audible that the whole street is out listening: sure enough the local guard arrive to quell the riot and set about arresting 'Lindoro'. But he takes the Captain aside and shows him his ducal birth certificate. The captain pulls his forelock and the act ends with everyone wondering what the hell is going on.

Act II Sc 1 Inside Bartolo's house

Bartolo boils with fury; he thinks 'Lindoro' is a spy sent by Almaviva to watch Rosina. A creepy music-master enters (it's 'Lindoro'/the Count in yet another disguise). He says he is a substitute for Basilio who is indisposed. He gives Bartolo the letter that Rosina sent him saying that Almaviva's mistress has been flashing it around. He proposes to show this letter to Rosina during the music lesson and to humiliate her. Bartolo is delighted. He introduces Rosina and the music lesson begins.

Rosina sings meaningful loverly songs to 'Lindoro' but is interrupted by Bartolo wishing to show off his singing talents. Figaro arrives: he prepares to shave Bartolo. With a view to elopement he obtains the balcony key by strategem: he unlocks the balcony door. Amidst all this business 'Lindoro' proposes to Rosina and is promptly accepted. Then – shock! horror! – enter Don Basilio, fit and well. There are concerted efforts by the Count, Rosina and Figaro to bribe Basilio to feign scarlet fever. They succeed – he departs to nurse his fever in private.

The Count and Rosina plot their elopement whilst Figaro unsuccessfully tries to divert Bartolo. Alas Bartolo smells a rat and explodes with anger. The three beg him not to give himself a heart attack.

Act II Sc 2 Another room in Bartolo's house

Bartolo alone worries himself sick. What are they up to? He sends for Basilio and goes to guard the front door: during his absence Berta chucks in her pennyworth of governessy philosophy. Basilio arrives, Bartolo asks him what about that music teacher? Never clapped eyes on him before says Basilio. Good God, says Bartolo, we'd better get the notary and get wed at once.

Meanwhile he gives Rosina back the letter to 'Lindoro' which he says was obtained from Almaviva's mistress. Rosina thinks 'Lindoro' is not true to her. An orchestral thunderstorm takes place.

Figaro and the Count arrive ready for the elopement. Rosina confronts 'Lindoro' with the letter. 'Lindoro' reveals himself as Count Almaviva – all is forgiven and unbounded joy ensues. They prepare for the elopement but the ladder has gone. But all is not lost – Don Basilio and the notary appear: the latter is forced to conduct the marriage of the would-be elopers at pistol point. Everyone happy except Bartolo. (How he wishes he had not taken the ladder away.)

MINUTES FROM START

LOOK OUT FOR

Act I Sc 1

Certainly the best known and equally certainly one of
0: the top two or three Rossini overtures,*** a form 0
which he pioneered and made his very own. And
there's been no better way of starting an opera invented since.

The opening scene with its whispered chorus leads
to the Count's florid (perhaps too florid for today's
3: *Ecco, ridente* tenors and audiences) serenade.* It fails to raise 3
Rosina and ends with the orchestral players im-
6: *Mille grazie mio signore* portuning their employer for more money* (with less 6
formality than they do today).

18: *Largo al factotum* Figaro's job description.*** Figaro here, Figaro 18
there, Figaro all over the world in what must be the
best known and most parodied cavatina in all opera.

The Count, encouraged by Figaro, serenades
27: *Se il mio nome* Rosina in a dreamy canzone.** She encourages him 27
on to a second verse, which is good news for us all.

32: *All'idea di quel metallo* The duet* in which the Count and Figaro cook up 32
the plot to billet 'Lindoro' on Bartolo as a drunken
soldier: a complete scene in itself including Figaro's
37: *Numero Quindici* one-note set of directions to find his shop** and the 37
final chortling reflections on money for the job
39: *Ah, che d'amore* (Figaro) and successful love (Count)** in a finale en- 39
livened by pulsating Rossinian crescendos and
cross-rhythms.

Act I Sc 2

42: *Una voce poco fa* Rosina's almost equally famous cavatina** is written 42
in high bel canto style, the first section andante – al-
most an introduction – but then gaining speed and
animation as she gets vicious about Bartolo and ending with some of the best known bits of bravura in the
operatic repertory.

52: *La calunnia* Don Basilio's lesson in dirty tricks*** – how to 52
start a rumour and discredit an enemy. He starts sotto
voce and ends with a bang (indeed a colpo di can-
none). A *tour de force*.

'Lindoro' loves R-O-S-I-N-A. She and Figaro en-
60: *Dunque io son* joy a duet** of pure happiness and the anticipation of 60
even more bliss to come with a lot of florid
semi-quavers.

Bartolo comes the heavy with Rosina: she's been
cheating and had better watch it: music of wonderfully pompous bluster with a cabaletta of breakneck
66: *A un dottor della mia sorte* patter.** There is a recurring leitmotif of consider- 66
able menace.

So into the twenty minutes of the finale: drunken
'Lindoro' and angry Bartolo exchange insults and
nearly blows: the room fills with Rosina, Figaro,
Basilio, Berta and then a pack of soldiers: all is in a
fever of musical excitement: barked out exchanges
between the men, snatches of melody: in a moment of
calm there is a magical sextet as Bartolo stands trans-
86: *Freddo ed immobile* fixed with fear*** and so into the hustle and bustle of 86
the final stretto, strongly reminiscent of the Act I

finale of *L'Italiana* (though lacking its disarming lunacy) with everyone's brain quaking, vibrating, shaking with fear and confusion.

Act II Sc 1

The Count as a substitute music teacher for Basilio gets on Bartolo's nerves with unctious good wishes
2: *Pace e gioia* repeated too often for him (and maybe for us).** 2

During the phoney music lesson the lovers sing in an uninhibited fashion about their love whilst Bartolo
7: *Contro un cor* snoozes.** He almost wakes up too soon for them. 7

After a bout of plot-heavy recitatif Basilio appears and in a quintet of medical concern the plotters persuade him he has scarlet fever and should go home to
16: *Don Basilio!* bed:** the insistent 'Buona seras' echo the 'Paces' 16
and 'Gioias' of the opening duet, leading to some sotto voce plotting and a splendid agitato finale as Bartolo in a noisy outburst rumbles at least part of the plot whilst the plotters advise calm, again for medical reasons.

Act II Sc 2

28: *Il vecchiotto cerca moglie* Berta has a little song* (agreeable enough) and there 28
is an orchestral thunderstorm* to cover the movement of the plotters who intend to elope. The Count reveals himself in his true blue-blooded colours to clear up an unfortunate misunderstanding with
36: *Ah! qual colpo inaspettato* Rosina: they are joined in a joyous trio** by Figaro: 36
everything is going to be fine. (But not so fine: the escape ladder has been removed by Bartolo.)

44.30: *Di sì felice innesto* And so the Finaletto,* a brief, cheerful and precise 44.3
farewell salute.

NOTES

The Barber of Seville	Rossini's sixteenth opera
First night	Teatro Argentina, Rome, 20 February 1816
Reception	Everything went wrong: the Count's guitar in the serenade was tuned to a different pitch to the orchestra's: whistles and catcalling: the evening never recovered. But at the next performance – all was well
Libretto	Sterbini

Source — Beaumarchais' Figaro trilogy (the second being *Le Mariage de Figaro*, the third *La Mère Coupable*)

NEWS AND GOSSIP

Mozart's *Figaro* had been premiered in 1786, some thirty years earlier. Thus Mozart's Count and Countess are Rossini's 'Lindoro' and Rosina; Berta is an alias for Mozart's Marcellina; Figaro, Bartolo and Basilio are the same, only considerably younger. The brilliant overture was not bespoke but off the peg: Rossini had used it twice before – for the operas *Aureliano* and *Elisabetta Regina D'Inghilterra*. It is said that Rossini wrote the *Barber* in a fortnight but claims of this sort are like fishing stories about the one that got away – they can never be proved or disproved. There is another fishing story about the *Barber* and the way in which singers were inclined to take over an aria and decorate it to suit their own taste. Rossini is said to have listened to the famous Patti doing her nut in her version of 'Una voce poco fa' and to have observed, 'What a pretty song. I wonder who wrote it?' The part of Rosina was originally written for a mezzo but today is often transposed to allow a high soprano to show off her paces.

The *Barber* took a little time to establish itself as probably the most popular and most performed piece in the whole operatic repertory.

COMMENT

The *Barber* has frequently been written up as the greatest of all comic operas. Beethoven admired it (despite his fury that everyone in Vienna was whistling Rossini's tunes and not his). Verdi thought it 'the most beautiful opera buffa there is' and there are loads of quotes from nineteenth- and twentieth-century critics hyping it up as 'Rossini's masterpiece', 'the model comic opera', etc. This is not quite true. The first act is quite splendid with its succession of all-time hits – Figaro's 'Largo al factotum', Rosina's 'Una voce poco fa', Basilio's scandal song, plus the wonderful Almaviva/Figaro duet and the helter-skelter finale (but not up to the Act I finale of *L'Italiana* either for musical or comic invention). Act II is musically overshadowed by what went before (Act I is twice as long – 90 minutes plus – and has more than twice as many notes as Act II) and depends for its success more upon Beaumarchais than on Rossini. (For all that, properly produced it is always bullet-proof in the opera house.) The twists and turns of the plot divert attention from the lack of substantial music. In the forty-five minutes of Act II there is the gloriously funny medical quartet and the happy Count/Rosina/Figaro trio before the intended elopement – but the rest is recitatif plus a number of agreeable short songs, the music lesson – which is sustained more on dramatic than musical tension – and the brief finaletto. Maybe Rossini inserted the orchestral storm to cover a scene change or a time-lapse, but it is a mild storm as orchestral storms go, with unimpressive lightning and not much thunder. The *Barber* is pure joy as music theatre but don't let the *Barber* fans have you think it is superior to all other Rossini. It isn't, but alpha of course.

Bluebeard's Castle
(A Kékszakállú herceg vára)

Hungarian fairy tale

Bartok

The one where Bluebeard's new bride insists on opening seven doors within his castle, each of which reveals a little more of his bizarre lifestyle.

CAST

Duke Bluebeard (A Kékszakállú herceg)	Baritone
Judith (Judit), his wife	Mezzo

1 act: running time 1 hr

STORY

Interior of Bluebeard's castle: a gloomy chamber with seven doors

We are in Hungarian Fairyland in Grimm time and a fellow slips in from the wings and delivers himself of a prologue which nobody can follow because it is full of metaphysical conundrums and you have only just sat down for Chrissake.

Bluebeard appears with Judith some distance behind. Are you sure you want to leave your folks and come here? asks Bluebeard. There's no central heating you know. Absolutely sure says Judith I love you so don't try to put me off. By the way why are there no windows? And why is there all this red stuff down the walls? [Blood: Ed.] This place needs redecorating Bluebeard my love and I am the one to do it. It's a DIY job. I don't want my castle looking like a Dutch interior says Bluebeard.

Hey what's behind those seven doors asks Judith. Nobody must see what's behind them says Bluebeard. Open them! Let in some fresh air! says Judith. She bangs on the first door and the whole castle moans in a thoroughly frightening manner. What was that? says Judith. This castle must be unhappy. Are you afraid? asks Bluebeard. Give me the keys and we'll unlock the first door says Judith.

Door 1. As Judith opens the door the castle moans again. There is a blood-red rectangle on the wall. I see branding irons, pincers, racks and electrodes says Judith. It is my torture chamber says Bluebeard. How horrible says Judith. Are you afraid? asks Bluebeard. Give me the keys to all the other doors says Judith. I must open them. Why? asks Bluebeard. Because I love you says Judith. OK for No. 2 go ahead says Bluebeard.

Door 2. As it opens all manner of lights flood through the door across the stage. What do you see? asks Bluebeard. Sub-machine guns, sawn-off shot guns, Colt .45s and semtex says Judith. It's my armoury says Bluebeard. Are you afraid? Gimme all the keys says Judith. Judith are you sure you want to see behind these doors? says Bluebeard. Yes I do she says I love you and must know all your secrets. OK here are keys Nos. 3, 4 and 5 says Bluebeard.

Door 3. Yellow light streams out. It's gold! cries Judith. Mountains of gold and of jewels. It's where I keep my ready cash and a few other odds and ends says Bluebeard. But the jewels have bloodstains on them says Judith.

Door 4. As the door is opened all manner of blossom-bearing branches shoot out. It's my secret garden says Bluebeard. It's lovely says Judith looking in but why are there bloodstains on those Iceberg roses?

Door 5. Judith flings open the door and finds a verandah lookout. I can see all your kingdom says Judith. It's all yours my love says Bluebeard. It's lovely but why is that blood-red cloud hanging about? asks Judith.

So that's the end of the show says Bluebeard. Give me a kiss Judith. I want to open the last two doors says Judith. Not possible says Bluebeard. They have a ding-dong. Judith wins. OK one more key says Bluebeard.

Door 6. Judith sees a pool of water. It is made up of tears, tears, tears says Bluebeard. Tell me Bluebeard says Judith about the women you loved before me and give me that last key. I know what I'll find there. Your wives. The tabloids have been saying it for years. You have murdered them. Here's the last key says Bluebeard. My earlier wives await you.

Door 7. As it opens some of the other doors shut. Moonlight shines out of the seventh door. Three earlier wives troop out dressed for a party. Good Lord they're alive! But they look a bit peaky says Judith. Bluebeard kneels before them. Aren't they stunners? he asks. Certainly more beautiful than poor little me says Judith. I found the first one at dawn, the second at noon and the third at sunset says Bluebeard. The fourth I found at midnight – you, Judith, the most beautiful of all. Every night is yours Judith. The wives retire to cell 7. Enough! Enough! cries Judith. Spare me! But Bluebeard goes and fetches her crown and robe and places them on her. Too heavy! she cries, too heavy! She walks through the seventh door bent under the weight of her robes into eternal darkness. It shuts behind her. Bluebeard is left alone.

MINUTES FROM START **LOOK OUT FOR**

2: Low strings creep in under the spoken prelude and 2
we know at once we are in pretty spooky territory.
After the two enter the happy home we hear a figure
4: in the woodwind (low–high–low) which is going to be 4
around a lot and then a walking string bass under the
5: vocal exchanges. Perhaps this is Judith's fear which 5
she keeps saying she hasn't got. It goes on, off and on.
Look out also for the high woodwind discords which
often crop up when blood is mentioned.

Judith is going to redecorate, clear the place up. A
9: *Nedves falát felszáritom* burst of sudden positive melody** makes it sound 9
possible.

Judith tries to open door 1 (bang! bang!) and hears
11: *A te várad* a really nasty noise.* Excitement followed by panic 11
and a lot of meaningful figures on the clarinet which
go on for quite a while.

16: *Hallod? Hallod?* Door 1.** The torture chamber. Excruciating high 16
tremolo on the strings. Ripples up and down on the
xylophone. Bumps and bangs. New figures from the
woodwind (solo clarinet first) just as meaningful as
the first lot.

20: Door 2.* The armoury. A trumpet. Martial sounds 20
from the woodwind. Judith wants to open all the
doors. She sees a stream of light like a river. Blue-
23: *Varam sötét töve reszket* beard sings lyrically about the blood that oozes 23
through his castle walls.

24: Door 3.* Gold. Piles of gold. Sustained scintilla- 24
tion by a shivering chord on the flutes, trumpets and
strings. A fiddle flits about. More bloodstained
semitones.

26: Door 4.** A garden pushes itself out. Relaxed 26
flowery music. A sudden collective pull together by
the whole orchestra. Sweet music. Judith sings
sweetly too. Until she finds spots of blood on the
white rose. The orchestra agonizes with her. Bloodstained semitones again.

31: Door 5.** A shower of light, a distant prospect, 31
loud pompous pentatonic chords. This is Bluebeard's
kingdom. An organ joins in to celebrate its majestic
size. Great chunky chords. Until Judith spots in the
far distance a blood-red cloud.

Bluebeard wants to kiss Judith. She wants to open
34: *Nyissad ki még* the last two doors.* The pace quickens into a very fast 34
waltz. The orchestra and Bluebeard both warn us – something terrible is going to happen.

37: Door 6.** Huge sweeps up and down. The whole 37
orchestra becomes a harp. Judith gazes on the pool of tears. What is it? The strings move uneasily in unison. More harp sweeps.

41: *Gyere, Judit* Kiss me Judith.** A tense exchange of love mess- 41
ages then a kiss. The orchestra is tense too. Close impassioned strings. Tell me Bluebeard who did you love before me?

45: *Nyisd ki a hetedik ajtót!* Judith's doubts grow and finally erupt.** Open 45
that last door! Now I know it's true that you killed all your wives! Turbulent, loud and pounding with fear and anger.

The seventh door. Hush. Quiet. The orchestra quivers with expectation. A long pedal bass under the chord of C minor. Judith looks on with amazement as the earlier wives walk out alive. Bluebeard sings in
49: *Szépek, szépek* awed triumph*** – see them the beauties. Judith is 49
broken-hearted. The first is dawn says Bluebeard in speech rhythm to quiet pulsating dawn music (tremolo strings). The second is noon. The third is sunset.

There is a burst of sound from the orchestra. The
52: *Negyediket éjjel leltem* fourth I found at midnight** he says. Spare me! 52
Spare me! shouts Judith overlaying his song. You are the best of all says Bluebeard. They gaze into each other's eyes as the orchestra billows up with a huge gust of emotion. It fades. From now on it will be all darkness says Bluebeard. The orchestra is playing the spooky music which opened the opera. It dies away until it is no more than two strokes on the timpani.

NOTES

Bluebeard's Castle	Bartok's one and only opera
First night	Budapest Opera, 24 May 1918 in a double bill with a successful Bartok ballet
Reception	Mixed
Libretto	Bela Balazs
Source	A fairy tale by Charles Perrault adapted from Maeterlinck

NEWS AND GOSSIP

The poet Balazs wrote the libretto for *Bluebeard* in a competition for one-acters set by the Budapest Opera. He hoped either Kodaly or Bartok would set it. Bartok opted in, but it didn't win the prize and hung around hoping for an airing for six years. In 1917 Balazs and Bartok had a big success with their ballet *The Wooden Prince*. So the prudent Opera management agreed to premiere *Bluebeard* in a double bill with the ballet. Balazs had pinched the story more or less from the masterly Maeterlinck's *Ariane et Barbe Bleue*. We don't know what impact *Bluebeard* had on Budapest in 1918 but today we can marvel that any selection committee failed to spot such an outright winner. *Bluebeard* is played less than it deserves for three reasons. It really has to be sung to the original Magyar words to make sense of the music. Any other language, and in particular English, has to be put through the mangle to match Bartok's notation. Second, it is half of a double bill that doesn't have any natural companion. If you play it first it tends to kill the second work stone dead and if you play it second it sends people home in a state of anxiety and gloom. Third, it is not a house-filler and for reasons just mentioned you can't really team it up with *Cav* or *Pag*. The original idea of coupling with a ballet is the best solution but then to have to pay a dance company and an opera company on the same night although it may fill the house is likely to empty the coffers.

COMMENT

Bluebeard is out there all on its own. There is no other opera like it. It could be the Hungarian *Pelléas et Mélisande* but for the fact that *Bluebeard* is Magyar modal and Magyar style and Debussy is French modal and French style. Also the story is inscrutable. It is a horror opera and one of the horrors is that we don't know why it is so horrible. Bluebeard didn't kill his wives. He has a nice garden. His kingdom is well-kept and pretty. But there is blood everywhere. What does he actually do? And why? The art of the opera is the way in which it uses text and music to pitch you into a frenzy of apprehension. Fear of the terrible unknown goes deeper into the bowels than fear even of death itself, and Boy!, doesn't Bartok make this work for him.

But in some ways *Bluebeard is* the Hungarian *Pelléas*. Bartok used the same format of declamation – first one character speaks then the other, but rarely do they speak together. The Magyar modes are different and (maybe because of Bartok's orchestration) not so easy on the ear as Debussy's and their sounds carry a different message. Whereas Debussy's music is soft, mellow and as warm as thermal underwear, Bartok's is tough, spiky and about as comfortable as a hair shirt. Both can be sinister in their fashion, both can write passages of piercing beauty, but beneath the surface East is absolutely East and West is unquestionably West.

Bluebeard, once the tiresome prologue is over, is good all through. There are no longueurs. There isn't time for them. There are great moments at the opening of every one of the seven doors: Bluebeard's song in praise of his wives is his finest piece: Judith's outburst of doubt her most dramatic. But it is the strange enigmatic ending where the music takes over the narrative that perhaps disturbs our nervous system as much as any other. Why does Judith walk into imprisonment? Why does Bluebeard want to cage her for life? The music tells us this is fate, he is terrible, she is the eternal sacrificial victim, unmentionable horrors, says the orchestra, lie ahead. So have a good day.

Even those who shy off *Bluebeard* because the music is not what they expect operatic music to be must, if they just listen to it once through, end up by realizing that whether they like it or not this is a little masterpiece. Bartok is a sorcerer whose music has more power than the words of Edgar Allan Poe or Boris Karloff films. Whereas they may make the flesh creep, Bartok terrifies the spirit. A hundred years ago they would have said the soul. But don't be wary of *Bluebeard*. Although it does not make for a jolly evening this Hungarian fairy tale has more power to move us than many a much longer and more worldly libretto. Definitely an alpha.

Boccanegra, Simon *see* Simon Boccanegra

La Bohème

Bohemian tragedy

Puccini

The one where a tiny hand is frozen, a sung waltz leads to a reconciliation, and a cold garret sees the death of our heroine by TB.

CAST

Rodolfo, poet	}	Tenor
Marcello, painter	all poor	Baritone
Colline, philosopher	all young	Bass
Schaunard, musician		Baritone
Mimi, a seamstress		Soprano
Musetta, a woman about town		Soprano
Benoit, a landlord		Bass
Alcindoro, a sugar daddy		Tenor
Parpignal toy seller, Customs officer, sergeant, boy etc.		

4 acts: running time 1 hr 40 mins

STORY

Act I A large attic

It is Christmas Eve not in the poorhouse but in a poverty-stricken attic in Paris 1830, the abode of four ex-student artistic types: two inhabitants, Marcello and Rodolfo, attempt to paint a picture and write a play respectively. It is very cold: they burn the MS of an old movie script to escape frostbite.

Third inhab Colline, philosopher, enters. Later also fourth inhab Schaunard, musician, with porters carrying food, wine, goodies, fuel. He has gained loot performing a gig for a rich eccentric. The goodies are put in the fridge. (There's some cash left over.) The four horse around: there is a knock on the door: the landlord Benoit seeking rent is grudgingly admitted. They ply him with wine: he gets pissed and admits he prefers young girls to his wife: mock prudish outrage by the four, and the immoral landlord is bundled out.

The four decide to visit Café Momus. They divide Schaunard's cash. Rodolfo stays behind to meet the deadline for his TV script: he is interrupted by a knock on the door: it's a stranger: a young girl Mimi seeking a light for her candle: she drops her key, and Rodolfo's candle also goes out: both grope on the floor for the key: their hands touch: Mimi's tiny hand is frozen!: Rodolfo seizes it: he gives Mimi an extensive C.V. also some poetic come-on stuff hoping for a closer relationship: Mimi responds with her C.V.: she works in a rag-trade sweat shop, she's fond of flowers, has a small bedsit. The three call outside window – 'Hey! Rodolfo!': he shouts, 'Just coming': he tells Mimi he loves her: mutual says she (seven minutes from their first hand touch). Both exit to join the party at the Momus.

Act II Street scene, in the Latin Quarter Paris: also section of Café Momus

Much street activity: students: hawkers: pavement traffic: gang of kids etc.: Mimi and Rodolfo join the other three: Rodolfo buys Mimi a bonnet. Musetta, an old flame of Marcello's, enters with butter-and-eggs man Alcindoro. Marcello says: Mimi see that Musetta – she's trouble. Musetta makes a bid to hook Marcello: he ignores her: she screams with a pain in her foot: she sends Alcindoro to get a fresh pair of shoes: she makes a determined bid for Marcello's attention (Waltz Song): Marcello keels over: they clinch.

A platoon of soldiers approaches: much street activity. The bill is presented: the four are short of cash: Musetta instructs the waiter to add the two bills together. The platoon passes: there is turmoil in the street: all exit. Alcindoro returns plus extra shoes: he finds a large bill but no Musetta.

Act III A tollgate outside Paris

It is dawn outside a customs post at the city gate. Traders, street sweepers etc. wait to enter. It is very cold. Rodolfo, Marcello and Musetta are at a nearby party. The gates open: the crowd enters, and so does Mimi (with a nasty cough): the customs man says Marcello is in the pub: he appears and says he is painting murals on the pub wall and Musetta is giving singing lessons. Mimi says things are not good: Rodolfo is jealous, they have many rows: Rodolfo exits from the pub, and Mimi hides.

Rodolfo says it is all over with Mimi: they have split up. Why? asks Marcello. She carries on with strange men says R. Come on, come clean says M. OK says Rodolfo, the truth is, I love her so much I can't bear the thought of her imminent death from TB. Mimi reveals herself, sobbing. Marcello enters the pub to continue his quarrel with Musetta. Rodolfo and Mimi recall their happy days and decide no split till spring. They continue singing loverly stuff as Musetta and Marcello exit the pub having a real ding-dong. The curtain falls.

Act IV As Act I

Rodolfo and Marcello mull over their respective love affairs. Problems, problems: Mimi has taken up with a Japanese stockbroker, Musetta is congenitally flighty. Colline and Schaunard enter with food. They all horse around again as in Act I: cod dances, mock duel etc. Musetta enters with bad news: Mimi is really sick. Rodolfo carries in Mimi: there is a loving reunion (the Japanese stockbroker has been discarded): Mimi is dying: Musetta gives up her earrings to pawn for money for codeine also to fetch doctor. Colline sings goodbye to his favourite bomber jacket (also going to the pawnbroker).

Rodolfo and Mimi (alone) recall their happy first meeting. Musetta returns with codeine, also muff (Mimi's tiny hands are frozen, again): she has a bad coughing fit: Schaunard spots that Mimi is going, going, gone. He tells Marcello: Rodolfo overhears, and throws himself on her bed: he cries Mimi! Mimi!

MINUTES FROM START

LOOK OUT FOR

Act I

The several and various tag-tunes or motifs which turn up from time to time throughout the opera: the very first as the curtain rises (bom-bom-bom) has something to do with the joys and hazards of Bohe-
1: *Nei cieli bigi* mian life: the next a long-breathed flowing melody* 1
from Rodolfo is taken up by Marcello, drifts away and disappears and then is heard in the orchestra from time to time notably when Rodolfo is alone before Mimi's arrival.

The arrival of the feast is celebrated by a Hooray
6: *Legna!* Hooray tune** which bounces along off and on for 6
some time. But one thing leads to another and it gets lost. But watch out – it will come back later.

One of the most famous tenor pieces in the opera
14: *Che gelida manina* rep.*** Rodolfo fancies Mimi: he tells her a romantic 14
yarn about himself – as young artistic persons are apt to do.

19: *Si. Mi chiamano Mimì* Seamstress Mimi responds:*** her account of her 19
work is more prosaic but nevertheless touching: then her aria flowers and takes wing as she tells Rodolfo how she longs for spring.

23: *O soave fanciulla* The love duet:*** Rodolfo: At last I've found my 23
dream girl, Mimi: I've fallen for him. Snatches from the earlier solos: Puccini at his most intense: a

dreamy ending as they drift off arm in arm to the Café Momus, and their voices fade into the distance.

Act II

An opening chorus with a difference:*** street scene with stallholders, passers-by, a gang of kids, students etc., all chorusing in character, interspersed with interjection, conversation etc. from our four plus Mimi. An operatic jam session with a texture, a sound, an atmosphere new to opera and once heard never forgotten.

3: *Ecco i gioccattoli* Parpignol the toy-seller's cry.* Heard twice, rau- 3
cous, in a remote key and followed by the swinging song of the gang of kids.

11: *Quando me'n vo* Musetta's waltz:*** all the fuss and by-play stops 11
dead as she takes the limelight and gives her all. Marcello is visibly affected: the scene fragments for a moment into side-plots and comment: Marcello takes up the wonderful waltz tune as Musetta fusses with her shoe and gets rid of Alcindoro. Climax in a passionate clinch.

16: *La ritirata!* The finale:** a fife and drum band approaches at a 16
very deliberate pace (slow march?) again in a remote key – there is a problem over the bill – the crowd gathers – Musetta adds the bill to her own – the soldiers come on stage, fife and drum fortissimo: the crowd joins in: all exit: Alcindoro comes on, sees bill – collapse of stout party – curtain. Bang! Bang!

Act III

0: Another unforgettable opening:** the icy cold dawn prelude (harps and flutes): the crowd stomping their feet and calling out to be let in to the city: the echo of Musetta's waltz: the pathetic figure of Mimi (again with a tug at the memory of the happy Mimi) creeping towards the inn: all is suspended animation until the bell of the hospice sounds out, the spell is broken and the day begins.

6: *O buon Marcello* Mimi's duet of despair with Marcello:** long 6
paragraphs: sustained melody: the regime with Rodolfo is breaking up: they must part. She sings with the anguish of a lover whose love is ending but not over.

The moment when Mimi shows herself, coughing and sobbing: the orchestra comes in with a great

16: *Ahimè, morire?* surge of love remembered.** 16

17: *Donde lieta uscì* Mimi's farewell:** musical reminders of happy 17
beginnings: she will be brave and go back to work alone: Rodolfo can keep the bonnet he gave her. Goodbye, no hard feelings she says again. Then the great final gust of passion. She doesn't mean any of that stuff – she loves him. Then the reconciliation duet – parting postponed: the edgy Marcello and Musetta shout abuse at each other whilst the dreamy music of the lovers drifts on in the background; it holds the ear until its final fade out, as in Act I, marred only slightly by a reprehensible solo violin.

Act IV

1: *O Mimi, tu più non torni* Rodolfo and Marcello mull over their love affairs – not going very well. Another long haunting tune.* 1
Then back to the spirit and some of the sounds of Act I: horsing around by all four ending in a dance and a mock duel – all very jolly.

9: *Intesi dire* Musetta's report:* how she found Mimi (to Mimi 9
music) rising to a great climax and fading as Mimi begins to speak for herself.

14: *Vecchia zimarra* Colline's farewell to his old coat:* a cod funeral ad- 14
dress followed by the most melting orchestral interlude** (the love motif again) as Mimi and Rodolfo are left alone.

17: *Sono andati?* The final love duet:** sweet memories recalled in 17
the face of death: hushed tones both calm and reflective.

25: *Che ha detto* The death of Mimi:*** no death scene in opera is 25
more touching and none uses simpler resources, from the first spine-chilling chord through the hushed and fearful exchanges to Rodolfo's final despairing cry of 'Mimi! Mimi!'.

NOTES

La Bohème	Puccini's fourth opera
First night	Teatro Regio, Turin, 1 February 1896 (Toscanini conducted)
Reception	The audience loved it but the critics were astonishingly negative. Not as good as *Lescaut* they cried (the idiots), this young man must stop fooling around and get back to some serious operatic work

Libretto Illica and Giacosa
Source Henri Murger wrote a series of sketches (Scenes of Bohemian Life), made them into a play (1849) then a novel (1851) – a big success

NEWS AND GOSSIP

When Puccini announced he was going to do *Bohème* there was immediately a row with Leoncavallo, the *Pag* man, whom Puccini had fired from the script team working on *Lescaut*. 'I thought of it first,' said Leon, 'have already approached artists.' 'OK, OK,' said Puccini, 'let's both write an opera and let the best man win.' So they both wrote a *Bohème* and the best man won. (Leon's *Bohème* came out a year after Puccini's and had a limited success.) Puccini also had problems with his own script team. He gave them a hard time. Even more picky than Verdi, he would cut, extend, argue over a phrase, change his mind, etc. Letters to Ricordi, the publisher, from all three make it plain that a bust-up was often only just round the corner. 'I am sick to death of this constant redoing, retouching, piecing together', wrote Giacosa, adding that he stuck it only because of his friendship with Ricordi and because he was 'fond of Puccini'. But stick to it they all did and the result was one of opera's smash hits. *Bohème* spread through the world of opera houses like the good news it is, demanding modest resources: singable by any good-class cast and sure fire box office. By World War I it was already amongst the top of the pops and has remained there ever since.

COMMENT

Bohème did to the world of Grand Opera what *Bicycle Thieves* did to world cinema. Both were something quite new, both deflated grandiose traditions and both employed a brand of romantic verismo that instantly won universal sympathy, except from the stony-hearted and the intellectual puritans. To some extent the ground had already been broken by *Cav* and *Pag*, two tales of romanticized low-life, but in *Bohème* the characters and their dilemmas are more sophisticated and the everyday nature of the story is coupled with an unashamedly romantic score. There are few set pieces, yet the music does not ramble on in an indeterminate fashion as per Wagner (often) or late Verdi (sometimes) but moves decisively from mood to mood and from tune to tune, many of which are loaded with special emotional messages and appear again and again. Puccini's tunes are not a matter of phrases, nor of sentences but paragraphs, some of them long, longer than Verdi, longer than Donizetti and sometimes longer even than Bellini. (Musetta's waltz, for instance, shorter than many and with a clear beginning and end, takes eight bars to unwind.) The vocal lines are grateful to sing, can immediately be grasped by the ear and live on in the musical memory long after the opera is over. The structure of the plot is taut: the story moves along at speed and there is no padding. Although manners and modes have changed a lot in a hundred years, we still feel at home with the four Bohemians as they fool around, we like their style, we are happy to see them happy in love, we are really upset when things go wrong and poor Mimi – it's almost like losing one of the family. It is no good being sniffy about Puccini: he is a great opera composer. He also shares with Bach, Mozart, Schubert and Verdi, and more recently the Beatles and Richard Rodgers, the ability to write a good tune. *Bohème* is one of the top ten operas for all but pedants and musical snobs. An alpha.

Boris Godunov

Historical drama

Musorgsky

The one where the Tsar gained the throne by killing the true heir when he was a baby, the memory of which drives him to madness and death.

CAST

Boris Godunov, the Tsar	Bass–baritone
Xenia, his daughter	Soprano
Fyodor, his son	Mezzo
Pimen, a hermit	Bass
Grigory, a novice monk	Tenor
Prince Shuysky	Baritone
Varlaam, a tramp	Bass
Missail, a second tramp	Tenor
Marina, Polish aristocrat	Mezzo
Rangoni, a Jesuit	Bass
An idiot	Tenor

The Secretary to the Boyar's council, an innkeeper, a nurse, a policeman, a peasant, two Boyars, two Jesuits

4 acts: running time 3 hrs 30 mins

Before we begin

Ivan the Terrible, the founder of pretty well everything in Russia including the OGPU, was succeeded by his son Fyodor who was unfortunately a bit of a wimp. This gave his pushy brother-in-law Boris Godunov a chance to muscle in on imperial matters. Ivan had had more than one wife and Fyodor's heir Dimitri was a much younger step-brother by a lesser and later wife of Ivan. The opera hinges on the belief that Boris in order to become Tsar had Dimitri done away with as a baby like the princes in the Tower (but there was only one Dimitri).

And another thing

There are at least seven published versions of *Boris Godunov* (see NEWS AND GOSSIP). The one described here is the Rimsky-Korsakov edition of 1908 with Act IV Scene 1 as edited by Ippolitov-Ivanov in 1925.

STORY

Prologue Sc 1 The courtyard of a monastery

We are in Moscow in the year 1598 and it is very cold as the crowd-control police beat up the citizens and force them to get on their knees. They are required to pray that Boris Godunov will decide to become Tsar. At this moment he is within the monastery allegedly torn with doubts but we all know the old trick of the hard-to-get Presidential candidate who won't stand unless he is drafted ho ho. Some blind pilgrims come on singing and a holy message is usually a good tip in opera but this time no one can make out what the hell they are on about. The Cabinet Secretary comes out and says no decision today lads, come round to the Kremlin tomorrow 11 o'clock.

Sc 2 The Kremlin. In the centre a staircase into the Imperial Palace

A procession passes up the staircase carrying the imperial crown. Boris has graciously accepted. He is the Tsar. The crowd is very pleased. Huzzah! Glory be! they cry. Boris comes out on to the imperial balcony and says I don't feel awfully good about this because I have psychological problems like fits of terror. So you will have to do your best for me God. Undaunted by this depressing speech the populace huzzah and hooray again like crazy.

Act I Sc 1 A cell in a monastery

Pimen makes the case for the huge importance of historians especially himself. Offstage monks chant. Grigory often has the same dream and apparently tells it to Pimen every time. It's about his getting to the top of a tower and then everyone throwing tomatoes at him. You eat too much says Pimen. How old would the Tsarevitch Dimitri be if he were still alive? asks Grigory. About your age says Pimen I know because I was there as a soldier when he was killed. I think I'll take a nap. God have mercy chant the monks. So says Grigory, now on his own, watch out Boris. No one dares to accuse you of killing babies but this old monk has got evidence in writing and sooner or later your number is up. [Clearly fancies his own chances: Ed.]

Act I Sc 2 An inn near the Lithuanian border

The lady who keeps the pub sings an irrelevant folk song about a duck. Two tramps Missail and Varlaam dressed as friars come round looking for money followed by Grigory in disguise. I want to get over the border to Lithuania says Grigory. Varlaam sings an irrelevant song about the battle of Kazan. Missail and Varlaam get smashed but Grigory says he's on the wagon. I want to get to Lithuania says Grigory again who is in danger of becoming a Lithuania bore. Quite easy to get through the sentries after dark says the pub lady. Sentries? says Grigory. They're after someone who is on the run from Moscow says the pub lady.

A policeman comes in and says Now then Now then anyone here who answers to this description which I can't read? I'll read it says Grigory. But he realizes it is a description of himself so he reads out a description of Varlaam instead. The policeman is about to arrest Varlaam when Varlaam asks to have a look at the document. This ain't me says Varlaam it's him. But Grigory scarpers out of the window.

Act II A room in the Imperial Palace

Xenia, Boris's daughter, is weeping because her fiancé is dead. I'll cheer you up says her old nursey and sings an irrelevant song about a flea. Except the flea dies. Fyodor, Boris's son, thinks this is tactless so he sings another irrelevant song about an owl. Father Boris comes into the nursery and says to Xenia there there dear you'll soon get over it and now please get out because I want to be alone with my son the Tsarevitch. See how good I am at geography Daddy says Fyodor running off all the main towns exports and production of wool in each region of Russia. You're a clever lad Fyo says Boris: now bugger off upstage because I want to do a spot of soliloquizing. Boris does a state-of-the-Tsar appraisal. On the one hand he has had four years high in the popularity ratings, a nice family life and the astrologers all give him A1 at Lloyds. On the other hand his daughter's fiancé dropped dead, he is slipping in the ratings, the economy is in bad shape what with pestilence and famine hindering productivity. People are putting the blame on him. But worst of all he has fits of the horrors. He dreams about a bloody child. He gives us some really nasty clinical details about the child's wounds. He sinks back in a daze of panic.

Meanwhile the nurses are having a life-and-death struggle with a parrot. A stray Boyar blows in and says by the way a messenger came to Prince Shuysky with details of a child's murder. It took place some time ago. The Boyar exits. Arrest him at once says Boris. Fyodor comes in to tell his dad the full story of the parrot.

Shuysky comes in. Listen Tsar something terrible's happened he says. There is this guy calling himself Dimitri who has raised an army in Poland and is coming to knock you off the throne. Get out Fyodor says Boris. Fyodor exits. Now Shuysky this can't be the infant Dimitri resurrected can it? People don't resurrect in real life do they? (He bursts into manic laughter.) now come on Shuysky when you visited that church at Uglich many years ago did you or did you not see that infant dead? No fooling or I'll have you castrated. I saw the child Dimitri stone dead in the church says Shuysky. It's true that the thirteen other children killed at the same time were in an advanced state of decomposition says Shuysky and he was as fresh as a daisy. But dead, yes certainly dead. (Exits.) I can't breathe says Boris I think I'm going bonkers. He is. The clock is one of those that have hideous little figures bouncing around it when it strikes. It strikes. Instead of the little figures Boris sees the dead baby. He's pretty well gone.

Act III Sc 1 A room in the Mnishek palace in Poland

A large number of Princess Marina's young female body-servants sing about her beauty goodness etc. no doubt hoping to improve their conditions of service. But she doesn't like flattery so it's no good nor does she fancy any of the numerous men who are making passes at her. She sends the women off and then says what she really fancies is this young Dimitri [Grigory of course: Ed.] coupled with the prospect of becoming Tsarina. A creepy Jesuit named Rangoni appears and says when she is Tsarina she must enforce Catholicism and he doesn't mind what sin she commits such as fornication to get the Tsarevitchship so long as once she gets in there she practises religious intolerance in his favour in the strictest manner.

Act III Sc 2 The garden of the Mnishek palace. Moonlight

Dimitri (Grigory) jumps out of the bushes saying he is in love with Marina. Rangoni saunters in [has been loitering with intent: Ed.] and says I have news for you Marina is potty about you. Bisto! Whoopee! Good-o! shouts Dimitri. Then he looks at the crafty Rangoni and says I don't believe you. You said that just to get me to admit I love her. No sir not at all good gracious me no never says Rangoni. In that case OK lead me to her says Dimitri. Look out says Rangoni guests are arriving. Sure enough they troop in. Marina is on the arm of some rich elderly Marquis. Let's go indoors says Marina, it looks like rain. They go indoors. Back comes Dimitri who has witnessed all, burnt up with jealousy because he saw Marina with another man. OK he says she can do what she likes I'll go off to war and be glorious.

Marina now steps back into the garden. O Marina I love you and I have been having a terrible time owing to jealousy says Dimitri. I don't want to hear all that lovesick stuff says Marina. Have you got a target date for getting to be Tsar in Moscow? So that's all you want says Dimitri how very disappointing. All right I'll wage a mighty campaign, beat Boris and when I'm Tsar I'll look down on you from a great height. You got me all wrong says Marina of course I love you carnally spiritually and all that. My Tsarina! he says. My Tsar! she replies.

Act IV Sc 1 A square in front of St Basil's Cathedral

The Moscow crowd are swilling around exchanging political gossip. A Deacon announces that Grigory the missing monk has been excommunicated. Inside the cathedral they have been singing a requiem for the dead baby Tsarevitch Dimitri. This is confusing say the crowd. Dimitri is alive and on the march: he'll thrash that bastard Boris and we'll have a decent Tsar again.

An idiot comes on singing holy riddles thereby letting us know he is an important idiot with extrasensory powers. The street kids take the mick out of the idiot and nick a rouble off him.

Boris's procession enters. Give us our Social Service payments! cry the crowd, they are overdue. And give us bread your gracious imperial majesty. Boris stops opposite the idiot. These street children are getting to be a menace the idiot says to Boris. Why not have them murdered like you murdered Dimitri? Arrest that man shouts Shuysky. No says Boris. Let him pray for me. Boris exits. I can't pray for Tsar Herod says the idiot. And what is more poor old Russia is in for a really dreadful time.

Act IV Sc 2 The great hall in the Kremlin

The Boyars' senate is passing a bill to deal with the rebel Dimitri. He is to be caught chained tortured cut up burnt etc. Shuysky arrives late with bad news. I spent the night looking through the keyhole of Boris's bedroom he says. He was sweating haggard shaking – Not true shout the Boyars. Enter Boris sweating haggard shaking also crazy. Go away you frightful ghost of a dead child! he shouts. It's not true that I murdered Dimitri! It's that Shuysky who put it about. Arrest him! May you be forgiven says Shuysky.

Boris comes out of his fit and addresses the senate. I want your advice he says. 'Scuse me your majesty says Shuysky there's a monk outside who has important news. Pimen comes in and tells a far-fetched story of a man whose blindness was miraculously cured by an angel who alleged he was the little dead Dimitri. This causes Boris to have a cardiac arrest. Get out everyone he cries. I'm dying fetch my son here at once. Fyodor comes on and Boris gives him his instructions as to how to run Russia look after the family and be holy too. Death bells start to toll rather too early. Boris hears them. Dies.

Act IV Sc 3 A clearing in a forest near Kromy

A crowd are molesting a captured Boyar. There is a lengthy display of class hatred. Missail and Varlaam come on saying that Boris has caused a deep recession in Russia but Dimitri is good news and go on with a load of anti-Boris propaganda. The crowd love it. Dimitri will set the people free they sing. Two Jesuits come on singing in Latin but the crowd turns ugly and they are dragged off to be hanged. Dimitri comes on with troops around him sounding trumpets waving banners *feu de joie* etc. Hurrah hurrah cries everyone. Dimitri has the Boyar released thereby showing clemency and rides off. Everyone follows him still cheering. The idiot stays on alone and repeats his dreary message about the blood and tears that lie ahead for Russia. Curtain.

MINUTES FROM START

LOOK OUT FOR

Prologue Sc 1

2: *Na kovó ty nas pokidáesh*

Bassoons start us off with a tune straight from the steppes and soon we are into what in most operas would have been the opening chorus. But this is no ordinary chorus.* Sometimes the crowd all sings to- 2
gether as in a football crowd only better, sometimes the men or the women or a fragment of the crowd do their own thing, sometimes there are three beats in a bar, sometimes five. The police shout to them to get on their knees and pray even louder for Boris to accept the crown. There are sotto voce conversations, eddies, incidents but mainly it is the huge volume of Russian voices that fills the ear. There are several insistent rhythms and we nearly always hear the strings standing behind the voices, sometimes the brass. It sounds very cold, many degrees below zero. The pilgrims also chuck in their pennyworth which is a more orthodox kind of holy singing.

Prologue Sc 2

6: *Da zdrávstvuet tsar Borís*

Boris is the Tsar of all Russias!*** Tocsins, bells, 16
gongs and all manner of deep Russian sounds tell us that this is a great day. A jerky woodwind tune (piccolos) comes in above all the booming like a glockenspiel made of treble bells. There are brass fanfares. It is a mighty noise. Shuysky shouts 'Long live the Tsar!' The crowd take up the cry. So do the Boyars. Different rhythms surge and sway through the mass of noise. There are sounds we have never heard in op-

era before. This is the chorus in a new role. It is the hero of the piece.

Boris is sad, fearful. He addresses the crowd. They are not daunted and respond with full-throttle hoorahs. The tocsins and bells respond too. The great sweeping tune of the earlier chorus takes the lead. There is a final burst of stupendous sound. All very unlike what happens outside Buckingham Palace after a coronation. The number of decibels is on a scale
25: to match the immensity of Russia. A knockout.***

Act I Sc 1

The long scene between Pimen and Grigory which sets up the plot and gives us a Reader's Digest of recent Russian history is the sort of thing that in traditional Western opera would have been handled mainly in recitatif. Here it plugs along in a low-gear Musorgsky style – almost non-stop singing, starting with a wriggling snake-like figure in the strings which continues under the earlier exchanges and the holy offstage chorus. The light orchestration lets the voices have a clear run. It ends more dramatically.
18: *A mnye porá* Pimen hears the sounds of day stirring,* a distant 18
tocsin sounds, the holy offstagers strike up again and once Pimen has gone Grigory's ambition becomes
20: *Borís, Borís!* clear.* Boris is guilty of a hellish crime. He will have 20
to pay for it.

Act I Sc 2

The short prelude has a tramping figure in the bass which was later pinched by Stravinsky to be the dominating motif of the *Rite of Spring*. The hostess
23: *Poymála ya* sings a rather intimate and very Russian song about a 23
duck.* Nice little fragments of melody float around.

The battle of Kazan – Varlaam's rousing party
28: *Kak vo górode* piece.** Plenty of Russian macho and jingoism. The 28
orchestra comes out of its closet and gives us a whizz-bang ear-filling accompaniment. It makes 'Hearts of Oak' seem like a dirge.

The dramatics in the inn go along well enough but only come to the boil when Varlaam reads the true
41: *A lye . . . lyet. . . .* description of the wanted man,* haltingly at first but 41
his reading skills seem to improve as he begins to twig that Grigory is the monk on the run. A hurry-scurry end to what has been a placid scene.

Act II

Gloom in the nursery. Xenia sings sweetly and sadly
0: *Gdye ty* to her dead lover.* The accompanying orchestra 0
sympathizes with her. Nanny tries to cheer her up
with a very four-square and simple-silly Russian folk
song; but she picks the wrong one for it ends in the
death of the hero – a flea. Fyodor sings an even simpler, sillier but undoubtedly jollier song this time
about an owl, a sparrow and a sexton (look out especially for the woodwind accompaniment). Both are
a bit nursery rhymeski.

Boris's arrival brings some gravitas to the scene.
After tender exchanges with Xenia and a quick appraisal of Fyodor's progress in geography he is left on
11: *Dostíg ya* his own to soliloquize as Fyodor moves upstage.** 11
výshey vlásti This is a fine piece, the music reflecting his thoughts
(which are pretty gloomy) by means of free writing
which in Italian might be called arioso. One thing
leads naturally to another, musical paragraphs being
structured much as are the words. No real tune, but
themes which will crop up again all forming an unbroken stream of 'thinks' music.

17: *Ay, kysh!* The parrot kerfuffle is nicely done* with shrieking 17
nurses and panicking strings and there is a lot of
charm in Fyodor's round-by-round account of the
bird's bad behaviour. But it does not help the plot forward one iota. A meander.

The interview with Shuysky. At first dark and
menacing. Boris tears into him with support from
heavy brass chords. Then the exchanges become
calmer until the mention of the name Dimitri causes a
26: *Dimítriya . . .* mild explosion.* Fyodor is sent away and Boris seems 26
Tsaryévich, to be losing his marbles as he grabs Shuysky by the
udalís! collar (upward phrases on tremolo strings) and laughs
crazily. But when Shuysky gives his grisly account of
what he saw in the graveyard the mood changes with
the woodwind choir sounding a decently reverential
note. But still a little spooky.

31: *Ukh! tyazheló!* The vision of Dimitri.*** Boris sinks back gasping 31
for air (discordant strokes from the strings). He raves.
The clock starts to tick (pizzicato violas and cellos).
He hallucinates. He sees the murdered baby before
his very eyes. The orchestra whips up his terror. The
other strings rush about in contrary motion. The

timp bangs out his final moment of panic. All goes quiet as he asks for God's mercy. Very frightening and one of opera's really great scenes.

Act III Sc 1

Marina listens to a chorus of gross flattery from her
0: *Na Víslye lazúrnoy* troupe of young ladies. The songs* are agreeable and 0
as mild as Russian milk.

Left alone Marina reflects on how boring is her present life and how glorious it will be when she becomes Tsarina. The boredom bit of her piece is fairly boring but as she begins to stoke up her ambition she
7: *Na prestól tsaryéy* moves into what could be called a sung mazurka* 7
which is really lively.

Marina's dialogue with the dread Rangoni starts with the exchange of compliments and his persuasive fervour being slowly (very slowly) applied to the lady. But she revolts. Why the hell should I do your missionary work for you? she cries, the music is jolted
15: *Krasóyu svoyéyu* out of its rut. Rangoni then gives her a lecturette* to a 15
slithery chromatic melody about how to seduce a prince which seems to imply he has had more sexual experience than one would expect from a Jesuit priest. Get out! she says. He doesn't and in a series of tense exchanges he wins. She falls at his feet. This is done with only a couple of noisy exclamations from the orchestra: the test of strength is between the two voices quietly supported by strings and woodwind with the odd blow struck by the horns.

Act III Sc 2

Dimitri (Grigory) gets fed up with Rangoni too. But again the Jesuit (who has a chromatic scale hanging about him in the background) oils his way back into Dimitri's favour.

24: *O, yésli ty nye lzhozh* Some passionate tenor singing from Dimitri* and 24
the same blend of smooth phrases and relentless pressure from Rangoni.

30: A polonaise strikes up.* It rumbles around in the 30
bass a little uncertainly at first, but wait, it soon warms up into a rousing Polish chorus and becomes a polonaise you could (almost) dance to. Meanwhile all the guests, who are Polish nationalists, forecast that Poland will overthrow Russia.

34: *Iezuít lukávy krépko* Dimitri is angry* (the tiresome Jesuit), jealous 34 (saw Marina with a rich old nobleman) and warlike (OK I'll get into battle and show them all) until – he meets Marina.

This important meeting is followed by an important ten-minute duet. Instead of greeting her with a cry of joy Dimitri tells her what a horrible time he has had owing to jealousy. Tortured phrases over a squirming string bass.

Keep all that stuff to yourself I don't want to hear it
she sings in a careless little bit of the polonaise
38: *Nyet, nye dlya rechéy* tune,** which is stopped dead by the horns. When 38
are you going to be Tsar? she asks. Oh dear so you
don't love me for myself says Dimitri, always ready as
are most opera Russians, to look on the gloomy side of
40: *Tebyá, tebyá odnú* things. He launches into some high passion.** Ur- 40
gent upward pushing phrases. She is dismissive. You creep she says. Hey hold on! he cries I am a mighty military man and we have the rhythm of a marche militaire and taps on the side drums. Wait till I'm Tsar then see what I do to you.

O but truly I love you Dimitri she sings in the most
44: *O, tsaryévich* lovely lyrical passage in the opera.*** I love you I do.
And a big warm tune creeps in under her singing line. He takes up the tune. At last they both appear to love each other. Climax. The long tune takes over in a (very) short symphony. She kneels (harp glissando): Hail Tsar says she. Rise Tsarina says he. They kiss. It's ecstasy. And now the guests get into the act to shout Hurrah (but how can they have known what was afoot unless they have been peeping through the bushes?). The duet has been a bumpy ride, but it ends gloriously.

Act IV Sc 1

A cold pizzicato prelude with a wavering figure above
leads to a lot of choral singing. The men outside the
2: *Shto otoshlá obyédnya?* cathedral are confused and sound it.* They ponder: 2
(1) Someone has been excommunicated – Grigory?

(2) Could Grigory be Dimitri? [Of course he pretends he is: Ed.]

(3) If so then why does the church pray for the soul of Dimitri who we thought died when a baby? The choral singing is as fine as ever but owing to the

confusion it is bitty and lacks the grand sweep of the Act I choruses.

The idiot has his first innings (verse 1). He sings in
5: *Myésyats yédet* a wavering whine* over a moving bass line and pretty 5
well sticks to this throughout (related to the wavering in the prelude). Moscow's street kids sing in that horrid nasal way that afflicts all children's choruses in opera.

Boris's procession passes and the people (the women have now been allowed out) sing movingly
8: *Tsar gosudár* asking him for bread.** Bread, bread, give us bread, 8
they sing. Poor Boris can do nothing about getting them bread. The scene ends with some more quavering stuff from the idiot (verse 2).

Act IV Sc 2

The assembly opens with loud Boyar-ish choral sing-
15: *Shtozh?* ing* and sonorous Boyar-ish brass chords. The 15
Boyars sound a savage lot and are much more interested in how Dimitri should be disembowelled etc. after death than in how he should be captured.

After Shuysky's account of how he saw Boris distraught (through a keyhole) Boris enters, distraught. But he collects himself – the music becomes stately,
20: *A? Ya sózval vas* regal and reassuring.* After so much noise and high 20
tension this pool of calm is a happy relief.

Pimen tells the tale to the same tune he used in Act
24: *Odnázhdy v vechérniy chas* I.* It's not remarkable but never boring and leads to 24
Boris's nervous collapse.

29: *Proshcháy, moy syn* Boris's goodbye to his son.** In this noble piece 29
Boris's voice gradually weakens to a whisper. Look out especially for the sneaky violin tune that creeps in high above Boris as he tells Fyodor that he will reign as the lawful ruler of all Russia and again the hushed string choir plus harp that plays under his final prayer. Whatever ghastly things Boris may have done in the past, his demeanour in dying is first class. The booming tocsin announcing Boris's imminent death gives us quite a shock.

Musorgsky, brilliant with bells, builds a terrifying clangour of death-knells (which could put the frighteners on anyone even in reasonably good health) from
35: *Zvon! pogrebál'ny zvon!* which the death scene*** spins out. It is terrifyingly 35
realistic with offstage chorus and Boris, struggling

with a death-rattle in his throat, crying for forgiveness. Then, as he expires – peace. Hushed chords from the orchestra and from the Boyars a whispered Amen. We are in the presence of death.

Act IV Sc 3

The crowd are giving the captured Boyar a hard time.
40: *Vali syudá* The chorus* starts rather conventionally with men 40
and women's voices segregated but it drifts towards the Volga and soon we are into pure Russian folk music with both sexes singing equally. It is a good enough chorus but musically the whole scene is a bit of a pudding.

We hear Missail and Varlaam singing an apparently rather tuneless and rhythmless chant, unaccompanied save for a sustained solo horn. But on the second and third verses it picks up an orchestral accompaniment and choral support and becomes a wild
47: *Gaydá !* revolutionary chorus.*** The chant is transformed 47
into a big stirring choral melody with a rhythm like a sledgehammer. Bang! Bang! Bang! – three heavy beats over and over again. Terrific.

The new Tsar approaches. Quite the best mini-
52: *Sláva tebyé* intermezzo orchestral in the opera.*** Two enor- 52
mous sweeps from top to bottom and back up again from the orchestra bring in a trotting march rhythm (Don't-you-get-it Don't-you-get-it). Chorded woodwinds. Side drums. Trumpets. Missail and Varlaam greet Dimitri. The chorus joins in. The trotting rhythm now has a great tune above it. The big drum speaks! Hail Dimitri!

Dimitri arrives: frees the Boyar: rides off to Moscow. All rather quick. Now we have the trotting chorus again but much slower. It fades away as we hear Dimitri's trumpet retreating into the distance.
56: *Lyéytes, lyéytes* The whine of the idiot starts up in the strings* then so 56
does he (his Verse 2 repeated). This dreary soul whimpers on about the disasters that lie ahead for Russia. A slow closing symphony, still wavering with the whine, and the opera fades away.

NOTES

Boris Godunov	Musorgsky's second performed opera
First night (Musorgsky's revised version)	Mariansky Theatre, St Petersburg, 8 February 1874
Reception	Warm
Libretto	Musorgsky
Source	A play by Pushkin

NEWS AND GOSSIP

In the Moscow of the 1860s opera was a state monopoly. Anyone who wanted to get an opera produced had to submit it to a selection committee who were of course state censors as well as judges of merit. A similar committee today would probably consist of nominees of the Prime Minister, the Home Secretary, the departments of Environment, Trade, Education and several others, and god knows which new operas, if any, would reach the stage. After a long delay *Boris* was turned down because it had no part for a leading female. This was indeed true of the original version, so Musorgsky set about writing a new act, the Polish act, about the encounter between Marina and Dimitri. This time it got by. The original version had been submitted in 1869, then revised in 1872 and the premiere took place two years later.

No opera has been more messed about with than *Boris*. Rimsky-Korsakov got in there first and re-orchestrated and re-arranged the whole thing, publishing two versions, one in 1896 and the other in 1908. That, with Musorgsky's own two, makes four. After that there were three more, one of them by Shostakovich in 1940. The Rimsky 1908 version which became as near to being the Standard Version as any was amended in 1924 when the Bolshoi popped in the first crowd scene in Act IV (the one outside St Basil's Cathedral) as well as the last one where Dimitri rides through in triumph. Musorgsky never meant both of these scenes to be played together, but today they usually are.

But all this pushing around doesn't matter too much because the opera was always a series of scenes rather than a running narrative. It was soon seen to be a majestic work and with Chaliapin singing Boris (the greatest ever) in the earlier part of this century it became a hit. Today it is performed widely but not often in international houses for the difficulty of getting a cast who can cope with the Russian language is formidable. In Russia it is of course a standard.

COMMENT

Boris overwhelms you with its Russian-ness. There is practically nothing so Russian in art save Eisenstein's great film *Ivan the Terrible*. By comparison Dostoevsky seems like a New York crime writer and Chekov a Western European country gent. Boris's gloom is Russian gloom, the plotting clerics are part of Russia's everlasting hang-up with religious hanky-panky, a lot of the music seems to come straight from the steppes and the chorus of bells stuns us with its absolutely one and only Russian sound. *Boris* is a new kind of opera. It has the same sort of relationship to Mozart's *Così* as Tolstoi's *War and Peace* has to Jane Austen's *Persuasion*.

The story is not so much a drama more a number of dramatic scenes (nine). Some of them – Boris in the nursery followed by Boris hallucinating – are Shakespearean. Some of them are an early form of verismo (the crowd scenes). The continuing thread is of course Boris's guilt but it doesn't do to try and give the opera an overall shape. Much better to take each scene on its merits. The reason for this is that after the first version had gone down the pan every change to the story (and there were plenty) made the scenes more independent.

It is unwise to get into a debate about the underlying meaning of *Boris* because the scribes have found all manner of really convincing interpretations e.g. that Musorgsky used history to make an undercover comment on the realpolitik of the day, that the opera has formal unity because the three main characters are the Tsar, Dimitri and the crowd and these three – wait for it – are balanced throughout the nine scenes in 'palindromic equilibrium'. And because the crowd are sometimes right and sometimes silly they represent 'the alpha and the omega'. Others see it as the people versus the Tsar. And similar.

At first it seems that Musorgsky's music has power but not beauty. A lot of the stuff from the steppes (the whole bundle of folk songs for instance) seem better fitted for something like the *Beggar's Opera* than grand opera, and indeed for those who don't like Russian folk-song stuff, they can be tiresome. But then Musorgsky's ability to symphonize Russian music comes to the rescue, as in the glorious orchestration of the bells, Missail and Varlaam's folk song in the last act, which Musorgsky takes by the scruff of the neck and pulls upwards and onwards into a tremendous choral job. Nowadays it's the fashion to prefer Musorgsky's own bleak orchestration to Rimsky's much more adroit arrangement. This will probably soon be reversed since just at this moment veneration for the Authentic has gone right over the top and in nearly every respect Rimsky's version wins. It depends whether you would rather spend a night on Balakirev's bare mountain or in the company of Scheherezade.

The great moments in *Boris* are of two kinds – the crowd kind and the

Boris kind. The coronation scene has the feeling of a great state occasion. The climax of this scene when the bells join in must be one of opera's top ten best noises along with the anvils in *Rhinegold*, the bells in *Parsifal* and the sharpshooting in *Freischutz*. Boris's greatest scene is when he hallucinates in front of the ticking clock. This is well up to the standard of the Shakespearean ghost-shock we get in *Macbeth* or *Hamlet*.

Boris's big solos lie between aria and recitatif and are quite a long way away from both. Musorgsky allows the voice to lead. It takes its own route, moving forward and doing its own thing, sometimes singing an actual tune. The orchestra follows and supports with its own stream of music. Sometimes it doubles the voice line but more often it gives the singer a solid base to sing from. It never conflicts. The orchestra, except in the short preludes, is seldom the star.

There are mottos for the main characters (Dimitri and the dead baby share the same one) but they are not important, as even Musorgsky came to realize, for when he revised the score he cut them down and indeed didn't put any into the new stuff he wrote.

It may not be a lovable opera but a good production of *Boris* is an event in the life of any opera-goer. It stuns you with its sheer size and weight which seem to match the power of Russia itself. It makes the Switzerland of *William Tell*, that most nationalistic of operas, seem like toytown. It makes Italian opera seem like light music. Its simplicity and directness make Wagner seem like Mad Max.

It is one of the great monuments of nineteenth-century Russian art and along with *Kovanshchina* is different, quite different, from any other opera in the book. An alpha.

Butterfly, Madam *see* Madam Butterfly

Carlos, Don *see* Don Carlos

Carmen

Spanish tragedy

Bizet

Carmen is unforgettable, but for opera amnesiacs it is the one with the tor-ee-a-dor song the gypsy Carmen and the simple soldier who stabs her to death.

CAST

Carmen, a gypsy girl	Mezzo
Don José, a corporal	Tenor
Escamillo, a toreador	Bass/baritone
Micaëla, adopted daughter of Don José's mother	Soprano
Zuniga, Don José's platoon commander	Bass
Moralès, another corporal	Baritone
Dancaïro, leading smuggler	Tenor/baritone
Remendado, rank and file smuggler	Tenor
Frasquita, a gypsy girl	Soprano
Mercédès, another	Soprano

Lillas Pastia, café owner; **Andrès,** an officer; gypsies, soldiers, guides, street sellers, etc.

3 acts: running time 2 hrs 40 mins

STORY

Act I A square in Seville

We are in Seville in the early 1800s outside W. D. and H. O. Wills wholly-owned Spanish subsidiary with guardroom opposite. Morales plus some squaddies observe the pavement traffic. Micaela sweet seventeen enters and asks: is Don José around? Not in our mob they say: the next shift is due any minute. Why not stay and chat? Not on your Nellie says she and runs. Some dead-end kids play soldiers. The guard changes: the old lot tell Don José that a nice-looking bird was enquiring for him. It must be Micaela says he. The kids go square-bashing again. Hey corporal says a new officer Zuniga is that a tobacco factory? with female labour? Sure is says Don José: the girls are a menace. They scare the bajesus out of me.

The tea-break hooter goes. Just look at 'em he says. Several voyeuristic layabouts plus soldiers take up positions to observe the display of female flesh. The girls erupt: chatter: smoke. Where's Carmen? all cry: Carmen enters on cue: the men shout Hi Carmen give us a break we love you. Carmen gives a habanera lecture on the nature of love. It's volatile she says. She spots Don José and fancies him. She chucks him a carnation. Cheeky pig says he but bajesus is she sexy.

The hooter goes: all in. Enter Micaela: she gives Don José a letter from his mother fresh socks a kiss and five quid. She hints his mother has a further message. Don José reads the letter and asks for the further message. It is Please marry Micaela. Well . . . er . . . um . . . says Don José this matter needs careful consideration. I will leave you to ponder says Micaela and call for answer later today. OK says Don José (thinks: hell, why not? But is troubled by lustful thoughts of Carmen.)

A riot breaks out in the factory: screaming girls run out: there was a knife fight between Manuelita and Carmen they say. José is sent in to fetch out the fighters. He comes back plus Carmen: she was fairly carving up Manuelita says Don José. What do you say to that Carmen? asks officer Zuniga. Tra la la answers Carmen. Insolent bitch says Zuniga. Tra la la says Carmen. Put the bracelets on her José says Zuniga. Tra la la says Carmen. Take her off to jail says Zuniga: all exit.

These bracelets are too tight lemme escape says Carmen. I fancy you Don José: you fancy me: let me free and you can have sex with me. She sings a big sexy number inviting Don José to meet her that night at Lillas Pastia's place. Don José is knocked all of a heap: he weakens: he agrees. He loosens the bracelets. Zuniga with a warrant plus an escort arrives: the girls sneak out of the factory to watch: the escort forms up: Carmen slips the bracelets. Don José does a dummy pratfall. Carmen ducks out. Tumult. Confusion: derision from the girls: curtain.

Act II Lillas Pastia's café

The gypsy girls Carmen Frasquita and Mercedes dance a sexy Spanish number for Zuniga and other officers. Tra la la for a wild free gippo life they sing. Time gentlemen please says Lillas Pastia: kindly get moving. The local pigs are hard on me I can't think why. I'll tell you why says Zuniga your place is known as the HQ for smuggling crack. Why don't you come on with us to a nightclub girls? Pastia signals negative. The girls say no. Come on Carmen you've got it in for me because I nicked you says Zuniga. Forget it. Incidentally that loon Don José your fancy man was sent down for aiding and abetting your escape. Is he still inside? asks Carmen. Out tonight says Zuniga.

A chorus of Escamillo's groupies breaks out offstage. Zuniga invites them inside. Escamillo sings pop song No. 1 in the Sevillian charts concerning the irresistible sexual power of men who kill bulls (e.g. himself). The fans go crazy. Pastia does his nut but Escamillo lingers. Hey sexy he says to Carmen doing anything tonight? Tonight I'm fixed up she says maybe some other time. All exit. Zuniga is still sexually hopeful. He tells

Carmen he will call back later. Thank God says Pastia: at last.

Enter the smugglers Dancairo and Remendado. There's a big lot of the stuff in today from our man in Ponders End they say. We are moving it tonight. Are you girls game? Is it physical labour? asks the girls. No: sexual persuasion of the boys in blue say the smugs. The job's not possible without the connivance of officialdom. I'll go says Frasquita I'll go says Mercedes. I won't go says Carmen. Why not? they ask. I'm in love says Carmen. Don't be a mug they say. I won't go says Carmen. It's that soldier isn't it they say. Bet he won't come tonight. Bet he will says Carmen. Don José is heard offstage dead on cue. Why not get the poor sod to join us? say the smugs: good idea says Carmen. Exit smugs enter Don José.

Where you bin? asks Carmen. In jankers says Don José released forty-five minutes ago and I adore you. Your officer Zuniga adores me too and I danced for him says Carmen. Oh Carmen! says Don José. OK OK I will dance for you now all on your own says she. She dances. Bugles signal it's time for roll call. I must get back says Don José. You're chicken says Carmen OK get out. She chucks rifle ammo and gas cape etc. at him. Hey Carmen have a heart says Don José I sniffed your flower daily in clink. I had loving thoughts pretty well incessantly. I love you Carmen I am quite gone on you. Not true says Carmen if you were truly in love you would share my gypsy life with me in the great outdoors. Steady on Carmen says Don José desertion is a disgraceful act. Also illegal. OK says Carmen goodbye. I'm not ever seeing you again. Geddit?

A knock on the door interrupts these interesting exchanges. Zuniga forces his way in. Good Lord Carmen he says are you consorting with riff-raff from the sergeants' mess when officers are available? Get out corporal. Shan't says Don José. They both pull knives. Carmen interposes. She shouts help! Smugs and gippos crowd in. They disarm Zuniga and give him the bum's rush. Carmen asks Don José so now are you coming with me? There's no choice now says Don José. Everyone sings in praise of gippo culture mountains freedom liberty etc. (No mention of wind rain and snow nor of persecution by the law being moved on by Rural District Councils and other gippo whinges.)

Act III Sc 1 A rocky mountain pass

The gang of smugs stagger on stage pretty well fagged out. They attempt to improve morale by singing bold songs about brave hearts never fear etc. But then sink to the ground in a stupor of fatigue. Dancairo and Remendado exit to make a recce. Don José says by God Carmen you treat me like dirt. I want to be free says Carmen. At least my mother still loves me says Don José. Then push off back to her says Carmen. You bitch says Don José.

Frasquita and Mercedes are at gippo fortune telling. The cards foretell nice things for both girls. Carmen joins them. She gets the black two spot. This means death. Carmen is not pleased. She tries again. Again the black two spot. Death! Carmen is really depressed. Dancairo returns. He has spotted three boys in blue guarding the pass he says. Go and get to work on 'em girls he says. OK says Carmen. Don José tries to interpose. Lay off you jealous sod says Dancairo. He tells the girls that there is no danger of violence only mild sexual persuasion will be required.

A guide unexpectedly ushers Micaela onstage. She is searching for Don José: the general situation up here is very scary she says and also I am scared of Carmen. But lo! Don José is just offstage and bang! he discharges his rifle. Bajesus that's enough says Micaela I'm off. Exits.

Enter Escamillo with a hole in his hat just above the brainpan. Enter Don José his knife at ready. Who are you? he shouts. I am Escamillo, registered Granada bullfighter 243674 says he. My dear old chap says Don José it's terribly dangerous wandering around these parts with no visa. I nearly shot you dead. I am here seeking a relationship with Carmen I believe she was potty about some boring soldier but now she has gone off him says Escamillo. Bajesus says Don José if you steal one of our gypsy girls you will have to pay the price. So you're the poor sod she chucked? says Escamillo OK let's fight for her. They fight: Don José is winning. Carmen interposes. Stop it at once she says. OK I'll be off says Escamillo I'll see you at a bullfight should you ever wish to pursue the matter of a relationship. By the way I will fight you Don José at any time to suit our mutual convenience. Carmen says Don José I've taken just about enough from you. Pack it in children says Dancairo on your feet and get moving.

There's a stowaway here says Remendado and brings out Micaela. Don José! cries she. Micaela! cries he. Please hear your mother's message says she. Your mother weeps and wishes you to come home with me. Shan't says Don José. I'm sticking with Carmen. I regret there is a further message says Micaela. Your mother has terminal cancer. In that case I will go says Don José and if you think you've seen the last of me Carmen think again. We shall meet again as sure as death. (Escamillo – cheerful chappie – heard offstage toreadoring his way down the mountain path.)

Act II Sc 2 Outside a bullring: the day of a bullfight

Fans arrive for the big fight. There is intense commercial activity. Oranges wine water cigarettes fans programmes etc. all on sale. The ritual procession preceding the death of a bull begins: cuadrillas: torreros: chulos: banderillos: etceteros: with local dignitaries interspersed: then the man himself – Escamillo. Carmen and Escamillo have a private moment to confirm their deep sexual bond. Watch out Carmen! says Frasquita: Don José has been sighted in the crowd. Who's afraid of the big bad wolf? says Carmen I will go and talk to him. All exit to witness the death of the bull.

So it's you says Carmen. It's me says Don José. You don't scare me says she. Come away with me Carmen says Don José. No. Absolutely no says Carmen our relationship is through finished ended caput. I adore you Carmen says he I will return to banditry I will do anything. There is still time to save yourself and me. I know you will kill me but the answer is no no no says Carmen. [Noises off from bullring.] Carmen attempts to get away. Don José interposes. That punk bullfighter is fucking you now isn't he? Eh Carmen? he says. Lemme go says Carmen. [Offstage the fans do their nut.] This is your last chance Carmen he says come with me. No. No. And no says Carmen. Here's your lousy ring back: she chucks it at him. OK says Don José: he raises his knife and stabs Carmen to the heart. [A triumphant chorus offstage.] Carmen dies. Arrest me for murder says Don José I did it. Carmen I adore you. Curtain.

MINUTES FROM START

LOOK OUT FOR

Act I

0 The overture* has the three main tunes of the opera – 0
the Bullfight Parade Toreador and the Death Theme – all fully formed and fighting fit. After all the jolly stuff that goes before, the Death Theme comes in with the shock of a cold douche. It will come like that again, and again.

The soldiers comment on life as it goes by in a laid-
4: *Sur la place* back chorus* and with a remarkable absence of four- 4
letter words.

The gang of dead-end kids do their send-up of par-
10: *Avec la garde montante* ade-ground drill to a sharp little number* introduced 10
by the woodwind imitating a fife and drum band, and indeed the woodwind has the whale of a time with this item both on its first and second outings.

The bunch of voyeurs who have come to eye the girls, the watching soldiers and the factory girls themselves drift lazily through this scene each with their own 'thinks' chorus, the girls singing a particu-
15: *Dans l'air, nous suivons des yeux* larly dreamy, smoky number* with the most delicious 15
coda squeezed out from the woodwind.

23: *L'amour est un oiseau rebelle* Very Spanish, very famous, the Habanera*** (sexy 23
sort of song from Havana, granddad of the tango) is a marvellous piece. It tells us that Carmen is quite a

girl, also offers a terrific test for any aspiring mezzo. The chorus adds powerfully to the effect. As she finishes the cheering fans crowd around her. She makes her first deadly approach to Don José and suddenly we are struck with the menace of the Death Theme.

The Micaela/Don José duet comes to life when she coyly hints she has a special message: then she goes
31: *Votre mère avec moi sortait* first in a set-piece** duet and delivers Mother's 31
Message, a touching item. The message gets more tuneful and more heartfelt as she proceeds. He replies with a different tune (Son's Reply), with cheerful memories of early home life – she joins in with his (Son's Reply) tune and he responds with hers (Mother's Message) and so they duet happily until the distinctly embarrassing moment when he realizes he is face to face with a proposal of marriage.

After the chatter of the cigarette girls Carmen's
44: *Tra la la la* languid insolence** in the face of Zuniga's ques- 44
tioning is wonderfully effective – as the scene plays on Bizet works a novel kind of magic, for the spoken word over music is not the usual form of 'melodrame' i.e. the music reflecting the sense/emotion in the text. Instead the orchestra picks away at Carmen's Tra La La La whilst the perplexed soldiers talk as they truss her up.

Carmen's second top of the pops solo number –
48: *Près des remparts* Seguidille*** (name for a traditional Spanish dance). 48
A scorcher. She uses all her sexiness to mesmerize Don José into accepting an invitation to form what nowadays we would call a relationship, and he, poor sod, falls for it. Again very Spanish (or what we non-Spaniards *think* is very Spanish), jerky rhythms, swoops, lingering in the middle of a phrase etc. – everything in fact except the castanets and the odd shout of olé. A terrific success. Followed by the runaway end to the act – Don José safely trapped, subdued excitement in the orchestra, Zuniga insulted once again, the escape – and then bedlam.

Act II

This act is made up of four stunning set pieces, every one a winner, plus the finale: the first, the Gypsy Dance, begins with the Entr'acte, now often played with the curtain up and the gypsies going at it in full swing: Carmen starts up with her description of the

2: *Les tringles des sistres*

gypsies' dance,** racy, heady and soon coming to 2 merge with the dance itself: the dance gets faster and faster and ends in a whirl – dancers all as high as kites. Packs a powerful Spanish punch.

Escamillo's fans can be heard belting out the Bull-fight Parade in the distance: they arrive and belt it out again: Escamillo uninvited treats the company to a vivid colour picture of the Toreador's public and pri-

10: *Votre toast . . . je peux vous le rendre*

vate life:*** one of opera's most hackneyed pieces, 10 played by brass bands, mangled by inadequate bari-tones, always round the corner on almost any middle-brow radio music programme, blaring out at agricultural shows, whistled, hummed by millions and unsparingly parodied – if a number can survive all this it deserves three stars and Toreador can – just – sur-vive with a top-class singer, although we may wish that Bizet had not opted to repeat the Toreador Toreador bit *four* times.

Now for a patch of inspired magic: perhaps the

18: *Nous avons en tête*

best item in the act – the quintet*** with the two 18 leading smugglers and the three gypsy girls: the men tell the girls they'll be needed for a job in fast darting exchanges which introduce the quintet proper (the

19: *Quand il s'agit*

men alone first then all five).*** This is not a 'thinks' 19 piece nor a plot-assister, it is a joyous celebration of woman's superiority to man in the matter of cheating, conning, double-crossing, lying, etc. and it should delight the heart of every ardent feminist. A catchy tune, fast, staccato, marvellous part writing and gen-erally just a little gem. But – we proceed. The men tell the girls they are wanted that night: Carmen refuses: the men plead with quite a new theme that would melt the heart of anyone but Carmen: she is adamant: they try again in yet another quite new and self-contained exchange: finally a reprise of the glorious racey fivesome chorus. Five minutes of delight.

24: *Je vais danser*

The Carmen/Don José duet*** is the centrepiece 24 of the act. Carmen dances for him, this time with cas-tanets and all (but no olés). It is a lazy beguiling tune and she la-la-las to it (no opera has more tras and las to the acre than *Carmen*): the regimental bugles play an unknown but apparently significant call: Don José

breaks into the dance in an embarrassed fashion: Carmen is goaded out of teasing into a flurry of anger and she goes for him in the most musically agitated passage in the scene: he pleads sweetly and mournfully – no good she tells him: get out. Then suddenly, as ever, the Death Theme forebodes something terrible to come. Don José in his longest and finest solo
30: *La fleur que tu m'avais jetée* piece*** tells Carmen of his longings for her in prison 30
(the Flower Song). A noble impassioned quasi-aria finishing with a tremendously urgent statement of I-Love-You. Carmen contradicts: if he loved her he would join her in the gypsy life: another wonderfully
35: *Là-bas – là-bas dans la montagne* apt melody*** – Away into the mountain – which 35
runs on amongst the argument.

42: *Suis-nous à travers* The finale is capped by a nomadic chorus** – it 42
sounds as if the mob was already tramping towards their beloved mountains until – at the very end – we have a short burst of the magical quintet, now in praise of Liberty rather than female criminality.

Act III Sc 1

0 The prelude** is another stand-alone gem, though it 0
fits perfectly the mood of moonlight, stillness and stealth. The flute has the first turn with the ingenuous little tune, which stays with the woodwind throughout.

The midnight march** of the smugglers, full of weariness and wariness and leading to their morale-
5: *Ecoute, compagnon, écoute* boosting chorus* and sextet, in spite of which they 5
continue to sound pretty well ready for a kip.

The card trio: Frasquita and Mercedes take the fortune-telling game lightly enough, notably in their
10: *Et maintenant, parlez, mes belles* delicious duet/refrain** asking the cards (very 10
nicely) to do their stuff. Not so Carmen: she draws a wrong 'un and dives into the darkest of dramatic reci-
12: *En vain pour éviter* tatifs then sings a doomy gloomy aria* in which she 12
seems convinced that a spade is a spade and means burial, preceded by death.

17: *Quant au douanier* The customs officers' trio and chorus.** The girls 17
say 'Leave 'em to us' to a catchy coquettish little number which if inverted is not a million miles away from 'Toreador'.

Micaela, wildly out of place amongst the rocks and smugglers, swears she will find Don José and con-

21: *Je dis que rien* front Carmen, whatever.* A free-moving, sometimes 21
affecting, piece with no great melodic strength.

The cunningly crafted finale works wonderfully well, though without any great musical landmarks. The confrontation between Escamillo and Don José
30: *Holà, José !* with its combative duet* winds up to the knife fight, 30
then Escamillo's dignified farewell accompanied by a sadly diminished Toreador tune, Micaela's repeat of Mother's Message from Act I leading to news of Mother's impending death, Don José's Goodbye – but we'll meet again to the Death Theme and finally the retreating Escamillo keeping his pecker up with the distant Toreador as he stumbles down the mountain back to the bullring.

Act III Sc 2

The last scene is Bizet's greatest *tour de force*.

39 The very Spanish fairground prelude** has the 39
woodwind playing the tune with the strings (pizzicato) giving a big-scale guitar accompaniment.

After the opening chorus and a good deal of quick operatic trading (no-one asks the price of anything; no-one haggles), the procession starts off to the glori-
43: *Les voici, voici le quadrille* ous strains of the Bullfight Parade*** in full fig. 43
There is a sort of double act: the chorus race-read the notables in the procession and between each dollop of information we have another orchestral helping of the Parade (four times, and always welcome). Then a brief pause for the 'I love yous' between Escamillo and Carmen, the Mayor's douce and decent little march, and the Parade dies away. So to the final
50: *C'est toi ? C'est moi* duet:*** Don José sweetly lyrical, still pleading, Car- 50
men cool, firm and declamatory.

Now the climax: Don José begins to break up: he shouts and bawls his passion for Carmen: the bullring huzzas break in with a savage irony – Escamillo has killed his bull – Don José's jealousy erupts: suddenly the Death Theme strikes home and the now half-crazed Don José seizes his dagger and strikes his blow, and offstage we hear not the Parade, but Toreador darkened by a sinister new theme in the lower strings. So back to the Death Theme and Don José's last broken utterances of desolation and despair.

NOTES

Carmen	Bizet's tenth (including operetta) and the last of his performed operas
First night	Opéra Comique, Paris, 3 March 1875
Reception	After the first act some applause, after the second less, during the third boos: last scene – debacle. This reception broke Bizet's spirit and stands as a lasting and terrible indictment of French musical taste
Libretto	Meilhac and Halévy
Source	A novel by Prosper Mérimée

NEWS AND GOSSIP

In Mérimée's novel Don José tells the story himself, how he lost his rank, his position and finally his life itself because of his crazy infatuation with the gypsy Carmen. Mérimée's Don José is a tougher more brutal type than Bizet's. He had already committed three murders before he met Carmen and there was nothing of the big soft Nelly about him. But even Bizet's Don José was too much for the Opéra Comique whose management believed in family viewing and fought a rearguard action against the sex and violence in the show from the date of commission right through rehearsals and up to the first night. We shall never know how much give there was and how much take and who gave and who took, but the final libretto still looks like a win for the home team over the Mary Whitehouses of the day. The librettists, Meilhac and Halévy, broadened and thickened the story: Micaela was no more than a one-line reference in Mérimée: a great deal of the colour (kids playing soldiers, smugglers' quintet, fortune-telling) was added to move the piece away from a single narrative line to something of a pageant of Spanish life with the original story still as a core of steel. Above all, there was the brilliant idea of setting the murder outside the bullring.

After the Paris disaster, *Carmen* was given the reception it deserved in Vienna in October of the same year. That conservative but truly musical city acclaimed it as a masterpiece and as a masterpiece it has been acclaimed ever since, standing right amongst the top of the most respected pops in every civilized country, including even France.

COMMENT

Carmen has a head start on most operas because of its libretto. The script team – Meil and Hal – did Bizet proud with a dramatization of Mérimée's story that could almost as well hold the stage as a play – and a gripper at that – but which they shaped into exactly the right article for Bizet's genius – lots of big numbers, not continuous music, plenty of colour, and with the story pounding along with a pulse like a cannon. They were a couple of real pros and even at this distance we should raise a glass to them as well as to Bizet for giving us this stunning piece. Indeed so artful were they that the spoken dialogue seems a natural part of the scene and not a leap into another idiom as it does so often in even the best *Singspiels*, e.g. *Fidelio* and *The Magic Flute*. And the lyrics themselves are as taut and as pointed as those of Rodgers or Lowe.

Carmen is perhaps the first true verismo opera, for *Traviata* still had the heavy aroma of romantic love hanging around it, *Cav* and *Pag* are in truth both barn-storming melodramas, but in Don José we recognize a real man, who self-destructs because of his infatuation with a real woman, Carmen, perhaps the first truly three-dimensional operatic heroine who becomes every bit as much of our lives as Anna Karenina or Madame Bovary.

Until the last scene *Carmen* can be misread as a succession of smash hits with talking in between. It is true that Carmen's set-piece solos, Toreador and Don José's Flower Song will bring the house down any day, but the real power of the opera lies in the contrast between the pomp and panache of the bullfight music (and the confident Spanish music of the gypsies) and Don José's tortured musical journey through the opera to his final 'O Carmen! Ma Carmen adorée.' The final scene, with what in film terms would be cross-cutting between the inside and the outside of the bullring, is even better in sound than it would be in pictures.

Carmen's impact is direct to the solar plexus, no doubt through the brain, but without requiring too much assistance from that quarter. It is clear, uncomplicated and, as Nietzsche said [Who he? Ed.], is the perfect antidote to the paranoia of Wagner. Bizet's sound too is a million miles away from that of Brahms and Wagner: he uses the woodwind as if they were a separate set of singers: nearly every piece has the singer or the woodwind in the lead and overall the sound is sparkling, clear and with no trace of German mud. The score is also exceedingly Spanish and despite all the De Fallas and Granadoses *Carmen*, along with Rimsky's 'Capriccio Espagnol', remains one of the two best-known pieces in the 'Spanish' repertory. How a Frenchman and a Russian came to make Spanish music more popular than the native Spaniards is a mystery. (No-one did it for England and any foreigner who tried to out-German the Germans would have been disembowelled by the Viennese musical mafia.)

Carmen is as near bullet-proof as any opera can be. It flourished in a recent splendid film, was transformed in an earlier film, *Carmen Jones*, and some would say enhanced, by Peter Brook, it even survived being set in a used-car lot by English National Opera. So *Carmen* is great, *Carmen* is a wonder, and anyone who don't like *Carmen* don't like opera and should look elsewhere for musical excitement and perhaps will find it in the works of Adlgasser, Scriabin or Thelonius Monk. Alpha-plus.

Cavalleria Rusticana

Sicilian tragedy

(A matter of honour)

Mascagni

The one about a Sicilian village with an Easter hymn and a terminal knife fight.

CAST

Santuzza, a village girl	Soprano
Turiddu, a soldier on leave	Tenor
Mamma Lucia, Santuzza's mother	Contralto
Alfio, a common carrier	Baritone
Lola, his wife	Mezzo
A peasant girl	

1 act: running time 1 hr 10 mins

STORY

An Italian village square, a church prominent

We are in Sicily in 1890 – real time for Mascagni, over a century ago for us. Before curtain up Turiddu serenades Lola. Church bells ring for Easter morning: we see the slow run-up to mass: people gather: they creep in to church. Santuzza asks Mamma Lucia: where's Turiddu? On a trip to Francofonte buying wine says she: not true says Santa he was seen here last night: he never came home says Mamma come into my house and talk. I can't says Santa I am excommunicated [so she can't visit? Ed.].

Their conversation is interrupted by jolly songster carter Alfio: he loves his horse also his wife Lola. He wants some Château Yquem 1882: where's Turiddu? Gone to get more Yquem says Mamma. Not so says jolly carter I saw him this morning. Santa shushes Mamma. Mass is beginning (at last): Alfio goes to church. The mighty Easter Hymn is sung by the whole village – half the population inside half outside the church – then all go inside conveniently leaving Mamma and Santa tête-à-tête.

Why did you shush me? asks Mamma. Because says Santa before Turiddu went on national service Lola made a solemn vow to marry him: once Turiddu was safely away soldiering Lola switched to jollio Alfio. Turiddu picked me up on the rebound: but Lola seduced Turiddu into her adulterous bed leaving me Santa high and dry (also we guess pregnant). My God says Mamma what a terrible earful for Easter Day. Mamma exits into church (resorting to instant prayer).

Lost boy Turiddu turns up. So where were you? Santa asks. Francofonte says he. Liar says she you bin with that tramp Lola. So you been tailing me? he asks: anyway you are my true love not Lola. Liar says she that bitch Lola stole you. The conversation is interrupted by Lola in person happily singing a little-girl song about flowers. Santa aims snide remarks at Lola. Let's go to mass says Lola. No Turi and myself are having an important conversation says Santa (Lola goes in). Santa turns on Turiddu. How can you treat a poor girl so? she says: get off my back says Turiddu (he goes into mass). Jollio Alfio arrives. Did you know your Lola's having it off with Turiddu? asks Santa. Thanks for the information says Alfio no longer jollio. By God I'll get them both. Mass is over. All exit.

Turiddu leads a communal booze-up, offers a glass to Alfio. No thanks says Alfio it's probably poisoned (insult!). All exit. Turiddu bites Alfio's ear (old Sicilian custom signifying You bastard I challenge you to fight to the death). Alfio responds You're on. Turiddu disengages his teeth and sings wimpishly – I am guilty: if I am killed poor Santa will be left alone. Alfio says see you behind the vestry: Turiddu half drunk bids a maudlin farewell to Mamma and begs her to look after Santa: he goes off behind the vestry. A crowd fills the square: a cry goes up 'Turiddu is dead!'. Santa faints. Mamma faints. Curtain.

MINUTES FROM START

LOOK OUT FOR

5: *O Lola, ch'hai di latti* — The prelude (a potpourri of tunes to come) is interrupted by Turiddu offstage singing a conventional but decent tenor aria (a Siciliana)* which speaks well of Lola and indeed says that unless she is in heaven when he dies he would prefer to go elsewhere – a gloomy thought so early in the evening. (Plot point: he is informing us of his adulterous love before we meet Santa.) 5

19: *Il cavallo scalpita* — Alfio sings a comic song about life as a carter.* Spirited. 19

23: *Regina Coeli* — The Easter Hymn,*** world famous, stately, irresistible, a real buster. Santa swings out nicely above the two choirs. 23

30: *Voi lo sapete, O mamma* — Santa explains her quite considerable problems to Mamma Lucia.* Dramatic outpourings to a suitable accompaniment. 30

37: *Fior di giaggiolo* — Lola's silly little song. It catches the ear.* 37

The furious exchanges between Santa and
42: *No, no, Turiddu* Turiddu end in a surging lyrical duet* (which still 42
carries faint echoes of the Easter Hymn). Powerful
stuff.

Santa, intense and at first a little more restrained,
tells Alfio that Lola is having it off with Turiddu.
48: *Turiddu mi tolse* They duet:* Alfio goes berserk. 48

52 The intermezzo:* a variation of the Easter Hymn, 52
with the same throbbing sentiment but not so compulsive in this second appearance.

57: *A casa, a casa, amici* The jolly scenes following the intermezzo* go with 57
a swing – first the hurdy-gurdy waltz chorus, soon to
a 4/4 vamped accompaniment (pom pom – chi chi).

59: *Intanto amici* Turiddu's solo** as he decides to get smashed (and 59
appears to be about to break into any one of half-a-
dozen well-known Neapolitan songs at any moment)
61: *Beviam! Beviam!* and finally the boozy chorus.* 61

Turiddu's two best solos come just before death –
64: *Compar Alfio* his wimpish pleading with Alfio* (Don't kill me: poor 64
Santa will suffer), a little slow at first (perhaps until
he gets rid of the taste of Alfio's ear) but leading to a
robust final flourish and his craven goodbye to
67: *Quel vino è generoso* Mummy** which again has two powerful bursts of 67
tenor angst before he runs off to be knifed.

NOTES

Cavalleria Rusticana	Mascagni's second
First night	Teatro Costanzi, Rome, 17 May 1890
Reception	A hit
Libretto	Menasci and Tozzetti
Source	A play of the same title by Verga

NEWS AND GOSSIP

Mascagni had seen Verga's play some time in 1884 and thought it would be a likely runner in a competition for one-acters set up by the up-and-coming music publishers Sonzogno. He was right. *Cav* won first prize in a field of 72. There was extra satisfaction in the fact that he had sent the score to Puccini in advance. Puccini thought it hadn't a chance. Wrong. Also his friend the publisher Ricordi thought the same. Wrong again. Sweet satisfaction for Mascagni, a winner, a hit, and egg on the faces of two frightfully important members of the musical establishment. The first performance was in a triple bill with the second and third prize-winners and it was clear at once that Mascagni had a world-class smash hit on his hands. So it was and so it is today. Twinned with *Pag* it is a sure-fire sellout.

COMMENT

Cav comes off because all the working parts are simple and effective as in a T model Ford. It has one great tune, lots of good little ones, standard but sound orchestration, conventional harmonic system and a high-voltage story of love and jealousy in the Sicilian outback. The parts are put together in a thoroughly professional manner and it works. There was a 1920s jingle about the T model as follows:

> There was a young fellow named Ford
> Who got a length of rubber and a board
> A little drop of petrol and an old tin can –
> He put 'em all together and the darned thing ran.

Translated into operatic terms and substituting Mascagni for Ford, this is an unfair but apt description of *Cav*. And the T model was, we must remember, the most successful and in many ways the most lovable car ever made. *Cav*'s strengths are the strengths of all traditional Italian opera: great bursts of melody, searing passion, high drama. Its weaknesses are in the huge ratio of padding to plot development (Prelude, Easter Hymn, choruses, Intermezzo – together half an hour out of less than an hour and a quarter). Indeed, what we have is not so much a plot, rather a situation (a quadrangle) leading to a fight (terminal). The hero is an exceptionally poor specimen of manhood, a coward, a sneaky adulterer, a thoughtless seducer of nice girls, a cry-baby and unreliable when it comes to buying wine. Not so much an anti-hero as a wet. The other characters are out of Mamma Lucia's book of stock opera types. It has a score that is orchestrated right on the nose (no depth and no richness of texture) and church music dripping with goo which is bugged with tiresome schoolroom progressions (tum tum: one-step-up: tum tum: one-more-step-up, etc.).

But, but . . . if *Cav* is put on with utter conviction (essential) and a full-blooded Italian cast (desirable) it is a knock-out. No doubt about it. Let the critics mark it as they may – a popular alpha.

La Cenerentola (Cinderella)

Romantic fairy tale

Rossini

Cinderella, of course, but not quite the British Cinders we know from our storybooks and pantos.

CAST

Cinderella (Angelina)	Contralto
Clorinda } her step-sisters	Soprano
Thisbe } her step-sisters	Mezzo
Baron Don Magnifico, their father	Bass
Don Ramiro, the Prince	Tenor
Dandini, his valet	Bass
Alidoro, a philosopher	Bass

2 acts: running time 2 hrs 25 mins

STORY

Act I Sc 1 A room in the Baron's decrepit castle

The frightful sisters are prinking: Cinders is crouching in the hearth singing her theme song of which the sisters have had quite enough: they tell her to belt up. A beggar comes in but no beggar he, rather one Alidoro variously described as the Prince's tutor, a philosopher, 'maestro' by the Prince and by himself as a pretty close associate of God. In truth he is probably a failed wizard (he does nothing recognizable as bona fide magic in the show) temping with Ramiro. The sisters are horrid to him: Cinders kind.

The Prince's men arrive with the announcement of a ball: father stumbles in: recounts a boring dream about future riches for himself and family: the sisters tell him about a ball where the Prince will select a bride. The sisters go off to their toilet.

Ramiro thc Prince arrives in person disguised as a servant: Alidoro has told him that there is a beautiful girl at this address: where is she? Cinders enters: makes eye-contact: drops her coffee cup and tells the stranger her life story. The sisters yelp for Cinders to help. The Prince in disguise tells father the Prince will arrive at any moment.

Sure enough Dandini disguised as the Prince tells of his hunt for a wife. He must get wed quick or else be disinherited: hence the ball. The sisters and father are all agog: Dandini camps it up like mad: the real

Prince wonders where is Cinders? The sisters, courtiers etc. go off to the ball leaving Ramiro eavesdropping on Cinders imploring father to let her go too. Father raises a stick to beat Cinders which makes the Prince and Dandini very uncomfortable. Father explains that Cinders is an uppity kitchen skivvy.

Alidoro comes in with the party invitation list: asks father about the third daughter? Dead, says he (I'll kill you Cinders he says behind his hand if you say a word). All go except the wretched C. Alidoro returns as a beggar and tells Cinders she will go to the ball and there will be a happy ending.

Act I Sc 2 A room in the Prince's palace

Dandini is conned into appointing Father chief butler: he is packed off to sample princely wines. The sisters compete for the 'Prince's' favours.

Act I Sc 3 Another room in the palace (in some productions the same)

Father roisters with some courtiers, he tastes thirty wines and dictates a memo on cellar management (pure padding: no relevance to the story). Ramiro asks Dandini in a secret conference: what are the sisters really like? Ghastly, says Dandini. But, says Ramiro, Alidoro told me one was a winner. Sod him says Dandini.

The sisters enter and renew their onslaught on the 'Prince': Ramiro offers himself to whomsoever should be the disappointed one. Like hell, they say, a common servant! But hark – a mysterious beauty has arrived. She enters and unveils, revealing a clone of Cinders, or is it indeed Cinders herself? How confusing. Everyone muses over this matter for some considerable time in a mild 'confusion' finale.

Act II Sc 1 A room in the Prince's palace

Father and the sisters take time out from the ball: they are disgruntled: will the mystery lady beat them to it? Father conjures up a rosy picture of a deluxe future life: he depends upon the sisters (which?) to get it for him.

Dandini (still as Prince) and Cinders drift in. Dandini says he loves her: she says she loves his servant. Ramiro who has been listening jumps out, reveals identity and proposes marriage. Not yet says Cinders not until you find me in my natural habitat: she gives him one of a pair of bracelets and runs for it.

The Prince asks Alidoro what he should do: up to you says the useless Alidoro. The Prince vows to find her. Father now begs Dandini (still the

Prince to some) to make up his mind: his girls are going crazy. Dandini lets the cat out of the bag, but slowly: he is no Prince he is the Prince's valet. Father bombs out.

Act II Sc 2 A room back in father's shabby castle

Cinders at it again (theme song): Father and the sisters return in an ugly mood. There is a storm: Dandini pops in with news. The Prince's carriage has crashed (and what was he doing belting off through the night with his ball scarcely over?). The Prince enters. Father's hopes are rekindled but the Prince glimpses the matching bracelet on Cinders's wrist. O joy! All six principals express private thoughts (some uncomplimentary) as if no one else were present. Alidoro completes the scene with a holy bromide.

Act II Sc 3 Throne room in Prince's castle

The finale: the courtiers hail the triumph of love, virtue and humility over pride and ambition. Cinders begs forgiveness for the bad behaviour of her dreadful relatives. This is granted. All rejoice.

MINUTES FROM START

Act I Sc 1

LOOK OUT FOR

La Cenerentola starts strongly, the first twenty minutes rolling out one vintage Rossini item after an-
0 other: first an overture of the top class*** (borrowed 0
from a previous opera, *La Gazzetta*) complete with the customary cheeky woodwind tune in mid-course, foot-tapping cross rhythms and bustling climaxes; then a pert duet between the sisters which is interrupted by Cinders's rendering of her really nice old
10: *Una volta c'era un re* ballad** about a prince who seeks a lady truly inno- 10
cent and good; next a quartet full of business with the phoney beggar, an agreeable chorus to announce the arrival of the prince Ramiro and then the scuffle and
15: *Cenerentola, vien qua* scuttle quartet** in which Cenerentola's role in life 15
clearly has some actual and musical similarities with that of Figaro, but ending (chorus and all) in a mighty climax more like The Heavens Are Telling than a buffa ensemble. Whew!

Things slacken off a bit – the sisters argue who should wake up Father in recitatif but he has already been awakened by their chatter (and what about The

Heavens Are Telling?) and after a cross quasi-
recitatif approach towards a cavatina he recounts his
20: *Miei rampolli femminini* farrago of a dream in a standard buffa manner.* This 20
piece of padding depends for its success more upon
its delivery than its musical inspiration.

And now the next big event of Act I – Ramiro
arrives, encounters Cinders wandering in singing her
26: *Un soave non so che* theme song: they embark on a duet,** at first in 26
snatches of private reaction to each other (love at first
sight!), looking fixedly in opposite directions so that
the audience knows neither can hear what the other
says, all of this very flowery; then they turn to each
other and swing along in continuous melody as
Cinders tries to explain her family situation. She is
interrupted by offstage yells for help from the sisters.

Ramiro greets Father in recitatif, and after another
beguiling entr'acte with a hunting horn (which will
recur), we enter one of Rossini's magical en-
38: *Come un' ape* sembles,*** in which Dandini (masquerading as the 38
Prince) takes the lead. This is all very busy buffa,
including a bout of patter, asides between Dandini
and Ramiro, interjections from the sisters and Father,
and a delicate and constantly varied orchestral accompaniment, climaxing with the chorus.

In a scene where Dandini in his role as Prince
butters up the two sisters we have an unusual event: a
44: *Or dunque, seguitando* patter recitatif.* 44

Cinders asks to go to the ball in a brief cavatina
46: *Signor, una parola* with a memorable phrase*** ('just one hour in the 46
Prince's palace'). This leads to a robust quartet,
father abusing Cinders, she pleading, Don Ramiro
furious, Dandini expostulating.

Alidoro appears and there is an uncomfortable
duet with Father in which the question as to whether
Cinders is alive or dead is debated. Now a 'thinks'
52: *Nel volto estatico* quintet** in which all five dreamily reflect on their 52
several confusions: this is resolved by each party
noisily asserting what they really do think: bustle and
rush.

Alidoro asks Cinders to come with him to the
palace: he reveals who he is [not at all clear: Ed.] in a
62: *Là del ciel nell' arcano profundo* cavatina* that starts glumly but ends with an up-beat 62
cabaletta as he assures Cinders her luck has turned.

Act I Sc 2

Dandini (as Prince) despatches Father to the cellars and continues to flatter the sisters in an extravagant fashion. All recitatif, padding rather than narrative.

Act I Sc 3

The courtiers in chorus acclaim their new Grand
Butler: Father dictates a proclamation in a buffa aria
82: *Noi Don* in which the melody is given to the violins** as he 82
Magnifico barks and growls below: beguiling orchestration
throughout.

The finale to Act I starts with one of Rossini's
84: *Zitto, zitto:* catchy tiptoe tunes,** as a duet when Ramiro quizzes 84
piano, piano Dandini about what the sisters are like (horrible says
Dandini) and continuing into a quartet as the sisters
squabble over who shall get 'the Prince'.

After an extended 'wait for it' scene the mystery
woman is unveiled – is it Cinders? Yes? No? The
matter is debated by all present in a breathless en-
87: *Parlar, pensar,* semble** which owes an unmistakable debt to the
vorrei great Act I quartet in *Fidelio*.

Everyone goes off to dinner but not before a big
92: *Mi par d'essere* and bold Rossini crescendo finale** that forecasts ter- 92
sognando rible turmoil ahead. If you think you have heard the
theme before you are right. (In the overture to this
opera and also in the overture to the *Barber*.) Really
big choral stuff at the end – The Heavens Are Telling
again.

Act II Sc 1

After some brief recitatif between the sisters and
Father, we embark on one of Rossini's monster comic
2: *Sia qualunque* songs* in which Father looks forward to the wonders 2
delle figlie and delights of being father-in-law to a queen. It is as
elaborate and as taxing as 'La Calumnia' in the *Barber*. First, a short introduction in jerky rhythm: a beguiling running tune in the violins introduces verses 1 and 2 (both with fantasy dialogue enacted in falsetto voice): then we move into a higher speed and finish with a patter-crescendo-climax as Father has a delirious mirage of the luxury life ahead. Exquisite orchestral accompaniment throughout and the running tune again at the close – with the right singer, always a resounding success.

Ramiro proposes to Cinders in recitatif, she gives him the bracelet in the same mode, and Ramiro then

9: *Sì, ritrovarla io giuro* embarks on an aria** with chorus swearing he will 9
find her again: an introduction – a melody – a sweet adagio section (as he kisses the bracelet) and then a bit of a bustle as they set out on the search.

After a long recitatif abounding with windows for comic business in which Father persecutes Dandini with questions (which daughter will he marry?) we
15: *Un segreto d'importanza* have an unusual item: a duet** for the two basses 15
which unrolls in fine style leading to yet another patter climax in which Dandini reveals himself as a valet (Father predictably shocked, outraged, horrified).

Act II Sc 2

Cinders, back in the fireplace, gives us a full rendering of her theme song. Father and sisters return:
23: *Storm* there is a storm* which never quite reaches Force 9 23
but is complete with a shepherd's hymn of thanksgiving à la Beethoven 6 and has force enough to overturn the Prince's carriage (good receding thunder). The plot proceeds in humdrum recitatif to the matching of bracelets upon which all six parties present are struck with wonder and after some opening declamatory lines sail into one of Rossini's happiest
27: *Siete voi?* inventions, a sextet,*** one singer holding the mel- 27
ody singing sotto voce, the others staccato, chorded, with one part or another shooting off from time to time into florid decorated lines. Next each character comes out in their own flowing solo: Cinderella is given the floor, and pleads touchingly for tolerance towards her frightful family. The pace changes: Ramiro claims Cinders as his bride: so dramatically to a climax of bliss (Prince and Cinders), consternation (Father and sisters) and wry amusement (Dandini). Alidoro throws in a philosophical bromide in recitatif and the finale begins with a lengthy orchestral flourish and chorus. So the happiness of the hero and heroine is confirmed, Father and sisters repent and
46: *Nacqui all' affanno* Cinders secures their forgiveness in affecting aria** 46
which develops into a splendid concerted rondo. Cinders has a sparkling solo episode: everyone harmoniously agrees she is just wonderful.

NOTES

La Cenerentola	Rossini's twentieth opera
First night	Teatro Valle, Rome, 25 January 1817 with Rossini (aged 25) at the keyboard
Reception	Very good
Libretto	Ferretti
Source	A fairy tale by Perrault. But all of Perrault's fairies and witches were dumped in favour of the unsatisfactory Alidoro

NEWS AND GOSSIP

In its first form *Cenerentola* had three numbers not by Rossini but by an unknown called Agolini but as the opera gained strength by repeated production Rossini threw them out and all the 'final' numbers are all his own (no opera score in Italy was absolutely final so long as the composer was alive and even after his death people fiddled). The recitatifs are not Rossini's, probably Agolini's. There are the usual stories about *Cenerentola* being composed in three weeks. Certainly Rossini did not seem to have time to write an overture since this one had already been used in an earlier opera, *La Gazzetta*. *Cenerentola* was a hit and for decades was more performed than even the *Barber*. It is difficult to cast, what with a mezzo or contralto heroine, a high tenor and two basses who must have voices that are distinct and yet match well.

COMMENT

Cenerentola in its good stretches (which is most of the time) is Rossini at his brightest and best. If, when one hears it out of the theatre, there are longueurs this is because the recitatifs (more of them than usual) are used to advance the very plotty plot rapidly and therefore need only minimal musical support. Another weakness is the dependence upon the Baron (Father) as a comic actor: he has three patter arias, only one of which is musically fresh ('Sia qualunquc delle figlie') – the other two having predictable vocal parts although one (the dictating of the memo on wine management) has the most bewitching accompanying figure. If the buffa bass is played by a worn-out but much-loved old hack, as, alas, is often the case, the results can be dire. There is also the irritating figure of Alidoro. But the good bits prevail: the glowing ensemble 'Come un' ape' which includes good tunes, patter, interjections, the usual speeding up and growing noisiness plus a really imaginative and inventive role for the orchestra: the catchy sotto voce scene 'Zitto zitto' where the Prince gets an earful about the sisters: the disillusionment duet between Dandini and Father: the Act II sextet which begins sotto voce again and develops into a short opera in its own right and the Rondo finale (lifted from the last act of an early version of the *Barber*). But what makes *Cenerentola* different from Rossini's other comic operas is his affection for the character of Cinders and the way he charts her development from scullery maid to queen. She does not have a dull bar in the whole piece: her theme song is simple and genuinely affecting, she pleads to be allowed to go to the ball in a phrase so poignant as to live in the ear, she gains dignity and self-confidence as the mysterious stranger, she deals with the Prince as an equal and in the finale comes right out of the closet and shows herself to be adorable, compassionate and quite capable of managing relations with her family, organizing the Prince and probably ruling the kingdom too.

Despite a few beta patches, *Cenerentola* is undoubtedly an alpha.

Cesare, Giulio *see* Giulio Cesare

Chénier, Andrea *see* Andrea Chénier

Cinderella, *see* Cenerentola, La

La Clemenza di Tito

Roman drama

(Tito the Magnanimous)

Mozart [K621]

The one where the Emperor Tito forgives everyone in sight including his best friend who tried to kill him but carelessly killed another man by mistake who as it turns out wasn't killed either.

CAST

Tito, Emperor of Rome	Tenor
Vitellia, daughter of the previous Emperor	Soprano
Sesto, friend of Tito, lover of Vitellia	Mezzo
Servilia, Sesto's sister	Soprano
Annio, friend of Sesto, lover of Servilia	Soprano
Publio, captain of the Praetorian Guard	Bass

2 acts: running time 2 hrs 20 mins

STORY

Act I Sc 1 A room in Vitellia's house

We are in the Rome of Tito better known to classical Brits as Vespasian in 78 AD and in the presence of Vitellia who wants some action. Hey Sesto she says to her aristo boyfriend will you kindly pull your finger out and get moving. You tell me over and over this plot of ours – to burn the Capitol and kill Tito – is all set up with Tiny Tim Lentulus standing ready but it's all talk talk talk. Remember this guy Tito killed my father the Emperor Vitellius? He also conned me into thinking he wanted to marry me? That he's now taken up with this Jewish slut Berenice?

Steady old girl says Sesto Tito is a very decent chap really hence my hesitation. Consider our engagement at an end says Vitellia unless Tito is killed tonight. OK I'll do it says Sesto. Thinks: nasty business having to kill your best friend but there that's life.

Sesto's mate Annio pops in. Tito wants to see you he says. So he's taking a few minutes off from humping with that Berenice? says Vitellia. Berenice has gone home. Tito refused to extend her visa says Annio. Aha! so he may still marry me thinks Vitellia. Hey Sesto I don't think we should start burning the Capitol yet hold on for now. Vitellia exits.

Sesto! says Annio: remember you promised that your kid sister would marry me? Sure says Sesto it was a very happy thought. Will you ask the boss for a special licence? Today? says Annio. OK says Sesto. Today.

Act I Sc 2 Part of the Forum

There is a big parade with reps from many conquered nations. The crowd cry Huzza for Tito what a nice chap and an exceptionally good Emperor too. I just wanted to tell you Tito says creepy Annio we Romans have just decided that you are God Almighty and we will construct an appropriate temple. And another thing Tito says Publio (C-in-C Home Guard) we've got all these colonials to cough up about half a billion denarii to cover your expenses. Jolly good of you says Tito but I would prefer to transfer all this loot to the Vesuvius famine relief fund.

Everyone exits stunned by the amazing goodness of Tito. Tito Annio and Sesto stay behind. I say I say Sesto old boy says Tito good news I have decided to marry your sister Servilia. Today in fact. You will become a royal in-law. Congratters. Um . . . Er . . . Well . . . says Sesto (thinks Oh Gawd poor Annio). What's biting you Annio? says Tito. Just indigestion says Annio suppressing terrible angst. OK Tito says Sesto you take her she's a lovely girl you'll be very happy together. What's more Sesto says Tito I will appoint you non-exec deputy Emperor. Oh Tito you are really too kind says Sesto. Not at all says Tito I am such a frightfully nice chap I get all my kicks out of being generous, kind, considerate etc.

Ah well that's my girl a goner thinks Annio. Pity, but that's life. Enter Servilia. Have I got news for you says Annio: you're booked to be Caesar's wife just when you and I were getting on so nicely. Oh lawks says she – but I love you still.

Act I Sc 3 A room in the Imperial Palace

Publio shows Tito list of tabloid editors noted for publishing nasty stuff about royals living and dead and seeks authority for consigning them to the wild beasts. Let 'em be says liberal Tito I believe in the freedom of the press. Enter Servilia. It's terribly kind of you to nominate me as Empress Tito says she but I love another. So now I know thank God someone speaks out says Tito my associates round here are all creeps full of double-talk: well done girl. Exits.

Vitellia comes on. I am so happy says Servilia. May I salute my new Empress? says Vitellia [she thinks she's happy for that reason: a mistake: Ed.]. Servilia exits. Sesto comes on. He takes earful from Vitellia. Idle pig says she no fire no murder no action. All right all right I'll do it says Sesto. Exits.

Enter Publio. The boss is looking for you Vitellia he says. He wants you for Empress. Holy cow! thinks Vitellia: what a turn up! She loses her marbles. She screams Sesto Sesto stop Sesto back to Square One. No burning. No murder. (But it's too late.)

Act I Sc 4 The Capitol

Sesto doesn't like doing it but he will do it just the same for love of Vitellia. Flames etc. are now visible. Annio comes on. You look terrible Sesto he says. You will soon know why says Sesto. Exits. Everyone comes on saying heard the news? The fire was not accidental. Political arson. Who done it? Who? they all cry. Sesto appears. Tito is dead! he cries. Oh what bad news shout the crowd.

Act II Sc 1 As last scene Act I

Annio tells Sesto you were wrong. Tito is not dead. They got the wrong guy. Goodness me! says Sesto: by the way – I done it. You done it! says Annio. Yes I done it says Sesto. I will fly the country. Nuts to that says Annio go and tell Tito you are terribly sorry it was a momentary aberration. Vitellia comes on. Fly the country Sesto she says and whatever else don't grass on me. Publio comes on and arrests Sesto for attempted murder treason arson etc: he says by the way the guy you thought was Tito was your accomplice Tiny Tim Lentulus and you didn't even kill him either. Not cut out for a hit man eh? Now get moving the Senate are in session awaiting your trial. Vitellia panics. She thinks he's bound to blow it.

Act II Sc 2 A grand Roman courtroom

The court passes a unanimous vote of thanks to the gods for Tito's safety also a lot of creepy stuff and adulation, Tito is just great etc. Fetch me Sesto says Tito. I can't believe him guilty. Want to bet? asks Publio. Exits. Annio comes on Sesto is guilty he says.

Publio comes back: I confirm he is guilty he says: he made a complete confession: subject to the Imperial OK Sesto will be offered to the wild beasts for lunch. The crowds are already gathering for a lively devouring. Lemme think says Tito. All exit.

On the one hand Sesto is a dastardly traitor thinks Tito yet on the other hand I don't want to damage my image as the world's most clement Emperor. Publio and Sesto come on with an armed guard. (Tito looks pretty grim thinks Sesto: Sesto looks terrible thinks Tito.) Leave us alone says Tito. All exit.

So you done it eh Sesto? says Tito. Yeah, I done it Tito says Sesto.

Please make it a quick death. Why you done it? asks Tito. Lordy! I must either drop Vitellia in it or keep mum thinks Sesto. He keeps mum. Hey guards take him away says Tito. All exit except Tito: he thinks – on the one hand – on the other hand. . . . After seven even-handed minutes he decides: clemency. He tells Publio to fetch Sesto. He sings to himself what a decent old softie I am. Exits.

Enter Vitellia. What news? she asks Publio. The Emperor Sesto and myself are on our way to the wild beasts says he. Sesto for lunch? asks Vitellia. Exactly says Publio. What did Sesto say to Tito? asks she. Dunno says he. He must have shopped me thinks she it's only human nature. Enter Servilia and Annio. It's up to you Empress to plead for Sesto say they. Me? Empress? says she. Sure they say there's a big marquee going up in the Forum for the wedding reception.

Then Sesto didn't shop me thinks Vitellia. All exit except Vitellia. Do I have enough bottle to tough it out? thinks she. To watch Sesto being eaten by lions tigers etc.? No. Maybe it would be more comfortable to confess all to Tito tho' that would turn him off marrying me. Indeed it's quite likely he would top me instead.

Act II Sc 3 A huge amphitheatre: wild beasts at the ready

Hail Tito sing the Romans you are the best thing before sliced bread. Thanks says Tito: bring on Sesto the prisoner. Go easy on him say Annio and Servilia. Tito begins: now Sesto – but Vitellia interposes. It was all my fault Tito she says. I masterminded the plot: I egged Sesto on: I'm so sorry. My God says Tito traitors keep popping out of the woodwork all around. OK since I am exceptionally magnanimous and since I brim over with clemency – I forgive you all every one without exception including Tiny Tim Lentulus. What a man! shout the Romans. What an Emperor! What amazing clemency! May Tito the magnanimous live for ever! No no says Tito not for ever: only for as long as I am doing a good job. Modest to the last.

MINUTES FROM START

LOOK OUT FOR

Act I Sc 1

0 The overture* is not in the show business style of *Figaro*, *Così*, etc., but it's a really good concert piece. The beginning is Tum-Ta-Tara and formal but the middle bit, which is developed from a single phrase, is great symphonic stuff. When we get to the reprise of part I the second subject comes first, followed by the first. It makes a change. 0

8: *Come ti piace* This duet* between Vitellia and Sesto is pretty 8 square so long as they sing one after the other, but when they sing together and we move from andante to allegro it picks up. Both parties now say that their emotions are raging, but the music doesn't rage all that much. Look out especially for a nice arabesque or flourish for both singers near the end.

13: *Deh se piacer* Vitellia's lecturette** to Sesto on the subject of 13
blind faith again starts out with a slow section which is good ornery Mozart. But the fast second bit gives her a chirpy tune which has the most bewitching phrase (upward semitones) near the end. This happens six times, and for this alone the piece must have two stars.

Act I Sc 2

Sesto and Annio, brothers-in-law-to-be and good
20: *Deh prendi un dolce amplesso* friends, sing this snatch of a duet* as they say good- 20
bye to each other. It has a friendly charm.

Tito gets his kicks from doing frightfully nice things for his friends, helping the poor, etc. Again
30: *Deh più sublime soglio* good standard serious Mozart* with most of the in- 30
terest in the orchestra. Keep your eye on the adventurous first violins, especially the staccato upward scale.

36: *Ah perdona al primo affetto* This stately tune** sounds more like Handel than 36
Mozart, but whoever might have written it, it is a good one. Annio's and Servilia's love is hopeless. They bear up with dignity and moralize a bit too. Apart from the wonderful melody itself, not much of interest.

Act I Sc 3

41: *Ah, se fosse intorno* This odd little number* has a humpty-dumpty ac- 41
companiment that leads you to expect something comic. But no, it is straight stuff. Tito is delighted to have someone around who isn't a toady and a creep. A fine clear vocal line but does not grab you as did the last duet tune.

47: *Parto, ma tu ben mio* And now for something on a much bigger scale* – a 47
seven-minuter from the wet and wimpish Sesto driven by love to murder his friend and patron Tito, and very unhappy about it he is. But he doesn't sound all that unhappy – indeed the music seems to be a total mismatch since the piece is a calm and agreeable duet for clarinet and voice, the clarinet part sticking firmly

to elegant clarinettish-type figures and not monkeying about with the vocal line at all. A lovely concert piece but about as emotional as a five-finger exercise.

54: *Vengo . . . aspetatte . . . Sesto!*

Vitellia is distracted and sounds it too:* she has 54
heard she is to be Empress just as she has despatched Sesto to kill the Emperor. Awkward. Here we have jumpy quavers in the violins, a tearaway vocal line with some very high stuff at the end that could be screams of anguish. Publio and Annio give no more than a bit of backing. How very unlike the number that went before.

Act I Sc 4

57: *Oh Dei, che smania*

The first and lengthy accompagnato.* It is made up 57
mainly of Sesto declaiming random thoughts (I'm scared: I'm a traitor: Tito's a saint: I'm a shit) punctuated by a curious sound of pumping in the strings sometimes abetted by the woodwind.

The finale – the best piece in the opera. Four stages:

60: *Deh conservate, oh Dei*

1. Sesto opens with a flourish:* May the glory of 60
Rome live on (I shall, of course, die). All of this to the cheeriest of melodies with the strings tripping up and down as if they were going to a picnic. He pops into the burning Capitol but other members of the cast creep on from the wings.

61: *Io Sesto non intendo*

2.** Now things get serious as reports of mayhem 61
come in. Ah! sing the offstage Romans (ten times). Sesto pops out again.

62: *Da me che vuoi?*

3. Now we go into accompagnato** as the dread 62
news of Tito's death is reported. The principals react in horror in a hushed sextet – very effective.

64: *O nero tradimento*

4. Finally the Romans come in with a dirge-like
chorus** – 'Black betrayal!' they sing and as their 64
anger gathers they shout 'Betrayal! Betrayal!' while the sextet, equally exercised, do their stuff around and above them. So the act ends with power and majesty.

Act II Sc 1

0: *Torna di Tito*

Annio persuades the guilty Sesto to stay and make a
clean breast of it. A mild little number,* strings only 0
in the orchestra with some nice things happening in the middle bit.

Sesto under arrest: Publio the officer of the law: Vitellia in considerable distress. A trio that rises
6: *Se al volto* above the general run:** the slowish first part nice 6
enough; each person doing their own thing. Then in the slightly faster second half Sesto becomes more melodious and as the voices overlap and towards the end sing in ensemble we have a very lovely piece of Class I Mozart. Poor Publio does not have much of a part: he shouts 'Get moving' to Sesto a dozen times but Sesto cannot, of course, move until we reach the double bar at the end.

Act II Sc 2

12: *Ah grazie si rendano* Just a touch of magic in this choral piece:** an attrac- 12
tive little symphony opens the scene: the chorus comes in hushed and reverential: Tito sings sweetly: the chorus does its repeat. There is a real sense of occasion and it is all quietly beautiful.

18: *Tardi s'avvede* A mildly pleasant snatch of an aria,* tuneful, sim- 18
ple, no middle bit and so very short. Mozart probably knocked it off in ten minutes flat.

20: *Tu fosti tradito* Another mild sweet piece,** quite perfect in its 20
own quiet way. After the opening declamatory stuff, Annio sets off on a long and rather lovely melodic line which provides a certain frisson when it dives into the minor key. Tito is just too nice a man to see villainy, says Annio, even when it stares him in the face.

After a long chat to himself about Sesto's sentence in an accompagnato, Tito sends for him. Publio brings him in and the three of them 'think' for some
26: *Quello di Tito il volto!* time in an interesting trio.** First each makes his 26
state of mind known (trembling in the strings for the scared Sesto, from Tito manly regret smoothly expressed, scooping runs in the strings for the watching Publio), then some declamation, then a faster bit in ensemble which gives Sesto a leading line with some delicious part writing. The trio fades away with some quiet rubbing in the strings. A remarkable piece.

A big one for Sesto, over seven minutes; along with Vitellia's to come, one of the longest arias in the
33: *Deh per questo istante* Mozart operas.* 33

1. Slow – gentle intro, simple noble melody, shortish minor middle bit repeat of melody – a decent piece but no great shakes.

2. Fast. Busy strings, a fast and firm melodic line. First some free-ranging stuff that takes to a jolly new subject in the first violins that might have come out of a Haydn symphony. More free ranging. Repeat of Haydn.

3. Still faster. A sort of long coda. Haydn once again. After part 1 the whole piece wildly adrift from the sense of the words, e.g.: I go to my death in despair – tortured by the fact I am a traitor – etc. Meanwhile the music is gathering nuts in May.

42: *Se all'impero, amici Dei* Another pretty long one, for Tito.* He wants to 42
rule by love but things aren't working out quite right. This time fast first with a four-square tune, then a slow and ruminative section in the middle, back to fast with a good development bit. It says something about this piece that what you most remember about it is (1) the fiery flourish by the fiddles, a punctuation mark used five times, (2) that the singer has a real struggle with the long run near the end, and most of them lose.

Something shorter, sweeter and with more feeling
49: *S'altro che lacrime* than what has gone before,* and in 3/4 time for a 49
change. Servilia tells Vitellia that sitting on her butt and weeping will get no one anywhere. Much in the same style as other arias in *Tito* but this one is warmer and more genuine. The mini-climax at the end is elegantly done.

After a tepid accompagnato something more con-
54: *Non più di fiori* siderable,** a rondo for Vitellia: which means a long 54
one whatever else, for a rondo in this context is a king-size formula for an aria and has nothing whatever to do with rondos in the concert hall. But it's something more interesting too, a duet for basset horn and Vitellia. This starts off in the rather splendid slow first section with the basset doing no more than doubling the violin and flashing around a few triplet figures and arpeggios, but come the faster bit and we do have the two voices working in a true duet and then comes a moment when the basset has the honour of introducing the main tune, a very good one. It then duets with Vitellia in the manner of a vocalized basset until we come to some bold brave string passages. But it picks up any stitches it can until it brings in the main tune

again, and so on to coda territory where there is a passage for basset and voice alone. Then a mighty finish.

Act II Sc 3

65: *Che del ciel* The chorus salutes Tito in a fine piece** that has a 65
strong whiff of Handel and gives the timpanist more work in three minutes than in all the rest of the opera put together.

After an accompagnata for Tito, much more interesting than Vitellia's, we are into the finale.** Sesto 70
70: *Tu, è ver, m'assolvi, Augusto* first: Thanks Tito, he says, good of you to forgive me: I'll never forgive myself. Better to sin and repent says Tito than never to sin at all [Funny one that? Ed.]. Then the gang of four join in for a snatch of a sextet. All good vigorous stuff. Finally the chorus lumber on, roaring out their platitudes and Tito says May I give up the crown the day I cease to be the wonderful fellow I now am.

NOTES

La Clemenza di Tito	Mozart's seventeenth and last opera
First night	National Theatre, Prague, 6 September 1791
Reception	Not much known, but not enthusiastic
Libretto	Mazzola after Metastasio
Source	Roman history

NEWS AND GOSSIP

Mozart was offered a commission to write an opera for the coronation of Leopold II as King of Bohemia. It was an offer he couldn't refuse, being broke, but one can be sure he was not in any way thrilled by the prospect of having to fish out some dreary old libretto that would be sycophantic enough to please the Royals. The one he settled on was a libretto by that wonderfully talented old bore Metastasio. It had already been set by forty (40!) lesser composers before Mozart got his hands on it. He cut it by a third in order to produce a 'vera opera' (real opera – his words). It was composed quickly (plenty of evidence for that) and alongside a strange bedfellow, the *Flute*. The first night seemed to pass off well enough but there was no enthusiasm until the last night of the run which Mozart missed, having already left Prague for the *Flute* in Vienna. *Tito* was soon performed all over Germany. It was the first Mozart opera to reach London (1806) and became top of the European Mozart pops in the first half of the nineteenth century, a position it quickly lost in the twentieth century and is now the most unpop of late Mozarts, except with Colin Davis, who really loves it, and about four other well-known musicos who rate it high out of sheer perversity.

COMMENT

It's clear that Mozart wrote a lot of *Tito* on the automatic pilot. If one wants proof of this there is telling evidence:

1. The number of notes – always an indicator of Mozart's involvement with an opera – half as many as *Figaro*, *Così* and *Giovanni*, less than *Idomeneo*, which was also a seria and ten years earlier.

2. Mismatch between music and words. When he was taking pains Mozart could fit every nuance in the text to a matching musical phrase. In *Idomeneo* he does this with amazing accuracy. In *Tito* several of the numbers don't reflect the mood of the text at all, never mind the words – notably in Sesto's rondo 'Deh per questo istante'. Also one feels he wrote the clarinet/basset arias to suit his old mate Stadler rather than the libretto.

3. Lack of characterization. Except for Tito, anyone could pretty well sing anyone else's aria without it noticing too much.

4. Sameness. Except for Servilia's minuet, the six lesser arias are alike in kind and character. The bigger ones tend to have the same form. Slow complete section first, faster second. Small climaxes, nobody sweating. Nothing like the variety of other operas.

5. Lacklustre orchestration. Just compare the wind parts with the da Ponte's, *Idomeneo* or the *Flute*.

Yet *Tito* has its fan club who will tell you that within its own limits, seen in proper perspective and taken in the right spirit, etc. etc., *Tito* has some of Mozart's most beautiful music. This isn't true. There *are* some good numbers: the finale to Act I, easily the best: the clarinet/basset items: the rather lovely Handelian tune in the duet 'Ah perdona': the trio 'Se al volto' and one or two others. Apart from these, the rest is beta, or second-gear Mozart. There is nothing shameful about this, the man was ill, in a hurry, didn't much care about the subject, had other things on his mind (the *Flute*). The sponsor undoubtedly got his money's worth, so why should we worry? Shakespeare wrote *The Two Noble Kinsmen*, Beethoven *The Battle Symphony* and Tennyson delivered himself of *Maud*. So beta for *Tito*, and one can be sure Mozart would agree.

Così fan tutte

Comedy of manners

(Never trust a woman)

Mozart [K588]

The one where two young blades go off on a bet that their girlfriends will be faithful, come back in disguise, make love to each other's girl and find that they aren't.

CAST

Fiordiligi, a well-to-do young woman from Ferrara, residing in Naples	Soprano
Dorabella, her sister	Soprano
Despina, their maid	Soprano
Guglielmo } officers in the Neapolitan army	Baritone
Ferrando } officers in the Neapolitan army	Tenor
Don Alfonso, an elderly amateur philosopher	Bass

2 acts: running time 3 hrs

STORY

Act I Sc 1 A tavern in Naples

We are in some sort of drinking house in Naples perhaps early in the eighteenth century and there are two officers Guglielmo and Ferrando arguing with busybody clubman Don Alfonso over the matter of female constancy. You can't ever trust 'em says he. I can trust my Fiordiligi says Guglielmo. I can trust my Dorabella says Ferrando. Baloney says Alfonso. The officers grab their swords (matter of honour). Don't be silly boys says Alfonso. Put those things away. Would you like to bet on it? 500 quid? You're on they cry. Two conditions says Alfonso: you don't tell the girls: you do exactly what I say. OK shake on it they say.

Act I Sc 2 The garden of a villa overlooking the Bay of Naples

Fiordiligi and Dorabella drool over photos of their chaps. I feel sexy says one. Me too says the other. We'll be married soon says one. Sooner the better says the other. Don Alfonso arrives. I have bad news girls he says very bad. About your fiancés. Very bad indeed. Dead? ask the girls. No says Alfonso. Wounded? Ill? No no says Alfonso they have been called up on active service.

Guglielmo and Ferrando enter in active service kit. Don't go say the girls. Must go, say the men. Tears. We can't live without you etc. say the girls. A boat arrives plus military band and chorus. The siren blows. Farewells. Promise to write say the girls. Every day say the men. Addio! Addio! The boat sails away. We wish you good weather and a calm sea sing the girls and Alfonso. Exit. (I must get off to organize the next scene in this pantomime says Alfonso as he goes.)

Act I Sc 3 A room in the girls' villa

Despina grumbles: life is hell below stairs. The girls come in looking (a) for a sword (b) for poison: suicide in mind. What's up? asks Despina. A ghastly catastrophe say the girls our boys have been called up. They may be killed. There are plenty more fish in the sea says Despina. We will die if they don't come back say the girls. No woman ever died of love says Despina. And don't expect your fellows to be plaster saints either: they will be chasing every bit of skirt in sight. Soldiers! The girls exit.

Alfonso enters. Hey Despina he says I want you. You can't have me says she. You're too old to give satisfaction. Stop that stuff says Alfonso I need your help. Money changes hands. I want you to persuade the girls to let these men console them. Look! Enter two Albanians (Guglielmo and Ferrando of course). Cor! says Despina. What freaks. They're about as sexy as two Aberdeen undertakers. Alfonso hides.

The girls enter. Get these ridiculous foreigners off the premises say they. Please! Please! Let us stay! plead the Albanians. We have fallen in love with you. Alfonso enters. Hello hello hello my very dear old friends he says. Let me introduce you. We think these lovely ladies are just sublime say the Albanians. What cheek says Fiordiligi. Don't go say the Albanians you are such beautiful sexy girls. You might at least show a little courtesy to my old chums says Alfonso. The girls leave. Ho ho ho say the Albanians. Silly old Alfonso see how wrong you were. Would you like to settle for 50% of the wager? Negative says Alfonso. Just you wait.

Act I Sc 4 The garden of the girls' villa again

The girls moan on about their chaps' departure. Horrid shouts are heard offstage. The Albanians rush on. You cruel females they yell. You have driven us to suicide you have. Each one drinks a slug of arsenic and rolls about in agony. My god how awful say the girls. What can we do? You might show them a little consideration says Alfonso. Exit with Despina to get doctor.

The girls kneel by the Albanians and make body contact through feeling pulses stroking brows etc. Alfonso returns with a doctor (Despina in disguise of course) who puts on a learned medico act produces a magnet and holds it over the patients. The Albanians make a miraculous recovery and as they come out of their trance they fondle the girls and ask for kisses. The girls are outraged. Alfonso and Despina think things are going well. The Albanians hope the girls will continue to be strong-minded.

Act II Sc 1 A room in the girls' house

Despina is fed up with the girls for being so prissy. Grow up she says you can have a really nice time there are lots of men around just be a bit clever. Fiordiligi is shocked but Dorabella thinks maybe she's got a point. Suppose we chatted up the Albanians just for a laugh? says Dorabella I'll go for the little dark one. OK says Fiordiligi I'll take the big blond. It could be a scream says Dorabella so it could says Fiordiligi. Hey girls! There's a party on at my place now says Alfonso come on!

Act II Sc 2 A garden beside the sea. A boat at the quay set up for a party – flowers, musicians, etc.

We offer you our love sing the Albanians. Yes they offer you their love sing the chorus in the usual boring repetitive fashion. So what's all this flash and fresco about? ask the girls. I can't speak: I have a mental blockage says embarrassed Ferrando. Me too says Guglielmo.

O gawd says Alfonso they'll never get started at this rate. Give me your hand Despina let's show them how it's done. They go through pantomime showing how to beg for a girl's forgiveness. The men clumsily attempt to join in the act. Let's go says Despina to Alfonso if they can't manage it now they never will. They exit. Um . . . er . . . warm for the time of year? says Ferrando. Er . . . um . . . lovely view? says Guglielmo. Take a walk? says Fiordiligi. Don't mind if I do says Ferrando. They walk off stage.

Let's walk too says Dorabella. Whatever you say says Guglielmo. They walk on stage. How are you feeling? asks Dorabella. Like death says Guglielmo. It's the poison says she: no it's love for you says he. Really? says she. Please accept this small token of regard says he. Coo! They're real diamonds says she I am yours. Loverly exchanges take place also exchange old token (pic of Ferrando) for new token (diamonds). They walk off.

Ferrando and Fiordiligi walk on. Why so cool? asks he. Push off and let me be says she. I am potty about you says he and all you do is treat me like dirt. Exits. He's made me all upset says Fiordiligi to herself. I do fancy him. Quel catastrophe. Exits.

Ferrando and Guglielmo come on. Good news old boy says Ferrando we've as good as won. She wouldn't give an inch. Very satisfactory says Guglielmo. My girl the same story I trust? says Ferrando. Not exactly says Guglielmo. In fact she was a pushover. Here's your photo (hands over old token). Zut! Bitch! Jezebel! I'll get her for this says Ferrando.

Steady says Guglielmo I have highest regard for the fair sex bless their pretty little faces but you must face it old boy they do sleep around a lot. O Lord: I love her and hate her at the same time I am getting psychologically disturbed says Ferrando.

Alfonso comes in. Ho ho says he. Dorabella fell for the Albanian Guglielmo. Well it's not altogether surprising says Guglielmo. I am noticeably sexier than some people not to mention any names. Pay up Ferrando says Alfonso. Meanwhile the experiment is not yet finished. Kindly continue under my orders until further notice.

Act II Sc 3 A room in the sisters' house

So you fell for him says Despina to Dorabella good for you. Enter Fiordiligi looking ghastly. I am all mixed up says she I truly love the old one: the new one makes me feel sexy. I am upset. Suppose you spurn the Albanian and your fiancé is killed in action there won't be much joy then eh? says Despina. Honestly sister it's best to pack in the honour stuff says Dorabella. Relax and go the Albanian way like me. Dorabella and Despina exit.

Never never never says Fiordiligi. I have Guglielmo's battle dress in the closet and I will dress up as a soldier and join Guglielmo in battle. Despina! she shouts fetch the master's uniform! Gawd what next thinks Despina (Alfonso and Guglielmo secretly watch all this pantomime: Guglielmo very chuffed). Guglielmo here I come! cries Fiordiligi. And leave me dying of night starvation? says Ferrando jumping out of the woodwork. Get out! says Fiordiligi rather indecisively. Either you give in or I die says Ferrando. OK I give in says Fiordiligi. They exit in a clinch.

Enter Guglielmo and Alfonso. Bitch! Whore! Female skunk! Toad! etc. says Guglielmo. Enter Ferrando. What's he going on about? he asks. Fiordiligi is now a goner too says Guglielmo. Listen boys says Alfonso why don't you marry these two? You must be mad say the men. Any woman would have done just what they've done and these are two sound healthy specimens as good as any you'll find says Alfonso.

Go on lads! Do it (he sings about women a bit). Now he says repeat after me: Così fan tutte (they do). Enter Despina. Hey gents she says the girls say they will marry you at 1600 hours. I have given instructions for the registrar to come, flowers, wedding cake etc. OK with you? OK with us say the Albanians.

Act II Sc 4 A room in the sisters' house set up for wedding breakfast

Despina is getting things ready. She bosses the servants, musicians etc. around. It looks good says Alfonso what a pantomime! The chorus sing the usual wedding rhubarb. The four enter. Everything in the garden is lovely they say. Thanks Despina. There are compliments on the outstanding beauty of the girls' eyes, ears, mouths etc.

Let's drink a toast to the future and forget the past they cry: begone all care. (Guglielmo is surly and does not join in: he has thoughts about disloyalty.) The notary arrives (Despina again of course) and embarks on a long marriage contract rigmarole. Give us a break say the four stuff all that legal rubbish just let us sign. The girls sign.

But hark! A regimental theme song from Act I is heard offstage. Alarm! Shock! Hide quick! shout the girls to the Albanians who run off stage. Good God! what now say the girls. Leave it to me says Alfonso. Guglielmo and Ferrando reappear as themselves. Hi girls they say. The order to embark has been countermanded. It's nice to see you again and so soon. Why so silent? (A servant puts their trunk into a closet forcing Despina out.) What the hell! A notary? say the men. Not a notary at all just me preparing for a fancy dress parade says Despina. Alfonso shows them the wedding contract. Zut! Donner and blitzen! say the men. Signed by Dorabella! Signed by Fiordiligi! You two-timing double-crossing bitches.

We are guilty guilty say the girls. Explain yourselves say the men. Alfonso can explain everything say the girls. The men go into the closet and come out dressed as Albanians. Shock of shocks! The men sing snatches of seduction songs [Ferrando sings the wrong number – from another show? Ed] and also some of Despina's doctor's patter. The girls are pulverized with shame guilt fear etc. It's all Alfonso's fault they cry. I fooled you sure enough says Alfonso but for educational purposes only [he omits to mention 500 quid: Ed.]. Now you are all much wiser, better, happier persons. So have a good laugh: kiss, forget, get married.

MINUTES FROM START

LOOK OUT FOR

0 The overture*** is a bright and brassy affair: lots of 0
loud chords also a figure in the woodwind which we get to know quite well since it is repeated 58 times (see COMMENT). Most conductors today drive the piece so hard that the poor ducks playing the flutes, oboes, etc. just don't have time to enunciate this thing properly and it all becomes a bit of a helter-skelter.

Both at the beginning and the end we have a formal statement of the Così Fan Tutte (CFT) motto.

Act I Sc 1

5: *La mia Dorabella*

The first trio:** Ferrando and Guglielmo are both 5
certain that their fiancées would never cheat on them – it's inconceivable. Alfonso has his doubts. This trio is a sprightly affair, the music doesn't make it seem a sword-drawing matter.

8: *È la fede delle femmine*

The phoenix trio.** Over a long pedal Alfonso 8
compares a woman who never cheats to a phoenix: neither exists. Yes, yes sing the lads: Dorabella is a phoenix, Fiordiligi is a phoenix. The CFT motto creeps in stealthily at the end. We know how to place our bets.

11: *Una bella serenata*

The final trio,** a more considerable affair: trum- 11
pets and drums. In a burst of confidence the two plan to spend their winnings on a party to celebrate their girls' true love. Can I come? asks Alfonso. Sure they reply and all three are off into a final gallop with a strong clear and catchy tune. But do we catch a hint of the CFT motif near the end?

Act I Sc 2

13: *Ah guarda, sorella*

A longish introduction leads to the lovesick duet** as 13
the sisters gaze soppily at pix of their beaus. A lovely florid run ends Fiordiligi's opener, varied a little when it comes to Dorabella's turn. The middle bit goes into the minor – melancholy happiness – then into a brisker allegro – long held notes by each girl whilst the other chunters. Their love will never change (close harmony). There is more than a whiff of send-up in the air.

Terrible news – so terrible that Alfonso can
19: *Vorrei dir*
scarcely get it out – a fleeting little aria,* almost an 19
aside.

21: *Sento, o Dio*

The Bad News quintet,*** a winner. Each of the 21
men stammers out their reluctance to get into the pantomime (broken phrases with chords between): Alfonso stiffens them up (a good firm bass line solo): the girls, silly things, say please plunge your swords into us (close harmony): the men go through the halting bit again, this time together – then we are off into the mainstream of the quintet (why is fate so simply horrid to us?) which flows sweetly and irresistibly to

its end. Look out particularly for the solo flourishes which spring out from the texture towards the end – first Dorabella, then Fiordiligi, then vice versa, then Ferrando. Guglielmo gets nothing. Just bad luck, there isn't time.

After the military chorus, a mild burlesque of the real thing, wc havc a short but great event, the Fare-
32: *Di scrivermi ogni giorno* well quintet,*** which, along with the trio to come, is 32
perhaps the most purely beautiful item in the opera. There is a rustling string accompaniment: it is expectant, and one by one the voices enter, hushed messages are passed and the girls swing out gloriously into a soaring top line: the men start the goodbyes to one of the best goodbye phrases in the business: goodbyes sweep through the score and in the later phases we have once again one of those ear-catching arabesques (Fiordiligi) that reach out from the texture and grab you by the throat. Magic. Then the ridiculous military march breaks in again.

35: *Soave sia il vento* The trio*** A Calm Sea and a Prosperous Voyage: 35
in the pure beauty stakes a match for the quintet that has gone before. All plotting and posturing are out of the window and the wicked old Alfonso and the two girls join together in a heartfelt wish for good weather. The sea rustles in upper strings: Fiordiligi leads the three in sweet harmony: the sea stops for a moment and the woodwind works with the voices to prepare for the sea's return and a climax of hope for sunshine and no wind: the intensity eases, the voices cease and the sea has the last word. Again, absolute magic.

Act I Sc 3

40: *Smanie implacabili* Dorabella's agitated little number* about losing her 40
love, again a bit of a cod. Nice enough but one has to admit that Dorabella gets the short straw in the matter of arias. All the heavy stuff goes to her big sister who has a slightly higher voice and is, of course, paid more.

If Despina were a man this would rate as an almost
45: *In uomini, in soldati* criminally macho aria.* As it is, it does something to 45
redress the anti-female balance. Men should be used to suit women's convenience she sings in her brash cheeky manner. A sort of 'thinks' start: reflection on

men. But then into a racy tune with some rather coy interplay with the orchestra. A traditional soubrette number. Can bring the house down.

51: *Alla bella Despinetta* The long and cleverly-worked piece** in a vest- 51
pocket version of a Mozart finale. It has three phases:

1. Don Alfonso introduces the two Albanians to Despina – the girl who can fix it for them. Hi Despina, do your best for us say they. Holy cow! what a pair of frights says Despina (but she doesn't recognize them). All of this in Mozart's best quick-fire dramatico style. No great tunes.

2. Fiordiligi and Dorabella come in. What the hell! they say. (Enchanting stuff: short phrases: the orchestra sounds crosser than the girls.) Despina get these tramps out! Despina and the men plead (soothing, slow, woodwind going along with them).

3. The girls are really mad. Trumpets and drums: the girls' angry runs versus the pleading phrases by the three ending in big striding unison stuff. Noisy.

After a bout of five-handed accompagnato, a rare
event, but in itself not remarkable, we come to the
60: *Come scoglio* biggest solo aria in the opera,*** and probably – bel 60
canto apart – the most taxing test of a dramatic soprano until Wagner. This is a send-up of a big opera seria piece with lots of low chest notes of great importance and lots of high notes too. A majestically slow introduction in keeping with her rock-like stance: a long clear melodic opening piece, a very short middle bit in the style of the introduction: back to the start again, but no, a change of gear into a higher speed and off we go on a new course: the strings race along in triplets, Fiordiligi catches on to the triplets and so to a climax and crashing end, triplets going on to the last bar. The lady's not for turning. Many attempt this mighty piece but few triumph.

Guglielmo points out to the girls in simple terms
65: *Non siate ritrosi* why he is such a sex bomb* (moustachios, etc.). Nice 65
one Guglielmo. The girls exit in a huff. Laughter
from the two Albanians. They mock Alfonso in a
67: *E voi ridete?* breathless hare-and-hounds sort of trio.* Their girls 67
69: *Un' aura amorosa* are staunch. Ho ho! (But they don't laugh last.)
A love song from Ferrando*** – roughly speaking 69

he is saying that love does for the heart what a large Scotch and soda does for the rest of the system – it's an effective refresher. He is in the same tenor territory as Don Ottavio in *Don Giovanni*, golden, winning phrases that would disarm a nun. Since there are no nuns around nor even his Dorabella his lovely, lovely song is wasted on the desert air. It goes like this: a full narrative statement of the melody (look out especially for the musical figure that expresses the words 'un dolce restoro': occurs twice); a middle bit not as uneasy nor minore as usual; then a repeat of the first part with a short coda. Thus you get the 'sweet refresher' phrase four times.

Act I Sc 4

The finale – some twenty minutes of non-stop activity – the crowning wonder of the act:

1. The girls reflect on life as it was before it was so
73: *Ah, che tutto in un momento* rudely interrupted by Albanians.** Placid vocal lines 73
duetting with an agreeable woodwind accompaniment in thirds.

2. Rudely interrupted: this time by Albanians
76: *Si mora sì, si mora* drinking poison.** The score is full of action, some- 76
times almost accompagnato but melody keeps breaking in, one tune after another. Dramatic.

78: *Giacchè a morir?* 3. The Albanians are dying.*** Send for Despina. 78
Yes, dying, says Despina. Look after them well she says and goes off to get a doctor. The amazingly inventive score keeps abreast of the action, one snatch of melody after another: changing patterns of accompaniment.

80: *Dei, che cimento è questo* 4. Now the girls are alone with the patients.*** 80
What to do? Get closer, but gingerly. Look out especially for a nine-note figure in the bass which eggs them on (Ta Ta Oom-pah Oom-pah Oom-pah Pom!).

82: *Eccovi il medico* 5. The doctor arrives talking Latin:** the music 82
steadies up to give the sort of formal greeting due to a professional man. Despina (for it is she) has a simple vocal line, no frills (and let's hope she doesn't do that horrible thing, sing through her nose, as was recently the fashion). The magnetic cure itself takes place to therapeutic trill.

6. The men wake up in a daze and hazily try to

85: *Dove son?* grope the girls,*** who don't know *what* to do. 85
Dreamy, muzzy music. Look out especially for a pretty arabesque (high flowery stuff) from Fiordiligi towards the end (twice in quick succession).

89: *Dammi un bacio* 7. Action! Change up two gears.*** Allegro then 89
presto. The Albanians ask for a kiss. This is going too far. Rebuffed, despite Despina and Alfonso pleading the medical advantage of a bit of osculation; this to a strong downward phrase, which stops the show for a moment each time it appears.

Now we get into a good old 'thinks' finale: Albanians (Hope they are really cross not just play-acting), girls (Go to hell you cheeky pigs), Alfonso and Despina (All this emotion means the girls soon won't be able to resist them). Buried deep in the knitting there are very fetching long runs from Fiordiligi and clarinets (twice) and Ferrando and bassoons (also twice). Final race to the tape as breathless as any.

Act II Sc 1

Despina tells the girls to grow up. Time they knew
2: *Una donna a quindici anni* how to handle men and sex.** A slow first bit – she's 2
giving them a lecture – then the fast second bit to a cheeky tune which runs its course twice and the third time (Oh not *again* you think) it fools you and stops. The end. A joke commonly played by Haydn.

Half in fun (perhaps less than half?) the girls ami-
7: *Prenderò quel brunettino* cably agree to a mild flirtation with the men.** 'I'll 7
take the little dark one,' says Dorabella. Of all the numbers in *Così* this is the one to test the maestro's feeling for tempo: too slow and it becomes a dirge, too fast and it loses its charm. A little faster than a guardsman's quick march, but nothing approaching the speed of the Bersaglieri. Look out especially for a long flowery run in which the girls sing together almost unaccompanied. Their voices and thoughts are in close harmony.

Act II Sc 2

10 An enchanting little symphony*** for the woodwind 10
band sets the scene for the Albanians singing seductively in thirds. They tell the breezes to carry nice messages to their loved ones. The chorus adds its authority to the message. Very mellifluous.

The tongue-tied girls stand and gawp. Alfonso and

Despina each take one by the hand and address
14: *La mano a me date* them** on behalf of the men, who echo their lines 14
from time to time like sheep. A flirty little figure in the woodwind starts the number off: Alfonso sings in the smooth insinuating phrases Mozart always uses for bogus sincerity. The pantomime ends with an accompagnato from Despina, speaking for thc girls (Let's forget the past); then we have part I again, presto, as Alfonso and Despina exit saying 'Now let them get on with it.'

Dorabella has succumbed in the recitatif that goes before. Now it's a matter of exchanging hearts, both miniature and metaphorical. Guglielmo's lovely mel-
20: *Il core vi dono* ody*** and Dorabella's reply are given the simplest 20
support by the orchestra until we come to the long pendant endpiece when we hear delicious frissons from the violins and some tremulous thirds from the woodwind. Perhaps the tenderest piece of love music in all Mozart, and both parties so wicked with it, Guglielmo conning Dorabella and she double-crossing Ferrando.

Fiordiligi fights against feelings that are growing warmer than friendship for Ferrando in an accom-
24: *Barbara, perchè fuggi?* pagnato.** This starts in a pretty ornery manner but 24
suddenly slips into a really moving passage when she says 'Please don't rob me of my peace of mind'. Fer-
26: *Ah, lo veggio* rando's aria which follows,* though good standard 26
Mozart, is the most ornery in the opera and is often cut.

31: *Per pietà* Fiordiligi's second big aria.*** She asks the absent 31
Guglielmo to forgive her if she falters just a little in the face of such a persuasive Albanian. A solemn start – a pure melodic line with huge leaps (an octave and a half). Respectfully accompanied the first time out but with interesting interruptions by the horns and then the woodwind on its second. Then a faster bit with a new melody: now lots of comments from the wind, getting more elaborate. A splendid climax and finish (with the horns still active).

After a biting accompagnato with cries of pain from the wounded Ferrando, Guglielmo slips into
42: *Donne mie, la fate a tanti a tanti* this jolly chauvinist ditty.** Why do all women ha- 42
bitually sleep around? I'm very fond of women, he

says, but this is not a nice characteristic. The cocky little melody has a continuous flibbertigibbet accompaniment for violins (sometimes with help) rushing around all over the place like the affections of those unreliable persons – women.

Ferrando, poor soul, now hates Dorabella, but un-
47: *Tradito, schernito* fortunately also still loves her. In this aria** both 47
emotions are fairly represented: hate in the opening broken phrases and love represented by a heavenly woodwind choir followed by some much smoother stuff from Ferrando. No matter we know it's all a bet, a joke and no more than codswallop, we are moved by this piece. Mozart treats Ferrando's feelings with total sincerity: this is a lover suffering as all true lovers have suffered.

Act II Sc 3

A thumbnail sketch of the nature of love by Dora-
53: *È amore un ladroncello* bella.** Light and flighty, again the woodwind have 53
an introduction to themselves and get very busy on the third appearance of what might reasonably be called the refrain.

Going, going, gone. Fiordiligi keels over in four stages:

56: *Fra gli amplessi* 1. Adagio. Fiordiligi** still in 'Come scoglio' or 56
rocklike mood. She's going to war to seek Guglielmo, her true love. Bold short phrases.

2. Allegro. But Ferrando will be broken-
57: *Ed intanto di dolore* hearted.** Now we have a battle of wills in a develop- 57
ing duet: no long melody sung over and repeated, rather a steady sequence of episodes piling on the tension. She weakens.

59: *Volgi a me pietoso* 3. Larghetto.*** Now Ferrando pleads in the 59
most beguiling phrases. Pretty well irresistible, and sure enough she ceases to resist.

60: *Abbracciami, o caro bene* 4. Andante.** They kiss at some length and finish 60
in a happy refrain with the strings wheeling around them in delight.

65: *Tutti accusan le donne* The nearest thing Alfonso has to a proper aria** 65
and a short one. We are back in the world of buffa: he tells the men that women are by nature polyandrous: if you expect constancy that's your mistake, not her fault: Così Fan Tutte (to the motto we first heard in the overture). The opera could end here, but luckily

for us it doesn't. (This is where Guglielmo usually pays up: nothing in the libretto.)

Act II Sc 4

The finale, and very eventful it is.

1. Despina and Alfonso fuss around getting the feast ready, also the chorus comes on singing the usual get-ready get-ready stuff. This is all pretty ornery and goes on long enough to allow the principals to change their costumes.

2. Now a big belter from the chorus, Hail the Bridal Pairs, etc., again nothing special, but then a quar-
70: *Come par che qui prometta* tet of the four,** happy, relaxed and really so prettily 70
written as to make you forget that there are anything but four innocent young folks approaching the altar. The belting chorus again.

The quartet continues: the men compliment the women: the women praise the men: all is sweetness and light and suddenly we are poised for:

3. One of Mozart's very specials – the Toast quar-
74: *E nel tuo, nel mio bicchiero* tet.*** Fiordiligi swings out in a long golden solo 74
line, next Ferrando in canon with Fiordiligi above, then Dorabella thickening the texture and adding interest to the emotional level, then – surprise! – in comes Guglielmo not in canon with the others, nor in accord, but grumbling to himself. Bitches! he says. Damnable bitches! This is odd behaviour, but he does not disturb the sweet music of the trio warbling on above. Dreamy.

76: *Miei Signori, tutto è fatto* 4. Alfonso brings on Despina* this time as a no- 76
tary and we drop back into buffa with something of a shock. Despina has a lot of stuff on one note but the scene works well enough so long as Despina does not affect some ghastly assumed voice, sneeze, sing out of tune or generally indulge in rubbishy business which some producers will, alas, permit and even encourage. The quartet, and the orchestra, get restive. For God's sake let's sign, say they.

5. But hark! The theme song of our heroes' regi-
78: *Bella vita militar* ment rings out. Stunned reaction** by the quartet in 78
fearful close harmony. Alfonso goes to recce – bad news from him and panic spreads through the orchestra. What to do? sing the girls choppily (the chaps have slipped off to make a quick change).

6. Guglielmo and Ferrando step in singing a sim-
80: *Sani e salvi* ple soldier's song** in fairly close harmony. Hey 80
folks, they sing, glad to be back. Discovery! Despina
first, the marriage contract next. Rage! (Allegro.)
With trumpets and drums and rushing figures in the
strings. Confession: (andante) the girls wish they
were dead, in thirds.
85: *A voi s'inchina* 7. The men reappear** as partly-dressed Alban- 85
ians (very quick change) and mock the girls by singing
the most tender bits of their seduction songs. Just a
jolly joke. Total disintegration of the girls – they gasp
out odd phrases, and the orchestra is panicky too.
8. Alfonso, the smug old prig, in a jerky little
87: *V'ingannai, ma fu l'inganno* solo,** says well that's a nice lesson for you all, now 87
kiss and be friends. Then a lovely forgiveness quar-
88: *Idol mio* tet,*** Despina chuntering on below, the 'thinks' be- 88
ing as follows: Girls (After this we'll never look at
another man), the men (I believe you and we won't try
any more tricks), Despina (Certainly they fooled me
but then I've fooled a lot in my time too). A final
chorus whose forced high spirits seem quite out of
place.

NOTES

Così fan tutte	Mozart's fifteenth opera
First night	Burgtheater, Vienna, 26 January 1790
Reception	No data. Count Zinzendorf, who had thought little of Mozart's earlier operas, liked *Così* a little better.
Script	Da Ponte
Source	Not known

NEWS AND GOSSIP

Figaro's revival in Vienna in 1789 was a big success and the musical Emperor Joseph II promptly commissioned Mozart and da Ponte for a new opera. A much simpler process than seeking sponsorship from industry or getting a grant from the Arts Council. It seems he offered double the usual fee, and if this is true we raise our glasses to him. Let this be a lesson to all sponsors today. No one knows where da Ponte found the story for *Così*. There is no evidence to back a popular legend that the plot was based on a real event, two Viennese officers betting that they would succeed in having it off with each other's girlfriends. It could have been a da Ponte original, although industrious scholars have beaten the bushes from Greek times onwards and found a dozen or more examples of a bet against chastity (always won) including Shakespeare, Boccaccio, Cervantes, etc. etc. But this is far-fetched stuff. Mozart and da Ponte were in a hurry to get the show on before the Emperor died, which was an odds-on bet at that time. This they did, but only just; Joseph died after the fifth performance and all theatres closed. But *Così* was brought back when they reopened later in the year. Haydn, a true Mozart fan, went to the rehearsals and must have had a lovely time. After the Viennese run a German version of *Così* was performed in Germany and practically nowhere else. Even in Germany it was cut about, rewritten, sanitized, etc. to avoid the stigma of immorality. During the whole of the nineteenth century it was played very little. Then early in the 1900s Richard Strauss 'discovered' *Così*, recognized it as a masterpiece and became its propagandist. There was a full-scale revival in Munich in 1910 and the sun began to shine on *Così* once more. Beecham revived it in London (but heavily Beechamized) before World War I, but the first great European production of this century was not until 1934 at Glyndebourne, where John Christie opened his first season with *Figaro* and *Così*. The Busch brothers and Carl Ebert put on what is for many people the definitive *Così*, which was recorded, acclaimed and is still available on CD today and *Così* is now, of course, in the repertory of all self-respecting opera houses.

COMMENT

From the start *Così* has been given a hard time because of its plot. 'Trivial and artificial' they said in Mozart's day. Beethoven loved the music but was shaken rigid by the immorality of the plot, as were his contemporaries. For over a hundred years this 'shocking and licentious work' pretty well disappeared from view. The twentieth century was not so much shocked as condescending. Even Blom writing in the *Master Musicians* series in 1935 (probably going to press just before the Glyndebourne production) says of *Così* 'ridiculous . . . preposterous situations . . . artificial intrigues . . . a show of marionettes', though he is decent enough to concede that it was 'a mildly amusing piece'. Then came the Glyndebourne and other revivals and the opera world took *Così* to their hearts and have been chattering about it ever since, mainly because of the plot. No one argues about the music, which has pretty well been canonized by every operatic sect. People no longer have hang-ups about the morality of *Così*, nor the rather strange conventions of the plot – time span 24 hours, outlandish disguises, seductions at the speed of lightning, etc. What interests them now is to poke about looking for the larger truths. There is a lot of pondering over who really loves whom. What does Mozart really MEAN? one serious *Così* student will say to another. The seduction music is so sincere, surely it MEANS that Guglielmo really loves Dorabella, not Fiordiligi? Would it MEAN more if the sisters knew about the plot all along? Didn't Mozart really want the couples changed around at the end? That would make it MEAN something much more significant. *Così* is commonly called 'the problem opera', but please believe that *Così* is no problem unless you want to make it into one.

For starters, you must accept that you can't explain the plot of *Così* in terms of twentieth-century psychology. We have read Freud, also *The Female Eunuch*. Mozart, by being born a bit earlier, escaped this experience. To the eighteenth-century man the plot of *Così* would seem to be neat, funny and true, quite in keeping with the current male view that women's proclivity to sleep around was widespread and reprehensible, whereas it was both natural and socially OK for men to sleep around whenever they felt inclined. The story of *Così* is given respectability, if any were needed, by its subtitle, *The School for Lovers*. This made it clear that *Così* was a moral tale teaching two lessons, one to men (don't trust your girlfriend an inch) and another to women (if you are unfaithful it can only lead to disaster). In eighteenth-century terms, all perfectly shipshape and correct and in line with the views of Mozart, da Ponte and all the gentry of Vienna.

So it was that Mozart's and da Ponte's approach to the plot of *Così* was nearer to that of Gilbert and Sullivan than of Harold Pinter. The important thing was to make each scene work. The silly infatuated sisters called for a degree of send-up so we get the cod-serious arias 'Come scoglio' and 'Per pietà'. The seducers must seduce successfully, so their love music had to be really persuasive. If each scene worked and the succession of scenes hung together and made a good shape for the act, then it was a success. There was no consideration of the credibility or morality of the story which arises when it is put under the microscope by scholars and other serious persons. Mozart's letters during the rehearsals of *Idomeneo* show that he is chiefly concerned with effect and motivation, not content (and this is borne out by the alacrity with which he included arias of sickening flattery in the made-for-royals operas). But there is one astonishing flaw in the plot which da Ponte skates over so quickly that it seems it has gone by largely unnoticed. This is after the game is up and just before the Così Fan Tutte has been sung in harmony by the three males. Alfonso says to Guglielmo and Ferrando: Why not marry the girls? Not on your life they say. Understandable. Do you still love them? asks Alfonso, clearly meaning the original pair. Well, yes they reply. A minute later Despina pops in and says the sisters are ready for the wedding, is this OK? Yes, say the men. This can't be right. They are the wrong girls. The men expect to marry their original loves. But the last scene shows us that the 'marriage' was a charade to achieve maximum humiliation for the wretched girls. The men must have been made privy to the plot. Shome mishtake shurely? Missing scene? Cut at the last minute? Scholars get your boots on.

The music in *Così* is of two kinds – sweet and buffa. The sweet music is the sweetest and most passionate Mozart ever wrote and unlike any music in any other opera: it includes the Farewell quintet ('Addio!') in Act I, the Fair Wind and a Calm Sea trio that follows it, all the seduction music in Act II also Ferrando's solo about the refreshing effects of love, and the final Toast trio (not quartet, because Guglielmo won't join in – and here *is* something that's worth pondering). These items haunt the ear more persistently than anything from *Figaro* or *Giovanni*, just as phrases from the love poetry of *Anthony and Cleopatra* and *Twelfth Night* will haunt the mind more persistently than any others.

The buffa music in *Così* is vintage buffa, all of it easy on the ear, witty and bright, with three-star items in the Bad News quintet in Act I, the finale to Act I and particularly from the moment when the Albanians are on the point of death to the end. Throughout *Così* the scoring, particularly of the woodwind, is stunning, as is Mozart's virtuosity in devising the right accompaniment at the right time for the right words.

The musical characterization in *Così* is not so strong as in *Figaro* or *Giovanni* but it is more subtle. Aside from Alfonso and Despina who are stock buffa types, we do gain a clear musical portrait of the different natures of the two girls, Fiordiligi the stronger character, the leader and more serious. Not far from Elizabeth Bennett or Emma Woodhouse in Jane Austen, but the Austen girls would, of course, have seen off any would-be seducer pretty smartly. Dorabella is a more flipperty type nearer Lydia Bennett or Harriet Smith, and without her sister at her side she would surely have given way in a trice. The men are less clearly drawn and less interesting. Ferrando is perhaps of quicker metal than the steadier Guglielmo – overall they are pretty well Tweedledum and Tweedledee.

All in all *Così* has the most perfect symmetry of plot and musical ground plan (key structure) of any of the operas: all the music is good and when it is very good it is perfect.

A final in-joke about the title and the overture. In the trio in Act I of *Figaro* (the Count, Susanna, Basilio) when the Count says he caught Cherubino having it off with the gardener's daughter – 'Così fan tutte le belle' (that's what all pretty girls do) sings Basilio. This phrase slightly pushed around is the basis of the whiffling bit the woodwind play in the overture 58 times. We also have the motto four times, so it could be said we have heard a version of the opera's title 62 times before the curtain goes up. One for the *Guinness Book of Records*. Alpha-plus.

Dido and Aeneas

Classical tragedy

Purcell

The one where Dido in her famous lament tells us to remember her but forget her fate.

CAST

Dido, Queen of Carthage	Mezzo
Belinda, her lady-in-waiting	Soprano
Second Woman	Mezzo
Sorceress	Mezzo
Aeneas	Baritone

2 Witches, a spirit, a sailor

3 acts: running time 1 hr 5 mins

STORY

Act I Sc 1 Dido's Palace

We are in Carthage Tunisia in the time of Aeneas which is very considerably BC but no one knows exactly how much B. Dido is in a state. Should she marry Aeneas or not? Belinda says cheer up and go on marry him it's a politically sound move. Carthage plus Troy is a solid power bloc. Also he loves you says she and he's such a pet (and I say the same says a Second Woman).

Aeneas arrives. Fate says you should not marry me says Dido. To hell with fate says Aeneas: marry me. Good for you good for me and enormously helpful in the matter of improved foreign relations for Troy. She's giving in! cries Belinda. (It's true.) Hoorah shout the courtiers: get going you cupids spread the news in all the national parks. Your side has won.

Act I Sc 2 A witches' cavern

Hey boys and girls says the head Witch let's screw things up in Carthage for that lady Dido. Good idea let's make her really miserable shout the coven. But how? Aeneas has broken his contract with the gods says she: Clause 17B says he must reside in Italy and here he is faffing around in Carthage we'll send a warlock (Inspector grade) disguised as Mercury and tell him there are direct orders from Jove for him to quit Carthage by

2359 tonight. And while they're all out hunting we will magic a storm on them just as an additional aggravation. Good idea we'll get working on the spells in our echo chamber right away say the coven.

Act II A grove

Nice here i'n't says Belinda. And plenty of game around. Yeah it's lovely says the Second Woman and historical too. Look at my dead boar says Aeneas. Looks like rain says Dido. A storm breaks. They all run for cover except Aeneas.

Inspector warlock dressed as Mercury appears. Jove says you gotta get out by midnight he says. Who? Me? says Aeneas. Yes of course. If that's what Jove wants I'll do it at once. [The creep: Ed.] Immediately. (Thinks) But how the hell am I going to break the news to Dido?

Act III Sc 1 Amongst the Trojan ships

Two-hour shore leave granted don't get too pissed we sail tonight sings a sailor. Got the message say the other sailors let's dance a hornpipe. They do. Sailors off. Witches on. Whoopee they cry our evil plan is working out just perfick and we'll blow the fleet off course and have a lovely cremation just to make a day of it.

Act III Sc 2 The palace

My god what terrible news says Dido. (She has heard on the grapevine.) Enter Aeneas: how can I tell you we must part? he says. Deceptive man I don't want any crocodile tears from you says Dido: get out! Just get out and let me die and let the Empire fall apart too. No I've changed my mind rather suddenly says Aeneas I'll stay. Go you traitor says she. I'll stay says he. Go! Stay! they shout at each other. He goes. I'm happy to die now says Dido. When I am dead and gone – remember me, but forget my fate.

MINUTES FROM START

LOOK OUT FOR

Act I Sc 1

The overture is in the French style, which is usually slow–fast–slow. But we have no second slow and so
1 the busy tick-tock fast section* runs straight into the 1
opening of the opera.

A cheer-up message for Dido from Belinda in a snatch of aria. She is backed up immediately by a firm
2: *Banish sorrow* and cheerful chorus.* 2
3: *Ah! Belinda* Dido is 'prest with torment' in an aria* that runs 3

high and sadly over a ground, that is a pattern of notes in the bass repeated over and over, in this case every four bars.

7: *When monarchs unite* Once again Belinda and then the chorus* give 7
common sense advice. It's a sound policy for monarchs to unite in marriage.

10: *Fear no danger* A delicately encouraging duet* – of course he loves 10
you say Belinda and the anonymous Second Woman. Of course he does echo the chorus.

Aeneas appears and puts his case in a fine firm arioso. Dido comes in. Now the chorus has something
12: *Cupid only throws the dart* more fancy,* a piece that starts in canon. Cupid's dart 12
flies about through the air deliciously. Belinda gives us the news that love has won and the chorus again confirm that love is indeed triumphant. Followed by
15 the triumphing dance.* 15

Act I Sc 2

16 The Witches scene:* a spooky piece indeed: the Sor- 16
ceress intoning her dire message: the manic laughter of the coven: the spiteful plot to frustrate the lovers: the echo chorus – a three-ring circus of evil in all of six minutes. By rather thoughtlessly giving away the plot at this early stage the witches do, however, rob the opera of any element of surprise.

Act II

0 A moment of repose after hunting: the whole scene* 13
is much of a piece. After a cheerful play-on Belinda and the Second Woman both have a relaxed aria neither of which has much to do with the plot. Each has its own charm, the second has a pretty vocal part spun out over a ground and for once it has no chorus.

6: *The skies are clouded* The storm breaks* with some fizzing in the strings 6
and the courtiers break into a hurry chorus in counterpoint giving tongue to the two most banal lines in the opera:

Haste, haste to town, this open field
No shelter from the storm can yield

Aeneas rather wimpishly agrees to leave Dido but
8: *But ah! What language can I try* worries about breaking the news to her. The opening
Ah!, repeated, leads into a fine burst of recitatif** 8
which makes him sound a lot more noble than he is.

Act III Sc 1

The jolly sailors have a short lively piece from the or-

chestra to set them going, the solo sailor sings cheerfully of telling the usual sailorly lies to the nymphs on
0: *Come away fellow sailors* the shore. The chorus concurs, heartily.** Perhaps 0
the most fetching chorus of the opera with its precise word-setting and clean-cut lines. A short sailors' dance follows.

The witches gloat and plot further mayhem. Their
4: *Destruction's our delight* gloating chorus (Ho Ho) is a little winner.** Their 4
dance, however, sounds eccentric but perfectly respectable.

Act III Sc 2

Dido waits for Aeneas: she seems to know her fate already which is not surprising considering the sailors had been chattering about it some time earlier. She
5: *Your counsel all is urged in vain* reflects on her fate in a powerful recitatif.* 5

The exchanges between Dido and the weak-minded Aeneas: rapid-fire overlapping cries of Away! and I'll stay. It sounds like real life. Very effective.

A sad chorus sets the scene for Dido's great lament. We hear a ground bass line of descending semitones:
11: *When I am laid in earth* Dido enters with her noble melody*** over a soft 11
string accompaniment. This is great music: it reaches out across the centuries and moves us today just as powerfully as if it had been written yesterday. Remember me, she sings and certainly once heard, her lament can never be forgotten. The final chorus scatters sad roses on her tomb and fades away to nothing.

NOTES

Dido and Aeneas	Purcell's only true opera
First night	Sometime before 1689. See below
Reception	Not known
Libretto	Nahum Tate
Source	A part of Vergil's *Aeneid*, already dramatized in a play by Tate called *Brutus of Alba*

NEWS AND GOSSIP

John Blow, the father figure of English music in Purcell's time, wrote an opera called *Venus and Adonis* which was performed at court and became the talk of the Carolean chattering classes. It is thought that this spurred

Purcell to write *Dido* in order to wipe Blow's eye. Whether or not it was ever performed at court we do not know, but we do know that it was put on by some lucky girls at a dancing academy run by one Josias Priest. He was a choreographer by trade and must have had a great time working out the dances for *Dido* and teaching the girls the steps. Although the text was handed down (or at least parts of it) in its original form, the earliest surviving copy of the music dates from 1777. So we have little idea how much of Purcell's original work we are hearing or how near it is to what he wrote. *Dido* just wasn't performed on stage in this country in between the years 1704 and 1895. This first revival was organized by the Royal College of Music and even after that it lay on the shelf for another quarter of a century. In the twenties and thirties it was occasionally performed in small theatres (once at Sadler's Wells) and then it was exposed to the world in all its glory in the Florence festival of 1940 and the Festival of Britain in 1951 when three separate productions were put on, one of them the version arranged by Benjamin Britten. Now everyone knows what a rare and lovely work it is.

COMMENT

Dido has the appeal of a primitive painting. The perspectives are different, the range of colours is small and it can seem to be rather a dim little work until suddenly with Dido's lament it reaches out through time and brings you a vision that is clear and strong and absolutely contemporary. The solos have two firm lines, the voice and the bass, often a ground bass, a device which becomes rarer and rarer as the opera form develops so we have pretty well forgotten all about it today. The choruses sound much more modern and could even have been written fifty years later. In both solos and choruses it is the setting of the words that shows off one of Purcell's greatest talents. The meaning of the word is reflected in the music, the shape of the word is preserved by the rhythm and by the musical emphasis, and as each word is treated with enormous respect so is the complete phrase and the sentence. No composer paid such meticulous attention to the setting of words until nearly two hundred years later when Wagner applied his very own very complex system to his own work. If Purcell were alive today and heard the way Opera in English forces 'funny' modern Anglo-Saxon words on to music carefully written for an Italian text, he would undoubtedly flee the country and settle in a place where the match between words and music was treated with proper respect. Unfortunately Nahum Tate's text for *Dido* is pretty crummy although some of the lines have a Simple Simon appeal, like:

Our plot has took
The Queen's forsook

but most of the text is made up of corny classical allusions, the clichés of the dramatic poet's trade. If only it had been Dryden who did the libretto for *Dido* and Tate for *King Arthur* how happy we would be, for Dryden brings out the very best of Purcell's word-setting skills.

It is of course the lament that puts *Dido* into the class of the greats, for without it (and the closing chorus) the piece would be no more than an interesting and attractive period item. But when we hear the sliding semitones of the ground bass and Dido's haunting phrases above we know at once that this is one of the great moments in music. And even Nahum rises to the occasion with the one really good line in the show:

Remember me, but ah! forget my fate.

An alpha.

Don Carlos

Historical drama

Verdi

The one where a royal lady marries her fiancé's father, where many heretics are burnt and where a dead king exits his tomb to save a living relative.

CAST

Philippe II (Filippo), King of Spain	Bass
Don Carlo (Carlos), his heir	Tenor
Elisabeth (Elisabetta), daughter of Henry II of France	Soprano
Thybault (Tebaldo), page to Elisabeth	Soprano
Rodrigue (Rodrigo), Marquis of Posa, a grandee	Baritone
Princess Eboli, lady-in-waiting to Elisabeth	Mezzo
The Grand Inquisitor	Bass

A monk, a herald, a count, a woodman, six Flemish deputies, a voice from heaven etc.

5 acts: running time – many versions, commonly something over 3 hrs

STORY

Act I The grounds of Fontainebleau. The palace visible

We are in France and later Spain in the sixteenth century. Once again operatic hounds are at work: at a hunt in the palace grounds the non-participant Don Carlos heir to Philip II of Spain (hung with mortifying soubriquet of 'Infanta' tho' a well-grown young man) gloats at the prospect of meeting French Royal Elisabeth his long-time fiancée: he is quite potty about her in true operatic style tho' they have never met. He has sneaked away from the Spanish court and the dreaded King father Philip.

Thybault the page is heard offstage wimping to huntsman: he is lost in the forest (within sight of the palace?): he enters in panic with Elisabeth. Who are you? she asks Carlos: I'm in the Spanish Diplomatic Service says he: OK Thybault she says, I am safe with this honourable government servant, go and get a rescue party. Carlos rubs two sticks together and makes a fire: he shows Elisabeth a locket with her photo inside: he reveals himself as Carlos: says I love you madly. So do I love you says she (quick decision).

Guns go off. Fireworks etc. Must be a peace treaty says she – goody.

But not goody. Thybault returns with the bad news that her father has promised that as the price of peace she will marry Carlos's father crusty King Philip II not Carlos. Crowds appear shouting Go on Elisabeth accept him girl: we're fed up with war. Elisabeth is in a fix: she eventually opts for 'Yes' (public duty): Carlos is cast down.

Act II Sc 1 The Chapel of St Yuste: tomb of Charles V prominent: garden behind

Monks at exercise pray for the soul of Charles V: Carlos arrives considering a monastic life: it's tough in here too says an elderly monk: sorrows don't vanish inside. Zingo! Carlos suddenly hears/sees the ghost of Charles V in sound and vision.

Rodrigo* arrives: he tells how the Flemish war is bogged down: Carlos is required to supply a better quality of leadership: I have a personal problem says Carlos: my father married my fiancée, I am still mad about her. Does your father know you love his wife? asks Rodrigo: no says Carlos: military service is the best remedy for the lovelorn says Rodrigo: OK I'll come along says Carlos. Bells chime. The King (retinue at his back) and Elisabeth arrive. Carlos's emotions run riot as the procession passes: Rodrigo and Carlos swear to be lifelong pals.

Act II Sc 2 A rustic/garden scene outside the gates of the monastery of St Yuste

Princess Eboli sings to Thybault and the Court females a song about a king with seven-year itch who courted a mysterious veiled lady and when the veil was lifted – it was his wife. (Irrelevant to this version: see COMMENT.) Elisabeth enters from the monastery. Rodrigo arrives from Paris with family news also a secret note from Carlos saying this Rodrigo is OK trust him. (Meanwhile Rodrigo gives Eboli the Paris Court gossip: Eboli lets slip she fancies Carlos.) Rodrigo persuades Elisabeth to meet Carlos. Carlos creeps on (waiting in the wings). Elisabeth dismisses all including her security woman Countess Aremberg.

Carlos tells Elisabeth he is going off to help the Flems: she says O my son: no says he wrong description: I am your lover: she is upset: Carlos passes out (excessive emotion): she is more upset: Carlos comes round and gets physical: he clinches her: she repulses him with the ambiguous remark 'can't marry until you have killed your father': both are upset. Carlos exits.

NOTE: *Rodrigo (Rodrigue in text) is referred to as Posa by several characters. Names are used in this story line in whatever form speaks most easily, e.g. Elisabeth not Elisabetta.

The King (retinue at his back) enters: he fires security woman Aremberg for dereliction of duty. Elisabeth fails to take the rap: she commiserates with Aremberg: the King and Rodrigo are alone: Rodrigo says call off the Flanders campaign: the King says no but I like your style: I will appoint you my personal adviser. I am worried: I suspect hanky-panky between Elisabeth and Carlos. Then he utters an obscure threat: beware of the Grand Inquisitor.

Act III Sc 1 The Queen's gardens: statues, fountains

Carlos checks an anonymous note which he thinks is from Elisabeth: it proposes a midnight meeting by the fountain: he is by fountain, it is midnight. A masked woman appears and Carlos goes into strong loverly stuff: the woman unmasks: it is not Elisabeth: it is Eboli. My God says Carlos: he goes white: Eboli is puzzled that Carlos has gone off her: she says there is a plot afoot, Rodrigo and the King constantly whisper about you: trouble ahead.

Suddenly she rumbles Carlos mistook her for another woman: she unleashes fury. Rodrigo walks on [prowling around at midnight? Ed.] and asks Eboli will she split? Eboli is equivocal: she will get Carlos one way or another. Rodrigo raises a dagger to ensure her silence: Carlos interposes. Rodrigo says your one way out is to give me all the incriminating papers [what papers? Ed.]: Carlos overcomes his unworthy suspicions of Rodrigo (King's man?) and hands over the papers.

Act III Sc 2 The square in front of Valladolid cathedral

The citizens are out for a fun event: a royal visit plus spectacular burning of heretics (auto-da-fé). The King enters from church: mighty huzzas. Six Flemish demonstrators rush on with Carlos in front: Peace for Flemland they cry. The King tells his security men to remove these terrorists but there is universal support for the Flems: the King makes for the exit. Carlos interposes and asks to be appointed Viceroy of the Low Countries. What? says the King, and give you the chance to uprise against me? You must be mad. Carlos draws his sword (intent uncertain): the King calls on the security men to disarm him: their reaction is sluggish. Rodrigo interposes: he takes Carlos's sword: Carlos is shocked at the double-cross. All turn to the serious business – a really good fry-up of heretics.

Act IV Sc 1 The King's study

The King is broody after a bad night: he is unloved by his wife etc. The Grand Inquisitor – old, blind and terrifying – comes on. The King asks how would it be with God if I killed my son Carlos? The Inquisitor says not so bad God did it to his son: anything else? No says the King. Then let me tell you we have bad intelligence on Rodrigo: he is a criminal, traitor, pushing you into bad ways, and I must also tell you that you are not doing so well with God yourself so watch it. He exits: the King thinks these priests are getting quite impossible.

Elisabeth rushes on in a panic – my jewel case is lost she says. I have it says King and what is this pray (photo of Carlos): he was once my fiancé says she, remember? Adulteress says he: she passes out. The King calls in Eboli: Elisabeth surfaces again: Eboli admits slipping the casket to the monarch. Eboli and Elisabeth are left alone: Eboli says I'm terribly sorry I shopped you: I was jealous and furious because Carlos has gone cool on me: also I used to sleep with the King, so that's it, sorry. Elisabeth says it's exile or a convent for you. Which? Tell me tomorrow. Eboli thinks maybe I can save Carlos before I go.

Act IV Sc 2 Prison dungeon: courtyard above

Carlos is in clink. Rodrigo visits him: he says Carlos's papers were discovered on his person so now he is in bad odour: the King is about to kill him but Carlos is to go free to Flemland. Two armed police creep in unseen: they shoot Rodrigo. The dying Rodrigo tells Carlos to meet Elisabeth tomorrow at the chapel of St Yuste. 'I am happy to die for my friend, Carlos farewell etc.' He expires.

The King enters (retinue at his back) and offers Carlos his sword back: he spurns it: you murdered Rodrigo he says. Alarum! Bells! Shouts! A mob attacks the prison demanding Carlos (put up to it by Eboli): the King says let them in: they enter in a frenzy. Eboli pops in and tells Carlos to scarper fast. The turmoil is quelled: the Grand Inquisitor tells the mob to get on their knees: they do. (Power of God.)

Act V Cloister of chapel of St Yuste: moonlight

Elisabeth addresses remarks to Charles V (entombed): she recalls her one-time happy meeting with Carlos: she asks Charles to pass an important message to God on her behalf. Carlos arrives: both reflect on the nobility of Rodrigo: Carlos decides he will be a valiant leader for the Flems: she agrees, praises his brave posture: their farewells are in progress but are interrupted by the King (inquisitors at his back) who seizes Elisabeth and hands Carlos over to the Grand Inquisitor. The tomb of watchful Charles V opens and a monk emerges: this monk (believe it or not) *is* Charles V: Charles V leads Carlos off [whither? Ed.].

MINUTES FROM START **LOOK OUT FOR**

Act I

A masterly opening act. After the usual operatic version of hunting noises, choruses off and some pantomime (in the proper sense of the word), we have Carlos talking to himself about Elisabeth and then an extended duet Carlos/Elisabeth passing through
9: *De quels transports* phases of recognition to her short cavatina of joy;* 9
12: *Ah! Ne tremble pas* then to a passionate love duet** (to the same tune). 12
After Thybault's bad news the final section** reflects 14
14: *L'heure fatale* their shock and fear, but ends with an easy-going happy cabaletta that we can only suppose shows confidence that their love will conquer everything.

The courtiers etc. march on (starting offstage in true Verdian style) to a sturdy determined sort of a
19: *O chants de fête* tune:** there is a great moment when after missing 19
three beats Elisabeth gives the faintest possible 'Oui' to the fatal question and then amidst the sturdy tune again and general rejoicing we hear cries of anguish from the two lovers as the whole ensemble*** builds into a thundering climax only to die away again and to leave Carlos alone uttering a few desultory and despairing thoughts. Stunning!

Act II Sc 1

Solemn horns are joined by a dry holy chorus of monks with a solo monk singing out about the vanity
3: *Il voulait regner* of pomp and power:* he gets worked up about this 3
matter and as the monks join him again the irrepressible Verdi brings in one of his big sweeping tunes,** not at all holy.

The duet between Carlos and Rodrigo is full of dramatic and musical action and it culminates in a
11: *Dieu, tu semas* duo,* not stanza about and then together, but in close 11
harmony from the start (unusual). They make a big thing out of swearing to be true to each other for ever (a topic not much discussed in real life) to a tune or motif which we shall hear again – and again (the Mates motif). Then, Lo! Philip and Elisabeth process into the chapel with attendant monks to exclamations
15: *Soyons unis* from the friends and the scene ends*** (splendidly) 15
with a resumption of the music of the duet backed by the Mates motif again.

Act II Sc 2

A divertissement. Ladies of the court pose and group
and sing about the beauties of nature to quasi ballet
19: *Au palais des fées* music: Eboli gives her big solo, the Song of the Veil.* 19
It sounds very Spanish and is souped up with Castil-
ian coloratura. Now for some pure magic. To a background of elegant Palm Court music Eboli and
25: *Que fait-on* Rodrigo size each other up** under cover of society 25
gossip. Meanwhile Elisabeth, trembling, opens and
reads the letter from Carlos: Rodrigo moves into one
of the most persuasive and beguiling baritone arias in
28: *L'Infant Carlos* all opera:*** he thinks Elisabeth really should see 28
Carlos and after humming and hawing a bit, she
agrees: the scene dies away as Rodrigo and Eboli
stroll off to the Palm Court tune. His work is done.

The tense duet Carlos/Elisabeth has no great sus-
32: *Je viens solliciter* tained melodies but one plaintive refrain** repeated 32
over and over as they agonize about their really bad
luck: for the rest it surges and flows in high emotional
style until Elisabeth rejects him, and he disappears
from view. Tremendously effective.

Elisabeth sings farewell to the unlucky Countess
Aremberg (unlucky too in having no singing part) in
43: *O ma chère compagne* what at first seems to be a sad simple song,** but un- 43
expected modulations and a rich orchestral accom-
paniment transform it into a sophisticated and very
effective little item.

46: *Restez!* A duet** Philip/Rodrigo finishes the act: again it 46
has no great set-piece arias/tunes but it brings out all
the conflicting emotions in the uncomfortable encounter. Disturbing.

Act III Sc 1

0 The lovely prelude** starting off with horns in fine 0
lyrical mood.

4: *Un tel amour* The duet** of mistaken identity gets going with a 4
fine lyrical sweep when Eboli reacts to Carlos's
loverly approaches: then when the mask drops they
drift into a state of stunned reflective exchanges until,
with the explosive 'Quel éclair' (My goodness me!),
Eboli realizes Carlos mistook her for the Queen.

8: *Redoutez tout* Two good trios: the first** vehement and arresting 8
as all three parties think strong thoughts: Eboli (Fear
my fury: I'll get him), Rodrigo (If you talk you'll have
some explaining to do yourself), Carlos (My God,

what have I done to Elisabeth's reputation?): the sec-
12: *Malheur sur toi* ond* (after some heavy stuff where Rodrigo tries to 12
knife Eboli) when Eboli, almost unaccompanied, puts a curse on Carlos and then building into the climactic moment with Rodrigo threatening her with dire retribution if she grasses and poor dazed Carlos wishing the earth would open up and swallow him. After the test of trust between Carlos and Rodrigo the scene plays out to the Mates motif.

Act III Sc 2

Mighty spectacle; resounding choruses: the clangour of brass: very big stuff indeed, a full dry run for *Aida* but the holy chorus a bit below Verdi's usual standard for singing monks and the grand march not up to snuff (circus music with a crummy cornet solo): but for the rest, terrific and look out especially for:

24: *Sire, la dernière heure* The Flemish prisoners' appeal.* 24

26: *Les Flamands sont des infidèles* The great ensemble,*** a jamboree of counterpoint, Flems, monks, soloists, people and all, in an overpowering burst of harmonious themes and contradictory feelings. 26

31: *O ciel!* The Mates motif is introduced sotto voce on two clarinets as a background to exclamations of surprise as Rodrigo disarms Carlos and then the theme of general rejoicing – belted out by all. 31

Finally the dying fall of the scene as the flames begin to toast the heretics and as the voice on high guides their souls in the right direction – upwards.

Act IV Sc 1

Stand by for one of opera's greatest scenes:*** a summit encounter between Church and State: compulsive, terrifying, memorable. First, an ominous string introduction with an uneasy solo cello doing a wordless recitatif – very spooky – then the king ruminates over the problems in his life (wife does not love him,
2: *Je dormirai* treason brewing) in a formal aria.* Not wildly excit- 2
ing but it sets the mood of vulnerability before the assault on him begins.

The confrontation: look out especially for:

9: *Le Grand Inquisiteur!* The Inquisition theme in the lower strings and bassoons which starts on the Grand Inquisitor's entry.* Unnerving. 9

11: *C'est donc moi* The outburst** of the GI when he starts the attack 11
on Rodrigo and the King: this music induces fear: whatever Philip may have felt at the time it can still scare the hell out of us today: it is followed by the thunderous exchanges of the climax*** and finally the attempt to return to a normal constitutional relationship.

The duet of the stolen casket: Elisabeth's defence of her innocence is set to one of Verdi's purest, sweet-
21: *Vous le savez!* est (and shortest) melodies.** 21
23: *Maudit soi* The subsequent 'thinks' quartet*** is pure magic: 23
King (What a suspicious bastard I am), Elisabeth (Wish I were back home in France), Eboli (I am guilty, guilty), Rodrigo (It's time I did something). A striking cello melody beneath (creeps in from time to time).

One great scene follows another: Eboli's confession of her three sins (secret love for Carlos, stealing the casket, sleeping with the king) and Elisabeth's reaction are set to very personal music, finishing with
30: *O don fatal* Eboli's bitter aria** of regret. It has a positive ending: 30
she resolves to save Carlos if she can.

Act IV Sc 2

Two good solos from Rodrigo: the first a simple mel-
37: *C'est mon jour* ody** as he foretells his death. The second carrying 37
the message to meet Elisabeth against a background of funereal brass. Then it flowers into a touching fare-
42: *Ah! je meurs* well to Carlos*** (another wonderful tune) with a 42
hint of the friendship theme in the orchestra, finally a climax, powerful for a dying man, but marvellously effective.

45: *Mon fils* The finale* is effective but seems unduly com- 45
pressed: a lot happens very quickly.

Act V

3: *Toi qui sus* Elisabeth's big moment: a huge solo:*** early on, a 3
melting legato tune, then a wander down memory lane (France!) and hopes of meeting Carlos – suddenly reality breaks in: she has nothing left: wishes to die, so switches to a high ethereal prayer. A set piece with a big climax. Exceptional.

10: *C'est elle!* The farewell duet*** Elisabeth/Carlos is the heart 10
of the last act: Carlos for the sake of Rodrigo's memory says he will be a stalwart leader of the Flems:

Elisabeth eggs him on, all of this to strong affirmative music: Carlos tells her that yesterday he would have ridden off into the sunset with her across the saddle but today he is noble, strong in honour, will give her up and go to war. So to the final dreamy, plaintive
12: *Au revoir* farewell section of the duet*** with its sad adieus and 12
the hopes for better luck in heaven: here Verdi makes an all-out assault on the emotions with that special clear, sustained high soprano line he provides for pure female souls in distress.

(Followed by the noisy tomb-opening *coup de théâtre* which ends the opera.)

NOTES

Don Carlos Verdi's twenty-fifth opera
First night Paris Opéra, 11 March 1867
Reception Very satisfactory
Libretto Méry and du Locle
Source *Don Carlos*, an epic poem by Schiller

NEWS AND GOSSIP

Verdi was a bit off–on about *Carlos* to begin with. Always attracted by big works and big names, he often fluttered around a Schiller or a Shakespeare but almost as often drew back. When first offered *Carlos* by the Opéra he turned it down but a new management moved in and pressed it on him again and this time he was 'bowled over'. Maybe this was a diplomatic reaction but he certainly set to work with the script team to make the piece bigger, better and grander – in short, the biggest operatic aspidistra in the land. *Carlos* was to be a knockout for the French public and critics. He would slay them. There was not enough spectacle in the script that he was offered, so he popped in two scenes from the original Schiller (the interview of Rodrigo by the King and the great confrontation between the King and the Grand Inquisitor), and invented a lot of new spectacle in the form of the big parade of Royal power, the demo by Carlos and the Flems and the burning of the heretics, a three-ringed circus all crowded into twenty minutes of mighty pageantry. Verdi's first shot at *Carlos* ran some five hours, too long even for Paris. It was endlessly cut, patched and rewritten during the long rehearsal period (some six months), which was not a happy time. Verdi walked out of rehearsals because of bitching between the Eboli and the Elisabeth and he found the Opéra production cold and lacking in heart. But the success of the first night must have cheered him up and he was much better pleased with a more red-blooded version at Bologna six months later. Still not satisfied he fiddled about with minor cuts for several Italian productions and ten years after the premiere when a production was pending in Vienna he decided to take drastic action. To save the opera from being cut about by managements who simply could not fit the monster into their schedules, he said he would 'prefer to wield the knifc myself'. So out went the first act, the ballets (hoorah!) and more. It was given in this form in Italian at the Scala in 1884. But there is no definitive version: opera houses still put it on in different forms. It can run from the five hours of Andrew Porter's careful reconstruction of the original Paris score (broadcast by the BBC) to reach-me-down mini-*Carlos*es of two and a half hours or less. The version described here is the Abbado/La Scala recording of 1985. *Carlos* has never been near the top of Verdi's top pops, perhaps because it needs such huge resources.

COMMENT

Carlos is perhaps Verdi's finest opera. Although the story is historico/romantic the characters come nearer to Shakespeare's historicals than the *galère* of stuffed dummies in Verdi's early works: we can believe in the ruthless King, the terrifying Grand Inquisitor, the tormented Carlos and the Rodrigo whose ultimate loyalty comes as such a relief, Eboli the liberated woman and Elisabeth whose sweetness is saved from insipidity by her Frenchness in a foreign land and by her tremendously inconvenient passion for Carlos. The plot trundles along at a good pace: even in the midst of spectacle things happen fast (the demo of the Flems; Carlos disarmed by Rodrigo; the heretics burnt). Indeed the grip of the narrative holds us in a way that is rare in Verdi (*Traviata* and *Otello* excepted). Disbelief is suspended and the music is built on a splendidly secure foundation. The only blot is the stroke of theatrical hokum which ends the opera. Charles V does nothing to resolve the story by stepping out from his tomb and taking Carlos into care. What is he actually going to *do*? Send his soul up to heaven to join Rodrigo (i.e. murder him) or keep him around in the monastery, in which case he can't expect much joy in life with the Inquisitor waiting for him outside?

For richness, depth and sheer enjoyability the score of *Carlos* is a phenomenon. Three things make it special in the canon of Verdi's work – the stupendous choral climaxes to Acts I and II and the sustained excitement of the choral jamboree of the auto-da-fé scene (more effective than anything of the kind except for *Aida*): the amazing number of goodies one after another (too many to name but just look at the succession of three stars in the section above): but most strikingly Verdi's change of gear into a style of operatic music that flows along without let or hindrance: no tee-ing up for a solo; no noisy applause points; very little recitatif; not one oom-pah in sight; the use of effective leitmotifs to key the subconscious as to what message the music is carrying; long passages of consequence following consequence in an unbroken chain. There are absolutely no longueurs throughout its marathon length and the only interruption to the dramatic flow (the Veil Song) is a leftover from the first version where Elisabeth and Eboli changed costume before the assignation with Carlos, thus making the Veil Song more relevant and the matter of mistaken identity more credible. *Carlos* is the grandest of grand operas and an alpha-plus through and through.

Don Giovanni

Tragi-comedy

Mozart [K527]

The one where the Don has already scored 1965 before the opera begins and makes four further attempts in the course of it before being consigned to hell.

CAST

Don Giovanni, a Spanish nobleman	Baritone
Leporello, his servant	Baritone
The Commendatore, a high official	Bass
Donna Anna, his daughter	Soprano
Don Ottavio, her fiancé	Tenor
Donna Elvira, aristo from Burgos	Soprano
Masetto, country fellow, a thickie	Baritone
Zerlina, his fiancée	Soprano

2 acts: running time 2 hrs 30 mins

STORY

Act I Sc 1 Outside Donna Anna's house. Night

We are somewhere near Seville sometime in the seventeenth century and Leporello is doing sentry duty outside a house within which his master is up to no good. He grumbles. Giovanni exits from the house with Donna Anna hanging on to him. She screams very loud. This wakes her Dad the Commendatore who stumbles on and challenges Giovanni to a duel. Anna exits to phone the police. Giovanni is not keen to slay an OAP but does so. Exits. Anna returns with Don Ottavio. Shock horror. She swears vengeance etc.

Act I Sc 2 A street in Seville. Dawn

Leporello asks Giovanni can he speak frankly. Go ahead says Giovanni. You are living a horrible life says Leporello. Belt up says Giovanni I smell woman. They hide: enter Donna Elvira. Wow! says Giovanni a good looker. Hey ho sings Elvira I am sad: I have been deserted by my lover. Poor sweet says Giovanni let me help. He steps out. Madam he says – oh shit says Leporello it's Elvira. Giovanni! you stinking double-crossing stoat says Elvira. Cool it cool it says Giovanni. You horrible man you says

Elvira you got me into bed promising marriage then stood me up. Leporello kindly tell the lady the facts of life says Giovanni. Exits.

Leporello reads a catalogue of Giovanni's score in the EU sex league: Italy 640, Germany 231, France 100, Turkey 91, Spain 1,003. He adds that Giovanni is also sexually democratic and will ravish any class of woman from aristos to beggars any type anywhere any time. Leporello exits. I'll get that Giovanni for what he done to me by God I will says Elvira.

Act I Sc 3 In the countryside. Morning

A gang of peasants enter going on about the wedding of Masetto to Zerlina who gives us a lecturette recommending marriage for the leisurely enjoyment of safe sex. Enter Giovanni and Leporello. Giovanni fancies Zerlina. He tells Leporello to cart off the whole gang to his country house. I'm not going says Masetto. You bloody well are going says Giovanni: Zerlina is safe with a titled gent like me. Ho ho says Masetto: watch it Masetto says Giovanni I am a person of some influence around here. OK OK says Masetto I hear what you say I'll go.

Giovanni chats up Zerlina: he does a stunning seduction act proposes marriage and says come and see my etchings my villa is quite close. Zerlina is quite overcome and agrees to view the etchings. Elvira bursts in. Don't believe that bastard she cries he's a double-crossing swine. Poor lady she is potty about me and has quite lost her marbles says Giovanni to Zerlina. Don't believe a word of it cries Elvira: come with me: Elvira and Zerlina exit.

Enter Anna and Ottavio (my God what next thinks Giovanni). I want your help says Anna. Giovanni (much relieved) replies Yes ma'am I'll do anything go anywhere to be of service to you. Enter Elvira: Watch it you folks says she this Giovanni is a snake in the grass, a crook, a liar, a seducer. The poor lady is in an advanced state of mental illness says Giovanni. She looks pretty sane to us say Otto and Anna. Elvira shouts you're as guilty as hell, you're a criminal, a liar, etc. Exits. Which one tells truth? ponder Otto and Anna. If I can help let me know says Giovanni just now I have to see a man about a dog. Exits.

Otto . . . says Anna . . . O my God . . . Otto . . . I've got it . . . That's him! Who? asks Otto. Him! she says him what killed my Dad him what tried to rape me. Tried? asks Otto. No measure of success I trust? Listen you dumbbell says Anna this is what happened (she gives him a detailed account: the surprise awakening: a man in her bed: thought it was Otto [Well! well! Ed.]: it wasn't Otto: her struggles: her escape: the murder etc.). So we must get him get him! she says. Revenge is a matter of prime importance to me. Exits. O Lord says Otto one simply can't relax when she's in a state like that. We will only get some peace when she calms down. Exits.

Leporello enters. I can't stick this job much longer the boss is just impossible says he. Giovanni enters: How's it going? he asks. Badly says Leporello. I took that lot home (Bravo! says Giovanni) I managed to get them to stay (Bravo!) I told Masetto a lot of lies (Bravo!) I got the whole lot pissed as newts – and who dropped in? Elvira? asks Giovanni. Right says Leporello and she rubbished you something horrible. So I pushed her out and locked the door (Bravo! Bravo!). OK says Giovanni now they're half smashed let's throw a big party tonight with dancing and all and just see if I can't make a few scores actually I have the figure of ten in mind.

Act I Sc 4 The garden of Giovanni's house

Masetto is dead jealous. You little tramp says he. He never touched me says Zerlina go on hit me do what you like to me – you still turn me on whatever you do. Wheedle wheedle I must be potty to weaken says Masetto (but he does). Giovanni is heard outside. We must hide says Zerlina. Why? says Masetto. Ahaaa . . . you don't want me to see you have made your number with Giovanni. Not true you bastard says she. Both hide. Giovanni enters plus servants peasants etc. OK folks he says we're going to have a great time! It's party time! Get moving! All exit.

Giovanni spots Zerlina and resumes his loverly stuff. Masetto jumps out. Hello my lad says Giovanni Zerlina is extremely anxious to rejoin you. Here she is old chap and let's all have a jolly good time at the party. (Masetto goes quietly but only just.) Enter Elvira Otto and Anna in masks. Gosh! they say a pretty tricky old job this one. It takes guts to get in there and expose the bastard in his own home. But we've got plenty of guts.

Leporello spots the maskers and checks with Giovanni. Hey there! you maskers! he shouts from window. Like to come to a party? Yeah sure thanks a lot says Otto. The boss will have a go at those females too thinks Leporello. God preserve us think they.

Act I Sc 5 A ballroom in Don Giovanni's house

The party is going great guns but sticky in patches. Masetto is crazy jealous: Zerlina is fearful. The maskers arrive. Giovanni is the perfect host. Everyone sings hurrah for freedom! [Why? Ed.] The dance restarts. Giovanni tells Leporello to mind Masetto. The maskers are very tense and not enjoying it much. Giovanni carries Zerlina offstage into a bedroom. Leporello follows to warn him that Masetto is brewing up. Zerlina screams. The dancing stops. All hell breaks loose. Giovanni comes on sword drawn dragging Leporello. The dirty skunk it was him that harassed her says Giovanni. But nobody is fooled.

The maskers unmask and shout Now we've got you you dirty beast. A timely thunderstorm breaks. Giovanni is cornered. There is suspense while all sing What a horrible man you are etc. Giovanni using Leporello as human shield makes a dash for it and escapes.

Act II Sc 1 A street. Night

Leporello tells Giovanni he's had enough. I'm off he says. Don't be a fool says Giovanni and slips him a couple of monkeys. OK I'll stay says Leporello if you promise to leave women alone. You must be mad says Giovanni I can't live without 'em. (Leporello stays.) Have you seen Elvira's maid? asks Giovanni. Whew! a sizzler. Let's swap costumes: the lower orders prefer sex with their own kind. (They swap.)

Elvira appears at a window and says Oh that terrible Giovanni I just can't wash him out of my hair. Ho ho thinks Giovanni: he shouts up to Elvira I love you still so I do. I'm really sorry for what I done. Get off says she I don't believe you. It's true he says Come on down please. You take her on Lep my boy says Giovanni I'm off after the maid. Hey! wait a minute! says Leporello. Belt up and get on with it says Giovanni. Exits.

Elvira enters. Leporello continues to court her as if he were Giovanni. Will you love me forever? asks Elvira. Sure thing says Leporello. Giovanni yells Murder! murder! just offstage. Elvira and Leporello run for it. Enter Giovanni. He serenades the maid's window. She opens but is interrupted by the arrival of a noisy gang led by Masetto.

Where's that bastard gone? he shouts. I am Giovanni's servant says Giovanni Can I be of service? Where's your horrible master? asks Masetto. Went thataway says Giovanni no maybe thataway suggest one party searches to the right one to the left. You stay here Masetto. The parties go off. Lemme see your cosh says Giovanni (Masetto hands it over). Giovanni hits Masetto on the head butts him kicks him in the groin etc. etc. Exits. Zerlina comes on. Are you sick or something? she asks Masetto. I've just been nearly beaten to death by that son of a bitch Leporello says Masetto. Come come poor lovey says Zerlina come up to my place and we'll do something to restore your health and spirits.

Act II Sc 2 A courtyard in Donna Anna's house. Night

Enter Leporello (still as Giovanni) and Elvira. Leporello tries to find a door to make an escape. Enter Anna and Otto both still girning on about love revenge etc. Leporello finds a door: Zerlina and Masetto come in through it. Here he is, shouts Masetto, the dirty skunk. Leave him alone! says Elvira he's my man. It's all a mistake folks says Leporello I am not Don Giovanni at all: I am his servant Leporello. Leporello? they echo. Gosh. All are bouleversé'ed. Anna exits [no reason given: Ed.].

So it was you who beat up Masetto says Zerlina. So it was you who fooled me says Elvira. Sorry folks I couldn't help myself I was only obeying orders says Leporello. He makes a dash for the door. Exits. Things are now quiet. Otto says it's now quite certain that it was Giovanni who murdered the Commendatore. We must get him. Meanwhile I'm off to sing another tenor aria to Anna.

Act II Sc 3 A graveyard. Equestrian statue of Commendatore prominent. Night

Giovanni scales the wall. Cripes! That was a close one! he says. He hears Leporello outside. Come in shouts Giovanni. Leporello scales the wall. Cripes! he says that was a close one! I was nearly killed owing to you. Listen to me says Giovanni I met a girl in the street who thought I was you and said Hey there old Leporello but when I start a little business with her she screams and raises the alarm so I escape here. How shocking says Leporello she could have been my wife. And what a laugh if she had been says Giovanni.

Suddenly a spooky voice echoes out: You will laugh no more, it says, after dawn. Whassat? says Giovanni. The voice booms out again. Show some respect for the dead it says. Mama mia says Don Giovanni what goes? He reads the inscription on the Commendatore's plinth. Vengeance it says.

Tell the old boy to come to dinner tonight says Giovanni to Leporello. Not bloody likely says Leporello I'm shit scared. Do it! says Giovanni. Leporello addresses the statue: the statue turns its eyes and nods its head. So you will dine with me? asks Giovanni. Yes says statue. Bloody queer goings-on says Leporello. We'd better get back home to get the dinner on says Giovanni.

Act II Sc 4 A room in Donna Anna's house

Otto and Anna going on about revenge as usual. Otto says Why not marry me it would cheer you up. At a time like this? says Anna you must be out of your mind. Certainly not yet. Ah well says Otto I only asked.

Act II Sc 5 A room in Don Giovanni's house

Giovanni is about to eat dinner. His house musicians play pops from contemporary ops. Giovanni particularly pleased by number composed by himself. He eats (rather disgustingly) a pheasant leg. Leporello scrounges food. Elvira rushes in: Giovanni she says I'm not asking for anything but that you change your immoral ways. Live decently. Giovanni sticks up two fingers. Wine women and women he cries that's my life. Elvira exits. She screams.

Go and see what hit her says Giovanni to Leporello. Leporello looks out of the door. He screams. He chunters with fear . . . stone man . . . in white . . . walking . . . tatatata . . . he says. You're off your rocker says Giovanni. A knock. Go and see who it is Leporello says Giovanni. Not likely says Leporello. He dives under the table. The Commendatore stalks in. You asked me to dinner and here I am says he. Incredible! says Giovanni: Leporello set another cover. I don't want food says the Commendatore I have a message. Will *you* dine with *me*?

Tell him to forget it says Leporello. I'm not chicken says Giovanni I accept your invitation. Shake on it says the Commendatore. (They shake.) Zut! says Giovanni his hand is dead cold. Repent! says the Commendatore. Shan't says Giovanni. Repent! says the Commendatore. No! says Giovanni. Your last chance to repent says the Commendatore. No! shouts Giovanni. Time's up! says the Commendatore (he fades away). Flames spring up also demons devils demoniac spirits appear singing. My God! My God! says Giovanni all the tortures of hell are closing in on me. And serve you jolly well right too sing the demons etc. Going . . . going . . . Ahhhh! shouts Giovanni as he drops into the pit. Ah! echoes Leporello as he sees his master go down for good.

Epilogue

Anna, Otto, Elvira, Zerlina, Masetto ask Leporello where's he gone? To hell says Leporello. You see it went this way: this stone man came into the dining room seized Giovanni's hand and chucked him into hell. So that's it. Anna will you marry me asks Otto (yet again). No says she. I'll take a raincheck for one year. [And what's the betting after that? Ed.] I'm going to get me to a nunnery says Elvira. Domestic bliss for us say Masetto and Zerlina. Off to the JobCentre for me says Leporello. All of them agree he was a bad man and he got his deserts.

MINUTES FROM START LOOK OUT FOR

0 The overture*** in its first few bars gives us fair warning that this opera is not going to be all giocosa (Mozart's word), that is not all froth and frolic. Even 0

after the dark introduction the fast bit is still full of menace. A long overture.

Act I Sc 1

After Leporello's opening whinge we go bang snap
8: *Non sperar, se non m'occidi* into action** in three stages: 8

1. Attempted rape: Donna Anna struggles with Giovanni: she leads the struggle duet in frightened breathless phrases, Giovanni follows and echoes, Leporello growls away below.

2. Confrontation, duel and murder. The Commendatore comes on shouting at Giovanni: the duel is short sharp and orchestral: it ends on a fraught long-held chord – is he dead?

3. Stunned reaction by Giovanni and Leporello. The Commendatore gasps out – yes, he is pretty well dead. All of this in three and a half minutes.

Mozart's accompanied recitatifs reach their zenith in this opera. Here we have the whole force of Donna Anna's shocked discovery of her dead father carried
12: *Ma qual mai s'offre* by an accompagnato** – biting strings for horror, 12
woodwind chords for grief. This speaks more directly than could an aria, and secco would, of course, be
15: *Fuggi, crudele, fuggi!* puny. Then we dive into the duet** Donna Anna/ 15
Ottavio, she again leading strongly and decisively, swearing to avenge her father's death and he limping along wimpishly below and behind her.

Act I Sc 2

Donna Elvira is looking for the man who abandoned
20: *Ah, chi me dice mai* her: a bold short aria** with strong outlines and lots 20
of unexpected sforzandos. Giovanni is sorry for her (but wait).

26: *Madamina, il catalogo* The Catalogue aria.*** Leporello reels off Gio- 26
vanni's score in each country (although he notches up ninety-one in Turkey, sadly he did not perform in England). A delicious allegro: Leporello unwinds the list with a rather ghastly relish with the whinnying woodwind mocking poor Elvira. Followed by a much less attractive andante, still mocking but without the bounce and charm of the first part.

Act I Sc 3

Masetto, suspicious (with good reason), warns Zerlina against the upper classes, reluctantly he agrees to leave her with the Don. Rather a square little num-

35: _Ho capito_ ber* with an angry beat. Typical Masetto music: we 35
will hear more like it.

Giovanni seduces Zerlina rather quickly (three
38: _Là ci darem la mano_ minutes 15 seconds). He wins her with a tune*** that 38
was later to win over the whole musical world. Simple, charming and memorable, it has been used for variations, musical competitions, translated into solos for piano, oboe, bassoon, etc. etc. In its proper form and place its freshness never stales. Look out for the doubling of the melody the second time it comes round, first by the flute then the bassoon.

43: _Ah! fuggi il traditor!_ Good advice from Elvira: this scrap of cavatina** 43
packs a punch that would have deterred any girl of good sense. Elvira's music is again decisive, firm and with big intervals and strong accents.

45: _Non ti fidar_ There are three things going on in this quartet:*** 45
(1) Elvira is determined to expose Giovanni as a double-crossing con man, (2) Giovanni explains that Elvira is out of her mind, (3) Anna and Ottavio are puzzled as to which story is true. The quartet starts with a firm sane statement from Elvira (He's a beast) followed by a wondering puzzled response from Anna and Ottavio (What a fine woman, she's clearly upset), a response which will crop up again later as they begin to get really fazed. Then things speed up as Giovanni comes in saying forcibly and pretty convincingly that she's potty. Even faster when Elvira rebuffs: now as both he and she get quicker and quicker, Anna and Ottavio get slower and more thoughtful (Mad? She doesn't look so mad), Elvira has quite hysterical little outbursts, patter-runs between breaths. The whole edifice swings into the minor – back to the major and on to the finish with Giovanni and Elvira shouting at each other in rapid fire whilst Anna and Ottavio linger over their doubts, which are now becoming very considerable.

48: _Don Ottavio, son morta_ The apex of Mozart's accompagnatos*** – the biggest 48
and best in the business. Down in Donna Anna's mind something stirs. Hey! she shouts, Good Lord! I know who killed my father! It was him! Huge dramatic chords. Then she recounts her story, much in the style of a witness giving evidence in a police court,

but more agitato. Ottavio acts as her feed like a professional stooge. The accompaniment thins out to let her get things off her chest. Lots of words – few notes. Then Anna sails majestically into her proud and
51: *Or sai chi l'onore* glorious aria.*** Long-breathed with a memorable 51
melody, lots of high notes (fourteen high As – three of them held for seven beats).

54: *Dalla sua pace* Ottavio's serene reaction*** to Anna's stormy 54
rampage. A honey-sweet tune, with its own mini-climax and cadentials (I want to be happy But I can't be happy Till I make you happy too).

60: *Finch'han dal vino* The jolly Giovanni.** He's just attempted to rape 60
a woman, killed a man, been abused by an old mistress, tried to seduce a peasant girl and to con two friends. Now he wants a really good party with lots of wine, women and song and the prospect of having sex with at least ten of his female guests. A short, noisy and coarse aria with plenty of gusto. Always gets a huge round from the house.

Act I Sc 4

Zerlina's music has simplicity mixed with knowing charm and here she makes her mock-innocent appeal
63: *Batti, batti, o bel Masetto* to Masetto to hit her.*** (It might have changed the 63
course of the opera if he had – and hard.) A lovely sweet tune with an exceedingly long solo cello weaving around it. Note especially how the woodwind take over the tune after Zerlina has sung it once and she then plays second fiddle, well second something, to them.

The wonderful finale, Mozart's most elaborate but not his longest, a music drama in itself. It moves through six stages:

1. Come to the party. Masetto hears Giovanni coming and there is a nervous whispered duet as he persuades Zerlina to hide. Giovanni strides in with a flock of servants and peasants and barks out instructions for the ball: the servants and peasants respond in the dullest twenty bars in the opera, grovel a bit and exit. Giovanni catches sight of Zerlina and immedi-
69: *Zerlinetta mia garbata* ately the score is alight.** Sweet loverly phrases until 69
Masetto jumps out: Giovanni softens him up, we hear a snatch of dance music in the distance and they all three decide to get in there and have a good time (a

surprise: we expected Masetto to clock him one).
2. And you come to the party too. The trio of antis
in masks stand outside Giovanni's house screwing up
71: *Bisogna aver coraggio* their courage to go to the ball* [and who told them it 71
was on? Ed.]. They are serious, even gloomy, in a
minor key and as usual Anna takes the lead with a
striking vocal line of her own. The other two are
72: *Signor, guardate* pretty well back-ups. Suddenly magic!*** The key 72
changes, the tune changes and we hear a distant minuet
and to its strains Leporello issues his invitation.
Giovanni backs him up: our trio reply in close harmony
(still minuetting), a few more courtesies and
73: *Protegga il giusto cielo* the episode is over. But more magic.*** A short 73
prayer put up by our trio, mainly in the interests of
Anna (Vengeance, please God, and keep us safe too),
gloriously scored for wind quintet and voices and
brushed with that special brand of gold dust that
Mozart reserved for wind ensembles.

Act I Sc 5

3. Welcome to liberty hall. We are into the bustle
75: *Riposate, vezzose ragazze* and bash of the party itself.* Rushing violins – no 75
dance rhythm yet. Hostly Giovanni chats up guests
but it's clear Masetto is going to be a problem. All
pretty well declaimed against orchestral jollity. A fanfare!
The maskers have arrived: greeting and a lot of
shouting about liberty, formal bang bang tonic–dominant
stuff.

4. Not so strictly ballroom. A stately minuet. Gio-
80: *Ricominciate il suono!* vanni and Leporello get everyone dancing.*** 80
Masetto still a problem. Look after that man says
Giovanni. A second orchestra (well, violins and
double-basses) strikes up and thickens the minuet.
Comments in character from several guests. Masetto
restive. Giovanni drags Zerlina offstage. Now we
have a third orchestra confusing things but in a very
decorous manner. Zerlina screams offstage! All orchestras,
all minuetting stop dead. Bedlam.

5. Explanations, explanations. A lot of shouting, a
lot of unison orchestra and all. Shock. Horror. Giovanni
comes on dragging Leporello. Noisy declamation.
He fools no one. The maskers unmask in a stern
81: *L'empio crede con tal frode* trio.** They enter in canon: Giovanni reacts boldly, 81
but he's had it.

6. In a single bound Giovanni faces the mob bay-
82: Trema, trema, o scellerato! ing for his blood.** They bay fortissimo and there is 82
thunder and lightning too, everything is very loud. But Giovanni does not lose courage. He slips away, jumps out of a window, into the orchestra pit, or whatever the producer has arranged for him, usually during the last eight bars of orchestral wind-up.

Act II Sc 1

Elvira comes to the window: Giovanni and Leporello
3: Ah taci, ingiusto core! below: she sails into a limpid, calm aria:*** begins by 3
talking to her heart, telling it not to carry on so, Giovanni is a horror: forget him. Giovanni and Leporello take the scene aboard in an up-and-down phrase of eight notes: Giovanni (unseen) takes over Elvira's aria tune and tells her he loves her. She can't believe it but wants to: he persists and she wonders. The eight-noter pops up again and again as one or another reacts or reflects. Elaborate, elegant, full of grace, it's impossible to square the mood of this piece with the mindless cruelty of what Giovanni is doing to the wretched Elvira. Giovanni shows no pity, neither does Mozart.

9: Deh vieni alla finestra Giovanni's serenade.*** Vocal line as smooth as 9
silk: mandolin accompaniment spicy and pert: short: quite perfect and very famous.

They went thataway. Giovanni gives instructions
12: Metà di voi to Masetto's gang.* A runaway piece that never 12
comes to anything much but there is some nice work in the orchestra. And one stomach-turning modulation.

17: Vedrai, carino Zerlina comforts Masetto,** badly smashed up by 17
Giovanni. A simple vocal line (as always for her) sweet as honey (but not saccharine) and as soothing as Friar's Balsam. The sexy, coy coda would surely turn on any Masetto even when half-dead.

Act II Sc 2

So now for the big stuff – barring the act finales, the
21: Sola, sola in buio loco biggest ensemble in the opera,*** rich, varied and 21
enormous.

1. Elvira fears Giovanni (Leporello of course) will leave her. Leporello searches frantically for the door. A fairly mild start – nice tune from Elvira, Leporel-

lo's answering piece mumbles around agreeably enough.

22: *Tergi il ciglio* 2. A majestic change of key.** Trumpets and 22
drums. In come Anna and Ottavio. He sings out (Sorry for Anna) in the bravest style ever and Anna replies (Only death will end my frightful grief) in typical Anna-music, strong line, free moving. Now we hear a fugitive figure hunting up and down in the strings and this will hunt with us and haunt us for a long time. Elvira and Leporello give vent to private thoughts.

24: *Ferma, briccone* 3. Things get tough for Leporello.** He is identi- 24
fied as Giovanni, cornered and confronted (a lot of the hunting figure). Elvira pleads for him. Loud harsh negatives from the other four.

4. 'Scuse me, says Leporello, I'm not Giovanni,
25: *Perdon, perdono* I'm Leporello.** Magical change of key. Hushed 25
amazement. Leporello!

26: *Mille torbidi pensieri* 5. Big brassy fanfare. Final molto allegro.** I 26
don't know what the hell's going on says Leporello. Nor I nor I nor I nor I say the other five very loudly, very chorally, for a very long time with Leporello pattering away below.

29: *Ah, pietà! Signori miei!* An agreeable buffa aria* from Leporello (I couldn't 27
help myself s'welp me God yer honour). Most of the interest in the orchestra.

31: *Il mio tesoro* Ottavio comforts Anna. A golden melody.*** In 31
the middle bit he will avenge her: now he gets as nearly fierce as the poor old thing can manage: back to the golden start: then a slightly ferocious end-piece. Lots of runs and sustained notes to show that whatever Ottavio couldn't do, he could at least sing.

Elvira still has problems. Can't decide whether she loves or hates the dreaded Don. Another magnificent
37: *Mi tradi* accompagnato followed by a quite stunning aria.*** 37
This number has one of Mozart's alpha-plus tunes, long, simple at first, but later running into all manner of decorative patterns. The short middle bit (she wants him dead) is a bit gloomy but otherwise the tone is remarkably cheerful. Lovely writing for the woodwind, perfectly shaped and a great coda. Brilliant.

Act II Sc 3

Giovanni and Leporello encounter the speaking
statue. At first he speaks to them in the middle of
42: *Di rider finirai* their secco recitatif.** Mozart, master of the uncosy, 42
as always uses three trombones to give gravitas and
spookiness to supernatural speech. Then we move
into a frightened scampering duet. The two ask him
to dinner. He replies with a monosyllabic 'Yes'.

Act II Sc 4

50: *Crudele? Ah no, mio bene!* Anna refuses Ottavio's proposal of marriage.* Here 50
we have first something between an accompagnato
and an introduction to the aria. It uses the tune of the
aria but speaks in the broken rhythms of recitatif.
Good, but not as good as the great accompagnato that
52: *Non mi dir* has gone before. Then the long aria itself,* slow at 52
first (Anna's usual downbeat mood), a faster section
with more spirit and then the best bit near the end,
terrific runs and some of Mozart's inspired cadential
writing (that is music that makes you think the end is
nigh but it isn't yet).

Act II Sc 5

The finale opens nicely enough with five minutes of
56: *Già la mensa* knockabout comedy* between servant and master. 56
Musically the most interesting items are the snatches
of tunes from current operas. Figaro's 'Non piu
andrai' (surprise surprise) gets the fullest treatment.

61: *L'ultima prova* Elvira's last throw.** She prostrates herself before 61
Giovanni but keeps her strong vocal line: perhaps it is
even more passionate than before. His replies are brutal in meaning and brutish in sound. Leporello chunters on with his customary running commentary.
Elvira screams in fear as she leaves. The emotional
temperature has shot up.

Now comes the hour of reckoning, perhaps
Mozart's own finest hour:

63: *Che grido è questo mai?* 1. Why did Elvira scream?** Giovanni asks 63
Leporello to find out. Leporello screams. Comes back
dithering with panic. Agitation in the orchestra too. A
stone man: he walks like TA TA TA TA (heavy
strokes in unison on the strings). You're potty says
Giovanni. The Commendatore enters.

64: *Don Giovanni a cenar* 2. Two tremendous chords.*** The Commenda- 64
tore speaks. He speaks slowly. His first 'Don Giovanni' has the ring of terror. Giovanni can't believe it:

the orchestra feeds our fear: Leporello is in a panic. The Commendatore forges ahead unstoppable favouring semitones but sometimes taking huge octave leaps. Scooping scales in the orchestra. Important things afoot, says the Commendatore. Leporello breaks into triplets. The orchestra starts to hammer under the Commendatore: he asks Giovanni to dine with him. I'm not chicken says Giovanni, I'll come. (Now for the first time in the opera we have a frisson of admiration for him.) You'll come? says the Commendatore (huge downward leap twice, rather like his first 'Don Giovanni'). Give me your hand says the Commendatore. Shit! it's cold says Giovanni: and now he starts to lose his marbles. Tremendous noise throughout the orchestra. Repent! says the Commendatore. Shan't says Giovanni. Basses rush about. Yes. No. Battle of wills.

69: *Da qual tremore* 3. Time's up! says the Commendatore.** Panic 69
for all. Chorus of evil spirits or something starts to hammer too. Flames. I'm going into hell shouts Giovanni (he's quite right), some hysterical phrases, then – Ah Ah Ah – and he's gone. Leporello adds his own Ah! as his master disappears.

The post-damnation sextet. (Epilogue.)

70: *Ah, dov'è il perfido?* 1. Leporello tells all. Fairly four-square stuff.* 70

72: *Or che tutti* 2. Slower section:* Ottavio proposes once again 72
(will he never get the message?). Anna postpones. A lovely duet, quite a lot of canon, quite a lot of sing-together. At this point in the opera a blessed patch of blue sky.

3. The other four reel off their career intentions,
73: *Io men vado* their vocal lines still very much in character.* 73

74: *Questo è il fin* 4. Fast, majestic final section.** They moralize 74
smugly. Sounds rather fugal but isn't really. Big climax for curtain fall.

NOTES

Don Giovanni	Mozart's fourteenth opera
First night	National Theatre, Prague, 29 October 1787
Reception	Enthusiastic
Libretto	Da Ponte
Source	Contemporary one-acter by Bertati (words) and

Gazzaniga (music) but this was only the latest in a succession of Don Giovannis. See below.

NEWS AND GOSSIP

Mozart was Prague's golden boy. The city had gone mad over *Figaro* when the stuffy Viennese had received it in a horribly condescending fashion. It had invited him on a special visit to hear their *Figaro* and had then commissioned him for a new opera for the next season. Well done Prague, say we. Mozart got da Ponte to do the libretto although he was up to his eyes writing two other librettos (one for Salieri) at the time. He pinched a lot from Bertati (different reports as to how much and surely someone could get their Mus.Doc. by laying the two pieces side by side and telling us exactly) but Bertati was only the top of an iceberg stretching back deep into time, actually to 1630. A Spanish gent, name of Tirso, produced the founding member of the Giovanni family. The story caught the fancy of writers in the same way as did Faust, Electra or Candide. There were dozens of Giovannis, usually with the Stone Guest to polish him off. Famous fellows – Molière, Goldoni – did it. Unknown fellows did it – they all did it, but da Ponte and Mozart did it best. (But this didn't stop Byron, Mérimée, Balzac and Bernard Shaw from doing it later on. But not yet Harold Pinter.)

There were the usual extraordinary precautions over censorship. When he submitted the text da Ponte left out Donna Anna's account of her rape (and certainly her calm acceptance of the man in her bed, even though it was Don Ottavio, seems a bit strange even today) and the attempted rape of Zerlina. Also the quite gratuitous shouts of 'Viva la libertà' were apparently popped in to please the Emperor who was fond of the idea of liberty. Mozart arrived in Prague on 1 October with the first night set for 14 October. Even today that looks like an impossible schedule and it was. The opening was postponed to the 29th and Mozart wrote out the overture on the night of the 28th which was therefore performed unrehearsed and must have been a mess. But the opera itself was an absolute wow. Not so a few months later in Vienna, where it was anything but. Too many arias, too chaotic, too unmelodic (!), too difficult. A reaction not comprehensible today, especially the word 'difficult' which meant difficult for the singers rather than the audience. One wonders how the poor dears would have coped with *Lulu*, *Bluebeard*, etc. Mozart shuffled the numbers around quite a lot for Vienna, adding some, deleting others. Two important changes were the addition of Don Ottavio's wonderful 'Dalla sua pace' and the cutting out of the post-damnation sextet, though whether he did this on grounds of taste (one hopes so) or because the opera was too long, we do not know. Anyway it was a flop and after a dutiful number of performances in its first run (fourteen), it was never again played in Vienna in Mozart's lifetime. After that people messed about with it. It was played quite a lot within the Austrian Empire in a German translation as a *Singspiel* (hideous thought). It reached Covent Garden in 1817 in a version titled *The Libertine* and 'arranged for the English stage' by Bishop, a really dim composer who had more than a dozen absolutely dire operas to his credit. *Giovanni* reached Italy in 1811 and France even later. During the nineteenth century it lay pretty low until the 1880s when at last the world began to realize that it was something pretty good. Today everyone knows it is a masterpiece and it stands high amongst Mozart's top four (the other three being *Figaro*, *Così* and the *Flute*).

COMMENT

Many people claim *Don Giovanni* is Mozart's best opera, even the best opera of all time. This cannot be so. It is true that it has perhaps Mozart's greatest operatic music but when it comes to the matter of plot it can't match *Figaro* or *Così*. All goes along nicely in Act I but in the first part of Act II we pretty well lose the main story altogether. There is no point in Leporello dressing up as Giovanni: it doesn't advance the Giovanni/Elvira relationship one jot. No point in Giovanni beating up Masetto except to liven things up with a spot of violence and to extract another wonderful number from Zerlina. The cornering of Leporello when assumed to be Giovanni is dead end. The truth is that Act I is one story which we pick up again in the graveyard and which is taken to its fearful end in the last scene. The only two players that are needed for the main story after Act I are Giovanni and Leporello. All the others have had it: they stick around in the same state as before, Elvira forlorn, Ottavio and Anna going on for ever about love and vengeance, Masetto and Zerlina together again after the disgraceful happenings at the ball. None of their stories pay off until the Epilogue. But the crafty da Ponte and the ingenious Mozart paper over these cracks and keep us on the ball by making the incidents so diverting in themselves and through the absolutely glorious music.

The score is pure gold, with as many or more solo winners as *Figaro* and *Così*, a three-star sextet, a brilliant finale to Act I and a last scene that knocks spots off anything in opera so far. The two act ends are also something entirely new. The finale to Act I starts with the little local difficulty with Masetto, pretty brash stuff, goes on to the invitation to the maskers with its whiff of ballroom music and their solemn little prayer to pull off their mission and then the turmoil of the ballroom scene itself. As the three plots thicken – restive Masetto, about-to-pounce Giovanni and watchful maskers – so does the texture of the dance music. The home team dance band plug away solidly at their minuet in 3/4 time, the second comes in with a sort of commentary in 2/4 and the third strikes up in another line of business altogether, again in triple time. Musically you lose your bearings, it gets like a bad dream – everything's going haywire, but in a most elegant fashion. Zerlina's scream wakes us out of the dream: everything stops dead and we are back on home ground – good standard Mozart finale stuff.

In the last scene of Act II Mozart brought terror to the opera stage for the first time. There had been lots of fear before, much of it female and tremulous, besides other popular emotions such as sorrow, joy, rage, love filial, love amorous and love parental. Natural disasters, especially storms, had featured often enough, but here, with the aid of trombones, semitones, octave leaps and a deep strong bass voice, Mozart pulled off something quite new, a *coup de théâtre* that can still raise the hairs on the napes of our necks. The growing tension of the confrontation with the Commendatore is tremendous. It is nemesis. It is awful. We are purged with terror and a little pity too for Giovanni, for in his final hour he shows pluck.

The Epilogue was composed to meet the eighteenth-century fashion for a cheery ending to an otherwise gloomy tale. It must be wrong to destroy the impact of the last scene by lining up the cast and letting them rip into their wind-up sextet. If producers must play it today, it is essential at least to allow applause to act as a sort of *cordon sanitaire* between the terror of Giovanni's final Aaah! and the chirpy account by the rest of the cast of their future plans.

One other great strength of *Giovanni* is the way each player is given a musical character. Also true of the other late Mozarts, but in *Giovanni* better defined and more precise. Elvira is defined in music as a strong-minded woman in torment, Anna as an even stronger-minded woman with an animal instinct for revenge, Ottavio as a sort of neutered tomcat, a foil to Anna and pretty useless except for his ability to produce the most golden sounds, Masetto has the music of a hulking brute, Zerlina's is full of guile, Leporello's that of the standard buffa comic but with a touch more insolence than we would expect. Which leaves the Don himself.

Millions of words have been written by clever people, including scholars, trying to pin down the true nature of Giovanni. This is not possible, for Giovanni is no more a real man than Tarzan, James Bond, or even the great god Zeus (who certainly shared some of his tastes). He is a mythological beast and like the man who encountered that other mythological animal, Thurber's Unicorn in the Garden, if you try and explain him away in rational terms, you are likely to end up in the funny farm. He did of course have human characteristics, quite a bit of Douglas

Fairbanks senior, something of Casanova (but better looking), a whiff of the Marquis de Sade, but in the end he is a manufactured man, a stereotype, Mr Supersex, who wanders through life doing one thing only and doing it pretty often. This is not to say that Mozart and da Ponte do not invest him with a lot of life, but even they cannot make this peripatetic bounder add up to a complete human being. From his music we learn that he can be seductive, coarse, arrogant and brave, but there is no musical core to Giovanni. If after the opera you were to shout down to hell 'Stand up the real Don Giovanni', at least three people would rise to their feet, not one.

The last scene gives *Don Giovanni* a stature. It has the power to purge us with pity and fear. It towers above the comic finales of *Figaro* and *Così* and whether or not *Giovanni* is Mozart's greatest opera, it is certainly his most powerful finale. Alpha-plus.

Don Pasquale

Farcical comedy

Donizetti

The one where the rich old bachelor is conned into 'marrying' an apparently nice young lady who makes his life hell until she gets what she wants.

CAST

Don Pasquale	Bass
Ernesto, his nephew	Tenor
Norina, Ernesto's girlfriend	Soprano
Dottore Malatesta, his alleged friend	Baritone
A Notary	Baritone

3 acts: running time 2 hrs

STORY

Act I Sc 1 Don Pasquale's house

We are in Rome (but it could be anywhere) in the early nineteenth century. Rich elderly crusty silly bachelor Don Pasquale has worked out a scheme. Fed up with his nephew Ernesto for refusing to get married and settle down, he has decided to marry a young wife himself, settle everything on her and disinherit Ernesto and serve him right too.

He awaits his doctor friend Malatesta, who is to procure a wife for him. Malatesta arrives to tell him he has discovered just the thing, beautiful, sexy, virtuous, etc. Who, asks Don P., highly excited, is she? My sister Sofronia replies the sly Malatesta (a lie of course). Just out of a convent. Exits.

Ernesto comes in: gets the bad news, agrees he has failed to obey instructions to marry, but for good reason – he loves girlfriend Norina. You've had it says Don P. I'm marrying Malatesta's sister. The double-crossing pig thinks Ernesto, I can't ask Norina to marry a pauper, Malatesta has ruined my chances.

Norina is telling us she is smart and sexy enough to hook any man, when she gets a letter from Ernesto saying the game is up and he is off to foreign parts. Malatesta bursts in and tells her the plot. She will become his sister, go through a phoney marriage service with Don P. then drive him so potty by bad behaviour that he will settle for anything – such as releasing her to marry Ernesto. Better tell Ernesto before he scarpers says

Norina. They then horse around rehearsing for the coming encounter with Don P.

Act II The same

Ernesto tells us he is feeling very low. Don P. bustles in all agog. Malatesta and Norina (now Sofronia) arrive and she goes through the pantomime of acting the bashful bride fresh from convent but in the end accepts his grotesque advances. A phony Notary draws up the wedding contract which favours the wife outrageously in every respect. Ernesto arrives shouting and carrying on: is apprised of plot: quietens down. As soon as the marriage is executed 'Sofronia' says she will require Ernesto as her constant escort. Don P. says on no account. 'Sofronia' gets tough: tells him to belt up: summons servants (three) and gives instructions for recruitment of more also for new furniture carriage and pair and in general all the trappings of a lavish lifestyle. Don P. astounded, outraged, upset. Is this a bad dream?

Act III Sc 1 The same: full of fashionable tradespersons offering jewels, hats, gowns etc. Don P. at a small desk with large piles of bills before him. Many servants

Don P. gloomily shuffles bills. 'Sofronia' appears in finery says she is off to the play. Don P. says no: she must stay home. Big row: 'Sofronia' slaps Don P. in the face giving an aside that this is a bit much but the plot must succeed. Don P. is suicidal. Is divorce possible? 'Sofronia' on leaving drops note of assignation with a lover. This is the last straw for Don P.: he sends for Malatesta. The servants gossip like crazy. Malatesta arrives conniving with Ernesto. Don P. attacks Malatesta: his sister is just terrible and is now plotting an assignation: they agree to trap the lovers in the shrubbery.

Act III Sc 2 The shrubbery

The lovers meet and sing the usual loverly stuff. Don P. and Malatesta apprehend 'Sofronia'. Ernesto slips away. 'Sofronia' denies anyone has been there. Malatesta tells Don P. that he will finally fix things. Informs 'Sofronia' that another woman is coming to live in Don P.'s house – Ernesto's Norina. In that case I'll leave says 'Sofronia', acting it up like mad. (Thank God says Don P.) You see says Malatesta the only way out is to have Ernesto and Norina marry and live in your house. Ernesto appears. The plot is exposed. Malatesta confesses. Don P. accepts force majeur: he agrees. Norina tritely remarks that it is unwise for old men to marry young wives.

MINUTES FROM START	LOOK OUT FOR	
0	The overture:** a string of good tunes (four), two of which we will meet again. Enjoyable.	0
Act I Sc 1		
	The first ten minutes: rarely has an opera been launched upon such a sea of melody: there is no recitatif: the story is developed in a quick-fire succession of catchy tunes, first in the accompaniment as Pas-	
7: *Son nov'ore*	quale awaits Malatesta:** then in the vocal line as	7
9: *Bella siccome un angelo*	Malatesta announces the good news** and Pasquale responds in two numbers, the first one vintage	9
13: *Per carita Dottore*	patter.*	13
	The long duet between Pasquale (a bit hang-dog) and Ernesto (amazed and outraged) has two high points, first Ernesto's sad recognition that his sweet	
22: *Sogno soave e casto*	dream is shattered*** and the final section with Ernesto railing against the man he thought to be his	22
26: *Ah! mi fa il destin' mendico*	friend.**	26
Act I Sc 2		
25: *Quel guardo il cavaliere*	Norina's big cavatina:** she gives us a full account of her accomplishments in ensnaring men's affections. In three parts: a succulent slow opening; the second based on the cheeky tune in the overture; the third a busy cabaletta.	25
	Malatesta and Norina rehearse how she will behave to Don P. in a wonderfully well worked rollercoaster	
32: *Pronto io son*	duet*** full of delights and leading to a resounding climax for Act I.	32
Act II Sc 1		
	The prelude features what sounds like a lugubrious cornet solo by Arthur Sullivan: Ernesto duly takes up this gloomy strain (thinks he is losing Norina) in a big	
2: *Povero Ernesto*	aria* which ends slightly more cheerily as he wishes	2
4: *Cerchero lontana terra*	Norina happiness without him.*	4
	The long pantomime of 'Sofronia's' introduction to Don P., mainly in recitatif, is interrupted by a rav-	
12: *Mosse, voce portamento*	ishing trio** (Don P., Norina/Sofronia, Malatesta).	12
	The business of the phony marriage service is	
19: *Fra da una parte eccetera*	spoken over another beguiling accompaniment.*	19
	'Sofronia' changes character: now nastily imperi-	
22: *Adagio un poco*	ous, she leads the attack on Don P. with verve** and malice.	22

27: *E rimasto la impietrato* One of Donizetti's magical 'thinks' ensembles:*** 27
Don P. (Good Lord, what's happening?), Ernesto
(Now I see what's afoot), Norina (I think Ernesto's
catching on) and Malatesta (Poor old Don P.).

The finale: again notable for a stunning stream of
30: *Riunita immantinente* melody in the accompaniment*** to 'Sofronia's' outrageous demands followed by a good, but standard, final burst of patter and confusion.

Act III

After a run-of-the-mill presto chorus from the servants and Don P.'s gloomy recitatif we have the battle
3: *Signorina, in tanta fretta* of wills duet** which has two special joys in it: the 3
sotto voce (asides) section (Don P. suicidal, 'Sofronia' slightly conscience-stricken) and the sparkling waltz finale when 'Sofronia' urges Don P. to give up and go to bed.

Second and much superior servants' chorus of
13: *Che internabile andirivieni!* tittle-tattle ending in another vintage waltz.* 13

Don P. and Malatesta concoct a phoney (on Malatesta's side) plot to entrap the lovers: the early ex-
21: *Cheti cheti immantinente* changes in their duet* lack Donizetti's usual felicity, 21
but soon things cheer up with a comic one-note presto patter song first by one, then the other, then
25: *Aspetta, aspetta* both.* 25

27: *Come e gentil'* Ernesto's serenade:*** quite lovely, but where *did* 53
the chorus come from?

41: *Tornami a dir' che m'ami* Touching loverly duet,** Ernesto and Norina. 41
The pantomime of the attempt to catch the lovers in flagrante takes place mainly to recitatif, as does the subsequent development and unravelling of the plot: once things have settled down, however, we have an
53: *Bravo, bravo, Don Pasquale!* elegant and cheerful little finale* in which everyone is 53
happy. Ernesto, prospects restored, Norina moralizing, Malatesta pleased with his little plot and poor Don P. glad to be shot of 'Sofronia'.

NOTES

Don Pasquale	Donizetti's sixty-third opera and last comedy
First night	Théâtre Italien, Paris, 3 January 1843
Reception	A hit
Libretto	Ruffini
Source	An earlier now unknown opera, but see below

NEWS AND GOSSIP

The story is alleged to be based on a play by Ben Jonson, *The Silent Woman*, which was, in the usual way, adapted, transformed, pillaged and pirated over the years and had last been seen thirty years earlier in the form of an opera by Pavesi. Ruffini, the poet (even hack librettists were given this agreeable title), suffered greatly from Donizetti's fiddling about with the text in order to keep up with his flow of fresh musical ideas. 'I hardly recognize my work as my own' said he finally and had his name removed from the credits. The original cast was strong and had been working together for some years as a star quartet of top names. The opera was altered to suit them during rehearsal and it seems Donizetti had not written the Act III finale when work began. In the end he popped in a piece from an earlier work, *La Bohémienne* (and also a number of concert pieces he had composed for other occasions). There are the usual stories of speedy composition – 'the opera cost me the immense fatigue of eleven days' wrote Donizetti, but he was boasting, for it is even easier than usual to prove that the composition took at least three months and was done with loving care. The recitatifs, for instance, often have a string accompaniment in place of the usual harpsichord. *Don Pasquale* was an immediate success and has held its position as one of the top of the pops in the Italian repertory ever since.

COMMENT

Don Pasquale is apt to be hailed as Donizetti's comic masterpiece, and judged on the music alone, maybe it could be so. But taken as a whole this claim will not stand, first because of the disagreeable coarseness of the plot which allows a stupid and harmless old man to be treated with unrelenting cruelty and second because the story itself is too thin and lacks any element of suspense or surprise. *Don Pasquale* shares with Verdi's *Falstaff* the ability to engender sympathy for the persecuted and dislike of the tormentors and this is not at all what Donizetti intended. It is true that both Norina and Malatesta make some feint at compassion, but this is crocodile-tear stuff and Malatesta comes out as a despicable cad, Norina as a minx and Ernesto as a prune. How unlike, how very unlike, the lovable Dr Dulcamara, the adorable Adina and the sweet pathetic Nemorino of *L'Elisir D'Amore*.

But in the music of *Don Pasquale* there is casual magic of a kind Donizetti never conjured up before. The set pieces are very fine, 'Come e gentil' is as good as the Furtive Tear ('Una furtiva lagrima' – the tenor solo in *Elisir* which is the daddy of them all), or nearly so, the pantomime duet between Malatesta and Norina in Act I is set to music as witty as anything he wrote, the ensembles are wonderful – but it is the *objets trouvés* strewn about in profusion on the margin of the score that particularly captivate the ear. Sometimes there are short orchestral asides of a few bars, sometimes they are leading melodies entrusted to the orchestra whilst the unlucky singers bark out their lines above them, as in Don P.'s anxious pacing about at the very beginning of Act I and during the mock marriage service. For those who don't much mind a bit of mental torture in a comedy plot, *Don Pasquale* must be an alpha, for those more tender-hearted it is still an evening of Donizetti at his musical best.

Dreigroschenoper, Die *see* Threepenny Opera, The

Dutchman, The Flying *see* Flying Dutchman, The

Elektra

Classical tragedy

Richard Strauss

The one where the half-crazy Elektra gets her brother Orestes to avenge her father's murder by killing her mother Klytemnestra and her mother's lover Aegisthus.

CAST

Elektra, Agamemnon's daughter	Soprano
Chrysothemis, her sister	Soprano
Klytemnestra (Klytämnestra), her mother	Mezzo
Orestes (Orest), her brother	Bass
Aegisthus (Aegisth), her mother's new husband	Tenor

Eight servants, one tutor, one companion to Klytemnestra

1 act: running time 1 hr 40 mins

STORY

The scene is set inside the palace of Agamemnon in Mycenae

We can still stand in the spot within the Lion Gate at Mycenae where the action of this opera took place. The time is soon after the Trojan war, father Agamemnon is murdered, brother Orestes is lost and the two sisters Elektra and Chrysothemis live on in the family palace with murderess mother Klytemnestra and her fancy man Aegisthus. A bunch of servants are gossiping round a well. Elektra shows at the doorway looking tatty and pretty well unhinged. A bit funny isn't she? says one servant. Always wailing and carrying on at tea time says another because her father was murdered at 4:27 precisely. She's like an animal says a third. I spoke to her the other day and she fairly went for me says a fourth. I think she's just lovely says a fifth she's bullied and beaten by that brute Aegisthus. Belt up you says the housekeeper she's a crazy bitch and that's that. Get into the house. They go in pinching and punching the maid who stood up for Elektra.

Elektra comes in looking pretty crazy and calling out her father's name. This is precisely the time they did for you in your bath Dad she says and she goes into the horrid details of what was clearly an unusually brutal crime, the murder weapon being an axe. Never mind Dad she says we'll get those murderous bastards: my brother Orestes and I will slaughter them and we will then dance on their graves.

Chrysothemis comes on. They're up to something those two Sis says she I think they plan to lock you up in a tower. To hell with that says Elektra come and sit down with me and have a hate session. Can't do it says Chrysothemis. I've got the fidgets. It's terrible in this place. I want to have a man, I want a white wedding, I want to have kids and lead a life like a woman can in Ruislip or Pinner. But we sit here like cagebirds and there's no news of brother Orestes either. What's that shindy going on in the house? asks Elektra. It's mother Klytemnestra says Chrysothemis she's had another of her bad dreams. I want a word with mother says Elektra. O Gawd I'm off says Chrysothemis and runs out.

Klytemnestra looks out of a window. Look at her, Elektra the spiteful cat says Klytemnestra. Hello lovely mother calls Elektra. She's in a good mood today says Klytemnestra I'll go down and talk to her. She enters the courtyard with her servants. I'm fed up with the medicos all telling me different things about my condition says Klytemnestra. If you my daughter will give me a bit of psychiatric advice that might be helpful. Get out all of you lot. Klytemnestra and Elektra are left alone.

It's these dreams says Klytemnestra how do I get rid of these terrible nightmares? You've got pretty effective supernatural powers Elektra, help me. In my dreams I feel my whole carcass is rotting away. It's very nasty. There must be a cure. Maybe it's finding the right sacrifice. You're spot on says Elektra. Find the right sacrifice and you're OK. Do you know what sacrifice is required? asks Klytemnestra. Is it animal vegetable or mineral? Is it a holy cow? No says Elektra. An unholy cow. One of the cows that is chained up? asks Klytemnestra. No. A free-ranging cow says Elektra. An actual cow? says Klytemnestra. No, a woman says Elektra. One of the female servants? A virgin? asks Klytemnestra. No says Elektra. One that has had considerable sexual experience? says Klytemnestra. Yes says Elektra.

How's Orestes? O my God says Klytemnestra, he has gone potty and lies in a kennel with the dogs. Not true says Elektra. I've set up a banker's order to pay for his keep says Klytemnestra. Not true says Elektra you sent a one-off payment for a contract killing. But he's still alive, Mother, he's still alive. Poof! says Klytemnestra. Faugh! I've got the best security police in Argos to guard me here. Nobody can get me. But you Elektra know perfectly well what sacrifice will stop my dreams and I'm going to have you locked up until you tell me who or what it is. Grrr! shouts Elektra springing at her mother's throat. Grrr! Listen to this Mum *you* are the sacrifice and the hunter will come when you are asleep and pull the covers off your bed. He and I will chase you upstairs downstairs till we get you cornered. We'll make you bend your neck to wait for the axe. We'll make you hang on there in panic for quite a while. And then PFT! the axe will fall. No more bad dreams after that mother. Elektra reels about as if she were drunk.

Ah! Oo! Oh my God! says Klytemnestra but just then Klytemnestra's secretary runs out and whispers in her ear (we can't hear it neither can Elektra) – Orestes is dead! Klytemnestra begins to laugh. The whole household creeps out and begins to laugh. They split their sides. Ho! Ho! What the hell are they laughing at? says Elektra. Chrysothemis runs on and tells her. Orestes is dead. I don't believe it says Elektra. It's not true. It's true all right says Chrysothemis. These two guys arrived, an old one and a young one. They saw it. He was savaged by his horse. The courtyard is full of servants. Get moving there shouts the butler. You Sophocles get onto a mule quick and get out there and tell the master Aegisthus the good news.

So it's true says Elektra. OK Chrys you and I will have to do it together says Elektra. Do what? asks Chrysothemis. Kill mother and her fancy man Aegisthus says Elektra. What what? says Chrysothemis. Did I hear you aright? Now listen Chrys says Elektra you are a very strong girl. And beautiful. I've always envied your thigh muscles. And your lovely biceps! She grabs her by the arm. Lemme go! cries Chrysothemis. Lemme go! Let's get out of here now Elektra. Now listen again Chrys I'm really going to look after you from now on, I'll find you a nice Peloponnesian boy and get you married. I'll tuck you up into bed with him Chrys and I'll babysit for you when babies come and you'll forget all about this little business we have to do tonight. No! Let's get away now! shouts Chrysothemis. Not before we do the deed Chrys says Elektra. No! No! No! shrieks Chrysothemis and wrenches herself free and runs off fast.

So it's me on my own-ee-o says Elektra. Now where did I bury that axe? She starts scrabbling in the dirt to find the murder weapon. After quite a bit of scrabbling to music Elektra notices a man standing at the door. Who are you? she asks. Who are you? he asks in return are you one of the skivvies here? I got a message for the lady of the house that her son Orestes is dead. Poor guy he didn't know his horse was a man-eater. I seen him dismembered before my very eyes says the man [it's Orestes: long time no see: Ed.]. So I'm left all on my own I don't count that Chrysothemis says Elektra. You got a family resemblance to Orestes says Orestes. Who are you? I'm Elektra says Elektra. You look pretty terrible says Orestes have they been torturing you? Listen to me Elektra, Orestes is alive. It's me. I'm Orestes. The dogs in the yard knew me. But you my sister had no bloody idea. How's that? Orestes hooray Orestes! Don't kiss me because I'm filthy and I've turned into a sort of scabby witch says Elektra. After Dad was murdered I gave up the refined life and lived like an animal and took up hatred as my main pastime. It was my way of honouring Dad. But your hand is shaking Orestes. It's shaking because I've got to kill, kill, kill says Orestes and the quicker the better. Good-oh says Elektra hooray! By the way, this old guy is Aeschylus my tutor quite a decent writer the Harold Pinter of his day says Orestes. Sh! Sh! says Aeschylus. She's inside with her maids. Not a man in the house. Now is the time.

The men go into the palace. O my God says Elektra I forgot to give them the axe. Zut! A terrible scream is heard coming from the palace. Chrysothemis and a number of servants gather in the courtyard. Something wrong? says Chrysothemis. It's those terrible dreams she has says a maid. I saw some men going in says another. My God here's Aegisthus coming we'd better clear off says a third. The courtyard empties. You idle sods. Why isn't the front door light on? shouts Aegisthus. Where are you Themistocles? Open the door for me and get some lights.

Allow me to help you says Elektra running down with a flashie. Thanks says Aegisthus where are the men with the news about Orestes? Inside the palace says Elektra dancing around him in a funny sort of way. Aegisthus the poor soul walks into the palace and about ten bars later we see him receiving grievous bodily harm at a window and screaming Murder! Murder! This is correct: another five bars and he screams his last scream. A body of unseen radio commentators within the palace take up the tale. The pro-Orestes servants are killing off the pro-Aegisthus lot like they were flies. There is a lot of blood. Three cheers for Orestes say the commentators and He's a jolly good fellow. A lot of women have crowded into the courtyard to listen to the commentary. Now they run off leaving Chrysothemis alone with Elektra. I want to lead the dance of death says Elektra but at the moment I have rather bad cramp so I'll sing a duet with you Chrysothemis first and see if that does the trick.

The servants who won are all really pleased says Chrysothemis. I was pretty well knackered before this happened says Elektra but now I'm a ball of fire. She starts to dance. Come on and join me she shouts. She dances like crazy. She drops dead. Chrysothemis runs over to make sure she is quite gone. She runs to the palace door and beats on it shouting Orestes! Orestes!

MINUTES FROM START	LOOK OUT FOR	
0	There is no prelude. Instead we have a shout from the orchestra: AGAMEMNON! This is his motto and it will pop up a lot. (The AGA is OK but the orchestra gets stuck on the MEM and we don't get much NON,	0
0: *Wo bleibt Elektra?*	if any.) We are into a prologue of gossiping servants,* but this is not the usual relaxed mood of gossip. They are all terribly jumpy and some seem to have the	0

bends. It is all about Elektra. She is wild she is vicious she is bullied. The brass come in with riff after riff. Everyone is frightfully upset especially the fifth maid who speaks up for Elektra and gets beaten for her pains.

The music which has been jumping about from key to key, if any, settles down a bit. Then from a calm start it begins to move forward. This is Elektra's music. Soon she begins to sing it in her first great solo. It is splendid and ** or *** throughout.

6: *Allein! Weh, ganz allein*

1. She calls on her dead father Agamemnon (we 6
hear Agamemnon's motto). It is the hour of his murder. Will he please show? Elektra is noble, regal and still calm.

9: *Sie schlugen dich im Bade tot*

2. But not for long. She rehearses rather disgust- 9
ingly the details of the act of his murder. The orchestra is naturally agitated by these horrible facts.

10: *So kommst du wieder*

3. But her father will come again in royal state. 10
Octaves echo up and down the brass section.

10: *Agamemnon! Vater!*

4. Agamemnon! Don't leave your little girl all 10
alone as you did yesterday. A wave of self-pity sweeps across the score. More octaves. There is a hint of a big romantic tune.

12: *Vater! Agamemnon!*

5. Agamemnon! You will be revenged. Blood will 12
flow. There will be blood everywhere. She goes blood crazy. Yet more octaves. Blood swills around in all parts of the orchestra, graphically.

13: *Und wir schlachten dir die Rosse*

6. And we will kill your horses and your dogs (we 13
hear the horses neigh and probably the dogs baying, although it may be the horses not yet quite dead) and then we three, Orestes my brother, myself and you will do a blood dance around your grave. (Terrific high note on the word 'grave'.) About now a sort of Ride of the Valkyries starts to swing and sway under the vocal line.

14: *Und über Leichen*

7. The Valkyries really get going and drive on 14
through the dance on the grave to a great feast. Agamemnon. Oh, my Agamemnon. She finishes, at last, worn out with bloodlust and just by singing such hard stuff for so long.

In the dialogue between Elektra and her sister, Chrysothemis' music is sweeter and simpler. What would have been recitatif in days gone by is now sung

dialogue, pointed and in character, riding on the back of a stream of orchestral sound. But Chrys is at her
18: *Ich kann nicht sitzen* wits' end and in a long and lovely solo** (a lot of it in 18
waltz time) she tells Elektra how she longs to have children, how happy she would be to live as a peasant. She breaks down and weeps. There is less intensity but more lyricism in the music than there was for Elektra and no attempt to make the orchestra mickey-mouse or mimic her words.

Klytemnestra has had a bad dream. She is ap-
25: *Ich will's nicht hören!* proaching* accompanied by a fearsome intermezzo 25
with a grunted figure in the bass repeated over and over again. Formidable.

In the opening dialogue Klytemnestra and Elektra are sparring with each other but when Klytemnestra
31: *Ich will nichts hören!* lets her hair down in her first long solo* we know 31
from the music that she longs for Elektra's love. Strauss has a special lyrical vein for self-pity and another for longing and here we have both. The rather disgusting passage about the sick exposing their ulcers is particularly lovely.

Klytemnestra hobbles down the steps to pizzicato chords on the strings. The stillness of the scene as the two women are left alone with a calm orchestra and whispered comments by the woodwind leads to Kly-
36: *Wer älter wird* temnestra's piece about her dream problem* which 36
starts calmly but soon we are into the heebie-jeebies. Strauss holds back on the volume for the nightmares but with spooky chromatic sweeps and nervous panic in the strings it's all quite scary. No sign of any fixed tonality, we are swinging around in a void where key signatures are unknown.

The long quiz between Elektra and Klytemnestra about finding the right victim to put an end to Klytemnestra's nasty dreams (which could almost have been taken as a model for Dostoyevsky's cross-examination in *Crime and Punishment*) starts playfully but the tension grows until it reaches a pitch of mad paranoia when Elektra springs at Klytemnestra's throat and delivers herself of her terrifying verdict – it's you who must die. She forecasts what will happen in some detail:

47: *Was bluten muss?* 1. The orchestra is a little manic. So is Elektra. 47

She gives a vivid account of how her mother will be chased out of bed by Orestes.

48: *Und Ich! Ich! Ich!* 2. She will follow at her heels like a dog. Frantic 48
burst of venom from the brass. The terrible fantasy rolls on.

50: *Alles schweigt* 3. Orestes holds the axe aloft and passes. The 50
timps mark time. Klytemnestra is trapped. But thc music gets going again and tells us that the death blow is coming. Elektra screams out her glee. Rather horrible, and it causes tremors down the spine.

4. Klytemnestra is pretty shaken, and no wonder,
poor old thing. An eerie piece by the orchestra. Skittering strings and woodwind flying all over the place.
A messenger whispers in the queen's ear. Demented
laughter from Klytemnestra. Very disturbing. The
52 orchestra howls and screams.* Why is she laughing? 52
asks Elektra. (She will soon find out.) This great climax marks the end of the first half of the opera.

Orestes is dead. Chrysothemis comes in howling like a wounded animal. Everyone knew but us. Elektra won't believe it. When she does she swings into action with a roll on the drums. She tells Chrysothemis she must help her to kill Klytemnestra and Aegisthus. Shocked horror from Chrysothemis. Elektra wheedles and persuades in what is something like a song of seduction:

60: *Du! Du! denn du bist stark!* 1. You are strong says Elektra. Beautifully strong. 60
And the music becomes warm and persuasive,** including a sinuous solo violin, not reprehensible for it is doing its best on its own to get the orchestra's message across.

2. Lemme go! shouts Chrysothemis. No says
Elektra I will pass my willpower from my body to
62: *Nein, ich halte dich!* yours.* A bit of an upset here but the orchestra does 62
not take it seriously.

3. Now Elektra pulls out all the stops in what is as
63: *Von jetz an will ich deine Schwester* near a love song as may be.*** She will cherish her 63
sister, will see her married, will be her midwife. A flow of lyrical phrases, one after the other, with sweeps on two harps below, the longest sweet passage in an opera that is mainly astringent.

4. The argument. I won't do it says Chrysothemis.

67: *Sei verflucht!* Agitation, confrontation.* The orchestra gets violent. 67
So do the sisters. It gets physical and very loud. Chrysothemis runs away. Curse you! shouts Elektra. And here Strauss's trick of ending every one of Elektra's purple passages on a towering high note stuns the listener if not poor Chrysothemis.

68 Elektra scrabbles for the fatal axe.* The strings 68
scrabble as if they are mad things and look out especially for a slow descending chromatic line from the violins down to all the scrabbly action below.

After the recognition scene (impressive but they really are a bit dumb not to catch on quicker), we have Elektra's glorious shout of 'Orest!' and then the orchestra sends her off into another of her great solo safaris.

1. Calm heroic music. A happy sea of wonder.
78: *Orest! Orest!* Orest! Orest! Then pure joy.** Soaring high notes. 78
The orchestra caresses and for once supports her lovely singing line without interfering.

82: *Nein, du sollst mich nicht umarmen!* 2. A cloud: she is ashamed: she looks like a tramp. 82
The cloud passes. She gave up all pride in order to avenge her father. This whole sequence is dreamy.** Elektra can now tell Orestes happily about her terrible life. It was worth it and the music is all lovely.

86: *Eifersüchtig sind die Toten* 3. Another cloud. Her hatred makes her into a 86
doomy prophetess full of despair who lives only to avenge her father.*

87: *Lass zittern diesen Leib!* Now the solo becomes a joyful duet.*** The brass 87
gives out what could be a call to arms. Orestes and Elektra exalt, they gloat, they go into a frenzy of excitement. They will do it! They will kill! O happy day. The orchestra is triumphant and ends the scene with a mighty bang, bang, perhaps the prospective deaths of Klytemnestra and Aegisthus.

90: *Es ist kein Mann im Haus* The high drama of Klytemnestra's death** is 90
played out mostly by the orchestra assisted by the odd scream. The entrance to the palace by the murderers goes quietly with a spiky figure played by the woodwind strings and brass and then fearful brass woodwind and timps building up an eerie atmosphere. Then the bassoons and low strings set off into a terrific scuttering figure which repeats and repeats rather as did the scrabble music. Elektra remembers

the axe. There is a bloodcurdling scream, then another. A crash from the orchestra and panic spreads like wildfire as the household decide to get the hell out of it.

Aegisthus turns up to a surprisingly cheery little
94: *He! Lichter! Lichter!* tune* and gets into conversation with Elektra who 94
cons him along something rotten. Brittle artificial music until Aegisthus gets inside and then Bingo! does it get real. Aegisthus screams blue murder from the window. The orchestra thunders. Elektra shouts 'Agamemnon'.

The finale:

1. Chrysothemis comes out of the palace carolling
98: *Elektra! Schwester!* in joy.** Orestes has done it. Unseen voices confirm 98
this fact. A mighty wall of sound.

2. Elektra is pleased too. Yes she knew. A happy
100: *Ob ich nicht höre?* melodious response.** She must dance. 100

3. Now the sisters, their earlier nasty row forgot-
102: *Hörst du denn nicht* ten, sing the most glorious happy duet.*** One melt- 102
ing phrase after another.

104 4. Elektra's dance of death.* The dance itself is a 104
turbulent orchestral piece with a driving rhythm, fragments of melody and noisy burps and bumps as it runs towards its climax. Elektra in her last soaring solo invites everyone to come and dance with her, but unfortunately expires before they can really get go-
108 ing. The ending is tremendous:*** Chrysothemis 108
leaves the dead Elektra, runs to the palace door and beats on it calling out 'Orest! Orest!' as the orchestra thunders out the Agamemnon motto and finishes with a huge major-key chord.

NOTES

Elektra	Richard Strauss's fourth opera
First night	Hofoper, Dresden, 25 January 1909
Reception	Partisan: more in favour and fewer against than for *Salome*
Libretto	Hofmannsthal
Source	Mainly Sophocles, a little Euripides

NEWS AND GOSSIP

When Strauss saw Max Reinhardt's production of *Elektra* he knew it was a snip. (He was at work on *Salome* at the time and went through mild phases of panic that the two subjects were too alike.) The author of *Elektra* the play, Hugo von Hofmannsthal, jumped at Strauss's invitation to turn it into an opera libretto and so a great partnership was born (five further operas – Strauss's five best). Strauss was really pleased with the result, as well he should have been, and let it be known that he thought Hofmannsthal was just the perfect librettist. Work started in 1906 after the launch of *Salome* and the opera was finished by September 1908. The premiere took place in January, under two years from first idea to first night, speedy work for a member of the big band fraternity. And what a big band, the biggest in opera to date, with eight clarinets, eight horns, four Wagner tubas and strings to match split into three separate sections with the front three desks of violas sometimes called on to switch instruments and to make up a fourth section of violins. This was surely a bit megalomaniac for it is not credible that even the sharpest-eared opera-goer could come out of a performance saying 'I loved that moment when the violas became violins', so long, that is, as they were hidden from view. Rehearsals and first night were in the hands of the same director/conductor team as *Salome* and went without any recorded disaster. Once launched, because *Salome* had been such a bombshell, *Elektra* was being played in many houses within months. Strauss himself as conductor shared with Beecham the first London performances in 1910. *Elektra* still split the critics, the new men were over the moon with another dose of such daring Strauss, but many of the old steadies found it gross, brutal and a little vulgar. At the Met in New York it was banned – God knows why, unless it was guilt by association with *Salome*. Today it stands on the fringes of the central repertory. Everyone knows that it is a good piece but there are very few voices that can cope with Elektra's part, the orchestra Strauss demands is enormous, it needs a lot of rehearsal time and since there is no interval, bar sales are always seriously down.

COMMENT

The orchestra is the star of *Elektra* but less so than in *Salome*, because Elektra herself has a much better singing part (but not such a good dance) than does Salome. She has four huge solos, first when she is talking to Agamemnon, or rather talking to herself about Agamemnon, second where she puts the frighteners on Klytemnestra, third when she tries to woo Chrysothemis into being an accessory to murder and the last when she is explaining her filthy appearance and tatty turnout to Orestes. They are all splendid pieces and not, as in *Salome*, tone poems using the voice as an additional instrument, but real true arias. They are heavily scored, sure enough, but you don't ever feel the lady's drowning in the waves of sound from the pit nor does she have to bawl her head off to make herself heard (except sometimes). Klytemnestra and Chrysothemis too both have a decent innings. All six of these long solos are entirely different in structure, in character and in mood. Together they make up almost half of the opera. The men have little to do, Orestes has a lot of one-liners and a nice duet with Elektra and Aegisthus has less than five minutes between arrival and death. There is no male voice heard (except for some shouting in the stables) until three-quarters of the way through the show.

The story is as strong as it has always been in its many versions through the ages and the poetry, even when twice translated (Greek–German–English), still gives off sparks with Sophocles' brilliant imagery and his power to shock and surprise. Strauss was indeed lucky for this is in a different class from the common run of opera librettos and a blessed relief from the turgid stuff that Wagner turned out for the *Ring*. It may be that it is the German response to the Greek imagination that makes *Elektra*'s libretto a specially good product.

The orchestra is enormous and the music can be sonorous and also sparkling with all the deft fancies which teemed in Strauss's brain. If it has a fault it is that there isn't a continuous line to get a hold of. No sooner have you heard a phrase that catches the ear than he drops it and offers another, then another, and just as you are reeling from the impact from that one, he's off again. My grandmother benevolently gave the village postmistress a copy of Chamber's Dictionary for Christmas. When asked how she liked it she said it was a very nice book but she found the subject changeable. So Strauss is expert in the strategic shape of *Elektra*, the paragraphs construe and the vocabulary is rich. It's just that the sentences don't tell a continuous story. Not as bad as *Finnegans Wake*, but worse than *Ulysses*. He drops into atonality sometimes, that is he abandons all relationship with a good old-time key structure, but he does this on purpose to disorient us and to make us feel thoroughly uncomfortable not because he is pursuing some frightfully important theory, as did Schoenberg. The bloodthirsty music and the angry music are both full of cordite and keep exploding with big bangs, lesser bangs and huge explosions. But it is the gentle music, the sweet music that catches us by surprise and takes us by the ears.

Elektra is a fine score riding on the back of one of the best of the gory old Greek horror plays. In good hands it is immensely powerful. There is still something of Sophocles in there, something that the Greeks looked for, a sense of being purged by pity and terror. An alpha.

L'Elisir D'Amore (The love potion)

Rustic Comedy

Donizetti

The one where our simple hero is about to lose his loved one when a quack doctor, a love potion and a furtive tear save the day.

CAST

Adina, a rich young woman: owns a farm	Soprano
Nemorino, a farm labourer	Tenor
Belcore, an army sergeant	Baritone
Dulcamara, a quack doctor	Bass
Giannetta, a peasant girl	Soprano

2 acts: running time 2 hrs 10 mins

STORY

Act I Sc 1 Adina's farm

The opera recounts the events in an interesting day in the life of a small Basque village perhaps 150 years ago.

It is dinner break on Adina's farm and the workforce (surely so large as to be uneconomic) loll around being happy and singing the usual opening chorus rubbish. Nemorino, handsome but poor, tells us he is deeply in love with Adina. She in a democratic way is sitting reading amidst the swirling workforce and now she edifies all present by reading aloud (singing) the story of Tristan and Isolde and the love potion or elixir. Indeed a very handy thing to have about the place say the chorus.

But is that a military band we hear approaching? It is indeed, and a small detachment (as large as can be spared taking into account the male members of the chorus acting as farm workers already on stage) of soldiers led by macho man Sergeant Belcore march into the farmyard. The preposterous Belcore instantly makes a pass at Adina, offers a bouquet and within 90 seconds a proposal of marriage. Adina, failing to recognize him for the bounder that he is and impressed by his virility, asks for time to consider. Nemorino panics – thinks what chance has a wimp like me in the face of this mighty military man?

Nemorino, alone with Adina, tells her – evidently for about the hundredth time – that he loves her. Push off she says you just don't turn me on and anyway you'd be better employed sucking up to your rich uncle who is ill and might leave you some money. And by the way, I believe in taking a number of lovers, not just one. (Pretty progressive stuff.)

Act I Sc 2 The village market place

Offstage trumpet again – but this time clearly a call to comedy – enter 'Doctor' Dulcamara complete with coach, assistant and stock in trade. He addresses the natives in a fairground spiel of overwhelming mendacity concerning his status in the medical profession and the qualities of his elixir which will cure toothache, asthma, dropsy, diuretic complaints, TB, rickets, scrofula, restore virility to the aged, ameliorate grief, etc.

The peasants buy in quantity and are then seized by a desire to leave the stage all at the same time (a common phenomenon in opera) leaving Nemorino and Dulcamara alone together. Do you have any good quality love potions in stock? asks Nemorino. Yes indeed says Dulcamara, slipping him a bottle of plonk, one that will cause hot pants all round, only one ducat, shake the bottle before use, drink at once and wait for 24 hours for the potion to take effect. But it is so strong as to be illegal [anabolic steroids? Ed.] so don't say a word for 24 hours by which time I'll be gone. OK and thanks a million says Nemorino (Dulcamara exits), sits down, drinks, gets drunk, starts bawling out inebriated snatches of song. Adina enters: is surprised. Nemorino, well gone, knowing she will fall for him next day, says forget all my loverly talk to hell with sighing and pining. Adina thoroughly perplexed.

It's the soldiers again. Adina, nettled by Nemorino's quaint behaviour, agrees to marry the outrageous Belcore on the next day: is infuriated to find Nemorino does not give a damn. A message comes: the troops must move to new quarters at ten o'clock next morning. So why not get married today? Yes? Yes. Now Nemorino thoroughly alarmed: marriage will take place before elixir has a chance to act. He pleads for delay. No good. So into the Act I finale – Nemorino forlorn, Belcore bombastic, Adina beginning to show that she is by no means indifferent to the rejected Nemorino.

Act II Sc 1 A room in Adina's house

The wedding feast. Dulcamara [why on earth is he there? Ed.] does a party act with Adina which deservedly brings the house down. The Notary arrives (Adina wishes to wait until Nemorino is present, ostensibly so that she can parade her triumph – but perhaps there is another reason . . .). Again there is a lemming-like exodus leaving Dulcamara eating. Nemorino drops in. He wants instant results from the elixir – tomorrow will be too late. Easy, says Dulcamara, buy another bottle and it will all happen. But I have no money says Nemorino. Sorry! says Dulcamara. Cheerio. I'll be at the inn for half an hour if you get the money.

Enter Belcore. Nemorino says he's broke. Why not enlist? says Belcore, twenty scudi on the nail. Nemorino enlists.

Act II Sc 2 The market place

Giannetta has heard a secret: Nemorino's uncle has died and left his millions to his nephew. She makes a meal of telling this secret to all the girls in the village who start to express a new interest in Nemorino. Nemorino staggers on having dealt with the second bottle and expecting amorous attention. Sure enough he is mobbed. This is witnessed by Dulcamara (amazed at what two bottles of vino can do – has he strange powers unknown even to himself?) and Adina who now feels pangs of jealousy turning to bitter regret that she has lost a good man. Dulcamara asks Adina would she like some elixir too? Not necessary, she says, I'm sexy enough to get any man I want without it (but not Nemorino).

Nemorino has spotted a furtive tear on Adina's cheek: he believes she loves him but he will continue to ignore her: it seems to work. Adina enters. She has bought him out of the army but evidently he has gone off her so she plans to go away. Nemorino is disillusioned: so the doctor's elixir does not work after all. But suddenly Adina caves in: she does love him, truly she does. She sustains the fiction that the elixir did work. Belcore is told the bad news and grumbles: Dulcamara sings the praises of his elixir to the tune of his party song: everyone rejoices, and Nemorino is told he is a millionaire to boot.

MINUTES FROM START

LOOK OUT FOR

Act I Sc 1

Not the full-scale overture – a short prelude made up of some vigorous show-biz bombast (Belcore and Dulcamara?) and in contrast a haunting slow melody, yearning for something (Nemorino?).

The rustic opening chorus is given a touch of class by Giannetta's high descant above it – then straight
5: *Quanto e bella* into love-sick Nemorino's first cavatina** – which 5
sets the tone for more to come. Adina charmingly tells
9: *Della Crudele Isotta* the tale of Isolde in ballad form,** with a catchy 9
cabaletta, seized on by the chorus.

Belcore and his stage army arrive: he makes a vocal assault on Adina with blustering proposals of intimacy: she replies coolly and as the ensuing duet warms up and speeds up, Nemorino joins in to make

19: *Un po del suo coraggio* it a trio*** which races away into double time, cres- 19
cendos, and a noisy climax. The first big ensemble
piece. Brilliant!

After a carefully composed and rather touching
stretch of accompagnata in which Adina gently tells
24: *Chiedi all'aura* Nemorino she can't love him,* she tells him why (she 24
is a free spirit). This forms the first verse (limpid and
lovely) of a duet which develops into a more passionate exchange (catchy tune with racy cabaletta and
force 8 climax).**

Act I Sc 2

The great Dr Dulcamara approaches to the sound of a
distant trumpet and an expectant chorus: he arrives,
32: *Udite, udite, o rustici* and embarks on his first mighty patter song*** intro- 32
duced by some declamatory stuff but soon rolling in
an easy canter to his emphatic sales pitch and ending
with a bout of persuasion (much more tuneful). He is
well received by a cheery chorus. And now we have a
marvel of sustained comic invention in the duet be-
41: *Voglio dire . . . Io stupendo Elisir* tween Nemorino and Dulcamara*** in which the 41
properties of the elixir are fully explored. The first
exchanges are short and brisk until we reach a catchy
refrain ('Obbligato, ah si, obbligato!') and from then
on the debate swings about freely to the final burst of
46: *Silenzio!* patter from Dulcamara* delivered under a lyrical 46
paean of joy and gratitude from Nemorino ('Ah! Dot-
tor, vi do parola'). The agreeable spectacle of Nemorino getting drunk is interrupted by the arrival of
54: *Esulti pur la barbara* Adina and then a duet,** with her very perplexed. 54
During this he sobers up rapidly, moving away from
his bibulous shouts of 'Trallaralala' to quite composed exchanges about what will happen tomorrow
and reaching a melodious, if mutually frustrating, climax and full close. (Look out especially for the lingering phrase on the word 'Domani', at the end of the
first section.)

The confrontation between Adina, Belcore and
Nemorino leads to a most enjoyable 'thinks' patter
64: *Che cosa trova a ridere* trio,** all sotto voce: Belcore (I'll hit this clown 64
soon), Nemorino (Wait for tomorrow), Adina (The
cheeky pig, why's he glad I'm to marry?).

The finale has action (the regiment to move at
once), drama (the wedding to be today) and in the

midst of flurry and confusion a streak of pure gold in
66: *Adina credimi, te ne scongiuro* Nemorino's touching plea for a postponement*** 66
which develops into a trio with Adina taking the melodic line, Belcore barking and shouting below and finally broadening out into a full ensemble including Giannetta and the chorus, and despite some internal patter, sustains its dreamy quality to the end. Top that? Impossible, but the cheerful finale keeps things going well enough to the first act curtain. Again, look out especially for a phrase in the orchestral accompaniment (which recurs in the final four bars of symphony). Once heard, never forgotten.

Act II Sc 1

Pretty standard choral rejoicing at the wedding feast
3: *Io son ricco, e tu sei bella* leads to Dulcamara's party act – the duet*** (barca- 3
rolle) with Adina about the rich old man and the smart young girl. You will find that this pernicketty little tune outlives all others in the memory. There is another outburst of the wedding chorus and all exit save Dulcamara. When Nemorino arrives looking for a second bottle he deplores his bad luck with plaintive strains, but Belcore is at hand and the two of them embark on the interesting and varied enlistment
10: *Ai perigli della guerra* duet** with Nemorino inclined to soar aloft in a high 10
tenor line whilst Belcore pumps out his patter below like a vocalized bassoon.

Giannetta imparts the 'secret' that Nemorino is now a millionaire in an agreeable sotto voce scene which is perhaps a shade longer than it might be for closet listeners deprived of a sight of the stage pantomime.

21: *Dell 'elisir mirabile* Nemorino drops by singing a cheerful cavatina** 21
and there are some nice chattering exchanges as the girls make up to the rich man and he congratulates himself on the good work done by the elixir. This develops into a running ensemble with Dulcamara (amazed at his own success) and Adina (perplexed) in which things happen very fast both as to plot and in the score and ending in a sequence in which everyone
26: *Si, tutte l'amano* asserts their own thing:*** Adina (I begin to feel jeal- 21
ous), Nemorino (So now she's longing for me), Dulcamara (Didn't know my own powers), Giannetta and chorus (He's going to be hard to get, but let's try),

but all come together in one of Donizetti's most sparkling and bubbly ensembles with two quite unexpected changes of key – each one giving an agreeable sensation in the lower stomach.

Dulcamara tells Adina that no female can resist
Nemorino (bad news for her) and presses the virtues
29: *Quanto amore!* of his elixir in a fizzing duet,*** Adina singing a sub- 29
lime melody high above Dulcamara's patter, also bassoon-like but highly individual. The pace quickens: Dulcamara very pressing: Adina tells him she can get any man she wants without his ridiculous elixir. Full speed finish.

36: *Una furtiva lagrima* Next the Furtive Tear*** (aptly called a Ro- 36
manza), with its dolorous real bassoon introduction: one of the most sung tenor cavatinas in the whole of the Italian repertory, and rightly so. Its tenderness and innocence speak directly to any opera-loving heart. Nemorino and Adina meet in a musical mood of puzzled mystery: Adina tells him she has bought
him out of the army. She has decided to go away and
42: *Prendi, prendi: per me sei libero* bids him farewell in a sad little ditty.** Nemorino 42
protests (if the elixir is not working he will die a soldier): Adina suddenly admits she does love him and so the duet takes a distinctly joyful turn and ends with a burst of lover's vows from Adina.

A roll of drums. The soldiers are back including the preposterous Belcore. After some plot-clearance
in recitatif Dulcamara launches into a paean of praise
51: *Ei corregge ogni difetto* for his elixir to the tune of his party song*** (a wel- 51
come return). All hail Dulcamara in a chorus which, quite frankly, is a bit of mashed potatoes. Dulcamara's coach moves off and as the great doctor departs the stage, the curtain falls.

NOTES

L'Elisir d'Amore Donizetti's thirty-seventh opera
First night Canobbiana Theatre, Milan, 12 May 1832
Reception A hit
Libretto The reliable Romani
Source See below

NEWS AND GOSSIP

Two months before the first night of *Elisir*, Donizetti and Romani had had a flop in that same city of Milan at La Scala with *Ugo, Conti di Parigi*. They accepted a quick commission for a comic opera no doubt to restore their reputations. It was alleged (as usual) that Donizetti wrote the score in two weeks. This for once can be proved to be almost certainly a lie since there is a letter to his father extant dated 24 April, a week before rehearsals started, saying the opera was almost complete. The libretto is based (pretty closely it would seem) on an opera of Scribe called *Le Philtre* and set to music by Auber about a year before, and this in turn was part of that interminable chain of borrowing, adapting, imitating, recycling plots that went on in the eighteenth and nineteenth centuries. An opera with an original plot was pretty well unknown. Donizetti did not think highly of the cast for the first night. He wrote: 'We have a German prima donna, a tenor who stammers, a buffo with the voice of a goat and a French basso who is not very much . . . Courage my dear Romani. . . .' And yet the first night was a wild success and ever since then *Elisir* has probably remained equal second in number of performances with *Don Pasquale* in the top ten comic operas. The *Barber*, of course, being first.

COMMENT

Elisir is the most lovable of Italian comic operas. It is truly 'comica' and not 'buffa', i.e. in the hands of Romani and Donizetti the characters are not cardboard cut-outs (as, for instance, in Rossini's *Barber*), but almost real people. We feel for Nemorino in his unswerving devotion (a sort of Candide of love), we come to love the brassy Adina as she gets her come-uppance and turns into a sentient, sensible woman. If the word had not fallen upon evil days, one would call *Elisir* a sentimental comedy but one which is tempered by irony (the elixir itself, the force enlistment, Nemorino's inheritance) and greatly enhanced by the huge Dickensian character of Dr Dulcamara and the stereotype of all amorous non-commissioned officers, Sergeant Belcore.

Musically *Elisir* is made up of several different strands – the yearning appeal of the tenor solos, climaxing in the Furtive Tear, Donizetti in his pathetic mood, which contrasts with everything else in the score; the patter songs which have such persuasiveness as almost to make us believe that Dulcamara is a pretty decent chap after all; the Adina line, seldom solo but always clear as crystal in duets and ensembles; the military band input and the rough, tough Belcore music; and finally the many concerted pieces in which Donizetti works his customary magic. But perhaps even more magic than usual, viz the Adina/Belcore/Nemorino trio which breaks into double time on Nemorino's entry, 'Un po' del suo coraggio', and the great ensemble in the finale of Act I in which Nemorino's plea for delay is rejected, an astonishing piece which seems musically to soar above the humdrum sentiments of the text. Tommy Beecham used to define a good tune as one which 'enters the ear with facility and quits the memory with difficulty'. If this definition were applied to all Donizetti's operas, *Elisir* would come out a clear winner. It is a little miracle, pure enjoyment from first to last and a sure alpha-plus.

Entführung aus dem Serail, Die *see* Seraglio, Il

Ernani

Romantic melodrama

Verdi

The one where a bandit dressed up as a monk hides in a cupboard and promises to kill himself if he hears his host blowing a horn.

CAST

Don Carlo, King of Castile	Baritone
Don Ruy Gomez di Silva, grandee	Bass
Ernani (Don Giovanni di Aragona), a duke turned bandit	Tenor
Elvira, young female relative of Silva	Soprano
Riccardo, squire to Carlo	Tenor
Jago, squire to Silva	Bass
Giovanna, squiress to Elvira	Soprano

4 acts: running time 2 hours 10 mins

STORY

Act I We have portentous titles for each act, here: The Brigand

Sc 1 Bandits' mountain hideout

We are in sixteenth-century Spain amongst bandits – not real-life bandits (criminal scum) but opera bandits – honourable, loyal, brave, etc. Their leader, an aristo gone native, trade name Ernani, tells the boozing brigands he loves Elvira: she is due to wed her elderly ugly guardian Silva tomorrow. How about an abduction? asks Ernani: you're on, they say.

Act I Sc 2 Elvira's room in Silva's palace

Elvira tells us she loves Ernani; she rejects jewels and gifts from horrid old Silva. Exits. King Carlo strolls in (poor security in Silva's palace), says he is potty about Elvira. He sends for her and makes a pass. Get off she says. Come on he says forget that brigand – I've carried a torch for you for years. That's no way for a royal to behave says she (ho ho). Carlo gets physical: Elvira snatches the gun from his hand but bingo! Ernani jumps in in person. Get out you revolting brigand says Carlo. Me? says Ernani. What about you? You royal turd you killed my dad (common reason for hatred in opera).

Silva enters. He is surprised to find the rivals harassing his fiancée (he does not recognize the king). Although ninety, he challenges them both to come outside. The courtiers reveal that Carlo is king. Golly! says Silva, terribly sorry – I had no idea. (Ernani aside to Elvira – I'll come and pick you up at sunrise tomorrow. Elvira to Ernani – get out quick you fool.) I happen to be standing for President of Holy Roman EEC says Carlo, and I came here to secure your vote: it'll be OK to stay in your castle eh Silva? I'll be honoured, sire says creepy S. This follower of mine (Ernani), says Carlo, will leave at once. 'Follower' thinks Ernani: sure I'll follow him till I stick a knife in his guts.

Act II The Guest
The Great Hall of Silva's palace

Operatic wedding feast (Silva–Elvira). A pilgrim at the gates is announced: Silva offers hospitality. The pilgrim sees Elvira: chucks his hood away. It's Ernani! [No dawn raid? Ed.] He offers Elvira a wedding gift – the reward advertised for finding and killing him (irony). Carlo is pursuing me he says. Silva's crazy code of honour dictates that guest Ernani must be protected. Ernani says Elvira you bitch you let me down marrying this old creep. Not so she cries: I was told by a usually reliable source that you were dead and anyway I was going to stab myself at the altar: look at this (she produces a dagger from her camisole)! That's all right then says Ernani. Clinch.

Silva catches them at it and goes for them with dagger upraised when the news breaks: Carlo is at the gates. Let him in says creepy Silva. Kill me now says Ernani. No says Silva I'll hide you from Carlo so I'll have the satisfaction of killing you personally at my convenience. Silva hides him in a secret laundry cupboard behind a picture of himself (irony). Where's the bandit Ernani? asks Carlo – I know he's here: search the castle, men: hand him over, traitor. I can't says Silva, he came in disguise, was offered sanctuary, it's a matter of honour. OK says Carlo either you get killed or him. Me, says Silva busting out with nobility.

We can't find him anywhere, King, say the troops. Elvira comes on – I'll take her instead of killing you says Carlo: No no says Silva, I'd rather be killed than lose her, please. (King Carlo takes her off without killing anyone.) Silva expresses strong dislike of the king.

Silva lets Ernani out of the laundry cupboard: come out and be killed he says: but I couldn't fight an old man of ninety says Ernani (matter of honour). Let me say ciao to Elvira. Elvira has been carried off by the king says Silva: by our rival? asks Ernani: rival? says Silva (a thickie) what rival? Carlo lusts after her you fool says Ernani. Gosh what next says Silva. Let's join forces and kill Carlo says Ernani. No I want to kill you first says Silva: why not Carlo first me second? says Ernani. Good idea says Silva but how can I be sure to catch you? Simple says Ernani: here is an occarina and if you blow one occ on it I will kill myself at once. Matter of honour? asks Silva: matter of honour says Ernani.

Act III Forgiveness
The extensive underground tomb of Charlemagne

King Carlo with Riccardo inspects the tomb where conspirators will meet shortly to construct a plot to kill the king (information passed by MI5). Meanwhile upstairs the electoral college is voting on the next President of Holy Roman EEC. Carlo tells Riccardo to fire three cannon if he is elected. He tells Charlemagne (dead of course) he is well qualified for the Presidency and would like his posthumous support. He hides.

The conspirators gather, including Silva and Ernani. They draw lots to be the hit man: Ernani wins. Silva says if you let me do it I'll never blow the occarina. I couldn't says Ernani: matter of honour. All the conspirators gloat for a little while. A cannon goes off – 1–2–3 bangs. King Carlo steps out. Trumpets blow: enormous numbers of people flood into the tomb including the electoral college released from toil, also Elvira [so where was she? Ed.].

The conspirators are arrested: send commoners to jail noblemen to the block says Carlo. Class-conscious Ernani chagrined at being graded as a commoner volunteers for the block. Matter of honour [surely a nutcase: Ed.]. Now speaks Elvira: forgive them King Carlo she asks. OK I will says Carlo in quickest conversion since St Paul on the motorway to Damascus.

Act IV The Masked Man
The terrace of Don Giovanni's palace

Another wedding party, now between Don Giovanni di Aragona (alias Ernani) and Elvira. The usual wedding stuff from the chorus: a masked man flits about amongst them. A duet of bliss between Ernani and Elvira is halted by the sound of a distant occarina. Ernani loses his marbles: what's up? asks Elvira. The occarina blows one occ nearer. It's all a bad dream says Ernani as they climb the stairs to the honeymoon suite. But no sir. Silva jumps out at the top of the stairs blowing the occarina like mad. Would you prefer poison or a dagger? he asks. O Lord says Ernani just as I was all set for a bit of bliss: this is too bad. Sorry says Silva, which? Dagger I think says Ernani. Please let him off says Elvira. No hope says Silva. Don't cry Elvira says Ernani I've got to do it. Matter of honour. He stabs himself: dies.

MINUTES FROM START

LOOK OUT FOR

Act I Sc 1

4: *Evviva! Beviam'!*
7: *Come rugiada al cespite*
10: *Oh tu che l'anima adora*

The opening chorus* indicates high morale amongst 4
the bandit gang, especially when they can get after
some booze. Ernani tells them of his troubled love life
in a good standard tenor aria** with a racey 7
cabaletta.* 10

Act I Sc 2

21: *Tutto sprezzo che d'Ernani*
25: *Qui mi trasse amor possente*

Elvira's first aria telling of *her* love problems seems a
little sub-standard until we come to the showy cabaletta.** Chorus plugs away meanwhile. 21
A good duet* between Carlo (fly with me) and 25
Elvira (not on your life) ending with violent exchanges as Carlo gets physical.

33: *Tu se' Ernani*

A rattling, rousing trio** – Carlo: Get out, you 33
nasty brigand, Ernani: I don't like you much either, Elvira: this is no way to behave in my house. Cheerful rather than angry: sounds as if they were all out for a ride on a roller-coaster.

38: *Infelice! e tu credevi*

An easy-on-the-ear aria* from Silva who is upset to 38
find two rivals standing around his intended – and a dramatic outburst from one and all when it is revealed that one of them is the king!

42: *Vedi come*
44: *Io tuo fido?*

The finale begins with an ensemble,** principals 42
and chorus, in which Carlo and Silva adjust their relationship whilst Elvira and Ernani stick to their guns:
then Carlo secures Silva's loyalty in solo exchanges
and so into the final** section where a multiplicity of 44
views are expressed – Ernani: I'll get you, Carlo, Elvira: I'll fly with you Ernani, Carlo: Gosh, I'd like to be the Holy Roman Emperor, Silva and Riccardo: Yes Sir, Yes Sir, Three Bags Full, Sir, Jago and chorus: Silva's sucking up to the king, Giovanna: Elvira doesn't fancy Silva at all.

Act II

0: *Esultiamo!*

Opens with a jolly chorus* of Silva's household em- 0
ployees singing O What A Beautiful Morning (little do they know).

5: *Oro, quant' oro*
6: *Ohimè, si perde*
10: *Tu, perfida!*

The pilgrim revealed as Ernani swings into a defiant aria,** leads into a trio* with Elvira and Silva 5
and then a duet** with Elvira, at first stormy – ac- 6
cusations – and later (almost unaccompanied but for a 10
harp) sweet – reconciliation – and finally ecstasy.

The high dramatics of the rest of this act begin
14: *No, vendetta più tremenda* with a furious trio** – Silva: I will hide you away and 14
kill you in my own good time, Elvira and Ernani:
Take it out on me let him/her go free. The frenetic
25: *Vieni meco, sol di rose* activity of one and all is steadied up by a love song* 25
from King Carlo who promises Elvira a golden future
with him. He likes it so much he sings it twice.

Towards the end of the act we dive into music hall,
30: *Tu m'hai salvato, uccidimi* enormously vigorous and cheerful oom-pahs** 30
whilst Silva and Ernani threaten to kill each other and
a brisk finale of knights making hunting noises as a
preliminary to battle.

Act III

Carlo, hopelessly hooked on Charlemagne, addresses
5: *Oh, de' verd' anni miei* his tomb in a noble aria** with a cello accompaniment 5
at the start and a fine burst of lyrical ambition at the
finish.

The conspirators give full-throated pledges of loy-
14: *Un patto! Un giuramento!* alty, belligerence, etc.* – until the first gun goes off. 14
After a lot of heavy stuff it is a relief to have some 14
14: *Un patto! Un giuramento!* jolly pleading** from Elvira – which succeeds in 19
19: *Ah! Signor, se t'è concesso* changing Carlo's mind and apparently character
almost immediately in his harp-accompaniment
21: *O sommo Carlo* thoughtful aria* 'I forgive absolutely everyone' fol- 21
lowed by a noisy and jubilant finale. No wonder: they
must all be quite relieved.

Act IV

We start with pretty standard on-stage dance music
plus pretty standard choral reaction to the man in the
4: *Cessarono i suoni* mask – but after that we have a virtuoso display** of 4
Verdi's skill in using his box of dramatic musical
tricks to heighten the histrionics of the plot (lovers
together at last – the call of the occarina (horn) – Silva
unmasked and threatening – Ernani pleads – Elvira in
shock etc.). We are kept on tiptoe throughout.

14: *Quel pianto, Elvira, ascondimi* If you heard the ensemble** leading up to Ernani's 14
death in isolation you would think you were out for a
trip on a fairly blue Danube – waltz time and very
gemütlich: this is a prime example of how the way we
read this genre of music has changed from Verdi's
day to ours. For him it was the right sort of stuff for
high tension drama. Whatever else: highly enjoyable.
In the opera's dying moments the music is effective
but conventional. No surprises.

NOTES

Ernani	Verdi's fifth opera
First night	Fenice Theatre, Venice, 9 March 1844
Reception	A huge success
Libretto	Piave (see below)
Source	Victor Hugo's stage play *Hernani* (big success in Paris some ten years earlier)

NEWS AND GOSSIP

When Verdi wrote *Ernani* he was thirty, at the beginning of his 'years in the galleys' and riding high on the success of *Nabucco* and *I Lombardi*. It was designed for the Fenice Theatre, with its small stage and Glyndebourne-sized auditorium and so is not encumbered by massive choruses. The subject of Ernani was chosen after a number of earlier runners had been discarded (Cromwell, Catherine Howard, Woodstock, Lear, Rienzi, a 'baritone opera' and others) and marked Verdi's first collaboration with the young Piave who was good news, for Verdi was to work with him on thirteen further operas including two of his biggest hits, *Rigoletto* and *La Traviata*. Whereas the lumbering *I Lombardi* was played mainly by Italian houses, *Ernani*'s appeal was wider and it quickly spread across the opera world. Even during the Verdi eclipse it was still played from time to time, standing well below the top six but above *Carlos*, *Forza* and the other later works. It is hard to sing, almost as tough as *Trovatore*, and so needs top-class voices. It is a bizarre thought that we might have had Ernani himself as a contralto part, for Verdi began his sketches by designing it as a trouser role for one Carolina Vietti.

COMMENT

Even Verdi's best friends would have to admit that *Ernani* is just a little bit over the top. Instead of toning down Victor Hugo's melodrama, Verdi seems to have hyped it up. Bottom and Snout could have done heroic things with Ernani's death by horn, dagger and poison. But the basic tensions of the plot do hold pretty well: Ernani's passion for Elvira coupled with his wild anger against Carlo and sexual jealousy of Silva make him a consistent fellow whom we rather like, though we do not learn why his second planned dawn raid to abduct Elvira never came off. Carlo is wonderfully kingly, especially in his gentle promises to Elvira of a life surrounded by roses and in his electoral address to Charlemagne. But he must have been a difficult man to work for if he habitually reversed decisions on major matters so irrationally as in the case of the sentenced/

pardoned conspirators. Elvira is a decent standard Verdi virgin. But Silva is more complex. Honourable to a ludicrous degree, he is prepared to partner Ernani in killing Carlo, is upset when his partner wins the raffle (which was surely the point of recruiting a younger man) and appears to want to use him/kill him in bewilderingly quick succession. The plot would not work without honour playing a part far in excess even of its role at the court of King Arthur. Self-preservation, normally regarded as a fairly strong instinct, comes second to ludicrously refined dictats of noblesse oblige, of honourable behaviour, like when you are conned by an enemy in disguise into offering him hospitality, you are still obliged to face death and destruction rather than hand him over to a potentially friendly king.

But when all the whingeing is over *Ernani* remains a really good evening in the theatre: it has melody (though nothing really unforgettable) and although much of the score is made up of inspired commonplaces, from time to time Verdi applies his magic touch to make the hair rise on the nape of the neck and the melting phrase to unlock the tear ducts. There are several top-class items: the trio for Carlo, Elvira, Ernani in Act I, Ernani's defiant aria when revealed as himself in Act II, Carlo's two arias mentioned above and several of the ensembles – all of these reach an alpha level. Overall a good try, workmanlike, enjoyable but not yet great. A beta.

Eugene Onegin (Yevgeny Onegin)

Russian romance

Tchaikovsky

The one where Tatyana takes all night to write a letter, Onegin kills his best friend and there is a lot of ballroom dancing.

CAST

Tatyana, a romantic girl	Soprano
Olga, her sister	Contralto
Madame Larina, their mother and a landowner	Mezzo
Eugene Onegin, landowner and playboy	Baritone
Vladimir Lensky, local squire and Olga's intended	Tenor
Prince Gremin, Tatyana's (last Act) husband	Bass
Filipyevna, Larin family's old retainer	Mezzo

Captain Buyanov (music by courtesy of), **M. Triquet** (entertainer), **Zaretsky** (Lensky's second and duel organizer), **Guillot** (Onegin's man)

3 acts: running time 2 hrs 30 mins

STORY

Act I Sc 1 Madame Larina's garden in the centre of her estate

We are in Chekov country in the seventeen-nineties with cherry orchards all over the place but only two sisters not three and Pushkin wrote the story. Sisters Tatyana and Olga sing an irrelevant Russian song. Mother Larina is making marmalade with Filipyevna aged retainer; she recalls her youthful flirty days and especially a Guards subaltern but Mum and Dad said No you must marry rich Grigovich next door. A humdrum marriage ensued also the death of Grigovich. Larina is now a contented widow mother to her girls and little mother to innumerable peasants.

Peasants arrive and greet little mother. They sing an even less relevant song also dance. There is some talk of harvest festivals. They bid farewell to little mother: exit. Freed from yelling capering peasants Tatyana says she is a romantic Olga says she is an outdoor girl.

But hark! A jeep is approaching. Men! They are Lensky Olga's chap plus glam new visitor Eugene Onegin at the sight of whom Tatyana instantly keels over. Onegin and Tatyana stroll offstage: Lensky and Olga take a more constricted stroll onstage. Lensky tells Olga he loves her (no news to anyone) Onegin returns telling a boring anecdote to wide-eyed Tatyana. Filipyevna says supper's up (thinks: maybe my little chicky has met Mr Rightovich).

Act I Sc 2 Tatyana's bedroom

Filipyevna says time for beddy-byes Tatyana says niet tell me of your early love life. Negative says Filipyevna I was a child bride: arranged marriage. Hey Tatyana are you sick or something? I'm upset says Tatyana. I'm in love. I want to be alone. OK says Filipyevna. Exits.

Tatyana confesses an acute infatuation. She sits down and starts a letter. No good: tears it up. Tries again. Reads the letter (pretty humble stuff: pity me etc.: you could disdain me etc.: please don't etc.). Stops: thinks: maybe I'm a mug to chance a letter: gets brave and writes on (why come in and upset my life?: maybe it's destiny or something: are you guardian angel or con man? Anyway I love you: take me or leave me). She finishes rambling but heartfelt letter: a whole night has passed (opera time).

Shepherds switch on trannies outside the window the sun rises etc. Filipyevna returns: Tatyana asks that the letter be delivered to Onegin via Filipyevna's grandson. Filipyevna (singularly thick) gets the message at last: the letter will be delivered.

Act I Sc 3 Another part of the Larin garden: Tatyana sitting on a garden bench

Peasant girls picking rhubarb sing Russian rhubarb song (in background): Tatyana waits and quakes. Onegin arrives. I got your note says he. I appreciate your sentiments but regret the role of husband and father is not compatible with my temperament. If I wed marital friction is inevitable. Brotherly love – yes OK I can offer modicum of that but let me tell you my girl don't try this 'I love you' lark on anyone else lest it be not so graciously received since I am exceptionally good-natured in this respect. Tatyana quinched.

Act II Sc 1 The Larin drawing room: a country house ball in progress

What a smashing party say the guests we never thought we'd have a band from the Depot. Thanks a lot Captain Buyanov super do Dom Perignon and all. The guests watch Onegin and Tatyana dancing. A bit close they think. They gossip of marriage. If that happened Tatyana would soon be ditched by a man of the world like Onegin they say. He overhears this and fumes: why did Lensky get me into this toytown? I'll show the bastard: I'll make a pass at his Olga. He dances with Olga although Lensky has the date. Lensky is cross. He dances with her again. And again. Lensky very cross calls Olga a double-crossing bitch.

Monsieur Triquet does his party piece: couplets for Tatyana's birthday. Onegin and Lensky smoulder. Onegin taunts Lensky. Why are you so sulky? You are trifling with Olga's affections when you have already destroyed Tatyana says Lensky. You stink. Whassat? says Onegin steady on old boy. I demand satisfaction says Lensky. The guests are agog: shock: horror: they attempt to interpose. M. Larina is devastated. Sorry to do this in your house Lensky says but I demand satisfaction etc. OK says Onegin I accept the challenge: it's a duel.

Act II Sc 2 The duelling ground: a water-mill in evidence

Lensky plus second Zaretsky waits. Onegin is late. Lensky has gloomy defeatist thoughts. He looks back on his golden youth and looks forward too: will Olga weep on his grave? Onegin arrives with a servant. Where's your second? asks pernicketty Zaretsky. My servant will act as second says Onegin [evidently bad form: seconds customarily gents: Ed.]. The duellists stand back to back: they both think what a funny old world: once we were great mates now we are out to kill. The duel ritual proceeds: the duel starts: Onegin shoots Lensky dead.

Act III Sc 1 Ballroom of a great house in St Petersburg some years later

The guests dance. Onegin (for it is he) broods: he is bored: I have no work: I am tired of golf: given up bridge: killed my best friend: no wife: travelling is too much sweat. Enter Prince Gremin with Tatyana on his arm. Gosh! Is it she? thinks Onegin: she's hatched out into a stunner.

Who is that man? asks Tatyana. A nutcase – Onegin – travels a lot – just back says a guest. Oh my goodness me thinks Tatyana. Who's that lady? asks Onegin. That lady is my wife says Gremin. Wife? asks Onegin. Sure: we married about two years ago says Gremin.

Let me tell you says Gremin there is nothing like a young wife to cheer an old chap up between you and me all the hangers-on round this court are a load of rubbish but – Tatyana is good: Tatyana is beautiful: Tatyana is young: Tatyana loves me. Happy happy happy me. Come and meet her. Onegin – my wife: says Gremin. We have met before says she. A long time ago says he. I must go now says she. Wonder of wonders thinks Onegin this glorious woman is the same country girl I lectured about love: now it's coming over me: dash it: *I* love *her*!

Act III Sc 2 The drawing room of Prince Gremin's house

Tatyana reads a letter from Onegin: she is emotionally upset: the old passion bugs her. Onegin enters: remember you gave me a hard time in the garden? she asks. I'd like to forget it says he. A loving girl of sweet seventeen was cynically brushed off – as no doubt were many others. Why pester me again? Do you want a cheap win over my noble husband Gremin? or what? Nothing like that says he straight up I love you.

It could have been so easy once she says (weeps) now I'm a married woman: go! Niet niet says he I love you madly I need you I want you. So do I love you too says Tatyana but I am true to noble Gremin. Go! (He goes.) Curtain.

MINUTES FROM START

LOOK OUT FOR

Act I Sc 1

The short prelude sets the mood for the opening scenes with the theme of Tatyana's Longing. This would seem to say she is a romantic lady by nature, for it appears on the scene before Onegin. But once smitten it focuses upon her longing for him.

2: *Slikhali l vi za roschei?*

Tatyana and Olga sing a pleasant song* in duet in 2
the near distance, on the hearing of which Madame Larina and Filipyevna stroll down memory lane. The folk song has a fetching chorus and Madame Larina gets quite agitato about her romantic past.

11: *Uzh kak po mostu*

The peasants open with a good deal of Russian
rhubarb, but the set-piece dance song* has zest and a 11
hammering Russian rhythm: it is developed into a mighty choral piece.

14: *Ya ne sposobna*

The second haunting melody of the opera – Olga's
song:* she says she is just a happy hockey girl, but the 14
music gives her the lie. She is a romantic too, or perhaps Tchaikovsky just couldn't help being one all the time. Her number is surrounded by quite a lot of Tatyana's Longing whenever she gets a look in.

21: *Skazhi, kotoraya Tatyana?*

The Sizing-Up quartet:** the gents sing to each 21
other loudly (fortunately the girls can't hear them) about the comparative attractions of the two sisters: Tatyana says (again inaudible to others) My Dreamboat Has Come At Last (Onegin of course). Olga, silly thing, fears gossip. An astonishing mixture but woven together with such skill as to make the overall effect one of wonder and amazement. A new love is being born.

23: *Kak shchastliv* Lensky's love song:*** at first just a happy greet- 23
ing for Olga, then it drifts away in the exchanges between Tatyana and Onegin: the second time Lensky gives us the love song full blast: I LOVE YOU.

Act I Sc 2

The unstoppable Wotan aside, this scene has probably the longest monologue (or monocant) in all opera. It is sandwiched between an opening and a closing duet with nurse Filipyevna (echoes of the Russian Dance still in her mind and lots of Longing in Tatyana's). The solo itself is a complete, self-contained music drama. After she is left alone, the orchestra delivers a heavy message – Look Out, Fate is Round the Corner, or something like that. We first heard this theme when Tatyana told Nursey that she was all upset and we could reasonably call it Tatyana's Fear. She nevertheless rushes into a delirious free-
40: *Puskai pogibnu ya* ranging burst of happy song** (roughly speaking: 40
'I'm in love'). Next a patch of recitatif as she takes her first shot at the letter (no good): she writes again to a new accompanying tune introduced by an expectant Ping Ping and the orchestra pretty well sticks to this as she reads aloud what she has written: she pauses, takes courage and sweeps into the third phase (Fate – indeed God – must have brought us together) to a
46: *Nyet nikomu na syvete* melody that runs and rises as it goes** and then the 46
scene reaches its climax as she passionately begs the absent Onegin to respond warmly, to put her mind to
49: *Kto ti?* rest, and this to a theme** of great intensity which 49
might have come from the Pathétique Symphony (and in fact pretty well does): she dashes off the final part of the letter to the Pathétique (which we can call Tatyana's Passion) fortissimo in the orchestra, is too scared to read it over and finishes with a distinctly Wagnerian-sounding last thought (He's a gent: I'm sure he'll be decent to me). So dawn breaks (but not without qualms – Tatyana's Fear again but not so intense) and shepherds begin piping. It has been a hard night's work, but by operatic magic what has seemed to last for hours has occupied just less than fifteen minutes from Good Night to Good Morning.

Act I Sc 3

Servant girls sing the usual kind of Russian rhubarb

in the background: Tatyana, scared to death, waits for Onegin with snatches of recitatif and one frightened reminder of the Letter Scene. Onegin arrives, declaims pompously for some time and then slips into
66: *Kogda bi zhizn domashnim* an easy superior sort of aria* (the cad) which has two 66
melodies, the first more tuneful, the second more patronizing. The scene works, but one can't help thinking Tchaik muffed this one a bit.

Act II Sc 1

The prelude opens with Tatyana's Passion, reminding us what the poor girl suffered, and then
3: *Vot tak syurpriz!* bursts into the great rumbustious waltz*** that 3
covers more plot in eight minutes than many operas can manage in a whole scene and with no waltz. What a party! say the guests. Jolly decent of you to bring along the band Buyanov old lad! Nice change from huntin' sing the squires in the middle section to the flurry of horns that break out in opera at the slightest mention of chasing the fox, and huntin' makes 'em pretty useless in bed sing the squires' wives still in the middle section and then we swing into gossip about Tatyana/Onegin's prospective marriage. What frightful provincial tittle tattle says Onegin. Why the hell did Lensky get me here (still in three-time)? I'll fix the bastard. Hey Olga how about dancing with me? Negative says Lensky: she's with me. Positive says Olga. Damned rude says Lensky. What a party! sing the guests and swing into a gusty reprise of the main waltz. It ends on a very full close. Whew! Not a dry shirt in the room.

12: *À cette fête convié* Monsieur Tricquet's couplets,* pretty dim in 12
themselves, are sent up by Tchaik rather nicely. As the one joke in the opera they deserve a star.

15: *Messieurs, mesdames* The Mazurka** starts off in fine style but soon 15
runs out of steam as it drifts on as a background to the start of the Onegin/Lensky quarrel (a trick Tchaik probably picked up from Verdi who used it twice with great effect).

Lensky reflects on past happy times in the Larina
20: *V vashem dome!* residence: now it's all gone sour:** his best friend is a 20
cad. A real whiff of nostalgia (Tchaik's strongest suit) in Lensky's half plaintive half angry address to M. Larina. Followed by the guests in full voice shocked

by the bad behaviour of the young gentlemen plus declamatory shouts from the two would-be duellists. Unless carefully handled this finale can easily turn into mashed potatoes.

Act II Sc 2

28: *Kuda, kuda, kuda*

Lensky's Farewell:*** we have already heard the 28
theme of this melancholy and affecting aria but now it is fully developed and flowers into a wonderful set piece. Lensky is a romantic too. (They all are.)

37: *Vragi! Davno li drug*

A strange and effective item:* as Onegin and Len- 37
sky stand back to back waiting for the signal to start shooting they have a little 'thinks' (Funny that old mates like you and I should be trying to kill each other). The scene ends with a reminder of Lensky's Farewell.

Act III Sc 1

0 The opening Polonaise:* the third great dance in the 0
opera showing Tchaik to be a dab hand in the matter of strictly ballroom as well as ballet. And the Écos-
9 saise,* the fourth. Fast noisy and not remotely Scot- 9
tish. Gremin thinks highly of married life with
11: *Lyubvi vsye vozrasti pokorni* Tatyana.*** Along with the letter scene this is the 11
most memorable item in the opera. It is a full set piece with a beginning, a middle section and then the beginning again. It is one of Tchaik's happiest inspirations, and a show-stopper. It also shows Gremin to be a much superior person to any other male in the cast. And as he takes Onegin over to introduce him we hear the Tatyana's Fear motif from Act I, but much modified, not much fear.

Onegin's rather surprising discovery to him (and
18: *Uzhel ta samaya Tatyana?* to us) that he loves Tatyana** starts pretty ornery but 18
then (happy inspiration) he tears into the same delirious melody that she sang about her love for him at the beginning of the Letter Scene.

Act III Sc 2

21: *O! Kak mnye tyazhelo!*

The last scene* is workmanlike and at times touching 21
but the Tatyana/Onegin duet has none of the magic of the Letter Scene and no big new tune to sweep us off our feet. Perhaps Tchaik had none left by this time. But in its own mild way it successfully carries the piece to its pathetic end.

NOTES

Eugene Onegin	Tchaikovsky's sixth opera
First night	Student production Malïy Theatre, Moscow, 29 March 1879 Professional first night, Bolshoi, Moscow, 23 January 1881
Reception	Respectful but not the wild enthusiasm that greeted the earlier *Maid of Orleans*. Some critical aggro that young Tchaik should have the gall to mess about with one of Russia's best-loved literary masterpieces
Libretto	Shilovsky and Tchaikovsky
Source	Famous verse novel by Pushkin 23

NEWS AND GOSSIP

When it was first suggested to Tchaikovsky that he should do an opera of *Onegin* he told his charmingly named brother Modest that the idea was crazy. But this didn't stop him from sitting up all one night and blocking out a treatment. He took this to his old friend Shilovsky and the pair of them worked out the seven scenes from the novel using as much of Pushkin's verse as they could, which in the case of the Letter Scene is nearly 100%. Tchaik composed the score in eight months in spite of emotional turmoil brought about by an astonishing debacle in his private life. A female ex-student wrote him a letter not unlike Tatyana's. Although a true-blue gay, he responded positively: they got married and the result was immediate disaster. One would like to think that it was his passionate affection for Pushkin's Tatyana (he wrote a lot of stuff about her) that unhinged his judgement and that it was Pushkin and not vanity that made him think he could be bisexual. Anyway he was wrong and the fact that he managed to compose this elegant and delicious score in the midst of a maelstrom says a lot for his compositional methods, which were rigid and precise.

Onegin was at first seen as one of those oddball items, a 'Russian' opera, and so was slow to spread to European houses outside Russia. Today although it is treasured by opera buffs there is still a whiff of patronage in the attitude of some managements who think of Tchaik as a composer of tuneful ballet music and heavy stuff for the concert hall. They are of course quite wrong. He wrote ten operas, more than Bizet and the same number as Bellini and Puccini. *Onegin* has always been amongst the top of the pops in Russia itself.

COMMENT

Onegin is one of the most lovable of operas, mainly because of Tatyana's music, and particularly the Letter Scene. Pushkin created in her a heroine as vulnerable as a Juliet or Ophelia, whose innocence is crushed before our very eyes, in this case by the ghastly Onegin. However he may come out in the novel, in the opera he is a most disagreeable figure, beastly to Tatyana, petulant at the ball, shoots his best friend dead and then wanders around as a clapped out playboy until the final meeting with Tatyana sparks some life into him. Yet Tchaikovsky gives him hero status musically and even when he is at his most horrible (lecturing Tatyana) he sings sweetly. This perhaps is how even an errant aristocrat was seen by Russian society and by Pushkin and in a strange way it adds to the pathos that Tatyana is destroyed by such a well-bred gentleman. The highlights in *Onegin* (the Scene 1 quartet, the Letter Scene, the ballroom dances, Lensky's farewell, Gremin on marriage) are balanced out by lowlights in that the peasant songs and dances sound to our ears like the standard stuff from the steppes, much of the duel scene is pretty ornery and musically the last act is not up to the level of the first. But the design of the opera into seven self-contained scenes with no continuous narrative pretty well saves the situation. We take each one as a separate course, and if some are more nourishing than others, together they make up a satisfying meal. The best, of course, is the Letter Scene and for this alone *Onegin* must be an alpha.

Falstaff

Shakespearean comedy

Verdi

The one by William Shakespeare where the merry wives of Windsor dump Falstaff in the Thames.

CAST

Shakespeare	*Boito*	
Sir John Falstaff: Jack	(same: often **John**)	Baritone
Bardolph } members of Falstaff's gang	**(Bardolfo)**	Tenor
Pistol } members of Falstaff's gang	**(Pistola)**	Bass
Fenton, a young fellow	(same)	Tenor
Doctor Caius	(same)	Tenor
Ford, alias **Brook,** rich tradesman	**(Ford,** alias **Fontana)**	Baritone
Mistress Ford, his wife	**(Alice)**	Soprano
Mistress Page	**(Meg)**	Mezzo
Mistress Quickly	**(Quickly)**	Mezzo
Anne Page, Ford's daughter	**(Nannetta Ford)**	Soprano

3 acts: running time 2 hrs

STORY

Act I Sc 1 Interior the Garter Inn

This is Shakespeare's *Merry Wives* speeded up. Some fringe characters are cut (Page, Shallow, etc.), several episodes are telescoped, some are plundered from *Henry IV* (the honour monologue etc.).

We are in Old England in the reign of Henry IV. Dr Caius accuses Falstaff (correctly) of breaking and entering the Caius residence. Falstaff is not impressed. Caius accuses Bardolph and Pistol of going through his pockets when he was drunk. Falstaff reprimands them not for the crime but for its amateurish execution. The bill is presented: Falstaff is broke: he tells his gang two rich women, Alice Ford and Meg Page, lust after him: he will board them. Bardolph and Pistol refuse to handle pimping letters: it's a matter of honour: Falstaff faxes the letters, and lectures B & P on matter of honour. He beats them up.

Act I Sc 2 A garden in Windsor. Ford's house in vision

Meg and Alice compare letters. They are identical. The two plus Anne and Mistress Quickly decide to trick Falstaff. Falstaff's gang (dirty dogs) tell Ford that Falstaff has evil intentions on his wife Alice. There is a loverly interlude between Anne and Fenton (kisses). The Wives of W. announce their plan: Mistress Quickly will tell Falstaff that Alice is dead keen to adulter. Ford announces a separate plan that he will visit Falstaff incognito to seek assistance with the seduction of Alice.

Act II Sc 1 Interior Garter Inn

Mistress Quickly tells Falstaff that Ford is absent from 2 to 3 p.m. daily: Alice will be ready to receive him. Meg sends a message that her husband is always around so Falstaff says he will follow up on the Ford intelligence. Ford, disguised as one Fontana (Brook), says he loves Alice from afar and needs Falstaff's help to seduce her: he hands over a large cheque. Falstaff says not to worry I will fix it for you I've got a date to seduce her myself this p.m. Left alone Ford bombs out.

Act II Sc 2 Interior Ford's house

The wives prepare the trap. A washbasket is filled with stinking washing and the servants are instructed to tip it into the Thames on cue. Falstaff makes a confident pass at Alice. Meg runs in saying Ford is returning. Falstaff hides behind a screen. Ford plus Falstaff's gang noisily search the house. The wives put Falstaff into the washbasket and conceal him under the dirty clothes. Loud osculation is heard behind the screen, which is overturned to reveal a slap and tickle going on between Fenton and Anne. Ford is cross (Fenton is a forbidden lover: rich Dr Caius is favoured): the gang rush out to continue the hunt: Alice summons the servants: Falstaff is tipped into the Thames.

Act III Sc 1 Outside the Garter Inn

Falstaff quite done up decides he must mingle wine with Thames water. Mistress Q. brings him a letter: Alice says she really does love Falstaff and suggests they meet at midnight at a well-known oak (Herne's) in the adjacent forest; Falstaff must wear a disguise as a black huntsman. Falstaff exits. Ford, the wives, Anne etc. lay a plot to scare the living daylights out of Falstaff.

Act III Sc 2 Forest scene. Herne's Oak centre

Fenton and Anne make brief loverly exchanges. The wives enter all in fancy dress as fairy queen, pixies, goblins, witches etc. Falstaff arrives disguised with horns on his head; he counts down the clock chimes to love-off. He meets Alice: he commences his odious attentions: Meg interposes saying the hoody-doodies are coming. Falstaff lies prone in panic (he has a strange belief that the sight of hoody-doodies brings death): the gang plus the wives plus casual extras flood onstage all in fancy dress to mock vilify humiliate and physically assault Falstaff: he squeals for mercy and undertakes to behave better in future: Bardolph's nose burns a hole through his mask: Falstaff twigs he has been set up. In unlikely circumstances Ford solemnizes a double marriage: Dr Caius with Anne, Fenton with an anonymous nymph. But no: Bardolph has swapped costumes with Anne so the couples turn out to be Caius and Bardolph (invalid since homosexual unions not legit in Elizabethan times) and Fenton and Anne. Ford accepts the inevitable: all unmask and sing everything is just a big joke. End.

MINUTES FROM START

LOOK OUT FOR

Act I Sc 1

0: *So che se andiam'*

The opening scene* dances its way through Dr 0
Caius' grumbles and the Amen antiphon to Falstaff's first solo which sets up his musical character. He tells Pistol and Bardolph they are just too expensive.

12: *L'onore!*

Then, at a trot, on to Falstaff addressing himself to
the matter of Honour: a marvellously witty setting** 12
to match the wit of the words – a superior burlesque number.

Act I Sc 2

17: *Fulgida Alice!*

The scene, as light as a soufflé, runs up to the reading
of the letters.* Although the women are sending up 17
Falstaff something rotten, several quite beautiful phrases** break in from time to time.

19: *Quell'otre!*

The two head-to-tail patter quartets** – words 19
unintelligible, music nondescript, or virtually unaccompanied, but still an exciting *tour de force*.

23: *Pst, pst, Nannetta*

The scene runs on at breakneck speed with two pauses for Fenton and Nannetta (Anne) to utter a few
sweet nothings.* 23

30: *Del tuo barbaro*

This time a patter ensemble with a difference:*** 30
eight vocal parts patter away like mad whilst the lovesick Fenton swings along in their midst with a sustained tenor line – all in all a bit of a miracle. Look out especially for the delicious cod romantic lines addressed to Sir John just before the company dissolves into laughter and the act ends.

Act II Sc 1

Throughout the opera, but particularly in this act, look out for the orchestral trimmings,** decorations, interjections. The orchestra lives a life of its own, commenting on the action, not merely accompanying it.

8: *Va, vecchio John* Sir John's song of triumph* – a sort of amatory 8
military march.

11: *Io l'amo* The Amor duet** Ford/Sir John, introduced by 11
Ford's song of woe (Alice doesn't love me) and then the duet swooping and swooning about in a romantic parody. Broken by Falstaff's questioning of Ford's motives and the mood taken up again in Ford's reply.

Act II Sc 2

18: *È sogno?* Ford's thoughts about jealousy:* so ferocious and so 18
convincing that it is hard to believe we are not meant to take them seriously. The whole of this scene moves along at lightning speed, the characters sing for their lives over a raft of orchestral sound, busy, delicate and mickey-mousing along with the action.

Alice's announcement that the play is about to be-
28: *Gaie comari* gin* is something of a set piece but is supported by a 28
flighty orchestra.

30: *Alfin t'ho colto* The duet* Falstaff/Alice is all tongue-in-cheek: 30
Alice conning Falstaff, Falstaff playing the heavy lover, Verdi mocking him, all wonderfully tuneful.

The general hurly-burly is steadied up by two in-
37: *Vien qua* terludes by the lovers Anne and Fenton, the first* 37
40: *Facciamo le viste* whilst Falstaff is being hidden and the second* in the 40
midst of the rumbustious finale. This begins with some staccato patter from Meg and Mistress Quickly
41: *Bella Ridente* then the sweet strains of the lovers** hold steady 41
amidst the riotous surrounding noise, but the scene ends once more in musical bustle and turmoil as the great mountain of flesh is tipped out of the window into the Thames.

Act III Sc 1

Falstaff's thoughts about the evils of the world and
5: *Io, dunque* the virtues of wine.* The music follows the route 5
taken by his mind. The milder pace is a welcome contrast to the rattle and push of the last act.

The confederates plot and scheme for the mas-
13: *Avrò con me* querade that night.** Dancelike, light, airy and 13
delicious.

Act III Sc 2

Horns, perhaps symbolic, echo around the forest and
Fenton opens the last act with the nearest thing he has
17: *Dal labbro* to an aria** in the whole opera. It is in the style that 17
has distinguished the young lovers' music through-
out, sweet, melodious and in the midst of such turmoil it strikes the ear gratefully.

22: *Una, due, tre* Falstaff counts down to lift-off* – and raises our 22
expectation for something heroic, only to dash our
hopes by saying that love turns a man into a beast
(accompanied by the most outrageous vocal and instrumental mickey-mousing).

32: *Sul fil d'un soffio* The address of the Fairy Queen* again steadies up 32
the tempo in a beautiful sustained set of instructions
to her cohorts as to how to make the night magic.

The climax of the last act comes with the turning
over and tormenting of Falstaff which goes on viol-
33: *Ahimè! tu puzzi* ently and noisily for some time.* One interesting item 33
is the quasi-liturgical plaint from the women for re-
pentance, but this is soon lost in a sea of abuse and
vituperation.

42: *Tutto nel mondo* The famous final fugue:** an epilogue with the 42
thesps lined up on the front of the stage as in Mozart's
Don Giovanni. A great set piece.

NOTES

Falstaff	Verdi's twenty-eighth and last opera
First night	La Scala, Milan, 9 February 1893
Reception	A masterpiece, said one and all
Libretto	Boito
Source	Shakespeare

NEWS AND GOSSIP

By the time of the first night of *Falstaff* Verdi was held in such veneration that if he had set to music the register of Paris cab drivers it would have had a great reception. But this was Verdi plus Shakespeare, the two greatest artists the world had ever seen. Wow! Verdi's lifelong love affair with Shakespeare was in the main platonic: he was an avid reader but only three times actually got into bed with the bard (*Macbeth*, *Otello* and *Falstaff*). He made tentative passes at several of the other plays, notably *Lear*, but shied off, perhaps because he felt that the mighty *Lear* was just too big even for him. But he must have been sorry to miss out on the putting out of the eyes and the shocking behaviour of Goneril and Regan. Verdi had worked with Boito first on the wash-and-brush-up to *Boccanegra* and then on to *Otello* so he knew he was a dab hand as a librettist. So he gave him the almost impossible task of turning a sprawling Shakespearean text into a taut opera plot and singable rhyming Italian verses. Verdi was right. When one looks at Boito's text for *Falstaff* one has to admit the man's talent was simply stunning. *Falstaff* was not commissioned. Verdi wrote it because, egged on by Boito, he wanted to, and he did it in under two years between the ages of seventy-eight and eighty, a pretty fair feat of concentrated creation at this time of life and a lesson to us all. For once he made no changes to Boito's draft libretto and instead of grumbling about the hard graft of composition, as he so often did, seemed to enjoy himself immensely. Since its first round of performances in the opera houses of the world *Falstaff* has been treated with respect but not much enthusiasm. Today it is harder to sell seats for *Falstaff* than *Ernani* or *Attila*, one reason being perhaps that except for Falstaff himself there are no star parts and baritones (bad luck for them) are just not as sexy at the box office as sopranos or tenors.

COMMENT

Do not expect to fall for *Falstaff* at first hearing. It is not grand opera nor a comic opera nor an opera at all in the Italian tradition we have come to know and love: it is something more like a musical fantasy based, of course, on an Elizabethan farce. The score is inventive, ingenious and rich, so rich in fact and presented at such breakneck speed that for the normal opera-goer listening to *Falstaff* is like being pushed through a gallery of Italian masters in a wheelchair at a trot. You know there is something great going on all around you but can't quite get hold of it. Most of the interest lies in the orchestration although there is still some life in Shakespeare's lines as (very cleverly) adapted by Boito. But things race along at such a speed you can't catch much of the text (and much of it is too fast for surtitles). Apart from the love music between Fenton and Anne, the Queen of the Fairies' song and the odd patch of melodious singing by other characters, the vocal lines are mostly declamatory and exclamatory. If however you have the time, the inclination and the knowledge to sit back at home with a score on your knee and play the piece over and over you will discover what a miracle of musical invention it is. Verdi clearly wrote it to please himself and let's hope it did, because if he thought it would please the general opera-going audience he was wrong. His musical invention travels at the speed of light and opera buffs are more comfortable with the speed of sound.

There are other negatives such as the musical tags or labels used to identify certain thoughts/emotions – not grand enough to be called leitmotifs – which become tiresome when obvious (the mock respectful greeting for Falstaff) and maddening when not obvious because the subconscious ear is distractedly searching for their meaning whilst the show gallops on, and continuity is lost. But the chief blemish of the opera lies in the distasteful spectacle of Jack Falstaff, one of the greatest comic figures in all literature, being reviled, assaulted and humiliated by a pack of quite unimportant people. We all despise Prince Hal for his rejection of Falstaff when he takes office, but that is high drama. It is with real sadness that we see such mindless cruelty inflicted on this prince of rascality. Shakespeare himself and the coarse susceptibilities of the Elizabethan court must take most of the blame, but Verdi and Boito should surely have known better.

Falstaff reveals something in Verdi that even his best friends would never have suspected – he had a sense of humour. Previous attempts to be funny (Melitone in *Forza* and the darkie plotters in *Ballo*) were absolutely dire, but here we have the octogenarian Verdi putting the orchestra up to all manner of whimsical conceits. There is, however, too much mickey-mousing which can become embarrassing, as when in the line 'Love turns me into a beast' the word 'beast' is given the sound of the braying of an ass.

Probably more people pretend to like *Falstaff* (and don't) than any other opera for it is always spoken of with great respect (with lowered eyes and a hushed voice, as for the Bach B minor Mass) but alas although something of a musical miracle and full of incidental musical delights, it has no sex appeal and no heart, and opera demands both these qualities. And so – a beta.

La Fanciulla del West

Wild Western melodrama

(The Girl of the Golden West)

Puccini

The one where a man escapes death through the love of a good woman and a woman escapes a fate worse than death by cheating at poker.

CAST

Minnie, owner of the Polka Saloon	Soprano
Mr Johnson (Dick), alias José Ramerrez, bandit	Tenor
Jack Rance, the sheriff	Baritone
Nick, barman at the Polka Saloon	Tenor
Ashby, Wells Fargo agent	Bass
Wowkle(!), Minnie's squaw servant	Mezzo

Sonora, Trin, Sid, Bello, Harry, Joe, Happy, Larkens, all miners

Billy Jackrabbit(!), Wowkle's intended; **Jake Wallace**, a touring folk and country singer; **José Castro**, one of Ramerrez's gang; a Pony Express rider

3 acts, 2 intervals: running time 2 hrs 10 mins

STORY

Act I The Polka Saloon

We are in the midst of the great Californian gold rush and our miners are forty-niners but our darling is not Clementine but Minnie. Hello! say the miners coming off shift into the boozer. Hello! Hello! Drink whisky (straight). Hello! Play cards (crooked). Hello! Some miners ask the barman: what's my chance of making Minnie? (Hello!) The barman's universal answer is: You're her favourite (Hello!). A folk and country singer gives a sentimental old-folks-at-home ballad: a wimpish miner Larkens is homesick and he blubs: someone organizes a sentimental whipround to pay his air fare home.

Miner Sid is caught cheating at poker: the general consensus is to shoot him dead. Jack Rance the sheriff says steady boys I've got a better idea: he pins a playing card to Sid's chest says if he takes it off then shoot him dead. The Wells Fargo guy Ashby blows in and says jigger that bandit Ramerrez: I'm worn out hunting his gang. Rance toasts Minnie as the future Mrs Rance. Bolloks Chink face! shouts the racist miner Sonora. Belt up you drunken bum! yells Rance pulling his gun. Enter Minnie: now now lads, she says, birds in their little nests agree: any more swearin' n' shootin' and you'll be debarred from my Sunday School. Aw Minnie! they cry. Several miners make up to Minnie with pathetic gifts, flowers etc. Ashby sees gold being used for payment, and says are you crazy? Gold in the open with bandits around?

Minnie commences her Sunday School: the miners are poor Bible scholars, Minnie an embarrassingly keen Biblephile. Mercifully the lesson is terminated by the arrival of the Pony Express. The miners soppily read letters from home. A stranger is announced outside (it is Johnson). Rance propositions Minnie: she says naff off. Rance launches into his autobiography, with loads of self-pity: Minnie gives her autobiography too but it is cheery.

Enter Johnson: Rance asks for his identity card, Johnson says he has mislaid it: he has just dropped in for a card game. Rance gets tough, insists on seeing his identity. Minnie and Johnson recognize each other: I'll vouch for him says Minnie: that's irregular but OK says sheriff Rance. Minnie and Johnson dance the miners' waltz together. Castro (a member of the Ramerrez gang) enters: 'Lynch him' is the cry. Not that says Castro: I'm a turncoat, I can lead you to Ramerrez. And that's the Boss's tackle there, he says, looking at Johnson's stuff [no-one takes action as a result of this extraordinary indiscretion: why? Ed.]. Then he tells Johnson sotto voce that the gang is outside ready to break in and steal the gold on a whistle cue from Johnson. Castro decoys all the miners to hunt Ramerrez.

Minnie and Johnson are left alone. They chat: Johnson makes mild passes at Minnie. Nick looks in: a nasty dago has been seen in the environs of the Polka Saloon, he warns. A whistle is heard. Johnson fails to give an answering whistle. So there is no raid. What about a visit to your place later? says Johnson. OK says Minnie but don't be disappointed, I am just a poor iggorant girl. Not so says Johnson you are angelic. Angelic . . . thinks Minnie; well darn it. (She fancies him.)

Act II Minnie's cabin: open loft with ladder above

The squaw Wowkle sings a lullaby to her papoose. Brave (perhaps not) Billy unfolds plans for their wedding. Minnie enters and dresses for best: she prinks (scent too!). Johnson says hello, and comes in. Minnie says: you sought me out at the Polka Saloon – why? Maybe you were seeking your moll Nina? Johnson ignores this: he says, you are pretty lonely high up here. Minnie, who is hot on the countryside, gives him an earful of the beauties of nature, her other activities, teaching the three Rs, reading pulp fiction: Johnson says Do you mind if I stay a bit? Wowkle and the papoose exit. Heavy petting commences. Johnson says he must go: Minnie says it's snowing outside, you must stay. They hear three revolver shots outside. Johnson says he will stay. They make loverly talk but Minnie says they must have separate beds; she learns that Johnson's name is Dick. Johnson listens at the door: no action is audible: it is bedtime.

Suddenly they hear 'Hello!': Johnson hides. Hello again: miners plus Rance enter. Thank God you are safe they say: that bastard at the Polka tonight was not Johnson but the evil bandit Ramerrez. That's not possible! says Minnie. But yes say the miners: his bandit colleague Castro fixed us a visit to his moll Nina, and she showed us lots of pix of Johnson, there's no mistake. Thanks lads, says Minnie, off you go. Johnson is not here, I'll be OK. They go.

So you bastard you came here to steal says Minnie. Not so says Johnson: I am a villain but I love you truly. Get out you skunk she says. He gets out: immediately he is shot: he is hauled in again bleeding: Minnie (she still loves him) hides him in the loft. Rance enters searching for Johnson: he's not here says Minnie: you love him you bitch says Rance grasping Minnie sexually. Get off she says. Drops of blood fall on to Rance's hand. Johnson is hauled down: he faints.

Minnie slips four aces into her knickers: she makes Rance a poker game proposition: if she wins Johnson goes free and Rance hops it: if she loses Rance shoots Johnson and has her. OK says Rance. Hand one goes to Minnie hand two to Rance and decider hand is won by Minnie (with a little help from her knickers). Exit Rance.

Act III A clearing in the forest. Camp fire. Miners sleep/ bivouac all round. Early dawn

Rance (jealous, and mad) chats up Nick. There are shouts and yells in the distance – Johnson/Ramerrez has been sighted. He must be taken alive says Ashby. Reports come in: they've got him – he's got away – they've got him again – here he is. Ashby formally hands over the prisoner to Rance: there follows some debate on the manner of execution – shoot him? – hang him? – both at same time?, and the miners now a lynch mob loudly shout nasty names: son-of-a-bitch etc. They recall the catalogue of Johnson/Ramerrez's crimes. A noose is prepared: a tree is selected. Johnson/Ramerrez makes a last request: don't tell Minnie how I died.

The request is unnecessary: Minnie arrives on scene: she interposes: Minnie is seized but says leggo or I will kill him and myself. They let go. Minnie makes a big appeal to the miners' better nature: she gives them a roll call of sentimental reminders of her past kindnesses: the big softies are much affected: they mutter they can't do this to their golden girl, also clearly God is behind her in this matter: take him back, Minnie, take him back, girl. She takes him back. They walk off into the sunrise.

MINUTES FROM START

LOOK OUT FOR

Act I

A vigorous prelude with a distant vocal salute to the Polka Saloon in the midst of it then away we go Hello! Hello! Hello! etc. swimming along over a dance-like melody but it disappears almost before you can grasp it. A wonderful opening.

7: *Che faranno i vecchi* The sad ditty* of Jake Wallace – what will the Old 7
Folks do if their sons never return?

15: *Hello, Minnie!* Minnie's entrance,* maybe not quite up to the 15
class of the Queen of Sheba, but mighty impressive all the same.

21: *Lavami e sarò* Minnie's Bible lesson:* the first set-piece aria: a 21
solemn melody and rather moving.

Jack Rance bears his soul to Minnie: the sad tale of
31: *Minnie, dalla mia casa* a loveless life:* Puccini gives him a deep soft melody, 31
really too nice for him.

You have to wait a long time for it, for the earlier part of Minnie's solo is quite bitty but when at last it
34: *Laggiù nel Soledad* takes wing it is wonderful.** She can reminisce too. 34
41: *La, la, la* Minnie's waltz:** at first to mouth music backed 41
by an accordion (woodwind) then the La La tune overtaken by a full-blooded Viennese-ish number: ends in the tumult of Castro's arrival.

The last quarter of an hour of Act I is made up of
45: *Mister Johnson, siete rimasto* the Minnie/Johnson duet** (interrupted for a mo- 45
ment by Nick's warning). The music feels its way from tentative beginnings to the full lyrical force of
51: *Quello che tacete* Johnson's first declarations of love.** The act dies 51
away gently as Minnie reflects on the matter of whether or not she has a face like an angel.

Act II

After the affianced Indians have done their rather boring stuff, there is another duet Minnie/Johnson, this time an eighteen-minuter. At first the conversation is conventional, but the music is not commonplace, rather romantic, and the temperature rises with increasingly passionate short lyrical phrases until
8: *Oh, se sapeste* Minnie bursts out with praise* for ponies, moun- 8
tains, pines, jonquils etc. and from then on the

dialogue runs into some purple patches such as
12: *Credo che abbiate* Johnson's thoughts* about women, then the kiss, 12
Johnson's false departure and so on to the love-in
15: *Dolce vivere e morir* climax** (then disappointingly slackening off to the 15
mutual 'goodnights').

26: *Sono un dannato!* Johnson's apology for himself* – the text is full of 26
self-pity but thc music is robust and he seems quite
cheerful in spite of his thoroughly disgraceful life.

37: *Una partita a poker!* The poker game:** tense, much of it played parl- 37
ando to no more than a faint excited pulsation in the
orchestra: ending with a gust of hysteria from
Minnie. (Makes your hair stand on end.)

Act III

A stunning start to Act III – one of Puccini's cold and
0 eerie preludes** followed by Nick and Rance quietly 0
1: *Ve lo giuro* chewing things over* (Rance: sexual jealousy, Nick: 1
Pity that dago busted into our lives). Suddenly the
4: *Ah! . . . Ah! . . .* hunt is in full cry and hunting noises** (man- 4
hunting) fill the valley in an earsplitting ensemble
whilst all sorts of side business goes on at the same
time (the miners race-read the chase: Rance: Sucks to
you Minnie, Nick bribes hangman Billy to fiddle
about with the noose).

13: *Ch'ella mi creda* Johnson's big moment:*** he asks the miners not 13
to tell Minnie that he came to such a shameful end: at
first slightly spooky, all in unison, then the old
Puccini takes over and OOMPH! we are into a big
warm lyrical lovely aria. The theme of Johnson's love
(heard before) comes in at the end.

16: *Ah, no! . . . Chi l'oserà?* The finale:* from the time Minnie appears on the 16
scene things go with a swing (but not Johnson). Big
argument with Rance (all miners against her) during
her first appeal she picks off Sonora, then with her
20: *E anche tu lo vorrai* second** (unashamedly sentimental, both thoughts 20
and music, but lovely) she begins to win them over
21: *Et tu mio trin* one by one in a *tour-de-force* ensemble*** which runs 21
up to her final victory (bully for Minnie) and then
walks off into the sunrise with lucky lucky Johnson.

NOTES

La Fanciulla del West	Puccini's seventh opera
First night	The Met, New York, 10 December 1910. Toscanini conducted

Reception	The audience loved it: the critics didn't
Libretto	Zingarini and Civinini
Source	A play by Belasco

NEWS AND GOSSIP

Once again Puccini was hooked by a Belasco play which he saw in the theatre (*Butterfly* was his too). He told his publisher, Ricordi, to get the rights. The creative team working on *Fanciulla* were an odd lot: Puccini himself, Zingarini the first librettist, who threatened to sue when Puccini suggested appointing a second one, Civinini. But he was appointed. Ricordi (publisher) and Belasco (writer) were the joint producers. Puccini himself suggested some of the more spectacular action, such as the manhunt and Minnie's final (and surprisingly successful) plea for Johnson's life. One wonders whether the first production would get by today. Musically and vocally (Toscanini conducted) it must have been terrific with Caruso (Johnson), Destinn (Minnie) and Amato (Rance) but it is known that none of these three could act and would stick firmly to the tradition that opera singers should move as far downstage as they could get, stand with legs braced and apart and belt it out. The first act waltz (Destinn and Caruso) must have been something rather special. The sets (of which we have photographs) were detailed down to the veins on the leaves on the trees and the costumes must have made the forty-niners look like guests at a provincial fancy dress ball. But *Fanciulla* survived and was seen in London in the following year and two weeks later in Rome with Maestro Toscanini once more at the helm. After that it languished and only began to be played again with the general Italian revival of the 1950s.

COMMENT

Do not expect the Puccini of *Bohème* and *Tosca*. This Puccini has been listening to Debussy and has moved with the times. Don't expect any attempt at the American folk and country idiom either. For some reason Puccini made a great thing over being Japanesy in *Butterfly* but didn't try to be American in *Fanciulla* whose score (except for Jake Wallace's party piece and some of Wowkle's stuff) is a million miles away from Scott Joplin or Home on the Range. Maybe he thought it would be too easy. There are references to Camptown Races and a couple of other ditties, but it's a good ear that can spot them. Also Jake's song (Old Dog Tray or whatever) does come back at the very end but considerably transmogrified. So what we have is Contemporary Puccini (whole tone systems: adventurous harmonies) stuck on to a true-love adventure story of the American West, primitive enough even for D. W. Griffith. Distinctly odd, even odder than Benjamin Britten's coupling with *The Beggar's Opera*.

But once you get used to the shouts of Hello, Son of A Bitch and Drinks on the House Boys, there is plenty to enjoy. The first act swings along at a great lick, much of the singing declamatory over orchestral writing that is almost always melodious, but in short bursts. Where the early Puccini tunes were a paragraph long here they are only phrases, sometimes just a couple of words. But the energy, cleverness and bubble of the piece grab your attention and fortunately the old Puccini keeps breaking through from time to time as in the waltz sequence and the final duet Minnie/Johnson.

The second act is the strongest dramatically (melodramatically) and the weakest musically with quite a lot of noises in the orchestra of a kind just to mickey-mouse along with the action. (One of the most prominent instruments is the wind machine.) There are at least two winners in Minnie's burst of girlish enthusiasm about the great outdoors and Johnson's apology for being such a dreadfully lawless fellow. In the last scene of the third act there is true operatic grandeur. The great ensemble where Minnie wins over the soft-hearted miners – believe it or not it doesn't matter – is tremendous. So there we are: a fascinating ingenious score with flashes of the old Puccini lighting the way, a simplistic but potentially heart-tugging story, and incongruous setting – it can't be an alpha but it is a pretty creditable beta.

Faust
Satanic melodrama

Gounod

The one where elderly Doctor Faust does a deal with the devil to be transformed into a young man with far-reaching consequences.

CAST

Dr Faust, a philosopher	Tenor
Mephistopheles (Méphistofélès)	Bass
Marguerite	Soprano
Martha (Marthe), Marguerite's minder	Soprano
Valentin, Marguerite's brother	Baritone
Siebel, one of Faust's students (male)	Soprano
Wagner (no relation), Valentin's friend	Baritone

5 acts: running time 2 hrs 50 mins

Note: The scenes in Acts IV and V are often treated in different ways. In the version described here the spinning scene in Marguerite's room has been dropped, the church scene comes first, followed by the scene in the town square where Valentin is killed. The Walpurgis Night scene is often dropped.

STORY

Act I Faust's study

We are in Germany in the fifteenth century and in the presence of an elderly and depressed Dr Faust. It is just before dawn. He is about to take an overdose of sleeping pills when he hears choruses of young girls and of farm workers singing cheerfully on their way to work about the glories of nature and calling for God's blessing. God has not been much good to me says Faust fingering the pills: I'd rather have the devil and POW! he's got him as large as life and dressed like Charles II as painted by Velasquez. Get out says Faust. Shan't says Mephisto: you called me I'm here to stay. What do you want? Money? Power? Fame? I want yoof says Faust. Yoof now yoof for ever I want to be able to have really good sex again. OK it can be done says Mephisto. What do I have to do in return? asks Faust. Sign this contract says Mephisto. What's it say? says Faust. Just says you will go to hell says Mephisto. Look! He conjures up a vision of a sexy girl spinning. I'll sign says Faust. Good man says Mephisto. Drink this. Faust drinks it and POW! again. He's transmogrified into a randy young man.

Act II A small-town fair

Several operatic social groups identified as matrons, soldiers, burghers, young girls, also first- and second-class students. All groups sing separately and severally the usual kind of choral allsorts associated with urban roistering. Valentin tells the folks that he is off to war with an insurance policy (a medallion) Marguerite gave him. Siebel (Faust's pupil whose voice never broke) and Wagner (no relation) say they will be Marguerite's minders while Valentin is on active service.

Wagner (no relation) starts to sing a song when he is rudely interrupted by Mephisto who sings a loud and incomprehensible ditty about the Golden Calf and up the sinners (an attempt at blasphemy). Mephisto goes around looking at hands and foretelling news: Wagner (no relation) will die: Siebel will poison all the flowers he touches: Valentin will be killed. He thinks the wine is plonk and magics Margaux 1482 out of the barrel on the inn sign. He insolently proposes a toast to Marguerite. Valentin challenges him to a duel. The wine which is running out of the barrel catches fire [why? just to show off? Ed.]. Valentin's sword falls apart. He makes a cross of the broken bits and Mephisto backs off.

Faust comes on. Where's that bird you showed me? he asks Mephisto. Wait here and she'll be along says Mephisto. But first the chorus gets waltzing then sure enough Marguerite trips in. May I have the pleasure of this dance? asks Faust. Get lost says Marguerite. Exits. What virtue! exclaims Faust. Everyone else waltzes on.

Act III Marguerite's garden

The boy soprano Siebel (potty about Marguerite) ponces around picking posies for her which instantly wither because of Mephisto's nasty spell. A rinse in holy water makes his hands wholesome again and he sings a love song. Enter Faust and Mephisto. Siebel ties his posy to a nearby lawnmower and exits.

Wait here says Mephisto to Faust I've left my casket behind. Exits. Faust sings an exceedingly chaste love song. Mephisto returns with his casket of jewels which he ties to the lawnmower next the posy. Faust and Mephisto hide. Enter Marguerite. She sings an irrelevant song but keeps breaking off to tell us she really fancied Faust when she saw him in the square.

She sees the stuff on the lawnmower. She is knocked all of a heap by the jewels and gets giggly as she puts them on. Enter Martha. Oh my God! You look wonderful she says: they must be from that pretty boy who made a pass at you in the square. Is Madame Martha at home? asks Mephisto coming out of the bushes. That's me says Martha. Your husband's dead says know-all Mephisto: sorry and all that but I'm now going to make a pass at you myself (he does so in a boring and long-winded manner). After a lot of hide-and-seek and other embarrassingly coy stuff by this quartet Faust and Marguerite at last think they are alone (Mephisto is hiding). She plays he-loves-me he-loves-me-not with a daisy. But he does love her and she loves him and they are getting quite sexy when she runs into her cottage to avoid things going too far.

What an amazingly chaste woman says Faust. But Mephisto pops out again and eggs Faust on to grab Marguerite's hand from out the window and then judging by Mephisto's hysterics standing outside the cottage Faust gets inside and grabs a lot more but since this happens offstage we don't really know what he did until the baby has arrived in the next act.

Act IV Sc 1 Interior of a church

Marguerite now an unmarried mother tries to pray but a choir singing something like a Dies Irae plus stray interruptions by Mephisto plus Gounod's organ music make it hard for her to concentrate. In the end she manages a short prayer but Mephisto lays a curse on her at the same time so it's about even stevens.

Act IV Sc 2 The town square

Soldiers sing the Soldiers' Chorus. Valentin arrives back from the wars. Siebel chickens out of telling him about Marguerite's disgrace. Valentin goes inside Marguerite's cottage. Faust and Mephisto arrive. I want to go in says Faust. Why? asks Mephisto: you've had that one let's look for another. He sings a song in very poor taste about the consequences of sex before marriage. Valentin comes out quite upset and ready to fight anyone. He chooses Faust who although certainly the worse fighter kills him owing to Mephisto's magic. But before dying he has (in true operatic style) a big number forecasting that Marguerite will become a *poule de luxe*. He delivers a brother's curse on her.

Act V Sc 1 A rocky valley in the Harz mountains

It is Walpurgis Night (a sort of witches' May Day orgy only not by day but by night). The souls of dead persons sing for a bit.

Act V Sc 2 A cave

Mephisto puts on his act presenting the great whores of history parading such figures as Cleopatra. There are seven dances presumably one each for the seven top-rating whores all tuneful but as an orgy Mephisto's party must be rated a flop. Faust sees a vision of Marguerite with a red slash across her throat.

Act V Sc 3 A prison

Marguerite is doing a stretch for murdering her child. Faust and Mephisto creep in. Faust tells Mephisto to get lost and he obeys. Faust and Marguerite go down Memory Lane and remember their nights of love. Mephisto returns and gazes balefully. Marguerite calls on angel-power to frustrate Mephisto and to save her soul. She sings to the angels ever louder and higher until she drops dead. A choir of angels says she is saved and reminds us that it is perfectly OK for sinners like Marguerite to go to heaven. So even though Mephisto had a very strong hand and played it strictly by the rules he lost. You can't win them all. (No further news about Faust.)

MINUTES FROM START

LOOK OUT FOR

Act I

0

The overture* opens glumly. Hammer blows fol- 0
lowed by sombre phrases which work their will a little
fugally until a harp ascending takes us up into a
celestial style of sweet melody (Valentin's farewell).
But still très sérieux and rather long.

6: *Rien! En vain j'interroge*

Faust broods.* Wordlessly, for quite a while. Then 6
he tells us that he is a manic depressive. Nothing
worth living for so he will top himself. Part recitatif,
some bursts of arioso and at the end of his soliloquy a
short determined sort of march towards death. Then
some rather dim rustic choruses of early-rising girls
and godly harvesters (we know they are rustic because
they are over a bagpipe-like drone bass). These do
nothing to cheer Faust up and he declares that God is
no good (a good bit this), he wants the devil. And
POUF! the devil appears.

18: *A moi les plaisirs*

After some market research to discover Faust's
requirements Mephisto hits the bullseye – yoof!
Faust sings a glorious free-ranging melody** which 18
has all the joy of yoof spinning around in it.

The vision of Marguerite spinning. Gounod man-
20: *O merveille!* ages quite a decent bit of magic here* – a horn 20
winding around solemnly. A bit of harp, of course.
The spell is broken and the act ends with a cheerful
duet Mephisto/Faust which is a reprise of Faust's
Yoof song.

Act II

0 A covey of choruses* open Act II, namely First 0
Students singing about drink, Soldiers eyeing the
girls, Burghers looking for gossip, Girls eyeing the
students, Second Students also interested in the girls,
and Matrons jealous of the girls. Each of the six
choruses has a separate innings to start with then they
combine, a little contrapuntally. It's all frightfully
jolly and tuneful – a halfway house between Offenbach and an amateur choir competition.

In the midst of all this there is a short solo for the
soldier by the name of Wagner (no relation).

Valentin's farewell. A celebrated but wimpish
6: *Avant de quitter ces lieux* piece with a good opening and closing tune* (asking 6
God to keep an eye on Marguerite) and some heroics
in the middle. Many calls on the deity throughout.

10: *Le veau d'or* Mephisto's wicked song about the Golden Calf.* 10
It's quite rousing but poorly calculated as propa-
ganda. The orchestra whips up a sort of witches'
carnival to support Mephisto's very feeble satanic
message. We are pretty close to operetta.

15: *De l'enfer qui vient* Mephisto checked.* A solo/choral scene as Valen- 15
tin makes a cross from his broken sword and the
chorus sing a holy chant with enough vigour to make
Mephisto sheathe his sword. It is effective melodramatic and incredible.

20: *Ainsi que la brise légère* The finale. A big build-up sets the waltz going.** 20
It goes and goes very well. Soloists interrupt to make
their plot points. Faust and Marguerite bring it to a
momentary halt as his invitation is offered and
refused. But soon we are spinning round again. The
crowd has no great message for us beyond 'Let's
Waltz'. Which they do to one of the best waltzes to
come out of opera.

Act III

2: *Faites-lui mes aveux* Siebel has bad luck with flowers, but overcomes. A
light number* with a clear fresh opening stanza, run- 2

ning on to some recitatif with Faust's 'A moi les plaisirs' beneath it all with an oom-pah accompaniment. This tuneful opening spreads into the exchanges between Siebel and Mephisto.

8: *Salut ! demeure chaste et pure* Faust's salute to Marguerite. A sweetish tune* 8
made pretty sickly by the well-intentioned support of a reprehensible solo violin. A more robust middle section does something to save the day.

13: *Il était un roi* The ballad of the King of Thule.* [Absolutely 13
irrelevant: Ed.] Quite charming in its rather aloof modal way. Interrupted by thoughts about the handsome stranger. Gives way to rapturous recitatif on opening the casket and leads to –

20: *Ah ! je ris de me voir* The Jewel Song.** Familiar, famous test-piece, 20
show-piece, mauled by aspiring sopranos etc. This sparkling number survives it all. It has dash, it has charm and it has the breath of Marguerite's girlish excitement as she dolls herself up in her devil-sent jewellery. It also has shape, a fine climax and stops in good time.

One of the best things about *Faust* is the easy melodious run of the recitatif/arioso. Here we have ten
24: *Seigneur Dieu, que vois-je !* minutes of sheer pleasure.* The oddly assorted 24
quartet (one virgin, one minder, one devil, one rejuvenated professor) unwind the plot with accomplished ease – the vocal line always elegant, the accompaniment full of good ear-catching ideas. Occasional ensembles. Two high spots: Marguerite's
29: *Mon frère est soldat* sad soppy song* about her dead little sister, a 29
31: *Je ne vous crois pas* splendidly crafted job; secondly, the 'thinks' quar- 31
tet:** Marguerite (I can't believe he really loves me), Faust (Listen to my loverly talk), Martha (He's probably laughing at me), Mephisto (Sorry I've got to see a man about a dog). Lovely intertwining parts.

33: *Il était temps* Mephisto reflects,* diabolically with his customary 33
chromatics. Solemn. Brass and harps. A powerful piece which adds a touch of darkness to a scene that was getting rather too jolly.

The Love Duet Faust/Marguerite. Long, varied and a *tour de force*:

36: *Laisse-moi, laisse-moi* 1. A serenade-type of spun-out melody* first from 36
him, then from her. Very fetching.

2. She loves me, she loves me not. The daisy game
breaks in fast and lively.
39: *O nuit d'amour* 3. The second big tune,** four times. Dripping 39
with love and longing (until death). Look out
particularly for the woodwind's contribution to
Marguerite's last strain.

4. Bang! We are into what might be a cabaletta (a
fast end piece). Agitato, the pain of parting spurs the
lovers to sing much faster. A nice bit of oom-pah
accompaniment creeps in to set our feet a-tapping.

5. But it isn't the end. One more impassioned
43: *Divine pureté!* loverly exchange,** as good as any that have gone 43
before. Now it is the end of the duet at last, but we
still have Mephisto's interference and Marguerite's
envoi from the window which leads to the mighty
sweeping tune that really does close the act.

Act IV Sc 1

This religioso scene in the church slips close to
self-parody, what with the pretentious intro with
strings and wind moving eerily in parallel motion, the
fumbling organ voluntary, the chorus of devils and
choristers, the latter singing the Dies Irae sound-alike
at the top of their lungs, and poor Marguerite praying
as best she can amidst these distractions, plus
Mephisto in person doing his nut. It is saved by two
3: *Souviens-toi du passé* splendid solos,** the first by Mephisto working on 3
Marguerite's sense of guilt. He makes a fine job of
being thoroughly beastly to her, rising phrases ever
louder, the organ grumbling away and the chorus
crashing in at the finish. The second, a great moment,
sandwiched between two bouts of Mephisto, is when
Marguerite finally gets praying and her prayer soars
above all the religious rhubarb in the finest lyrical
8: *Seigneur, accueillez la prière* passage in the opera.** This is Gounod at his best – a 8
splendid tune, beautifully crafted, with a tear-jerking
climax. Bravo! And to be fair, the theatrical hocus-
pocus of the generality of the scene is pretty enjoyable
too.

Act IV Sc 2

The soldiers are returning! The orchestra gives us
advance warning by playing one of the most famous
13: *Gloire immortelle* march tunes in the world.*** Soon it is going 13
strength 9, stage band and all. The later strains are

every bit as good as the bluff starter. Sousa would have been proud of it. It fades away into the distance.

After Mephisto's thoroughly disagreeable, taunting song with its bursts of heavy diabolical laughter (laughing devils being even more of a pain than
22: *Redouble, O Dieu puissant* laughing policemen) we have a trio* Mephisto/ 22
Faust/Valentin. The fraught situation is in no way reflected by the cheerful nature of the music which is as bright as a May morning (including a solo to an oom-pah accompaniment from Valentin). Meanwhile they are thinking: Mephisto (How funny, Valentin thinks he can beat the devil), Faust (Valentin looks really steamed up), Valentin (I'll kill either or both). The trio is followed by a musically rather feeble swordfight.

The finale. Valentin is found dying in the street by
25: *Par ici* a respectful and horrified chorus.* He makes the 25
customary brave gestures of a soldier in the face of death and turns on Marguerite rather nastily (first in recitatif and then in a short aria) saying that the only course open to her now is to become a hooker for the rest of her life. This unbrotherly thought is delivered in solemn, almost holy, tones. Even the chorus thinks Valentin is going too far. Throughout all this poor Marguerite utters only two words – high and piercing – 'O Dieu!'.

Act V Sc 1

Will-o'-the-wisps tell us they are the souls of dead
0: *Dans les bruyères* persons but seem quite happy about it in a chorus* 0
that starts as if it might become Mendelssohn's *Midsummer Night's Dream* rather than Walpurgis Night.

The arrival of Faust and Mephisto leads us into the most genteel Walpurgis Night on record with a polite recitatif from Mephisto to introduce the pantomime array of the great tarts of the past. This is greeted by
5: *Que les coupes s'emplissent* an agreeable chorus* from the girls who are in a very 5
jolly mood. No one seems to be Walpurging at all.

Act V Sc 2

7 The ballet music** is all tuneful and elegant and 25
orchestrated with more imagination and variety than the heavy stuff in the opera itself. This is Gounod on his home ground. No call for gravitas. The best numbers are rated as under:

1. Les Nubiennes**
2. Adagio
3. Danse antique
4. Variations for Cleopatra*
5. Les Troyennes***
6. The March Variations**
7. Phryné's dance.

This last noisy dance is the nearest we get to Walpurgis and is also said to represent an orgy. With all the great tarts of history present and only two gentlemen of quality one wonders how they can orge without letting class distinctions go hang.

Act V Sc 3

25 A long introduction of solemn brasses alternating 25
with a sweet clarinet solo gets Faust and Mephisto into Marguerite's cell. Mephisto leaves Faust to sort things out. Marguerite wakes up and sings a sweet
32: *Oui, c'est toi !* happy little aria which she shares with Faust.* They 32
recall their first meeting to a waltz tune which starts with Marguerite singing one note for 30 bars, then slows to allow her to take a stroll down Memory Lane. Faust urges her to run away with him, but no go. Mephisto joins in and tries to eject the pair before God can claim Marguerite. But she has a secret weapon, an appeal to God through an heroic melody in steps rising to a great climax which evidently does the trick for when she dies (just before we reach G major) the heavenly choir claim her as their own. Their reasoning may be obscure, but they have done well.

NOTES

Faust	Gounod's fourth opera
First night	Théâtre Lyrique, Paris, 19 March 1859
Reception	A success
Libretto	Barbier and Carré
Source	A play *Faust and Marguerite* by Carré loosely based on an episode from Goethe's *Faust*

NEWS AND GOSSIP

Gounod had the idea of an opera based on the Faust legend some ten years before he started serious work on his *Faust*. In its first form it was wildly overwritten, some say an hour longer than at the first performance

Whole chunks were chucked out, some new ones put in, including a number from an earlier opera that had been aborted (*Ivan The Terrible*). This was the Soldiers' Chorus, a number that would soon sweep the world and would have made Gounod a millionaire had mechanical rights been operative in his day. At this stage the opera had spoken dialogue not recitatif and its shape, especially Act IV, was pretty fluid. *Faust* caught on at once. Gounod popped in recitatifs for the productions in French provincial houses and soon it became the most favoured opera of the French repertory. He revised it for a big production at the Opéra in 1869 with the ballet music as we now know it. It was thought to be more modern than Meyerbeer (true), did not imitate Wagner (also true), a fine exemplar of French aesthetic taste (if true, an awesome comment on French aesthetic taste). In fact it lies on the borderland of operetta. *Faust* had a good run as one of the top of the pops for nearly a century but after World War II enthusiasm waned and today it lies resting for long periods. In Germany it is thought to be an impertinent gloss on Goethe's great work and is called *Marguerite*.

COMMENT

One of the problems with Gounod's *Faust* is that the Devil is no more impressive than a conjurer at a children's party. Maybe Goethe's original could summon up some of the terror felt for the Prince of Darkness in the Middle Ages, but Gounod's librettists aimed much lower. Marguerite's downfall and Valentin's death could have happened in any opera without Mephistopheles' assistance and as for the main theme – the rejuvenation of Faust – it doesn't pay off. All that happens is that transformed into a young man he has a bad time. So was it a mistake to change ages? So does he change back? Or go on seducing?

With the Devil reduced to the role of a naughty prankster the contest between good and evil is pretty one-sided and results, of course, in a pushover for God. Perhaps this is just as well because there is nothing in the music to make us think Gounod could have coped with a challenge between good and evil in the grand manner. The two scenes where a conflict does take place – the church scene and Marguerite's final appeal to the angels – are good theatre but hardly in the class of Bach's B minor Mass.

So we have not quite a flippant but definitely a lightweight treatment of a great romantic theme but alas one that gets lost towards the end in the distractions of Walpurgis Night and Cleopatra etc. Marguerite's death is stuck at the end like a postscript.

None of this matters too much because the farrago of a story gives Gounod a chance to show what he can do best and it is quite a lot. For one thing he could build a scene. His theatrical touch is sure and his scenes run with a zip and end with a bang. The church scene, for all its phony oozing sentiment, is a tremendously effective *coup de théâtre*. The end of Act II with Mephistopheles laughing his head off as Faust and Marguerite find true love is nice conceit. There are few if any longueurs.

Gounod could also write a tune. Faust's 'A moi les plaisirs' in Act I is a lovely fresh melody, Valentin's farewell is a hit, the Act II waltz still holds its charm although we may have heard it a hundred times, and so does the Soldiers' Chorus which we have heard a thousand. These last two are great popular tunes with an international currency as great as the 'Dance of the Hours', 'Liberty Bell' and 'Deutschland, Deutschland'. There is also of course the Jewel Song which can't be played but only sung, and it is still sung a lot. The ballet music is not far behind and deserves its popularity. Not so high in the charts but worth a detour is the 'thinks' quartet in Act II where Faust and Mephistopheles first encounter Marguerite and Martha, and the Faust/Marguerite duet which ends the act with a really big tune.

It is because it is so full of good tunes, because all the music is easy on the ear, because many of the scenes (although a bit kitschy) are brilliant theatre, that *Faust* was such an enormous favourite for nearly a hundred years. Today we are a bit more picky about our operas. We can grumble that the Faust story, in itself a bit bogus, is made trivial by Gounod, the music is light and dripping with sentimentality, the opera has no form and the ballets stop the show in its tracks. But if we are not snobs (and of course none of us will admit to that), if we have an ear for a tune, are fond of golden syrup, then we can sit back and enjoy our *Faust* almost as much as the French Opéra public did in the days when it was their darling. But it's a beta.

Fidelio

Human drama

Beethoven

The one with the prisoners' chorus and where a woman disguised as a prison worker liberates her husband and strikes a blow for freedom, feminism and prison reform.

CAST

Rocco, senior warder at Pizarro's prison	Bass
Marzelline, his daughter	Soprano
Jaquino, menial prison employee	Tenor
Fidelio, Leonore, disguised as an assistant warder	Soprano
Florestan, her husband, a political prisoner	Tenor
Don Pizarro, prison governor and fascist	Bass–baritone
Don Fernando, Home Secretary	Bass
Solo prisoners	

2 acts: running time 2 hrs

STORY

Act I A composite set including a prison courtyard, a gatehouse and the warders' quarters

We are looking at life in a prison near Seville Spain in the eighteenth century. [*Sing*] Marzelline irons her Dad's vests: security guard Jaquino pesters her to marry him. She rebuffs him: you promised he says: not quite promised says she. Jaquino exits to investigate a mysterious knocking. Marzelline exposes a strong fancy for assistant screw Fidelio (Leonore of course).

[*Spiel*] Fidelio returns from the repair shop with chains fetters etc. Rocco quizzes him about quality and price. Good lad he says you will get your reward: slyly glances at Marzelline. [*Sing*] The silly girl is falling for me what a bore thinks Leonore: Jaquino thinks: her Dad wants to see those two fixed up. Zut! [*Spiel*] I will set up marriage for you two soonest says Rocco but you will need some cash. [*Sing*] Adequate money supply is an important matter in life says he (tritely). [*Spiel*] That's true boss says Fidelio but there's another thing, let me assist you in the care of the political prisoners.

Steady boy says Rocco the boss is funny about them: maybe the fellow travellers but not the Commie leader in the deep hole dungeon with big security around him. Bin there two years. The boss ordered starvation ra-tions poor sod. Don't take Fidelio to any scene too shocking says Marzelline. Nuts says Leonore: I'm a toughie: take me. [*Sing*] You got guts boy says Rocco I will ask the boss for permission today. Good-o says Leonore (hopes to find Florestan of course). Good-o says Marzelline (thinks promotion means a quicker route to marriage).

[*Spiel*] Pizarro and security guards parade in: Pizarro sorts through the mail and finds a fax informing him that a surprise visit from the Home Sec is imminent. Home Sec suspects there are men imprisoned improperly. Crumbs! He'll discover Florestan! thinks Pizarro. [*Sing*] I'll kill him that's what I'll do and with some satisfaction too. [*Spiel*] Post a sentry to watch the Seville road he says: as soon as the Minister's black limo appears sound a trumpet! Geddit?

[*Sing*] Hey Rocco says Pizarro here's two hundred quid. What for? asks Rocco. To kill that Communist toad in service of our country says Pizarro. Couldn't says Rocco. OK if you chicken out I'll do the murdering you dig the grave says Pizarro. Well says Rocco a merciful release for him I suppose (both exit murderwards).

Leonore jumps in: God what a bastard she cries what dastardly plot is afoot? (But she sees a hallucinatory rainbow which calms her down.) [*Spiel*] Let's let the prisoners up for a breather she says to Rocco (returned). Without the boss's permission? says Rocco. Marzelline pops in. You and Pizarro are as thick as thieves she says to Rocco. You keep him in play while we let the prisoners out. Jaquino and Leonore do so.

[*Sing*] Appreciative sentiments are expressed by the prisoners: keep it down boys says the leading prisoner or the boss will hear you (but a spying officer observes them and runs off to Pizarro). Rocco comes on and tells Leonore: Good news the boss agrees you can visit the dungeons also marry Marzelline: now we are going to go down to the special prisoner. To be released? asks Leonore. No killed says Rocco. By you? she asks: no by Pizarro he says: you and I dig the grave (maybe for my husband she thinks): she weeps. There there says Rocco you stand behind. Not on your life says she I am OK it's just a fly in my eye.

Let's go says Rocco. But Jaquino and Marzelline run on shouting that Pizarro has found out about the prisoners. Get 'em in fast says Rocco. Pizarro storms in: abuses Rocco. It was a treat for the King's birthday today says Rocco [very weak: Ed.] anyway your priority is killing the chap down the hole not bothering over perks for prisoners [stronger: Ed.]. Get down and dig that grave says Pizarro.

The prisoners are herded back into the cells. Grumble grumble they say only just got out and it's back again into the dark.

Act II Sc 1 The deep dungeon and the staircase down into it

[*Sing*] Florestan tries to equate his frightfully unfair situation with ideas of divine justice (fails). He hallucinates: thinks he sees an angel: the angel is Leonore. [*Spiel to music* i.e. *melodrame*] Rocco and Leonore arrive: Florestan is asleep: they prepare to dig the grave in an old well: Leonore is nervous: [*Sing*] Keep at it boy says Rocco: I will try to save that poor sod whoever he is thinks Leonore.

[*Spiel*] Florestan wakes up: tell me he asks Rocco who runs this frightful prison? (Leonore recognizes his voice!) Pizarro says Rocco. That bastard says Florestan send for the wife to help me. Can't do that says Rocco. Got anything to drink? asks Florestan. Drop of wine says Rocco. [*Sing*] Thanks a lot says Florestan that young 'un looks a bit peely-wally eh? (She sure is peely-wally.) Can I give him this piece of bread? she asks Rocco. No says Rocco. Come on says she. OK OK says Rocco give it to him.

[*Spiel*] Rocco gives the signal for Pizarro that the grave is dug: all ready for murder. Pizarro enters. Pizarro confronts Florestan. [*Sing*] I'm going to kill you you punk informer Commie bastard he cries: he draws his dagger: Leonore interposes: you must first kill his wife she says: he Florestan me Leonore. Pizarro is about to kill both – the trumpet sounds! [*Spiel*] The Home Sec is here! shouts Jaquino down the hole. Coming up! says Rocco. [*Sing*] Pizarro exits Florestan and Leonore exult.

Act II Sc 2 Castle parade ground: statue of King visible

Hail and hooray shout the crowd of locals. Justice at last! The King has sent me to sort things out here says Fernando. Here's Florestan says Rocco. Good Lord I thought you were a goner says Fernando. Also his wife Leonore: she came as a boy assistant screw says Rocco then saved her husband Florestan. Pizarro was about to murder him, you see. Pizarro you horrible man you are under arrest says Fernando. All is well I love you says Florestan to Leonore. I will recommend Leonore for DBE says Fernando. All is well says everyone and well done Leonore.

MINUTES FROM START	LOOK OUT FOR	
Act I		
0	The overture** is the fourth out of four – the perfectionist Beethoven doing his nut to get it absolutely right. One and Two are OK, Three an absolute knock-out but too powerful for the opera's low-key opening number. It (No. 3) is sometimes played before the last scene – a mistake, because even there it	0

climbs to such dizzy heights that the opening of the final scene cannot really top it. Also you feel you have had a complete meal and have no appetite for any more Leonoring. The last effort does its job nicely.

6: *Jetzt, Schätchzen, jetzt sind wir allein*

In the opening duet** Jaquino pesters Marzelline 6
to marry him, but she has gone off him and on to Fidelio. The piece has the air of a number that has strayed in from the concert hall and tells us at once that we are not in an opera but a Singspiel and that this is one of the sings before the next spiel. It is a neatly structured piece, precise and tuneful. Marzelline does, however, flower into some looser and more romantic stuff when Jaquino leaves the stage for a moment. The singing is interrupted twice by a mysterious knocking by the orchestra (Fate knocking at the prison door? Prisoners rattling the bars? Builders? Faulty central heating?).

12: *O wär ich schon*

After a short spiel the next song** is Marzelline 12
having hopeful thoughts about Fidelio. Love and marriage not impossible she thinks (Ho Ho). It is a sparkling piece coming straight from the heart and almost painfully innocent. Again, although formally structured, it breaks into a bit of a romantic whirl at the end of each verse.

16: *Mir ist so wunderbar*

And now the world stops. Not only the stage world but the world of the listener, whatever he may be doing and wherever he may be. The grave string introduction casts its spell ahead of the first entry (Marzelline) and then the magical canon*** grows and 16
swells as next Leonore then Rocco and lastly Jaquino, join in. Wonder heaped on wonder as the other three voices weave a free pattern around the last entry. Suddenly the shades lengthen and the light fades and we have a hushed coda over a lingering tonic pedal. Then a forceful, final full close. The strands in the 'thinks' combo are as follows: Marzelline: (conning herself of course) Fidelio loves me for sure, goody, Leonore: Bit of a problem here, she thinks I'm a chap, Rocco: They'll make a stunning couple, Jaquino: O dear, o dear, Marzelline's gone cold on me. After the tic-toc, tic-toc of each entry in the canon we can hear the anguish, hope, joy, etc. in each part as it stands

against the others. This Olympian piece surpasses all the 'thinks' ensembles in Donizetti and Verdi. Theirs may have been longer, more complex and have called on mighty choral and orchestral support, but better they could not be.

26: *Gut, Söhnchen, gut* After the quartet this trio** has something to live 26
up to and good though it is, it can't quite do it. It is Beethoven at his most brave and bouncy but our characters have once again become singing actors not living people. The middle section sounds like a symphonic development and the burden of the piece is quite plotty. Rocco: You need guts to go down into the frightful torture cells, Leonore: I have loads of guts, Rocco: Happiness is built on fearing God and respecting justice, Leonore: That's me, Rocco: I'll ask the boss today if you can go with me, Marzelline: Yes do, it may speed up our marriage, Rocco: I'm getting on a little and if I hang up my dinner pail Fidelio could take over, Marzelline: Don't talk like that; all, again and finally: You must have guts to get on in life.

Pizarro (one would have thought unwisely) trum-
35: *Ha! Welch ein Augenblick!* pets his delight in revenge* and in the agreeable pros- 35
pect of murdering his old enemy Florestan. His troops listen to him a bit bemused. A robust 'rage' aria: the strings work away to good effect in a properly furious accompaniment.

Now we get nearer to opera. Pizarro asks Rocco to
39: *Jetzt, Alter, jetzt* partner him** in his dread design to murder Flor- 39
estan. Rocco demurs, but only mildly, because he cons himself into thinking death for Florestan would come as a merciful release. This duet makes compulsive listening: never a dull bar and every thought driven home with clarity and despatch. Tremendously workmanlike.

44: *Abscheulicher!* Leonore's first solo** – a powerful recitatif of hate 44
against Pizarro until she sees a rainbow and turns a bit soppy: there is a sweet intro to her aria and three horns range along in company with her in good style until we reach what one would hesitate to call the cabaletta, but which is certainly a fast bit at the end. This is really good: she is urged on by the friendly horns, now panting hotly beneath, to fine sentiments

of duty and devotion and twice strikes a memorable high note.

52: *O welche Lust* The prisoners' chorus.*** A grave strophe from 52
the strings tells us that something serious is about to happen and then, as the prison gates are thrown open, a sinuous little motif in the woodwind weaves its way around the voices of the prisoners, distant at first, but rising to full-throated shouts of delight in the sunlight and fresh air. A solo prisoner tells them to keep their peckers up and they respond so noisily that a second has to tell them to belt up a bit. They heed his advice for a while, but finish by repeating their greeting to the sunlight pretty loudly. Here, interestingly enough, is a piece which in an oratorio would seem only pretty good but when coupled with the sight of the poor wretches groping upwards into the light, is quite overwhelming.

59: *Nun sprecht, wie ging's?* Now at last we are into true opera country:** the 59
dialogue between Leonore and Rocco, the arrival of Marzelline in a mucksweat, the fury of Pizarro: this sequence flows along unchecked, part recitatif, some melody, lots of orchestral colour, and we take aboard the drama and the music as a single message. No stop–start, no spieling.

67: *Leb wohl, du warmes Sonnenlicht* The final ensemble:** under cover of chivvying 67
the prisoners back into the cells each character has his 'thinks' line: Pizarro: Get a move on Rocco and let me get murdering, Rocco: OK I'm going but I'm scared stiff, Leonore: Will no-one stop this bastard?, Marzelline: Poor dears, they were so enjoying themselves, Jaquino: Some funny stuff going on between Pizarro and Rocco, eh?, prisoners: Here we go, down again. Although each part in itself is fine, the finale doesn't quite come up to snuff. There is no real climax, catharsis, orgasm or whatever. But onstage the sight of the poor devils being herded back into darkness is a great help, also the calm little orchestral coda.

Act II Sc 1

The first bars of the introduction tell us that we are now into a pretty gloomy mood. This sombre piece is interrupted by a fearful shout of 'Gott!' from the trapped Florestan, who then tells us what a hard time he has had in exchange for doing his duty. A pure,

4: *In des Lebens* clear little motif introduces his aria** which is force- 4
ful, but halfway through changes gear, for he sees a vision of an angel, Leonore, leading him up to heaven. There is a piquant oboe accompaniment – maybe it is Leonore's spirit or something.

13: *Nur hurtig fort* The digging duet* is interrupted by powerful 13
gusts of emotion as Leonore wonders if the prisoner is Florestan. This impedes her spadework considerably and poor old Rocco has to keep nagging her with an eerie underground sort of tune, but her voice soars up into the light. The combination is both fearful and rather wonderful.

And now another piece of pure magic – the trio
18: *Euch werde Lohn* Florestan, Rocco, Leonore*** – half 'thinks' half ac- 18
tuality. Florestan starts with a suave main theme, saying to the other two thanks a lot for being so decent to me, Rocco replies don't mention it but Leonore tells us, not them, that she is all of a flutter. Florestan notices Leonore is acting a bit funny, Rocco and she debate the propriety of giving Florestan a bit of bread, and the pulse of the music stops as she offers it to him. So back to the main theme with Rocco and Leonore joining in a most glorious ensemble (again with a mixture of 'thinks' and duet dialogue) and finally a quick coda and lingering final notes before Florestan actually eats the much-sung-about piece of bread. A really strange jumble of noble thoughts and ornery chitchat to inspire music of a sort that people used to call 'sublime', a word we don't use but we know what it means.

Now things get moving, high drama as Pizarro en-
24: *Er sterbe! Doch er soll* ters the cell and viciously confronts Florestan.* He 24
tells him he is going to kill him, Leonore interposes, shouts that she is his wife and pulls a gun on Pizarro. Then the great *coup de théâtre*: the distant trumpet. So often in opera when things get physical and go fast the music makes no more than stock melodramatic gestures, but Beethoven here supports the action with gutsy stringent stuff that makes the air crackle. After the trumpet, a moment of calm: each one reflects what the news means. After the second trumpet and Jaquino's shouted message, all hell breaks loose again and Pizarro and Rocco exit.

30: *O namenlose Freude!* Shouts of joy.** It's you! Yes it's me! (or I! if you 30
prefer it). Florestan! Leonore! What bliss! Etc.! Pent-up emotion escaping like steam released through an opened valve. Beethoven is particularly strong on joy (as the European Union has reason to know).

Act II Sc 2

The orchestra opens the finale as if it were going to play a dance tune, but soon switches to Pomp & Cir-
33: *Heil sei dem Tag* cumstance. In comes the chorus Hailing* away and 33
we are off into Fernando's recitatif as he begins winding up the plot for us with the occasional but noisy assistance of the chorus. Then a moment of calm. An
40: *O Gott! Welch ein Augenblick!* oboe leads into Leonore's entry;*** she sings a gentle 40
melody and is joined by Florestan, then Fernando, Rocco and Marzelline, this time not in canon but conjuring up the same magic sense of wonder as in the Act I quartet. The chorus quietly slips in behind them and the spell holds until the mood changes and the chorus bursts in with gusty and noisy shouts of jubilation. From here on it is all gas and gaiters, the soloists tripping along on top, everyone going for bust, a little hectic perhaps, but then that's Beethoven, and indeed it is hard not to think of the finale of the Choral Symphony.

NOTES

Fidelio	Beethoven's one and only opera
First night	Mark 1: Theater an der Wien, Vienna, 20 November 1805 Mark 2: ditto, 29 March 1806 Mark 3: Kärtnertortheater, Vienna, 23 May 1814
Reception	See below
Libretto	1. Sonnleithner 2. (Revision) Breuning 3. (Revision) Treitschke
Source	French play by Bouilly 1794

NEWS AND GOSSIP

Fidelio had a rocky start in life. In 1805 Napoleon was on the move and Vienna was packed with French soldiers. Most of opera's regular clients had pushed off into the country and the run-up to the first night had been bugged by threats of censorship (the statue of 'the good monarch' which originally stood centre stage in the last scene was designed with the pathetic hope of softening the Emperor's attitude). Also the rehearsals had been chaotic. The opera was too long (exactly how long we don't know) and ran for only three performances. Beethoven, no doubt with his well-known bouts of fury and despair, cut the three acts to two, junked a couple of first act numbers and shortened the dialogue. The second version was put on six months later and went a little better. But he immediately got at it again, revising, cutting, patching, rewriting, and eight years later the third version was staged, again in Vienna, and this is the one we know and love today.

As a revolutionary work *Fidelio* caught the mood of the day and was played all over Europe as something of a political shocker. Rather as John Osborne's *Look Back in Anger* torpedoed the run of Aunt Edna plays in the London of the 1950s, so in 1805 did *Fidelio* discredit the stuffy and pretentious baroque opera tradition that was still hanging around in Vienna. But the old order was probably doomed anyway, for as well as Napoleon, Rossini was soon to be on the march.

Fidelio was soon seen to be a masterpiece and it has held a hallowed position in the opera repertory ever since. And here's a note to clear up the confusing matter of the overtures:

Leonore No. 2:	composed for the first performance in November 1805.
Leonore No. 3:	composed for the first performance in March 1806. The big one. Sometimes (mistakenly) played before the last scene.
Leonore No. 1:	adopted as a concert piece 1807.
Fidelio:	(quite different) composed for the 1814 performance and nearly always played before the opera.

COMMENT

Beethoven would be the first to admit that *Fidelio* is a bit of a mess. For one thing the *Singspiel* form never really worked. It had been forced on the Viennese houses by Imperial decree because the Emperor was mad at the Italians and the French for their dominance in opera. Mozart suffered from it and Beethoven picked up the fag end of this hybrid old thing, which was bad luck on him. So *Fidelio* starts with alternate bursts of singing and spieling and the songs seem to have come in from outside and do not form a part of a living and breathing music-drama. Beethoven himself said, when he chucked out a couple of numbers from the first version, that they were too like concert pieces. But so are the ones that stayed in, including even the wonderful, wonderful quartet. What is more, the spieling is pedestrian stuff. Sonnleithner's lines have no spring in their step, and read about as well as a telephone directory. Traditionally, the job of the recitatif was to tell the story and of the arias to reflect the sentiment, but in *Fidelio* the sing bits do a lot for the plot and the spiel bits tend to stop the action dead in its tracks and let all the steam out of the mood built up by the marvellous music. It's not until the prisoners come lurching out of their cells that we are gripped by the power of true opera. Again the story up to this point has been toy-town stuff – scenes from the family life of an elderly prison warder – with no hint of the passion and nobility of what is to come. Except that the music is wonderful, the first scene of *Fidelio* is, in fact, a pretty fair old disaster. But the music wins us over, for here is Beethoven at his greatest and best. It does not matter that the forms are symphonic and the style instrumental, he bowls us over just the same. And as the opera progresses and we climb the true operatic peak of Act II all the awkwardness and irrelevances (it couldn't matter less whether Marzelline wants to marry Jaquino or Fidelio) are forgotten. From the prisoners' chorus (one of the most moving scenes in all opera) onwards, the piece holds its power, we can tolerate the spiels and, indeed, the melodrame (spoken word against musical backing) between Rocco and Leonore is a positive plus. The tension builds through the trio and quartet leading up to the trumpet call and then the joy and the passion of the Leonore/Florestan duet makes it the real climax of the opera. It is Beethoven's ability to make his absolute music pack such a dramatic punch that lends such enormous power to *Fidelio*: his passionate advocacy of liberty, his hatred of tyranny speak to us directly through the music and make *Fidelio* one of the greatest of all operas. Only the weakness of the beginning stops it being an alpha-plus: a mighty alpha.

Figaro *see* Marriage of Figaro, The

Die Fledermaus (Fledermaus)

Viennese farce

Johann Strauss

The one where there isn't a bat but only a ball at which everyone pretends to be someone else until their true identities come into the open at a police station next morning.

CAST

Herr von Eisenstein, a member of the Viennese idle rich	Tenor
Rosalinde, his wife	Soprano
Adele, Rosalinde's maid	Soprano
Ida, her sister	Soprano
Falke, a friend of Eisenstein	Baritone
Frank, a prison governor	Baritone
Alfred, an Italian tenor	Tenor
Prince Orlofsky, a Russian prince	Mezzo
Dr Blind, a lawyer	Baritone
Frosch, a prison officer	Speaking part

3 acts: running time anything from 1 hr 45 mins to 2 hrs 15 mins

Note: In recent years producers have felt free to mess around with the text of *Fledermaus*, to put in topical jokes, to cut some of the bits that don't work, to rewrite the Frosch part for some famous comic of the day, etc. and those music directors who are avid for a free chance to improve an opera have also sometimes permed the numbers and waltzed the old thing up in other ways. The version described here is the 1960 Karajan recording with the Gala (ballet) items left out.

STORY

Act I A room in the Eisenstein residence

It is 1874 in old Vienna city of wine women and Johann Strauss and Adele the maid runs in with a letter from her sister Ida. I've got a spare invitation to the biggest ball of the season at Russian Count Orlofsky's tonight she writes. Why not pinch one of Madam's Dior creations and come along disguised as a lady? Meanwhile a weedy tenor is singing pops from

Verdi in the street outside. In comes the fabulous Rosalinde. No Adele you can't have the evening off to visit a sick aunt she says the master is going to jail tonight and I shall need you and who is that singing *Simon Boccanegra* outside the window? It isn't *Simon* says Adele it's *Ballo* and it's one of your ex-lovers Alfred the cut-price tenor. Adele exits. Alfred enters. Get out says Rosalinde I'm a married woman. OK says Alfred but only if you swear I can see you again. I swear says Rosalinde but only so long as you promise not to sing Verdi. Alfred exits.

Enter husband Eisenstein and lawyer Blind slagging each other off because they have messed things up in court. Eisenstein's sentence has been extended from five days to eight. After a very long trio Blind exits. Falke enters and Rosalinde exits. Eight days old boy bad luck says Falke but I have this great idea. Come to the great Orlofsky ball tonight in disguise. I can fix Frank the prison governor it will give you a wonderful send-off. Lot of gals there old boy. You're on says Eisenstein but the wife must not know. Rosalinde returns. Why are you two looking so cheerful? she asks. Falke runs for it. What is the right thing to wear in prison I wonder says Eisenstein. Got it! I'll wear full evening dress. You must be mad says Rosalinde (Eisenstein exits Adele enters) and by the way Adele you can have the evening off after all. Eisenstein enters in full evening dress. Goodbye my dear sweet faithful wife he says. Same to you says she. Eisenstein exits.

Alfred enters a bit smashed and starts to sing. What an ugly jacket says Rosalinde why don't you put on my husband's dressing gown? OK says Alfred still singing in an Italian fashion. Frank the prison governor arrives to escort the distinguished prisoner Eisenstein to jail and assumes that Alfred is he. (At least he got the dressing gown right.) I'm not Eisenstein says Alfred. Yes you are you fool says Rosalinde fearing scandal. Oh yes so I am says Alfred. Of course. Frank carts him off to prison.

Act II Count Orlofsky's ball

My my say all the guests look at the caviar the chandeliers the tiaras isn't it grand (thereby confirming the suspicion that despite all the glitter the old Vienna mob were a pretty provincial lot). Who is that female impersonator over there? says Adele. That's the young Prince he's a very rich mezzo soprano says Ida. Can I have some money to gamble with please Prince? says Adele. Take my Barclaycard the limit is ten thousand thalers says the Prince. And will you lend me some your English Lordship says Ida to Lord Palmerston. Piss off you cheeky pig he replies. Falke struts around making it clear he has set up some great joke but can't reveal it yet because it would spoil the plot but he does tell the Prince that Adele is no great lady but a lady's maid. Eisenstein arrives as the Marquis de Renard.

Falke gets on the phone and asks Rosalinde to come along too but in disguise. Hello Marquis says the Prince let me tell you about myself. I'm a rich horribly spoilt brat of eighteen always bored and usually drunk and if I don't care for one of my guests I have him slung out. I seldom laugh but Falke tells me that tonight I'm going to have a good laugh at you. At me? says Eisenstein. Good lord.

Adele comes back having lost all her money. Gosh you're the living spit of our maid Adele says Eisenstein. (And you are my master Eisenstein poncing around at a ball when you should be in jail thinks Adele.) I'm not your maid says Adele and passes the matter off with a song and a laugh. Enter Frank disguised as Le Chevalier Chagrin. You two Frenchies had better get together says the Prince and they do and there is a big laugh in the fact that neither can speak French.

Eisenstein takes Adele into the garden. Rosalinde arrives in a mask. There he is says Falke in the garden with your maid Adele. Not in prison at all. Zut! says Rosalinde. The traitor! Eisenstein comes back. Let me present this Hungarian countess says Falke. Oho says Eisenstein I do fancy you. He flirts. What a pretty watch says Rosalinde sounds as if its tick is metronomically coincidental with my heartbeat. Let's prove that says Eisenstein laying an eager finger not quite where her heart could be assumed to be. They fiddle around counting. Rosalinde takes the watch and drops it down her front. Zut says Eisenstein that's my watch gone.

Rosalinde sings a Hungarian song. Tell us the story of the bat say the guests for no reason at all. Well it was this way says Eisenstein. Falke and I went to a fancy dress ball together and got drunk. He was dressed as a Fledermaus, in English a flying mouse better known as a bat. On the way home I dropped off Falke the distinguished QC on a public bench in front of the Law Courts where he slept for two days as all his clients and colleagues filed past having a good laugh. They thought he had gone batty! Ha Ha Ha. How very funny says everyone Ha Ha. Doesn't he want to get his own back on you? they ask. Sure does but I keep my eye on him says Eisenstein (and Ha Ha now say we).

From now on nothing much happens to the plot. They drink champagne and sing about it in their bourgeois way. They waltz a lot. They give a toast to comradeship as if they were at the dinner of a branch of the British Legion. Eisenstein asks Rosalinde to unmask but she won't. The clock strikes six. Eisenstein and Frank depart, unknown to them to the same destination.

Act III The reception area of a prison

Frosch the comic prison officer holds the stage with a monologue for some time. He is joined by a drunk and dishevelled Frank who tries to get into his Governor's uniform. He asks for coffee. The coffee machine explodes. He goes to sleep. Adele and Ida arrive. I want you to help me to get on the stage she says to Frank and goes into a series of excruciatingly awful acts though it is hard to see why she thinks an audition in front of a drunk prison governor will do her any good.

Eisenstein arrives. Why have you been locked up Chevalier? he asks. I haven't says Frank I run this place. I'm the Guv. And I'm not a marquis but about to be an inmate of your place. I'm Eisenstein says Eisenstein. Don't try that funny stuff with me says Frank. I arrested Eisenstein last night as he was having it off with his wife. Whassat? says Eisenstein. Blind arrives. Who sent for you? asks Eisenstein. You did says Blind. Zut! says Eisenstein it must have been the imposter they have in cell 12. Gimme your wig jacket and glasses and I'll pretend to be you and then perhaps I'll find out what the hell is going on.

Rosalinde and Alfred come in. I'd like to break this Neapolitan ape's neck thinks Eisenstein but maybe I'd better wheedle his story out of him. Mother of God! he's wearing my dressing gown. It was all perfectly respectable says Rosalinde this gentleman was having supper with me and was arrested in mistake for my husband. What is more she says I have since discovered that my husband was pursuing young girls at a ball and I'm going to give him a hard time when he comes back. I AM EISENSTEIN says Eisenstein. You faithless bitch you randy wop I AM EISENSTEIN. Here. In front of you. Fear me! So. So says Rosalinde how about this? (she digs the watch out of her front).

The Prince arrives with everyone else who is not already in the prison. What's going on? says Eisenstein. Let me explain says Falke. This is my revenge for that corny bat trick you played on me. I set the party up with the Prince. I faked Ida's letter to Adele. I got you to come to the party. I got Frank to come as a chevalier because the poor sod is so class conscious he wouldn't come as a prison governor. I got Rosalinde to come and fool you. Very clever says Eisenstein but how about this Neapolitan songster having it off with my wife? Just an invention says Rosalinde. And the dressing gown? I saw him wearing it on stage and got a duplicate for you says Rosalinde. And I will pay for you to go to RADA so long as you are appropriately grateful says Frank to Adele. Oh well says Eisenstein I suppose funny things happen in Viennese operettas let's all sing that champagne number again. They do.

MINUTES FROM START

LOOK OUT FOR

Act I

0 The overture** – a sampler of most of the best tunes in the opera including the great waltz. A slice of chocolate cake from Old Vienna. 0

14: *Ach, ich darf* A surprisingly amiable duet* considering the two 14
parties are a mistress, Rosalinde, refusing her tearful
lady's-maid Adele a night off. Short and just not too
sweet.

Herr Eisenstein is displeased with his legal adviser.
A rapid-fire trio Eisenstein/Rosalinde/Blind which
races through patter, some recitatif, several pages of
one-liners, a couple of attempts by Rosalinde to calm
17: *Ach, mein armer* them down (the second a moment of real charm)* and 17
ends in a helter-skelter cabaletta. Snatches of good
tunes abound.

Falke persuades Eisenstein to come to the party
20: *Kommt mit mir zum Saufer* (old chap).* An opening solo with a nice accompani- 20
ment from Falke as he makes the proposition then a
long bout of musically aimless duetting as they gloat
rather disagreeably over the fun of deceiving Rosalinde (poor little mouse). They end with a tuneful
galop to the finishing post. (Let's get off to the gals.)

25: *So muss allein ich bleiben* Rosalinde sings a solo** full of crocodile tears for 25
Eisenstein in prison. It's a haunting tune that sounds
sincere but isn't. Eisenstein and Adele join in a trio of
phony grief. All three, from time to time, can't resist
barking out their excitement at the thought of free-
27: *Oje, oje, wie rührt mich dies* dom to one of the catchiest items in the piece.** 27

Alfred gives up singing snatches of Verdi for a
while to serenade Rosalinde in a very Austrian
29: *Trinke, Lieben, trinke* fashion,* waltz time, yodelling and horns, Mantovani 29
strings and those slow scoopy waltz bits that all Vien-
nese composers (and certainly all Strausses) thought
were absolutely essential clinchers to make the heart
flutter. In its final throes it becomes a duet, for Rosalinde, of course, joins in. Not much of a tune and one
star only because it is a prime specimen of vintage
Viennese glühwein.

The arrival of Frank. The orchestra continues to
hum Viennese tunes under its breath. Alfred tries
from time to time to sing an encore of his last number
but this is squashed by Rosalinde. Instead the invitation to drink, always irresistible in Old Vienna, leads
to scoopy waltz bits, much more fetching this time,
and finally we get Rosalinde's pert and pretty num-
34: *Mein Herr, was dächten Sie von mir* ber** swearing Alfred is indeed her husband. A 34
show-stopper.

The finale. Alfred at last gets off to prison with delays for goodbye kisses and in order to give a decent
38: *Folgen Sie nun schnell* run to the rattling good trio** started off by Frank 38
and building up to a fast, furious and satisfactory end to Act I.

Act II

After an opening chorus that could have been written by Strauss's copyist, and perhaps was, the first musical event of interest is Orlofsky's song about his ungracious behaviour as a host. Banal at first, it eventually brings on a tune that sneaks into your af-
4: *Ich lade gern mir Gäste* fections* and deserves a mild star. 4

Adele laughs at the Marquis in waltz time to one of
10: *Mein Herr Marquis* the top tunes in the show.** The ha-ha-has are pret- 10
tily set. Most operatic laughter is a pain. This isn't.

The watch duet starts pleasantly enough as Rosalinde and Eisenstein size each other up. Then a rather boring middle section as the heartbeat/watchtick contest is set up. But all is forgiven as soon as the
21: *Ein, zwei, drei* counting starts. A catchy tune,** lots of sparkle and 21
finally a shower of wordless coloratura from Rosalinde as she leaps and bounds about above Eisenstein who chug-chugs away beneath.

24: *Klänge der Heimat* Rosalinde's Hungarian number,* with all the 24
gypsy tricks in the book. As a czardas it may not be the real McCoy but it makes a terrific climax to her party piece.

30: *Im Feuerstrom der Reben* The Champagne Song.* Veuve Clicquot in an or- 30
dinary year perhaps, not Dom Pérignon. It is jolly enough, fast enough and just bubbly enough to please.

This is something dangerously near to a solemn
33: *Brüderlein, Brüderlein* number* in which Eisenstein asks everyone first to 33
kiss each other and then to be friends for life. But it's not really serious and soon we are in the land of waltzy schmaltzy and the guests rally to move into the final infectiously waltzy waltz – the great Fledermaus
37: *Genug, damit, genug!* waltz** which we first heard in the overture. 37

Act III

Adele is a woman of many parts. In a dainty little
10: *Spiel' ich die Unschuld vom Lande* number* with plenty of vocal gymnastics she tries to 10
show she is a versatile actress.

The legal triangle. Rosalinde, Alfred and Eisenstein sort things out.

19: *Ich stehe voll Zagen* 1. A sotto voce 'thinks' trio* – Rosalinde (I'm 19
scared stiff), Alfred (Maybe I'll have to come clean), Eisenstein (I'd like to break his neck).

2. Eisenstein in character as Blind. Recitatif complete with stammer. He asks for further and better particulars of last evening.

3. Alfred tells the tale. They drift into a beguiling
21: *Was ich erfahr' verwirrt* 'thinks' trio,** the 'thinking' being much as above. 21

4. Rosalinde takes up the story. We are now in an easy-going jog trot mode. Eisenstein has an outburst. But we drift safely back for a final jog trot until the trio ends.

5. Eisenstein now begs for a full confession. Wonderful Fledermaus things happen in the orchestra.

6. Rosalinde makes her pitch. Her husband was out on the tiles last night. Slow to start but picks up power and charm as it goes along.

7. Eisenstein reveals himself to be himself in Grand Opera style and all three run into one of the
25: *Ja, ich bin's, den Ihr belogen* great tunes of the opera.** Worth waiting for, and we 25
have waited quite a while.

28: *O Fledermaus, o Fledermaus* The finale** starts with everyone imploring Falke 28
to stop being beastly to Eisenstein, and sure enough through a mixture of telling lies and the truth (but mostly lies) they manage to cheer him up mainly through a reprise of many of the best tunes. They finish with the Champagne Chorus.

NOTES

Die Fledermaus	Strauss's third opera
First night	Theater an der Wien, 5 April 1874
Reception	Rapturous
Libretto	Haffner and Genée
Source	A French farce. See below

NEWS AND GOSSIP

During the nineteenth century the Strausses were famous as bandleaders who had their own family polka and waltz factory. Father Johann started the business and Johann II carried it on. But the Viennese impresarios feared that Offenbach was going to take over the musical theatre in Vienna and egged on Johann II to compete with true Wiener Blut operettas. Which he did, leaving the bandleading job to his brother Eduard. His first two operettas were not much cop but the third, *Fledermaus*, was a hit from the word go. He wrote it fast, allegedly in forty-two nights, which is surely possible for once he had thought of the tunes the actual settings for each number need not have taken much more than forty-two minutes and some could almost have been left to his copyist. He got the script from a famous French farce by Meilhac and Halévy, the wonderful couple who wrote much of their best stuff for Offenbach. This was translated into German for the stage by one Carl Haffner. He started to adapt the piece for Strauss's libretto but for one of the thousand reasons (now forgotten) that cause divergence between writers and producers, he walked off the picture and Genée took over. From its first night *Fledermaus* has never looked back. In Austria it holds a position hallowed by generational nostalgia, rather as does *Peter Pan* in London. New Year's Eve is especially favoured for a special *Fledermaus*. And the maus has fledered pretty well all over the operatic world although the Italians are a bit sniffy about what they think of as Viennese kitsch. But the French sink their pride and revel in it.

COMMENT

What happens if you put together a top-class French farce with the composer of the very best Viennese dance music? The answer is *Fledermaus*, a terrific popular success and maybe one should just leave it at that. But the truth is that the music slows down the farce and that the farce provides neither good song opportunities nor words of any distinction for the music. So *Fledermaus* is more dependent than almost any other opera on the verve, the skill and the casting of the production. A sparkling *Fledermaus* can send you home feeling as if you'd drunk some of the champagne that swills about on stage in such huge quantities, a damp *Fledermaus* makes *Parsifal* seem a riot of fun.

As we all know, Strauss was the best of all Viennese tunesmiths and *Fledermaus* has at least six of his very top numbers. But once he had got the tune he did not have much more to offer. The structure of a scene is usually to move from a fairly slow tune to another tune a little faster, then a third, faster still. When in doubt Strauss reverts to a waltz, and when he is really stumped, to the Fledermaus waltz, one of the great tunes of all time.

So we should look to a man of the theatre, and indeed a man who can produce farce, a class of person who is becoming very rare, to make the most of *Fledermaus*, also a writer as witty as John Mortimer to beef up the book. Then, and only then, do we need the music director. But he must have booked at least three top star singers and have the band play the score as if they loved it even though they may be hankering for Schoenberg all evening. There is no point in debating whether *Fledermaus* is music theatre, operetta or grand opera. It is what it is, and done right will deliver an evening full of laughs and good tunes. A beta.

The Flying Dutchman (Der Fliegende Holländer)

Nautical fantasy

Wagner

The one where the Dutchman seeks a good woman to release him from sailing the high seas for ever: he finds one who jumps off a cliff and they both ascend to heaven.

CAST

Daland, a Norwegian skipper	Bass
Senta, his daughter	Soprano
Mary, Senta's old nurse	Contralto
Erik, a young Norwegian in love with Senta	Tenor
Smith, Daland's helmsman	Tenor
The Dutchman	Bass–baritone

3 acts: running time 2 hrs 30 mins

STORY

Act I A harbour in a rocky bay: cliffs beetle

We are in the Norwegian fiord of Sandwigen at some unspecified date and the weather is bad. Skipper Daland has brought his ship in for shelter: he is vexed because he has seen his home but missed making a landfall at his home port by seven miles owing to a mighty storm. Relax lads he says to the crew and stop singing that halloyoho stuff for Chrissake: the storm is dying out. Go below. Smith he says you take helmsman's watch see and keep awake: exits.

Smith sings soppily about his girlfriend. He requests the south wind to propel the ship in her direction. He goes to sleep. The Dutchman's ship sails in alongside. Smith wakes up. The Dutchman goes ashore. Smith nods off again. The Dutchman says Heigho so that's another seven years gone: I am permitted by my curse contract with the superior powers one landing each septaquennium to try to negotiate my release from perpetual sea voyaging: boy am I sick of this compulsory touring. I tried suicide but the conditions of the curse contract forbid it. Roll on Judgement Day. And you can say that again sing the Dutchman's crew (invisible ghosts).

Daland comes up: You asleep again Smith? he says. Nothing happened Boss honest says Smith. Then how about this bloody great ship lying alongside? says Daland. Sorry Boss it escaped my attention says

Smith. He shouts ahoy. The Dutchman appears. You all right old boy? asks Daland. Ship and tackle OK says the Dutchman: just one thing do you take paying guests at your nearby home? I have large quantities of loot aboard. What kind of stuff? asks Daland. Gold bars, pearls, specie, diamonds, platinum and heavy water says the Dutchman – you can have the contents of chest 67BX in return for one night's lodging (he opens 67BX and displays contents). Cripes! says Daland be my guest. I always admired the Dutch.

Have you a young girl preferably a daughter about the home? asks the Dutchman. Indeed I have an excellent daughter says Daland. May I marry her? asks the Dutchman. Of course of course of course you can says Daland. The terms of my curse contract are stringent says the Dutchman. I must travel perpetually so wealth is of no value to me. If I marry your daughter you can take the lot. My daughter is sexy virtuous industrious honest and beautiful says Daland. OK it's a deal says the Dutchman can I take her over today? As soon as we get clearance for take off from Met. says Daland.

Will this marriage meet the conditions of the escape clause in my curse contract? thinks the Dutchman, if so goody. Lucky old storm, lucky encounter, lucky old me thinks Daland. Fax in from Met. Captain sir says Smith: South wind force 5 about to commence. Fine great OK says Daland. You go first I follow says the Dutchman. Daland's sailors (after a rest of only 45 minutes) cheerfully rig for departure.

Act II The spinning room in Daland's house

Mary supervises the midday shift of spinning operatives working in Daland's house for West Norwegian Home Industries. All the girls sing as they spin except Senta who gazes at the portrait of a romantic-looking but pasty-faced man. Get spinning Senta says Mary, looking at that pin-up all day is disgraceful. She's acting funny because she's in love with Erik the Animal Conservation Officer say the girls. Sing us the ballad of the Flying Dutchman Mary please says Senta. Negative says Mary. Then I'll sing it myself she says: gather round girls.

Yohohojehohijaho she sings to put them in the mood there was this ship with blood-red sails in serious need of maintenance owing to endless voyaging round and round the world. The skipper was a gaunt man from Schipol who once uttered a blasphemous four-letter word when in extreme nautical difficulties rounding Cape Horn in a force 12 gale. The tetchy superior powers laid a curse contract on him namely he must sail the seas for ever until he finds good woman who is eternally faithful to him. He is permitted access to dry land once every seven years to contact marriage bureaux etc. How interesting say the girls.

Hey hey girls shouts Erik, I've seen Senta's Dad's ship coming in. Oo! Oo! The men will be home any minute say the girls. And what was that rubbish you were going on with? says Erik to Senta. You know your Dad plans to give permission for our wedding this visit? I can't talk now I'm busy says Senta. I am upset Senta says Erik your Dad wants a rich son-in-law and my pay as an Animal Conservation Officer is not good and is indexed to the cost of living. Also you seem to have gone potty about that pin-up picture guy who looks like a corpse. Listen: I dreamt a dream that I saw a strange ship and two men came ashore one your Dad the other the guy in that picture. You fell at his knees and then there was a big cuddle and the two of you went off together.

The door opens: Daland and the Dutchman enter. Senta is stunned. It is he! Hello Senta I brought this bloke along with me – do you mind if he stays the night? says Daland: by the way he wants to marry you and I've agreed. He's very rich. Now I'll leave you both to get on with it. Exits.

Good Lord! This is the girl of my dreams thinks the Dutchman. Good Lord! This is the man in the picture thinks Senta. Will you do what your father wants? asks he. I always do what my father wants says she. You may be the means of activating the escape route clause 17B in my curse contract says he. I will do my utmost to oblige says she actually I am overwhelmed by romantic passion and will be true to you unto death. Sounds like pretty good news says he. 'Scuse me says Daland popping in I can't hold up the end-of-trip party any longer the crew are battering on the door for booze: have you two fixed up that marriage? Yea, fixed it says Senta. I confirm that says Dutchman.

Act III A cove: the two boats moored alongside each other, Daland's with the crew on deck, the Dutchman's deserted. Daland's house visible, also a steep cliff. Night

The sailors on board Daland's ship rollick on deck singing nautical rhubarb. A bevy of local girls arrive with picnic baskets alcoholic refreshments etc. They approach the Dutchman's ship. Hey there you lot they shout: like a snack? No response. You asleep or something? say girls. No response. Must be dead say sailors. Funny they say this ship is very similar to the legendary vessel of the Flying Dutchman. The girls leave the Dutchman's ship and present their picnic baskets to Daland's crew: exit.

Daland's crew dance and sing nautical rhubarb once again. Blue fireworks explode round the Dutchman's ship. The sea seethes and the wind howls in a very localized storm which is confined to the immediate area around the Dutch ship. The Dutchman's crew come to life and sing a ghostly chorus. Let's hope the skipper really is fixed up they say then our endless voyages are over. We can't see a soul say Daland's crew. They must be ghosts. They start off on rhubarb again. The Dutchman's crew interrupt Daland's crew with cries and shrieks of ghostly rhubarb. Choral contest develops Daland's versus Dutchman's. The Dutchman's wins. The localized storm stops.

Senta runs on Erik in pursuit. It can't be true says Erik. You are dumping me for this total stranger? It's my duty says Senta also destiny also father's instructions. Hold on Senta says Erik remember when we went fell-walking together? When cuddling you said 'I love you' over and over. The Dutchman eavesdropping in the rocks jumps out. That's torn it! he cries. Unfaithful! Goodbye Senta! Hold on says Senta where are you going? To sea for ever says the Dutchman. Right boys get ready to sail. No need! Stop! A mistake! I am faithful! says Senta. Not so says the Dutchman you are proven to be unfaithful had you claimed faithfulness on oath you would have suffered eternal damnation. A lot of women have gone down that way. You have had a lucky escape.

He jumps on to his boat and sails off to sea. I can prove I am faithful unto death shouts Senta. She jumps off a cliff and kills herself. The Dutchman's ship sinks instantly. The sun rises. The Dutchman and Senta hand in hand float heavenwards to sort out his release from clause 17B of the contract with superior powers.

MINUTES FROM START **LOOK OUT FOR**

0 The overture,*** full of salt and spray, is a splendid 0
concert piece. Mainly stormy, up to force 9, it has patches of calm when the redemption motto and the Sailors' Chorus from Act III break in.

Act I

A heavily skittish figure featuring the bassoons intro-
17: *Mit Gewitter und Sturm* duces the steersman's song to his absent girlfriend* 17
but his thoughts about her are not exciting enough to keep him awake. After the first stanza of agreeable tenor music he comes out with a sort of seaman's yodel which HOJOHOHOs around for some time. As he drops off we hear the approaching Dutchman's boat playing his motif on its foghorns.

The Dutchman is gloomy, and not without
23: *Die Frist ist um* reason.** 23

1. He talks to the sea (for which he has formed an intense dislike) for a while in recitatif and then launches into:
2. A vigorous account of his roving life which we have already heard instrumentally in the overture.

The sea swirls and washes about in the strings in a wonderfully pictorial fashion. This is quite the best bit of the Dutchman's rather long message about himself and his problems.

3. A quieter piece follows where he asks to be let off from eternal wandering. (But he must know it's no good.)

4. Then ranting again against fate: he looks forward to Judgement Day when it will surely be curtains for everyone. Look out for the very loud Last Trump – three heavy blows delivered by the brass. He ends noisily: an unhappy man.

The second half of this act is made up of a duet between Daland and the Dutchman:

1. This suddenly gets animated when the Dutchman offers all his treasure in exchange for a wife and a
43: *All' meinen Reichtum* good home.** Romance is in the air: we can't smell 43
the sea any longer, it's all roses and waltz time as the men gyrate with delight at the thought of (a) riches and (b) a fixed abode. This section ends with a neat little symphony.

2. It's still springtime but now we move on to
47: *Wohl Fremdling* more practical matters.* Pretty four-square phrases: 47
a deal is done: and there is metaphorically a very long handshake: everything most melodious, and wholly harmonious.

49: *Wenn aus der Qualen* 3. Still they go on:** what great luck, I'm rich 49
says Daland (but the Dutchman can't hear him). Hope for me at last says the Dutchman (and it doesn't matter whether Daland can hear him or not). The pair of them swing and sway together in rounded lyrical lines urged on by the strings and towards the end what sounds like a battalion of horns.

Action! The south wind gets up (so what wind was blowing the hell out of everything twenty minutes ago?). Daland decides to get moving to the steersman's skittish figures, now transformed into a strange
54: *Du siehst, das Glück* little circus dance* and we move into a sailors' choral 54
version of the steersman's song. Although they have only had a very short rest the crew are keen to get to their girlfriends. If it weren't Wagner one might say some of the progressions in the sailors' music were definitely ornery. The concluding symphony fades

away to a bit of the Spinning Chorus – to be continued in the next act.

Act II

The spinning wheels hum and buzz along in the strings: an oboe sings out a tune you can't forget although after its tenth repetition, you will probably
0: *Summ' und brumm'* want to. The girls take up the tune*** to its treadmill 0
accompaniment. There is an interruption by Mary. Then they sing it all over again. For some reason the girls seem to think that a good bout of spinning will hasten their lovers' return. Wagner does an immaculate job here – the spinning sound picture, the tune, the choral and orchestral writing all neat, precise and satisfactory. A winner in its own class.

9: *Johohohe!* Senta's ballad** is introduced by the Dutchman's 9
motto swinging about in the orchestra. She opens with a touch of the JOHOHOs like the sailors in Act I but soon settles into a conventional three-stanza ballad, each strophe organized into three parts:

1. Opening strain repeated four times telling the story of the Dutchman and his curse.

2. Sea music accompaniment as in the overture and the Dutchman's first big piece. Continuing the story but with the interesting exclamation HOOEY! popped in at the head of each of the three phrases.

3. A sort of holy calm with a simple tune (three blind mice, the third one with a hiccup: the Redemption motto) doubled in the woodwind. Hopes of redemption. At the end of stanza 2 the chorus whisper along with the end bars and in stanza 3 they take it over completely until – Senta bursts out in a wild free-ranging coda (quite a relief after the straitjacket of the ballad form) 'I'll do it myself' she cries 'I'll be his woman'. This stretches credibility a bit because she hasn't yet met him, but if you can accept that Satan would condemn the poor fellow to a wandering life for ever just for using a four-letter word in bad weather, then you can believe anything.

17: *Ach! Wie viel hab' ich* The girls' exit chorus.* Suddenly we have a scut- 17
tering scampering piece of theatre music that might have been lifted straight from an Offenbach opera. Bizarre.

After a lyrical duet in which Erik tells Senta at

some length that he loves her in an agreeable but
26: *Senta hass dir vertrau'n* rather ornery fashion we come to Erik's Dream.* 26
Spooky music: hushed tones: a stranger comes to take her away (Dutchman's motto: no doubt who it is): she went with him: she never came back (Redemption motto). This is more like the later Wagner we know and admire: not desperately exciting and with not much tune, but moving freely into new ways of writing continuous dramatic music without stop–starts, without recitatif, without set numbers. Senta finishes off the piece thoughtfully, with more Redemption.

As Daland introduces the Dutchman something
33: *Mögst du, mein Kind* happens in the strings* – a new kind of music with a 33
yearning sweet-water tune, quite different from the salt-and-spray stuff or anything else we have heard so far. It never gets into the main action but stays in the accompaniment surfacing from time to time as Daland sings his very four-square four-lines-at-a-time stanzas. He recommends Senta as a suitable marriage prospect.

Senta takes the Dutchman aboard, a big set-piece duet in three parts:

40: *Wie aus der Ferne* 1.*** Both in a dream. The Dutchman starts 40
slowly almost unaccompanied (This is the girl of my dreams) but when Senta comes in (This is the man of my dreams) things warm up considerably and as they sing together we have the first great love duet climax in Wagner. Very fine. (A whiff of the Redemption motto at the end.)

45: *Wirst du des Vaters Wahl* 2.** Now down to practicalities. Will you have 45
me? he asks. I always do what Dad tells me, she replies. Hope I can redeem him she thinks aloud (actually very loud). What an angel says he (Redemption motto) but you must be always faithful says he, if not (amidst a lot of the sea music) I'm off on the trail again. It will be my pleasure says she.

51: *Ein heil'ger Balsam* 3.** Together they exult: bliss: joyful union: the 51
curse is off. Another good climax.

The short trio that ends the act is made rather
55: *Hier meine Hand!* special by the conviction of Senta's promise to be
faithful sung in a high soprano line.** She gives her 55
fidelity bond.

Act III

Between the acts there is one of those musical transformation scenes at which Wagner was going to be frightfully good. As the musical mood changes so imperceptibly do the mottos. From the high emotion of the last trio to carousel on deck in about fourteen stealthily taken steps.

The sailors' chorus – the orchestra does it first so it
2: *Steuermann, lass' die Wacht!* is no surprise – is rousing.** There are in fact two 2
associated mottos around in here, the second a variation of the first sung by the girls. The scene ploughs on as the male and female choruses duet and marvel at the Dutchman's ghostly ship lying alongside. Daland's crew try to reassure themselves with a full repeat of the opening chorus.

11: *Yohohoeh!* A sort of choral contest* between the Dutchman's 11
ghostly crew and Daland's robust Norwegians. The ghosts win. Powerful stuff, mottos flying around, perhaps a little crude, but effective.

A mildish reproof for Senta from Erik in a low
17: *Willst jenes Tag's* voltage but agreeable tenor aria.* He reminds her he 17
used to risk his life climbing cliffs to get her flowers – and she said she loved him.

As the Dutchman gives orders to hoist sail we have
23: *Segel auf! Anker los!* an impassioned trio from three tortured people,* the 23
Dutchman (She broke her word: back to sea), Senta (You're wrong, I'm very reliable: stay!), Erik (Senta! That's an evil fellow). There is real urgency and bite in this stormy section which fades into something more ornery as we get nearer and nearer to the melodrama of the last scene, when the music finally becomes the sort of stuff used to support a D. W. Griffith silent movie, but a grand one, let's say *Intolerance*.

NOTES

The Flying Dutchman	Wagner's fourth opera
First night	Königliches Sächsiscles Hoftheater, Dresden, 2 January 1843
Reception	Mixed, which means pretty bad
Libretto	Wagner

Source Several: Sir Walter Scott, Captain Marryat, Fenimore Cooper, but mainly on a book of fictional memoirs by Hein

NEWS AND GOSSIP

In 1839 Wagner made a sea crossing to London which should have taken eight days but lasted three and a half weeks. Storms drove the boat – the *Thetis* – into a Norwegian fiord where Wagner was deeply impressed by the sounds of the crews' shouts echoing around the rocks. The experience he said, unreliably, led to the concept of the *Dutchman*, but there is no evidence that he started work on it until eighteen months later. He wrote the libretto (the 'poem') in Paris and because he was broke sold a prose version to the management of the Paris Opéra where an opera called *Le Vaisseau fantôme* was developed and put on by people of whom we now know little, care less, and which was a total flop. Wagner then completed his own version and sent it to Berlin. No takers there. Meanwhile, his *Rienzi* had been a big success and as a result he got the *Dutchman* staged in Dresden. He had dickered around with a Scottish setting (in which Daland was called Donald!) before settling for Norway and had written the opera as a continuous piece without act breaks, which must have posed an impossible problem for the technical staff. By the time it was ready to put on it was pretty well in its present shape, but after a rough first night it had only three performances before it was withdrawn. The *Dutchman* then lay around for a decade or so until Wagner had made his name with *Tannhäuser* and *Lohengrin*, when it was put on in Zurich. Wagner kept tinkering with the score and a later version reached London and America in the 1870s and spread to all those operatic parts of the world where Wagner was OK. The *Dutchman* came to be reckoned as a true Wagner opera, which it probably isn't (*Rienzi*, of course, was thought to be a Wagner opera written before Wagnerization set in). The set pieces have a concert life equal to any in Wagner partly because they are not 'bleeding chunks' but self-contained pieces of the sort that well-balanced operas had offered to the concert hall ever since opera began. The *Dutchman* is now an occasional piece in the rep of any major opera house and is enjoying a healthy life.

COMMENT

With the *Dutchman* we find Wagner moving down the road towards a new kind of opera, but he hasn't got far. What is best about the *Dutchman* is the stand-alone traditional numbers – the overture, the Spinning Chorus, Senta's Ballad, Erik's Dream. There are stop–start items with quite a lot of old-fashioned recitatif around them. Then we have the sailors' choruses the last act with quite a lot of dramatic ding-dong and big free solos for the Dutchman and Daland – all of which are fine. But to present the old thing as a continuous music drama, even with the act breaks rubbed out and musical links played through the scene changes, is a bit of a con. We don't find Wagner's mesmeric power in the *Dutchman* as we do in the *Ring*. We don't get sucked in. No spell lies across the whole opera, and although the good bits are very good, the gear changes are obvious and jolt us from one mood to another almost like a roll on the drums between music hall acts.

The story is strong in its central idea of the Dutchman condemned to sail the seas for ever in his phantom ship until redeemed, but weak in detail, not to say ludicrous. Why should Satan, presumably in favour of sin and bad behaviour, take exception to blasphemy? Anyone who blasphemed, one would have thought, was batting on his side. And if all blaspheming sailors were treated equally the seas of the world would be teeming with nautical peripatetics. Senta's fixation on the man in the picture is incredible but permissible under the normal operatic ground rules. But for the Dutchman to shy off her like a terrified mustang because she had a teenage cuddle and kiss with the boy scout Erik seems strange, also his requirement that faithfulness should be retrospective into a time before any two parties meet seems against reason and certainly against common law, otherwise nearly everyone would enter the state of marriage with grounds for divorce already established. Finally, the heavenly assumption of the Dutchman and Senta is risible because the opera is simply not grand enough to carry this sort of supernatural happening – *Götterdämmerung* perhaps, but not this simpler saga of seafaring folk.

But when all is said and done, the *Dutchman* has a top-class overture and patches of splendid music where Wagner demonstrates that he can not only write a good tune but make it work for him dramatically in a way no one else knew how. An alpha.

La Forza del Destino (The Force of Destiny)

Spanish melodrama

Verdi

The one where a marquis is killed by an exploding pistol and his daughter in monk's costume finds her lover has murdered her brother just outside the front door of her cave.

CAST

Marchese de Calatrava, Spanish Grandee	Bass
Leonora, his daughter	Soprano
Don Carlo, his son	Baritone
Don Alvaro, a young Peruvian aristo	Tenor
Curra, Leonora's maid	Mezzo
Preziosilla, a gypsy camp follower	Mezzo
Padre Guardiano, Father Superior	Bass
Fra Melitone, comic monk	Baritone
Trabuco, pedlar	Tenor
A mayor, a surgeon	

4 acts, 2 intervals: running time 2 hrs 45 mins

STORY

Act I A bedroom suitable for a marquis's daughter

We are in eighteenth-century (or thereabouts) Spain: moving in high social circles. Marquis Calatrava fusses around his daughter Leonora's bedroom shutting windows etc. Leonora is upset: she weeps and hugs Daddy who says there, there, goodnight: he goes off to bed. The maid Curra briskly opens the window, says come on, stop mooning get ready for your elopement (due any minute). Horses' hooves are heard: eager eloper Alvaro (incognito Peruvian prince) swings over the balcony. Leonora says I can't do it. Alvaro says rubbish: she says postpone it for 24 hours I must see Daddy again. Alvaro says Now: Leonora says Well, OK. Footsteps on the stairs. Panic.

The Marquis enters with sword drawn (servants at his back): he rages: makes insulting remarks: he orders the servants to arrest Alvaro. Alvaro totes a gun: he says Leonora is innocent I am guilty – I am willing to sacrifice my life to be murdered by the Marquis not by servants. Go ahead: he chucks his gun at the Marquis: the gun hits floor: spontaneous combustion: the shot kills the Marquis (million to one?): the dying Marquis makes a terrible curse on both parties. He expires.

Act II Sc 1 A room in an inn designated 'kitchen' but appears to be of general resort

A chorus of taxi drivers and riff-raff waiting for dinner also the town's mayor sing a hostelry-type chorus: Carlo disguised as a student obliges with grace before meat. His sister Leonora disguised as a boy looks in: she sees vengeful brother: she hides.

Preziosilla, a gypsy girl, sings an idiot song about how war is beautiful: she tells Carlo's fortune, says you are no student: your future outlook is poor. Some pilgrims (offstagers) pass singing operatically. Leonora peeps out – escape is not possible. The pilgrims' chorus induces prayer throughout the inn.

Carlo quizzes taxi driver/pedlar Trabuco about the nature of his recent passenger (he suspects it was possibly Leonora): the mayor says who the hell are you anyway? I am Pereda says Carlo I have a doctorate from Harvard, I am a graduate of Oxford and Florence (all lies of course): an evil man attempted the seduction of my best friend's sister: he killed my friend's father: his sister died in the mêlée: the seducer is on the run. I have hunted the seducer with my friend: the seducer escaped to New York. (Leonora overhears all.) Bedtime says the mayor: all disperse.

Act II Sc 2 A monastery set in rocky landscape: church centre

Leonora has escaped from the pub unrecognized and is upset to learn Alvaro is solus in New York. She prays: monks (offstagers) are heard chanting: Leonora decides to seek sanctuary. The admissions clerk Melitone gives her a hard time: he fetches the Father Superior: Leonora (still in male disguise) says she is female. O Lord! says F.S. Did you get Father Cleto's letter with my C.V.? asks she. O Lord again! says F.S. So you are Leonora di Vargas. Any chance of accommodation here? she asks: a simple hermit's cave will suffice. I will dedicate my life to God. This is not a mixed community says F.S. but I will stretch a point so OK.

He gives her a monk's costume and tells her she can inhabit the vacant hermit's cave. Leonora takes communion as the monks troop into the church now open to view: F.S. tells the monks the hermit's cave is off limits but absolutely: anyone messing around there is subject to a terrible curse, got it? Got it they reply. (All accompanied by much prayer.)

Act III Sc 1 A forest near Velletri, Italy: night

We are at war: Spain and Italy v. Germany. Offstagers play cards noisily. Alvaro (for it is he), Captain of the Spanish household cavalry, is very low: he talks to himself: he recalls his royal Peruvian parents dethroned: now with no Leonora he seeks death etc.

His gloomy thoughts are interrupted by a cardroom scuffle offstage: he goes off and breaks it up: he returns with grateful Carlo (for it is he) who says you just saved my life brave friend. Why such mayhem? asks Alvaro. They suspected me of holding five aces says Carlo. Who are you? asks Alvaro: Felix the Don says Carlo who are you? Fred of Herreros says Alvaro (both lying of course): they swear eternal friendship.

Act III Sc 2 A room in a house in Velletri commandeered by Spanish officers (temporarily a field dressing station)

Medical officer (surgeon), orderlies etc. observe the battle. Herreros (Alvaro) is exceedingly brave: he is wounded: the battle ebbs and flows: each side scores: the result at full time is Spain/Italy 1 – Germany 0: Huzza! Alvaro (Herreros) enters stretcherborne: the M.O. says it's touch and go. Carlo (Felix) says he will recommend Herreros for the Calatravian V.C. Alvaro (Herreros) winces at the mention of Calatrava (Leonora's family name – remember?). Alvaro entrusts a key plus his briefcase to Carlo: will Carlo destroy his secret papers if Alvaro expires? Carlo agrees: Alvaro exits on stretcher.

Carlo disgracefully opens the briefcase: then he honourably decides not to open the papers but a photo of Leonora drops out. O god, so it's him says Carlo. The surgeon reports Alvaro will pull through. Good thinks Carlo: when he's well enough I'll kill him.

Act III Sc 3 The base camp of the Italo-Hispanic army: NAAFI stalls etc. all closed down: night

The dawn patrol passes through. Alvaro and Carlo come on: they recognize each other: Carlo asks Are you passed fit for active service? A1 says Alvaro. OK says Carlo I challenge you to a duel. You bastard! says Alvaro, you opened my papers: not so, says Carlo, that tell-tale photo fell out. I won't fight says Alvaro: her father's death was a shooting accident and Leonora was still a virgin then but now alas she's dead. Not so says Carlo Leonora lives but not for long. I will make it my business to kill her too. Come on says Alvaro, let me marry Leonora: my family is socially equal to yours though slightly coloured. Nothing doing you dago says Carlo: she must die. I'll kill you first says Alvaro. Swords are drawn, the duel commences: the patrol returns: interposes: the duel is stopped. Carlo exits and Alvaro decides to enter holy orders and seek seclusion.

A divertissement. Soldiers sing a soldierly chorus. Preziosilla (again) is touting her fortune-telling business. NAAFI personnel dispense booze: customers drink toasts to Felix and Fred (little do they know): Trabuco (again) is peddling like mad: next starving peasants come on also a platoon of tearful young soldiers (lack of moral fibre): the cowardly soldiers are rallied by gung-ho Preziosilla: enter Melitone the monk (what next?) preaching fire and brimstone. A final idiot song of the glory of war is sung by Preziosilla plus chorus: now all are universally eager to get at the Hun.

Act IV Sc 1 Interior of monastery seen in Act II

Melitone is doling out stew: he is really mean to a chorus of persistent beggars: the beggars say Father Raffaele is nice, you are nasty. The Father Superior says tone it down there Melitone: play it Raffaele's way. Raffaele? says Melitone, he's potty: probably the devil in disguise. Not so says F.S. but perhaps he's had a nervous breakdown. (Raffaele is the ecclesiastical alias of Alvaro of course.)

Carlo arrives seeking Raffaele: he is offered two Raffaeles and selects the right one. Confrontation: Carlo makes racist remarks and says let's duel: Alvaro is not keen, he begs, pleads, kneels, etc. Carlo gives Alvaro a straight left to the jaw: Alvaro stung at last seizes his sword and both exit. They duel offstage.

Act IV Sc 2 Leonora's cave

Leonora, still pining for Alvaro, goes to collect her daily ration from a rock: she hears the duel offstage: she retires to her cave. Alvaro the victor knocks on the cave door: he asks for last rites for his dying opponent: Leonora says it's not possible: you must says Alvaro: Leonora exits cave and sees Alvaro: recognition! Cripes! Don't touch me: I have bloody hands says he: Whose blood? she asks: Carlo's he says. O God, my brother, cries Leonora: she runs offstage: she screams as the dying Carlo knifes her: she returns, also dying, with the Father Superior. She expires to await Alvaro in heaven.

MINUTES FROM START

Act I

LOOK OUT FOR

0 The very good overture:* opens with the Destiny motif (we will hear a lot of it: four hammer blows followed by a Beethovenish bit of angst): this introduces other main themes. o

This act is slow to start but livens up with the ar-
14: *Ah, per sempre* rival of Alvaro* and his exchanges with Leonora (to 14
elope or not to elope) finishing with a brisk elopement
18: *Son tua* duet* (She: I will fly with you after all, He: I love you 18
hurry up). After that, dramatic encounter music as Father comes on, is shot, dies etc.

Act II Sc 1

After Preziosilla's drumbeat song (pretty ordinary)
7: *Padre Eterno* we have the first great music of the opera:** off- 7
stagers (pilgrims this time) crescendo towards us: the motley crew in the inn kneel and pray and Leonora sings a clear and touching private prayer above the choral mass.

17: *Holà! Holà! È l'ora* Quite a jolly finale* to the inn scene as everyone 17
wishes each other goodnight in so noisy a fashion as to make sleep impossible.

Act II Sc 2

19: *Sono giunta!* We hear Leonora's opening conversation with God* 19
to the accompaniment of the Destiny motif (in various forms) then as she addresses her remarks to the
21: *Madre, pietosa* Virgin she sails into her own lovely theme*** (Leon- 21
ora's Prayer) and continues whilst offstagers (monks) give her backing in the form of the Venite. Very fine.

27: *Infelice, delusa* The long duet** in which Leonora applies for and 27
is granted admission to the monastery: two high points – the end of her first application (sinuous duetting with the Father Superior) and the tailpiece in march time. Pretty joyful: she has been admitted and the Father has given her his blessing (and her monk's costume).

47: *Maledizione!* The Curse chorus:* the monks take up (with sur- 47
prising enthusiasm) the idea of a terrible curse falling on anyone who visits Leonora's cave. A nice little adieu from Leonora (choral accompaniment) ends the act.

Act III Sc 1

Alvaro gloomily reflects life is hell and swings into an
7: *O tu che* address to Leonora amongst the angels:* a bit of a 7
stop–start affair but with a fine lyrical burst at the finish.

Act III Sc 2

17: *Solenne in quest'ora* The sombre duet** in which Alvaro (wrongly) thinks 17
he is going to die and gives deathbed instructions to

Carlo. Grave and stately.

Two good solos from Carlo: the first a reflective
23: *Urna fatale* unshowy lyrical piece* as he overcomes his disgrace- 18
ful impulse to open the secret papers: the second a
27: *È salvo* paean of joy** on hearing that Alvaro will live (so that 19
he can kill him).

Act III Sc 3

37: *Non io, fu il destino* Again a good Alvaro/Carlo duet:** Alvaro tells Carlo 37
in sweet persuasive tones he didn't do nothing wrong: discovers Leonora is still alive (big shout of joy), goes into the persuasive bit again: Fool, says Carlo, in a Rossinian counter rhythm, I'll kill her. So to the climax: both swearing death and destruction.

The very long divertissement which ends this act is slightly enlivened by two patches of good stuff: a
42: *A buon mercato* light dancing tune* (a touch of the Offenbachs) for 42
the joshing of Trabuco by the soldiers and again when the NAAFI staff comfort the whingeing weeping recruits, and Preziosilla's second solo which has an
46: *Che vergogna* agreeable tune.* For the rest it is ornery, and the last 46
rataplan quite embarrassing. Something between *William Tell* and *White Horse Inn*.

Act IV Sc 1

The opening scene (beggars at the gates) begins with socially acceptable solemnity but then becomes a knockabout argument between Melitone and the
4: *Il resto* chorus: a lively buffa aria for Melitone:* faster ex- 4
changes, still faster and a racing finish.

The final encounter between Alvaro and Carlo:
15: *Le minaccie* Alvaro starts the duet** with the Pity motif (one of 15
the three great tunes of the opera) and when his appeal fails there is high drama including the face-slap and the rush offstage to get a-duelling. Vintage Verdi.

Act IV Sc 2

Leonora, assisted by the Destiny motif, finds her fate
20: *Pace, pace* to be really awful:** she still loves Alvaro: would like 20
to join the angels (anticipatory harp accompaniment). One of the pure, soaring celestial arias and a fine one.

28: *Non imprecare* Leonora's departure. The final trio** (Alvaro: I 28
am redeemed, Leonora: I await you in heaven, Father Superior: Pious exhortations). Calm, reflective, a good death (harps now appropriate).

NOTES

La Forza del Destino	Verdi's twenty-fourth opera
First night	Imperial Theatre, St Petersburg, 10 November 1862
Reception	Some report enthusiasm, others 'a moderate success'. See below
Libretto	Piave
Source	A play by the Duke of Riva, also one scene pinched from Schiller

NEWS AND GOSSIP

After *Simon Boccanegra* Verdi said he was giving up composing and taking up farming. He settled on his country estate and no doubt farmed in a gentlemanly fashion, though one can't see him actually getting his boots dirty nor suffering much from blisters. No one knows why this happened. After three years of this country life he got a letter inviting him to do an opera for the Imperial Theatre in Leningrad. We don't know if a figure was mentioned, but maybe it was an offer the money-conscious Verdi couldn't refuse. He dickered about a bit with Victor Hugo's *Ruy Blas* but the thought of a valet becoming a royal was a bit rich for the Imperial censors. So he picked up this wild romance, *La Fuerza del Sino*, by a Spanish nobleman (probably Piave's idea) and the old firm set to work on *Forza*. It was ready by the end of 1861 and the Verdis made the long trip to St Petersburg, only to be told that the Leonora was ill and the show would be put off until the next season. (No substitute? No earlier date? Something funny about this.) So back again to St Petersburg nine months later, and *Forza* was launched at last. Some accounts say 'a moderate success' but the music scribe of the St Petersburg main broadsheet reported '. . . wild cheering . . . prolonged applause . . . to comply with insistent demands the celebrated composer was dragged on stage on several occasions . . .'. Hit or no hit, Verdi didn't like it much. The structure bothered him (with good reason) and he thought the original ending was a bit off. It was in fact even more bizarre than the current version: after Leonora's death Alvaro confessed he was a messenger from hell and yelled out frightful things like Let mankind perish! Annihilation for all! and then jumped over a precipice. Very odd. So Verdi reworked the old thing with a new librettist, Ghislanzani (Piave had been put out of action by a stroke), made a number of major changes to the score and the new *Forza* was premiered at La Scala, Milan, in February 1869. This time everyone agreed it was a big success. *Forza* was played quite a lot in the next thirty years when the Gothic taste was still quite acceptable, but in this century its popularity fell away, though today it still pops up surprisingly often. Surprisingly when you consider what the other fifteen Verdi operas listed in this book have to offer.

COMMENT

Forza is much inferior to *Boccanegra*, which came before it, and *Carlos*, which came after: it is hard to decide whether Verdi was just out of practice, wasn't really trying or had temporarily lost his marbles, at least in the matter of opera construction. The narrative itself is both scanty and bizarre. Bizarre elements: two officers swearing eternal friendship on the battlefield, both incognito, both principals in a family feud; a young woman admitted to a monastery; a man slain outside her cave who turns out to be her brother, etc. Because so brief, the story is padded out with three lengthy roustabout scenes (and other minor bits of padding) that do nothing to advance the plot, and most surprisingly two of them are placed head to tail (end of Act III, beginning of Act IV). Thus there is no forward movement of the plot whatsoever for nearly forty minutes. The goings-on in the soldiers' camp include a tarantella, a rataplan and some heavy attempts at comedy (never Verdi's forte). The sentiments are distressingly banal and Verdi's class II ballet music is light, harmless and pointless. But the opera has its great moments, including three of the most memorable tunes Verdi wrote – but too far apart for comfort. The first act is thin, the second, after the roistering in the inn, is held together by Leonora's breathtakingly beautiful prayer and her long duet with the Father Superior, Act III has the great duets between Alvaro and Carlo, Act IV has another good duet, Alvaro/Carlo, and the final very effective trio, but this is not a lot in an opera which runs for nearly two and three-quarter hours. Great moments, but patchy. Beta.

Freischütz (Der Freischütz)

Horror opera

Weber

The one where our hero seeks the help of the powers of evil to ensure that he shoots straight with the result that he nearly kills his bride-to-be.

CAST

Kuno, the head forester	Bass
Agathe, his daughter	Soprano
Ännchen, her cousin	Mezzo
Max, forester Grade II	Tenor
Kaspar, also forester Grade II	Bass
Kilian, a rich farmer	Baritone
Ottokar, the Prince who owns the forest	Baritone
A Hermit	Bass
One **Black Huntsman (Samiel)**, four **Bridesmaids**	

3 acts: running time 2 hrs 10 mins

STORY

Act I In front of an inn in a forest

[*Sing*] We are in Bohemia, land of forests gamekeepers and sharpshooters, in the commonest of opera times which is somewhere in the seventeenth century and it is all gas and gaiters outside the village pub. Kilian (a character who disappears immediately) has won a shooting contest and the nasty yokels jeer at forester Max who has had an off-day. [*Spiel*] More like an off-month for his boss Kuno is worried that on current form he won't win the sharpshooter cup next day which would (a) ensure that he would succeed him as head forester (b) permit him to marry Agathe, Kuno's daughter. That's a lot to be riding on a single shot say the peasants: how come this contest was set up anyway?

The Prince was out hunting one day says Kuno and he saw a poacher who had been chained to a stag [*Sing* and *Spiel*] as a punishment and as a great animal lover he offered a prize for anyone who could shoot the man without hurting the stag [you got it wrong way round: Ed.] and someone did it and he set up this annual shootfest as a result. But the rumour got around that this guy had used Fryshot to make sure he hit the mark.

What's Fryshot? ask the peasants. It is shot fried in black magic with a little cinnamon says Kuno as a result of which the first six bullets in each batch are guided by radar and are guaranteed to hit the mark but the seventh is on a different frequency and under the control of that frightful chap Samiel alias the Black Hunter who is now known to be enemy agent 247. He can make the seventh go wherever he likes. That's how they got President Kennedy. Good Lord say the peasants. Fancy that. The evil Kaspar rolls his eyes meaningfully.

[*Sing*] I feel very low says Max missing things all the time. Maybe I have the evil eye of 247 on me or something. Be a man Max! Brace up! says Kuno shaking him by the hand. Oho! oho! Fryshot! Fryshot! says Kaspar darkly and, at this point in the plot, incomprehensibly.

The peasants merrymake, waltzing for a while. They all go into the pub leaving Max to whinge on alone. As he does this 247 the Black Hunter is seen in the bushes by us but not by Max. [*Spiel*] Kaspar comes on. Have a drink old boy he says aloud and behind his hand he says Now's the time Samiel 247. [Kaspar wants to escape from Samiel's spell by substituting Max for himself: Ed.] Here's to Agathe who stood me up to go with you he says to Max. [*Sing*] Kaspar sings a coarse drinking song.

[*Spiel*] Kaspar you stink says Max. How would you like it if I could guarantee you hit the mark tomorrow? asks Kaspar. Lemme show you take my gun and shoot at that eagle. Can't see it says Max. Look there! says Kaspar. Out of range says Max. Have a try says Kaspar. BONK! The eagle drops from the flies. Holy cow! says Max. Was that No. 5 or No. 4 shot? Fryshot says Kaspar. Fryshot? says Max. Can you get me some? Meet me in the Wolf's Glen at midnight says Kaspar. Max exits. [*Sing*] Now I've got Max where I want him sings Kaspar.

Act II Sc 1 Inside Kuno's house

[*Sing*] Ännchen is putting back a picture that fell on the third stroke of seven o'clock precisely. She sings a scatty song to let us know she is a skittish person whereas Agathe is a *femme sérieuse* who is getting anxious because Max has not called in yet. [*Spiel*] Also we hear that when Agathe went to see the Hermit he gave her roses and also a warning of some dire event about to take place. Ännchen goes and Agathe has a long brood [*Sing*] but whose step is that she hears? Why Max's of course so it's cheer up time.

[*Spiel*] Agathe he says I'm back in form. I got a high eagle down by the pub. He throws his hat down and smashes the lamp. My my says Ännchen who has come back now you smash the lamp and at the third stroke of seven o'clock precisely the picture fell down (Max thinks – third stroke precisely . . . that's when I shot the eagle. Or was it the fourth stroke?).

I got to be off again says Max. Why? you're just back say the girls. Shot a stag a sixteen-footer earlier today [impossibly large and the whole thing a lie of course: Ed.]. Where? they ask. The Wolf's Glen he says. [*Sing*] O holy mother of God says Agathe don't go there! The whole place is radioactive with evil spirits and the HQ of the Black Hunter 247. A man has to do what a man has to do says Max. Exits.

Act II Sc 2 The Wolf's Glen

[*Sing*] It's All-Spooks Benefit Night. The spooks are singing spooky songs on spooky topics such as blood on spiders' webs, moonmilk and a bride being shot [Agathe: Ed.]. Kaspar is doing his nut arranging human skulls, transistors, eagles' wings, oscillograph tubes etc. in a circle. OK 247 he shouts [*Sing*] Samiel! I'm ready. What is it tonight? asks Samiel 247 invisibly. Don't want to give up my soul tonight: can I have an extension? asks Kaspar. No says Samiel 247. Not even if I give you a substitute human sacrifice? asks Kaspar. What does he want? asks Samiel 247. Fryshot says Kaspar. Six for him the seventh for me? asks Samiel 247. Six for him and one for you says Kaspar. You could use it to shoot his bride. That would be an interesting way to use No. 7. Is it a deal? Lemme see him first says Samiel 247. Oh come on Sammy it's a nice deal says Kaspar. You'll get his soul as your property, shoot his bride dead and all that just for three-year extension for me. It's a doddle. Lemme think says Samiel 247.

A fire springs up in the middle of the magic circle. The spooks howl wail go bump and generally hype things up. Max looks down from over a flat on stage left. [*Sing*] It's a big drop he says and it's thundering and the spooks are very numerous. Well done mate says Kaspar. Come on down. [*Sing* and *Spiel*] Just a moment says Max I am having a problem with a vision of my dead mother in her coffin. Come on! shouts Kaspar. Oh Lord it's Agathe now with a beard and no legs says Max. Jump man! shouts Kaspar. I'm not chicken says Max. He jumps. [*Spiel*] Let's get frying says Max. OK says Kaspar here's the frypan.

[*Melodrame* – speech over music] First you put in the bat's blood and cinnamon with a bouquet garni (Hey Samiel 247 see I do it right he says behind his hand) then the black lead [he goes on, favouring the Constance Spry recipe: Ed.]. After three-and-a-half minutes of full frontal frying he shouts: They're Ready! At this point all sorts of spooky things happen to the lighting for this scene is the Lighting Director's night out too. Amidst phosphorescent flashes Kaspar shouts
ONE OUT!

A grunt from the orchestra
TWO!

A bigger grunt!
THREE!
A short intermezzo
And so on to a stupendous climax on SEVEN!!! when Kaspar is thrown to the ground by an unseen chorus and literally all hell breaks out, thunder, lightning, red puffs of smoke, Chinese crackers, gales of wind, multiple spookies right left and centre.

Samiel! Samiel 247! calls Max.

Here I am says Samiel appearing as the Black Hunter.

Act III Sc 1 In the forest

[*Spiel*] Nice day after the storm says a huntsman. I hear there were terrible goings-on in the Wolf's Glen again last night says a gamekeeper. Old Samiel 247 at it again says a forester. Max comes on. Good luck with the trial shot says an earth-stopper. Have you got any of the Fryshots left? Max asks of Kaspar. I took three and left you four says Kaspar. What have you done with yours? asks Kaspar. That prince made me shoot off three says Max. All bulls-eyes. I only got one Fryshot left. Lend me a couple like a good chap. Not on your life says Kaspar. Use your last for the trial shot. (Thinks: Ho Ho Ho.) Max exits. Kaspar blows off his remaining Fryshots. OK on your marks shouts a military policeman.

Act III Sc 2 Agathe's room

[*Sing*] Agathe sings a sad song. [*Spiel*] You've been crying says Ännchen to Agathe. I had this scary dream says Agathe. I was a white dove and Max shot me. Pshaw! says Ännchen. Dreams! [*Sing*] I had a cousin who dreamt a man jumped on to her back and she shot him dead with her bedside pistol only to wake up and find that she had shot the spaniel. Here come the bridesmaids! The bridesmaids curtsey smile coyly and sing a bridesmaids' song. [*Spiel*] Agathe opens a gift box from Harrods. It has a wreath inside! Gloom and doom until the unquenchable Ännchen chucks it away and makes a garland from the Hermit's roses instead. The bridesmaids sing again.

Act III Sc 3 A tented fairground

[*Sing*] A posse of huntsmen do their party trick learned from the Swingle Singers to make a chorus sound as if it were all done by horns. [*Spiel*] Prince Ottokar says OK folks let's start. Where's the bride? With due respect your Principality says Kuno I suggest shoot first welcome the bride second. Max tends to get the shakes when she is around. Meanwhile

Kaspar climbs a tree. OK says Ottokar. See that white dove there Max? Shoot! Don't shoot! cries Agathe coming out from the tree where the dove is perched. [But surely a long way below? Ed.] The dove flies past Kaspar's tree. Max swings through the line. He shoots. Both Kaspar and Agathe drop. Is it a right and a left? No: the Hermit appears from nowhere and assists Agathe to centre stage.

[*Sing*] O Gawd cry the crowd he's shot the bride. Not so says Kuno she's alive but he certainly winged this one (Kaspar). It must be that holy hermit who fouled things up groans Kaspar. He saved her and put the bullet into me. I'm OK says Agathe. Just a passing fit of the vapours.

Samiel 247 appears behind the gasping Kaspar visible to us and to him but not to anyone else. So you've come to get me Sammy says Kaspar. A curse on all hermits. Ah well it's a fair cop. He dies in considerable agony. He was a bad lot anyway says Kuno. Chuck his body into the Wolf's Glen.

Now Max just tell us what the hell has been going on. Well boss you see it was this way says Max: Kaspar led me on. We fried magic bullets together. I got four and the first three worked a treat but the fourth went off on an exponential curve. You're fired says Prince Ottokar. You're out. You're finished. You're banished. OK says Max that's a fair verdict.

Steady Prince says Kuno this is a good man here. Handy with an axe and diligent. Don't take him away from me Prince says Agathe. He was a good guy really he was Prince say the foresters. Yes, a good guy Prince echo the peasants. Have some mercy. No! says the prince. No! my last word.

Is this really the right sentence? asks the Hermit moving steadily downstage. O Reverend Sir please forgive me says the Prince. You know best of course. God knows best. Anything you decide will be all right with me Sir. We can all make a mistake says the Hermit and isn't it a bit silly that the happiness of two persons should depend on a single shot? Supposing he had hiccups? Mind you he has behaved in a horrible unholy way but how about giving him a conditional discharge and binding him over on good behaviour for one year, eh Prince?

A very good suggestion says the Prince. An excellent suggestion. Thank you sir. That's my decision Max.

I'll be of unblemished character from now on says Max. O goody says Agathe. Praise God says everyone else. Yes that's right says the Hermit God done it all really. So it's him you should thank. (They do. But you may be sure old Samiel 247 is still lurking there in the Glen waiting for the next gook coming around looking for Fryshot.)

MINUTES FROM START

LOOK OUT FOR

Act I

0 The overture* starts slow and gloomy but soon we 0
move into the light with a bout of cheerful horns. Then some Beethovenish minor stuff for quite a while (we will hear it again later in the opera) and into the happy major-key tune which we will welcome back in Agathe's aria in Act II. So into a pretty athletic development and finally back to a reprise of the big tune with decorative pendants.

Bang! Bang! Sharpshots ring out as we hear hunting noises and the first very jolly chorus gets under way, followed by a truly rural stage-band march. And
12: *Schau der Herr mich an als König!* so into the sequence of Kilian and chorus** teasing 12
Max (hee-hee-hee-hee).

The foresters' trio. This intriguing number runs through a number of changes of mood:

18: *Oh, diese Sonne!* 1. Max is very low.* Kuno says your fate lies in 18
your rifle barrel. The evil Kaspar urges Max to take a chance. Each sings in character.

2. The chorus who have been umming and awing
20: *O lass Hoffnung* in the background break into a sort of hymn* of hope 20
that Max will do well. Max swings out saying he must be in the power of some evil force. Kaspar says it's a good idea to be in league with the devil. Max fears he will lose Agathe. All very tuneful but undoubtedly fraught.

It all stops. Kuno grasps Max by the hand and tells him (in recitatif) to trust in God. There is a loud and
23: *Das wild in Fluren* thumping chorus* with a vocal imitation of hunting 23
horns while real horns are hunting away like anything. The whole scene has a vaguely ritualistic air.

25 The Tanz.** A very Tyrolean waltz with a rousing 25
tune and lots of yeast. It dies away.

The tormented Max has two arias amidst bouts of
27: *Durch die Wälder* heavy recitatif. The first a Simple Simon of a tune* 27
recalls happy days now gone. The second in two parts is serious: first wistful, Agathe – she is waiting for
31: *Doch mich umgarnen* him, and then into a savage allegro** (the Beethoven- 31
ish stuff first heard in the overture). Fate is against him.

34: *Hier im ird'-schen Jammertal* Kaspar's drinking song.* Three verses: crude and 34
rather nasty, but then it's meant to be. Immensely

heavy pulse that beats the hell out of the orchestra. Piccolos to the fore.

Kaspar gloats over poor Max who will become Samiel 247's victim in place of him. A splendid force-

38: *Schweig, schweig* ful aria:* four-square, clear-cut and melodious. 38

Act II Sc 1

0: *Schelm, halt fest!* The duet* between Agathe and Ännchen starts do- 0
mestically but as it swims along with its neat and tuneful accompaniment it gets just a little involved in more serious matters such as the palpitations in Agathe's breast caused by anxiety over Max. It's easy-going and easy on the ear. Ännchen's pert and pi-

5: *Kommt ein schlanker Bursch* quant aria about love and marriage,** introduced and 5
ornamented by an oboe, is buoyed up by a bassoon and is truly rurally rustic. A charmer.

10: *Wie nahte mir der Schlummer* Agathe's big number.*** 10

1. She can't go to sleep. A clarinet introduces a slow sweet air over a closely chorded string backing. It is a lovely night outside. Look out especially for the glorious way she reaches up to and dwells on the word 'schöne'. The slow melody continues.

2. A storm is brewing over the distant mountains. Varied recitatif. Let's pray the angels will look after us in storms. Second verse of the sweet air.

14: *Alles pflegt schon* 3. She listens for Max's arrival. Arioso,** a little 14
disturbed. She sees him! A cry of delight. The music gets faster.

15: *All meine Pulse schlagen* 4. And into the fast final part of the aria,*** in 15
which we get the happy tune first heard in the overture.

20: *Wie? Was? Entsetzen!* The farewell trio.** 20

Max tells the girls it's a quick turn-around: he's off to the Wolf's Glen. Agathe is shocked. Ännchen sounds unimpressed and sings a little song of innocence. So into the debate. Max says he must go. Agathe begs him to stay, Ännchen too. He is tempting fate. This part of the trio again sounds Beethovenish in its force and vigour. Never a dull moment and Weber's inventiveness takes the ear by surprise over and over again. We reach a full stop with slow and soft farewells all round. Followed by loud and fast farewells. Then we start up again with a slow sad envoi and a final fast burst of Beware and Be careful.

Seven minutes of Weber at his best.

Act II Sc 2

27: *Milch des Mondes* One of opera's truly spooky scenes.* The ghostly 27
chorus intone a ghostly chant whilst frenzied voices add hair-raising cries above it. Very frightening.

The dialogue between Kaspar and the invisible
29: *Samiel! Samiel!* Samiel.* Mainly melodrame (words spoken over 29
music). Still very spooky: Samiel's voice echoes nastily around the glen. It thunders. The strings run little frissons of fright around the dialogue.

From the time Max appears the main burden of the spookerie is taken over by the stage-effects department but throughout all the astonishing happenings the music gives high-voltage atmospheric support, mickey-mousing where appropriate, thundering, shushing, susurrating in the most sensational fashion. The climax comes in the casting of the bullets where the orchestra provides a series of increasingly tense
39: *Eins!* intermezzos*** between the counting out of each 39
bullet. Between the fifth and sixth bullets extra forces are called in and we have a chorus to swell the mighty climax. Between bullets 6 and 7 we have Beethoven (from the overture) as well. A knockout. Weber with his modest classical orchestra gets better effects than do some of the wilder composers today with 120 players including seven on percussion.

Act III Sc 1

0 In the Interlude** we have a prince amongst operatic 0
hunting tunes, of which there are dozens all with horns pumping away in hunting thirds and hunting fifths. But there is even better still to come.

Act III Sc 2

A solo cello leads sweetly into Agathe's serene cava-
4: *Und ob die Wolke* tina to greet her wedding morning.*** Her song has 4
something of the purity of the Countess's two arias in *Figaro*. The melodic line is fresh and clear with a touch of pathos lurking behind it because we must all by now think she is going to be shot.

Ännchen does her best to cheer Agathe up.

1. A flourish on a solo viola introduces an agree-
11: *Einst träumte* able romanza* with the ridiculous story about the 11
ghost dog Nero. Lots of girlish charm and some mock heroics from the orchestra and a nice turn into the

major key at the end.

2. Tender recitatif with some fancy stuff from the viola again, pleading phrases from the tearful Agathe.
14: *Trübe Augen* A carefree melody comes tumbling out.** Very girl- 14
ish, with the solo viola still doing tremendous business in the gaps in the vocal line. A little cabaletta, or end piece, and a touch of coloratura to finish with. A great day for the leader of the viola section.

Concerted folksy stuff for four solo bridesmaids
17: *Wir winden dir den Jungfern-kranz* and a chorus* which has some small mite of rustic 17
charm. It comes back again (and again) amidst the dialogue that follows and by then its sixth appearance has quite definitely worn out its welcome.

Act III Sc 3

22: *Was gleicht wohl auf Erden* The huntsmen and their horns again.*** But now it 22
is the full works. Chorus and horns belting it out with a scoopy middle section over a la-la-la bass. Terrific. These Bohemians are definitely in favour of field sports.

The finale, a mighty eventful one and started by gunfire.

26: *Schaut, O schaut* 1. Shock horror. Max has shot his own bride.* 26
The chorus move into some powerful Miserere stuff until Agathe opens her eyes which causes them to switch into a rather nice short Gloria.

29: *Ich atme noch* 2. Agathe tells one and all she is still alive.** A 29
simple high solo line that knocks us all of a heap. One of Weber's best. Very short.

3. Kaspar gets his come-uppance. Kuno leads the chorus of condemnation into what sounds as if it were going to be a big choral last number but it doesn't last
32: *Nur du kannst* long. Max pleads his cause,* ably assisted by a tearful 32
bassoon. Everyone pleads for mercy in a lovely pass-
35: *Er war sonst stets* age with two answering phrases** that for a moment 35
steal the show. But Ottokar is a hard man. He's not for turning.

4. The Hermit gives judgement. Pretty ornery
36: *Wer legt auf ihn* stuff but saved by an enchanting flute descant* which 36
floats in like a happy bird once we know that the sentence is going to be a light one.

5. Max, Agathe, Ottokar, the Hermit, Kuno and
41: *Die Zukunft soll mein Herz* Ännchen move into a sextet** that swings and sways 41
its way into happiness after which the Hermit obli-

gingly modulates to an appropriate key for the chorus to bang in with a mighty crash (rejoicing now of course). The flow of their final bit of bellowing is stopped in its tracks by an injection of the happy tune (a happy stroke) sung by six happy soloists who are once again joined by a deliriously happy chorus.

NOTES

Der Freischütz	Weber's fifth performed opera
First night	Schauspielhaus, Berlin, 18 June 1821
Reception	Very good
Libretto	Kind
Source	A number of plays/operas were around that used elements of the Freischütz story which had recently been published in a book by Apel and Laun

NEWS AND GOSSIP

Weber had a powerful voice in the lobby agitating for a school of German opera and when he got the job of Music Director in Dresden in 1817 he immediately floated the idea of an opera based on the Freischütz story. The Schauspielhaus in Berlin was just rebuilt and he managed to do a deal with Count Brühl, the Intendant, to premiere it there. (In those days the chaps who ran opera houses were Counts before they started not Sirs after they had finished.) But poor Carl Maria failed to get a steady run of *Freischütz* partly because his duties at Dresden kept distracting him with events like royal premieres and partly because his TB (of which he died four years later in London) was now getting pretty serious. But he finished on time and produced exactly what the German public wanted – a German Singspiel with good German tunes, loads of good German hokum and some really wonderful German music. The fame of *Freischütz* spread like wildfire and it became easily the most often performed German opera in the repertory. It also spread to opera houses all over the world and has never really gone out of fashion. Today it could not be called a resident in any rep outside of Germany, but it is a frequent seasonal visitor.

COMMENT

A lot of people like to think of *Freischütz* as high camp but the truth is that it is pure hokum. Hokum of the very best quality, not quite up to Mary Shelley's *Frankenstein* nor Carl Dreyer's *Vampyr* but miles ahead of

Edgar Allen Poe. At first glance it might appear to be nothing more than a fairy tale with a sinister twist. But if you were to have cast James Cagney as Max, George Raft as Kaspar and Boris Karloff as Samiel, you could have had a world-beating horror movie on your hands. As hokum goes it is the real McCoy, for the Wolf's Glen has a whiff of the genuine saltpetre.

The more mundane part of the story is pretty ornery with a cast-to-style heroine and heroine's friend, a kindly boss, an imperious prince and the usual chorus which merrymakes, rejoices, bemoans or praises God to order. But the music is not ornery: it is amazing. Weber can write wonderful tunes, no doubt about that, and he can make the orchestra work for him as effectively as Beethoven. But he can also surprise us in a way that Beethoven couldn't or didn't (no disrespect meant).

Early on in the opera we have the teasing chorus (Hee-hee-hee-hee) then Max's wild heroic aria 'Doch mich umgarnen', Agathe's long solo as she waits for Max passing through three or four different territories before she hears his step and bursts into her happy tune, the theatre music for the Wolf's Glen, the razzmatazz of the horn chorus, and the sharp drama of the Act III finale. We have never heard anything so daring before. Think of Gluck. Think of Mozart and think even of *Fidelio*. That music, however splendid, stays within the stately enclosure labelled 'Opera'. But Weber doesn't, he breaks out all over. Perhaps it was his boyhood spent as a member of a troupe of travelling actors that gave him his astute sense of theatre, for his ability to write for theatrical effect is uncanny. The Wolf's Glen scene is carried almost entirely by music and effects, especially effects. At the same time he writes for the Singspiel form as well as anyone ever did and minimizes its lumbering style by putting in just enough speech to carry the story forward without the least possible delay.

Along with *Hansel and Gretel*, *Freischütz* is probably the least worst Singspiel on the books for we don't ever get impatient with the spoken word as we do even in the *Flute* (no disrespect meant). And when we do come to the music it is music of high quality. Weber has only to strike a chord to let us know that he has authority. He is always the master of what he is doing. No padding, no unnecessary notes, always the maximum of effect with the minimum of fuss. Indeed, we could almost paraphrase a famous conversation as follows: 'Too few notes Mr Weber.' 'No your Highness just the right number.' Weber gets his effects through his thorough knowledge of the orchestra. As Chopin was a man of the piano and Schubert a study composer, Weber was constantly on the rostrum beating his way through the operatic repertory of the day. Although pretty fair to all sections he had his favourites, clarinet first and flute perhaps second with a strong penchant for a solo viola.

This extraordinary opera still works on the stage at a time when the magic in several much more famous pieces (Lohengrin's swan, Sister Angelica's resurrected baby) has faded. This must be because Weber wrote it with intense conviction. He really believed that once he got us into the Wolf's Glen he could scare us out of our wits. And, with the right production, he still can. An alpha.

Gianni Schicchi

Farcical comedy

Puccini

The one where a dead man dictates a will which disappoints every single member of his family.

CAST

Bereaved relatives of newly expired Buoso Donati:

Zita (La Vecchia), cousin, aged 60	Contralto
Rinuccio, nephew, 24	Tenor
Gherardo, nephew, 40	Tenor
Nella, Gherardo's wife, 34	Soprano
Gherardino, their son, 7	Contralto
Betto di Signa, brother-in-law, uncertain age	Bass
Simone, cousin, 70	Bass
Marco, Simone's son, 45	Baritone
La Ciesca, Marco's wife, 38	Mezzo
Gianni Schicchi, Buoso's neighbour and friend	Baritone
Lauretta, his daughter, 21	Soprano

A doctor, lawyer, cobbler, painter, no chorus

1 act: running time 50 mins

STORY

The bedroom of Buoso Donati, a reasonably well-to-do Florentine small landowner, proprietor of three mills etc. The said Buoso Donati dead in a bed, centre stage

We are in Florence 1299. The family mourns the death of beloved Buoso. Their grief is very intense but what's that? A rumour is whispered around – in Signa (where Buoso's mills are sited) they are saying Buoso bequeathed his entire estate to the monks. Deadly fear grips the family. What to do? Bad news for us if the will is still with the notary says senior citizen Simone: if the will is still in this room – bad news for the monks. Frenzied search: false alarms: finally success – Rinuccio discovers the will: he claims approval for his marriage to Lauretta as the price for releasing the will to the family. For God's sake yes they cry (but not Auntie Zita).

All gather: they read the will. Groans. Expletives. Shock. Horror. It *is* all going to the monks. Strong views unfavourable to the monks are expressed. Now real tears are shed. Could the will be altered? There is general agreement that the only person with sufficient I.Q. to tackle this is – Gianni Schicchi. Schicchi? says Zita: that peasant bastard from out of town? – not on your life. Hey steady says Rinuccio, Florence is a top city because it showed hospitality to bastards from out of town like Giotto, the Medicis, Mussolini, Brunelleschi, the Ford Foundation, now Schicchi.

Schicchi arrives: he says ba goom you all look glum – has Buoso recovered? No, they say, he's dead: we're disinherited. And the Rinuccio/Lauretta wedding is now off says Zita: no legacy to the Schicchi family: no dowry to Lauretta: no wedding so there. Schicchi is cheesed off: you mean cat Zita he cries. Lauretta says Lovely daddy I want my fella Rinuccio please please fix it – the alternative is suicide. OK OK OK says Schicchi, gimme the will. Let's see if it's fixable. (A lot of bated breath.) Negative he says (morale drops) yet maybe . . . (morale soars). Listen! says he: does anyone outside know Buoso is actually defunct? Not a soul they say. OK OK OK says Schicchi – do what I say (he is interrupted by a knock at door – it's the doctor): keep him out says Schicchi. Buoso is resting, say the relatives. Have his bowels moved? asks the doctor. 'Come later' says voice of Buoso (Schicchi, an amateur ventriloquist, gives a perfect imitation of Buoso) 'just now I am overwhelmed with fatigue'. The doctor turns tail.

Schicchi issues his plan as follows: the corpse is removed: the bed is made: Schicchi is inserted: he impersonates Buoso: the notary arrives: a fresh will is dictated. All the relatives are deeply impressed. They sing God save our gracious Schicchi. They talk among themselves and parcel out minor possessions – no problem. But there is no accord on the mule, the house, the mills in Signa. Deadlock. A death bell tolls. Panic. Gherardo runs out and reports the unfortunate demise of Captain Smith's Filipino servant. Eventually all agree that Schicchi should have complete discretion in disposing of the mule, house, mills. Each relative in turn secretly attempts to bribe Schicchi to assign the mills etc. Schicchi secretly says OK OK OK to all.

The women undress Schicchi and put him in pyjamas. Excitement rides high. Schicchi warns that if the deception is rumbled hands will be chopped off and the offender will wave goodbye to Florence with a stump. The notary arrives plus witnesses: initial legal mumbo jumbo takes place. Early minor bequests go to plan. The mule? asks the notary. To his great and good friend Gianni Schicchi says G.S. Eh? What's that? Come again? whisper the relatives (all in shock). And the house? The same says G.S. The mills? Also to Gianni Schicchi says G.S. You double-crossing skunk the family shouts. Quiet quiet says the notary do not disturb the testator in the course of dictating his last testament. Schicchi reminds the family of chopped off hands if they are rumbled. Things quieten down.

So that's it says Schicchi and Zita would you please pay off the notary – in cash. The notary exits. Schicchi leaps from his bed and wields a cudgel: fracas: Get out of my house he yells. The relatives attempt to loot: Schicchi ejects them. The lovers Lauretta and Rinuccio sing of life and love in Florence. Schicchi solus addresses the audience 'Well folks howdya like that?' (Thunderous applause)

MINUTES FROM START

LOOK OUT FOR

The prelude – a few bars – instantly gives us a theme that is to dominate the first fifteen minutes of the piece: it is anxious, naggingly insistent and a bit of a whine. You will hear it over and over (and over) in many forms.

Rinuccio has found the will Hooray! He celebrates in a snatch of what could have been a Neapolitan love
6: *Zia, l'ho troato* song.** 6

The study of the will (momentous occasion) has an
10 introduction* that sounds like a Scottish paraphrase 10
(Selkirk, Kilmarnock, Old Hundredth, or something).

After the dreadful impact of the will the whine re-appears as a walking bass and soon the whole party moves from a state of shock into a bout of hysteria. They think of all the lovely grub the monks will get. A
12: *E con le facce rosse* lively chatter chorus.** 12

Rinuccio does a great PR job for Gianni Schicchi
14: *Avete torto!* and for Florence.* Starting conversationally we are 14
soon into high flown stuff (with a hint of Lauretta's
15: *Firenze è come un albero* song to come),** a lovely florid Puccini purple patch, 15
vintage 1900. Wallowable.

19: *O zia! io l'amo* The half-way ensemble:* a semi-finale not so 19
much of confusion as of contest: starts staccato, everyone cross, speeds up into patter, good climax and then Plonk! into Lauretta's song.

22: *Oh! mio babbino caro* Lauretta's song.*** A hit. Heard and played all 22
over the world and deserves it – a beautifully haunting melody. The fact that Puccini (tongue in cheek) laid on the sentiment with a trowel doesn't matter. One of the Maestro's Top Ten.

From the moment Schicchi undertakes the job of
24: *Datemi il testamento!* reorganizing Buoso's will we are launched on a roller
coaster of quick-fire farce.*** The comedy is pointed 24

and supported by a marvellously adroit score which has tunes, effects, noises, atmosphere for every occasion. Almost impossible to find high points – it's all on a rarefied plane and stays there.

Schicchi's script for the deception of the no-
30: *Il testa la cappellina!* tary.*** A staccato Hungarian gypsy-like start mov- 30
ing on into an heroic Grand Opera final flourish.

35: *Ecco la cappellina!* 'I hear you':** each member of the family offers 35
Schicchi a prospective bribe in turn. 'I hear you' says Schicchi. Gypsy accompaniment again.

37: *Spogliati, bambolino* The bedtime trio.* Nella, La Ciesca and Zita un- 37
dress Schicchi and put him to bed. Sweet soothing lullaby music suitable for an innocent child (Ho! Ho!).

51: *Lauretta mia* Surprisingly, at this late stage a lovers' duet* in the 51
uninhibited Neapolitan manner. Lauretta and Rinuccio can get married after all and they're going to live (guess where) in Florence. The combination of this honeyed duet followed by Schicchi's spoken epilogue gives the opera an abrupt but punctual and absolutely convincing ending.

NOTES

Gianni Schicchi	Puccini's eleventh opera, counting the Trittico as three
First night	The Met, New York, 14 December 1918
Reception	A palpable hit (see below)
Libretto	Forzano
Source	Remotely from Dante (see below)

NEWS AND GOSSIP

Schicchi is one of the very few operas which was not based on some existing book or play. Opportunist writers used to whizz these around to broody composers rather as scripts for the remakes of old classic films are touted round the remake market today. *Schicchi* was the original idea of Forzano with the slenderest acknowledgement to (of all people) Dante. Apparently Buoso Donati and Gianni Schicchi were real people. Dante was married to a Donati and his mention of Schicchi is not favourable, being described as a low-life scoundrel who played some dastardly legal trick in changing Buoso's will in his favour. So Forzano started pretty well from scratch and shortly after he had offered *Angelica* to Puccini he sent along the idea for *Schicchi* to make up the third leg of the Trittico.

Puccini had already started on *Angelica* but was cock-a-hoop with *Schicchi* and put everything aside to work on it. But he found *Schicchi* tough going and went back to the softer option, finishing *Angelica* by July 1917 and *Schicchi* not until April 1918. Puccini missed the New York premiere where *Schicchi* stole the evening, as it did later in Rome and London. This made Puccini cross because he wanted each leg of the Trittico to be seen as equally good (which of course they aren't) in order to keep the three horses in the troika running as a team. But it was no good. *Schicchi* is so far the best that it was inevitable it should have a life of its own, and be paired with other works – sometimes lamentable new one-acters. No matter how weak a partner *Schicchi* has in front of it, it can be relied upon to save the evening, for no first half can be bad enough to rub the sparkle off the wonderful wonderful *Schicchi*.

COMMENT

Gianni Schicchi is a little miracle. It must be placed alongside *Bohème* and *Tosca* as one of Puccini's top three (a trittico in another sense). Gone is all the Japanese Chin-Chin exotica, gone is the dire influence of the whole-toners (absit Debussy) and with *Schicchi* Puccini sticks two fingers up at the modernist critics and writes music on a harmonic structure that would scarcely cause Papa Haydn to bat an eyelid.

The miracle does not lie only in Puccini's reversion without shame to his earlier style, but in the revelation that musically he is a comic genius. He had a bit of fun with the Bohemians' horse play, some (not so good) comic stuff with the Sacristan in *Tosca* and in *Turandot* some whimsical high jinks with Ping, Pang and Pong (but the attempt at sophisticated comedy in *Rondine* is a flop). Then suddenly we have in *Schicchi* pure farce set with gusto, zest and an expert sense of timing, a feeling for the comic phrase, for the repetitive joke ('Sta bene') for the cod sentimental piece (the bedtime trio) and above all the breakneck speed of events (one disaster chasing on the heels of the last) which is the essence of farce. If only, if only Puccini had coincided and got to work with that great farceur Feydeau instead of messing around with the grandiose *Turandot* and the incongruous *Fanciulla*, what riches we might have had.

Schicchi has no longueurs. Within two minutes the family grief for Buoso turns into panic at the rumour that the monks are going to get everything and from then on we have the discovery of the will (6 minutes), the ghastly news confirmed (9 minutes), the decision to call in Schicchi (13 minutes), Schicchi's arrival (17 minutes), Schicchi agrees to collaborate (23 minutes), removal of the corpse (26 minutes), arrival of the doctor (27 minutes), Schicchi's operational orders (29 minutes), funeral bell (false alarm) (33 minutes), arrival of the notary (40 minutes), Schicchi's bombshell (45 minutes), concluding rites, love duet, Schicchi's farewell (53 minutes). Whew! This is express speed for any plot and one that would certainly have made Wotan stir his stumps. Equally astonishing is the punch packed by the few short stretches of calm water in the course of this torrent. They are Rinuccio's ode to Florence (3 minutes), Lauretta's song (2 minutes), the bedtime trio (3 minutes) and the lovers' duet (under 2 minutes) – every one a hit. The orchestration is always a delight and often a surprise, there are no tiresome incipits (or tags of music which promise a tune and then fade right away), the opening theme (the whine) is worked through half the piece but never to death, the mock solemnity and the phony grief are sent up in the nearest thing to deadpan comic notation you can get in music and all in all *Schicchi* is just brilliant. An alpha-plus.

La Gioconda (The Street Singer)

Venetian melodrama

Ponchielli

The one where a lion's mouth is used as a letter box, where a ship is torpedoed on stage, a dead woman comes to life and a live woman prefers death to a fate worse than.

CAST

La Gioconda, a street singer	Soprano
Her mother, the blind woman (La Cieca)	Contralto
Alvise Badoero, Venetian big shot, member State Security Commission, etc.	Bass
Laura, his wife	Mezzo
Enzo Grimaldo, Genoese aristo	Tenor
Barnaba, State Security agent	Baritone
A gondolier, public scribe, pilot, monk, etc.	

4 acts: running time 2 hrs 35 mins

STORY

Act I The Lion's Mouth (Ponchielli gave each act a title)
The courtyard of the Doge's palace

We are in seventeenth-century Venice and it is carnival time. Sailors, monks, fancy-dresses (harlequins etc.), maskers, Moors, other ethnics, tourists, etc. all carnivalize like mad. A gondola race is announced by MI5 man Barnaba. He gloats over the prison cells in the adjacent palace: he is ambitious to fill them (a thoroughly disagreeable person).

La Gioconda is visible plus her pious blind Mum. Gioconda makes to go and fetch boyfriend Enzo. Barnaba makes a pass at Gioconda: she rebuffs him. The gondola race is over: Barnaba tells the loser that Gioconda's Mum put a curse on his boat (a lie) also tho' she has no eyes she can still see (a lie, and ridiculous too) also she's a witch says Barnaba. The idiot crowd believe him. Burn the witch they cry. Mum is dragged to centre stage. Enzo disguised as a sailor interposes: he takes on the crowd single-handed: big fracas: Enzo exits.

Alvise and Laura appear at the top of a grand staircase. Stop it you scum says lordly Alvise: Barnaba my man, who is this woman, is anything known? A witch m'lord says Barnaba: not so says Gioconda: she must die shout the crowd: Enzo returns with the crew of his yacht at his back: the woman is good says Laura – save her Alvise. Get off you lot says Alvise, let her stand trial. Thanks ma'am says Mum to Laura please accept this rosary as a token of gratitude.

Enzo and Laura recognize each other (big plot point): everyone goes into the church except Enzo and Barnaba. Barnaba says you are no ship's captain you are Enzo one of those Grimaldis exiled for too close a relationship with Alvise's wife Laura: tonight when Alvise is chairing the board meeting I will deliver Laura to your yacht (shows his MI5 badge); I hate you but I also want revenge on Gioconda: it would be easy to kill you but more painful for her if you betray her. Enzo goes off to scrub up his yacht.

Barnaba dictates a letter to Alvise telling him Enzo and Laura plan to elope. He places the letter in the unhygienic mouth of a stone lion for the six o'clock collection. Gioconda hiding behind the lion hears it all: Barnaba gives the lion a lecturette on the state of the nation (Venice) and the importance of MI5 to the health of the state. Gondola, Vespas, etc. arrive for vespers: Gioconda is upset at Enzo's desertion but still holy. She and Mum pray.

Act II The Rosary
A brigantine moored to an island in the Venetian lagoons

Many sailors, midshipmen, etc. 80 in all [grossly overmanned: Ed.] lounge on ship. The frightful Barnaba comes alongside telling fishing stories (in fact making recce). Enzo is on deck. All shipshape? he asks: aye aye cap'n they reply. Bristol fashion? aye aye, etc. He sings poetic stuff to while away the time waiting for Laura. She comes alongside in Barnaba's boat. Big reunion. Nasty bastard that Barnaba she says. Forget him we sail at moonset says he (moon begins to set but slowly). Enzo goes down the hatch.

Gioconda creeps out from stowaway position. Who are you? asks Laura. Your rival says Gioconda: I love him more than you do. Not so says Laura I love him more than you. Don't says Gioconda: Do says Laura: Don't Do Don't Do, etc. My intention is to stab you to death anyway says Gioconda: she pulls a knife: she sees Alvise's boat approaching: she stops stabbing: Good Lord! she says Alvise's here. Holy cow! says Laura this is it. Gioconda sees the rosary and recognizes Laura as Mum's saviour: her attitude changes. Hey take this mask says Gioconda and jump ashore: scarper! The ever-lurking Barnaba sees her go. Zut! thinks he.

Enzo comes up the hatch. Laura has run away says Gioconda: she has gone off you somewhat also she's chicken but Gioconda loves you Gioconda is brave. You bitch says Enzo. Watch it says Gioconda. Police launches are closing in: rat-tat-tat: machine-gun fire. Run for it Enzo says Gioconda. Run? says Enzo (rat-tat-tat) run?? (rat-tat-tat) A Grimaldi run? You must be mad. He sets light to the ship and jumps into the sea: the ship sinks in flames (in two metres of lagoon water).

Act III Ca' d'Oro

Sc 1 An antechamber in the Ca' d'Oro (the Golden House), the Badoero residence

Alvise broods: he thinks: it's a pity she got away last night but of course she must die. I will arrange a really good party to accompany her dying groans (nice one Alvise). Laura enters and is greeted with false politesse. So you want a second marriage? says Alvise. Come and see your marriage bed. He shows her a coffin/catafalque. (Idiot voices are heard singing a happy pop number on the lagoon – dramatic contrast.) Alvise says to Laura take this poison. He exits.

Gioconda comes in: she says here's a short-time knockout pill – gimme that poison and you take the pill in water. Exit. Alvise comes back and sees the empty glass. So you took it, good girl, he says. Exit Alvise. Gioconda comes back on. I am making a monumental sacrifice she says I am saving her for Enzo!

Act III Sc 2 Ballroom in the Ca' d'Oro

Welcome to one and all says Alvise. Very nice of you to invite us say the guests. Let's watch the Dance of the Hours says Alvise – but it's not hours it's 8 minutes 57 seconds. Barnaba drags in Mum. What's this? all cry. I caught her lurking to practise witchcraft says Barnaba. I was praying for the dead says Mum: hark at the death bell (sure enough it tolls). Who's dead? says Enzo. (Wait and see.) That man is not revelling says Alvise turning to Enzo. Revel! And who the hell are you anyway? The exiled Prince Enzo Grimaldi none other says he. How dare you show up says Alvise.

That's torn it say the guests. All express appropriate shock horror at this outrage. One thing's for sure they say the party's over. Meanwhile Gioconda promises Barnaba if he springs Enzo from prison he can have sex with her (ugh!). Alvise draws the curtains and reveals the apparently dead Laura lying in state. Enzo leaps at Alvise in fury: servants interpose.

Act IV The Orfano Canal
A corner of a ruined palazzo on a canal

Two guys deliver the seeming corpse of Laura to Gioconda's humble home. She pays them off and says Mum's lost too would you have a look for her? Sure lady they say. So it's suicide for me I guess says Gioconda: I've lost my lover: lost my Mum: I don't wish to witness the loverly reunion of Enzo and Laura: but hey! maybe Laura really is a stiff? Or suppose I pitched her into the lagoon? What then? Her evil thoughts are interrupted by a gondolier's voice saying there are dead bodies in the canal (one could be Mum?): enter Enzo: you got me sprung he says what do you want? Only to give you sunshine happiness joy etc. says she. You sound potty he says. What are you going to do Enzo? she asks: Top myself on Laura's tomb says he. The tomb is empty says she: Laura lives. Lies says he: no true says she: where's the body says he: tell me (he pulls a knife): there is no body says she. Enzo understandably fed up is about to strike when Laura pipes up weakly from behind a screen crying 'Enzo': she revives: stupendous reunion. Gioconda is a saint says Enzo: an angel says Laura.

Idiot voices (again) approach. Here are your idiot friends to transport you two in a motoscafo to distant parts says Gioconda. Off you go to the happy land. Oh Laura she says you've got Mum's rosary round your neck too: that's good luck. Arrivederci Gioconda they say, you've really been decent thanks old bean thanks a lot. (They sail away.)

So what price suicide now? says Gioconda fingering the unexpended portion of real poison. Oh Lord! she remembers the deal with the dread Barnaba: starts to pray. Dirty dog Barnaba observes her praying and stomps in demanding sexual satisfaction. Cool off Samson she says I must tart up first. (Horrible Barnaba slavers with lust.) So you want my body says Gioconda – here it is – she sticks a dagger† into a vital place – dies. Well now isn't that disappointing says Barnaba: but at least I had the satisfaction of drowning her Mum.

† Dagger count:	unused:	Gioconda on Laura
		Enzo on Alvise
		Enzo on Gioconda
	used:	Gioconda suicide
Result: unused 3 – used 1		

MINUTES FROM START

Act I

LOOK OUT FOR

The early scenes of carnival junketing around the Doge's palace are noisy, festive, plotty in patches and

a little breathless. After the very decent prelude with
two motifs that will be around a bit – big sweeping
tune (rosary), little fidgety thing (bad man Barnaba) –
5: *Noi cantiam!* comes the best chorus. It has one good sturdy tune* 5
then after a musically uncomfortable attempt at sex-
ual harassment (Barnaba) we are back again with the
post-boat-race chorus shouting, gambling, witch-
17: *No: Dio vuol ciò* hunting, even trying a bit of fugato,* etc. until 17
Alvise's entrance quietens things down. Whew!

Grateful Mum gives her rosary to Laura: a simple
25: *Voce di donna* aria* hushed, holy and with a melody sweeter than 25
butterscotch. The sort of thing that works wonder-
fully with a Latin audience (Gounod's 'Ave Maria')
and does not leave us northerners entirely unaffected
either, perhaps against our better judgement.

Barnaba confronts Enzo with his past and present
30: *So tutto! so tutto!* and then reveals that he works for MI5, etc. A duet** 30
develops to a catchy tune as bright as a May morning
and in no way matching Barnaba's sinister machina-
tions. Enzo, who should be scared to death, responds
in an equally debonair and tuneful fashion.

36: *Carneval! Baccanal!* The last scene* – Godawful in many ways – offers 36
an irresistible bundle of well-worn operatic tricks.
First the populace carnivalize once again to music
that is half roads between Sir Roger de Coverley and
White Horse Inn (allegedly it is a dance named the
Furlana); this stops dead to let in a holy organ: holy
offstagers chorus in impressive fashion and above
them La Gioconda goes up like a rocket and sings a
saccharine high soprano line whilst her old mum
chucks in her pennyworth to thicken the mixture.
Only half an inch away from self-parody, but a really
enjoyable wallow.

Act II

5: *Pescator, affonda l'esca* Barnaba (disguised) gives us a jolly fisherman's song* 5
backed by the very numerous crew of the yacht/
brigantine including the middies who give vent to
lines such as 'We are the squirrels of the sea' and 'See
how the nimble boys jump' – all of this at one o'clock
in the morning.

Now we hit quite the best patch in the opera. As he
waits for Laura, Enzo sings his first big set piece, a
11: *Cielo e mar!* fine aria** and a real test for any tenor with its long 11

legato lines and a lot of stuff pretty high up. Then
Laura jumps aboard and there is a great musical em-
18: *È l'uomo che ci aperse* brace and so into the first section of their duet** 18
which flows along nicely to a reassuringly happy tune
20: *Laggiù fra le nebbie* and finishes with a moonset number,* both singing 20
together as they watch this amazing phenomenon of
the natural world.

In the fraught duet with Gioconda Laura has two
nice pieces: the first her prayer to the Virgin to pro-
23: *Stella del marinar!* tect her* (though at this stage it is difficult to see from 23
what) and second her very beguiling statement of love
25: *L'amo come il fulgor* for Enzo which pops out like a Neapolitan song* and 25
underlies and steadies up the exchanges with
Gioconda.

Never in the history of opera has so much happened on the quarterdeck of a brigantine in the space
of ten minutes and amongst the welter of melodra-
matica there is some good stuff, notably the final ex-
29: *No, più non t'ama!* changes* between Gioconda and Enzo, who finishes 29
strongly. For the rest it is musical helter-skelter. The
cannon shots give a good deal of satisfaction.

Act III Sc 1

Alvise's opening thoughts and the duet that follows
have a 'Dance of the Hours'-ish tune skittering
around but the music is mostly ornery until Laura responds to the news of her impending death with a de-
8: *Morir! Morir!* lightful little aria,* as sunny and happy as can be. 8
Odd. Shock and horror do come on when she sees her
10: *La gaia canzone* coffin, but the idiot voices on the lagoon don't really 10
do their work for they sound too much like a send-up
by the King's Singers.

Act III Sc 2

The chorus of grateful guests goes with a swing and
leads to the most parodied piece in opera – the 'Dance
17: *S'inneggi alla Ca' d'Oro* of the Hours'.*** Anyone who has seen Walt Dis- 17
ney's ostrich performing to this picky little tune will
have difficulty forgetting it. But the final galop is
irresistible.

31: *O mia stella d'amor* The finale to Act III is a really good ensemble.** It 31
begins with Enzo saying that if anything happens to
Laura he'll top himself. The others respond to his arrival severally and variously – Gioconda (Poor chap),
Barnaba to Gioconda's Mum (I'm going to get you).

Later, Barnaba to Gioconda (What about a deal?), Alvise (Bloody fool to come spoiling my party), Gioconda's Mum (Barnaba is really nasty), the guests (What a cheek). This agreeably convoluted piece wends its way to and fro for some five minutes before Alvise draws the curtain – and the catafalque/coffin is revealed.

Act IV

The best of the last act lies in the Enzo/Gioconda
duet and the following three-handed scene with
Laura. Gioconda tells Enzo that she wants to make
12: *Ridarti il sol* him a happy man in a happy snatch of melody.* It 12
takes Enzo some time to grasp what a saintly street
singer she is, but after Laura's revival (distant idiot
voices again) she punches it home at the sight of the
24: *A te questo rosario* rosary and with one of those pure little hushed arias* 24
that shine out like a good deed in a noisy world.
31: *Vo' farmi più gaia* Gioconda's flighty flirty little song* to con Barnaba 31
into thinking she is going to relish their impending
sexual encounter is the last item of interest before the
opera reaches its disappointingly scrappy end.

NOTES

La Gioconda	Ponchielli's eighth
First night	La Scala, Milan, 8 April 1876
Reception	Cordial
Libretto	Tobia Gorrio, an anagram for Arrigo Boito (Interesting. Was the great man ashamed of working on *Gioconda*? Probably)
Source	A Victor Hugo play

NEWS AND GOSSIP

Ricordi thought Ponchielli a promising lad (of forty) and commissioned him to write *Gioconda* in 1874. Unfortunately Ponchielli followed the Parisian style of Grand Opera developed by the composer Meyerbeer and the writer Scribe. Their alleged motive was to raise the art of opera to a higher plane, but more likely they wanted to keep an unmusical public happy in spite of having to spend an evening watching opera. The Paris style meant that an opera should be long but with many intervals (*Gioconda*: four acts, five scenes, four intervals, which allows for generous alcoholic intake but makes the whole session about four hours). Next, the dreaded ballet had to take place, usually in Act III. Here it is mercifully short (nine minutes). There also had to be massive crowd scenes (Act I, the carnival, Act III, the ballroom scene), spectacular effects (Act II, naval battle, and the ballroom and catafalque). Verdi's *Aida* survived the dead weight of all this paraphernalia but not many others. *Gioconda* was popular in Italy and has stuck around since then up to the present day. Elsewhere it can only be put on properly by the big houses and they tend to think twice before assigning such huge resources to so moderate a piece. As a concert and media bon-bon the 'Dance of the Hours' is top of the pops. If Ponchielli were still alive his PRS on this piece alone would rival any single by the Beatles.

COMMENT

The most astonishing thing about *Gioconda* is how good the good bits are and how bad the bad. Enzo's aria 'Cielo e mar' is a winner, the duet and trio from Act II and the long intricate finale to Act III are all clever stuff and really enjoyable (although the Act III finale muffs an important plot point by allowing the sex deal between Gioconda and Barnaba to be inaudible under layers of warbling voices). But against this there are cheap melodies, schoolroom orchestration, a conventional style of recitatif lurching along on crutches, high sentiments set to the operetta-ish music and bathos lurking round the corner all the time. There is also a lot of mismatching. The Enzo/Barnaba duet in Act I should be sinister but sounds like the lark ascending. Alvise's opening thoughts have a short orchestral end-piece that must surely have been stuck on the wrong page (but perhaps not?). Laura greets the news of her death with a happy little chortle. And so on. One is forced to think that musically Ponchielli had no idea what matched with what, and when the sentiment of the words and the mood of the music do coincide this is due to sheer good luck. So *Gioconda* is a pretty rum old piece, but there are nuggets if not of pure gold, of a very good class of traditional operatic metal. Alas, a beta.

Giovanni, Don *see* Don Giovanni

Giulio Cesare

Opera seria

(Giulio Cesare in Egitto – Julius Caesar)

Handel

The one where Pompey's widow is sent to gather flowers in the garden of a harem, where Cleopatra is imprisoned by her brother and Caesar takes a dip in a harbour.

CAST

Romans:	
Caesar (Guilio Cesare), First Emperor of Rome	Alto (castrato)
Curius (Curio), his steward and a Roman Tribune	Bass
Cornelia, Pompey's wife	Contralto
Sextus, Pompey's son	Soprano
Egyptians:	
Cleopatra, Queen of Egypt	Soprano
Ptolemy (Tolomeo), King of Egypt	Alto (castrato)
Achillas (Achilla), an Egyptian courtier	Bass
Nirenus (Nireno), an Egyptian courtier	Alto (castrato)
Roman soldiers, Egyptians	

3 acts: running time 3 hrs 45 mins

STORY

Act I Sc 1 Egypt. A bridge over a branch of the Nile near Alexandria

We are in the Nile Delta in September 48 BC and Julius Caesar is chasing his old rival Pompey and getting a big Hello from the Egyptians. Pompey's wife Cornelia and son Sextus jump out and say our man is ready to call it quits. Good show says Caesar I am ready for a bit of pax myself. And what's under the dishcover those Gyppos are carting in? A sight to gladden your heart sir Emperor says the Egyptian General Achillas it's Pompey's head (whips off the cover). A present from Ptolemy. Cornelia faints. How disgusting says Caesar and against the Geneva Convention too. Please inform your king I won't tolerate this.

Cornelia comes to and tries to commit suicide. Stop that says Curius and why not marry me instead? Faugh! says Cornelia: one of Caesar's men? No thank you. O dash it says Curius. Exits. We're in a nasty fix Mum says Sextus: in the middle of Caesar's army and Dad decapitated.

You must avenge him son says Cornelia.

Act I Sc 2 A room in Cleopatra's palace

Bad news Ma'm says Nirenus your brother Ptolemy topped Pompey and sent his head to Caesar trying to suck up to him. I'll go to Caesar and see if my sexiness doesn't work better than sending dead heads says Cleopatra: I'll get even with that scheming rat my brother. I'll get to be the one and only monarch you wait and see. Oh yes says Ptolemy stepping out from behind a screen. Indeed. You get back to raffia work and leave the ruling bit to me. And you get back into your massage parlours and leave it to me says she. Exits. So how did Caesar like my little joke? asks Ptolemy. A frost says Achillas. A flop. He didn't like it at all. Listen. Why don't you murder him too? I'll do it in exchange for guaranteed sex with Pompey's widow Cornelia. OK not a bad idea says Ptolemy. Is Cornelia really as sexy as all that?

Act I Sc 3 Caesar's camp. The ashes of Pompey's head in an urn

Caesar is brooding over Pompey's minimal remains when Cleopatra arrives with Nirenus disguised calling herself Lydia. Whew! what a stunner thinks Caesar, Pompey forgotten. Whew! thinks Curius: if I can't get Cornelia then this one will do pretty well. A favour please sir Emperor she says. Lovely hair says Caesar. Nice boobs says Curius coarsely. Sure I'll help you lady says Caesar but I'm busy just now. Exits. He's got hot pants for you Cleo says Nirenus you got him fixed.

Enter Cornelia and Sextus. Cleopatra and Nirenus duck behind a screen. We can pick up a sword here to kill Ptolemy they say but how can we find him? I'll help you says Cleopatra I'm Lydia and I work at his place. He's been a dirty dog to me and I shall be very happy to see him murdered – Nirenus: kindly show these persons to the palace.

Act I Sc 4 An antechamber in Ptolemy's palace

Ptolemy and Caesar meet. Hail Caesar you're doing pretty good says Ptolemy. Not doing so badly yourself says Caesar but that Pompey's head was a nasty trick. Thanks a lot says Ptolemy these guys will see you into another room. Does he think I'm stoopid thinks Caesar. Exits with his own posse. Enter Cornelia and Sextus. You cut off my Dad's head you weasel you I challenge you to a duel shouts the silly Sextus. Lock him up lads says Ptolemy and put the woman on to cleaning the harem loos. Exits. The frightful Achillas says to Cornelia if you will give me a nice time I'll let you both escape. Faugh! says Cornelia. Goodbye Sextus I'm off to the loos.

Act II Sc 1 A grove of cedars with Mount Parnassus in the distance

Caesar coming? Cleopatra asks Nirenus. Yes says he. All stage effects ready and working? Yes says he. OK says she after the pantomime take him to my apartment and say Lydia is coming to see him with some big news. Exits. Caesar arrives sweating (Parnassus a long hike from Alexandria). Where's that girl? he asks. Coming shortly says Nirenus. A heavenly orchestra plays. The clouds open revealing Cleopatra sitting on a throne dressed as Queen Victoria. My God what a beauty shouts Caesar: she looks like Lydia. He starts clambering up Mount Parnassus. The vision vanishes. Like to go to Lydia's place Caesar? says Nirenus nudge nudge. You bet says Caesar.

Act II Sc 2 The garden of the harem

God how I hate this job says Cornelia. You only have to say the word says lecherous Achillas and I'll let you go free. Faugh! says Cornelia and runs for it but Ptolemy interposes. Lemme go shrieks Cornelia. Did you make it with her Achillas old boy? asks Ptolemy. No but I've got everything fixed for Caesar's exit says Achillas behind his hand to Ptolemy and exits. If you don't fancy Achillas says Ptolemy to Cornelia how about me? I'm a king. And I'm a Roman woman says Cornelia, faugh! and exits. Pity she won't go quietly. I shall have to rape her what a nuisance says Ptolemy. Exits.

Cornelia re-enters. Am I fed up with these sex-mad Egyptians she says I think I'll end it all. She prepares to jump into a conveniently adjacent cageful of lions. Stop stop shouts Sextus running on: I've come to rescue you Mummy. Enter Nirenus. Ptolemy wants you in his bedroom line-up with the other girls on duty tonight says he but don't worry we'll all three go along there and wait until Ptolemy has his trousers down then Sextus here can stab him to death and no sweat. Good idea says Cornelia. I'll make a good stab at it says Sextus.

Act II Sc 3 Cleopatra's garden

I guess I'll pretend to be asleep when Caesar comes says Cleopatra. He comes. There's Lydia asleep he says: I'd like her to be my wife one day. Accepted says Cleopatra promptly waking up. Thanks. Steady: Cleopatra might not like it says Caesar. Curius runs in: you've been betrayed again Caesar Ptolemy's on your trail. Don't go Caesar says Cleopatra. By the way I am not Lydia I'm Cleopatra. Gracious me says Caesar. I'll see off any traitors that come after you she says strolling to the wings. I'm Queen you know. Oh no! My God! There are millions of Ptolemy's men. Run Caesar! Run! I'll stand my ground says Caesar and runs off. Sounds of mayhem. I hope he's OK says Cleopatra.

Act II Sc 4 A room in the harem

Ptolemy is lining up the girls for the night shift including Cornelia. You've drawn the short straw Cornelia he says: you open the batting. No she don't! shouts Sextus jumping in. But Achillas jumps on Sextus and takes his sword. I got news for you boss he says: Caesar gave us the slip but he jumped off the pier and drowned. Also Curius. Cleopatra's now mustering Caesar's troops to march against us. Now can I have a nice time with Cornelia please? No you can't you randy dog says Ptolemy. I'm off to defeat Cleopatra. Will be back shortly. Well I made a fair bugger of that says Sextus, I think I'll kill myself. No don't says Cornelia: follow after Ptolemy and strike him down. Go on. All right I bloody well will says Sextus.

Act III Sc 1 A harbour near Alexandria

Achillas comes on with men at his back. I'm on Cleopatra's side now and we'll fix that bastard Ptolemy well and good he says. Exits. A musical battle rages offstage. Enter Ptolemy. I've won he says: those first violins did a splendid job and you're my prisoner now young Cleopatra so there. Things sure are pretty bad says Cleopatra, Caesar dead, me a prisoner, Cornelia and Sextus a busted flush, but even when I am dead I'll still go after that terrible Ptolemy and haunt the wits out of him. Exits under armed guard.

Caesar comes on. God that water was cold he says I wonder where that Cleopatra might be? Lot of corpses round here he adds. Nasty smell. Very depressing. Sextus enters on the opposite side of the stage still looking for Ptolemy in his wimpish way. He finds Achillas with a nasty wound. Take these secret operation orders to Dugout 99 says Achillas: there is a platoon of SS guards there who know the secret passage into Ptolemy's study, rescue Cornelia kill Ptolemy and good luck because I think I'm slipping away. (Dies.) Caesar crosses the stage: Gimme that seal he says. Good Lord it's the boss says Sextus: we thought you were dead. I was an Olympic standard swimmer you know says Caesar. Come on to the palace men and save the lovely ladies Cleopatra and Cornelia. Exits. Things are looking up says Sextus. He follows Caesar.

Act III Sc 2 Cleopatra's apartments

Cleopatra is really down. But hark! it's Caesar at the door. My God it's a ghost! says Cleopatra but it's no ghost and some pressing to the breast takes place. Meet you at the port says he. OK don't fall off the pier again she replies.

Act III Sc 3 Ptolemy's throne room

Enough of this fooling around Cornelia says Ptolemy: get your toga off. Leave me alone says Cornelia: you can't rape me: I'm a Roman woman and I happen to have this dagger. She makes to strike: Sextus appears and interposes. Oh let me do it please Mum he says I'm a man you see. He has a swordfight with Ptolemy and kills him. Look! I avenged my Dad Mum says Sextus. You sure have done avenged him says Cornelia good lad.

Act III Sc 4 The harbour at Alexandria

Now we've won I can tell you that you all done well says Caesar. My boy Sextus done exceptional says Cornelia killed Ptolemy in the act of raping. Let's all be friends now. Here Caesar take Pompey's crown and share certificates. Thanks says Caesar: Cleopatra can have the crown. Now Cleopatra let's sing a love duet and get the opera off to a really nice finish. They sing accompanied by a chorus of war-weary Egyptians who say that everything is now just absolutely perfect.

MINUTES FROM START

LOOK OUT FOR

Act I Sc 1

0

The overture. In the style of the day it has a stiff and slow first section (repeated), a fast middle then, when you expect a return to the slow it runs straight into the opera. The fast section is exceptionally merry and bright. 0

After a respectful but not very enthusiastic welcome from the assembled Egyptians we have a short, fast and firm opening aria* from Caesar. Let's see what you fellows can do, says he, in the matter of honouring a conquering hero like me. 5

5: *Presti omai l'egizia terra*

Caesar is outraged by the sight of Pompey's head served up on a plate. This is a 'rage' aria** with the fiddles flashing with anger. Indeed for much of the time it is a two-part piece – violins and voice. A good tune and some breathtaking runs. 11

11: *Empio, dirò, tu sei*

Cornelia, calm in her sorrow, has a quietly beauti-
16: *Priva son d'ogni conforto* ful aria.* Seven minutes of Handel in his *Largo* gear, 16
but this number, good though it is, will never make the top ten.

Sextus in fiery mood is determined to get his own back on the horrible Egyptians. A fast and furious re-
23: *Svegliatevi nel core* venge aria* with a slow middle bit when the ghost of 23
his father tells him he really must get in there and do some good avenging.

Act I Sc 2

Cleopatra rather cheekily wishes Ptolemy as much good luck as king as he has had with women. Apparently he has a tremendous sexual reputation. A flighty
30: *Non disperar, chi sa?* piece,* fast, fleeting and agreeable with a more lyrical 30
middle bit which has longer and smoother phrases.

35: *L'empio, sleale, indegno* Ptolemy sings a petulant little war song.* He's out 35
to get Caesar, no doubt about that, but Handel makes him sound like a puppy barking at a Great Dane. TUM-TI goes the very firm rhythm and TI-TUM-TI again.

Act I Sc 3

Caesar recalls Pompey's greatness as he gazes at the
40: *Alma del gran Pompeo* ashes of his head in a noble accompagnato.* 40
Impressive.

45: *Non è sì vago* Caesar is struck all of a heap by Cleopatra's beauty* 45
(in disguise as Lydia). She is more beautiful than the flowers of the field. A free-ranging melody over a steady walking bass. This is no passionate outburst, indeed Caesar's reaction to this knockout beauty is a bit staid.

Naughty Cleopatra instantly sees a chance of using her sexual powers to get Caesar to do down brother
50: *Tutto può donna vezzosa* Ptolemy. A pert and confident aria* backed by the 50
violins swinging up and down an arpeggio figure like crazy.

After a bout of arioso gloom from Cornelia as she gazes at Pompey's tombstone, Sextus tells us he is determined to avenge his father Pompey. This is an odd
61: *Cara speme, questo core* number.* A solo cello gives out what sounds like the 61
subject for a fugue, Sextus enters and we have what is almost a canon. The two of them swarm along together, one always a step or two behind the other. As a piece it works well but it does not sound as if Sextus

had much stomach for revenge.

68: *Tu la mia stella sei* Another perky aria** from the unquenchably op- 68
timistic Cleopatra. She hopes her lucky star will assist her in all the mayhem and skulduggery she so cheerfully plans to inflict on her brother Ptolemy. This number is a cut above the general run, its spirits are so high.

Act I Sc 4

So now we have the tramp tramp of a march rhythm
and a horn, first with the tune and then floating
77: *Va tacito e nascosto* around with scoops and scallops.* Caesar thinks Ptol- 77
emy is a tricky fellow. A whiff of Onward Christian Soldiers in the air.

83: *Tu sei il cor* A stern love song from Achillas.* Blackmail really. 83
Marry me or else be condemned to pick flowers in the garden of the harem for ever. A muscular tune, vigorous, with vicious little stings from the violins. Does not endear Achillas to the listener one bit.

Cornelia and Sextus have to part and this gives rise
88: *Son nata a lagrimar* to this lovely duet.** The opening symphony sets the 88
tone of yearning sadness. The way the two female voices (Sextus is still very young) echo each other's phrases and then come together is wonderfully effective. So nice to hear two voices in an aria and it is really a shame that owing to the conventions of opera seria we have no ensembles: Handel could have served them up a treat.

Act II Sc 1

As Caesar waits for Lydia (Cleopatra of course) he hears 'harmonious sounds from the spheres'. But not so very harmonious to our ears, the Parnassian onstage combo is sonorous but thickish. Then Cleopatra/Lydia/Goddess of Virtue takes up the refrain
5: *V'adoro, pupille* and turns it into a ravishing aria,** clear, simple and 5
direct. Caesar interjects an 'O My!'. Cleopatra continues. The middle bit of her piece is particularly fetching.

It's not often that an Emperor has a duet with a
11: *Se in fiorito ameno prato* bird,* but that is what we have here. The bird is rep- 11
resented by a solo violin – Caesar plays himself – and both tell us that Lydia can brighten the scene by being a sort of bluebird of happiness. The bird can sing in both the major and minor modes and has some nice

little cadenzas. A curio.

Act II Sc 2

Cornelia is very sad amongst the flowers in the harem.
19: *Deh piangete, O mesti lumi* Her short but touching lament* is one of those tunes 19
that lives on in the ear.

Achillas tells Cornelia if you let me love you everything will be OK but if not – look out! A brisk and
24: *Se a me non sei crudele* tuneful number* with a precise accompaniment 24
which has a mind of its own: it starts in unison and runs throughout like clockwork.

Ptolemy is really upset at being spurned by Cornelia.
28: *Sì spietata, il tuo rigore* In one of the most tuneful and forceful arias** of 28
the opera he gets thoroughly spiteful with venomous little twirls to tell us what a nasty man he is.

Cornelia faces the prospect of Ptolemy being murdered
33: *Cessa omai di sospirare!* with some satisfaction.* A curiously halting 33
and indeterminate piece for such a strong resolve.

Sextus shows his determination to slay Ptolemy.
37: *L'angue offeso mai riposa* This number* has a firm walking bass which marches 37
on relentlessly beneath the fine phrases of Sextus's vocal line.

Act II Sc 3

43: *Venere bella* A prayer to Venus.* Cleopatra wishes to look excep- 43
tionally seductive. The middle section has some adventurous passages which contrast happily with the formality of the opening strain, which is repeated quite often enough for comfort.

51: *Al lampo dell'armi* Well, not quite a patter song,** but rapid fire in- 51
deed from Caesar as he hypes himself up for the encounter with the conspirators. Speed, bustle and a bass that races rather than walks. An oddball and a winner. Ends with shouts from the conspirators in the wings.

And now the opera moves on to a higher plane.
54: *Che sento? Oh Dio!* Cleopatra's accompagnato** is suddenly dramatic 54
and full of real feeling, especially when she so sweetly begs the gods to protect her lovely Caesar. Then, as soon as we hear the symphony before her aria, we know we are to have one of those serene and beautiful
56: *Se pietà di me non senti* arias*** which were Handel's greatest gift to opera. 56
Partly because the style of the accompaniment falls more gratefully upon our ears today than the frenzied figuration of the faster numbers, partly because of the

sheer magic of the melodic line, this aria strikes home with all its power, just as no doubt it did in Drury Lane two and a half centuries ago. Look out especially for one high note which is not at all the one you expect.

Act II Sc 4

A fidgety little figure introduces a sort of accompag-
64: *Belle dee di questo core* nato from Ptolemy* who is once again making a pass 64
at Cornelia. It fidgets on as Ptolemy climbs into something approaching aria and then relapses into secco as he gets serious about sex with Cornelia. But enter Sextus!

70: *L'aura che spira* A bold and fierce aria* from Sextus who is once 70
again hyping himself up to kill Ptolemy. The middle section, as is often the case, has some agreeable free-ranging ideas, for the rest the aria is satisfactory enough within the straitjacket of its precise measures, but scarcely big enough to end an act.

Act III Sc 1

Another hype-up to mayhem, this time by Achillas.
2: *Dal fulgor di questa spada* Good vigorous standard stuff* with a strong finishing 2
burst.

5 The battle! A stirring symphony full of fight and 5
fury. Ptolemy does not care for his sister and proposes
6: *Domerò la tua fierezza* to humiliate her in another vicious little aria* with 6
sprigs of malice thrown out by the violins in abundance. Another good standard piece.

Act III Sc 2

11: *Piangerò* Another great aria from the desolate Cleopatra.*** 11
First the sad and slow 'Piangerò' – I shall weep – she is desolate and tells us so in the most lovely sorrowful phrases. Then her spirit flares up and she swears her ghost will give Ptolemy a hard time after she is dead. Fast and furious. So back to the sad 'Piangerò' and a dying fall.

Caesar, having swum the harbour, is not well placed. He has no troops and spends the next few minutes bemoaning the fact, first in an accompagnato
19: *Aure, deh, per pietà* then in a long and rather dismal but effective aria.* It 19
has a slightly more sparky middle section when his thoughts turn to Cleopatra.

A much more cheerful Caesar thinks he is going to win every battle. The opening symphony tells us he

29: *Quel torrente che cade* has got his bottle back and he carols away* with a clear 29
tune and some real breath-testers towards the end. A good number.

Act III Sc 3

34: *La giustizia ha già sull'arco* Another upbeat item,* this time from Sextus who is 34
out to get Ptolemy. This strain of warlike hype (of which we have had quite a lot) is generally based on quick tempo, a firm vocal line and a lot of running around by the violins, which here are exceptionally active. Again a good standard piece.

After some dramatic accompagnato as Cleopatra's sad thoughts accompanied by a solo oboe are interrupted by the sound of battle (fizzing strings), Caesar appears. Rescued! She sings a really happy little
41: *Da tempeste il legno infranto* number** with chortling trills and bubbling runs. 41
Hooray! And quite a long Hooray! it is.

Cornelia immensely cheered up by the death of
50: *Non ha pui che temere* Ptolemy sings a sweet and swinging number* to cel- 50
ebrate her release. It has the usual clear top and bottom lines with the violins doubling the voice part more than usual (except in the middle bit): this gives it a strong forward impetus.

Act III Sc 4

53 The celebratory symphony.* A noisy affair with the 53
pairs of trumpets and horns extremely active. Interesting rather than beautiful and as explosive as a fireworks display.

59: *Caro, Bella* The Love Duet.** Opening with each lover enun- 59
ciating, very slowly, the words 'Caro' and 'Bella', they both run on into a rumpty-tumpty tune, which stretches into a more measured and loverly middle section. Then we go back to a longer and dreamier 'Caro' and 'Bella' – a great stroke. Followed by rumpty with some lovely decoration.

64: *Ritorni omai* Finale.* The grossly underworked chorus have a 64
suitably celebratory salute to the lovers and then we swing into a concertante section, Cleopatra and Caesar singing in duet. After the formality of the choral writing, this is a delight and ends the opera with a fresh, light touch. Everybody happy.

NOTES

Giulio Cesare	Handel's seventeenth opera and fifth full-length opera for the Royal Academy of Music
First night	King's Theatre, London, 20 February 1724
Reception	A hit
Libretto	Haym based on Bussani
Source	Roman history hyped up and reconstructed for the opera stage by a succession of seventeenth- and eighteenth-century scribes

NEWS AND GOSSIP

The Royal Academy of Music was founded in 1719 to put on Italian opera in London and so in many ways was the forerunner of the Royal Opera House. All well brought up young aristos in those days did the Grand Tour and had therefore seen Italian opera on its home ground in Naples, Venice, etc. So the Academy was set up as a joint stock company by the gentry for their pleasure. To their subscriptions the monarch added an annual grant of £1000 (rather nicely called a 'bounty') and it would be interesting to know how this compares with the level of subsidy granted to the Royal Opera House today in real terms (which by the time they have been pushed around by statistics are nearly always pretty unreal terms anyway).

Handel was one of the composers on the Academy's books, as was his big rival Bononcini. But in those days composers were not thought of as creative artists whose work was holy and immutable. They had to do what best suited the really important people, the singers, who then, as now, brought in the money at the box office. *Giulio Cesare* was a big success for the Academy and ran for thirteen performances, apparently well above average. It had a few performances in Germany in the next ten years or so and after that it lay on the shelf for pretty well two hundred years until revived in (of all places) Göttingen in 1922. Early operas with their primitive scoring offer a huge temptation to arrangers to arrange them to such a degree that there is not much left of the original piece except the tune (an extreme case – the *Beggar's Opera*, roughly contemporary with *Giulio Cesare*, and see what Frederic Austin did with it on the one hand and Benjamin Britten on the other). So poor old *Giulio* was mauled about considerably during the early years of the Handel revival and only when we all had to be frightfully authentic did it return to something nearer to the form in which Handel wrote it. This happened fairly recently with a production in Birmingham in 1977 and was reinforced by the ENO production of 1980. This was an enormous hit, and at the time of writing still runs.

COMMENT

Giulio Cesare is not an opera to set the pulse racing. Indeed, the word opera today as commonly used only just stretches back to cover the staid spectacle and disciplined sound of opera seria. There are no Valkyries, Bohemians, Pavarottis, and not a single trombone. And yet, and yet, within its smaller scale passions do rage, tears are shed and lovers do swear undying love. Not much of this emotion comes through to us from *Giulio*'s highly formalized music. The rage arias don't affect us personally as does the rage of the Count in *Figaro*. What we hear is a nice lively aria in the convention of rage music. The battle music is remote and a little ludicrous, rather like the battles on the Bayeux tapestry, where angular cardboard men strive to kill each other with toy swords. All rejoicing, especially choral rejoicing, sounds much the same. But there are emotions that can still strike true through the conventions of the day and they are mainly the emotions of courage, joy and sorrow. Sorrow, always one of Handel's strongest suits, is an easy winner in *Giulio*.

Cleopatra has the best music throughout but her two great arias of sorrow, 'Se pietà di me non senti' and 'Piangerò', reach out through the centuries and can affect us afresh with the nobility of her grief. Her perky numbers have verve and excitement, her seductive music is less persuasive. But quite aside from the music as a conduit for emotion, there is another pleasure in *Giulio* and that is in the music itself, as 'absolute' music. Many of the three dozen or so numbers in *Giulio* could be changed around and no one would notice much [and no doubt many were: Ed.]. Nearly all have a strong bass line and a strong top line with not a lot between. Many share the same mood; the decorations are different, the tunes are different, but to a normally musical person on the Clapham omnibus they are pretty well indistinguishable. Yet if you hear them over and over they begin to grow on you. Soon you will give in to the subtlety and charm of Handel's art and may, unless you are careful, become a Handel addict, and from there it is a short run to becoming a Handel bore.

Although the numbers are by no means all similar, their quality is pretty even. Once you have taken out the three or four greatest hits nearly every other item gets one star. The accompagnatos are effective in raising the dramatic temperature and giving a springboard for the oncoming aria and the secco recitatif is a joy throughout. Handel took greater pains over his secco passages than did most eighteenth-century composers, including Mozart, who was happy to leave the secco recitatif to his assistant. Many of the big dramatic moments – the presentation of Pompey's head, Cornelia's several suicide attempts, Lydia's revelation that she is Cleopatra – are covered by secco and Handel doesn't try to make a big deal out of them. But the secco is always written close to the sense of the text with melody and speech rhythm working together in a pretty miraculous way. All of this can be ruined if the underlying cello line is taken too seriously. Cellists tend to go mad if given a chance and will add their own twiddly bits at the drop of a hat. If there is any cello at all it should be gossamer light in tone. The orchestration of the numbers themselves is usually described as sumptuous, though after an earful of Wagner it sounds scrawny and honestly it is hard to brew up much enthusiasm for the sonority of *Giulio*'s score, which with its four horns, oboes and bassoons, may have been a wonder in its day but has sort of been overtaken by Mahler. The Symphony of Various Instruments performed on stage is an interesting oddity, having a part in it written for the theorbo, a sort of long-necked lute.

Giulio Cesare, of all of Handel's operas, is the most performed today. Of the libretto there is little to say since it is one of those stock constructions loosely based on history which has no credible story and no real dramatic interest. It has four or five of his very best numbers, it is melodious, and musically always very satisfactory, it is amongst all opera seria perhaps the least remote before Gluck began to transform the old thing into something more human. Beta.

Girl of the Golden West, The *see* Fanciulla del West, La

Godunov, Boris *see* Boris Godunov

Götterdämmerung *see under* Ring, The

Hänsel and Gretel

Gingerbread opera

Humperdinck

The one where Hansel and Gretel nearly get eaten by a gingerbread witch but turn the tables and cook her in her own oven (Regulo 4). Loads of angels and a couple of fairies.

CAST

Hänsel, a boy	Mezzo
Gretel, a girl	Soprano
Gertrude, their mother, very poor	Mezzo
Peter, their father, a besom-maker	Baritone
A witch, carnivore and cannibal	Mezzo
Sandman, a fairy, dispensing sleeping pills	Soprano
Dew fairy, a fairy in the wake-up-call business	Soprano
Angels	

3 acts: running time 1 hr 45 mins

Two points: 1. The first and second acts are joined together by an orchestral piece – the witch's ride – so no interval there. 2. The parts of the Mother and the Witch are often doubled by the same singer, which gives both characters interesting psychological overtones.

STORY

Act I Interior of a poor cottage: the forest visible through the window

We are in a German besom-maker's cottage in the time of Hans Anderson. Hansel and Gretel are horsing around singing nursery rhymes and whingeing because they are hungry. They hope for a rice pudding when Mum comes home. They dance an action-packed dance (klapp klapp klapp) as taught them by Auntie. Mum catches them prancing around and gives them hell for not chore-ing, besom-making, stocking-knitting, etc. Mum breaks the milk jug and gets tearful (no supper no money etc.). She drives the children out to p.y.o. strawberries in the forest. She moans on alone. She sleeps.

But hark! Ral-la-la-la – our jolly neighbourhood besom-maker approaches. A good day on the besom market. I dropped in at Tesco's (also Joe's place) on my way home he says dumping the shopping on the table. There is a warm welcome for the arrival of garlic sausages etc. Where are the kids? asks Dad. In the forest p.y.o. strawberries in Squire's copse says Mum. Squire's copse? says Dad you must be mad. Why? asks she. It's the habitat of an exceedingly dangerous cannibal witch says he. She decoys children by means of gingerbread lollipops then minces them into sandwich fillings and eats them. He takes a swig of Schnapps. Both exit to save the children from the cannibal witch.

Act II In the forest

Gretel sings another goo-goo nursery rhyme. Hansel fills his basket with strawberries. Both fool around making a daisy chain. A cuckoo cucks. The children eat all their berries. Darkness falls. They are lost. They shout. They are terrified by the echo. They panic. They hallucinate and see a Sandman arriving to administer soneryl. He wishes them sweet dreams. They pray to angels. They sleep. A number of angels obligingly carry out interesting manoeuvres ex the sky down to the forest. They provide a security guard round the children.

Act III Sc 1 The same

The wake-up fairy makes a call. The children wake. They compare dreams about angels carrying out interesting manoeuvres ex the sky etc.

Act III Sc 2 The same: but – the mist lifts and so does a drop curtain exposing a gingerbread house

The children goggle at a house constructed of Mars bars Kit Kat etc. They start eating the outer walls. The Witch calls. Did you break wind just now? asks Hansel of Gretel. The Witch calls again. And again? asks Hansel. The Witch calls again and so on. The children make a big joke over the matter of wind. The Witch lassos Hansel. Get off he cries. You look yummy says she. She sweet talks the children offering all kinds of child-attracting foodstuffs. The children are uneasy.

The Witch casts an immobility spell. She pushes Hansel into a cage for fattening. Gretel is immobile. The Witch feeds Hansel and runs through some tasty recipes suitable for a plump male infant. She lights a fire under the oven. She changes her mind: she decides to eat Gretel first and to put Hansel on the back burner. The Witch rides her broomstick bawling out the witch's motto song. Gretel fetches almonds for the further feeding of Hansel. Whilst the Witch is feeding Hansel the almonds Gretel shakes the magic hocus pocus juniper branch.

The Witch edges Gretel towards the oven and tells her to look in. How do I get up? asks Gretel. Like this says the Witch incautiously leaning into the oven. Whoops! The Witch is bundled into the oven by the two muscular children (Regulo 4). Great rejoicing. The oven explodes revealing numbers of children coated in batter awaiting insertion into the microwave. Gretel wields the magic hocus pocus juniper branch again and the children step out of the batter: all rejoice: Mother and Father drift in. The rejoicing continues full strength until it is modified by Father introducing a somewhat irrelevant Christian message.

MINUTES FROM START

LOOK OUT FOR

Act I

0

The overture** trots out three of the catchiest tunes 0
in the piece – the Angels' Prayer, the Dew Drop Fairy and the Liberated Children – first presented one after the other, then pushed around a bit in the development and finally called back in combo. A great beginning.

8: *Suse, liebe Suse*

The hungry duet* which opens the first act rolls 8
out with a continuous flow of melody – never a dull moment and a tiny foretaste of the Angels' Prayer.

14: *Brüderchen, komm, tanz mit mir*

The Hansel and Gretel dance sequence*** has 14
three nice tunes, the introductory one, Come Dancing, then Klapp, Klapp, Klapp and the third, Tra La La – these build up to a foot-tapping climax with an artful descant over Tra La La and a gradual increase in volume, sonority and rhythmic push. Brilliant! And with all this cleverness it remains childish and innocent.

22: *Ral la la la*

Dad's jolly return home.* We may have a surfeit of 22
Ral La La Las before the scene is through, but again it is simple, vigorous and marvellously orchestrated. Dad describes the lifestyle and appalling cannibalistic

32: *Eine Hex', steinalt*

practices of the Gingerbread Witch – a robust set 32
piece,** atmospheric and mildly frightening.

Act II

0

The witch's ride* – at first you might think Fasolt 0
and Fafner had popped in from *Rhinegold* (the giants' motif) but soon a powerful witchlike figure (descending scale) dominates this not very spooky interlude which is joined to the next scene by a reprehensible solo violin.

14: *Hast du's gehört?*

The frightened children:** after they hear the 14
cuckoo-echo (and this is a really spooky effect) the children panic into a frenzied musical climax which

strikes home with great effect after the pretty mild stuff they have been serving up for the last ten minutes.

16: *Der kleine Sandmann* The travelling Sandman's song,* perhaps too sim- 16
ple to start with but once we get to sweet dreams and angels it does indeed go dreamy in a very satisfactory fashion.

18: *Abends, will ich schlafen* The Angels' Prayer*** fully deployed as a duet. A 18
bit soppy in this simple form (although beautifully orchestrated and with its heavenly closing cadence fully exploited) but wait and see what it can do once the angels get a bit of wind in their wings.

21 Foolishly known as the Dream pantomime,** this 21
great splurge of orchestral sound accompanies the antics of the Guardian Angels (fourteen in number and an incompetent lot they turn out to be). It is a rich mix, this one, with the Angels' Prayer pounding out strength nine, but dying away and with a quiet angelic coda.

Act III Sc 1

0 Another prelude** with a snatch of the Dew Fairy, 0
first since the overture. So competent, so well written, so *good*.

The whole of this scene is a bit of a treat. First the
3: *Der kleine Taumann* Dew Fairy with her enchanting sinuous melody*** 3
(not unrelated to the Sandman's) rising to a peak just before she exits to continue her dew duty elsewhere – then Gretel's sleepy awakening to the mood and mel-
5: *Wo bin ich?* ody of the Dew Fairy*** (marred, alas, by the intru- 5
sion of a reprehensible solo violin), next the children wake themselves up by uttering agreeable farmyard animal noises and finally Gretel (who pretty well hogs this part of the show) recalls the vision of angels of the
7: *Mir träumte* night before.** Dreamy. 7

Act III Sc 2

The hungry pair encounter the gingerbread house and are amazed – as they inform us in a swinging
11: *Wie duftet's von dorten* waltz,** another catchy tune which grows rather 11
slowly from its first two notes but before long is rollicking. (And rollicks on in the next scene, even the witch joining in.)

The Witch pretty well has the best of it musically for the whole of this scene as she slavers over the

scrumptious-looking children and indeed right up to the time of her terminal visit to the oven. All melodious mickey-mousing stuff. There is a particularly be-
24: *Nun Jüngelchen* witching passage** as she fattens up Hansel with 24
raisins and almonds.

26: *Hurr hopp hopp hopp* The Witch's motto song:* now we get the Witch's 26
tune full blast and at full length, and as witches' motto songs go, it is in the top rank.

30: *Juchhei! Nun ist die Hexe tot* Hansel and Gretel's duet*** of triumph as the 30
witch frizzles inside the oven – first we have a fun version of the witch's theme and then we go back to the rollicking waltz for now there is cause to rollick and Humperdinck fairly lets it go.

Once the boys and girls get out of their breadcrumbs we have the Liberated Children's theme which we first heard in the overture and from there the finale goes with a swing. Nearly every one of the tunes we have got to know and love makes an appearance – especially effective is Hansel and Gretel's
38: *Ihr Englein die uns so treu* duet*** (Dew Drop Fairy), Father's Ral La La La 38
and then leading the chorus of children to a variation of Klapp Klapp Klapp and then at the very end a hushed and positively last appearance of the Angels' Prayer.

NOTES

Hänsel and Gretel	Humperdinck's first opera
First night	Hoftheater, Weimar, 23 December 1893 (Richard Strauss conducting)
Reception	Good
Libretto	Humperdinck's sister, Adelheid Wette
Source	Grimms' fairy tales

NEWS AND GOSSIP

Humperdinck was asked by his sister to write four songs for a production of Grimms' fairy tale *Hänsel and Gretel* which she was putting on as an amateur children's show. He did it, everyone liked them and so he wrote a bit more for a fuller production. Again, terrific success within the Humperdinck circle. Why not make it into a full-blown opera, Engelbert? they cried. So he did and now it became a public success and one of the smash hits of all time. Richard Strauss said 'Masterpiece' and if Richard Strauss said that of any work in Germany at that time it *was* a masterpiece. After the first production in Weimar *Hänsel and Gretel*s sprang up like mushrooms in every German opera house, especially at Christmas. Then it spread across the world, but it must be admitted that its Grimm Teutonic nature means that it is better loved in Munich than in Naples.

COMMENT

Humperdinck could certainly write a tune. *H & G* has at least a dozen that are memorable and whistleable. He could also develop a tune as ingeniously as any composer living or dead: thematic material was putty in his hands, he could squeeze, shape, stretch, contract, combine – a thematic prestidigateur extraordinary. He was also one of the few, the very few, supreme orchestrators, purged of all Wagnerian grossness and capable of the transparent clarity of Rimsky-Korsakov and the sonority of Berlioz. Harmonically agreeable, not venturing an inch beyond his master's (Wagner's) range and with a good sense of theatre – all of these reasons help to explain why *H & G* is such an outright winner. It is no more a children's opera than *Alice in Wonderland* is a child's book. The absurd simplicity of the story appeals because of its genuine naivity. It has something of *The Young Visiters* about it, something of Grimm and something of *The Lion, the Witch and the Wardrobe*. The angels would be truly dreadful if they were not seen as the vision of the children, the Witch would be a target for the anti-violence lobby if she were not a fairyland person. Yet Humperdinck is never schmaltzy and presents murder by baking not as an act of violence but as a joke. Somehow he manages to avoid all hazards, perhaps because (perish the thought) he was just a little simple himself and was blissfully unconscious that he was anywhere near a danger area. Maybe what makes *H & G* so special is that it is a children's opera written by an adult child.

But we don't need to get tangled up in this sort of stuff to enjoy one of the most endearing and musically adroit operas in the book. It does not sag anywhere (although the Witch's solo scene goes on for quite long enough) but it does have many great moments – the dance sequence in Act I which transforms a banal little folk tune into a wonderfully crafted musical event, the Angels' Prayer and the Dew Fairy's themes in their many appearances, the jubilant duet after the witch is safely in the oven and the potpourri finale – all of them are red rosette, blue chip numbers. Perhaps not quite an alpha-plus, but easily an alpha.

Idomeneo

Classical drama

Mozart [K366]

The one where Neptune tries to make Idomeneo kill his son and causes mayhem with storms, earthquakes and a monster.

CAST

Idomeneo, king of Crete	Tenor
Idamante, his son	Soprano
Arbace, Cretan court official	Tenor
Ilia, a Trojan captive, a royal	Soprano
Electra, visiting Greek princess	Soprano
High Priest of Neptune	Tenor
Neptune, voice only	Bass

3 acts: running time 3 hrs 15 mins*

STORY

Act I Sc 1 Ilia's apartments in the Cretan royal palace

We are in Crete shortly after the fall of Troy and Ilia is all alone with several problems: (1) Her Trojan father and family have been killed by the Greeks (wooden horse etc.); (2) She is now a prisoner of the Greek king Idomeneo; (3) She should hate the Idomeneo family but doesn't because (a) Idomeneo saved her life; (b) she loves his son Idamante; (4) Final problem: she fears that Idamante fancies Electra (a Greek royal) better than her.

Idamante arrives and says good news: father Idomeneo's fleet has been sighted offshore: we will free all Trojan prisoners. He also says to Ilia you are my ideal woman. Steady on says she your lot killed all my lot and now you want to form a relationship. It's not at all *comme il faut* (but secretly she is delighted). Don't blame me for the Trojan defeat says he. It was those gods what done it.

The Trojan prisoners troop onstage. Set 'em all free says Idamante. Thanks a lot Prince say the prisoners really nice of you. Electra (Greek chauvinist) pops up and says Idamante what the hell are you doing? Gone soft or something? These Trojans are our enemies: war crimes etc.

*NOTE *Idomeneo* has no authorized version: there are several optional items which Mozart cut or rearranged for the original production and for a later court performance in Vienna. The version described here is the one used by John Eliot Gardiner in his 1990 recording.

Arbace comes on with really bad news: father Idomeneo has been drowned at sea. [Of course not true otherwise no more opera: Ed.] Electra (alone) asks herself why Idamante runs after a low-down Trojan slave like Ilia when an eligible Greek royal is available, like her. Thinks: I'll get her the bitch by God I will.

Act I Sc 2 A rocky seashore

The weather is not good. A nasty rough sea batters the remains of Idomeneo's boat. The sailors beg the gods to turn it in. Neptune emerges in person. Hey there Neptune says Idomeneo give us a break. Neptune turns a steely eye on Idomeneo (implies remember your vow old son) calms the sea, submerges. Nice to be back on shore says Idomeneo but how I regret I took that damfool vow in panic, namely that I must kill the first bloke encountered: such a pity: also bad luck on him.

Idamante appears and spots Idomeneo: hello old fruit he says (doesn't recognize him: he hasn't seen his father since he was in short pants) are you shipwrecked or something? Can I be of help? O Gawd thinks Idomeneo this is the poor guy I must murder. Do you know an old bloke named Idomeneo? asks Idamante. Why do you ask? says Idomeneo. He's my Dad! says Idamante. Believed lost at sea. I am he! says Idomeneo. Hello son!! My dad!! says Idamante. Best get away from me says Idomeneo. Exits fast. What the hell's this? says Idamante. No joyous reunion? What's bitten the old man?

Orchestral Intermezzo

The Cretan women give a big hello to Idomeneo's disembarking troops. All sing to Neptune a first class god they say leads an interesting blameless life saved us from force 9 gale thanks a lot old Neptune really good of you.

Act II Sc 1 Inside the royal palace

You see it was this way says Idomeneo to Arbace: there was a terrible storm: Neptune let me off drowning on condition I offer a human sacrifice. And you picked – who? asks Arbace. The deal with Neptune was that I would kill the first bloke encountered on Cretan soil says Idomeneo. And who was he? asks Arbace. Idamante my son says Idomeneo. Cor stone the crows says Arbace my my well rotten luck. Idamante'd better hop it fast says Arbace and we'll find some other way to pacify old Neptune. I'd do anything for you Idomeneo I would [a creep: Ed.].

Ilia blows in. I've come to pay my respects – happy to meet you she says. Delighted to have you stay with us says Idomeneo. A second father to me you are says Ilia. She blows out. So why suck up like that? thinks Idomeneo. Maybe she has fallen for Idamante: another one to suffer when I kill him off. What the hell Neptune you're a hard bastard you are. Exits. Electra in. Whizzo! she cries. Going home! and with Idamante! Now he'll be mine.

Act II Sc 2 Sidon (Crete) harbour: many sailors, Greeks, Cretans

The weather is much better. What ho for a calm sea and a prosperous voyage sing all. Hurry up and push off says Idomeneo. Addio, farewell, goodbye, cheerio, etc. Suddenly another storm blows up. Thunder: lightning. A frightful sea monster appears. My god says Idomeneo: Neptune is after me again this monster will slay thousands: OK I'll volunteer for the chop myself. Is that any good Neptune? (No it isn't.) The storm continues. Everyone runs for cover.

Act III Sc 1 The garden of the palace

Ilia thinks Idamante has gone overseas. She sends him tender messages via the wind. But blow me down Idamante has not gone. He pops in and says Ilia before my departure I must undertake a high risk job: namely kill the monster. Are you insured? asks Ilia: you are the heir to the throne you know: if I must go away I don't mind death says he. I must tell you something says Ilia though you are a taboo man because your family are my enemies – I love you Idamante. Oh how nice says Idamante. Hip hooray. Let's get wed fast.

Idomeneo and Electra come on. Idomeneo acts funny. He says I have problems with you and Neptune. I can't explain. You'd best get away fast. How awful says Ilia – Electra comfort me. Me comfort you? says Electra what a laugh. Lemme come too says Ilia. No: you stay here says Idamante [why? Ed.].

Arbace comes on and says there is a big demo going on in the main street. Neptune's priests are carrying on something dreadful because their god has been cheated. All exit except Arbace who says what's hit this town? The gods are destroying it but completely. If the death of one guy is required please accept me as the human sacrifice: spare King Idomeneo.

Act III Sc 2 A square in front of the royal palace

Idomeneo plus retinue enter the square and face a demo fronted by priests of Neptune. They point to the corpses blood devastation etc. all around. The High Priest says to Idomeneo: how about it? Are you going to make a human sacrifice or not? Who is to be your victim? Response to this question is urgently required. It's Idamante says Idomeneo. Now a father must kill his son. Gosh what a terrible vow the old man took sing the mob: the poor lad done nothing wrong. They creep off dabbing their eyes.

Act III Sc 3 Outside the temple of Neptune

The mob has reassembled to see the killing. Priests sharpen axes etc. Enter Idomeneo in state robes leading a procession. Call it off Neptune please he cries: no more storms monsters etc. But hark! There are off-stage shouts of: Well done old lad! Nice one Idamante! Whassat? asks Idomeneo. Good news says Arbace: Idamante tackled the monster and killed him stone dead. Good news hell says Idomeneo Neptune will be even more mad now Idamante has killed his pet. Idamante makes a hero's entry. I am ready for slaughter father he says: Don't worry I know you have to do it. Idomeneo has a trial swing. Bombs out. Can't do it boy he says. Go on Dad says Idamante don't be chicken have another go and by the way take care of Ilia won't you. OK son says Idomeneo: takes his stance and raises the axe. Ilia interposes kill me instead she cries [third substitute on offer: Ed.]. Earthquake occurs.

Neptune (invisible) speaks in person: I am an old softie he says and can't resist young love: I will cancel the vow on the following terms: Idomeneo resigns all office: Idamante takes over as Chief Executive and King: also marries Ilia. Great! say Idomeneo Idamante Ilia and Arbace. Terrific! Thanks Neptune! Electra enters in high dudgeon. Zut! Hell! she cries. I am a woman scorned. She rages: carries on something dreadful: hysterics. Exit. Now listen all you Cretans says Idomeneo I appoint Idamante King and Ilia Queen see and treat them proper (and incidentally I now feel much better in myself). Hooray sing chorus may they live happily ever after. Hooray.

MINUTES FROM START

LOOK OUT FOR

Act I Sc 1

Idomeneo starts conventionally with a somewhat stiff
and starchy overture followed by unexceptional recitatifs and arias from Ilia and Idamante. But the first
22: *Godiam la pace* chorus* of freed Trojans and happy Cretans sets the 22
pulse stirring with its rushing semiquavers in the
strings and its solo voices telling us rather movingly
how nice it is that hostilities are over.

Electra's fury against Ilia can be heard in the bub-

29: *Tutte nel cor vi sento* bling of the bassoons in the introduction to her aria.* 29
Her anger is less consistent as the piece goes on:
spurts of fury, sure enough, but some quite calm legato phrases too. A spirited piece.

Act I Sc 2

The roaming Idomeneo encounters a man. Suddenly
35: *Spietatissimi Dei!* as the accompagnato starts* the scene darkens and we 35
feel the horror of his discovery that this is his son.
Vivid use of accompagnato – one of Mozart's strongest cards.

Idamante, puzzled, uncertain, wonders why his
37: *Il padre adorato* Dad deserted him.* As so often in this opera, the or- 37
chestra does much of the work in setting the mood,
the voice much less. The feeling of lost-ness in this
number is powerful and appealing.

The Intermezzo. Noisy stuff with a modicum of
tunefulness and rather longer than necessary to get
everyone disembarked, one would have thought. But
51: *Nettuno s'onori* leading to the stunning Neptune chorus.** Again, 51
immensely effective use of solo voices, especially the
quiet section when Neptune blows on his golden
53: *Su conca d'oro* shell.** A chaconne, that is the whole piece is written 53
over a ground bass (a repeated pattern of notes).

Act II Sc 1

2: *Se il tuo duol* Arbace's somewhat creepy sentiments of loyalty etc.* 2
sound quite respectable as he belts them out amidst
the very busy strings which surround him.

Ilia is sad to have lost her father, but finds in Idomeneo a good substitute. She is determined to be
happy in this new life, but does not sound much like it
7: *Se il padre perdei* yet. This is a lovely slow aria,** sweet, melodious and 7
with gorgeous work in the woodwind going on above
and around Ilia's vocal line.

Idomeneo asks Neptune so why save me from shipwreck, eh? Having to kill my son is worse. A wonder-
15: *Fuor del mar* ful piece:** the sea rustles disarmingly, the strings, 15
busy again, spin a sort of cat's cradle around the vocal
line, which is firm, brave and manly with lots of taxing runs and twiddly bits. The woodwind has a lot of
the action too, and the horns. Mozart vigorous,
breezy, going at a gallop.

And now for a patch of relatively calm water. Electra, in an unusually mild mood, says she is quite pre-

pared to take Idamante second-hand from Ilia should
Ilia graciously decide to give him up. This plaintive
23: *Idol mio, se ritroso* little aria* is accompanied by strings alone and leads 23
straight into a quiet but businesslike march* as the
Act II Sc 2 scene changes to the port of Sidon (Crete) where an
31: *Placido è il mar* embarkation is taking place and a chorus* of seafaring 31
folk pray for a calm sea and a prosperous voyage (Ho
Ho). This choral piece is as mild as milk and especially beguiling when Electra takes over the middle section with a nice solo in which she says much the same thing.

And now, during the last ten minutes of Act II,
Mozart shakes the old opera seria form into dramatic
33: *Pria di partir, o Dio!* life. First we have the Farewell trio,*** by far the 33
most considerable piece in the opera so far. It has an andante opening section in which each voice has its pointed and very satisfactory entry: Idamante (Goodbye Father), Electra (Thanks), Idomeneo (You got to go) and then after numerous farewells they break into a brisk allegro in which they all devoutly hope that things will get better.

37: *Qual nuovo terrore* So into the storm,** briefly orchestral but soon a 37
cause for considerable choral agitation. The monster
appears (no precise musical cue for him): Idomeneo
40: *Eccoti in me, barbaro* pleads with Neptune in a fine accompagnato,** but 40
it's no good: the storm continues and so does the splendid chorus. It fades away in a brief coda as the terrified seafaring folk flee the stage.

Act III Sc 1

Ilia (wrongly) thinks that Idamante has sailed away
and sends him sad love-lorn messages by way of the
1: *Zeffiretti lusinghieri* winds.** Although it may not instantly catch the ear, 1
this is an aria you will come to love with its simple opening melody and rich middle bit in the minor.

And now a second change of gear. Suddenly we are spirited into a new world. Gone are the four-square melodies, the standard harmonies, the routine tonic–dominant forms. As soon as we hear the sinuous chro-
15: *Andrò ramingo e solo* matic bass line of the great quartet,*** we know that 15
the old world of opera seria is vanishing before our very eyes and that Mozart is leading us into a new and glorious age where opera has moved out of the salon and into the theatre. Against a rich and sequential

musical background we start by each character saying their own thing: Idamante (I'll go away, sure, but only to look for death), Ilia (I'll come too), Idomeneo (Have a heart, Neptune), Electra (Revenge!): in this section the message of each character has its own distinct musical setting. It ends with Idamante and Ilia telling Idomeneo to calm down. Then all together they agree that their degree of suffering is above limits (the word 'soffrir' being emphasized in the most astonishing fashion – the first syllable forte and the second piano) and that on the whole death would be a happy release, the thought of death being introduced each time by a series of sinister stings from the strings. Next we have a reprise of the opening thoughts sung by all voices almost simultaneously with the music belonging to each one most miraculously combined and finally back, rather grandly and at some length, to the idea of death being better than suffering. The piece ends with Idamante casually dropping his opening phrase again – 'I'd best be off'. Wonderful!

With Arbace's accompagnato and aria we are back in the old world of opera seria. The accompagnato is
21: *Sventurata Sidon!* of sterling stuff,* but for some non-opera-seria-goers 21
the aria will outstay its welcome.

Act III Sc 2

The High Priests give a rundown of the mayhem done by the monster in an orchestrally adventurous
35: *Oh voto tremendo!* recitatif and we are into another huge chorus.** What 35
a terrible vow, the people sing, lugubriously. Let him off, Neptune, pleads the High Priest. No sign of this, so the chorus gloomily and magnificently proceeds. But in the end, with the help of the horns, we slip happily and sweetly into the major mode.

Act III Sc 3

After a modest little march to allow the fraught Idomeneo to make his state entry, he pleads movingly with Neptune to be decent to him. The priests, although their words seem to support him, stick to a recurrent monotone which makes it sound as if they were on Neptune's side.

49: *Padre, mio caro padre!* The extended accompagnato* dialogue between 49
father and son is a marvellous example of Mozart's

ability to make the music speak the meaning of the words. There is not one thought, nor one inflexion, that is not reflected in the (strings only) accompaniment.

54: *No, la morte io non pavento*

A noble aria* from Idamante in traditional form. 54
He does not fear death.

60: *Orsù mi svena*

The high drama of Ilia interposing between filicidal father and victim son and saying 'Kill me instead'* is interrupted by an earthquake (in practice 60
usually a crash on the timps, but nothing in the score) followed by a choir of trombones (always a sign of the supernatural in Mozart) introducing the offstage

61: *Ha vinto Amore*

voice of Neptune. This is solemn stuff indeed* and 61
mighty effective too. Love has worked the trick once again.

63: *Oh smania! oh furie!*

Electra spoils it all. In the most vividly dramatic
accompagnato*** of the opera she says 'Misery! 63
Hell! Zut! I want to die!' But she is more mad than sad (anger bursts out fortissimo in the orchestra). Then the poignant moment when she stops and says 'O well: I suppose I'd rather slip off to join brother Orestes in Hades than stick around with you lot.' [For those who follow things closely, this recitatif is to be found in the Appendix, not in the main score.] So into

67: *D'Oreste, d'Aiace*

her great rage aria,*** and what rage it is. Semi- 67
quaver bites and stings in the strings, the fortissimo outburst again, an even more venomous middle section, then back at it again with a couple of final outbursts of hysteria in the coda. Top that.

77: *Torna la pace al core*

Mozart doesn't try. A simple slender canon amongst the strings introduces the now calm and reflective Idomeneo who abdicates gracefully in an accompagnato, wishes the young couple well and slips into his peaceful, mildly agreeable but rather
long last aria.* He's feeling a lot better. 77

84: *Scenda Amor*

The noisy cheerful final chorus* sung right 84
through twice with a pleasant (mainly woodwind) intermezzo sandwiched into the middle. So into the dreaded ballet.

NOTES

Idomeneo	Mozart's tenth opera, third opera seria
First night	Hoftheater, Munich, 29 January 1781
Reception	Well received
Libretto	Varesco
Source	70-year-old libretto by one Danchet

NEWS AND GOSSIP

A commission for an opera was something Mozart longed for all his life, and in the summer of 1780 he got one, for the Munich Carnival of 1781. He picked the Idomeneo story and hired one Varesco, a cleric in his home town, Salzburg, to adapt it, maybe because father Leopold could keep an eye on him (Mozart was in Vienna) and he would certainly be cheaper than any Viennese poet. This was a lucky arrangement for us because Mozart and father Leopold had to keep in close touch and from their letters we get the most wonderful insight into Mozart's mind as he creates, prepares and rehearses an opera. But not, alas, the performance, for Leopold popped over to Munich for the first night.

From the letters we learn that Mozart was thinking all the time of getting the opera to work dramatically, cutting, linking, speeding things up, until he felt he had got some momentum into the old thing: that he felt offstage supernatural voices should only be given a short innings if they were to be effective – the ghost in *Hamlet* was too long – and so cut his Neptune to only nine bars: that he took enormous pains to push and pull the arias around to suit the voices of the singers, the once-great Raaff, an ageing Pavarotti whose last stage appearance this was to be, a clapped-out old trouper singing Arbace and a novice castrato for Idamante whose performance was 'as stiff as a board': that the two sisters singing the female parts were really good: that he wanted and was sent trumpet mutes: that the orchestra (the Mannheim) was 'the best in the world': that Varesco was a pain in the neck (he turned up on the first night looking for his money) – and much more.

The first night went well: there were only two more performances scheduled – and then nothing for five years when there was some sort of amateur concert performance in Vienna. For this Mozart switched the part of Idamante from castrato to tenor – one would have thought a great idea for present-day productions since now (happily for them) we have no castrati, but no. Either the directors don't know about it (as is certainly true of one great opera house) or they feel that to transfer Idamante's part down an octave messes up the texture of the ensembles. After Vienna there was no production for another twenty years and after that *Idomeneo* was performed pretty well only in Germany until a concert performance took place in Paris in 1902. In the UK it was first heard in Glasgow in 1934 and not in the USA until 1947. This is pretty amazing when you look at the dozens of *Idomeneo*s playing all over Europe in the Mozart-mania year of 1991 to cries of 'Masterpiece!' 'One of Mozart's greatest hits!' etc. etc. Anyway, *Idomeneo* is now OK worldwide.

COMMENT

Most opera buffs find opera seria a pretty boring old thing. New recruits to Mozart's operas bubbling with enthusiasm for *Figaro* and *Così* come out of *Idomeneo* and *Clemenza* a bit bemused. The succession of concert arias strung together with secco recitatif is a million miles away from the kind of opera they know and love. Seria was produced, of course, for the courtly old world where Princes ordered up operas to massage their egos and to fill a blank evening for a visiting royal. But *Idomeneo* is roughly only two-thirds opera seria and one-third something new. Mozart had seen opera in the French style with scenery, choruses and, alas, a ballet. But there was something else: Mozart's inner drive to write opera as a continuous music drama was busting out. In *Idomeneo* the old stop–start one-thing-after-another opera seria begins to take on a momentum and become living breathing opera, but not until the end of Act II, and then again pretty well throughout Act III. And then things begin to roll – no interruptions from seccos, no full stops, no applause points, no repeats. Arbace does get into the act, it is true, with a splendid but old-style turn (accompagnato and aria) and this is a pity. But apart from that it's all go and fizz up to Electra doing her nut at the very end, and this is OK too for she nicely caps the big stuff of the climax. Here Mozart is composing an opera like the young genius he was. The invention, the number of good tunes, the sheer cleverness of the writing, all of them propel the old form along like a rocket. The orchestra is given a star role, especially the woodwind, and often the singers sound like bit part players as the action moves into the pit.

The accompagnatos are hugely dramatic, again with the orchestra doing its stuff to create the drama, not just to support it, and, although it would be some seventy years before it disappeared altogether, the dividing line between recitatif and aria is becoming blurred (as in Electra's last furious spiel). Alas, the characters are not yet living and breathing people. Ilia and Idamante are routine characters without a flavour of their own. Why Mozart didn't chuck out Arbace is hard to understand, since he does nothing except hold up the plot. But some of their emotions are real. We can share in the panic of the trapped Idomeneo, in the jealous paranoia of Electra. The choruses move us too, but in a different way, perhaps more like our reaction to Haydn's *Nelson Mass*, or to *Messiah*.

Because *Idomeneo* has such great music in it many people call it a masterpiece, which it isn't. Like *Fidelio*, it is a hybrid between a non-dramatic form of opera and the real thing. Much of the first two acts is good ornery Mozart. What comes later is great Mozart, but that's a bit late in the day. But then what is good is so glorious that *Idomeneo* must be an alpha, no less.

Iphigenia in Tauris
Classical drama

(Iphigénie en Tauride)

Gluck

The one where a sister is almost forced to kill her brother who has already murdered their mother in revenge for her having killed their father.

CAST

Iphigenia (Iphigénie), high priestess of Diana	Soprano
Orestes (Oreste), Iphigenia's brother	Baritone
Pylades (Pylade), Orestes' friend	Tenor
Thoas, King of Tauris	Bass
Diana (Diane), goddess of hunting	Soprano
A priest, priestesses, a Scythian, a Greek woman	

4 acts: running time 1 hr 45 mins

STORY

Act I A wood sacred to Diana: Diana's temple visible behind

We are in what is now roughly the Crimea at the time just after the Trojan War whose date gets earlier and earlier as archaeologists dig deeper and deeper and the weather is bad. A number of priestesses of the goddess Diana led by Iphigenia pray for the storm to abate. It abates. I have a nasty feeling something horrid is going to happen says Iphigenia. I dreamt last night I saw my dad Agamemnon covered in blood being killed by my mum Clytemnestra who handed me a sword and I killed my brother Orestes with it. What did you eat before turning in? asks one priestess. Woe misery I am doomed blast it says Iphigenia and my brother Orestes has been carried off by our enemies. Woe misery etc.

Enter King Thoas. Listen you priestesses he says, the gods have decreed that my life is at risk unless every stranger who enters this country is instantly sacrificed to them. Two young Greeks have just come ashore Your Royal Highness says a local. Get them off to the altar says Thoas and you Iphigenia and your priestesses get sharpening those knives. I am getting no job satisfaction from this thinks Iphigenia.

A crowd of Scythians come and explain they get some comfort from killing all strangers because although bad for the tourist trade it helps the gods to forgive them their crimes. [The logic of this is not clear: Ed.] They then dance a ballet. Pylades and Orestes come on. Why did you come to my country? asks Thoas. It's a security matter says Pylades. You won't talk? OK I was going to kill you both anyway says Thoas.

Act II The temple of Diana

Stop blubbing Orestes says Pylades. Remember you are a hero. But I've run you into trouble says Orestes namely certain death. Never mind says Pylades let's die together with stiff upper lips. A messenger priest arrives. I've got to split you two up he says. Oh no! they cry. But yes he says. He splits them up taking Pylades away. This is terrible says Orestes. He hallucinates. He sees a crowd of furies. Murderer! Mother-killer! they yell at him. They drag in the ghost of Orestes' dead mother Clytemnestra. O dear he says this is most distressing. But the vision of his mother turns into Iphigenia who has come on stage while he is dreaming. He wakes up. This lady is the dead spit of my poor dead sister Iphigenia he thinks. [A long time since they met: Ed.]

Take the bracelets off him girls says Iphigenia. Where do you come from young man? From Mycenae says he. Mycenae! says she. How is King Agamemnon going along? Dead says he. Murdered. Murdered? says she: who done it? His wife Clytemnestra done it says he. And what's more her son Orestes then murdered her. What a lot of killing says she: so what happened to Orestes? Dead he says (a lie of course). His sister Elektra is the only one left now. (Exit Orestes.) Well that's my family pretty well wiped out says Iphigenia. What bad news. I am most depressed but at least let's have a little funeral ceremony for my brother Orestes. Poor Iphigenia say the priestesses, by all means we'll join you in a funeral service.

Act III Iphigenia's quarters near the temple

I will send off a messenger to my sister Elektra thinks Iphigenia one of these two prisoners will do. Maybe the one who reminds me of Orestes: yes I'll send him. Orestes and Pylades are brought in. Great to see you again mate they say to each other. Sorry I have to kill you says Iphigenia but if I don't do it Thoas will kill all three of us. But I have good news. One of you can escape by carrying a message to Argos. I have decided it should be you, the big one. What me? says Orestes. Yes you she says. Exits.

I can't let you be killed says Orestes to Pylades. It will be my pleasure to be killed says Pylades if it saves your life. No no let it be me says Orestes. No me says Pylades. Me says Orestes. Me says Pylades and so on for some time.

Iphigenia returns with some priestesses. Take him away she says pointing at Pylades. Not him! Me! says Orestes. Me says Pylades and we are into the same old routine again. If he gets killed I'll top myself says Orestes. OK says Iphigenia since you are so tiresome let's try it the other way round. You the big one for the chop she says. You the little one take this letter to Elektra. (Funny thinks Orestes why this interest in my sister Elektra?)

Act IV Inside the temple of Diana. An altar ready for a human sacrifice

For some reason which must be psychological I don't feel up to killing this particular man thinks Iphigenia. The priestesses lead on Orestes. Hooray I'm going to be killed says Orestes just what I wanted. I admire your bravery greatly says Iphigenia. Very nice of you says Orestes I haven't had much sympathy lately. The priestesses get the knives altar etc. set up in accordance with the Scythian sanitary regulations governing human sacrifice. Time for the first incision say the priestesses.

Strike! This is the way they killed my sister Iphigenia in Aulis says Orestes apropos of nothing. Whassat? says Iphigenia, why you must be my brother Orestes! The very same says he. I'm your sister Iphigenia and not dead says she. They embrace. A Greek woman rushes on: hey look out you lot she cries the dreaded Thoas is on his way he's mad that you let one of the foreigners go off to Argos he's out for blood I can tell you. Thoas comes on men at his back. Get that man up and onto the altar for immediate carving up he says to the guards. He's my brother! shouts Iphigenia. Don't care if he's Pontius Pilate says Thoas: up guards and at him. Stand back cries Iphigenia. The guards ambivalate. OK I'll do it myself says Thoas and I'll rid me of this troublesome priestess at the same time. Pylades [he never left: Ed.] rushes on men (Greeks) at his back [survivors of the shipwreck? Ed.]. He kills Thoas very smartly and the Greeks chase all Scythians into the wings. The goddess Diana appears in person. Listen to me she says you Scythians must return to Greece all the wartime loot you pinched. You Orestes and your sister Iphigenia can return to Argos. Gosh! says Pylades are you two brother and sister? How amusing. Well that's everything pretty well tied up say the priestesses and indeed that is the case.

MINUTES FROM START

LOOK OUT FOR

Act I

0 The opening scene* gives us a brisk account of a short storm. The prelude starts with a smooth sea, as is made clear by means of a suave minuet played by the strings. But not for long. The storm breaks with fizz- 0

ing strings and thunderous timps. Iphigenia politely asks the gods to call it off. She has low-voltage support from a posse of priestesses who don't sound as if their hearts are in their work. Between stanzas the
6: *Ces Dieux que notre voix implore* winds rage on. Then comes a lovely moment* as the 6
storm dies away and tranquillity returns to the weather, the sea, the orchestra, but not, alas, to Iphigenia's heart.

Iphigenia sings to the goddess Diana in a sweet sad
14: *O toi qui prolongeas mes jours* aria:** life is unbearable, could Diana please arrange 14
for her to die. This is Gluck at his most appealing. Iphigenia has a lovely vocal line and the accompaniment is respectful and gives the singer every chance to wring our withers. The aria is put to rest by a soft chorus from the sympathetic priestesses.

19: *De noirs pressentiments* Thoas's song of panic.* He is scared out of his wits, 19
because there are strangers around. Under his deal with the gods he should have killed them. He declaims his vocal line over fluttering strings and moody woodwind.

21: *Les Dieux apaisent leur courroux* The chorus of Scythians* is an interesting curio. It 21
follows the rather silly eighteenth-century fashion for 'Turkish' music (piccolo, cymbals, tambourines and drums) and has an insistent rhythm rather like Hollywood Red Indians.

24 The individual numbers of the dance music* are 24
attractive if a little simpering but the ballet as a whole is rather a dire little event. It starts French and drifts eastwards to finish 'Turkish' (as above plus a triangle).

The introduction of Orestes and Pylades is carried over recitatif and the act ends tamely with a repeat of the Scythians' chorus.

Act II

After some gloomy parley with Pylades in accompag-
2: *Dieux qui me poursuivez* nato Orestes has a good aria* in which he begs the 2
gods to let him die (a common sentiment in this opera). Orestes' music sounds neither guilty nor suicidal singing out briskly as he does with a good deal of firm backing from the strings in unison.

5: *Unis dès la plus tendre enfance* Pylades replies in a calm and tuneful aria,** one of 5
the best in the opera. He is happy to die in the company of his mate Orestes.

As Pylades is marched off after another bout of fairly ornery accompagnato suddenly we have a mo-
10: *On te l'enlève, hélas!* ment** where the music reaches out and touches us 10
with real feeling when Orestes sings: Alas they have taken you away – Pylades has died for me. But the spell doesn't hold, the following recitatif and aria fall away into fidgeting gloom, which is effective enough but outstays its welcome.

13 The dance and chorus of the Furies or Eumenides 13
(agreeably described as the Pantomime) is not very furious. The Furies start their capers with a KNOCK-KNOCK-KNOCK which sounds as though it might be menacing but then they whirl into a decorous dance sequence which would do very well for the end-of-term jolly at a seminary for young ladies. Despite Clytemnestra's ghostly appearance their chorus sounds no fiercer, though the text threatens bloody revenge.

After the long recitatif in which Orestes tells Iphigenia of the family upsets at Mycenae, she sails into a
22: *O malheureuse Iphigénie!* serene aria** high above a repeated figure in the bass. 22
This is one of Gluck's loveliest tunes and the fact that its gentle beauty is wholly at odds with the despairing sentiments of the words should not be allowed to bother us too much. A soothing chorus rounds off this piece nicely.

A fresh melody is introduced in the short symphony that covers the preparation for the funeral
28: *Contemplez ces tristes apprêts* rites, then it is taken up first by the chorus* then by 28
Iphigenia and then by the chorus again. Thus we hear it over and over again both in the major mode and in the minor. Its charm just lasts the course and it makes a nice calm end to Act II, although it is only very faintly funereal.

Act III

The third act starts slowly with standard recitatif and a run-of-the-mill aria from Iphigenia but in the following trio things begin to move. This is something
5: *Je pourrais du tyran* of a curio.* The two men argue the toss with Iphi- 5
genia as to which should be killed. She referees in slow sustained tones: the men constantly break in: she chooses Orestes to stay: the argument goes on between the men in recitatif: then they swing into a

9: *Et tu prétends encore* duet* which starts and ends chirpily but generates 9
considerable gravitas in the middle.

Pylades implores Orestes to give up his desire for
14: *Ah! mon ami* death. An aria* that starts fetchingly but whose halt- 14
ing accents don't really allow it to take wing.

Now the agitated debate over which of the two volunteers should be selected for sacrifice continues. Orestes feels so strongly that he threatens to kill him-
18: *Quoi? toujours à mes vœux* self anyway in what promises to be rather a nice aria,* 18
but he gets his way and so breaks off, and we are cheated of what might have been something more considerable.

The last aria in Act III starts as if Gluck had suddenly gone minimalist. A fiddly little figure races up and down. Seemingly Pylades has gone demented. But no he hasn't, and the aria turns into a robust af-
20: *Divinité des grandes âmes* fair** with a bold Pylades, assisted by trumpets and 20
drums, swearing he will save his friend come what may. Nice interjections by the woodwind.

Act IV

1: *Je t'implore* The last act opens with a good recitatif and aria* from 1
Iphigenia. The aria is dogged by a nagging figure in the lower strings which seems to be struggling against the voice part. Iphigenia does not want to kill Orestes. [Gluck pinched this number lock stock and barrel from a Bach partita: Ed.]

4: *O Diane, sois-nous propice!* A nice quiet chorus* politely asks Diana to be satis- 4
fied with what is going to be a very satisfactory human sacrifice.

The final drama begins.

1. After a routine female chorus that could be a standard item in the Church of Diana order of service, we have the high drama of the priestesses urging Iphigenia to strike, she unable to do so, the revelation that the victim is her brother, all to recitatif that is no better than ornery until at last we come to a happy lit-
12: *Ah! laissons-là ce souvenir funeste* tle aria* from Iphigenia as she savours the joy of the 12
family reunion.

2. Now the drama quickens. Thoas trundles in furious to find them all still fooling around with the
14: *De tes forfaits* victim still alive. There is a lively cross man's aria** 14
and it runs straight into an ensemble with Orestes being dragged to the altar, Iphigenia explaining he is her

brother and Thoas singing he will kill them both. This is lively stuff and in quite a different gear from the languid recitatif/aria of the earlier scenes, fizzing strings, basses banging away like timps.

3. The marines arrive led by Pylades. A sturdy
16: *De ce peuple odieux* chorus* of Greeks routs the Scythian household cav- 16
alry amidst frenzied shrieks from Iphigenia and the priestesses.

4. The goddess Diana puts in an impressive personal appearance and in a burst of authoritative rec-
17: *Arrêtez! écoutez? mes décrets* itatif* sorts everyone out. 17

5. Pylades' final short and sweetly wistful arietta
18: *Dans cet objet* of brotherly love for Orestes** leads to a four-square 18
bang-about final chorus.

NOTES

Iphigenia in Tauris	Gluck's forty-fifth opera (including short operas) and his last but one. The sixth of the seven operas he wrote for Paris
First night	Paris Opéra, 18 May 1779
Reception	Big success
Libretto	Guillard
Source	Euripides, and several earlier adaptations of the Iphigenia story

NEWS AND GOSSIP

In the 1770s Gluck and one Piccini were rivals for No. 1 in the Paris opera charts. The Académie Royale thought it was good for the box office to hype up the competition between these two and actually commissioned an *Iphigenia in Tauris* from both at the same time. Gluck went first and had a knockout success. Piccini went two years later and flopped.

Although his work was now geared to commissions from the Paris Opéra, Gluck was by no means a Frenchman. He lived in Vienna and made the trip to Paris just in time to sort things out before rehearsals started. The Opéra company was large, riddled with bad old conventions and its singers sang in a style that did not suit the modernist Gluck. He had bad health and a bad temper and the rehearsal period must have been hell for everyone. But he did succeed in forcing his new model operas onto the stage in the way he wanted and did thereby advance the speed of the evolution of French opera which always tended to be the slowest in the European operatic convoy. From the first, *Iphigenia in Tauris* was performed a lot. It reached London in 1796 and as one of what were reckoned to be one of Gluck's best operas it was often the preferred candidate when a management felt it was time to do a Gluck. Gluck's disarmingly sparing use of his resources to get his dramatic effects attracted the attention of meddlesome big-band composers, namely Wagner and Richard Strauss (also Berlioz), both of whom arranged one of his *Iphigenias*, Wagner going for *Aulis* and Strauss for *Tauris*. Strauss had the gall to introduce leitmotifs of his own and to Straussify the poor old thing until it was unrecognizable. He forced his version on some opera houses early in the century but for the last sixty years it has been laid peacefully to rest. Today *Iphigenia* is still heard from time to time in the opera circuit, although it is usually mounted out of veneration for Gluck as an important figure in the history of opera than from any burning desire on the part of a producer to show what they can do with it.

COMMENT

Gluck's later operas are the chamber music of the opera house. They are classical through and through but lack the punch and power of the original Greek tragedies. Euripides set out to seize you by the throat and purge you with pity and terror. Gluck makes no attempt to seize or purge. In *Iphigenia* the tragedy is refined, restrained and distanced from the blood and violence of the Greek original. If operas were steaks, *Iphigenia* would be a minute steak well done and *Elektra* would be a Chateaubriand pretty well sanglant.

But only a fool will belittle chamber music. In its own quiet way it can say things just as profound, think thoughts just as beautiful and reach through to the musical sense with as much penetration as can the much noisier big-scale music. The route it takes is more through the brain and not so much by way of the viscera and this cuts down the number of chamber-music fans to a pretty select few. But there are many who put Handel's operas above all others and who get their most enjoyable vibes from operas written before *Figaro*. For such people *Iphigenia* is a very wonderful opera indeed. Its plot is simple and runs straight. It is structured in the most professional manner with recitatifs, arias, choruses and ballets perfectly balanced. In its own operatic terms the drama works beautifully and is the crowning example of Gluck's theory that in opera all the individual pieces should be subordinate to the dramatic flow of the whole thing. The music is always of good quality and sometimes quite beautiful. The recitatifs, sometimes long, are all accompagnato and set with loving care (much more care than Mozart gave to his secco recitatifs in his opera serias). Gluck could write a tune and does so in pretty well every aria. Although there is no show-stopper, Iphigenia's first act aria

'O toi qui prolongeas mes jours', Pylades' memories of boyhood 'Unis dès la plus tendre enfance', and Iphigenia's lovely song of desolation 'O malheureuse Iphigénie!', are all touching, and have that purity of sound and spirit which makes Gluck superior to the multitude of run-of-the-mill opera composers who were turning out similar operas by the dozen for the kings and princes of Europe.

It is interesting to reflect on the limited range of emotion covered by the arias in *Iphigenia*. Six of them are about grief or misery, two are happy (although the reason for happiness in one is the prospect of death), one is sung in terror, one in anger, one in a mood of resolve, and one is calm. These are the stock attitudes of opera seria with grief/misery always top of the charts, but seldom with such a huge lead. Maybe Gluck felt most at home in the misery mode or perhaps it was what the clients enjoyed most.

Gluck's orchestration is always adroit. There is one thing about his music that is especially interesting and that is his habit of writing in horizontal lines. The orchestra, most often the lower strings, frequently has a figure that moves along in the accompaniment parallel to the vocal line. This can become something like a duet. The orchestral effects (the storm, etc.) are, however, a little toy-town and the choruses mostly conventional.

It is hard to remember when you listen to this classical piece that Gluck was seen as a bit of a tearaway in his day. His ambition was to reform the stiff and boring old forms of French opera by making the words and music work together to give a dramatic flow as opposed to the stop–start succession of numbers in the old style. Hardly an eighteenth-century Wagner, but with some of the same aims and ideals.

It scarcely seems possible that *Iphigenia* is by the same composer as *Orpheus*, of seventeen years earlier. *Orpheus* makes an immediate impact on the senses yet in its own quiet way *Iphigenia* is a little beauty. Although the music reaches us from a long way off through time, for those who like their opera cool, classical and distant, *Iphigenia* is one of the best. A beta.

Julius Caesar *see* Giulio Cesare

L'Italiana in Algeri (The Italian Girl)

Lunatic comedy

Rossini

The one about the sex-mad Pasha trying to make it with an Italian Girl who effects her escape by appointing him a Pappataci.

CAST

Mustafa, Bey of Algiers	Bass
Elvira, his wife	Soprano
Lindoro, an Italian slave, loves Isabella	Tenor
Isabella, the Italian girl	Contralto
Taddeo, an elderly hanger-on of Isabella's	Baritone
Zulma, Elvira's lady-in-waiting	Contralto
Haly, Captain of the Corsairs	Bass

2 acts, 1 interval: running time 2 hrs 10 mins

STORY

Act I Sc 1 A small room in the Bey's palace

We are on the Barbary coast of Algeria two hundred years ago. Elvira tells the assembled eunuchs that her husband Mustafa has gone off her, but completely. The eunuchs respond sympathetically (surprisingly they are all tenors and basses). Mustafa appears and confirms in no uncertain terms that he has had enough of Elvira: tells his sidekick Haly (Italian for Ali) he will marry her off to the slave Lindoro and pack the pair of them off to Italy. Meanwhile will Haly please provide him with a strapping Italian girl pronto, for this is his current fancy. Haly points out the difficulties: Mustafa gives him six days to find a suitable girl or be impaled.

Lindoro's sentimental mooning over the girl he left behind him is interrupted by Mustafa who briskly informs him that he is going to get a wife. Steady on, says Lindoro, I'm very choosy about wives. Nonsense says Mustafa you'll just love this one, she's got everything.

Act I Sc 2 A pirate ship has landed on the seashore

Isabella, along with elderly hanger-on Taddeo, has been captured by Haly's corsairs. There is lots of booty and girls including this outstanding Italian girl, Isabella, just the thing for Mustafa. A chorus of hoorays. Isabella reacts coolly. She sorts out the tedious Taddeo. He knows she is in love with one Lindoro (surprise in store). Taddeo is to stop making passes at her: he must adopt the role of uncle.

Act I Sc 3 Back at the palace: a small room

Mustafa is busy despatching his reluctant wife plus Lindoro to Italy: Haly arrives with the big news – he's got the boss his Italian girl. Mustafa gloats in anticipation in a rather disgusting manner. Lindoro tells love-lorn Elvira he won't marry her but there are plenty of suitable boys in Italy: they decide to bid a formal farewell to Mustafa.

Act I Sc 4 A grander room in the palace: the balcony of harem visible in rear

Isabella is ushered in: she recoils in horror at Mustafa's lecherous ogling: she plans to play a game with him. The tiresome Taddeo intervenes: Mustafa orders him to be impaled at once. This is prevented by Isabella: she announces that he is her uncle. Lindoro enters with the farewell party and recognizes Isabella as the girl he left behind him, and so into the finale where everyone expresses his/her confusion/frustration except for Mustafa who is crazy with lust: he alone is quite clear what he wants.

Act II Sc 1 A small room in the palace

The general view of eunuchs is that Mustafa has gone potty. Once a tamer of women now an Italian girl is taming him. Isabella hears about Lindoro and Elvira: she is displeased. Unfaithful? No no says Lindoro let me explain. This was forced on me by Mustafa. The lovers plot escape together by ship. Tedious Taddeo complains to Mustafa that Haly is still running around with a stake in an unpleasant way. No sweat, says Mustafa, I'll make you a Kaimakam (High Court judge), which he does. Taddeo not certain that this is a good thing: he is fearful of his duties as a Kaimakam but reluctantly accepts the honour. He is congratulated by the eunuchs.

Act II Sc 2 Another part of the palace. Isabella dresses in front of a mirror

Elvira tells Isabella that Mustafa would like coffee with her, tête-à-tête. Isabella says you have got to stand up to men – watch me. Mustafa secretly watches Isabella dress until he can hold out no longer: he tells Taddeo to conduct her to him at once and exit when he sneezes. Coffee à deux becomes coffee à quatre (plus Lindoro as waiter) for Isabella insists Elvira joins them and Taddeo won't go no matter how much Mustafa sneezes. Mustafa explodes in anger: the scene ends in chaos.

Act II Sc 3 The small room again

Lindoro soothes Mustafa – Isabella loves him so much she has decided to create him a Pappataci. What's that? he asks. [What indeed? Ed.] A very special order with very singular rules says Lindoro. Isabella aided by Lindoro and Taddeo plots their escape.

Act II Sc 4 The grand room in the palace

The ceremony of Mustafa's induction into the Pappataci order begins. Mustafa strictly observes the rules (eat like mad and keep your eyes shut) whilst Italian party steals aboard ship that conveniently stands backstage. Mustafa sees he is licked: philosophically he decides to take Elvira back as his wife. The Italian party – presumably – depart.

MINUTES FROM START	LOOK OUT FOR	
Act I Sc 1		
0	Overture:*** a full-length concert piece, perhaps the best of all in a genre where Rossini excelled.	0
8: *Serenate il mesto ciglio*	Superior opening scene:** Elvira tells the eunuchs of Mustafa's court that he no longer loves her. (They know this already): tuneful solos and chorus: brutish Mustafa	8
13: *Oh! Che testa stravagante*	joins in a patter trio* with Elvira and Haly confirming this to be the case.	13
16: *Languir per una bella*	Lindoro's first and very fetching cavatina:** he longs for the girl he left behind him. Fancy work by a solo horn.	16
23: *Si inclinassi a prender moglie*	Mustafa informs Lindoro he is to marry Elvira: Lindoro lists his requirements in a wife (very exacting): Mustafa says Elvira has them all: witty patter duet with agreeable bursts of lyricism.**	23
Act I Sc 2		
27: *Qua ci vuol' disinvoltura*	After a sotto voce chorus (pirates stunned by such a rich opportunity for plunder) Isabella gives us her version of Kipling's 'If' in a fast patter song.**	27
32: *Ai capricci della sorte*	Isabella and Taddeo progress through impatience with each other then reconciliation and finally hit on the plan of playing uncle and niece: a wonderfully pertinent orchestral accompaniment and the whole duet a huge success.***	32

Act I Sc 3

44: *Già d'insolito ardore* Mustafa's intriguing song of anticipatory lust.* 44

Act I Sc 4

The encounter between Mustafa and Isabella gives rise to some vocalizing not a million miles away from
48: *Oh! Che muso, che figura!* a yodel, or a crazed cuckoo clock.* Things begin to 48
move: Taddeo's uncle-dom gives rise to a catchy quartet: a hushed trio ushers in the recognition of Isabella and Lindoro who modulate dramatically: fol-
58: *Confusi e stupidi* lowed by the jolliest of septets.** 58

So to the speeding up into top gear and the miracu-
62: *Va sossopra il mio cervello* lous finale*** – the ultimate in confusion – in which 62
with a myriad of cross-rhythms each character emits his own signal of bewilderment (Elvira: Din Din, Lindoro and Haly: Tac Tà, Taddeo: Crà Crà, Mustafa: Bum Bum, respectably pronounced Boom Boom) all of which together with the appropriate pantomime can make this the pottiest, funniest buffa finale in opera. A phenomenon.

Act II Sc 1

0: *Uno stupido uno stolto* The act opens with a sprightly chorus* of the eu- 0
nuchs who together with Elvira, Zulma and Haly marvel at the taming of Mustafa by Isabella.

4: *Oh, come il cor* Lindoro's happy cavatina:* very cheerful to be in 4
Isabella's good graces once more. Listen for the duetting oboe.

Taddeo, with greatness thrust upon him, deplores
8: *Ho un gran peso sulla testa* his fate in the face of salutations by the chorus, ending
in a lively climax with Rossinian cross-rhythms.** 8

Act II Sc 2

As Isabella dresses for her meeting with Mustafa she knows him to be watching her, also Taddeo and Lin-
13: *Per lui che adoro* doro. She sings a sly cavatina* about her great love for 13
him (with interjections from the watching men).

The meeting takes place and gives rise to an easy-
29: *Ti presento di mia man'* going quartet* – Mustafa, Lindoro, Taddeo and Isa- 29
bella – which becomes a quintet when Elvira joins them: Mustafa explodes in a furious solo followed by a sotto voce finale of confusion and frustration which blazes out into an accelerando ending.**

Act II Sc 3

33: *Pappataci! Che mai sento* The agreeable Pappataci trio** in which Taddeo and 33
Lindoro cheerfully explain the mysteries of this bizarre order to Mustafa.

Isabella addresses the Italian slaves in an elaborate
41: *Pensa alla patria* scena and rondo which includes a patriotic song,* a 41
rousing chorus and an oom-pah finale.

Act II Sc 4

The finale runs its course through the induction of
Mustafa as a Pappataci in a comic patter duet in
which Mustafa repeats the Pappataci oath after Tad-
53: *Di veder e nor veder* deo* (the word Pappataci itself has its own little leit- 53
motif) and then to more patter as the Italians steal
away and leading to the celebration of Isabella's triumph over Mustafa in the happiest possible final
60: *La bella Italiana* jingle.*** If this finale overall lacks the sustained in- 60
vention and gathering momentum of the finale of Act
I, it is redeemed by this happiest of Rossinian inventions to round off this opera of 'organized madness'.

NOTES

L'Italiana in Algeri	Rossini's eleventh opera (but first buffa masterpiece and second popular success)
First night	Teatro San Benedetto, Venice, 22 May 1813
Reception	Wild enthusiasm
Libretto	Anelli
Source	Previous opera same story (1808)

NEWS AND GOSSIP

Italiana was commissioned as an emergency stop-gap to replace an opera that had fallen through. It is said to have been written in 27 days and this is pretty well par for the course for Rossini during this period (*Barber*, three weeks). But such statements are pretty meaningless. We know that Mozart stored music in his head but could *set it down* very quickly. Rossini may have been walking about with bits of the Italian Girl in his mind for months, though he didn't have much free time in the run-up to it, turning out as he did some six operas in the twelvemonth from May 1812 to May 1813. *Italiana* caught on quickly and was widely played across Europe (the first Rossini to be staged in Germany). Even during the Rossinian eclipse (1880–1930), it held its place in the repertory pretty well.

COMMENT

Italiana with its fantastic plot, lunatic finale to Act I and farcical Pappatacian order is an hilarious romp, but a romp held together by considerable dramatic discipline and theatrical nous.

The musical ingredients are many and various – Lindoro's sweet love songs, Isabella's patriotic ballad, the buffa duet in which Mustafa and Lindoro run through the essential attributes of an acceptable wife, the Pappataci trio, the mellifluous, if deep-toned, chorus of eunuchs, the barking and shouting of the sex-mad Mustafa as he tries to make his way into bed with the Italian girl, the imperious recitatifs of Isabella, an early champion of feminism – all of them succeed each other in a craftily laid plan, each sequence leading inevitably to a Rossinian climax – his great gift to opera buffa – with their catchy tunes, pulse-stirring shifts in rhythm, their breathless accelerandos and ensembles calling for a troupe of vocal acrobats. By such means did Rossini shift opera away from the world of Mozart and *Figaro* towards that of Offenbach and *Orpheus in the Underworld*. No wonder that Beethoven was cross because everyone in Vienna whistled Rossini's tunes.

Rossini may have written another dozen operas, some more serious (*Tell*), some more popular (the *Barber*), but he never did better than in this jeu d'esprit of his salad days. An alpha in anybody's language – but beware, it needs an alpha production, and if the fizz and sparkle are missing it can go flat and you will wonder what the hell I am going on about.

Khovanshchina

Historical drama

Musorgsky

The one where Boyars, Princes, would-be Tsars and a Tsarina all plot and scheme for the leadership of poor old Mother Russia.

CAST

Prince Ivan Khovansky	Bass
Prince Andrei Khovansky, his son	Tenor
Prince Golitsyn	Tenor
Shaklovity, a Boyar	Baritone
Dosifey, leader of the Old Believers	Bass
Marfa, a widow, a young Old Believer	Soprano
Emma, a German girl	Soprano
Susanna, an old Old Believer	Soprano
A Scribe	Tenor
A priest, a sentry, three Streltsy, two servants, the Tsar's messenger	

5 acts: running time 2 hrs 50 mins

The version of the opera described here is the arrangement made by Shostakovich in 1960 and adapted by Claudio Abbado for his 1969 recording (see NEWS AND GOSSIP).

Before we begin

At the time that the opera starts the Tsar situation in Russia is decidedly dicey. There are two learner Tsars, young lads of sixteen and ten named Ivan and Peter, serving under the regency of their big sister Sophia, the acting Tsarina. The two learner Tsars are step-brothers with different mums who dedicate their lives to plotting and scheming to ensure that their boy and he alone should succeed to the Tsarship. The elder of the two, Ivan, has the support of the Khovansky family and the Streltsy (of whom more below) and also the goodwill of the Tsarina Sophia. Step-brother Peter and his lot have been booted out of Moscow and are plotting and scheming some distance away. The Khovansky/Sophia/Ivan party want to preserve the way of life and values of Old Russia. The Peter party want to turn it into a modern Western European state (although nothing in Russia in those days was as simple as that).

There are two organized groups:

1. The Streltsy, a military body having something in common with the Household Cavalry (but no horses and employed by a political grandee and not the Crown), Popski's Private Army and Hitler's Blackshirts.

Less well disciplined than any of the above; often on the razzle; always brutal. Regard Ivan Khovansky as their Führer and their father calling him (God knows why) the White Swan.

2. The Old Believers. Something on the lines of Scotland's Wee Frees but they sing a lot better. Whatever they believe in it is something the Peter party regard as an obstruction to progress.

There are also the Boyars, a group of barons almost as powerful as the British barons at Runnymede, the Tartars, always a threat from the Steppes, and the Muscovites, not ducks but people and the citizens of Moscow.

It's not always easy to read the political allegiances of the main characters, so here is a ready reckoner.

1. Prince Ivan Khovansky (historical). At the beginning of the opera the most powerful man in Russia and dead at the end. Head of the Streltsy. Led a revolt against the religious reforms supported by the Peter party. (This was 'the Khovansky affair' – the 'Khovanshchina'.) Supporter of sub-Tsar Ivan and Tsarina Sophia who is the ruler of Russia when the opera begins. (But she changes sides in Act IV and has Khovansky murdered.)

2. Prince Andrei Khovansky (historical). More interested in young girls than politics. It is thought father Ivan has ambitions to make him Tsar. Redeemed by the love of Marfa and persuaded to burn himself to death, all in the good cause of the Old Believers.

3. Marfa (fiction). A rabid Old Believer. Ex-mistress of Andrei. Saves an unimportant German girl Emma from his clutches. A very good woman throughout.

4. Dosifey (fiction). The John Knox of the Old Believers. Although upset to see his followers driven to mass suicide by the Peter party he tends to fold his hands and trust in God (who let him down atrociously). Not so much an opponent of the Peter party, more a victim. A very good man. (The sympathies of the opera are with the Old Believers and against reform.)

5. The Boyar Shaklovity (historical). Works with Sophia and the Peter party to murder Khovansky and is later installed as his successor to lead the Streltsy (but after the opera is over).

6. Prince Golitsyn (historical). Tsarina Sophia's chief minister. In the past has had access to her bed as well as to her political schemes and plots. [Note: 'Prince' was a courtesy title in Russia which does not imply any relationship with Royals: Ed.]

STORY

Act I Red Square Moscow

We are in that part of Red Square that has not changed over the centuries at sunrise on a cold winter's day in the 1680s and there is a Streltsy sentry asleep at his post before our very eyes. He is singing in his sleep. A group of Streltsys who have been passing thc night raping pillaging and murdering come on and torment the sentry until the city square stenographer or scribe comes on and they torment him instead. Shaklovity appears and says to the scribe Take a letter. It's top secret so keep mum about it or you will be disembowelled. He dictates 'Calling all Tsars Ivan Khovansky is going to start a rebellion to push all you lot out, to pass local government over to the Old Believers and to set up young Andrei Khovansky as Tsar.'

Here Shaklovity's business is interrupted by a pack of Muscovites who pass by singing folk songs. The Streltsy follow them shouting and singing 'We Are The Masters Now'. When he gets a little peace Shaklovity continues 'We are your friends. We are in hiding just now but once the whistle blows we'll be out of the closet like a flash.' Get that to the Tsarina quick says Shaklovity. It's anonymous. Exits. But the Muscovites return, pull the scribe's hut to pieces and make him read them a public notice which lists the ghastly crimes the Streltsy have committed.

A big procession comes on stage. It is Khovansky père having a mini Nuremberg rally. After a lot of shouting and salutes to the White Swan he makes a two-faced speech saying that there is a lot of treason about (ho ho) and it must be stopped. Everyone must be loyal to the Tsar (ho ho again). The procession exits.

Emma comes on trying to escape from young Andrei Khovansky who is hanging on to her blouse. Leggo! she shouts. Rapist! Come on Emma old girl let me love you please says Andrei. Marfa (no lisping here she really has an 'f' and not a 'th') comes on. So Andrei she says you promised to be true to me and now here you are trying to have it off with this Fraülein. Don't you worry my dear she says to Emma I'll look after you. Get off you bitch cries Andrei and leaps at Marfa with a dagger. Marfa pulls a knife as quick as a flash and parries Andrei. I won't kill you now she says I have other ideas in mind for your exit.

Trumpets and drums sound out and we are back with another Führer's procession. Khovansky père comes on sees Emma and says There's a sexy piece. Get a hold of her Streltsys and after a gang rape or two pass her on to me. Lay off! cries Andrei. She's mine! Stand back Andrei says father Khovansky. Shan't says Andrei. Get that girl Streltsys says father. Then take her dead says Andrei (tries to stab her).

Dosifey comes on with a lot of parsons and vicars behind him. Now now he says calm down. Marfa take the young German lady home.

Andrei cool off. God is good. We must save our ancient faith and he is off on a party political for the Old Believers. Khovansky père breaks in: Streltsy – 'Shun! he shouts to his troops. To the Kremlin – Quick March. And by the way Andrei I appoint you second lieutenant in charge of the bicycle shed. Off they march while the Old Believers continue to sing their holy stuff for some little time.

Act II The summer house of Prince Golitsyn

Golitsyn reads a sexy love-letter from the Tsarina Sophia. What's she after now? thinks he. Can't trust that woman an inch. He then reads a letter from his mum. Be a good boy Golly she says don't think evil thoughts and be sure to wear your thermals in this cold weather. The fortune-teller's here M'Lud says a valet. Send her in says Golitsyn. Enter Marfa (a bit of a surprise but her main job is to join up all the far-flung strands in the plot). A lot of your security chaps around she says. Nervous? One has to be careful these days says Golitsyn. OK get going. Marfa puts on the gear. Black cloak etc. and gazes into a bowl of water. Pretty bad news Prince she says. Disgrace. Exile. Estate sequestered. Stop it! Get out! shouts Golitsyn. Marfa exits. Drown her in the Home Bog at once Golitsyn says to a valet. Dear dear he thinks to himself. So I'm going to be disgraced after all I did for Russia in the Polish war.

Khovansky père forces his way in. Howdy my little man how is it in Toytown? says Khovansky. Been plotting a lot lately? Satisfied with what you've done to destroy the Boyars? And the Old Believers? Get off says Golitsyn I remember when you broke down in tears when the Tsar didn't favour you in the placement at a feast. You stink says Khovansky. You pick your nose says Golitsyn.

Dosifey creeps on. Come come gentlemen he says. Birds in their little nests agree. Prince Golitsyn do you know what will save Russia? I will tell you: God's love. Certainly, precisely, exactly, I agree says Golitsyn but I find your Rockers the Old Believers a little old-fashioned. I have more modern ideas. All right says Dosifey why don't you get out there and lead the German Mods against Russia? Dosifey is right says Khovansky you are a menace to Russia. And what about your Streltsy running amok all over the place? says Dosifey you're no better than he is. At this point the Old Believers rock on singing like crazy while the three Russian noblemen continue to exchange insults.

Marfa runs on. Prince Golitsyn she says your man tried to drown me in the Home Bog and what is more he said it was your orders and he would have done it but for Tsar Peter's soldiers who stopped him. Tsar Peter's soldiers?! say Khovansky Golitsyn and Dosifey in unison. Holy cow!

Shaklovity runs in. An edict has been issued in Murmansk he says to the effect that the Khovanskys are making a putsch to dethrone the Tsars! And what does Tsar Peter say to that? asks Dosifey. He says he thinks there may be something in it says Shaklovity.

Act III The Streltsy quarter of Moscow

The Old Believers are at it again. They troop by singing propaganda numbers. Marfa slips out of the crowd and sits in the garden of the Khovansky residence. She sings a folkish song about a woman (herself) abandoned by her lover (Prince Andrei). A very old Believer named Susanna quite unreasonably attacks Marfa as an evil woman and possibly a witch. Once again peacemaker Dosifey pops in and comforts Marfa perhaps rather more intimately than befits a man of God.

Shaklovity comes on singing drearily about the fate of poor Russia who has suffered so much from Godlessness, Tartars, Germans, bad Boyars etc. [not to mention congenital depressives like himself: Ed.]. Shaklovity is interrupted by stirrings amongst the Streltsy. Let's get out there and smash a few heads in they sing. But the Streltsy women have had enough and have formed a Feminist Group to form an anti-Streltsy female lobby. The battle of the sexes goes on in choral terms until the scribe runs on rigid with panic. Tsar Peter's troops are in Chinatown! he cries. I saw dozens of them queuing outside Ley On's takeaway. Mama Mia! cry the Streltsys. Let's report to the White-Swan-Führer and ask him what we should do. But the White Swan is ahead of them. Did you want me children? he asks. Peter's troops are about to attack us Father! they cry. Lead us into battle! Not today says Khovansky we saved Moscow three years ago. Once is enough. He goes off to bed, leaving the Streltsy thoroughly puzzled (and not only the Streltsy but opera audiences ever since) as to why he has chickened out.

Act IV Sc 1 A reception room in the Khovansky residence

Khovansky's household girls' choir sings folk songs, the liveliest one being entitled Haddock the Footman. His Persian dancers do Persian dances. His private secretary whispers in his ear saying Golitsyn tells you to watch it. Ridiculous says Khovansky. I am safe in my own home which is in fact literally a castle. Get those Persian girls dancing again and a bit more décolletage please. Shaklovity bursts in. The Tsarina has real problems he says. She has asked me to summon you to give her advice. What's that? The Tsarina wants to consult me? says Khovansky. Why of course. Certainly. Delighted to do anything I can. Bring me my second-best ermines at once. The girl choir bursts into a song about a White Swan swimming to have sex with a female white swan. Shaklovity stabs Khovansky. [As instructed by Sophia? Or just to create a vacancy for himself as head of the Streltsy? Ed.] Look at the White Swan now says Shaklovity with his foot on the dead Khovansky's chest like a big-game hunter. It's not swimming so well tonight eh? Ho ho ho.

Act IV Sc 2 Moscow. The square in front of St Basil's Cathedral

Crowds of Muscovites wander around the stage looking very Russian. A carriage goes by carrying Golitsyn off to exile. Look at that says Dosifey who has crept on again. The mighty Khovansky dead and the great Golitsyn booted out of Moscow. Enter Marfa. Holy father she says to Dosifey Peter's troops have surrounded the convent where I reside and we are done for. Ah yes I see says Dosifey. Right. The time has come for self-immolation. We will now all burn ourselves alive. But it is essential that you persuade Andrei to be burnt in tandem with you on a two-person pyre. Andrei comes on. Marfa he shouts give me back my lovely Emma. Don't be so childish says Marfa she's already back with her folks in Frankfurt. And anyway I want you and me to be burned together. Your dad is dead and they are out hunting for you all over Moscow. You are a witch says Andrei. I will have you burnt at the stake. OK if you want to arrest me call the Streltsy says Marfa. Andrei puts out a signal calling all Streltsy. No response. Again he tries. Negative. Andrei is terrified. Don't worry Andy says Marfa I'll look after you. The Streltsy now march on each one carrying his own electric chair. The female Streltsy are delighted by this turn of events. That's right, kill 'em all the dirty toads they cry. But no. A personal Boyargram arrives from the collective Tsars. The Streltsy are forgiven. [Why? Ed.]

Act V The HQ of the Old Believers in a pine wood near Moscow

Dosifey sings dismally about the fate of poor Mother Russia. The Old Believers could have saved her if allowed to do so but now they are going to be exterminated. The Old Believers troop on expressing a lot of holy thoughts about death. Andrei comes on looking for Marfa. Where are you my darling? he asks with a quick change of attitude towards her. [Why? Ed.] I'm here my love let's burn together says Marfa. The Old Believers troop on again dressed as Druids. They build a fire. The last trump sounds. As Tsar Peter's troops arrive on the scene they all jump into the flames.

MINUTES FROM START **LOOK OUT FOR**

Act I

0 Dawn breaks over the river Moscow in the prelude* 0
with solo woodwind arabesques trying to hasten the sun to rise. It rises to a flowing melody on oboe and strings that sweeps along until the church bells start to ring out. Things go quiet and we have the melody several times more on strings and as it fades, on a clarinet and finally a horn. A really nice quiet opener with such a noisy opera to come.

After the brutal soldiery pass on there is a long
9: *Ėj . . . Ėj ty stročilo!* dialogue* between the scribe and his client Shaklov- 4
ity before dictation actually begins. There are booms from the brass for Shaklovity and pirouettes from the woodwind for the scribe. The letter itself is highly confidential but is dictated pretty loud considering that a crowd of Muscovites are chattering in an agreeable chorus not too far off. The transaction is interrupted by alarums and excursions, the greatest alarm being an excursion by a band of Streltsy singing
13: *Goj vy, ljudi ratnye* their version of the Horst Wessel song.* 13

The Muscovites give the scribe a hard time. They force him to read the notice posted on a pillar. But although rough they are decent lads at heart and become, as it were, a single person, an Everyman chorus. Appalled by what they hear from the scribe
23: *Och ty rodnaja matuška Rus'* they launch into a solemn hymn** addressed to the 23
Motherland. This is in no way a national anthem but becomes an unaccompanied chorus of sympathy for poor troubled Russia (a century later to become a showpiece for the Red Army Choir). It is very fine in its fashion.

A crowd gathers and gives a tremendous build-up to the entry of Prince Khovansky senior. The Streltsy sing him in in Blackshirt style. The orchestra gives
27: *Deti, deti moi!* him a bang-bang-bang introduction. He speaks.** 27
He is their father and their Führer. He is melodious, smooth. They love it. A tremendous response. Heil Khovansky! We must support the young Tsars he says by killing the wicked etc. Sure must they say. You ready for action you Streltsy? he asks. Ready Chief! reply the Streltsy. Now sing a patriotic song he
29: *Slava lebedju* says. They sing to the White Swan** alias their great 29

white chief Khovansky. The noise is enormous, the tune irresistible, the woodwind goes mad with great shrieks and whirls and the brass pounds out deep sonorities, the Streltsy chunter on with Heil Führers. Quite a to-do.

After Andrei has tried everything just short of
on-stage rape to get possession of Emma, Marfa
33: *Tak, tak knjaže!* comes on the scene and cools it.** She takes Andrei's 33
desertion as a matter of course. Now she offers to protect Emma. Her steady low mezzo holds the centre of the trio between Andrei's ranting tenor and Emma's terrified shrieks. Andrei, backed by coarse sharp brass chords, attacks Marfa. She parries. Andrei does his nut, but hark – the Streltsy trumpets sound, the pulse of the music quickens and the Chief is on his way. It has been an eventful trio with 'acts' in it as well as 'thinks'.

After the musically stormy and very public quarrel
between Khovansky senior and his son the arrival of
Dosifey calms the family fury and gives the orchestra
40: *Stoj! Besnovatye!* a bit of a rest.* He sings in the mode of all 40
Musorgsky's good priests, slow, steady, not much tune, in a sort of dogged Greek Orthodox version of plainsong. Just as we have had about enough of him BOOM goes the great bell (orchestrally, a gong) of
Ivan the Terrible in the Kremlin. Dosifey tells his
45: *Bože vsesil'nyj* followers to pray, which they do, conventionally* but 45
movingly, between the regular booms of Ivan's bell.

Act II

1: *"Svet moj bratec Vasen'ka"* Golitsyn reads a love-letter from the Tsarina* over a 1
light accompaniment. Can he trust her? Probably not if we are to believe the heavy negative string bass we hear under his thoughts. An agreeable opener to the act. What do the heavy drum rolls mean? Perhaps Shostakovich just popped them in because he was partial to drums.

A sweet clarinet introduces Marfa, but her forecast
of the future is not sweet. After a bit of mysterious
stuff in the orchestra she gets stuck into the matter of
7: *Sily potajnye* Golitsyn's future.* Things look bad. He's going to 7
get the boot. Banished to some far-off land. All of this to a steady beat in the orchestra and a winding vocal line for her. Get out! Drown her! shouts the Prince.

Loud explosions from the brass. Too bad thinks
Golitsyn after winning the DSO and Bar in Poland.
(And we have musical memories of past battles in
some stirring martial stuff rather like the Greek
national anthem.)

The furious row between Ivan Khovansky and
12: *A my bez dokladu* Golitsyn has some surprisingly lyrical music* besides 12
the orchestral bangs and grunts that naturally punc-
tuate a Russian argument orchestrated by Shostakovich. It gathers heat and pace until Dosifey arrives on
the scene and once again calms things down. He
sings, as usual, in a holy mode supported by an air
cushion of soft brass. But when he loses patience with
Golitsyn and tells him all right then go and lead the
Germans against us, he breaks into an unholy
19: *Nu čto ž* rumbustious tune** which is very unlike his usual 19
douce mode of expression.

Golitsyn replies using the same tune. Dosifey
replies to that and so luckily we get three full verses of
it. The argument continues to the chanting of the Old
Believers who seem to have done pretty well in
beating up some sect who believe in the wrong things.
Look out especially for the wonderfully deep brass
punctuation between the verses of the Old Believers'
number.

Musically, Marfa's escape from drowning doesn't
amount to much but the announcement that Tsar
Peter's troops are around gets an instant and thunder-
24: *Petrovey* ous reaction from our trio.* The final minutes of the 24
act are splendid theatre. A Boyar jumps in and says
with evident relish that the Khovanskys have been
declared enemies of the state (big dramatic chords).
Stunned silence. The music fades away. Sometimes
you will hear, before the curtain falls, trumpet calls
and a foretaste of the Peter Party music to come in Act
III. Sometimes you won't. It depends on whether the
producer decides to follow Musorgsky's outline or
Rimsky's 'improved' version.

Act III

The Old Believers are at it again. They sing their way on and then off the stage with a tune not quite right for the Salvation Army but nearly. They leave Marfa on stage to give her situation report of what has hap-

pened since the murder attempt in the marshes. Her tune sounds weedy at first but by verse three it soon
4: *Už kak podkralas'* picks up a swinging accompaniment* and begins to 4
fill the ear nicely.

9: *Esli b ty togda* The duet** between Marfa and Susanna starts 9
metaphysically complex but musically ornery (same tune but boring accompaniment). But when Marfa tells us about her lost lover she sings with real feeling and some of the final high duetting is lovely.

After the Marfa/Dosifey consolation scene which has some nice music during its long and depressing course (same tune again but treated more generously), the stage is left to the Boyar Shaklovity who
18: *Spit streleckoe gnezdo* sings a splendid Boyar's concert piece** saying ex- 18
actly what you would expect a good class of Boyar to say, namely look at poor old unhappy Mother Russia, the Tartars gave you a hard time the Boyars were kicked out by this bastard Tsar Peter, the Germans are just around the corner and only God can save you. Come on God! Save Russia! The vocal part is built with great skill gaining in authority and Boyar-power as it goes along and reaching a really fine climax.

The Streltsy men strike up their rough and brutish
26: *Podnimajsja, molodcy!* chorus* which has the sentiments of a skinhead set to 26
coarse street-life music. The women take them on, stridently. The orchestra fans the row, the strings sometimes doubling the vocal line above with violas sometimes below. It becomes tit for tat, men, women, men, women, a silly sort of peasant songfest idea but Kuzka, one of the Streltsy, saves the situation with his ballad about the big bad woman with a taste for
28: *Zavodilas' v zakoulkach* slander. Now we have a tune that is a real goer*** and 28
as it spreads through the community it has them all good friends and jolly good company in no time. This is top-class gypsy music and very noisy.

The scribe rushes on and warns that Peter's armies are approaching. The Streltsy men and also the women are much more sympatico when scared. They sing a rather nice choral invitation to Father Khovan-
35: *Batja, Batja* sky to come out and look after his children.* He 35
comes out, but is feeble. We saved Moscow once he says but not this time. That Peter there has a lot of clout. Not what is expected of a Führer, but the

Streltsy take it quietly and indeed sing a soft little
hymn as if butter wouldn't melt in their mouths. A
dim ending to the act.

Act IV Sc 1

0: *Vozle rěcki* The peasant song that opens the act* is likely to 0
please the audience better than it pleases Khovansky,
to whom it sounds like a dirge. He asks for something
more up-beat and gets it but is almost immediately
interrupted by bad news.

5 The ballet.* This is agreeable but pretty dim 5
snake-charmer music of the 1870s (cor anglais).
Shostakovich does what he can by arranging it nicely
and having the percussion work overtime. The last
minute is good fun.

Khovansky orders the girls to sing a song in his
14: *Plyvet, plyvet* praise. This second one* is even more like a dirge 14
lebeduška than the first and rightly so for Khovansky is stabbed
to death during the third verse. Look out especially
for premonitions of death in the brass while the girls
are still singing.

Act IV Sc 2

Golitsyn goes into exile. More than any other scene in
20 the opera this long intermezzo* with its quiet 20
choruses gives the impression of the break-up of the
old Russia. Towards the end the sad strong phrases
fade downwards over a long, long held bass note. This
is desolation.

Once Dosifey and Marfa come on things get
moving.

Dosifey realizing the game is up advises Marfa to
jump into the flames when her convent is burnt.
23: *Tak vot čto?* Andrei should be at her side.** Roughly the principle 23
is that if you can't be anything else, be a martyr. His
speech is as bold as brass and loudly supported by
brass too. Marfa replies in holy ecstasy that she will
do it.

24: *A, ty zdes'* Andrei bursts in on the scene** with a tremendous 24
bustle on the strings. He is his usual violent and
unpleasant self. Where's Emma? he asks. Give me
Emma back. Marfa, who is rapidly becoming a saint,
replies sweetly that Emma has gone back to her
fiancé. Andrei rages.

Now Marfa gives him the bad news in a dirge-like

25: *Vidno ty ne čujal* holy chug-chug.** Your Dad's dead. He lies un- 25
buried. You are a wanted man. Andrei still blusters, tremolo strings and all. I'll have the Streltsy burn you for a witch he shouts. Call them sings Marfa. Andrei blows his Strelts-horn. Ivan's great bell sounds out from the Kremlin. No Streltsy come.

28: *Ne daj poščady* The Streltsy march on,*** each one carrying his 28
own private execution block. Oh my God! I'm done for says Andrei. Marfa leads him off to deep rumblings in the brass. The Streltsy women are really pleased that their menfolk are going to be beheaded and we have a turmoil chorus, tocsin, brass, men and women all together.

30 But now we have a trumpet voluntary* from Peter 30
the Great's top troop of trumpeters, all Kneller Hall trained. Then turmoil and the trumpeters again. Peter's messenger makes an announcement – all Streltsy are pardoned. Final climactic turmoil. Stupendous.

Act V

After the excitement of Act IV the opening of Act V is a bit of a come-down. You might almost as well be in
0 church. But look out for the fugitive string melody* 0
that flitters around Dosifey's opening address and the lovely deep brass burps that come humping in from time to time. Alas, the prayer itself refuses to get airborne.

10: *Bozě, grech moj* A touching duet* between Marfa and Andrei still 10
pining for Emma but understandably much tamed by ill fortune. It is mostly Marfa remembering the days they were in love. She is out of her saintly mode now and sings like a loving woman. We have echoes of one of the earlier folk songs, but very much slower and more richly harmonized.

A sinister death march stalks with a regular beat on
16: *Slyšal li ty* the timps. Marfa bravely defies fate.** Andrei is not 16
so sure. Look out especially for the lovely ending to Marfa's message to Andrei (plus a subdued tocsin beneath: just before the bugles sound). As the chorus enter we have some melting harmonic shifts.

The finale opens with what sounds like an Orthodox chant. At first it is sung by the female Old Believers unaccompanied but it slowly gathers support from chorus and orchestra. Then there is a short but mighty climax of bells, voices and brass which fades as the flames shoot up, the Old Believers jump to their death and the curtain falls.

NOTES

Khovanshchina	Musorgsky's third performed opera
First night	Kononov Auditorium, St Petersburg, 9 February 1886
Reception	Politically correct
Libretto	Musorgsky
Source	Russian history

NEWS AND GOSSIP

It must be a bit of a facer for any composer squaring up to a big historical subject to know that none of the leading characters (in this case no member of the Romanov family) may appear on the stage. This was the ruling of the Russian censor at the time of the composition of *Khovanshchina*. *Hamlet* without the Prince, *Macbeth* without the Macs, *Henry IV* and *V* without a single Henry would have made things pretty difficult for Shakespeare. Nothing daunted, Musorgsky dived into *Khovanshchina* with the idea of making prime movers of the Streltsy, the Old Believers and the Muscovites and of using proxies for the Royals (Golitsyn and Shaklovity). He never finished the opera, starting work in 1872 and dying in 1891 before he had done much more than assemble most of the numbers in performance order in his 'Blue Book'. Rimsky-Korsakov got in there almost at once and orchestrated, 'corrected' and cut the opera to his taste, no doubt taking pretty big liberties in the process. In particular he favoured Tsar Peter by popping in Peter Party music at the end of Act II. This gives the whole opera an upbeat twist which was certainly not Musorgsky's intention. He preferred the noble gloom of the Old Believers and spoke darkly of 'the power of the Black Earth' which was read to mean that the old Russian culture was strong enough to resist Peter's reformist notions of making Russia a member of the EU.

After Rimsky had worked his will on *Khovanshchina* next came Diaghilev. He got Stravinsky and Ravel (strange bedfellows?) to improve on Rimsky's version for a production in Paris in 1913. Finally, Shostakovich had yet another go starting from scratch and the Musorgsky 'Blue Book', but clearly taking a lot of leads from Rimsky. This version had its premiere at the Mariansky in Leningrad (as it then was) in 1960 and is basically the one described here with the important exception of the last scene which is from the version by Stravinsky.

Khovanshchina is a big aspidistra to pack into any but the major houses. It needs a lot of people on stage to get the full effect of the choruses and since their appearances overlap you can't double (or treble) a singer as a Strelt, a Muscovey or an OB. Also it needs Russian voices to make it come off well and, if sung in Russian, as it should be, singers who can at least cope with the Russian language to make it come off at all. So it is a fairly rare bird in the aviary of international opera. A giant vulture, perhaps, morose, broody, but powerful.

COMMENT

Like *Boris*, *Khovanshchina* is not so much an opera more a number of scenes of Russian history. Alas the plot, if any, is even less coherent and (like *Simon Boccanegra*) it demands a pretty detailed understanding of a complex and completely unfamiliar political system. For a novice, trying to get a grip on the story of *Khovanshchina* is as tough as a first encounter with mahjong. The language is foreign, the symbols don't seem to have any sense in them and you can't find out what the hell the game is about anyway. It does not help at all to know that it is a work of faction, that owing to the prohibition on using real-life Royals, Musorgsky had to insert Dosifey as a sort of listener's friend to guide the clients along the plot line. Alas, Dosifey fails in this enterprise almost as certainly as he did in trying to save the Old Believers. Also the Andrei/Marfa love interest is so awkwardly spatchcocked on to the main story as to be faintly ludicrous.

But with all its faults *Khovanshchina* has one great virtue, it throbs with a very Russian love of Russia. Everyone loves Russia in a different way. Khovansky, the Old Believers, every Muscovite and Musorgsky himself. Other nations have a problem in showing their love of their country in acceptable terms – the French are chauvinistic, the British were jingoistic, the Americans are brash – but for some reason, to love Russia is a lovable thing in itself, although one does get a little deaved with the constant keening about poor Russia's terrible past, unfortunate present and catastrophic future.

This is the heart of the opera and much of the best music is inspired by it. Apart from the stand-alone folksy numbers, of which there is an even bigger helping than in *Boris*, we have the Muscovites' national hymn in Act I, Dosifey's patriotic outrage when he taunts Golitsyn about leading a German invasion into Russia, Shaklovity's Boyars' scene in Act III and all of the Old Believers' better choral numbers.

There is also good dramatic music in the Marfa/Andrei relationship. This bizarre sub-plot justifies itself in the Marfa/Emma/Andrei scene in Act I and the Andrei/Marfa duet in Act IV which ends in his futile attempt to call out the Streltsy. The wholly irrelevant Susanna/Marfa scene also shows what Musorgsky can do in what is the nearest thing to a showpiece operatic number.

No one knows how Musorgsky's own orchestration would have sounded. Bleaker than Rimsky's, one would guess, perhaps nearer to Shostakovich. But both versions bring us the sound of Russia at full strength, for it is the mighty choruses and the emphatic use of the orchestra that give *Khovanshchina* its power to stun us. Here is a slice of Russia served up in the raw and if we can't quite follow why the chief minister should so suddenly decide to murder his Empress's chief supporter, we are clear that Russia is great, Russia is in trouble and that blood will continue to flow long after the curtain comes down. But as an opera it only rates beta.

Lakmé

Oriental romance

Delibes

The one where the daughter of a Brahmin priest falls in love with a British officer and kills herself when duty calls him back to the regiment.

CAST

Nilakantha, a Brahmin priest	Bass–baritone
Lakmé, his daughter	Soprano
Hadji, their servant	Tenor
Mallika, their slave	Mezzo
Gerald, an English officer	Tenor
Frederick, ditto	Baritone
Miss Bentson, a governess	Mezzo
Rose, an English girl	Soprano
Ellen, ditto	Soprano

3 acts: running time 2 hrs 20 mins

STORY

Act I The garden of a secret Hindu temple

We are in India in the 1880s when the British Raj ruled the roost and there was no subversive talk about Independence. Nilakantha a Brahmin priest has been forbidden by the beastly Brits to practise his religion but he continues to do so in secret, indeed a few of the faithful are worshipping at this moment led by his deaconess daughter Lakmé. After divine service Lakmé carelessly leaves her jewellery on a bench and goes off downstream with her maid Mallika for a dip.

An unlikely party of Brits namely two juvenile officers (Frederick and Gerald) one comic governess (Miss Bentson) two silly debs (Rose and Ellen the latter the fiancée of Gerald) break into the temple compound. Frederick tells them it's the base for an underground terrorist organization led by a frightful fanatic called Nilakantha. They move on.

Gerald stays to make a sketch of the jewellery for his fiancée Ellen. Lakmé and Mallika return: Gerald hides. Whew! What a jolly pretty girl he thinks. Lakmé spots him. You bounder! she says. Get out! Just lemme look at you please says he. I've got a feeling I'm falling says Lakmé (to us not to him). Get out! she says again (to him) what gave you the right to bust in on me here? Love he says. Love found a way. Love? she says. Yes: I've got a feeling I'm falling: love is the sweetest thing and I rather think it's two for tea but hark what is that? Fanatical Dad is back. Who done bust through my fence? he asks. Oh it's this guy here is it? Right: he must die.

Act II A busy Indian bazaar

Miss Bentson and her girls are not much at home in a bazaar and provide some crummy comedy. A bell rings and the market closes. Now we are into a festival with pseudo Indian temple dancers doing their stuff. Nilakantha comes on got up as a beggar with Lakmé rattling a can. He unwisely sings about revenge although the English party are within earshot. But they don't hear him. He also says he is worried about Lakmé (who has gone gloomy out of love for Gerald). He gets Lakmé to sing in order to attract some trade. This she does with a ditty in the style of a Neapolitan coloratura soprano but fails to get any money in the tin.

Suddenly she sees Gerald and faints. Aha! thinks Nilakantha that's my man. I'll get him. Gerald rushes over to Lakmé. Leave her Gerry leave her shouts Frederick we are due to rejoin the regiment (a body of soldiers passes by). Exit all the English. Nilakantha plots and plans with confederate priests how to murder Gerald. Exit Nilakantha.

Gerald returns and sings a pretty long love duet with Lakmé in the square which has emptied for this purpose. Lakmé suggests they skip off to a love-nest in the jungle. Once they are sure the love duet is over a festival procession of Brahmins comes on as do the English to spectate. But they do not care for Hindu spectacle and leave, all except Gerald. Nilakantha and his mob steal up on Gerald and kill him. But no: Lakmé discovers he's not dead only severely concussed.

Act III A love-nest in the jungle

Gerald has come to but has a bad headache. There is a lot of love-nest talk. Unseen lovers go by to get magic water from a well. Frederick breaks into the love-nest. He has followed a trail of blood. You know where your duty lies old boy he says and strangely enough we can hear parade ground noises and the patriotic songs of soldiers from this ill-chosen love-nest. I'll be there to serve my Queen and country old boy says Gerald.

Lakmé sees she has lost Gerald and eats some poisonous mangel wurzels growing conveniently near the love-nest. They drink some magic water from the well and swear eternal love. But it won't be all that long says Lakmé because I'm dying. She tells Nilakantha who has turned up for the finale that he must forgive Gerald because he has drunk holy water. She tells Gerald he has given her a sweet dream. She dies.

MINUTES FROM START

LOOK OUT FOR

Act I

0 The prelude* is a bit of a musical switchback: loud 0
and vulgar opening then one tune on the heels of another. By the time it ends we know we are in a land of
placid harmony with would-be oriental pretensions.
Just a star, mainly for bizarrité.

6: *Blanche Dourga* Lakmé's prayer.* After some oriental chirps and 6
burps a rhubarb opening chorus and a nice but wholly
European recitatif from Nilakantha we hear Lakmé
praying to three selected Hindu gods. She sings like a
caged linnet, warbling, trilling, bel-cantoing. All very
high and very pretty-pretty. A soft chorus below, off
and on.

10: *Lakmé c'est toi* A tune for Nilakantha.* Relaxed and beguiling. 10
But as he duets with Lakmé it gets lost and we pro-
gress through recitatif to the gentle ensemble of farewells that closes the scene. As mild as milk, spiked
with golden syrup.

14: *Dôme épais le jasmin* The barcarolle duet.* Why two Indian girls should 14
sing a duet in a form commonly used by Venetian
gondoliers is puzzling. Perhaps it is because they are
going boating. But it is very agreeable and pretty and
makes no demands on the listener whatsoever. Sort of
close harmony, repetitive and eventually fading away
down the river.

The English ensemble. The famous five throw out
a jumble of views and expressions about India and
22: *Quand une femme est si jolie* about women in a flighty ensemble* leading to two 22
agreeable ditties, one from Frederick and the other
from Ellen. Frederick thinks Indian women are just
little pets. Ellen thinks they compare poorly with
modern women of Europe. So back into the flighty
ensemble and we have to pinch ourselves to remember we are not listening to Gilbert & Sullivan.

Gerald's fantasy. He builds a sexy/romantic image
29: *Fantaisie aux divins mensonges* of what Lakmé might be like in an agreeable aria* 29
which meanders along very pleasantly without any
apparent structure, without form and made up of a
number of dreamy phrases each one the consequence
of the last. Or rather the inconsequence, for they have
no discernible relationship.

37: *Pourquoi?* Lakmé's happy song.* A reprehensible solo violin 37 introduces a high and at first halting solo piece for Lakmé which builds cleverly into a mini-orgasm of happiness. A sweet piece.

The encounter. The duet which comes at the end of Act I is a rum affair. Lakmé has her various melodic ideas, Gerald sticks to a strange figure which rises and falls like a five-finger exercise and Delibes has great difficulty in combining them. But relief is at hand – a
44: *C'est le dieu* tune,* the best in the piece, breaks out as Gerald is 44
smitten by love for Lakmé and she in turn is smitten by love for him. This builds into the usual lovers' climax where both smite and are smitten at the same time. Unfortunately the last chorus has both voices and the orchestra plugging out the tune in unison. Puccini could pull this off. Delibes can't.

Act II

The entr'acte is another curio, but tuneful. A covey of fifes, Mantovani strings and the brass section each has
2: *Allons avant que midi sonne* a short innings. Followed by a chatter chorus* that 2
could have come straight from *The Mikado*. Three
7 dances.* Although obviously intended to carry the 7
flavour of the East, the first sounds Russian peasant, the second Russian Tchaikovsky, the third circus snake-charmer. But Delibes could write for ballet and all three stir the limbs. Followed by a singularly dim little chorus.

Nilakantha addresses Lakmé with the most un-Brahminlike sentiments imaginable in a mildly agree-
17: *Lakmé, ton doux regard* able number.* 17

The Bell Song. Lakmé tells the tale,* and in a very 23
23: *Où va la jeune indoue* odd way. Patches of recitatif with bursts of bel canto
between. Could be practice hour backstage in a Neapolitan theatre and the poor Indians must have been a little surprised to hear fioritura and Italianate vocal gymnastics echoing round their market place. Used to be popular as a show-off piece for aspiring sopranos. A star for bizarrité. Both before and after the thing itself Lakmé has outbursts of wordless coloratura gargling.

Having got rid of a fife and drum band rather quickly, the conspirators lay their plot in one of the
33: *Au milieu des chants* most nearly operatic scenes in the piece.* The dark 33
background of undulating strings and the sotto voce

plotting are effective.

The love duet. This is a pretty piece, perhaps at its
41: *Dans la forêt* best in Lakmé's dreamy vision* of a little hut in the 41
jungle.

The closing scene of Act II with its distinctly ornery chorus (with interruptions) and the melodrama of the grievous bodily harm applied to Gerald would soon fade from the mind were it not for the
53: *Ils croient leur vengeance* genuinely touching envoi* from Lakmé as she 53
crouches over his body. 'May God protect our love' she sings (diplomatically avoiding any mention of which god is being addressed).

Act III

0 Entr'acte:* a nice one to the tune of 'Dans la forêt'. 0
Suitable for a slow pas de deux in any ballet of the period.

Owing to being asleep, Gerald doesn't hear Lakmé's number that opens Act III. He doesn't miss much. Having shaken off slumber, he sings about
9: *Ah! viens dans la forêt* love in the forest in perhaps the most grown-up aria* 9
in the score. It has a character of its own both in the melodic shape and in its novel-sounding harmonies. Nice one, Leo.

21: *Ce n'est pas plus toi!* The break-up. An effective scene* where Lakmé 21
suspects Gerald's treachery and tries to get him to swear to be true to her against a background of military noises (so close to the jungle love-nest?). Fifes. Shouted orders. Unlikely exclamations from the Tommies such as 'Courage!' 'March with a song!' 'Let our soldierly songs fly to mother England!!'

The final duet. This runs its course sweetly and variously, snatches of melody constantly holding out hope for a stretch of sustained inspiration. This almost happens once when Gerald drinks the magic
27: *Qu'autour de moi tout sombre* water* but it drifts on into a chocolate-box climax. 27

The final melodrama gets by on a succession of stock operatic gestures but is once again saved from
32: *Tu m'as donné le plus doux rêve* total banality by a sweet high soprano farewell* (for- 32
ever this time) from Lakmé.

NOTES

Lakmé	Delibes' twenty-third and last performed opera (including operetta)
First night	Opéra-Comique, Paris, 14 April 1883
Reception	A big success
Libretto	Gille and Loti
Source	A novel by Pierre Loti variously called *Rarahu* and *Le Mariage de Loti*

NEWS AND GOSSIP

Delibes read Pierre Loti's novel on a train journey. He liked it and composed the score between the summers of 1881 and 1882. He had spent his life producing ballets and operettas with a good deal of success, some of them at Offenbach's famous theatre Bouffes-Parisiens, though how any audience who really liked Offenbach could put up with Delibes' brand of soft soap it is hard to understand. He went for the big one with a serious opera *Jeu de Nivelle*, now happily forgotten. So on to *Lakmé* which was right in the centre of the current and unfortunate fashion for exotica about the Far East (Meyerbeer's *Africaine*, Bizet's *Pearl Fishers*, Massenet's *Le Roi de Lahore* et al.). It had a vogue at the time and was played at the Opéra-Comique until the 1930s. Now it lies in a state of well-deserved obscurity.

COMMENT

It is hard to understand how *Lakmé* got under the wire into the field of Grand Opera. It certainly isn't grand nor is it an opera, except in the sense that any piece staged with singers and a full orchestra is an opera. It is in fact a musical romance of the kind that Ivor Novello produced so successfully fifty years later, with the difference that *The Dancing Years* had spoken dialogue and *Lakmé* has recitatif (though with patches of parlando, or speech over music, when Delibes ran out of steam).

It is not being toffee-nosed to recognize *Lakmé* for what it is – undemanding light music of the kind that was played by Palm Court trios all over Europe in the first half of this century. But opera – no. The music doesn't have the power, the characters don't have the credibility and the unconscious comedy of Delibes' vision of India make it a pretty ludicrous old thing. Or if you take it in any way seriously, insulting, not to the Raj which has, God knows, been caricatured enough and deserved it, but to Hindu culture and the Hindu religion, a lot more venerable than French Catholicism.

The music is not without charm. Delibes could write a moderately good short tune but never a long one. So you get in the best pieces a sort of haphazard parade of good melodic ideas which beguile the ear but don't satisfy that craving for shape, form, structure or whatever it is that tells us when a piece of music is music and not muzak. The best numbers are Lakmé's 'Pourquoi?' in Act I and Gerald's 'Ah! viens dans la forêt' in Act III. The orchestral pieces are much more professional and it is odd that Delibes, who could write ballet music with the best (well, nearly the best), seemed to lose his sense of direction when he wrote for the human voice. The famous Bell Song is a particularly awful piece of kitsch.

So I would advise against spending the price of an opera ticket on *Lakmé*. Indeed, if the sale were challenged on the grounds of infringing the Trades Descriptions Act, I would not be surprised. Gamma or worse.

Lecouvreur, Adriana *see* Adriana Lecouvreur

Lescaut, Manon *see* Manon Lescaut

I Lombardi (alla prima crociata – The Lombards on the First Crusade)

Mediaeval tragedy

Verdi

The one with lots of singing crusaders, a hermit in a cave and a brand of mineral water with supernatural powers.

CAST

Arvino, son of Folco, Lord of Rò	Tenor
Pagano, his brother	Bass
Pirro, Arvino's A.D.C.	Bass
Viclinda, Arvino's wife	Soprano
Giselda, Arvino's daughter	Soprano
Acciano, Tyrant of Antioch	Bass
Oronte, his son	Tenor
Sofia, his wife	Soprano
A priest, etc.	

4 acts: running time 2 hrs 2 mins

STORY

Act I (Each act has a rather pompous subtitle – Act I is called: The Revenge)

Sc 1 A square in Milan

We are in the eleventh century outside a church in Milan with an unusual service going on within: purpose – to celebrate the happy reunion of two feuding brothers. Outside the church the citizens are doubtful, not to say sceptical, about the bona fides of brother Pagano. A chorus of women less well-informed than the men (unusual) ask questions in order to trigger a now-read-on rundown: they are told that Pagano and brother Arvino were both dead set on marrying Viclinda: Arvino got her: Pagano laid ambush to kill brother Arvino on the way to church: he messed it up: was exiled: now he's penitent, returned, forgiven: but can he be trusted?? Now read on.

Everyone is pleased about the reconciliation but Pagano lets drop (only to us) that indeed he is by no means sincere. An irrelevant priest pops in and says Arvino has been appointed C-in-C of next Crusade by Peter the Hermit [who he? Ed.]. A band of singing nuns stroll on singing for peace:

Pagano sneers at them thus clearly signalling himself to be a really bad man: he tells Pirro (brother Arvino's A.D.C.) he's going to kill Arvino properly this time and get Viclinda for himself. Pirro, disloyal bastard, says great I'll go with that: he conjures up a gang of thugs ready for any mayhem that offers.

Act I Sc 2 A gallery in Folco's palace, bedrooms off

Viclinda feels a bit funny about Pagano: maybe he's about to double-cross? Arvino says I hear footsteps: you keep cave, look after father Folco. Pagano comes on: Pirro tells him Arvino has turned in: the thugs set the palace alight: Pagano drives his sword into a sleeping body (off-stage): Viclinda intervenes: Arvino shouts: jings! Pagano has killed the wrong man, namely his dad Folco. A serious error. Arvino tries to kill Pagano, is stopped by daughter Giselda: Pagano tries to kill himself, is stopped by guards. Pagano, still alive, is banished by general consent.

Act II The Man of the Cave
Sc 1 A hall in the palace of Acciano in Antioch

Another country, another set of royals. A chorus of ambassadors (so many?) tell Moslem supporter Acciano that Christian Crusaders (reported to be behaving frightfully badly, raping, etc.) are on their way.

Crown Prince Oronte pines for love of Lombardette Giselda, surprisingly already a prisoner in Antioch. Mum Sofia (a Christian) tells him: the girl loves you. Hooray says he. If you marry her you must become a Christian says wily proselytizing Sofia: OK by me says broad-minded Oronte.

Act II Sc 2 A hermit's cave

The Hermit (Pagano of course) is ridden with guilt but is rooting for the Crusaders. (Sound of distant battle.) Pirro appears: he seeks divine forgiveness for being an accessory to patricide. Also (despicable dog) he has reneged to the Moslem side for fear of being shot for cowardice by the Lombards. Hermit says forgiveness is certain if Pirro leads a fifth column and opens the gates of Antioch to the Crusaders.

Arvino arrives: he asks the holy Hermit to bless his enterprise and by the way, he says, my daughter's a goner. Not to worry good sir says the Hermit, you'll get your daughter back and be inside Antioch by tonight. Wizzo! says everyone.

Act II Sc 3 Inside Acciano's harem

The harem inmates tell Giselda she's a lucky pig to have bagged Oronte. But against this her family and the other Lombards will of course be wiped out. Too bad. As Giselda prays a bit Lombards chase Turks across back of the stage (so the Lombards have won). Sofia comes on: she says a traitor (Pirro of course) let the Lombards into Antioch: her husband Acciano says their son Oronte is dead. Enter Crusaders, Hermit and Arvino: Giselda repulses dad (he's killed her Oronte): gives him a lecture on pacifism: goes mad and prophesies nasty things for the future. Arvino (very cross) tries to kill her: the Hermit stops him.

Act III The Conversion
Sc 1 By the Mount of Olives

Pilgrims sing about Jerusalem (for a long time). Giselda wanders on – so does Oronte, not dead at all. A mirage? Not so, reports of death grossly exaggerated. Come fly with me he says: sure thing she says: they fly, to sounds of distant battle.

Act III Sc 2 Arvino's tent

Arvino is still cross because Giselda was rude to him. Crusading knights rush in: they report sighting of evil brother Pagano lurking amongst the Lombards. I'll get him says Arvino.

Act III Sc 3 Mouth of a cave: River Jordan visible outside

Oronte, weak from (much delayed?) effect of wounds, is brought into the cave by Giselda. He says he is dying: no, stick it out, says she: your death would diminish my respect for God. Belt up says the suddenly appearing Hermit, wash out your blasphemous mouth. He recovers his composure: your proposed mixed marriage does not look good but all will be well he says if Oronte is baptised with water from the River Jordan. Oronte is baptised. All is not well: Oronte expires. Much talk of reunion in heaven.

Act IV The Holy Sepulchre
Sc 1 Another cave

Giselda dreams she sees Oronte who gives her a tip, namely that if the Crusaders drink a special brand of mineral water (Siloam con gaz) it will make them strong and mighty and they will win.

Act IV Sc 2 The Lombard camp

The Crusaders grumble about leaving lovely Lombardy for this God-forsaken desert. Giselda and Arvino give the troops a pep talk: advise them to drink Siloam con gaz. They do.

Act IV Sc 3 Arvino's tent

The Hermit arrives badly wounded and is taken into Arvino's tent for first aid. He reveals himself as Pagano (no surprise) but is about to die. He asks forgiveness: gets it: asks to see the Holy City: is shown it (curtain pulled aside!) full of victorious Crusaders cheering like mad: dies.

MINUTES FROM START

LOOK OUT FOR

Act I Sc 1

Lombardi opens with a series of choral-concertante set pieces, the first giving us a now-read-on précis to a
7: *T'assale un tremito!* cheerful fairground tune: the second (and best),* 7
with spirited contributions from the hopefully reconciled principals (Arvino, Pagano, also audible Giselda, Viclinda), lurches to a noisy conclusion in waltz time: the third is tuneful but by now we have had quite a lot of the singing citizens.

But yet more: this time females only: a solemn prayer put up by some nuns, interrupted by Pagano talking about revenge and murder (unwisely surely – but then in true operatic style no-one but his mate
19: *Sciagurata! hai tu creduto* Pirro can hear him): ends with a nice solo.* 19

Yet another chorus, this time all-male, Pirates-of-Penzance style, very fast, from Pagano's gang of hired
21: *Niun periglio* thugs.* 21

Act I Sc 2

28: *Salve Maria* A nice little prayer to the Virgin from Giselda:* slow 28
to start but flowers to a pretty conclusion with attendant flute accompaniment.

Another helping of principals/chorus concer-
38: *Va! sul capo* tante* ends the scene with a noisy condemnation of 38
Pagano's frightful act.

Act II Sc 1

0: *È dunque vero?* A good standard chorus and bass duo*opens the act: 0
it improves to one-star level in a final hymn to Allah in which presumably not all of the ambassadors join.

4: *La mia letizia infondere* The first of two splendid tenor arias** for love-sick 4
Oronte in close succession: seven golden minutes.

Act II Sc 2

14: *Ma quando un suon' terribile* The Hermit (Pagano) struggles with his guilt.* 14
22: *Stolto Allhà!* The Crusaders' By Jingo! final chorus.* Light cav- 22
alry stuff very offensive to Islam: it would certainly have earned them a Fatwa if they had not had one already.

Act II Sc 3

The scene opens with a 'Turkish' prelude and an unexciting chorus of women of the harem reflecting no doubt their pretty unexciting lives. Giselda makes a prayer to her mother which moves into a nice lyrical
28: *Se vano è il pregare* vein with some really flowery stuff to end it.* 28
Giselda goes mad, and thereby gains her big chance to do a mad scene, the forerunner of many
32: *No! No! Giusta causa non è* mad scenes to come. She starts her aria* a little stick- 32
ily but as dementia begins to bite she has a nice oompah lyrical passage which spirals upwards into some pretty potty coloratura with a slightly other-worldly quality.

A below-standard end to the act.

Act III Sc 1

A big succession of set-piece choruses starts the act off: pilgrims this time, so we have a full-voiced Hail
0: *Gerusalem! Gerusalem!* to Jerusalem first:** next the females sketch out some 0
of the more notable events that took place in the city: then the men do the same and finally together. A little heavy and holy but mighty impressive.

And now for something entirely different and really good – a marathon duet between Oronte and Giselda. First Giselda, much saner, roams alone giving vent to recitatif: she meets Oronte: they declare
8: *Per dirupi e per foreste* their love: a fine sweeping aria from Oronte** mov- 8
ing into a racy duet taken at breakneck speed: Giselda now has her turn and steadies things up with a very
11: *Oh belle, a questa misera* decent little aria:* next a fetching section of duetting 11
to throbbing harps finishing in a gallop as the distant Crusaders hype themselves up for battle.

Act III Sc 2

Good vigorous stuff: nothing remarkable.

Act III Sc 3

20 The prelude* is a brief violin concerto: double stop- 20
ping at first then a sweet/soppy tune: runs into an
24: *Qui posa il fianco* agreeable presto. Ends with gravitas.
A great trio, part one effective (no more)* (Oronte: 24

I'm dying, Giselda: No you aren't, if so God is no
28: *Qual voluttà trascorrere* good, Hermit: Don't blaspheme), part two*** quite 28
wonderful (Oronte: I feel much better but in a funny way: I'm still dying, Giselda: You mustn't leave me, Hermit: Never mind: if you don't get it here you will have it good in Heaven). The solo violin of the opening concerto hovers around the whole scene and is probably Oronte's soul (or something) ascending to heaven. Very affecting.

Act IV Sc 1

Giselda's dream, celestial spirits, vision of Oronte
(now defunct) is not at all spooky or holy. First a vivid
5: *Oh! Di sembianze eteree* acrobatic piece** with an unnerving change of key as 5
she sees the dead Oronte and then (after some good
6: *Non fu sogno!* declamatory stuff) a jaunty display aria:** easy on the 6
ear if a little common (lots of oom-pahs).

Act IV Sc 2

It's the chorus again; this time the Lombards tell God they have done him proud by swapping the beautiful plains of Lombardy for this frightful Middle East. They do it in what sounds like a lurching Tyrolean
10: *O Signore, dal tetto natio* drinking song* with twirls on the flute and all. Bizarre 10
17: *Guerra! Guerra!* but tuneful. A second powerful chorus* calling 17
everyone to fall in for battle (with Arvino and the Hermit in amongst it too) is more effective.

Act IV Sc 3

21: *Un breve instante* One last good ensemble – a trio* between the Hermit, 21
now revealed as Pagano, Giselda and Arvino (Pagano: Now it's me that's dying, Giselda: Forgive him, Dad, Arvino: Yes, I do) before the final impressive but rather lumpen outing for the chorus.

NOTES

I Lombardi	Verdi's fourth opera
First night	La Scala, Milan, 11 February 1843
Reception	A wild success
Libretto	Solera. See below
Source	An epic poem by one Tommaso Grossi

NEWS AND GOSSIP

The librettist, Temistocle Solera, had already worked with Verdi on *Nabucco*. This bizarre figure had run away from school to join a circus, had two operas accepted by La Scala before he was twenty-four and was thought to be a spy for Queen Isabella of Spain. As usual, there were problems during rehearsal: the Bishop of Milan found the baptism in the waters of the Jordan to be blasphemous [why? Ed.] and forbade its performance. But his powers must have been limited since Verdi paid no attention to this edict and nothing untoward happened to him either politically or spiritually. The touchpaper of Italian nationalism was set alight by one or two items in *Lombardi* that were thought to be coded revolutionary messages, but then one is forced to believe that if someone had set the telephone directory of 1843 to music the restive politicos in the audience would have cheered any reference to Freedom Travel p.l.c., Liberty's, or even Victoria Station.

COMMENT

I Lombardi catches Verdi fairly low on his learning curve. The libretto is dreadful and some of the music coarse, bombastic or just plain awkward. The story starts well enough with the reunion of the brothers and the unlikely murder of their father. But just as our adrenalin begins to run we are switched to another court, darn it, another tyrant with another family and we have to start pretty well all over again. The Hermit fools no-one, Pirro is unbelievably venal, the Crusaders teeter on the brink of self-parody and two deaths (Oronte and Pagano) so similar, so holy and in such quick succession is surely one too many.

As we reach Act IV there is such an overkill in the matter of holiness that one's sympathies tend to veer to the side of the Turks. As to the music, it is chorus time in Lombardy – even more choruses than *Nabucco*, though some are not so good. The Scala chorus must have been quick-change artists since they had to appear as citizens, nuns, cut-throats, ambassadors, Crusaders, concubines, Crusaders again, pilgrims, celestial spirits and finally pilgrims and Crusaders mixed. Some of the choruses, particularly the ones that open Act I and Act III, plus the fierce call to arms – 'Guerra!' (Act IV Scene 2, a real little stinger) – are Verdi in full fig, but others verge on the ornery. But . . . there are sections of *Lombardi* where Verdi's genius breaks through the mists with music as beguiling as any we shall get from him in his later years. The Oronte/Giselda duet in the first scene of Act III, also the trio Oronte/Giselda/Hermit in the next scene, show Verdi at his young best, though admittedly we have to wait a long time for them and the burst of inspiration does not last long. Overall, with its clumsy plot and musical longueurs, we must mark *Lombardi* down as a beta. Can (and will) do better.

Lucia di Lammermoor

Historical tragedy

Donizetti

The one where our heroine's wicked brother cons her into believing her fiancé is unfaithful so that he can make her marry a rich man, which she does but it's no good because she goes mad and murders him.

CAST

Lucy Ashton (Lucia)	Soprano
Henry Ashton (Enrico), her brother, Lord of Ravenswood	Baritone
Edgar (Edgardo), dispossessed heir to Ravenswood	Tenor
Arthur (Arturo), Lord Bucklaw	Tenor
Raymond (Raimondo), Chaplain at Ravenswood	Bass
Norman (Normanno), Captain of the Guard	Tenor
Alice (Alisia), Lucia's companion/minder	Mezzo

2 acts: running time 2 hrs 10 mins

STORY

Act I Sc 1 The grounds of Ravenswood Castle

We are in the seventeenth century and in the land of Sir Walter Scott about 40 miles south of Edinburgh and Henry Ashton and his security man Norman plus retainers are conducting a manhunt before dawn. Henry is afeared that reports of a lurking stranger mean that Edgar whose father he killed (and then pinched Ravenswood) is the lurker. Also he suspects Edgar is indulging in loverly meetings with his sister Lucy. He has heard a rumour that one morning Edgar did a toreador act and saved Lucy from a charging bull. He tells Norman that he is broke and only if sister Lucy marries rich Lord Arthur Bucklaw can things be set to rights. But she won't have him. Because she is in love with Edgar?

Henry's suspicions are confirmed by the chorus prancing in: they have sighted Edgar. So it's true says Henry. I'll fix both sister Lucy and her lover. Just wait and see.

Act I Sc 2 By a fountain in Ravenswood Park

Lucy tells her minder about an apparition she had: she saw a dead girl in the fountain, but cheer up – she is shortly going to meet her lover Edgar. Edgar arrives: Alice keeps watch: all three in a bit of a panic lest discovered. Edgar says before he goes back to France (acting as a sort of fifth-columnist for the Stuarts) he will humbly ask Henry to bury the hatchet and let him marry Lucy. No, no, she says: that'll blow it: we must keep our love secret. This makes Edgar very cross: he gave up all ideas of revenge he says for love of Lucy now she shilly-shallies: she soothes him: they take a solemn vow to marry and exchange rings. Please remember to write every day she says.

Act I Sc 3 A room in Ravenswood

A crowd of wedding guests are assembled at Ravenswood but it would seem prematurely for Lucy has not yet agreed to the marriage. Henry and Norman have intercepted letters between Edgar and Lucy and have concocted a phoney compromising letter from Edgar to another woman.

Lucy enters: she tells Henry she is not free to marry. She is pledged to another man. Henry shows her the forged letter. Lucy is completely thrown. So now you can feel free to marry says Henry and please get a move on. I'm in trouble all round – King William the head of my party is dead: Queen Mary the leader of the rival party [Shome mishtake surely? Ed.] is coming to the throne: I'm in hock all round and only a good marriage can save me. (Exits: enter Raymond.) Father, what should I do? asks the agonized Lucy. Forget that worthless Edgar and marry Arthur says the priest (thinking it all for the best). Lucy, now in a highly emotional state, gives way.

Act I Sc 4 A hall in Ravenswood

The Ashton household and friends are gathered to greet bridegroom Arthur who arrives and starts asking awkward questions. So what's this I hear about Edgar and Lucy? he asks. Why is Lucy so pale? She was quite knocked out by the death of her mother says Henry, think nothing of it. Lucy, after a good deal of vocal agonizing, signs the marriage contract. Pow! Edgar bursts in. Lucy faints. Edgar claims Lucy's hand: turmoil: bewilderment. Henry is struck with pity for Lucy [a little late surely? Ed.]: Raymond is horrified: Lucy wishes she were dead etc. Edgar and Henry draw swords: Raymond interposes. Edgar learns Lucy has signed the marriage contract with Arthur. He chucks the ring back at her: everyone shouts for God's sake go. He goes.

Act II Sc 1 The Wolf's Crag (a desolate spot)

It thunders. Edgar is thoroughly upset. He sits brooding in a lonely tower. Henry arrives [how did he know Edgar was there? Ed.] and gloat-ingly tells him Lucy is now in bed with another man. Bad feeling on both sides leads to an assignation for a duel at dawn.

Act II Sc 2 The hall at Ravenswood again

Back at the ranch morale has miraculously recovered. Lucy's wedding night celebrations go with a swing until Raymond arrives with shocking news from the bridal suite. Lucy has stuck a dagger into bridegroom Arthur! He is dead! Consternation – Lucy enters, clearly mad – runs through several fantasies – the dead girl in the fountain again – visions of a happy marriage to Edgar etc. Henry returns to witness final stages of dementia, everyone in tears: as the most famous mad scene in opera ends Raymond turns on Norman and tells him (quite unfairly) that it is his plotting that has caused this misery – begone.

Act II Sc 3 Amongst the family tombs at Ravenswood

Edgar, awaiting the duel, is dripping with self-pity and wishes to die. Passers-by from the castle tell him Lucy is mad. She constantly calls out his name and is certain to die. Suddenly the death bell tolls. Raymond arrives and confirms that Lucy is dead. Edgar prays that he and Lucy will meet in heaven, stabs himself and expires, but not before completing his farewell cavatina.

MINUTES FROM START

LOOK OUT FOR

Act I Sc 1

0
2: *Percorriamo le spiagge*
12: *La pietade in suo favore*

The prelude has high drama,* a rousing opening 0
chorus,* some tense recitatif-ish exchanges between 2
Norman and Henry and then two cavatinas from
Henry, both bristling with hatred. In the second** he 12
works himself up into a fine lather of fury and despite
choral attempts to restrain him (quite useless), he
ends with a swingeing cabaletta.

Act I Sc 2

18: *Regnava nel silenzio*
22: *Quando, rapito in estasi*

Lucy tells Alice about the frightful dead girl in a
fountain** and then embarks on one of the best- 18
known cavatinas*** in the opera – she tells of her pas- 22
sion for Edgar spinning out a clear melodic line which
on the second time round sparkles and flashes with all
manner of fireworks.

29: *Ah! verrano a te sull'aure*

Edgar arrives and the pair swing into a tortured
duet. One good thing after another especially the long
sweet and melodious farewells.*** 29

Act I Sc 3

We are into high tragedy at once. First some exchanges between Norman and Henry leading to Lucy's arrival and then 15 minutes of duetting between Henry and Lucy on a rising tide of emotional tension – Lucy attacks him for treating her so lousily-
43: *Il pallor, funesto, orrendo* ** – she is stunned by Edgar's reported double- 43
45: *Soffriva nel pianto* cross.** Henry pleads with her to stick by him or else 45
47: *Se tradirmi tu potrai* he goes bust.*** Ends in one of Donizetti's most ex- 47
citing climaxes.

Raymond now comes the heavy with poor Lucy, first in the recitatif ('you must give him up') and then
52: *Ah! cedi, cedi* in a solemnish cavatina** leading to agitato ex- 52
changes. Lucy yields: Raymond trumpets his tri-
54: *Al ben de'tuoi qual' vittima* umph in a cavatina** which is not a million miles 54
away from the Soldiers' March in *Elisir*. Lucy supplies some wild shrieks from time to time and the galumphing march tune ends the scene in high style.

Act I Sc 4

After an off-the-peg wedding chorus Arthur makes his hellos and starts asking awkward questions over a delicious phrase on the violins that seems to come
61: *Se in lei* straight out of a Rossini overture.** Tension builds 61
as Lucy dithers (will she/won't she sign the wedding contract?) over sweeping strings: all hell is let loose as Edgar bursts in and things move forward as follows:
66: *Chi mi frena* first a duet** in close-ish counterpoint with Henry: 66
next a trio with Lucy and then a broadening out into a glorious sextet with all the principals,*** finally joined by the chorus. High melodrama as Lucy admits she did sign (a bit of the Rossini again) and then the final choral turmoil – effective enough but a bit of a pudding compared with the power and clarity of the earlier climaxes.

Act II Sc 1

Orchestral thunder (very good) carries through to become a sort of continuo to Edgar's recitatif preceding his unpleasant encounter with Henry which occupies the whole scene and is again full of good things. It starts stealthily over a walking bass and continues with a series of duets: first, Edgar rages as Henry taunts him with visions of Lucy in bed with another
3: *Qui del padre ancor respira* man:** next the challenge to a duel at dawn and ex- 3
pressions of mutual hatred to strangely inappropriate

9: *Ah! o sole* military air.** A good-going finale. 9

Act II Sc 2

10: *D'immenso giubilo* A better than usual jolly chorus** ushers in party 10
night at Ravenswood. This is stopped in its tracks by
Raymond's announcement of mayhem in the bed-
chamber. He recounts the horrible scene in a melodi-
13: *Ah! dalle stanze ove Lucia* ous cavatina.** 13

Lucy enters for her great mad scene: a flute hovers
around throughout like a familiar spirit: she starts
with incoherent but heartbreaking recitatif: she
19: *Ardon' gli incensi* bursts into her first sweet/sad cavatina*** ending 19
with the tragic echoes and coloratura fireworks that
have been incompetently sung probably more often
than any other music in opera: she indulges in several
fantasies: the onlookers pity her: she finds just
enough spirit to embark on her mad/happy Ophelia-
34: *Spargi d'amaro pianto* like farewell song*** before she sinks senseless into 34
Alice's arms. Very affecting.

Act II Sc 3

Menacing horns usher in dawn amongst the Ravenswood tombs: Edgar tells us he is really upset about his
40: *Fra poco a me ricovero* fate in recitatif and then in a doleful cavatina.** He 40
learns of Lucy's death: he gives us a bigger and more
47: *Tu che a Dio spiegasti l'ali* powerful cavatina*** as he declares he will commit 47
suicide and join Lucy in heaven.

The ghost of this melody hangs over his dying utterances and the opera ends with the chorus requesting divine forgiveness presumably for his felo-de-se. Perhaps the wicked Henry would seem to need it more.

NOTES

Lucia di Lammermoor	Donizetti's forty-sixth opera
First night	Teatro San Carlo, Naples, 26 September 1835
Reception	A hit. Donizetti wrote 'It pleased the audience very much . . . every number was listened to in religious silence and then hailed with spontaneous cheers.'
Libretto	Cammarano
Source	Sir Walter Scott's *The Bride of Lammermoor*

NEWS AND GOSSIP

In the 1830s Walter Scott's historical romances were all the rage on the Continent and *Lucia* had been used as a libretto no less than three times before Cammarano got his hands on it. He did a really professional job and as a result of *Lucia* went on to become the most sought-after librettist of the Italian opera trade (seven more operas with Donizetti). Donizetti had problems with the San Carlo theatre management who were short of money to pay for rehearsals and although the opera was written in six weeks and completed on 6 July, the first night was delayed for three months. For some ten years after its first appearance *Lucia* became the vogue opera ('Donizetti's masterpiece') whenever Italian opera was performed, but then it had a bad time, becoming merely a vehicle for prima donnas to show off their fioritura in the mad scene. It was often cut about and today we have at least two different performing versions. It came back to health with the bel canto revival and is now always treated with proper respect. Today it is the most performed of Donizetti's serious operas.

COMMENT

Lucia is special amongst Donizetti's tragic operas because it is written with such skill and such conviction that can suspend disbelief even in this ultra-romantic tale. This is saying something when one looks in cold print at Henry's Gothic anger, Edgar's excessive and undergraduate passions and Lucy's lack of wit and feminist spunk in being conned and bullied by her frightful brother. Nevertheless we are won over, we share Lucy's fear of Henry's rage, we sigh for love with Edgar and weep for Lucy, that is to say if we are the sort of people who can succumb to opera; there are many, poor things, who can't. What makes *Lucia* superior to *Lucrezia Borgia*, *Anna Bolena* and *Maria Stuarda*? First, the libretto, which is cleverly extracted and adapted from Sir Walter's sprawling novel and tells the story with clarity and pace, giving just the right balance between action and reflection to allow the music to flower. Second, the power of the big set pieces, two of which are amongst the towering monuments of all opera, the sextet early in Act I and Lucy's mad scene. Third, outside of the set pieces the score has a constant spring and drive which keeps the drama on the boil: musically there is a succession of good things one after another with a very low quota of operatic dross and practically nothing (one chorus and a little recitatif) out of the stock-pot. In *Lucia* Donizetti moves further away from Rossini's reliance on set forms and gets nearer to the continuous flow of dramatic music which was to become the stock-in-trade of Wagner. Indeed the score is so much a part of the narrative that if (fantastic thought) the opera were to be performed without words as a ballet the story would still come through with absolute clarity.

But beware. *Lucia* requires not only four top-class singers but singers who can act. Without some histrionic ability in the heroine the mad scene is an embarrassment. Henry has got to be more than the stock baddy. Edgar must be a bella figura.

If you are lucky, if the cast is good and the production at least sensible then you are in for one of the most glorious evenings that Italian opera can offer. An undoubted alpha.

Luisa Miller

Romantic tragedy

Verdi

The one where the hero is an imposter, the heroine is thought to have double-crossed him and they both drink poison too soon to enjoy what could have been a happy ending.

CAST

Count Walter, wicked landowner	Bass
Rodolfo, his son, first known as Carlo	Tenor
Wurm, evil steward to Count Walter	Bass
Miller, an old soldier	Baritone
Luisa, his daughter	Soprano
Duchess Frederica, Rodolfo's cousin	Mezzo
Laura, a country girl	Mezzo
A peasant, etc.	

3 acts: running time 2 hrs 14 mins

STORY

Act I (Acts have romantic titles. This one: Love)
Sc 1 A Tyrolean village with a church in the centre

We are in seventeenth-century Tyrol: the Tyroleans are merrymaking like mad as operatic Tyroleans do in any century: the reason – Luisa's birthday. After an opening jolly chorus and setting-up stuff Luisa's lover Carlo arrives: he says he's just crazy about her and she says she's crazy about him. Father Miller suspects Carlo is a phoney carefree seducer. Luisa and Carlo plus lustily singing villagers disappear into church for divine worship.

The Wurm arrives; he lusts after Luisa and bullies Miller: why is her marriage with me not fixed? Miller says he disapproves of arranged marriages as a matter of principle: Luisa is to decide. Carlo is not Carlo at all but Count Walter's heir Rodolfo, says the Wurm: I knew it says Miller, a seducer. [How come the young laird is not known by sight? Ed.]

Act I Sc 2 A room in Count Walter's castle

The Wurm tells wicked Count Walter that Rodolfo is courting a village girl, very common, name Luisa Miller. Tiresome brat says Count W. I've just fixed up a fine match for him: fetch him here pronto. Rodolfo comes.

Lordly dad tells him he must marry his childhood sweetheart Frederica now a widow: her husband the old Duke is defunct, left broad acres, good contacts, oodles of dough: the Duchess is also still soft on Rodolfo. I don't want all that stuff says Rodolfo, I don't want the lady. She's outside now says Count W.: do what you're told – get in there and get engaged. Exit Count W. to see a man about a hunting dog.

Enter Lady Frederica with several female helpers who exit discreetly: Hello Rodolfo she says remember the good old days? Sure I do Duchess he replies (call me Freddie says she) but I'm really sorry to tell you that today I love another. Another? she says. Just that he says: Dad was crazy to set this up. You bastard she cries I'll get you for this (very angry: a woman scorned).

Act I Sc 3 A room in the Millers' cottage

The most confused sporting event in all opera takes place offstage ('let slip the greyhounds': 'Let us drive the covers'). Luisa awaits her lover Carlo: father Miller comes in: he has bad news: Carlo is indeed a phoney, his actual identity is Rodolfo son of wicked Count Walter and he is marrying his rich Duchess cousin that day. Yes and no says Rodolfo bounding in with ears aflap: I am Rodolfo, I am not marrying cousin Frederica. I'm true as a bell to you, Luisa, and I confirm our official engagement. Count W. will be mad says Miller. Never fear says Rodolfo I've got something on him that will keep him in line.

Enter Count W. (men at his back): I have come to exercise the law he says: arrest that woman as a common seductress. Luisa pleads: leave her alone says Miller. Arrest him too says Count W. (Bad luck Luisa sing the villagers crowding in to see the fun.) Do you see that Rodolfo? says Count W. I do says Rodolfo and unless you let Luisa go I will publish some interesting facts about your past: let her go says ashy-faced Count W. (The hunt is now forgotten by all.)

Act II Intrigue
Sc 1 The Millers' house

Bad news for Luisa: the villagers saw her father in chains etc. en route to the castle dungeon. The Wurm appears and says the axe is hovering over Dad's neck: there's only one way to avert decapitation – Luisa must write a letter as dictated by him. He spouts a letter swearing Luisa's love for Wurm also proposing their elopement. Luisa much put about prays etc.: on balance she decides to write the letter and save Dad's life.

Act II Sc 2 A room in Count Walter's castle

Count W. is broody about pig-head Rodolfo. The Wurm reports that the matter of Luisa's letter has been effected. The two have retrospective thoughts about the disappearance of the last Count, believed rubbed out by the Mafia but actually murdered by this dreadful pair. Count W. tells the Wurm Rodolfo knows all: Wurm is very scared.

Frederica arrives and Count W. tells her Luisa is not really in love with Rodolfo and he can prove it. The Wurm produces Luisa through a secret door and forces her to say she loves the Wurm not Rodolfo. Frederica is delighted: Luisa shattered: the dastardly duo well pleased.

Act II Sc 3 A hanging garden (come again?) in the castle

A peasant hands Rodolfo Luisa's letter: he sends for the Wurm all a-tremble: he thinks how awful, I can't believe it. When the Wurm arrives Rodolfo challenges him to a duel: Wurm panics and involuntarily and harmlessly discharges his pistol. Count W. arrives (men at his back) and says he was badly advised: Rodolfo can now marry Luisa. What that slag heap? says Rodolfo (he shows the letter): Count W. says, Then why not marry Frederica to spite her? Rodolfo says, Don't mind if I do: Count W. says, There there, come come, good boy.

Act III The Poison
The Millers' cottage

The villagers are in the cottage again showing their sympathy for Luisa as offstage preparations for Rodolfo and Frederica's wedding are proceeding. Miller returns: Luisa shows him a letter proposing a suicide pact for herself and Rodolfo. Miller says what a silly idea: drop it, wander the country with me. He exits.

Luisa prays: Rodolfo enters unseen and pours poison in a jug of lemonade. He confronts Luisa: is her letter to the Wurm authentic? She says, Yes I wrote it. Both take a swig. Rodolfo presses Luisa who reveals all: she loves him truly (too late): Miller arrives: they sing an agonized trio: the villagers get in again, then Count W. (men at his back) also the Wurm: Luisa expires: Rodolfo kills the Wurm just before he passes over himself. Curtain.

MINUTES FROM START — LOOK OUT FOR

Act I Sc 1

A full-scale symphonic overture (main theme reappears in last act): an introduction with a cor anglais

7: *Ti desta, Luisa* to the fore, a rustic opening chorus* with poppling 7
woodwind as fresh as fresh can be – Tyrolean maybe
but not the dreaded leather-slapping gemütlich kind.

11: *Lo vidi* Luisa's first outing: a young girl's cavatina* as 11
clear as crystal with trills and some spirited stuff at
the finish.

What would have been a simple and sweet 'I love
14: *T'amo d'amor* you' duet* is given a sinister twist by Miller mutter- 14
ing his base (bass) suspicions about Rodolfo. The
chorus have no such inhibitions and all go into the
church singing a jolly tune in double time.

Miller tells the Wurm he does not believe in arranged marriages in a benign and rather touching
19: *Sacra la scelta* cavatina* followed shortly by a much bigger event: a 19
23: *Ah! fu giusto* fine aria of rage–despair** on learning that Rodolfo is 23
an imposter.

Act I Sc 2

Count Walter reflects on his son's tiresome
29: *Di dolcezze* behaviour:* a sad sorry affair, too gentle perhaps for 29
so thoroughly wicked a man.

A great duet: (1) Rodolfo and Frederica recall
34: *Dall' aule raggianti* happy days in the nursery* (very agreeable), (2) 34
Rodolfo tells her I love another (forceful strokes from
the orchestra compel them to face up to the facts), (3)
some dramatic recitatif stuff, (4) the final and musi-
38: *Deh! la parola* cally quite delicious resolution** (Rodolfo: Terribly 38
sorry, I could not tell a lie, Frederica: Hell hath no
fury . . .) and all to a debonair little tune in whose
mouth butter would not melt.

Act I Sc 3

This whole scene is masterly, from the hunt noises at the opening to Luisa's sudden release at the end. For the most part the plot races ahead in powerful recitatif in which the Miller, Rodolfo and Count Walter successively pile turn upon twist: high quality stuff which flowers often into bursts of lyricism, a delight.
45: *Fra' mortali* All of this a preamble to the grand concerted piece*** 45
– forward drive, subtle changes of rhythm – in which every character sings as if for their life (Miller: I won't grovel to this monster, Rodolfo: Woe woe, Walter: Father knows best, Luisa: Wish I were dead, Peasants: Poor thing too, Soldiers: Just obeying orders Guv.). Soloists sing out and do their thing: then

some closely knitted stuff for all – finally a chorus of overwhelming sympathy for Luisa. Really wonderful finale and the short end-scene with a twist does nothing to diminish its grandeur.

Act II Sc 1

A narrative chorus tells Luisa her father is having a
0: *Ah! Luisa* hard time. Luisa interjects. A telling scene.* 0
Two star solos from Luisa: the first her protest
5: *Tu puniscimi* against signing the letter** – direct, free flowing, elo- 5
quent: the second her outburst of hatred against the
11: *A brani, a brani* Wurm** – musically more in sorrow than in anger 11
until the horrid Wurm joins in, when the music turns nasty too.

Act II Sc 2

Two big numbers dominate this again very effective scene:

18: *L'alto retaggio* 1. The duet** in which Count Walter tells the 18
Wurm Rodolfo knows their dread secret, a surprisingly easy-going set piece with only occasional outbursts of terror.

23: *Presentarti alla Duchessa* 2. The four-handed scene*** Walter/the Wurm/ 23
Frederica/Luisa – insinuating intro from the Wurm, flashing dramatic exchanges between the women and a final unaccompanied quartet (rare in Verdi) which adroitly reflects the feelings of each party – Luisa (I'm at the end of my tether), Frederica (Whoopee!), Walter and the Wurm (Gloat gloat). A wonderfully effective finale (but we must bear in mind that owing to operatic magic, Luisa's very private thoughts expressed fortissimo are audible to us alone and not to fellow thesps).

Act II Sc 3

Rodolfo is really low because (as he thinks) Luisa has
double-crossed him: he voices his pain and grief in a
32: *Quando le sere* top-class tenor solo** (nineteenth-century torch 32
song).

38: *L'ara, o l'avello* The final duet and ensemble:** desperate excited 38
stuff from Rodolfo (Life not worth living without Luisa), Count W. (much cooler: You will come to love Frederica), Chorus (Father knows best). Not quite up to Act I finale but runs along very well.

Act III

0: *Come in un giorno* The opening choral scene** uses a haunting melan- 0 choly theme from the overture: very affecting.

7: *La tomba* The big duet** between Luisa and her father. 7
Opens with a feathery light coloratura piece – almost mad heroine stuff – telling him of suicide pact: persuasive riposte from Miller in a smooth melody with accompanying twirls from the strings: big dramatic bit (he persuades her): the final marvellous section
13: *Andrem, raminghi* (we will take the open road) a ballad-like tune** sung 13
in turn then with Luisa's high descant over the Miller plugging on below: a final and more cheerful cabaletta (open road not so bad after all). Big close.

17: *Ah! l'ultima preghiera* Luisa's prayer:* could be an Ave Maria but for the 17
ominous bustling bass: slender but effective (sandwiched between two rather doughy bits of organ voluntary).

Two sterling Rodolfo/Luisa duets: the first the
24: *Piangi, piangi* clock-chime duet:* slow to catch fire but later power- 24
27: *Ah! maledetto* ful: second* the final desperate recognition that it's 27
all a big misunderstanding: fast underneath slower
32: *Padre, ricevi* above: big climax. The closing trio** – Luisa (expires 32
in last bar), Rodolfo (lives on to kill the Wurm), Miller sobs: My daughter, my daughter. A moment of magic when Luisa's soul appears to be going aloft to the accompaniment of harps, followed by the heaviest mortality rate amongst principal singers in 30 seconds in any opera (one murder, two deaths by poisoning).

NOTES

Luisa Miller	Verdi's fifteenth opera
First night	Teatro San Carlo, Naples, 8 December 1849
Reception	Surprisingly hard to find any evidence
Libretto	Cammarano
Source	Schiller's play *Love and Intrigue*

NEWS AND GOSSIP

Verdi didn't want to write *Luisa Miller*. He had a contract with the San Carlo management in Naples to deliver an opera but he had moved to Paris, where he hoped to become an operatic lion, and didn't want to go back. He did suggest some subjects but they were blocked by the censors as too political (1848 was of course the year of revolutions and demos all over Europe). The management got fed up and threatened to put Cammarano in jail unless he and Verdi delivered. Cammarano quickly came up with the pretty bland story of *Luisa Miller* and Verdi agreed. From then on things went along well enough, though Verdi (the scourge of librettists) found Cammarano a tough cookie compared with Piave and Solera whom he could push around pretty much as he wanted. But the show went on and must have done well for it was soon playing all over Italy. Later in the century it was pushed almost out of sight by *Trov*, *Rig* and *Trav* and today, because opera managements tend to follow the fashion like a flock of starlings, it's seldom seen. It deserves better – but one posh revival that sets the critics cheering will bring it back soon enough, for it is a sterling piece.

COMMENT

Luisa Miller is the most underestimated of Verdi's operas. The libretto has pace, clarity and a succession of the sort of 'strong situations' which were meat and drink to Verdi. The first act is beautifully constructed with duet finales to the first two scenes and a masterly third scene with a brilliant and original finale tailed with a surprising appendix. The second act runs equally powerfully and if the third is a little slow at the beginning over the double suicide and very quick at the end with murder and death in seconds, we can live with that because the good bits are very good. There are minuses. The characters are cardboard cut-outs, wicked Count, evil steward, father-dominated hero, good old soldier, standard heroine daughter, but at least they are recognizably human and more like us than Druids, Roman generals or Spanish brigands. Again, although the characters are stock, their emotions are closer to real life than in the earlier Verdi operas.

Musically *Luisa* is a surprise and a joy. Gone are the pomps and pretensions of the heroic operas: the chorus is not overworked (and has one number at the start of Act III with a new kind of choral magic), the recitatifs are less bombastic, the tunes better, the accompaniments less routine and never vulgar. It is true that the third act has not got the same sustained rich musical stuffing of the first two, with long stretches of declamatory/exclamatory/explanatory recitatif, but it works, and after two such glorious acts who could grumble about a third act that is no more than good? An alpha.

Macbeth

Historical drama

Verdi

The one you expect to be Shakespeare's *Macbeth* but it isn't quite.

CAST

Macbeth, Thane of Glamis (for a start)	Baritone
Lady Macbeth	Soprano
Banquo (Banco), a Scottish general	Bass
Macduff, a Scots nobleman	Tenor
Malcolm, son of King Duncan	Tenor.

Witches, lady-in-waiting, murderer, apparitions (3), physician, servant – all small parts

Also non-singing walk-past characters: King Duncan (Duncano), Fleance (Fleanglo, son of Banquo), etc.

4 acts, 1 interval: running time 2 hrs 10 mins

STORY

This is Shakespeare's *Macbeth* skilfully cut down to the size of a two-hour horror thriller and given a happy ending.

Act I Sc 1 A blasted heath

We are in Shakespeare's Scotland and Macbeth and Banquo encounter witches – professional forecasters – who say Macbeth has a big future: first as Thane of Cawdor then King of Scotland, but after that no joy, Banquo's sons will take over. A messenger promptly tells Macbeth he has been promoted to be Thane of Cawdor. M. is much impressed.

Act I Sc 2 Glamis Castle

Macbeth has written to the wife with all his news: she thinks the witches' forecasts promising. Macbeth returns: Lady M. eggs him on to murder their weekend guest King Duncan: M. is not too keen but agrees to have a go. He does it. Now he is deeply upset: he turns chicken: will not go back to smear the sleeping guards with incriminating blood. Lady M., impatient with wimp husband, does it herself. There are bloody hands all round.

Duncan's murder is discovered: the castle is in turmoil: Prince Malcolm, Duncan's son, scarpers to London.

Act II Sc 1 Glamis Castle

Macbeth is now king but he's moody: he fears Banquo's line will benefit from the murder, not his: the ghastly couple decide Banquo and son must die too.

Act II Sc 2 In the park of Glamis Castle

Macbeth's hit men lie in wait for Banquo. He comes on with his son Fleance: Banquo is murdered: Fleance flees.

Act II Sc 3 The banqueting hall in Glamis Castle

Macbeth's accession party: lots of people. Lady M. urges the guests to drink up. A hit man reports to Macbeth: we had only partial success: Banquo is dead, but Fleance escaped. Macbeth injudiciously tries to sit down in Banquo's empty chair. Banquo's ghost (only seen by M.) sits down first. M. loses his marbles: he addresses the ghost: general perplexity: Lady M. covers for him: the ghost appears again! This time M. blows it, and everyone is suspicious: Macduff decides Scotland is getting too hot for comfort and exits. Lady M. is mortified by M.'s poor performance and lack of moral fibre.

Act III Sc 1 The witches' cave

The witches are busy preparing an absolutely disgusting brew-up. Enter Macbeth on the look-out for further and better particulars concerning his future. The witches say – Macduff: watch him – he's dangerous. Then they move into the apparition business, presenting (1) a bloody child (2) a child with a crown holding a branch (3) a procession of kings – the last being Banquo with a mirror in his hand reflecting the whole troop of his descendants.

Macbeth reports this bad news to the wife (who has followed him) also that the witches have thrown him two bits of encouragement: he will not be licked (1) by any man born of woman (2) until Birnam Woods come to Dunsinane. That's pretty hopeful stuff. Nevertheless Lady M., to be on the safe side, decides on another brace of murders – Macduff and Banquo's boy Fleance a.s.a.p.

Act IV Sc 1 A barren moor in the Border Country (sic) surprising since Birnam and Dunsinane are 100 miles further north

A chorus of miserable Scots families, apparently mobile members of the Macduff clan, girn and grumble about their lives and hard times. Macduff appears and says sorry he wasn't there to defend them and his own family from horrid King Macbeth. Malcolm marches on at the head of an English army. He tells the troops to adopt field camouflage by holding Birnam Wood branches in front of their advancing bodies.

Act IV Sc 2 Inside Glamis Castle

A doctor and a lady of the court observe Lady M. walking and talking in her sleep. She has horrific nightmares: blood – blood on her hands.

Act IV Sc 3 A battlefield

Macbeth is not happy with himself (with good reason) as he forebodes: he is told (1) Lady M. is dead – a piece of news he takes calmly – (2) Birnam Woods are on the move: so into battle. He engages Macduff who reveals he did not enjoy natural birth: 'torn from his mother's womb': he kills Macbeth: victory for Malcolm and Macduff: general rejoicing: all prophecies are punctiliously fulfilled.

MINUTES FROM START — LOOK OUT FOR

Act I Sc 1

The Prelude: full of storm, menace and one sweet melody (most of the themes turn up again later). Witches etc. dramatically and musically vivid but the first event of real note is the Macbeth/Banquo duet
11: *Due vaticini compiuti* — on the matter of the prophecies.* Witches finish the 11
scene in a more tuneful mode.

Lady M. decides to hype up her sluggish husband
19: *Vieni! t'affretta* — in a debonair little cavatina,* interrupted by some 19
forceful hurry music and then continues to summon up his courage for Duncan's murder.

Act I Sc 2

The duet of terror between Macbeth (loses his marbles) and Lady M. (practical to the end): high
33: *Fatal mia donna!* — drama throughout and two soaring lyrical passages.** 33
41: *Schiudi, inferno* — The finale – a tremendous chorus*** with en- 41
semble filtered into it making a powerful appeal to the

Almighty to identify and punish the criminal (which He does in Act IV).

Act II Sc 1

3: *La luce langue*

Lady Macbeth sings a sunset song about the prospects of power, calmly at first but ending in ecstasy.* 3

Act II Sc 2

10: *Come dal ciel precipita*

After the murderers' chorus (too close to the comedy chorus in *The Pirates of Penzance* for comfort), Banquo has a sombre and impressive aria* full of 10
foreboding.

Act II Sc 3

16: *Si colmi il calice*

26: *Biechi arcani*

A mood of hectic jollity from the start of the scene:
Lady M. has a bizarre set-piece aria* to an oom-pah 16
accompaniment (which is later repeated): the second appearance of Banquo's Ghost much more effective than the first: the scene ends unusually with a 'thinks'
ensemble** in waltz time, calm, reflective and effec- 26
tive: Lady M. (My husband is chicken), Macduff (I'm going to get away from this lot), Chorus (Violent crime is on the increase).

Act III

7: *Dalle basse e dall'alte regioni*

11: *Fuggi, regal fantasima*

16: *Vi trovo alfin!*

Amongst all the opera's high dramatics nothing is more effective than Macbeth's second encounter with the witches, especially the parade of the apparitions
and his response to them:** his address to the 7
phantom kings** and finally the fraught duet*** with 11
Lady M. in which their frenzy of plotting and 16
scheming borders on hysteria.

Act IV Sc 1

2: *Patria oppressa!*

9: *Ah, la paterna mano*

The entr'acte is full of funereal brass and leads to a
fine chorus** in which the wretched Scots clansmen 2
sing menacingly of their miserable life and times.

Macduff – to a surprisingly cheerful accompaniment – sings eloquently** of his grief over his 9
murdered family. (Malcolm then arrives to a brisk marche militaire.)

Act IV Sc 2

16: *Una macchia e qui tuttora*

25: *Pieta, rispetto, amore*

Lady M. sleepwalks.*** Quietly obsessional at first; 16
then soaring onwards and upwards in a bewitching vocal line to a great climax. Horrible, unspeakable woman!

Macbeth reflects that nobody loves him.* Indeed 25
he is much disliked.

The excellent final scene: a lively fugal piece for trumpets: Macbeth and Macduff fight: Macbeth's
31: *Mal per me che m'affidai* death song:** rousing addresses by Macduff and new 31
king Malcolm: a splendid and unexpectedly moving
36: *Salgan mie grazie a te* final chorus:*** no routine bang-bang ending this. 36

NOTES

Macbeth	Verdi's tenth opera
First night	Teatro della Pergola, Florence, 14 March 1847
Reception	A success
Libretto	Piave
Source	Shakespeare

NEWS AND GOSSIP

Verdi was always fiddling about with plans to do Shakespeare, most of which didn't come off, but *Macbeth* did, and with a bang. He was always bugged by an itch to do something new and he wrote to Piave 'This tragedy is one of the greatest creations of man! If we can't do something great with it let's at least try to do something different. . . .' As rehearsals went along he gave Piave a hard time, jobbing, patching and reworking, determined no doubt to make the opera as outré as it could be. And indeed it must have seemed pretty strong stuff in its day. Nearly twenty years later Verdi reworked the opera for a production in Paris and for this version he wrote the two stunning last act choruses and Lady Macbeth's sunset song. He also changed the ending to a happy one and agreed to write some ballet music, though it's hard to imagine what kind of a ballet could possibly survive after the last act of *Macbeth*. Anyway, the Paris revival was a flop. Although *Macbeth* was widely performed especially in Italy it never joined *Rig*, *Trav* or *Trov* as top of the pops. Along with the general run of Verdi, *Macbeth* languished until Italian opera bounced back in the last sixty years. Rudolf Bing, that great standard-bearer for Verdi, put *Macbeth* back in favour with a production at the Met in the 1960s and since then it has come up in the world to become a fairly rare but well-regarded item in the repertory of the opera world.

COMMENT

Macbeth has a taut fast-moving libretto which takes the plot racing along clearly and decisively from point to point. If you cut out Shakespeare's poetry (if!) his plots often benefit from concentration, thus the Mac-

Millan ballet of *Romeo and Juliet* moves more inevitably to the last sad scene than does the play. This *Macbeth* is very fast and piles on the agony in the most effective fashion. (Nor is the libretto without its own modest brand of poetry.)

Verdi makes the most of this bloody story with music that is on the go all the time, vivid, theatrical, just stopping short of melodrama. The witches' music is not so much spooky as demoniac (except in the scene of the apparitions): Macbeth's inner turmoil features less than his brutality and his cowardice: Lady M. on the other hand is wonderfully reflected in all her music, whether she be acting a part to jolly up the party with 'Si colmi il calice' or appearing like a zombie in the sleepwalking scene – which is the great dramatic moment of the opera. Verdi rises above the crude brutality of the plot in two surprisingly beautiful and moving choruses – that of the miserable Macduffs at the beginning of Act IV and the people's song of thanksgiving at the end. These reach beyond the confines of a story about warring Scots nobles and carry a message of compassion.

Macbeth is great early Verdi, a big step forward from his earlier stuff, and because it is not so well known as *Rig*, *Trav* and *Trov*, for most people it comes as something of a surprise. And indeed it is surprising that such a vivid opera is not more performed. An easy alpha.

Madam Butterfly (Madama Butterfly)

Japanese tragedy

Puccini

The one with a Japanese wedding, the Stars & Stripes and a puff of smoke on the horizon.

CAST

Madam Butterfly (alias **Cio-Cio-San**), teenage geisha	Soprano
Suzuki, Butterfly's devoted servant	Mezzo
Bonze, Butterfly's uncle	Bass
Goro, one-man escort and marriage agency	Tenor
Pinkerton (B.F.(!) – Benjamin Franklin), US naval lieutenant	Tenor
Sharpless, United States Consul	Baritone

Kate Pinkerton, Prince Yamadori, Imperial commissioner, Registrar, Butterfly's family (numerous)

2 acts: running time 2 hrs 20 mins

STORY

Act I A Japanese house set in a Japanese garden on a Japanese hill overlooking Nagasaki

This is Japan in real time for Puccini, a century ago for us. Goro who is a marriage agent and also apparently a house agent shows Pinkerton around a very Japanese house and parades the servants. Pinker is contemplating marriage that day: he asks Goro for the guest list: Goro reels off a lengthy family roll call.

Sharpless arrives: Pinker says he's buying the house on a 999-year lease which he can cancel any time: he sings a male chauvinist imperialist ditty about macho American males (Have a Scotch Sharpless old boy) travelling world picking and choosing women: he has chosen his child bride Butterfly: as with the house he can chuck her any time. Yes but why marry? You must be mad says Sharpless. I've fallen for her says Pinker. She is an attractive lady says Sharpless, she called at my office yesterday: but it's a bad show to abandon a trusting girl. Priggish sod (Another Scotch?) says Pinker, I'll teach her good sex, great advantage to her. Here's to the Pinkerton family back home says Sharpless. Here's to a real American wife one day says Pinker.

Butterfly and friends are heard approaching. The Americans and the

Japanese make polite exchanges. Butterfly explains that her family was once rich but owing to the Stock Exchange crash are now poor and she a geisha. She has no brothers or sisters only her mother. What about your father? asks Pinker. Dead says Butterfly (everyone is embarrassed: there was something rum about father's demise). Your age? he asks. Fifteen she says. The Registrar of Marriages plus Butterfly's friends and relatives (numerous) arrive. (What a farce says Pinker aside: all this ceremonial stuff: I could be off in a month.) The relatives and friends size up Pinker as prospective husband: some for (he's rich and handsome) some against (Butterfly's charm is fading: he'll divorce her soon).

Butterfly unpacks belongings from her capacious sleeves including a sword (Goro informs Pinker the sword was a present from the Mikado inviting Butterfly's father to a disgusting act of hara-kiri: father's response was positive) also dolls (the souls of her ancestors) but Butterfly says now she will give Pinker's God a trial run. The marriage ceremony takes place. The officials plus Sharpless depart. The family toasts the couple.

Suddenly in bursts nasty Uncle Bonze, a frightful senior Buddhist clergyman who accuses Butterfly of deserting the family religion: he curses: he excommunicates. The family is much impressed: they side with Bonze, saying OK Butterfly you're on your own: now we will all cut you dead. They all go: Butterfly is very weepy: Pinker comforts her. It is bedtime: Butterfly is embarrassed at stripping off before male Pinker: Pinker reassures her: they make long loverly exchanges: they walk into house together. . .

Act II The same. Part I

Suzuki and Butterfly wait and pray. They are nearly broke. Pinker's return is much desired. Suzuki is doubtful he'll come back: Butterfly says shut up: one fine day puff atomic fission – Pinker will be back. Goro lurks without. Sharpless enters with a letter from Pinker: Butterfly asks when robins nest in the USA? Sharpless is ornithologically nonplussed. Butterfly explains that Pinker promised to return in the robins' nesting time – maybe American robins are triennial nesters? Sharpless is foxed. Butterfly says Goro pesters her to take a rich fellow Yamadori as her new husband: it's just not on.

Goro enters followed by Yamadori. Butterfly says get off I am still a married woman. Not so says Goro: in Japanese law desertion equals divorce. Phooey says Butterfly: I'm the wife of a US citizen, so I am subject to American law and divorce requires a court order and all that. She exits to brew tea. Gorblimey says Sharpless Pinker's ship has been sighted but he doesn't want to meet Butterfly – what a bugger's muddle. Butterfly comes on with the tea. Yamadori goes off.

Sharpless attempts to read Pinker's letter: Butterfly is excited, and keeps on interrupting him. Sharpless gives up and chickens out of telling her the bad news point blank: instead he asks what if Pinker never came back? Either geisha or death says Butterfly: probably death. Why not team up with rich Yamadori? says Sharpless. Wash your mouth out, says she, and what about baby? [This baby is 2 years 3 months minimum: Ed.] Is it Pinker's baby? asks Sharpless. He's got blue eyes and flaxen hair so by Mendel's laws he must be Pinker's, says she, but Pinker doesn't know about him. She addresses the baby: do you see this terrible fellow she says, he thinks your dad walked out on me. Cad. Sharpless asks the baby's name: Sorrow, says she, but on Pinker's return we will have a fresh christening and rename him Buster.

Sharpless goes out: Suzuki comes in dragging Goro by the ear: this dirty dog's been spreading a story that Pinker's not the father says she: an illegitimate child is bad news in the USA says Goro: belt up or I'll kill you says Butterfly. Goro goes off: the harbour cannon goes off. Here comes a ship flying the American flag: Pinker's ship! Whoopee!: joy: rejoicing: love triumphant.

Butterfly and Suzuki ransack the garden for the best blooms: they decorate the house: Butterfly applies her make-up and thinks sucks ya boo to Uncle Bonze and the priggish family: she makes a hole in the wall to survey the scene and await Pinker's arrival. Mood music begins.

Part 2

The mood music goes on and on including birds. Butterfly waits and waits. The baby (Sorrow) has dropped off. Then Suzuki drops off. Butterfly is still awake. Suzuki awakes and sends Butterfly and baby off to take a nap. Sharpless and Pinker arrive and see all the flowers etc. Pinker says don't wake her.

Suzuki spots a strange female in the garden (it is Mrs Pinker): Pinker and Sharpless tell Suzuki all. Suzuki is devastated: Pinker says she waited three years for me – what a shit I am. He chickens out: exits. Enter Mrs Pinker she requests Suzuki to inform Butterfly that the Pinkers require custody of the baby. Butterfly approaches. Mrs Pinker exits into the garden. Suzuki tearfully tells Butterfly that Pinker has gone off her. Butterfly sees a strange female and correctly guesses it is Mrs Pinker. Sharpless confirms that the Pinkers require custody. Mrs Pinker shouts in through the window: Please confirm the custody will be OK. Butterfly says send Pinker back in 30 minutes and he will find the baby ready for collection. Mrs Pinker goes off plus Sharpless.

Butterfly sends Suzuki to play with the baby. Butterfly unsheaths the suicidal sword: Butterfly makes a passionate farewell to her baby: Butterfly sets him to play with a doll plus a toy American flag (Stars & Stripes forever): Butterfly retires discreetly behind a screen: Butterfly cuts her throat: Butterfly gestures weakly towards the baby to Pinker rushing on to collect his son. Butterfly expires.

MINUTES FROM START	LOOK OUT FOR	
Act I		
0	The short prelude: a tremendously busy contrapuntal piece* not at all Japanese, not at all atmospheric.	0
6: *Qui verran l'ufficiale*	Goro lists the likely attendance at Pinkerton's wedding:** the catalogue starts to the accompaniment of a jokey bassoon tune which by the time of Sharpless's arrival grows into a sweeping orchestral dance sequence. Very attractive.	6
8: *Dovunque al mondo*	The first of many tunes that haunt the ear:** Pinkerton's character sketch of the typical American male (unlikely to endear him to feminists or one-time colonials), punctuated by The Stars & Stripes and continuing in a musically agreeable dialogue with Sharpless.	8
14: *Ah! Ah! Quanto cielo!*	A moment of magic:*** we hear Butterfly and her friends approaching up the hill but with enough breath left for her to float out her happy thoughts (to the Butterfly theme) over a backing of good wishes from her mates. Rises to a pretty climax. Dreamy.	14
22: *Che burletta*	Another rich ensemble* uncomfortably Japanesy at first but soon bedding down into the well-loved Italian idiom: a variety of views expressed: Isn't the bridegroom handsome?: He's not so handsome: He looks like a king and very rich: Goro offered him to me and I turned him down: Butterfly looks wonderful: Butterfly's beauty is already fading: Is there any booze?: There'll be divorce for sure, etc. etc.	22
37: *Bimba, bimba, non piangere*	The last eighteen minutes of Act I is taken up with the Pinkerton/Butterfly duet** which has many high points (and some low ones, notably Butterfly's rather boring request for love – 'Vogliatemi bene' – accompanied by a reprehensible solo violin). Some of the high ones are: one of the opening rounds when Pinkerton notices that evening is coming (observant	37
40: *Viene la sera*	chap),** another huge juicy melody which we're	40
48: *Vieni, vieni!*	sorry to lose so quickly – the same big stuff** as Pin-	48

kerton tells Butterfly not to be afraid (The Bonze and all that) and the final grand climacteric which starts with the Happy Butterfly theme and gusts up to force 9 as the lovers linger on the threshold of their love-nest.

Act II Part 1

8: *Un bel dì vedremo* Butterfly's famous forecast** of Pinkerton's return 8
one fine day. At first more appealing for its pathos
than its melody which is rhapsodic but settles into a
9: *Ed egli alquanto* fine firm line*** before its fortissimo ending. 9

Butterfly constantly interrupts Sharpless as he
22: *Amico, cercherete* tries to read her Pinkerton's letter* (over a bass figure 22
almost as persistent as Butterfly herself). He gives up
and says: What if he never comes back? (Boom!) He
25: *Di strapparvi assai* tries to get her to consider Yamadori:* she (to a tre- 25
mendous fanfare) produces her trump card: the
27: *E questo? E questo?* baby.** An effective sequence. 27

Butterfly prefers death to the geisha's trade: a big
35: *Che tua madre* aria** which takes time to shake off its very Japanesy 35
beginnings, but once again the real Puccini stands up
and gives her a terrific final whirl. Followed by a big
burst of 'Vedremo' (hope for Pinkerton's return) before Sharpless exits.

An American ship! Butterfly gives us what is to
42: *Bianca . . . bianca* some extent a replay* of 'Vedremo' leading to a tri- 42
umphant Stars & Stripes then she dives into a glori-
45: *Scuoti quella fronda* ously happy lyrical duet** with Suzuki: poetic stuff 45
about Spring as they fill the house with flowers (the
flower duet).

Act II Part 2

8: *Dormi amor mio* Butterfly's lullaby* as she goes up the stairs with the 8
baby: sweet and soft.

13: *Io so che alle* Another moment of magic: the trio*** Sharpless/ 13
Pinkerton/Suzuki: they grapple musically with the appalling dilemma of telling Butterfly about Mrs P., the three anxious voices moving over a grave and solid tune that gives them a firm base for their worrying thoughts. There is a considerable climax.

22: *Tu, Suzuki* Butterfly's realization of the dreadful truth** and 22
her agreement to give up her son are handled coolly: the pace is slow: metaphorically you could hear a pin drop, then the pathos of this unfortunate lady's plight strikes you full in the midriff. Marvellously effective.

But now all restraint goes to the winds: over a deafening drumbeat Butterfly pushes Suzuki out, addresses the suicidal sword (now sotto voce), bids an hysterical farewell to her son, sets him to play and
30: *Lascialo giocar* commits hara-kiri.** Great stuff if your melodrama 30
count is sufficiently high.

NOTES

Madam Butterfly	Puccini's sixth opera
First night	La Scala, Milan, 17 February 1904
Reception	A disaster. Howls of derision. But three months later in Brescia a big success
Libretto	Giacosa and Illica
Source	See below

NEWS AND GOSSIP

The original *Butterfly* story was written by an American lawyer, one John Luther Long, and is said by people who have seen it to be so simple as to be embarrassing. This was the unlikely basis for a one act play by David Belasco which retained a lot of the Jim Crow (or Him Clow) Japanesy dialogue and which Puccini saw in London in the summer of 1900. He smelt an opera in it and immediately asked a reluctant Ricordi (his publisher) to get the rights. There was the usual scrapping over the libretto with Puccini winning most points. What caused the most aggro was his decision to drop the original second act set in the American Consulate (contrast between East and West). At this point work stopped because Puccini was very badly hurt in a car crash. But he was back at the piece by August 1903 and from then on was confident he had a winner on his hands. He was, of course, right, for after the Milan debacle and some fairly hefty revision, *Butterfly* never faltered, taking off and flying round the opera houses of the world at almost record speed. And it has stuck at the top of the rep along with *Bohème* and *Tosca* ever since.

COMMENT

Butterfly is an enormously sexy opera but it lacks the certainty of step of *Bohème* and *Tosca*. Its charms lie in the pathos of the story and the listener-friendliness of the music plus one or two stunning set pieces. It has weaknesses. In the first act Butterfly's little-girlishness begins to get tiresome and indeed one wonders whether she is not rather seriously mentally retarded (but in the last act she shows the steely courage of one of those fanatical teenage saints, becomes a pathetic figure and arouses true compassion). Pinkerton himself has not enough stature to become an interesting figure (Sharpless much better). Butterfly's wait is too long and the appearance of Mrs Kate Pinkerton in a Japanese garden in a New York coat and skirt verges on the ludicrous (Puccini was queasy about this himself). But the main drawback is that Puccini's Japan is seen as a tragicomic Third World country where funny little people have quaint little customs. All right before the imperialist ethos was smashed to smithereens but today it is Puccini, Illica and Giacosa that look rather funny and ignorant little men, not Goro the marriage broker nor the Bonze. Also much of the music is in a phoney Japanesy idiom (comparable to Sullivan's Miya Sama chorus in *The Mikado*) rather than any part of a real oriental cultural tradition. (It is alleged that Puccini based his Japanesery on 'seven original Japanese folk melodies'. Further and better particulars are required before we can swallow this one.) Indeed it is only when the score shakes off its Japanesy trimmings and becomes truly Italian that the pulse begins to quicken and the senses begin to respond.

Musically *Butterfly* tends to move in fits and starts; gone are the long gloriously unfolding melodies of *Bohème* and *Tosca*, and although always easy on the ear, there is not much in *Butterfly* that is easy to whistle. There is a lot of coitus interruptus: the fragments are teasing, too short to give satisfaction. The action hangs about a bit too: the long vigil and the interminable intermezzo that splits the two halves of Act II is tedious. We know what's coming and we want to get it over with. But pick away as you like, *Butterfly* wins you over in the end. Puccini's instinct was absolutely spot on. His music and her predicament together are pretty irresistible and the great set pieces – the chorus of Butterfly's friends as they climb the hill, One Fine Day, the flower duet, the Pinkerton/Sharpless/Suzuki bad news trio, all of these break through the critical barrier. And why is it that in Puccini's hands the Stars & Stripes can raise the hairs on the nape of even non-American necks? An alpha, but not plus.

The Magic Flute (Die Zauberflöte)

Masonic extravaganza

Mozart [K620]

The one with three temples, three ladies, three boys, a birdcatcher, the Queen of Night and a serpent.

CAST

The Queen of Night		Coloratura soprano
Three Ladies, her employees:	**First**	Soprano
	Second	Soprano
	Third	Mezzo
Three Boys, ditto	**First**	Soprano
	Second	Soprano
	Third	Mezzo
Pamina, her daughter		Soprano
Tamino, an Egyptian prince		Tenor
Papageno, a birdcatcher		Baritone
Papagena, a mate for Papageno		Soprano
Sarastro, Priest of the sun		Bass
Monostatos, Guardian of Sarastro's prisoners		Tenor
Speaker, an elderly priest		Bass
First armoured man		Tenor
Second armoured man		Bass
Priests, slaves, acolytes etc.		

2 acts: running time 2 hrs 40 mins

STORY

Act I Sc 1 A rocky gorge with a temple in view

We are in a mythological age and a magic land where there are wild animals African slaves professional birdcatchers classical temples Egyptian gods and western music. [*Sing*] Enter Tamino in a panic pursued by a serpent. He faints. Three Ladies appear and kill the serpent. They find Tamino inert: all three are instantly sexually attracted to Tamino – they compete for solo sentry duty while the other two go to report the incident: impasse: all three Ladies exit through the temple.

[*Spiel*] Tamino comes to: he inspects the defunct serpent. He hears a mouth organ. Papageno an ornithological nutcase enters dressed as bird carrying cages of birds etc. [*Sing*] I'm a cheerful birdlike chappie he says and I'm fed up with catching boring forest birds. I fancy birds of another kind for sex romps domestic bliss etc. [*Spiel*] Who are you? asks Tamino incidentally I am very classy royal son of important foreign king. Me? says Papageno. I am a totally ignorant bum employed by the Queen of Night as an assistant birdcatcher. I supply birds in exchange for food and drink. The Queen of Night? says Tamino didn't I read about her in my dad's Financial Times? By the way are you a human being or a bird? A human says Papageno also I'm very strong. Hey, is that serpent dead? Yes, says Tamino. In that case I killed it says Papageno.

The Three Ladies pop out from behind a rock. Papageno you stinker they say no food for you today, no wine and also we will zip up your lying mouth you never done killed that dragon we done it. (They padlock his lips together.) And Tamino they say here's a presie from our Queen for you. A pic of her daughter Pamina. Exit Ladies.

[*Sing*] What a stunner! says Tamino. I would like to find this lady. Enter Ladies again. [*Spiel*] Tamino they say you are Lucky Jim: madam has decided to send you on a mission to rescue her daughter Pamina who was snatched away by an evil man. I'm on says Tamino what's all that thunder? Madam likes to make a big entrance say the Ladies. [The rocks open/trapdoor is sprung/palette lowered from the flies (or some magic device) to bring the Queen of Night into prime singing position.] [*Sing*] You look a decent chap says she if you rescue my daughter you can marry her [exit through rocks, trap, upward or whatever].

Down on earth Papageno hums to get unzipped. The Queen forgives you says First Lady: no more lying see? Unlocks him. And Tamino here's a magic flute from the Queen. It can do pretty well anything. Mind if I push off? says Papageno. Certainly not. You're part of the Tamino mission to rescue Pamina from Sarastro say the Ladies. From whom? says Papageno. Sarastro? That gangster? He'd put electrodes on my ears and other parts if he caught me. I'm not going. Belt up you are going, say the Ladies, and here is a magic bellophone to protect you. Also we have assigned three singing boy scouts to guide you to Sarastro's castle. So cheerio, get going.

Act I Sc 2 The Egyptian room in Sarastro's palace

[*Spiel*] Sarastro's slaves chatter. Pst! says a slave. Old Monostatos has got it coming to him. Pamina's escaped! Enter Monostatos you slaves there go and fetch the bracelets, he shouts. Pamina is recaptured. Pamina is carted on all chained up. [*Sing*] You're for it now says Monostatos. Pamina faints away on a divan. Get out all of you shouts Monostatos preparing to rape.

Hey anyone at home? says Papageno peeping in. (For it is he.) That's a pretty thing says he looking at Pamina but pale. He sees the blackamoor Monostatos. Gawd what's that? he says. Monostatos sees the birdman. Gawd what's that? he says. Exits in terror. [*Spiel*] Are you Pamina? asks Papageno: I know your Mum. My mother! Ah! sighs Pamina. She packed me off here with a Royal Johnnie to rescue you says he. Where is he? asks Pamina. He sent me ahead to do recce says he. Thc boy scouts who were meant to guide us here never turned up. I hope he comes soon says she. Sarastro is out shooting and will be back at noon. Tamino's lucky, says Papageno, there's no girl for me. There there, I'll find you someone says Pamina [*Sing*] both agree that love is really a frightfully nice thing.

Act I Sc 3 A grove: three temples facing the audience with titles: WISDOM, REASON and NATURE

[*Sing*] The Three Boys (preferably suspended in a balloon basket) conduct Tamino to the temples. This way old boy they say and to get by here you must be brave bold wise discreet patient etc. How about Pamina? he asks. Never mind about her yet you just be brave bold wise discreet patient etc. say the insufferable Boys. Well I get the message says Tamino. It seems I have to be brave bold wise etc. to get her.

Let's have a go at one of these temples. Knocks. Get off! shout voices within. Tries temple no. 2. Again shouts of temple closed! Nobody at home! Tries no. 3. A Spokesperson appears. What do you want? he asks. I'm looking for a criminal type says Tamino. None here says the Spokesperson. Everyone here is brave bold wise good . . . OK OK says Tamino. Does a chap called Sarastro live in these parts? he asks. Yeah he does says Spoker. In the temple of Wisdom? asks Tamino. In the temple of Wisdom replies Spoker. That's a big laugh says Tamino Sarastro and wisdom! You must be joking. I'm off.

Hold it says Spoker you got something you want to get off your mind about Sarastro? Only that he's a monster egomaniac practising violence, cruelty and also holding persons in detention in contravention of the Geneva Convention Section 17 says Tamino. Section 17? says the Spoker. Someonc told you something? Some lying bitch? Listen son, never believe what a woman says they are all liars every one. Sarastro could explain everything. Explain why he snatched Pamina? says Tamino. Sure he could says Spoker. Is she alive? If so where is she? asks Tamino. I'm not telling you son says the Spoker. You got to get wise and become a mason first. How long is the course? asks Tamino. Not all that long shout a lot of unseen persons clearly eavesdroppers. Is Pamino alive? Tamino asks the unseens. Alive yes they shout back. Good news says

Tamino. I think I'll play the flute for a while. He plays.

Wild animals creep out in large numbers (one lion says to another: We got the wrong night this should be *Orpheus*. No it isn't stupid says the other, it's the animal walk-on in the *Flute*. Oh my God says the first lion, I've got my *Orpheus* make-up on). [*Sing*] These animals are fine thinks Tamino but I wish it were Pamina. He hears Papageno's mouth organ. Thinks: maybe he knows where she is. He exits in wrong direction (bemused by animals).

Papageno and Pamina enter. Where is he? they ask. He must be near, I could hear his flute with that dud B flat says Papageno. Enter Monostatos with slaves. Got you! he says. Chain 'em up lads! Papageno starts up his bellophone. Magic! All coloured persons instantly enter dance-trance cutting bizarre capers and exit prancing. If everyone had a bellophone like ours trouble would dance out of their lives say Pamina and Papageno sententiously.

Voices off are heard shouting Sieg Heil Sarastro! Sarastro? say Pamina and Papageno, we're trapped! Enter Sarastro plus many Sarastrians. Mein Führer says Pamina it's all true I tried to run away but only because I was sexually harassed by your servant a wog. Cheer up says Sarastro no forced sex in my outfit also I happen to know you are potty about A. N. Other. But I'm afraid I can't let you go. I want to go back to Mum says Pamina. Negative says Sarastro it's not a good idea for you to go to her. I want my Mum says Pamina. Young females need male guidance says Sarastro women are quite incapable of rational thought.

Monostatos brings in Tamino. It's him! says Pamina. It's her! says Tamino. Clinch. Break it up instanter says Monostatos. And let me tell you Sarastro this Papageno tried to nick Pamina till I stopped him. Thanks Monostatos I award you 77 strokes of the cat on the soles of your feet for lust and lechery says Sarastro. O gee boss says Monostatos have a heart. And bring Tamino and Pamina into the disinfectant tent to be purified for temple testing says Sarastro. Heil! Heil! shout the Sarastrians. Curtain.

Act II Sc 1 A palm-grove. A meeting place for the priests

A number of priests march in and settle at a board-room table. [*Spiel*] I have called this E.G.M. to propose an important foreign royal for immediate membership says Sarastro, name Tamino Smith: rank Prince: age 25. Decent sort of chap? asks one. Very decent says Sarastro. Financially sound? asks another. Banks at Coutts says Sarastro. Public school? asks a third. Eton and Trinity says Sarastro.

And another thing says Sarastro this lovely girl Pamina to be his bride, a matter arranged by the gods and myself. I abducted her for this purpose from her politically unsound queen mother. This frightful female terrorist plots and schemes against our company. It sounds all very fine Sarastro says a priest but royals are often softies will Tamino stand up to the tests without starting to talk to the flowers and things like that? Tamino is no softie says Sarastro. What if he gets killed in the tests? asks another. He's fully insured says Sarastro.

Sarastro reckoning that the priests are now favourably disposed addresses the gods Isis and Osiris and [*Sing*] politely requests them to assist Tamino also in the case of the candidate's death to ensure a safe passage to the other world.

Act II Sc 2 Forecourt of a temple. Night

[*Spiel*] Tamino and Papageno are led on by priests. How do you like this? Tamino asks. I'm dead scared says Papageno. Spoker and assistant Spoker come on. Why are you here? Spoker asks. I want to be a good man says Tamino. Are you prepared for high risk and possibly terminal tests? asks Spoker. Yessir says Tamino. Shake on it says Spoker. How about you Papageno? Tests are not much in my line says Papageno I require only simple life and an agreeable wife. You won't get a wife unless you take the tests says Spoker. Are the tests tough? asks Papageno. Very tough says Spoker. Then I will stay single says Papageno. But Sarastro has selected a wife for you by the name of Papagena says Spoker. OK I'll have a go says Papageno.

Right says Spoker we're off. No talking from now on. [*Sing*] And don't weaken if any representative of that monstrous regiment of women try to chat you up. Exit Spokers. The Three Ladies come up through a trap. Hello hello you're in a pretty fix say the Ladies. We can tell you that the priests plan certain death for you both. Papageno chatters in panic and Tamino tells him to belt up. Our Queen is in the temple and will protect you from these evil clerics say the Ladies. Come on Tamino says Papageno let's do a bunk. Tamino shushes Papageno that's rubbishy women's talk he says belt up. So you won't talk? say the Ladies. The priests offstage shout it's the frightful three again to hell with them. The Ladies drop through a trap. The Spokers come on: [*Spiel*] Well done chaps they say you passed that test OK.

Act II Sc 3 A garden. Pamina asleep. Moonlight

[*Spiel* then *Sing*] Monostatos comes on moody about racial discrimination – no sex for me because I'm black? He says it's not fair: I have the same sex drive as whites so look out Pamina: he prepares to rape her. The Queen of Night enters: [*Spiel*] get off blackie she cries. (Mother! says

Pamina.) Where's that guy I sent on the rescue mission? asks the Queen. Gone into Sarastro's theological institution says Pamina. That's torn it says the Queen your dad did a deal with that Sarastro that his lot would rule the world by day and yours truly by night. He told me that women were too stupid to rule by day. Unless you get your man to leave before dawn he'll become one of them and you've lost him.

Why? They seem decent people says Pamina. Decent? They are a shower of stinking rats says the Queen. Listen: here's a knife: you go and stick it into Sarastro and you will rid the world of bad rubbish. Then I will get back the power to rule in daytime. If you fail to kill Sarastro you are no longer my daughter. So there! (Sings.)

[*Spiel*] So Mum wants me to be her hitperson? says Pamina. It's not possible. Hey Pamina says Monostatos if I tell Sarastro your Mum is in these precincts he'll bump her off instanter. Now if you give me a good time I'll keep quiet. Never! says Pamina. Monostatos advances lecherously. Enter Sarastro. Get off you banana boat scum he cries. Monostatos runs out mumbling so I'll join up with the Queen so I will. Please Sarastro don't go after my mother says Pamina. My dear girl says Sarastro [*Sing*] in these halls any thought of revenge is quite unknown.

Act II Sc 4 A vast room

[*Spiel*] The Spokers lead in Tamino and Papageno. Wait here for the next cue they say and remember no talking. Papageno chatters on regardless. I could do with a drink of water he says. Presto! Disabled OAP appears by magic with water. Papageno chats her up. How old are you? he asks. Eighteen she says (big joke), my husband Papageno is 10 years older says she. Your husband Papageno??? says Papageno. Who's he? You are! says she.

Punitive thunder stops this conversation. [*Sing*] The Three Boys float in: Hi again they say you forgot your instruments – here's 1 flute 1 bellophone also some grub for Papageno. You're doing well Tamino cheerio. [*Spiel*] Papageno tucks in while Tamino plays the flute. Pamina runs on. O Tamino she says. No response. You sick or something? she asks. No response. [*Sing*] O Lord he's gone off me I think I'll go and top myself says she. No response. [*Spiel*] You see Tamino I too can keep mum when required says Papageno.

Act II Sc 5 A vault shaped like a pyramid

[*Sing*] The priests are singing their morning song. Good morning sun they say Tamino is through to his finals. [*Spiel*] Sarastro and Tamino come on. So far so good my boy only two more to go says Sarastro. Bring on Pamina! He wants to say his last goodbye says Sarastro. [*Sing*] Last goodbye? says she. Last goodbye says Sarastro. Last goodbye says Tamino. Well, it's just possible we may meet again says Sarastro. All exit.

[*Spiel*] Papageno comes on with the assistant Spoker. Where's Tamino? asks Papageno. I wish to God I'd never started this trip. Papageno says the Spoker you have failed. Oh have I says Papageno then I'd like a large Scotch. Very good says Spoker. He gets it.

There's only one other thing I'd like says he – a wife. [*Sing*] The OAP appears again: [*Spiel*] Hi-de-hi sweetheart here I am nice little wifey says the crippled OAP. Just a minute . . . steady on . . . says Papageno. Marry me now or else go to prison with a bread-and-water diet forever says the OAP. OK I will says he. Bam! Zizzo! The OAP is transformed into a gemütlich young girl. Sorry old man: you're not worthy of her yet says the Spoker. Papagena, kindly disappear (she disappears).

Act II Sc 6 A garden

[*Sing*] The Three Boys float on moralizing as usual. Look here comes Pamina pretty well gone potty with stress they say. I think I'll kill myself now says Pamina fingering a dagger. Farewell Queen Mum. The Boys interpose. Stop it Pamina they cry. Tamino loves you. Loves me? she says then why won't he talk? Aha that's a security matter say the Boys, we can't say but follow us and meet him. They go.

Act II Sc 7 Two mountains: one spouting water, the other fire

Two armoured men tell Tamino they invigilate the final tests by fire and water. OK I'm hyped up and ready says Tamino. Pamina shouts 'Tamino' offstage. Is she coming too? asks Tamino. Yip say the armoureds. Pamina comes on: big reunion. Together we will go they say. Give us a tune on that flute of yours says Pamina its magic powers may reduce the danger. Tamino and Pamina pass through fire with no problems but a bit slow also through the water even slower. You done it! sing offstage priests. You done it! Both now certified Sarastrian masons!

Act II Sc 8 Back to the suicide garden of Sc 6

Papageno comes on: I think I'll top myself he says: life without a wife is not worth living. He puts a rope round a tree branch and screws up courage. One . . . two . . . thr— . . . the Boys (keen Samaritans) are here again. They interpose. Play your bellophone you fool they cry. He plays: Papagena materializes: both are very pleased but become afflicted with Papageno's stammer. They discuss family planning. Exit.

The Queen of Night plus the Three Ladies and Monostatos creep on conspiratorially. Quiet! says everyone (quite loudly) quiet! If our plot succeeds ma'am do you undertake that I marry your daughter Pamina? asks Monostatos. I undertake says the Queen. Let's get after those Sarastrians and kill the lot they say. Suddenly there is atomic thunder and laser lightning. Also cosmic rays. Help! Help! we have gone all weak! they cry. Ow! Ow! (They are overcome.)

Act II Sc 9 The temple of the sun

Tamino, Pamina and the Three Boys (the turncoats), priests and, of course, Sarastro all give thanks: the sun's rays have routed forces of night (and we thought it was thunder) beauty wisdom etc. have triumphed. A passing vote of thanks to Isis and Osiris too although they have nothing whatever to do with the solar system. Curtain.

MINUTES FROM START — LOOK OUT FOR

0 The overture*** – a great show-business piece. A fidgety fiddle tune comes in right after the slow introduction and keeps going off and on pretty well right through. There is a pause and we have the Three Chords from the horns, and for a while the strings fidget fugally and in the minor. Back home again to the sunny major key for the reprise of the first bit (or rather bits of it, for quite a lot is new). 0

Act I Sc 1

Action!

1. Enter Tamino pursued by a serpent, singing a little wimpishly and passing out almost at once.

2. Enter the Three Ladies who promptly kill the serpent (fanfare) and go on to boast about it.

3. Now look out for a lovely strain in the lower

9: *Ein holder Jüngling* strings** as the Ladies focus on sexy Tamino and sing in turn What a dreamboat! Then together: Let's tell Madam about him. Here the Three set their style, which doesn't change throughout. It is close-ish harmony, sometimes the top Lady leading, sometimes one of the lower Ladies moving around snakily below. They have their own tempo too, never very fast, never very slow. 9

4. Each one competes for solo sentry duty over Tamino whilst the orchestra goes CHUCK CHUCK

CHUCK below. Then they realize (singing together) how unsafe it would be for any one to be alone with this man and the scene ends with a longish and sweet-
12: *Du Jüngling schön und liebevoll* ish arrivederci** in one of their favourite rhythms – 12
TI-TUM, TI-TUM, TI TIRALEE TUM – with a little fancy stuff at the end.

14: *Der Vogelfänger bin ich ja* Papageno's comic number** complete with pan- 14
pipes. He is cheerful but sex-starved. A neat little item, perhaps on the coy side.

Tamino gazes on the likeness of Pamina and in true operatic fashion falls for her though the picture must be very small and show only her face. [How does he know that she is not a hunchback with rickety legs? Ed.] He sings his heart out in a pure noble and finally
21: *Dies Bildnis ist bezaubernd schön* passionate tenor aria.** 21

The Queen of Night has a sweeping accompagnato – she tells Tamino that he has made a good impres-
28: *Zum Leiden bin ich auserkoren* sion and settles in to part 1 of her aria*** which is 28
slow and grave and then dramatic as she gives a tabloid account of how Pamina was snatched. Part 2 (fast) is all fizz and fireworks – if Tamino can rescue Pamina he can keep her for good. Tough vocal gymnastics for the Queen – if she wins, magic; if she is struggling, quite awful, like a Monday morning singing lesson in Aberdeen.

32: *Hm! Hm! Hm! Hm!* The quintet** of the Ladies, Tamino and Papa- 32
geno, varied, wonderful, packed with plot and with an unbroken stream of fascinating music.

1. Unlocking Papageno. He hum-hums his appeal to get rid of the padlock. Pure buffa. The Ladies appear and unlock him and then with Lady-style music all five moralize about the benefit to the world if no one told lies.

2. Fitting out the expedition. The magic flute itself is presented with a description of its powers (which don't tally at all with its future use as an animal attractor/deterrent). The same harmonious mood as above, but with a continuous flow of new melodic ideas. A short pause over a pedal as the Three reflect on the magic powers of the flute. Some knockabout exchanges when Papageno tries to chicken out.

37: *Silberglöckchen Zauberflöten* 3. He gets his bells. Now a lovely trio*** as the 37
Three prepare to go. This wonderful scrap of music

comes from nowhere and disappears in a trice. Some composers would have made it work for half an hour.

4. News about the Boys and – something new – an
38: *Drei Knäbchen, jung, schön* introduction to the Boys' music.** Fragile, a little 38
spooky, high, close harmony, amazing. So to the farewells.

Act I Sc 2

Papageno, fresh from his terrifying encounter with Monostatos, finds Pamina coming to from her black-out. This unlikely couple sing the praises of married life, of which neither of them has had any experi-
46: *Bei Männern, welche Liebe fühlen* ence.** Which perhaps is why this duet is what the 46
Victorians would have called sublime – simple, perfect and quite beautiful. Look out especially for Pamina's farewell arabesque (sung twice).

Act I Sc 3

The finale ranges freely over the whole palette of *Flute* music from A to Z.

1. First the Boys with their weird superboy
49: *Zum Ziele führt* music,** a little holy, haunting and supported by 49
wind and timps, it verges on Mozart's Masonic. They have two short innings, give Tamino some excellent advice and float off.

2. Tamino has a long – surely too long – accompagnato as he fumbles around knocking on doors and chatting up the Speaker. At last he gets the message that Pamina is alive and decides it is time for a short flute recital.

59: *Wie stark ist* 3. This gentle tune*** is greatly liked by the local 59
fauna who turn out in numbers (well – numbers depending on the size of the budget) and it can cast a spell over us humans too. Tamino takes over the burden of the melody and personalizes it into an appeal to Pamina to turn up – quickly. Then a shout of joy as he hears Papageno's pipes and he runs off in the wrong direction (perhaps deaf in one ear). But in our ears the flute tune lingers on.

4. Now we have a scampering search sequence: Papageno and Pamina look for Tamino – flute and pipes exchange signals but the level of fieldcraft is poor and they can't find each other. Instead – interception by the ridiculous Monostatos. And here we must pause for the great glockenspiel scene. The little

tune for Papageno's bellophone is enchanting (unlike his panpipes which get on your nerves early in the op-
63: *Das klinget so herrlich* era) and the sotto voce chorus*** by the bad black 63
men and the ballet to its toy-town jingle are about as far as you can get from the crashing and terribly serious choruses that are about to break out. This is the *Flute* and its magic runs all over.

5. A little cheerful moralizing from Papageno and Pamina (in the *Flute*, as in *Alice in Wonderland*, everyone moralizes at the drop of a hat). The first big Sarastro chorus (military rather than Masonic) makes the temples shake on their foundations. Now we have a dramatic and quite lovely dialogue between Pamina
67: *Herr, ich bin zwar Verbrecherin!* and Sarastro.** She pleads with him, singing pretty 67
high, and his replies get very low indeed. He is not pleased by her desire to get back to her Queen of Night mum. She pluckily keeps asking. After the frightful Monostatos has been dealt with we have the final chorus with a bit of vintage Sarastro sandwiched
72: *Es lebe Sarastro* into it. It is a stunner,*** a great occasional piece for 72
full forces, fit for a coronation or a grand mass but equally welcome in this extraordinary jumble of wonderful music that makes up the finale to Act I of *The Magic Flute*.

Act II Sc 1

0 The march of the priests,*** solemn, calm and quite 0
beautiful. Trombones, flutes and bassets help to give it its very special sound. In a stretch of secco recitatif punctuated by the triple chord Sarastro gets the approval of his board of governors for Tamino and Pamina to enter for their Higher Certificate in Endurance. Now he politely asks two Egyptian gods to see
6: *O Isis und Osiris* they have a decent chance. A deep bass aria*** which 6
has gravitas, power and, the second half especially, a memorable tune.

Act II Sc 2

0: *Bewahret euch vor Weibertücken* A short duet* between two priests, gratuitously of- 0
fensive to women but easy on the ear.

12: *Wie? Wie? Wie?* A quintet,** the Three Ladies, Tamino and Papa- 12
geno. The Ladies are distressed to find the chaps in dangerous circumstances: why not obey the instructions of their Queen and escape? Papageno chatters, but Tamino tells him to belt up and explains to the

Ladies he can't talk, all of which causes him to talk quite a lot. The Ladies are clearly disturbed and flutter around with anxious phrases. As the piece races along we get one delicious snatch of melody after another, thick and fast. The scene ends with thunder and offstage shouts, but Tamino has done well and qualified for his next test.

Act II Sc 3

18: *Alles fühlt der Liebe*

Monostatos's furtive aria* before settling down to 18
rape Pamina. Is it really so awful for a black man to have sex with a white woman? he asks. The accompaniment is 'Turkish' (without the drums and cymbals), the sort of thing given to Osmin in *Seraglio*. Fluttering piccolo and strings.

22: *Der Hölle Rache*

The Queen of Night's second aria,*** full of 22
passionate defiance. This remarkable and very difficult piece is a knockout if the singer can ride it with ease and conviction. This does not always happen.

26: *In diesen heil'gen Hallen*

Another stately and splendid bass aria*** from 26
Sarastro, even deeper and more melodious than Isis and Osiris and benefitting greatly from elegant support mainly from the strings which do their own thing in measured counterpoint to Sarastro and take over the burden of the melody when he goes plunging down to the lower depths.

Act II Sc 4

33: *Seid uns zum zweiten*

The Boys bring half-time refreshments** and return 33
the magic flute and bells. A rather brisker tempo, but the same close harmony and reedy texture. A short visit.

36: *Ach, ich fühl's*

Pamina's song of desolation** – Tamino has de- 36
serted her – in Mozart's saddest key, G minor. The simplest of accompaniments allows Pamina to give every pathetic phrase its full weight. Some quite difficult stuff for her too.

Act II Sc 5

40: *O Isis und Osiris!*

The priests chorus on in a holy fashion.* They think 40
Tamino looks like a promising candidate. Not so striking as other choruses, but good noble stuff.

44: *Soll ich dich*

The Goodbye trio** – Pamina's farewell to 44
Tamino before he goes over the top. Tamino in good heart, Sarastro deep down and encouraging, only Pamina in a bit of a panic. Again a resourceful accom-

paniment and a stream of good musical ideas.

50: *Ein Mädchen oder Weibchen* Papageno's Volksong with bells.** He is still going 50
on about finding a wife. The song is in two parts, part 1 flows, part 2 keeps halting, both very volksy. The bell bit comes in between verses and is varied.

Act II Sc 6

The finale:

56: *Bald prangte* 1. The Three Boys say the sun will soon rise*** 56
(big news). Perhaps the most heavenly of all their utterances, it speeds up and breaks into an agitated trot when they see the desperate Pamina about to stab herself.

2. Duet, Pamina and the Boys, speaking as one which is their practice. She says Tamino has gone off her but they tell her (they take their time about it) that he still loves her and that they will take her to him. Not so much dramatic as pretty and persuasive. We know Pamina's not going to top herself anyway.

Act II Sc 7

3. A menacing contrapuntal string intro leads us to expect something momentous. Sure enough the
62: *Der, welcher wandelt* two Armed Men come in strong** about the appal- 62
ling difficulties of the final test. Quite frightening: the strings keep at their exercise until Tamino responds in manly fashion – and hark! what do we hear?

69: *Tamino mein!* 4. It's Pamina! And her cry of joy*** is one of the 69
great moments in music (a sideways slip into another key is part of the trick). A sweet and soothing bassoon and string intro lets Tamino show her the horrendous prospect, then in a solo full of telling phrases and with a bassoon in attendance she advises him that the magic flute will come in handy. This ends in a quartet with Tamino and the Armed Men with another of the
72: *Wir wandeln durch des Tones* *Flute*'s (short) great tunes.*** 72

5. The trials by fire and water.* The magic flute, aided by timps, keeps the dangers at bay and there is a short burst of rejoicing from the chorus (and where did the females come from?).

Act II Sc 8

6. The second attempted suicide. Papageno, de-
75: *Papagena! Papagena!* prived of Papagena, thinks to top himself.* A lot of 75
the dreaded panpipes but easily the most attractive thing about this buffa piece is the skirmishing of the

strings in a figure that punctuates the bouts of Papageno's misery. But hold! The Samaritans to the rescue again, namely the Three Boys. They pipe away with great urgency and advise him to try his magic bells. This does the trick, Papagena appears and we
79: *Pa-Pa-Pa* etc. are into the Pa-Pa-Pa-Pa-Pa bit.** Simple fun, but 79
neat and melodious.

7. Monostatos, the Queen of Night plus the Three Ladies advance on the temple with evil intent to a sin-
83: *Nur stille, stille* ister staccato little march.* But thunder and Sarastro 83
put paid to their plot (whatever it may have been).

Act II Sc 9

And so, rather suddenly, it's all over. The good people have triumphed over the forces of night and we close with two choruses, the first solemn and mighty
86: *Heil sei euch Geweihten!* impressive, the second*** bright and cheerful as be- 86
comes the end of this extraordinary opera and with a final piercing phrase that lives in the ear long after the curtain has come down.

NOTES

The Magic Flute	Mozart's sixteenth and penultimate opera
First night	Theater auf der Wieden, Vienna, 30 September 1791
Reception	No reliable data but word of mouth must have been good, for it played to packed houses from the second night on
Libretto	Schikaneder
Source	Many sources, at least eight, alleged or real. Certainly the title (and a bit more) was taken from a play by Wieland, *Lulu, or the Magic Flute*

NEWS AND GOSSIP

Because the *Flute* was the biggest success of Mozart's life there were plenty of people claiming a hand in writing the libretto, including members of Schikaneder's company. This was a scratch collection of singers, craftsmen and musicians kept together as a big theatrical family by the fact that they lived and worked in a suburb just beyond easy commuting range of central Vienna. Mozart lived there too while working on the *Flute* (March to July 1791 plus a few hectic days before the first night on September 30) and must have taken part in script conferences. Scholars have dug up at least eight literary ancestors of the *Flute* (some of them going back to the twelfth century) and have gone to huge pains to prove that all of them could quite easily have been faxed to Schikaneder from the universities, libraries, etc. where they lay. It is clear that Schikaneder was at least chairman of what could well have been a script committee and this would account for the *Flute* being, if not a musical camel, an operatic animal with eccentric features. Schikaneder was by no means a literary man, but rather a travelling showman who was now going almost posh because he could see money in it. He was also an actor, a singer, a designer and a stage-machinery freak. We can see his hand behind the serpent, the bellophone, the wild beasts, the two draught lions, the fire and water machinery and the Three Boys, if they were suspended in a balloon basket, as seems likely, for a real hot-air balloon had achieved lift-off in a Viennese park some weeks earlier and the tabloids were full of it. It must also be likely that at least some of the less relevant props (the serpent, the animals) reflected a prudent use of existing stock. Anyway, Schikaneder, for once, with the help of Mozart, got it right and the fame of the *Flute* soon spread all over Europe. But the language barrier kept it to German-speaking houses until the end of the century, when it was translated into French and Italian and suffered the usual mutilation in the process. The Italian version played in London in 1811. But in the nineteenth century the *Flute* cast its magic far and wide until today it ranks amongst Mozart's top four.

COMMENT

Many people find the *Flute* a pretty rum old item, but one thing is for sure – it has the most glorious music. What's more, it has its own kind of music, or rather its own several kinds of music, which just don't happen anywhere else in Mozart. There is the solemn priestly music complete with trombones and bassets which has all the sonority of Mozart's Masonic music but none of the gloom. Indeed it is not gloomy at all, it is profound and peaceful, the music of a brotherhood of frightfully good men who are so wise as to be in danger of becoming gods. No music like it before or since: a couple of bars and you know – that's it, that's them, that's Sarastro's lot. Then there is the Tamino/Pamina music – the purest love music Mozart ever wrote, not passionate like *Così*, not playful as in *Figaro*, not despairing, as is Elvira's in *Giovanni*, but sometimes sad, sometimes happy, straight from one trusting heart to another and luckily caught by us on the wing. Next the music of Papageno, juvenile Simple Simon stuff. It catches the ear at once and would certainly have won the Eurovision Song Contest of 1791, but is the only music in the *Flute* that wears out its welcome with repetition, especially the dreaded panpipes which gets as tiresome as a child's musical toy at Christmas. Monostatos is a *type* and is given typical blackamoor music à la Osmin, the Three Ladies have their own personal style and the Three Boys (they must be boys and not females), fluting away in their other-worldly fashion, have the power to disturb and unsettle us with their rather spooky music from another sphere. The Queen of Night and Sarastro are firmly type-cast in their own kind of music. Sarastro's two numbers could belong to no one else and the Queen, although her first number is benign and her second vitriolic, also has a personalized style, regal, icy clear and as high as the stars.

As for the story – well. First one has to recognize that the Singspiel format – so often a disaster – suits the *Flute* down to its folksy foundations and that nothing else would have served it so well. Continuous music or even recitatif could not have coped with its switches in mood nor would they have made the plot any clearer, indeed rather the reverse, if that is possible. There have been many brave attempts by scholars, philosophers, psychologists and *Flute* fanatics all over the world to make sense of the *Flute*. They go to incredible lengths to prove one of two things, or both:

1. The *Flute* has a logical story line.
2. The libretto of the *Flute* has within it a system of signs and symbols which can be decoded to reveal some great Masonic parable.

Of course you can make a case for anything to be a logical narrative, whether it be *Finnegans Wake*, *Jabberwocky* or the book of Revelation, and there is no doubt that the *Flute* offers a pretty good challenge. For instance: the relations between the Queen of Night and Sarastro in the *Flute* are not good and this is because her father left daytime to him and nighttime to her. But Sarastro seems to do pretty good right throughout the twenty-four hours whilst she does no better at night than by day. In the early scenes there is no doubt that both Tamino and the audience believe the Queen and her lot to be decent respectable people and then find out they have been conned. They are not goodies, they are very bad baddies. There is no dramatic point in this. The all-wise Sarastro has on his staff an unreliable Moor who is given three opportunities to rape a prisoner in his charge. This argues both a poor recruitment policy and slack middle management and therefore casts doubt on the quality of the chief executive. The Three Boys, employed by the Queen, are assigned to help Tamino rescue Pamina. So what do they do? Instead of leading him to Pamina, they dump him in the middle of Sarastro's temples, give him a short lecture on morality and disappear. Double agents perhaps? Right up to the moment he appears on stage, we still believe Sarastro to be an evil man. But then he is terribly nice to Pamina and the chorus tell us he is pretty well the best thing since Jesus Christ, or at least Albert Schweitzer.

And so on through a load of contradiction and discrepancies, most of them appearing in the spoken dialogues.

The other conundrum lies in the Masonic bit. We have to ask ourselves are Mozart and Schikaneder really serious? Is there some deep Masonic meaning? Or are the Masonic trimmings there just to make the show a bit more sexy? There are certain facts:

1. Mozart and Schikaneder were both Masons.
2. In 1791 Masonry was headline news in all the broadsheets because the Imperial court was trying to suppress it.
3. The trials and tests that Tamino and Pamina had to undergo are pretty similar to the rituals for entry into the Masonic order.
4. The triple chord which pops up all over the place probably does represent the Masonic triple knock, one of those boy scout tricks which Masons enjoy, like their funny handshake.
5. When Sarastro talks about wisdom, etc., he uses Masonic jargon.

These facts have given lift-off to all manner of *Flute*/Masonic theories, many of them fascinating (especially to their authors) and ranging from the lunatic to the almost credible. The Masonic number of three, for instance, is discovered all over the place. So we have three ladies, three boys and the triple chord: twice three is six, and three times six is eighteen and we have eighteen places for the priests' meeting and the priests' march is eighteen bars long. And so on.

But both the narrative problem and the Masonic problem can be easily explained if you look not at the text but at the way the *Flute* was put together and by whom. It has all the marks of a piece made to meet a deadline and based on a book (in the sense of a pantomime book).

Technically, putting on the *Flute* must have been pretty like the putting on of a pantomime which has to be adapted from rehearsal to rehearsal to meet new timings for scene changes, to cut gags that don't work, to rewrite a scene to cover a weak artist, to put in all the new ideas that are better than the old ideas, to reshape an act to meet the lighting cues – in all of this ad hoc activity the success of each scene becomes paramount and the mainframe story, unless the producer is a genius, will get a bit lost. Neither Schikaneder nor Mozart was this kind of genius. Schikaneder was not a serious writer, rather something between P. T. Barnum and Donald Wolfit, Mozart, though certainly a musical and probably a mathematical genius too, was not a literary man and certainly no Masonic John Bunyan. To think that these two, whilst working against the clock and trying to cope with all the problems of composition and production, could have evolved some great philosophical masterpiece, is just potty. It may be true, for instance, that they changed the plot-line late in the day to avoid damaging comparisons with a show about a magic bassoon (!) which opened just before them.

As to the Masonic things, during its long life pantomime would often haul in references to real life events to stir emotions already strongly held by the audience – The Kaiser and Hitler in the two world wars, all manner of royal events, from Queen Victoria's jubilee on and, when we had it, the Empire in all its glory – and one can see that at the time of the *Flute* the Masonic thing must have been good box office. That is not to say that our two Masons did not treat the order with respect – they did, but it is not easy to believe, certainly of Schikaneder, that holy thoughts came first and that their effect on the box office was entirely absent from his mind. And many of the clues to a deeper significance are rubbish. The Masonic three, for instance, are found in *Don Giovanni* just as frequently as in the *Flute* – three maskers, three selections from operas in the last act, three orchestras at the ball, two of them playing in three-time etc.

When all is said and done, the *Flute* is the *Flute*, and who minds? Certainly not the audience, who leave the theatre happier people and with a belief that the world might be a slightly better place than they thought it was three hours earlier and who do not much care whether Sarastro and the Queen of Night are paradigms for members of the ruling Hapsburg family, nor whether the E flat phrase on the horns represents the sound of a novitiate Mason rolling up his trouser leg or whether it is just a good tune. Alpha.

Manon Lescaut
Sentimental melodrama

Puccini

The one where a government minister has his mistress jailed for common prostitution and which ends with two people dying in a desert.

CAST

Lescaut, an officer in the Guards	Baritone
Manon Lescaut, his sister	Soprano
Chevalier des Grieux, student, also a baronet	Tenor
Geronte di Ravoir, Treasurer-General, government official, very rich	Bass
Edmondo, a commoner student	Tenor
Publican, Dance Master, Wig Maker, Lamplighter, Police Officer, Naval Captain, etc.	

4 acts: running time 1 hr 45 mins

STORY

Act I The courtyard of an inn: outdoor tables etc

We are in eighteenth-century Amiens. The beer garden of the inn is full of students goosing local girls returning from work. The student leader Edmondo (a commoner) quizzes student des Grieux (an aristo). Why is he withdrawn? Is he in love? Des Grieux says no: he starts joshing the girls.

A coach arrives with three interesting characters: a laid-back Guards officer Lescaut, his sister Manon (a stunner), and an elderly rich VIP Geronte. The students wolf-whistle Manon: des Grieux chats her up: she says she is en route to a convent. Golly! a real beaut like you he says: will you meet me later? OK she says: she enters the inn.

The students rib des Grieux. Lescaut tells Geronte his sister is about to take the veil. Geronte says join me for dinner. Yessir! says Lescaut (he smells money). The chorus rabbit on watching a card game. Geronte who has evil designs on Manon tells the publican he wants fast horses and an M.O.T.-tested carriage on standby in one hour. Yessir! says the publican. That old lecher is ahead of you Edmondo tells des Grieux. Waddya mean? says des G. He's got a coach and horses on standby says Edmondo: des G. says OK just you keep her minder brother in play (he is at cards with the students).

Manon appears: des G. persuades her to fly with him. Geronte comes in: Edmondo tells him Manon has flown with des G. Geronte is quite thrown. Zut! after them – zut! he cries. Lescaut is cool: there's no point chasing them, they had too long a start he says: she'll come to heel in Paris: students have no money. (Geronte thinks: Zut! And zut! again.)

Act II An elegant salon in Geronte's Paris house

Manon prinks before the mirror. Lescaut drops in and preens himself on his success in switching Manon from des Grieux's student poverty to Geronte's luxury. Manon says she is sex-starved and wants to go to bed with des Grieux. Lescaut says he has just launched des G. on a career as a professional gambler, when he's rich cohabitation will be OK. A vocal group sings a piece composed by Geronte (terrible) for a dancing lesson for Manon: Geronte plus other old lechers including clergy observe: Lescaut decides Manon is deeply bored: he will fetch des Grieux after all: Manon dances with Geronte (ugh!): Geronte and clergy etc. exit for stroll: Manon is to follow.

Des Grieux arrives! At first he is resentful of her desertion: soon he clinches Manon. Geronte enters: he sees all: exits. Des Grieux and Lescaut say get away quick: Manon fiddles around hunting out her most favoured jewels. Security men surround the house: they barge into the room: des Grieux draws his sword: Lescaut interposes: Manon is arrested: her jewels spill on to the carpet. Geronte is greatly amused.

INTERMEZZO

(A bit of musical padding designed to cover another huge hole in the plot, namely Manon has been tried, sent down for prostitution and condemned to be extradited as slave labour to America: des Grieux tried everything: failed to get to appeal court (Lescaut apparently did nothing) so here they now are on the day of embarkation.)

Act III The quay at Le Havre: a boat about to sail. Dawn

Lescaut and des Grieux pace the quay; Manon is imprisoned in the adjacent barracks. The sentry is bribed. Des Grieux is in a highly nervous state. A guard duty squad passes, the bribed sentry in the midst. Des Grieux contacts Manon at a window of the barracks: an irrelevant lamplighter sings simplistic ditty (to add atmosphere) while des Grieux briefs Manon on the escape plan: OK I've got it says she.

Rifle shot rings out: all hell breaks loose: Lescaut runs on and says it's a total cockup: indeed S.N.A.F.U.: des Grieux makes a suicide attempt but Lescaut interposes. Manon advises des Grieux to go: he doesn't.

A crowd gathers. A drum-roll sounds: women are paraded for roll call and embarkation. The voyeuristic crowd gloats, much taken with Manon: Lescaut tells the crowd a romantic tale about Manon, all lies: he says des Grieux is her wronged husband: des Grieux makes a feeble attempt to snatch Manon: the crowd supports him: forces of law and order prevail: Manon is embussed: des Grieux makes a tearful appeal to the captain to take on an extra deckhand. The captain (old softie) agrees. Manon and des Grieux are quite delighted (little do they know . . .).

Act IV A deserted plain near New Orleans. Hot

Manon and des Grieux struggle on both pretty well scuppered. They have no water: no food: no sense of direction: no hope. We hear constant reminders of their great mutual affection: Manon passes out: she recovers: des Grieux goes on recce: he finds zilch: more mutual affection: Manon expires: the curtain falls on des Grieux about to expire.

MINUTES FROM START — **LOOK OUT FOR**

Act I

In the early stages of the opera des Grieux has all the
5: *Tra voi, belle* — best tunes: he chats up the girls* to an easy-going 5
number soon to lead to a cheery undergraduate
20: *Cortese damigella* — chorus: his first approaches to Manon in a duet* 20
where he is poetical and she matter-of-fact and then
24: *Donna non vidi* — we have his reflections** on what a stunner she is. 24

25: *Vedete? Io son fedele* — Des Grieux leads Manon in a duet* that begins 25
sedately but blows up into a considerable head of steam to the question – will she, won't she fly with him? Eventually she will, and concedes with the same word as does Mozart's Zerlina when conquered by the Don – 'Andiam'.

The students, who have kept at it off and on pretty
31: *Venticelli ricciutelli* — well throughout the act, have a catchy last chorus* to 31
accompany the cool philosophizing of the hoodwinked Lescaut.

Act II

5: *In quelle trine* — Manon remembers past passion:* she remembers her 5
romps with des Grieux to swooping phrases that reach a very decent climax: something here of the Puccini to come.

13: *Vi prego, signorina* — The dancing lesson – this genteel scene* trips 13
along to a pastiche minuet etc. Manon gives a sardonic commentary on her dance with Geronte, end-

ing with a flourish. The subsequent elaborate business of exiting the company has an elegant accompaniment.

21: *Tu, tu, amore?* The stormy reunion duet,*** Manon/des Grieux, 21
breaks through into (early) vintage Puccini passion. Real feeling: big climax.

33: *Lescaut?!* The panic trio,** Lescaut/des Grieux/Manon, 33
rushes and bustles as they skitter around, leading to the arrival of the police and Manon's arrest. A rousing end to Act II.

Intermezzo

A good enough piece but dreary; a mood of gloom is settling over the opera.

Act III

2: *Manon!* The duet* des Grieux/Manon as he gives her 2
instructions for her escape, interrupted by a bizarre ditty from the lamplighter and also by clock chimes: brought to an abrupt end by a rifle shot. Some bursts of lyrical song, bags of atmosphere.

So now here's something really good.

8: *Rosetta!* The roll call:** at first the chorus provide no more 8
than an obbligato, commenting on each woman, but Manon takes their fancy and Lescaut stokes up their pity for her until the crowd take over fortissimo and pretty nearly drown the passionate farewells between Manon and des Grieux. But suddenly the ensemble slackens in intensity and dies away. This is something new in the way of choral writing; dramatic, surprising and it works wonderfully well.

14: *Guardate, pazzo son* Des Grieux's impassioned appeal* to the captain to 14
take him aboard (unlikely to have much effect on most old sea dogs, but this one evidently likes lyrical tenors). A good soaring, wildish piece.

Act IV

The long duet that makes up pretty well the whole of the last act has its purple passages punctuated by outbursts of terror. Look out especially for (purple)

2: *Vedi, son io* des Grieux tries to arouse Manon to consciousness:* 2
(terror) Manon left on her own looks back on her past

10: *Il mio passato* and finds it quite horrible.* 10

The final double death is affecting, especially

17: *Non voglio!* Manon's last farewells.** 17

NOTES

Manon Lescaut	Puccini's third opera
First night	Teatro Regio, Turin, 1 February 1893
Reception	Unanimous praise, a better reception than any other Puccini opera was to get
Script	Praga (resigned), Leoncavallo, the *Pag* man (fired or resigned), Oliva (squeezed out and retired hurt), Illica, who pretty well took over: contributions from Giulio Ricordi and Puccini himself
Source	A novel by the Abbé Prévost

NEWS AND GOSSIP

As can be seen above, Puccini had a rough time in getting *Manon* to the stage. From the start his publisher and adviser Giulio Ricordi had been against the project mainly because Massenet's *Manon* had been a huge success some ten years earlier. (Auber's 1856 version was pretty well forgotten.) But Puccini was dogged. 'Why not two operas?' he asked. 'A woman like Manon can have more than one lover.' So he struggled on trying it this way and that way and driving everyone mad. In the end it was the old pro Illica who sorted things out, but the libretto is not good. Puccini's *Manon* has a worse script than Auber's, a much worse one than Massenet's, and all three fail to mobilize the original Prévost's story, which is full of good stuff and could make a rattling good television series today. When at last it was finished, there was no room for *Manon* at the Scala, which was being prepared for Verdi's *Falstaff*, so Ricordi got it on in Turin. When we compare the wild enthusiasm of its reception to the much less warm reaction to Puccini's later masterpieces, we can only be puzzled. Maybe everyone was waiting for the advent of a second coming of a talent like Verdi's. Bernard Shaw spotted the possibility that Puccini could be his successor, but he should not get too much credit for this since the surrounding talent (the Young Lions that failed to roar) didn't offer much competition. *Manon* was played all over Italy and made at least a first appearance in every major opera house. Since then it has been played about as much as it deserves, which is not often.

COMMENT

In comparison with Puccini's blockbusters, *Manon* seems rather a dim little affair. It is made up from scenes from the Abbé Prévost's long novel and whole chunks of the narrative take place between acts. This is dramatically inept because we lose any sense of continuity in Manon's downward spiral and the agony does not pile on as it should. Why did she leave des Grieux for Geronte? What happened at the trial? Why in the last act are the lovers suddenly legging it through a desert? (Because des Grieux had fought a duel with the colonial Governor's nephew and thought he had killed him – but we are never told that.) There are other weaknesses. The intermezzo is a poor gloomy thing: two major characters in the first act disappear – Edmondo after Act I, Geronte after Act II: Lescaut drifts off into the mist at Le Havre: there is no plot development in the last act except Manon's death (widely anticipated). But each scene after the first act has a strong situation, the music is adroit and, when required, intense, the use of the chorus, especially in the roll-call scene, is something new and successful. There are high points when the lovers come together again in Act II and in the rush and bustle of the arrest, but *Manon* never packs the punch one expects from it. Maybe one day we will get a production that opens our eyes and ears to a work that is lurking somewhere behind a score and libretto that seem to have many of the ingredients of an alpha opera but which obstinately refuses to come to the boil. Barely a beta.

Maria Stuarda
(Mary Stuart)
Donizetti

Historical tragedy

The one where Elizabeth I arranges to meet Mary Queen of Scots in a park but goes on to have her topped just the same.

CAST

Mary Queen of Scots (Maria)	Soprano
Elizabeth I Queen of England (Elisabetta)	Soprano
Robert Devereux (Roberto), Earl of Leicester	Tenor
George Talbot (Talbot), Earl of Shrewsbury	Baritone
William Cecil (Cecil), Lord Treasurer	Bass
Hannah Kennedy (Anna), Mary's lady-in-waiting	Mezzo

2 or 3 acts (different versions): running time 2 hrs 20 mins

STORY

Act I The environs of the court at Whitehall

We are in the London of Elizabeth I who has taken a strong fancy to Robert Earl of Leicester. He, alas, is indifferent to Elizabeth, but infatuated by Mary Queen of Scots, Elizabeth's political prisoner. Act I opens with a power-sharing offer (incorporating marriage) to Elizabeth from the King of France (irrelevant to our story).

Elizabeth then gets down to her problem: what to do about Mary? Talbot, a very decent fellow, advocates clemency, hard-liner Cecil, decapitation. Elizabeth dithers. Leicester gets a letter from Mary suggesting an historically outrageous meeting with Elizabeth hoping for a rapprochement. Elizabeth makes a meal of agreeing to a meeting.

Act II Grounds of Fotheringhay Castle

Sad Mary awaits Elizabeth. After a bout of extensive doubtful duetting with advisers by both queens, they meet. There is no rapprochement. Quite the reverse, an exchange of unqueenly insults and vulgar abuse including five- and seven-letter words, namely whore and bastard.

Act III Sc 1 Whitehall

Elizabeth agonizes. The death warrant – to sign or not to sign? Her jealousy over Leicester overcomes her sense of pity: she signs and maliciously orders Leicester to witness the execution.

Act III Sc 2 Mary's chamber, Fotheringhay

Talbot and Cecil tell Mary she must die. Mary confesses her sins (numerous) to Talbot.

Act III Sc 3 A room adjoining the execution chamber

Mary, guilty, remorseful, pathetic but uttering sentiments of great nobility approaches the block in the presence of Leicester, Talbot, triumphant Cecil and anguished friends. As the executioner enters the curtain falls.

MINUTES FROM START

LOOK OUT FOR

Act I

6: *Ah! quando all' ara*
12: *Ah! dal ciel discenda*
17: *Ah! rimiro il bel sembiante*

The first fifteen minutes of Act I are table d'hôte
Donizetti (rum-te-tum overture, standard opening
chorus, recitatifs, etc.) except for a couple of pretty
cavatinas for Elizabeth, the first about her love for
Leicester* and the second** mulling over the Mary 6
problem and followed by a rousing ensemble. 12

A nice cavatina for Leicester romanticizing about
Mary,** leading on to quite a lively duet with Talbot. 17
Elizabeth catches Leicester red-handed with Mary's
letter: after some pretty standard recitatif things get
moving when she accuses him of being in love with
Mary which he admits in a sweet if slightly soupy
aria.* Good duetting to the end of the act. 28

28: *Era d'amor l'immagine*

Act II

4: *O nube che lieve per l'aria*
8: *Nella pace del mesto riposo*
12: *Ah! non m'inganna la gioia!*

An incongruously cheerful little prelude introduces
the miserable Mary recounting her woes to Hannah:
a touching cavatina.* After the noisy arrival of Eliza- 4
beth's hunt another cavatina** in which she decides 8
that for her the royal meeting is off. (Leicester shortly
persuades her otherwise.)

Splendid tuneful duetting between Leicester and
Mary,** loverlike at first and then animated as Leic- 12
ester gets macho about getting her out of prison
(which of course he doesn't, the wimp). Amazing

23: *È sempre la stessa*

'thinks' sextet** for principals observing the well- 23
known operatic convention that no one seems to realize that anyone else is on stage. All give vent to private thoughts in ingeniously worked ensemble.

26: *Morta al mondo*

32: *Figlia impura di Bolena*

Dialogue of the Queens:*** appeal for mercy by 26
Mary. No hope! Repudiation by Elizabeth in a cheery
oom-pah cavatina. Mary's outburst of Billingsgate
insults** leading to extremely lively finale, everyone 32
agog, including courtiers, defectors it would seem
from the hunt.

Act III Sc 1

4: *Quella vita a me funesta*

8: *Ah! Deh! per pietà sospendi*

Agreeable duet* between Elizabeth and Cecil, sur- 4
prisingly debonair in the light of subject matter – the
death warrant. Leicester has fine opening passages in
a melodious trio*** which starts mildly enough, 8
changes gear twice, and ends in a blazing presto with a
cheerful ump-ti-ti accompaniment.

Act III Sc 2

17: *O mio buon Talbot!*

24: *Quando di luce rosea*

The 'Grand Confessional Duet'** between Talbot 17
(revealed as a priest) and Mary. Starts with run-of-
the-mill recitatif but gains momentum and is transformed into a great tragic scene as Mary admits her
catalogue of sins.*** 24

Act III Sc 3

36: *Vedester? Vedemmo*

47: *Deh! Tu di un' umile preghiera*

53: *D'un cor che muore*

58: *Roberto! Roberto! Ascolta!*

60: *Innocente infamata*

The complete scene is a dramatic and musical
masterpiece. Marvellously unnerving prelude and
sotto voce chorus of Mary's friends.*** 36

Mary's prayer for forgiveness*** is taken up, 47
thickened and spread through the chorus (the 'Hymn
of Death') with Mary's high soprano above. One of
the great haunting melodies of Italian opera.

Mary prays that Elizabeth be forgiven:*** 53

She asks Leicester to lead her to her death:** 58

The courtiers and friends greet the arrival of the
executioner in an ensemble*** in which pity, menace 60
and exaltation are combined. Mary's high soprano
soars above. Terrific!

NOTES

Maria Stuarda	Donizetti's forty-third opera
First night	La Scala, Milan, 30 December 1835
Reception	Not good

Libretto Bordoni
Source Schiller's play *Maria Stuart*

NEWS AND GOSSIP

Donizetti wrote *Maria Stuarda* for the San Carlo theatre in Naples but the King vetoed it, presumably because it was not the thing to have royals slanging each other like fishwives (he can hardly have objected to one queen killing off another for this was a well-known historical fact). Maybe the Church had a voice in it too for the story can be read as a win for the Protestants. Donizetti then pillaged the piece unmercifully to supply numbers to other operas and when it was put together again for Milan the score was a hotch-potch of Donizetti's original plus reworked versions of the bits that had been used elsewhere. The original score was discovered in Bergamo in 1958. An arresting but quite unimportant fact about Bordoni the librettist (who was only seventeen when he did *Maria*) is that he later became the Chief of Police in Naples where his sympathies would be likely to switch to supporting the censor, not opposing him. He based the script on the wildly inaccurate play by Schiller who once admitted that 'History is only a storehouse for my imagination and its subjects must put up with what they become in my hands.' *Maria Stuarda* was performed from time to time in Italy last century but lay dormant in the twentieth century until it reappeared through a revival at Bergamo in 1958 to celebrate the discovery of the original score.

COMMENT

Maria Stuarda is no unflawed masterpiece with its fictional history, slow start, ignominious hero and some measure of stock-pot recitatif, but it abounds in glorious passages of vintage Donizetti. In the two-handed scenes where emotion runs high the recitatif bursts into spontaneous snatches of melody like birdsong. The tragedy builds inexorably to the last scene although even here the orchestral accompaniment often sounds more like music hall or circus than a tragic grand opera. Today this oom-pah rum-ti-ti style seems to trivialize the serious moments in an opera and bel canto composers seem to be like the musical counterparts to Dr Johnson's friend who wanted to be a philosopher 'but cheerfulness keeps breaking in'. The truth is that Donizetti wrote his vocal lines with such power and such conviction that they can work their magic despite the tum-ti-tum that is going on in the pit – indeed make it sound perfectly complementary. It is, after all, the intensity of passion in the vocal writing that raises *Maria Stuarda* to the level of an alpha, if a spotty one.

The Marriage of Figaro (Le nozze di Figaro)

Comedy of manners

Mozart [K492]

The one where the Count and the page hide behind the same chair, where the Countess's maid makes a surprise exit from a closet and where Figaro discovers the woman who wants to marry him is his mother.

CAST

Count Almaviva, a Spanish nobleman	Baritone
The Countess Rosina, his wife	Soprano
Figaro, the Count's major-domo	Baritone
Susanna, the Countess's lady's maid	Soprano
Cherubino, a page	Mezzo
Dr Bartolo, the Countess's one-time guardian	Bass
Marcellina, Bartolo's housekeeper	Soprano
Don Basilio, a music master	Tenor
Don Curzio, a notary	Tenor
Antonio, a gardener	Bass
Barbarina, his daughter	Soprano

4 acts: running time 2 hrs 30 mins

NOTE: The version described here omits, as is the usual practice, the dramatically irrelevant arias of Marcellina and Basilio in the last act.

STORY

Act I Sc 1 A room in the Almaviva house in the country

We are in an empty back room in the servants' quarters of the Almaviva country residence in Spain near Seville in the seventeenth century. Figaro measures up the space for the marriage bed: Susanna trims a bonnet says do you really think this room is a good idea? Sure says he: if Madam rings you are close to her room similarly myself and the Count. Thickie! says she it's also possible that the Count sends you down to Sainsbury's and in one bound he's in my bed. He's quite gone off the Countess and the other available females and is pursuing me. Unobservant twat she goes on why do you think the Count gave us so generous a dowry? Was he grateful for good service? Grateful hell. And by the way Don Basilio is the go-between who presses me to let the Count have his bit on the side. Oho says Figaro it figures. The Count plans to visit London with me as his courier and you as his whore. Watch it Count! From now on you dance to my tune. Exits.

Bartolo plus Marcellina enter. Marcellina says I can stop this wedding between Figaro and Susanna. Here is an IOU of Figaro's. It's past redemption date and the contract says either he pays up or marries me. Excellent says Bartolo: I would like to fix that bastard Figaro anyway he stopped my marriage to Rosina by helping the Count to steal her. Revenge! Nothing like it for moral satisfaction! I love it. (Exits.) Here's that little bitch Susanna coming says Marcellina I'm off. They meet at the door: after you says Susanna: after you says Marcellina: age before beauty says Susanna: the Count's pet has precedence says Marcellina and so on for two minutes fifteen seconds. Exit Marcellina.

Enter Cherubino. Hell! he says the Count found me in a compromising situation with Barbarina and says I must go. Alas Susanna I will see you no more he says. I thought you fancied the Countess not me says Susanna. That too says Cherubino and thoughts of you dressing and more particularly undressing her fairly turn me on. Is that her ribbon? Yep says Susanna. Cherubino snatches the ribbon and sings a song explaining that he feels sexy about women in general. He describes the more genteel symptoms.

The Count enters: Cherubino hides behind a chair. I'm taking Figaro to London says the Count. Meanwhile how about it? Nothing doing says Susanna. Come on says the Count meet me in the garden tonight. I'll make it worth your while. He hears Basilio talking outside. Zounds! says the Count I must hide. He goes to the chair. Gawd help us thinks Susanna. Cherubino creeps round chair to the front and hides on the seat. The Count crouches behind the chair. Susanna covers Cherubino with a dust sheet. Basilio enters: Hey Susanna have you seen the Count? he asks. Negative says Susanna. The Count is potty about you says Basilio. I'm not interested she says. But he's rich powerful and surely a better bet than that teenage sex maniac Cherubino says Basilio. What'ya mean? says Susanna. He was seen leaving your room at dawn says Basilio. Not true says Susanna. Have you heard that he gives the Countess lecherous looks when waiting at table? says Basilio it's the talk of the household.

The Count jumps out. The little bastard he says I'll chuck him out instanter. I'm sorry I evidently dropped in at an inconvenient time says Basilio. Gawd help us says Susanna. She faints and nearly sits on Cherubino. She recovers. What I said was only loose talk m'Lud says Basilio. Cherubino must go says the Count. I caught him at it under a table with Barbarina. I lifted the tablecloth like so (he lifts the dust sheet and reveals Cherubino). Zut! says the Count go and get Figaro at once and you Susanna are a slut. I am innocent says she Cherubino hid on your arrival. He crept round when you hid. You heard my conversation with Susanna? the

Count asks Cherubino. I tried not to says Cherubino. Lecherous little bastard says the Count.

Enter Figaro holding a bridal veil plus numerous peasants. The peasants sing we have jolly decent Count hoorah for him. What's this pantomime? asks the Count. We are all delighted that you abolished the right of first night sex with your employees' brides says Figaro so I request you hand this veil to Susanna as a pledge. Crafty sod thinks the Count: the ceremony can take place later he says now I must see a man about a dog. I promise a wedding party in due course. The peasants sing again and exit.

Why so down? Figaro asks Cherubino. The Count has sacked me says Cherubino. Oh please Count say Susanna and Figaro he's only a young boy. In some ways he's too grown-up says the Count. OK he can stay on as a subaltern in the Horseguards but you must get out of this house. Now. Hey Captain Cherubino says Figaro there'll be no more sex romps for you now. Route marches – bayonet practice – assault courses – there'll be blood sweat tears and maybe death. Have a good day.

Act II The Countess's bedroom: closet adjoining

The Countess is really depressed. The Count has gone off her but completely. Susanna enters. Has the Count tried to make it with you? asks the Countess. Oh sure says Susanna but it's a matter of sex for money not love. There's a typical husband for you says the Countess he sleeps around like a stoat then he's jealous of his wife for no reason. Figaro enters. Susanna won't play so the London scheme is off he says: the Count is now teaming up with the dreaded Marcellina to do us down.

So I have a plan to send the Count a note via Basilio saying his wife is meeting a secret lover in the garden tonight and also that Susanna is willing to meet him. Shall we dress up Cherubino as female impersonator and give the Count a bit of his own medicine eh? Good idea say Susanna and the Countess. The Count is out hunting we have plenty of time for a dress rehearsal with Cherubino now says Figaro.

Enter Cherubino: he sings the Countess a song (he says that teenage love life is a very confusing experience). The Countess and Susanna begin to undress/dress Cherubino: he shows his newly arrived commission. Susanna points out that it lacks a seal and so is invalid. Susanna exits.

Cherubino makes sexual advances to the Countess. A knock on the door! The Count! Lemme in! he cries. Who's in there with you? Nobody not a soul shouts the Countess. Cherubino runs into the closet. The Countess lets in a very suspicious Count. Why lock the door? Why so flustered? he asks anyway look at this. He shows her Figaro's letter. There is a noise in the closet. Whassat? he asks. Susanna I think says the Countess. Susanna comes in and stands in the background unseen. Lemme look in that closet says the Count. That would be quite improper says the Countess Susanna is stripped to the buff in there trying on new undies. It's your lover that's in there open up! says the Count. No says the Countess. I'll get the servants halloo halloo shouts the Count. You want a public scandal? says the Countess. OK OK I'll do it myself. I'll get the tools. But you will come with me. We'll lock bedroom to make sure there is no hanky panky says the Count. Both exit.

Susanna lets Cherubino out of the closet. The bedroom door is locked. Cherubino jumps from the window. Susanna goes into the closet. The Count and Countess return. It's all right really says the Countess but I must tell you that it's Cherubino in the closet. Zut! says the Count that little weasel again. It's all quite innocent but you'll find him stripped to the waist says the Countess: we're dressing up. Gimme the key says the Count: he draws his sword and opens the closet. Susanna comes out. Surprise surprise. Were you alone in there? asks the Count. Look in and see says Susanna. Sorry Rosina says the Count I made a mistake. But why this damfool joke eh? Why all that stuff about Cherubino? Just to steam you up says the Countess.

So now we come to this letter about some lover meeting you tonight says the Count. How about that? A joke by Figaro and Basilio says the Countess. Enter Figaro. The town band is standing by he says. The peasants are agog. Is it time to start the festivities? Just a minute says the Count what about this letter? I've never seen it before says Figaro (I wish Marcellina would hurry up thinks the Count who has been plotting).

The gardener Antonio enters and says that a man has just jumped from the bedroom window and broken his flowerpots. Pay no attention to that old lush he's smashed out of his mind says Figaro. My story is true says Antonio. Actually it was me says Figaro. It didn't look like you says Antonio it looked more like Cherubino. Cherubino is in transit to Seville says Figaro it was me and actually I sprained my ankle (Ow!). Then these papers must be yours says Antonio producing Cherubino's commission. The boy gave me them says Figaro. Why? asks the Count. To get . . . (the Countess and Susanna signal to him) . . . to get the seal. (Too bloody clever thinks the Count.) Enter Bartolo Basilio and Marcellina who deploy the case of Figaro's IOU. The only fair settlement is for Figaro to marry Marcellina says the Count. Turmoil: confusion. Judgement deferred.

Act III A room in the castle

The Count paces about. Thinks: those were pretty rum goings-on this morning. (The Countess and Susanna appear backstage but by means of opera magic the Count can't hear/see them and vice versa.) Go on make a date with him says the Countess. The Count thinks if Susanna won't play then I bloody well will make Figaro marry Marcellina. (Countess exits.)

Susanna asks the Count for some aspirin for the Countess. So Marcellina will get your Figaro? says Count. Never says Susanna I will pay her off with the dowry you promised me. Dowry? What dowry? says the Count. Come on says she a deal is a deal. What about your part in a deal? asks he. Shall I meet you in the garden tonight? says she. For sure? says he. Cross my heart and spit in my eye says she. (The Count can scarcely believe his ears.) Figaro walks through to fetch Susanna: as they exit she says (too loud) we've got the case sewn up: he fell for it. The Count overhears. Tantrum. These frightful servants are constantly scheming plotting to do me down he rages. I'll get them. Why should an upper-class gent like me have to watch menials pleasuring each other when I require to have sex with one of them myself?

Enter Curzio, Marcellina, Bartolo and Figaro. The case is settled says Curzio pay up or marry Marcellina. Shan't says Figaro. I must get parental consent. Who are your parents? asks the Count. Dunno says Figaro I was kidnapped when a child and my only means of identity is this horseshoe birthmark on left forearm. Horseshoe birthmark on your left forearm? cries Marcellina. Little Raffaello my son! Bartolo here is your father! Susanna enters to see Figaro embracing his Mum and swings a left hook: explanations. His mother? His mother. His father? His father. Etc. (Quite a surprise after all.) So there will be a double wedding – Figaro/Susanna and Bartolo/Marcellina. The Count and Curzio are exceedingly cross: everyone else is delighted.

Enter Barbarina and Cherubino (who is still hanging around). Come to my place she says and dress up as a girl so you can join the girl guides' presentation of floral tributes to the Countess. OK says Cherubino but watch it that Count is a menace. Exit.

Enter the Countess still mournful: the Count is no longer turned on by her: not one bit. But she still hopes . . . Exit.

Enter the gardener Antonio plus the Count. Antonio tells the Count that Cherubino is at his house dressing up as a female. Exit.

Enter Countess and Susanna. I've made the date says Susanna. Better confirm it in writing says the Countess. They seal the letter to the Count with a pin writing 'Please return the pin to register receipt'. Susanna exits.

The girl guides arrive with their floral tribute. Who is that one with nice eyes? asks the Countess (it's Cherubino). Enter the Count and Antonio: they expose Cherubino. Zut! says the Count disobedient little toad you will suffer for this. But Countie says Barbarina when cuddling on sofa at my place you said little me can have anything she wants. I want Cherubino for my husband.

Enter Figaro: break it up he says we're running behind schedule. It's time for the dancing. Can you dance with your sprained ankle? says the Count. It's much better thanks says Figaro. I don't believe a word of your story this a.m. says the Count. The Count and Countess take up their position. Gamekeepers haymakers milkmaids etc. process dance and sing. Apparently it's an old Spanish pre-marital custom. Susanna slips the letter to the Count: the Count pricks his finger with the pin. Figaro spots this. Ladies and gentlemen says the Count I wish to announce a big party at 2000 hours tonight. Fireworks to follow. Curtain.

Act IV The Almaviva gardens: night: two summerhouses, one left, one right

Barbarina looks for the lost pin (the Count told her to return it to Susanna). Figaro and Marcellina enter and learn from Barbarina of the Count's planned meeting with Susanna. Bad news Mum says Figaro she's double-crossed me. Show some bottle boy says Marcellina it may only be a joke. Joke hell says Figaro I'll get those two. Exits. Barbarina goes into summerhouse I. I'll wait for Cherubino here she says.

Re-enter Figaro also Bartolo and Basilio plus gamekeepers haymakers etc. Stand by lads says Figaro and when I give the signal come out fast (they hide). It's a pity that Susanna is not a good girl and true says Figaro. I am vexed: I suppose all women are pretty immoral when it comes to the bit: oh dear oh dear: what a world. Enter Susanna dressed as the Countess also the Countess dressed as Susanna (Marcellina also wanders through and settles in summerhouse I). Real Susanna spots Figaro suspicious bastard why does he suspect me? [Why did she not tell him all? Ed.] I'll have some fun and give him a hard time. She sings a teasing song full of sexy anticipation of her date with the Count. Figaro hears but can't see her: he is much put out.

Cherubino enters and flirts with 'Susanna' (really the Countess). The Count arrives. He, Figaro and the real Susanna watch Cherubino sexually harass the assumed Susanna (really the Countess). The Count interposes with a left uppercut to Cherubino which catches Figaro who was also interposing (but the Count thinks he made contact with Cherubino so Figaro is not exposed). The Count softens up 'Susanna' (the real Countess) and suggests a little sex together: as both exit they bump into Figaro and rush off in different directions.

Figaro now alone says if the Count and Susanna think they can have it off together I'll lay a trap for them. The 'Countess' (the real Susanna) shows herself. Cripes! says Figaro here's the Countess seeing for herself what the Count gets up to. The 'Countess' says I'm sticking around till I get my own back (that's Susanna's voice!! says Figaro to himself Oho oho now I get it). Figaro puts on a big act pretending to make a serious pass at the 'Countess' (the real Susanna). She gets cross: she hits him: she drops disguise. Take it easy old fruit says Figaro I knew it was you all the time.

The Count returns still seeking 'Susanna' and sees Figaro making love as he thinks to his wife. He calls out for help. Gamekeepers haymakers etc. emerge. The assumed Countess (Susanna) runs into summerhouse I. I've got him says the Count. He goes to summerhouse I hauls out Marcellina Cherubino Barbarina and Susanna (still as Countess). Figaro and the 'Countess' (the real Susanna) ask for pardon. Negative no never not on your life says the Count. The real Countess emerges from the summerhouse II as herself. The penny drops all round especially with the Count. (So he's been making love to his own wife.) Maybe I can now ask you to pardon them? says the Countess. Oh Lord God help me Rosina please please forgive me says the Count. OK says she: forget it. So that's all over sings everyone. Let's get off to the fireworks.

MINUTES FROM START

LOOK OUT FOR

Act I

0 One of Mozart's four quite special overtures*** (oth- 0
ers *Giovanni*, *Così*, *Flute*). Not musically related to anything in the opera but it sets the mood of the mad midsummer day even before the curtain goes up.

We drop in on below-stairs life in the Almaviva residence on what is so far a normal morning – perhaps the most casual start to any opera before Strauss (R.). Figaro measures up, Susanna trims her cap in an
4: *Cinque . . . dieci . . . venti . . .* easy-going duet.** 4

The bells and what they might lead to. A catchy tune, orchestrally witty, a small but perfectly formed
6: *Se a caso Madama* duettino.** Din Din! 6

11: *Se vuol ballare* Figaro declares war against the Count:** bold firm 11
and musically a little more threatening than one would expect in an opera purely buffa.

Doctor Bartolo still wants to get Figaro in revenge
14: *La vendetta* for what he did to him in *The Barber of Seville*.* He 14
barks out his hatred in stark biting phrases, but in planning his campaign he moves into patter. Malice and determination in the vocal line, charm in the orchestra.

18: *Via, resti servita* This fidgety, bitchy little duet* has an orchestral 18
accompaniment as light as a soufflé and as bright as

spring sunshine. On their own the vocal parts would mean little.

22: *Non so più* Cherubino is in love with all women.*** He quakes 22
like a jelly before the range of femininity that surrounds him. Tender, precious and genuinely sympathetic to the problems of teenage love.

27: *Cosa sento!* An action-packed trio.** The Count comes round 27
from behind the chair as Basilio is scandalizing everybody to Susanna: Cherubino must go he says (fierce blunt musical lines). Didn't mean what I said whines Basilio (downwards-sliding pleading phrase). Now I'm done for says Susanna (fluttering); she faints and nearly sits down on Cherubino (ministered to by Count and Basilio, close harmony); recovers: he must go barks the Count (poor lamb plead the other two). I'll tell you another thing says the Count (recitatif) I caught him at Barbarina's under the table: lifts cloth to illustrate, exposes Cherubino: hushed surprise: noisy surprise. Now I know what sort of a woman you are, says the Count to Susanna. Women are all the same says the loathsome Basilio. Gawd help us says Susanna. All sing strongly in character. Exit.

Cherubino must give up his sex-obsessed court life to become a soldier – hard living and a good chance of being killed. Figaro puts the boot into him. The hit
38: *Non più andrai* number of the show*** in its early years. Not a 38
straight aria, not a patter song, but a gloat, vicious and ironical. A big bombastic tune and look out especially for the way the orchestra join in to taunt poor Cherubino.

Act II

The Countess's lament for a love that has disap-
0: *Porgi amor* peared. A short cavatina*** with a long melodic line. 0
Sad, nostalgic and so beautiful as surely to penetrate the heart of even that callous brute the Count. (But he doesn't hear it.)

Cherubino, composer and poet, sings his set piece to the Countess about the agony and ecstasy of teen-
8: *Voi che sapete* age love.*** It has an innocent and wonderful mel- 8
ody: starts in the major: moves into the minor in the middle bit (love's agony) and back into the major for a repeat of part 1. Accompanied by pizzicato strings

(Susanna's guitar) with a lot of help from the woodwind. A little miracle

Susanna's running commentary on the dress-
11: *Venite inginocchiatevi* ing-up of Cherubino.** Not so much a tune, more a 11
continuous flow of tunefulness with the woodwind doubling, echoing, anticipating and duetting with Susanna's vocal line.

17: *Susanna, or via sortite* An agitated trio:** the Count suspicious, the 17
Countess scared out of her wits, Susanna hiding, visible and audible to us but not to them. Starts with some abrupt shouting from the Count but soon sweeps into a canonic bit with all three voices urgent and alarmed. From then it runs and runs. Look out especially for Susanna's tripping top-line run (three times). Vigorous and nervous throughout, lots of sforzandos.

The miraculous finale:

23: *Esci ormai, garzon malnato* 1. Confrontation.*** The Count and Countess 23
face the locked door: he outraged, violent, barks out his lines, growing ever more sinister: note the build up and speed up (Get out of my sight, woman) and the threatening woodwind runs in thirds (He must die): she flutters around in panic – stricken little phrases.

26: *Signore!* 2. Astonishment.*** Susanna comes out of the 26
closet. A hush. A cheeky little speech from her (molto andante). The Count and Countess try to collect their wits (sliding scales in the woodwind).

27: *Susanna son morta* 3. Repentance.*** The Count asks for forgive- 27
ness. The women are hard and haughty. The Count sticks to his barked-out lines, the women declaim and exclaim: sometimes it's almost recitatif: the tunes (two very catchy ones) are in the orchestra.

31: *Signore, di fuori* 4. Interruption.** Figaro pops in not knowing 31
what's afoot (big introductory flourish: we slip into triple time). He says everything's ready for the wedding – let's get going. The Count says wait: the musical excitement fizzles out. We wait.

32: *Conoscete, signor Figaro!* 5. Inquisition.** What does Figaro know about 32
the letter? Nothing. A stealthy, picky tune for the inquisitor: brusque replies from the victim: look out especially for the wonderful chorale-like ensemble over a deep double bass pedal.

33: *Ah! Signor, signor!*

6. Episode.** Antonio makes his statement – a 33
man jumped from the window. Pretty tense atmosphere – fragments of melody.

36: *Vostre dunque saran*

7. Contest.*** The battle of wits between the 36
Count and Figaro (supported by Susanna and the Countess). A perpetuum mobile figure ticks away in the strings like a time bomb – but each time it is about to go off Figaro defuses it.

40: *Voi signor, che giusto siete*

8. Climax.** Marcellina, Bartolo and Basilio ar- 40
rive to press their case for Marcellina to marry Figaro. Aggressive fanfares: each one says their piece, starting sedately but running away into patter. The Countess, Susanna and Figaro recoil in horror: the Count feels better: calls for silence (three times): then faster, each group gloats/laments together and separately as the ensemble becomes almost a choral piece, faster again to prestissimo and a helter-skelter final burst to the tape.

Act III

2: *Crudel! perchè finora*

Susanna agrees to meeting the Count in the garden
that night:** the Count begins gruffly (almost reci- 2
tatif) in the minor: Susanna slips sweetly and persuasively into the relative major for her reply. Then the delighted Count relaxes into a new and cheerful tune and so the duet ends with the two as happy and harmonious as budgies.

5: *Hai già vinta*

The Count's recitatif and aria of rage and revenge.** Both are so intensely emotional as to be 5
frightening. Big stuff, fit for a high tragedy. The aria in two halves: the first more exclamatory (Zut!), the second with more of a tune (Zoot).

11: *Riconosci in quest' amplesso*

The Mia Madre sextet (Mozart's favourite).*** 11
Marcellina starts with a motherly melody (to which she returns later): this celebration of filial love is interrupted by Susanna with a more stringent tune: she finds it hard to grasp what's going on: this is explained in old-style music hall one-liners (Not his mother? Yes his mother. His mother? His mother, etc.). Then into a final dreamy ensemble full of wonder, though not everyone wonders in the same way (Susanna, Figaro, Marcellina and Bartolo all filled with delight: the Count once again in a rage, with Don Curzio for some reason taking his part). Half the

comedy lies in the score.

After a powerful accompagnato telling us she really
is having a bad time, the Countess recalls the golden
17: *Dove sono* moments of her love affair with the Count.*** The 17
opening is sweet, sad, nostalgic – it moves into an
agitated middle bit in the minor – then back to the beginning and finally a faster and more florid end piece.
She still has hopes, but one can't give much for her
chances. Brings a tear to the eye.

23: *Che soave* The letter duet:** the Countess and Susanna echo 23
zeffiretto and overlap each other's sentences as one dictates and
the other writes. 6/8 time with a swinging rhythm in
the upper strings. Rather like learning to type to a
Sousa march. Lots of charm.

30: *Ecco la marcia!* The finale:* the march begins: the Count and 30
Countess more or less speak over it as they square up
for the official reception: two girls do their stuff to a
weakish tune of the kind Mozart reserves for fairly
routine occasions: the formal but twitchy dance
music begins (a fandango): the Count gets the letter
(almost recitatif, sotto voce), Figaro notices the pin
(all of this very effective): the Count promises a terrific party that evening: the chorus repeat more noisily the rather ornery piece that the two girls sang
earlier. Curtain.

Act IV

Figaro disillusioned: Susanna's given in to the
Count! Women are totally unreliable sings he in a bit-
5: *Aprite un po'* ter, biting aria.* The strings frisk around, seeming to 5
quegli occhi rub salt into his (self-inflicted) wounds. [Silly of him
to jump to such a wrong conclusion: Ed.]

Susanna teases the listening Figaro. A calm and
9: *Deh vieni* easy-going little aria:** it's going to be really nice 9
meeting the Count and the conditions are perfect.
Some echoes of the letter duet: a swinging see-saw
melody: pointed comments from the woodwind.

So now the dramatically hard-to-follow but musically wonderful finale.

14: *Pian pianin, la* 1. Confusion.** Cherubino approaches 'Susanna' 14
andrò più presso (the Countess) to a purposeful march tune which is to
do good service off and on throughout this section.
The Count appears and watches. Now we have an extremely busy all-singing 'thinks' ensemble, some-

times solos, sometimes overlapping parts, sometimes all together. The Count aims a straight left at Cherubino, hits Figaro.

17: *Partito è, alfin l'audace*

2. More confusion.** The Count alone with 17
'Susanna' (the Countess) makes loverly advances: Figaro growls unhappily. A new smooth tune in the violins builds into a busy trio with Figaro hammering away at his own personal phrases in the bass.

20: *Tutto è tranquillo*

3. Ultimate confusion.*** Figaro and Susanna 20
(the 'Countess') at odds. Figaro opens with a little pastoral song as mild as milk: notices 'the Countess' (Susanna), recognizes her and strikes up a mock serenade in over-the-top poetic style with over-the-top tune. Things warm up: Susanna belts him round the ear. Fierce aggressive stuff in her vocal line and rumbustious orchestration.

23: *Pace, pace, mio dolce tesoro*

4. Peace.*** Peacc between Figaro and Susanna: 23
everything explained. A smooth pacificatory duet: a moment of calm. But the Count breaks in shouting mayhem and murder: Figaro caught spooning with his wife. Shocking!

25: *Gente, gente all' armi*

5. Pardon.** The Count calls up his cohorts to 25
catch Figaro (loud chords) and hauls a miscellany of persons out of summerhouse I (orchestral excitement with a couple of violin trills per person). Susanna (still thought to be the Countess by the Count) and Figaro beg for mercy: strong vocal negative from the Count (five times): everyone pleads for pardon solemnly and seriously (but the violins seem to be sending them up a bit): the real Countess, in best grand opera style, reveals herself as herself and pleads for them in a majestic phrase: the Count, stunned and ashamed, repents, repeating the Countess's phrase (all rather quick, this bit) and then everyone moralizes in a chorale-like and solemn ensemble: but things perk up: let's have a really good party they sing (much more quickly), with fireworks.

NOTES

The Marriage of Figaro	Mozart's thirteenth performed opera, fifth comic opera (including short works)
First night	Burgtheater, Vienna, 1 May 1786

Reception	Now known to have been pretty good, though for many years there was a tradition that it was a flop
Libretto	Da Ponte
Source	Beaumarchais: *La Folle Journée ou Le Mariage de Figaro*, the second play of a trilogy

NEWS AND GOSSIP

Mozart himself may have lighted on Figaro as a possible opera subject. He had seen Paisiello's setting of *The Barber of Seville* (part one of the Beaumarchais trilogy) which had been a big success in Vienna in 1783 (though today it seems a pretty boring old thing compared with Rossini's knockout *Barber* of some thirty years later). The play, thought to be terribly daring (servants getting the better of their masters!), was banned from the stage in Vienna. Da Ponte and Mozart had to job around the censor before starting work (in late 1785). The first cast was stunning and we know a little about the rehearsals and backstage life from the journal of Michael Kelly who doubled Basilio and Curzio. (He persuaded Mozart to give Curzio a comic stammer. Did it come off, we wonder?) The opening run in Vienna of nine performances was about par for the course. The Emperor forbade encores except for solo arias, maybe because the applause tended to get out of hand, but more likely because the work (with the inclusion of the two Act IV arias now usually left out) must have lasted a minimum of three and a half hours and with too many repeats would run on beyond the imperial bedtime. The first smash hit performance was in Prague in January 1787 and after that *Figaro* became popular in Germany, but mainly in a German translation. Outside of Germany it was not widely performed in Mozart's lifetime. (In Florence in 1787 the management decided to dump Mozart's last two acts and have them composed by an unknown by the name of Tarchi.) In the nineteenth century it had limited circulation but not until the 1930s did the Mozart revival lift *Figaro* into the top ten. And who would dare to ask a contemporary composer to rewrite a single note today?

COMMENT

For some people *Figaro* is just the best. It has a stream of good tunes, a certainty of step, a story that keeps us on the edge of our seats (at least the first time), characters we love and some we don't, two ensemble finales that are just out of this world and something else besides – magic. *Figaro's* magic is a special magic that gives it a charmed place in the opera buff's heart, mind, brain, or whatever organ it is that opera buffs use to register their feelings for opera. If we try to look at *Figaro* as an artefact – not easy – we can see some of the reasons why it is such a triumph. First, its brevity. The units (especially in Act I) are on average shorter than in any other Mozart opera – indeed in nearly all operas except the *Beggar's Opera*. No development section in the overture. Short middle bits in the arias. Arias nearly all short, nothing like 'Come scoglio' in *Così* (four and a half minutes), all solos in Act I last less than three minutes (except the curtain aria 'Non più andrai' – three minutes 45 seconds). Recitatifs also are all short and tightly packed with plot/information. The effect is to whizz the viewer/listener along at a terrific speed on a switchback journey that delivers him already dizzy with pleasure into the finales – and then things begin to move even faster. The action of the finales has been split into sections in the 'Look Out For' bit, but in performance they move seamlessly through the twists and turns in the plot until they break into the mad gallop of the final presto.

Second, the libretto. *Figaro* has a firm base in Beaumarchais' play, which, having no music, had room for more characters, more plot and more jokes. But da Ponte did a great job in cutting it down. The main line of the story rips along as clear as crystal until confusion takes over in Act IV. And this is not disaster for the upshot is clear – the Count was caught out making sexual advances to his own sexually abandoned wife. (Incidentally a good party game is to ask a group of learned musicos to recount just exactly what happens in Act IV of *Figaro* and if two out of ten get it right then that's good.)

Third is the attraction of the characters, who can be set up much more firmly in an opera than in a play where the producer and the actors can (and do) push and pull a character around at will. You will never see two Lears the same and there are plenty of Violas who would not recognize another producer's Sebastian as coming out of the same play, never mind as their twin. But Mozart has defined his characters with music. Even if Cherubino had rhubarb words we would know from his two arias just what sort of a lad he is. We get to know Figaro and Susanna through the saucy rough-and-tumble of their music. The Countess, poor love, tells us more about the nature of her sadness through her music than any actress could manage by means of mugging, gesture and voice alone. The Count's rage bowls us over in shock. Even if he did his nut on the legit. stage he could never make his frustration so real. Mozart could define character through music as no-one ever did before, and very few since. In *Figaro* he created a galère of characters to match (not in their nature, but in their power) Jeeves, Tom Jones, Jane Eyre and Jorrocks. Mozart's Figaro, as well as being the great fixer, is a more complex character than Rossini's Figaro, the ingenious factotum. He is jealous, insolent, hates his master and beats him at his own game. Not a standard buffa character at all.

Fourth, the two finales are the best-ever comedy Mozart. (But not the first in this form. The finale of Act II of *Finta giardiniera*, ten years earlier, was a model for the *Figaro* finale and was, surprise surprise, four minutes longer.) In both the Act II and Act IV finales the plot moves on in pretty bold steps. Sometimes things stop for a bout of wonder or confusion, but not for long. Nothing like the more static finales of Verdi and Donizetti, where a single dilemma will keep everyone on the go for a long, long time. Mozart's finales are in fact an early form of continuous music drama. One wishes, perhaps, that he had done the same thing right through opera and transformed the recitatifs into living and breathing operatic language.

Figaro is not perfect. There are an awful lot of comings and goings in Act III (eighteen comings, fifteen goings, counting the chorus as one). Probably it seemed better to deploy the plot in lots of short scenes than in fewer and longer recitatifs which would unroll the story in reported speech, as in the boring old opera serias. But at times it becomes a bit fidgety – there is the occasion when Barbarina and Cherubino, for instance, are on stage for only one minute and make one single plot point. Then there is the confusion of the last act. It takes a really good producer to keep us properly informed of who is serenading whom, who can hear but not see whom, who is in each summerhouse and why. More cues for the audience (God knows the cast give each other plenty) would be a help. Bartolo and Basilio seem to be stock opera characters mixing with real people. Even if you cut the two irrelevant arias, the last act starts slowly with Barbarina hunting for that tiresome pin. Figaro's failed letter of Acts I and II is confusing when there is a real letter to come in Act III (Susanna to Count).

But these piddling points are swept away before the glorious but by no means straightforward progress of Figaro and Susanna towards the consummation of their marriage, one presumes after the fireworks at the close of that long, mad midsummer's day. Alpha-plus.

Masked Ball *see* Ballo in Maschera, Un

Miller, Luisa *see* Luisa Miller

Meistersinger

Human comedy

(Die Meistersinger von Nürnberg)

Wagner

The one with a disagreeable town clerk, a noble cobbler, a street brawl and a prize song.

CAST

Veit Pogner, goldsmith and Mastersinger	Bass
Eva, his daughter	Soprano
Magdalene, her maid	Mezzo
Hans Sachs, cobbler and Mastersinger	Bass
David, his apprentice	Tenor
Sixtus Bechmesser, Town Clerk and Mastersinger	Bass
Walter von Stolzing, a knight	Tenor
Mastersingers (nine), a night watchman	

3 acts: running time 4 hrs 30 mins

STORY

Act I Sc 1 Inside the church of St Katherine's Nuremberg
In which our hero declares his love for a lady but fails to sing his way into the club of Mastersingers whose members will be allowed to compete for the lady's hand

We are in Nuremberg mediaeval city of song and there is a church service in progress. Handsome knight Walter sidles up to pretty young woman Eva and says excuse me but are you spoken for? Eva recognizes Walter as overnight houseguest. Well no not exactly says her maid Magdalene not actually engaged but father Pogner has booked her as the prize for an upcoming song contest. Whoever wins gets her as wife. I see I see says Walter to Eva let me escort you home. No stay here says Magdalene, here's Mastersingers apprentice David (sure enough David is fussing about resetting the church as venue for a song contest) he'll teach you the tricks of the Mastersinging trade: you stay and get your Master's certificate and then you can compete for her. Eva I love you says Walter [a bit sudden? Ed.]: see you tonight. OK says Eva. Exits.

Act I Sc 2 A makeshift arena

So you think you can get your certificate at first try? says David. Ho ho. How much do you know about the Meister method? Zero says Walter. OK listen to this says David. He launches into a farrago of rules regulations admonitions prohibitions. Meanwhile the apprentices set up the singers' dais all wrong. David sorts them out: they take the micky out of him.

Pogner and Beckmesser enter. You are odds-on favourite to win my girl Eva says Pogner to Beckmesser: such a good singer you are. But if I win and she won't have me will you push it? asks Beckmesser. No I will not push it says Pogner. Excuse me says Walter would the Masters accept me as a late entry? I must propose you for the Masters' club first old friend says Pogner. The Masters assemble: roll call: Pogner makes the opening address. In my travels he says I found Nuremberg's image very poor. We are generally perceived as stuffy starchy stingy also philistine so I dreamt up this song contest to improve the image of this great city of ours and I offer my daughter as wife to the winner. Nice one Pog! shout the Masters. Viva Veit! cry the apprentices. But just one thing says Pogner if she doesn't like the winner she has power of refusal.

Why not allow the people to exercise their democratic right and judge the contest? asks Social Democrat Sachs. Subversive left-wing talk say the Masters. Order! back to the agenda says Pogner: we have this late entry my friend Sir Stolzing. I propose him as candidate for the Masters' Guild. Excellent C.V. noble parents property owner Name at Lloyds member of the Athenaeum banks at Coutts. Vocal education? asks the baker Kothner. I studied these classic LPs of Caruso Gigli Chaliapin says Walter (All dead says Beckmesser). But what actual educational establishment? asks Kothner. School of Nature says Walter (He learnt from the birds says Beckmesser). Are you prepared to submit a trial song? asks Kothner. Yes says Walter (poetically and at some length). Right! Into your marker's box Beckmesser says Kothner and remember Sir Stolzing seven faults and you're out. Take a look at the conditions of contest (apprentices show a video to Walter whilst Kothner sings the soundtrack).

Cue! shouts Beckmesser. Walter takes off into a romantic rhapsody. Beckmesser jumps out. Seven faults already he cries gleefully: do you want any more of this rubbish? It's funny sort of stuff say the Masters. Is this what they call minimalist? asks one. More atonal I would think says another. Perhaps it's tone rows says a third. Can't stand this modern stuff says a fourth. I liked it says Sachs: the marker is clearly biased jealous and emotionally upset. His intervention is unfair. I say go on Sir Stolzing to hell with the marker. Walter sings. Sachs and Beckmesser slag each other off: the Masters argue. Pogner tries to cool it: the apprentices dance:

chaos. Beckmesser yells let's take a vote. Big majority against Walter's admission. Curtain.

Act II A street in Nuremberg. Evening
In which an elopement is frustrated and a serenade leads to an altercation which becomes a riot

The apprentices shut up the shops for the night. Lena comes on asks David how did Sir do at the trial? Flunked it says David. Lena is quite thrown by this news and flounces out. Getting on OK with your bint eh David? shout the apprentices. David goes after them: he gets physical. Enter Sachs: stop that mauling you impudent dog he cries and set me up for the night shift. Pogner plus daughter Eva come on. Excited about tomorrow? he asks. Yes but must the winner be a Master? she says. Sure says he but remember you have power of veto. He retires indoors. Lena comes on. Any news? asks Eva. David says he was ploughed says Lena. O my God I must get the full story from Sachs later says Eva. Both exit.

Sachs comes out to cobble but monologues instead. That Sir Stolzing sang pretty good today he muses but the Masters hated it. Funny. Eva comes on. Come for your shoes my love? asks Sachs. Not for my shoes says she. To ask you who will win tomorrow. Search me says Sachs. Why don't you have a go yourself? asks Eva (a new idea to Sachs: for a moment he sees a glorious vision. But it fades). How did the trial go? asks Eva. Badly says Sachs this knight didn't make it. He's out. No chance? asks Eva. No chance says Sachs. (He spots that Eva is unduly concerned.) Lena comes on. That Beckmesser's going on about serenading you she says. What a bore says Eva why don't you sit in my window. I'm staying here. Lena exits.

Walter enters. Hi! says Eva: bad luck. Bad luck? says he: so I'm not good enough for that po-faced toffee-nosed poxy lot of Mastersingers. Bastards! The watchman's foghorn sounds. Let's fly together whispers Walter. All withdraw as watchman passes singing at his work. Once he is out Walter and Eva immediately clinch. Let's go let's go now they say but Sachs shines a preventive torch up the ally. They cower. Beckmesser slinks in tuning his banjo. I'll get that toad says Walter. Shurrup: wait till he goes says Eva.

Wise clever Sachs taking aboard all of Wagner's plot quite easily embarks on a very loud cobbler's song. Jerum! Jerum! etc. Bugger that noisy cobbler thinks Beckmesser. In an intermission between verses he goes up to Sachs. Working late tonight eh Hans? he says. Working on your shoes for tomorrow says Sachs Jerum! Jerum! etc. Shall we make a run for it? says Walter. No keep still says Eva. (Halloolaloola yells Sachs.) Beckmesser sees a female at the window. Sachs gimme a chance for Chrissake he says I wish to rehearse this song: a dry run for tomorrow: I would welcome your views. Strums on his banjo. OK OK says Sachs you sing away I'll mark your faults with my hammer. Beckmesser sings (a lot of banjo too) Sachs hammers. More and more. David spots Lena being serenaded. Neighbours open their windows. David sets on Beckmesser with a sand wedge. Neighbours in night clothes pour out and join in the fracas. Full-scale civil disorder ensues. Walter attempts to make a path for himself and Eva. Sachs rushes out seizes Eva and pushes her into her father's house. The riot continues until the watchman's foghorn sounds again. The street empties. Our friendly neighbourhood songster watchman holds the stage alone. Curtain.

Act III Sc 1 Sach's workshop
In which our hero rehearses his bid for winning a song contest, a journeyman is promoted and an unscrupulous town clerk makes off with someone else's poem

Sachs sits brooding during a broody prelude. David enters fearing a wigging for last night's fight. He messes around: Sachs is oblivious – still brooding. At last he wakes up and asks David to sing his trial verses. Bemused David starts off to Beckmesser's serenade tune: corrects himself: sings nicely: asks Sachs why he doesn't have a go in the contest? Stoopid says Sachs go and get dressed for the festival. David exits.

Sachs is broody again. He goes on for some time delivering irrelevant and opaque thoughts on the nature of madness. Walter enters saying so you see I had this dream-song but it's no good I can't compete. Those bastards won't let me in. They are not bastards says Sachs. They are decent conventional elderly gentlemen who dislike the passion of youth modern music whole-tone systems and the like. Sachs and Walter debate matters of musical taste etc. Sachs says sing me your dream-song I'll make notes. Walter sings his song: Sachs offers some advice: Walter sings again: Hey Walter Sachs says you have a good number there we might be able to do something with it meanwhile go and get changed. Both exit.

Enter the loathsome Beckmesser with a black eye limping etc. Prying around he spots Sachs's transcript of the words for the dream-song. He reads it and deduces Sachs is a competitor for Eva. Enter Sachs dressed to kill. Hey Sachs you deceitful skunk so now I know why you hounded me last night says Beckmesser. My rival eh? But I'll beat you you bastard. Mistake mistake says Sachs I'm not competing. Then what's this? says Beckmesser. Oh that old dream-song says Sachs if you want it my friend keep it, keep it. A poem by Sachs! Goody! thinks Beckmesser. Thanks Sachs very decent of you always knew you had a heart of gold he says: my number and your lyric will make me a certain winner. Exits.

Eva enters saying her shoes don't fit (a lie). After some persiflage Sachs cobbles. Walter enters in his Sunday best unseen by Sachs. Eva gives a great cry. Sachs cobbles on. Walter launches into the third chorus of the dream-song. Listen to this girl says Sachs pretty good stuff eh? Sachs you are a sweetie says Eva if you were twenty years younger I would really go for you. Enter David and Lena. Sachs gives David left uppercut the traditional way of signifying his promotion to junior manager. All quinque sing glorious quintet about their hopes and fears for the coming day.

Act III Sc 2 A meadow outside Nuremberg set up for a fair In which our hero triumphs, Sachs is acclaimed by all Nuremberg and we are given a lecture on the holy nature of German art

Craft guilds compete in song and friendly insults. Shoemakers first bakers next then tailors each with a buzzword – Streck, Me-e-eh and Beck respectively. The girls arrive: they dance with the apprentices including David (on the run from Lena). The Mastersingers are sighted and greeted with a welcoming chorus for all and especially for the song contest president Sachs. Much obliged says Sachs I'd like to thank Brother Pogner for putting up Eva as first prize and remember it's all about art.

Beckmesser is seen in a mucksweat trying to sort out Sachs's lyric to his tune. The crowd is amused. Beckmesser is called: begins: gets his knickers in a twist: the poem is totally confused and ludicrous: the crowd laugh: Beckmesser flounces off the podium. It's that bloody cobbler he shouts he conned me. Believe me folks that poem was authored by Hans Sachs. Sachs? says the crowd: it's not possible: he writes good stuff. There's nothing wrong with the song says Sachs if it's sung right. Anyone here volunteer? Walter steps forward. This is the chap who was wrongly refused entry into the Masters' Guild says Sachs and actually it was him what wrote the song. Would you like to hear it sung proper? Yes yes cry one and all.

Walter steps up and starts. He sings his very beautiful very romantic number. The Masters and the general public are amazed. It's new! It's good! It's magic! It's a wow! they say. Give him the prize Sachs! OK says Sachs. He puts the crown on Walter's head. Walter rejects it. I don't want to be a stuffy old Mastersinger he says. Listen to my advice young man says Sachs and incidentally it will also serve as a brief Party Political Broadcast on behalf of German art. Listen folks: we must keep it pure. Don't let any foreign stuff foul it up. Keep out the wops and the frogs. Do you get the message? Got it shout the crowd. Hurrah for German art!

Best art in the world! Hurry up Hitler!

Walter accepts the crown. Everybody happy except the miserable Beckmesser.

MEISTERSINGER – THE MAIN MOTTOS

Number	*Name*	*Description*
1	Masters	Taa-ta-ti-taa. Decent, worthy and important
2	Prize Song	Four golden notes vaulting downwards with the melody flowing on after them. Becomes the third verse or Aftersong of the final version
3	Pomp	A fanfare, tum-ti-ti-tum, then a sequence of pompous chords rising and rising
4	Apprentices	Jerky downwards steps in the woodwind, ti-ti-tum
5	Festival	A short sweet phrase, could be birdsong
6	Satisfaction	Dotted quavers going downwards: ti-tum/ti-tum/ti-tum
7	Cobbler	Je-rum Je-rum followed by a downward scale
8	Wahn	I've-lost-my-mar-bles. Two slow notes, a kick and two quicks
9	Sachs/Eva	An eight-note phrase, beginning with two clear high notes

MINUTES FROM START

LOOK OUT FOR

Act I Sc 1

0 The overture:*** one of the great milestones in music. It begins with a full statement of the Masters motto [1] reflecting the decency, the worthiness and the importance of the Masters guild in the life of the community. We will hear it again and again. Next is a yearning motto in the woodwind which has to do with the mutual attraction of Walter and Eva (Love, unlisted). This is followed by the fanfare of the great brassy Pomp and Circumstance tune which displays the Masters in all their pageantry and glory [3]. This reaches a climax: after some fairly drastic modulation we are into the theme of the last verse of the Prize Song [2] of which we are going to hear a lot too. Suddenly the thick welter of sound explodes into a cheeky and piquant variant of the Masters in the woodwind with a fragment of the Prize Song in counterpoint. 0

Then back to the Prize Song main theme [2] with a swinging accompaniment and chattering woodwind above. But what is this we hear in the bass? It's the tune of the Masters [1], used as a foundation. Now Pomp [3] joins in and these three run as a troika until Pomp wins, takes over and dominates the final stretch up to curtain rise. Wonderful: if Wagner had written nothing else this one would have put him up there with the greats.

9: *Da zu dir der Heiland kam*

The chorale** might well be an authentic period 9
piece and not ersatz: it is really fine. Delicious instrumental solos are poked in between the heavy choral phrases: and look out especially for a snaky solo cello, for once not reprehensible, also for the organ chord which sits above the long long pedal point as the congregation file out.

12: *Verweilt! Ein Wort!*

Walter makes his enquiries. This really lovely
three-handed scene,** Walter, Eva, Magdalene, 12
flows along with lots of bubble and squeak: all three in lyrical mood with Love (unlisted) and a soufflé version of the Masters [1] and Pomp [3] fizzing away in the background from time to time. To mark David's presence (he is messing about with the furniture upstage), we have the first full statement of the Apprentices theme between these two – downward steps in the woodwind in threes, ti-ti-tum [4]. There is a short final trio in which Walter seems to have worked out pretty well what the Prize Song is going to be even before he knows he is going first to dream it and then to sing it.

Act I Sc 2

After David's very thorough tutorial in which he gives poor Walter a rundown of the rules and regulations of a song contest (references to both Masters [1] and Pomp [3] throughout and an odd hint of the Prize Song [2] plus a forecast of the Cobbler's song to come) we have some jolly knockabout stuff between

34: *Was macht ihr denn da?*

David and the apprentices* who have put up the plat- 34
form all wrong. They wonder – will the stranger knight make it? (As well as the Apprentices we have a new theme here – Celebration: with a jerky rhythm, unlisted.)

After Pogner's entry and the roll call (Pogner's

motto, a four-noter played over and over, unlisted),
45: *Nun hört, und versteht mich recht!* Pogner makes his address.** He opens with the 45
lovely Festival motto [5], a short sweet phrase of four notes which could be birdsong. He sings it to the words 'Das schöne Fest'. He goes on with something more like recitatif as he turns to foreign affairs but gets poetical as he approaches his climax 'Eva my only child' whom of course he is offering as the prize (Masters [1] lurking around in the background quite a lot, but mainly Festival [5]).

The act rolls on splendidly in a sort of free-fall rhapsody – arioso-recitatif (quite a lot of the Masters [1] and Festival [5]) with no great musical landmarks until Walter gives the Masters his account of how he
60: *Am stillen Herd* learnt to be a poet.** 60

The Masters chatter a lot between the three stanzas of this number. It has a fine lyrical sweep and phrases that linger in the ear, but lacks the higher voltage of the Walter songs to come.

A minor event but worth a mention: Kothner reads
68: *Ein jedes Meistergesanges Bar* the rules in a pedantic tongue-in-cheek set piece* 68
which might almost persuade one that Wagner had a sense of humour. (Some Masters [1].)

More impassioned than 'Am stillen Herd', not so
72: *Fanget an!* disciplined as the Prize Song, this trial song** is writ- 72
ten to give us an idea of Walter's natural talent (it has the fragment of the Prize Song mentioned in the overture accompanying it). It is a real set piece and although Beckmesser thought little of it, we relish this patch of uninhibited Wagner in an otherwise plotty first act.

80: *Singt dem Herrn Merher* The finale is an ensemble** of confusion – not the 80
confusion of Rossini's finales with each character wondering what the hell to make of things, for here everyone knows exactly what he wants – Sachs and Walter to finish the song, Beckmesser to sabotage it, the Masters to restore order, Pogner to see his man does not finally lose out and the apprentices jumping for joy at the general chaos. Act II ends with a better class of chaos than this one which is musically too thick a mass for everything to register. Although we desperately want to hear Walter struggling through his last verse and can't, the general effect of all the

cross-currents of sound is very satisfactory.

Act II

After the rowdy start to the act (nearly all new music), Pogner and daughter Eva stroll on for five minutes of
4: *Lass seh'n, ob Meister Sachs* enjoyable dialogue,* too one-sided to be called a duet, 4
for Eva, like a good Nuremberg daughter, only speaks when spoken to. Pogner is really pleased with life except for that little matter of the knight at the singing contest which went wrong. He tells Eva tomorrow she is going to have a nice day. The scoring is light with the woodwind darting around in the most melodious fashion and there is one new short motto (dotted quavers going downwards – ti-tum ti-tum etc., a first cousin of the Love motto in the overture) which seems to describe his pride in Nuremberg – Civic Satisfaction [6].

Sachs sits and thinks under his elder tree and we
11: *Was duftet doch der Flieder* are into the Flieder monologue.** Why don't I give 11
up all this poetic stuff and just stick to my last? he asks himself (a lot of bustle in the orchestra and quite a big dose of the Cobbler's song to come). Then he worries over the trial held earlier in the day: Walter's singing had natural beauty but was so strange as to make it hard to size up. Funny. He made the others mad but I loved it. So ruminates Sachs. (Some of the Trial Song around, with its accompanying fragment of the Prize Song.) This is a great piece: it seems to flow out effortlessly and from it we begin to learn what a generous big-hearted character Sachs is going to become.

Eva calls on Sachs for news of the song contest.
17: *Gut'n Abend, Meister!* This *is* a duet,** freely written, leaping from point to 17
point. At first they fence with each other. She taunts him: why doesn't he have a go himself? But in the end his concern over the contest and hers for Walter break through and they become passionately involved. Eva is really disgusted that the petty-minded Masters have rejected her man and unfairly gets after Sachs as party to the crime (ending with bits of Cobbler's music).

Eva sees Walter approaching and Wagner gives us
27: *Da ist er!* one of those great surges of orchestral sound* that so 27
wonderfully reflect the quickening of the pulse when

lovers meet. But ecstasy does not last long. Walter breaks into a tirade against the frightful Masters: the whole thing was a nightmare he says. Turbulent violin music with some satirical side swipes at the Masters [1] and Pomp [3]. As Walter and Eva plan to elope they are interrupted first by the night watchman with his splendid ditty and then by Beckmesser tuning his lute.

36: *Jerum! Jerum! Hallahallohe!*

The Schusterlied*** – Sachs's rollicking Cob- 36
bler's Song [7], in three stanzas and an outright winner. Walter, Eva and Beckmesser all chunter over it a bit and although helpful to the plot, this does become tiresome and one longs for the clear concert version which gives Sachs a chance to belt it out without let or hindrance. One of the four items in the opera that are complete set pieces.

50: *Den Tag seh' ich erscheinen*

Beckmesser's Serenade.* The tune is a parody, 50
some say, of the style of a Jewish cantor. After the long argument with Sachs the first and second stanzas of Beckmesser's serenade seem even longer and the hammer blows from Sachs begin to lose their charm, when – hey presto! – they start singing at the same time and in double time, and as the neighbours pop their heads out of the windows, things cheer up amazingly.

55: *Zum Teufel mit dir*

Turmoil.** Everyone out and all singing very 55
loud. If it turns into mashed potatoes (which it often does) it will seem to go on too long. But if it comes off (and Toscanini had it rescored to make this more likely) then it is one of the best welters of sound in the business. Whatever happens earlier on, the end piece always works like a dream. The busy street is hushed, Sachs pushes Eva back to safety, the night watchman's horn booms out as he sings his comforting night lines once again, this time conclusively.

Act III Sc 1

0

The prelude*** is a pensive piece with noble 0
thoughts delicately expressed. First a full-bodied strong tune in the cellos – the Wahn motto (see next page for a definition of this crazy word – starts I've-lost-my-mar-bles, two slow, a kick and two quick [8]) which we have already heard in the Schusterlied bit of Act II but only in a fugitive form. This theme swells

upwards to be taken up by the strings in counterpoint and leads to a sort of brass choir chorale, which will return as the chorus that greets the Masters in the last scene. This solemn fanfare is followed by a sequence of strong new tunes, then the brass choir again, and so back to Wahn [8]. One must suppose that it has something to do with the serious side of Sachs, although he reads a book right through it and pays not the blindest bit of attention to what is going on in the pit.

Nowhere in Wagner is there more mickey-mousing of the action to the music than in this scene between the dreamy Sachs (Wahn [8]) and the jumpy David (Apprentices [4]): it is lively but can be embarrassing unless David is kept firmly under control. There are nice moments, as when David after his false
11: *Am Jordan Sankt Johannes stand*
start sings his well-tailored verses** to the Master in 11
the form of a Bach chorale.

Slice it how you may, it is not easy to make much
14: *Wahn! Wahn! Überall Wahn!*
sense of the Wahn monologue* in which Sachs gives 14
us the benefit of his thoughts on this midsummer morning. The word Wahn itself is a bit of a block since it does not mean simple madness but some combination of divine discontent, illusion, inspiration and mania for which naturally enough there is no one word in English and indeed the whole notion is very German, very philosophical and very Wagnerian. The monologue can be split into three parts:

1. There is Wahn all over the world causing war and mayhem. Quite a lot of reference to Wahn [8] but mainly free and running up to a sharp climax over the frightful persistence of Wahn.

2. Smug reflections on wonderful wonderful
17: *Wie friedsam treuer Sitten*
Nuremberg* Civic Pride (unlisted) Festival [5] so 17
comparatively Wahn-free – but – but last night there was a riot. A lot of riot stuff from Act II.

3. Some sentimental thoughts about how the riot
19: *Ein Kobold half wohl da:*
was caused* and then some constructive thinking 19
about how this quality Wahn can be harnessed to do good (as, one imagines, in inspiring song contests, but honestly by now one is beginning to give up). References to Festival [5] and to the Prize Song [2].

So there you have it: one of the most celebrated pieces in the opera, musically coherent, aspiring to philosophical profundity but in truth just a bundle of old Wahn, and cobbler's Wahn at that. (Especially the bit about hunting which is quite impenetrable.)

The duet Sachs/Walter which leads up to the re-
22: *Gruss Gott, mein Junker!* hearsal of the Prize Song is a phenomenon.*** It does 22
not advance the plot one inch and for ten minutes the two men discuss the nature, quality and appeal of romantic music. Not, one would have thought, a particularly lively topic. But the whole duet is set to music that is quite ravishing, a flow of lyrical ideas, most of them free, although Festival [5] (one of the most heavily worked mottos in the piece) is there at the start. Rhapsody takes over altogether when the duet reaches the point where Sachs gives Walter ad-
26: *Mein Freund, in holder Jugendzeit* vice about the need for stamina in a composer.** 26
Clearly this was a subject close to Wagner's heart and he throws all his energy into the discussion of this matter.

Sachs coaches Walter in the art of winning a song
31: *Morgendlich leuchtend im rosigen Schein* contest.*** Actually his help does not go beyond a lit- 31
tle strategic advice, for Walter seems to have got the first two verses of his dream song pretty well pat. Sachs is deeply moved, and so are we by the first full hearing of this glorious piece. Sachs responds to the song with his reflective Wahn theme [8].

Beckmesser picks around in Sachs's workshop and finds the Prize Song poem. Wagner goes over the top here with motto after motto from last night's brawl used to mickey-mouse Beckmesser's actions as in a
46: *Ein Werbelied! Von Sachs!* Tom & Jerry cartoon. But the duet* with Sachs has 46
an amazing flow of fresh and sprightly melodic invention. But it is much too long. Musical references all over the place, especially to Beckmesser's lute music from Act II and the beginning of the Prize Song.

Now we move into the clear upper atmosphere. Eva comes in. Her shoes don't fit. This touching
58: *Gruss Gott, mein Evchen* scene*** has a new motto – hinted at before – the 58
Sachs/Eva motto, introduced by an oboe and developing into a ravishing eight-note phrase starting with two high clear notes [9]. The two duet together with quick give and take over an orchestral accompaniment of tenderness and simple clarity. Then as Eva sees Walter (Sachs doesn't) she gives a great cry.

Sachs busies himself with the shoes until Walter
comes in with the third verse of the Prize Song
(which this time he has apparently dreamt up whilst
awake). Then a great emotional moment – Eva weeps
on Sachs's shoulder, Walter seizes his hand and all
three stand in a tableau before a mighty orchestral climax. Sachs defuses the tension with some jolly stuff
about the shoemaker's life (Cobbler [7]) and this mar-
66: *O Sachs! Mein Freund!* vellous scene ends with a set-piece solo*** from Eva 66
telling Sachs how much she loves him, but not as a
prospective husband. Sachs replies briefly, and affectingly (textual and musical references to *Tristan*
here), the spell is broken and we are into the hustle
and bustle of Midsummer morning.

After Sachs has celebrated (to the tune of the opening church chorale in Act I) the birth of a new master-
song and the promotion of David from apprentice to
journeyman (Masters [1] and the Prize Song fragment), we are into the most magical moment of the
73: *Selig, wie die Sonne* opera, the quintet.*** It is a 'thinks' piece as follows: 73
Eva (Such a good song it's bound to win), Sachs (So I
really must give up any idea of marrying Eva), Walter
(Here's hoping), David (That was sudden promotion
for you!), Magdalene (A journeyman! We may be
married soon!). All these disparate thoughts are expressed most harmoniously. The opening themes of
the quintet are new, look out especially for a long
smooth phrase first heard in the accompaniment and
then passed from voice to voice. The music drifts into
the Prize Song [2], and spreads into a chorus of happiness and hope. Something the like of which you
have never heard before and which must be counted
amongst the greatest moments in opera.

Act III Sc 2

The transition from Sachs's workshop to the Festival
meadow is managed orchestrally by a bustling
build-up of excitement with fanfares and flourishes
and references to Festival [5] and the Masters [1] and
80: *Sankt Krispin, lobet ihn!* so we are into the sing-about* of the rival guilds, the 80
Shoemakers to the tune of the Schusterlied (Cobbler
[7]), the Tailors and Bakers each to something new.
The repeated monosyllabic war-cries (Shoemakers

'Streck', Tailors 'Meck', Bakers 'Beck') become a little embarrassing.

83 The Dance of the Apprentices* – a little mincing 83
for such rough lads but tuneful. Some horseplay with David. Followed by more fanfares, the Masters [1] and Pomp [3] and the Masters arrive on stage.

90: *Wach auf* A rousing chorus*** – first heard when played by 90
the brass choir in the prelude to Act III. All Nuremberg rises to greet the Masters and especially Sachs. They give us the surprising news that dawn is near although they are standing in a brightly sunlit meadow. This is Wagner at his most civic, the sort of anthem that could have been made to order for the City of Birmingham at the height of its municipal glory.

After Sachs has said Thank You for this tribute (Wahn [8]) we have the painful farce of Beckmesser's attempt to sing Sachs's words to the tune of his
109: *Morgendlich* serenade in Act II with its ghastly lute accompani- 109
leuchtend im ment. And now the Prize Song proper.*** Walter has
rosigen Schein done a lot of work on it since morning for although the musical inspiration is the same, the poem is different and more relevant. Now we have it in all its glory and as it casts its dreamy spell over the assembled citizenry it makes us believe for a moment that we too are standing in a meadow in Nuremberg overwhelmed by the beauty of song. Or if we remain aware that we are sitting in an opera house, there is something wrong with the production, for this is one of opera's most magical moments.

The crowd take up the reprise of the Prize Song and Walter is acclaimed the outright winner. He then rather rudely rejects membership of the Masters
117: *Verachtet mir* guild. This provokes an outburst of rather nasty 117
die Meister chauvinism from Sachs,* much of which is sung (at
nicht the beginning and the end) to snatches of the Prize Song [2] above Masters [1], plus several other references including Pomp [3]. The opera ends with all stops out. Walter relents. Everyone sings the praises of Glorious German Art, coupled with the name of Hans Sachs, to positively the last and easily the noisiest rendering of the Masters [1].

NOTES

Meistersinger	Wagner's seventh opera
First night	Königliches Hof- und Nationaltheater, Munich, 21 June 1868
Reception	A tremendous success
Libretto	Wagner
Source	Research into sixteenth- and seventeenth-century history of Nuremberg. But no previous version of the story itself

NEWS AND GOSSIP

Surprisingly, Wagner first thought of *Meistersinger* as a short comic item to be performed immediately after *Tannhäuser*. Admittedly, after four hours of *Tannhäuser* one is ready for some refreshment, but most people would feel more like a glass of the strong stuff than another Wagner opera. Also his idea of 'short' would probably mean starting *Tannhäuser* off at noon. Luckily he dropped this curious notion. In 1845 he started delving into the history of Nuremberg in the seventeenth century and discovered quite a lot about the singing guilds and the civic poet Hans Sachs who wrote plays (one of them about the death of Siegfried). He linked the historical story with his own pet propaganda lines, such as:

1. Art is/should be about the most important thing in life
2. German art is in danger of being taken over by foreigners and Jews like that frightful Meyerbeer
3. It's about time that the establishment gave a decent hearing to modern music. Music like mine, for instance
4. Music critics who don't like my stuff are small-minded malicious bastards, especially that Hanslick who writes in the Vienna Sunday Times.

All of these thoughts went into the hopper and Wagner worked on the *Meistersinger* libretto for seventeen years, in clear spaces during the writing of *Lohengrin*, *Tristan* and *The Ring*, finishing it in 1862. He completed the score three years later.

The huge success of the premiere (under Hans von Bülow) set all the musicos in Europe a-talking but *Meistersinger* did not immediately sweep the opera stages of the world. Although it was mounted in the German number two provincial houses in the following year it did not make it to Vienna and Berlin until 1870. Then London in 1882, the Met in 1886, Bayreuth in 1888. It seems incredible today that this great masterpiece should have hung fire. *Meistersinger* is not 'difficult' Wagner. Certainly expensive and hard to mount, but so wonderful, such a crowd-puller, that one would have thought that urgent faxes would have been flying in all directions – 'Maestro, I've seen a show we just got to put on!' But no.

Today *Meistersinger* is the best-liked Wagner opera, not such a monster as *The Ring*, clearly better than the slightly ludicrous *Tannhäuser* and *Lohengrin*, less holy than *Parsifal*, not so taxing as *Tristan*. So it is played a lot, and loved by not only Wagnerites, but a lot of the generality of mankind as well.

COMMENT

Meistersinger is the acceptable face of Wagner. There are no hang-ups with sex and sin, no power-mad dwarfs, no sprouting staves, no swans and not a holy grail in sight. Even the racial propaganda mentioned in the notes above can be played down to zero effect except for the unavoidable and disagreeable final outburst about the ethnic cleansing of the arts.

The story is simple, strong and rather slow. Its strength lies in Walter's struggle and success in pushing romantic or impressionist art in the face of the sort of hatred that always springs up amongst the arts establishment in the face of anything that is good or new. Although Walter is the front man in this contest, it is really Sachs's support for him that gives the opera its gravitas. Indeed the smart way in which Sachs outwits Beckmesser and makes Walter into No. 1 in the charts at a single blow is something that even Brian Epstein would have envied when he launched the Beatles. The sub-plot with Beckmesser is not so strong and there is too much of it. In particular the long dialogue with Sachs before his serenade in Act II and the encounter with Sachs in his workshop in Act III Sc 1 could be cut pretty heavily.

David and his apprentices pad out the work with their Rolf Harris-boy-scout antics, but the music is so good not a second of this could be cut and the producer has to do with it what he can (but not too much, please). Again, it is the music that saves the long discussion between Sachs and Walter in Act III Sc 1 about the nature of poetic inspiration and Nuremberg's musical politics for it does nothing to advance the plot. The street riot and the blaze of choral singing in the last scene both come off very well, but it is of course the Prize Song itself which is the high peak of the show and it is brilliantly managed.

Unlike *Lohengrin*, *Tannhäuser* and co., the characters in *Meistersinger* are recognizably human. Sachs, of course, sensible, wise, a little radical and clever with it, wins you over pretty soon, although after listening to the Wahn monologue we can see a club bore in the making and in his final utterances about German art a potential fascist. His sudden fantasy of winning the contest himself and taking Eva to be his wife gives him an extra dimension (and her too, for why does she suggest it?). This is not the sort of stuff you find in Verdi or Puccini with their raging black and white passions. It shows both characters with a genuine tenderness for each other and so when Walter enters in the shoe-fitting scene and we rejoice with Eva in her cry of ecstasy, we also feel a stab of pain for Sachs. Walter is a good standard romantic knight and a top-class artist to boot, but he does not win our hearts as does Eva. Beckmesser is less successful, partly perhaps because Wagner was keen to use him as an agent to vent his spite. He is too near a caricature to be taken seriously and too essential to the plot to be just a witless clown. It is an uneasy role which seldom comes off in performance. Pogner, on the other hand, is in kilter with real life: one meets at least one Pogner on every respectable borough council, and long may they pontificate – civic do-gooders, decent through and through.

But the great glory of *Meistersinger* is its music. The rich sonorities of the Masters' two themes full of pomp and circumstance fill the ear in a highly satisfactory way, the Prize Song beguiles as do few other songs, prize or otherwise. There are some great set pieces – Walter's account of his learning processes ('Am stillen Herd'), the Schusterlied, the last act choruses, the Prize Song itself and above all the Act III quintet which for sheer lyrical invention stands alone in Wagner's huge operatic output in the same way as does Beethoven's Act I quartet in his single opera *Fidelio*. The pastiche pieces are immaculate – the opening church scene, David's verses and Pogner's address. With such variety and apparently endless flow of melody, it comes as a bit of a surprise to discover that the use of thematic material in *Meistersinger* is very economical. The two Masters themes do a tremendous amount of work, as does the Prize Song. These three plus another six or seven much shorter mottos generate the music over most pages of the score, set pieces excepted. The music of *Meistersinger* is closely knit, there is nothing flabby about it and although perhaps twenty minutes too long, it is never really boring, as are patches in *The Ring*. It has no vulgarities, as has *Tannhäuser*, is not pretentious like *Parsifal*, and what pomposity it has is delivered with more than a whiff of send-up.

It is also nearly producer-proof. It cannot be set in a used-car lot nor in Hiroshima after the bomb. It demands a church, a street, a meadow and although these can be reduced to black drapes (when the opera can still survive), they cannot be transmogrified into symbolism without destroying the piece entirely.

So it's three hearty cheers for *Meistersinger*, a noble life-enhancing work which, although a long sit-down, can give you one of the happiest and most rewarding of evenings in the opera house. Alpha-plus.

Norma

Druidical tragedy

Bellini

The one where everyone is either a Druid or a Roman and priestesses have the greatest difficulty in adhering to the vows of chastity.

CAST

Norma, high priestess of the Druids	Soprano
Oroveso, Norma's father, leader of the Druids	Bass
Adalgisa, junior Druid priestess	Soprano
Clotilda, a friend of Norma	Soprano
Pollione, Roman Proconsul in Gaul	Tenor
Flavio, Roman centurion	Tenor

2 acts, 1 interval: running time 2 hrs 15 mins

STORY

Act I Sc 1 An open-air Druid temple

We are in Roman-occupied Gaul in 50 BC amongst lots of Druids. Oroveso, Druid headman, exhorts the Druid community to drive the Romans out. Pollione, the Roman commander, reveals to Centurion Flavio a penchant for female Druids. He has already seduced top priestess Norma and fathered two children by her. Now he fancies junior priestess Adalgisa.

The Romans hide as Norma, the headman's daughter, arrives for the big mistletoe ceremony: Norma decrees no putsch against the Romans yet: her father Oroveso and all the Druids grumble: they would much prefer to get after the Romans now. All exit.

Adalgisa says she is torn between priestly duty and love for Pollione: favours the former. Pollione appears and passionately advocates the latter: Adalgisa capitulates: they plan to elope to Rome.

Act I Sc 2 Outside Norma's home

Adalgisa seeks Norma's permission to leave the priesthood for love of a man, which Norma, with a good deal of fellow feeling, readily concedes. But the man is Pollione! This is too much. Norma tells Pollione what she thinks of him and tells both him and Adalgisa to get out of her life.

Act II Sc 1 Inside Norma's home

Norma thinks it best to kill her children rather than let them face disgrace. But she just can't do it. She begs Adalgisa to adopt them and take them to Rome. Adalgisa refuses: remorse sets in: she says she will give up Pollione to Norma. The two women are now great friends.

Act II Sc 2 In the forest

Headman Oroveso tells the Druid army to cool it. No attack yet.

Act II Sc 3 The Druid temple again

Norma who was convinced Pollione would return to her arms (Why?) learns he has no such intention, indeed he is plotting to abduct Adalgisa by force. Norma gongs up all the Druids and tells them that things have changed: they can get after the Romans now, at once, with maximum ferocity. But wait: Pollione is caught lurking in the sacred precincts intending to abduct Adalgisa.

Norma in a private interview with Pollione says she will spare his life if he will abandon Adalgisa. No he says. OK I will kill Adalgisa says she. Pollione says no no kill me not her. Norma gongs up again and tells all the Druids a priestess has betrayed her vows. Who? Who? they cry. I, me, Norma, says she. Sensation. The opera ends with penitents Norma and Pollione mounting their funeral pyre. Father Oroveso is left to mind the children.

MINUTES FROM START LOOK OUT FOR

Act I Sc 1

After an overture tuneful but pregnant with gloom
the curtain goes up on Oroveso working the Druids
into a frenzy against the hated Romans. Excellent:
though the Druids sound rather too jolly to be
6: *Ite sul colle, o Druidi* warlike.** 6

Pollione explains the problems of his love life to
15: *Meco all' altar di Venere* Flavio. Two good cavatinas.* 15

After Norma has attempted to persuade the Druids 20
20: *Me protegge, me difende* that now is not the time to drive out the Romans, she
addresses a hymn to the moon in what is perhaps Bellini's greatest, certainly his best-known, coloratura
30: *Casta Diva* aria.*** The scene continues with Norma's shining 30
soprano swooping and diving above the chug-chug of
a supportive chorus.**

Adalgisa, poor soul, after much anguished recitatif

47: *Deh! proteggimi, O Dio!*

has a touching cavatina.* 47

51: *Va, crudele, al Dio spietato*

The scene ends with a great duet of persuasion:*** 51
Pollione and Adalgisa alternating in two arias each of

55: *Vieni in Roma, ah! vieni, o cara*

two stanzas followed by free arioso duetting** to the 55
curtain.

Act I Sc 2

After the longest spell of unrelieved recitatif in the
opera (7 minutes) during which the plot unfurls
somewhat sluggishly we are rewarded with the lovely

7: *Oh! rimembranza!*

duet between Adalgisa and Norma.*** The melody, 7
lovely on its first appearance, lengthens and strengthens in its three successive appearances, building a
platform from which springs the late-flowering
phrases that complete Bellini's long lyrical line. The

11: *Ah! sì, fa core, abbracciami*

duet ends with a joyful cabaletta.** 11
After some dramatic recitatifs in which Pollione is
identified as the lover of both priestesses (shame! trai-

15: *Oh non tremare*

tor! etc.) Norma has a brief aria** which is shortly 15
followed by a great trio of vituperation, shame and
despair from Norma, Pollione and Adalgisa respectively. This starts, perhaps surprisingly, with a persistent tune in waltz time with an oom-tum-tum horn

17: *Oh! di qual' sei tu vittima*

accompaniment,** goes on through some dramatic 17
recitatif to a cavatina for Norma which sets off the final burst of anguish à trois. It concludes with a summons from the Druidical gong and from the chorus for Norma to return to her ecclesiastical duties.

Act II Sc 1

Again the scene opens with a lengthy spell of recitatif
lightened by an agreeable burst of arioso as Norma re-

6: *Teneri, teneri figli*

flects on the brighter side of motherhood.* 6
The scene plays out with a series of duets, the first

12: *Deh! con te, con te li prendi*

of melting beauty*** in which Norma tries to per- 12
suade Adalgisa to take over her family responsibilities
(which Adalgisa will not do), moving into a faster

30: *Si, fino all'ore estreme*

pace as the two swear everlasting friendship.** 30

Act II Sc 2

A choral intermezzo* contrasting in scale and mood with the last long two-handed scene. Does its work well enough, but not remarkable.

Act II Sc 3

The last scene is one of almost continuous high drama

with chorus and principals on stage and hard at work almost throughout, and to great effect.

11: *In mia man' alfin' tu sei* An emotional duet between Norma and Pollione** 11
with the first part of the theme repeated three times before its final flowering. The duo changes gear twice before reaching its grand climax and the reappearance of the chorus.

21: *Qual cor tradisti* Norma's last great aria.*** 21

28: *Deh! non volerli vittime* Norma sings a short cavatina** in a minor key 28
asking her father to be good to her children and then we enter the grand climacteric of the whole opera and the ascent of the funeral pyre.

NOTES

Norma	Bellini's eighth opera
First night	La Scala, Milan, 26 December 1831
Reception	A flop ('Fiasco!!! Fiasco!! Absolute fiasco!!!' wrote Bellini to a friend)
Libretto	Tried and trusted partner Romani
Source	A French play of the same name. Opened only in January 1831. So *Norma* became an opera very promptly

NEWS AND GOSSIP

After the ghastly first night, things looked up. The second night went OK and *Norma* was played thirty-nine times in its first season against strong opposition (*Anna Bolena*, *Otello*). *Norma* soon became Bellini's most pop opera though it has always divided critical opinion down the middle – Wagner loved it, Berlioz hated it. Northern Europeans and the clever Dick musical Brits have always sniffed at Bellini and point to *Norma* as the most ludicrous of bel canto operas in a field which contains some pretty rum items. But with the opera-loving public *Norma* has a clear win over her critics.

COMMENT

If you like Bellini at all you will like *Norma* best. Long sweet melodies, raging emotions, high theatricality – all the tricks of the bel canto trade and practically no longueurs. It is his masterpiece – no doubt about it – and can overcome the dangerously comical sight of a stageful of Druids in what looks like Ku Klux Klan gear without the hoods. The story majors on strong situations rather than credibility (how come that no one in the village ever knew that their chief priestess had two children?) but then that's opera, or rather Italian opera before verismo. There are passages of pure magic ('Casta Diva', 'Rimembranza', 'Deh! con te, con te li prendi') and the hurricane force of the last act is irresistible except to the musically stormproof. An alpha for all seasons.

Onegin, Eugene *see* Eugene Onegin

Orpheus and Eurydice

Classical drama

(Orfeo ed Euridice)

Gluck

The one where Orpheus looks back with fatal results.

CAST

Orpheus (Orfeo)	Contralto (Castrato)
Eurydice (Euridice), his wife	Soprano
Cupid	Soprano

3 acts: running time 1 hr 45 mins

NOTE: There are several versions of *Orpheus* (see NEWS AND GOSSIP). The one described here is the production directed by Sir George Solti at the Royal Opera House Covent Garden) and recorded by him in 1969 with Marilyn Horne as Orpheus.

STORY

Act I A grove of cypresses: the tomb of Eurydice in the centre

We are in Thrace long before history began and attending the funeral rites of the lovely Eurydice. Orpheus weeps for his lost love. Shepherds and nymphs (a class of person hard to identify) weep too. He is like a turtledove that has lost its mate they say. Suddenly Orpheus rounds on the gods in fury. Why did you take Eurydice away? he asks. Why? Why? I want her back. Cupid pops in. Good news Orpheus he says the gods will give you an audition and if you play your lute up to Grade VIII standard you can make the trip to Hades and bring Eurydice back. What wonderful news says Orpheus. Steady, there is one condition says Cupid. You may not look at her until you cross the frontier with Hades on the way back. I can do it! I will do it! says Orpheus. She's going to think it's a bit funny and it's going to be tough fighting off those furious Hell's Angels but I'll do it so I will. Hooray! Eurydice alive again!

Act II Sc 1 A cavern in Hades

A group of Hell's Angels are lounging around. Who's that playing classical music? they growl. (It's Orpheus of course. He has passed his test and has come to claim Eurydice.) They go into a rock-and-roll routine. If it's not a god we'll fairly turn him over they say. Let me by says Orpheus. In no way say the Hell's Angels crowding him. Come on lads says Orpheus lemme plead for a while. He pleads. OK say the Angels you plead pretty good: pass: they rock and roll again.

Act II Sc 2 The Elysian fields, the upmarket neighbourhood of Hades

Dead Heroes and Heroines (now alive again) are dancing a classy sort of ballet. Nice here isn't it? says Eurydice. Yeah it's lovely say the Heroics. She exits. Orpheus comes on. Golly he says isn't this just beautiful. Come in old chap say the Heroics: make yourself at home. I am looking for Eurydice says Orpheus. Hi Eurydice you're wanted shout the Heroics. She comes on. Orpheus leads her away – but without looking at her.

Act III Sc 1 A rocky valley in the mountains

Come on follow me says Orpheus. What a nice surprise says Eurydice: is it really you my lovely husband? (Orpheus keeps stumping along with eyes on the ground.) What the hell's the matter with you? says Eurydice: we have this happy reunion and you don't even look at me. Sorry, can't do it says Orpheus. Are you mad at me or something? says Eurydice. No kiss no cuddle not even a look. It's important we get out of here quick says Orpheus. There'll be plenty of time to cuddle later. Why in God's name are you so cruel? says Eurydice. (This is terrible thinks Orpheus.) I'm fainting says Eurydice. Oh my God I can't stand it any longer says Orpheus and turns to help her. She dies. What have I done? says Orpheus [well, blown it actually: Ed.]. What shall I do without Eurydice? How can I live without Eurydice? I shall kill myself. (Holds dagger at the ready.) Stop that! cries Cupid popping up from nowhere. You have suffered enough you poor old thing. You can have your Eurydice back. Look here she is. Sure enough she is amongst us again as large as life. They clinch. Joy. Rapture. Bliss. Etc. And Cupid joins in to congratulate them on such a happy outcome.

Act III Sc 2 The Temple of Love

Shepherds and shepherdesses always quick to hear of a good party dance and caper. May love triumph they sing. May love triumph says Orpheus. Indeed it may says Cupid and so say I too says Eurydice.

MINUTES FROM START

LOOK OUT FOR

Act I

0 The overture is a lovely concert piece.* Compact, tuneful, perfectly crafted and nothing whatever to do with the opera. As was the custom in those days. 0

3: *Ah! se intorno* The opening chorus** plangent, sorrowful and made the more affecting by Orpheus' cries of 'Eurydice' which punctuate its solemn course. The choral writing with its low soprano line and support from three cornetts and trombones has a solid modern sound that could make us think it was composed fifty years later. The funeral symphony which is played whilst flowers are strewn on Eurydice's grave sustains the mood until the sad chorus returns. The momentary switch back into the major key just before the end has an uncanny effect. A great opening scene. 3

14: *Chiamo il mio ben così* Orpheus' lament,*** something unique in opera. For ten minutes Orpheus holds the stage singing of his love for the lost Eurydice. It is a formal piece, three stanzas to the same heart-rending melody, interrupted by the cry 'Eurydice! Eurydice!' after which there is a free-ranging section which is almost too melodious and too richly supported by the orchestra to be called accompagnato. It is indeed something new in opera, two bouts of accompagnato inserted between three refrains, the accompagnato becoming more and more passionate, the refrains calm and sad. But there is not one orchestra but two, the second (offstage) made up of strings and oboes and acting as an echo to the first and also to the voices, especially during the refrains. This echo-magic, so much a part of the Eurydice legend, takes us into a new and mysterious world of sound where Orpheus' grief resounds around the hills and dales of Thrace and so too within our minds. Gluck uses a different solo instrument or instruments in each refrain (flute, horns and English horn respectively) and clearly took enormous pains to support his wonderful vocal line with just the right texture of orchestral sound. 14

Look out especially for a phrase that penetrates the ear with its beauty when Orpheus sings 'Eurydice is dead and I still live' ('Euridice non è più').

The lament ends with a traditional recitatif in

which Orpheus asks the gods why they carried off Eurydice and, in language that is far from respectful, says he will damn well try and get her back. A great, great piece.

Cupid has a message for Orpheus and he passes it
24: *Se il dolce suon* on (twice) in a pretty aria.** Orpheus may get Euryd- 24
ice back. Hooray I will see her again he interjects (twice). The length and airy nature of Cupid's piece is wonderfully effective after the preceding gloom.

Cupid has further and better particulars for Orpheus. There are ground rules which he spells out
27: *Gli sguardi trattieni* in a more formal piece* with the most delectable 27
woodwind accompaniment.

Orpheus ends Act I with something entirely
31: *Addio, addio o mei sospiri* different – a bullish bravura aria* that could have 31
come out of quite a different opera, and indeed it does – Gluck had used it twice before in earlier operas and a rival composer, one Bertoni, claimed he had written it anyway. No matter, although it is no great shakes, it brings the act to a rousing end. Orpheus says he will overcome.

Act II Sc 1

The prelude is called a dance (for the Furies) but it sounds more like the gloomy introduction to an unwritten Beethoven symphony. Then we hear Orpheus approaching strumming on his lute (harp
2: *Chi mai dell' Erebo* and pizzicato strings). Next a nasty angular chorus* 2
from the Furies with the voices singing in octaves. Then Bang! – we are into a real dance with flashing strings and still a lot of runs in octaves. Another dose of the nasty chorus, Beethoven again and Orpheus starts to plead. Six minutes of Gluckian allsorts.

Orpheus pleads, and very fetchingly. His sweet
6: *Deh! placatevi con me* persuasive tones* are at first rejected roughly. But the 6
Furies weaken: their second chorus is less hostile, their third, to soft repeated chords in the strings, has them in two minds. The fourth is a shout of 'Carried Unanimously'.

12 The ballet of the Furies* is furious indeed. The 12
fiddles playing as fast as they can and soon the lower parts are scuttering around for dear life too. Booms and bombast from the horns. But it ends calmly. Pacified, or perhaps tired out.

Act II Sc 2

16 The languid minuet* (the ballet of the Blessed 16
Spirits) that opens Scene 2 is an agreeable piece (but surely too slow for a dance by Heroes and Heroines), with a long and beautiful flute solo in the middle. It is pastoral rather than dreamy and one can see real shepherds and shepherdesses gyrating around in Arcadian slow motion rather than the Heroics. The pastoral mood goes on into Eurydice's solo and the chorus that follows, the general drift of which is to tell us that the Elysian fields are a pretty nice place.

A sumptuous symphony plays as Orpheus approaches. A sweet and memorable oboe tune, pizzicato accompaniment, twirls in the woodwind. This
28: *Che puro ciel!* carries on under Orpheus' greeting*** to the lovely 28
Elysian landscape and his song of longing for his Eurydice. As the aria progresses the accompaniment flowers into the most gorgeous rich patterns of sound. A stunner.

The Heroics greet Orpheus respectfully in a
33: *Vieni ai regni del riposo* charming chorus,* but things are moving too slowly 33
for him. Please bring on Eurydice he asks. Come in Eurydice sing the Heroics in a repeat of the same gentle chorus which fades away to nothing as the act ends with Orpheus (eyes averted) and Eurydice standing alone on the stage.

Act III Sc 1

A burst of agitation from the strings leads to the long accompagnato during which it becomes clear that the lovers are in a terrible fix.

5: *Vieni, apagga il tuo consorto* Then the fraught duet** of confrontation. Why so 5
cruel? asks Eurydice. Can't tell you, says Orpheus. Which under the circumstances must seem a little unreasonable. Neither the duet nor the recitatif before it quite rises to the drama of this scene. The duet with its one- and two-liners lacks a continuous melodic idea but it is powerful and, as always, beautifully crafted. Eurydice is suspicious and jealous.

Eurydice pours out her frustration in an aria of
11: *Che fiero momento!* noble anger.* Orpheus puts in a clattering obbligato 11
(for Chrissake what can I do) but Eurydice roller-coasters over him and finishes in a fine burst of fury.

14: *Ecco un nuovo tormento!* The accompagnato that covers the denouement* 14
(the look, the faint, the death) and Orpheus' half-

crazed reaction are not the most dramatic in the opera and since it was not yet the practice to handle scenes of this kind in a fully-fledged ensemble, I suppose we must be satisfied with what we have got. Which is pretty good.

18: *Che farò senza Euridice?* The most famous of all Gluck's arias.*** And a 18
wonderful tune it is. In the later French version he dolled it up with a larger and more important setting but in truth it is, as Dr Johnson would have said, a melody that needs no sauce. In form it mirrors Orpheus' lament in Act I, three refrains and two verses (accompagnato) between and with the same cries of 'Eurydice! Eurydice!' at the start of each verse.

Once again the drama of Eurydice rising from the dead is treated in accompagnato but celebrated in a
26: *Gaudio, gaudio son al cuora* trio* of sombre joy. The part writing is so wonderful 26
that one tends to think how mean it was of Gluck to give us so little. This piece with the insistent catchphrases running on in the strings is a little wonder. Cheerfulness breaks in towards the end and at last all three sound thoroughly happy about love and its effects.

A stiff little ballet leads to a formal final chorus introduced by Orpheus. Cupid and Eurydice are both
30: *Talor dispera* allowed to sing out into individual solos* which help 30
to lighten this rather pompous close.

NOTES

Orpheus and Eurydice	Gluck's thirtieth opera and the first of his three 'reform' operas
First night	Burgtheater, Vienna, 5 October 1762 on the birthday of the Emperor Francis I
Reception	A great success
Libretto	Calzabigi
Source	The classical myth: many subsequent versions

NEWS AND GOSSIP

In the year 1761 Gluck was lucky to meet the two partners who joined with him in his campaign to reform the old opera seria of Metastasio and

Co. into something more human. The serias were elaborate, long and really little more than a succession of arias stuck in a story of classical gloom to show off the voices of the Pavarottis and Callases of the day. In Calzabigi Gluck saw a kindred mind. He (Calzabigi) was quite a fellow, successful businessman, theatre administrator and writer, and it was he who formulated the 'reform' theory and pushed it around with the appropriate degree of hype. He also wrote the libretto for *Orpheus*, and it is a masterpiece. It has the 'noble simplicity' which was the aim of Gluck's reform movement. The other collaborator was one Angiolini, a choreographer, who was happy to bust up the old ballet traditions of the operas of Rameau. Anyone who has tried to reconstruct the dances used in the French opera of those days will have every sympathy with Angiolini because with their mincing steps and mechanical movements they must, even then, have appeared ludicrous to the modern men of what was called the Enlightenment. Whatever Angiolini did was apparently a huge success, but alas we shall never quite know what it was.

These three created *Orpheus* together. Its first performance set all Vienna talking and soon the rest of the opera world. It was revived in Vienna in the next season, travelled to Paris in 1769 and then was rewritten in a grander and longer form in French for a production at the Paris Opéra in 1774. Everyone recognized it as a masterpiece and one or other of these versions was performed pretty frequently. For some reason Gluck's operas were irresistible to big-band composers: both Wagner and Richard Strauss 'arranged' one of his operas and no doubt damaged them irreparably in the process. *Orpheus* fell foul of Berlioz who confused the hell out of everyone by 'arranging' a composite of the Italian and the French *Orpheus*es. So now an eager beaver of a music director has three versions to choose from – the Italian, the French and the Berlioz – and this gives him a fine opportunity to move in and produce a fourth – his own.

Another variable in this most fluid of operas is the pitch of Orpheus' voice. Gluck wrote it for an alto castrato. Since then it has been adapted for a soprano castrato, for a tenor and in 1813 finally, one hopes, for a contralto, though I suppose it is possible we shall have a baritone Orpheus sooner or later.

Orpheus is one of the operas which have never died. It has had its quiet periods and its flushes of fashion, but it is universally seen to be a great piece and hence will find its place in every centre of opera when its turn comes round and when a contralto who can do justice to the part of Orpheus can be found.

COMMENT

If *Orpheus* had never been written and somebody told you that an opera with three characters, two female and a castrato, could have changed the course of opera history and become an accepted masterpiece besides, what would you have said? Harrison Birtwistle to you? But it's true, *Orpheus* did help to push opera seria into the grave (although Mozart was still sweating away with the old Metastasian form even twenty years later). *Orpheus* did the trick because it was great as well as new. Its 'noble simplicity' reaches out through time and can move us today, so its effect on the opera world when it was new must have been sensational. There is no surer way of changing people's minds than by winning their hearts, which *Orpheus* has the power to do. The head presents a bigger problem.

Orpheus has a flying start because of its subject – one of the myths that linger in the mind and have caught the attention of dozens of poets from Vergil up to the present day. The happy ending is a terrible mistake. No doubt it was required by a custom so strong that even the reforming Gluck could not buck it. But alas for the original where the disconsolate Orpheus is torn apart by the Furies and his severed head floats down the Averno still crying 'Eurydice! Eurydice!' and 'the reverberate banks respond – Eurydice'. So we have to make do with a disappointingly jolly finale and the triumph of love. For the rest the story is simply and elegantly told and even in translation we can spot that it is high-quality stuff. Although the structure of the two laments looks highly artificial, the performed work seems a natural, almost spontaneous, outpouring of grief. But that is what good writing can do.

Musically *Orpheus* starts and finishes conventionally: a separate sinfonia in front and stock happy chorus at the tail. But between, aside from some of the ballet music, there is hardly a single routine bar. Sometimes we are carried along on the stream. Sometimes we are engulfed, as in the two great laments. Often we are surprised, and always we marvel at the adroit setting of the words and the variety and richness of the accompagnato. In the first two acts there is a good deal of action for both chorus and soloists. Act I opens with fifteen minutes of glorious music, the funeral chorus and the first great lament and then we have recitatif and aria ending with the cheerful imported piece 'Addio, addio o miei sospiri'. The second act has the taming of the Furies (tamed more by argument and not solely by the power of music as in some versions of the myth), the placid country scene with Eurydice and the Heroes, recitatif for Orpheus' arrival and a final chorus for the Heroes. But the last act is no more than a duologue between Orpheus and Eurydice until Cupid pops in to sort things out and we are into the final rejoicing. It is quite a feat to carry the burden of the drama in accompagnato without the listener noticing that the resources are so small.

Gluck is ingenious in setting a mood. The heavy sorrow of the first scene hangs like a cloud on the music until at the flap of a wing Cupid's good news cheers everyone up. Then we are as bright as can be. Act II starts uncomfortably with harsh mood music for the fury of the Furies, but it mellows as they weaken. Then we have a pastoral scene (in F major which was *de rigueur* for all pastoral scenes, no one knows why). This is tremendously pastoral and continues to be so right up to Orpheus' arrival and his wonderful song in which he shows he is really a very pastoral chap at heart. But then his mind turns to Eurydice, the pastoral mood is blown away and the Heroes get into the act. Act III is something quite different. The music follows the sense of the words like a shadow fish following a shark. And now we marvel at the delicacy of the music's response to each shade of meaning. We are piloted along the emotional path that leads to the disastrous look back: we are hooked: we are in there with the wretched Eurydice's frustration and with Orpheus in his terrible dilemma: the music is telling us everything: this is living drama, living opera, before Mozart had even started.

So much for Gluck's power. We had a whiff of the same thing from Monteverdi but that was long long ago. Handel was fine in his fashion, but he is not this sort of modern man. *Orpheus*, with its noble libretto and its generous helping of great music, stands high above all eighteenth-century operas until Mozart (including Gluck's zillion other works). Now opera as we know and love it has begun. Hooray! Alpha.

Otello

Shakespearean tragedy

Verdi

The one where the story of Shakespeare's *Othello* with music is clearer and an hour shorter than it is without.

CAST

Otello, Governor and C-in-C Venetian forces Cyprus (coloured)	Tenor
Desdemona, his wife (white)	Soprano
Jago (Iago), his personal Staff Officer	Baritone
Cassio, an army captain	Tenor
Emilia, Iago's wife, Desdemona's companion	Mezzo
Lodovico, Venetian envoy	Bass
Montano, retired Governor of Cyprus	Bass
Roderigo, a Venetian	Tenor
A herald	

4 acts: running time 2 hrs 10 mins

STORY

Pretty well Shakespeare's *Othello*, with the first (Venetian) act omitted and the rest condensed and adapted on Verdi's basis of 'brevity clarity and truth'.

Act I Outside a castle abutting on the sea. An inn. A storm. Evening

We are in fifteenth-century Cyprus. A crowd is on the lookout for the arrival of a ship carrying Governor Otello: it is sighted: it makes a difficult landing: Otello springs ashore and says the Turks are licked: good lad hooray says the crowd. Otello exits: the crowd exult.

Staff Officer Iago chats up a young Venetian blade Roderigo: says so you fancy Otello's Desdemona? Hang about she'll get bored with him soon: I will aid and abet your affair owing to my hatred of Otello who promoted Cassio – that clown – over me. The storm abates: a bonfire is lit and general roistering begins.

Iago toasts Desdemona: Cassio responds warmly: Desdemona is the tops says he: see that, Roderigo, says Iago, Cassio the young lecher has his sights on Desdemona: get him drunk and his disgrace will follow. A competitive drinking session begins: much wine is consumed.

Montano the retired Governor orders Cassio on guard duty but Cassio is too pissed to respond. Roderigo jeers: Cassio is belligerent: he attempts a duel: Montano interposes: Cassio turns on Montano: Iago tells Roderigo to sound the alarum: general confusion: Otello appears and asks Iago what the hell? He sees Cassio drunk and Montano wounded. (Desdemona is now awake too.) Otello is very cross: Cassio is cashiered (Iago is delighted): the streets are cleared. Otello and Desdemona are alone. They make loverly talk: kiss. Curtain.

Act II A room in the castle: terrace and garden beyond

Iago suggests Cassio asks Desdemona to work on Otello: Cassio thinks it's a good idea so he awaits Desdemona on the terrace. Iago introspects: he tells us what a horrible piece of work he is. Otello arrives: Desdemona and Cassio are promenading in garden. Iago says see those two together? Nudge nudge wink wink.

Brief divertissement. Albanian and Cypriot sailors, women, kids, serenade Desdemona and give her bouquets knick-knacks etc. Desdemona asks Otello to go easy on Cassio, he's a good chap really. Otello negative. He complains of a headache. Desdemona attempts wet hanky treatment: he tells her to get off and chucks her hanky away. Emilia retrieves it but Iago snatches it from her (with a view to planting it on Cassio): Desdemona is upset.

Otello's jealousy is stoked up by crafty Iago. Otello demands some proof: Iago responds with a cock-and-bull story of how he saw Cassio dreaming about having it off with Desdemona. He has also seen her hanky (a present from Otello) on Cassio's person. Otello's jealousy is now terrifically strong: he swears vengeance: the frightful Iago promises to help.

Act III Great hall of the castle

A herald tells Iago and Otello that Venetian state officials are arriving. Iago sets up a stratagem: he is to walk and talk with Cassio on the terrace: Otello to listen unseen. Iago reminds Otello to apply the hanky test. Desdemona tries the headache remedy with an M & S hanky. Otello says where's my gifted hanky? At the laundry says Desdemona. It will be a serious matter if that hanky is lost says Otello – go fetch. Not now silly says she . . . and about Cassio. . . . Go fetch! cries he: and you've been sleeping around too. Not on your life says she. You whore says he: he pushes her out. Otello, losing his marbles, rants wails etc.

Cassio turns up on the terrace: Iago makes their conversation seem sinister (though in truth it is innocent). He plays the planted hanky-panky game, with Otello busting out with jealousy behind a pillar. Cassio exits. Otello and Iago discuss what forms of murder would be most appropriate for Desdemona. Suffocation is selected. Iago says he will look after Cassio.

The Venetian officials arrive and get a good reception from the Cypriots. Otello studies the court circular. Suddenly he lunges out at Desdemona for no reason (he is going potty) and reads the court circular aloud. He Otello is recalled to Venice: Cassio is appointed Governor as of today's date. Desdemona is upset and weeping but Otello gets physical and throws her down. Under cover of the general consternation alarm amazement etc. Iago tells Otello sotto voce that he had better hurry up with that killing and leave Cassio to me.

He also points out to Roderigo that if Cassio is rubbed out Otello plus his beloved Desdemona must stay in Cyprus: good idea says Roderigo. Otello, now barking mad, falls on the floor: he gets up: he orders all out except principals: he falls down again, while the crowd outside still cry 'Viva Otello Lion of Venice'. Look at the lion now says the gloating Iago (Otello lying senseless on the floor).

Act IV Desdemona's bedroom

Desdemona says Otello is a little better and he told her to wait for him in bed. She asks Emilia to lay out her wedding dress. Desdemona sings a sad song about a willow and says goodnight to Emilia: she has some premonitions of danger: she prays: sleeps. Otello enters and gazes at Desdemona: he kisses her three times: she wakes up: he accuses her of being Cassio's lover, of giving him the hanky etc. Not guilty says she, really not: Cassio is dead says he: God have mercy says she don't kill me Otello: let me live a little longer. No! says he. He smothers her.

There is a knock on the door and Emilia enters to say Cassio is alive and Roderigo dead (wrong way round for Otello). Desdemona shows signs of life: I am guiltless says she. Who did it? asks Emilia: it was suicide says Desdemona (she dies). Liar says Otello: I did it because she's Cassio's whore, Iago said so. And you believed that crook? says Emilia: she cries murder, help etc. Enter Cassio, Iago, Lodovico: Iago's lies are exposed also the hanky-panky business: Montano enters and says the dying Roderigo blew the whistle on Iago. Iago runs for it: he is pursued but not retrieved: Otello appalled gazes on the dead Desdemona: he stabs himself: kisses the dead Desdemona: dies.

MINUTES FROM START **LOOK OUT FOR**

Act I

The whole opening storm chorus complete with
0: *Una vela!* interjections, thunderclaps and a tang of the sea.** 0

9: *Fuoco di gioia!* The Fire chorus:** a *tour de force*: artful but not 9
too clever.

15: *Chi all'esca* The drinking song,*** Iago bamboozles Cassio 15
into indulging too heavily to the amusement of one
and all. Irresistible, rollicking, opera's number one
alcoholic number.

21: *Già nella notte* The love duet** that so satisfactorily ends the act: 21
free-ranging, high voltage, passionate with a dying
fall and romantic exit (but leaving us with a slight
hankering for a good old-fashioned Verdi tune?).

Act II

The plot is propelled along forcefully by harsh,
urgent music in the case of Iago whilst he sets up
3: *Credo in un Dio* Cassio and reflects on what a horror he is himself.* 3
Effective but uncomfortable. After the aggro and
agitation of Iago stirring up Otello's jealousy, har-
13: *Dove guardi* mony and grace are restored in the pretty chorus** of 13
the several groups who offer flowers, compliments
and bric-a-brac to Desdemona to a refrain with
mandolines picking about and a hurdy-gurdy bass
which seems set to go into perpetual motion. There is
a glorious conclusion as Otello and Desdemona join
in, charmed by what they see.

19: *Forse perchè* The quartet*** that follows Desdemona's at- 19
tempts to appease Otello – Desdemona (Tell me
what's wrong, my love), Otello (She's gone off me,
why? Because I'm getting old? Am non-white? Not
good in bed?), Iago (Gimme that handkerchief),
Emilia (You're up to some dirty work: No!) (but he
snatches it). Not quite a 'thinks' quartet because Iago
and Emilia develop the action as they bark away at
each other, Otello rambles on magnificently in the
centre and Desdemona, pure and sweet, soars above
the pettiness and evil of the world. Stunning.

24: *Ora e per sempre* The act ends with the extended duet** in which 24
Iago fuels Otello's jealousy: effective and quite
upsetting. Two high points: Otello's first outburst of
grief to a military accompaniment as he retrospects
past glories: Otello's vow to avenge himself, sung first

by him then by both in a frenzy of excitement.

Act III

3: *Dio ti gioconda* During his duet** with Desdemona Otello gets 3
progressively nearer to madness: she remains calm,
7: *Esterrefatta fisso* sweet and outraged. The climax** leads on from her 7
horrified reaction to his rage and her 'first tears' solo. Tremulous and fearful.

Otello teetering on the brink of jealous mania pours
12: *Dio! mi potevi* out his grief:** powerful stuff: declamation mixed 12
with wild bursts of melody.

Desdemona introduces the massive finale*** with
28: *A terra!* another of her pure soprano appeals,** this time for 28
pity as she lies in the slime: this gets a big response from everyone in traditional 'thinks' style, as follows: Desdemona (I'm in agony), Emilia (She's wonderful: not one word of reproach), Cassio (O what a beautiful morning), Roderigo (Hell! Desdemona, my secret love, is leaving the country), Lodovico (This is a rum do: Otello's gone all queer), Female Cypriots (Did you see him belt her one? For pity's sake!), Male Cypriots (What the hell's going on (later) Otello is carrying on something awful).

As if this were not enough we have two plot developments knitted into the texture: Iago urges Otello to speed up his revenge and says he will take care of Cassio: Iago tells Roderigo that if Cassio is rubbed out Otello and Desdemona will have to stay: Will he kill Cassio? OK says Roderigo. The final histrionics take place as the hall empties and Iago's moment of triumph closes the act.

Act IV

The prelude with its bare harmonies and plangent cor
5: *Piangea cantando* anglais prepares us for Desdemona's Willow Song.** 5
This celebrated item is sad, unearthly and makes us uneasy until it modulates into comfort on the word 'Cantiamo!'. The setting is un-Verdian, almost modal with bare, spare accompaniment. Instructions to Emilia are artfully woven into the ballad and the masterstroke is to delay Desdemona's climactic scream of terror until *after* the song has ended with a calm full close.

11: *Ave Maria* Desdemona's prayer:** an above-standard pious 11 soprano address to the Virgin, notable for its intensity rather than its charm.

From here on the tragedy storms to its conclusion
24: *Niun mi tema* pausing only for Otello's solo of stunned horror*** as 24
he realizes what he has done – all expressed in Verdi's noblest dramatic vein – then his address to the dead Desdemona and the final kiss bestowed to an echo of the kiss motif we heard at the end of Act I when kisses were still sweet.

NOTES

Otello	Verdi's twenty-seventh opera
First night	La Scala, Milan, 5 February 1887
Reception	A big success. With the 74-year-old Verdi in the house, the most honoured man in Italy, it could not have been anything else
Libretto	Boito
Source	Shakespeare

NEWS AND GOSSIP

What or who made Verdi return to composition more than ten years after *Aida*? Probably the smart young Giulio Ricordi, son of Tito Ricordi who had for many years been Verdi's adviser and friend. Giulio had the wit to enlist Boito, a really talented up-and-comer whose opera *Mefistofele* had recently been revived and who was in a fair way to becoming a popular poet. The pair of them dangled *Otello* before Verdi's eyes and he, always a sucker for Shakespeare, decided he had been resting long enough. Verdi first arranged to have a trial run with Boito on a revision of *Simon Boccanegra*. These two vain and complex characters must have got on all right for they stuck together and started on *Otello* in March 1884. But Verdi was getting on a little, he was composing in a new style, Shakespeare had to be treated with respect, and it was two-and-a-half years before the score was completed, a sluggish pace for a man who had written fourteen operas in nine years. But when it came out its success was enormous: applause all round, except from Bernard Shaw who thought that Verdi's 'well is running dry'. A truly crass remark, but then Shaw, although an adroit writer about performance, was a poor judge of music. Since its first round of the opera houses of Europe, *Otello* has held a respected place in the repertory and is played pretty frequently, partly because it is greatly admired both by managements and aficionados. But it doesn't sell tickets like the famous three – *Rig*, *Trav* and *Trov*.

COMMENT

Otello is a masterpiece, no doubt, but it is a masterpiece written by a composer different from the Verdi of *Traviata*, *Don Carlos* and *Aida*. Verdi had heard Wagner and pondered (though he slept peacefully during the Vienna production of *Tannhäuser*). What we have here is not a series of arias, duets and ensembles separated by recitatif and free arioso writing, but a continuous stream of music, powerful, passionate and responsive to the meaning of each line, with few set-piece items popped in here and there.

These do, however, include the drinking song in Act I, the choral offering to Desdemona in Act II and the Willow Song in Act IV – all of them wonderful. But now they are islands in a stormy sea of music which drives along the burden of the tragic plot and fuses music and drama more completely than Verdi had ever done before. There are a couple of near-miraculous ensembles (the Act II quartet – Desdemona, Otello, Iago, Emilia – and the finale to Act III) which have added to Verdi's 'thinks' technique a new ingredient – plot development by one or more characters in the midst of reflection by others. The Act III finale (a scene not in Shakespeare) is quite the biggest aspidistra in this line of business – seven independent vocal parts over a busy chorus and an active orchestra and its effect is electric. Admittedly, unless it is brilliantly produced, this mighty edifice can turn into mashed potatoes (it can be given a clarity in the recording studio it can never have on stage) but when it comes off the effect of Verdi's final and most majestic ensemble is overwhelming.

Partly because of this new technique the pace of the opera is fast which in its way is a plus for it is true that purely in plot terms Shakespeare often benefits from compression (MacMillan's *Romeo and Juliet* ballet, Verdi's *Macbeth*). Thus *Otello* has the drive and compulsion *Othello* does not have as a play, but although Boito does very well, the power of the poetry, of course, is gone. *Otello* is magnificent, an opera to marvel at. Perhaps it inspires admiration rather than affection. An alpha.

I Pagliacci (The Comedians)

Fairground tragedy

Leoncavallo

The one where the broken-hearted clown has to put on the motley and then stabs his wife.

CAST

Canio, travelling showman (stage name Pagliaccio)	Tenor
Nedda, wife of Canio (Columbine)	Soprano
Tonio, hunchback clown trouper (Taddeo)	Baritone
Beppe, trouper (Harlequin)	Tenor
Silvio, Nedda's local lover	Baritone

2 acts: running time 1 hr 10 mins

STORY

Act I A common on the edge of a village

We are in a Calabrian village, August 1870 and Canio's travelling troupe (four actors – limited budget) are putting on a show tonight. Tonio sticks his head through the curtain (prologue) and tells us the old custom was to assure the audience the play was all phoney the actors not real: this play contrariwise is about true life and the actors *are* real.

Drumroll: bugle call: a crowd gathers with amazing speed (it is a feast day): Canio's company in a donkey cart appear in the parade: they are well received. Canio as barker gives the spiel: tonight's show doors open 11 p.m. (late but it looks like a sellout). The crowd reacts operatically huzzas caps in air etc. Tonio attempts to assist Nedda from the donkey cart: Canio rebuffs him: the crowd is intrigued: a yokel yells out watch out somebody'll steal your girl: Canio delivers a surprisingly frank speech concerning his intimate marital affairs: the play is one thing real life another he says: on stage husband surprises wife adultering and thrashes her lover: all laugh: in real life if anyone lays a finger on my wife Nedda watch it boy watch it.

Bells cause the crowd to move off churchwards in a crocodile boys and girls in pairs (old Calabrian custom). Canio and Beppe accompany locals to the nearby boozer. Nedda thinks: Canio is a jealous bastard, bad scene if he catches me adultering. She sees birds flying by: gives a long ornithological soliloquy (irrelevant).

Tonio boards Nedda says I am a sexually repulsive hunchback but I love you. Nedda derides him: Tonio gets physical: attempts a lecherous grab: she strikes him in the face with a horse whip: you'll pay for this says he: exits. Enter Silvio. Are you mad? says Nedda. Poncing around at this time of day? It's safe enough says he: Beppe and Canio are in the boozer. You might have run into a half-wit clown attempting rape one minute ago says she. He says Nedda – skip out of this bunch of wandering googoos when they move on: stay here with me. Can't she says. (Tonio spies on them through a slit in the canvas. Aha!) Oh come on says Silvio. OK she says I will. They talk loverly: they make an assignation for escape.

Silvio exits: Canio fetched by Tonio gives chase: Tonio gloats: Canio returns having failed: no Silvio. What's the adulterer's name? he asks Nedda. I'm not telling says Nedda. Canio pulls a knife on Nedda. Beppe interposes. The house is filling: the show must go on says Beppe. How can I give a decent performance when I'm emotionally disturbed? says Canio. Nevertheless he vestis la giubba.

Intermezzo (3 minutes) Act II The same

The audience make a fair old meal of getting to their seats. Silvio slides on: psst! he says remember tonight? I'll be there says Nedda. Opera within opera begins. Columbine/Nedda awaits her lover Harlequin/Beppe: husband Pagliaccio/Canio is absent. Servant Taddeo/Tonio makes passes at Columbine/Nedda (reflecting real life of course). Harlequin/Beppe leaps through the window and kicks Taddeo/Tonio out. The lovers plot over supper to drug Pag./Canio and to escape together. Husband Pag./Canio blusters in: athletic Harlequin/Beppe jumps out through the window. Two covers set? Oho! says Pag./Canio: a man: his name? Not telling says she (reflecting real life again!).

Zut! says Canio I've had enough (loses his marbles) I'm not Pagliaccio at all he cries: I am Canio the poor sod who dragged you up out of the gutter launched your stage career (Blimey! what a play! say the audience) you slut whore bitch get out says Canio. Suits me says Nedda (but sensing danger she tries to get the show back on rails: fails). Before you go off with your fancy man says Canio tell me his name. Shan't says Nedda. OK says Canio: he pulls a knife and stabs her. Hey! hey! help! Silvio! she cries. Silvio rushes on and Canio knifes him neatly too. Jesus and Mary cry the audience (certainly getting their money's worth). Canio announces the comedy is ended.

MINUTES FROM START	LOOK OUT FOR	
Act I		
6: *E voi, piuttosto*	The Prologue, a well-known party piece, does its work well and flowers into an attractive lyrical patch towards the end.*	6
8: *Eh! . . . Son qua!*	The chorus comes on prancing and shouting quite a bit* but steady up and give us two foot-tapping tunes, the second an oom-pah.	8
10: *Un tal gioco*	Canio delivers a lecturette* to the rustics on the relationship between life and art. A little out of place, one would have thought, but it is beguiling in its lyrical turn of phrase and homespun philosophy.	10
15: *Don, din, don, din*	The Ding Dong chorus.** Cheerful rather than holy, with some very secular advice to young lovers. Fades away nicely. Quite a treat.	15
20: *Qual fiamma avea nel guardo*	Nedda has adulterous thoughts* which are swept away by the sight of a flock of birds, resulting in a lengthy ornithological aria. It has verve and style, and sussurates.	20
24: *So ben che difforme*	Tonio makes a determined pass at Nedda:** his opening plea is sweet and persuasive: her reply tinkling and amused: things hot up dramatically and musically until he is struck in the face: high tension as he threatens and goes.	24
29: *E fra quest'ansie*	The Silvio/Nedda love duet** warms up when Silvio urges her to stay put with him when the caravan moves on. It's all agreeably passionate and lyrical and from time to time the tenor line blazes out gloriously. It fades out dreamily – until Silvio has to run for his life.	29
42: *Vesti la giubba*	Canio's tearful bit about clowning with a broken heart.** The most popular number in the piece – why? It's not the best, but perhaps it's the sentiment and the sob at the end that make it such a draw.	42
Act II		
0: *Ohè! Ohè! Presto!*	Not many opera audiences could manage to sing this chorus* as they take their seats; it starts with a simple oom-pah but a strong tune builds it up to a stirring finish trumpets and all.	0
4: *Oh! Colombina*	The first item to lift the cod melodrama out of parody is Harlequin's serenade* which is neat and tuneful.	4
	The next item of note is the pretty-pretty little	

12: *Guarda, amor mio* tune* in the Harlequin/Columbine duet. Nedda 12
reverts to it later on when she tries to get the show back on the rails. It has just the right music-box, china doll sound.

The great moment in *Pagliacci* comes when reality (well, stage reality) breaks in. This is signalled by Canio's interjection 'Nome di Dio' and takes a
16: *No, Pagliaccio non son* complete grip in his great tirade*** of jealousy, 16
frenzied, overpowering and wonderfully singable. And from there, in spite of Nedda's attempts to cool it, it runs on in fine high dramatic style to the two stabbings. Did ever an audience before or since see a real double murder before their very eyes?

NOTES

I Pagliacci	Leoncavallo's first published opera (and only success)
First night	Teatro dal Verme, Milan, 21 May 1892
Reception	A wow (Toscanini conducted)
Libretto	Leoncavallo
Source	Leoncavallo got the idea from a court case tried by his father who was a judge

NEWS AND GOSSIP

Ricordi thought Leoncavallo, although a good libretto writer, was pretty dodgy when it came to composing. He took options on two early operas but did not put them on. He added him to Puccini's team of five librettists on *Manon Lescaut* but they quarrelled and Leoncavallo was fired. The poor man was by now pretty sick of operatic life. Nevertheless he locked himself up for five months and wrote the libretto and score for *Pag.* He had seen Mascagni's *Cav* and thought he could do just as well in the verismo stakes. He sent the script to the publisher Sonzogno who backed it and put it on to huge applause. *Pag* was written as a one-acter but the applause after 'Vesti la giubba' always stopped the show. So Leoncavallo popped in a formal stopper in the shape of a short Intermezzo to quieten the house down. Now we have the heading Act II before the play within a play begins. In the manuscript the last line ('La commedia è finita!') was given to Tonio but such is the overpowering vanity and leverage of tenors that it was pinched by successive generations of Canios and today his name is printed in. Quite wrong of course. Tonio did the prologue and should have the last word.

Pag caught on at once and sped around the world operatic circuit in quick time. As early as December 1893 it was twinned with *Cav* and the relationship has since become Siamese. Today still probably the two most performed operas in the whole repertory.

COMMENT

Pag is a much superior article to its twin *Cav*. It has a plot instead of a situation and characters who although pretty well off-the-peg are credible and quickly grab our interest. But its claim to be the first verismo (or true-life) opera is pretty phoney. The prologue tells us that what we have is not a bunch of actors playing in a fantasy but real people acting out scenes from real life. But in real life it can't often happen that a play reflects precisely the actors' own marital/domestic scene. Parables, in short, are for fiction. Second, Canio's little troupe are figures of stage romance taken up with affairs of the heart and nothing else. Verismo people shave, eat, go to the lavatory and keep their feet on the ground. Verismo drama happens in the low key settings of ordinary life, in the kitchen, the office, in the street. *Pag*'s *mise en scène* is exotic. (More of this sort of stuff in OPERATICA under *verismo*.) But pshaw to all that – *Pag*'s appeal has nothing to do with theories. It speaks directly and powerfully to any musical person and builds to a terrific musico/dramatic climax of jealousy and violence. The chorus has good tunes, varied, ingenious and never treacley, as in *Cav*, nor on-the-nose obvious as in early Verdi, the narrative is taken along its stormy route by means of music that has a powerful forward drive and all recitatif has gone, the set pieces bring the house down, and the combination of the power of the drama pushing along with an urgent and effective score make *Pag* a really punchy one-acter. A very popular alpha.

Parsifal

Holy melodrama

Wagner

The one where a simple-minded teenager by shooting a swan gets involved with a religious sect whose king is permanently wounded and whose official messenger is a convertible woman, sometimes witch, sometimes houri.

CAST

Titurel, semi-retired king, father of Amfortas	Bass
Amfortas, acting ruler of the Kingdom of the Grail	Baritone
Gurnemanz, a senior Knight of the Grail	Bass
Kundry, a woman under a spell	Mezzo
Klingsor, failed knight of the Grail, now evil	Bass
Parsifal, a foolish boy	Tenor

Knights of the Grail (tenors and basses), **Squires** (some trebles), **Flower Maidens** (sopranos and mezzos), voices from above

3 acts: running time 4 hrs 40 mins

BEFORE WE START

Some Angels, we hope with due authorization, gave to King Titurel the Grail, the cup from which Jesus had drunk at the Last Supper, and the Spear, which had pierced His side on the cross. The motive for this transaction is not known, but the Angels certainly thought they had put the things in safe hands. Alas no. Titurel recruited a body of knights to guard the castle where the relics were sited but one applicant for the job, Klingsor, was blackballed because he failed to pass the safe sex test. Indeed, his sexual history showed him to be quite unfit to consort with knights who were so pure in mind they had never had it off with anyone, ever. Klingsor foolishly castrated himself, thinking that would lessen his sex drive and get him in. But no, the blackball stood. In a fury he set up a lavish brothel close by Titurel's place in the guise of a castle with the park full of hookers, who in order to spare the blushes of the Bayreuth set were called Flower Maidens. By these means he hoped to de-purify Titurel's knights one by one, get them fired and, when there were none left, to seize the Grail; though why such a loose-living chap should want a grail, even when castrated, is a mystery. So many of Titurel's knights slipped off for a short time at Klingsor's open-air massage parlour that his operational strength fell dangerously low. He therefore sent his son Amfortas to close down Klingsor's house but unfortunately he fell for the chief hooker, one Kundry, and Klingsor took the holy Spear off him while he had his trousers down. He then gave him a nasty wound with it just below his rib cage which went septic and for lack of penicillin which had not yet been invented, would not heal. Kundry while continuing as a hooker by night lived a double life, becoming by day a sort of down-at-heel witch who acted as a runner for the Grail knights whose staff-vetting procedures were poor. Now read on.

STORY

Act I Sc 1 The grounds of Titurel's castle
In which Kundry rides in with some medicine for the wounded King Amfortas who graciously receives it on the way to his bath

We are in the land of myth vaguely located in Spain and the time is AD but not much. Hey lads get up and pray says Gurnemanz to two young sleeping sentries and good day to you he adds to a couple of stray knights how's HRH Amfortas this morning? Much the same say the knights temperature 101° pulse normal wound still suppurating. He's on his way to his morning ablutions. There's only one cure for him says Gurnemanz and I'm not telling at this stage for fear of spoiling the plot.

A witch is seen riding fast. She rushes in. Here's some Friars' Balsam for Amfortas she says: it's the last bottle left she says nothing like it. Enter Amfortas groaning on a litter. God what a terrible night says he. Sorry that new prescription from Professor Gawain didn't work says a knight he's gone off by the way. AWOL? says Amfortas. Probably sneaked off into Klingsor's whorehouse. None of these damn medicos are any good I just have to wait for the arrival of the holy fool. Remember I told you that I got this holy fax saying only some innocent fool who had come to see the light through some terrible experience could cure me. But meanwhile says Gurnemanz try some of this Friars' Balsam. Kundry got it for you. Thanks Kundry says Amfortas (exits).

Ho ho look at Kundry nasty dirty brutish thing say the squires. Leave her alone says Gurnemanz she does a good job for us and has the misfortune to be under a curse. By the way Kundry where were you the day we lost the Spear? (Kundry looks at the ground.) Why not send her to get it now? say the squires. That would be against the Grail rules section 17B says Gurnemanz mysteriously. How well I remember the day Klingsor nicked it off Amfortas while he was bonking. A disastrous bonk that was. Tell us more say the squires. Gurnemanz tells them a whole heap more about the blackballing of Klingsor etc. and also that when the wounded

Amfortas got back to the Grail Hall and was praying like crazy the Grail spoke and read out to him the fax about waiting for a holy fool (and the cleaners found the hard copy on the floor next morning).

Act I Sc 2 The same
In which a swan is shot and Parsifal discovered to be of subnormal intelligence

A dead swan falls from the flies and a squire shouts up to the flies Hey it isn't Swan Lake tonight that's on Thursday. Shut up you fool it's in the script says another. Who done this dastardly act? says a third. Some knights enter giving Parsifal the bum's rush. He done it they cry this big loony done it with his bow and arrow. You done this? asks Gurnemanz. Yeah it was a great shot he was coming really high says Parsifal. You feel no shame murdering a beautiful animal? says Gurnemanz the birds and the beasts have as much right to this forest as do you.

He goes on to give him severe anti-blood-sports lecture and ends by asking him how could you do such a thing? Dunno says Parsifal. Who's your father? asks Gurnemanz. Dunno says Parsifal. Where are you from? Who do you work for? What school did you go to? University? What's your blood group? asks Gurnemanz. Dunno dunno dunno dunno says Parsifal. What's your name then? asks Gurnemanz. Dunno. Lordy Lordy we have a real thickie here says Gurnemanz and maybe one for the men in white coats. Look to it lads and give this swan a decent Christian burial (they knock up a small coffin and reverently bear the swan to its final resting place).

So what *do* you know? Gurnemanz asks Parsifal. How to make bows and arrows and I know I had a mum called Gloomy Kate. Enter Kundry. [Is she his mother? Ed.] I can tell you more says Kundry: his dad was killed in battle before he was born. And one day I saw soldiers says Parsifal. And he kills giants and poachers and any other wicked person with his bare hands says Kundry. What's wicked? says Parsifal. This poor loony certainly should be inside says Gurnemanz. And your mum took it very badly that you ran off and left her says Kundry. Parsifal leaps at Kundry's throat. O God and a violent one too says Gurnemanz as he separates them.

I think I'll take a nap says Kundry (disappears into the bushes). You come with me son says Gurnemanz the Grail might do you a power of good. What's Grail? asks Parsifal as they start trudging along a moving walkway while scenery rolls past (if it's a traditional production) until they are in the Grail Hall.

Act I Sc 3 The Grail Hall in Titurel's castle
In which Parsifal is subjected to Holy Communion apparently to no effect but we are tipped off that he is going to be Amfortas's saviour

An all-male Holy Communion is being celebrated by boys youths acolytes squires knights etc. You do the honours Amfortas says Titurel. No you do it Dad says Amfortas my ribs are killing me and I think all this stuff about Christ's blood plus my guilt is giving me a nervous breakdown. O my God it's started bleeding again. He passes out. Whilst Amfortas is in dreamland the boys sing about the promised coming of the converted fool though it's hard to see how that could have worked its way into the Liturgy. Amfortas did you hear me? says Titurel. Amfortas comes to and jacks himself up and does the priest's office for the whole stageful of choristers extras etc. The hall empties and Gurnemanz goes up to Parsifal and asks well how did that grab you? Dunno says Parsifal. OK you loony says Gurnemanz and – stand by folks for the only attempt at a joke in *Parsifal* – since you are such a gander get out there and look for a goose. Heavenly voices are heard by us – maybe not by anyone else – singing That's the boy! that's the converted fool elect! watch that man!

Act II Sc 1 On the ramparts of Klingsor's magic castle
In which Klingsor summons Kundry to his castle to seduce Parsifal who kills a number of Klingsor's security police in forcing an entry

Klingsor is sitting looking in his magiscope: aha I see this loony is on his way he says. Wake up Kundry you idle bitch report for duty. Now! At once! Kundry appears in a haze of blue light. You been working for that Grail mob again? asks Klingsor. Kundry screams very loud and writhes too. Yes she says. So you like to think the good you do for them there makes up for the harm you do them when you are with us here says Klingsor. A likely story. OK get your war paint on. No! No! spare me wails Kundry. Not likely says Klingsor I got you well magicked into my power. And yet you used to sleep around yourself says Kundry. Belt up! says Klingsor I don't want any of that stuff. You get on with your job of seducing your way through those Grailers so I can get my hands on the Grail. That Parsifal's nearly here now get into your tart's togs quick. Must I? asks Kundry. For Chrissake give over says Klingsor he's a sexy chap you'll enjoy it.

My God there's Parsifal laying about him like crazy – there's Jimmy Ferris gone – now he's got his sword through Claude – there's Jack Beauchamp's arm off. An unforced error there – oops! right through Charlie's thigh on the backhand – they're leaving the court – game set and match Parsifal. Are you ready Kundry? As for you my lad one bedroom bout with her and you'll be magicked into my power. He presses the garden release button and the castle shoots to the back of the stage. A garden springs up in front.

Act II Sc 2 Klingsor's garden
In which Klingsor's hostesses make minor attempts on Parsifal's virtue and Kundry launches a full-scale seduction but all fail in the face of the impenetrable stupidity of our hero

Klingsor's full establishment of hostesses come in whingeing about the death and mayhem caused amongst their playmates by Parsifal. Jimmy Ferris was the biggest tipper in the business says one. Charlie won't be able to do much with only one thigh says another. Some of them will need weeks in hospital before they can perform again says a third. Who done it? they all ask: who is this murderous bastard?

Parsifal jumps over the fence. It's him they cry. Why did you do it? In order to get to you says Parsifal I had to clear the way somehow. You killed our men. Who'll be our playmates now? they ask. I will says Parsifal. O goody say the girls we're not greedy it's only fifty dollars for half an hour. I saw him first says one he's mine. Bollocks says another he took my card let's have some harmless foreplay and dance a-ring a-ring of roses before anything else happens says a fly one.

They dance but the girls start pushing shoving and kicking each other in the groin trying to get their hands on Parsifal. Stop it he shouts and pushes them off. An eerie voice rings out: Parsifal! it says P..A..R..S..I-..F..A..L. Whosat? says Parsifal. Stay here says the voice. The girls run off. Are you speaking to me? says Parsifal. Yes says Kundry (for it is she – now transformed for seduction duties) your Pa called you Parsley before he died and your Ma called you that parsley fool but things got mixed up in the word processor and . . . OK OK OK says Parsifal.

Whew! you look sexy are those the things they call suspenders? Do you live here? No I came a long way just to see you says she. I knew you when you were a kid living with your mum Gloomy Kate. She thought the world of you and died of sorrow when you walked out on her. Oh my God! I never thought of that! I killed my mother! I am guilty guilty guilty! cries Parsifal. Never mind I bring you this message from your Mum says Kundry and gives him a long sexy kiss. Parsifal reels back. Help! Amfortas! he says save me from sin which this must surely be because of the funny feeling I have in my trousers. I must think of the Grail like mad.

He has a fit and when he comes to he goes on I should not be consorting with a high-class tart in this garden. I am guilty guilty guilty . . . and he goes off again. Hey Parsifal can't you keep your mind on the business in hand says Kundry. You whore says Parsifal you must be the one who got Amfortas into trouble. Get off! Get out! Get lost! If you're off sex and on to redemption says Kundry what about me? You know I'm under a curse because I made a joke in front of Jesus about his Father and in his infinite compassion he is now giving me hell.

I have an idea if we had a nice time together that might just lift the curse. No it wouldn't says Parsifal you stand a much better chance if I follow the holy option. If one kiss gave you such a lift says Kundry just think what the full personal service could do. Leave it to me says Parsifal I will fix your redemption without any full personal service. Just show me the way to go home – the way to Amfortas. Never! Not on your life! says Kundry he's a wimp I'll get after you with that self-same Spear if you start trying to help that weasel. Come on Parsifal just a short time and with your clothes on if you like . . . Get thee behind me evil woman says Parsifal. Hi! Klingsor jumps out holding the Spear. This Spear will stop you in your tracks my boy says Klingsor. But no Parsifal seizes the Spear and makes the sign of the Cross with it. This activates a destruct button within the castle which promptly falls down in ruins.

Act III Sc 1 In the grounds of Titurel's castle. Early morning. Some years later

In which Kundry goes into domestic service and Parsifal turns up in a dark suit

Kundry lies groaning in a bush. Gurnemanz pulls her out. Springtime Kundry he says wake up. But there's not much messenger work now owing to the recession. How about a cleaning lady? asks Kundry could I do for you for instance Mr Gurnemanz? OK says he – who's that coming onstage in black armour? (It's Parsifal of course.) Hey you do know this is a no-armaments area? And that it's Good Friday which is a no-armaments day? (Parsifal strips off.) My God it's that loony what shot the swan! and he's got the Spear! says Gurnemanz.

Nice to see you again says Parsifal. I wanted to help that nice Amfortas but I got lost for about ten years. I rather think there was a curse on me says Parsifal. I now see you are the converted fool who is to be our saviour says Gurnemanz: you've arrived in the nick of time for things are pretty bad in the Grailhouse. Titurel dead Amfortas refusing to do his bit with the Grail low morale generally grafitti on the castle walls also mass visitations to the massage parlour. My God it's all my fault says Parsifal if I'd got to Amfortas right away all this could have been avoided I'm guilty guilty guilty and he's off again. Never too late to mend says Gurnemanz we can get along there and sort things out shortly.

Would you please purify me first? asks Parsifal. My feet are a bit smelly after ten years of wandering. Certainly says Gurnemanz. Kundry! The gentleman's feet. I'll do your head says Gurnemanz. Parsifal sprinkles holy water on to Kundry as she wipes the engine oil off his feet. She is thus released from her curse. Nice day for a Good Friday says Parsifal. I see the birds and the bees are all at work. Yes that's what Good Friday's all about says Gurnemanz. Parsifal kisses Kundry on the head to make quite sure she's curse-free. Gurnemanz puts a spare set of Grail-knight's ermines onto Parsifal. Avanti! says Gurnemanz and they trudge off into Scene 2. Probably past the same forests rocks etc. as in Act I for few houses can afford two such huge panorama cloths.

Act III Sc 2 The Grail Hall
In which Titurel is taken to his grave, Amfortas is cured and a pigeon flies over Parsifal

By a lucky stroke of timing Gurnemanz and Parsifal arrive just as a procession of knights comes in carrying the body of Titurel fronted by the Grail. This will be your last Communion old boy they say. They open the coffin in front of Amfortas and there is a brief ululation by one and all at the sight of the body. True to form Amfortas starts whingeing noisily about wanting to die too. Serve the sacrament Amfortas shout the knights: go on. Do it. It's your job. It's what you're paid for. Can't do it says Amfortas look at my wound it's bleeding (he rather disgustingly shows it) besides I have this psychological block. Kill me please do but no serving of the sacrament.

Parsifal steps up and touches Amfortas's wound with the Spear. I think this might help your problem he says (and it does): this is the Spear he adds I've brought it back. (Sensation.) Uncover the Grail please he says. He kneels down before it. Kundry lies down at his feet. She expires. The Grail begins to give off sparks. It's a miracle that's what it is say all the knights etc. A pigeon flies in and hovers over Parsifal's head. Clearly everyone including God thinks Parsifal has done a good job.

PARSIFAL MOTTOS

Number	*Name*	*Description*
1	Sacrament	First item in the prelude. Slow, solemn, aimless.
2	Grail	Alias the Dresden Amen. Upward phrase and A-MEN.
3	Faithful	O come all ye faithful – but not quite. First heard as a clarion call repeated three times.
4	Spear	The end of Sacrament [1]. Three shorts run up to a long and it trails away.
5	Kundry	Downward sweep in the strings from very high to very low – four octaves.
6	Amfortas	Two slow opening notes with a long tail behind them.
7	Klingsor	A fleeting figure up and down sloped like the arch of a bow.
8	Innocence	Slow and hymn-like, much longer than most.
9	Parsifal	Soft horns in thirds, bouncing gently upwards.
10	Bells	Not quite the first four notes of Big Ben.

MINUTES FROM START — LOOK OUT FOR

Prelude

0 The prelude is intensely serious but lacking in charm. 0
It begins with a parade of mottos as follows: Sacrament [1], Grail [2], Faithful [3]. Then Grail [2] again. Then some powerful stuff building up (Faithful [3]) in sequences. The rest of the prelude pushes around these mottos in a stop–start fashion until we reach a new one, Spear [4] – the end of Sacrament [1]. We wait for the thing to come together and to give us some nice ongoing music but it never does. No star.

Act I Sc 1

Gurnemanz wakes the two squires. All pray. Grail [2] and Faithful [3]. Two knights appear, outriders of Amfortas's bathing party. Mostly recitatif but then some arioso trying to get out. A sluggish start. Mainly Hellos and How is hes? No star.

Kundry is spotted by one of the squires, surprisingly a soprano (arranged for choral duty? or else is very young) and Kundry arrives in a fluster of strings. We hear that her horse is not flying through the air today but crawling (very odd because the fiddles are certainly giving us fly-music not crawl-music and it is not all that common for a horse to crawl). Anyway Kundry comes in to her motto [5]. She gives Gurnemanz the Friars' Balsam and he greets Amfortas on arrival. Quite nice exchanges. Things are looking up but still no star.

21: *Recht so! Habt Dank* Amfortas to the rescue.* As he gives the bulletin on 21
his overnight health we hear his motto deep in the strings [6] (we heard it first at the beginning of the act) and he sings splendidly for so sick a man, calm sweet music in three stanzas, although in the second he has a moment of bad temper in hearing that Gawain has gone AWOL. He is looking forward to his morning ablutions.

As the invalid's procession moves on there is a
27 short orchestral symphony* passing Amfortas [6] 27
from instrument to instrument in the most beguiling fashion.

The squires start to pick on Kundry but Gurnemanz, in a strong bid to become a Wotan for Christ, starts to tell us about her extremely unusual past life and then goes on to tell the tale of the Grail.

29: *Hm! Schuf sie euch Schaden je?* 1.* Kundry is a good woman. Provides a reliable 29
messenger service. May be under a curse. May have been reincarnated. Old Titurel first found her lying about in the bushes. Where were you Kundry the day we lost the Spear? (Kundry looks at the ground.) This is bold recitatif with some fragmentary tunes. Bits of Sacrament [1], Kundry [5] and Faithful [3].

36: *Das ist ein andres* 2.* Why not send her to get the Spear now, ask the 36
lads. No that wouldn't do. It's forbidden, Amfortas had it nicked off him by a woman – well, sort of a whore – I was there. Tell us more say the squires. A lot of Spear [4] and stuff distantly derived from Sacrament [1].

40: *Titurel, der fromme Held* 3.** Let's start at the beginning (after ten min- 40
utes!). Titurel was given charge of the Grail and Spear [4] also Grail [2] and Sacrament [1]. He knew Klingsor who applied for membership of the Grail club. Much as 2. above.

44: *Klingsorn, wie hart ihn Müh'* 4.** Klingsor was blackballed! Change of gear. 44
The easy-going narrative gets rumbustious. We have a new motto, Klingsor [7], first heard on a clarinet

doubling a bassoon – a spooky sound. After the agitato about Klingsor (with a bit of the sexy music to come) things settle down as the aged Titurel hands over to his son Amfortas. And you know what happened to him. Derivatives of Sacrament [1]: Grail [2] pretty well its old self.

48: *Vor dem verwaisten Heiligtum*

5.** To get the Spear back Amfortas was told by 48
some angelic means that only a fool (with certain other qualifications) could get it back. Solemn, quieter, almost sotto voce. Now the motto of simple fools, Innocence [8], is sung twice first by Gurnemanz and then by the prefects. Trembling strings, soft brasses and the apparatus of hush. (Grail [2].)

Throughout this twenty-minute account of past history the vocal line gives no great pleasure. Gurnemanz is telling us the plot, not singing about it. It is in fact a marathon recitatif with scraps of melody for the voice but accompanied by gloriously rich orchestral backing. Although a shower of fresh ideas lie thick on the ground the texture is not so dense as in the earlier Wagners. There are lots of striking phrases floating around which sound as if they are important new mottos, but they aren't. Many are distant relatives of bits of Sacrament [1] and of Grail [2]. The woodwind has a big piece of the action. The interjections from the listening prefects (most of whose voices have broken – what a relief) come as welcome breaks.

Act I Sc 2

Now it's all go. A swan! Dead! Who done it? Parsifal done it. (Knights and squires solus and in chorus.) This gives Gurnemanz an opportunity for a short
53: *Du konntest morden* Party Political Broadcast** on behalf of the World 53
Wildlife Fund. The thought of the birds and the beasts unleashes some of Wagner's loveliest nature music, as did the forest in *Siegfried*. This is something really different, fresh, outdoor and not in the least holy. But after he has spoken sharply to Parsifal we have holy lift-off again with the Parsifal motto [9].

56: *Wo bist du her?* Gurnemanz quizzes Parsifal.** Gentle probing 56
and innocent replies from our Candide. There is something strangely touching about these exchanges which happen over a sweet accompaniment. (Amfortas [6] and Parsifal [9].)

Getting to know our hero. Parsifal tells us some of
60: *Ja! Und einst am Waldessaume vorbei* the things he *does* remember.* He saw a troop of sol- 60
diers and knocked off the odd robber and giant. We have a jolly musical ride in the background and then some brisk adventurous music. After which the motivation of the scene is hard to follow, especially when Parsifal assaults Kundry for telling him of his mother's death and indeed his general mode of behaviour is incomprehensible. But Gurnemanz thinks he may be spotting a champ in our Candide. Musically scrappy, but always on the go (Parsifal [9], Kundry [5], Grail [2] and Klingsor [7]).

Gurnemanz marches Parsifal through caves and rocks to the Grail Hall [2].

Act I Sc 3

67 This transformation scene* is pleasant enough but 67
not on the same scale as the great transformers in *The Ring*. Wagner seems inhibited by an excess of holiness and the great hall steals in in a discreet fashion not in any way dramatic. No bang, no wallop but quite a sizeable climax built out of Amfortas [6], Grail [2] and Bells [10], a new motto (not quite the first four notes of Big Ben, with a hitchkick on the first note when played on the strings or the timps, but losing it when the bells become real). The male chorus that
73: *Zum letzten Liebesmahle* follows* is sung almost entirely against a combination 73
of Bells [10], banged out on the timps, and Grail [2] in counterpoint above. This goes on so long as to make you think there is a spectral stage army marking time in the wings. The last of the choruses (the boys alone) makes some play with Faithful [3]. The choruses are all very decent and they come off better on stage with the holy sets and props than they do in the study where they sound a little dim.

The old Titurel tells Amfortas to serve Communion. Amfortas agonizes for seven minutes and then faints. Again it is hard to find satisfaction with the words (there is too much about holy blood) and the vocal part is much what we have become inured to.
82: *Nein! Lasst ihn unenthüllt!* But the orchestral scene is full of interest** and of 82
beauty. (A lot of Amfortas [6] now so developed as to be quite unlike its old self, and of the inevitable Sacrament [1] and Grail [2].)

We are now into something like a full-dress communion service conducted partly by divine agencies and partly by humans. One divine stroke is to shine a ray of light onto the Grail, like Tinkerbell in *Peter Pan* (but the Grail doesn't move). The introductory music is melodramatic – Wagner at his phoney holiest – it then passes through some standard religious voluntary stuff (Sacrament [1], Grail [2], Bells [10]) to a
101: *Nehmet vom Brot* surprise – the college song of Grailers,* which breaks 101
in, sung with gusto first by the knights on one side then by the knights on the other side then by all the knights together and it goes with as much of a swing as the Eton Boating Song. This unholiest of tunes comes as blessed relief. The words are of course still part of the service so what we have here is the opposite of the rugger song which sets bawdy words to Hymns Ancient and Modern. Here we have holy words to Grailhouse Rock. But it lapses back into the holiness of Grail [2] with treble voices and high fiddles. Faithful [3]. And a bit of Amfortas [5] and Innocence [8] still clinging on. This is a processional, and very effective it is, right up to Bells [10] dying away at the end.

Act II Sc 1

0 The opening orchestral piece* is a mildly effective rush-around mainly by the strings telling us that evil men are afoot (Klingsor [7] and Kundry [5]). 0

Klingsor is looking in his magic mirror and knows all. Parsifal is approaching (Innocence [8]). Klingsor calls Kundry. She awakes dramatically.

There is some cross-talk between Klingsor and Kundry which doesn't advance the plot and is probably the musical low point of the opera. But hark! Parsifal's call rings out [9]. Action! Klingsor race-reads to rousing battle music based on Parsifal [9] and
14: *Ho! Ihr Wächter!* Innocence [8]).* His knights get knocked out one by 14
one. Klingsor magics his castle into a pleasure-garden.

Act II Sc 2

This surprises Parsifal, especially when a lot of hostesses run out of the bushes. The music is superior theatre-music. Now we have something very close to the Act II ballet of the old French opera – a complete change of mood, light tuneful music and lots of girls, only they don't dance.

1. The girls are sad. They have no playmates, Parsifal has killed them all. Sad music, not too sad, close harmony singing, no mottos.

2. They parley with Parsifal. Is he friend or foe? Pert dialogue, music cheering up.

3. Friend! Fluttery cheerful music, dead playmates forgotten, leading to –

22: *Komm, Komm, holder Knabe!* 4. Sexual harassment of Parsifal in waltz time.** 22
This is enchanting. No holy blood around, no holy anything, everything quite quite human and a rattling good tune too. And Klingsor's hookers all sound like the sweetest of young things. But they quarrel over Parsifal and, alas! we are back to four in a bar.

Now we strike gold. We hear Kundry offstage calling 'Parsifal'. Her voice floats in asking Parsifal to stay and the girls to go, which they do with a final flutter and giggle.

1. Kundry appears (Innocence [8]) and gently tells
Parsifal about his father and more especially his
31: *Dich nannt' ich* mother,*** how she doted on him and how she pined 31
for him and died when he left her. This is Wagner spinning a web of stunning beauty. No mottos, but a recurrent ear-catching phrase that starts each fresh section (long higher note smoothly down to the second, a beautiful and enlarged cuckoo call). As she tells him of his mother's grief the smooth flow is interrupted by the Frustration motto imported from *The Ring* (a buzz like a bee – unlisted). But up till then, dreamy.

2. Parsifal is really cut up to think of what he did to
his mother. Kundry seizes this mother thing as an aid
41: *War dir fremd noch der Schmerz* to seduction** and moves decisively into the sexual 41
assault. Then the kiss. Wagner muffs this one. It is not as big an event as it should be. (It has the 'Tristan chord' embedded in it: there is also some clever work with Sacrament [1].) But Kundry's wily approach still holds the dreamy magic of 1. above. Look out especially for the fancy patterns from the solo woodwind.

45: *Amfortas!* 3. Parsifal jumps back like a startled mustang.* He 45
rejects her. At first tumultuous, then noble and holy

(Grail [2] and Sacrament [1]). Kundry is really surprised but goes on trying to seduce him (aided by a reprehensible solo violin). Parsifal re-enacts Amfortas's seduction and rejects her even more firmly, using fairly strong language.

4. Kundry tells Parsifal of her hard life and the
53: *Grausamer!* reason for it.* (Quite a lot of the borrowed Frustra- 53
tion.) Lower voltage, sad, halting. A shriek of shame when she gets to the bit about her laughing at Christ. She just can't seem to get holy again (Grail [2]). Can Parsifal bail her out? What about just a bit of short-time sex?

5. I can only save you by being a goody says Parsi-
60: *Auf Ewigkeit wärst du verdammt* fal in a short lecturette on the nature of salvation.** 60
Powerful, free-ranging stuff. Kundry suggests that a full personal service now would be very helpful to Parsifal's career. She is now getting desperate and the music has lost all its early control, it goes into waltz time. They get into a ding-dong. Parsifal wants to find Amfortas, Kundry still wants Parsifal. Quite
66: *Hilfe! Hilfe! Herbei!* hectic. Kundry calls to the boss for help.* She is now 66
hysterical and the music is surging about like the Dutchman's sea, but not so well ordered. Klingsor throws the Spear to a sweep on the harp. It hits holy air above Parsifal's head and stops dead. Grail [2]. Parsifal hauls it down and is triumphant. He is also full of magic and uses it to destroy the Klingsor residence and policies. Bang! Crash! Crumble! Deeply descending bass. Exit.

Act III Sc 1

0 The prelude* in its wild chromatic meanderings is 0
telling us that Parsifal has wandered for a long time (but with the Grail [2] in mind). It is a nice mild piece, not ambitious.

It takes Gurnemanz some time to drag Kundry out of a bush (Kundry [5]). He finds her much improved and suitable for domestic service. This is mostly quasi-recitatif and pretty ornery music-to-suit-the-action.

A black knight comes on (Parsifal [9] in the minor mode: he's tired). He is fully armed. It's Parsifal! Gurnemanz tells him it's not the thing to wear full battle order on Good Friday. Parsifal strips off. Gur-

nemanz recognizes him, and his Spear. The first half of this scene moves haltingly from line to line of thinly accompanied recitatif. Sometimes it seems as if it would peter out altogether. Certainly it would win any operatic slow-bicycle race. But after recognition the music flashes out in one of those spellbinding patches of slow wonder that are one of Wagner's
17: *Erkennst du ihn?* trademarks.* Mottos abound (Parsifal [9], Spear [4], 17
Amfortas [6], Grail [2]).

The wheels begin to turn. Parsifal gives a spirited account of his wanderings and in the next half hour we are to see his progress from roving lunatic to king.

22: *Zu ihm, des tiefe Klagen* 1. Parsifal's report* flows freely and with a strong 22
pulse. Mottos: Innocence [8], Grail [2].

2. Now it's Gurnemanz's turn to give his sitrep,
24: *O Gnade! Höchstes Heil!* and pretty gloomy it is – but easy on the ear.* Before 24
his opening phrase we have a long sweet melody extracted from Sacrament [1] and towards the end we hear the music of the prelude to this act. (A derivative of Sacrament [1] is worked pretty heavily and there is a smidgen of Bells [10].) Parsifal replies that he's frightfully sorry to have caused so much grief.

3. The rituals. The washing of the feet, anointing
36: *Du wuschest mir die Füsse* of the head, etc. Six minutes of magic.*** The music 36
is gentle, caressing. A sense of Parsifal's simplicity and goodness reaches through to us, perhaps for the first and only time. Gurnemanz tells Parsifal he will meet Amfortas (Parsifal [9]). As Kundry deals with Parsifal's feet we have a reminder of the Flower-girls music. (Does Parsifal recognize Kundry as the Other Woman and do evil thoughts cross his mind just for a moment?) Gently and tenderly with a cushion of soft sound we get to the crowning and now we have Parsifal [9] triumphant and Grail [2] very triumphant indeed to end the ceremony.

42 4. The Good Friday music*** heralded in by 42
Faithful [3]. Then a fresh piece with no mottos (to start with anyway). It is calm and melodious with woodwind solos swinging out very agreeably. Parsifal nearly spoils it all by harking back to the gloom of the Crucifixion but Gurnemanz brings happiness back. According to him all the birds, beasts and flowers are well briefed in the story of the Resurrection. This

lovely piece has a reference to Grail [2], otherwise it is pretty well its own man. Parsifal adds a pretty coda.

Time to get moving says Gurnemanz and the long
52 march* begins to Bells [10] and a stalk-about figure in 52
the bass which this time builds to an ear-splitting climax as they reach the Grail Hall.

Act III Sc 2

The two processions of singing knights start off sounding like any old anthem for two choirs but the texture is artfully thickened and once Bells [10]
60: *Ach, zum letzten Mal!* comes backing in on the timps we are won over.* It's a 60
good piece and a perfect preparation for Amfortas's miserable solo.

Amfortas's miserable solo. He really is very unhappy and in great pain. Snatches of melody but a glum piece on the whole that fails to arouse much sympathy until the very last few bars which do strike a chord (a touch of Sacrament [1]). The knights get stroppy. Amfortas stands firm (variants of Amfortas [6]). Parsifal interposes (Grail [2], Amfortas [6]). Heals Amfortas (Parsifal [9], Innocence [8] and Spear [4]). Takes the Grail (Faithful [3]). Kundry drops dead. Tinkerbell again. A pigeon appears above his head. This pantomime is accompanied by glowing
75: *Höchsten Heiles Wunder!* ethereal music, of which the last chorus** and the 75
closing symphony are of great beauty and we have farewell references to Innocence [8], Sacrament [1], Faithful [3] and Grail [2].

NOTES

Parsifal	Wagner's thirteenth and last opera
First night	Festspielhaus, Bayreuth, 26 July 1882
Reception	Awed
Libretto	Wagner
Source	Mediaeval poems *Titurel* and *Parzival* by Wolfram von Eschenbach

NEWS AND GOSSIP

Like most of Wagner's operas, *Parsifal* was a long time in the making. First thoughts are recorded as early as 1845, the first prose sketch was completed in 1857, the libretto by 1877 and the score by 1880 – thirty-five years from the immaculate conception to the reverential delivery, during which time it must be remembered he wrote six other operas including the monster *Ring*. *Parsifal* was aimed to be the opening event for Wagner's custom-built opera house at Bayreuth. Only a major religious-cum-artistic event would be big enough to open the Festspielhaus and only the new house would be good enough for *Parsifal*. It was a PR man's dream and Wagner, always ready with a snappy slogan, labelled *Parsifal* a Bühnenweifestspiel, or a Play Specially Composed For The Consecration of The Theatre. Early in 1882 the whole of Bayreuth entered into a period of advent and the rehearsals took place in an atmosphere of holy anticipation. The event itself was greeted with the usual angry debate but this time it was not so much about the music as about the propriety of going through what was pretty well a full-dress communion service on the stage of a theatre, even a consecrated Festspielhaus. Megalomaniac to the last, Wagner put an embargo on any performance of *Parsifal* anywhere other than Bayreuth, and then died. His dutiful widow Cosima kept this embargo in force until the copyright ran out in 1913. Although it was challenged by one or two operatic productions, and was cheekily put on at the Met in 1903, the embargo held pretty well. King Ludwig was permitted the treat of a couple of private showings in Munich, but for the Wagner fan who just had to see *Parsifal* it was Bayreuth or nothing. *Parsifal*'s most prosperous decade was probably the 1920s when every major opera house had to put it on. Since then it has settled down near the bottom of the Wagner popularity ratings and this can be explained by the current level of interest in grails and the fact that the Italians absolutely hate it. The Good Friday music is played quite a lot on radio stations on Good Friday.

COMMENT

Even today there are probably some devout Christians who can find in *Parsifal* a sublime experience, but for most of us it is a bit of a pill. It is not so much that we resent Wagner's hypocrisy in lecturing us on the virtues of innocence and purity of heart – as if Robert Maxwell had written a book on business ethics – it is because it is so staggeringly pretentious. Wagner sets himself up as a sort of musical Pope who has produced a work pretty well as important as the Crucifixion itself. He expects us to speak about *Parsifal* in hushed tones and to take our shoes off before we go in to hear it. Many clever and serious writers have spoken of Wagner as a seer and visionary who foresaw all the discoveries of those important Viennese doctors who were to tell us about sex-dreams, mother fixation, the ego, the id and things like that. This may well be true, but those of us who have a sturdy view of European culture find Wagner's claim to have put together bits of Schopenhauer's philosophy with bits of Buddhism, pagan myth and Christian doctrine, pretty irrelevant to the fact that the finished work is a bundle of pretentious nonsense tinged with morbid sentimentality. Even devout Christians were a bit sickened by the banal symbolism of the Amfortas/Christ Kundry/Mary Magdalene relationship when the opera first appeared.

So how does this simply awful libretto affect the music? Unfortunately quite a lot, because the music, however beautiful, and a lot of it is very beautiful, cannot entirely escape its association with the words. The assumption that you are in the presence of great holiness makes even the preludes to Acts I and III overblown and at the moments of extreme holiness (the voices in the dome of the Grail Hall) the pantomime on the stage makes the music sound ludicrous. By far the most enjoyable act is the naughty one, Act II, both the Flower Maidens with their unholy waltz and the seduction scene with Kundry first telling Parsifal of his boyhood (in one of the most beautiful passages in the opera) and then trying to seduce him (how one wishes she had made it: this indeed might have saved him from being such an insufferable prick). Time and again we have a long solo passage (as in Gurnemanz's narration in Act I) where the vocal part, although it may be doing wonderful things in reflecting the sense of the words, doesn't have much musical interest but the orchestra behind it is playing away in the most heavenly fashion. The scoring is rich and the mood mostly relaxed and gentle. Even in the Act I and Act III transformation scenes Wagner didn't go for the huge effects he had pulled off so brilliantly in *The Ring*. There is, however, a lingering smell of incense over even the most rumbustious music in both acts. The one occasion when this is (surprisingly) shaken off is at a very holy moment at the end of Act III when the knights break into Grailhouse Rock as they sit down to supper. This is very jolly.

There is ten minutes of magic in Act III where Gurnemanz and Kundry give Parsifal his wash and brush-up before his entry into the Grail Hall. For once we feel that these are three people with normal human feelings and not just Wagner's creatures acting as mouthpieces. The Good Friday music is not a bit holy and wonderfully refreshing – as good as any of Wagner's nature music, which is saying a lot, for as we know from *The Ring*, this strange man had a real feeling for mountains, forests and rivers.

Wagner's use of mottos has gone a stage further even than in *Tristan*. They are now associated with ideas and moods more than with things and people. People still have them, but Parsifal's motto, which is used more than any other, is still a rare bird compared with Siegfried's in *The Ring*, which comes pumping out every few minutes, and the mottos for the other characters hardly recur at all. By far the most heavily worked motto is the Grail [2] which crops up whenever the conversation moves grailwards and which has a field day when the spotlight is on the Grail itself. As in *Tristan*, the opening phrases of the prelude become a sort of quarry from which a lot of subsequent material is extracted. But often it is so worked and processed on the way that only a motto bloodhound would want to trail it back to its origins. *Parsifal* has one great musical plus. Wagner's orchestration, always brilliant, here moves into its final and rather wonderful phase. It is rich and at the same time clear, reflective, mellow and at ease with itself, producing lovely effects without seeming to try. As ever, he favours the wind band above the strings as spokesmen for his messages, but there is more equality in the treatment of the orchestra than in the earlier works and in *The Ring*.

The odour of sanctity which hangs around *Parsifal* is not always one of frankincense and myrrh. For one thing he has this ghoulish fascination with blood generally, and especially with the blood of Christ. Those of us who recoil even from the idea of being blood donors and have difficulty, as wine lovers, in accepting the idea of Christ's blood being turned into wine, can take a certain amount in the cause of opera, but this is surely too much:

I feel the fount of divine blood
Pour into my heart
The ebb of my own sinful blood
In mad tumult
Must surge back into me
To gush in wild terror
Into the world of sinful passion
It now rushes out
Here through my wound like His
Struck by a blow from that same spear

This, surely, is pretty disgusting and when coupled with Tristan's similar performance in tearing a wound open on stage, it must be more than a coincidence that the word 'blood' appears with such distasteful frequency.

But perhaps there are still a few for whom *Parsifal* is pure gold, as it was for the great and good Gustav Kobbé, who wrote of the Grail music after the first performance in Bayreuth: 'For spirituality it is unsurpassed. It is an absolutely perfect example of religious music . . . without the slightest worldly taint.' Even today Barry Millington, a famous Wagner scribe, though using longer words, still seems to like it pretty well. He says: 'The juxtaposition of sublimity with richly ambivalent symbolism and an underlying ideology disturbing in its implications creates a work of unique expressive power and endless fascination.' So that's it really. An alpha.

The Pearl Fishers (Les Pêcheurs de perles)

Exotic melodrama

Bizet

The one where two pearl fishers love the same priestess with the result that two members of the triangle are nearly burned to death by the third until happily for them he repents.

CAST

Zurga, leader of the pearl fishermen	Baritone
Nadir, a fisherman	Tenor
Leila (Leïla), a Brahmin priestess	Soprano
Nourabad, a Brahmin priest	Bass

3 acts: running time 2 hrs 10 mins

STORY

Act I A beach in Ceylon. A Hindu temple visible

We are in Ceylon long before it was renamed Sri Lanka amongst pearl-fishing folk. They are singing and dancing in a pearl-fishing fashion. They have to choose a leader. They choose Zurga. A young one-time pearl fisherman Nadir comes out of the bushes. He says he has been on a long safari hunting tigers. Zurga is happy to meet up again with his old mate Nadir. They take a trip down Memory Lane to a moment where they both fell for a girl and then both swore to keep away from her so that they might stay friends.

A boat arrives with a veiled holy woman (Leila) hired by the pearl fishers to ward off the spooky-wookies and other evil spirits. She has with her Nourabad who is a Hindu priest and her minder. She gets a big hello from one and all but Nadir recognizes her as the girl they left behind them. Zurga does not recognize her. She has to swear to carry out her duties assiduously and to the satisfaction of her employers. She and Nourabad pop into the temple for a spot of prayer and Nadir left alone owns up to us that he was on no safari but on the trail of Leila about whom he is still potty. He drops off for a snooze. Leila returns still singing a bit of the Brahmin Mass. She sees Nadir. They gaze. They might as well admit it – they are in love.

Act II A ruined Hindu temple

It's night. We know that because the chorus tell us it's night also the stage is dark. Nourabad posts Leila on her anti-spookies duty. Apropos of absolutely nothing except assisting Bizet with the plot Leila tells Nourabad that when she was a schoolgirl she hid a man in her room and saved him from a heavy mob who were after him. So he gave her this pearl necklace and told her to wear it always even in the bath. She is left alone and thinks about lovely Nadir.

Pow! Lovely Nadir is here amongst us. They love each other and say so for some time. Nadir says see you at the same place tomorrow night and exits. Bang! A shot. Did they get him? No. He's dragged on by the crowd and it starts to thunder too. Kill 'em both shout the crowd. Canoodling on duty and on holy ground too. Stop! cries Zurga for he has emerged. I am your king and you will kindly obey me. Stand back! The fisherfolk pause and whisper. Scarper now fast! says Zurga to Leila and Nadir. See who she is before she goes says Nourabad and tears off her veil. Holy cow! cries Zurga: it's the girl we left behind us. They're both traitors. Kill them both! Kill! Kill! Kill! And it's thundering like mad too.

Act III Sc 1 Zurga's tent on the shore

Zurga is pretty vexed that he has had to condemn his best friend to be topped. Leila comes in with an escort. Nadir is such a decent guy she says why not let him off? I'm happy to die in his place if that's any good. We didn't have an assignation honest we didn't Nadir was just looking for tigers (a lie). Good news! says Zurga maybe I can let him off after all. Oh goody! says Leila I love him you see. Love him! shouts Zurga. You love him? The treacherous double-crossing dog! I love you too! I'm jealous! That's it then! It's curtains for both of you. As Leila is led away by Nourabad to be burnt she hands her necklace to a young lad saying please post that back to my Mum 44A Main St Candy. Zurga snatches the necklace with a cry.

Act III Sc 2 A funeral pyre in front of a statue of Brahma

The fisherfolk dance around stoned out of their minds and looking forward to an enjoyable double burning. Nadir prays that Leila should be saved. She is led on. They sing bravely about facing death together. At dawn the execution squad is about to seize them when Zurga interposes. It isn't dawn yet at all! he yells. It's your huts. They are on fire! Everyone runs off to the burning huts. Zurga frees Nadir and Leila. He shows Leila the necklace. So he was the man on the run. They are all friends now. Nadir and Leila walk off into the dawn singing prettily. Zurga watches the pearl fishers attempting to save their children and belongings. Not one of them suspects arson by the hand of their good-natured king.

MINUTES FROM START

LOOK OUT FOR

Act I

From the first bars of the short prelude we know we
are in safe hands. It is grave, it is melodious and it
2: *Sur la grève en feu* leads into a chorus* which opens with some phoney 2
exotica but turns out to be much better than most
opening choruses with a fine middle section for male
voices only. The impetus of the chorus is kept up by
the election (unanimous and no nonsense about a card
vote) of Zurga as leader, the arrival of Nadir with a
9: *Des savannes et des forêts* brief but attractive solo* about hunting big game and 9
then friendly acceptance of him as an honorary pearl
fisher. This seals off the very satisfactory scene-setting opening section. Look out especially for the activities of the woodwind in filling gaps, making introductions and generally decorating the scene.

Zurga and Nadir tell the tale turn and turn about of
how they were smitten by love for a mysterious
15: *Au fond du temple saint* woman at a temple. The easy and elegant duet** has a 15
tune to remember. At first it is hard to catch (from the flute accompaniment) but it comes out of the closet twice when they sing together, and it is glorious (the theme of the Triangle). There is a burst of agitato stuff in the middle as the woman flees which makes the return of the tune even more satisfactory.

Zurga explains how the veiled woman comes each
year to give spiritual assistance to the business of
21: *Une femme inconnue* pearl fishing. This short piece* is brought alive by a 21
snaky clarinet which works its way into the texture and incites the orchestra to take over its tune, which becomes the centre of attraction.

23: *C'est elle, elle vient* The arrival of Leila.** We hear the theme we first 23
heard in the prelude, grave, mysterious, a little holy, followed by the Triangle theme. The crowd greets her in another rather special chorus, women only, then men, then both. Zurga swears her in in a heavy dramatico style until he gets to the bit when he prom-
28: *Si tu restes fidèle* ises her a pearl if she is a good girl, when he surprisingly swings into a cheerful little waltz,** but back to 28

the dramatico as she recognizes Nadir (Triangle theme again), decides to stay and is sung off on her way to the temple by another rather special
31: *Brahma, divin Brahma* chorus.*** A great scene, with Triangle theme and 31
thereabouts to the end.

36: *Je crois entendre* Nadir's confession.* Nice enough but not a tune to 36
catch the ear. A persistent rocking figure helps him along on his way.

39: *Le ciel est bleu!* The finale.* Three things are going on. Leila is ad- 39
dressing the gods. Nadir is asleep. The chorus makes restful noises in the background. Everything pretty calm. But now Nadir wakes up and Leila turns her attention from the gods to him. They get into a love duet with some high coloratura stuff from Leila. The chorus remains calm. Although there is magic in the air the finale is a little disappointing. The final tune is too like a nursery lullaby to rise to the occasion and we have none of the sense of end-of-act climax we expect.

Act II

Leila left alone. The ten-minute scene that opens Act II is micro-drama in itself. It begins and ends with a chorus over a la-la pedal bass that is the men la-la-ing away on a single note. Then the recitatif between Nourabad and Leila, very satisfactory in itself, twice lifts off into melodious bursts of arioso which greatly
4: *Si ton coeur reste pur* adorn the scene. The first* is when Nourabad tells 4
her to keep her promise and go to sleep, the second* is 6
6: *O courageuse enfant* in the course of Leila's flashback.

9: *Comme autrefois* Leila's happy cavatina.* No earth-shaker but 9
lovely in its own dreamy way. Horns to start it off and a busy clarinet warbling away with rapid chest notes in the quick middle bit.

15: *De mon amie* The love duet.** 15

1. Nadir is heard approaching. A serenade on the hoof to harp accompaniment, fading up until:

2. Cries of recognition, fast fugitive music. Excitement, racing pulses. Line and line about. To part or not to part.

20: *Ton coeur n'a pas compris* 3. A verse each of the big one.** Just the tune we 20
wanted. Memory Lane.

21: *J'avais promis* 4. Yet another agitated tune:* how can we ever 21
part? Verse about.

5. The big one again.

The finale.

25: *Ah! revenez à la raison* 1. The alarum.** Thunder. An outbreak of the 25
delicious big melody we have just heard in the orchestra accompanying the lovers' farewells. More thunder. Shots. Nourabad agitato. Chorus very agitato.

29: *Voici les deux coupables!* 2. The chorus of death.** Building from a quiet 29
start to a menacing climax. The culprits must die. Leila and Nadir make observations on this verdict. Quite frightening: very vivid: the climax.

3. Hold it! Zurga orders release. The chorus sadly and slowly agrees.

4. Leila exposed (to a reminder by the flute of the theme of the Triangle). Zurga furious. Back to the chorus of death. Really terrible thunder.

5. Everyone on their knees praying in a repeat of
34: *Brahma, divin Brahma* the Brahma chorus*** which any god would have 34
been delighted to receive. A really fine piece, sonorous, rich and giving the second act the climactic finale that was missing from the first.

Act III Sc 1

A short anxious intermezzo leads to Zurga's troubled recitatif. After the storm he thinks more calmly about
1: *L'orage s'est calmé* the terrible discovery of Nadir and Leila's love.** 1
The strings steal in with sorrowful phrases – the recitatif builds to a burst of grief and runs into an aria of sad anger and remorse in which the words 'O Nadir – O Leila' are repeated over and over again. He regrets the death sentence. His emotions break out into a paroxysm of shame and guilt. A big climax. From the first note of the intermezzo to Zurga's last 'Forgive me' this is all of a piece. Very fine.

The Zurga/Leila duet. A small opera in itself, running for all of a quarter of an hour, and what a good run.

1. Leila comes to Zurga asking for a one-to-one
7: *J'ai voulu te parler* talk.** Zurga has a surge of his old love for her. All 7
over a tiptoe accompaniment of the theme of the Triangle.

2. Each one has a 'thinks' piece, inaudible to the other. Leila is scared: Zurga quivers with love for her. Not recitatif, not aria, just Bizet moving things on with perfect judgement.

3. Leila's pleas, sweet and short. Nadir is innocent. Is that so? maybe I can let him off thinks Zurga. He is getting excited and the temperature rises.

4. Punctuation mark. Kill me save him says Leila
12: *Pour moi je ne crains* in sincere and sweet tones** above a sympathetic 12
cello line and pizzicato accompaniment. Ends with a bit of coloratura special pleading.

5. So you love him, do you? (Agitato, stormy.) Then I'll kill the bastard says Zurga. My old jealousy is really warming up, says he, in a swinging solo.

6. Delicious answering pendants from Leila as she pleads. Climbing higher and leading to:

18: *Eh bien, va* 7. The final together bit:** faster, swinging tunes, 18
dramatics with all the gunpowder and shot needed for the final fusillade in a big and splendid set-piece duet such as this.

Leila gives her necklace to a young pearl fisher to
20: *Ami, prends ce collier* be returned to her mother after her demise.* The 20
theme of the Triangle in the accompaniment, a tiny bit of it sung. It works wonders.

Act III Sc 2

22: *Dès que le soleil* The dawn chorus* of the mob, highly excited by the 22
prospect of a public burning. Bits where men and women alternate. Good orchestration, strong rhythms, effective interpolation by Nadir about to fry.

Sombre woodwind and brass and a sombre address to the gods by Nourabad – Leila arrives: a fearless
25: *Sombres divinités* duet** by Nadir and Leila, interpolations by Noura- 25
bad and chorus. We are happy to die together they sing. This is a venturesome piece of music for Bizet particularly in Leila's contributions. But the refrain itself is solid enough and it is finally plugged out by the chorus with Leila doing some nice work above.

An unusual end to an unusual opera. Zurga frees the lovers in a welter of high-voltage recitatif. The
33: *Plus de crainte* lovers walk offstage singing their last duet** to the 33
theme of the Triangle. Strangely effective.

NOTES

The Pearl Fishers	Bizet's seventh opera (including operettas)
First night	Théâtre Lyrique, Paris, 30 September 1863

Reception	A success
Libretto	Cormon and Carré
Source	The adaptation of a similar libretto, *Les Pêcheurs de Catanes*

NEWS AND GOSSIP

Bizet was twenty-four when he was commissioned to write *Pearl Fishers* for the Théâtre Lyrique and he wrote it fast, probably in less than six months. The earlier versions had spoken dialogue in place of recitatif and there was a great to-do about the form of the ending. Even for the 1863 opening performance, several different options were tried and after that a lot of people had a shot at improving Bizet's final choice (which any good producer can make really effective and is a happy relief from the usual boom-boom-hurrah final chorus). *Pearl Fishers* had a good opening run of eighteen performances and then dropped dead, mainly because of the cranky clique of French music critics who encouraged Meyerbeer and Delibes (good) and did their best to suppress Berlioz and Bizet (bad). French musical taste in opera has always been quite dreadful and remains so today. The fact that of Bizet's thirty operatic works only six are still available in a performing version is a national disgrace.

Despite the French, *Pearl Fishers* has climbed into the affections of the international opera public and is now more or less a repertory work. And, to be fair, it did have some circulation in provincial France in the second half of last century.

COMMENT

Pearl Fishers is one of the two most underestimated operas in this book (the other: *Adriana Lecouvreur*).It is a young fellow's opera, just past being a student and not yet an *homme sérieux*. Thus, although the patches of high emotion (terror, love, guilt, etc.) are all mightily effective, they are not yet deeply felt. Perhaps this is a good thing, because the story is quite clearly in the realms of the science fiction of its day and not homely stuff about people who live do and say like us, the members of the audience. Nevertheless, the writers did a good job, for the libretto is simple, fast, clear and in its incredible way quite believable. Also original, because there are not many operas hung on an *amour à trois* such as this one. Zurga loves Leila. Nadir loves Leila. Leila loves Nadir. Zurga, in a different sense, loves Nadir. An algebraic equation of relationships you don't meet with too often. The music is amazingly good. Bizet could write a tune. And he could make a tune work for him. The recurrent use of the theme of the Triangle maybe owes something to Wagner, maybe not. But one thing is certain, that Wagner, with all his panoply of power, could never have invented this haunting fugitive melody. Maybe its closest parallel is the 'Mates duet' in *Don Carlos*. Some of the *Pearl Fishers*' numbers are stunningly good. The Zurga/Nadir reminiscent duet in Act I, the arrival of Leila, the Nadir/Leila love duet in Act II and the finale to Act II, almost the whole of Act III Scene 1, parts of the Zurga/Leila duet in Scene 2, all of them are great operatic writing. In addition to his heaven-sent gift of melody, Bizet at twenty-four was orchestrating like a wizard, organizing his material into scenes and acts like a veteran and showing that overall grasp of form which eluded Verdi sometimes and the Russians always. These qualities make *Pearl Fishers* a very special opera.

It is still a pretty rare event, so grab any chance you may have to see it. Alpha.

Pêcheurs de perles, Les *see* Pearl Fishers, The

Pelléas et Mélisande

Romantic tragedy

Debussy

The one where Melisande lets her hair down a long way to her lover Pelleas who is killed by her husband leaving her so grief-stricken that she too dies.

CAST

Arkel, king of Allemonde	Bass
Pelleas (Pelléas), a grandson of Arkel	Tenor
Golaud, his half-brother, also a grandson of Arkel	Baritone
Genevieve (Geneviève), their mother	Contralto
Yniold, Golaud's son	Treble or soprano
Melisande (Mélisande), a young woman	Soprano
A doctor, a shepherd	

5 acts: running time 2 hrs 30 mins

STORY

Act I Sc 1 A forest

We are in the mythical kingdom of Allemonde in some indeterminate period but probably about King Arthur's time and Melisande is dabbling her hands in a fountain. Golaud comes on (lost whilst hunting). What have we here? he says: a little girl crying by the spring? He approaches. Get away she says. Let me help you he says. Get off says she. Who are you where do you come from what are you doing? he asks. Fishing for a crown that fell in the water she replies. I'll get it for you he says. Don't want it who are you anyway? she says. I'm Golaud says he. You're an ugly old man says she. What's your name? he asks. Melisande she answers. Come with me he says. No she says. Oh, come on he pleads. OK I'll come she says.

Act I Sc 2 A room in the castle

Some months later Genevieve reads a fax from Golaud to his half-brother Pelleas. Grandpa Arkel listens. I met this Melisande in the forest he says and married her. She cries a lot. Won't tell me a thing about herself. I'd like to come home and I know that Mum will be all right but Grandpa Arkel could cut up crusty. Try it out on him and if he's OK hoist a lamp on the flagstaff. I should be sailing by and if the light is there I'll make harbour. If not I'll sail on to Liverpool and never come back.

How about it Arkel? asks Genevieve. Well I had meant him to marry Tommy Dewsbury's girl says Arkel but maybe this one will be all right. He's been a good lad since his first wife died and a good father to little Yniold says Genevieve.

Pelleas comes in blubbing. My old schoolfriend Mark is dying he says can I go and visit? No says Arkel. Your dad is ill. Your brother is coming back with a new wife. Your place is here. Be sure to put that lamp up the flagstaff says Genevieve.

Act I Sc 3 In front of the castle

Genevieve and Melisande come on. It's pretty gloomy here with all them trees says Melisande. There's more light on the sea side says Genevieve. Pelleas comes on. They watch a ship leave harbour through a symbolic mist. It is the ship that brought Melisande. Pelleas says there's going to be a symbolic storm. He is going to go away. Oh dear says Melisande.

Act II Sc 1 The well of the blind men in the castle park

Pelleas and Melisande are chatting by the well of the blind men. It can restore sight. Melisande's hair tumbles down into the water. It is very long. They get it out with a landing net and chat on. Melisande's wedding ring drops in the water as the clock strikes twelve. They can't get it out. Melisande is upset. What shall we tell Golaud? she asks. The truth says Pelleas.

Act II Sc 2 A room in the castle

Golaud is in bed. As the clock struck twelve his horse knocked him off and rolled about on top of him. He is now pretty badly squashed. Melisande ministers. She starts to cry. What's the matter? asks Golaud. Nothing she says. Golaud pesters. What is it? His family being beastly? The dark and gloomy castle? Poor little Melisande. He takes her hands. Where's your wedding ring? he asks. Lost she says. Lost? he says: bloody hell where was it lost? In a cave by the sea says Melisande (a lie). Get down there at once and look for it says Golaud. But it's dark says she. Don't raise irrelevant objections says he. Get searching. Now.

Act II Sc 3 In front of a cave by the sea

Pelleas and Melisande wander about in the cave. But Pelleas didn't bring a torch. He thinks the moon will give enough light [!: Ed.]. The moon comes out. They see three sleeping beggars. They give up the phoney search.

Act III Sc 1 One of the castle's towers

Melisande sits in a window combing her hair. Pelleas appears at the bottom of the tower. Melisande you look smashing he says. What stunning hair. They chat. Melisande tries to reach down to touch his hand. Her hair falls down. There is a lot of it. He struggles in the middle of a cascade of hair. Let me go! shouts Melisande. No replies Pelleas and ties her hair to a willow tree with a reef knot. Somebody will catch us together cries Melisande. [Too damn right they will and it's Golaud: Ed.] You two are just a pair of kids says Golaud. Why don't you grow up?

Act III Sc 2 The cellars beneath the castle

Been here before Pelleas? asks Golaud. Not for some time says Pelleas. See that deep hole that smells of death? says Golaud. Yes but let's get out says Pelleas.

Act III Sc 3 A terrace outside the entrance to the vaults

Whew! that's better says Pelleas. I just about passed out down there. There's Melisande in the tower window. See here Pelleas says Golaud I know you're just kids but I'm warning you. No more hanky-panky with Melisande. Get it? We must take great care of her. She is in an interesting condition.

Act III Sc 4 In front of the castle

Golaud takes Yniold on his knee. Do Mummy and Uncle Pelleas spend much time together? he asks him. Yes says Yniold. Do they quarrel? What do they talk about? Do they talk about me and keep your fingers out of your mouth? What do they say about me and I'll give you a bow and arrows? Do they kiss? Do they send you away? Look Yniold I'm going to hold you up to look through the keyhole. Are they both there? Are they fully dressed? Has Pelleas got his trousers on? I'm scared Daddy: let me down or I'll kick your face in says Yniold.

Act IV Sc 1 A room in the castle

Pelleas tells Melisande his father (never seen or heard, Mycroft Allemonde) is better. So he can go away to visit his schoolfriend if not dead by now. He says let's meet tonight at the well. It's my last night.

Act IV Sc 2 A room in the castle

Arkel comes in and says to Melisande things are going to cheer up in the castle now Pelleas's father Mycroft is getting better. You've had a pretty dull time of it so far. And how about letting me fondle you a bit he says it does wonders for an old man. Enter Golaud with symbolic blood on his forehead. Let me wipe it off my lord says Melisande. Don't touch me says Golaud and gimme my sword. I'm not going to kill you – yet. She looks as if butter wouldn't melt in her mouth. Playing the innocent bitch. You are sexually rank and revolting. Get down on your knees. He seizes her hair and bashes her about. Stop it Golaud says Arkel. OK OK says Golaud very calmly you can sleep around as much as you like and I will then do what is customary. He exits. He must be stark out of his mind says Arkel. I don't think he is but he's certainly gone off me says Melisande.

Act IV Sc 3 The well of the blind men

Yniold tries to move a big stone in order to get at his golden ball which is stuck behind it. A flock of sheep passes. They are all weeping. Where are they going? Yniold asks the shepherd. Not back home to beddie-byes says the shepherd. You can be sure of that.

Act IV Sc 4 The same

Pelleas waits for Melisande. I must take a careful note of how she looks he thinks because I won't see her again. Melisande arrives, late. Why so late? asks Pelleas. Golaud was sleeping lightly and I got my dress caught in a mousetrap she says. I'm going away he says. I love you. So do I love you she says. Pelleas goes ecstatic for some time. They hear the rumble of the castle gates being closed. Good! says Melisande. Now we can't go back. Hark! Pelleas! There's someone in the bushes. You're getting jumpy says Pelleas. It's Golaud says Melisande. He's got a sword with him. More than I have says Pelleas. He's coming after us says Melisande. Let's have one last really good kiss. They kiss. Golaud kills Pelleas. Melisande runs away.

Act V A bedroom in the castle some months later

Her wound is so slight she can't be dying from that says the doctor. Yet we all keep our voices down that's a bad sign says Arkel. They were just innocent little children and yet I killed him says guilty Golaud. Melisande wakes up and wants some air. Who is in the room? she asks Arkel. The doctor and me says Arkel – also Golaud. Please leave us alone says

Golaud. Arkel and the doctor exit. Please forgive me Melisande says Golaud I love you. Will you tell me the truth? Were you and Pelleas just in love or did you make love? In love no more says she. Don't tell lies when you are at death's door says Golaud. It is the truth says Melisande.

Arkel and the doctor return. What have you been doing to her Golaud? asks Arkel. You will bully her to death. Melisande's mind is wandering. Arkel asks her if she would like to see the baby. What baby? she asks. Why yours says Arkel and her baby is held up in front of her.

The bedroom fills with women, the castle servants. What's going on? asks Golaud. Who said all these women could come in? Not me says the doctor. Why are you here? Golaud asks the women. No answer. Golaud wants to be alone with Melisande again but no one moves. She's awake. She's asleep. Speak quietly says Arkel the human soul likes silence when it is time for it to depart. Suddenly the servants fall on their knees. Is it over? asks Arkel. Yes – they are right says the doctor. She's gone.

Come away Golaud. Leave her in peace says Arkel. She lies there as if she were her baby's elder sister. Bring the child too. It's her turn now.

MINUTES FROM START

LOOK OUT FOR

Act I Sc 1

0 The prelude is short and opens with a plainsong-like 0
theme immediately followed by a second theme – two firm notes followed by a series of triplets – both of which are to crop up again in the body of the act. It could really be the prelude to anything and leads straight into Golaud finding Melisande at the spring.
1: *Je ne pourrais plus sortir* He addresses her in arioso* but the airs are whole- 1
tone and not whistleable. Melisande responds like a frightened wild animal (her first response is unaccompanied like many more to come) and it becomes more like recitatif. A solo oboe tells us of her grief. So they quiz on, Golaud giving a straight answer to a straight question but Melisande hopelessly evasive, e.g. when Golaud asks her 'How old are you? she replies 'I'm feeling cold.' This is symbolism.

The music rolls on, full of tiny incident, sometimes an outburst of fury from the strings sometimes a flighty pirouette from the woodwind but always the thick, rich, chorded mainstream lives a life of its own beneath the Q & A of the two characters.

10 The interlude* starts with a whirring figure in the 10
strings like a very slow flight of the bumblebee related to the triplet theme in the Prelude. Calls and cries

from the woodwind and squirming horns suppress the bee and we have a series of chords mounting to a climax with a flourish of trumpet at the end.

Act I Sc 2

12: *Voici, ce qu'il écrit*

The letter scene.* Genevieve reads Golaud's letter to Arkel. She sings almost at reading speed with a light and simple accompaniment. Arkel replies in much the same way. There are fugitive phrases of love and affection, not in the vocal parts but in the orchestra. The whole scene is quiet, hushed and makes us feel that here we have two wise and caring people dealing with bad news. 12

Act I Sc 3

Nothing much happens (except for a new melody that is to pop up a lot, usually on an oboe) as this conversation piece outside the castle walls swims calmly along.

24: *Hoé! Hisse Hoé!*

The ending is effective.* The three spectators peer through the mist at a ship leaving the harbour, we hear the sailors singing, the music gives a surge of joy as Melisande recognizes it as the ship that brought them, but this is quickly followed by a frisson of fear for its safety (force 9 gales forecast) and then, when Pelleas and Melisande are left alone we hear tender phrases from the woodwind signalling that feelings warmer than those of friendship are springing up between them. 24

Act II Sc 1

0: *Vous ne savez pas*

Pelleas and Melisande by the fountain. Her long hair and the ring fall in the water.** The music perfectly catches the mood of two people already in love when casual conversation is brushed with lovers' magic. Many points made by the words have a quick reaction from the music. But it's not mickey-mousing, it's instant illustration, usually impressionistic (except when a sweep on the harp tells us the ring is sinking). The whole scene has a gentle charm that casts a spell that is irresistible, except to the Debussy-proof. 0

6 An interlude* that speaks to us in more traditional musical language. The strings forbode, and soon the whole orchestra is telling us there is stormy weather ahead. 6

Act II Sc 2

Melisande is by Golaud's bed, not so much a duet,

10: *Ah! Ah! Tout va bien* more a musical conversation.* 10

1. Golaud tells his story. He came a cropper at twelve noon precisely and we hear some clock-chimes on the basses. Natural speech-rhythm to a descriptive musical background.

2. Melisande tends Golaud. The orchestra is all
11: *Voulez-vous boire?* tenderness and love.* 11

3. But Melisande is crying! We hear the sharpness of her grief on the oboe just as we did when she first wept by the fountain at the start of Act I. Why so sad? Golaud quizzes her over an anxious restless accom-
12: *Qu'y a-t-il Mélisande?* paniment* for a long time, ending with sweet 12
pleading phrases as he takes her hands.

4. The ring is missing! Golaud is alarmed, Melisande panics. Now, as Golaud rages, the strings whip themselves into a suppressed frenzy which dies away as Melisande goes on her unlikely mission to look for a ring that isn't there in a cave in the dark. The music fades away and the scene ends with a sense of hopelessness as Melisande weeps again to her solo oboe.

20 A calm and springlike interlude* gets the bends in 20
its final stages and warns us of terror to come.

Act II Sc 3

Pelleas does his boy scout bit about moonlight in a monologue over a very satisfactory rolling accom-
23: *Oui, c'est ici* paniment.* Melisande sees the beggars and every- 23
thing drifts away into aimlessness, especially the music. They'll come another day.

Act III Sc 1

Melisande lets her hair down. Almost unaccompanied (light strings, harp and flute only), Melisande sings like a minor-key linnet as she lowers her enor-
1: *Mes longs cheveux* mously long hair.* 1

Pelleas, to animated and then almost ecstatic noises
2: *Holà Holà* in the orchestra, sees her hair and lusts after it.* Her 2
hair falls to a downward sweep on the violins and
5: *Oh! Oh! Mes cheveux* engulfs Pelleas, who goes hair-mad.* Even though a 5
hair-fetishist, he manages to spare some attention for Melisande herself and becomes quite lyrical and loverly towards her.

Golaud anticipated by a thumping timp stumps
10 by. Children will be children he opines. And his 10
down-to-earth reaction to the spectacle of his half-

brother entangled in twenty feet of his wife's hair is remarkably cool.

11 The interlude before Scene 2* is intense, with 11
dreary tunes struggling to assert themselves. It ends quietly with a hint of menace.

Act III Sc 2

15: *Prenez-garde* The whole of this scene is played to dungeon-music.* 15
A squirming figure starts in the lower strings and bassoons and never lets up as other parts of the orchestra support it including towards the end the brass. It goes on and on and the voices do their thing separately and above it. Quite spooky.

In an interlude, Debussy gives a marvellous musical impression of escape from the claustrophobia of the dungeons into clear sunlight.

Act III Sc 3

17: *Ah ! je respire enfin !* We have two monologues,* Pelleas spotting the 17
women on the ramparts to a nice trotting rhythm and then Golaud giving him a solemn little lecture. Stop fooling around with my Melisande. Golaud's music is not so square as his character, but it is serious and less fantastical than the music of the other characters.

Act III Sc 4

Golaud and Yniold. The most effective scene of the opera.

1. Golaud starts his cross-examination coolly
22: *Viens, nous allons nous asseoir ici* enough. His opening questions are ingratiating. 22
Yniold replies briefly in a clear treble. An excellent child witness.

2. But when we get to the matter of the closed
23: *A propos de la porte* door, Golaud's jealousy begins to smoulder.* The 23
orchestration gets deep and dark, the phrases rough. He boils over. He is like a blind man groping for evidence. But he still tries to soften up Yniold with bows and arrows and buttery legato phrases in the strings.

27: *Rien, rien, mon enfant* 3. The enquiry about kissing* excites them both: 27
Yniold demonstrates how they kiss by kissing his father on the lips.

29: *Ne fait pas de bruit* 4. So things go on until Yniold is held up to do his 29
stuff as a Peeping Tom. The strings go pumping on with the triplet figure rising higher and higher. Golaud pushes things too far. He is in a frenzy. High tension. Yniold doesn't quite scream but God knows

how the couple in the bedroom don't hear the frightful shindy going on just outside the window.

Act IV Sc 1

Act IV Sc 2

After a hurried meeting between Pelleas and Melisande, given a surreptitious air by the music, some sweet strains bring on Arkel and the longest mono-

3: *Maintenant que le père de Pelléas*

logue in the opera.** He tenderly says how sorry he is 3
that Melisande had to live in a house of death for so long and now seeks to kiss her. This speech has all manner of short but lovely lyrical phrases breaking out around it from the orchestra which is quite clearly on his side.

Golaud enters in an ugly mood. He asks Melisande

9: *Eh bien, mon épée?*

for his sword,* roughly. Great gouts of bile surge up 9
inside him and we can hear them surging throughout the orchestra. He gets physical, seizing Melisande by the hair. The orchestra is as agitato as we are. Really rough stuff.

13: *Vous ferez comme il vous plaira*

Arkel calms him down.* He is like a man after an 13
epileptic fit. Trembling, abashed. Soft horn chords. Maybe he did have an epileptic fit. Is he drunk? asks Arkel. No, says Melisande but his love for me is dead. There is calm after the orchestral storm. We don't just listen to this scene, we feel along with it.

14

This interlude makes a mark. A noble tune* (a 14
variant of the triplets) builds to a huge climax, it slows and quietens with a touch of the oboe only to blow up once again. One wonders why it goes on like this: it must have some programme of which we know nothing.

Act IV Sc 3

Yniold tries to move a boulder to get at his lost golden

19: *Oh! Cette pierre est lourde*

ball.* The orchestra makes pushy noises. A flock of 19
sheep go by. The orchestra makes bustling noises. But they are going to the abattoir. Yniold sings innocently. This little diversion is really effective.

Act IV Sc 4

23: *C'est le dernier soir*

The final duet.* 23

1. Pelleas waits for Melisande. Is she coming or is she not? Many fleeting thoughts. Agitated.

2. Melisande arrives. Breathless exchanges. Why she is late? Suddenly the uneasy orchestra relaxes

into love music. This is their last meeting. They exchange unaccompanied messages of love.

28: *On dirait que ta voix* 3. Pelleas sings something quite near to an aria.** 28
It starts sweetly, full of gentle love but moves into passion. He has found his ideal. The orchestra fades away.

4. The castle gates close with a sound like a clap of thunder (timps bassoons and lower strings). The die is cast. They are on their own. Hooray! But wait.

5. Someone is around. Golaud. Nervous and hushed at first, they overcome their fear and the or-
34: *Il ne sait pas que nous l'avons vu* chestra builds to a great climax** as they fling them- 34
selves into a passionate clinch. Golaud jumps out and kills Pelleas very quickly. The act ends with a bang bang on the timp.

Act V

0 The act opens with a lightly scored introduction* 0
(violas and harp) which ticks like a clock. There are some sensible exchanges between the doctor, Golaud and Arkel. Melisande wakes and wants the window
3: *Ouvrez la fenêtre* open.* She is out of her delirium. Arkel points out 3
that everyone is talking in the hushed tones suitable for a terminal ward. The orchestra too shows restraint: fragile, beautiful music.

8: *Mélisande, as-tu pitié* Melisande and Golaud alone. Fraught exchanges.* 8
Golaud demands the truth. Melisande tells it in short sweet replies over a flute and harp accompaniment. Golaud will not believe that she and Pelleas did not make love. We only were in love she says. Golaud gives up.

Arkel and Melisande. He gives affectionate
13: *Qu'avez-vous fait?* answers to Melisande's fairly scatty questions.* Does 13
she want to see her baby? The words take the lead over the music which is light and supportive.

The solemn servants tramp in over pizzicato strings. The guilty Golaud wants to put things right between Melisande and himself. A flurry – raised voices, the orchestra leaps out of the background.

17: *Attention, attention* Melisande's death.*** Hush. Arkel asks that her 17
soul be allowed to depart privately and in silence, quietly accompanied by high strings and a trumpet with both the triplet theme and the oboe tune in evidence. The servants fall on their knees. Echoing

pizzicato chords, very eerie. They're right says the doctor, she's gone. Arkel delivers his epilogue supported by a sorrowful orchestra which, after his last words, lets the opera slip away to a background of high strings and harp. This last scene carries with it a sense of the reality of death that has rarely been caught in opera. It is masterly.

NOTES

Pelléas et Mélisande	Debussy's only performed opera
First night	Opéra-Comique, Paris, 30 April 1902
Reception	Mixed. See below
Libretto	Debussy
Source	A play by Maeterlinck

NEWS AND GOSSIP

Debussy saw Maeterlinck's play *Pelléas* in 1893 and it evidently reached parts of him that no other literary work had reached before. He was stunned. All other work in the pipeline was gazumped whilst he worked on the score and the libretto. He cut and cut again at the play and his judgement was good for there can have been few first-time opera composers who have come up with such a good libretto which was all their own work. By 1895 he had pretty well finished *Pelléas* in short score (that is on two staves with ideas for orchestration in coloured ink) but didn't get it accepted by the Opéra-Comique for three years. Then a wait of another four years for performance. Opera schedules moved no faster in those days than they do today. In rehearsal it was found, amongst other things, that the interludes did not run long enough to cover the scene changes so Debussy, much against the grain, had to write them longer. It is not hard to imagine the effect on Debussy's nerves of a nine-year wait followed by two months of turmoil. But even the most symbolic opera has to meet the practicalities of production, so his carefully polished masterpiece had to be messed about to meet the needs of the Opéra. He was not happy.

The first night divided the critics. The literary scribes found it 'sickly', 'lifeless' and didn't like the 'impressionism' of the work. The composer Paul Dukas liked it, saying that 'each bar exactly corresponded to the scene it portrayed', and d'Indy, the grand old man of French musical life, thought it was just great.

Pelléas soon caught on. Its beauty and power won through over the strangeness of its form and of its music. It became a standard in the

French rep. for most of the first half of this century and is now played regularly by all major opera houses.

COMMENT

It is hard to race-read any opera in a meaningful way, but with *Pelléas* it is pretty well impossible. Part of the reason is that Debussy uses a foreign musical language. While the general impression of his music is easy on the ear and nice to listen to, most of the grammar and syntax is difficult if not impossible to describe because he is working in an unknown territory with modes, whole tones and the like instead of the good old diatonic scale which had served music so well for over two hundred years. As with dogs who can hear high frequency sounds inaudible to humans, so learned musician can hear the set of mottos that Debussy uses in *Pelléas*. Most of us can't. There are personal mottos for Golaud and Melisande for sure, others less certain. There is a motto for the forest, but no, maybe it's not the forest, it's timelessness. Even if you can hear these mottos, it is not easy to describe them in prose without getting into a thicket of ten-syllable words. *Pelléas* is a score of enormous subtlety. Words, phrases, thoughts are reflected with instant sensibility. We don't often catch this because the idiom is so strange. As the Chinaman said, all whites look alike to me. Any ten bars of *Pelléas* could be transposed for any other ten bars, said one musical right-winger, and you wouldn't notice. Which is nonsense, of course, but with a grain of truth in that to most people Debussy's range of emotion sounds as if it stretches no further than from A to B, A being pleasant, soft après-midi music and the B being agitated, angry, frightened.

It is fair to say that Debussy can be so impressionistic that it is hard to know what the impression is meant to mean, which is fine for concert music but not so hot when you are telling a story. The Debussyan blur can be rather like a late Turner. You can't easily tell whether it's a train crossing the Tay bridge or the Fighting Téméraire.

Quite apart from the musical language, Debussy uses an entirely new form for his opera. There are no numbers. The orchestra plays a main part. Some scenes are like orchestral tone poems with the voices playing the part of additional instruments. The words are mostly in monologue or conversation. There is no chorus. There are no ensembles. There is practically no singing in the operatic sense. The words are usually declaimed or spoken. At the centre of the stage is the *décor orchestral*, or the orchestral setting. But alas it's not on the stage at all, it's in the pit and you can't see it. So the main protagonist, as with Wagner, is impersonal and invisible and the figures on the stage are diminished to accessories accompanying the fact of opera.

Behind Debussy's music lies the strength and beauty of Maeterlinck's play. This has poetic imagination of rare quality, the story itself, both so much more delicate and more moving than that of *Tristan*, the business of darkness and light better managed, the characters as vivid as can be, symbolic touches – the ring, the sheep, the misty boat, the hair – always a true poetic vision and neither twee nor silly-whimsical. You are never for one moment embarrassed by the symbolism of *Pelléas* nor do you have the slightest inclination to sneer. The death scene is unique in opera.

There is no other opera like *Pelléas*. Most people catch a little of its magic, some people are bowled over. At the very least you can sit back and listen to the wonderfully mellifluous score, the sonorous orchestration, the constant fresh flights of fancy by woodwind instruments, the refreshing new noises he makes by working in a novel tonal system. And having let these sounds sweep over you for four acts, you will find in the fifth that Melisande's story suddenly has you by the throat and that the dignity, pathos and dramatic mastery of the last scene will leave you with that sense of having been hit in the solar plexus that is the desideratum of every opera buff. An alpha.

Porgy and Bess

American folk opera

Gershwin

The one where the cripple Porgy wins Bess away from the macho-man Crown only to lose her to the bright lights and drug scene of New York.

CAST

Porgy, a crippled beggar	Bass–baritone
Bess, a girl	Soprano
Crown, a stevedore and macho-man	Baritone
Sportin' Life, a dope pedler and smart guy	Tenor
Robbins, a man	Tenor
Serena, Robbins's wife	Soprano
Jake, a fisherman	Baritone
Clara, Jake's wife	Soprano
Maria, boss of the cook shop	Contralto

Other Catfish Row persons, **Jim, Peter, Lily, Nelson, Annie Scipio** (a boy), **Frazier** (a phoney lawyer), a **policeman, Mr Archdale** (a rich white) and not forgetting **Jasbo Brown,** jazz pianist

3 acts: running time 3 hrs 15 mins

STORY

Act I Sc 1 An open court in Catfish Row

We are in the midst of what when the opera was written was still called the Negro quarter but which today is known as the black community. The Catfish Rowers make their living mainly by fishing and the sea is only just offstage. Jasbo Brown is playing a blues number and some Catfishers dance. Clara sings a lullaby to her baby. There is a crap game about to start. Sportin' Life has his own bones (dice) but they are known to be fixed. The crap school builds up. Porgy arrives in his goat-cart and joins the school. They think it best to wait for Crown who is on his way ('takin' the whole sidewalk').

Crown arrives with Bess. He takes a long swig from Sportin' Life's flask. So does Bess (and scandalizes the ladies of Catfish Row). The crap game starts. It is interrupted by a good deal of singing about the nature of woman from which it is clear that the respectable Catfish Rowers think Bess is a tramp.

The crap game gets serious. Crown is almost too drunk to read the bones. Porgy craps out. Robbins craps out but Crown won't let him take his money. They fight. Crown kills Robbins with a cotton hook. Panic. Serena flings herself on the body. Everyone slinks off. Bess tells Crown he'd better get off quick before the police arrive. Crown says OK but whichever man may pick you up when I'm away I'll come back to claim you back. Sportin' Life sneaks up and gives Bess what he thinks she most needs, a sniff of Happy Dust. Come with me to New York Bess he says. I haven't sunk as low as that yet says Bess. Sportin' Life exits. Bess knocks on one door then another. Nobody will let her in. She knocks on Porgy's. He takes her in.

Act I Sc 2 Serena's room. Robbins's body on the bed

The room is full of Catfishers singing a spiritual. There is a saucer for money for the funeral, not yet enough. Porgy and Bess come in. Bess offers money. Serena says she doesn't want her money. Bess says Porgy gave her the money. Serena accepts it. The saucer now holds 14 dollars and 50 cents. There is a good deal of confidence that the Lawd assisted by Jesus will make sure that there is enough money in the saucer. A detective and a policeman come in. The detective picks on Peter. You done it I know you done it he says. Not me boss says Peter, Crown done it. I seen him. What about you Porgy says the detective. You seen it? I seen nuttin' says Porgy. OK says the detective we'll take old Peter along until we catch Crown. Exit the law.

That villain Crown runs free and they lock up poor old Peter says Porgy. That's Life. There is some choral mourning for Robbins. The undertaker arrives. Can't bury him for fifteen dollars says he. He'll have to go to be chopped up by the medical students. O Gawd no, please! says Serena. OK I'll do it at a loss says the friendly liberal undertaker. Everyone is pretty pleased with this and they now (chorally) set about taking their tickets for the promised land.

Act II Sc 1 Catfish Row as in Act I

Jake is going fishing and it's going to be a long pull to get there (huh!) and surprisingly he plans to drop anchor not in the Blackfish Banks but in the Promised Land. Clara reminds Jake that the September storms can be bad around Blackfish Banks. Annie reminds everyone that the ETD for the picnic on Kittewah Island is 10 a.m. Porgy who has plenty of nuttin' is happy. What he has got is his gal. Sportin' Life comes on and meets his match in Maria who blows away his Happy Dust and tells him to get lost and stay away from Catfish Row.

Frazier the phoney lawyer comes on and offers Porgy to divorce Bess from Crown for a dollar. It transpires Bess was never married to Crown. Then it will cost 1 dollar 50 says Frazier. Mr Archdale comes on to tell Porgy he is standing bail for Peter who will be released at once. He gets into the divorce debate and sends Frazier packing. A buzzard buzzards overhead. This is a bad sign. Porgy and chorus tell it to keep on flying for if it lands on any house it brings death.

Sportin' Life makes another pass at Bess with promises of Happy Dust and life in New York. Porgy chases him off. He tells Bess she is his woman now. Bess tells Porgy he is her man. The picnic crowd sing a holiday chorus. Bess says she ain't goin'. Porgy persuades her to go. She goes.

Act II Sc 2 On Kittiwah Island

The picnickers sing and dance. Sportin' Life questions the veracity of certain passages in the Bible. Serena a Christian fundamentalist breaks in scandalized by this show of godlessness and tells them the boat is just going. They go, all but Bess. Enter Crown. Glad to see you says Crown. Got any Happy Dust? I'm a clean living gal now says Bess and I'm going back to the boat now. Damn the boat says Crown I'll be leaving here in a couple of weeks and we'll go off together. Who are you living with now? Porgy says Bess. Ho ho ho says Crown. I'm living decent with him and I want to go on living with him and there are plenty of other women you can get says Bess. No cripple's going to take my girl away from me says Crown. You ain't leaving. He kisses her. Get off says Bess, weakly. Get into that thicket says Crown. She gets.

Act II Sc 3 Catfish Row

Jake is warned that the Met say there will be a storm. He musters his crew for the long pull (huh!) and they set off for the Blackfish Bank/Promised Land. Bess is sick. Serena says her prayers will save anyone. She leads a community prayer to Doctor Jesus. Street vendors vend strawberries, honey and crabs. Bess recovers [Dr Jesus having had just time enough – five minutes – to diagnose and treat her ailment: Ed.]. How long have I been sick? she asks. Over a week says Porgy. I know you've been with Crown. How are things between you? He says he's coming to take me away says Bess. And you'll go? asks Porgy. Yes I will says Bess I'm not worthy of you. But it's you I love. OK says Porgy stay with me. Just you leave Crown to me. Clara and Maria discuss the weather. It begins to blow up as they speak.

Act II Sc 4

So Met were right. It's a terrible storm and most of the citizens of Catfish Row are in Serena's room as usual imploring the Lawd to do what they want which is a variety of things (to be lifted to the bosom of Dr Jesus, to be led into the Golden Meadows, to have Professor Jesus give some orders to his Met office, for Captain Jesus to make sure they will continue to live sweetly etc.). Bess and Porgy think smugly that no one could survive on Kittiwah Island in a storm like this – but there's someone knocking at the door and it is not Dr Jesus, Professor Jesus nor Captain Jesus nor Death itself but Crown.

I've come for Bess he says. You're not my man says Bess. I'm Porgy's. Are there no whole men left? says Crown and seizes Bess. Porgy interposes. Crown knocks him flat. Everyone prays. Crown mocks them. He sings an irrelevant song about a red-headed woman. Through the window Bess sees Jake's boat floating upside down. Clara rushes out. Crown says he will go out and get Clara and then he will come back for Bess. No you won't says Porgy. All right, see you on another day says Crown. Exits. Clara does not return. Everyone immediately addresses their attention again to Doctor, Professor and Captain Jesus.

Act III Sc 1 Catfish Row. The storm is over. Dusk

The citizens tell the dead Clara not to be downhearted for Jesus is walkin' on the water [more than Jake could manage: Ed.]. Sportin' Life lurks around looking for Bess. Maria chases him off. Bess sings Clara's lullaby to her baby. The citizens turn in for the night. Crown creeps on and crawls to Porgy's door. Porgy reaches out and knifes him in the back. They fight. Porgy throttles him and chucks his body into centre stage. Bess, he shouts, you got a man now.

Act III Sc 2 The same

The detective comes on. He quizzes Serena Robbins as the prime suspect. She has an alibi. He gets Porgy and Bess out and asks Porgy if he knows Crown by sight. Yes Porgy does. Then Porgy must come along to identify the body. Oh no! cries Porgy I couldn't look on that face again. You got to says the detective. No says Porgy. OK I'll send a cop round to pick you up says the detective. Porgy you got to go says Bess. Two cops arrive and pick Porgy up.

Sportin' Life sidles up to Bess. They'll lock him up for at least a year maybe three says Sportin' Life. What you need is some Happy Dust. Bess says no, then yes. There's a boat leaving soon for New York he says.

Come and live it up there with me Bess. Have another shot. Get off you rattlesnake she cries. OK he says I'll leave some of the stuff here in case you change your mind.

Act III Sc 3 The same

It's good mornings all round. Everyone merry and bright until Porgy is brought back in a patrolwagon. The reception committee is uneasy. He tells them he refused to look at Crown and was sent down for contempt. Now he's back with a surprise for Bess and presents all round. He cleaned up at the jailhouse crap game. A big build up for the Porgy/Bess reunion. He crawls to his door. No Bess. Where is Bess? Is she dead? Tell me quick where is Bess? They tell him, but not quick. Bess has gone off to New York with Sportin' Life. Where's New York? asks Porgy. A thousand miles away to the north past the Customs House they say. Bring me my goat-cart says Porgy. I'm off to New York. He addresses the Almighty Oh Lawd he says I'm on my way. He's on his way sings everyone and he certainly is on his way. He is goat-carted off upstage and the curtain falls. But how far he got we shall never know.

MINUTES FROM START LOOK OUT FOR

Act I Sc 1

0 A *Rhapsody-in-Blue*-ish flourish* with the Doo-de-dah-doh rhythm in the brass choir and the curtain is up and we are listening to Jasbo Brown rendering the same piece on a honky-tonk piano whilst citizens of Catfish Row dance dreamily around intoning both a Da-doo-da and also a Wa Wa which gets louder and louder. And louder. Then stops. 0

4: *Summertime* Summertime.*** Gershwin's most inspired melody and one of the greatest numbers of all time. 4

8: *Roll dem bones* A crap game spiritual,** followed by some roustabout stuff leading to a reprise of Summertime floating above the crap game, now in progress. 8

14: *A woman is a sometime thing* It is Jake's view that men are more reliable parents than women.** 14

17: *Here come de honey man* Look out for the first street-seller music.* More to come later. 17

18: *You Scipio! Here comes Porgy* Look out for Porgy's entrance and Porgy's music.* 18
Porgy tells us what it's like to be a cripple.* Gershwin melodious, sentimental. 21

21: *No, no, brudder* Reprise of A Woman is a Sometime Thing.* 25

25 The crap game ends in a fight. The ensemble

32: *Oh, stop them!* works up to a rowdy climax* (the orchestra alone is 32
fugal and not so pugnacious).

Act I Sc 2

38: *Where is brudder Robbins?* Requiem for brudder Robbins.** Not a spiritual this 38
time nor is it jazz. It's Gershwin going straight and it is truly moving with its refrain 'Gone Gone Gone' leading to the final chorus 'Overflow, Overflow'.

48: *My man's gone now* Serena keens for her man** and is comforted by 48
the citizens. A pure melody that picks up a limping rhythm as it goes on towards a show-stopping climax.

54: *Oh, the train is at the station* The Promised Land.** First Bess in a fairly four- 54
square set of verses plus chorus, then a whispered chorus, unaccompanied, and finally the works, Bess, chorus and orchestra stomping it out fortissimo with cross-rhythms. Train noises an added bonus.

Act II Sc 1

1: *Oh, I'm agoin' out* A long pull.*** Like the Volga boat song this has all 1
the surge and flow of a traditional worksong and its own special punctuation. Huh!

One of the numbers that has had a prosperous life
4: *Oh, I got plenty o' nuttin'* outside of the show.*** The steady oom-pah (banjo) 4
accompaniment and breaks from the solo instruments help it along. But it is the tune itself that is the star.

7: *I hates yo' struttin' style* Maria takes on Sportin' Life in a jog trot number* 7
set to a gem of a lyric.

9: *Mornin', Lawyer* The recitatif scene** concerning the lawyer Fra- 9
zier's visit is classy stuff especially the piano breaks and the wandering Porgy music. The short sharp bursts from the chorus work a treat too.

The buzzard song. Something more operatic. It
17: *Buzzard keep on flyin'* comes off but only just.* The chorus helps to give it a 17
little buzz.

20: *Picnics is all right* Sportin' Life, persuasive, has a fetching style and a 20
tune in whose mouth butter would not melt.*

23: *Bess, you is my woman now* Porgy and Bess's love duet.*** The most original 23
number in the piece and perhaps the best. The tune is a version of *the* Gershwin tune to be found also in the piano concerto and *Rhapsody in Blue* but this is by far its best appearance. Look out particularly for the lovely two-part writing as they sing together. This number can stand against any love duet in opera.

29: *Oh, I can't sit down* An up-beat pre-picnic number* followed by the 29
emotionally fraught coda, Bess's loving goodbye to

Porgy and Porgy's reprise of Plenty of Nuttin'. But he's got his girl. (He thinks.)

Act II Sc 2

After perhaps the Catfishers' weakest chorus we have
36: *It ain't necessarily so* — another of the great numbers*** that were to become 36
standards worldwide. It's not only the number itself nor the lyric that catches the fancy but the way both of them turn upside down the usual sweet smiling faith in holy writ typical of most spirituals.

47: *Oh, what you want wid Bess?* — Bess tells Crown to get another girl.* Crown says 47
no. This number has a galumphing accompaniment that sounds quite ornery until we get to the climax of the duet when it turns menacing. Crown is not a nice person at all. Quite frightening in fact.

Act II Sc 3

59: *Oh dey's so fresh and fine* — The Street Vendors.*** The action stops and we 59
have one of the most telling strokes in the piece. Over a pedal bass the strawberry lady spins out her high song with its uppity end phrase. Next Peter the honey man, last the crab man with his hiccuppy call. Still the pedal bass.

67: *I wants to stay here* — Bess and Porgy's second big duet.* Bess wants to 67
stay but Crown will take her. A lovely opening melody for Bess but not such a big event as duet no. 1.

Act II Sc 4

75: *Oh de Lawd shake de Heavens* — The storm starts in the orchestra.* Panic in Serena's 75
(very crowded) room. Four solo prayers combine over a confused choral/orchestral backing but everything comes together with the happy spiritual chorus** 'An' where you goin' stand'. Followed by good show-business thunder and lightning.

Clara tells her baby it will go to heaven to a reprise of Summertime, Porgy and Bess confer, the chorus goes spiritualling on, the wind whistles and we are
79: *Oh, dere's somebody knockin' at de do'!* — onto the next great invention:** 'Somebody Knock- 79
ing at the Door' with a lot of freelance shouts and suggestions from those within. (It's Crown of course.)

83: *You is a nice parcel of Christians!* — The finale:** the temperature rises as Crown 83
storms in, sings romantically to Bess and defiantly to everyone else including God whilst the chorus plays along with 'An' where you goin' stan', my brudder?'.
87: *A red-headed woman* — Crown tells us that no woman can make a fool of him
in an upbeat number** with chorus and clarinet 87

breaks pushing it along. Clara runs out. Crown delivers some majestic recitatif and goes out to save her. Prayers again, as at the beginning of the scene. Mighty powerful stuff.

Act III Sc 1

A short prelude in Gershwin's Modern Music mode
leads us nicely to the chorus of comfort for Clara. It
starts still as Modern Music but it swerves into an-
1: *Jesus is walkin'* other lovely spiritual.** Played out with a nice flute 1
on the water obbligato.
6: *Summertime* The second reprise of Summertime*** (this time 6
sung by Bess) and if ever a number deserved two repeats it's this one. Then (maximum contrast) the very
noisy fight and death of Crown.

Act III Sc 2

After Porgy has been carted off by the law and Bess
succumbs to Happy Dust, Sportin' Life swings into
11: *There's a boat* his swanky show-business number** which surely 11
dat's leavin' has enough charm to persuade a lot of girls seriously
soon to consider taking the train to New York. A big flashy
orchestral end-piece.

Act III Sc 3

The prelude opens with Gershwin in his piano prel-
14 udes mode.** Very beguiling. He gives the flute al- 14
most a concerto role. But it grows into something
nearer to a Broadway intro and leads into the cheery
17: *Good mornin'* Good Morning chorus** with its catchy cross- 17
Sistuh! rhythms.
Porgy's return, very happy, poor sod. Reprise of
22: *Now dat's de* Plenty of Nuttin'** to new words. 22
style for my Bess A reprise of the first love duet as Porgy senses
something is wrong. Suddenly he gets really scared
27: *Bess, Oh,* and we are into the final trio:** Porgy (Where is 27
Lawd, my Bess! Bess?), Maria (She's gone off with Sportin' Life),
Serena (You're better off without her). The three
voices twist and weave together as Porgy slowly gets
the message. It's an original way of resolving a plot
and it comes off in truly operatic style.
So we slip into fairyland as Porgy demands his
goat-cart and sets off for New York. And we end with
31: *I'm on my way* the showbusiness number I'm on my way.* 31

NOTES

Porgy and Bess	Gershwin's only full-length opera
First night	Colonial Theatre, Boston, 30 September 1935
Reception	On balance, favourable but many Doubting Thomases
Libretto	Heyward and Ira Gershwin
Source	See below

NEWS AND GOSSIP

At some date in the 1920s a black American named Goatcart Sammy murdered a woman and was pursued by the police who, being provided with Cadillacs, not surprisingly overtook the goat-cart and put him in jail. This story caught the fancy of one DuBose Heyward who put it into a novel called *Porgy*. This caught the fancy of George Gershwin when he was touring in 1926 with one of his earliest and best musicals, *Oh, Kay*!. He wrote to Heyward suggesting an opera. Heyward put him off because he was dramatizing the book for Broadway. The play was a hit and in 1932 Gershwin propositioned Heyward again. He saw in *Porgy* a chance to write an opera where he could find the middle ground between classical music and American jazz, one of his lifelong desires and by now a fixation. The deal was done; Heyward was to do the libretto working along with George's brother Ira, widely known as a top-class lyricist.

George put in a lot of homework living on an island off Charleston, South Carolina, studying a community of Gullah negroes whose music was thought to be the nearest thing to the real McCoy in the matter of spirituals, 'shouting' etc. He wrote the opera in twenty months. The piano score was entirely his own work but how much of the orchestration he did himself has always been a bit of a mystery. (One Will Vodery had orchestrated his early one-act opera *Blue Monday* and Paul Whiteman had certainly had a hand in some of the orchestral pieces, notably the piano concerto.) The Gershwin brothers were the impresarios as well as the creators of *Porgy* and they took great pains to audition and select their all-coloured cast. Todd Duncan got the role of Porgy and was to sing the hit numbers all over the world for the next forty years (perhaps just a little too long). After the out-of-town run the show had its real first night in the Alvin Theatre, New York on 10 October 1935. It ran for 124 performances – not enough to recoup the investment on a Broadway musical but surely a candidate for the *Guinness Book of Records* as an opening run of consecutive performances of a new opera. It was not a hit. Well liked by some, musically pretentious and politically Uncle Tom to others, it faded from the scene until it was revived by Merle Armitage in 1938 and again by Cheryl Crawford in the early 1940s when most of the recitatif was replaced by spoken dialogue. There was a hugely successful production in 1952 which starred Leontyne Price and toured America and Europe (Milan, Leningrad, London) but it was not until the 1980s that opera managements took *Porgy* seriously. Houston and then the Met revived it in the 1980s and in 1986 it was given perhaps its first musically sensitive and dramatically slap-up production by Glyndebourne which then transferred to Covent Garden. At last *Porgy* was respectable, *Porgy* was an opera, *Porgy* was a hit.

COMMENT

Porgy gave the twentieth century some of its all-time standards ('Summertime', 'I got plenty of nuttin' ', 'It ain't necessarily so' etc.) but it is more than a 'numbers' opera and more than a play set to music. There are sequences – the ending to Scene 1 of Act II ('Bess you is my woman now') and the whole of Act II Scene 4 (the storm scene in Serena's room) – where *Porgy* has lift-off into true opera. The recitatifs are no worse than many of the early Mozarts, except that they are all accompagnato and although Gershwin motors along pretty well for most of the time, there are some stretches where he runs out of gas, as, for example, when Sportin' Life makes his first pass at Bess at the end of Act I Scene 1 and when Bess encounters Crown on Kittiwah Island in Act II Scene 2. Although there are good stretches Gershwin didn't always get his recitatifs right. They are full of ear-catching and distracting scraps of melody which don't grow big enough to be satisfying and get in the way of putting the message across quickly and clearly. The old secco recitatifs pattered out the story at a rate of knots, Gershwin's sometimes wallow about as if the engine had stopped. They are also enormously repetitive and bits of *Rhapsody in Blue* and the piano concerto keep popping up. All of this makes you wonder whether it wasn't a good idea to turn the opera into a *Singspiel* by replacing the recitatifs with spoken dialogue as in the Cheryl Crawford production in the early 1940s. But on balance it is surely better to leave the recitatifs in because they keep us continuously in Gershwin-land and it is sort of essential to the opera to hear His Master's Voice all the time. Also the impact of the white men who can only speak and not sing (a really telling stroke) would be lost.

Porgy's strengths lie in the stunning quality not only of George's numbers but also of Ira's lyrics. Never before or since has the wonderful but almost unsingable English language been handled better, except possibly by Dryden for Purcell or Gilbert for Sullivan – and neither of *them* ever did anything so neat as Ira's description of Jonah's domestic situation when

'he made his home in
that fish's abdomen'.

Many of the lyrics have the appeal of nursery rhymes or folk poetry – 'Summertime', 'I'm on my way', 'Dere's somebody knockin' at de do' ', 'An' where you goin' stand' etc. – all of them do something to stir some nostalgic part of the human spirit.

All in all the book for *Porgy* is excellent but for two things, the cop-out ending, and its length. As to the first, De Sica had much the same problem in his film *Miracle in Milan* when the only solution he could find to a verismo story was to have the poor people of the streets turn into angels and fly into the never-never over Milan cathedral. Similarly, Porgy's departure for New York in his goat-cart, although it may draw a furtive tear, is a terrible chickening out from verismo and so does serious damage to the credibility of the story.

From time to time *Porgy* has been found to be politically incorrect, Uncle Tom or just patronizing to the black community of Catfish Row. The same charges can be laid against dozens of operas, plays and films made in times before we were taught to be more politically wary. Although *Così* may be passionately condemned by today's feminists and the two Negroes in *Ballo* turned into Mafiosi by tender-hearted producers, it is of course a lapse in common sense for anyone today to think that a composer or writer could possibly foresee that political correctness would come to make him seem an unfeeling brute. It is as silly to condemn Mozart for male chauvinism as it is to grumble about Jesus Christ having no female disciples or to blackguard Shakespeare for inventing Shylock. There were many folk plays and films following the Uncle Tom tradition – *Green Pastures*, *Cabin in the Sky* – which were made by good-hearted sympathizers with the black cause who were only seen to be politically ignorant when the black community itself became politically aware. Gershwin was on the side of the Catfish Rowers just as John Steinbeck was on the side of the Cannery Rowers – if both were politically naive then too bad. Maybe in the fullness of time Political Correctness will be seen to be just as silly as the Chauvinists are now seen to be clearly wrong.

Gershwin hoped that *Porgy* would combine 'the drama of *Carmen* with the beauty of *Meistersinger*'. Some hope. But musically he was not so pretentious, sticking pretty well to his own kind of stuff – liberated jazz – and making it work operatically as well as could be. The leading characters have, if not leitmotifs, their own personal musical labels. There are also passages in his own Modern Music style which are tremendously effective, such as the street vendor scene – a moment of magic – as well as the Act III preludes to Scene 1 and Scene 3. It is this sort of thing that helps to move *Porgy* away from the world of musical plays and towards real opera.

If *Porgy* were half an hour shorter it would send the audience home in an even happier mood. But it is a hard work to cut, for the bits that are musically weakest cover the most important sections of the plot and the places where we pause and have a bit of a rest (e.g. the street vendors scene mentioned above) are musically amongst the best bits. But for all its length, its occasional lapses and its narrowish range of musical expression, *Porgy* is something entirely different, an event and a great night in the theatre. Undoubtedly an alpha.

I Puritani

Historical romance

(The Puritans)

Bellini

The one where the Puritan bride goes mad when her Cavalier bridegroom stands her up in order to save the life of a royal Royalist.

CAST

Protestants:	**Lord Walton (Valton),** Governor of Plymouth Castle	Bass
	Sir George (Giorgio), Walton's brother, retired colonel	Bass
	Elvira, Walton's daughter	Soprano
	Sir Richard Forth (Riccardo), colonel in Cromwell's army	Baritone
	Sir Bruno Robertson (Bruno), captain in Cromwell's army	Tenor
Catholics:	**Lord Arthur Talbot (Arturo),** Cavalier officer	Tenor
	Queen Henrietta Maria (Enrichetta), widow of Charles I	Mezzo

3 acts, 2 intervals: running time 2 hrs 20 mins

STORY

Act I Three scenes in and around a seventeenth-century English castle

We are in Plymouth Castle and it is pretty near to the end of the Civil War. Puritan Elvira is pledged to marry Puritan Richard but loves Catholic Arthur. Friendly Uncle George tells Elvira's father that if he forces a Puritan marriage on Elvira she will certainly die for love of Arthur. Father relents, Arthur is delighted, Richard not so pleased. All assemble for the wedding. Amongst the wedding gifts a bridal veil is prominent.

A new character appears: no Puritan she but Henrietta widow of Charles I, apparently allowed out for the wedding as a final treat before decapitation. Arthur's Cavalierly chivalry is aroused: when the wedding veil is playfully placed on Henrietta's head Arthur carries her off thus thinly disguised through the guards to safety.

The wedding party assembles, but no bridegroom. Elvira, deprived of her intended, begins to go mad. Everyone deplores this sad turn of events.

Act II Interior: Plymouth Castle

Elvira is now quite mad. Richard swears vengeance on Arthur. George, the great persuader, tries to induce Richard to forgive Arthur: he succeeds on the grounds that Arthur's return will be beneficial to Elvira's mental health.

Act III A garden near Plymouth Castle

Arthur returns three months later (what *was* he doing?). He lurks outside Elvira's residence: sees her walking about quite mad. Arthur then has a dangerous game of hide-and-seek with some Puritan soldiers. Elvira appears again: Arthur explains all and declares his everlasting love: Elvira is restored to sanity. Puritan troops arrive and seize Arthur. Decapitation looms. Elvira goes mad again. But hark! – a herald approaches. The Stuarts are defeated: a (surprisingly) magnanimous Cromwell pardons all top Cavaliers, including Arthur. Universal rejoicing especially by Elvira, now as sane as sane can be.

MINUTES FROM START

LOOK OUT FOR

Act I Sc 1

8: *La luna, il sol, le stelle*

After a short and unexciting prelude and two soldierly opening choruses, one sleepy and one warlike, we hear the Puritan family holding household prayers
in a very un-Puritan but agreeable quartet.* 8

14: *O Elvira, o mio sospir' soave*

16: *Ah! per sempre io ti perdei*

20: *Bel sogno beato*

Richard, very sick at his treatment by his putative father-in-law, indulges in self-pity at some length with three powerful lyrical passages all worth at least
one star* apiece. 14
16
20

Act I Sc 2

24: *Sai com'arde in petto mio*

Elvira, who still does not know the good news, has a cavatina of great conviction, saying she would rather
die than marry Richard,* followed by some excellent 24
duetting between Elvira and Uncle George, especially –

25: *Piangi, o figlia, sul mio seno*

1. When he tells her about her father's change of
heart.* 25

2. After a very full report of how brilliantly he
32: *A quel nome, al* argued her case there is a stirring build up to the finale
mio contento and the arrival of Arthur.** 32

Act I Sc 3

The wedding assembly: a quartet over the chug-chug
of a choral accompaniment. Arthur and Elvira soar
36: *A te, o cara,* above in long and lovely bel canto lines.** 36
amor talora Gripping duet, very agitato: Arthur recognizes
45: *Figlia a Enrico* Henrietta as the widow of Charles I.** 45
He promises, in an aria of great bravura, to save her
47: *Non parlar' di* life.***Followed by a charming mini-aria from Elvira 47
lei che adoro (who has no idea what is going on) which leads into
48: *Se miro il suo* the glorious ensemble*** (Arthur, Elvira, Henrietta, 48
candore Uncle George) during which Elvira (fatal move) puts
the wedding veil on Henrietta.
Strong declamatory encounter between Arthur
and Richard threatening revenge for stealing his
52: *Ferma! invan',* intended.* 52
rapir pretendi Chorus of confusion as wedding party discusses
absence of Arthur: Elvira rapidly going mad, sings
sweet Ophelia-like song inviting invisible Arthur to
59: *O vieni al* accompany her to the altar.** 59
tempio Final ensemble:* Elvira trips and trills away in her 63
63: *Misera figlia* madness over a chorus humping along in desolation at
morrà d'amor her dreadful fate.

Act II

After drab extended opening choral scene Uncle
George gives the latest bulletin from the sickroom in
8: *Cinta di fiori* a touching aria.* 8
From here on almost to the end of the act we have a
continuous stream of music in Bellini's best mode of
sweet melancholy: the melodies are long, the pathos
cumulative:
18: *O rendetemi la* 1. Elvira's first sad mad aria*** which leads into a 17
speme trio with Richard and Uncle George.
26: *Vien', diletto, è* 2. Elvira's silly-mad song (leading to exit).*** 26
in ciel' la luna 3. Duet (Richard, Uncle George)** opening with 30
30: *Il rival salvar* a simple folkish melody repeated three times and
tu dêi developing into a free-ranging exchange, Richard
slowly and sadly persuaded to forgive Arthur.

Finale: Both men hear the trumpet calling them to
war and end the act with a brisk outburst of soldierly
macho.

Act III

After some opening recitatif and a nice little cavatina
10: *Corre a valle, corre a monte* from Arthur,* lurking outside Elvira's house, the act 10
comprises two great scenes:

1. The long duet of reunion – Arthur and Elvira – drives along its course with several changes of gear:
18: *Nel mirarti un solo istante* Arthur's first lovers' aria** 18
20: *Ti chiamava ad ogni istante* and Elvira's reply** 20
and finishing with Arthur's second passionate
28: *Vieni fra questi braccia* aria*** leading to an intense and ecstatic duet to 28
conclude the scene.

2. The Puritan troops arrive to arrest Arthur: a lengthy choral scene with interpolations notably a cavatina from Arthur (surprising orchestral introduction reminiscent of a soft-shoe shuffle) but first the
36: *Credeasi, misera!* aria** then an ensemble over the chorus, persisting in 36
the soft-shoe rhythm, work magnificently. Big stuff, until the tension is broken by the joyful news that Arthur is pardoned and the opera ends in muddled
44: *Suon d'araldi?* shouts of general rejoicing.** 44

NOTES

I Puritani	Bellini's tenth and last opera
First night	Théâtre Italien, Paris, 25 January 1835
Reception	A triumph
Libretto	Pepoli
Source	A contemporary French play by two unknowns – Ancelot and Boniface

NEWS AND GOSSIP

Bellini wrote *Puritani* to capture what was then the high ground of the opera scene – Paris. He was 32 years of age, had just had a flop in Vienna, a bust-up with his long-time librettist partner Romani and been cited as co-respondent in a big divorce scandal. So getting out of Italy seemed a pretty good idea. He met Pepoli in the salons of Paris and liked him: they had a smooth partnership and the opera went on stage well rehearsed and with a top-notch cast. Bellini was particularly chuffed because his rival Donizetti's opera (*Marino Faliero*, now dead and buried) was a comparative flop with five performances while *Puritani* was a hit with seventeen. Shortly after the success of *Puritani* Bellini was given the Légion d'Honneur and shortly after that (September) he died of an inflammation of the lower intestine. *Puritani* spread quickly across the opera scene and has always been recognized as one of Bellini's best. Yet during the bel canto eclipse *Puritani* was not heard at Covent Garden for seventy-seven years – until Joan Sutherland revived it there in 1964.

COMMENT

The second act of *Puritani* is Bellinissimo – Bellini at his best, spinning out long sweet melodies in a mood of romantic melancholy. He shared the fascination of his age with the state of romantic madness, especially madness in pure, sweet young women, which was treated as if the patient were in a trance, in and out of which she could slip according as to whether the news was good or bad, rather than as a clinical state of mental illness. However that may be, sadness (and sleepwalking) brought out the best in Bellini, also the ecstasy of lovers in an extreme state of loving each other, as with Elvira and Arthur in their wonderfully inventive duet early in Act III. Bellini is also good in the several confrontations between male characters but his military music is muffled and lacks the sparkle and panache of Donizetti. The plot, strongly influenced by Sir Walter Scott's approach to English history, is told in terms of a boy's adventure story with risible details, such as the Puritan household rehearsing their prayers to the sound of an organ and bells and Cromwell's troops shouting 'Viva la libertà' (popped in no doubt for the Paris groundlings). But for the Belliniphile *Puritani* is a treasure and an alpha, though for the generality of opera buffs it may not rate quite so high.

Rigoletto

Horror melodrama

Verdi

The one where the hunchback jester hires a hit man to murder his boss but finds the resulting corpse is not his boss but his daughter.

CAST

The Duke of Mantua	Tenor
Rigoletto, court jester	Baritone
Gilda, his daughter	Soprano
Giovanna, her minder	Mezzo
Sparafucile, assassin for hire	Bass
Maddalena, his sister	Contralto

The Duke's courtiers etc. as follows:

Count Monterone	Baritone
Count Ceprano	Bass
Countess Ceprano	Mezzo
Matteo Borsa	Tenor
Cavaliere Marullo	Baritone

Also more very small-part courtiers, pages, servants.

3 acts: running time 2 hrs

STORY

Act I Sc 1 Public rooms in the Duke's palace (Verdi's own set instructions are very detailed and almost always ignored by today's set designers)

We are in sixteenth-century Mantua: a big party is being thrown in the Duke's palace. The Duke himself (chauvinist, womanizer and cad) strolls on with courtier Borsa talking about this mysterious girl he fancies and visits nightly in a slum. He sings a little song which reveals him as an utter bounder: he turns his attention to females present at the ball: makes a mild pass at Countess Ceprano whilst Rigoletto (officially the hunchback jester, but his real function is to give the Duke a thrill by maliciously insulting the Duke's chosen targets) mocks the Count.

Another courtier Marullo bounces in: he says they have discovered Rigoletto has a mistress. It's a big joke because R. is sexually repulsive. The Duke continues to chat up La Ceprano: he discusses the possibility of abduction – get rid of her husband, says Rigoletto, by imprisonment or murder. This annoys the husband who draws his sword on R. – steady, says the Duke, Rigoletto you go too far – Ceprano sotto voces the other courtiers to plot a comeuppance for this offensive creature: everyone hates him: everyone's keen to join in.

Count Monterone lurches on stage really upset: the Duke has seduced his daughter: Rigoletto is cheeky: the Duke orders Monterone's arrest: Monterone curses both the Duke and Rigoletto in a most impressive manner.

Act I Sc 2 A dark alley, Rigoletto's house above

Rigoletto has a strange chance encounter with Sparafucile, professional hit man. I have no work for you just now, he says, but if anything crops up I've got your card. Lengthy soliloquy by R.: he compares his tongue to the hit man's dagger – both are lethal weapons. He reveals himself as a nasty spiteful piece of work bugged by class hatred. He has got the curse on his mind too.

Gilda comes in: they sing a lot of loving father-and-daughter stuff. She asks about her Mum but R. will say nothing. He's very nervous about security. The doors are locked? Does she go out? (only to church): he checks with the minder Giovanna: then he pokes about outside, allowing the frightful Duke to slip on to terrace and chuck a bribe to minder Giovanna. R. comes back still grinding on about security. He goes in.

Gilda admits to us that she has told a lie. There is a fella who follows her to church – good Lord here he is! Standing on her terrace! They discover they are in love and the Duke gives nom de guerre as poor student Gaultier Maldè. Footsteps! The phoney student runs for it. Gilda reflects.

Courtiers assemble in the street below with the purpose of abducting Rigoletto's mistress (a mistake of course – it's Gilda they've seen). Rigoletto surprises them but they tell him they are after abducting Ceprano's wife and there is some stuff about him feeling the Ceprano crested key. He is given a mask and at the same time is blindfolded without his twigging it is being done (you must believe this): he is told to hold the ladder. Meanwhile Gilda is seized and carried off: Rigoletto cannot hear her screams because the blindfold covers his ears (you must believe this too): at last he tears off the blindfold, finds Gilda gone, remembers the curse, bombs out.

Act II A room in the Duke's palace

The Duke is uncharacteristically upset because when he returned to Gilda's house there was no Gilda. The courtiers come on stating they have captured Rigoletto's mistress: the Duke twigs it is Gilda and slips off stage to seek her out. Rigoletto comes on, gloomy: the courtiers mock him: he reveals that Gilda is his daughter: twigs she must be in an unsafe place – namely with the Duke.

He tries to get after her: the courtiers bar his way: he blubbers and beseeches but no need – Gilda freshly ravished rushes on, tells her father all. Rigoletto says let's get out and by God I'll get that Duke. They pass Monterone (of the curse) in the hall.

Act III A lowlife tavern on the riverbank

Rigoletto takes Gilda to see an exhibition that will kill her love for the Duke. The Duke arrives disguised as a subaltern in the Horse Guards: he orders wine from Sparafucile (for it is he): he sings about mobile women to Spara's sister (hooker Maddalena), then gets down to heavy petting. Gilda and Rigoletto view all this from outside. Gilda is upset. Rigoletto sends her off to set out for Verona dressed as a man. He does a deal with Sparafucile – twenty scudi down to kill the Duke and the rest at midnight on proof of results. Rigoletto insists he personally will throw the corpse into the river.

A storm starts. The Duke is offered a bed in the tavern, and accepts. He sings a repeat of mobile women. Gilda arrives dressed as a man and spies through a crack. Maddalena, potty about the Duke, says don't kill him: lose ten scudi? says Spara: no, kill Rigoletto when he returns and take the money off him says Maddalena. Gosh that's my Dad they're talking about says Gilda. I am a fair trader, it's absolutely against my principles says Spara. But . . . If any odd client should pass by I might knock him off instead.

Gilda, still in love with the frightful Duke, decides to make the supreme sacrifice: she knocks on the door and is stabbed to death in the midst of mighty orchestral thunder. Rigoletto returns on the stroke of midnight: he is given a body in a burlap bag. He pays up. As he drags burlap bag towards the river he hears – no! It can't be? Yes! It is – the Duke singing his mobile woman song. Rigoletto opens the bag – it's Gilda, dying. She sings a bit and dies. Rigoletto remembers Monterone's curse, and this time he really does bomb out.

MINUTES FROM START

Act I Sc 1

LOOK OUT FOR

The prelude – a short burst of menace – followed by slightly anaemic offstage dance music and rapid-fire plotting exchanges until the naughty Duke sings his

4: *Questa o quella* first little male chauvinist ditty* to a mildly agreeable 4
tune.

The ensemble of courtiers celebrates the pleasure and gaiety of the court over an undercurrent of gen-
10: *Buffone, vien qua* eral dislike for Rigoletto* – until interrupted by the 10
about-to-curse Count Monterone.

Act I Sc 2

A strikingly long-winded melody in the middle strings provides an eerie accompaniment to the
15: *Quel vecchio maledivami!* bizarre dialogue between Rigoletto and Sparafucile.* 15
A spooky encounter.

The long duet between Rigoletto and Gilda passes through a phase of sickly remembrances of dead wife and mother to one of the great lyrical pieces of the op-
30: *Ah! veglia, o donna* era*** – Rigoletto's orders to Giovanna to look after 30
his pure flower and Gilda's response – this lovely passage is repeated twice, the last time with all sorts of coloratura trimmings from Gilda.

39: *E il sol dell'anima* Another burst of intense lyricism,** this time from 39
the Duke with a creditable semblance of soaring passion – he goes up and up, and Gilda responds again with cut-crystal patterns of high sound.

43: *Caro nome* Gilda's great show aria (very famous).*** She is in 43
love and at first sings like a bird, then like a coloratura soprano really going it. The last phrases float over the sotto voce approach of the horrid courtiers.

Act II

The Duke's solo of anguish at losing his girl has alternating declamatory and lyrical passages – the lat-
0: *Ella mi fu rapita!* ter* (wholly out of character) quite touching. 0

The courtiers report their midnight escapade in an
5: *Scorrendo uniti remota via* oom-pah chorus to end all oom-pah choruses.* The 5
Duke, now he knows his girl is safe, responds cheerily.

The tormented Rigoletto pleads with the courtiers
14: *Cortigiani, vil razza dannata* to give him back his Gilda* – the last tearful pleas are 14
sobbed out over a fugitive cello accompaniment.

Again a long Rigoletto/Gilda duet, full of incident, in its early stages a somewhat maudlin prayer of thanks to the Almighty, but after the passing through of Monterone (of the powerful curse), finalizing in a much more manly style at a jog-trot and in the
26: *Si, vendetta* pleasant anticipation of revenge.** 26

Act III

3: *La donna è mobile* Opera's ultimate sexist ditty,** the Duke sings about female volatility. 3

7: *Bella figlia dell'amore* An item of pure magic: the quartet*** in which the Duke makes his play for Maddalena in melting tones: she replies skittishly, whilst Gilda in a high soprano line suffers the hurt of recognizing him for the double-crossing shit he is and Rigoletto rumbles on about vengeance. Four minutes of pure gold. 7

From this point to the final curtain the high drama of action on stage dominates the scene: the dialogue is supported by adequate oops, bumps and other timely gestures from the orchestra (including an erratic thunderstorm), echoes of the great quartet and a repeat of the Duke's sexist ditty (twice) but there are also two great musical moments:

26: *Se pria ch'abbia* 1. An impassioned trio,*** Gilda, Maddalena, Sparafucile, in which all three are screwed up to the point of decision (different decisions); this occurs twice, lasts only for seconds but its climax will not easily be forgot. 26

30: *Ah, ch'io taccia!* 2. The final ethereal duet** in which Gilda passes over and Rigoletto brings down the curtain with his tortured shout of 'AH, LA MALEDIZIONE!' 30

NOTES

Rigoletto	Verdi's seventeenth opera
First night	Teatro La Fenice, Venice, 11 March 1851
Reception	Wild enthusiasm
Libretto	Piave
Source	Victor Hugo's play *Le Roi s'amuse* (Paris 1832)

NEWS AND GOSSIP

It is hard for us in the late twentieth century to understand the apparent paranoia of kings, ministers and governments in the last century over matters of censorship. They apparently really believed that any 'subversive' notion in a stage work would threaten the social fabric of their, in many cases, potty little states – Naples, for instance, being at the same time a great place for commissioning operas and then stopping them in their tracks because of some irrational fear. The working of the censor's mind in those days was as pathologically suspicious as it is in our MI5 today and it is there maybe we have to look to find any parallel degree of fantasy about the potentially dire effects of free speech. In Paris Victor Hugo's play *Le roi s'amuse* had been closed down after its first night (immoral: subversive). Even twenty years later this gave Verdi the shivers because Victor Hugo's plot had bowled him over and he was dead keen to get *Rigoletto* on in Venice. He wrote to Piave 'I have in mind a subject which if the police would allow it is onc of the greatest creations of the modern theatre.' The police (the Austrian censors) didn't allow it. The play was obscene. So Verdi went to work and after a tremendous struggle and by changing the king to a duke and making other meaningless concessions, he got it through. Verdi's passion for *Rigoletto* paid off in box office terms. It was an immense and immediate success. The operatic grapevine worked at full speed and within months *Rigoletto* was playing all over Italy, soon all over the world. From the first night on it was clear that *Rigoletto* was going to be Verdi's No. 1 hit and so it has been. One of the half dozen most performed operas in the repertory.

COMMENT

If *Tosca* is a 'shabby little shocker' (it isn't), what is *Rigoletto*? At best a rattling good melodrama. Pay no attention to higher pretensions for this piece – psychological insights, profound study of humanity etc. – nor to Verdi's own claim that Rigoletto 'is one of the greatest characters ever created in the theatre'. In the opera (maybe not in the play) Rigoletto is an odious little toad, brutish and malicious in the way he goes about his work. We dislike him at once. His long apology for his nasty behaviour does not wash. He loathes the courtiers and clearly gets a buzz out of being spiteful to them. Not nice, and being a hunchback is no excuse. Thus we can't have much sympathy for his fixation on Gilda which, granted his nasty nature, seems more like an incestuous perversion than pure paternal love.

Nor does the character of the Duke hold together all that well. In the second act he would have us believe he is romantically in love with his mystery girl and really upset that he has lost her. We can't go along with that. Just look at the record and consider that after all this mushy stuff he goes on to rape her in seven minutes six seconds. (Incidentally, Monterone's curse, so effective in Rigoletto's case, misses out on the Duke completely.)

But these are quibbles in face of Verdi's wonderful score which brings gusts of really powerful romantic passion to the operatic stage for the first time. Here we have energy and intensity such as we have never heard before. The plot, though corny, is bullet-proof, the tension of the last act terrific, the two great ensembles mind-blowing. *Rigoletto* is a great evening in the theatre and if you have heard the two top numbers too often you can console yourself by reflecting that 'La donna è mobile', for so long the testing ground for inadequate tenors, has at last been pushed out of the No. 1 spot by 'Nessun dorma'. A slightly deformed alpha.

THE RING

Contents

A General Hello

There is no need to be frightened of *The Ring*. Gone are the days when a pilgrimage to Bayreuth ranked equal in holiness with a visit to the Passion Play at Oberammergau. Today there is no need even to leave your office at three o'clock, for *The Ring* is now accessible on CD, which is the perfect medium for getting acquainted with it. Most people will want to job about amongst the tracks for a while before tackling the old thing in its enormity in the opera house. But if you are one of those who is content to let the music wash over them with only the vaguest idea of what the words are saying, and find it enough to know that Siegfried is good, the dwarfs are bad and there is something about the ring having a curse on it – don't bother to read on. If, on the other hand, you are an eager beaver who wants to hunt each motto to its lair and feel it imperative to find out the whole truth about the Norns, then you will have to buy some proper opera books. But if, like most of us, you feel a spot of homework is required in order to get reasonable customer satisfaction, then do read on.

The Ring is of course the biggest aspidistra in the world of opera and for a newcomer the voyage of discovery can be tough. But if you are *Ring*-prone or even just *Ring*-tolerant, it is quite a thing to hear this mighty work of genius unrolling before your very ears. But don't expect a lot of laughs.

It is of course the music that makes the *Ring* experience different from just going to the opera. With the Italians, including Verdi at his greatest and even with Mozart, we are looking at and listening to the opera from outside. Brilliant, wonderful, marvellous they may be, but it's a performance. The music of *The Ring* engulfs us. We get right in there – into the saddle in the Ride of the Valkyries, we march in step amongst Siegfried's funeral cortège. We are in the middle of that ring of fire with Brünnhilde. It is possible to get too far in and get singed, like Bernard Levin. But *Ring* mania is only a mild inconvenience and it really does no harm. Nevertheless, it is a medically certifiable mental state and whereas there is no danger of anyone suffering from the bends after coming up from *Figaro* or *Aida*, *The Ring* can have you wandering around in a daze for a week.

It is not possible to explain why some music is great and some isn't. You can point out technical things as you can with a great painting. But what you can't do is to put your finger on why Rembrandt pulls it off and Jimmy Brandt who rents your attic doesn't. In *The Ring* Wagner pulls it off. He commands mighty forces. To compare his orchestra with Haydn's is like comparing the Albert Hall organ with a harmonium in a Friends' meeting house. In particular he unleashed the power of the brass section and packed it with sonorous instruments, some of which he invented himself. He could write a good tune. He pushed the language of music (which had stood still for nearly two hundred years) into new territory. Like Debussy after him, he could make pictures with music, in particular fire, water, various states of the weather and the sort of scenery you get in national parks. He could write music of great intensity about love, hate, horror, happiness and bravery. He could construct a climax that climbed from peak to peak: and each time you thought you had got to the top he surprised you with something higher. He could build a scene with perfect judgement of tempo and contrast. But although he was a superman in all other departments and the great panjandrum of orchestration, this still does not explain the chemistry that makes him the great musical magician he was. You can only learn by listening. But you have to listen for a long time for, alas, he had no wit, nor any part of the soul of wit, brevity.

When it comes to the words, he was not so great. The best you can say about the story of *The Ring* is that its setting of myth and mystery and its huge imaginative scope doesn't let the music down. It is the sort of work where the tone is lofty, where nobility is truly noble and where evil is unspeakably bad, where a giant can turn into a dragon at the drop of a magiçap and a dwarf into a toad. Wagner's judgement was spot-on in using a phantasmagoria of myth as a basis for *The Ring* for it is much easier to make heroes out of gods and villains out of dwarfs than to cope with human nature. Also any awkward plot points can be magicked out of the way in a trice.

The story itself is not all that hot. The three-tier system, as we would now call it, that Wagner built up out of those depressing old sagas – gods, humans, dwarfs – isn't complete and isn't rational. Although parts are worked out in great detail – far beyond their importance to the plot – there are great holes in the middle. And the detail is often otiose. We hear a lot, for instance, about the Valkyries who were bred by Wotan out of Erda to carry the corpses of dead heroes to Valhalla where they would be revived and retrained as stormtroopers. This is picturesque but silly. Wotan surely had enough magic to call the corpses up to Valhalla without the bother of a platoon of Valks. Indeed, why not recruit them whilst still alive and cut out the costs of resurrection which must have been considerable? At the centre, the motivation for the collapse of the system is unclear. Why does Wotan wander? Why does he lose his bottle? Is it the effects of the curse? If so, it has taken a long time to act. If it's not the curse, what is it? There are now plenty of the medicinal apples around in Valhalla. Maybe he had Alzheimer's and we weren't told. And why do the gods Downfall? Once the Rhinegirls get the ring back all should be gas and gaiters up there. But no, even when she knows she is going to give up the ring, Brünnhilde sends Loge off to arsonize Valhalla. Why?

But faults in the system – which is a pretty crazy one anyway – don't matter so much as the faults in telling the story. Here by far the biggest bugaboo is Wagner's habit of constantly regurgitating the *Rhinegold* story. Somebody tells us a bit of the story and half an hour later someone else tells us the same bit again, only for a third telling to surface in Part III. Even when a part of the story takes place before our very eyes – e.g. Alberich's theft of the gold – we are told about it again on four separate occasions. Meanwhile, all action stops. The narrative drive goes into neutral. Sometimes it seems like reverse. If it weren't for the soothing effect of the music it would drive us all potty. You could say that retelling No. 2 or No. 3 usually gives more detail and you could also say that the telling opens a door for some wonderful music (and some pretty ornery music too) but the balance of advantage must be against so much retelling, which is fine in Homer or a Strauss tone poem, but in a music-drama – no.

The handling of the main characters is the second great weakness. Wotan, who we thought was going to be the king pin of the whole piece, fades out completely after Part III and is not up to much in Part II. We don't know why he fades out. He has no payoff except having his spear broken by Siegfried. So why doesn't he go back to base and have it repaired? Siegfried did it to Nothung. If it is a symbol that his magic power is running out of gas, again why? Siegmund passes over in Part II and Siegfried doesn't arrive on the scene until Part III. Only Brünnhilde is central to the story after *Rhinegold*. The story also suffers from the characters being such an unattractive lot. With Wotan one loses patience very early on. Ill-tempered, indecisive, cowardly and much too talkative, he is not a person one would want to invite into the home. The truth is that Wagner packed into Wotan so many different roles (chief god, hen-pecked husband, loving father, orbital strategist, power-mad plotter, Don Juan, dwarf-oppressor) that the result is an unfocused character who never really comes off. And why is he wandering? We don't know, and apparently he doesn't either. Maybe Fricka just wanted him out of the house.

The two heroes of the Strength Through Joy movement, Siegmund and Siegfried, are a couple of boneheads who in the real world would be best employed in the boxing ring ('My boy doesn't know what fear is'), the Gibichungs are brutish, the dwarfs abhorrent, and thus we have only one major character – Brünnhilde – with whom we can have some fellow-feeling. She is quite splendid and gives us hope that there is some spark of decent feeling in Wagner after all. But with all of these faults, the story and the characters have power and the sort of power that Wagner in his slightly obscene way was aiming for. By dealing in blood, death, incest, necrophilia, deformity, etc., he can touch those deeper and darker instincts that we have within us and wish we hadn't got. Occasionally he can make the music help him enormously in this rather disagreeable task. One feels he gloats over the dirty bits and particularly incidental items such as Alberich raping a human female in order to produce the ghastly Hagen. Not the sort of thing Barbara Cartland would put in her books. But for those who want snuff movies, *The Ring* can offer a worthwhile beginners' course. (See **The Death Toll** page 563.)

Amidst all this death and doom Brünnhilde pretty well saves the day. She is brave, she is good, she is true, she is lovely, and the only thoroughly respectable person in sight. We rejoice with her in her love for Siegfried and we share her grief at his death. She also gets the best music, and deserves it.

The story of *The Ring* is told not only in words but in mottos (see page 558). Wagner made a big thing of the motto system in composing *The Ring*. It doesn't always work. For instance, in *Valkyrie* Act II Sc 2 when Wotan does one of his tedious recaps to Brünnhilde the mottos respond to the text like a pack of Pavlov's dogs. Each one sits in its kennel and only pops its head out when it hears His Master's Voice. You mention the ring, you hear the Ring; you think of Valhalla, you hear Valhalla. It gets close to parody. At the other end of the scale the mottos can work splendidly in the orchestral pieces where they are turned over and developed, and in the great duets too. Here they become part of the fabric and not silly little labels being offered by Wagner, 'like a madman at a party constantly handing everyone his calling card'. It is best, however, not to get too deep into mottology because it is easy to get lost in the mist. Everything can be related to everything and everything can have a deep and sometimes elaborate message. Some quotes from a musico:

Loge as the ambivalence of primal energy (Loge [8])
First stirring under the Rhine as a premonition of consciousness (Rhine [1])
The Valkyrie as the masculine element in women (Valkyrie [16])

Beware of writing too much on the labels.

There is a general belief that in the motto idea Wagner invented a wonderful new system for composing operas. Certainly all the Wagner scribendos, and they are legion, tend to give him good marks when he is laying on the mottos thick and fast and poor marks when he forgets about mottos and just writes a good tune. I quote from a scribendo who is worried about the master's performance in *Götterdämmerung*: '. . . retrogressive elements of grand opera exist side by side with mature passages of motivic integration'.

It is the word 'retrogressive' that tells the tale. This scribendo does not take account of the fact that a lot of the best music occurs when Wagner uses very few mottos or chucks them altogether (retrogressive) and some of the most boring music when it is tremendously well motivically integrated and bouncing along from one old motto to the next. No one can tell how Wagner's work would have developed if someone had persuaded him to junk this whole apparatus as a load of theoretical rubbish, or at least to have kept it within the sort of bounds set by *Meistersinger*. For the trouble with the motto game is that when you get really deep into it it is great fun for the composer and for the musicologist but not for the client. Like Bach's mirror fugue, which can be played backwards, forwards, upside down, in a mirror and in braille, it is not such a satisfactory piece for the listener as, for instance, that old warhorse the Toccata and Fugue in D minor, which can only be played one way – forwards. One of the problems for the aficionado of *The Ring* is that you keep thinking you hear a relationship between one motto and another and the other problem is that you are usually right. So whilst you are occupied with this mental/aural struggle the dragon is killed and you miss it. However that may be, the composition of the motto itself is often a small-scale work of genius (as for example Fate [19], Anvils [9], Ecstasy [21]).

There is another part of the Wagner product that is beyond the reach of most clients and certainly all non-German-speaking clients, and that is the relationship between words and notes. When Wagner worked on the script he started with a prose draft. This he converted into a poem. There aren't any rhymes, but the lines scan and there is a lot of alliteration. Even without knowing the German, one can guess pretty safely that Wagner was no Keats, for words that filter through in translation such as Wishmaidens, Battlefather and the constantly recurring Wondrous send a shiver down the spine. But in fitting music to the words he went to extraordinary lengths. Let me just quote a short passage about this from one of the best Wagner scribendos, Brian Magee:

> If, says Wagner, he writes a line like 'Liebe giebt Lust zum Leben' (Love gives delight to living) the concepts involved are obviously consonant and therefore no change of key is called for. But suppose the line is 'Liebe bringt Lust und Leid' (Love brings delight and sorrow) then delight and sorrow are opposites and the music should modulate between them. What should happen is that the key in which the phrase begins on the word 'love' should remain the same through 'delight' and then change on the word 'sorrow'. But the modulation must express the interrelationship of delight and sorrow in the state of love, at the same time as their difference; it must articulate their conditioning of each other. . . . Now supposing the next line is 'Doch in ihr Weh webt sie auch Wonnen' (which might be very freely translated: 'Yet even its pain gives us joy'). Then the key of 'sorrow' from the end of the previous line should be carried through as far as 'pain', because the emotional mood remains the same. But then the verb in this second line starts a shift of the mood back towards that of the first half of the previous line; therefore the music should begin to change key on 'gives', and on the word 'joy' should arrive back at the key of 'Love gives delight'.

Or:

> Sieglinde enters. She tells how an old man dressed in grey had thrust the sword into the tree at the wedding ceremony of herself and Hunding. This narration, 'Der Männer Sippe sass hier im Saal', is a choice example of the musico-poetic synthesis – the practical application of Wagner's principles of word-setting – that finds its most consistent expression in *Die Walküre*. Particularly noteworthy are the low-lying vocal line depicting the old man's low-brimmed hat, the shape of the melodic line portraying the flash of his eye and then its 'threatening glance', the falling chromatic intervals for his lingering look of yearning, the expressive appoggiatura on 'Tränen' ('tears') and the final rise to a top G for the physical act of implanting the sword in the tree. The sounding of the Valhalla motif by horns and bassoons announcing the real identity of the stranger, is one of the classic uses of leitmotif to comment on the action.

Amazing, isn't it? But no good unless you understand the German. And so all this intensive labour really goes for nothing unless you are an insider in the Wagner club.

In moderating this and others of his excesses, what Wagner badly needed was an editor. Until our Richard came on the scene the opera composer was a pretty workmanlike fellow. Verdi, for instance, and especially Mozart, would adapt and adjust to suit the needs of the house, of the sponsor and of the singers. They also had a librettist who was always a talking block and sometimes a critic, occasionally a partner. Wagner was his own librettist, his own manager, his own editor and his own hero. He thought he was pretty good in all of these capacities. In the writing and putting on of a show no other opinion mattered. The composer was always right, which we now see he very often wasn't. Just as it was a happy accident that Mozart had da Ponte, Strauss had Hofmannstahl and Hart had Rodgers, so it was a bit of a disaster that Richard had no one to work with but Wagner, for he was not only self-indulgent but also a megalomaniac. It is of course quite possible that a sensible partner would have persuaded him not to touch anything so outlandish as *The Ring* at all, and where would we be then?

Even today *The Ring* could be much improved if the longueurs were cut out, some of the sillier script points straightened out and the whole thing reduced to more manageable proportions. This would allow the big houses to put it on without the total disruption it now causes, or at the very least give them more time for rehearsal, the evening could be organized more sensibly for the clients who would not have to suffer from an undigested chicken salad bolted down at half-past five and timed precisely to ruin the love duet. Alas, this will never happen because a cult of religious veneration for the wishes of the composer now rules the musical roost. Wagner himself played a big part in promoting this by putting out a lot of self-serving propaganda about art being pretty well the sole purpose of life and the wickedness of tampering with the work of an artist, especially a great artist such as himself. To be authentic, to do exactly what the scholars say Scarlatti, Schubert or Monteverdi would want you to do, if necessary going to the length of building a sixteenth-century ophicleide – this today is pretty well the holy grail. Never mind that the piece would sound much better played another way or that modern acoustics are different, that pitch has gone up, musical taste changed, musical marathons don't fit into our culture – never mind anything at all, just stick a harpsichord into the Albert Hall and not on any account a Steinway. If you can't hear it at least you know what you're not hearing is authentic. The real obstacle to producing a sensibly revised version of *The Ring* is not the chorus of outrage that would go up, but the difficulty of finding a musician of genius to do it.

But the thought of what we might have had can't dim the glory of what we have got. There was a time when Wagner and especially *The Ring* divided mankind into the Wagnerites and the rest. Today the war is won. There are a few I-can't-stand-Wagners still around and these are usually people who confuse Wagner the nasty little man – and he certainly was racist, chauvinistic, a liar, a megalomaniac with fascist tendencies – with Wagner the composer of genius. They may also be people whose defences are too weak to withstand the sort of visceral attack Wagner makes upon them. But most of us can now be cool about Wagner and even the coolest must stand back and regard *The Ring* with wonder. It has been called the greatest feat of human imagination in the nineteenth century, and that is a statement that it is hard to deny. You can find in it what you like. Bernard Shaw found a socialist tract, others have called it fascist propaganda. Robert Donington saw it as an early statement of Jungian philosophy. The ecologists find in it a parable about polluting the world. No doubt equestrians, metallurgists, pyromaniacs and undertakers recognize some special message in it too. There had been nothing like it before and there has been nothing like it since. It is large, it is complex, it rides through the opera house like a juggernaut. Not much of it is lovable, some of it is repugnant. But when it makes its way through the ear and spreads across our sensibilities we know that we are listening to something that is a considerable event in the affairs of mankind and one that will stay with us to marvel at and to puzzle over for the rest of our lives.

After a performance of the last act of *Götterdämmerung* at a Prom in the mid-sixties the promenaders cheered for half an hour, then when the artists went home and the lights went out they stayed on and cheered in the dark. This could happen for no other piece of music.

Leitmotifs, Mottos and All That

In planning their history of England, *1066 And All That*, Messrs Sellar and Yeatman decided to include only those dates that were memorable. As a result of careful research they finally included only one – 1066. Deryck Cooke in his Companion to Decca's *Ring* quotes 191 leitmotifs. He is careful to say that deep down there are many more than this and he has just picked up a few of the more showy ones lying about on the surface. Robert Donington in his book on *The Ring and its Symbols*, by heavy pruning, gets the number of motifs down to 93. In the following section 29 main mottos are listed, all of them memorable, plus roughly an equal number of others which are mentioned but not thought to be memorable.

There are three ways of listening to *The Ring*:

1. Lie back and let it sweep over you. Don't bother about the plot too much, just . . . Ahhh . . . the Rhine . . . lovely music . . . Don't bother about the mottos at all. A lot of clients get their buzz out of *The Ring* in

this way. Perhaps most.

2. Hunt every motto to its lair, if necessary reading books, even getting the piano score. Seek out family relationships. Set up your own theory of motto evolution. In fact, go motto mad. The trouble is that in the advanced stages of motto mania the patient ceases to hear the music as music. *The Ring* becomes a gigantic crossword puzzle – a quarry for new clues.

3. There is no need to go poking about in the viscera of *The Ring* to get the maximum mileage from it. But you can't listen to it without noticing the mottos and you can't get a handle on the old thing unless you have some idea what the main mottos mean. So each individual in this third class, according to the sharpness of their ear, the efficiency of their musical storage capacity and their determination, will sort out for himself the level of motto-recognition that he must reach to give himself satisfaction. The number of mottos selected in this guide is calculated to suit an intensely musical child of ten or an intelligent but unmusical retired airline pilot of sixty.

So what the hell is a motto anyway? Some carry in notes messages like Love is the Sweetest Thing or Every Silver Lining Has a Cloud. Others are personalized. Walk-on parts have no mottos. Supporting roles may have only one motto (the Giants, when both are still in human, or gigantic, form). Erda, Gutrune and the stars get several. Siegfried has half-a-dozen and more. Each motto is telling you something, though sometimes it is pretty hard to make out just exactly what Wagner had in mind. In some cases one suspects he didn't really know himself, but just liked the noise. Valkyrie [16], Anvils [9] and Valhalla [5] are easy and indeed not far from the system of *Peter and the Wolf*. A tune for everyone: the jolly hunter, the evil wolf, etc. More mysterious are ideas like Fate [19] or Ecstasy [21], which probably mean something different to each listener.

A motto can be as short as two notes or can be stretched out like chewing gum to cover half-a-dozen pages of the score. In their virgin form mottos are seldom more than two or three bars. A motto can change into another motto. A motto can split in two like an amoeba and then the split bits can split again: and it is also like a chameleon for it can change its colour in a trice. All mottos are related to other mottos, say the Mottologists, indeed all mottos can trace their family tree back to the great Mother Motto, the chord of E flat with which the piece begins. Here a sceptic will suggest that with enough changes of gear, as in those funny fade-throughs of the early cinema, you can transform Winston Churchill's face into that of Madonna, but that when it's all over they still look different people. Pop Goes the Weasel to the Grand March in *Aida* can be done in ten easy stages but that doesn't mean the tunes have any real relationship.

Many people find the mottos a bit of a nuisance. Conscious or subconscious groping for mottos can take your attention away from the game that's going on before your very ears and Wagner may be scoring a series of goals whilst you are grubbing about motto-hunting.

The matter of mottos is treated in the following pages as follows:

1. Longlife mottos. Can be recognized without difficulty. Are important. Crop up off and on throughout the show. These have a number.

2. Short Stay mottos. Can be recognized. Can be important in a single scene or within an act. May be referred to in other parts of *The Ring*, but seldom, and when they are they don't matter that much. These have a letter.

3. Momentary mottos. Can be recognized, but more difficult because they don't happen so often. They seldom crop up outside their own patch; some of them, although very insistent when doing their stuff, fade away completely. These are unlisted.

It is probably unwise for the lay listener to burden his memory with the unlisted lot or for that matter any of the 130 further mottos indexed by the scholarly Deryck Cooke but not mentioned in these pages at all.

The Mottos

Longlife	*Short Stay*	*Motto*	*Sounds like*
Rhinegold			
[1]		Rhine	A smooth flow of water with eddies going up and down jerkily
[2]		Gold	A bugle call that flies upwards and stops (played on a trumpet)
[3]		Rhinegold	One long note – Rhine – down to the adjacent note – Gold – shorter
[4]		Ring	Woozy chords rotating around in a vague way
	[a]	Rejection	A slow yearning sort of thing hanging on to an early high note
[5]		Valhalla	Pompous brass going down then up: very civic (related to [4] above)
	[b]	Stress	Jerky downward steps
[6]		Giants	BRRM-TI-TA (TA). A scoop up and the following notes hammered out in unison
	[c]	Apples	Slow horns with triplets towards the end. Rather nice

[7]		Spear	Downward scale that could go on for ever, often punched out by trombones
[8]		Loge	Flickering semitones and more. A sort of motto grouping which hangs together. No sweat
	[d]	Bad News	A two-note cry of grief, WOE-WA, twice
[9]		Anvils	Clinketty Clinketty Clinketty Clinketty
[10]		Tarnhelm	Or magicap. Horns moving about (but not that much) rather close to each other
[11]		Curse	The rhythm of DAMMIT-ALL rising to a high note – with a nasty low afterthought
[12]		Earth or Erda	An upward sweep in chords moving unevenly. Sometimes settling on the top note
[13]		Destruct	Earth [12] upside down

Valkyrie

	[e]	Sieglinde	A bass line going down followed by chords going up
	[f]	Lovers	A long, smooth, sweet, string melody
	[g]	Self-Pity	A slow item climbing upwards and ending with an unusual harmony
	[h]	Volsung	A majestic melody with dotted rhythms
[14]		Sword	Trumpet octave and arpeggio. Shining bright
[15]		Nothung	A downward octave twice, with a tail-piece
[16]		Valkyrie	Rocking-horse rhythm punched out by trombones. Unmistakable
[17]		War-Cry	A ferocious inverted yodel. Can be followed by a trill and peals of laughter
[18]		Frustration	Starts with a buzz like an angry bee, then fades away
[19]		Fate	A doomy three-noter. Long – short (down) – long (up). Often followed by ominous drumbeats

[20]		Siegfried Heroic	A call (often horn) with three upward steps and a tail. Can be confused with Curse [11]
[21]		Ecstasy	The sheer beauty of this phrase makes it impossible to miss
	[i]	Sleep	Semitones poncing around usually downwards (the first time they squirm)
[22]		Trance	A smooth downward phrase of five notes. Repeated over and over

Siegfried

[23]		Fafner	Grunting, sometimes squirming, tubas
[24]		Horn I	The daddy of them all. A horn call that winds about and can go on almost for ever
	[j]	Longing	Strings – sweet and slow
	[k]	Wanderer	Even-paced chords: semitones
	[l]	Blacksmith	Downward runs in the bass
	[m]	Muscle	Five-finger exercises taken from the schoolroom piano to the orchestra pit
[25]		Forest Murmurs	Shimmer shimmer
[26]		Birdie	Birdlike piping
	[n]	Heroic Love	A tender hiccup, soon smoothed out
	[o]	Sigh	A downward sigh, then pretty

Götterdämmerung

[27]		Horn II	Son of Horn I but regal
[28]		Brünnhilde	A sweet phrase – low note, twiddle, high note then three more
[29]		Gutrune	A gentle sighing woodwind phrase, soft and sweet
	[p]	Gibichungies	Brassy chords in a swoop up and down. Start and finish on the same note

The Gods – A Family Tree

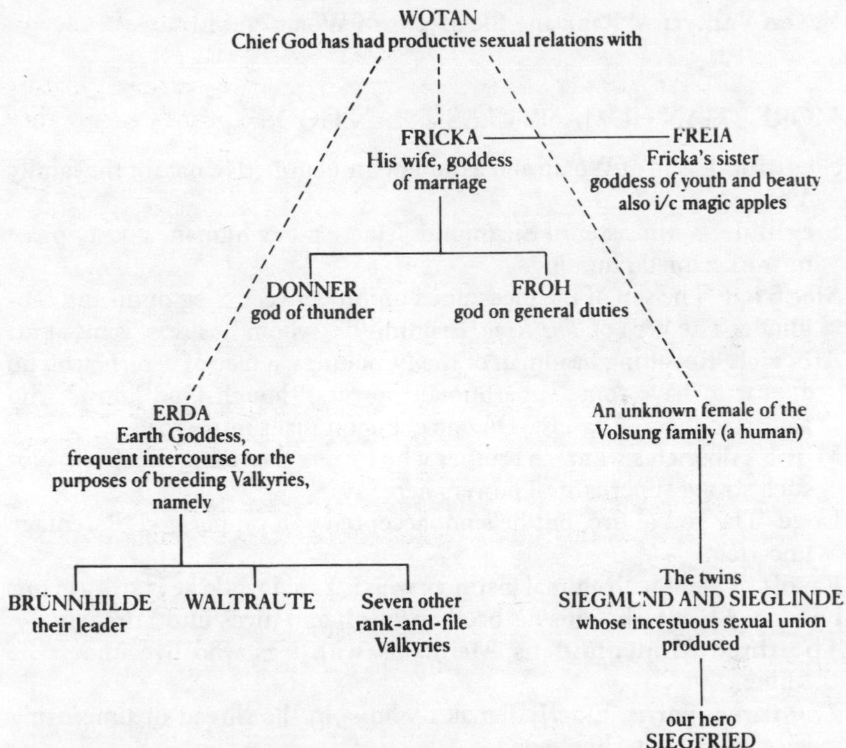

Who's Who (and What's What)

GODS

Wotan Chief god, sometimes wanders on earth where he is known, unsurprisingly, as The Wanderer. Sponsor of Valhalla and has a finger in most pies but fades out in the last act of *Siegfried*.

Fricka His wife, goddess of marriage. Role model for Mary Whitehouse.

Freia Fricka's sister, goddess of youth and beauty, she guards the apples that give the gods everlasting life. Important only in *Rhinegold*.

Donner Son of Wotan and Fricka, god of thunder. Not important.

Froh Son of Wotan and Fricka, god on general duties. Even less important.

Erda Goddess of the Earth. An important god. Related to no one. Has had frequent sex with Wotan.

Brünnhilde Daughter of Wotan and Erda. Leads a flying squad of light cavalry under the command of Wotan.
Waltraute Brünnhilde's no. 2. Same parentage.
Seven Valkyries Rank and file illegits of Wotan and Erda.

MORE THAN HUMANS LESS THAN GODS

Siegmund Son of Wotan and a human unidentified female of the family Volsung.
Sieglinde Twin sister of Siegmund. Married to a human, a nasty piece of work named Hunding.
Siegfried The son of the incestuous union between Siegmund and Sieglinde. The hero of *The Ring*. Brünnhilde, whom he loves, is his aunt.
Alberich Revolting headman of the Nibelungs, a race of dwarfs who do appear to have some superhuman powers, though God knows who gave it to them. A fascist. On one occasion turns into a toad.
Mime Alberich's wimpish brother who fosters the young Siegfried. Not such strong supernatural powers here.
Loge The god of fire, but he's not accepted as a proper god. Parentage uncertain.
Fasolt A giant with animal instincts who is killed while he is still a giant.
Fafner A giant who kills his brother Fasolt and turns into a dragon.
The three Rhinemaidens Mermaids with legs who live under the Rhine.
The three Norns Elderly females who spin the thread of time using very primitive technology.
A bird A creature with whom Siegfried can communicate after a dose of dragon's blood and who is helpful in that it has a good knowledge of the local topography.
Hagen Son of Grinhilde (see below) and the awful Alberich, therefore only just superhuman, indeed his behaviour marks him out to be subhuman rather than super.

HUMANS

Hunding Husband of Sieglinde. An ape.
Grinhilde (Grin Hilde) Wife of a senior Gibichung. Seduced by the dreaded Alberich resulting in Hagen (see above).
Gunther Legitimate Gibichung.
Gutrune Gunther's sister.

GROUPS

Nibelungs The race of dwarfs who live mainly below ground. Main occupations mining, smelting, being bullied by the ghastly Alberich.

Gibichungs Members of the disagreeable Gibich family. Landowners on a big scale. Country seat on the banks of the Rhine which sometimes overflows.

Valkyries Wotan's flying squad of female equestrians. Main duty to carry corpses up to Wotan's HQ for heart transplants and subsequent resurrection into warriors.

THINGS

The Tarnhelm or **magicap** Headgear made by Mime to a formula known only to Alberich. Whoever wears it can change his form (toad, snake, etc.)

Nothung Wotan's sword which was pulled out of an ash tree by Siegmund, shattered on Wotan's spear, put together again by Siegfried and used to kill the dragon and finally to shatter Wotan's spear. [Though why the shatter-power of the two weapons should have switched so decisively it is hard to know: Ed.]

The Ring: Death Toll

(Characters in order of disappearance)

Victim	*Cause of Death*	*Person or Persons Responsible*
Fasolt	Battered by a blunt instrument, perhaps his brother's fist	Fafner
Siegmund	Sword wound	Hunding
Hunding	Unknown	Wotan
Sieglinde	Died in childbirth	Natural causes, but surely the appropriate god could have saved her?
Fafner	Sword wound	Siegfried
Mime	Unprovoked attack: sword wound	Siegfried
Siegfried	Spear wound in the lumbar region	Hagen
Gunther	Sword wound	Hagen
Hagen	Death by drowning	Rhinemaidens

Brünnhilde	Burnt alive	Suicide while the balance of her mind was disturbed
Wotan Fricka Freia Donner Froh	Immolation	Loge

TOTAL 15

Rhinegold
Part I of *The Ring*

(Das Rheingold)

Wagner

The one where we start under water, where a goddess is walled up in gold blocks, one giant kills another and a dwarf turns into a toad.

CAST (see **Who's Who** page 561)

Wotan, chief of the gods	Bass–baritone
Fricka, his wife (goddess of family affairs)	Mezzo
Freia, her sister (goddess of youth and beauty)	Soprano
Donner, her brother (god of thunder and meteorology)	Bass–baritone
Froh, another brother (god on general duties)	Tenor
Loge, a demi-god appointed by the gods as their official diplomat, wheeler-dealer and agent on all matters concerning fire	Tenor
Woglinde } Rhinemaidens	Soprano
Wellgunde } Rhinemaidens	Soprano
Flosshilde } Rhinemaidens	Mezzo
Fasolt } giants	Bass–baritone
Fafner } giants	Bass
Alberich, head Nibelung	Bass–baritone
Mime, his brother	Tenor
Erda, earth-mother, a goddess	Mezzo

1 act: running time 2 hrs 40 mins

STORY

Sc 1 Under the waters of the Rhine

In which the sun rises on the gold beneath the waters of the Rhine, Alberich renounces sex, nicks the gold and leaves the three Rhinemaidens in deep distress

We are submerged in mythical time and in the mystical waters of the Rhine and these three Rhinemaidens are swimming around like fishes wearing no diving gear whatever. Waga Woge? says Woglinde to Wellgunde. Yes, I'm coming replies Wellgunde. Sisters says Flosshilde watch over that thar gold girls: watch it.

A revolting dwarf Alberich appears through a crack in the Rhine: Hi sexy! he shouts. Who's that? ask the girls. From Greater Nibelheim says Alberich. Any chance of having sex with you girls? Dirty beast says Wellgunde. Let's teach him a lesson says Woglinde. Alberich slips over rocks scutters sneezes trying to get after the girls. The girls make provocative passes: dwarf-teasing. Alberich spurned.

The sun rises and lights up the Rhinegold. What's that stuff? asks Alberich. Ignorant pig say the girls it's the Rhinegold of course. It gives absolute power to anyone who swears to give up all forms of sexual satisfaction forever. Works best when formed into a ring. Great Scott I see I see says Alberich. OK I swear to give up all forms of sex forever. He seizes the gold. He runs/swims off with hollow laugh. The Rhinemaidens yell help! Stop thief! etc. No good.

Sc 2 A mountain top. The newly-built city of Valhalla visible in the clouds
In which Fricka gives Wotan a hard time for doing a foolish deal, the giants come to take away Freia and Loge suggests a way of saving the situation

Wakey wakey Wotan cries Fricka. Get off says Wotan I'm having a lovely dream [and why two gods should be sleeping rough on this mountain top I do not know: Ed.]. Wotan – says Fricka – it's about that Valhalla. Oh yes? says Wotan. Mad extravagance says she and Wotan what possessed you to offer my sister in payment to those building contractors? Crazy coot. I had to offer the giants something says he. If only you'd mentioned it I would soon have stopped you says she. Hell, woman, says he, it was you that egged me on. Only to get some fixed abode to make it more difficult for you to sleep around says she and anyway you stink. Hey – didn't I lose an eye for you when courting? says he anyway I'm not going to give Freia up to those giants. We depend on her for those apples that keep us young.

Enter Freia in panic. They're coming to take me away she cries those bleeding giants. Relax says Wotan relax. Seen Loge around? That tricky Dick? says Fricka. He's no good. When he did the deal with the giants says Wotan he promised me to get Freia out of it. I don't trust you Wotan I'm sending for my brothers says Freia: Heyup Donner: Heyup Froh.

Enter giants. Job completed boss they say. We want our pay. What did you have in mind? asks Wotan. Don't come funny Wotan they say: Freia of course that was the deal. Not Freia says Wotan you clots that was just a joke. Joke was it? say the giants. OK if you won't deliver we'll just take her now. Enter Froh and Donner. Hands off our sister you big bullies they cry. Take it easy boys no physical stuff says Wotan.

Enter Loge. Where have you bin? says Wotan kindly sort out this mess right now. You got us into it. Now now now says Loge steady on I negotiated this contract very very carefully Clause 17B says best endeavours will be used to find a substitute for Freia no more no less. So what? says Wotan. We're taking Freia say the giants. Loge you're a double-crossing bastard say Froh and Donner.

Wait wait wait says Loge I travelled the world to find a sex substitute for these giants better than Freia and I found these Rhinegirls who had lost their Rhinegold. This stuff gives absolute power to any chappie who forswears sex and makes a toolie out of the gold. Nasty Albert Alberich the circus dwarf from down under, swore the sex oath, nicked the gold, made a ring out of it and now queens it over everyone down there. He might be up here soon too. By the way Wotan I told the girls I'd ask you to get it back for them.

I want that ring says Wotan. How can I get it? Nick it from Albert says Loge. We like the sound of that gold say the giants: Wotan – get us the gold and we'll give you back Freia meanwhile she comes with us as a hostage. They trundle off. A fog falls. The gods go grey. What's the matter? cries Loge. Radioactive fallout? Ah no of course it's apple deficiency caused by carting off Freia who made those medicated apples with monkey gland effects. Oh Gawd Wotan look what you done to us now says Fricka.

Hey Loge says Wotan on yer bike we'll go get that thar gold from the horrible Alberich now. Which route down? says Loge the water route or the sulphurous cleft? Sulphurous cleft says Wotan. They go down a hole and it's intermezzo time.

Sc 3 The underground workshops of the Nibelungs
In which we learn of the powers of the magicap and the ring and Alberich is persuaded to turn himself into a toad in which form he is apprehended

Alberich drags on Mime by the ear. Has he met production targets? Did the night shift meet its quota? He pulls his hair and pinches him in little boy bully fashion. He grabs the tarncap from Mime. Says Abracadalberich: disappears. Where did you go? asks Mime. I'm still here says invisible Alberich whipping biting and kicking the poor sod. Ho ho. So you made the magicap so good now I can spy on you idle bastards at work. Exits.

Loge and Wotan creep out. What is this whimpering mess? asks Wotan finding Mime. Who done this to you? My brother done it says Mime he bosses everyone around something terrible since he got this ring. Before that we were just one big happy family of admittedly revolting dwarfs making toys for the Japanese market. Now it's bang bang bang all the time. Why did your brother beat the hell out of you? asks Loge. Well you see I make this invisibility headgear to his formula and when it's done I put it on to get invisible and escape him. So? says Loge. No good says Mime I forget the codeword. So he snatched it and disappeared on me. Who are you folks anyway? We have come to help you says Loge.

Alberich comes on shouting and screaming at the workforce something horrible. Whaddya want you two? he asks. We heard you are now the big man dictator of Nibelung County We wished to pay our respects says Wotan. Cut all that crap says Alberich you two are up to no good. Steady on Alberich says Loge: who devised that new carbon ignition system for you? Also I am your second cousin once removed. You're just a tricky dicky says Alberich. Look at that pile of loot. Ever see anything like it? Never says Loge. Nothing to what it's going to be when my chaps really get extracting from them thar gold seams says Alberich and once I reach fifty billion I will conquer the world I'll come up into your territory and I'll take over you lot. Having rejected sex I am all-powerful so look out you posh godly lot I'm on my way to conquer pillage and rape. [Rape? Howzat? Ed.]

Keep cool Wotan says Loge: now Alberich you've really done frightfully well starting with practically no capital and an unmotivated workforce but suppose some villain were to nick that ring? What then? Aha I've thought of that says Alberich I have this magic tarncap: when in danger I disappear. My my says Loge just think of that what an amazing thing I can't believe it. I'll show you says Alberich: turns into a cobra. Squirms. God you terrified me says Loge. Very clever Alberich says Wotan. I don't suppose you can do small ones as well as big ones says Loge. Sure thing says Alberich how small? Let's say a toad says Loge. Alberich becomes a toad. Wotan puts his foot on it. Alberich is captured and trussed up by Wotan and Loge.

Sc 4 The mountain top again
In which the ring and the magicap are traded for Freia, the giants fall out with fatal consequences and the gods move into new premises

Wotan and Loge come on with Alberich (no longer a toad) in chains. So we got you Alberich say Loge and Wotan now we want a pretty good ransom to let you go. What you got in mind? says Alberich. All that gold says Wotan. Gawd! says Alberich well I suppose even if you get the gold I can make a fresh lot by keeping the ring [a most injudicious speech: Ed.] OK you can have it. I will issue instructions to my chaps. Could you get me a portaloo I'm embarrassed to be seen all chained up or maybe set me free now? Not until every penny is paid says Wotan. The nasty dwarfs bring on many tons of gold. OK now? says Alberich. Gimme the magicap says Loge. All right I suppose they can make me a duplicate says Alberich. OK now? Gimme the ring says Wotan. O Lord help us Mary Mother of God expletive deleted says Alberich not that. The ring says Wotan. No no no says Alberich you bastard you I do all the dirty work you pick up the ring no bother. No no no. The ring! says Wotan. He gets it. Now I am the Lord of Creation says Wotan I gloat – hear me. Let the dwarf go. All right but before I go I will put the curse of death on any owner of the ring present or future says Alberich. [So who gave little Albert Alberich the power to curse? Ed.] He curses. Goes.

Froh, Donner and Fricka are amongst us once again. Fafner and Fasolt are on their way says Loge. How did you get on? says Fricka. Mission accomplished says Loge. Hooray I could do with a few of those apples says Froh. The giants and Freia enter. Money's ready says Wotan. Here it is. Look Wotan I really fancy this girl says Fasolt. I couldn't leave unless the gold blocks conceal her entirely one glimpse and I'm back like a yo-yo. The junior gods and Loge brick up Freia in gold blocks. I can still see her left tit says Fafner coarsely. (Oh dear says soppy Fasolt such a sweet girl so sorry to lose her.) All the gods are upset.

What a disgraceful scene says Wotan why did I ever get those crazy giants on the job? Donner thunders. Shut up says Fafner. More gold! cry the giants I can still see it. There is no more gold says Loge. OK let's chuck on this here item says Fafner. My God that's the magicap gone says Loge. She's still visible! says Fafner: get that crack blocked or else. Stick that ring into it pronto. What! says Wotan this ring!!! No. Negative. Not never. It's mine. It belongs to the Rhinemaidens anyway says Loge. Finders keepers says Wotan. Stuff it in that crack or we carry off Freia says Fasolt. Help! Help! cries Freia. Give it up Wotan says Fricka. Give it up says Froh give it up says Donner. Shan't says Wotan.

The earth opens and an elderly lady namely Erda the Earth Mother is elevated to a prime position centre stage. As you know Wotan she says my family send you a fax every night with advice about future strategy but today this is a matter of such importance I bust out of the earth in person to tell you: *Leave that ring alone*. Most impressive says Wotan. Anything else? No says Erda: *Now mind what I say Wotan* (she sinks without trace).

OK giants says Wotan. Here's the ring. Take it. Fafner starts shovelling gold into a burlap bag. Hey steady says Fasolt leave some for me. Push off says Fafner if we'd kept Freia you would have been humping day and night so it's only fair that since it's gold not Freia I get more than you. Not fair says Fasolt. Is fair says Fafner leggo that ring. Shan't says Fasolt. OK then take that says Fafner: kills him. My God that curse is really hot stuff says Wotan. You did well Wotan says Loge. Let's get up to your Valhalla then says Fricka. Oh Lord I feel guilty again says Wotan maybe I should have a Fernet branca or a session with my shrink.

Meanwhile Donner gets to work on the weather to produce:

1. a sultry haze
2. pale clouds
3. lightning
4. mist and drizzle
5. thunder

all pretty simple so far but now wait for it:

6. a rainbow pedestrian bridge to Valhalla.

The gods tramp up the bridge to Valhalla. Whassit mean 'Valhalla'? asks Fricka. Riddle-me-ree says Wotan. An odd bunch these gods says Loge; think they know everything. In fact they are doomed. I might burn them up myself one day if I have time.

Rhinemaidens strike up from the valley below. We want our gold back they sing we want our gold. Tell those Rhinemaidens to belt up says Wotan to Loge. Pack it in girls shouts Loge. You're not getting your gold. But they don't pack it in and go whingeing on until the curtain comes down.

MINUTES FROM START **LOOK OUT FOR**

Sc 1 (For motto numbers see the Table on page 558)

0 The prelude** takes us back to the beginning of time 0
even before the Rhine began to flow. But at last above
the famous long-held chord of E flat we hear something stirring: soon the Rhine is on the move and
amongst its waters we hear the Rhine motto (a smooth
flow of water with eddies going down and up jerkily
[1]): now we are engulfed and out of the watery ar-
4: *Weia! Waga!* peggios Woglinde's morning song floats up.* The 4
girls on sentry duty exchange tribal cries like sea-lions. Rather nice.

Alberich and the girls. Although it goes on a bit, this scene is full of watery magic. After the girls have identified Alberich he scrambles over the rocks slipping and sneezing (you hear this mickey-moused in the score). He slavers with lust: each of the girls in turn teases him by singing sexily as they swim towards him and then darting away at the last moment.
7: *Heia Du holder!* Perhaps Wellgunde's love music is the nicest.** 7
Then all three together mock him in close harmony with a good deal of ringing laughter – really rather an unpleasant way to treat a person of restricted growth

and not at all politically correct.

The sun rises on the Rhinegold. This is a big event and perhaps the finest moment in the opera. First we hear lazy horn arpeggios floating around with water susurrating above. This is the Gold motto and as the first rays of the sun strike the gold we hear it more powerfully (a bugle call that flies upwards and stops, here played on a trumpet [2]). The girls sing a hymn
15: *Heiajaheia!* to this morning miracle*** with a lot of Heijaho Heia 15
stuff in it then the Rhinegold motto [3]: one long note – Rhine – down to the adjacent note – gold! – shorter. (There has been quite a lot of it around already but not so you would notice much.)

17: *Des Goldes Schmuck* Now the girls tell Alberich the tale:** 17

1. The gold is all-powerful if forged into a ring (the Ring motto [4] – woozy chords rotating around in a vague way – hard to pick up here but no sweat, lots of it shortly).

2. But to make it work you've got to give up sex (Rejection motto [a] – a slow yearning sort of thing hanging on to an early high note – Easy).

20: *Der Welt Erbe* Alberich does it.* No more sex he swears. High 20
drama. To a great scoop on the horns he seizes the gold and exits with hollow laughter (much hollower in the recording studio than on stage). The girls go frantic. And so they should for they have really messed it up.

24 The linking intermezzo** between deepest Rhine 24
and highest mountain top plays over two pretty important mottos: firstly the Ring [4] (already heard) – here it's clearest on the horns that move about in
Sc 2 thirds – and Valhalla [5], pompous brass going down then up (over a harp): very civic. (It's related to the Ring motto.)

After some early morning bickering between Wotan and Fricka (Wotan in trouble for the mad extravagance of Valhalla and the idiocy of promising Freia in payment), Freia herself comes on the scene in
33: *Hilf mir, Schwester!* panic.* The giants are coming to get her! Quite a lot 33
of the Stress motto [b] – jerky downward steps. Wotan tries to calm her: but what is this we hear? The coarse, brutal motto of the giants [6] – BRRM-TI-TA-TA (sometimes without the last TA), a scoop

up and the following notes hammered out in unison – unmistakable. This booms out as Fasolt and Fafner

35: *Sanft schloss Schlaf dein Augen*

come on. Now there is a parley,* musically rewarding 35
but not much cop for Wotan. Although the giants' utterances – really quite melodious – are quite at odds with their motto, they are tough guys. We done a good job for you boss, says Fasolt, now we want Freia. Without those apples she manufactures you will all die Ho Ho says Fafner. Apple motto [c] – rather nice, slow horns with triplets towards the end.

But the marines, in the shape of Froh and Donner,

42: *Zu mir, Freia*

are coming.* Wotan tells the boys not to get rough – 42
Spear motto [7] – downward scale that could go on for ever, we've had it before as punctuation but now it's punched out boldly by the trombones and incidentally Wotan's spear symbolizes about a dozen things including power, authority, doing deals, his problems, his inhibitions (and probably his thoughts on the ERM too). Just behind Froh and Donner, Loge – motto [8] – flickering semitones in the strings, and more. A sort of motto grouping which hangs together. No sweat. So now we are into a dramatic patch, Wagner in his forceful driving mood: no longueurs.

After Loge, in true shyster fashion, has disclaimed liability for the Freia/Valhalla deal the giants begin to come the heavy and demand their rights. This leads to a lengthy debate:

48: *Umsonst sucht' ich*

1. Loge tells the tale.** He looked all over the 48
world for something the giants would like better than sex and by chance lighted on the story of the ring. A piece that begins as recitative, is then interrupted by the orchestra and continues in something more like an aria, ending with lots of Gold [2] and Rhinegold [3]. Everyone muses rather quietly for some time.

56: *Den Ring muss ich haben!*

2. I must have that ring says Wotan.* How to get 56
it? Steal it says Loge in a shout. We would consider a barter deal say the giants – the ring in exchange for Freia. Not likely says Wotan. Very good say the giants and trundle off dragging Freia with them. Lots of Giants [6] around. Vigorous and tuneful stuff but the confrontation not so gigantic as one might have hoped.

61: *Was sinnt nun Wotan so wild?* 3. You gods don't look so well says Loge.* Oh my Lord, it must be for lack of Freia's apples. Here the stage goes into a sort of grey mist and so does the music. The Apple stuff at the start [c] is brisk enough but the gunpowder runs out of Loge's boots as he watches the gods wilt. Lots of Loge [8] about. 61

4. Let's get that thar gold cries Wotan who has more stamina in the face of apple deficiency than the
66: *Auf, Loge, hinab mit mir!* others. Loge come with me.** They set off to one of Wagner's quite magical transformations (the intermezzo between Scene 2 and Scene 3). First we have lots of Loge [8] then a motto indicating Bad News [d] – a two-note cry of grief WOE-WA, twice – (this time from Alberich: we heard it first but only incidentally when Alberich failed to catch the Rhinemaidens); next a heavy dose of Gold [2] and then, with a carefully calculated shock, into Anvils in Action motto 66
69 [9]*** – clinketty clinketty clinketty clinketty. For a little while, as the Nibelungs' production line becomes visible, we have nothing but clinking (from a battery of eighteen backstage anvils, if Wagner's wishes are respected) and no orchestra at all. By now we are well below the Rhine and the disgusting Nibelungs are all around us. 69

Sc 3

Alberich bullies Mime and extracts the Tarnhelm from him – Tarnhelm motto [10] – horns moving about stealthily, but not that much, rather close to each other. Loge and Wotan arrive and listen first to Mime being bullied by Alberich and then to Mime's sob story. All of this is pretty low voltage and too
74: *Sorglose Schmiede, schufen wir sonst woh!* long, but there is one lively reminder of the Anvils* as Mime recalls the good old days before Alberich's productivity campaign. Alas this scene is not a gripper. There is no way in which we can get emotionally involved in the spectacle of two singularly unpleasant dwarfs having a family quarrel. The music is as clever as ever but for a while we seem to be watching a puppet show. No star. 74

Alberich becomes power-mad, cracking his whip and screaming at his revolting gang of gold workers.
78: *Hieher! Dorthin!* He tells them to get moving again fast,* orders Mime back to his bench. He flaunts the ring – Ring motto 78

[4]. Musically this scene is compulsive but nasty.

83: *Die in linder Lüfte*
Alberich boasts he will take over upstairs,* kick out 83
the gods and rape their women. Recitatif-ish at first
but he works himself up into a pretty fair frenzy. Lots
of Valhalla [5] about.

89: *Riesen-Wurme winde sich ringelnd!*
Alberich's party piece:* first the transmogrifica- 89
tion (Tarnhelm motto [10]) into the serpent (unison
squirming in the tubas) and then the toad (toadish
leaps in the woodwind). We have another crafty
transformation intermezzo which plays around with a
parade of mottos, including Anvils [9], Giants [6],
Valhalla [5] and Loge [8]. Fascinating, but not as
good as the earlier intermezzos.

Sc 4

After an opening exchange to strangely ill-fitting
light-hearted music the trussed Alberich agrees to
trade in the gold so long as he keeps the ring [4] and
summons his frightful horde to drag in the loot. This
99: *Wohlan, die Niblungen*
is an effective little episode* to a rumbling back- 99
ground of Anvils [9] and a good deal of Bad News [d]
too.

The business of getting the ring off Alberich is
played in hushed tones, almost sotto voce. This is
really effective, for when he lets loose his storm of
106: *Bin ich nun frei?*
hatred it has all the more power** – Curse [11] sung 106
twice at the beginning and end of this piece; the
rhythm of DAMMIT-ALL rising to a high note –
with a nasty low afterthought. It is Alberich's swan-
song: frightening in its animal-like ferocity.

On Freia's return we have a welcome patch of blue
sky. Froh, a god of little consequence, gives vent to
the first decent sentiments we have heard this last
112: *Wie liebliche Luft wieder uns weht*
hour.* A sweet burst of melody based on Apples [c] – 112
Nice to have you back, he says to Freia. And Fricka
greets her politely too. This oasis of lyrical music disappears slowly as the vocally gentle giants parley
about screening Freia with gold blocks. This to a
walking bass and a good deal of Giants [6] and Anvils
[9].

Fasolt, the more decent giant, is going to miss
118: *Freia, die Schöne*
Freia. He sings to her rather fetchingly.** Then we 118
have the debate about the next destination for the ring
with music that is – considering the raging passions

all around – surprisingly light and airy: Rhinegold [3], a little Anvils [9] and Ring [4]. This ends in the impasse between Wotan and the giants.

Erda's solemn warning. First we have the primaeval Earth motto [12] – an upward sweep in chords moving unevenly and here settling on the top note – all deep down on Wagner tubas and then Erda's
122: *Wie alles war* sombrc and beautiful aria.** The Earth motto [12] is 122
around pretty well throughout as is a new motto, Destruct [13], forecasting the final downfall, or twilight of the gods, or Götterdämmerung, or whatever. It's the Earth motto [12] turned upside down. Dust to dust, earth to earth. (Nice one, Richard.)

128: *Zu mir, Freia!* Now things happen rather more quickly.** Wotan 128
gives up the ring: Spear [7]. The giants, no longer gentle, quarrel. One kills the other noisily with a lot of banging on the timps. Wotan marvels at the power of the curse (very loud rendering of Curse [11], twice on the trombones).

The biggest and best of all the transformation
134: *Schwüles Gedünst schwebt* scenes.** Donner, who has not yet had much to do, 134
swings his hammer and the violins shoot up like rockets to create a shimmering upper-air world – not unlike the opening water music. In the midst of this Rhine in the Sky a fanfare breaks in (which clever musicos have related to half a dozen of the earlier mottos, but let's just take it as a fanfare). Bang! Thunderclap! The Rainbow Bridge has sprung up. Well done Donner we say, and the orchestra shimmers and purrs in recognition of his good work. Now there is a sort of brief symphony – Valhalla [5] – followed by Wotan taking possession of the premises. Another resounding trumpet fanfare which again we would be wise to take on its merits here because it really belongs to *Valkyrie*. And now it must be confessed that things hang about a bit. Why is it called Valhalla? asks Fricka. Dunno says Wotan. Tell you later. These gods, says Loge, think they've got it made. Poor silly things. I might burn them up sometime if the fancy takes me.

142: *Rheingold! Rheingold!* In the final scene** we hear the Rhinemaidens 142
whingeing away in the valley, asking for their stolen gold back – Rhinegold [3] and Gold [2]. Wotan tells

Loge to shush them. But they carry on and sing us out of the opera, moaning on about their terrible loss. Though less than climactic, this makes a satisfactory end to the great prologue and the orchestra winds things up by playing on magnificently beneath the Rhine.

NOTES and NEWS AND GOSSIP See **The Birth of *The Ring*** page 632

COMMENT See also **The Ring – A General Hello** page 549

The general effect of *Rhinegold* is far finer and bigger than would seem to be the case just by looking at the number of stars. Apart from the transformation scenes there aren't many big set pieces like the Ride of the Valkyries, Siegfried's Journey down the Rhine, or the anvil-splitting bit, and again, except for the intermezzos, there are not many big climactic moments. The prelude is stunning and after that the watery scenes swim along very nicely so long as they remain innocent and jolly, although they tend to wear out their welcome as each of the sportif ladies makes much the same pass at Alberich. But the sun striking the gold is a stupendous event and the Rhinemaidens' hymn that follows lifts our spirits to rejoice with them in this great hullabaloo over sunrise. Freia's music is a joy, the giants are melodious. But in Scene 2 there is nothing to make us sit up much until Loge appears. His report bringing us up to date with the Rhinegold situation, although too long, is a musical journey of some interest, as is the following parley with the giants. But perhaps the greatest moment of the opera comes when we are shot into the Nibelung workshops and are half deafened by the eighteen anvils, each of a size carefully specified by Wagner. This liveliest scene is followed by the most tedious, the power-mad Alberich bullying his brother. Even when Wotan and Loge arrive, the opening exchanges are less than thrilling and here in particular you feel you are looking at the rough cut of a film before it has been brought down to anything near its right length. Wagner is of course up against a problem that bugs all dramatists – a wily person must be given enough time to show that he is wily and persuasive (although we don't seem to mind too much when Don Giovanni talks Zerlina round in two minutes flat).

The sound pictures that Wagner conjures up in *Rhinegold* are vivid. To start from the beginning of time is a really good idea. We are in an empty world, static, asleep, waiting for something to happen. Then when the flow of the Rhine starts it is truly majestic, and the underwater music is as underwatery as music can be. When we recollect the taste of the spume and spray of the *Dutchman* we must see in Wagner a water composer extraordinary. Sunrises are pretty easy, but the early sun lighting up the gold makes this one special. The mountain top music has no picture power whatever but the Valhalla references do. We can see the towers and turrets floating about up there amidst the high cirrus. The greatest sound-blow is of course the Nibelung workshop. The snake, toad and gold building-blocks don't come through visually despite Wagner's Disneyland attempts, but Donner's great trick of throwing the rainbow with the appropriate props of thunder, lightning and a crash in the wings works a treat. Strangely enough it is perhaps the dying fall of the opera that has strongest visual magic: the petulant Wotan striding up to his new home, the disaffected Loge lurking, the three Rhinemaidens singing plaintively in the valley below.

Rhinegold gains its power from its size, its length, its intensity and its sustained invention. When it flags it is not because the music is particularly weak but because that kind of music has gone on in the same mood for just a bit too long. But this is a small complaint in the face of this great feat of musical imagination, the curtain-raiser for the mighty saga that is now on the road and which casts its spell over everyone who isn't Wagner-immune. And bad luck on them we say because we are going to have a great time.

Valkyrie (Die Walküre)

Part II of *The Ring*

Wagner

The one about a sword being pulled out of a tree, the ride of the Valkyries and a ring of fire being ignited around our heroine.

CAST (see **Who's Who** page 561)

Wotan, chief of the gods	Bass–baritone
Fricka, his wife (goddess of marriage)	Mezzo
Brünnhilde, Wotan's daughter, chief of the Valkyries	Soprano
Siegmund, Wotan's son	Tenor
Sieglinde, twin sister of Siegmund	Soprano
Hunding, her husband	Bass
Eight Valkyries	Sopranos and contraltos

3 acts: running time 3 hrs 50 mins

STORY

Act I Interior of Hunding's house

Sc 1 In which Siegmund meets his twin sister to whom he is magnetically attracted

Time and place are both mythological but Siegmund's problems look real enough as he staggers in and slumps down in a heap by the fire. What's this then? says Sieglinde: it looks like a case for casualty. Water water cries Siegmund. You look scrumptious he says: who are you? This says Sieglinde is the Hunding residence and I am Mrs Hunding pray make yourself at home. Thanks says Siegmund by the way I am wounded. Had a bit of a scrap. Here's a large scotch says she. Thanks says he that's better now I'd best be off. Why not stay on here? says she. OK thanks says he. Stays. By the way, he says, I call myself Dismal.

Sc 2 In which Siegmund meets his brother-in-law who says he will kill him

Enter Hunding. This guy Dismal dropped in in pretty poor nick says Sieglinde. Get him and me a meal right away woman says Hunding. You can stay here Dismal owing to the laws of holy hospitality. I lost myself getting here says Siegmund just where exactly am I? Is it somewhere near Basingstoke? This is the Hunding residence says Hunding and who pray are you?

Well I can't call myself Homebird nor Happy nor Smiler says Siegmund because I am prey to self-pity so Dismal is the name I go by. My father was a wolf and I had a twin sister. One day our home was vandalized my mother murdered and my sister abducted. After that my wolf father and I became free-range hunting wolves and I enrolled as a wolf cub. Then the same hooligans got my father. I found his wolfskin but his credit cards and watch had gone. After that I had a hard time wolfing on my own. It makes you very unpopular you know does wolfing. That's why I've called myself Dismal.

Who are you running away from now? asks Sieglinde. Another gang who tried to make a girl marry a bloke against her will. I went along and killed them all says Siegmund. Then their relatives arrived and quite unreasonably tried to kill me. That's why I'm not called Homebird Happy or Smiler. Great Scott! says Hunding I was one of that girl's clan. You killed two of my second cousins once removed: you can stay here tonight Dismal owing to the laws of holy hospitality but tomorrow I will kill you. Hey Sieglinde get my horlicks goodnight all. Exits. Also Sieglinde.

Sc 3 In which Siegmund gets his name, a sword and carries off his twin sister with conjugal intentions

Gosh thinks Siegmund that girl is a knockout. She gives me funny vibes. Apropos of nothing he says my dad promised me I would always find a sword somewhere around if I got into a fix. Like I am now. I see nothing. But yes – what's that shiny thing stuck in that there tree trunk?

Enter Sieglinde. I spiked his horlicks with soneryl so you can get away she says and there's an old sword you could use stuck in this tree if you can get it out. An old man stuck it in there years ago [Wotan of course: Ed.] and so far nobody's been able to shift it. Must be a knack. I'll take the sword and you too if I may says Siegmund you see I love you (sings loverly song about spring with heavy hints about brothers carrying off sisters). You look very like me says Sieglinde and you look very like me says Siegmund. You must be my sister. Golly! I don't like your name Dismal says Sieglinde nor is Smiler suitable nor any of that wolf stuff: I name you Winner which since this is a German opera will be translated as Siegmund.

OK says Siegmund and pulls the sword out. I will call this sword Nothung he cries [obsessed with names: Ed.] for nothing can be done without it and now nothing remains but to carry you off my twin sister and make you my bride. OK she says. Let's go.

Act II A wild rocky mountain ridge

Sc 1 In which Wotan is worsted by his wife in a marital disagreement

Wotan and Brünnhilde are on this mountain top together and he says to her get down there right away Brünnhilde and see that Siegmund wins against Hunding in this fight that's billed for 1600 hours. Oho says Brünnhilde better wait until you've had a word with the wife and she's on her way now.

Enter Fricka furious in a sheepcart. What's this Wotan are you on the side of adultery and incest? Steady on old girl says he love is love – as minister responsible for marriage I must insist that you stop favouring those bloody wolf cubs of yours says she and what about you anyway sleeping around in the most brazen fashion embarrassing the hell out of me. Listen woman says he in this crisis we have over the ring I need a hero to return the blasted thing to those Rhinemaidens. I need Siegmund. And trample underfoot the sacred laws of marriage? says she. I demand you withdraw magic from that Nothung sword and let Hunding kill the adulterous lecherous incestuous – OK OK OK says Wotan you win. No magic protection of any kind – you swear? says Fricka. I swear says Wotan. Good says Fricka.

Sc 2 In which Wotan unburdens himself of a great deal of the plot of *The Ring* to his daughter Brünnhilde

How'd it go? asks Brünnhilde. Badly says Wotan. It's the pits. I'm knackered. Fricka has done for me. How come? asks she. Well let me tell you all says he. He embarks on a lengthy narration from which the following are the main points:

1. I won the world by making some pretty dodgy deals with certain doubtful operators. Loge was of course a bad influence. And all the time I longed for love.
2. That Valhalla business stank a bit. I eventually paid off those tiresome giants with the gold I nicked from Albert Alberich and he put this curse on the ring he had made from the gold.
3. Erda told me to get it back to the Rhinemaidens but didn't tell me how to do it.
4. This bothered me so I went down below the earth and had a good deal of sexual intercourse with Erda resulting in you and your eight Valkyrie sisters.
5. The purpose of all this begetting was to produce an elite corps of female cavalry to haul up the corpses of dead warriors to Valhalla where they would be revived and retrained as stormtroopers to defend my HQ.

6. All this went pretty well but now I'm in a panic lest Albert Alberich gets the ring back from Fafner [Fafner now a dragon: Ed.] and takes over all my corporate affairs.

7. I can't attack Fafner because the deal I did with him specifically excludes aggression.

8. So I need a hero who is a free agent not my son not a part of my establishment not created by me not in any way complicit to get the ring back. Bugger it! How do I do that?

OK I get your problem says Brünnhilde [more than most of us can manage: Ed.] how about that young wolfperson Siegmund? I wolfed along with him as a kid says Wotan and that Nothung sword has some of my stainless steel magic on it. But he's my son and not a free agent. Fricka rumbled that blast her.

Will you let Siegmund be killed then? asks Brünnhilde. It's all hopeless says Wotan. It's the curse of Alberich. Erda said a son of his would smash me up and now I hear a dwarf has made a woman pregnant. He's the one that will get me. It's all simply terrible (he bombs out). Pull yourself together Wotan says Brünnhilde *what do you want me to do*? Don't protect Siegmund says Wotan. Fricka has won. Shame on you cries Brünnhilde. I won't do it. You mutinous bitch you'll do what you're told says he. I've never seen you chicken out before says she. But OK I'll do what you say.

Sc 3 In which the runaways pause for a moment to allow Sieglinde to panic about pursuit by dogs

Hey! Steady! Not so fast stop! says Siegmund to Sieglinde we're both knackered. You must leave me my love says Sieglinde for I am guilty guilty guilty I made love to my brother whilst married to Hunding. Never mind I'll kill him shortly with this Nothung sword says Siegfried. No sweat. Listen! That's the baying of his hounds says Sieglinde (going a bit potty) they'll tear your flesh to ribbons. Faints.

Sc 4 In which Brünnhilde tries her best to obey her father's disgraceful instructions but is overcome by her noble nature

Look at me Siegmund says Brünnhilde [whatever happened to those dogs? Ed.] I want you to follow me to Valhalla please. Will I meet my wolffather there? asks Siegfried. You will meet your wolffather says she. Who else? asks he. A lot of dead soldiers she says officers of course now revived and retrained as stormtroopers. Any girl guides? he asks. Several girlguide troops says she. Can I bring along my sister and wife same person? asks he. Negative she says. Then I won't go says he. If you don't go that Hunding will kill you says she. Faugh! says he – that ape? My magic Nothung sword will soon polish him off. I've got news for you says Brünnhilde Wotan has de-magicked that sword. The treacherous sod says Siegmund, OK I'll fight, die and go to hell rather than oblige him by trundling up to this Valhalla place. At least let me look after your wife says she. If I'm going to die I'll kill her first says he. Madman she says think of the babby. [Sieglinde now pregnant: Ed.] My mind is made up says he: we will both die. Siegmund she says you're wonderful! I can't resist your chutzpah. I will re-magic the sword and you will kill Hunding and to hell with Wotan.

Sc 5 In which Siegmund expects to kill Hunding with his magic sword but is killed himself owing to Wotan's intervention and Hunding also drops dead from shock

Siegmund watches over Sieglinde in a deep sleep. She is having a terrible dream. Save me Siegmund! she cries just as the dreaded Hunding appears. Hey Dismal come out and fight he shouts. You think I'm still unarmed or something? says Siegmund I got this sword from out your ash tree boy: watch out. Stop it you two, kill me first before you kill each other says Sieglinde. (They pay no attention.) Attaboy Siegmund says Brünnhilde. Kill! Kill! Kill! Wotan materializes and holds out his spear which shatters Nothung. Hunding attacks. Siegmund falls down dead. OK Hunding says Wotan run off to Fricka and tell her what a good boy am I. But Hunding falls down dead. [Why? Ed.] Brünnhilde will pay for this says Wotan, snarling.

Act III A mountain top

Sc 1 In which Brünnhilde returns to barracks with Sieglinde across her saddle and a council of war discusses plans for her escape

The Valkyries are at their exercise: a vigorous form of airborne dressage combined with the transportation of dead bodies. Hoyoyoho! cries one. Heiaha! replies another. I gotta nice dead second lieutenant here cries a third. I got the tank captain that killed him cries a fourth. So it's all go with plenty of innocent girlish fun and laughter in Valkyriland plus a lot of horsey talk with sly jokes about mares and stallions. Hey shouts Helmetwig looking up from her pocket calculator, there's only eight of us. Should be nine. Brünnhilde's missing. Better wait for the captain says Walltrout.

But who is this they spy? Why it's Brünnhilde galloping split-arse with a female across her pommel. She arrives. Get up there and watch out for

Wotan he's after me she yells. What's the matter? they all cry. I got in there to protect Siegmund in a fight, she gasps, against Wotan's instructions: he turned up and caught me at it. Siegmund was killed this here female is his wife. Wotan's not far behind.

My God! Defying the boss! You're in real trouble Brünnhilde! they all say. Don't worry about me please says Sieglinde just kill me quietly and I'd really much prefer that. But what about the babby? asks Brünnhilde have you the right to deprive a half-human embryo of life? O Lord I hadn't thought of that says Sieglinde please save me. Right you slip off on your own says Brünnhilde and mind the dragon on the left and the nasty thick forest on the right. And by the way I'd keep these broken bits of Siegmund's sword. Could be useful. Thanks a lot B you're really kind says Sieglinde. Exits. Wotan's coming yells a Valk. Hide me girls! shouts Brünnhilde.

Sc 2 In which the Valkyries fail to protect Brünnhilde from Wotan's wrath and he pronounces a terrible punishment

Where's Brünnhilde? asks Wotan. Stop messing about I know she's here. Cool it Wotan they cry. She's here sure enough but calm down a bit please before you see her. She's for it girls I tell you says Wotan she'll be chucked out of Valhalla without a penny to her name and without a roof to her mouth. D'ye hear me Brünnhilde? Yes I do father says Brünnhilde appearing quietly. This hurts me more than it hurts you says Wotan: you're cashiered from the service. You're out. You're finished. You're done.

What exactly does that mean? asks Brünnhilde. Well banished from Valhalla for a start says Wotan, no more dragging up corpses no more serving the drinks no more family fun. How awful! cry the Valkyries poor Brünnhilde! And I will put you to sleep on this mountain top and – wait for it – whatever fellow finds you first and wakes you up will take you for wife and you will skivvy for him in some peasant's hut for the rest of your life. Got it? Hey Wotan! Steady on! Be reasonable! Please! say the Valkyries. Get off you lot says Wotan (they get off).

Sc 3 In which Brünnhilde makes a powerful case in defence of her conduct leading Wotan to decide to reduce her sentence in such a manner as to ensure that her future consort will at least be a hero

So was it so terrible what I did? asks Brünnhilde. I only did what you really wanted to do yourself. You wanted to stand by Siegmund. It was only after that terrible Fricka had argued you into a trance that you caved in. I did you a favour. And another thing when I saw Siegmund was such a dreamboat and so feisty a fighter I knew I couldn't let him down. So that's it says Wotan you see this guy about to be killed and you disobey me because he's cute. I had a hard time I will tell you in reaching that decision – I didn't like it at all – so what do you do? Jump in there with a light laugh and do it your way.

I couldn't believe my ears when you gave those orders says Brünnhilde. Not like my Dad. Not worthy of you. Nonsense says Wotan you just fell for that guy. Look father if this sleep business is on then OK but I don't like the waking up bit. Suppose some wimp like John Major were to find me? I come of a good family I have the DBE the DSO and Bar you made me an OM I am in fact a gallant honourable and very distinguished person. Can't you arrange things so that only a good class of man preferably brave would find me? You're asking too much and anyway I must be going says Wotan.

Dad how can you do this to your little girl? says Brünnhilde. Please please Dad throw a ring of fire around me so that whoever it is that gets through must have nerve and may even be Mr Right. OK good point I'll do it says Wotan and I'm really sorry to have to say goodbye to you my darling girl. Loge! Come here. A ring of fire round this lady at once please. (A ring of fire springs up.) Curtain.

MINUTES FROM START

LOOK OUT FOR

Act I Sc 1

(For motto numbers see the Table on page 558

0 The prelude* is stormy, indeed a storm, with the 0
middle strings buzzing on one note whilst the lower strings range up and down restlessly. They repeat a figure based on Spear [7] over and over. This builds up until the brass give out the cue for thunder (the same as Donner used, to get thunder at the end of *Rhinegold*: unlisted) and the timps bang out the thunderclap. Now we have a bit of peace after the storm and the music softens and sweetens as the curtain goes up.

Love's Awakening. The hunted Siegmund staggers in and collapses to his motto – cellos moving purposefully in a firm short phrase (unlisted). Sieglinde fetches him water and as they make eye contact and get into each other's C.V.s we have some of the ten-
4: *Ein fremder Mann?* derest music imaginable.*** In particular there are 4
short orchestral passages amidst the action which speak softly of their sudden strange mutual attraction

using mainly two mottos, the first Sieglinde's very own – a bass line going down followed by chords going up [e] – and the motto for their mutual love, Lovers, a long romantic smooth sweet melody [f] heard first on a solo cello when Siegmund is brought the water (we will hear a lot of this one). Until Siegmund gets active about leaving, the whole of this scene is played in a dreamy cocoon of romantic music, much of which is woven by the woodwind.

Act I Sc 2

But hark! What is that we hear? Hunding the hunter with his huntsman motto (a brassy hunting fanfare – unlisted). But, alas, when he enters the temperature drops and we are into a patch of quasi-recitatif as Hunding quizzes Siegmund – quite a lot of Hunding – and then we have Siegmund's dreary account of his early life – three long instalments, none of them by any means thrilling, but some lovely references to the Lovers motto [f] poked into the chinks in this sombre
29: *Ein trauriges Kind* tale. The last bout of autobiography is the best,* 29
when Siegmund describes a second massacre largely conducted by himself. He ends up with a rather ghastly burst of self-pity: now, he says to Sieglinde, you know why I'm not called Smiler. This to a Dismal Desmond of a motto – Self-Pity [g], a slow item climbing upwards ending in an unusual harmony. Almost immediately after this we first hear the noble Volsung theme – a majestic melody with dotted rhythms [h].

Hunding's challenge to Siegfried is surprisingly gentlemanly. It is followed by a lot of business onstage as Sieglinde goes to prepare Hunding's spiked nightcap. This has a gentle but portentous or-
35 chestral accompaniment* (Sieglinde [e] but only the 35
last part) ending in a prospective burst of the Sword motto (trumpet octave and arpeggio [14] – unmistakable, shining bright, first heard at the very end of *Rhinegold*).

Act I Sc 3

Now for something more considerable. A fine lyrical
39: *Ein Schwert verhiess mir der Vater* soliloquy** from Siegmund. He remembers his 39
father promised him a sword (a lot of Sword [14]) and this is mingled with excitement about Sieglinde –

Lovers [f].
45: *Der Männer Sippe* An equally good reply from Sieglinde.* She tells 45
the tale of how some mysterious old guy (Wotan of
course, and we hear a bit of Valhalla [5]) stuck the
sword into the tree. And towards the end we get a
blessed break in the tempo, which has been going at a
slow canter for the last zillion bars. Suddenly it's fast.
A lot of Sword [14] throughout, some of it pretty
triumphant.

The Spring Song. Something that nearly amounts
51: *Winterstürme wichen dem Wonnemond* to a set-piece aria from Siegmund.** He sees a con- 51
siderable affinity between love and springtime. This
is a fresh lyrical inspiration (in triple time – what a
nice change) and one feels it sprang from Wagner's
pen with some relief after the workshop labours of the
earlier pages. We are in the same territory as Walter's
'Am Stillen Herd' in *Meistersinger.* Virile, heroic, and
very very romantic.

The last part of Act I consists of a rather wonderful
54: *Du bist der Lenz* duet,** though true to Wagnerian principles the two 54
duettists do not sing together but turn and turn
about. It is an impassioned and freely written piece
gaining in intensity as it goes along and taking aboard
the dislodgement of the sword Nothung in its stride.
Siegmund and Sieglinde are brother and sister – so
what? Love is stronger than the taboos of consan-
guinity, much much stronger, if this cataract of passion is admissible evidence. Valhalla [5] crops up
when Wotan is mentioned and during the actual
sword-pulling bit, as well as the Sword [14] and Rejection [a], we have a new motto, Nothung (it means
the sword is needful or needed), consisting of a slow
downward octave twice, sung by Siegmund to 'Nothung, Nothung!' plus a tailpiece [15].

Act II Sc 1

0 The prelude starts with the Sword [14] and Lovers [f] 0
echoing around all over the place. Then what is this?
Do we hear the sword beginning to turn into a Valkyrie? Perhaps a little but then Ta-tum-titi-ta-ra and
the horses begin to run. This is the Valkyrie motto:
rocking horse rhythm rolled out by the trombones
4: *Hojotoho* [16]; unmistakable. Hojotoho!* The great war-cry of 4
Wotan's female warriors first sung by Brünnhilde

herself (War-Cry, a ferocious inverted yodel [17] often followed by a trill and a peal of laughter). Brünnhilde warns Wotan that there will be trouble with the wife. There is trouble, sure enough. Wotan and Fricka embark on a twenty-minute argument, much of it dry and recitatif-ish but with some appealing passages. The course of events is roughly as follows:

1. After the opening formalities Fricka says it's quite disgraceful about these Volsungs (see **Who's Who** page 561): adultery and incest, what next? I don't consider marriage without love a binding contract says Wotan – some Spear [7]. Quite appalling says Fricka. All the above to pretty ornery run-along Wagner.

2. Love will always find a way says Wotan. So let these two be. Rather nice references to Siegmund's
9: *Heut hast du's erlebt!* Spring Song.* 9

3. Fricka gives him a real earful. You're going to pot, Wotan, she says. And just look at the record of your own adulteries. The second part of this out-
11: *O, was klag' ich um Ehe und Eid* burst* shakes off all mottos and takes wing into free 11
writing. It runs along ferociously and grabs the attention.

4. The argument now becomes metaphysical (when is a hero not a hero) and the music less interesting. A good deal of the Sword [14].

5. Fricka is winning. Well what do you want? asks Wotan. No more protection of Siegmund says Fricka. OK says Wotan to a new and insistent motto – Frustration: starts with a buzz, like an angry bee, then fades away [18]. So Nothung will lose its power (lots of Sword [14]). Brünnhilde yodels offstage (War-Cry [17]). Collapse of Wotan, game set and match to Fricka, who celebrates her victory with a calm and
23: *Deiner ew'gen Gattin* dignified request** that Wotan goes on oath to keep 23
his word. He does so. We hear Spear [7], but it is broken up, also Curse [11]. A thoroughly eventful and musically satisfactory ending to the long, long debate.

Act II Sc 2

26: *O heilige Schmach!* Wotan bombs out.* He explodes with anger, shame, 26
guilt, misery, etc. Lots of Frustration [18], and an upside-down Sword or two [14]. Lively and dramatic.

Wotan on the couch. An extended self-analysis taking in a lot of his life and history. This dismal monologue addressed to poor Brünnhilde runs for some fifteen minutes in a dry sort of quasi-recitatif, almost parlando, with little help from the music. This is nondescript stuff, except for a generous sprinkling of mottos which pop out like cuckoos from clocks, mickey-mousing punctually with Wotan's thought processes and including Frustration [18], the Ring [4], Valkyrie [16], Valhalla [5], Sword [14], Curse [11], Earth [12] and a new one, an amalgam of Earth [12] and Frustration [18] (unlisted). Things do perk up a bit when Wotan works himself into a fury over
44: *Und für das Ende* Alberich's role in the ring saga,* and when, after that, 44
Brünnhilde brings him to the point, asking him Well, what now? The final exchanges have real feeling and we are left with something of the same sense of desolation as are Wotan and the mutinous Brünnhilde.

Act II Sc 3

50 There is a short orchestral prelude* before Siegmund 50
and Sieglinde arrive on this popular mountain top. It is based on Lovers [f] and you could be excused for not noticing this. But love in any form is a relief from a gloomy Wotan.

52: *Raste nun hier* With the Siegfried/Sieglinde duet* we are back in 52
the land of the lyrical Wagner although all is by no means sunshine and sea air. Sieglinde is running away in panic. Siegmund tries to stop her – lots of Lovers [f]. I'm your brother, husband, companion, minder, etc., etc., he cries, with no sign of breathlessness. I'm guilty, guilty, she replies in sweeping rushing phrases. Don't worry, I'll deal with Hunding says he: Nothung will see him off nicely – Sword [14] – and the whole musical texture stiffens. No! No! she screams, Hunding and his dogs are out after you now (loud hunting horns, real or imagined). She faints into an orchestral trance which dies away, but it takes an unconscionable time a-dying.

Act II Sc 4

The encounter between Brünnhilde and Siegmund – a really good scene.

1. The Wagner tubas speak out with a new motto – Fate [19], a doomy three-noter – long – short

(down) – long (up). It is sombre and sonorous and
64: *Siegmund! Sieh auf mich* very pregnant. Brünnhilde accosts Siegmund:** she 64
tells him of her mission. Enormously impressively paced, with the deep, deep tubas sounding Fate [19] and the brass choir putting in quite a lot of Valhalla [5] with just a whiff of Valkyrie [16] from time to time, plus references to Lovers [f]. This sounds like a bran tub but it isn't. The mottos fall into place in the context of the music's flow. There is plenty of air, plenty of room. Everything works wonderfully well.

71: *Zu ihnen folg ich dir nicht* 2. Siegmund's negation.** I won't go. Lots of 71
Fate [19] (and Fate extended to four bars). The pace quickens. Brünnhilde comes the heavy: You've got to go. Siegmund is stoical: I won't go. This piece is lyrical and uninhibited.

76: *Der dir es schuf* 3. The argument.** The tempo speeds up, the 76
volume grows, the number of notes per minute increases – there is a splendidly controlled accelerando and crescendo – or speed up and sound up – as the two parties get really dogged with each other. Although there are a few references – Lovers [f], Fate [19], the inevitable Sword [14] – and the tubas are still there in full voice, we are now into really great lyrical writing and it is thrilling.

80: *Halt ein, Wälsung* 4. Brünnhilde converted.*** In agony and at the 80
same time in ecstasy, she defies Wotan and tells Siegmund it's OK she will be on his side: he will win. This wonderful outburst from Brünnhilde raises the hairs on the nape of the neck, and not a motto in sight (or if there is it does not notice).

Act II Sc 5

83: *Zauberfest bezähmt ein Schlaf* Siegmund and Sieglinde alone.* After the storm of 83
Brünnhilde's departure we have the soft sweet music of the orchestral prelude that began Scene 3 with some of Fate [19] but more of the love music, Lovers [f], which runs under Siegmund's address to the sleeping/fainting Sieglinde. But suddenly – bang crash – he hypes himself up for battle, Sword [14]. He makes such a racket as to wake Sieglinde who is having a bad dream. This leads to musical turmoil as Hunding turns up blaring his horn all ready for the
88: *Wehwalt! Wehwalt!* fight. He bleats bloodthirstily.* Action! A lot hap- 88
pens very quickly. Hunding and Siegmund square up

for battle in rather a muffled manner except for the Sword [14] shining out clearly. Kill me first! shrieks Sieglinde.* Get after him with Nothung! yells Brünnhilde – Sword [14] again and Valkyrie [16]. Watch me do the spear trick! says Wotan – Spear [7]. He does the spear trick: Siegmund falls dead (BONK!) – Bad News [d] followed by Volsung [h] and Fate [19]. Jump on my horse love, says Brünnhilde to Sieglinde – Valkyrie [16]. Now everything stops as slow trombones give the scene some gravitas. Then (CRASH! POW!) Hunding drops dead (cause of death unknown) and we are into a furious endpiece; Wotan very cross with Brünnhilde – Frustration [18] – and then a noisy orchestral finish. Rousing stuff, but this finale lacks the expert pacing of the great Siegmund/Brünnhilde scene that has gone before.

Act III Sc 1

0 The Ride of the Valkyries.*** As famous as any mu- 0
sical ride in history. We start off orchestrally with only reasonably light forces engaged. After the opening trill (wonderfully exciting), we have both Valkyrie [16] and soon, as the girls join in, War-Cry [17] as well. The Valkyrie tune drives along its course relentlessly until it lets up to allow the girls to have a little gossip about their horseys. But then BINGO and we're off again with greater force than ever and some nice girlish laughter (a pendant to War-Cry [17]) until we get to BANG! WHAM! the final rendering of the ride with all the massed fire-power of the brass section pounding out the tune in unison. A really big noise, and very satisfactory. Now we have some more stable-yard chatter and lots of laughter until we get to the count, when, after careful calculation, the girls find they are only eight, not nine. Brünnhilde is missing.

7: *Nach dem Tann lenkt* The Valkyries' meeting.** Brünnhilde rides in 7
over some sweeping scales, deriving from Earth [12]; although they do a lot of work in this scene, they don't appear again. She explains herself and Sieglinde to the waiting Valks in breathless recitatif; all very fast. Oh Brünnhilde! say the Valks, disobey father Wotan? Yer on yer own lady. Good exciting stuff. In earlier

days this section might have been called arioso, but it is arioso in fast forward, faster than any of the Italians – even Verdi – could have managed.

Brünnhilde plots Sieglinde's escape. After some discussion about escape routes and some plotty stuff updating us on Fafner's change of lifestyle (now a dragon), we reach one of the most lovely passages in the opera and one that decides the future course of the whole saga: Brünnhilde tells Sieglinde to push off
14: *Fort denn eile* quick:** she is pregnant with Siegfried: she must 14
take the fragments of Nothung for future reconstruction. This is Brünnhilde at her best – heroic, prophetic and at the same time a kind, decent woman. In this fine piece she sings an important new motto (doubled by horns), Siegfried Heroic: it starts with three upward steps, a heroic call with a follow-
16: *O hehrstes Wunder!* through [20]. This leads to Sieglinde's reply,*** the 16
most inspired melody in the whole pantechnicon, Ecstasy [21]. Too long and too beautiful to be called a motto, it reappears again at the end of the whole *Ring* and its message in both places is to tell us what a glorious woman is Brünnhilde.

Wotan's arrival, with his habit of never saying in ten bars what can be said in a hundred, heralds some boring stuff to come, and indeed his verdict on
Act III Sc 2 Brünnhilde paid out inch by inch in recitatif/arioso
(Spear [7] prominent) is tedious, but the situation is saved by the Valks who panic on his arrival in the most pleasing fashion and who once again revive interest when they plead for mercy for Brünnhilde in
25: *Halt ein, o Vater!* eight-part counterpoint.** Their disappearance to 25
strains of Valkyrie [16] and with the descending scales of laughter turned to tears, is also agreeable.

Act III Sc 3

So we enter the forty-minute marathon duet between Brünnhilde and Wotan that runs us through to the final curtain.

1. Brünnhilde pleads with Wotan: What I did was what you really wanted me to do. She starts with rather a lovely melody perhaps derived from Spear [7] – but then anything can be derived from anything else if put in enough gear-changes – which stays with her until the end of the round. Wotan's utterances

tend to be pretty dry, but hers are sweet and persuasive and particularly when she tells Wotan that it was sympathy for Siegmund that compelled her to help
40: *Scheu und staunend stand ich in Scham* him.* (Frustration [18], Valkyrie [16], Curse [11] and 40
Spear [7] around early in this section.)

2. The debate continues at much the same musical temperature, Wotan (dry recitatif-ish) saying he has renounced the Volsungs, Brünnhilde (more lyrical) saying they are great and that there is a new Volsung hero to be born (Siegfried Heroic [20]). No stars.

3. Now Wotan turns to the matter of Brünnhilde's punishment. He decrees sleep and whoever wakes her up – finders keepers. Reference to Fate [19]. A new motto, Sleep [i]: slow chords poncing around in semitones, usually downward, but on this first appearance they squirm. Brünnhilde wants her waker-up to show he's up to snuff and her passionate
49: *Soll fesselnder Schlaf fest mich binden* appeal** to Wotan pays off. Very fine, Wagner at his 49
stormy imperious best – Siegfried Heroic [20], some Spear [7] and Valkyrie [16]. Brünnhilde gets her ring of fire.

4. Wotan's farewell. At last he comes out of his corner singing like a loving father rather than a crusty
52: *Leb wohl, du kühnes, herrliches Kind* Victorian paterfamilias. Goodbye my girl he says:** 52
you shall have your fire. He warms to his work; only a warrior shall have you, he says (Siegfried Heroic [20]). Then as he puts his magic on Brünnhilde we
55 move into a splendid orchestral intermezzo.*** A 55
lovely motto here (we have had a hint of it before) – Trance [22]: soothing five-note downward phrase. It carries on under Wotan as he squares up for his last kiss. This is a different Wotan, quieter and quite touching (Rejection [a] and some of Sleep [i]). Now
66 another intermezzo – mainly Trance [22].*** Peace- 66
ful, sleep-inducing and quite beautiful. Suddenly both Fate [19] and Spear [7] break in harshly and Loge music [8] starts spurting out all over the place as Wotan calls on him for fire. As the fire laps over the rock we have a last forecast of Siegfried's heroism [20] and as Loge [8] dissolves into Sleep [i] the opera glides away, trance-like [22], into the distance. But not without a reminder of Fate [19].

NOTES and NEWS AND GOSSIP See **The Birth of *The Ring*** page 362

COMMENT See also **The Ring – A General Hello** page 549

The story of *Valkyrie*, if not exactly humdrum, is simple and straightforward. Man runs into hut, falls in love with long-lost twin sister. They elope. Gods disagree as to whether or not the man should be sponsored in duel with sister's husband, senior god withdraws sponsorship, man killed. Wife/sister, now pregnant, saved by junior god. Senior god punishes junior god by dumping her in a ring of fire to sleep until Mr Right comes along to wake her with a kiss. If the script had been kept down to the narrative and the digressions, in particular the metaphysical arguments, dropped, *Valkyrie* would have come out at something between two-and-a-half and three hours, instead of nearly four – about the same length as *Rhinegold*. The main hold-ups are Wotan's now-read-on stuff, which is an immense amount of retrospective detail explaining the whole saga of the ring, and also two lengthy debates, Wotan/Fricka on the nature, function and status of a hero and the Wotan/Brünnhilde debate about crime and punishment. We also have a shorter now-read-on from Siegmund himself in Act I. These digressions are a drag on the show because:

1. They hold up the forward thrust of the narrative.
2. No one can understand them without doing a lot of prep. Even German-speakers are unable to catch this sort of stuff when it's sung over an orchestra of a thousand, and surtitles can't properly cope with anything beyond fairly straightforward narrative and dialogue.
3. The actual subject matter is deeply boring. The ring saga told as a tale could be magic, but synopsized in a scrappy sort of flashback to justify Wotan's conduct, it is hardly a gripper. As for the arguments, they are legalistic if not donnish, a million miles away from the direct emotional clashes that were the stuff of Italian opera. We listen with impatience to clever points being made in slow time.

This is not to say that the music of the slow bits is boring too. It is true that Wotan's ramble through the past in Act II is musically tedious, but the two arguments are not. But even Wagner can't write consistently thrilling music for singers who are scoring debating points off each other and therefore in these sections the voltage drops and so does the listener's interest.

In the rest of the opera the music is always gripping and often quite wonderful. Wagner deploys his best romantic/mystical strain in the love music in the first scene (and in lots of later references), in the Spring Song and in the final duet. This is the music of sexual magnetism and also of the tearaway romantics, not unlike Walther's music in *Meistersinger*. The heroic music that is the most powerful in *The Ring* is the stuff written for the collective of the Valkyries which musters more force than ever Siegfried could drum up on his own. The Valkyries are quite wonderful in sound and concept, and their music has as much zing as any that has been written for the opera house. Pity the poor designer: how can he possibly match such majestic pictorial music?

On the softer side, the best scene in *Valkyrie*, both dramatically and musically, is Act II Scene 4, between Siegmund and Brünnhilde. The opening exchanges in this confrontation are marvellously impressive with Wagner's very own tubas doing exactly the work for which he had designed them, and then we have a slow build-up to the climax with mottos abounding yet adding to the rise and rise in the tension up to the final explosion. If only every page of the score had the forward drive and absolute command of pace as does this one, how happy we would be.

The other great scene in *Valkyrie* is the last. The forty-minute duet between Wotan and Brünnhilde is too slow and too long and does not really warm up until she makes her appeal for a more honourable sentence, but then it takes wing and carries us with it to the glorious end with fire lapping the stage and the five-note Trance motto repeated mesmerically over and over and over again, but not once too often.

There are two short items of pure joy in *Valkyrie*. The first is Sieglinde's farewell to Brünnhilde – 'O hehrstes Wunder!'. Suddenly Wagner pulls out of the bag a phrase more striking and more beautiful than anything else in the opera. It is one of those rare moments of musical elation that may occur only once in a month's listening (and Wagner uses this piece of magic only once again – at the very end of the road). The second is when the eight Valkyries beg Wotan not to be too rough with Brünnhilde. This is clever stuff – eight separate parts in counterpoint – and it sounds dense and tightly-knit, but it catches the ear and sticks in the mind, as great music should, whether it be clever or just good.

So there it is, *Valkyrie* sprawls, has its longueurs, its miracle patches, its scenes that are compulsive and scenes not so compulsive, also, of course, the Ride itself, but whatever your reservations and vexations with the opera may have been, if you are a fair listener you will acknowledge it as a work of genius, and you will leave the opera house or stow away your CDs marvelling that the human imagination could stretch to such a huge enterprise and should then, more or less, pull it off.

Siegfried

Part III of *The Ring*

Wagner

The one where Siegfried turns blacksmith and forges a sword with which he kills a dwarf and a dragon and then walks through fire to discover eternal love.

CAST (see **Who's Who page 549**)

The Wanderer, Wotan, chief of the gods, in disguise	Bass–baritone
Siegfried, a hero	Tenor
Mime, a dwarf	Tenor
Alberich, his brother, chief dwarf	Bass–baritone
Erda, Earth goddess	Contralto
Brünnhilde, chief Valkyrie, suspended from duty	Soprano
A bird	Soprano
Fafner, once a giant, now a dragon	Bass

3 acts: running time 4 hrs

STORY

Act I A cave in some rocks in a forest

Sc 1 In which Mime fails to piece together the magic sword Nothung and our hero learns the story of his early life

It seems I've been at this forging bit forever says Mime to himself and every time I produce a sword from these sodding fragments that bastard Siegfried smashes it up. In talkative mood Mime goes on to tell us:

1. Siegfried is fearless
2. Fafner is now a dragon and guards the Rhinegold in his cave (adjacent)
3. Siegfried is very strong
4. He plots to have Siegfried kill the dragon and get the gold for himself.

Enter Siegfried leading a bear. Why the hell do you keep bringing in bears? says Mime climbing up the scenery. I prefer their company to yours says Siegfried. Is the sword ready? Yip says Mime. Siegfried smashes it. Another dud he says. You're hopeless. Ungrateful boy says Mime: have some minestrone? Not your pigswill says Siegfried I ate an antelope in the forest. You are horrible to me Siegfried says Mime and yet

I did all the work of mother nurse tutor P.T. instructor skivvy chef barber religious adviser and you hate me. Because you are a revolting deformed dwarf says Siegfried also because you smell. I can't think why I come back here. Parental affection says Mime.

Nuts says Siegfried and talking of parents who was my mum? There wasn't one says Mime. Parthenogenesis. Did it all myself. Liar says Siegfried a pretty person like me couldn't have a toad like you for one parent never mind both. He beats Mime up. Stop it you're killing me screams Mime. Who were my parents? asks Siegfried screwing Mime's neck. OK OK I'll tell you says Mime: you see I came on this woman giving birth. Name? asks Siegfried. Sieglinde says Mime.

Where is she? asks Siegfried. Dead says Mime she said if it's a girl call her Mary Lou if a boy Siegfried. Expired. Father? asks Siegfried. Not known says Mime that's how I became your mother nurse tutor. . . . Belt up says Siegfried any other material facts? Your mum gave me these bits of your dad's sword says Mime. Get moving you disgusting dwarf says Siegfried, make me a decent sword and I'm off hunting and wish I could never see you again. Exits. Dear dear says Mime. This is not how I had planned it at all.

Sc 2 In which Wotan in disguise challenges Mime to a quiz game in which the stakes are high

How do? says Wotan strolling into Mime's cave. Get off says Mime no travellers. But I am not a commercial says Wotan I am a consultant. No consultants required says Mime: get out. Wotan doesn't go. OK says Mime we'll play this game. Rules as follows: I ask you three questions. You get 'em right you stay. You get 'em wrong I kill you. OK? OK says Wotan.

Your starter for ten says Mime what kind of persons live under the earth? Nibelungs says Wotan. Correct says Mime. No. 2: what class of persons live on earth? The giants says Wotan. [No one else? Ed.] OK No. 3 says Mime: who lives in heaven? The gods says Wotan. OK you win says Mime. I won't kill you.

But now for the second leg says Wotan it's my turn. Go ahead says Mime. Your starter says Wotan: what is the family Wotan loves best and punishes most? The Volsungs says Mime. Good enough says Wotan. What was the name of Siegmund's sword? Nothung says Mime. OK says Wotan No. 3: who will weld Nothung back into shape? Dunno says Mime. So I win the right to kill you says Wotan. The correct answer is 'The man who never knew fear' and I hereby delegate to him whoever he may be the right to murder you in his own time. Cheerio. Exits (Mime wets his pants).

Sc 3 In which before our very eyes Siegfried forges an excellent sword and tests it upon a defective anvil

Mime is having a nightmare about the dragon. Siegfried wakes him. Is the sword ready? he asks. Napoo says Mime a man told me no one can do it except someone who never knew fear. Fear? says Siegfried whassat? Makes you wet your pants says Mime. I'll take you to visit the dragon. He should do the trick.

OK says Siegfried but let's make the sword first. You can't do it says Mime the instruction manual got burnt in the forge. Stuff that says Siegfried I'll do it somehow. He starts. Want some solder? asks Mime. No says Siegfried no patching up this time. A complete re-forge. By the way what's the sword called? Nothung says Mime. Nothing attempted nothing done says Siegfried. He forges on singing Ho Ho Ho quite a lot and hammering the sword on the anvil. Mime thinks (out loud) hey this guy doesn't know fear yet let's hope the dragon scares the hell out of him. If not he could be the one Wotan delegated to knock me off. He could pinch the treasure too. I'll poison him after he's killed the dragon, that's what.

Ho Ho Ho sings Siegfried forging on. He gives a running progress report. At last (Ho Ho Ho) the sword is finished and for some incomprehensible reason he strikes the anvil a mighty blow. The anvil splits in two (Ho Ho Ho).

Act II Deep in a forest

Sc 1 In which Wotan the Wanderer has a disagreeable encounter with Alberich outside the dragon's cave and nothing much happens

Alberich is watching over the dragon's cave to make sure no one else pinches the gold. Enter Wotan thinly disguised. Go away Wotan says Alberich you've already played one dirty trick on me: I don't want you stealing the gold a second time. Ho Ho wait till I get that ring Wotan and I'll fairly sort out you gods. I'll be the king of the castle I will. Anyway I know your tricks. All this stuff about an earth-born hero. Have you got one yet?

If you want to pick a fight says Wotan do it with Mime that nauseating brother of yours not with me. Did you know he was double-crossing you and will pinch the gold himself? And he was bringing a hero with him to do it? Why don't you tell the dragon he'll be killed unless he gives you the gold now? Fafner wakes up. Alberich puts the proposition. Be quiet *please* says Fafner lemme sleep. Well that was a no go says Wotan. Exits. I'll get you gods in the end says Alberich rather feebly.

Sc 2 In which Siegfried kills the dragon and gets good advice from a bird

Enter Mime and Siegfried. Is this where I learn about fear? asks Siegfried the simple soul. If you don't learn it here God knows where else says Mime. In there lives the most horrendous beast sabre-toothed lethal claws deadly tail saliva of vitriol urine of nitric acid breath of phosgene . . . . OK OK does it have a heart if so where? asks Siegfried. Usual place says Mime. Noted says Siegfried. I'll take a little nap by the stream says Mime you go ahead and kill that beast when you come out then wake me up. Exits.

Siegfried muses what a revolting little dwarf is Mime I'm so glad he was not my dad. Wonder what my mum was like (gets all soppy) I wonder if that bird could tell me (also crazy) maybe I could talk to it if I made similar sounds? (And ridiculous too.) He tries blowing on reeds and makes embarrassing noises. Tries his horn which he can play to about standard Grade IV. The bird is not impressed but the dragon wakes up. Stop making that bleeding noise he shouts can't a fellow sleep? I've come to learn fear also to kill you says Siegfried. Pshaw says the dragon I'll eat you for breakfast first. Will you indeed? says Siegfried and plunges sword into the dragon. Mother o'God says the dragon fancy being killed by a fresh-faced lad like you mark my words you'll suffer for this: what's your name? Volsung, Siegfried V. Volsung says Siegfried licking the dragon's blood off his fingers in a rather beastly fashion.

Hey Siegfried says the bird: a German composer called Wagner made that dragon's blood an enabler to the comprehension of ornithological linguistics – God knows why – so we can now talk to each other so long as you don't use long words and I'm telling you for starters that there's gold in that thar cave also the Tarnhelm magicap and the laser-ray ring that could make you Superman Batman or whatever. Thanks says Siegfried be my Robin.

Sc 3 In which the two dwarfs quarrel, Siegfried avoids being poisoned, kills Mime and follows the bird in search of a lovely lady

Alberich slinks on also Mime. Keep your thieving fingers off my gold says Alberich. My gold says Mime. Mine says Alberich. Mine says Mime I made the tarncap and the ring you lost them. Anyway it belongs to the boy now says Alberich he won it. Let's split says Mime you take the ring I take the magicap. Not bloody likely says Alberich no deal. (Withdraws.)

Siegfried exits the cave carrying the ring and magicap. What the hell do I do with this stuff I don't know says Siegfried. Don't give it to those devious dwarfs says the bird. Did you learn fear? asks Mime. Don't think so says Siegfried. You need a drink says Mime: take this it will kill you. Whassat? says Siegfried. It's poisoned says Mime and for some reason which neither I nor anyone associated with this show can fathom I'm blurting out the truth all the time although I mean to conceal it. You think you're funny or something? says Siegfried. Cuts his head off. Pushes corpse into the cave. Drags the dead dragon across the mouth. Sits under tree. Pity poor lonely me he says no brothers no sisters mother dead father unknown – hey you bird could you please find me a mate?

I know just the girl says the bird but there's a slight disadvantage. What's that? asks Siegfried. She sleeps all the time says the bird also a permanent bushfire rages round her. Any hope for me? asks Siegfried. Only if you have never known fear says the bird. Snap! says Siegfried that's me never had a tremor. Would you kindly fly towards this lady at the pace of a rather slow marathon runner? Only too happy to oblige says the bird.

Act III The foot of a mountain
Sc I In which Wotan the Wanderer has a pretty unsuccessful interview with an old associate, namely Erda the earth mother

Wakey wakey Erda cries Wotan get your feet on the floor. Whosat? says Erda. It's me I'm an incognito VIP traveller says Wotan. Lemme be says Erda. If you want anything go to Norman's office it's full of Norms they're paid to give information. I'd rather have it from the boss if you don't mind says Wotan.

Go and ask my girl Brünnhilde says Erda: it may interest you to know that she's the result of my liaison with HRH the King of Greece alias Wotan a distinguished god. She's in trouble says Wotan she went against her dad Wotan. He punished her by putting her to sleep in a bushfire. Who's that pig to punish anyone for being uppity? says Erda he's been getting above himself this last two million years. Excuse me I want to drop off again. Hey Erda wake up your old lover Wotan's in trouble and he wants to know how to stop the end of the world. Whassat? says Erda kindly stop bothering me with foolish questions. She goes to sleep.

She's gone off says Wotan but I could tell her something namely that I'm not that much bothered about the end of the world any more for I'm going to duck out pretty soon and hand over to that young Volsung grandson of mine he's got his hands on the ring already. He's a good chap and will sort out that bastard Alberich good and proper. It would be nice too if he married his aunt Brünnhilde. Such a fine woman. Have a good sleep Erda.

Sc 2 In which Siegfried is extremely rude to his grandfather and breaks his spear

That bird goes too bloody fast I've lost it says Siegfried but here's an old man. Hey you have you seen a female asleep on a rock in a bushfire? he asks. What's all this? asks Wotan. Well you see there was this dwarf who got me to kill this dragon whose blood made it possible for me to understand birds so I asked one to bring me here which it did but I've lost it says Siegfried. How did you kill the dragon? asks Wotan. With a sword says Siegfried. Who made the sword? asks Wotan. I did says Siegfried. From what? asks Wotan. Splinters says Siegfried. What splinters? asks Wotan. Oh for Chrissake stop it you tiresome old bastard says Siegfried. Kindly show some respect for age says Wotan. The last guy who lectured me had his head cut off says Siegfried get out of my way. Shan't says Wotan. Lemme past says Siegfried. My spear will stop you says Wotan. Faugh! says Siegfried. He smashes Wotan's spear with Nothung. Walks by: arrives at a rockface which slowly starts to move downwards until we reach –

Sc 3 The mountain top
In which Siegfried walks through fire and learns about the female shape through waking up an extremely attractive female with whom he falls in love

What's that? says Siegfried passing through the fire unsinged, why it's a sleeping horse! And there's a sleeping fella. His armour looks a bit tight better cut it open. Somewhat riskily he uses Nothung as tin-opener and cuts a slit down the person's chest. Peers inside. Good Lord he says – Lord bless me – looking very carefully at the contours of the person's chest – well I'll be damned that ain't no fella. I've got a funny feeling all over and especially in my trousers – why I know what it must be – it's – it's a woman! How impressive! God I'm terrified! Scared rigid! I have learned fear at last! Doesn't she look just stunning?

Whassa time? What year is it? Who woke me? says Brünnhilde. I did. Me. I'm Siegfried says Siegfried. Thanks Siegfried says Brünnhilde I knew you before you were born when your mum was pregnant I was her best friend. Good to see you Siegfried I always thought my dad would make things work out right. You've got lovely lips says Siegfried. O Lord there's my old Sam Brown and my Smith & Wesson .310 says Brünnhilde now I no longer hold HM's commission I am no longer a royal I am just a mortal. Zut! How ornery!

This Siegfried looks a sexy fellow best not to get involved. I'm scared stiff of human sex having been for many centuries above that sort of thing. Brünnhilde I love you says Siegfried employing quite a lot of poetry. Actually I love you too says Brünnhilde weakening. They clinch. Rapture. Bliss. I'm on fire. I'm no longer afraid. Yours forever. Forever mine. You are sublime. You are lovely. You are just a pet they say to each other. They are in love. Curtain.

MINUTES FROM START

LOOK OUT FOR

Act I Sc 1

(For motto numbers see the Table on page 558)

0 The prelude* opens dark and very deep, first with a 0
couple of bassoons soon joined by a double-bass tuba, a startling sound indeed. It moves upwards from the bowels of the earth, first giving some play to Frustration [18] and then, rather hesitantly, to Anvils [9], gaining speed and strength all the time. So on to Bad News [d] on the cor anglais, Ring [4] and finally Sword [14] rings out loud and clear. Quite a story in sound and an effective curtain-raiser.

After a bit of solus forging and brooding by Mime – one new motto, Fafner (as dragon): four notes on grunting tubas [23] – we hear a hurried burst of Siegfried's Horn: a winding horn call, unmistakable [24] and he bounces in with a bear. The poor creature has no motto, something that must distress the Animal Rights fraternity. Siegfried tells Mime how he came
8: *Nach bessrem Gesellen* by the bear in a fine lyrical burst,* Siegfried Heroic 8
[20].

Siegfried tells Mime he doesn't think much of him as a metal-worker and rejects Mime's offer of a nice roast beef breakfast. (A new version of the Anvil motto [9], Mime the tiresome, Mime the nanny: fidgety fiddles – unlisted.) Mime replies in a set-piece
12: *Als zullendes Kind* saga of pained self-pity* – I done everything for this 12
lad and he spits in my eye. This is a particularly attention-catching patch in a scene that swims along at a good pace and melodiously.

Siegfried replies that he just can't stand Mime and then a tiny miracle. Wagner turns Mime's longing for affection into an orchestral phrase of melting beauty which for a moment stops the show in its tracks (Longing – strings sweet and slow [j]). Mime begs for
17: *Ei Mime, bist du so witzig* love but Siegfried is more interested in the birds and the bees. He indulges in a brief wildlife rhapsody* 17

(you can hear the birds fluting away) which has a fine careless rapture.

When he asks about his parents (Siegfried Heroic [20]) Mime won't tell him until Siegfried gets physical (climax) and forces the story out of him (an unlistcd motto of the Volsung family here in the woodwind, not to worry with it) and Longing [j] then in hushed tones Mime tells of his birth and Sieglinde's death – Siegfried Heroic [20] again. Persistent quizzing of Mime extracts from him the news of the fragments of Nothung and now we go into a fine flurry as the excited Siegfried tells Mime to get for-
27: *Und diese Stücke* ging fast* (a lot of free writing). He goes and Mime 27
sits dolefully at his anvil (sad version of Anvils motto [9]).

Act I Sc 2

Wotan drops in to Mime's cave with a noble new motto – Wanderer (even-paced chords: semitones
31: *Heil dir, weiser Schmied!* [k]). His stately greeting* is answered by Mime in a 31
pert fashion and they parley on until the incomprehensible guessing game begins (Spear [7]). Wotan's answers are mickey-moused punctually by the motto for every item mentioned including Anvils [9], Giants [6], Fafner solus as dragon [23], Valhalla [5] and Spear [7] – this last very loud. Wotan keeps things on the boil all the way, but the one star at the head of the scene will have to do for all this riddle-me-ree stuff.

Now it's Mime's turn and he runs through his catalogue of mottos until Wotan asks him the sixty-four thousand dollar question which he can't answer. Mime explodes into a frenzy and Wotan addresses
53: *Dreimal solltest du fragen* him in a good final burst* of the sort of running arioso 53
he has been dealing out for most of the scene. He tells Mime that:

1. Your head is in hock to the guy who does the remake of Nothung
2. And he will be a man who never knew fear.

There is a good deal of Siegfried Heroic [20] around at this point.

Act I Sc 3

56: *Verfluchtes licht!* Soon we have the rippling fire music of Loge [8] as
Mime has some sort of brainstorm.* He also halluci- 56

nates up Fafner the dragon breathing down his neck. Vivid.

After Mime's rather feeble attempt to make Siegfried's flesh creep by goosing him with forest fears,
60: *Sonderlich seltsam muss das sein!* Siegfried replies manfully* that he'd love to be scared 60
but finds it frightfully difficult. This is a good burst of natural song which traffics mainly in three mottos – Trance [22], quite a lot of this distorted at first but soon smoothed out, Siegfried Heroic [20], Loge [8] and then a lot more Trance [22].

Siegfried brushes Mime aside and in a scurry of excitement prepares the fragments of Nothung for the
65: *Her mit den Stücken* forge.* This is sung to, around and within a welter of 65
sound in which the strings play around with Siegfried's Horn motto [24] in a dozen different ways.

68: *Nothung! Nothung!* Siegfried's forging song – a set piece.** Well, not 68
all that set, for each strophe tends to drift off into highways and byways. But it is all one continuous piece of rolling anvil-hitting music fifteen minutes long with interjections by Mime and not a million miles away from Hans Sachs's Schusterlied in *Meistersinger*. But this is heavier metal with Nothung [15] and two new mottos: Siegfried Blacksmith [l]: rolling downward runs in the bass with some fancy trimming on top (octave leaps), this last so heavily used that it is almost hammered to pieces; and finally Siegfried's Muscle [m]: a motto which comes in various forms, here a five-finger exercise played not on the piano but thumped out in the bass in octaves by all manner of instruments. This mighty outpouring ends noisily and in great triumph with Siegfried bursting the anvil in half (Horn I [24]).

Act II Sc 1

0 The prologue* growls and booms along its sluggish 0
passage to curtain up. The bass tubas play basso profundo with that deep rasp that sends a frisson down the spine. We have the rhythm of Giants [6] (before Fafner's transformation) on the timps and besides Fafner's squirm [23], quite a lot of the Curse [11].
7: *Zur Niedhöle fuhr ich bei Nacht* The long confrontation between Alberich and Wotan 7
is not exactly musically dull, it just doesn't seem to be getting us anywhere. There are patches of quasi-recitatif but some arioso as well, some little climaxes

and some big climaxes. They rake over old ground. They threaten. They finish up exactly where they started. References to Wanderer [k], Curse [11], Spear [7] and for Wotan a little Frustration [18]. No stars.

At last Wotan threatens Alberich with Siegfried's
13: *Mit mir nicht* arrival and calls to Fafner in his cave.* Now we have 13
some mildly diverting pantomime stuff, timps still sticking to the old Giants [6], some squirming [23], Fafner singing out of an echo chamber. Alberich flings the Curse [11] after the retreating Wotan. But all a little below par, only just a star.

Act II Sc 2

This scene opens with brisk exchanges between Sieg-
22: *Wir sind zur Stelle!* fried and Mime in a sort of recitatif,* heavily dotted 22
with mottos – Blacksmith [l] on a solo horn, the old Giants [6] on the timps, Fafner [23], a reminder of Anvils [9]. Siegfried's interest in the dragon's anatomy is to discern the position of its heart which we hear beating rather revoltingly for a few bars.

At last the evil Mime goes and we are into Forest
28 Murmurs:** shimmering strings [25]. This has an 28
outdoor sound like the music of the waters of the Rhine or the clouds around Valhalla and it comes as a wholesome change from loathsome dwarfs and dragon's heartbeats. The rest of the scene goes as follows:

1. Siegfried wonders about his parents. Who was his mum he asks himself in soft and melodious
30: *Aber, wie sah meiner Mutter* tones.** Lovely, and related to Longing [j] and an 30
unlisted Volsung motto.

2. More Murmurs [25], very agreeable. A bird springs out of a bush and sings (Birdie [26]: birdlike piping).

32: *Du holdes Vöglein* 3. Siegfried in a really nice lyrical free passage* 32
debates whether birdtalk can be understood by humans. Tries to ingratiate himself with the bird by blowing on reeds. Horrible results. Tries his horn instead. Lengthy and taxing solo* which has every First Horn in a state of panic until it is safely over – Horn I [24], Siegfried Heroic [20].

4. Fafner makes disgusting noises – growls and rumbles – from his cave. O Boy! shouts Siegfried,

he's coming out. Now a dialogue between Fafner and
38: *Haha! Da hätte mein Lied* Siegfried,* pretty witless but it helps to build up the 38
tension. Shouts and growls – lots of Fafner [23] of
course and the old Giants [6].

42 5. The battle itself** – Fafner [23] played against 42
Horn I [24], Giants [6] banging on in the timps and in
victory a whiff of Nothung [15]. A rousing encounter.

44: *Wer bist du kühner Knabe* 6. The dragon's deathbed speech.* As well as the 44
above mottos, the old Giants [6] played full and
proper and the Curse [11].

7. Siegfried licks the dragon's blood off his fingers and can now understand the bird, who has a
47: *Hei Siegfried* message for him. A novelty number* with quite a bit 47
of charm.

Act II Sc 3

And now for something entirely different – a change of mood, change of music, a queer scene. Alberich and Mime lurch on to a lumbering syncopated accompaniment arguing the toss about who gets the treasure. Few mottos – a little Anvils [9], Ring [4] and Rhinegold [3]. Then Siegfried comes out of the cave wondering what to do with the pretty stuff. A nice re-
53: *Was ihr mir nützt* flective piece* with a cushion of horns heaving about 53
below Siegfried's voice and leading into Murmurs [25]. Out pops the bird again singing in perfect German [26] and gives its anti-dwarf warning. Then (surprise) Mime muses to some sweet and rather dreamy
55: *Er sinnt und er wägt* version of the motto for the Volsung race* [h] inter- 55
rupted by Frustration [18]. Mime's version of this motto is shorter than Wotan's – of a size more suitable for a dwarf.

Mime meets his end. The dialogue between Mime
57: *Willkommen Siegfried!* and Siegfried is strange indeed:* the music is halting 57
and uncertain, making its own path as it goes along. And as for the words – one has the awful suspicion that Wagner thought he was being comical in making Mime blurt out his true thoughts very much as did Basil Fawlty on the memorable night when the German guests died at Fawlty Towers. Whatever the intention, the scene doesn't work. A star because it is such a curio. Mottos – Frustration [18], fleeting references to Birdie [26], Anvils [9]. Mime's subsequent death and Alberich's echoing laugh do, however, give

a measure of satisfaction.

Siegfried triumphant. After he has pushed Mime's body into the cave, dragged the dragon's body across its mouth and said Thank You to Nothung – whew! – Anvils [9], Giants [6], Horn I [24] and the Curse [11] – whew! again Siegfried settles down to a little quiet
66: *Da lieg auch du* meditation.** This is Siegfried lyrical, and very nice 66
too; he wonders did he have brothers? Sisters? Who was his mum? He asks the bird, how about a suitable wife? References to Mime's Frustration [18] and, of course, a lot of Birdie [26], who now has an additional motto as a bonus for having done so well – a two-bar musical rocket (unlisted). So now the bird steers him towards Brünnhilde and for a moment the downward scales in the orchestra seem to be going to break into the Trance [22]. Siegfried is told to be brave, the bird flies off to pilot Siegfried to his next adventure and Siegfried brings down the curtain with a lyrical outburst that might almost be birdsong too.

Act III Sc 1

0 A stormy prelude,* going at a fast canter and pretty 0
loud. The main subject is the dotted downward bit of Spear [7], and two others that stick out are Earth [12] and Earth upside down, which is Destruct [13], also a hint of Frustration [18]. We are also treated to a welcome clap of thunder to allow the earth to open up and release Erda.

A duet for Wotan/Erda takes up the whole scene (seventeen minutes) which advances the action not one whit and could be summarized as follows:

Wotan:	Erda, wake up, I need some advice.
Erda:	Don't bother me. Try the Norns. Try Brünnhilde.
Wotan:	OK, then let me tell you something: our number's up. We gods are doomed. Got it? (Erda sleeps on.)

But musically this long meander by the Wanderer is rich, sensuous and a little marvel in itself. It goes something as follows:

2: *Wache, Wala! Wala!* 1. Wake up.* Wanderer Wotan tries to rouse 2
Erda: Spear [7], Erda [12], Destruct [13] and Sleep [i] before Erda says Whosat? Help me, says Wotan, I

need advice – Erda [12], Wanderer [k] and Spear [7]. Erda: Get off; ask the Norns. Wotan: I'd rather ask their boss – a new motto for the Norns ending with two notes and a jump (unlisted, echoes of both Stress [b] and the Ring [4]). All of this nothing dialogue rests on a cushion of the most ravishing orchestral sound. One wishes one could listen to it without the singers. (Some enterprising recording manager might try this one day.)

2. Down Memory Lane. Erda recalls she once had
9: *Männertaten umdämmern mir den Mut* sex with a chap called Wotan* (although all-wise, she 9
apparently fails to penetrate Wotan's somewhat flimsy disguise – that eye-patch wouldn't fool a child) and the result was Brünnhilde. Ask her, she says. Wotan goes into a now-read-on about Brünnhilde's unusual situation and pesters Erda again, as she tries to go to sleep (Trance [22] and Sleep [i]). Again the music rages and soars under this low-level, low-interest dialogue. Now there are fewer mottos, less mickey-mousing, although Erda [12] and Spear [7] are still around.

13: *Du bist nicht* 3. Wotan's final oration: a fine piece.** Don't be 13
fooled by an important-sounding motto (two long string notes and an upward run), it's a one-off and has no special meaning. Minor mentions of mottos about, but they don't impede Wotan's rapturous sweep as he sings Stuff it then! OK it's all going to fall apart. So what? (Big climax.) His elation dies away after easily the best session he has given us so far. A scene to relish – in the study.

Act III Sc 2

Now it's Wotan/Siegfried for fifteen minutes and quite a change in mood and sound. The early exchanges between the two are brisk, dry and tuneful, all now-read-on stuff (with appropriate mottos) until Siegfried begins to get rude and uncouth. In an open-
23: *Was lachst du mich aus?* ing passage of great musical sweetness** he asks the 23
stranger why he laughs at him? Words and music do
not seem to fit at all, but they lead to an excited out-
24: *Das wär' nicht übel!* burst from Siegfried* and the row between the two 24
warms up, the most prominent mottos being Spear [7] versus Sword [14]. The war of words and mottos ends in a clap of thunder and in the clatter of the shat-

tered spear. (Last time remember it was the other way round: Spear 1 Nothung 0, so now it's 1–1. But the spear seems to be out of it for good.) Good action stuff.

So Wotan disappears and Siegfried looks hungrily towards the fire. He exclaims a bit and we are into a
30 busy noisy intermezzo,** a real buster in which every 30
motto tells a story and there are a lot of them – Siegfried Heroic [20], Rhinegold [3] [Why is this here? Shome mishtake surely? Ed.], Horn I [24], Loge [8] and associated fire music, Sleep [i], Trance [22] and Siegfried Heroic again [20]. Got it? But this does not prevent the pieces being all of a piece and there is a magic moment that causes a frisson down the spine when the Trance floats in serene and calm as ever at the end.

Act III Sc 3

At the end of the intermezzo the first violins all alone climb up the rock to where Brünnhilde lies. They are slow climbers, and towards the end it sounds as if they could do with a whiff of oxygen. Siegfried pokes around singing a bemused sort of recitatif over a bed
35: *Selige Öde auf sonniger* of rich orchestral sound* (some snatches of Valkyrie 35
[16]). Here again is a section that would surely play better without the vocal lines. Siegfried opens Brünnhilde's breastplate with Nothung (tricky). But, goodness me, who and what is this man with bumps on his chest? The woodwind wanders around describing the contours of Brünnhilde's bust. Then POW! Musical
37: *Das ist kein Mann!* Explosion!*** Sex in all its mighty power hits 37
Siegfried full in the solar plexus. Really quite a knockout with Siegfried shouting excitedly amongst the whirling strings. He comes out of his delirium and things quieten down. Motto-spotters may have an anxious time because it seems there are a lot moving around, but most are freelances on short-term contracts and the only long-serving staff member is Trance [22] which steals in as beautifully and as quietly as ever. We are now into a magical orchestral
48 poem:** awakening, sunrise, wonder and finally – 48
love. Shimmering strings, melodious woodwind, bold brassy chords held for a very long time.

Now things get ecstatic. Brünnhilde says who

woke me? It was I says Siegfried. Siegfried she says.
Oh goody, and for once in the height of their ecstasy
Wagner breaks the groundrules and both sing at the
52: *O Heil der Mutter* same time.*** This duet is pretty overwhelming and 52
with twenty-five minutes to go one wonders how he
can top that. But without actually topping it he successfully pulls us off the climax with some full-
54: *O Siegfried! Siegfried!* blooded godlike love music** based on a new motto, a 54
tender woodwind figure followed by a smooth ending
(Mutual Heroic Love [n]). This, first heard on the
woodwind and infinitely changeable, rolls on and out
as the two gaze into each other's eyes, spellbound.
Variously orchestrated.

Now for a bit of a rest. There's my old horse Grane
grazing over there says Brünnhilde – snatches of Valkyrie [16]. My trappings of power have gone. She
muses a bit sadly and Siegfried too, although he has
his bursts of fire, decelerates gradually into recitatif
until, great moment, he swings into his second love
tune – Lover's Sigh (a downward sigh, then pretty
67: *Sangst du mir nicht* [o]).** My eyes grow dim I cannot see I have not 67
brought my specs with me sings Brünnhilde in a
panic. [Why? Ed.] But Siegfried soothes her with
Lover's Sigh.

Now Brünnhilde sings an important number – better known as the Siegfried Idyll. An outpouring of
young love to music that is older and wiser than
70: *Ewig war ich* young love.*** The combination of the two tells us 70
what a glorious woman Brünnhilde is. Siegfried
jumps in with all his boyish charm and we are into the
73: *Dich lieb' ich* final and miraculous stages of this marathon duet.*** 73
Mottos can go by the board now (though there are
several) as we are swept along by Wagner doing the
thing he does best, piling on the agony and generating
wave upon wave of passion each one higher than the
last until we are overtaken by the surging climax of
Siegfried's love for Brünnhilde and hers for him.
Stunning.

NOTES and NEWS AND GOSSIP See **The Birth of *The Ring*** page 632

COMMENT See also **The Ring – A General Hello** page 549

The trouble with *Siegfried* is that when it is good it is very very good but when it is bad it is boring. The same can be said, of course, of *The Ring* as a whole, but in *Siegfried* we get the extreme case. The problem lies mainly in the script. There are at least two scenes which have no dramatic value whatsoever and one of these is just plain silly. Why should a host suddenly suggest to his guest that he should play a word game with him with death as the penalty for losing? And why should any guest accept such a ridiculous challenge unless he is a loony? The game itself is so poor that it would not have survived even on the tackiest local television channel in Nibelungenland for more than a second and turns out to be no more than a cover for yet another regurgitation of the Nibelungen saga. This is also true of the second scene – Wotan's unsuccessful try at interviewing Erda. Again there is nothing here but a churning-over of past history and we get no fresh news until the interviewee goes to sleep and the interviewer addresses her with a monologue which he might just as well have addressed to us in the first place and have saved poor Erda the annoyance of being woken out of her delicious eternal slumber. But this scene is musically rich and although the crassness of the libretto may be a pain, the music makes up for it.

Several of the other scenes wear out their welcome – the terribly slow speed at which Siegfried finds out about his parents, Wotan's predictable ding-dong with Alberich in the first scene of Act II, the two dwarfs quarrelling over the gold in Act III Scene 3, and the scene in the last act where Siegfried is so gratuitously rude to Wotan.

In the first half of the opera these dramatically damp patches seem more draggy because some of the music is fairly ornery, but in the second half where Wagner was a more advanced pupil (see **The Birth of *The Ring*** on page 632), the richness of the score beguiles us into feeling that things are going along pretty well. So we have an opera with a three-star final half-hour, two two-star episodes – forging the sword and the forest scenes – plus elsewhere a lot of gorgeous music, so let's just revel in that and for the rest be a little thankful.

For the good music in *Siegfried* is brilliant. It has no stirring set pieces for the concert hall, like the Ride of the Valks (although Forest Murmurs used to be played quite a lot in a mildly effective concert form), but Act III, especially, is full of great orchestral writing and the orchestration has its own special brand of sonority throughout the dragon-related parts.

The opera offers tuba-lovers a field day and whereas *Valkyrie* has the loudest music Wagner wrote, *Siegfried* has the deepest. The dragon's noises are really something to frighten the horses. The two set pieces – the forging song and the Siegfried Idyll – work well, but for those who know the Idyll in its orchestral form, it sticks out as a bit of an import, like the 'Stars & Stripes' in *Butterfly* (well, perhaps not quite like that). The musical character of the bird is as cute as the dragon is grotesque; Erda's music is even more beautiful than it was on her first appearance (but sleepier); Brünnhilde is as glorious as ever; the two dwarfs as tiresome, except for the moment in Act I Scene 1 when Mime (inexplicably) for a moment becomes a beautiful person. The Wanderer has a noble entry but after that his musical persona is even more unfocused than when he was himself. This may be because he doesn't seem to know why he is wandering or what he is supposed to be doing.

Siegfried himself has all the musical panache needed to make him the brave bonehead he has to be, although when first heard his absolutely memorable horn tune may be a little too close to operatic fox-hunting for comfort. But with his love music he becomes a grown-up human being – or almost, for his panic is still adolescent. He gives the impression of being a Wagnerian Cherubino who, if he had found Tosca, Desdemona, Carmen or even the Marschallin in the middle of the fire, would have fallen for any one of them just as madly. He was, after all, and a little late in life, discovering sex for the first time and this quite naturally made him very excitable.

But it is not the thing to question the bona fides of one of the parties in what is (possibly excluding the one in *Tristan*) the greatest love duet in Wagner. It is a *tour de force* and at the same time something more genuine than that. Wagner believed in this sort of passion as a central item in his scheme of things and with his genius for building a climax he raises this scene to an incredible pitch of emotion, emotion truly felt by him, by Siegfried, by Brünnhilde and so by us. Or rather most of us, for there will be those anti-Wagners, poor souls, plus that quite large section of mankind who have the misfortune to have tin ears who will fail to be moved by this great climacteric. But in the opera house where aficionados gather, as the curtain comes down you will hear the applause start hesitantly, in a whisper, as the clients slowly haul themselves back, as from an anaesthetic, into the land of the living. In the closing minutes of *Siegfried* Wagner deploys the full power of opera and if you are not overwhelmed, too bad – go and listen to Vivaldi – but if you are, it is the experience of a lifetime – and it will not do you the slightest harm.

Götterdämmerung (The Twilight of the Gods)

Part IV of *The Ring*

Wagner

The one where Siegfried makes new friends who stab him in the back, where Brünnhilde is very brave and Valhalla goes up in flames.

CAST (see **Who's Who** page 561)

Siegfried, a hero	Tenor
Brünnhilde, one-time chief of the Valkyries	Soprano
Waltraute, a Valkyrie	Mezzo
Alberich, chief of the Nibelungen	Bass–baritone
Hagen, son of Alberich and a human female	Bass
Gunther, his half-brother, King of the Gibichungs	Bass–baritone
Gutrune, Gunther's sister	Soprano
Three Rhinemaidens	One mezzo, two sopranos
Three Norns	Soprano, mezzo, contralto

Prologue and 3 acts: running time 4 hrs 15 mins

RELATIONSHIPS IN GÖTTERDÄMMERUNG

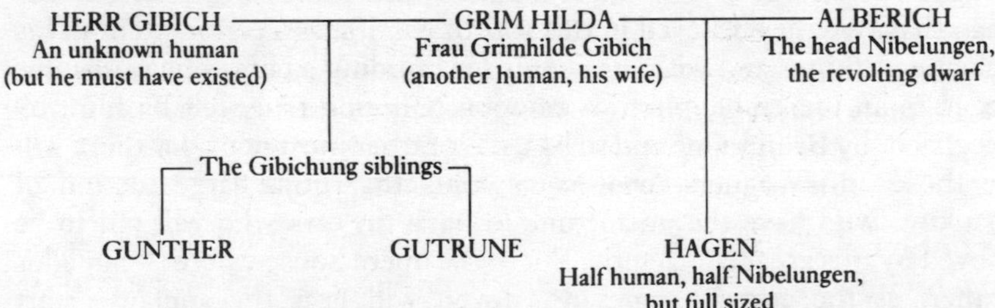

Subsequently: Siegfried when doped marries (or nearly) Gutrune
Gunther when pushed by Siegfried marries (or nearly) Brünnhilde

STORY

Prologue The Valkyries' rock: the same as the last scene in *Siegfried*

In which the Norns tell us rather more than we want to know about the past, have some interesting information about the future and meet with an industrial accident, Siegfried and Brünnhilde swear eternal devotion, he gives her the ring, she gives him a horse and he sets off for his musical journey down the Rhine

In the vague timescale of *The Ring* we move into timelessness. Three Norns sit spinning the Rope of Destiny and recall amongst many irrelevances that Wotan (having no filofax) cut his spear from a very superior ash tree nearby in order to record on the shaft in extremely small writing details of deals done. Siegfried smashed the spear: Wotan's employees chopped up the ash tree and piled the logs round Valhalla. Meanwhile Wotan has preserved the bits of his shaft to use as firelighters to ignite the logs round Valhalla in case he wants to arsonize it.

At this point the Rope of Destiny snaps which is lucky for us since otherwise the opera would never have got started. The Norns vanish: day breaks: it is some twenty-four hours after the last scene in *Siegfried*. Siegfried and Brünnhilde come on exchanging sweet somethings. OK I love you too much to stop you going on this business trip says she and anyway I'm not really good enough for you. Yes you are says he and sorry if I wasn't all that hot in bed last night you see I'm a little inexperienced. Think of me when you're away says she. Sure says he. Must be off thanks for the sex lessons now here's a ring (*the* ring!) for you. Thanks says she. Here's my horse as a present for you. Very nice of you says he. Together we are one they sing and more fancy stuff in this vein. Siegfried moves off.

Act I Sc 1 The hall of the Gibichungs on the banks of the Rhine

In which Gunther and Hagen plot and scheme to get Brünnhilde as Gunther's wife and to get Siegfried to assist them

Hey Hagen says Gunther – how's my popularity rating this week? Not good says Hagen, about the same as Clinton's. How can I raise my profile? asks Gunther. Royal wedding says Hagen nothing like them I know just the girl – name of Brünnhilde – only one snag she lies in the middle of a bushfire. Oh I see says Gunther am I brave enough to get in there and fetch her? Frankly no says Hagen you must get someone much braver than you to do it for you. Who? asks Gunther. Young Siegfried Volsung is probably as good as any. Comes of good stock and he killed a dragon [also Hagen's uncle Mime: Ed.], says Hagen owns the ring which makes him Lord of Creation.

Listen says Hagen: suppose Siegfried fetched in Brünnhilde to be your wife and we got him to marry your sister Gutrune. Good idea eh? How could we do that? say Gunther and Gutrune. Remember that stuff in the magic medicine chest? asks Hagen: forget-all pills and love philtres and stuff like that? Make a magimix and dose Siegfried. Great idea say the other two – Hagen you're a genius. I wish Siegfried was here says Gutrune. On this cue Siegfried sounds his horn for he is drifting down the Rhine in a punt with a horse.

Sc 2 In which Siegfried after drinking a magimix potion loses his memory and falls for another woman, namely Gutrune Gibichung

Hey Siegfried the Gibichungs shout. Hey to you he says can you direct me to Gibichung Hall? I believe it is near Basingstoke. This is it they cry. Siegfried gets out. Welcome welcome welcome says Gunther: are you *the* Siegfried? That's me says Siegfried. Owner of the Rhinegold? asks Gunther. Now you mention it yes says Siegfried I only kept this yellow balaclava that's the magicap Tarnhelm: I gave the ring to a nice girl called Brünnhilde.

Gutrune comes on with magimix medicine. Like a scotch? she says to Siegfried. Don't mind if I do says Siegfried here's to Brünnhilde (quaffs) magimix has instant effect: do I fancy *you*? he says what's your sister's name Gunther? Gutrune says he. Gutrune I am getting good vibes. Grabs her. Will you marry me? he asks (Gutrune exits indicating assent).

Have you a wife Gunther? No says Gunther but I know who I want: it's Brünnhilde but she's in a circle of fire and I'm not very brave so I couldn't get in there. I'll get her for you says Siegfried. I'll give you Gutrune in exchange says Gunther: let's be blood brothers says Siegfried. They go through a nauseating routine of mixing blood and wine and quaffing. How about joining our blood brotherhood Hagen? they ask. Sorry my blood is of an extremely rare blood group and will not mix says Hagen. Sullen bastard let him be says Gunther.

OK says Siegfried let's get going. Like a bit of a kip first? says Gunther. No sir says Siegfried on on on. Oho says Hagen as they disappear let the happy lads go wife-hunting so long as they bring back what I want – the ring.

Sc 3 Brünnhilde's rock
In which through the agency of the Tarnhelm magicap Siegfried as Gunther carries Brünnhilde off for a second time and for a different purpose

Who's that arriving? says Brünnhilde. Sounds like one of the old Valkyrie gang thunder and all. Hey Brünnhilde shouts Waltraute wake up it's me. What's up? asks Brünnhilde by the way I'm in love with Siegfried. Trouble at t'mill says Waltraute the governor's lost his marbles. Wotan's stopped sending us corpse-gathering. He took a sabbatical and travelled incognito as A. Wanderer. He came back with his spear broke. He has stacked up wood around Valhalla as if for a Guy Fawkes Night bonfire. He called a staff meeting won't eat won't talk sits there everyone around him waiting for Godot.

I asked him what was bothering him. That ring he said. Brünnhilde has it. Unless she gives it back to those Rhinemaidens we're all for the old heave-ho. Brünnhilde honey give it back please do love. Not on your nelly says Brünnhilde. Are you crazy or something? This ring is the cream in my coffee it's holy sacred love it's the tops it's the Mona Lisa. Valhalla can go to blazes: I keep the ring. Get off. (Waltraute exits in an electric storm.)

Nice evening says Brünnhilde the ring of fire is burning nicely. Whoops! is that Siegfried's horn? Siegfried magicapped appears through the flames as Gunther. Who the hell are you? says Brünnhilde. It's me I'm Gunther the Gibichung says he. You must come and be my wife. God help us how did this creature get past the flames? says she: Wotan you let me down you sod.

Let's go to bed in your cave says he. Stand back! says she this ring will stop you in your tracks. Will it hell says he. Jumps on her. After an ugly struggle wrenches off the ring. Get into that cave says he and we'll put Nothung down the middle of the bed to prevent any hanky-panky. I promised to deliver you to my blood brother a virgin. [Siegfried is, of course, suffering from sexual amnesia: Ed.]

Act II The bank of the Rhine outside the Gibichung hall
Sc 1 In which Hagen and his singularly unpleasant dwarf father chat about the ring, its past history and its future ownership: it will be theirs

Are you awake Hagen? asks the revolting Albert Alberich. What'ya want? asks Hagen. You're a clever lad Hagen says Alberich. Listen: did you know that Wotan and his lot have pretty well packed it in? Broke his spear or something? Who's going to take over? asks Hagen. We are says Alberich we nick the ring off this young bonehead Siegfried and Bob's your uncle. I have the matter in hand says Hagen. Relax. I will get the ring. But it's mine says Alberich you wouldn't let your old dad down would you son? Mind your own business says Hagen.

Sc 2 In which Siegfried returns to Gibichung Hall and reports the success of his mission

Hi Hagen says Siegfried. Hi Siegfried says Hagen how did it go? OK says Siegfried I fetched out Brünnhilde and passed her on to Gunther they're coming along behind. C'mon out Gutrune shouts Hagen Siegfried's here. Everything OK? asks Gutrune did Gunther get singed at all? He didn't go near the fire says Siegfried I went in as his ringer thanks to the magicap. Got her out slept with her – whassat? says Hagen you had sex? Never a tickle says Siegfried I put this great thing between us [Nothung of course: Ed.] then early this morning I magicapped the changed Siegfried/Gunther into Gunther/Siegfried. So that's it and here they come now I hear them. Fine good say Gutrune and Hagen blow the foghorn to get tenants together and let's have a double wedding.

Sc 3 In which the gloomy Hagen makes the tenants laugh at a joke and Gunther and Brünnhilde arrive

Alarum! Emergency! Stand to your weapons! shouts Hagen. Here we are boss is it the mob from up the river again? they ask. Gunther is coming back with a wife says Hagen. Yeah yeah say the tenants so are her folks trying to get her off him? We shall kill a cow, horse, pig, sheep or a cock as a sacrifice today says Hagen – but no humans. OK OK boss they say so what? A big booze-up says Hagen. Ho Ho Ho what a good joke Ho Ho say the easily amused tenants. Here come the bridal pair says Hagen. Nice to see you back Gunther shout the tenants.

Sc 4 In which Brünnhilde is shocked to find Siegfried planning to marry another woman: she reminds him that they are in German opera parlance man and wife (means they had sex together) and this sets the cat amongst the Gibichung pigeons

Welcome to our place Madam shout the tenants. Listen folks she's a very superior person is my fiancée says Gunther. Hey Siegfried old bloodie how about a double wedding? Is Siegfried here? My God! says Brünnhilde. And with Gutrune? I'm going to marry her says Siegfried. Brünnhilde blacks out: comes to. That's my ring he's wearing she says the one that you Gunther wrenched off me. I never says Gunther. I didn't get this ring off any woman says Siegfried I got it off a dragon. (Tenants signal to each other that the gent is a little funny in the head.) Not so says Hagen Siegfried got that ring off Gunther by trickery (a dastardly lie of course).

This is too much screams Brünnhilde he pinches my ring and makes to marry Gutrune well she's getting soiled goods anyway because Siegfried had a night of sex with me so there! My my gee whizz fancy that say the tenants. Shut up Brünnhilde says Siegfried. That's not true not true at all. We had the sword Nothung between us all night (he only remembers second night when he was Gunther anyway). Liar says she Nothung was hanging above the washbasin (she is recalling their first night of love).

Hey folks this is a serious matter say the tenants. A fiancée of a Gibichungy sleeping around with Volsungs. Come and swear to the truth on my spear says Hagen. I swear I never touched her swears Siegfried. I swear he gave me the full works says Brünnhilde.

Gunther your fiancée needs psychiatric help says Siegfried or maybe that Tarnhelm didn't do its job on some important parts of my body anyway women change their minds at the drop of a hat so let's just carry on with this wedding party. Exits on a high with Gutrune. The tenants follow tongues hanging out for booze.

Sc 5 In which Hagen secretly lusting after the ring plots to kill Siegfried. Brünnhilde tells him how to do it and Gunther is enlisted as an accomplice

This is a real old puzzle says Brünnhilde. I don't know what's come over Siegfried. I'll fight him for you says Hagen. You? says Brünnhilde. Poof! Not a hope I magicked him swordproof. All over? asks Hagen. Well now you come to mention it I didn't magic the rear portion because his style was always face to face. Thanks for the tip-off says Hagen.

Fancy Siegfried cheating on me like that I feel dirty says Gunther. All your fault for going in for that magicap stuff says Brünnhilde you were too chicken to go in there and get me yourself. Only Siegfried's death will make you feel better says Hagen. How about all that blood brother stuff? says Gunther. Never mind that if you killed him you could get your hands on the ring says Hagen. How about Gutrune? says Gunther. Tell her he was gored by a rhinoceros says Hagen. Agreed? Agreed says Gunther. Yes agreed says Brünnhilde.

Act III Sc 1 A valley on the Rhine, with a cliff beetling and Rhine waters visible
In which the Rhinemaidens beg Siegfried to give them back the ring but to no purpose

Nice morning isn't it sing the Rhinemaidens what a smashing sunrise – it would be even better if we still had the gold. Weialala! Isn't that the heroic hornblowing hunter on his way? (It is.) Maybe he'll give us back our gold. Seen a dog fox? asks Siegfried I lost him. Give us that ring on your finger say the girls and maybe we'll tell you. I killed a dragon for that ring says Siegfried worth more than a fox besides the wife wouldn't like it. Gee! Isn't he cute say the girls.

OK girls I'll give it to you says he come here. Before you hand it over they say you should know that there's a curse on it so if you'd kept it you would have been killed today anyway. Don't you bloody threaten me says Siegfried the deal's off. On your own head be it sing the girls you'll be rubbed out today. What tiresome females says Siegfried.

Sc 2 In which Siegfried tells us his life story which we already know and is killed by Hagen

Halloo Siegfried shouts Hagen. Halloo to you says Siegfried. Any luck? asks Hagen. Went after pheasant but finished up with waterfowl and a lost fox gimme a drink says Siegfried. Somebody told me you were psychic with birds says Hagen. Lemme tell you all says Siegfried.

He embarks on lengthy C.V. including: Mime – forging sword – Nothung put together again – death of dragon – tasted dragon's blood (ugh) – understood birds – helpful bird advised on Rhinegold – took Tarnhelm magicap ring etc. – bird advised Mime a wrong 'un – Mime killed – bird directs to Brünnhilde – walk through fire – wins Brünnhilde.

Here Siegfried is interrupted by ravens: he turns to look at them: Hagen inserts a spear into his back. Hey Hagen what are you at? cry the tenants you're killing that man. Revenge for perjury says Hagen arcanely. Siegfried badly wounded jacks himself up for goodbye message to Brünnhilde: Brünnhilde he says my life my love I went through fire for you Brünnhilde and wakened you with a kiss. I'm coming to you. . . . (Expires.) So now we have an extempore procession to the crematorium accompanied by the great funeral march.

Sc 3 Gibichung Hall and beyond. Night
In which Gutrune learns of Siegfried's death, Hagen kills Gunther in a squabble over the ring, Brünnhilde rides her horse into Siegfried's funeral pyre, Hagen is drowned by the Rhinemaidens and Valhalla goes up in smoke

Siegfried is late back from the hunt says Gutrune. Panics. Hagen and all return. Sorry Gutrune says Hagen I'm afraid Siegfried's dead. A rhinoceros got him. Not so says Gunther it was Hagen what done it. So I did too says Hagen because what he swore on oath on my spear was a lie. By the way I claim that ring in return. Get off you dwarf-begotten bastard says Gunther it's mine. Want to bet? says Hagen. Kills him. As Hagen goes to take the ring from Siegfried's finger the corpse raises its arm scaring the hell out of everyone.

Quiet please listen to me says Brünnhilde the two Gibichungies plotted his death. You were in it too you jealous bitch shouts Gutrune. Hush you poor miserable thing says Brünnhilde he was my lover before he met you. Blast and damn you Hagen for making me give him those forget-all pills says Gutrune she was his true love and I done her wrong.

Pile up a bonfire fit for a hero's cremation and bring on my horse Grane says Brünnhilde. Goodbye Siegfried great hero my lover perfect man the Rhinemaidens have told me all. Listen Wotan you evil man you used Siegfried to rid you of that curse and sure enough it passed on to him so he has destroyed himself and destroyed my life. Now I know everything. The ring I shall give back to the Rhinemaidens (she takes it off Siegfried's finger) and now get off you ravens (they are circling around again) and tell Loge to put the match to Valhalla.

So now I'll light the pyre (does so) and listen to me old Grane – jump right into the flames with me on your back (he jumps in obediently). Fire breaks out all over the stage (as widespread as fire regulations will allow). Tenants cower by the footlights. The Rhine rises rather suddenly and overflows onto the stage putting out the fire. The Rhinemaidens appear. They take the ring from the ashes of the quickly burnt-out bonfire. They return to the Rhine. Hagen dives into the Rhine to get the ring. The Rhinemaidens drown him.

In the distance Valhalla burns up nicely with all the gods visible as they fry until smoke blots them out. All is over and the mighty saga has reached its end. (Whew!)

MINUTES FROM START **LOOK OUT FOR**

Prologue (For motto numbers see the Table on page 558)

A loud brass chord – the chord of doom – opens the

action (we heard it when Brünnhilde was woken up). Then we are immediately taken back in time into Rhine music [1] – next a sharp reminder of Fate [19] and the prelude is over.

The three Norns tell the tale, past, present and fu-
2: *Welch Licht leuchtet dort?* ture. This is calm music, the sort of thing suitable for 2
priests, priestesses and seers. It's more alive than recitatif, in no way stunning, but it reaches its small climax effectively enough. As at the beginning of a marathon film you are prepared to sit through a fairly slow-moving first reel, so here you feel this is a very fair introduction for big things to come. (Fate [19], Valhalla [5], Spear [7], Loge [8].) The rope snaps (Fate [19] again), not a moment too soon. No star.

17 Prelude for Siegfried and Brünnhilde.** Fate [19] 17
is followed by a long recitatif for the lower strings and then two shining new mottos break the surface, the first (which has the same notes as Horn I but in an entirely different rhythm: Horn II [27]) answered immediately by the second (glorious Brünnhilde [28]: low note – twiddle – high note and three more, making a sweet phrase, this time on a solo clarinet) and the two work together to make a wonderful thing of this second, bigger and better prelude.

The Siegfried/Brünnhilde duet. It would be wrong to say that this duet takes over where the later scenes of *Siegfried* left off, for nothing could top that great climacteric. But the music of this duet is of the same kind and has both a sexual and romantic intensity. It is topside Wagner – and so early in the opera too. The piece goes something as follows:

21: *Zu neuen Taten* 1. Brünnhilde:** I wouldn't properly love you if I 21
didn't let you go and do your heroic business (Brünnhilde [28]). Anyway I'm not really good enough for you. She sings all this to a superior sort of freestyle recitatif and sounds so joyful as to give the lie to the humble line she is taking.

23: *Mehr gabst du* 2. Siegfried:** Don't be cross if I'm not yet very 23
good in bed. The main thing is we love each other madly. This is a poem of happiness and again he does not seem cast down by his poor sexual performance. Introduced by Horn II [27].

3. Now he gives her the ring and she gives him her

26: *Lass' ich, Liebste* horse Grane.** Not a very fair swap because by any 26
standards Grane must be aged and unlikely to show any turn of foot. [But he has no curse attached to him: Ed.] There are changes of rhythm and style here, but it all remains pretty ecstatic with references to the love music at the end of *Valkyrie*, to Siegfried Heroic [20] and Valkyrie [16]. They finish with a bout of saying Hail! to each other, both still on a high. The accompaniment is luscious and the climax terrific. Siegfried rides off on his journey (Horn II [27]).

31 Siegfried's journey down the Rhine.** A rich and 31
varied orchestral *tour d'horizon* starting with Horn II [27] and Brünnhilde [28] and moving out into the big world with Horn I [24] which after some busy traffic gets the concerto treatment, first for horn and then oboe and is developed into a mighty string tune which makes way for – wait for it – the Rhine [1]. Now we are back amongst the Rhinemaidens and we have Rhinegold [3], Gold [2], the Ring itself [4] and a bit of a rumble in the bass which could be Loge's fire music still smouldering away. Anyway the end is portentous (Bad News [d]) and it portends something pretty dire.

Act I Sc 1

So we are back on earth and at rest, indeed inside Hagen's hall where for the next fifteen minutes there is to be nothing but plotting and scheming. Hagen himself is given a rather physical motto – a sweep up then a jump down, twice – unlisted. The story is de-
0: *Nun hör, Hagen* veloped in Wagner's grown-up vocal style,* that is to 0
say the music moves along very close to the sense of the story, sometimes in VSR (Very Superior Recitatif), sometimes picking up a fragment of melody when required building up into little puffs of excitement. The orchestration is strong, rich and clear and the orchestra is, as usual, the spokesman for the relevant mottos, which include Valkyrie [16], Loge [8], Volsung [h], Horn I [24] and the Ring [4].

After a conspiratorial whisper from Hagen about the nasty drug they are going to inflict on Siegfried, Gutrune says 'I wish I could see Siegfried' and right
11: *Möcht' ich Siegfried* on cue we hear Curse [11] immediately followed by all
of Siegfried's horn calls which break out in a jumble,* 11

but soon, thanks to some heavy work from the strings, Horn I [24] wins and excitement builds as Siegfried is sighted spinning down the Rhine in his punt with a horse. Once again a little unfair to animals, Wagner gives Grane very poor musical recognition (Valkyrie [16]), but by now Siegfried's horns are busting out all over. An entry fit to make the Queen of Sheba send for her court composer.

Act I Sc 2

After the preliminaries (for some arcane reason a whiff of the Curse [11]) Gunther welcomes Siegfried
16: *Begrüsse froh, O Held* in a good set piece* and Siegfried replies in an equally 16
traditional fashion with a fair bit of Siegfried Heroic [20]. After so much go-as-you-please it is quite a relief to have things steadied up into an old-fashioned operatic exchange.

But soon we are off again chatting about the Tarn-
20 helm and Gutrune comes in with a new motto (a 20
gentle sighing woodwind phrase: soft and sweet [29]) to offer Siegfried the magic medicine. Here we have the music of witch doctors, spells and curses – sotto voce – until Siegfried looks up and Wham! falls in love with Gutrune.

The blood brothers duet. After Siegfried has announced that he will marry Gutrune in two minutes flat (Gutrune [29] and Curse [11]) he gets into finding a wife for Gunther. Why not Brünnhilde? A most suitable choice and I'll get her for you says Siegfried (Loge and fire music [8] and Horn I [24] as developed on the journey). Use the Tarnhelm? Yes, I'll change myself into you Gunther old boy. So let's be blood
26: *Blühenden Lebens labendes Blut* brothers.* Now we have the disgusting spectacle of 26
two men mixing their blood into a wine cocktail. Whilst this job is being done we have a shower of mottos (Curse [11], Siegfried Heroic [20], Spear [7]).

(Now a digression. It must be said that in the matter of mottos, from now on it becomes pretty hard to explain Wagner's thought processes. Why does he keep dredging up mottos from the past that seem to have nothing to do with the matter in hand? What the hell is the Spear doing here? Is it because it symbolizes deals? But surely only Wotan's deals. Is it because the whole house of cards is built on deals?

Including the blood brother deal being done now? No doubt the Wagnerian scribendos will find an answer to it.)

Anyway, to get back to blood-brothers, they drink
the revolting liquid and sing a little blood-brother
26: *Treue trink' ich* ditty* in thirds which simply must have been sug- 26
dem Freund gested by the palship duet in *Don Carlos*. It's an odd-
ity in Wagner and rather nice (Curse [11] and Spear [7] still around). It's interesting that this duet should have a collegiate, even a Masonic, ring to it. (Hagen disassociates himself from these goings-on with the Ring [4] booming away behind.)

30: *Frisch auf die* A burst of mad excitement.* Let's go! shouts Sieg- 30
Fahrt! fried. It's all hustle and bustle. Gutrune can't stop
him. So he jumps in a boat and leaves after a visit of twenty minutes, having swigged a forget-all potion, got a new wife, drunk blood, sworn blood-brotherhood and planned an expedition to abduct a lady surrounded by a ring of fire from a mountain top. Even the Harvard Business School would regard this as a productive use of time.

Hagen sings a doomy gloomy farewell. It's all going
35: *Hier sitz' ich* to end in tears.* Impressive. 35

zur Wacht The intermezzo* to cover the scene change back to 36
36 the rock is agreeable but scrappy compared to Sieg-
fried's Journey down the Rhine which we have already had. It has an air of mystery (a little thunder in the background) and bristles with mottos – Rhinegold [3], Ring [4], Horn I [24], Siegfried Heroic [20], Spear [7] and finally and gloriously, Brünnhilde [28]. Now the thunder is close.

Act I Sc 3

Idyll music, thunder, Valkyries [16] and War-Cry [17] open the duet Brünnhilde/Waltraute.*

42: *So wagtest du* 1. First, some free writing. Brünnhilde tells Wal- 42
traute what happened to her. Although the thunder is now very close there is a feeling of mountains and fresh air in the music which moves swiftly from point to point (Valkyrie [16], Siegfried Heroic [20] and, as we get to the matter of how Wotan is going along, Frustration [18]).

2. Waltraute's report on the state of Valhalla is paid out in inches. It is not exciting: packed with

mottos, some of which are Frustration [18], Spear [7], Valhalla [5], Ring [4], Rhinegold [3] and Curse [11].

3. But when Brünnhilde asks her what she wants things take wing, nearly all mottos are shaken off and we are into a spell of fresh free music. Brünnhilde's assertion that she is going to stick to the ring
54: *Ha ! weisst du, was er mir ist ?* whatever** is quite splendid (Ring [4]). In a quiet 54
moment it takes us back to the love music at the end of *Valkyrie* – Sigh [0], also Brünnhilde [28].

Now for one of Wagner's great musical/spectacular *coups de théâtre*. Claps of thunder. Waltraute
68: *Blitzend Gewölk* disappears in an electric storm.** The surrounding 68
fire (Loge [8]) goes all funny and creeps nearer. Siegfried's horn! [24]. Fire blazes up (Curse [11]). Siegfried jumps out. Rapture! But it's not Siegfried. Significant chord. Owing to the magicap it's Gunther. Horrors! Who the hell are you? gasps Brünnhilde. It's as good as the movies. And musically a knockout.

The final scene is all flash! bang! pow! Brünnhilde reacts with horror to the advances of Siegfried/
71: *Wer ist der Mann* Gunther.** Due to the magic of the magicap every- 71
thing is distorted – Siegfried's voice and also the mottos. Only Brünnhilde stays straight (Tarnhelm [10], Horn II [27], Curse [11]). After the noisy scuffle over the ring (she loses) there is an oasis of soft sound, the Idyll and Brünnhilde's own haunting motto [28]. Soon to be wiped out by the brutish Siegfried/Gunther, instructing his sword (in his natural voice) to act as a chastity barrier between himself and Brünnhilde in case he feels inclined to indulge in any funny stuff before delivering her intact to the real Gunther. A quaint note on which to end an act that has turned the world topsy-turvy. (Frustration [18], Brünnhilde [28], Nothung [15].)

Act II Sc 1

A gloomy prelude based mainly on Hagen's motto (unlisted) is interrupted by the unspeakable Alberich with an onrush of nasty Nibelungen music. He goes on and on about getting the ring back (many sidelong glances at many mottos). Hagen shows his good judgement by treating his father with complete disdain. In this scene we are in the doldrums – but wait:

a flush of horns break cover and weave about to greet the dawn as it comes up over the Rhine. This is a pleasure. Suddenly Siegfried's personal horn bursts in [24] as bold as brass and as brisk as can be and we are off into Scene 2.

Act II Sc 2

A rollicking scene as Gutrune and Siegfried get acquainted. Uneasily she asks him how went the day
17: *Euch beiden meld' ich* and he,* as always in *The Ring*, gives her a very full 17
account of what we the audience know already. You ask a silly question, you get a long answer. Gutrune may not be the great and glorious soulmate that Siegfried found in Brünnhilde, but she certainly sounds good for more laughs. The main mottos: Tarnhelm [10], Nothung [15], Loge [8] and Horn I [24]. One of Wagner's jolly scenes and only a little galumphing.

Act II Sc 3

Hagen blows his emergency foghorn several times. It makes a noise in questionable taste but does its job of rousing the tenantry. Wagner now goes horn mad and a variety of horn noises in various horn keys boom
20: *Hoiho! Hoihohoho!* out.* The tenants pour in all eager for the fray and 20
singing something between Rufty-Tufty and the chorus from a particularly bloodthirsty oratorio. Hagen tells them it's not war, it's a wedding party. Big joke. The tenants laugh dutifully and chorus on. Two new mottos here: Rufty-Tufty, a skittering dancing figure usually in the bass, unlisted; and We Are the Gibichungies, a brassy swoop down and up in thirds, starting and finishing on the same note [p]. Although this crowd scene goes with a swing and is very welcome at this point, since for most of the preceding fourteen hours we have been gazing at two hominids on an empty stage, it is not one of Wagner's best efforts. If he was going to the expense of having a chorus of thousands brought in for this one item plus the odd shout or two hereafter, he might have given us something more on the lines of the choruses in *Tannhäuser* or *Meistersinger*. This is not value for money. The Sieg Heils! at the end would not have been out of place at the Nuremberg Rally.

Act II Sc 4

Brünnhilde Bouleverséed.

The would-be wedding scene opens with the near-
29: *Brünnhild', die hehrste Frau* est thing to a song* we have had for a long time, 29
accompanied by what, if it were not Wagner, we
might call a vamp. After Gunther has set things going
we get into the high dramatics of poor Brünnhilde's
struggle to cope with this nightmare situation.
Mainly exclamatory and high recitatif (with a distort
of Valkyrie [16], the Gibichungies [p], Fate [19], a
snatch of Brünnhilde [28], the Curse [11] and a little
Frustration [18]).

The dam bursts. Brünnhilde can contain herself no
longer. *J'accuse* Siegfried of taking the ring off me she
39: *Ha – Dieser war es* sings** in a furious outburst. He done it! Traitor! 39
Now we soar and swoop along with her anger and
Siegfried's rebuttal. But the subject changes to the
matter of whether or not Siegfried had sex with her
and now everyone gets into the act – the stage army,
the women and all, and in the general mish-mash the
voltage drops (Frustration [18], Nothung [15],
Sword [14]).

Now we are treated to the sort of ritual dear to
myth and ancient lays. This time it's spear-point
swearing, the spear-point being a substitute for the
Bible, which has not yet reached these parts. Hagen
goes first, Siegfried second, then Brünnhilde. The
matter at issue is whether when first they met Nothung hung on the wall (bad) or was placed between
them in the bed (dangerous, but good, because this
will prove Brünnhilde's virginity). Her swearing is
49: *Helle Wehr! Heilige Waffe!* easily the best** and as a woman wronged her out- 49
bursts of passion ring true and clear amidst all the
musical skulduggery around her (Valkyrie [16],
Nothung [15]). Siegfried, well out of character, ends
the scene by saying Well let's be friends anyway and
have a jolly party. But the playout doesn't sound all
that jolly, ending as it does with variants of the Gibichungies [p] and a little reminder of the Curse [11].

Act II Sc 5

The scene opens with Brünnhilde pensive and then rolls on to allow the trio Gunther/Hagen/Brünnhilde to consider how to dispose of Siegfried in what sounds the most surprisingly laid-back and lyrical fashion (Fate [19], Siegfried Heroic [20], Sword [14],

Bad News [d] and Brünnhilde [28]). Only when
Brünnhilde has a stab of jealousy for Gutrune do
68: *Was riet mir mein Wissen?* things wake up** and the final trio, the three singing 68
together (against Wagner's general ground rules) is
glorious indeed. Siegfried shall die! That's one thing
settled. And to keep things on a high the playout
makes merry with the Gibichung motto [p] as the
wedding procession comes on.

Act III Sc 1

0 Horn calls start off the prelude,* Siegfried's first [24] 0
answered by the moody call of the gloomy Gibichungs. Then, serenely, the Rhine music that opened
the whole cycle breaks in [1] – and what a relief it is to
hear the cool water music again after such a dose of
the noisy domestic life of the Gibichungies. The prelude (Rhinegold [3]) runs on into some watery dance
3: *Frau Sonne sendet Lichte* music for the Rhinemaidens as they sing*** a sur- 3
prisingly cheerful song about their lost gold (Gold
[2], Rhinegold [3]). A nice new motto here – Happy
Rhinemaidens, lingering phrases in the woodwind in
close harmony – unlisted. This is a delight. It is interrupted by Siegfried's horn [24] and then his arrival.

The Rhinemaidens ask Siegfried for the ring – he
7: *Ein Albe führte mich ihr* refuses.* Bits of the old Horn around [24]. This is all 7
done in a spirit of persiflage with peals of laughter
from the girls; not what one would expect when so
serious a matter is at stake – like the end of the world –
but let us be thankful, for Wagner is here in a wonderfully unbuttoned mood.

The exchanges become more agitated as the debate
14: *Siegfried! Wir weisen dich war* goes on* – you'll be cursed Siegfried say the girls. 14
Pshaw! says Siegfried. OK on your head be it say the
girls, moving delicately into a synchronized trio and
swimming offstage. Great play is made of the new
motto but we have reminders of Spear [7], Gold [2],
Rhinegold [3], the Ring [4] and Curse [11]. This is
lively, buoyant music. No stodge at all.

Act III Sc 2

After the Hails and Hellos, mostly spoken by the
horns (lots of [24] and [24] developed) and after the
24: *Mime heiss ein mürrischer Zwerg* drinking horn stuff (the new motto from the last
scene still around), Siegfried moves into a musical
autobiography,** with appropriate mottos, Anvils [9] 24

as he runs through his early days with Mime, then the forging of Nothung [15], the death of Fafner [23], the death of Mime, all with the Forest [25] giving a background to a lot of the story as the bird trills it out [26]. There is a break for refreshments: Hagen slyly slips some anti-amnesiac into Siegfried's drink and when Siegfried carries on we get to the Brünnhilde bit (Brünnhilde [28] and Loge [8] and more Bird [26] and so on) and up to the rock (Trance [22]) and references to the Brünnhilde love music. Suddenly – two frightfully important ravens interrupt the proceed-
32: *Was hör ich!* ings.* As Siegfried looks up at them he is speared in 32
the back (Curse [11], Siegfried Heroic [20] and Fate [19]). One can't but think that Wagner muffs this bit. The music, although tense and mildly dramatic, really doesn't seem to rise to the occasion. After all, this is *it*. The death of Siegfried! Or almost, for he yanks himself up on his elbow and delivers his fare-
34: *Brünnhilde, heilige Braut!* well message.* This is introduced by the brass chord 34
of doom and is then delivered in hushed tones. (Siegfried Heroic [20], Brünnhilde [28] and Fate [19].) This farewell piece is calm, peaceful and moving. At last he dies. And now, to assure us that his death is a frightfully important event, we have the mighty Fu-
40 neral March.*** This stunning piece opens with a 40
chord punched out twice on the brass (insistent, upsetting and to dog us throughout the whole course of the march), which turns out to be a musical retrospect of Siegfried's life. Every motto tells a story, and there are plenty (listed below) but the two that blaze out in their full glory are Sword [14] and Horn II [27]. These are the mottos of a hero and they are given the full treatment. Other funeral marches (Handel's, Chopin's) can be used for quite modest funerals of Class I and Class II VIPs, but this one is too grand even for a Prime Minister and too glorious for a royal. It would have done well for Charlemagne or – perhaps – de Gaulle. As it dies away it leaves one problem behind it – how to get the opera started again. (Prominent mottos besides Sword [14] and Horn II [27] are: Self-Pity [g], Siegfried Heroic [20], Brünnhilde [28], Curse [11] and Ring [4].)

Act III Sc 3

So things do start moving again in a quiet but effec-
46: *War das sein Horn?* tive recitatif* by Gutrune as she waits for the return 46
of the hunters. Does she hear Siegfried's horn? No,
but *we* do (also Brünnhilde [28] and Fate [19]).

Now it's all go; the hunters return; no Siegfried;
he's dead; he's carried in on his shield. Gutrune
bursts into an agony of hatred for Gunther and
50: *Siegfried, Siegfried erschlagen!* Hagen* (introduced by the two funeral chords): there 50
is high drama as Gunther and Hagen fall out over the
ring and get into their swordfight.** Gunther is 52
52: *Nicht klage wider mich!* killed. Siegfried raises his dead hand with the ring on
it to music of immense power. It sweeps us along
from shock to shock. (And incidentally look out for
the tenants' oohs and aahs when Siegfried's dead
hand comes up – they send a shiver down the ver-
tebrae.) Mottos: Curse [11], Sword [14] and Destruct
[13]. Gutrune sees the light (a bit late), namely that
the forget-all magimix that she had given Siegfried
made him forget his true love Brünnhilde – the duet
between the two is ennobled by a shining lyrical pass-
55: *Armselige, schweig!* age from Brünnhilde.** (Mottos: Gutrune [29], Fate 55
[19].)

The finale. In the short intermezzo before Brünnhilde's final spiel we have reminders that she was once
a Valkyrie. Now she sings once again with author-
57: *Starke Scheite schichten mir dort* ity,** telling the lads to pile up the logs on Siegfried's 57
funeral pyre and declaring she will ride along with
him to wherever it is he is going. (Heaven? Hades?
Not Valhalla.) (Loge [8], Siegfried Heroic [20].) She
goes on to muse, beautifully and quietly, on Siegfried's nobility. Now she knows why he broke his
word. (Heroic love [n], Sword [14], Nothung [15],
Fate [19], Curse [11].)

She contemplates the ring, taken from Siegfried's
finger, and promises to return it to the Rhinemaidens.
She is now into her stride. Noble heroic Brünnhilde
music, still poppling with mottos (Rhine [1], Curse
[11]).

68: *Fliegt heim ihr Raben!* The climax.*** Brünnhilde tells the ravens to get 68
back to the rock and tell Loge that the time has come
for his great act of arson, namely to put a match to all
those logs stacked up against Valhalla. Then instructions are sung out in queenly fashion, the music sur-

ging and billowing beneath with mottos now a living part of the noble stream of sound (introduced by Spear [7] and leading to Loge [8] and Destruct [13]). Grane appears and Brünnhilde tells the poor beast its next and final job is to leap into the fire. Now Ecstasy [21] (unheard since Act III of *Valkyrie*) rises up and stuns us with its sheer loveliness. Brünnhilde, in a blaze of glory, jumps onto Grane and rides into the fire, and that for her is pretty well it. (Loge [8], Valkyrie music [16] and [17], Ecstasy [21] and Siegfried Heroic [20].)

72 The playout.*** Even the grandeur of Brünn- 72
hilde's exit is topped by this mighty final symphony. This is Wagner at the top of his bent with all the stops out and with a compendium of mottos to complete the story: Valkyrie [16], Loge [8], Sleep [i], Rhinegold [3], Rhine [1], Curse [11], Valhalla [5], Siegfried Heroic [20] and, of course, Ecstasy [21]. Even if the stage effects can't rise to the occasion (they never can), nothing can dim the glory of this knockout finale. Finally Ecstasy takes over and the mighty *Ring* dies away in a rare moment of sweetness and beauty. Thank goodness for Brünnhilde, say we. She may not have saved the day for the gods but she has made the night for us.

NOTES and NEWS AND GOSSIP See **The Birth of *The Ring*** page 632

COMMENT See also **The Ring – A General Hello** page 549

Although *Götterdämmerung* is the longest of the four legs of *The Ring*, it has the fewest longueurs. The Norns at the start are not madly exciting. We could well do without all that stuff about the World ash-tree. Also the scene between Alberich, dwarf father, and Hagen, human son, both of them deeply repugnant figures, is no fun. But the re-caps and now-read-ons are no longer a bore. Brünnhilde bringing Waltraute up-to-date and Siegfried telling the by now well-worn tale of his life, although dramatically as tiresome as ever, are both musically rather splendid. But the main thing about *Götterdämmerung* is that the good bits far, far outweigh the mediocre. The early Siegfried/Brünnhilde duet takes us back into the heady upper air of the last scene in *Siegfried*, the scene between Siegfried and the Rhinemaidens is full of delights, the Gibichungs, especially

Gutrune, have surprisingly civilized music, no grunts and uncouth tuba noises here; the two orchestral pieces, the Journey and the Funeral March, both come off a million dollars and the finale – well – the finale is one of Wagner's greatest achievements. It gains its strength dramatically from the heroic nobility of Brünnhilde. Here we have music not, as so often in *The Ring*, sung by or about people for whom we do not care a fig, but by a woman we have come to love and venerate. By now Brünnhilde is a true heroine. The final stretch of *The Ring*, from Brünnhilde's message to the ravens to the end, and the orchestral symphony that follows generate opera power of a kind we have never known before. It is as if the opera, which had up till now been driven by steam, had suddenly discovered how to use atomic energy. Well, perhaps not quite like that, but Wagner would be pleased with the comparison.

THE BIRTH OF *THE RING*

The Ring	Four operas, **Rhinegold, Valkyrie, Siegfried** and **Götterdämmerung**. The chief work of Wagner's life, for the pattern of composition see below
First nights	
Rhinegold	Königlich Hof- und National Theater, Munich, 22 September 1869
Valkyrie	As above, 26 June 1870
Siegfried	Festspielhaus, Bayreuth, 16 August 1876
Götterdämmerung	As above, 17 August 1876
	First performance of **The Ring** as a complete cycle: 13, 14, 16, 17 August 1876 at the Festspielhaus, Bayreuth.
Reception	Always mixed: see below
Libretto	Wagner
Sources	See below

It took Wagner 26 years to complete *The Ring* from first draft to putting the final touches to *Götterdämmerung*. He wasn't a slow worker, he just kept getting involved in other operas. His first idea was for a single opera, *The Death of Siegfried*. But as he got hooked on the Sagas the size of the story ballooned up. He realized there would have to be too much now-read-on to make the thing dramatic, and if Wagner reached this conclusion then it must indeed have been true. So he decided on two operas, *Siegfried's Death* and *Young Siegfried*. Then these two got a bit crowded so he split the *Death* into two by adding *Götterdämmerung* and put some of the now-read-on stuff into a prologue, *Rhinegold*, which he tiresomely and insistently called 'a preliminary evening'. The four pieces in approximately their present form were in draft script by the end of 1848.

The main sources for the gloomy tale were the Icelandic sagas. These were not at all ancient, being written about a hundred years after our own Norman Conquest. Siegfried etc. were remembered historical characters, like our Alfred and the cakes, but even more unfortunate. They also supplied some of the Who's Who of the gods, Wotan = Odin, and so on. Another source were some German–Nordic poems, no doubt equally brutish. When one reflects that only a couple of hundred years later the witty and sophisticated Chaucer was writing stuff that would have rated a fourteenth-century *New Yorker* we can be thankful we lived in warmer climes.

Wagner set about writing the librettos for *The Ring* in reverse order, *Götterdämmerung* first, *Rhinegold* last. But he took his eye off the ball to write *Tristan*, finished in 1857, and *Meistersinger* ten years later, two walloping great works that finally and decisively put him to No. 1 in the German opera ratings and equal No. 1 to Verdi in the international league.

Wagner's method of working was first to write a prose version of the story. He then translated this into his own kind of poetry – scansion, alliteration, high-flown words, but no rhymes. Those in a position to judge, most of them pro-Wagner, will reluctantly admit that this is not great poetry, so we are probably right in thinking that *qua* poetry it is pretty dreadful. (Surprisingly, this was perhaps the only area where Wagner was not vain: he never claimed to be a great poet, so why did he take such enormous pains to give second-rate words such careful treatment when setting them to first-rate music?) He then went on to a sketch score on three staves – one for the voice and two for the orchestra. Sometimes he went to a second sketch score, sometimes straight to the full score. Then a bit of fiddling around and into rehearsal.

Wagner had practically no income and spent a lot of money and so required sponsorship to keep the wheels turning. He found this in a small way from a number of female fans and in a big way from a young man of eighteen who was potty about his music and was, fortunately for Wagner, a king and could therefore divert state money, regardless of the wishes of the taxpayers, into Richard Wagner Enterprises. So it was that under the admiring eye of King Ludwig of Bavaria *Rhinegold* and *Valkyrie* were premiered in the King's Theatre Munich in 1869 and 1870. Bits of the unfinished works had been performed at a concert in Vienna some seven years earlier and this had already got the adrenalin running in musico and critical circles. This first full helping of *The Ring* fuelled the civil war that was to rage amongst musicians for a quarter of a century after Wagner's death. Those against were led by one Hanslick, a leading Viennese music critic, and those for by Wagner. Three of Hanslick's main planks were: Wagner was pushing music beyond the bounds of what music should properly be asked to do (wrong), Wagner paid far too much attention to the setting of the work – music should come first, words second (right) – and Wagner was wrong to be lurching around in the area of myth and legend: opera should be about people (half right). And many other things too, for as a great classicist Hanslick found Wagner desperately untidy. So did the Wagnerites and anti-Wagnerites rage against each other until the war began to peter out about the middle of this century.

Wagner had many theories about how to write music for opera. He was extremely strong on theories and plucked ideas from all over the place and especially from Aeschylus and Schopenhauer and put them into his operatic magimix formula.

Some of the novelties were:

1. Motivic integration. The whole idea of musical mottos telling you what to think while you listen. Cues without words. Plenty about this on other pages.

2. Musico-poetic synthesis (!). Making the words and music fuse into a single experience. Further and better particulars on page 554.

3. Tonal structure. The overall strategy of key relationships and the (to us) rather crazy emphasis on the association of a musical idea (often a motto) with a particular key. Scribes will report with triumph that he brings back motto *xyz* IN THE ORIGINAL KEY. So bully for him.

Wagner the theoretician had the unusual capacity to put his theories into practice. He certainly made it hard for himself, but after some pretty dour early stuff (the dwarf bits of *Rhinegold*, *Valkyrie* Act I) and after *Tristan*, his learning curve speeded up and in the music of *Siegfried* (second half) and the later additions to *Götterdämmerung* he is really motoring with all the computer controls showing positive. But whether or not this huge apparatus of musical technology improved or impeded his performance as an opera composer, we shall never know.

It was Wagner's dream to have a Festival Theatre designed by him to perform his works. This would ensure that they were 100% proof. Written by Wagner, composed by Wagner, cast by Wagner, produced by Wagner, performed in a Wagner-designed theatre, where the programme notes and even the notices in the gents' advising clients to adjust their dress before leaving, would be written by Wagner himself. Amazingly enough he delegated the musical direction of the first full cycle to Hans Richter but we can be sure there was some pretty imperious back-seat driving.

At first he tried to site the Wagnerfestspielhaus in Munich but Ludwig was getting such a hard time from his civil servants (most of whom were probably crypto-Hanslickers) for spending money on a megalomaniac composer that he had to switch to the Glyndebourne concept and set up a Festspielcountrykindofhaus at Bayreuth. To finance it he opened a fund to which all big-hearted supporters of the arts (i.e. of Wagner) were invited to contribute. It flopped, and the opening *Ring* cycle had to be postponed. Once again the Wagner-crazy King Ludwig picked up the tab. (You can imagine the scene when this news reached the permanent secretary to the Treasury.)

The two Munich productions had passed off reasonably well. The house had a firm management and Wagner, as an old opera house pro, respected the musical standards and the technical team. But the rehearsals for the full cycle at Bayreuth must have been murder. By nature Wagner was a dictator and at Bayreuth he was also a god. Added to this, he was now into an advanced stage of megalomania, and who would like to have been the person responsible for the anvil splitting in half while Siegfried's sword was still up in the air (which did happen)? Wagner must have come to realize that his vision of *The Ring*'s scenic effects was not going to come off and – worse still – could never come off. Sitting in his study, he was complete master of words and music, but when it came to opera's third estate – the *mise en scène* – he could not by sheer brainpower make flats, backdrops, gaslight and stagehands do magic things. This must have been a terrible blow to him, like when he found he couldn't walk on water either.

So the Bayreuth theatre was built, the full cycle of *The Ring* performed, the dream realized, and Wagner didn't like it much. He thought the sets looked crummy and Richter took the gloomier bits too fast, The Ride of the Valkyries too slow.

But the first full cycle of *The Ring* was a sensation. It had made its mark and during the 1890s it was given in Vienna, London and New York and, liked or loathed, it was universally recognized as the Everest amongst operas that it is.

Since then it is staged from time to time when the major houses can afford it and, whereas the announcement of other operas may be news, a production of *The Ring* is still a headline event.

It is impossible to grade this Xtraordinary and Xceptional work as if it were an ordinary opera so let us therefore just give it an X.

La Rondine
(The Swallow)

Parisian romance

Puccini

The one about Gay Paree where a society woman turns grisette and a maid dresses up as her mistress.

CAST

Magda, society woman with a past	Soprano
Lisette, Magda's maid	Soprano
Rambaldo, Magda's butter-and-eggs man, precise relationship uncertain	Baritone
Ruggero, rich and innocent young man	Tenor
Prunier, a Bohemian-ish poet	Tenor

Périchaud, Gobin, Crébillon (business friends of Rambaldo), **Bianca, Suzy, Yvette, Gabriella, Georgette, Lolette** (Parisian girlettes).

Lots of grisettes whorettes demi-mondettes etc. Plus similar male riff-raff also students painters and everyone who you would expect to meet on a night out in Montmartre with Toulouse-Lautrec

3 acts: running time 1 hr 15 mins

STORY

Act I A luxurious Paris salon 1850

Magda is throwing an at-home party. Boring bankers discuss Bourse news in the background. Silly girls cluster round the poet Prunier. Magda hostesses: Prunier sings his latest party piece but breaks it off saying it is unfinished. Magda supplies an extemporary finish. Rambaldo gives Magda a necklace (there is no plot point for this – indeed no point at all). Lisette cheekily announces that a young man has been waiting hours to see Rambaldo: send him up says Rambaldo. That girl is too pushy says Prunier, she needs slapping down: not so says Magda, Lisette is my little ray of sunshine. Magda has a fantasy of escaping social duties to pursue sexy encounters with students etc. She recalls one dreamy past experience.

Prunier starts reading palms gippo fashion, while Rambaldo lazily interviews the young man Ruggero in the background. Prunier divines that

Magda has the soul of a swallow: she will migrate to warmer climes (but will return). All discuss which is the best café for Ruggero's first night out in Paris: opinions diverge. Majority vote – Bulliers. All go to bed except Prunier and Lisette who commence a period-style flirtation. Lisette dresses up in Magda's clothes and both exit. Magda floats across the stage dressed as a grisette (whatever that may be).

Act II Bulliers: grand Second Empire café

A crowd mills around: high society fashionable whores students flower-girls etc. The students fancy Magda as a grisette: they mob her: she pretends she has a date with Ruggero who is sitting alone. They dance: they make enjoyable body contact. Prunier and Lisette turn up. Lisette thinks that grisette is a dead spit of her mistress – dang it, it's her she says. Rubbish says Prunier. But Lisette is absolutely correct.

This unlikely quartet make a party of it, each pair noisily in love (Magda and Ruggero have been acquainted only fifteen minutes: this is speedy even for opera). Enter Rambaldo: Ruggero and Lisette fade into the background. Rambaldo asks Magda if she's coming home? Negative she says: I have found true romance. Rambaldo makes a gentlemanly exit: Ruggero and Magda a loverly one.

Act III Idyllic scene in the grounds of an hotel on the Côte d'Azur

Ruggero and Magda bask in sunshine and happiness. Ruggero mentions his financial embarrassment, he also says he has written to Mum and Dad for permission to marry Magda. Exits. Magda is worried what the hell to do: tell him about her other life or keep mum? Lisette and Prunier enter. Lisette has just bombed out as a vocal act at the local music hall in Nice and now says she wishes to return to domestic employment. There is plenty of aggro between Prunier and Lisette: they ask the pageboy to announce to Magda that two Paris friends await her.

Magda comes on: Prunier asks, Are you happy? Sure am says she: I don't believe it says he, you'll soon be back in Paris solus: will you reemploy Lisette? Sure will she says. Exit P & L. Ruggero rushes on with a revoltingly soppy letter from his Mum saying OK my darling get wed. Magda, cast down, tells Ruggero she cannot accept. Why? Why? he asks: because I am soiled goods she says. Oh shucks he says, come on, I don't mind a bit of soil. Negative she says. Both very sad. End.

MINUTES FROM START

LOOK OUT FOR

Act I

0

The short opening prelude* is agreeable, frothy café 0
music. It is followed by some five minutes of the same sort of stuff, much of it in waltz time.

5: *Chi il bel sogno*

Doretta's dream, Prunier's latest party piece* at 5
first to piano accompaniment. It gets much better

6: *La conquista mi tenta*

when Magda takes up the story** and gives the 6
dream (which is pretty boring up to this point) a sexy ending.

15: *Denaro! Nient' altro che denaro!*

Magda's fantasy of low life.* In a diverting piece 15
that wanders all over the place she sees herself as a grisette (whatever exactly that was).

30: *Le Bal Mustard!*

A sparky little ensemble* in which the assembled 30
company run through the four-star night spots with the intention of giving Ruggero a good night on the town.

Act II

After a heavy dose of fun, frolic, champagne and chatter Magda's first duet with Ruggero takes us back near to the old Puccini and we begin quite the best sequence in the opera:

5: *Scusatemi, scusate*

1. 'Scuse me says Magda.* Please stay, says Rug- 5
gero to a sweet barcarolle-like tune. Let's dance?

8: *Vuoi tu dirmi*

2. So the waltz starts* and judging by the tone of 8
the conversation, it must be dirty dancing (amor, boci vibrante, ardor, etc.). At first tentative, the waltz

10: *Dolcezza! Ebbrezza!*

bursts out into a full Viennese oom-tum-tum,** with 10
all the trimmings.

3. The waltz oom-tum-tums on under dialogue

15: *Perchè mai cercate*

for some time. Then the second good duet** Magda/ 15
Ruggero. She: Don't try to find out who I am, He: I know who you are: you are my heart's desire.

21: *Bevo al tuo*

4. The third and most memorable love duet** 21
Magda/Ruggero. Sweet nothings really, but such a good tune. It swells into an ensemble (all loverly stuff) and ends dreamily with the revellers sprinkling flowers all over the lovers, all four of whom, disregarding public decency, are in a clinch. Nice, but a little Ivor Novello, as is the last love-in duet before the curtain.

Act III

4: *Ah! ti ricordi*

Yet another very amiable duet** Ruggero/Magda 15

with a catchy tune that switches down into the pit to become an accompanying figure and stays there and thereabouts for some eight minutes.

30: *Ma come puoi lasciarmi* Positively the last duet* Magda/Ruggero: they accept the need to part (Ruggero without question, the wimp) in a gossamer-light cloud of sadness. Soppy tunes, no passion, all very genteel but, in its too simple way, quite touching. 30

NOTES

La Rondine	Puccini's eighth opera
First night	Monte Carlo Opera House, 27 March 1917
Reception	Good, but see below
Libretto	Adami
Source	Storyline offered to him by the management of the Vienna Opera

NEWS AND GOSSIP

After *Fanciulla* Puccini cast about in a hectic search for the right subject, chucking out nearly a dozen prospects in favour of *Rondine*. On a visit to Vienna in 1913 he was offered 200,000 kronen by the management of the Karlstheater for ten numbers for a musical comedy. He said no; but back in Italy his ever-present business sense asserted itself and in March he offered instead an opera on the libretto of *Rondine* which two of the Vienna Opera writers were working on. In May 1914 he got down to it. The outbreak of World War I delayed things and Puccini went off the whole idea – 'a load of rubbish' he wrote (and honestly he was pretty near the mark here). However he called in a trusty librettist, Adami, and by Easter 1916 the job was done. But there were complications: the contract called for a first performance in Vienna – Austria was at war with France; old Ricordi, Puccini's impresario and business manager, had died and his son was not up to snuff. Eventually Puccini did a deal with a new publisher, Ricordi's rival Sonzogno, and the premiere was arranged for Monte Carlo. After the good reception at Monte Carlo came Buenos Aires (fair) and Bologna (bad) and finally Milan (disaster and a real hammering from the critics). In 1920 *Rondine* was performed in Vienna and went down like a lead balloon. After that the poor thing was pretty well laid to rest and today is only revived as a curio.

COMMENT

And now for something entirely different: not quite a Light Opera, for it has no laughs: not operetta, for it lacks the zing and zizz of true operetta: almost a musical comedy but too refined: in truth a sentimental journey through a Viennese tea room. And what's wrong with that? Nothing really, except to ask why the composer of *Bohème* and *Tosca* should waste his time on a rather dim little number like this? Partly money, for he was offered a deal he could not refuse by Viennese impresarios to write something operetta-ish, partly because he had nowhere else to go: he could not job backwards to *Tosca/Bohème* territory: the modernism of *Fanciulla* had not pleased and Puccini (like Verdi) was critic-sensitive to an almost pathological degree. So why not try something old, something new and something, if not blue, then a sort of faded lavender? *Rondine* is saved from oblivion by three of Puccini's great qualities: his ability to write a good tune, adroit orchestration and consummate stagecraft. Without these three *Rondine* would instantly sink below even the Lloyd Webber line and become a junk musical. Despite its small pluses, there is a lot of stuff in *Rondine* that is ornery, but the best of it (about twenty minutes) is a really nice sound to have about the house when, for instance, cooking. Easily thc best music comes from the duets, every one with a whistleable tune, the waltzes have lots of oomph, as do some of the chatter ensembles. Strangely, too, the spirits of both Richard Strauss and Franz Lehár occasionally stalk the pit – Strauss in his less pretentious domestic chit-chat mood and Lehár just as Lehár. Not an alpha, not a beta – some lower category according to taste.

Rhinegold *see under* Ring, The

Rosenkavalier

Romantic comedy

(Der Rosenkavalier)

Richard Strauss

The one where a Field Marshal's wife sends her lover to assist in the wedding of her cousin with the unforeseen result that he falls in love with the cousin's bride and she loses him.

CAST

The Marschallin, Princess Marie Thérèse Werdenberg	Soprano
Octavian, Count Rofrano, nicknamed **Quinquin**	(Mezzo-) Soprano
Baron Ochs (of Lerchenau), the Marschallin's cousin	Bass
Herr von Faninal, a rich tradesman	Baritone
Sophie, his daughter	Soprano
Marianne, her minder	Soprano
Valzacchi, an Italian private eye	Tenor
Annina, his side-kick	Contralto

A lawyer, an Italian singer, three orphans, a milliner, an animal trader, two major-domos, a police inspector, four abandoned children, four footmen, four waiters

3 acts: running time 3 hrs 25 mins

STORY

Act I The Marschallin's bedroom

We are in old Vienna during the reign of Maria Theresa and Octavian a young Viennese blade is crawling out of the Marschallin's bed having had an orgasm during the overture and we are not quite sure what kind of sexual coupling has taken place since he is not a young blade at all but a mezzo-soprano in trousers, or rather shortly to be in trousers once he puts them on. It turns out to be an amicable relationship between a woman – let's guess – in her mid-thirties and a boy of seventeen. They bill and coo and he hides as an only slightly politically incorrect little black boy brings in the breakfast chocolate and then they bill and coo again. A second alarm! It's the Field Marshal in person! Octavian hides again, but it isn't the Field Marshal at all it's the Marschallin's ghastly country cousin Baron Ochs forcing his way into her room. My God Quinquin says the Marschallin (her rather precious pet name for Octavian) do you remember we were given a letter from him in the coach and I never opened it? Octavian dresses up as the Marschallin's maid (now he/she's in drag × 2) and the Baron bursts in. He bumps into Octavian and enjoys it. The Marschallin receives him and between bouts of ogling her maid he states his business.

I'm going to get married to Sophie Faninal daughter of a very rich and common grocer he says. (But he takes much longer than this to say it.) Ah yes! Of course! What you said in the letter says the Marschallin. And I want someone to take the Silver Rose to her that is the rather poncy habit of the Viennese gentry says the Baron. He then gives a disgusting account of his sexual antics with milkmaids etc. and instead of throwing him out on his ear the Marschallin offers her cousin Octavian to act as Rosebearer. Meanwhile there is all sorts of farcical by-play as Ochs tries to get near the maid who has assumed the name of Mariandel. The Marschallin shows the unspeakable Ochs a miniature of Octavian and he spots the likeness with Mariandel. She must be his bastard sister he says. Indeed it's a good idea to keep family bastards as body servants I have my bastard son working for me in that capacity. Could you provide me with a lawyer too? he asks. Yes OK says she (God knows why). Let in the lawyer and the rest of the queue to my morning levée she says to her Major Domo.

A flood of beauticians, musicians, Asiatic carpet-sellers, insurance agents and double-glazing salesmen pours in. An Italian tenor sings. Ochs consults the lawyer. The Marschallin has a rinse and set. Three orphans ask for charity, also a distressed gentlewoman. It is one of those opera scenes that writers, composers and directors just adore, which is why they usually go on too long as does this one. The only plot point to come out of all this hullabaloo is that amongst this riff-raff there is an Italian private eye and his side-kick looking for work. Ochs engages them to procure Mariandel for him. The whole gaggle are shooed off the stage. Ochs's piggish bastard son hands over the silver rose in its case to the Marschallin.

Left alone, the Marschallin reflects that she is getting on a little. Octavian now returns dressed male. Why so sad? he asks. Time, time, time is against me says the Marschallin. Sometimes I get up at night and stop all the clocks. Sometimes I put the calendars on rewind. Sooner or later I'll be too old for you Quinquin. She sighs. Don't talk like that I'll love you for ever says Quinquin. He leaves in a slight huff. O God I never kissed him goodbye says the Marschallin. James! John! Archibald! Theophilus! she shouts: Go catch the young master before he rides off! But they are not sufficiently fleet of foot. He's got away. She sends the little black boy off to take the rose to him and sits and thinks until the curtain falls.

Act II The reception salon in the Faninal residence

Sophie waits in a state of panic while her minder Marianne race-reads the arrival of Octavian. He does it in style – two carriages, many servants, etc. Octavian does his formal bit and while it is going on it is clear that the couple are falling in love at a speed and with an intensity that is only known in operas and silent movies. They have a conversation. Sophie shows that she has spirit and wit and has done a pretty thorough research job on Octavian in *Who's Who* and *Debrett*. They are now even more in love. Herr Faninal brings on the Baron, who behaves even more odiously than usual, poking Sophie like a prize cow, ignoring her minder, patronizing Faninal. Sophie tears herself away from him. Octavian silently rages. The Baron goes off to settle the contract saying that if Octavian feels like slinging a leg over Sophie that's OK with him. It might warm her up nicely in readiness for her wedding night.

You're not going to marry that toad are you? asks Octavian. No. Never. Not on your life says Sophie. Will you help me to escape a fate worse than death? There is an interruption: the Baron's retinue of illegitimate sons and rustic skinheads are all drunk and trying to rape Faninal's maids: they are ejected. The answer is Yes says Octavian. Together we will set you free. I love you. Reciprocated says Sophie. They kiss.

Valzacchi the private eye and Annina his helper leap out shouting loudly and pinion the lovers. The Baron comes on. What's up? he asks. This person – Octavian says but the Baron keeps interrupting. This person he shouts at last refuses to marry you. Come come don't be silly she'll soon get used to me don't worry I'll tame her I know the sort says the Baron. I challenge you says Octavian. Not now says the Baron I'm busy with the marriage contract. You'll not get past me says Octavian drawing his sword. Anyway you are a lecher, an evil bastard and a sewer-rat. Well well what a cheeky little chappie says the Baron. Draw! says Octavian. They both draw, Octavian scratches the Baron on the upper arm. Help! Murder! Police! I'm dying! screams the Baron. All the servants rush on. Chaos. Turmoil. Bandages antibiotics and brandy for the Baron. Faninal tells Sophie to get out and never darken his door again. Annina comes on with a letter for the Baron, supposedly from Mariandel, suggesting a meeting. This cheers the Baron up no end and the act ends with him complacently humming one of his favourite waltzes. But he has made a fatal mistake. He didn't tip Annina.

Act III A private room in a hotel. Dinner for two is set. There is a bed in an alcove

Valzacchi who has been bought out by Octavian is masterminding the trap to be set for the Baron. Annina has disguised herself as a widow. Extras are being rehearsed to appear through trapdoors or at hidden windows. It's country house amateur theatricals. Octavian is dressed as Mariandel. He leaves and returns on one arm of the Baron, the other being in a sling. A lot of business as the landlord waiters Valzacchi fuss around the Baron. Music starts to play backstage. The Baron tells everyone to get out. He tells Valzacchi to be sure to keep the bill down. He offers Mariandel some wine but she says she's on the wagon. Mariandel plays the innocent, sees the bed and is scandalized.

So you just got engaged Baron? says Mariandel. When a gent is out with a lady they don't talk about things like that says the Baron. My God he adds you are the living spit of that little sod who tried to murder me. One of the men playing the spooks comes out too soon and gives the Baron a turn. Whassat? he says. Nothing says Mariandel, nothing there. Mariandel starts boozing. She gets maudlin. The Baron thinks he can fix her up by undoing her bra. Spooky faces again. The Baron takes off his wig. A widow walks in through the wall. The Baron rings for help. The landlord and servants etc. rush in. The widow says That's him! That's my husband. Never seen her in my life says the Baron. Is everyone crazy? Four kids appear Papa Papa Papa Papa they sing in that particularly nasty nasal tone adopted by operatic children. Listen to your kiddies says the widow. So you were thinking of bigamy? says Valzacchi. Watch out that the Purity Police don't get you. A Purity Policeman walks in. What's this What's this What's this he says. This man is a Baron says the landlord. Anyone confirm that? asks the Inspector. Yes this man says the Baron indicating Valzacchi. Never seen him in my life says Valzacchi. Who's that female anyway? asks the Inspector pointing at Mariandel. My fiancée says the Baron. Name of Faninal. Faninal arrives on the scene. Are you the father of this female? asks the Inspector. Never seen her before in my life says Faninal. Sophie arrives. It's a scandal says everyone. He had four kids by this widow and now he's trying to marry Sophie Faninal. The Baron looks desperately for his wig. The Inspector gets stroppy. Octavian jumps behind the curtain into the bed and dresses male again. Faninal collapses. Sophie takes him out. Octavian chucks female garments out between the curtains à la stripper. Riot bedlam and confusion.

There is a fanfare. The landlord announces that the Marschallin has arrived. She makes a regal entrance. Ah yes my man she says to the Inspector I think you once worked as a bodyguard for my husband? Yes Ma'am. I did I did says he slapping up a smart one. My God it's the Marschallin says Octavian/Mariandel putting his/her head out between the curtains. The Baron signals her back. Sophie comes on again. My father says you can naff off and never come near our house again she says to the Baron. The Marschallin sorts things out. The Baron is to give up any idea of marrying Sophie. It has all been a Viennese masquerade, no more.

Octavian shows up dressed male. The Baron does a double take. Then he remembers when he first saw Mariandel and puts two and two together. The Marschallin looks at him piercingly. OK he says I will keep quiet about that one. [But is certain to use it at the first blackmail opportunity: Ed.] Gradually they all leave. The Baron is pressed to pay the bill but has left his credit card at home. The Marschallin is left alone with Sophie who is sad because she thinks everything must be over between Octavian and herself and Octavian who has the tough problem of introducing the girl he loves to the woman who is his mistress. Octavian and Sophie are phazed with embarrassment. The Marschallin who is familiar with the ground rules of Viennese amorous adventures realizes her number is up quicker than she expected and like the gracious and good lady she is she lets Octavian know that he is off the hook. She quizzes Sophie to make sure she is a suitable gal and then gives the thumbs up to their affair, not without a furtive tear. To mark this important occasion all three sing a very fine trio. The Marschallin leaves to do a PR job with Faninal.

Octavian and Sophie are left alone. They are happy lovers. The Marschallin and Faninal pass through benevolently. Octavian and Sophie exit. The almost politically correct little black boy runs on looking for the Marschallin's specs which he finds and runs off again thereby providing a cute little final flourish before the curtain comes down.

MINUTES FROM START — LOOK OUT FOR

Act I

0 The overture* is famous for starting the opera off with an orgasm, but honestly if nobody told you you would never know. After the rufty-tufty in bed with the *moment de joie* signalled by whooping horns we have a post-coital calm. Pleasant thoughts from the woodwind. A retrospective glow from the strings. Then Strauss, an inveterate mickey-mouser, makes the birdies sing. Ornithologically less precise than Messiaen. 0

7: *Du bist mein Bub* Sweet nothings whispered between the Marschallin and Octavian. Some gorgeous phrases float in.* 7

The birdies again. Some embracing to soft strings.

9 Elegant ballet music* as the little black boy serves breakfast, rather slowly. 9

11: *Jedes Ding hat seine Zeit* The breakfast waltz.* A little stiff and old-fashioned for such a moment. They exchange endearments between sips of chocolate. 11

16: *Quinquin es ist ein Besuch* After the false alarm of the Feldmarschall's return the music slips into an easy waltz.* It's only Cousin 16

Ochs, no threat. Octavian slips into something loose and becomes Mariandel.

The Baron's double game (trying to catch Octavian/Mariandel at the same time as conducting his business with the Marschallin) is played against an-
18: *Pardon, mein hübsches Kind!* other dance tune,* or rather a dance tune in snatches 18
for between whirls we have what used to be recitatif but in the hands of Strauss becomes a sort of speak/sing resting on a cushion of orchestral sound. The scene is every bit as sweet as the hot chocolate called back by the Baron in the hopes of seeing Mariandel's ankle.

Now we have tantalizing snatches of waltz leading up to the Baron's lengthy and moronic account of his methods of satisfying his animal instincts. It's a repulsive performance and could only be thought to be funny in a leather-slapping Bavarian beer hall or in a British rugby club. Unfortunately both the Marschallin and Octavian seem to be amused and snigger
33: *Weiss mich ins engste Versteck* away like anything. The bright and cheerful trio* that 33
ends this dreary monologue seems to have a Russian folk theme thumping away in its midst. Isn't he awful? sings the Marschallin. I can always get sex somehow says the Baron. Oo a nice young girl like me wouldn't go anywhere near a chap like that says Mariandel coyly.

37: *Drei arme, adelige Waisen* The levée goes with a swing** although the Mar- 37
schallin's security arrangements seem to be lax in allowing entry to such a horde of unwanted riff-raff. Musically the members of the service industries seem to be at least fifty to a hundred years behind the gentry. The orphans, it is true, do have some shifting tonality in the first of their several beguiling verses but the flautist is a virtuoso in the style of the 1780s and the Italian tenor's song could have been written by Bellini in a spare moment. But the Baron in his argument with the lawyer waxes quite Wagnerian.

Suddenly we move from farce into opera. The Marschallin reflects on youth and maturity with
49: *Da geht er hin* special reference to herself. This is nearly an aria,** 49
the sung line is accompanied lightly and in no way smothered by the orchestra as can happen in Strauss. It is a melodious piece harmonically with nothing that

could cause Schubert to cock an ear and it is a little touching.

54: *Ach! Du bist wieder da?* The long love duet** between the Marschallin and 54 Octavian.

1. She is amused to see him stride in again, as a man. They pick up the tender bantering mood that was there in the opening exchanges and pick over the alarums of the morning to music like warm pink cotton wool. A tiny cloud floats in (trombone and bass tuba). Don't be like other men she says. What do you mean? he asks fearfully. The cloud cover thickens. Sooner or later you will slip away she says. He weeps.

2. The music is sad but still sweet and dreamy as
60: *Die Zeit* she gives him a short lecturette** on the effects of 60
time on a woman's physiognomy. Sometimes she stops all the clocks. But we hear them chime on the harp and celeste. Then with a ravishing phrase she says it doesn't do to be afraid of time.

63: *Mein schöner Schatz* 3. Octavian is upset.* The music climbs out of the 63 cotton wool. He is agitated. One day you will find a girl younger and prettier than me she says. It is the beginning of the end. Back into the cotton wool but now it's tinted with blue. The Marschallin gets dangerously sentimental as she moves into her farewell mode.

66: *Sie spricht ja heute* 4. Now it's clearly moving towards goodbye.** 66 She tells him her plans. It has been fifteen minutes of Strauss in his worldly/tender mood and a real good wallow.

72: *Da drin ist die silberne Ros'n . . .* The act ends artfully,* Octavian goes, the forgot- 72 ten kiss, the little black boy, the silver rose and a dreamy last message from the Marschallin followed alas by a brief last-wicket stand by six reprehensible solo violins.

Act II

0 The build up of the prelude,* the buzz in the house- 0 hold, Sophie at prayer while her minder race-reads the goings-on in the street, all help to make Octavian's arrival into a good theatrical event. We hear his motto (first heard at the start of the overture: rather like a very short national anthem) just before he shows and soon after we get the eerie Rose motto (celeste, harps, three flutes and three solo violins) which

sounds like water dripping off icicles.

The encounter duet:

6: *Mir ist die Ehre* 1. Octavian and Sophie go through the ritual* of 6
giving and receiving the rose in a state of charmed
embarrassment. The icicles drip. Suddenly Sophie
surprises us by bursting into song about roses in
9: *Wie himmlische* heaven.*** She is happy. She sings like a bird, but 9
much more beautifully. Octavian falls under her
spell. It is an enchanted moment. They are in love.

11: *Dahin muss ich zurück* 2. They sing together*** but neither hears the 11
other. They are both a little delirious with delight.
Sophie's soaring melody winds on.

3. But now real life breaks in. Things have to be
done with the rose. They become aware of the servants and Marianne the minder. They sit down to
make polite conversation. The music passes from
13: *Ich kenn' Ihn schon* magical to agreeable humdrum.* Sophie is pert, just 13
short of cheeky. Octavian, staggering from the *coup de
foudre* that has knocked him stupid, begins to respond
with some spirit. The music is full of happy phrases
but it does not force the pace; it is gentle, and as helpful as it can be in allowing these two young persons to
fall in love as quickly and as pleasantly as possible.

The early comedy of the Baron's ghastly behaviour
is played over a bright oom-pah orchestral accompaniment, but when the adrenalin starts to run the
angry ensembles make the orchestra uneasy and the
strings in particular sound strained and tense. But
things relax when the unspeakable Baron comes in
25: *Mit mir* with the big waltz tune*** (though one can't help 25
wondering why Strauss allowed such a glorious tune
to be mauled about by this oaf on its first appearance).

After the noisy intermezzo that accompanies the
attempted rape of the Faninal domestic staff there is a
hush. Sophie and Octavian are alone (Rose motto,
Octavian's motto). They agree that the thought of
marriage to the Baron is impossible. Octavian's motto
rings out, boldly. Then the music softens and melts as
they kiss for the first time. Now they walk on air each
32: *Mit Ihren Augen* one cheerily singing their own thing** – he: she 32
needs me to stand up for her; is that all, or does she
really fancy me?, she: I want you to protect me. O I
do! I do! The pulse of the music beats faster than in

the first love duet, we are in dreamland again but now there is a hint of reality when Octavian's reai-world motto breaks in again over the long happy melodic line that the orchestra has been spinning.

The Baron enters, and from the deliberate pace of
35: *Eh bien, Mamsell* the early comic exchange* the speed and excitement 35
build up, first when he lays his big meaty hands on
Sophie then faster still on Octavian's challenge to a
duel. Then presto when all the household joins in.
Now there is bedlam. It is craftily done, the comedy
being wonderfully well pointed by the orchestra.

51: *Da lieg' ich* The Baron cheers up.* Alone with the servants and 51
the doctor at first he is full of spleen. He thunders
against Octavian. He thinks Vienna stinks. His band
of thickies sing a slightly spooky threatening chorus
(Octavian! Wait till we get him!). But here's a letter –
from Mariandel – and the wonderful waltz 'Mit mir'
56: *Ohne mich, ohne mich* creeps in.** The Baron is a changed man. He's not 56
bothered any more by his wounded arm nor by
thoughts of Octavian's impudence. All he can think
about is how soon he can get to bed with the lovely
chambermaid. Annina reads the letter. The waltz
floats on. The Baron will dictate an answer later. The
orchestra comes in with a full fortissimo version of
the waltz. As it fades the Baron toddles off to bed.

Act III

The prelude to Act III is panicky and conspiratorial
but as the curtain goes up it changes character and becomes a background piece for pantomime. A lot of
people are very busy laying a trap for the Baron. We
hear Octavian's motto first en clair and then in waltz
form. More waltzes creep in with excited furbelows
from the woodwind, but as the noise dies down we
find they are coming from the stage, or rather just offstage. It's the hotel band. They play off and on for
some ten minutes sharing the honours with the or-
10: *Nein! Nein!* chestra in the pit. An especially fetching waltz* 10
accompanies Mariandel's refusal to take a drink. (The
12: *Ach, lass' Sie schon einmal* 'No' waltz – more of it to come later.) And another* 12
as the Baron squares up to take his first kiss.

15: *Die schöne Music!* And 'Mit mir',** again, from offstage. 15

The Baron sees a ghostly face. And another. And a
19: *Jetzt wird's frei mir* widow in black. There is a struggle* between heebie- 19

jeebie music and the rose-tinted waltz. The heebie-jeebies win. Waltz time is over.

With Annina's arrival a chug-chug-chug starts in
the orchestra which goes panting on as the crazy
20: *Er ist es!* ensemble* builds up until the entry of the inspector 20
puts a stop to it.

After some fifteen minutes of unremarkable knockabout music there is a mighty fanfare. The Marschallin has arrived. The farcical romp is over. We are back
35: *Ihre hochfürstliche Gnaden* in the land of opera.* 35

The big orchestra fades away. There are no
waltzes. For some ten minutes we have bewilderment
and shock as the Marschallin unravels the terrible
39: *Mon cousin bedeut' Er ihn!* mix-up.* Solo woodwind takes the lead over a back- 39
ground chamber orchestra quietly doing its best to
help. It is an enchanted scene of suspended animation. Even the Baron becomes almost human and look out especially for the moment when the Marschallin reflects on the disappointing nature of all men and the exchanges with the Baron that follow.

Farce music and waltzes reappear in a glorious
46: *Leupold, wir gängen!* riot** as every character in the plot pesters the Baron, 46
most of them asking for money. This puts paid to the sub-plot in style and we are free to return to more serious matters.

In this scene with the Marschallin, Sophie and Octavian we come to the heart of the opera. Once again the big orchestra has disappeared and there is the lightest accompaniment of wind soloists and strings.

48: *Mein Gott!* 1. An embarrassed triangle,* Octavian ashamed 48
and guilty, Sophie devastated and the Marschallin a bit thrown that her forecast has come true so soon. She speaks to Sophie in gentle phrases. Don't be so upset. But she is angry with Octavian for playing it so dumb. He has the guts (just) to show that he wants Sophie rather than her.

50: *Heut' oder morgen* 2. They sing together,** tender, hurt and all won- 50
dering how the other two will jump. The Marschallin: I knew it would happen, I will be brave (cries a little), Octavian: I love *you* Sophie, Sophie: You'd best forget me.

52: *Ich muss hinein* 3. The Marschallin gently chats to Sophie.** 52

How long have they been in love? [About twelve hours? Ed.]

55: *Hab' mir's gelobt*

4. The glorious soprano trio.*** This is a great operatic event on a par with the quartet in *Fidelio* or the *Meistersinger* quintet. The three parties 'think' as follows: Marschallin (It has happened very quickly. He will be happy with that girl that stands there), Octavian (I want to consult her but I can't. But I do know one thing – I love Sophie), Sophie (I would like to kneel and thank her, she is giving him up for me). The trio rises to the heights because we feel the sentiments to be true and touching. The blend of the three voices makes a fresh sound. Although all in roughly the same soprano range the parts are clearly independent and together make a new sort of operatic magic. 55

61: *Spür' nur dich*

The dreamy mood continues. Octavian and Sophie sing a sweet boy-and-girl duet,*** Faninal and the Marschallin pass through the room. Ah well they say, boys and girls will be boys and girls. Octavian and Sophie sing their duet again this time with the icicle chords of the silver rose hovering above them, the music plays out the opera in the same mood but Strauss can't resist a final appearance of the little black boy to give the same cute ending to the last act as he did to the first. 61

NOTES

Rosenkavalier	Strauss's fifth opera
First night	Königliches Opernhaus, Dresden, 26 January 1911
Reception	A triumph
Libretto	Hofmannsthal
Source	French comedies by Molière and others for episodes, but the main story original

NEWS AND GOSSIP

Strauss wanted to write a comedy after *Salome* but got stuck into *Elektra* instead which has no laughs in it whatsoever. But it gave him the chance to find out that Hofmannsthal was his ideal partner. Now he had done his two shockers Strauss was even more avid to show that he could do drawing-room opera too and the pair of them set to work on *Rosenkavalier*, like two boffins discovering the atom. At first the opera favoured Ochs and farce only, plus the romantic Octavian/Sophie strand but gradually the Marschallin came out of the cupboard and grew to be the centre of gravity. Work started soon after the premiere of *Elektra* (January 1909) and the new opera, longer than the first two put together, was ready for performance within two years. There was trouble with the second act. Strauss pointed out that if it didn't come off the whole opera would flop. They did not see in advance that the farcing up of Act III went on too long and was a much bigger threat, but they were quick to admit it after the opening run.

Once in rehearsal it became clear that the Dresden house producer could not cope with such a monster and the great Max Reinhardt was called in and evidently did a great job. He refused a credit not out of pique but in consideration for the feelings of the staff man he had replaced.

Rosenkavalier was a big hit. If not as big as *My Fair Lady* some fifty years later, it was a success on a showbusiness scale, for its appeal went far beyond the circle of the opera buffs. It had fifty performances in Dresden and thirty-one in Vienna in its first year. Special *Rosenkavalier* trains were run to the theatre towns. It gave its name to brands of champagne and cigarettes. Although there is not much named after it today, it is still hugely popular in the opera houses. Alas it is a bit of a pig to put on (big cast, huge orchestra, a running time of at least 4 hours with intervals, which means overtime all round). So although the smaller companies are pushed to run a *Rosenkavalier*, in all the big houses it is there or thereabouts. If not quite a part of the central repertory it is a desirable bon-bon and always a good star vehicle and house-filler.

COMMENT

It is not easy to mix broad farce with serious sentiment, but in *Rosenkavalier* Hofmannsthal and Strauss pull it off. But only just, because the farce is too long and too broad and certainly in the last act the old thing teeters (for a long time) on the brink of pantomime with not a credible character in sight. But the Marschallin comes to the rescue in the nick of time.

She, of course, is not only the saviour of that scene but of the whole opera. Without her it would be a musical farce with some good waltzes and a scattering of sentimental songs. It is almost unbelievable that the Marschallin was something like an afterthought and not the central inspiration. As it turned out, she is one of the great lovables of all opera. There are few agreeably sophisticated women in opera at all and none that have her wit, her mastery of affairs and her understanding of the society around her. The other great character is Ochs, but he is flawed. As a butt he is better cast than Falstaff because he is not so nice. So we don't resent too much the cruel way he is hounded and bullied in the last act. But his grossness is too brutish to be funny and certainly it is impossible to believe that the Marschallin would have put up with his nasty talk in her house. Some nationalities are better at making dirty talk funny than others. The Brits are a bit uneasy with it, the clear winners are the French who can be absolutely disgusting with such wit and style as to get away with anything, but the Germans can have a yokelish beery way of telling their dirty jokes so bluntly as to be embarrassing. Ochs does this to the nth degree and loses a lot of charm in so doing. But for all that he is a mighty fine comic figure, as cowardly, vain, lecherous and deceitful as the very best.

Because of the fine balance between farce and sentiment, *Rosenkavalier* is tricky to produce. The newly founded firm of S & H had a great sense of theatre – all the right touches are there, the business in the Marschallin's bedroom, the build-up of the second act, the wonderfully effective final scene including the dinky little black boy, but they failed to realize two things – the farce in the last act gets tedious and the whole opera goes on for perhaps half an hour too long. Cuts could be made in all three acts which would speed things up nicely and there would be no great musical loss. The Baron's bedroom conversation with the Marschallin in the first act is an example.

The opera has three overlapping but distinct classes of music, the music of sentiment, the waltzes and the back-up music. The last, for all its force and variety, does no more than support the action on the stage during the spells of farce. The waltzes are wonderful, and at least three of them are world-beaters, the theatre music does its work efficiently but it is in the music of sentiment that we find the true glory of *Rosenkavalier*. Strauss has an astonishing ability to tug at the heartstrings through his gentle, tender brand of music. In this territory he was a musical psychiatrist with a romantic bent and the best passages in *Rosenkavalier* have in their recipe a dash both of Freud and of a very superior Barbara Cartland.

The soprano trio in the last act is one of the great events of opera and must have a place in everyone's top ten from Kobbé to Maestro Levine. There are two sweet duets between Octavian and Sophie. Perhaps most touching of all is the sad duet when the Marschallin delicately tells Octavian that time will take its toll, their love cannot last. In moments like these the music runs the danger of being almost too sweet, but it never quite crosses the frontier between crême brulée and marshmallow. Schmaltz is always just over the horizon, but never quite appears.

The back-up music is of the early sound-movie kind, a lot of orchestral oohs and ahs to match the action. Lots of melody too but now only in scraps and sometimes infuriating in that good tunes keep slipping away through your fingers almost before you can grasp them. The orchestra is not quite such a monster as for *Elektra* but it is still big (ninety-three in the pit) and with a stage band too, but since this is offstage it can now be put on tape. The orchestration is masterly, as ever, and there are some strokes, such as the icicles over the end of the Rose duet, that live in the ear for ever. The parts of the opera that would in the old days have been recitatif are handled better by Strauss than by Wagner. He can break off a big concerted piece and slip into narrative more nimbly than the master (no disrespect meant) who tended to go wallowing on with great waves of sound even though someone was just asking what time was dinner. He also sensibly reduces his forces to chamber size when he wants to give the centre stage to the singers. Wagner never learnt this trick.

Rosenkavalier is sophisticated, knowing and at the same time moving and this is what gives it its chance to be a great opera. The waltzes are wonderful, on a level above the waltzes of the other Strausses. The farce works if it catches on and sets the clients rolling in their seats, not so good heard cold in the study. But taken all together, *Rosenkavalier* is something of a phenomenon, and also probably the most popular opera written in the twentieth century. Alpha.

Salome

Biblical melodrama

Richard Strauss

The one where Salome does the dance of the Seven Veils and gets the head of John the Baptist in return.

CAST

Herod (Herodes), Tetrarch of Judaea	Tenor
Herodias, his wife	Mezzo
Salome, his stepdaughter	Soprano
Narraboth, captain of the guard	Tenor
John (Jochanaan), St John the Baptist	Baritone

A page, five Jews, two Nazarines, two soldiers, one Cappadocian, one slave

1 act: running time 1 hr 40 mins

STORY

A terrace of Herod's palace on Lake Galilee

We are in Roman-occupied Palestine between BC and AD and Herod the local ruler is throwing a big party inside his palace. Outside on the terrace a captain, Narraboth, and two soldiers are guarding St John the Baptist who is imprisoned in a hole known as a cistern although there is no water in it. How beautiful Salome looks tonight says Narraboth (he is crazy about her). What's all that shouting? asks one soldier. It's those frightful Jews at Herod's nosh-up says the other. When they argue about religion you can hear them a mile off. John pipes up from his cell. After me Jesus will come he says in fine biblical language. Tell him to belt up says one soldier. He's quite a decent guy says the other. Nice manners. Always prophesying. Trouble is you can't make out what the hell he is going on about.

Salome comes on. Whew! she says it's nice to get away from those frightful Jews and that lecherous old stepfather of mine who keeps eyeing me as if I was a piece of meat. John pipes up again from below. Whassat? asks Salome. It's the prophet Your Highness says Narraboth. We've got him in a hole underneath us here. Is he the one who keeps slagging off my mother? asks Salome. Fetch him up I want to speak to him. Sorry Your Highness says Narraboth. No one may speak to him. Herod's orders. Fetch him up! says Salome. Impossible says Narraboth. Look Narraboth says Salome if you fetch him up I will let you watch me take my bath tomorrow. All right fetch him up says Narraboth (thereby starting off a load of trouble). John comes up the stairs very slowly in order to give Richard Strauss time to write a powerful intermezzo.

Salome looks at John and you can see she gets strange vibes from him. Where is that womanizer Herod? he says and that whore of a wife? My God he's speaking of my mum says Salome. And are you the daughter of Sodom? he asks Salome. [Shome mishtake surely – sodomy not commonly thought to result in childbearing: Ed.] My goodness how I lust for your body says Salome. It's white as snow, ivory, roses. No it isn't she says looking closer it's absolutely filthy and that gives me even more of a buzz because I am as kinky as a coot. And your hair is quite disgusting. Oo what a thrill. And look at that snotty mouth with clags of clotted beard around it. I want to kiss that. I must kiss that. Your Highness I can't bear to hear you talk so dirty to this loony says Narraboth: kills himself (but nobody notices). Go and seek Jesus says John to Salome. Lemme kiss you John says she. Not on your life says John. He goes down to his cistern slowly giving Richard another intermezzo opportunity.

Herod comes on. Where is Salome? he asks. Ah! there she is. Move the party out here varlets he cries. Don't keep looking at Salome in that bedroom way says Herodias. You're always doing it. Why is there blood on my Bokhara rug? asks Herod. The captain did a hara-kiri says a soldier. O pity. Nice chap. Get the body removed says Herod. That wind blew up suddenly he adds. There is no wind says Herodias. It's all that Jewish food you ate. Salome looks peaky says Herod. Salome! come here. Have a glass of wine. Not thirsty Sir says Salome. Some fruit? asks Herod. Not hungry Sir says Salome. Come and sit down next to me Salome says he. Not tired Sir says she. This daughter of yours has really bad manners says Herod to Herodias. It's just that she thinks you're a lecherous old toad says Herodias. John pipes up from below. That awful little man is at it again Herod, says Herodias: can't you have him stopped? Why don't you hand him over to the Jews? Shouts of Oyez! Give him to us! from the numerous Jews in the party who then get into a furious argument over religious matters. John keeps at it from below going on about incestuous wives. Herod for Chrissake stop him says Herodias. He didn't mention you by name says Herod. Let him be.

Salome! says Herod: dance for me! Don't do it Sal says Herodias. Dance for me Salome says Herod again. I won't dance says Salome. Oh come on says Herod. No says Salome. I will give you anything you want up to half my kingdom if you dance for me says Herod. Are you serious? asks Salome. I swear says Herod. Anything you want. I'm not having my daughter dance while that holy gook in the dungeon keeps prophesying and while you go on eyeing her in that lustful manner says Herodias. OK Herod says Salome. It's a deal.

She dances. Seven veils. A strip number. Sensation, especially from Herod. Super! Superb! Superlative! he cries. Now my Salome what do you want? John the Baptist's head on a plate she replies. O crikey! not that my love. That's impossible. I want John's head she says. But hold on says Herod he's a holy man and a prophet and it's impossible. (It's a very good idea says Herodias.) I WANT JOHN'S HEAD says Salome. No! No! says Herod. Steady old thing, how about the Koh-i-noor diamond? Half my kingdom? JOHN'S HEAD says Salome. O Lordy Lordy what an obstinate child says Herod. How about my white peacocks? Lovely animals and good layers too. JOHN'S HEAD says Salome. You are on oath. Make you Deaconess of the Jews? asks Herod. Is that any good? JOHN'S HEAD says Salome.

OK OK I give up. Chop his head off officers says Herod. Herodias insinuates Herod's ring off his finger and sends it to the executioner (Royal Authorization). Everyone listens for the chop, especially Salome. Get down there and tell them to get moving says Salome to a page. But it's already done. John's head neatly chopped off is held up on a silver salver through the opening of the hole. Salome does her nut. She seizes the head and (disgustingly) kisses it on the lips. She goes into a fit of sexual epilepsy getting rid of inhibitions and complexes right left and centre by singing for a long time about the sort of stuff that Dr Freud would have found of great interest. She's a monster says Herod. Look at her. I approve of everything she has done says Herodias. It's suddenly got dark let's get inside says Herod. Salome still kissing says your lips taste bitter John. Is it the taste of death or the taste of love?

Herod has had enough.

Kill that woman he says.

The soldiers kill her.

MINUTES FROM START

LOOK OUT FOR

From the first clarinet flourish and the first line – 'How beautiful is the princess Salome tonight' – the scene rises on a sea of calm music interrupted only by the distant shouts of the Jews. We get a sense of the starry night, of the boredom and small talk of guard
3: *Nach mir wird Einer kommen* duty. Look out especially for John's contributions* 3
from below. He strikes his own style at once and sticks to it throughout the opera.

5: *Ich will nicht bleiben* Salome is intrigued. She wants to see John.* The 5
pulse of the music quickens. She sings to three beats in a bar. There is something desperate in the soldier's refusal. John sings on with his prophetic stuff regard-

less, to four beats in a bar. Riffs from the brass. Salome looks into the deep dark cistern and the orchestra goes deep and dark too. John's music is like plain prose. Salome's is flighty, poetic and chromatic. Each has their own set of mottos. Salome wheedles – so does the woodwind – seductively. A harp lends a hand. Narraboth hasn't a chance. As John climbs into
13: *Ah!* view the orchestra is struck full of wonder,** the 13
horns being particularly amazed. Two minutes of miraculous music, ending with a succession of intervals we recognize from the tone poem *Also sprach Zarathustra*.

John makes a heavy attack on Salome's stepfather
15: *Wo ist er, dessen Sündenbecher jetzt voll ist?* and on her mother.* Salome is more struck by his 15
appearance than by the rude things he is saying about her mum. Look out especially for a thrilling high note as she says he looks as chaste as the moon. John is told who she is and thunderously rages against her.

A huge cry of ecstasy and Salome is off into paroxysms of sexual desire for John (helped along by
24: *Jochanaan, ich bin verliebt* harp, horns and strings).*** 24

1. She compares his body to pure poetic images – lilies, snow, roses etc. Dreamy.

2. John tells her to get back. Now she goes all kinky. She sees his body as leprous, loathsome, but even more desirable. Rough shouts of revulsion from the brass. Salome gets dreamy again in waltz time, especially about his lovely black hair.

3. Even more ecstatic about his hair being clotted and filthy. But now she homes in on the real cause of her desire, his red mouth (tambourine and celeste). She must kiss it. The stream of wonderful melody ends.

John says never! Narraboth says Don't please talk dirty like that, and kills himself (a useless thing to do). Salome sticks to her guns. Kiss your mouth she repeats. Turbulence throughout the orchestra.

33: *Tochter der Unzucht* John cools it.* He tells Salome to seek Jesus. His 33
main motto is triumphant. Then the *Zarathustra* sequence again. It seems an unlikely thing to ask and sure enough she pays no attention whatsoever and continues to repeat that she must kiss his mouth. It has become a fixation. You are accursed says John

(*Zarathustra* again) I'd rather not look at you any more. His revulsion is pegged home by the orchestra in a series of convulsions as he goes down the steps to the dungeon. His mottos and hers are mixed. The intermezzo dies away.

Herod feels a great wind where there is none. But it is there in the orchestra. He sings to Salome like a
44: *Salome, komm, trink Wein* lover.* Will she drink? (Triangle and pizzicato 44
strings.) Not thirsty. Eat? Not hungry. Sit on her mother's throne? Not tired. John's clear steady voice is heard from below. This is it, he says. The time has come.

Better hand him over to us says one of the Jews. A furious scrap breaks out amongst a quintet of Jews over doctrinal matters. Confusion. Once again the
50: *Siehe, der Tag ist nahe* clear noble tones of John cool things down.* Jesus has 50
come he says. To take over. It's true say two Nazarenes (decent chaps). We saw him. Tell him to keep quiet says Herodias, several times, as his comments become more and more insulting.

Herod has some fetchingly lyrical lines as he pleads
58: *Und wärs die Hälfte meines Königreichs* with Salome.* Herod and Salome do the deal, against 58
Herodias's wishes. Yes Salome will dance. Dance music begins. Turbulence, especially when Herod takes rather a nasty turn (it's wind again). John prophesies death and destruction.

60 The dance of the Seven Veils,* alas quite the 60
weakest item in the opera. It sounds like the film score for a D. W. Griffiths silent movie with wrong notes. There is an attempt to be exotic with a snake-charmer bit at the start and a big swanky romantic tune just after half way. But it fails to build. Mottos from the opera proper popped in all over the place. Richard really muffed this one. But worth a star if only as a curio and for the small army of percussion people who start pinging and banging in bar 1 and keep at it throughout.

Herod is just thrilled. Bravo Salome! An excited
69: *Herrlich! Wundervoll!* outburst* richly supported by the orchestra. What 69
would she like? The head of John the Baptist. Salome is icy cold and look out especially for the way she sings the word 'Jochanaan'. Shock, horror. Especially in the brass section.

73: *Still, sprich nicht zu mir!* Herod pleads.** He makes every effort he can 73
think of from half his kingdom to a hundred peacocks. He goes on and on, he is almost unhinged. The music is febrile. The orchestra becomes unstable. Salome will not budge. She repeats her demand again, and again. Herodias gloats. A wonderfully effective sequence.

79: *Man soll ihr geben* Herod gives up. OK she can have John's head.* 79
The horns howl in triumph. Trumpets shriek. Then a hush over a fearful long-held bass pedal as everyone listens for the sounds of death. Salome hears nothing. A nagging high note on the double-basses is repeated over and over as she waits. She hears a crash (low strings). Have they fouled it up? Send in the marines to finish him off. The timps thunder.

John's head appears, duly severed. Salome in
83: *Ah! Du wolltest mich nicht* rapture.*** High-voltage rapture at first but soften- 83
ing and sweetening, and a lyrical orchestra shares her rapture. In her exalted state Salome's mind passes from fancy to fancy and the music flows along with her, miraculously sweet and melodious. The main mottos of the opera all appear but do not bother us in the least. The great lyrical climax of the piece.

Herod can take no more. Salome is a monster. He starts to move off. The moon goes dark: the earth trembles. Salome still in ecstasy sings her envoi. The kiss is over. Strauss writes a soft, beautiful line for Salome and the orchestra (assisted by an organ)
95: *Ah! Ich habe deinen Mund geküsst* responds, touching it with magic.*** Herod shouts. 95
Kill that woman. She is killed.

NOTES

Salome	Richard Strauss's third opera
First night	Hofoper, Dresden, 9 December 1905
Reception	Thirty-eight curtain calls but the critics hated it
Libretto	Lachmann's translation of Oscar Wilde's play
Source	The unlikely combination of Oscar Wilde and the Bible

NEWS AND GOSSIP

Richard Strauss's first two operas had been flops, but flops d'estime within the small circle that thought he was the greatest thing since

Richard Wagner. This was not many people and certainly not the critics. He was casting about for a subject for his next opera that would really slay the critics when he came across Wilde's play *Salome*. It was just what he wanted. The play was banned by the Lord Chamberlain in London, had flopped in Paris (Wilde wrote it in French) but the great Max Reinhardt had scored a spectacular success with it in Berlin in a version translated by the poet Hedwig Lachmann. Strauss made cuts but otherwise used the libretto almost verbatim. He wrote the score in about a year and then had a terrible time when the opera went into rehearsal. The singers had never seen anything like it before and grumbled that their parts were impossible. The Salome did not care – or perhaps could not manage – to appear as a kinky sex-mad girl of seventeen, to say nothing of stripping off. But it was all right on the night. It had just that blend of decadence, novelty and lovely lush lyricism to hit the Dresden middle-classes smack in the solar plexus.

Salome caught on both within and outside of Germany at once. Toscanini put it on at the Scala. Strauss conducted premieres in Graz and Turin. Mahler wanted to play it in Vienna but it was banned there as it was in London and New York. *Salome* became news. Everyone talked about it. To have seen *Salome* was the peak of one-upmanship. Now it is seen to be a masterly work if not a copper-bottomed masterpiece. It is performed all over the opera world whenever a vocally sound and visually credible Salome and an orchestra of 105 players can be brought together. But most Salomes have chickened out of the Seven Veils and let in a ballet dancer sometimes of less than half their weight.

COMMENT

Oscar Wilde's play still has the power to shock and Strauss makes the most of it. He gives an already dramatic text a supercharge of even more dramatic music. Some people find it a little too much, and in one way it probably is. The sheer noise of Strauss's orchestra, with its army of brass, heckelphone and quadruple woodwind can pretty well drown everything else, especially the singers. It seems to have escaped the attention of the big-band maniacs like Strauss and Wagner that there had to be a balance between singer and orchestra. Since the day of Beethoven's *Fidelio* the numbers in the pit had almost trebled which meant they could make roughly three times as much noise. But the human voice was still the same size which meant that most human voices couldn't be heard, only voices like foghorns. It was no good shushing down the orchestra because then you lost a lot of the most important stuff, for unlike in a Bellini opera where the orchestra accompanied the singer, *Salome* is really an orchestral tone poem with an additional part for the human voice. There have only been three or four sopranos since World War II who could really make it with *Salome* and that for all practical purposes is too few.

Never mind. Even if the orchestra drowns out the singers, *Salome* is still a knockout. It is basically old-style diatonic music with a lot of wrong notes and, with its amazing inventiveness, quicksilver reactions and luscious scraps of melody, the score of *Salome* is a stunner. Wilde's wonderfully good text gives it a head start. The way he repeats key lines – 'I want the head of John' and there are many more – is something new in opera. The poetic trips taken by the music reflect the still-fresh poetry of the text. Salome's first rapture when she sees John, Herod's feverish wheedling, Salome's final ecstasy, all of these are set to ravishing music. The darker side of the work, Salome the necrophiliac, Herod the crazy teenophile, Herodias the psychotic Johnophobe, etc., come across with the rather obscure intensity that we get from Wagner in the nastier bits of *The Ring*. Clearly Strauss was excited by writing music about kinky sex. Contrasting with all of this the steady nobility of John's utterances offer a sheet anchor of decency. It is he who makes the opera a moving work. But for him it would be no more than a cheap sensation.

Strauss uses mottos à la Wagner quite a lot. But unlike Wagner's mottos they don't sit up and beg all the time. Ah yes, you say, that's John's kind of music, or Salome's, and you are happy that the mood and the actual notes together give you a music picture of the person. This is rather a nice way of doing things.

The orchestra is the star of *Salome*. Other composers may have written differently for the orchestra but no one ever wrote better. Whether it be through the screaming brass, the ever-active woodwind or the strings (including a solo violin for once not reprehensible but spot on), Strauss gets to parts of the listener that other composers cannot reach. His sounds are fresh and not staled by a thousand repetitions as in the final chords of a classical symphony, especially Beethoven (no disrespect meant).

For a lot of people the music of *Salome* does have one rather big drawback – its inability to hold any line of thought for more than a few seconds. It is a musical switchback with the switches very close together. The shape of the paragraphs is fine and the words are wonderful, it's just that the musical sentences don't construe into continuous narrative. Many of them are unfinished. At this stage in his life Strauss is brilliant at raising an appetite but he doesn't always satisfy it.

The senses recoil from this horrid story but maybe it is this that jerks us into the mood of wonder that the ancient Greeks looked for in a tragedy – the sense of being 'purged by pity and horror'. So there are not many laughs in *Salome* and persons of a nervous disposition should think carefully before buying a ticket, but for those with strong nerves and a love of rich sonorous music, *Salome* is something special. An alpha.

Schicchi, Gianni *see* Gianni Schicchi

Sicilian Vespers, The *see* Vespri Siciliani, I

Siegfried *see under* Ring, The

Il Seraglio (Die Entführung aus dem Serail, The Escape from the Seraglio)

Turkish farce

Mozart [K384]

The one where two Spaniards are caught trying to rescue their girls from a Turkish harem and would be for the chopper but for the benevolence of a non-singing Pasha.

CAST

Constanze, a Spanish lady bespoke by Belmonte	Soprano
Blonde, her English maid	Soprano
Belmonte, a Spanish aristo	Tenor
Pedrillo, Belmonte's servant	Tenor
Osmin, the Pasha's security chief	Bass
Pasha Selim, a benevolent ruler	Speaks only

3 acts: running time 2 hrs 10 mins

STORY

Act I A square in the garden in front of the Pasha's palace

We are in some part of the Turkish Empire sometime before Turkey lost it. Location pretty vague but definitely near the sea coast. [*Sing*] Belmonte tiptoes on stage seeking Constanze (his imprisoned fiancée). He accosts a fig-picking Turk Osmin who is singing lustily about the need to lock up girlfriends lest flirty guys pick them up. At last he gains Osmin's ear: this Pasha Selim's place? he asks. Yip says Osmin. Pedrillo here? asks Belmonte. That toad stinker creep says Osmin so you consort with bums like that who hang around to get a sniff of our harem girls? Get off the premises (Belmonte gets off). [*Spiel*] God not another bloody Hispanic says Osmin one Pedrillo is enough. Hey Osmin is the Pasha back yet? shouts Pedrillo. Gawd! says Osmin find out yourself. Why so bloody-minded old fruit? asks Pedrillo. Because you stink and get lost will you says Osmin. Sings I-hate-Pedrillo song. Exits in fury.

[*Spiel*] Belmonte pops up: Hey Pedrillo he cries. Hello boss long time no see replies Pedrillo. So what goes? asks Belmonte: is Constanze here? Locked up with Blonde says Pedrillo. We three escaped together: myself I was appointed the Pasha's head gardener: Constanze is top of the pops in the harem. Wazzat? says Belmonte. Is the Pasha pleasuring himself with my Constanze? Probably negative says Pedrillo: Pasha Selim is a real gent he never forces unwanted intentions. I have a catamaran at the ready in the harbour, says Belmonte: Get me a job as the Pasha's interior decorator so I can get inside and slip the girls onto the boat and push off. A good plan – but for that bastard Osmin says Pedrillo. Belmonte sings about his love for Constanze.

The Pasha comes on with his followers (in full chorus). [*Spiel*] How about it Constanze? says he. Not tonight Selim says she I love another. [*Sing*] Mad about the boy. [*Spiel*] OK I give you till tomorrow then it's torture or else says he (thinks: admirable but inconvenient girl).

Hey Pasha you want a decorator? says Pedrillo, this guy's pretty good. OK says Pasha sign him on. Exits. Great says Pedrillo: now let's both slip into the palace. Stop there! you bastards! shouts Osmin. [*Sing*] Clear off says Osmin. We wanna get in say Pedrillo and Belmonte. Off says Osmin. In say B. & P. Off: In: Off: In: they yell. Finally B. & P. do a yorker on Osmin – they get in.

Act II The garden of the palace

[*Spiel*] Blonde tells Osmin she won't take orders from any man least of all a stinking Turk. [*Sing*] You treat me nice – I'm nice. You treat me rough – look out. [*Spiel*] Remember you are my slave says Osmin. Slave? Slave? I am a Brit says she: Rule Britannia. [*Sing*] Shut up and get out says she (he gets out).

[Still *Sing*] Constanze enters very low: no luck no Belmonte no hope. [*Spiel*] Come on Constanze old girl buck up says Blonde never give up maybe the Marines are coming any minute. Enter Pasha. Time's nearly up Constanze says he. Any decision yet? Negative says Constanze [*sing*] I have an unshakable love for Belmonte: torture will do no good and death would be quite a relief so there! Both exit sadly.

[*Spiel*] Hey Blonde shouts Pedrillo have I got news for you! Belmonte's here! Catamaran in the bay! Escape at last! Collect you both midnight! OK? Goody! says Blonde, but what about Osmin? This spiked liquor will fix him says Pedrillo. [*Sing*] Blonde: Hooray [*spiel*] I must tell Constanze [*sing*] Pedrillo: into action: hooray.

Enter the dreaded Osmin. [*Spiel*] Why all this gas and gaiters? he asks. Wine says Pedrillo: it's good stuff. Wash out your mouth says Osmin wine is forbidden to all in Islam. Have a try says Pedrillo: We . . . ll says Osmin. [*Sing*] Wine is good stuff sings Pedrillo: both sing: wine very good stuff: Osmin drinks whole bottle. [*Spiel*] Wine is really excellent stuff (Pedrillo leads him into house smashed out of his mind: wine also spiked with soneryl). Hey Belmonte the coast's clear says Pedrillo and here are Constanze and Blonde. [*Sing*] Nice to see you again Constanze says Belmonte: indeed so it is says Constanze. Everything is fixed for tonight says Pedrillo.

Everything just hunkydory sings everyone but just one thing, says Belmonte, how did you react dearest Constanze when Selim Pasha got fresh with you? Icy disdain? Or just a little of the come-on? Pig skunk cad, says Constanze, you suspect me? And how about you Blonde? asks Pedrillo, did Osmin exercise his droit de slavemaster? (Blonde executes a neat right hook to Pedrillo's jaw.) Sorry girls sorry they say: didn't really mean it. A mistake: please forgive us. OK say the girls we forgive you. All hunkydory again.

Act III Sc 1 As Act I Osmin's house visible

[*Spiel*] Belmonte and Pedrillo are at their escape stations. [*Sing*] Belmonte says love is a mighty powerful force. [*Spiel*] Where are the ladders? asks Belmonte: steady: we must give the song signal first says Pedrillo. ([*Sing*] Song signal ballad about an abduction duly sung.) [*Spiel*] Let's get moving say the girls: hold the ladder still will you? Descent commences. Osmin comes out half smashed. He raises the alarm. Guards seize the escapees. [*Sing*] Osmin gloats.

Act III Sc 2 Interior of Selim Pasha's palace: Selim holding court

The prisoners are held before the Pasha. [*Spiel*] So this is the reason for delay, eh Constanze? asks Pasha. Not so m'Lud says Constanze. I knew nothing of the plans then. M'Lud says Belmonte I done it for love of Constanze I am no interior decorator I am a Spanish aristo named Lostados.

Lostados? Lostados? says Pasha. Not related to the victorious General of the Battle of the Bulge? My father says Belmonte. Your father lied swindled stole the mess funds incriminated me and had me imprisoned says Pasha. How do you expect me to treat his son? eh Belmonte? Badly says Belmonte. Judgement adjourned says Pasha.

[*Sing*] Gosh we're in it up to our necks sing Constanze and Belmonte. Still – better to die together than to go to the block alone. [*Spiel*] Pasha returns with surprise judgement namely Belmonte's father was such a pig that he has no wish to act in the same manner. So clemency is the order of the day. All is forgiven: all go home: let everyone be happy ever after. [*Sing*] Hooray and mercy is a good thing they sing (all except Osmin who has no interest in mercy but merely thinks Zut! Zut! Zut!). Janissaries sing the National Anthem. End.

MINUTES FROM START

LOOK OUT FOR

Act I

0

The overture** starts as if it were a standard 'Turk- 0
ish' concert piece: halfway through it stops dead and
we hear Belmonte's tiptoe introductory music: then
Bang! back to the Turkish rough-and-tumble and a
formal close: then, my goodness, Belmonte on tiptoes
again, this time in the major mode and for real. He is
ready to burst into song, and a nice mild little tenor
4: *Hier soll ich dich* aria it is.* 4

The Belmonte/Osmin duet opens with Osmin's
fig-picking folksong about the advisability of keeping
7: *Wer ein Liebchen hat gefunden* one's mistress locked up:** with its lugubrious mel- 7
ody and dirge-like refrain (Trallalera etc.), it makes
him sound about as cheerful as an Aberdeen undertaker. But things change: as the two get into their
cross-talk we float off into snatches of tuneful duetting, much of it in canon, and then a final emphatic
agreement to disagree.

15: *Solche hergelaufne Laffen* Osmin's aria* in which he makes it clear (at great 15
length) that he does not care for Pedrillo one bit. In
music-hall days this would have been called a novelty
number and Mozart wrote it so as to show off the
original Osmin's (one Fischer) deep bass voice.

Between the crash and clatter of the Turkish
27: *Singt dem grossen Bassa Lieder* chorus* and its repeat is a sweet and soft filling of solo 27
29: *Weht ihm entgegen* voices** wishing Pasha Selim nice weather and a 29
happy trip. Lovely!

The first female solo voice after half an hour of
singing men – Constanze's lovely and fully formed
31: *Ach ich liebte, war so glücklich* aria** with two beautiful melodies and a fiendishly 31
difficult high bit at the end.

36: *Marsch, marsch, marsch!* The March, March, March trio.** Perhaps the 36
shortest finale to any Mozart first act: Belmonte and
Pedrillo want to get in, Osmin wants them to get out,
and after some vigorous counterpoint and a presto
coda, they win, he loses.

Act II

Blonde's instructions to Osmin on how to treat Euro-
1: *Durch Zärtlichkeit und Schmeicheln* pean women are simpler and sweeter when sung* 1
than when spieled. A very decent little item.

5: *Ich gehe, doch rate ich dir* The knockabout Osmin/Blonde duet* in three 5
parts: first he shouts Do as you're told; second, Don't

know why these Englishmen allow their women to get so uppity (to an almost sotto voce patter); third, the debate threatens to get physical and noisier. Blonde remains pert and cool throughout.

11: *Traurigkeit ward mir zum Lose*

Constanze's desolate aria** of longing for Bel- 11
monte. It starts with a cry of anguish and when it reaches the words 'I am torn away from you' we have the nearest thing to a great sad sigh that music and Mozart can provide. A big aria and heartfelt, with basset horns, always a sign of something special in Mozart.

19: *Martern aller Arten*

Constanze's earlier arias are as foothills to this
towering number,*** Constanze's 'Come scoglia', 19
and indeed in some ways the predecessor and model for Fiordiligi's big aria in *Così*. Constanze defies torture and will brave even death, so she will. This outburst of heroism is preceded by an introduction complete in itself, a concertante for solo flute, oboe, violin and cello and throughout the aria this group shares delicious intimacies with Constanze and in a way adopts her as a fifth and leading member of their group leaving the rest of the orchestra to do the heavy stuff. It is a formal set piece but with such variety and versatility within as to astonish the conventional ear and to tax the brightest and best Constanze right across the full range of her voice, for although she has some difficult high stuff there are some very important low notes too.

37: *Vivat Bacchus!*

Pedrillo persuades Osmin to break the pledge in
the jolliest of Turkish jingles* complete with triangle, 37
cymbals and big drum. And on top of it all a piccolo whistling away like a demented starling.

42: *Wenn der Freude Tränen*

Belmonte sings of his happiness at being with Constanze once again:* the first half with its chromatic 42
slide sounds happier than the second, but both are as mild as milk and very agreeable.

47: *Ach, Belmonte!*

In this final quartet** they all start friends and fin- 47
ish friends but there is a nasty bust-up in the middle. Yet on the whole the music is joyful, the part writing elegant, almost concert-hall Mozart. We do not feel that the tiff is going to lead to anything much, and indeed it doesn't. Tuneful and effective throughout, but this finale does not raise the dramatic temperature

as will the great finales to come.

Act III Sc 1

1: *Ich baue ganz auf deine Stärke*

Belmonte's aria** addressed to the power of love 1
takes us right out of the world of harems, Osmin, and pushes into the clear upper air of one of Mozart's purest inventions. The aria is formal and melodious with ample room for the woodwind to make their own special contribution, the opening melody is easy and elegant but the tune that lives in the ear comes in about halfway through.

8: *In Mohrenland*

Pedrillo's Romance;** as distinctive and as mem- 8
orable as Don Giovanni's serenade, with the orchestral strings collectively playing at being a mandolin.

12: *Ha, wie will ich triumphieren*

Another novelty number from Osmin.* Lots of 12
rage, lots of bluster and again a chance to show off his lowest register, this time down to D natural, which is low indeed.

Act III Sc 2

Belmonte and Constanze comfort each other in the face of death, and successfully, for the opening reci-

17: *Welch ein Geschick!*

tatif*** (very beautiful) is downbeat and the last sec- 17
tion is a paean of joy. By this time they have gotten round to the idea it would be really nice to die to-

19: *Ha, du solltest für mich sterben!*

gether. The body of this big formal duet** moves 19
tunefully from stage to stage, getting more confident at every step. Perhaps the last joyous section does go on a bit. We get the idea quicker than they think.

28: *Nie werd' ich deine*

This magical Vaudeville*** shows that Mozart 28
was already a master of the operatic finale. First we have each member of the cast saying 'Thanks Selim' in the Vaudeville (a form of French popular song) which has the catchiest possible tune. Each person sings the tune twice and then the ensemble sing it through again in chorus. The whole ensemble is through-composed, that is to say each verse is varied in notation and in orchestration to suit the character of the singer. All goes well until we reach entry number 12 and Osmin, who starts on course but explodes into his rage music which accelerandos the tune into smithereens as he runs off the stage. Now we have the sentiments of the Vaudeville song in ensemble in a sort of Mozartian chorale which obliterates the effect of Osmin's really bad behaviour. Good order and vir-

tuous values are restored once again. Finally Bang! Wham! we have the chorus of Janissaries singing in unison a very loud God Save The King, Turkishly assisted by the triangle, the cymbals and the Big Drum. Whew!

NOTES

Die Entführung aus dem Serail	Mozart's eleventh performed opera
First night	Burgtheater, Vienna, 16 July 1782
Reception	Good
Libretto	A libretto by Bretzner already used in an earlier opera
Source	Not known. There were a lot of escape-from-the-harem stories around, e.g. Mozart's earlier unfinished opera *Zaide*

NEWS AND GOSSIP

Mozart got the commission to write *Seraglio* in July 1781 shortly after he had been fired from his job as a staff musician to Archbishop Colloredo. It must just about have saved his bacon, for he was now a freelance and had no other major commission. The performance was planned for a visit of the Russian Grand Duke, but the visit was postponed and the show was no longer wanted when the visit did at last take place. The commission came from one Stephanie, the boss of the new National Singspiel opera house which had been set up three years earlier by Emperor Joseph II to encourage German opera. (Shades of English National Opera – but then a 'German' opera meant a new opera composed in the German Singspiel style, not a translated text.) Stephanie and his company must have liked *Seraglio*, because after messing about with the structure and the text quite a lot they put it on in their next season of their own volition. It was an immediate wow in Germany and played some forty cities in the Austrian Empire within a few years. It also caught on all over Northern Europe but not in Italy where the first performance was given in Florence (believe it or not) in 1935, later than England (London 1827). But then operatic Italians would naturally regard a comic Singspiel, even by Mozart, as a load of old German rubbish. Today it is played a lot: too much, perhaps, if it be at the expense of earlier Mozart operas, so many of which lie on the shelf un- or under-performed.

COMMENT

Seraglio has the bad luck to be a Singspiel. This bastard form of German opera never worked and should surely have been left in its rude volksy state for peasants and mechanicals to put on in village halls. The idea of Singspiel was that the story should be told in spiels and the singers should sing the songs about the situation in which the spiel had put them. Mozart pushes that on a bit in that some songs have a degree of plot movement, namely the final trio to Act I, March! March! March! (in which the plot movement admittedly does not take place until the last few seconds); the Bacchus duet in which Osmin does actually get smashed and passes out as the thing proceeds; and (the only real example) the final quartet of Act II when the lovers all quarrel and make friends again. All the rest of the singing leaves matters after the song just exactly as they were before it. To cap that, *Seraglio* is a singularly silly Singspiel with a plot that can be told in thirty seconds, stock characters (not at all politically correct by today's standards) and only one surprise, the Pasha's unexpected burst of clemency in the last act. In addition to this we have the then fashionable 'Turkish' setting with its slightly naughty harem, the tedium of Osmin's rage and fury, thought to be a peculiarly Turkish characteristic, and very few jokes, none of them good. So even when Mozart applies some of his most enchanting music to this rather primitive piece we should expect no miracle.

In those days the word 'Turkish' when applied to orchestral music meant the addition of a big drum, cymbals and a triangle to the normal orchestral strength and a lot of crash bang music which need not have much of a tune but which must be noisy and have an enormously emphatic first beat in the bar. It occurs in patches throughout the whole of *Seraglio* and although Mozart's *alla Turca* is less bombastic than most, it is still no Turkish delight.

But after so many bad things, the good – and they are very good. The arias of Belmonte and Constanze, although curiously placed (Constanze has two big ones treading on each other's heels, Belmonte has no less than four, each one popped in wherever there is an opening), are amongst Mozart's best, in particular Constanze's (ten-minute) gutsy refusal to kowtow to the Pasha's threats. This huge elaborate aria could have been lifted from the most serious of opera seria: it is noble, quite lovely and soars above the silliness of the plot and the low-life stuff of Pedrillo and the choleric Osmin. We enter the upper air again with Belmonte's two big ones – his thoughts about Constanze in Act I, so sweetly expressed, and the joyful number before the quartet at the end of Act II. Some of the pop numbers are winners, Osmin's fig-picking dirge, Pedrillo's serenade, the March! March! March! trio, the drunk duet. It must be admitted, however, that Osmin can rant too loud and too long and that much of his music is the coarsest Mozart ever wrote. The final prize is the Vaudeville, a really wonderful Mozartian creation and unique – there is nothing remotely like it anywhere else. Although we have the tune twelve times (until Osmin runs away with it) and the chorus repeated four times, it is still not enough. We could do without the interruption of the noisy Janissaries and go on far, far into the night listening to this enchanting Vaudeville going round and round and round almost for ever.

So we have a gamma stage work with music that is alpha and sometimes alpha-plus. A beta would seem to be the mark, which may undervalue Mozart's sing but would certainly flatter the spiel.

Simon Boccanegra

Political tragedy

Verdi

The one with patricians, plebs and a doge who rediscovers his long-lost daughter, quells a riot and dies by poison.

CAST

Simon Boccanegra, pirate, subsequently Doge	Baritone
Maria, his daughter, known throughout Act I as **Amelia Grimaldi**	Soprano
Jacopo Fiesco, a Grimaldi and a Patrician, Maria's grandfather	Bass
Gabriele Adorno, a Grimaldi and a Patrician, Maria's lover	Tenor
Paolo Albiani, a Pleb, and evil	Baritone
Pietro (no surname), another Pleb	Bass
A small-part Captain	Tenor

Prologue and 3 acts: running time 2 hrs 15 mins

STORY

Stand by! This is the most complex, contrived and convoluted plot in all opera. So first some background.

The domestic story

Simon is a successful pirate. He is common, therefore a Pleb. This does not stop him putting patrician Maria Grimaldi in the family way. The resulting baby is dumped by Simon on a 'foreign shore': a crone is put in charge of her. Unluckily the crone is set upon by bandits and killed. Infant Maria cries for three days and disappears. Meanwhile back in old Genoa her mother, also Maria, dies. On the same day Simon is elected Doge. He meets Fiesco, Maria senior's father, who rages at his dead daughter's seducer. He will only forgive if his little granddaughter is returned to him. That's not possible says Doge Simon: she's lost.

Twenty-five years on: a charming girl Amelia is living with the Grimaldis: Gabriele, a remote Grimaldi, loves Amelia, and asks Fiesco for permission to marry her. (At this point Fiesco changes his name to Andrea (for a while). Please don't ask why. The change is unimportant and the reasons inscrutable.) Fiesco tells Gabriele another Grimaldi infant died in Pisa in a convent and in order to secure the succession (death duties or something) the next-door convent baby was switched across (Maria of course). Amelia (Maria) is therefore common, not a Patrician. I don't give a stuff says Gabriele.

Doge Simon calls on Amelia (Maria). If she marries his nasty colleague pleb Paolo he will pardon all the Grimaldis who have been plotting against his dogedom. She tells him I'm bespoke and anyway I'm not a Grimaldi – I'm an orphan whose old Nanny was killed etc. Soon in true operatic fashion they exchange lockets etc. and prove that Amelia (Maria) is Doge Simon's daughter. Big deal, lots of rejoicing. Doge Simon tells nasty pleb Paolo no luck mate: your marriage plans are off. Paolo is bitter. He lays plans to abduct Amelia but his gang foul it up and she escapes. Amelia's lover Gabriele is hauled up before the Council and wrongly accused of attempted abduction. He then falsely accuses Doge Boccanegra of planning the same. Swords are drawn: Amelia (Maria) interposes: all charges are withdrawn.

Amelia (Maria) joins her father in the Doge's palace. Nasty Paolo tells Gabriele that this proximity has been arranged because Doge Simon is having it off with Amelia (Maria): Gabriele foolishly falls for this and jealously seethes. Amelia tells Doge Simon she loves one Gabriele. A frightful Grimaldi, says he, one of my enemies. O please, says Amelia. OK says big softy Doge Simon, you can have him and he snoozes off, reacting to early symptoms of death by poisoning (Paolo had done it). Jealous Gabriele arrives to kill Simon: Amelia (Maria) interposes. She explains Simon is her father, not lover: apologies all round. Gabriele agrees to fight for Simon: Simon agrees to the marriage. As Simon expires he names Gabriele as the Doge Elect.

The political story

We are in fifteenth-century Genoa: there is a lot of aggro between Patricians (not many) and Plebs (numerous). It is election time: two plebs Pietro and Paolo plot and scheme: rich pleb Pietro says to hell with patricians, he will fix it for pleb Simon Boccanegra to become Doge: and will fix Paolo with a job at court. Simon is elected Doge but is bothered by dissident patricians especially the Grimaldi family, not without reason since he killed Adorno, father of Gabriele (see above), and seduced the daughter of another, Fiesco.

Maria (Amelia) is revealed as Doge Simon's daughter and a Grimaldi. He reneges on his promise to let evil Paolo marry her. Forget it he says: Paolo does not forget. He plots with the Grimaldis to abduct Amelia (Maria) and to depose Doge Simon. The abduction is a flop – Amelia (Maria) escapes. The anti-Simon faction is licked by a loyal mob. Grimaldis Fiesco and Gabriele are put in clink. Doge Simon makes Paolo (as government minister) curse all the plotters and swear to bring them to justice. Paolo is upset because he has cursed himself: he turns spiteful and puts poison in Doge Boccanegra's Perrier water. Then he hauls Fiesco and Gabriele out of jail, makes them confess to their part in the plot and urges Fiesco to kill Doge Simon there and then (to make assurance doubly sure); he tells Gabriele Amelia (Maria) is the Doge's mistress, so why not kill him too? (Trebly sure.) The Grimaldis both refuse (but Gabriele subsequently tries it – see above).

A second rebellion starts. Gabriele is reconciled to Doge Simon, and refuses to join it: he agrees to take a message of peace to the rebel leaders. The second rebellion is quelled: all the leaders are pardoned except Paolo who is very properly condemned to death. We see the reconciliation of Doge Simon and Fiesco Grimaldi. Peace in our time.

The story as it happens on stage
Prologue A square in Genoa

Pietro and Paolo plot to have Simon Boccanegra elected Doge. They persuade him to stand. A crowd assemble. He is elected in an informal poll. Fiesco exits sadly from palace: his daughter Maria is dead. He meets Doge Simon and rages at his daughter's seducer. He tells the story of his lost granddaughter. Fiesco swears his eternal feud. The square fills with plebs celebrating Simon's election victory.

Act I Sc 1 Garden of the Grimaldi outside Genoa

Amelia (Maria) sings of her childhood. She tells Gabriele to stop political plotting and to get on with making love. Fiesco enters and tells Gabriele the yarn of Amelia (Maria), the convent, etc. Doge Simon arrives and says he will pardon all the Grimaldis if Amelia (Maria) will marry Paolo. Amelia (Maria) says she loves Gabriele. She tells the story of her infancy: father and daughter are revealed! What a surprise! Paolo is told no dice: the marriage is off: he plots to abduct Amelia (Maria).

Act I Sc 2 The Doge's council chamber in his palace

Doge Simon on the throne proposes peace with Venice. He is voted down. There is a riot outside: Gabriele is surrounded by the crowd (the abduction failed) and guilty Paolo thinks to scarper: Doge Simon prevents him. Shouts of 'Down with the Pats also Doge Boccanegra' from outside. Doge Simon has the doors opened: crowd rushes in: Fiesco and Gabriele are presented as traitors. Gabriele and Doge Simon each think the other is behind the abduction: they fight: Amelia interposes.

So who did plan the abduction? all ask. It must be a Pat say the Plebs. A Pleb say the Pats: swords are drawn: mêlée: Doge Simon calms the tumult with an impressive show of leadership. Gabriele apologizes (but is held in custody), Paolo is told he must discover the identity of the would-be abductor.

Act II A room in the Doge's palace

Paolo puts poison in Doge Simon's Perrier. Then acting officially he quizzes Grimaldis Fiesco and Gabriele: he asks whether they will kill Doge Simon: he tells Gabriele that Doge Simon has an intimate relationship with Amelia (Maria). Both refuse. Alone Gabriele rages. Joined by Amelia (Maria): he accuses her of sleeping around: she explains she and Doge Simon are intimate relations of a different kind.

Amelia (Maria) tells Doge Simon she loves Gabriele: he is at first outraged, later acquiescent. He takes a draught of poisoned Perrier: he sleeps. Gabriele enters: he is about to stab him when the great interposer Amelia (Maria) gets between them. Doge Simon awakes: he and Gabriele are reconciled. Another rebellion is heard outside: Doge Simon asks Gabriele to bear a message of peace to the rebel leaders.

Act III A room in the Doge's palace

The rebellion is over. Fiesco is brought in. Paolo on his way to the scaffold tells Fiesco he has poisoned Doge Simon. Doge Simon comes in. Fiesco tells him he is dying: there is a lengthy reconciliation between father (Doge Simon) and grandfather (Fiesco) of Maria. Maria and Gabriele enter. Maria is told Fiesco is her grandad: Gabriele is nominated Doge-elect thus at last ending the Grimaldi feud. Everybody is happy: peace in our time.

MINUTES FROM START

LOOK OUT FOR

Prologue

0 The theme of the Prelude** – unmistakably sea music – runs through the first six minutes of the opera. 0

Fiesco's lament for the dead Maria starts in
9: *Il lacerato spirito* declamatory mode* but turns lyrical** as he implores 9
11: *Il serto a lei de' martiri* her, freshly arrived in heaven, to pray for him. 11

The long duet between Fiesco and Simon is full of
22: *Oh de' Fieschi implacata* incident:* some lyrical passages: some shouting: all of 22
it vibrating with hate, pity, recrimination, etc. Lively.

Act I Sc 1

More (pretty calm) sea music for the prelude: Amelia
2: *Come in quest' ora bruna* sings about the past in a nostalgic aria.** Gabriele 2
arrives and they duet tunefully as Amelia tries to turn
his thoughts from politics to love.

20: *Favella il Doge* The great duet*** in which Simon finds a daugh- 20
ter and Amelia (Maria) a father. The scene takes wing
23: *Grave d'anni quella pia* with Amelia's (Maria's) aria** about the very trying 23
events of her girlhood. The duet ends with both
parties quite delighted.

Act I Sc 2

After the tumult of the early part of the scene Amelia
(Maria) quietens down with her account of her
48: *Nell' ora soave* abduction in a simple and affecting aria:* accusation 48
and counter-accusation are quelled by the Doge's
51: *Plebe! Patrizi! Popolo!* (Simon's) impressive address** requiring the council 51
to behave itself, and followed immediately by the sec-
ond piece of pure magic in the opera – a 'thinks'
52: *Il suo commosso* quartet*** with chorus: Amelia (Maria) supporting 52
the Doge's (Simon's) plea for peace: Pietro and Paolo
scared and uncertain what to do: Gabriele rejoicing in
Amelia's (Maria's) safety and Fiesco thinking – well,
what do you expect if you appoint a pirate to head the
state?

Act II

Gabriele's agony of hatred against Simon (the
5: *O inferno! Amelia qui!* Doge):* emotional stuff followed by a prayer for 5
7: *Cielo pietoso* Amelia's (Maria's) innocence.** Sublime. 7

18: *Parla, in tuo cor virgineo* The fraught duet*** between Gabriele (thinks she 18
is sleeping with the Doge/Simon) and Amelia/Maria
(innocent): fine lyrical passionate writing.

Another ensemble that transports us into the
11: *Perdon, Amelia. Indomito* stratosphere – the trio*** between Gabriele (Sorry I 11
made a terrible mistake), the Doge/Simon (Should I
forgive him?) and Amelia/Maria (prays for forgiveness for Gabriele). Affecting: really beautiful.

Act III

The dying Doge thinks of his early piratical days: a
7: *M'ardon le tempia* wonderful musical evocation of the sea.* 7

Fiesco and Simon the Doge make it up at last in an
14: *Piango, perché mi parla* affecting duet.** 14

The final glory of the opera: the goodbye quar-
20: *Gran Dio, li benedici* tet.*** Doge/Simon, Gabriele, Fiesco and Maria 20
(Amelia) plus chorus gently and with solemn beauty

take Simon to his death and the opera to its final curtain.

NOTES

Simon Boccanegra	Verdi's twenty-first opera
First night	Teatro La Fenice, Venice, 12 March 1857
Reception	Pretty cool, but the critics liked it
Libretto	Piave
Source	Unknown Spanish play by one Gutierrez

NEWS AND GOSSIP

There are two *Simon Boccanegras*. Only the scholars know the first, which was so badly received in Venice. We know Mark II which was produced nearly twenty-five years later by Verdi and the very talented Boito (he later did the libretto for *Falstaff*) after a lot of heavy work. They made the opera less gloomy and put in the stormy council scene as the finale to Act I. Mark II was a big success when it opened in Milan in 1881, whereas Mark I had been a total flop. During the composition of Mark I Verdi had the usual censorship problems, though what they could have found to pick on in *Simon* it is hard to see. Sex? Nothing except a suspicion of a relationship which, if true, would have been incestuous. Violence? A few unsheathed swords, but not nearly so many as in most historicals. Subversion? Well, whose side are you on? The Pats win pretty well game, set and match. Perhaps Piave wanted to use a few four-letter words, the Plebs, after all, were *very* common.

Simon Boccanegra, though it has its own fan club, has never really caught on. It is respectfully treated by the major opera houses but in box office terms it is in the mid to low Verdis. Miles behind *Rig*, *Trov* and *Trav*, and even *Attila* can lick it.

COMMENT

The plot of *Boccanegra* might have been devised by Torquemada. Those gallant few who master it have the big plus of understanding the motivation of each scene (although even then there are plenty of oddities – why on earth did Simon refuse to let Paolo marry Maria? What made Gabriele and Simon switch from deadly enmity to eternal friendship? Etc.). Those who find it too much of a sweat just have to take each situation as it comes and enjoy the music. But this is a poor second best, for throughout the opera the intensity of the drama and the strength of emotion are almost always at level 9 and without knowing what the hell it's all about, interest can flag. *Boccanegra* Mark II has a wonderful score, great mature Verdi, rolling on from one powerful passage to another. It has the ability of all great opera music to *evoke*: we can smell the sea, feel part of the riots, shrink before the admonitions of Boccanegra: the music speaks clearly. There are few set-piece arias and only one great solo for Boccanegra himself (the calming of the council) and the glory of the vocal writing lies in the duets (Fiesco and Boccanegra in the Prologue, Amelia (Maria) and Boccanegra in Act I, Gabriele and Maria (Amelia) in Act II) and in the ensembles, in particular the great quartet that leads up to Boccanegra's death. Alas no masterpiece. The power and drama of *Boccanegra*'s score is harnessed to a story few can follow and is pretty boring to those who can. But as a crib to the musical action it's worth having a go. Even though the story could only rate a gamma, the music must bring it up to alpha.

La Sonnambula (The Sleepwalker)

Somnambulist drama

Bellini

The one where our heroine is discovered in a strange gentleman's bedroom but manages to prove that she is a congenital sleepwalker and didn't know what she was doing.

CAST

Amina, an orphan	Soprano
Elvino, a landowner, her fiancé	Tenor
Teresa, her step-mother and owner of a mill	Mezzo
Count Rodolfo, lord of the manor	Bass
Lisa, an innkeeper, loves Elvino	Soprano
Alessio, a local lad, loves Lisa	Bass
A notary	

2 acts: running time 2 hrs 20 mins

STORY

Act I A village square

We are in an anonymous part of Switzerland nearly 200 years ago. A village rejoices in the celebration of Elvino and Amina's nuptials – but not everyone – Lisa, a juvenile local innkeeper jilted recently by Elvino does not rejoice. Elvino arrives late owing to a visit to his mother's grave (excuses, excuses). Alessio (a minor figure) vainly pining for Lisa continues to organize the rejoicings which go on for thirty-four minutes and deal with such matters as the notary, the wedding ring, vows, happiness etc.

A mysterious Count Rodolfo arrives asking his way to the castle. Too far they say: you must overnight at Lisa's inn. The stranger is strangely familiar with the local tourist features: Amina is presented to him. Gallantries are exchanged: Elvino jealously thinks the count takes too much interest in Amina. Teresa says it's time to break it up before the frightful frightening phantom appears. What phantom? asks the count. A fearful phantom that terrifies all humans and animals say villagers. What rubbish says count and exits to the inn. Amina and Elvino, left alone, forget their jealousy and become good friends again.

Act I Sc 2 A hotel bedroom

The count, now revealed as the long-lost son of the Lord of the Manor, makes a mild pass at innkeeper Lisa who drops her hanky on a hasty exit as a ghostly apparition appears, namely somnambulist Amina in white nightie. The count now considers making a pass at the apparition. Lisa assuming that immorality is about to take place runs off to fetch Elvino and let him see what his beloved gets up to when she is assumed to be tucked up in bed. The count hears the voices of forelock-tugging villagers coming to suck up to their new master. He jumps out of the window: the villagers arrive, also Elvino and Lisa: Amina awakes and finds herself in a gentleman's bedroom: everyone is quite shocked: Elvino says the wedding is off.

Act II Sc 1 In the forest

A troup of villagers plan to force the count to come out and declare Amina innocent (so the wedding would be on again) or not innocent (then the count must see her right). Amina and Teresa meet Elvino and plead for the wedding to be reinstated. Elvino is adamant. The villagers come tumbling down the forest path: the count says Amina is innocent they say. Elvino is sceptical: the wedding is still off.

Act II Sc 2 The forest square again

Elvino is going to marry Lisa! Now! This is bad news for heartbroken Amina and insignificant Alessio. The count appears: stop everything he says, Amina is innocent, and he gives a lecturette on nature of somnambulism: this is poorly received. All are determined to carry on with the second wedding until loyal Teresa produces the hanky Lisa dropped by Count Rodolfo's bed: so what about that? Another wedding down the pan? But see!: an apparition is walking a tricky course over the village rooftops: Amina? Why yes: her innocence is proved, all is forgiven and the rejoicing starts again. Back to Square One.

MINUTES FROM START

LOOK OUT FOR

Act I Sc 1

2: *Tutto è gioia*

After a cheery introduction and a Viva chorus, Lisa sings a pleasant, pensive aria.* Rustic chorusing 2
thereafter for some time.

11: *Come per me sereno*

Amina's pre-nuptial aria** develops into a sort of 11
concerto for soprano and chorus with some tough vocal gymnastics for the soloist.

23: *Prendi: l'anel' ti dono* Elvino has his first big aria* which moves into duet 23
with Amina** full of nuptial clichés and then a
double concerto with chorus (almost overcome by
weight of nuptial sentiments): changes gear twice,
becoming livelier and faster.

Rodolfo comes and goes: this gives rise to the jeal-
52: *Son geloso del zefiro errante* ousy duet* between Amina and Elvino which leads, 52
for those who like it, to an Olympiad of coloratura to
end the scene.

Act I Sc 2

After a wealth of plot-developing recitatif sleepwalking Amina enters Rodolfo's chamber and they
6: *Oh ciel'! che tento?* indulge in a gentle, delicate duet** with a persistent 6
woodwind accompaniment.

After a clockwork-like chorus leading to the discovery of Amina in Rodolfo's room there is a slow en-
17: *D'un pensiero e d'un accento* semble* reflecting the pained surprise etc. of each of 17
the participants (Elvino, Amina, Lisa, Teresa and
chorus). This speeds up as Elvino tells Amina that the
wedding is off and the scene ends with a vocal mêlée
20: *Non più nozze* of outrage all round.** 20

Act II Sc 1

After a slightly weird prelude, designed no doubt to
let the chorus have a bit of a stamp around the stage
on their way to the castle, there follows an unusual
event in the Bellini repertoire – a lengthy scene for
2: *Qui la selva è più folta ed ambrosa* the chorus alone* in which (after opening with a 2
sweet strain to rhubarb words) they go on after con-
siderable thought to write the script of what will happen at the castle, what they will say to the count, what
he will say to them, etc. Interesting drama within a
drama.

12: *Vedi, o madre, afflitto è mesto* Amina and Elvino in a desperate duet:* he tells her 12
what a pain she is: Amina says I am innocent: lively
stuff: then the chorus gets involved, having seen the
count: they report that he too says she is innocent and
tell him to give over. But no, he is confused and unable to hate her or forgive her. We move into a spark-
17: *Ah! perchè non posso odiarti* ling finale,*** Elvino rejecting, Amina pleading, 17
chorus interceding, with very fetching hurry music.

Act II Sc 2

The scene opens with stock recitatif and choruses,
but then Lisa gets her big moment with an endearing

2: *De'lieti auguri a voi son grata*

aria* incorporating a modicum of fireworks: she now 2
believes Elvino and she will be married.

Rodolfo explains Amina's apparent perfidy is due

7: *V'han' certuni che dormendo*

to innocent somnambulation** (again a delicious 7
woodwind accompaniment). The bombshell of Lisa's
handkerchief found in the Count's room. So she is

12: *Lisa mendace anch'essa!*

perfidious too. All reflect on this, led by Elvino.** 12

After the pantomime (in the proper sense) of
Amina sleepwalking over the roofs etc. we have a gentle cavatina from her, which becomes a recitatif and

20: *Ah! non credea mirarti*

29: *Ah! non giunge uman' pensiero*

then an aria** both broken by grief. (But all's well in 20
five minutes.) Amina's final cheery aria** would seem 29
to belong to operetta, as would the chorus, but both
are irresistible, and the coloratura flies high.

NOTES

La Sonnambula	Bellini's seventh opera
First night	Teatro Carcano, Milan, 6 March 1831
Reception	Terrific: 'Not a dry eye in the house' reports Glinka [What the hell he doing there? Ed.]
Libretto	Romani (five earlier librettos mostly hits)
Source	Lots of previous plays/operas. Somnambulism was very popular in the theatre of the early 1800s

NEWS AND GOSSIP

Because of a switch from *Ernani* to *Sonnambula* (caused by fear of the censors) we have the usual report of helter-skelter composition. The first night was postponed for a couple of weeks, maybe because the opera just wasn't written in time. Bellini wrote Elvino's part for a tenor (one Rubini) who could sing very high and he goes up to high D in the manuscript but in the printed score the part is transposed down a tone lower. This sort of fiddling about with pitch meant that someone had to fix the required changes in key, and a bag of nuts for anyone who can spot them in *Sonnambula*. Although such a hit on its first night, *Sonnambula* spread comparatively slowly in Italy but became something of a pet with Victorian audiences in London. It suffered of course from the anti bel canto snobbery of the earlier part of this century but it came back to public notice through the stunning performances given by Callas in Milan and Edinburgh in 1957.

COMMENT

Sonnambula has some of the best of Bellini – but not so generous a helping as in *Norma*, perhaps about equal to *Puritani*. The plot hangs about for the first half hour and after that goes swiftly though predictably through to the incredible final fraught sleepwalk where the poor soprano is called upon to walk a plank. The imagination boggles at the gradation of plank-thickness that would be required for Callas, Rita Hunter, Caballé, etc. Musically the best events are the duets and the ensembles (Elvino, Amina and chorus, the 'ring' ensemble in Act I Sc 1, the finale to Act II Sc 1). The arias are as beautiful and heart-searching as ever in Bellini but in general they lack the long unwinding and sophisticated form of *Norma*'s 'Casta Diva'. The role of the woodwind is more adventurous than usual (and to a lesser extent the horns, but the horns always have one or two favoured spots in a Bellini opera): the first sleepwalking scene has an accompaniment more memorable than the tune. *Sonnambula* makes a good evening in the theatre: if the plot is a little too Maria Marten to lift it to the level of a *Puritani* or a *Norma*, once it gets started it is full of drama (well, melodrama perhaps) with scarcely a dull moment. It just scrapes an alpha.

Stuarda, Maria *see* Maria Stuarda

Suor Angelica
(Sister Angelica)

Religious fantasy

Puccini

The one where a dying nun is visited by the Virgin Mary accompanied by the nun's dead illegitimate child.

CAST

Suor Angelica, a nun	Soprano
La Principessa, the Princess, her aunt	Contralto
La Badessa, the Abbess	Mezzo
La Maestra Delle Novizie, The Mistress of the Novices	Mezzo
La Zelatrice, a monitor	Mezzo
Suor Genovieffa, Suor Osmina, Suor Dolcina, nuns	Sopranos

Many other small-part sisters, medical, fund-raising etc., some civilians, nearly all sopranos except for two mezzos one medical and one civilian.

1 act: running time 1 hr 10 mins

STORY

The garden in the centre of a cloister in a nunnery

We are in the seventeenth century and a highly religious atmosphere – there are sisters (nuns) everywhere. It is a typical nunnery morning: not much headline news but a lot of things happen such as one sister is punished for laughing in church, another is punished for concealing flowers in her habit, another is entranced by a fountain turning gold at sunset, another (then all) sadly recalls it is the anniversary of the decease of a well-loved sister, another (Angelica, secretly an unmarried mother) gets philosophical about the nature of desire, another says that all desire is off limits for nuns, another (an ex-shepherdess) says still she desires to fondle lambs' cool noses, another (glutton) desires good food, Angelica is thought to desire news of her family.

A nun is stung by a wasp. Angelica prepares a herbal remedy. It's all go down at the nunnery. But hark! Two alms sisters set up a sort of NAAFI tea bar: they dispense provender: Goodness, they say, what a smart carriage at the gate. What carriage? everyone asks. The Abbess tells Angelica her auntie a royal princess has arrived to see her.

Enter this aged elderly ebony-sticked dowager who tells Angelica her sister Anna is soon to marry an aristocratic gent despite the shocking disgrace brought on the family by Angelica. Angelica must now sign a deed of conveyance for all her worldly goods to her sister Anna. Angelica says OK but how is my beloved baby? Dead says the aunt. O! O! O! thinks Angelica. She signs the deed: she collapses (grief): she recovers: another lengthy burst of grief. All exit.

Angelica returns plus a tot of homebrew poison. She drinks it. She realizes (a bit late) that suicide is a mortal sin: she prays. Doors open: enter a susurration of angels with the Virgin Mary in the van leading by the hand (wait for it) Angelica's little dead blond bambino.

MINUTES FROM START	LOOK OUT FOR	
0	A spellbinding opening.** Distant bells sound out a four-note motif: this is taken up by the strings and then is rolled out fully and variously orchestrated with the pious sisters singing Ave Maria above. Delicious Hello from the piccolo and farewell from a flute.	0
12: *I desideri sono i fior*	Sister Angelica's thoughts about the nature of desire.* Short and sweet, soaring up in true Puccini style to a passionate final burst of oomph.	12
22: *Da gran signori*	The plot thickens. One of the alms collectors tells about a mystery coach in tones of suppressed excitement: the conversation swings along over a long and recurrent melody** until the Abbess makes her announcement. Angelica is disturbed and there is a brief but lovely Requiem sung by the sisters to calm her down.	22
41: *Senza mamma, o bimbo* 48: *La grazia è discesa*	Angelica's nauseatingly mushy address to her dead baby* – set to a series of nice melodic sequences. Pentatonic-ish. Followed by easily the best sequence in the piece: the sisters comfort Angelica who moves onward and upward into a state of exaltation** (courtesy of the Virgin Mary) – ethereal exchanges: high soprano floating out – all the old Puccini magic.	41 48
53: *È discesa la grazia* 54: *Una madre t'implora*	The final death scene has its moments notably when Angelica informs her dead son that she will be meeting him shortly* and again in the early after-effects of the poison.* But the angels sound half-hearted and CD listeners can be thankful they are	53 54

spared the ghastly sight of the dead infant picking his way towards his dying mama.

NOTES

Suor Angelica	Puccini's tenth opera, counting the Trittico as three separates
First night	The Met, New York, 14 December 1918
Reception	Not much data. Thought to be OK
Libretto	Forzano
Source	Original

NEWS AND GOSSIP

Forzano thought up this rather dreadful story as the basis for a play but hearing that Puccini was in the market for shorties, he offered it to him as an opera. Puccini snapped it up, maybe because he was getting pushed to find a third leg for the Trittico. He composed fast and it was finished in six months, but first he visited the convent at Vicepelago where his sister Igenia was the Mother Superior, to pick up some local colour. Maybe he picked up too much.

As a package for a single evening the Trittico soon fell apart. For one thing it was too long, 3½ hours of music with two major re-sets, say 4½ hours minimum, and the first to go, very properly, was *Angelica*. This amazed Puccini, for composers always seem to think very highly of their most criticized work. After a decent reception at the premiere and in Rome and London the Trittico was seldom played complete and *Tabarro* and *Schicchi* tend to be teamed up with other composers' work as often as with each other. *Angelica* languishes. (A really enterprising festival impresario would put on a two-night stand for *Cav* and *Tabarro* followed on the next night by *Pag* and *Schicchi* with a concert performance of *Angelica* on Sunday.)

COMMENT

Angelica moves forward in three gears: sweet nothings in the nunnery: emotional exchanges between aunt and niece: the pantomime ending. One would have thought that Puccini would have seen that a dead mother, a resurrected child and a grand march led by the Virgin Mary was pushing it, and indeed even in Italy where both Puccini and the Virgin Mary are greatly revered, there have been sniggers in the house when this toytown masquerade steps out. There are three lovely passages: the calm opening Ave Maria to the theme of the bells: the long low melody that unwinds beneath the chatter about the carriage: the exaltation of Angelica when the Virgin Mary encourages her to sing a beautiful descant line above the chorus. For the rest, the girls'-school frolics in the convent are set to music that is agreeable enough though it has patches that are definitely ornery (the wasp sting, the shepherdess) and the exchanges between La Principessa and Angelica are out of the later Puccini stock pot which bubbles away with scraps of pentatonic Debussy.

But the thing that really turns you off *Angelica* is the saccharine sweet patches in the score. Puccini tends towards pretty sticky stuff when he writes about sweet distressed young things, about mother love or about the Virgin Mary. All three at once prove absolutely lethal, and *Angelica* leaves an aftertaste as cloying as a milk-chocolate lollipop. Definitely a gamma.

Il Tabarro (The Cloak)

Horror one-acter

Puccini

The one about low-life Paree where a bargee hides a corpse under his cloak.

CAST

Michele, bargee, 50 years of age	Baritone
Giorgetta, his wife, 25	Soprano
Luigi, stevedore, 20	Tenor
Tinca, stevedore, 35	Tenor
Talpa, stevedore, 55	Bass
Frugola, Talpa's wife, 50	Mezzo

More stevedores, a street singer, organ-grinder, rag trade girls, two passing lovers

1 act: running time 55 mins

STORY

A barge moored to a quay. The Seine. Dusk

We are in Paris in 1910. Stevedores unload sacks of cement from a barge. Loads of low-life Paree atmosphere. Giorgetta offers the stevedores a refresher (plonk). A passing organ-grinder performs: Giorgetta and Luigi waltz on deck: it is slightly dirty dancing. Michele (the boss) puts a stop to the frolics.

A passing singer sings. His repertory includes grand opera notably *Bohème*. Some passing sweat-shop girls listen. Frugola drops in and drones on about raiding trash bins her boring old cat etc. The cement is all unloaded: the stevedores appear on deck: Tinca goes off to the boozer (he's been stood up by his wife), Luigi moans about the tough stevedoring life. Giorgetta and Frugola nostalgize: Giorgetta goes on about a poncy suburban maisonette, Frugola about a rose-tinted cottage. Luigi joins in: he clearly fancies Giorgetta.

Frugola and Talpa push off: Luigi and Giorgetta left alone are having good vibes but Michele interposes. Drop me off tomorrow at Rouen says Luigi. Don't be soft says Michele: there's no work there. OK I'll stay aboard says Luigi. Michele goes. Why the hell do you want to leave me?

asks Giorgetta: I can't stand that Michele pawing you says Luigi. They fix a meeting on board late p.m. – the signal will be a lighted match on deck. Luigi goes off. Michele and Giorgetta have a long conversation about times gone by: he recalls love and affection, and remembers how they jointly rocked the baby's cradle (baby now demised), and how they nestled together under his cloak (the tabarro) etc., etc. – why has she gone off him? Giorgetta evades the question: she retires below. Double-crossing whore, he says.

Late-night Paris atmosphere: several natural sounds: lovers sing. Michele works himself up into a jealous frenzy: he runs his mind through a list of likely adulterers. He lights his pipe. The signal! Luigi hoves into view: Michele seizes him by the neck: he forces him to admit he is Giorgetta's lover: he strangles him and conceals his corpse inside his cloak. Giorgetta comes up: she asks him to take her under his cloak: he opens the cloak: the corpse rolls out. He forces her face against the face of the dead Luigi.

MINUTES FROM START — LOOK OUT FOR

0 — The swaying swinging prelude* takes us into Debussy-like waters. Restful. 0

7: *Ballo con la padrona* — The dance to the organ-grinder's tune.* Très Parisienne with wrong notes. René Clair-ish. 7

10: *Primavera, primavera* — The street singer does his worst:* a soufflé made up of his ballad about a girl called Mimi (*Bohème* reminders) whilst Michele and Giorgetta carry on talking and the seamstresses add a coda. 10

21: *Ho sognato una cassetta* — The opera takes wing: first Frugola's fantasy* of a country cottage, cheerful and agreeable, then Giorgetta's longing for a life in the Paris suburbs. She gets 21
25: *Ma chi lascia* — passionate about this and Luigi joins her*** in a lyrical outburst (the old Puccini) which must have to do with love of something more sexy than bricks and mortar. Huge climax and wonderful coda to a fateful theme in the brass. It dies away. 25

After Michele goes to put up the lights the duet continues in fits and starts – sotto voce, agitated, pas-
35: *Folle di gelosia!* — sionate, up to Luigi's final jealous outburst** – both orchestra and soloist wrought up to breaking point. Lyrical phrases but shortish because they are choked by passion. 35

The uneasy conversation between Michele and Giorgetta begins to bite after Michele mentions their

dead baby: she gets soppy about the time when they
40: *Erano sere come queste* were in love together on the boat.* He starts rather 40
dismally but warms to his work and his nostalgic
whingeing (more lyrical every minute) gets into Giorgetta and she screams Stop it! We feel for her. He more or less stops.

47: *Nulla ! Silenzio* Michele fuels himself up with anger and jealousy* 47
for an unknown rival. He gets almost incoherent with rage (goodness knows why Giorgetta doesn't come and shut him up).

51: *Avevo ben ragione* The last scene* leading to Michele's ghastly rev- 51
elation of what is under his cloak, is more music theatre than opera, for the shock effects come from the stage and not the pit, but Puccini here shows that he could have written a masterly score for a horror film.

NOTES

Il Tabarro	Puccini's ninth opera, counting the Trittico as three separates
First night	The Met, New York, 14 December 1918
Reception	Not much data but certainly OK
Libretto	Adami
Source	A Grand Guignol play *La Haupelarde* by Gold and recently performed

NEWS AND GOSSIP

Puccini had wanted to do a three-handed evening for long enough but his publisher and minder Ricordi wouldn't let him. Bad box office, he said (and was proved quite right too). Ricordi died in 1912 and Puccini was a free man. When he saw Gold's play, which must have been dreadful, he grabbed it. (He described it as 'apache . . . almost, no, more than almost, Grand Guignol'.) There had been some sort of a row with his old librettist Illica, so he hunted around and eventually settled on Adami. Meanwhile he was busy composing *Rondine*. *Tabarro* was finished in 1916 and Puccini wanted to put it on in Rome twinned with his very first opera *Le Villi* which had never been performed. Perhaps it was the only way he could get *Villi* out of the cupboard and onto the stage. But, alas, some of the singers he wanted had been called up to serve in World War I (war does such terrible things to us) and the plan fell through. Two years later Puccini had completed the other two one-acters (*Suor Angelica* and

Gianni Schicchi) and the premiere was set for the Met. Puccini wasn't there but no doubt the transatlantic telephone line hummed.

COMMENT

'More than almost Grand Guignol' said Puccini and indeed Michele's final act of pushing Giorgetta's face down against that of the dead Luigi is brutal, vicious and would not have been allowed in the early French sound films of fifteen and twenty years later that dealt so exhaustively with Paris low-life, its raffish argot complete with flics, prostitutes and desperadoes and all. *Tabarro* gets by because its low-life verismo is strong on passion – the passion of jealousy – and the power of its music elevates its savagery into something nearer tragedy. The early scenes hang around a bit – only just diverting enough to hold our attention – but once we realize there is murder in the air (Luigi says it first) we are hooked. *Tabarro* is a long short story that might be better as a short short story but it packs a mighty final punch. The music is mature Puccini: no exotica, no clash between the native culture and the setting of the story (as in *Fanciulla*), no twee oo-là-làs. Not much of the old soaring lyrical stuff but very good when it briefly appears. The Giorgetta/Luigi duet is perhaps the high point, although in the Michele/Giorgetta duet the musical progression of his mood from nostalgia for the past to violent jealousy in the present is rather marvellous. Musically *Tabarro* is less of a sing-piece and more of a film score. The score supports the drama and does not stop and flaunt itself saying: 'listen to me'. The effect is a one-acter that is powerful, moving and quite a little frightening too. Alpha, just.

Tannhäuser

Religious fantasy

Wagner

The one where the Pilgrims sing their Chorus, where Venus loses her man, and where runner beans start to grow out of the Pope's staff.

CAST

Heinrich Tannhäuser, errant knight and minstrel		Tenor
Venus		Soprano
Hermann, Landgrave (ruler) of Thuringia		Bass
Elisabeth, his niece		Soprano
Wolfram, knight, minstrel and former friend of Tannhäuser		Baritone
Walther	Thuringian knights and minstrels (Minisingers)	Tenor
Biterolf		Bass
Heinrich		Tenor
Reinmar		Bass
A shepherd's boy		Treble

3 acts: running time 3 hrs plus

STORY

Act I Sc 1 Venusberg

We are in Venus's country place: rocks, cascades, lakes, bowers and all that stuff. The time is the thirteenth century (Venus herself aged at least 6000 but wearing well). A variety of classical wildlife is on view including fauns satyrs nymphs bacchantes all revelling. Sexy dancing all round leads to a terrific orgy but before anyone can really orge the Three Graces call in Cupids to clean things up. Volleys of arrows cause casualties.

But soon all activity is taking place offstage. Tannhäuser is having a nap centre stage. He disentangles himself from Venus stretches yawns. What's up with you? asks Venus. Homesick says Tannhäuser. You must be mad says Venus. There's nothing like this life: top-class porn available free and you can have it off whenever you feel inclined. Cheer up Tan give us a song do.

Tan sings that it's all lovely super sexy dreamy in Venus's place but he wants out. Ungrateful beast says Venus stay on and I'll give you a specially nice time. Must go says Tan I miss green grass bells birdsong. OK get out you puritanical pig says Venus but come back. Shan't says Tan. This debate continues until Tan invokes the name of the Blessed

Virgin Mary. Venus (she knows when she is licked) disappears.

Act I Sc 2 A green valley in the Wartburg. A shrine to the Virgin visible

Tan kneels at prayer. A traditional operatic shepherd's boy plays his customary pipe and sings a conventional rhubarb song about spring. Enter Landgrave Hermann with flock of hunting Minisingers at his back. Hey! Who is that praying guy? he asks. The Minisingers approach Tan. Why if it isn't Harry Tannhäuser! says Wolfram. Are you all right old boy? Where have you bin? What have you bin up to? ask others. I prefer not to tell says Tan. But I'm glad to be back. Welcome come with us say Minisingers. No: I prefer to go it alone says Tan. Remember that female Elisabeth? asks Wolfram. After you left she pined and went solitary if you come back she will socialize again. OK I'll come says Tan. Jolly good show say all the Minisingers. Hunting commences to another outbreak of horns.

Act II The Festival Hall, Wartburg

Hello hall! Elisabeth says: this is the venue where Tan used to sing so nicely and now he's coming back! Tan and Wolfram enter. Long time no see says Elisabeth what have you bin up to? Can't remember says Tan I had a blackout. I had a nervous collapse says Elisabeth. Nice to have you back Harry. Nice to be back says Tan. (Bang goes my chance of making it with Elisabeth thinks dejected Wolfram.) Exit Tan and Wolfram.

Enter Hermann. What were you and Harry saying? he asks. Private matters says Elisabeth. OK says Hermann remember this song contest I mentioned? It's starting now and you are president. There is a big parade with lots of noisy brass band music. The hall fills. Hermann explains the rules and hints coyly that Elisabeth can give the winner any prize including herself in marriage.

The first competitor Wolfram sings a standard song contest number about romantic love employing the adjectives enraptured sublime virtuous radiant dazzled etc. Pretty good say the lords and ladies. Bloody rubbish says Tan. Nuts to pure love copulation is the thing – nothing like it. Shock horror! How can you be so disgusting and in front of ladies too? says Biterolf. You horrible depraved vulgar man get your sword out I challenge you. Me too cry several Minisingers unfurling swords. You sex-starved sparrow Biterolf says Tan you've never even done it. You're not worth stabbing.

Steady lads steady says Hermann. Let sublime love drive out pollution from our Miniclub says Wolfram. Nuts to sublime love give me the real stuff like I got in the Venusberg massage parlour says Tan. Gawd! they cry in shock he's been to the Venusberg massage parlours! All females leave in disgust.

The Minisingers crowd Tan with prodding swords. Elisabeth interposes. Stand back she cries. Give poor Tan a chance to repent before death. Crumbs! she must be an angel of God say the lords and ladies. We'd better treat her with respect. Elisabeth influences me greatly says Tan now I see I am a sinner and really should repent. Get off the premises you loathsome toad says Hermann: get on a pilgrimage at once with them there pilgrims. Yes good idea says everyone get in there with the pilgrims. Some pilgrims with treble voices are heard outside (either very young or not entire). OK says Tan – to Rome! To Rome! shouts everyone else. Curtain.

Act III Green valley, as Act I Sc 2. It is getting dark

The prelude offers a tone poem of Tannhäuser's pilgrimage to Rome. Elisabeth prays at the shrine of the Virgin. Wolfram watches. He thinks: she's praying for Tan to return with a clearance certificate from the Pope. The pilgrims are heard offstage. We got our chits they sing good news we can all repatriate. Elisabeth watches but sees no Tan. Hail BVM says she I'm coming to join you. Pardon me says Wolfram might I have a word before you go? Negative signals Elisabeth who then slowly disappears up a path to heaven.

Wolfram pulls out his harp and requests the evening star to pay its respects to her as she passes en route to becoming an angel. It gets dark. Tan enters in rags. Why if it isn't Harry Tannhäuser again says Wolfram what now? I'm looking for Venusberg says Tan. Didn't you get to Rome? says Wolfram. Got to Rome says Tan. Did you attend the holy feast? asks Wolfram. Attended holy feast says Tan. Got your clearance certificate? says Wolfram. No clearance certificate says Tan. Why? asks Wolfram. Well there is this Pope says Tan pardoning thousands all around but when it comes to Joe Soap not a word. Not an if or a maybe. If you've had it off with Venus in person says this Pope then nothing doing. No certificate unless my staff sprouts with runner beans. It's very disappointing. So I say to myself say I this holy lark's a dead loss I'm off to Venusberg again. Funny: I can't seem to find the way: it was easy enough last time.

You're mad to go there says Wolfram: Aha! Venusberg approaches cries Tan as a pink mist plus the aroma of cheap scent engulfs the stage. Venus appears in person: welcome back old thing she says. 'Swounds how could a decent chap like me get mixed up in such goings-on says Wolfram. Leave her Harry leave her. Let me be says Tan. Remember Elisabeth says Wolfram.

Darkness suddenly falls as a chorus of Minisingers is heard offstage. Elisabeth – now an angel – is praying for you on high says Wolfram: Harry you're saved. (Zut! Lost another says Venus: she disappears.) A funeral cortège enters bearing Elisabeth's corpse: Pray for me Elisabeth cries Tan: he falls down dead. It gets light. Soprano pilgrims march on carrying the Pope's staff now sprouting runner beans. Here's salvation for all they sing. Including our Tannhäuser (but it's just too late). Curtain.

MINUTES FROM START

LOOK OUT FOR

Some of the best music in the opera lies in the first
0 twenty minutes, made up of the overture*** followed 0
by the ballet music of the Orgy. In the overture,
which is a sort of reader's digest of the whole opera,
we have first the Pilgrims' Chorus reverently presented by the brass choir and answered by a sad string
tune: this section builds to a very loud restatement of
the Pilgrims with the trombones doing their nuts. It
fades away and we are into something naughty – wild
arpeggios in the strings, flutters in the woodwind and
more pretty sexy stuff. Then the clear statement of
Tannhäuser's plea to be let off the chain (coming
shortly), more mildly orgiastic stuff, then a window
for a brief glimpse of the blue skies of the good life
(quiet, in the woodwind): more orgy: a big statement
Act I Sc 1 of Tannhäuser's plea and so into the orgy proper, and
10 a pretty good orgy it is.** Wagner uses four main 10
themes to whip up a mighty turmoil of excitement, although, as always in orgiastic ballets, there is a lot of delirious foreplay but no actual consummation. Judging by the crashing and thwacking by the percussion there is a certain amount of sado-masochism about too. The Three Graces restore order. After all this excitement there is a rather long patch of calm with the Sirens calling OO-AH before we get into the action.

22 The mists have cleared away: Tannhäuser and 22
Venus begin a sometimes acrimonious dialogue that is to run for the rest of the scene: at first it is mainly recitatif under another name, striking, powerful recitatif with a rich accompaniment and much modulation, but recitatif just the same, ending with a spirited burst from Venus as she asks Tannhäuser for a song.

27: *Dir töne Lob!* His song** is a set piece in two stanzas to a harp ac- 27
companiment and to the tune we have already heard in the overture (Tannhäuser's plea). It sounds a bit strenuous for the boudoir. Maybe it is telling us that Tannhäuser was a great sexual athlete. As well as praising Venus as the tops in bed he has another message – I want to go home.

32: *Geliebter, komm!* Venus wheedles. A seductive ramble* around 32
Tannhäuser's ego amidst a sensual welter of strings and woodwind with harps later plus, alas, a reprehensible solo violin. Tannhäuser rebuffs her with stanza 3 of the song above.

Venus lets him have it. Get lost! she cries to an absolutely furious orchestral accompaniment (strings really angry; downward staccato scales). Then she goes soft again. Then another outburst. Then a bit of
44: *Wie hätt' ich das erworben* sweet self-pity** (What have I done wrong?) 44
wrapped in a cloud of ravishing accompanying sound with the woodwind working some effective magic. But she gets cranky again and the duet finishes with the two of them definitely at cross purposes. Finally Tannhäuser cheekily quotes the Virgin Mary as his sponsor, at which Venus disappears in a puff of holy smoke with an immense orchestral crash.

Act I Sc 2

A pretty rum old scene, this one. First we have the Shepherd's Boy and his versatile pipe, with a range of four octaves, but with a song which is pretty ornery stuff (surely Wagner could have done better). Then the pilgrims creep up on us chorusing away mighty
51: *Zu dir wall ich* impressively** and finally Tannhäuser gets in there 51
amongst the pipe and the pilgrims, clearly a changed man.

No composer can resist a hunting horn but here Wagner goes mad and bombards us with horns to the right of us, horns to the left of us, horns solo and
55 horns in chorus.* (In Paris he wanted twenty-four 55
horns but only got sixteen. Short commons.) For those listeners who like horns it's great. (But today you usually get only twelve.)

Suddenly, as happens so often in Wagner, we strike a patch of sparkling water in the middle of a fairly turgid run. Wolfram welcomes Tannhäuser

58: *Gegrüsst sei uns* back to the ranch.* Tannhäuser's interest picks up 58
when he hears the name Elisabeth! The Minisingers
come in one by one, we have a happy ensemble,
soothing, melodious and, as it should be, welcoming.

Wolfram recalls Tannhäuser's days as No. 1 in the
62: *Als du in kühnem* charts.** A formal piece, the second stanza holding 62
what emerges as the tune. This is introduced by a
really fetching few bars of strings and woodwind but
the tune itself (which has to do a lot of work before the
scene ends) has an unfortunate whiff of schmaltz
about it. The ensemble which follows is very satisfactory up to a sudden and coarse change of key just
before Tannhäuser's final capitulation. The finale
speeds up a little jerkily towards the end (the Maestro
can help greatly here) but it is joyful, enjoyable and
ends with another absolutely frenzied outbreak of
horns.

Act II

Elisabeth's greeting. After a short prelude (agreeable
woodwind solos) with tantalizing snatches of a big
string tune and eight lines of recitatif (I was really sad
when Tannhäuser left) we are into the clear straight
3: *Wie jetzt mein Busen* line of Elisabeth's aria.** And at the end, at last, we 3
get a full statement of the big tune. But even now it is
elusive.

12: *Gepriesen sei die Stunde* The duet* that follows the Greeting warms up as it 12
goes along. Elisabeth, the simple soul, is pretty well
thrown by Tannhäuser's return, she doesn't know
why, but perks up when she recalls the songs of the
sixties. A series of excited flourishes in the violins
move them into an exultant mood,** the duet takes
off and races to a brilliant finish as our two carol away
happily over the gloomy asides from Wolfram.

This time it's trumpets, simply bursting out all
over the place. Introductory of course, for trumpets
in large numbers are nearly always used fanfarishly.
20 What they introduce here is the Grand March,*** 20
three catchy tunes one after the other at first orchestral and then, as American academics would say,
choralized. Grows in volume to become quite deafening. Marvellous: vulgar: irresistible, especially the
third tune over the I'VE-GOT-FOUR-NOTES
accompaniment.

34: *Blick ich umher* The song contest begins.* Wolfram first, a rather 34
limp recitatif-ish entry, but then he's only allotted
harps and then violas and cellos. Well liked in the
Hall of Song but no prizes from us. Tannhäuser's
contribution is sung in something of a sexual trauma,
and is more interesting but Biterolf's shocked response lowers the temperature again. Now we sail
into the fourth stanza of Tannhäuser's address to
43: *Dir, Göttin der Liebe* Venus from Act I.** But this time the accompani- 43
ment is full of naughty Venusberg music and the
message is reversed: instead of wanting out he's
wanting to get back. (What a relief to return to a good
tune.) At this point, incidentally, the song contest finally gets lost in an argument about sexual morality.
And it's very heated stuff because in those days a
Minisinger found in Venusberg must have been like
discovering a bishop in a massage parlour.

And now for something much more substantial,
perhaps the best sequence in the opera. After the dramatics of the drawn swords, Elisabeth makes her plea
46: *Zurück!* for Tannhäuser to be spared** so that he may repent. 46
There is no great Wagnerian tune here nor any mu-
sical excitement but suddenly the scene becomes
serious and moving. We respond to Elisabeth's courage, nobly expressed, and so do Landgrave Hermann
and the Minisingers in a profound, reflective cho-
51: *Ein Engel stieg* rus*** which anticipates the melody of Elisabeth's 51
prayer in the next act: Tannhäuser sings in an an-
guished tenor line amidst this and Elisabeth soars
above in a radiant descant.

A very decent recitatif from Landgrave Hermann
which keeps up the high tone of what has gone before: it breaks into a trot (in the accompaniment : the
strings get highly mobile) and becomes arioso if not
61: *Versammelt sind aus meinen Landen* an aria.* He tells Tannhäuser to get in amongst the 61
pilgrims.

62: *Mit ihnen sollst du wallen* The final chorus:** still on the same elevated 62
plane: the burden of the melody (a long winding one)
is taken first by the tenors, then by Elisabeth solo.
Everyone is saying roughly the same thing: it's a good
idea for Tannhäuser to turn pilgrim. There is a lot of
counterpoint about with busy voices all around:
everything stops dead whilst we hear teeny teenage

pilgrims warbling in the valley. A good idea, but Wagner lacked Verdi's certainty of touch with off-stagers, and it sounds a bit Hollywood. Melodramatic shouts of California Here I Come! from Tannhäuser. Curtain.

Act III

0 Prelude.* Solemn and rather aimless chording in the wind begins to take the shape of part of the Pilgrims' Chorus, but we lose it, get a cascade of descending notes in the strings plus the sad string tune (which we have heard in the overture) for the redemption of Tannhäuser, which goes on both loud and soft for some time. 0

After Wolfram's uninspired comments about Elisabeth at prayer, we hear the Pilgrims' Chorus*** swelling up proper (all grown-up pilgrims and entire, no trebles) and very fine it is: the final burst with the full orchestral treatment sounds more secular than holy, but it would still stun a priest at fifty yards. Then it fades. Tannhäuser is not amongst them.

11: *Begluckt darf nun dich* 11

16: *Allmächt'ge Jungfrau* Elisabeth's prayer.** Calm, intense and again with a firm outline. The woodwind embellish and accompany the vocal part ingeniously but do tend to slow things up towards the end where they become aimless. Rather like the stuff which the organist plays when he has run off all the music billed for the voluntary and has to fill in time until the bride arrives. Meanwhile Elisabeth is ascending to heaven, but very slowly. 16

26: *O du mein holder Abendstern* O star of eve** (not of Eve as some have mistakenly thought). Well! Arresting, certainly, popular, very, but isn't it just a little too much? Those scoopy chromatic bits? Isn't that snatch of throbbing cello pretty ghastly? 26

34: *Inbrunst im Herzen* Tannhäuser's long narration.* We start with two stanzas accompanied by the winding string figure that was in the Prelude to Act III. This takes the lead and dominates the scene as Tannhäuser tells us what a hard time he gave himself on the road to Rome. Then a long stretch of unremarkable recitatif. Things chirp up with the entry of the Venusberg music and the piece ends strongly. 34

(After the formal opening this nine-minute stretch

of narrative is freely written with no set forms and hence is generally thought to be a step forward for Wagner to greater things. That must be good, but one wishes he had taken shorter steps or walked a bit faster, or both.)

The final stages. Tannhäuser's narrative is fol-
43: *Halt ein! Halt ein!* lowed by a lively argument** between Wolfram (You 43
would be mad to go back to Venus) and Tannhäuser (I'm going just the same) which becomes engulfed in an orgy of Venusberg music coming to a climax as Venus appears in person, pink fog and all, very ready to have Tannhäuser back. Now we have an exciting tug of war between the forces of good (Wolfram) and evil (Venus) for the soul of Tannhäuser, by now one would have thought not a particularly attractive item. Wolfram scores an easy win by just invoking the name of Elisabeth. Tannhäuser echoes 'Elisabeth!' as he did in Act I and this appears to have much the same effect on Venus as did the introduction of the BVM into the conversation in Act I. Now we hear male off-
48: *Ihr ward der Engel* stagers approaching singing a magnificent chorus** 48
about Elisabeth's soul. This is the *coup de grâce*: Venus concedes, fades away into the pink and Elisabeth's funeral cortège comes on to centre stage, her corpse prominent on a bier. 'She's praying for Tannhäuser' sing the pilgrims, knights and Minisingers, making a wild guess in order to be as helpful as possible to the plot. 'O Elisabeth, pray for me' sings Tannhäuser, and expires, cause of death unknown. Meanwhile the teenage pilgrims strike up a much weaker chorus reporting the issue of runner beans from the Pope's staff, which means that pretty well everyone is pardoned, including Tannhäuser. The musical situation is saved by a final sonorous rendering of the Pilgrims' Chorus and the curtain falls with everyone really pleased that Tannhäuser's soul, thanks either to the love of a good woman or to the greenery sprouting from the Pope's staff, or both, has safely gone aloft.

NOTES

Tannhäuser	Wagner's fifth opera
First night	1. Königliches Sächsiscles Hoftheater, Dresden, 19 October 1845 2. Opéra, Paris, 13 March 1861
Reception	1. Uncomprehending. 2. Fiasco
Libretto	Wagner
Source	Two unrelated mediaeval legends

NEWS AND GOSSIP

In 1843 Wagner went to the Dresden court as assistant Intendant, musically a young lion and politically a revolutionary. He had already done quite a lot of work on *Tannhäuser* and, now an insider, he persuaded the management to put it on. It didn't go down well. The singers found it too tough and neither the Tannhäuser nor the Elisabeth had the vocal stamina to last out the evening. Also the Dresdeners were somewhat stunned by this new kind of music. Four years later Wagner was involved in the Dresden uprising. It failed and he pushed off to Paris where in 1860 (he was by now quite famous) the Emperor Napoleon III invited him (good news) to put on *Tannhäuser* at the Opéra. There were two snags:

1. All operas at the Opéra had to be in French.
2. A ballet in Act II was a must.

Wagner said OK to the translation but insisted the opening Venusberg stuff should serve as the ballet and set about expanding and rewriting it. He was warned this would not do and it didn't. The first night was a disaster. Not from lack of rehearsal – there were 163 of them – nor from any skimping on production values – an outsize orchestra: sixteen horns, six horses and ten dogs on stage in the hunting scene – but because of the Jockey Club. The young aristos of the Club were apt to stroll into the opera after dinner to look over the girls in the second-act ballet and then to stroll out again. They did not expect to stroll in on something like a Pilgrims' Chorus and took steps to teach the management a lesson by turning up in huge numbers at the point where the ballet should have been and by whistling, catcalling, booing and carrying on as high-spirited young gentlemen will do when indulging in tribal customs. There was also a conspiracy theory, namely that the whole debacle was staged to spite the politically unpopular Princess Metternick, who had persuaded Napoleon to have the opera put on. After three nights of hooliganism the opera was taken off and no doubt there was a second-act ballet in every show for the rest of the season. Even before the Paris debacle, *Tannhäuser* had played in some sixty German houses and now with this scandal behind it, it spread even faster and quicker. Early this century, along with the *Dutchman* and *Lohengrin*, it was amongst the most popular Wagners, but as taste swung towards late Wagner *Tannhäuser* probably suffered most. Opera managements now think of it as something of a curiosity and as a wasteful use of that rare commodity – a Wagner tenor.

COMMENT

Anyone seeking proof that Wagner had no sense of humour need look no further than *Tannhäuser*. It begins with the spectacle of a well-built Wagnerian soprano lying on a couch with a Wagnerian tenor, likely to be no sparrow either, in a rosy-pink brothel-like light, both of them in a post-coital trance, whilst an orgy rages around in which a large number of the sex-mad throng are half animals. Later we have the spectacle of the bodily assumption of Elisabeth to heaven, although today she is generally spared the hike up the rainbow staircase to the skies. There is also the bodily return of Venus to the Thuringian countryside – although even Wagner became queasy about this and in later productions Venus was heard but not seen. If Wagner's pompous solemnity about Tannhäuser's moral welfare were good for a laugh and no more, we could sit back and enjoy the good things in the show. But enjoyment fades as his false religiosity becomes more and more nauseating. Wagner was not a believer and wrongly thought that the spirituality which had inspired Bach's B minor Mass, the painting of the Florentines and Dante's *Inferno* could be used by any good pro. as a mechanism to wheel out a holy plot. Which it can't, because when false piety is rumbled there is nothing left but kitsch. That is why the pilgrims trudging to and from Rome are cardboard figures, why Elisabeth is no more than a nutcase, why the Minisingers are a comical band of prefects at a pious public school and why Tannhäuser himself is a ludicrous figure. The other great plot motivator, the belief that an evil man can be saved by the love of a good woman, already one of Wagner's obsessions, is not so silly. But here it doesn't work so well as in the *Dutchman*, because he was a wild romantic figure who gripped the imagination whereas Tannhäuser, although maybe a good singer, is an unattractive man who is making a terrible mess of his life. Not worth praying for, much less dying for.

So what's good about *Tannhäuser*? Well, certainly the tunes and the orchestration. The tunes are striking and memorable, but not all of them pass muster. The Pilgrims' Chorus, although noble and holy when sung offstage, loses its solemn charm as it gets louder and when brayed out fortissimo by the trombones it tends to parody its own quiet and more decent self. Tannhäuser's first act aria is vigorous, Elisabeth's two big numbers effective, the Venusberg music – later Wagner grafted on to earlier Wagner – is wonderfully sparky and the big climax a real banger. O Star of Eve has a sort of ghastly attraction. But secretly many of us relish a bit of a wallow, rather like the two old ladies on holiday in the Riviera who would say to each other 'Let's go down to the beach and be scandalized'. The three best bits are the overture, which Wagner worked over and over to make it an effective concert piece, the Grand March in Act II Scene 2, and the finale to this scene (from the point of Elisabeth's plea to save Tannhäuser to the final ensemble) when for a moment real values and true feeling take over.

Musically *Tannhäuser* is still made up of a succession of striking musical numbers linked together by recitatif-type material of a much lower voltage. It is still a long way away from the seamless musical flow that Wagner was aiming for and finally achieved in *Tristan* and *The Ring*. On the credit side there is not much that is dull: Tannhäuser's narrative in Act III, although hailed by the musicos as a great leap forward in Wagnerian technique, is dreary listening: the Minisingers tend to go on a bit and the song contest could have been organized with more pace and better songs, but on the whole, although you may not be delighted by *Tannhäuser*, you are unlikely to be bored. A beta.

Tell, William *see* William Tell

The Threepenny Opera (Die Dreigroschenoper)

Low-life ballad opera

Weill

The Berlinized version of Gay's *Beggar's Opera*.

CAST

Peachum, organizer of a gang of beggars	Baritone
Mrs Peachum, his wife	Contralto
Polly, their daughter	Soprano
Macheath (Machie Messer), underworld gang leader	Tenor
Brown, Metropolitan Commissioner of Police	Baritone
Lucy, his daughter	Soprano
Jenny, a hooker	Soprano
A ballad singer	Baritone

3 acts: running time approximately 2 hrs 15 mins depending upon the production. Music alone: 1 hr 15 mins.

STORY

Prologue London. Soho. A fair

We are in London shortly before a coronation and rubbing shoulders with pimps, hookers, pickpockets, beggars and villains of every kind.
Song: The Ballad of Mac the Knife.

Act I Sc 1 Peachum's beggars' kitchen

Song: Peachum's Morning Hymn (Peachum).
Peachum learns from Mrs Peachum that their daughter Polly is having it off with the gang leader Mac the Knife.
Song: You can't stop them (Peachum and Mrs Peachum).

Act I Sc 2 The HQ of Mac's gang, a stable stacked with stolen goods

Mac and Polly are holding their wedding reception.
Song: The wedding song (four gang members).
Mac is not pleased with the low standard of efficiency and poor productivity of his gang. He thinks they should go to the Harvard Business

School. To cheer things up Polly sings.
Song: Pirate Jenny (Polly).
The Metropolitan Commissioner of Police arrives, name of Brown. Hi Mac he says congratters old man and as a married man I will of course continue to let you do anything you bloody like so long as I get my cut.
Song: The Cannon Song (Mac and Brown).
Brown pushes off to see about the coronation which is happening next day. The gang disappear. Polly and Mac bill and coo.
Song: Lovers' Song (Mac and Polly).

Act I Sc 3 Back at the Peachums'

Peachum doesn't want to lose Polly who is a nice little earner.
Song: The Barbara Song (Polly).
Then the First Threepenny Finale (Polly, Peachum, Mrs Peachum).

Act II Sc 1 Mac's HQ

Mac leaves Polly to take a walk in Parliament Hill Fields. Peachum wants him arrested. Mrs Peachum thinks he is in Cable Street with his harem of hookers. She wants to bribe one of the girls to give him away. Polly says he is so close to the Metropolitan Commissioner nothing could happen to him. But to be on the safe side she advises Mac to scarper. She will run the gang while he is away.
Melodrame (words spoken over music): Polly and Mac say goodbye.
Song: Polly's Song.
Song: The Ballad of Sexual Obsession (Mrs Peachum).

Act II Sc 2 A brothel in the East End

Mac sits with a large number of prostitutes and remembers the good times he had when pimping for his old girlfriend Jenny.
Song: The Song of Immoral Earnings (Mac and Jenny).
Whilst duetting with Mac most affectionately Jenny gives a signal to the waiting cops who arrest Mac.

Act II Sc 3 A prison

Brown says he is sorry to inconvenience his friend. Mac finds his standard of living has dropped.
Song: The Ballad of Good Living.
Brown's daughter Lucy, one of Mac's earlier fancy girls, plans to let him out of jail. Polly turns up.

Song: Jealousy Duet (Polly and Lucy).
Lucy rounds on Polly and slags her off.
Song: Lucy's Aria.
Mrs Peachum comes on and pulls Polly away. Mac escapes and runs back to Cable Street. Peachum arrives to see Mac and finds only Brown. He threatens Brown that he will mess up the next day's coronation by injecting his beggars into it.
The Second Threepenny Finale (Peachum, Mrs Peachum and chorus).

Act III Sc 1 Peachum's beggars' kitchen

Peachum makes plans for his gang of professional cripples and beggars to get in there amongst the horses' hooves and really foul up the coronation. Brown arrives and arrests him.
Song: The Insufficiency of Human Endeavour (Peachum).
Peachum tells Brown that unless he is freed he will deploy six hundred cripples to lie down in front of the royal coach. Brown gives up. Releases Peachum. Peachum says he'd better get after Mac again.

Act III Sc 2 The prison

Mac is back in jail.
Song: Solomon's Song (Jenny).
He has been betrayed once again. He is to be hanged. He tries to bribe his way out.
Song: Call from the grave (Mac).
All his old friends come to visit him. The coronation bells ring.
Song: Epitaph (Mac).
Song: Walk to the gallows (Peachum).
Third Threepenny Finale: The king's messenger arrives to say that a happy ending to the opera is preferred and Mac is pardoned. The opera ends with a hymn, led by Peachum, which solemnly declares that criminality should not be prosecuted. Life itself is punishment enough.

MINUTES FROM START — LOOK OUT FOR

Prologue

0 — The overture** has two halves: the first with a bang bang (four times) figure which seems to be saying Wake up! Wake up! Listen to our show! and the second a really nice Bach-like bundle of fugality. The subject is given out by an alto sax, taken up by a trumpet and passed on to a clarinet. 0

3: *Und der Haifisch* — The ballad of Mac the Knife.*** In many ways the 3 motto song of the 1930s, and certainly one of the landmark tunes of the century. The orchestration of the later verses, especially when the piano comes in, is an added bonus.

Act I Sc 1

6: *Wach auf* Peachum's hymn.** It is of course, as always with 5
Brecht/Weill, the words and music together that make this wicked little item such a winner, the scurrilous words being set to a cod Lutheran chant suitable to accompany the holiest of thoughts.

7: *Anstatt dass* The 'You can't stop them' song.* Polly is out on 7
the tiles. They all do it sings Peachum, with a trumpet and then a sax giving him a run for his money.

The Moon over Soho sings Mrs Peachum, romantically, to a persistent vamp accompaniment.

Act I Sc 2

10: *Meine Herren* The Ballad of Pirate Jenny.* The words, the tune and 10
the rhythm when put together contribute about equally to make what is really nothing into a ballad that catches the attention – for a while (for it does go on a bit).

14: *John war darunter* The Cannon Song.* By no means politically cor- 14
rect but with loads of zing and the best refrain-tune in the opera, a pounding piano and incidental curlicues from the trumpet.

17: *Siehst du den Mond über Soho?* The Love Song.* Begins as speech over music but 17
when they sing together it is one of the sweeter of Weill's bitter-sweet pieces. The words, of course, take the piss out of any idea that the sentiment in the music is real.

Act I Sc 3

19: *Einst glaubte ich* The Barbara Song.* The chirpy chorus is not a mil- 19
lion miles away from Mac the Knife nor, for that matter, the Volga Boat Song.

24: *Was ich möchte* The First Threepenny Finale.* A pert opening 24
from Polly – why the hell shouldn't I be allowed to have a man? Peachum comes the heavy: Mrs Peachum is melodious and motherly. Peachum gets faster and faster and eventually all three singing together tend to agree that everyone is a punk at heart.

Act II Sc 1

Look out especially for the ridiculously beautiful ac-
0: *Ach Mac* companiment* to the melodrame of Polly parting 0

with Mac and his amazingly beautiful farewell flourish. It could be Gounod on a good day. Followed by
1: *Hübsch als es währte* Polly's sad little song – he'll never come back.** 1

3: *Da ist nun einer schon* The Ballad of Sexual Obsession. Mrs Peachum's big moment.** She tells us what gentlemen do at 3 night. She isn't coming the acid, she is reporting. It is so cool she might be reading a short address to the Law Society. A doleful tenor sax doubles the voice part. This is one that can haunt the ear for weeks.

Act II Sc 2

6: *In einer Zeit* The Ballad of Immoral Earnings.* Tender memories 6 of life in a whorehouse. It taps away in tango rhythm in typical Weill style but it's not one of his specials. Just good. Three verses, one each and one together. A nice instrumental tailpiece (first time two saxes: next time two Hawaiian guitars!).

(Note: sometimes Pirate Jenny pops up again here because in the early days Lotte Lenya grabbed the number away from a less formidable Polly and made it her own. It should either be Polly's or Jenny's; to play it twice must be wrong and it is more of a Polly song than a Jenny song because the singer is clearly a skivvy in a hotel and not a whore.)

Act II Sc 3

15: *Ihr Herrn, urteilt jetz selbst* The Ballad of Good Living. A cheery piece* going 15 along at a comfortable jog-trot with a more tuneful tune than most with trumpet and sax fooling around the main vocal line pretty freely.

18: *Komm heraus* The Jealousy Duet.* Bitchy one-liners – they work 18 well enough on the stage but would become tiresome played back in the home but for the sweet joint refrain 'He loves me and me alone'.

20: *Eifersucht. Wut.* Lucy's Aria.* Nearly a grand opera item but not an 20 aria, more arioso with patches spoken (parlando). But with a truly grand operatic climax – and the orchestra jack themselves up to give very high-class support; the descending figures that keep coming in the intro and then throughout could have been written by Gluck.

24: *Ihr Herrn, die ihr uns lehrt* The Second Threepenny Finale.** It's food that 24 makes the world go round. The first half is a heavy meal, slow and lumpy. The answer to the question asked from off-stage livens things up – and it has a

good tune too. We finish operatically, rather dim
chorus and all.

Act III Sc 1

0: *Der Mensch lebt durch den Kopf* Ballad of the Insufficiency of Human Endeavour.** 0
Peachum explains that man just isn't clever enough to
cope with life in the neatest, smartest and funniest
number in the piece. The patter-like speech is accompanied by the orchestra pretty well in ensemble.
For once the saxes and trumpets don't stray around
doing their own thing.

Act III Sc 2

2: *Ihr saht den weisen Salomon* Solomon's Song.* This dreary number is only worth 2
looking out for because of its strange accordion ac-
companiment. Jenny's singing line is doubled an octave lower and the usual accordion cha-chas are
chucked in above.

After his hectic Call from the grave Mac dives into
7: *Ihr Menschenbrüder* another nearly operatic number – Epitaph.* He asks a 7
wide variety of persons to forgive his sins, sardoni-
cally one hopes, for it would be a shame if he had lost
his bottle at this stage in the game. He starts the ballad
with the lightest of wind accompaniments over a pizzicato string bass. But it builds to a full chorus of support and in the last verse dies away again as Mac
makes a quiet and sincere plea for the police to have
their faces bashed in.

10 Third Threepenny Finale.* 10

1. After the news from Peachum that we are not to
have a hanging after all but a happy ending, we are
12: *Horch, wer kommt?* into a chorus of welcome to the king's messenger. 12
This is thin and repetitious and needs a lot of stage
business to help it get by. Nice part for the piano.*

2. A cod grand opera recitatif from the messen-
13: *Anlässlich ihrer Krönung* ger.* Rather good. Mac is ennobled. 13

3. Mac responds in true operatic style.* He always 14
14: *Gerettet, Gerettet!* knew things would turn out well in the end. We get
into a running lyrical line. Polly chucks in her
pennyworth.

16: *Darum bleibt alle stehen* 4. A march,* not, after all, to the gallows. The 16
Peachums make their statements, Mrs simply saying
well isn't that nice, but Peachum himself preaching a
little sermon on the text that all crime should be
spared from prosecution.

5. A hymn with overtones and echoes of the real
17: *Verfolgt das Unrecht* old Lutheran stuff.* Injustice should never be pur- 17
sued and soon it's going to be winter and very cold and we are going to die. Holy sounds (harmonium and all).

NOTES

The Threepenny Opera	Weill's second successful collaboration with Brecht. Many earlier musical ballets, plays, quasi-operas etc., some performed, some not, many lost.
First night	Theater am Schiffbauerdamm, Berlin, 31 August 1928
Reception	Ecstatic
Libretto	Brecht and Elisabeth Hauptmann
Source	Frederick Austin's revival of John Gay's *Beggar's Opera* at the Lyric, Hammersmith in 1920. Song material from François Villon, Rudyard Kipling and others

NEWS AND GOSSIP

Everyone in the musical world was talking about the phenomenal success of Frederick Austin's *Beggar's Opera*. Brecht decided that after treatment the piece would be just right for the cabaret/theatre world of Berlin. He translated it. Then he did more – he Berlinized it. He got an impresario to agree to put it on, sent a fax to Weill, his team-mate on *Mahagonny* which had only just opened and eight months later after chaotic rehearsals *The Threepenny Opera* hit the stage. There are recordings still available of the original cast and we can therefore tell that the original show was quite unlike the show we see today. Here are some of the reasons:

1. Weill after the first run re-orchestrated it from a seven-piece jazz combo to a pit band of twenty-three.

2. The parts were played by actors who could sing (rather as Rex Harrison 'sang' in *My Fair Lady* but without his charm and none of them quite so tone-deaf).

3. Brecht revised the whole thing in 1931 to keep pace with his changes in ideology (he was of course a Marxist). This is the version used now.

4. Lotte Lenya (Weill's wife) outlived him by some thirty years and used her position as owner of the rights to create all manner of mythology about how the piece had been done and (more difficult to contest) how the

master had *wanted* the piece to be done. She would only license performances that reflected her enormously egotistical views.

The first production of *The Threepenny Opera* touched a spot that galvanized the whole German nervous system, rather as did Hitler in a bigger way a year or two later. For two years *Threepenny Opera* fever had Germany rolling about in ecstasy. And it spread. By 1933, 133 separate productions had been licensed. Pabst made a famous feature film. There were eight separate English translations/versions. The show ran for 2611 nights in New York, at that time the longest running musical in history. But the fever cooled and by the end of World War II most people could take it or leave it. Today *The Threepenny Opera* is not in the regular opera repertory. It crops up from time to time in opera festivals and more often in the legitimate theatre, which is where it really belongs.

COMMENT

The Threepenny Opera owes more to Brecht than to Weill. Brecht gave it that whiff from the sewers that was the popular smell for all art in Berlin and in Vienna at that time. His lyrics exploit the mood of despair brilliantly. He does not invert moral values quite so neatly as does Gay in the original *Beggar's Opera* and indeed, as his Communist friends told him, it is scarcely a social satire at all. In *The Threepenny Opera* it is not the rich, the powerful or the pompous who are pilloried. All mankind is in a pigsty where all pigs are equal and struggling not to drown in their own pigshit. The Brecht text is only just saved from being boringly depressing by his wit, which is deadly.

Weill, on the other hand, wrote one top-class tune (Mac the Knife) and a lot of pretty good cabaret numbers. Pretty good, that is, if you take each one on its merits, not so good if you listen to them head to tail on a CD, much better when sandwiched between bouts of spoken dialogue as they are on stage. The tunes themselves do not have the direct appeal of the ballads of Tin Pan Alley nor of the American musical of the same period and their orchestrations are often a bit dreary. Weill has two aggravating habits, one to keep doubling the vocal part with an orchestral line an octave lower, the other to chuck in dozens of chirpy little interjections from the trumpet and sax soloists which are all predictable and repetitive. He was in fact a computer composer before computers were invented. Today if you gave your Omaha automatic harmonium a Weill stop you could apply the *Threepenny Opera* sound to almost any piece of music.

Weill was a passionate anti-Wagnerian and had picked up ideas about the future of opera from his tutor Busoni and from a study of Schoenberg's theories. There is no doubt that he and Brecht took opera back into the theatre and took it back to the people (their kind of people), but they also took it back over a hundred years to the old Singspiel form that had been the bugaboo of German opera since it was imposed by the decree of the old chauvinist Emperor Joseph II. The ballads stop the action dead. The plot moves not in recitatif but in speech. There are few ensembles and the choruses are dire. All the work of Mozart, Verdi and Wagner in putting music and drama together into that glorious thing opera goes for nothing.

The best way to enjoy *The Threepenny Opera* is to forget all the political and cultural luggage that Brecht, Weill, Lenya and their followers tried to pile into the old thing and to see it as an extended cabaret act. Strangely enough, if taken at its face value, it has a naivety and an innocence that is rather touching. It is like schoolboys talking dirty to shock their parents. But the schoolboys are clever, funny and original and they still have the power to shock, if only just. Beta.

Tito, La Clemenza di *see* Clemenza di Tito, La

Tosca

Political thriller

Puccini

The one where the prima donna sticks a knife into the chief of police and her lover goes before a firing squad who shouldn't shoot him but do.

CAST

Floria Tosca, opera singer and star	Soprano
Mario Cavaradossi, her lover, a painter	Tenor
Cesare Angelotti, freedom fighter, political prisoner	Bass
Barone Scarpia, Chief of Police	Baritone
Spoletta, plain-clothes detective	Tenor
Sciarrone, Police Sergeant	Bass

A Sacristan, a Cardinal, **Roberti** (another policeman), an executioner, a Judge, a shorthand writer, a shepherd boy, a gaoler, etc.

3 acts, 2 INTERVALS: RUNNING TIME 1 hr 45 mins

STORY

Act I The Church of St Andrea Rome: interior

We are in Rome during the Napoleonic Wars: the goodies in our story are on old Boney's side hoping to liberate Rome from the nasty Fascist regime. Angelotti an escaped freedom fighter enters and furtively searches for the key to the Attavanti family chapel: he discovers the key by the Madonna shrine: he scuttles into the chapel.

Enter a comic Sacristan with painter's brushes thinking Cavaradossi has arrived (a painter currently working on an official portrait of Mary Magdalene). No Cav; his snap tin is untouched. The Angelus bell rings: the Sacristan prays: Cav enters and pulls off a sheet: he reveals a pic of a stunning blonde with golden curls and blue eyes: the Sacristan thinks it is too near Page 3 and also the dead spit of a known woman parishioner. Cav explains the picture is a combo of two women, Floria Tosca and another.

The Sacristan goes: Angelotti comes out: Cav slowly recognizes his old political colleague ravaged by prison life: they share a warm reunion: I've just been sprung from prison says Angelotti. From distant parts Tosca yells Hey Mario! Wait a sec says Cav till I get rid of the woman: I am bloody starving says Angelotti: here take my snap tin and scarper pronto says Cav: Tosca appears: what woman were you talking to? she cries: no woman says Cav I love only you: he makes sexual advances: not in front of the Virgin Mary says Tosca, meet me tonight after my gig: we'll go to your place (thinks: one day I will have cottage with roses round door etc. better than Cav's place).

I've got to get back to work says he: he turns to the pic. Tosca sees the pic. Just tell me, she says, who the hell is that broad? Mary Magdalene says he. Not on your life is that Mary M. says she it's that Attavanti woman with those piddle blue eyes. Well actually um er yes he says but your eyes are superior. I will forgive you if you paint in black eyes says she and no whoring after strange women if you please. Their mutual attraction is fuelled by this jealous spat, and they indulge in mild petting despite the Virgin Mary. Tosca exits, Angelotti comes in.

What now? asks Cav. I will stay till dusk then run for it in drag says Angelotti: my loving sister left female gear fan and all in the chapel. I am determined to outwit that bugger Scarpia says Angelotti. That's a dangerous bastard watch it says Cav. Best if you scarper to my place now, just over wall: jump into the well, there's a secret closet halfway down. Boom! The cannon signals an escaped prisoner. Leg it man! says Cav – Scarpia will be on your tail soon.

The Sacristan and choristers come on and horse around and chatter: great news – Boney is defeated: there will be a big show tonight with fireworks for a royal gig featuring Floria Tosca. Another boom boom – but more sinister. The dreaded Scarpia is amongst us: his henchmen at his back: the Sacristan and choristers chatter.

Scarpia says an escaped prisoner has taken refuge here, search it boys: he goes into the Attavanti chapel: he finds a fan with the Attavanti crest and sees the pic the likeness of Lady Attavanti: who done that? he bellows. Why Cavalier Cavaradossi says the Sacristan. What him says Scarpia Tosca's politically suspect boyfriend? That's his empty snap tin we found in the chapel says the Sacristan: so Angelotti guzzled it says Scarpia: what ho there's Tosca creeping in. Congrats on your holiness Tosca, he says: you come to pray, other women come in to consort with painters (he points at the other woman in the pic). Prove it says she: look at this fan says he, I found it in the painter's snap tin. My God says she it belongs to that Attavanti woman: I came here (church filling up with worshippers) to cancel my date with Cav owing to the royal gig and now you tell me this. Those two are probably humping away at his place now: she weeps: exits.

Scarpia says tail her. (Thinks: I'll kill him and have her before the day is out.) A Cardinal leads a procession down the crowded aisle big ceremonial stuff chanting incense loads of clergy etc. Scarpia kneels in an act of prayer.

Act II Scarpia's apartment Level 3 Farnese Palace (Levels 1 & 2 Queen of Naples)

Scarpia at table thinks with luck by dawn both Angelotti and Cavaradossi will be hanged. He asks Sciarrone (Acting Butler in the Metropolitan Police Force) is Tosca at the gig yet? As he listens to the gig going on below he has a lengthy lecherous gloat about his prospective rape of Tosca. Spoletta enters: he has tailed Tosca to Cavaradossi's: no Angelotti (Zut! says Scarpia) but he has arrested Cavaradossi. (Bully for you says Scarpia.)

The torture gang enters – Cavaradossi, judge, torturer, shorthand writer, executioner, four bruisers (Tosca's voice in full throttle is audible below). You harboured an escaped prisoner says Scarpia; you gave him clothes food shelter. I deny everything says Cav. Tosca rushes in, embraces Cav. Keep mum girl he whispers. For last time says Scarpia, will you talk? Negative says Cav. OK boys take him down and get to work says Scarpia. The torture gang exits through a trap door.

So did you catch them humping? asks Scarpia. No, alone says Tosca: it is useless to quiz me or him. Wait and see says he what he does under torture says Scarpia (O my God says she): but if you talk, the torture stops says he. Stop! she cries: stop! he orders. Say nothing gal shouts Cav from below under stress. The torture proceeds: yells and screams from below pile the pressure on to Tosca until she gives way – Angelotti is in the well she says. Lay off boys shouts Scarpia.

Cav, a shocking sight bruised and bleeding, is brought up. Did you talk? he asks Tosca. No she says (a lie). She talked says Scarpia. Bloody bitch says Cav. There's a sudden diversion: a fax comes in saying Boney not licked but victorious at Marengo. Huzza shouts Cav: now you're for it Scarpia you pig. You'll be dead anyway says Scarpia: take him away.

Scarpia and Tosca are alone: Scarpia makes creepy advances: realistic Tosca asks how much? Not money says he: I want you. I'll jump out of the window first says she. You let me have you, Cav goes free: you say no, he dies. That's not a very nice proposition says she: Scarpia gets physical, chases her round the sofa. Drumbeat! Hear that? Cav is on his way to the gallows says he.

Tosca takes a breather to pray: I have been a good girl: why do I deserve this? Spoletta looks in saying Angelotti is dead – suicide. Hang him from the gallows just the same says Scarpia. And Cav? asks Spoletta; what orders? Well Tosca? asks Scarpia. She nods 'Yes I will' (ugh!). He must be seen to die: a phoney execution is the only way out says Scarpia. Hear that, Spoletta? execution à la Palmieri. Yessir à la Palmieri says Spoletta. (Encoded message: Palmieri was promised a phoney execution then shot just the same. Tosca smells no rat.) Spoletta exits.

Tosca says she and Cav must have letter of safe conduct. OK says Scarpia. He sits down to write. Tosca spots a flick knife on the table: she surreptitiously seizes it. Scarpia rises and attempts an embrace. Slooch! He gets the knife between the shoulder blades – 'the kiss of Tosca': Scarpia expires: Tosca extracts the safe conduct from his hand: she conducts later than last rites, putting candlesticks and a crucifix around the torso of his corpse. Exits.

Act III Castel Sant' Angelo: appropriate offices: walkways: courtyard etc. Dawn

A shepherd boy sings, bells chime all over the place. Cav signed in for execution asks for pen and paper and writes a nostalgic letter to Tosca. Tosca rushes on and shows him the safe conduct: she gives Cav a drama lesson on how to feign death by firing squad. She tells Cav about her recent triumphant murder of Scarpia. Both anticipate a lovely hol together in sunny climes. They exchange loverly thoughts and more drama school stuff: Tosca gets impatient.

At last the firing squad squares up: shoots: Cav drops. Very good! cries Tosca. The squad exits. Tosca runs to Cav – he's been shot dead for real. Mother of God! Shouts and cries outside indicate the news of Scarpia's death is spreading fast. Tosca is the prime suspect. Spoletta rushes at Tosca. She jinks: she runs to parapet: jumps to her death. End.

MINUTES FROM START LOOK OUT FOR

Act I

The opera opens with the motif of the dreaded Scarpia (Oom-pah Ti Boom-crash) and this is the front end of a pair of brackets that will hold together the whole work.

3: *E sempre lava!* The Sacristan fusses about to a flighty little tune* 3
of his own (he and his choristers give the first act the sort of light relief we get from David and the apprentices in *Meistersinger*) but several other motifs, important-to-be, poke their way in.

Cavaradossi bursts into song about the two gor-
10: *Recondita armonia* geous models for his Madonna.** Careless rapture, as 10
per a mistle thrush in exceptionally good form.
14: *Non la sospiri* Tosca's vision of rural happiness:** look out espe- 14
cially for a tripping cadential figure (tailpiece) which cropped up first a little earlier (when Tosca prays to the Madonna) and now begins to dominate the scene (appears four times in quick succession).

The great Cavaradossi/Tosca duet (the Black Eyes

23: *Quale occhio* duet). The first two strains are nice enough* then 23
suddenly we are into one of the greatest of Puccini's
24: *Mia gelosa!* tunes*** (of all tunes) which says something about 24
the sweetness of love overcoming jealousy. It is long-phrased, repeated four times (not once too often) and finally dies away in the orchestra. But you will hear echoes of it again and again later in the opera and it will live in your ears' memory forever.

28: *Un tal baccano* From Scarpia's dramatic appearance,** through 28
his excited sleuthing on the trail of Angelotti and then his savage encounter with Tosca – all as vivid and as frightening as can be – look out for orchestral delights, musical references and especially the final orchestral recap of the love/jealousy theme as Tosca exits.

As Scarpia gives orders to his bruisers to follow
38: *Tre sbirri, una carrozza* Tosca a great processional theme sweeps in.** It 38
surges and swells to the end of the act beneath Scarpia's horrid anticipation of a right and a left – Angelotti's head and Tosca's body – all this runs alongside the slow movement of the Cardinal's procession through the now crowded church and the singing of the Te Deum – until the curtain falls abruptly to the crash of Scarpia's theme.

Act II

The prelude with its echoes of the love/jealousy and the Scarpia themes does not forbode: it reflects Scarpia's suppressed excitement: he thinks it is going to be his lucky evening: one rape and one murder.

In Act II up to the entry of Tosca there are no set pieces, no great tunes, but the plot is moved along wonderfully effectively. Look out especially for the eerie combination of the dreaded Scarpia's lustful
2: *Alla cantata ancor* and murderous thoughts* against a backing of high 2
society dance music (and later a posh cantata and Tosca's party piece), for the doom-laden tune that follows Cavaradossi around like a shadow and for the way the orchestra 'talks', setting the mood, pointing the action, telling us what Scarpia feels, what Cavaradossi feels: light years away from the 'orchestral accordion' of the early bel canto operas.

10: *Ed or fra noi parliam* The torture scene:*** no need to alert anyone to 10
anything here, because you will be transfixed – but do

spare a thought for the pacing of each step towards Tosca's breakdown, the dialogue Tosca/Scarpia, the exchanges between the separated lovers, the orders barked out by Scarpia and the yells of pain from Cavaradossi. The build-up is intolerable. No wonder Tosca could stand no more.

The turmoil following Sciarrone's breaking of the
news (true this time) of Napoleon's victory: a brave
20: *Vittoria! Vittoria!* patriotic outburst** from Cavaradossi: Tosca is con- 20
cerned only with her betrayal and its effect on Cav-
aradossi: as he is hustled out she screams 'Ah! Mario! Mario!'.

The rest of the act is taken up with a duet Scarpia/
Tosca (with the interruption by Spoletta) until she
terminates it with the fatal stab. Scarpia tries to ingratiate himself and proposes his loathsome deal in a
27: *Se la giurata* passionate solo.** 27

Along with One Fine Day and Your Tiny Hand,
30: *Vissi d'arte* the most famous of Puccini's big soprano pieces.*** 30
Tosca's question (why is this happening to me?) and prayer. Building up wonderfully to its big climax, and touching.

The final scene: Scarpia sits down to write the
phoney letter of safe conduct to a sweeping mel-
33: *Si adempia il voler* ody,** calm but full of menace, giving us a breathing 33
space between the storms past and the storm to come: then the 'kiss of Tosca' with all the stops out – and the calm melody plays the scene out (All Rome trembled before him) ending with a sonorous funereal version of Scarpia's theme accompanied by a death rattle of drums. Stupendous.

Act III

0 A magical opening*** – solo horn, then some of Puc- 0
cini's 'cold dawn' music (as the dawn in *Bohème* Act III), the shepherd boy's song and the chorus of bells*** orchestrated around the love/jealousy theme.

As Cavaradossi sits down to write his farewell note
to Tosca overwhelming memories crowd in – there
are memories for us too in the score: the love/
jealousy tune (solo cello) and the tripping tailpiece –
9: *E lucevan le stelle* he soars into his great tenor aria*** and sings his 9
heart out. Then he breaks down and weeps.

14: *Liberi!* The Freedom duet:** both very chuffed, excited, sung over a lurching dance rhythm accompaniment like a very slow cake-walk. The duet ends in a mighty 14

19: *Parlami ancora* burst of ecstasy.*** 19

22: *Così!* A dirge-like march** accompanies the business of the mock execution but of coursc it isn't mock and after the salvo is fired the trombones bray out the ghastly theme until it sinks away to a whisper: Tosca finds Mario dead: all hell breaks loose and she makes her last leap to the harsh echoes of Scarpia's villainy. 22

NOTES

Tosca	Puccini's fifth opera
First night	Teatro Costanzi, Rome, 14 January 1900
Reception	The public acclaimed it: some critics found it too crudely violent
Libretto	Illica and Giacosa
Source	*La Tosca,* a play by Sardou

NEWS AND GOSSIP

Puccini had seen Sardou's play way back in the 1880s and had asked his publisher Ricordi to get a lien on the rights. This Ricordi had failed to do and when Puccini had got *Manon* and *Bohème* out of his system and was casting about for a new subject he thought of Tosca again. By now an unknown named Franchietti had got the rights, so he sent Illica and Ricordi to con the poor Franchietti out of the rights by telling him the opera was far too violent (rape, torture, execution) and too political for the Roman taste. It was a pushover. Next day Puccini had a contract with Sardou and he was off, adding Giacosa to the script team – now the same as for *Lescaut* and *Bohème*. The Illica draft was as usual put through the mangle by Puccini (*Bohème* was all poetry and no action, said he, whereas *Tosca* should be all action and no poetry) and the finished book went into rehearsal in the Autumn of 1899. *Tosca* caught on at once and has been amongst the very top of the pops ever since, just second to *Bohème* but a neck ahead of *Butterfly*.

COMMENT

The sniggering description of *Tosca* as 'a shabby little shocker' says more about English musical snobbery than about this ferociously effective melodrama. *Tosca* grabs the attention from the first bar and races on to its terrible end with only two slight pauses for breath (the high jinks of the Sacristan and Co. and the shepherd boy singing in the stillness of the dawn). Those who used to find it vulgar (not many would dare to join this camp today) were probably too intellectually frail to stand up to its savage assault on the emotions. *Tosca* is craftily designed with a sure-fire theatrical touch. The first act with the instant appearance of Angelotti moves steadily to its love climax in the Cavaradossi/Tosca duet and then to its climax of hate, Scarpia triumphant in his beastly plans, this last played against the stately pomp of the Cardinal's procession.

The second act is zip and zap, never a pause. We too are subjected to torture along with Cavaradossi until Tosca gives way and then everything follows its inevitable course until the fatal stab (those who doubt the ability of a prima donna to deliver a death blow with such an implement should have worked with Callas. Sometimes it seemed quite likely she would do it to her producer). If the pace slackens too much at the opening of the last act, it picks up immediately Tosca appears on the scene. Only Tosca's last leap over the parapet gets a little near the borders of credibility and despite a slight sense of fudge it is probably best for her to take the plunge offstage. *Tosca* is the most vivid of Puccini scores. The labels or tags he used to signpost certain ideas/states of mind through the music are many and they stick in the ear. Indeed he does something Wagner often fails to do with his more on-the-nose leitmotifs – he can alert the subconscious to a musical memory without the brain having to go through the mental processes of saying 'Ah yes, that's the Angelotti doom motif'. We *feel* the message without having to decode it.

Tosca has at least four of Puccini's greatest set pieces: the love/jealousy duet and the final Scarpia/processional scene in Act I, Tosca's 'Vissi d'arte' in Act II and Cavaradossi's 'E lucevan le stelle' in Act III. The dawn of Act III is clearer, calmer and colder than the *Bohème* Act III dawn and the chorus of bells an eccentric stroke which comes off a million dollars.

Some people understandably shrink away from the sadistic streak in Puccini, which was undeniably there, as he himself admitted (his 'Neronic inclinations'). But other great artists have not been afraid to use violent cruelty as a means to a dramatic end, including the author of *Lear* and *Timon of Athens*. In the end it must be the temperament of the individual that decides whether or not they can take the Cavaradossi torture scene. If you can, and unless your taste is too refined even for melodrama or your susceptibilities too tender to face raw emotion, *Tosca* is one of the greatest. An alpha-plus for all but the cowards.

La Traviata (The Fallen Woman)

Tragic romance

Verdi

The one where the call-girl is a social embarrassment to her lover's family so she gives him up, her golden heart is broken and she succumbs to terminal TB.

CAST

Violetta Valéry, courtesan and heroine	Soprano
Annina, her maid	Soprano
Alfredo Germont, lover of Violetta	Tenor
Giorgio Germont, his father	Baritone
Baron Douphol, Violetta's stand-by lover	Baritone
Gastone de Letorières, man about town	Tenor
Flora Bervoix, friend of Violetta, society woman	Mezzo
Marchese d'Obigny, elderly socialite	Bass
Doctor Grenvil	Bass
Servants, a messenger	

3 acts, 2 intervals: running time 1 hr 50 mins

STORY

Act I Violetta's house: suite of reception rooms

We are mixing with high society in Paris in 1850. Violetta, *poule de luxe* (socialite whore, a type of woman unknown today), greets the guests to her party. Her old friend Gastone introduces a new friend Alfredo: at dinner Gastone says Alfredo is potty about Violetta: he worships her from afar: he visited her house every day for a bulletin when she was recently sick. Alfredo is called on to sing a toast to love, wine etc. and pulls it off nicely.

As the company moves off to dance (it was a very brief dinner) Violetta signals her illness: Alfredo lurks: a tête-à-tête ensues. Alfredo says he has loved her for a year. Violetta says forget all that love stuff, I've quite gone off it. But she gives him a camellia and says come up and see me sometime, maybe tomorrow.

The company returns: everyone says their farewells: Violetta is left alone: now she's not so certain she has gone off love altogether: she hears Alfredo singing distant farewells (no double glazing): now she's definitely uncertain.

Act II Sc 1 A room in a French country house

Alfredo comes in from shooting: his happy thoughts about rural bliss in his *ménage à deux* are shattered by Annina announcing that Madam sent her to Paris to keep the brokers' men at bay by selling the family silver: a thousand ECUs required a.s.a.p. Alfredo is confounded: thoughts of money never entered his mind (sweet man!) – gosh! Zut! Quel blague! He resolves to go to Paris to sort things out.

Violetta gets an invitation to Flora's party in Paris. A visitor arrives, namely Germont, Alfredo's Dad. He accuses Violetta of living on immoral earnings namely Germont family money. She refutes this: she never took a centime. He tells her Alfredo's sister's wedding is threatened by the disgrace of Alfredo consorting with a high-class whore: she must give him up. For a short time? asks Violetta. For ever Germont replies. Anguish, shock, despair, tears, concession: yes she will give him up. Good girl says Germont, goodbye. Alfredo enters. He has a confused encounter with Violetta but he (sweet, but a bit of a thickie) does not twig. Love me forever and goodbye says Violetta. Isn't she a darling says he.

Alfredo reads the bad news in Violetta's letter: gone for good (true motive for departure concealed): he is devastated. Germont reappears: come back and join your loving family says Father: naff off, you interfering old sod says Alfredo: he sees Flora's invitation: I'll catch up with her there he says.

Act II Sc 2 A party room in Flora's house

Flora's party is in full swing: what in ballet terms would be a divertissement – namely colourful padding, gypsies, toreadors. Alfredo arrives: Violetta comes in with Baron Douphol: tension builds: Violetta wishes she'd stayed home. Alfredo plays cards (nature of game obscure) with Gastone: he wins: the Baron challenges Alfredo to a game: Alfredo wins a fortune.

Then it's supper break: Violetta slips out and Alfredo joins her at her request: she says hop it the Baron is out for your blood: he says not on your life and do you really love that ghastly Baron Douphol? She says yes (a lie of course). Alfredo calls everyone in from supper: he says this woman spent all her money on me now I pay her back: he chucks all his winnings at her feet. Germont is outraged at such appalling behaviour in a member of his high-class French family: Alfredo is remorseful: the Baron breathes fire and revenge: Violetta hopes one day Alfredo will have the full story: the guests think this is the act of a cad: he should be slung out.

Act III The bedroom in Violetta's house

Violetta is dying of TB: Annina nurses her. Doctor Grenvil visits her and tells traditional doctorly fibs about how she will recover soon: Violetta is not fooled. The carnival is on: Annina is sent to give money (not much left) to the poor. Violetta reads a letter from Germont: the Baron has been wounded in a duel, Alfredo has gone abroad: he is coming back to see her.

A masked [how do we know? Ed.] chorus passes under the window: Alfredo arrives. The lovers are in ecstasy: they make plans for a new joint residence in the country: Violetta attempts to dress: she falls back weak as a kitten clearly dying: the lovers rage a bit against fate.

The doctor and Germont (appropriately guilty) arrive: Violetta gives Alfredo a portrait of herself and generously says if he finds another woman to give it to her [Is this a good idea? Ed.] then gently and pathetically expires. One of the most famous deaths in all opera.

MINUTES FROM START

LOOK OUT FOR

Act I

0 The great brooding melody* of the prelude moves into an oom-pah can-can-ish accompaniment to the arrival of the guests and it continues to bang on under all the opening hellos. 0

8: *Libiamo ne'lieti calici* The brindisi** (a song ending in a toast to something or other): very lively, very catchy, very well-known. It drifts on with an ensemble chorus for some while. 8

13: *Un dì felice* Alfredo's first love song,* agreeable but dim: Vi- 13
14: *Ah, se ciò è ver* oletta's reply** much more sparky; duologue continues over ballroom muzak in waltz time.* 14

19: *È strano! È strano!* Violetta's big set-piece emotional recitatif* followed by her aria** which climaxes in a burst of bird-like melody plus fireworks and finishes with a rousing cabaletta: Alfredo bleating in the distance very effective. 19

Act II Sc 1

Alfredo still in shooting togs is remorseful about his inattention to the matter of housekeeping money; a
4: *O mio rimorso!* nice vigorous cavatina.* 4

After elegantly phrased exchanges in recitatif the great duet between Germont and Violetta: at first a number of short solos: next Germont's statement of
9: *Pura siccome un angelo* his case in measured tones** then Violetta's shocked 9
response first in broken phrases soon leading to a passionate lyrical outburst: Germont's second innings,

14: *Un dì quando le veneri* again to a restrained refrain of great beauty:**Vi- 14
oletta concedes in a tearful and hushed solo** leading 20
20: *Ah! dite alla giovine* to tender exchanges between both in a marvellously
crafted duet:*** now they lapse into recitatif as the 22
22: *Imponete* enormity of the decision sinks in: after that a final
25: *Morrò!* bout of duetting** (Violetta: If I die please tell him 25
why I did this, Germont: You're a wonderful girl and
virtue will bring its reward), then the coda made up of
the final affecting goodbyes.

The confused scene between Alfredo and Violetta
ends in her passionate demand: LOVE ME! ex-
29: *Amami, Alfredo* pressed in a phrase of great intensity*** as she runs 29
into the garden.

Germont's attempts to win over his son do not
match his recent and much better performance with
Violetta. This time, the call to Alfredo to rejoin the
35: *No, non udrai rimproveri* family nest sung to a debonair little tune,* fails – and 35
the scene ends with Alfredo's noisy walkout.

Act II Sc 2

Gypsies, toreadors, etc. perform and sing to ballet
music: then once this pantomime stuff is out of the
way crafty Verdi builds the tension adroitly through
terse exchanges over an excited orchestra: Violetta
44: *Ah, perchè venni* several times interjects her prayer for mercy:** as 44
things are about to climax the announcement of sup-
per lets the air out of the balloon.

The tense scene between the star-crossed lovers:
47: *Invitato a qui sequirmi* emotional exchanges* over a walking bass. 47

51: *Di sprezzo degno se stesso* The wonderful 'thinks' finale:*** original, subtle, 51
tuneful and rhythmically varied as never before. Germont has a sweet sad plaint (Can this be my boy?), Alfredo quite fed up with himself (What a shit I am), the chorus hushed, shocked, embarrassed (Poor Violetta: my God how awful), Germont in a second coming (The girl's a brick), the Baron (I'll get you yet Alfredo), Violetta (If only he knew how I love him). It begins softly and variously with many of the asides whispered: it gains vigour and begins to swing; it ends in surging mezzo forte of shame, regret, despair with public sympathy expressed by one and all.

Act III

0 The prelude:** plangent strings with a strong mess- 0
age of grief set the mood and continue as background

support to the exchanges between Annina and Violetta in the early part of the scene.

After reading Germont's letter Violetta has a surge of energy: is Alfredo leaving it too late? Those were really happy times we had together – a touching nos-
12: *Addio del passato* talgic little song.** 12
Alfredo appears: a duet of pure happiness:** first 14
14: *O mia Violetta* the breathless joy of being together and then plans to set up house together (a mirage) in more measured tones.

Violetta's slow march to her death – there is a brave adieu to life by the lovers in music that makes as if to
19: *Ah! Gran Dio!* defy death:** the last hushed ensemble begins with 19
Violetta's gift to Alfredo of her picture over a funeral march accompaniment; Alfredo urges her to live: Germont is overcome by guilt: and Violetta soars into
23: *Se una pudica vergine* her last aria*** generously urging Alfredo to find 23
happiness with another: with one final exclamation ('GIOIA!') she dies and the last muttered words of grief fade into the final curtain.

NOTES

La Traviata	Verdi's nineteenth opera
First night	Teatro la Fenice, Venice, 6 March 1853
Reception	'Complete fiasco,' wrote Verdi. But the critics liked it
Libretto	Piave
Source	Alexandre Dumas' play *La Dame aux camélias*. See below

NEWS AND GOSSIP

There is a legend surrounding the *Traviata* story, namely that Alexandre Dumas the younger met a courtesan, one Marie Plessis, at a party in Paris; went to bed with her that night and set up a *ménage à deux* in a country house near Paris. Dumas then wrote his novel in which a young man meets a courtesan at a party in Paris etc. (Marie did not have TB, did not pay Dumas' bills but did swan off back to Paris and her Baron Douphol and did die at the age of 23.) Dumas turned his novel (*La Dame aux camélias)* into a play: a huge success. Verdi may have seen the play. (He was in Paris on 2 February 1852, the night of the premiere, certainly.) He must have read the reviews which were raves. Nothing further is known until January 1853 when we find him and Piave working on the libretto two months before the first night. *Traviata* eventually became one of the top ten in Italy and even during Verdi's eclipse a regular in the rep. of most international houses. Dumas' original story has spawned a huge brood of operas, films, ballets, etc., and star Violettas (Marguerites) have included Bernhardt, Garbo, Callas and Fonteyn, all of them splendid realizations of the legendary whore with a heart of gold.

COMMENT

Traviata is the first grown-up opera about contemporary life and thus a milestone in opera history. Verdi made no PR fuss about the fact that he was abandoning historical subjects (*Nabucco*, *Lombardi*, *Ernani*, *Attila*) period drama (*Macbeth*, *Rigoletto*) and farrago plots such as *Trovatore*, for real-life verismo. Not that *Traviata* is a drama-doc but it is first in a stream of stories of romantic realism that he passed on to Puccini and were to become the main stock in trade of Hollywood for over half a century. It is a lovely story, aimed directly at the heart, and it is one of those properties (handled with even a modicum of talent) that is bullet-proof in print, on stage or on the screen. Verdi clearly fell in love with Violetta and indeed with the whole opera and he deployed all his now formidable powers as an opera composer to produce one of his most perfect scores. Violetta has the best music, from her first big aria in Act I ('È strano!'), the great duet (the heart of the opera) with Germont in the second act, to the last desolate scene which brings us close to death itself and takes us towards her own death in a wonderfully well devised and varied series of steps, each one musically deepening the sense of pity we feel for this very unfortunate lady. It is a long death but it does not seem a slow one. It is true that the gypsies and the toreadors at Flora's party break the narrative flow and that, thinly supported by Verdi's Class II film/ballet music, their purpose can only be to add six minutes to an already short opera, or to fall in with the dreadful French practice of ruining good operas by packing bad ballets into them. Apart from this there are no longueurs. Two very similar parties are perhaps one too many and the final confrontation between Alfredo and the Baron Douphol is fluffed (on purpose? to avoid distraction from the main story line?) but overall the dramatic structure of *Traviata* works like a dream and a dream supported by some inspired musical ideas, such as the 'thinks' finale to Act II, and the use of the prelude theme throughout the beginning of Act III. So *Traviata* is a great opera: the music speaks to us directly: Verdi's feeling for Violetta finds an instant echo in our feelings: we believe in the characters – ordinary people like you and me, not queens, troubadours or warriors. We can take the opera to our hearts lock, stock and barrel with any picky reservations overwhelmed by the warmth and pathos of the story of *La Dame aux camélias*. Alpha-plus.

Tristan and Isolde

Erotic music-drama

Wagner

The one with two lovers, a love potion and a love death.

CAST

Tristan, a Knight, and nephew of Mark, king of Cornwall	Tenor
Kurwenal, Tristan's ADC	Baritone
King Mark	Bass
Melot, a courtier of the Cornish court	Baritone
Isolde, an Irish princess	Soprano
Brangäne, Isolde's lady-in-waiting	Mezzo
A sailor, a helmsman, a shepherd	

3 acts: running time 3 hrs 30 mins

STORY

Act I On the deck of a ship at sea

Sc 1 In which Isolde expresses her wish that the boat should sink with all hands and thereby bring her life to an end and Brangane is worried lest her mistress be unwell

We are in the Dark Ages on a small boat en route from Ireland to Cornwall and there is this sailor up in the rigging singing modern music. Who's that and where are we? says Isolde waking from a nap. That's Nutty George singing says Brangane and we are in sight of Cornwall. Everything has gone to pot says Isolde my life is in ruins. I'd like a storm to sink this ship and all who sail in her. You feeling all right m'lady? asks Brangane. A paracetamol? Or is it a mental problem? Air! More air! shouts Isolde. Brangane pulls open the curtains and we see the whole of the deck and it is Scene 2.

Sc 2 In which Isolde sends Brangane to ask Tristan to come to see her and she receives a dusty answer

See that Tristan skulking up there in the bow? asks Isolde as Nutty George sings his number again. Yes sure says Brangane he is very well spoken of. The stinker says Isolde he daren't face up to me just you wait and see. Ask him to come here. Brangane goes. Kind sir she says to Tristan my lady awaits you. We're nearly there says Tristan I'll take Isolde ashore when we arrive. I rather think she'd like to see you now says Brangane. I can't leave the wheel just now says he. Quit fooling around says she it's an order.

Get back interjects Kurwenal and tell Isolde that Tristan takes orders from no one. He goes on to sing a nasty song recalling Tristan's brave but unhygienic behaviour in chopping off Morold's head (Isolde's one-time fiancé) and wrapping it in a parcel and posting it to her. Ho ho sing all the sailors this is the way Tristan pays his respects to ladies. Ho ho.

Sc 3 In which Isolde tells Brangane the previous history of her relationship with Tristan and decides to end it all for both of them

Well what did he say? asks Isolde. He says he can't leave the wheel says Brangane. I heard it all says Isolde including that vicious send-up song. Let me tell you that once a guy called Tantrum sailed into Cork sick as a pig and yours truly nursed him back to life.

I saw his sword had a suspicious nick in it plus hairs like Morold's. I went to the fridge and got out Morold's head and sent the head and the sword to forensic. Sure enough they found a fragment of sword above Morold's left ear that fitted also the hairs were identical. So Tantrum was Tristan see? I could have killed him then. Missed my chance. I forgave him instead. And he said he loved me and then he went off bragging that he'd carry me off to be the bride of his Uncle Mark. I'm sick, sick, sick. I hate him. I wish he were dead and that I was too.

Steady on m'lady says Brangane you are going over the top really you are. Tristan behaved within the Cornish code of Courtly Conduct Section 17B in fetching you out for his uncle. He's done nothing wrong. Honest. He's just out there breathing 23 feet away says Isolde *and he doesn't love me*.

Oho! Aha! Now I get it thinks Brangane. But m'lady she says no man could not love you. You are such a peach. But if he needs a bit of a shove how about that stuff your old Mum brewed up and left in the medicine chest which I happen to have by me quite handy? You mean the love potion? Not on your life says Isolde but the instant poison – yes good idea. Get it out. At this point the crew whose discipline is poor start singing and shouting because the ship is entering harbour.

Sc 4 In which Isolde tells Kurwenal she must see Tristan for a special purpose before disembarkation and instructs Brangane to get a death draught ready for them both to drink

Enter Kurwenal. Get your bags together ladies he says we're nearly there. Take a message please my man to your master says Isolde: say I require him to come and solemnly beg my pardon before we land. Very good Ma'am says Kurwenal I'll do it but it is quite likely he will tell you to get lost. Right Brangane farewell for ever get the drink ready says Isolde. Which drink? says Brangane. The poison of course stupid says Isolde. So who's going to drink this? asks Brangane. Tristan and I says Isolde. O God no! says Brangane. But yes says Isolde this is just the sort of occasion for which my mother gave me the travelling medicine chest. Enter Tristan.

Sc 5 In which Isolde recounts to Tristan past events, suggests that he says Sorry and they drink to letting bygones be bygones which they do with momentous results just as King Mark comes aboard the ship

So why didn't you come when you were told? asks Isolde. It's laid down in the Manual of Court Procedure says Tristan that a knight escorting a royal bride should never be alone with her within fumbling distance. It's also in the Manual that before you accept an enemy as a friend he does the pardon ritual including the toast-drinking says she. Enemy? says he who is the enemy? You are my enemy says she: you killed my man and you done me wrong. When I nursed you under that silly name Tantrum I swore I'd get you in the end.

Be my guest says he take my sword and do it now. That wouldn't be a nice thing to do to kill one of your king's best knights says she. Now let us do the pardon drink. (The sailors start shouting and carrying on as the ship docks.) Tristan goes broody. Come on Tristan says Isolde drink it. The pardon procedure will put you straight with King Mark with yourself and with me.

Hey there two points starboard shouts Tristan to the sailors his mind elsewhere. OK. Right. Last time you did a good job as a physio to get me well let's hope this time this drink will help my psycho [he means his love for Isolde which is a great aggravation and which he has to hide because it is his duty to escort her to marry his Uncle Mark – too bad: Ed.] so here goes. He drinks. Steady on says Isolde leave some for me. She drinks. They both go funny. They gaze into each other's eyes. They call out each other's names. It's love! [Chemically induced: Brangane switched the bottles: Ed.] Meanwhile it's all go on the ship. Brangane tries to get a pretty limp Isolde into her ermines. Sailors shout and bustle, King Mark arrives amidst an outbreak of royalist fervour. Huzza!

Act II In the garden of King Mark's Cornish castle

Sc 1 In which Isolde is anxious to give the signal for Tristan to join her and Brangane is unable to prevent her

I can't hear that hunting mob now can you? Isolde asks Brangane. Yes I can says Brangane they're still quite close and it would be crazy to switch that light off and give the signal now. You want to keep Tristan away from me don't you? says Isolde. You must be careful says Brangane everyone noticed something funny when Tristan handed you over on the boat.

And watch that Melot he's up to no good. Melot? says Isolde he's Tristan's best friend. Melot is a treacherous toad and Mark's informer and this hunting lark is no more than a trap to catch you two together says Brangane. Not true says Isolde Melot organized the hunt to give us a chance to have a good time together. Put out the light! No leave it alone says Brangane I should never have given you that love shot. You didn't know the power of Mrs Minne the goddess of love did you? says Isolde she's telling me now to give the signal. No for Chrissakes no! shouts Brangane. But it's no good. Isolde puts out the light [which is the signal of course: Ed.]

Sc 2 In which Tristan arrives and after a great deal of loverly talk we are meant to think they are lovers in the carnal sense although we don't actually see them do it.

Tristan appears. Isolde he says. Tristan she replies. So we are off into unimagined rapture sublime bliss overwhelming joy and similar. Day is our enemy night is our friend says Tristan. Yes the day is really a drag says Isolde. Yes isn't it? says Tristan and the night is tremendously friendly? Yes tremendously says Isolde. Let's personify them and for a little while sing about them plotting for and against us says Tristan. Good idea says Isolde let's. They do.

For quite a long while they recap the past (remember the night you put antiphlogistine on my wound instead of Friars' Balsam?) But suddenly Tristan gets an unusual idea: wouldn't it be nice to die together? But how do we know we'd be allowed to stick together in the great unknown? asks Isolde. (Hey look out you two it's past six, shouts Brangane.) Couldn't split us says Tristan not enough power. OK let's do it then says Isolde what a terrific idea. Tremendous says he. Terminal says she. Everlasting love says he. Eternal bliss says she. Die in your arms says he. Never to wake says she. Let's go on like this for about five minutes says he. Even longer says she. They go on for six minutes thirty seconds. But then –

Sc 3 In which Tristan and Isolde are discovered in a highly compromising situation by King Mark and his court

A scream from Brangane. A shout from Kurwenal. No good. The hunters with King Mark at their head have arrived (without making a sound): Tristan and Isolde exposed! There you are Your Royal Highness says

Melot what did I say? I've saved you from a disgraceful marriage and should get an earldom or at least the OBE. Saved me from what? says Mark. This is the most terrible thing. Tristan is my best friend and he done me wrong. My belief in human nature is seriously at risk. (It's all just a bad dream says Tristan hopefully.) I have something to say to you Tristan says Mark and he certainly has for he goes into a full appraisal of Tristan's army record his career as a courtier his behaviour as a friend (and all of this with poor Tristan lying amongst the gladioli with his trousers down). You are a great disappointment Tristan he says what made you do this to me? I can't answer that Uncle says Tristan. I'd best be off to my old home in Brittany. Will you follow me there Isolde? I'll come says she.

Melot draws his sword. Traitorous rat he cries. Melot I thought you were my true mate says Tristan but you sneaked on me to Uncle Mark because you lusted after Isolde yourself. Take that! But he drops his sword God knows why and Melot gets in with a fairly good thrust and inflicts not a mortal but a stretcher-case wound. Tristan flops back onto Kurwenal Isolde onto Tristan and King Mark gives Melot a sharp slap on the wrist. Curtain.

Act III Outside Tristan's castle in Brittany. A huge lime tree centre stage

Sc 1 In which we find Tristan at home and not at all well and soon to be anxiously awaiting the arrival of Isolde which eventually takes place

Tristan is asleep beneath the lime tree. A shepherd pipes as best he can whilst trying to keep clear of his sheep. How's the patient, Kurwenal? he asks as he reaches the double bar. Poorly says Kurwenal I wish Isolde were here. I'll play my Mazurka in E flat as soon as I see her ship says the shepherd. Make it the one in G sharp minor says Kurwenal the fast one. OK says the shepherd. He plays on.

Tristan stirs. That sounds like my Dad's old bass clarinet says he. Where am I? Here says Kurwenal. Brittany. Kareol Castle. Your old home. Tristan surfaces. Kurwenal tells him what's happened since he flaked out in Cornwall. I can't remember a thing says Tristan except for Isolde. I keep thinking I see her but it's only a dream. I wish she was here. She'll be here today says Kurwenal. It struck me that she did a good job on you after you had tangled with Morold and she might do it again so I arranged for your UK solicitor to bring her over.

Isolde coming! Great! Terrific! Good man Kurwenal you done well you are this man's best friend get up that lighthouse, look out for the ship look out look out look. . .! There it is! [No it isn't he's just hallucinating:

Ed.] No boss says Kurwenal no ship. So meanwhile I'll tell you of my extremely unhappy boyhood says Tristan (he does so) so you see he says I was brought up to yearn and I've yearned a lot since then and I am particularly good at yearning to die. (He now hallucinates again about Isolde, the wound, death and mixing a poison from lover's tears. He's really pretty well gone.) He passes out and Kurwenal thinks he has expired. But no. I see the ship! he cries. Isolde's on it!

Oh no not that again thinks Kurwenal but suddenly he hears the G sharp minor mazurka. It's a real ship. Told you so! shouts Tristan. She's coming in fast cries Kurwenal and she's flying the Cornish duster. Oops! she's gone behind some rocks. Not aground I trust? asks Tristan. No I don't think so says Kurwenal look there she is again I can see Isolde. They're landing. She's coming. I'll go and fetch her says Kurwenal.

Sc 2 In which Tristan tears the dressings off his wound and expires from loss of blood just as Isolde arrives

Oh what a beautiful morning sings Tristan Oh what a beautiful day I've got a beautiful feeling Isolde is coming my way. I feel great I'm going to take up my bed and walk. I won over Morold with a wound so I'll win over Isolde with a wound too [Not quite right in the head: Ed.]. He tears his wound open. Look at all the lovely blood he says streaming out all over. He gets up and staggers around. Tristan! cries Isolde offstage. Sounds like her says Tristan. Isolde rushes on stage: Tristan! she says. Isolde! he replies (expires). Wake up Tristan says Isolde I've come to die with you. Let's look at your wound. My God – no breathing – no pulse – you're dead! It really is too bad of you Tristan to die on me like this. She passes out.

Sc 3 In which Melot and Kurwenal are killed, King Mark says he now knows the whole story and Isolde joins Tristan in death

A second ship is sighted. Kurwenal and the shepherd plus local unemployed agricultural workers barricade the gates against King Mark and his men. No good. You are heavily outnumbered says a spokesman give yourselves up now and you will be well treated. Not bloody likely says Kurwenal brandishing his sword. Get back cries Melot (for it is he). Kurwenal kills him. You madman says King Mark. Hold back. But no there is a general mêlée. Kurwenal is wounded and lies down to die next to Tristan. My God! Everyone's dead round here says King Mark: Tristan Kurwenal Melot Iso . . . Isolde's come to! cries Brangane. Thank God there's someone still breathing says King Mark. Isolde I have to tell you I now know the whole story. I came to arrange for you and Tristan to be happily married but now everyone's dead and it's quite spoiled my plan. You all right Isolde? asks Brangane. Isolde clearly in a trance gazes at Tristan. Look at him she says he's coming alive again! He's opening his eyes! He's breathing! He's incandescent! He's levitating! Listen – do you hear that heavenly choir? They are singing for him! And that wonderful smell of sal volatile! There are clouds of it all around me . . . all around me . . . I think I'm going . . . going . . . going . . . (She goes. Sinks onto Tristan's body. Dead.)

TRISTAN MOTTOS

Number	*Name*	*Description*
1	Tristan	A leap and a slow descent to the 'Tristan chord'
2	Isolde	Four notes going up and leaving you hanging in the air
3	Stab	A variant of Isolde, a stab of emotion: a long note followed by a short note over a notable chord
4	Gaze	A five-note motto (Tum-ta-ti-TA-ta) with a sizeable drop in the closing TA-ta
5	Sea	A downward waver followed by a triplet run up
6	Death	Long loud first note dropping a long way (an octave) to a muttered ending
7	Wound	A downward sliding phrase – semitones
8	Doom	Two strident opening notes and a third that fades away
9	Tragic	First a brassy fanfare, later strong and simple, a musical clove hitch
10	Day	A boom then a drop followed by an upward jerky phrase
11	Frustration	A snaky upward scale with semitones
12	Ecstasy	Sweet high smooth phrases – really nice
13	Minne	A slow downward sweep, twice, the same pattern
14	Night	Slow, dreamy, long first note, down and a tum-tum-ti-ta
15	Love at Peace	Sweet lyrical melody, longer than a motto, unmistakable
16	Love in Death	Hymn tune, notes of equal values, deliberate
17	Mark Disappointed	Very deep in the bass clarinet: long opener slipping down in semitones
18	Angst	A hitch upwards, down again to the starting note and a two-note tack

MINUTES FROM START

LOOK OUT FOR

Act I Prelude

0

The Prelude** opens with two mottoes that are Siamese twins. In a hushed voice and in four bars this twin motto sets the mood of the love story we are going to hear. Its first phrase descends (from an initial leap) to a chord that grabs you by the throat (the 'Tristan chord') and the second rather plaintive phrase goes up and leaves you hanging in the air. We can call the first Tristan (his love for Isolde) [1] and the second Isolde (her love for him) [2]. They are followed at once by a variant of the end of the Isolde motto, the Stab (of emotion), centring on a long note resolving on to a shorter note and here ending over a notable chord [3]. We shall hear a lot of these three, the first two are so much part of the work as to be mentioned only when they stand out, but the Stab is hardly mentioned at all because it is used as a sort of emotional punctuation mark. (It comes into its own at the very end of the opera.) 0

These mottos don't hold the stage long for next on the scene is a five-note motto (Tum-ta-ti-TA-ta, with a sizeable drop on the closing TA-ta, the Gaze [4]). This, as we are to hear later on, catches the moment when Tristan and Isolde first looked into each other's eyes and knew it was goo-goo between them. The Gaze is worked over intensively by the orchestra, mainly the strings, for nearly ten minutes and it is amazing that this modest little thing can offer enough stuffing to carry this rather wonderful piece almost to its close. After the climax we close with Tristan [1] – Isolde [2].

Act I Sc 1

A young sailor sings a song about the girl he left behind him – unaccompanied and unmemorable but for a phrase (a downwards waver followed by a triplet run up), the Sea [5].

11: *Wer wagt mich zu höhnen?*

Isolde wakes up* (a reminder of [4], she was dreaming of that magic moment). She is pretty cross owing to frustrated love and hopes the ship will run on the rocks and everyone will drown. Brangane tries to soothe her. This passage runs out in a sort of ongoing arioso at an easy speed somewhere between the 11 pace of the 2,000 and the 10,000 metres, occasionally breaking into a sprint. There will be a lot of this in *Tristan* carrying the calmer part of the plot with the orchestra doing most of the work and having all the tunes. Lots of Sea [5] churning about.

Act I Sc 2

Brangane throws open the curtains and we see nautical life on the deck beyond. The young sailor repeats his number, this time with some rubbing strings beneath, and Isolde, still in a black mood, sees Tristan at the helm. She wishes him dead. Here we have the motto of Death for the first time, sung by Isolde (long loud first note dropping a long way – an octave – to a muttered ending [6]). Isolde asks Brangane what she
thinks of Tristan (Brangane thinks he is lovely) and
17: *Was hältst du von dem Knechte?* sends her to fetch him.* There are nice exchanges. 17
But Isolde gives away her true feelings when we hear
Isolde [2] – love for Tristan – in the middle of some
loud anti-Tristan stuff.

Brangane's errand. Some swirling horns (Sea [5])
tell us of the manliness of the crew as they fiddle with
lanyards, mainstays, etc. Brangane's first exchanges
with Tristan are in a polite quasi-recitatif and his
21: *Grämt sie die lange Fahrt* replies are full and melodious* but as she gets stroppy 21
the tempo changes and we move into a brisk set-piece
24: *Das sage sie* ballad from Kurwenal.* As so often in a Wagner set 24
piece, the voice takes a clear lead over the orchestra which drops back to become a mere accompaniment for a while. The nasty mocking tone of this piece carries through to the short chorus that closes the scene. At the end of Kurwenal's song and in the sailors' chorus we hear the Fighting Knight motto, Tristan the feisty warrior, a military flourish, up down up (Knight (unlisted), and if you happen to know Tchaikovsky's *1812 Overture*, you will be greatly helped by recalling the brassy tune in that).

Act I Sc 3

Isolde tells her story:

She is miffed by Tristan's snub. So she will tell all
to Brangane and starts by recounting Tristan's first
27: *Wie lachend sie* Irish trip* including the disgusting stuff about 27
Morold's head being sent through the post and the
good job that forensic did in fitting the splinter to the

hole in Tristan's sword. She was going to kill him but their eyes met and the Gaze took place. Wagner's free-style writing at its best with a lot of Tristan [1] and Isolde [2] around and in various forms. Tristan was wounded (Wound motto, a sliding downward phrase, semitones [7]). She gazed at him and, of course, Gaze [4] comes in strong on cue.

She healed the wound and he swore to be her true love, now he has the brass neck to come to fetch her to
31: *Sein Lob hörtest du eben* marry his uncle for political reasons.* This section 31
goes marching on, Isolde's fury is rising all the time with the earlier mottos, especially derivatives of Wound [7], and Knight (unlisted) also in evidence.

So now she really thinks very little of Tristan and
34: *O blinde Augen!* we have a cataract of abuse** in descending octaves 34
leading to a great musical and dramatic climax – Traitor – Revenge – Death – Death for us both. (More free singing but Death [6] still prevalent.) Here Wagner really piles it on and holds us spellbound as the distressed lady pretty well bombs out before our very ears.

It is a wonderful fifteen minutes, but tough going for the Isolde – as taxing a bout of soprano singing as you will find anywhere.

39: *Was meinst du Arge?* Brangane tries to calm Isolde** and is doing a good 39
job until she says How about your old mum's aphrodisiac? (a variant of Gaze [4] followed by Isolde [2]). What about the other bottle, the poison? says Isolde. (Death [6] and a new motto deepish in the bass, too noble to be called a squirm, two strident opening notes and a third that fades away, Doom [8].) These are dreamy exchanges as if the two ladies were already into some magic trance, out of which they are rudely brought to earth by the O-Ho-Hoing of the crew. They have sighted land.

Act I Sc 4

Kurwenal brings in a breath of sea air with some
44: *Auf! Auf! Ihr Frauen!* cheery stuff about going ashore.* A change of tempo, 44
a break in the intensity, the orchestra cheerful too (an upbeat version of Sea [5]) and only a little galumphing.

The potions – which one? Highly charged ex-
47: *Nun leb wohl, Brangane!* change between Isolde and Brangane:* sometimes 47

excitable with strings rushing all over the place, but later sotto voce and doomy. Quite a gripper. Lots of Death [6] and Doom [8] and Isolde [2].

Act I Sc 5

The first Tristan/Isolde duet:

51 1. Tristan presents himself with a new motto, 51
Tristan Tragic [9] – a tremendously important four-note brassy fanfare here but after this much diminished to something strong but simple, like a musical clove hitch. Opening exchanges never descend to ornery but no star.

55: *Nicht da war's* 2. Isolde's indictment.** In two long solo pieces 55
she tells Tristan about Morold, Tantrum's wounds, oaths, etc. and makes him feel pretty awful. He offers her his sword to let her kill him. Here one marvels at Wagner's resourcefulness: the music unwinds sticking close to the sense of the text all the time but spinning along with fresh delights and surprises at every turn. Few mottos – Wound [7], Tragic [9] and Doom [8], not high voltage, but good.

3. Have a drink? Isolde says it would be bad form
59: *Wie sorgt' ich schlecht* to slay one of her future husband's best knights* (also 59
his nephew). Let's make friends and have a drink on it – Gaze [4]. (From now on the duet is subject to interruption from the manic crew who seem to be unable to go about their business without yelling Ho! He! Mizzen! Bowsprit! etc.) She then goes skittish and does a send-up of the coming meeting with Uncle
64: *Du hörst den Ruf?* Mark,* not without a little Doom [8], but mainly jolly 64
with a tripping, mocking accompaniment. Tristan is momentarily distracted by navigational matters but returns to the duet with a not-too-impressive oath of atonement – he drinks, she drinks, and as the liquor is doing its work the orchestra builds up expectations as to the effect. Is it a poison? An aperient? An aphrodisiac? A hurricane of strings susurrating up and down and all over is followed by breathless tension in the woodwind, [1] and [2].

An aphrodisiac! POW! And does it work fast! Tristan! she cries. Isolde! he moans, and they gaze [4] into each other's eyes then embrace, and the orchestra
70: *Tristan!* billows up to embrace them too.** 70

Now several rather important things happen at

72: *Wehe! Weh!* once.*** The lovers go into a feverish love trauma, 72
King Mark arrives, Brangane tries to get Isolde into her ermines, the manic crew go mad with excitement (Sea [5]), Kurwenal tries to get Tristan to attend to his duties, Brangane admits she swapped the bottles, Isolde faints. Musically this builds into a bustlingly effective finale, with the sailors doing their nut and the orchestra making huge *Meistersinger*-like noises and the dopey lovers still crying out feebly to each other, unable to relate to real life. Very satisfactory.

Act II

Prelude The prelude is a beauty** and with no effort at all manages to give birth to three entirely new mottos, first the opening motto Day [10], which keeps breaking in on the lovers' dream world, a boom then a drop followed by an upward jerky phrase – immediately followed by Frustration [11], a snaky upward scale, semitones and here followed by a hiccup and, again overlapping with Frustration, something really nice – Ecstasy [12], sweet high smooth phrases (here on the flute) swimming around in a state of great pleasure. The prelude is a midsummer night's dream and a winner.

Act II Sc 1

So to the unmistakable sounds of an operatic hunt
2 (horns in their hunting mode)* and although they are 2
mainly open notes, it must be hard to play them out there stumbling about in the brushwood in the dark. And what, for Chrissake, are they hunting *for*? Foxes, out of season and at midnight? Meanwhile, Brangane and Isolde have a great duet:

5: *Der deiner harrt* 1. Brangane tells Isolde Melot's a wrong 'un.* 5
Watch him. This is free-flowing with references to Ecstasy [12] and distant cousins of [1] and [2] are never far away. The whole of this section holds the ear pretty well enthralled.

2. Isolde tells Brangane that the aphrodisiac was only a little help to her love for Tristan, which was al-
10: *Dein Werk? O tör'ge Magd!* ways there. Late in her call to the Love Goddess,** 10
delightfully named Mrs Minne, we have a persistent new motto – a slow downward sweep, two legs the same pattern, one after the other, the second lower (Minne [13]). Now she works up to the great climax

of giving Tristan the signal by putting out the torch. This is swashbuckling loverly stuff, emphatic, committed and tuneful, with some of Ecstasy [12] and Minne [13].

Act II Sc 2

15: *Isolde! Geliebte!* The first love duet*** – twenty minutes of Wagner at 15
the top of his bent. As the lovers see each other we have a case of extreme orchestral excitement. The word climax has been used from time to time on these pages for quite minor storms. This one is a hurricane. The lovers ride into it with an exchange of rapturous one-liners (Bliss! Mine for ever! Sublime joy! etc., etc.) and then launch into loverly outpourings in which the music and the emotion take a strong lead over the text. Such content as there is covers:

1. Night is our friend, day our enemy (O bliss!)
2. A recap of past events. Do you remember? (O joy!)
3. Hooray for the aphrodisiac (my beloved)
4. More night-versus-day stuff (my treasure)

The music in the early part of the scene gusts along in a mood of high passion (Ecstasy [12], Minne [13]) but when we move into the night and day, the storm blows itself out and from here on the exchanges, although still rapturous and high voltage, become more orderly. From time to time the lovers sing together, a rare event in Wagner and a signal of something special. The Day motto [10] is worked pretty heavily here and later a new motto, Night (slow, dreamy, a
29 long first, down and a tum-tum-ti-ta [14]). The duet 29
ends with a coda, a sort of grace before meat, or rather in this case, before love (introduced by a variant of Stab [3]). After the tearing passion of the love-in this quiet hymn-like piece comes in with good effect. This duet, together with part two that follows, is the centrepiece of the opera, it is wonderfully vivid, powerful and will sweep all but the Wagner-proof off their feet. A stunner.

35: *Einsam wachend* Brangane's warning.** Useless of course. A lovely 33
slow-moving piece with words and phrases stretched out over a ravishing orchestral accompaniment.

38: *Lausch, Geliebter!* So to part two of the duet,*** which starts in a very 34
different manner, indeed one would say in a relaxed

post-coital mood but for the fact that the poor things being continuously on stage have had no coital opportunity as yet (and never get one). But the climax in the first duet was pretty well as good as an orgasm. The lovers lie calmly developing the rather sick idea of dying together to music about as far away from the smell of death as can be imagined. (A sweet lyrical melody much longer than most mottos and unmistakable, Love at Peace [15].) As they begin to get keen on the idea, another motto, destined to become the theme that opens the Liebestod, is sung by Tristan (starts rather like a hymn tune, notes of equal length, deliberate and strong, Love in Death [16]).

Brangane gives another warning (no good). Now things work up into a second mighty climax, not the great flurry that opened the first part of the duet, but a slow build-up, a lesser climax followed by a greater climax (Ecstasy [12], Love in Death [16] the chief themes) until the great joy in the idea of death together reaches a point of no return. Here we have a foretaste of the climax of the Liebestod.

This second half of the duet is every bit as good as the first. Although the emotions range only from A to B (Death to Love), their intensity is considerable, ingenious, melodious and the music is quite beautiful.

Act II Sc 3

51 Suddenly the lovers are exposed. Not in flagrante del- 51
icto, for there has been no delictus, but things look pretty bad to King Mark. There is no saying what any one of us would do if we were a king who on returning from a night's hunting discovered his best knight having it off in the gladioli bed with his bride-to-be. A muffled oath perhaps or a quick swipe with a sword. But no: King Mark tells us at great length how very disappointed he is to find Tristan with his trousers down and what bad luck it is for a king to have so treacherous a best friend. He does a lot of this to a new motto (long opener slipping down in semitones – played very deep on a solo bass clarinet – Mark Disappointed [17]). The temperature drops. This is a little boring.

Nothing to say Your Honour, Tristan replies (Tristan [1], Isolde [2], Love at Peace [15]). Then he

asks Isolde if she will follow him to his home coun-
66: *Wohin nun Tristan scheidet* try.* This trance-like appeal works around with the 66
original Tristan [1] and Isolde to [2] good effect. Isolde says yes she will (Isolde [2] and Love at Peace [15]). The world of the King and court are suspended motionless while these tender exchanges take place. But not for long. Tristan tells Melot what he thinks of him. Tristan attacks Melot. Melot wounds Tristan with noisy support from the orchestra ending with the Mark motto [17] punched out by the brass section. Musically this is a scrappy act end and indeed during the concluding twenty minutes the spell falters and we begin to consider the matter of a large scotch in the interval.

Act III

Prelude The prelude** opens gloomily, as indeed it should, for things are looking pretty bad. We hear a variant of the Isolde motto [2] (over minor-key harmony) and this is ridden hard by the strings in a desperate fash-
Sc 1 ion until we hear the shepherd's pipe. This shepherd is no country-and-western fan and his piece sounds something like a pibroch arranged for the cor anglais by Debussy. Followed by some desultory dialogue between Kurwenal and the shepherd. Tristan sur-
11: *Wo bin ich?* faces. By careful questioning of Kurwenal* he finds 11
out who he is, where he is, etc. There is general rejoicing in the orchestra and Kurwenal too, greatly cheered by signs of life in his master, gives his answers accompanied by a cheerful little polonaise (Tum-ti-tum-tum like any polonaise), followed by bustle and fuss.

17: *Dunkt dich das?* Tristan delirious.* Tristan's sick-bed thoughts 17
start grottily (Isolde [2]) but once he gets into his stride with the night versus day bit (again), the wild raving nature of the music carries us along with it (Night [14], Day [10]). He then works himself up into a mucksweat, cries out for Isolde and sinks back exhausted. Kurwenal says she is coming. He has sent for her.

26: *Mein Kurwenal* So Tristan launches into Round 2.* He tells Kur- 26
wenal what a good chap he is and then spins into another whirl of anxiety. Where's that ship? Is it coming? There it is! I see it coming! (Mad of course:

it isn't there at all.) Here we have a motto first heard at
the start of the act – Angst; a hitch upwards, down to
the starting note and a two-note tail [18]. This is repeated obsessively, faster and faster. The shepherd
signals No Boat gloomily on his cor anglais, this time
more like a dispirited yodel. The yodel reminds Tristan of his father's death, the cor anglais melts into the
orchestral texture and we move into Round 3 with sad
30: *Muss ich dich so verstehn* thoughts about childhood.* But he soon gets back to 30
yearning, yearning for death, yearning for Isolde,
yearning for her healing touch (Wound [7]). He
yearns on in similar vein with climaxes, calm patches,
sometimes up but mainly down with remarkable
stamina for a man so badly wounded. At last he sinks
back unconscious (Tristan [1], developed and
transformed).

Kurwenal thinks Tristan is dead. But he isn't. Up
and out of his blackout and into Round 4. Here we
41: *Das Schiff? Siehst du's noch nicht* have an oasis of calm.** Tristan fantasizes; he thinks 41
he can sense the ship coming towards him (and this
time he's damn right: if Kurwenal was up that watch
tower he'd see it too). He has a touching awakening
(to Isolde [2]) and then we hear again the sweet motto
of the goddess of love Minne [13]. But what's that?
The shepherd is piping like crazy and the message
clearly is Ship Ahoy! Now it's all go, Kurwenal goes
up the watch tower and gives a running commentary
as she comes in safely. She's here! He runs off to fetch
Isolde. Music apt to the scene and on the ball all the
way.

Act III Sc 2

50: *O diese Sonne!* Tristan bombs out.** In a fever of excitement he goes 50
over the edge and tears open his wound (a disgusting
thing to do). Clearly he's a goner. Isolde rushes in as
he flakes out. She calls out 'Tristan' (Ecstasy [12])
and once again 'Tristan' and almost with his last
breath he whispers 'Isolde' (Isolde [2], Stab [3] and
Gaze [4]). This is a special moment: all the world
stops and in the sudden hush the music speaks to us
person to person very quietly.

Tristan is dead. Isolde discovers this with exclama-
52: *Ha! Ich bin's, ich bin's* tions of shock as she examines his body and then with
bewildered reproaches.* How could he let her down 52

like this? She has not yet taken aboard the fact of death. Grief (or perhaps joy?) is still to strike. The music tells us her emotions are still in suspense. Isolde moves from quasi-recitatif to broken phrases and then into a run of unanswered questions with the orchestra sounding uncertain and indecisive beneath (Angst [12], Love in Death [16]).

Act III Sc 3

Now the rough and tumble of the second lot arriving. Kurwenal kills Melot and is then killed himself. All supported by high-class theatre music or, as they used to say in the film studios, hurry music. King Mark steadies things up by addressing the dead Tris-
63: *Warum, Isolde, warum mir das?* tan and then Isolde, explaining his good intentions.* 63
This dignified short aria is moving in its solemn way. It also prepares the ground for Isolde's big piece.

65: *Mild und leise* The Liebestod,*** death for love or love in death. 65
Isolde's finest hour and one of Wagner's greatest inspirations. The Love in Death motto [16] steals in quietly in the orchestra and Isolde, almost certainly, as one would think, in a trance, sees all manner of things happening to the dead Tristan – smiles, opens his eyes, gives off sparks. She hears a sweet melody, surely the one she is singing. So far the Liebestod has had only one theme, using only the wonderful Love in Death phrase [16], all the time building it higher, broader and stronger as Isolde's voice climbs with it and (now together with a variant of Stab [3]) then soars out on the topmost peak of this great climax. Great waves of sound surge out and break over the Stab [3] as Isolde sees celestial waves in her trance. The music fades into a peaceful coda as she expires (Isolde [2]). Nothing else like it in all music.

NOTES

Tristan and Isolde	Wagner's seventh opera (but see below)
First night	Königliches Hof- und Nationaltheater, Munich, 10 June 1865
Reception	Intense hostility by one faction, stunned admiration by the other
Libretto	Wagner
Source	Celtic legend, mainly as recounted by a

twelfth-century German writer, Gottfried von Strassburg

NEWS AND GOSSIP

During the early 1850s when he was still struggling with *Siegfried*, Wagner fell in love with Mathilde Wesendonck. She was the wife of one of his patrons and the affair seems to have been purely romantic, maybe because Wagner was wary of losing a really useful sponsor through adultery. Because of this affair he stopped work on *The Ring* and began to toy with the idea of an opera based on the legend of Tristan and Isolde. He set five of Mathilde's poems (she was quite a good poet) to music. That was to become the essence of *Tristan* and it is clear that he began to identify his feelings for her with Tristan's feelings for Isolde (but there is no record of their planning a love-death together). In 1857 he dived into a bout of intensive composition. By the end of the year he had finished Act I. Then there was a domestic row (over Mathilde?) and he wrote Act II in Venice in 1858 and Act III in Lucerne, completing the whole opera by August 1859. Two years for an opera that had no model, no antecedents, was very complex, very long and initiated what was pretty well an entirely new system of harmony. Not bad.

The run-up to performance was not so quick nor was it trouble-free. It took six years before his sponsor King Ludwig of Bavaria could get *Tristan* put on in Munich. Even then it was postponed. On the day fixed for the premiere the bailiffs walked into the Wagner residence and took the furniture (he was always in debt), also the Isolde lost her voice. No wonder. Even today when it has been proved that Isolde is a singable role, if only by a handful of very strong women, it is still a terrifying prospect. To face up to it before anyone knew whether it was singable at all must have been enough to frighten the voice out of anyone.

The premiere caused a lively row. Those in favour were affected pretty well as Bernard Levin is today. Wagner was a crusader as well as a man who wrote operas. He stood for enlightenment – political, philosophical, aesthetic and musical. Of those against, some were anti-Ludwig, a king who squandered taxpayers' money on the arts, and modern art too which nobody wanted and nobody understood. Some found they couldn't stand up to the blitzkrieg that *Tristan* unleashes on the emotions. Some were anti-modernists, some pro-Jewish and some just thought his music a load of old (or rather new) rubbish. The argument filled the arts pages of the Sunday supplements for years to come and was good for a silly-season feature right up to the turn of the century.

But as the years rolled on, and excluding the monster *Ring*, *Tristan* came to hold second place to *Meistersinger* amongst the serious Wagner public. They began to rumble the overblown pretensions of *Lohengrin* and *Tannhäuser*, and *Dutchman* was not real Wagner and *Parsifal* was too long and too holy. It also came to be No. 1 in the quality stakes – fully integrated musico-poetic synthesis and stuff like that. Today opera managements draw a deep breath before pencilling *Tristan* in on the schedule and this is for two reasons: it is almost impossible to cast and it takes an age to rehearse it properly. But it sits in the CD catalogue with several splendid versions and if the Liebestod were picked as the theme for the next Olympic games, it would, like 'Nessun dorma', undoubtedly get into the Top Ten. But preferably not sung by three sopranos.

COMMENT

Tristan was something of a musical time bomb. At first the musical world was stunned. Here was a way of writing music that was entirely new. The classical key structure and harmonic system had been chucked. Here there was a sort of stock pot full of motto-like fragments which were pulled out from time to time and slid about all over the place in a sea of chromaticism. A fellow could scarcely tell what key he was in never mind get a grip on the shape. There were no arias, no recitatifs, only one set piece. Etc. It wasn't until the next century that the time bomb exploded. A little preliminary burst from Debussy and his fellows, but the big bang came with Schoenberg and the Second Viennese school who picked up the baton from *Tristan* and chucked out the whole diatonic system as well. A lot of people (misguided of course) will wish that Wagner had stuck to Flying Dutchmen. In many ways *Tristan* is a bit of a wonder. For one thing it is all of a piece. In the much earlier trio *Tannhäuser*, *Lohengrin* and the *Dutchman*, Wagner was trying to shake off old operatic forms and force his way into his own very private world of Music Drama. In all three there are bits of old and bits of new. During the twenty years it took for Wagner to compose *The Ring* his style was growing up through adolescence to maturity. This means that *The Ring* is patchy, with items fit for the old grand opera in *Götterdämmerung* (written first) and with *Rhinegold* (written last) the nearest to his new ideal of Music Drama. *Meistersinger*, thought his best by many, is still more or less a series of set pieces with other bits between. *Tristan* comes in the middle of all this and he struck a style that was quite distinct and had a perfect unity. It's a style that many find hard to take, especially when ladled out in such huge doses. But the sheer beauty of the music holds most people under its spell and the use of mottos is not nearly so distracting as in *The Ring*. Here the mottos are about ideas rather than things. There are no mottos about such things as anvils, dragons, fire. Indeed it is often hard to know what the mottos are about, if they are about anything definite at all. There is one that has been variously labelled by the Wagner scribes as 'Tristan's Honour', 'Morold' and 'Isolde's Anger'. A pretty wide choice. But the mottos work their way into the texture in a highly satisfactory manner. There is no need to be a motto spotter to enjoy *Tristan*. The mottos can become subliminal.

Tristan also scores on the matter of plot. It is simple, it moves at a steady pace. The central characters are all strongly drawn. Along with *Meistersinger*, it has the most convincing cast with not one dud, if one excludes the unimportant Melot. King Mark is a wimp, it is true, but he is an honourable if long-winded wimp. His headmasterly speech to Tristan when caught with his trousers down is the only real longueur in the piece. Otherwise it trundles along with hardly a pause. Kurwenal's quasi-comic song in Act I is a welcome break and does its work well.

The high spots in *Tristan* are high indeed but they rise from an already high plateau and not from sea level. Thus they don't stand out as much as do the three-star items in the other operas. But the preludes to Acts I and II are both wonderfully compact, closely-knit orchestral pieces. The Tristan/Isolde duet in Act I is a bit of a marvel in its variation of pace and mood and the finale to Act I gives it a resounding finish. Act II holds the great love duet between Tristan and Isolde. It is the central item of the opera and in it Wagner reaches maximum thrust. Some would say it is the greatest love duet ever written. There is less high-voltage music in Act III, but we are of course moving steadily towards the great climacteric – the Liebestod. Even if you can't stand the sentiment, you have to admit that this number has a great tune. As a finale it lacks the earth-shaking size of the last ten minutes of *Götterdämmerung* but although smaller in scale, it has the same manic intensity of feeling and we leave the opera house suitably stunned.

And yet there are reasons why *Tristan* can't be counted amongst the select group of alpha-plus operas, and they are three. The first is that the world of knights, ladies, honour and romantic love à la Alfred Lord Tennyson doesn't grab us as it did our great-grandfathers. Their eyes would grow misty as they read aloud the tale of Lancelot and Guinevere. Today we find Norman Mailer a more convincing read. Jung, Freud and Germaine Greer have done terrible damage to the great lovers of history as recorded in saga and story book. *Tristan* is therefore only wholly acceptable to those persons who like their operas clothed in white samite, mystic, wonderful. There are not many of them left.

The second is about the vibes we find in the music. Whilst *Tristan* will bowl over most first-time listeners pretty soon, as they lie emotionally prone listening to the second, third and fourth hour of this music of power and beauty, there begins to lurk at the back of the mind – aside from more normal reactions such as The mixture is too rich, I can't stand it, I'm suffocating, bring me a brandy and ten minutes of Scarlatti quick, or What time is tea? – apart from these, the question that grows is one that challenges the foundations of belief in Wagner and it is this: isn't this all just a little Hollywood? Hollywood in the sky, of course, but still with the phoney sentimentality of Hollywood at its core.

The last bugaboo about *Tristan* relates to Wagner's close interest in sex and death. The two treated separately are of course the stuff of all drama, but it does seem that Wagner himself got a sexual kick out of putting them together and creating a musical orgasm out of a love-death. This is moving towards the territory of the snuff movie and whereas in *Tristan* there are only three deaths compared to *The Ring*'s fifteen, and two of them are military, there is a sort of sublime gloating over the central death that is disagreeable. It is no good the Wagner lobby making the case for Wagner as a genius who had the guts to attack our primitive instincts through dwarfs, incest and magic sex instead of making operas about polite society. It is not that at all: the death-love in Wagner is decadent, not primitive. This is the Wagner that liked to spend time stroking velvet, the Wagner that invented Venusberg and Kundry and amongst the clouds of scented emotion Isolde describes in the Liebestod we pick up a whiff of perfumed obscenity. So, at the end of the day, alpha, no plus.

Il Trovatore (The troubadour)

Exotic melodrama

Verdi

The one where the gypsy woman throws the wrong baby onto the bonfire and thus causes the grown-up unburnt baby to be killed by his brother.

CAST

The Count of Luna, General in the King's army	Baritone
Ferrando, a Captain, ditto	Bass
Leonora, a lady-in-waiting	Soprano
Ines, her companion	Soprano
Azucena, a gypsy woman	Mezzo
Manrico, her presumed son, rebel commander	Tenor
Ruiz, one of Manrico's NCOs	Tenor
Servants, messengers, gypsies etc.	

4 acts: running time 2 hrs 20 mins

STORY

Stand by for the most confused baby-swapping plot in the business. So let's get that sorted first.

Count Luna II had a younger brother called Garcia. One day when Garcia was a baby an old gypsy woman was found breathing over the cradle. Garcia fell ill. Garcia's father Count Luna I believed the gypsy had cast a spell on the baby. Disregarding the due processes of law he had her hunted down and burned at the stake. The gypsy's daughter Azucena understandably mad for revenge seized – as she thought – the wretched baby Garcia and chucked him on the fire. Mistake! It was the wrong baby – her own (and nobody noticed). Thus she was left with Garcia and brought him up as her son under the name of Manrico, our hero, true brother to our villain, Count Luna II. Get it? Then the rest is a pushover.

Act I: The Duel
Sc 1 Count Luna's palace

It is fifteenth-century Spain: there is a revolt against the king whose general Count Luna (baddie) is asleep whilst numerous soldiers and Captain Ferrando snooze on guard. They gossip: Luna is jealous of rival anonymous street singer (troubadour): Ferrando tells the story of baby Garcia (see above) but doesn't of course get the baby-swap bit, reports only that Garcia was burnt to death. Also that the old gypsy still haunts quite a lot.

Act I Sc 2 Night scene: the garden of the palace

Leonora lurks with intent – waiting for the troubadour? She tells Ines she fancies him greatly. Ines says watch it. Count Luna besotted by love gropes towards Leonora's staircase – his intent is uncertain. Troubadour Manrico arrives and sings a serenade: Leonora listens: the Count confronts the troubadour: the rivals exit with swords drawn: Leonora passes out.

Act II: The Gypsy
Sc 1 A gypsy camp

The gypsies are at their early morning shift. Azucena tells the gypsies of her mother's dreadful death (maybe for the hundredth time): the gypsies exit. Azucena tells the story again in full detail to Manrico who says golly so I am not really your son. Yes you are says Azucena the crazy lying gimp (and by saying this she confuses everyone including Manrico and the audience). Manrico tells her some uncanny power prevented him killing Luna during their recent duel.

Despatches arrive: Manrico has been posted to newly captured town Castellor. News comes that Leonora believes Manrico was killed in the duel: she is entering a convent in Castellor (coincidence). Azucena tells Manrico don't go but he goes, thus leaving his mother to save his lover.

Act II Sc 2 Courtyard of convent in Castellor. Night

The dreaded Luna and his men are laying an ambush to abduct Leonora as she arrives with loads of nuns on her way to sign on for Christ. Luna seizes her but Manrico suddenly appears. He is generally thought to be a ghost (reports of his death grossly exaggerated). Manrico says he's not dead and just then Ruiz and the Manrico Marines arrive: they frustrate the Count's ambush, carry off Leonora and the nuns have never seen anything like it in their lives before.

Act III: The Gypsy's Son
Sc 1 A camp site outside Castellor

Another camp and the Count again. A suspicious civilian is brought in for questioning – Azucena. Ferrando identifies her as the daughter of that burnt lady who breathed on baby Garcia. She admits she is Manrico's mother (stupid). Luna says lock up this foul and wicked gypsy.

Act III Sc 2 Waiting room outside a chapel in Castellor

Leonora and Manrico are waiting at the church door: their intention, marriage. News comes that Luna has got his hands on Azucena and a suitable bonfire is being built for her. This time Manrico forsakes fiancée for Mum: he rushes off to save her.

Act IV: The Execution
Sc 1 A prison room in the castle of Aliaferia

Manrico's defence of Castellor has failed: he is in prison. Ruiz and Leonora appear with vague thoughts of saving him but no, the dreaded Luna turns up (as usual with men at his back) and orders that Azucena and Manrico both go for the chop on the next day. Leonora offers Luna a deal: if he lets the prisoners go free she will let him have a nice time with her. It's a deal says Luna and lets her go to tell Manrico that he's off the hook. On the way Leonora decides to avoid a fate worse than death by taking a shot of arsenic from a small reservoir in her ring which she carries around in case of emergencies like this.

Act IV Sc 2 A prison cell

Azucena and Manrico are chained up. Azucena is gloomy at the prospect of being burned like her mother: Manrico recalls happy gypsy days of yesteryear. Leonora comes to tell them the good news: Manrico realizes how she got them their freedom and tells her he can't do with unfaithfulness (ungrateful pig) and it is all over between them. Leonora says she is dying anyway. Manrico is now stunned by her purity, devotion etc.

But they have dallied too long! The dreaded Luna appears (men at his back) and as Leonora dies he has Manrico topped: he dags Azucena to the window so she can watch this nasty scene. Azucena tells him with some glee that he has just executed his own brother and at last everyone has got the story straight.

MINUTES FROM START — LOOK OUT FOR

Act I Sc 1

4: *Di due figli* — Ferrando's full account of the old gypsy's doings – the Ballad of the Burnt Baby* – has at its heart a jaunty refrain with what Verdi may well have intended to be a gypsy lilt. 4

Act I Sc 2

Leonora has two solos about her love for her blessed
troubadour: in the first she is conventionally agree-
20: *Di tale amor* able, but in the second* as chirpy as a caged linnet. 20
27: *Qual voce* A good roustabout trio:** Leonora infatuated, 27
Luna crazy with jealousy, Manrico manly.

Act II Sc 1

The opening singalong climaxes in what is known as
7: *Chi del gitano* the Anvil Chorus** in which the gypsies (not nor- 7
mally celebrated as primary producers) strike anvils
as they sing about the value of gypsy girls as motiv-
ators of higher productivity. Lots of zing and a good
tune. Recurs after Azucena's description of an execution by fire.

Azucena gives Manrico the full works – relives the
horror of the dreaded night and tells the truth in a
9: *Soli or siamo!* duet** of high drama. 9

The duet gets airborne again (after a patch of
pretty heavy stuff) when Manrico tells of his inability
to kill Luna when he was at his mercy and Azucena
17: *Mal reggendo* says go on do it next time:* it continues in high style 17
to the end of the scene.

Act II Sc 2

As so often in Verdi the nasty Luna is given a beauti-
25: *Il balen del suo sorriso* ful solo** fit for an unblemished hero. This is fol- 25
lowed by further bursts of lyric beauty which sound
pure enough but which can only be inspired by his
bestial lust for Leonora (as opposed to Manrico's
pure love).

The final ensemble: Manrico turns out not to be a
38: *E deggio e posso* ghost: look out especially for Leonora's descant.*** 38

Act III Sc 1

The soldiers face the prospect of battle with a zest
known only to soldiers in opera. Two choruses: the
2: *Squilli, echeggi la tromba* second very strong.*** 2

A great concerted piece:*** first Azucena sings of 7
7: *Giorni poveri vivea* gypsy life: is recognized by Ferrando: the Count decides to avenge his dead brother: high emotion: great
pace and tuneful with it.

Act III Sc 2

Manrico sings of marriage and death in a mildly beau-
13: *Ah sì, ben mio* tiful fashion.* 13

Manrico reacts vigorously to the sight of the flames
18: *Di quella pira* on the funeral pyre: a memorable tune** and a rous- 18

ing ensemble finale to the scene (but meanwhile the flames must be getting a real hold).

Act IV Sc 1

Leonora sends a sigh through the walls of the prison
3: *D'amor sull'ali rosee*
to her lover. A sad little aria* with taxing final sighs in 3
altissimo.

Next an impressive scene: mysterious voices
within breathe a requiem: Manrico sings his farewells
8: *Ah! che la morte*
from his cell.** Leonora replies over a dead-march 8
accompaniment and ends the exchange with a pas-
12: *Tu vedrai che amore*
sionate declaration of her love*** in a big and lovely 12
aria again with a display-piece ending.

Luna arrives: the rest of the scene is marvellously
vivid duet: Leonora pleads for mercy in a passage that
sets the pulse racing: a final impassioned plea from
22: *Mira di acerbe*
her** then (Verdi having inexplicably fluffed the 22
great moment when she offers him sexual satisfaction
in exchange for Manrico's release) a wonderful paean
26: *Vivrà! . . . contende il giubilo*
of triumph from her*** and a prospective gloat from 26
him.

Act IV Sc 2

The long (too long?) gloomy two-handed opening
scene is musically impressive – especially when
mother and son recall happier days gypsying around
34: *Riposa, o madre*
in the mountains.** 34

The final scene is a triumph of sustained inspiration: first the reunion duet between Leonora and
38: *Che! . . . non m'inganna*
Manrico,** then his accusation of unfaithfulness: 38
their exchanges halted by Azucena's 'AH!' followed
41: *Ai nostri monti*
by a golden trio*** in which passion and fear melt 41
away into soft persuasion: then when Manrico realizes the truth (she's a martyr not a whore) they
joyfully reconcile: and finally Leonora's death and
the rough brutality of the last scene – though whether
Luna has time to take in the full import of Azucena's
message ('You've murdered your brother') is doubtful: certainly no supernatural urge restrained *him*.

NOTES

Il Trovatore	Verdi's eighteenth opera
First night	Teatro Apollo, Rome, 19 January 1853
Reception	Stupendous. See below

Libretto Cammarano, completed Bardare
Source An original Cammarano

NEWS AND GOSSIP

On the first night, although the streets around the theatre were flooded and the prices had been pushed up to Pavarotti level, *Trovatore* was a sell-out and got so much applause that the last act was encored in its entirety. The libretto was that rare thing – an original, written by Verdi's old partner Cammarano, the doyen of Neapolitan librettists and a tough old dog. Verdi kept asking Cammarano for 'something new and fresh' from the libretto, which he didn't get, so when Cammarano died in the July of 1852 before the libretto was finished, Verdi injected some ideas of his own – for instance, making the Act IV Sc 1 offstage chorus, Leonora's aria 'Tu vedrai che amore' and Manrico's troubadour's song 'Ah! che la morte' all happen at once (they had been planned to follow each other in succession), cutting the conventional ensemble finale to the second act and ending instead with shouts, curses, yells of rage, etc. There is the usual stuff about the opera having been written 'in one month'. Unlikely. The notices were raves and picked out its 'Castilian characteristics' as being distinctive – a quality we don't much notice today. Coming between *Rigoletto* (hunchback) and *Traviata* (call girl), *Trovatore* reverts to old-style operatic types plus gypsies. The topic of filial and maternal love was also picked out as a new thing for opera. It was more usual for fathers to kill (or nearly kill) beloved sons (*Idomeneo* etc.). *Trovatore* immediately moved up to the top in the Italian repertory and has remained there ever since.

COMMENT

Verdi could not have foreseen that almost within his lifetime baby-swapping plots were to become ludicrous through over-use, thanks particularly to W. S. Gilbert. Nor perhaps was he to blame for thinking that weirdo gypsies would give the opera a Spanish flavour (none of the music sounds in the least bit Spanish today). But surely he could have sorted out the baby-burning bit (a) with less repetition (b) with more clarity. When, on the third time out, Azucena tells the true story and then denies its truth, she really cocks things up for all and sundry except old *Trovatore* hands. It is also strange that Azucena does not tell Luna that Manrico is his brother before and not after he has killed him, thus certainly saving the life of her 'son' and probably her own as well, matters which had been concerning her greatly throughout the early part of Act II. People who say 'What do you expect of an opera plot?' should get the answer – credibility, as in the best operas, such as *Figaro*, *Carmen* and *Meistersinger*, etc.

But no plot weakness can undermine the power and drive of the *Trovatore* score. After a slow start (Ferrando's account of the baby-burning is a bit of a bore) the opera gathers pace with the trio that ends Act I and never looks back. The gypsy camp with its choruses and campfires may be too close to parody for comfort but it is great popular music and soon we are into more serious stuff with the duet between Azucena and Manrico and from then on the tension does not flag right up to the last act whose first wither-wringing scene prepares us for the last glorious fifteen minutes of the opera where the wily Verdi deploys his uncanny sense of staging high drama to utterly convincing music. Whilst not pure gold all through, the high spots of *Trovatore* must ensure it an alpha and its high quota of pop music has put it permanently amongst the top of the pops. Warning: *Trovatore* demands four top-class singers. With three out of four it gets by, with only two or less it can be a pain.

Turandot

Chinese extravaganza

Puccini

The one where a prince avoids decapitation by winning a word game, and nobody sleeps.

CAST

Altoum, Emperor of all China		Tenor
Turandot, Princess and Altoum's Heir Apparent		Soprano
Ping, Chancellor	whimsical Privy Councillors	Baritone
Pang, Minister of Supply	whimsical Privy Councillors	Tenor
Pong, Minister of Food	whimsical Privy Councillors	Tenor
Timur, exiled King of Tartary		Bass
Liù, his (female) slave and devoted servant		Soprano
Calaf, Timur's son, also in exile		Tenor
A mandarin		

3 acts: running time 2 hrs 20 mins

STORY

Act I The Imperial City: dawn

It's Peking, China, in the Middle Ages also fairyland. A mandarin reads a decree to the populace: Princess Turandot will marry any available male royal who can pass the I.Q. test (three riddles). Failed candidates will be decapitated. This announcement stirs the populace to blood lust and mob violence: the police get tough: an old man is knocked over (Timur disguised): Liù calls Help! A young man (Calaf disguised) helps. Thus father and son both on the run meet by (fairytale) chance.

The populace await moonrise when the last failed candidate, a Persian prince, is due for the chop. The moon rises: the crowd are struck by the peely-wally appearance of the Persian prince. Turandot enters: the crowd shout 'Mercy on this poor shrimp': Don't be such softies she says, go ahead, chop him. Calaf intending to curse Turandot as the cause of family misfortunes is now bowled over by her beauty, sadistic sex appeal etc.

Calaf decides to go for the riddle test: he runs towards the great gong (candidates gong up for entry): Pingpongers interpose and attempt to dissuade him: that riddle test serves as a conduit to the slaughterhouse they say (the severed heads of previous contestants are on display all around: quite disgusting): best push off young man they say. Turandot's court ladies interpose: kindly belt up they say: Princess Turandot is taking a nap.

Pingpongers continue to attempt to dissuade Calaf from the riddle test: they call up ghosts of failed contestants: Calaf is steadfast in his intention: the snuff squad file through carrying the head of the peely-wally Persian. Timur and Liù join in entreaties to Calaf: they all say drop it you madman. Calaf remains stubborn: he strikes the gong three times.

Act II Sc 1 A pavilion: interior Imperial palace

The Pingpongers natter on in the manner of quaint operatic Chinamen. Life was OK they say until Turandot got active: now she's chopping off heads right left and centre: it's becoming repetitious, this year's count is thirteen already. They all desire a sabbatical in their country cottages: much preferable to organizing state butchery. They run over the characteristics of some outstanding victims. All wish Turandot could find a lusty husband. They chatter on. (Note: no plot development whatever in this scene.)

Act II Sc 2 Large square adjacent to the Imperial palace

Eight wise men come on each carrying three scrolls containing answers to the I.Q. test [twenty-four scrolls for answers of only three words? Ed.] Emperor Altoum says that refereeing the riddle test is a disagreeable but legally necessary task. He tells Calaf to get out from under: the odds against success are a hundred to one.

Turandot appears: she explains that her feminist grandma Lou-Ling a top-class empress was dethroned raped and killed by men: her revenge on men is death by riddle. Turandot asks riddle one: Calaf's answer 'Hope': bullseye say the wise men: one nil to the challenger. Second answer 'Blood' and third 'Turandot' both correct. Three nil. How provoking! says Turandot: Daddy don't make me marry this clever dick, please not. We must play by the rules Turandot says Emperor Dad. Sporty Calaf makes a gratuitous counter challenge (crazy fool): if Turandot discovers his real name by dawn she can chop him. Emperor says I sanction that deal.

Act III Sc 1 The garden of the palace: night

Heralds proclaim Nessun Dorma: universally understood to mean – wakey wakey – no sleep (until Calaf's name is discovered). Calaf estimates his chances of success as odds-on. The Pingpongers fear Turandot's reaction to a forced marriage: they offer Calaf sex orgies, a huge cheque, anything to get him off the premises.

Liù and Timur are hauled in: Liù admits she is aware of Calaf's name. Turandot is called to hear it. Liù is tortured: she keeps mum: Turandot asks why is she so brave? Liù says it is the power of love: Turandot sets the torturers on again: Liù stabs herself fearing she will break down. Calaf and Turandot are left tête-à-tête. Calaf gets physical: he embraces Turandot: she succumbs to the power of love. Calaf tells her his name but Turandot has gone off the idea of murder. The lovers go before the Emperor: Turandot says 'I now know Calaf's identity: his name is love.'

MINUTES FROM START

LOOK OUT FOR

Act I

One of the longest sequences of chorus–solo–chorus in opera to date – nearly 20 minutes off and on and never a dull one. After three explosive chords and some Chin-Chin stuff we plunge into a sea of Italian sound. The mob are baying for blood and strewn amongst this we get plot-setting exchanges (Timur/Liù/Calaf) which ride melodiously on the surface of

10: *Perchè tarda la luna?*

the ongoing chorus. So to the moonrise chorus,** 10
hushed, expectant, sustained until the old thing heaves over the horizon. Finally we have the pleas for mercy (useless) again with solo lines above. It gets more Chin-Chin as we go along. There is one main Chin-Chin theme which catches the ear (to do with Turandot's bloody-mindedness).

The first set-piece solo. Liù's heart is breaking: an affecting appeal to Calaf in something like the old

25: *Signore, ascolta!*

Puccini style.** 25

28: *Non piangere, Liù!*

Calaf's response,** firm sympathetic and with a 28
fine lyrical line and climax. Leading to the surging ensemble in which everyone tries to stop the fool from beating the gong – which of course he does. Big stuff over an insistent four-note motif.

Act II Sc 1

The whole of this scene is taken up with a trio by the Pingpongers. These three volatile characters seem to encourage Puccini's most tiresome Chin-Chin streak: they reminisce, fantasize but also indulge in a

3: *Ho una casa*

rather lovely bout of nostalgia* for their country cot- 3
tages. Quiet and dreamy (harp, celeste and flutes).

Act II Sc 2

12: *Prelude*

A noisy start.* Lots of pomp and circumstance veer- 12

ing between Chin-Chinery and a German brass band on its day out.

22: *In questa reggia* Turandot's first utterance:* heavy going at first (a lot of Chinese history) but suddenly switching to 22
26: *Mai nessun m'avrà!* sunny Italy with a lyrical burst and a big big tune,*** taken up by Calaf and rounded off by the chorus. 26

36: *Turandot! Turandot!* The final sequences of Act II:* a rousing 'Good Luck Boy' for Calaf from the assembled throng; the big Chin-Chin tune back again from Act I; Turandot's request to be excused marriage and dad's negative; all strength 9. Calaf comes in with a foretaste of 'Nessun dorma' and then a final powerful Chin-Chin salute to the emperor. A terrific finale. 36

Act III Sc 1

Made famous by football, three tenors, and its entry
3: *Nessun dorma!* into the Top Ten, this wonderful aria*** shines out, pure Italian gold, amidst all the surrounding exotica. It has a sweeping line, a great climax and if you don't fall for this you might as well give up hope of a good relationship with Italian opera. 3

14: *Tanto amore segreto* Liù's big number** before she kills herself. Vivid and really moving. With a lush string accompaniment. Turandot is beginning to weaken by the end of 14
25: *Principessa di morte!* the duet** with Calaf. Three longish solo chunks to start with, not all that easy on the ear, then things improve greatly with a series of one-liners. Finally the big duet tune from Act II ('Mai nessun') comes storming in and sweeps us along with it. 25

Act III Sc 2

We have a battery of earsplitting fanfares to prepare us for Turandot's surprise package – 'His name is Love' – then we can sit back and revel in a choral
40: *Amor! O sole!* replay of 'Nessun dorma'*** until the curtain comes down. 40

NOTES

Turandot	Puccini's twelfth and last opera
First night	La Scala, Milan, 25 April 1926
Reception	See below
Libretto	Adami and Simoni
Source	An eighteenth-century play by Carlo Gozzi – adapted by Schiller

NEWS AND GOSSIP

Just after World War I Max Reinhardt was the wonder boy of the European theatre, rather as Peter Brook is today (and both of them strangely enough produced stunning *Midsummer Night's Dreams*). Max Reinhardt put on a stage version of *Turandot* which set the chattering classes agog, including Puccini. He got together with librettists Adami and Simoni saying let's make an opera which will 'modernize and bring human warmth to the old cardboard figures' (which they failed to do, see COMMENT below) and off they went on the long, long trail of creating a new type of opera. The story appealed to Puccini's sadistic streak. (Gozzi's play had a lot of mayhem in it but not the scenes of Liù's torture and death, which came out of the Maestro's own and at times rather nasty imagination.) The construction of the libretto ran its usual nit-picking course then work on the score began and by March 1924 Puccini had finished everything up to Liù's death scene. In November he died of a heart attack. His sketches for the last twenty minutes of Act III were completed by a good competent pro chosen by Toscanini, one Alfano. At the premiere in Milan Toscanini laid down his baton at the point where Puccini's work ended, saying 'This opera ends here because at this point the Maestro died' (sensation!), but in later performances he took it through to the end. There was the usual kerfuffle over how true to Puccini's intentions Alfano's final bit might be. Toscanini cut his stuff by some five minutes (Toscanini's version is described here) but to most of us today it sounds as if the boy did pretty well (actually he was over fifty). Anyway, as with Sussmeyr's and Mozart's *Requiem*, we simply don't know and can't know how near the understudies got to what the masters might have wanted. On the first night *Turandot*'s first act got a good hand, the second not so good and the third was stopped dead in its tracks by Toscanini's antics. The critics tried desperately hard to like it, and some succeeded. *Turandot* did not catch on immediately. Only after World War II did the major houses start to revive it. But now it probably rates halfway down the Puccini popularity scale. Only big houses can put it on.

COMMENT

Some find *Turandot* tough going, but even if you have a life-and-death struggle with the old thing, you know that there is some great stuff here. It is a very odd piece, for aside from the excuse it gives producers and designers to go mad with spectacular Chinoiserie, the story itself is more the stuff of ballet than of opera – and a crazy mismatch, one would have thought, with a composer who had made his name by bringing verismo into traditional story-book opera. Of verismo there is none: the fairy story is as conventional as *Cinderella*, the only interesting adjustment being Puccini's treatment of Liù (which incidentally makes her into a rival heroine to Turandot and a much more cuddly one). The twist given to the plot by Calaf's totally unnecessary vow to put his head on the block if Turandot can find out his name seems a bit silly even for a fairy story. The Pingpongers are a tiresome trio who don't exist as separate characters but remain as Siamese triplets, not funny nor contributing anything to the plot. (Again they would have been a good act in ballet.) But the story is full of 'strong situations' of the kind the Italian maestros were always seeking and it gives Puccini plenty of openings for his brand of *Aida*-like big stuff and for cliffhangers (will he/she won't he/she?) and a dose of the Neronics as well. (When accused of liking sadistic plots he admitted to 'a Neronic streak'.) The score is ingenious, complex and neurotically active most of the time, not many patches of sweet tranquillity. It is also immensely powerful and keeps hitting you in the solar plexus just as he intended it should. But it is not always easy on the ear and the intrusive Chin-Chin flavour is hard to live with. This is not real Chinese music, as anyone who has been to China can tell, indeed although he is reputed to have used several tunes he heard on a Chinese musical box (!) it has no audible relationship to the music of the Dizi, Suona, Pipa, Yanquin or Banhu etc. Only the big gong, which produces a noise, not a musical note, sounds truly Chinese. So why did he encumber himself with all this phoney Chin-Chin paraphernalia? There is some discussion about this in the composer section, but briefly it may have been because he wanted to avoid the charge of the Same Old Stuff Again (*Bohème*, *Tosca*) and also of being Old-fashioned (Verdi with wrong notes) so he strove to keep up with the whole-toners, the pentatonickers, the Bergs, Schoenbergs and the Jonesbergs, at the same time shying away from an encounter on their home ground. Thus he moved the playing field to Japan (*Butterfly*), California (*Fanciulla*) and China (*Turandot*). Some of the pentatonic, modal and whole-tone stuff comes off wonderfully well and all of it is artful, but it is only when he jacks in the Chin-Chin and reverts to his native idiom ('Mai nessun', 'Nessun dorma') that we really warm to *Turandot*. Otherwise we admire but do not greatly love nor do we have any real feeling for any of the characters, except possibly Liù. But it is a monumental piece of work and the finales to Acts I and II can bring the house down. It is absolutely dependent upon its production values. Where you can put on *Bohème* in a barn, *Turandot* needs, if not Wembley, at least a Grand Opera House, loads of dancers, dozens of extras, a huge chorus and stunning spectacle. And at least three great singers. Given that, it can be an alpha.

Twilight of the Gods *see* Götterdämmerung *under* Ring, The

Valkyrie *see under* Ring, The

I Vespri Siciliani (The Sicilian Vespers)

Historical drama

Verdi

The one where a boatload of thirteenth-century gentry sail by whilst licentious French soldiery sexually assault Sicilian women and where wedding bells don't and then do start a bloody massacre.

CAST

Monforte, French Governor of Sicily	Baritone
Arrigo, his long-lost son, Sicilian patriot	Tenor
Elena, Sicilian noble lady, also a patriot	Soprano
Procida, patriot leader	Bass
Danieli } Elena's servants	Tenor
Ninetta } Elena's servants	Contralto
Béthune, senior French officer	Bass
Vaudemont, junior French officer	Bass
Tebaldo } French soldiers	Tenor
Roberto } French soldiers	Baritone
Manfredo, a Sicilian	Tenor

5 acts: running time 3 hrs 20 mins

STORY

Act I The main square Palermo with Elena's palace, Governor's palace and army barracks in view

We are in French-occupied Sicily in the year of our Lord 1282 precisely. Some French troops boozing and horsing around arouse the resentment of native Sicilian drinkers. The French are given a warning by Béthune against fraternization with Sicilian women since Sicilian men are exceedingly jealous.

The beautiful Duchess Elena exits from the chapel after prayers for the soul of her brother killed by the French when taken hostage. The licentious soldiery demand a song: she obliges with a patriotic ditty, a thinly disguised call to arms. Mayhem breaks out quelled by the immensely impressive appearance of Governor Monforte: natives and soldiers slink off. Monforte and Elena plus well-educated servants Danieli and Ninetta indulge in a philosophical singsong.

Arrigo comes in mighty pleased at being acquitted of charges of treason: good old Sicilian legal system says he, I got a fair trial: not so says Monforte I fixed it. Others exit and Monforte quizzes Arrigo about his C.V., family background: Arrigo is riled when Monforte offers him service in the French army: you can stuff that up for starters says Arrigo: I dislike you intensely for strong political plus personal reasons so stop this stuff. Watch it boy says Monforte and one word of advice leave that Elena alone. Why? asks Arrigo. Never mind why, says Monforte, do it. Shan't says Arrigo.

Act II Sicilian countryside scene. Chapel of St Rosalia near, sea behind

The exiled patriot leader Procida disembarks glad to be back from fruitless worldwide search for allies, arms, men: he whips up revolutionary fervour with the reception committee. Elena and Arrigo come on: the three plot an uprising that evening nearby the (onstage) chapel of St Rosalia where a multi-wedding event is already billed. Procida goes off to pursue revolutionary business. Arrigo tells Elena he is stuck on her and promises to avenge her brother's death. Do that boy she says and it's a deal – I am yours.

Béthune arrives with an invite for Arrigo to the Governor's ball that night. Not likely says Arrigo: you rude sod says Béthune you are under arrest. They exit. Procida comes on and is told Arrigo is in clink. The wedding parties assemble and start dancing a tarantella: the lecherous French soldiery come on: they fraternize egged on by crafty Procida pretending his friendship for the French. Things get physical: there's sexual harassment: some soldiers hustle off selected girls with rape clearly in mind. Sicilians are chicken says Procida: the French pinch their girls: the Sicilians show no action no guts: he stirs up revolutionary fervour: suddenly a boatload of gentry sails by singing madrigals: this further infuriates the now seething natives. Procida says if the revolution gets under way he will stab Monforte to death at the ball tonight.

Act III Sc 1 Monforte's study

Monforte recalls his separation from his wife: he fingers the deathbed letter from her telling him Arrigo is his son. Broody and paternally deprived he sends for Arrigo, shows him the letter: Arrigo shock horror exits in disarray.

Act III Sc 2 Hall in Monforte's palace: a ball in progress

Enter Monforte: he signals the proceedings to commence. Ballets! The four seasons: usual paraphernalia: zephyrs naiads fauns satyrs etc. etc.:

the guest dancers thank the pros: good show! Masked Elena and Procida tell Arrigo the plans to assassinate Monforte. They give him a secret conspirator's badge. Arrigo is upset, does not wish to condone patricide. Monforte enters: Arrigo tries to warn him in coded double talk: Elena steps up with dagger poised: Arrigo interposes: Monforte calls out the military: everyone wearing a conspirator's badge is arrested. Monforte tries once again to recruit Arrigo for France: no good. Meanwhile all the conspirators shout abuse at Arrigo – traitorous dog etc.

Act IV The castle courtyard: portcullis, galleries, etc.

Arrigo gets a pass from Monforte to visit the conspirators: he hopes to persuade Elena to forgive him: she is adamant until she learns of the father/son relationship: she softens. A love duet ensues. Hard man Procida is led on: Monforte orders the execution of Elena and Procida. Arrigo begs for mercy: if no mercy would Monforte please execute him with his mates. Procida says he does not wish to be executed in company with a disreputable person such as Arrigo. A chorus of offstagers (friars) lends gravitas and atmosphere.

Monforte says OK I will spare them if you enter into filial relationship. Elena and Procida say don't do it: better we die. Arrigo is in a fix. The portcullis ups to show the executioner flexing his muscles sharpening axe and all. Arrigo tries to rush the executioner: Monforte interposes. Arrigo cries 'Father' three times: Monforte is satisfied the terms of his deal have been fulfilled so he frees the prisoners also decrees that Arrigo marry Elena that night: everyone is quite delighted except hard man Procida.

Act V The castle grounds: a chapel visible

The wedding guests sing usual wedding stuff: Elena is as happy as Larry: Arrigo is also happy to marry Elena but still broody. Procida comes on and tells Elena his secret plan: when the wedding bells sound uprising natives will fall on the French and slaughter them. Elena is in a fix: she feels she cannot reveal Procida's plan to Arrigo who says What's up you dumb or something? Elena decides: the wedding is off. Arrigo is upset. Procida is cross at double-crossing Elena (no wedding bells no uprising). Monforte arrives and says nonsense give me your hands you are now married: the bells ring out: a highly successful massacre commences.

MINUTES FROM START	LOOK OUT FOR	
Act I		
0	The overture: perhaps Verdi's best** (why so seldom heard outside the opera house?). As usual it contains	0

many of the main themes of the opera.

The first act is slow to start with a standard chorus (French v. Sicilians) and plot-setting exchanges between the French military men. The first musical
17: *In alto mare* event is Elena's indirect call to arms* – an introduc- 17
tory section; then the ringing cry Be of Good Courage; then a stalwart aria taken up by the crowd who work themselves into a fine patriotic frenzy.

Suddenly we get a piece of almost casual Verdi
23: *D'ira fremo* magic, a 'thinks' quartet,*** almost unaccompanied, 23
almost sotto voce: Elena (I'll revenge my brother, wait and see), Ninetta and Danieli (She's on about her brother again), Monforte (*Oderint dum metuant* – Let them hate so long as they fear).

The last part of the first act is made up of an extended duet of confrontation between Monforte and Arrigo. It all goes well enough and there are two especially attractive items: one, the sweet and beguiling
28: *Qual' è il tuo nome?* cello tune** which lies under Arrigo's quizzing by 28
Monforte, and then Arrigo's splendidly vigorous and
30: *Di giovine audace* ear-catching solo** (or rather leading part, for Mon- 30
forte is growling away appreciatively throughout), saying more or less I don't give a damn for you – do your worst. The duet ends with only a slight outbreak of act-end climax.

Act II

Procida's version of Napoli, only it's Palermo and
3: *O tu, Palermo* he's a bass. A typical patriotic song** with a catchy 3
tune. Followed by some jolly oom-pah conspiratorial stuff.

The chief glory of the second act, the Arrigo/Elena
13: *Quale, o prode* duet:** she thanks him for his promise to fight for 13
freedom: he says he's potty about her in an urgent and persuasive cavatina: she says (to a funereal accompaniment) that although grieving for her brother, yes, she does seem to have a thing about him and then in a unique pendant echoing the spirit of the duet proper, she makes her deal: if you avenge my brother's death I am yours.

The tarantella, riot, presumptive rape etc. Here Verdi is pushing it a bit. To be outraged to the same tune (and a boring one) as that used for wedding celebrations seems a bit off: the sotto voce chorus of

shame doesn't work. Finally the natives screaming 'revenge' at the boatload of gentry on their way to the
29: *Ah! Del piacer* ball singing their beautiful barcarolle** is really 29
pretty funny and even when we hear it at home we raise our eyebrows. Can do better.

Act III Sc 1

2: *In braccio* Monforte's big moment: a huge aria* about making 2
friends with his son. Extensive, worthy rather than lovable but with a bizarre cabaletta not a million miles away from the Dance of the Hours.

Once again the second part of this scene is a duet, Monforte/Arrigo. It gets going when Monforte asks
12: *Quando al mio sen* Arrigo** 'Aren't you grateful to me for being so de- 12
cent?', to which he replies 'You're a monster and I hate you', and then it really takes off when Monforte tells him he is his son. One of Verdi's big sweeping
15: *Mentre contemplo* tunes*** that surely must have been top of the barrel- 15
organ pops. It reappears in the final stretto as Arrigo pushes off Monforte's paternal embraces (with an accompaniment that is pretty near to a boogie bass).

Act III Sc 2

Once again the dreaded ballet. Nothing shows off Verdi's amazing fecundity more than this succession of cheerful, bouncing tunes. The four ballets together have more than twenty individual dances, some of them a little picky others brilliant with stunning solo parts for clarinet, cor anglais and flute.

The third act, after the ballets, drives forward remorselessly to a majestic finale: the early plotting is done over a background of dance music which continues right through Arrigo's warning dialogue with Monforte and only packs up when the conspirators attempt their coup (a device used equally tellingly in *Ballo*), then the great finale: first all parties recoil in
57: *Colpo orrendo* shock in a sotto voce reflective chorus** (conspir- 57
ators: What a treacherous bastard, Arrigo: I'm really ashamed, Monforte and the French: Thank God – a narrow shave that one), next Elena, Danieli and Pro-
59: *Ah! O patria adorata* cida move into a patriotic hymn** very nicely ac- 59
companied, followed by a full 'thinks' ensemble – Arrigo (My God what have I done?), Monforte and the French (Arrigo, you'd be well advised to join us), conspirators (patriotic stuff, echoed by Sicilians).

Then some brief dramatics as Arrigo appeals to the conspirators for mercy (no hope) and finally the full works with all the stops out. Powerful.

Act IV

2: *Giorno di pianto* Arrigo's doleful aria of self-reproach* improves as 2
passion rises.

The long and eventful duet: Arrigo/Elena. He
pleads for mercy in some agitation, but no good until
he tells her that his father is Monforte (musical ex-
13: *Che far dovea* clamation mark!) then a more lyrical relationship** 13
as she weakens: some recitatif as they assess this
15: *Arrigo! Ah* rather appalling situation: an aria** pure and sad 15
from her (I, about to die, forgive you) with a colora-
17: *È dolce raggio* tura finish: he replies affectingly** Let's die together 17
– with celestial harp accompaniment (perhaps a little
premature). The duet dies away quietly and this is
uncommon.

27: *Addio, mia patria* The magical quartet*** Procida/Monforte/ 27
Arrigo/Elena starts with a solemn measure from Procida (His son! Then that's the end of the revolution) over an inoffensive oom-pah and develops dreamily into four strands of thought, the three others being Monforte (When these two are dead Sicily will be safe), Arrigo (All my fault, and if you die Elena so will I), Elena (Goodbye my lovely land of Sicily). They drift together and apart with Elena taking the lead in a soaring soprano line. The ensemble dies away to nothing.

So to one of Verdi's most effective tricks – the offstage chorus, in this case the offstagers are monks
31: *De profundis* chanting a De Profundis.* Immediately we have an 31
other-worldly slightly spooky feeling which runs right through the high dramatics of the near-execution and pardon. Everything seems to happen in a sort of dream-like slow motion.

The massive finale starts with everyone (except
Procida) terribly happy and Elena and Arrigo spring-
34: *Omai rapito* ing off with a jolly tune** and leads to a final roust- 34
about with the basses singing an umti-tum-tum in double time below the old tune – a triumph of virtuosity but not perhaps quite the thing for so dignified an occasion.

Act V

And now for something entirely different. After a fairly ornery opening chorus we have a dainty/
3: *Mercé, dilette amiche* delicious siciliana/bolero** from Elena in waltz time, 3
full of loving thoughts and good wishes. Elegantly supported by the chorus and capped by a bout of swinging coloratura stuff high above them.

7: *La brezza aleggia* A sweet little duet* Elena/Arrigo. Everything is 7
OK: trouble a thing of the past (ho ho).

Perplexity: which side should Elena take? Why won't she tell Arrigo what bothers her? A gentle
17: *Sorte fatal!* trio** which reflects the agony of indecision far better 17
than Verdi in his high dramatic mode.

20: *Più a lungo* The pre-finale ensemble* is pretty hectic: Elena 20
can no longer conceal the truth from Arrigo (but she never gets round to telling him about the bells). Procida is bouleverséed by Elena's treachery, Arrigo, poor sod, hasn't the faintest idea what's afoot: they declaim and shout in an everlasting chorus until Monforte appears and imposes a minute or two of calming recitatif. But once the bells ring out all hell breaks loose again and things happen very fast indeed. A bit of a scramble.

NOTES

I Vespri Siciliani	Verdi's twentieth opera
First night	The Opéra, Paris, 13 June 1855
Reception	All Verdi could desire
Libretto	Scribe
Source	Perhaps original but more likely to have been based on some old unknown piece

NEWS AND GOSSIP

The story of *Vespri* had been written for Donizetti by the neatly named French librettist Scribe under the title *Le Duc D'Albe* and set in Holland. Since Donizetti was now dead, Scribe offered it to Verdi, who was a bit sniffy at first but eventually accepted it. He insisted that it should be set in 'warmer climes', hence its transfer to Sicily where it could be adapted to take aboard an old legend that during the French occupation a French soldier had sexually harassed a Sicilian woman as she was making her way to attend Vespers. Her husband immediately knifed him. This led to a general mêlée which spread across the island. Allegedly 2000 French were killed in what became known as the Massacre of the Sicilian Vespers. Verdi composed *Vespri* very slowly for he was dead nervous of the French critics. In one of his letters he writes that 'to write an opera for the Opéra with five hours of music is enough to fell an ox'. (A typical Verdi exaggeration: even with the ballets the present Italian version runs only 3 hours 20 minutes and allowing for translation and cuts, the opera would never have exceeded four hours.) Its success was, however, enormous. *Vespri* played for many more performances than contracted, the critics went over the top and even Berlioz (an unlikely admirer) said it bore the mark of 'grandeur and sovereign majesty'. Partly because it demands huge resources, after an early vogue *Vespri* pretty well disappeared from view until the famous revivals with Callas in Florence and Milan in 1951. Even so its performance record since then has been patchy. The later Italian version (supervised by Verdi) is now nearly always used.

COMMENT

Vespri suffers seriously from the French taste. The fashion established chiefly by the pompous Meyerbeer dictated that an opera should have five acts, a ballet and run for most of the evening ($3\frac{3}{4}$–$4\frac{1}{2}$ hours exclusive of intervals). Verdi surprisingly accepted all these requirements in his contract with the Opéra and the result is that an already long and unwieldy opera (3 hours 20 minutes) is stopped dead in its tracks by 30 minutes of ballet and has two hugely demanding spectacular scenes, one of which – the rerun of the Rape of the Sabine Women followed immediately by a boatload of gentry on a sea trip in evening dress – is too near the caricature for comfort, and the other, the massacre itself, which can only be a bit of a bun fight on stage. The construction of Acts I and III is too similar, the second half of both taken up by lengthy duets between Monforte and Arrigo (good in themselves) whose constant wrangling becomes tiresome. Some of the orchestral scoring in the later acts sounds sketchy, lots of arpeggios and standard operatic gestures.

And yet, and yet, as ever in Verdi, there are wonderful things in *Vespri* from the overture, which is Verdi's best, to the ballet music (which has been used over and over by great choreographers from Petipa to Kenneth MacMillan), the little 'thinks' quartet in Act I ('D'ira fremo'), the gentrified barcarolle in Act II, the last big tune in the duet Arrigo/Monforte in Act III Scene 1 ('Mentre contemplo') and the second 'thinks' ensemble in the following scene ('Colpo orrendo'), the magical quartet in Act IV ('Addio, mia patria') – all of these show Verdi at his melodious and dramatic best. That said, the opera lacks a continuous style: it is strange that as well as the ballets we have a barcarolle and a tarantella (neither of these forms is associated with either France or Sicily). The three 'constant' characters (Monforte, Elena, Procida) steady things up a bit when they are on stage (Arrigo is musically all over the place).

A massive opera containing some of Verdi's best and finest work but overall no masterpiece. Beta with lots of alpha spots within it.

Werther

Sentimental tragedy

Massenet

The one where a young poet falls in love with a girl who is about to marry someone else. He says unless she leaves her fiancé he will kill himself. She doesn't: he does.

CAST

The Bailiff (50 years old)	Bass–baritone
Charlotte, his eldest daughter (20)	Mezzo
Sophie, his second daughter (15)	Soprano
Albert, Charlotte's fiancé (25)	Baritone
Schmidt, a friend of the Bailiff	Bass–baritone
Johann, ditto	Bass–baritone
Werther, a poet (23)	Tenor
Brühlmann and **Käthchen** (guests), six additional children of the Bailiff	

4 acts: running time 2 hrs 10 mins

STORY

Act I The garden of the Bailiff's house. Summertime

We are in Wetzlar 50 km from Frankfurt by the M73 in the 1780s in the garden of the Bailiff who has a large family – eight to be precise – but alas their mother died some years ago. The Bailiff who is apt to get the seasons confused is coaching the younger children as they sing Christmas carols.

Schmidt and Johann pass by in order to set out some useful plot points namely that Charlotte is going to a ball that night: that another guest will be the melancholy poet Werther: that Charlotte's fiancé Albert is away on a business trip. They exit towards the Golden Grape.

Werther arrives pretty well knocked out by the beauties of nature which he describes for our benefit. He observes the Christmas carolling and says children are lovely things thereby proving that however badly he may behave in the acts that follow he is a decent fellow at heart.

Charlotte comes out dressed for the ball and the children cluster. What a scene of love and innocence says Werther and my goodness how I fancy that lady. The ball party depart (Werther, Charlotte and two walk-on players who make an inscrutable joke by uttering the word 'Klopstock').

Sophie packs the Bailiff off to the Golden Grape and who should creep into the garden now? Why Albert! Where's Charlotte? he asks. Gone to a ball says Sophie. Keep mum about my return Soph says Albert and we'll surprise 'em all tomorrow. By the way does Charlotte still love me? Sure thing says Sophie. Goodnight.

Werther and Charlotte are returning from what appears to have been a very short ball. Well cheerio goodnight and thanks Werther says Charlotte. Hold on a minute says Werther I love you and as a poet by profession it will take just a little time for me to go through the routine . . . Rapture! Joy! Celestial smile! Gorgeous eyebrows etc. You must be mad says Charlotte. The Bailiff stumbles in shouting Hey Charlotte Albert's been sighted. He's back! Albert? Whosat? asks Werther. My fiancé says Charlotte. I promised my mum as she was dying that I would marry him. If you marry another man I'll top myself says Werther. He stays behind as the others go into the house. He is really gloomy.

Act II The town square of Wetzlar three months later

Johann and Schmidt are sitting outside the Golden Grape and pad out the show with some irrelevant cross-talk before exiting into the pub. Albert and Charlotte stroll on. They have been married for three months and still have a high regard for each other. They go into the church. Werther appears and watches them which makes him feel quite upset. Schmidt and Johann plus one of the walk-ons lumber through to no purpose. Albert comes out of church alone (seeking a comfort station?) and lays his hand on Werther's shoulder. Sorry old chap and all that he says I know you fancied my wife. Just wanted to say – hard cheese. Too true says Werther but not your blame. Let's remain good friends. Sophie, singing and dancing, comes on with a bouquet of flowers for the Minister. She takes Albert off to the no doubt dazzling party to celebrate the Minister's Diamond Jubilee.

Werther now alone has a good chance to be really gloomy. He thinks he will go away. But then Charlotte goes by on her way to the Minister's rave-up. I love you he says as usual and at considerable length. Hold on! says Charlotte I'm married to Albert. You should go away. Impossible! says Werther (changed his mind). Well at least until Christmas says Charlotte. She exits. I think I *will* top myself says Werther. God might be quite pleased to see me earlier than expected [a whimsical fellow: Ed.]. Sophie runs on again: we're all at the party waiting for you Werther she says. Not coming says Werther. I'm going away. Now. For ever. Ciao. Guests from the Minister's party (evidently a bit of a flop) flood on to the stage. Werther's gone! shouts a tearful Sophie. For ever. For ever? repeats Charlotte thoughtfully. I think she must have feelings for him warmer than those of pure friendship says Albert to himself.

Act III The drawing room of Albert's house. Christmas Eve

Charlotte sits reading a whole pile of letters from Werther. Quite a lot of poetic stuff also nasty threats of suicide. Sophie enters. Are you OK Charlotte? she says. You're not as jolly as you used to be. O Soph I might as well tell you I'm just bloody miserable says Charlotte. Come and spend Christmas at our place says Sophie. Christmas! says Charlotte if he doesn't come back by tomorrow it means he's dead. I'll come with you. Sophie exits. O Lord says Charlotte I've been a good girl why do you do this to me? The door opens. In walks Werther.

It's me! says Werther. So I see says Charlotte. That's fine. Everyone is expecting you. Everything here is just as it was when you left. Yeah, I see those pistols are still there says Werther in a nasty meaningful way. Meanwhile I'll sing you a song by the Scottish poet Rabbie Ossian. He does so. He then gets a bit pressing. He asks for a kiss. Charlotte gives way. They kiss. I love you says he. I love you says she. Then she breaks and runs. I never want to see you again she says and exits. Right, that's decided it says Werther. It's a bullet through the brain for me. He exits too.

Albert appears. Hey Charlotte he cries Werther's back! Charlotte runs on pretty confused. Oh . . . Ah . . . Yes . . . she says. You all right? asks Albert. A servant walks in with a message from Werther. Could he please borrow Albert's pistols? Albert makes Charlotte hand over the pistols. They all exit, Charlotte racing after the pistols to prevent felo-de-se.

Act IV A tableau or vision of Christmas Eve in Wetzlar. Snow. Moonlight. Nothing happens. Fade through to Werther's study

Werther has done it but not all that well. He has enough life left to see him through to the final curtain. Charlotte rushes in. Shock horror. Forgive me Charlotte says Werther. No, all my fault honestly says Charlotte I'll ring for an ambulance. Don't bother says he I'm a certain goner. I love you. So do I love you says she. Let's forget everything and be happy for a few moments. Yes, let's forget everything they both say. The children start singing outside the window the Christmas carols that they have been rehearsing since July (but not much improvement). Sophie joins them. Werther says if they won't bury me in holy ground put me in a nice place and plant two *Tilia reticulata* at my head. He dies.

MINUTES FROM START

LOOK OUT FOR

From the first bars of the overture we know we are into romantic territory. There are soft sweet tunes, harp accompaniments and a reprehensible solo violin.

Act I

At the start of Act I the carol singing bit has a sort of
5: *Jésus vient de naître* off-key charm* but then the scene runs on indeter- 5
minately plotting the plot and setting the scene until
it reaches a jolly and slightly contrapuntal end. Goodnight they all say.

Werther arrives (to the accompaniment of an agonized cello) absolutely knocked out by the beauties of
11: *O Nature, pleine de grâce* nature. In a good but general-purpose sort of aria* 11
(we heard the tune in the overture) he begs nature to
receive him, which, having no option, she no doubt
does.

For the next ten minutes nothing much happens
except a series of bromides from Werther (of chil-
16: *Chers enfants!* dren:* Nothing on earth is more precious) and the 16
entry of Charlotte. There is then a slow march
through the domestic routine of the bailiff's household. The two things that are worth looking out for are the skittish orchestration that accompanies the action and the one tuneful outburst from Werther when he is going on about children.

We are still waiting for something to happen when
Albert arrives and delivers himself of a rather dim
27: *Quelle prière de reconnaissance* little number* which is followed by a limp interlude 27
(time lapse for the ball to take place).

32: *Il faut nous séparer* After the ball is over the Werther/Charlotte duet* 32
does begin to get things moving. It is introduced by a slow waltz scored for musical-box (harp, solo cello, solo violin) as Charlotte says they must part. Werther brings some passion to the scene and declares his love. The temperature drops as we move into a patch of recitatif as they debate family problems and Charlotte's memories of her mother, this last to a nondescript tune. But now, with a great deal of build-up, we return to the musical-box tune turned into a big sweeping melody in the orchestra as Werther gets into some heavy loverly stuff. This is interrupted by the return of the Bailiff and the act ends with a reflective reprise of the musical-box waltz and a final shout of despair from Werther. He has learnt Charlotte is intended for another.

Act II

Act II opens with a mildly agreeable scene when Johann and Schmidt sit drinking. The music has an

0 antique flavour,* the snatches of melody are four- 0
square and the men sometimes sing and sing about in staid alternation. The orchestra (horn trill) is really the thing to look out for. The organ enters to remind us that we are near a church.

After some sweet exchanges between Charlotte and Albert as they enter the church Werther is very suddenly amongst us again telling us in a vivid arioso/recitatif how upset he is that Charlotte is not to be his bride and then diving breathlessly into easily
9: *J'aurais sur ma poitrine* the best number** so far. It is fast, it is tuneful, it 9
flows along without let or hindrance to its final cry of depair.

Albert says 'Bad luck old boy' to Werther in a num-
12: *Mais celle qui devint ma femme* ber* as sweet as syrup of figs and Werther replies 'Yes 12
it is bad luck but I'm not bitter' in a less beguiling fashion. Just that: a stanza each, symmetrical and precise and ending punctually.

Sophie brandishing a bunch of flowers sings a
16: *Frère, voyez le beau bouquet!* gushing girlish song.* She is frightfully happy, as the 16
flighty accompaniment tells us. She slows up a bit at the sight of gloomy Werther but in her last exchange with Albert she's fizzing again. A nice episode.

The wimpish Werther after a terrific outburst of nobility decides, in agonized recitatif, to leave Charlotte for ever. He remembers their first meeting (musical-box again), sees her and decides not. The dialogue between them debating this matter – to stay or not to stay – (it is hardly a duet) runs along very
23: *N'est-il donc pas d'autre femme* nicely,* Charlotte giving her lines to a series of sweet 23
but fragmentary snatches of melody: Werther replying more roughly. So they compromise: part until Christmas.

Another baring of the soul by Werther. This one starts nicely and although it lacks any continuous melody it builds into a sort of frenzy of self-pity that
29: *Lorsque l'enfant revient* is pretty overpowering.* This time he's on about sui- 29
cide but we know that if he did it now it would make the opera end too quickly. Layer upon layer of intense string tone plus other instruments combining to pile on the agony.

Act III

0 A biggish prelude* with a fidgety start but soon set- 0

tling into a smooth string tune that, for once, runs its full course.

3: *Werther! Werther!* Charlotte reads the letters: her big solo.* 3

1. Werther still obsesses her. Recitatif. Broken phrases. The cellos and basses fidgety again, as in the prelude.

2. She reads the letters. The first is a whinge (alone, sad, grey sky, etc.) to an eerie set of parallel chords going up and down like ghost music.

6: *Des cris joyeux d'enfants* 3. Cheerfulness breaks in.* Children beneath the 6
window remind him of the children at the Bailiff's house. Fast flourishes in the strings over a syncopated bass.

4. Will he come back or won't he? That is the question. Big climax.

7: *Tu m'as dit: A Noël!* 5. The last letter* threatens suicide, a most 7
ungentlemanly thing to do. Fraught and tense.

Sophie consoles Charlotte,** perhaps the best scene in the opera.

1. Sophie arrives as happy as ever and full of girl-
10: *Bonjour grande soeur!* ish coloratura.** (Twittering woodwind.) What's the 10
matter sister? she asks. And the strings poke in a persistent and haunting phrase between the sung lines.

2. Sophie moves from snatches of recitatif/arioso into a short, at first cheerful but soon questioning style: it's Werther, isn't it? The haunting phrase comes in again.

3. Charlotte breaks down. She weeps. She tells
13: *Va! Laisse couler mes larmes* Sophie of her pain to a slow, poignant melody* 13
dogged by a dismal saxophone.

4. Sophie (she must have won every heart by now)
15: *Tiens, Charlotte* persuades Charlotte to come back home.* Again mel- 15
odious recitatif with the same haunting theme. And then, as she leaves, Charlotte cries – come back and kiss me once again. Not a dry eye in the house.

Charlotte refers her problems to higher authority
18: *Ah! mon courage m'abandonne!* in a stormy address to the deity.* She is very upset 18
and the strength and volume of the orchestral climax at the peak of her prayer must surely have got through to Him up there.

19: *Ciel! Werther!* Werther returns.** A lot of small talk. An attempt 19
to keep things on a humdrum level. Musically adroit, hesitant phrases, flashes of melody in the orchestra.

25: *Pourquoi me réveiller* Werther sings Ossian's song.* A fine well-con- 25
structed piece. Effective but could have been composed by a computer geared to the Massenet model with automatic harp arpeggios.

Now the big stuff. They love each other. A kiss?
28: *Ah ! ce premier baiser* No, no. But yes, after a huge build-up,** splendidly 28
managed, and reaching a really fine musical orgasm when the kiss takes place. But Charlotte runs away and Werther once again gets onto the suicide bit with an impressive and sombre last goodbye in which he rather grandly asks all nature to mourn for him.

Albert returns and supported by a menacing little buzzing figure in the strings, he starts to find out just
33: *Werther est de retour* what is afoot.* The terrified Charlotte exclaims from 33
time to time as Werther's note arrives and is read by Albert to a solemn and slightly holy accompaniment. It is all hush and expectancy. The pistols are handed over. Then POW! Charlotte springs into action and rushes out with a huge orchestral crash and we are into the flurry-worry of the intermezzo (a fairly stock

Act IV piece) with a lot of trombones. This transforms itself
0 into moonlight music with a long streaky tune* and 0
snow falling from the harp and a wind machine blowing force 9 against which we see the vision of a sleeping village. Then back to Sturm und Drang in Werther's study.

The long death of Werther.* Werther has shot himself so accurately as to allow Act IV to run its full course before he dies just before the curtain (twenty minutes in all).

1. Going. Charlotte finds him. Distress. He loves her. She admits she loves him. Some nice lyrical snatches. And we have a return of the musical-box
10: *Oui du jour même* waltz* as Charlotte tells him she loved him from the 10
very first day.

2. Going. Children are singing carols offstage. This is irony, which Charlotte is not slow to point out. Werther, sinking very slowly, utters another bromide or two.

3. Still going. Charlotte sees the end is near. Werther gives instructions about his burial arrangements. Dreary stuff.

4. Gone! The usual susurration by the orchestra

to mark the passing of a soul. The children, who have a somewhat macabre sense of humour, go into fits of laughter.

NOTES

Werther	Massenet's fifteenth opera including operetta and short operas
First night	Hofoper, Vienna, 16 February 1892
Reception	A success
Libretto	Three now forgotten Parisian scribes Blau, Milliet and Hartmann
Source	Goethe's novel *Die Leiden des jungen Werthers*

NEWS AND GOSSIP

When Massenet finished the score of *Werther* in 1887 the Opéra-Comique turned it down as too gloomy, and certainly a theatre billing itself as Comique which put on *Werther* would probably have infringed the Trade Descriptions Act. So it lay around for some years until in 1890 *Manon* had a huge success in Vienna and the management then asked Massenet to come again. So *Werther* saw the light of day in a distant capital and before an audience very different from the one for which it was composed. It went down well with the Viennese who were perhaps better conditioned to gloom than the giddy Parisians. Indeed, when it was finally put on at the Opéra-Comique, it was pulled from the rep after the first season. It was also a flop in London but hit the headlines in 1903 when the Opéra-Comique put on a sparkling new production. Suddenly it was top of the pops with 1300 performances in Paris alone. Along with *Manon* it became the first choice for houses who wanted to put on a Massenet opera. For fifty years it was all the rage. But after World War II the French romantic school of opera fell into disrepute and was sneered at a good deal by the bright young toughs of the new European music. It is not often played today. Without absolute conviction it doesn't come off and not all that many contemporary producers are convinced.

COMMENT

Werther has one of the simplest stories in all opera. Boy one meets girl – girl marries boy two, boy one kills himself. No more than that except a lot of padding. But Massenet carries off the mainline story in a high romantic style and fills out the fringes so artfully that boredom is kept at bay, though sometimes, as when two irrelevant characters spend five minutes praising Bacchus, impatience isn't. The chief weakness of the story lies in Werther being such a pill. Romantic love on a suicidal scale is hard enough to take even with the noblest of heros, but when the suicide is committed by someone you would have been glad to have got rid of in Act I, the impact is negligible. Werther is both a wet and a selfish bore. Let's hope he was at least a half-decent poet, but the way he drools over a lavatory-calendar quote from Ossian (who never existed anyway) doesn't give one much hope. Bring on the pistols!

The music is always well-mannered and would cause no offence to the most ardent Gounod-lover. Indeed, Massenet's nickname 'la fille de Gounod' is apt. But *Werther* has much of what it takes to make us sit contentedly through a couple of hours of opera. Massenet could write a tune, although he is economical with big ones, there being only three or four major events, one of them – the musical-box – in the nature of a main theme. But the orchestra is full of good melodies weaving around the vocal line though these are elusive and don't often consummate. Here Massenet has one thing in common with Wagner at his most tiresome, namely the practice of the singer singing in a dry exclamatory mode whilst all sorts of gorgeous things are going on in the orchestra which you can't properly hear because your ear is occupied in trying to make out what the hell is being said/sung. Between the set-piece numbers much of *Werther* is conversation resting on an air-cushion of light music, beguiling, amusing, undemanding and very cleverly contrived. It is a relief to have no chorus on duty.

The serious stuff is conventional, professional but only once or twice does the music break out to assault our emotions or delight our ears. Sophie is always enjoyable and endearing: the first big reprise of the musical-box tune in the Charlotte/Werther duet in Act I is fine: Werther's troubled aria at the beginning of Act II – 'J'aurais sur ma poitrine' – the Sophie/Charlotte scene in Act III and the love duet Charlotte/Werther that follows, are all really enjoyable and all have some real opera-power.

But when all is said and done it is not a high-voltage signal we are receiving. *Werther* is a romance, what, if operas were novels, would be classed as a novella, miles above Barbara Cartland but based on the same quasi-religious belief that romantic love is pretty well the only important thing going on in the world.

One enormous plus is Massenet's adroit orchestration. Here he was, in his own limited field, a genius. His handling of the woodwind can be as light as a soufflé and as delicious (but chocolate rather than cheese) and his heavy stuff, gloomy lower strings and mournful brass, can almost persuade us that this is really serious music. Also good with harps, but rhythmically a bit of a jog-trotter.

Werther takes a long time to get started, about half an hour in fact, and if it never climbs higher than the foothills of serious opera, there are patches of sunlight on the way up and one or two spiffing views. It is an opera to pass the time away pleasantly rather than to sear the soul. You will leave the opera house as you would leave a Chinese restaurant, satisfied for the moment but soon hungry for more, and with absolutely no fear of indigestion. Beta.

William Tell

Patriotic drama

(Guglielmo Tell)

Rossini

The one with the apple, the arrow and the overture.

CAST

Guglielmo Tell, a Swiss patriot	Baritone
Edwige, his wife	Mezzo
Jemmy, his son	Soprano
Melchthal, elderly wise Swiss person	Bass
Arnoldo, his son	Tenor
Gessler, Hapsburg local governor	Bass
Rodolfo, junior officer under Gessler	Tenor
Matilde, Hapsburg princess, Gessler's sister	Soprano
Leutoldo, fugitive from Gessler's forces	Bass
Gualtiero, friend of Tell	Bass
A fisherman (tenor) A hunter	

4 acts, 2 or 3 intervals: running time 3 hrs 55 mins

STORY

Act I Sc 1 Rustic Swiss scene including Tell's house, a river and a boat

We are on the shores of Lake Lucerne in the thirteenth century. The Swiss people in general are happy and praise God but the more politically aware Tell family resent Switzerland's loss of freedom to the hated Hapsburgs. Weddings are to take place in the village: the wise man Melchthal tells his son Arnoldo to get moving too: it's time he were wed. But guilty Arnoldo loves the Hapsburg princess Matilde. Despite this Tell bullies Arnoldo into promising to join the freedom fighters.

The wedding ceremonies start in full operatic style. Arnoldo slips off to bid Matilde farewell: Tell tails him. The weddings get going: Jemmy wins a bows-and-arrows prize: but suddenly one Leutoldo, fleeing for his life from Gessler's men, staggers on. Tell (having failed to find Arnoldo) is back and bravely ferries Leutoldo across the river to safety.

The Hapsburg minion Rodolfo storms in at the head of a posse: he demands the name of the man who saved Leutoldo. Nobody will grass on Tell: Rodolfo seizes the unlucky Melchthal as hostage and his men begin to break up the village.

Act II A wild place: pine trees: mountains encircling the Rütli: Lake Lucerne

Huntsmen and shepherds sing bloodthirsty and pastoral choruses respectively. Matilde comes on in search of Arnoldo. He arrives. They discover they are in love but being on different sides things look tough. So Arnoldo decides to change sides and fight for the Hapsburgs: Matilde leaves. Tell and Gualtiero appear and inform Arnoldo the Austrians have killed his father Melchthal. Arnoldo decides he must avenge his father which means he must change sides again and fight for the Swiss. The men of the cantons muster and sing patriotic choruses.

Act III Sc 1 Inside a ruined chapel near Altdorf (a Hapsburg) Castle

Arnoldo tells Matilde he must change sides again to avenge Melchthal's death. They decide they must part forever.

Act III Sc 2 The market square, Altdorf

The dreadful Gessler imposes forced merrymaking on the Swiss who must bow before his hat stuck on a pole. Tell and Jemmy refuse to bow and are arrested. Tell tries to get Jemmy away to signal the start of the revolution. He is caught in the act. As a punishment he has to shoot the world-famous apple off Jemmy's head. He does it, thereby ensuring freedom for himself and Jemmy and a fourth act to the opera.

But Gessler discovers Tell had a secret weapon – a second arrow to kill him had the apple shot gone astray. Both Tells are arrested again. Matilde pleads for Jemmy's release (and privately swears to free Tell too). Hard man Gessler says Tell will be thrown to the reptiles [what reptiles? Ed.] in nearby castle: tumult: the Swiss plead, the soldiers cheer. Matilde escapes with Jemmy.

Act IV Sc 1 Another village square outside Melchthal's house

Arnoldo guides Swiss patriotic troops to an arms dump set up by Tell and Arnoldo's father Melchthal: everyone determined on vengeance.

Act IV Sc 2 The shores of Lake Lucerne: Tell's house visible

Matilde returns Jemmy to Edwige: she says she will offer herself as hostage against Tell's safety: but Edwige says Tell is in a boat on the lake with Gessler on his way to death. There is also a frightful storm brewing – Lord save us! Jemmy unilaterally decides to light the beacon to start the revolution: but with a single bound Tell has freed himself: with Tell at the tiller the boat makes a crash landing on stage (or sometimes just off): Tell jumps ashore leaving the inefficient Gessler and Co. aboard. Tell is reunited with family and friends: Gessler, now disembarked, falls dead from an arrow from Tell: news comes that the castle is taken! Victory! Triumph! The storm gives way to calm sunshine. God's in his heaven and all's well with Switzerland. Even the Tells are pleased.

MINUTES FROM START

Act I Sc 1

LOOK OUT FOR

0 The overture:** a concert piece bigger and longer 0
than Rossini's standard model: three sections (none repeated – not sonata form), the last section featuring the famous galop.

12: *È il ciel seren'* The opening chorus** is a spacious hymn to 12
nature: a new Rossini to opera buffs: choral writing not a million miles away from his church music.

The high tenor of the happy fisherman soars above a harp accompaniment: Tell is not so happy and utters dark forebodings, cow-minders sound horns and in a second wonderfully crafted chorus all (save the Tells) express satisfaction at the state of the world,
21: *Salute, onore, omaggio* moving into a sort of quadruple concerto** with 21
chorus and the two Tells, Arnoldo and Melchthal. Ending in a mighty paean of joy.

31: *Ah! Matilde, io t'amo* A lyrical duet Arnoldo/Tell:** Arnoldo agonizes 31
(is a patriot: hates the tyrant: loves the tyrant's sister) whilst Tell bombards him with patriotic propaganda.

42: *Ciel che del mondo* Yet another great chorus** celebrates the wed- 42
dings (three) about to take place: Arnoldo in an obbligato thinks – 'I'll sneak off and see whether I can find Matilde.' A less lofty chorus with a Tyrolean flavour leads to a dramatically disastrous but tuneful ballet.*

The chorus to celebrate Jemmy's successful sharp-
57: *Gloria e onore* shooting has an attractive hurdy-gurdy bass* (to re- 57
mind us we are amongst rustic folk).

The splendid finale to Act I: the Swiss people, always on the lookout for a chance to address the Al-
64: *Nume piëtoso* mighty, thank Him for Tell's escape to safety:** the 64
evil soldiers sing death and destruction in a sinister sotto voce chorus: Rodolfo starts his inquisition –

who helped the murderer escape? Jemmy and Edwige give vent to appropriate interventions, Melchthal is arrested, the houses smashed up, all with the solo voices spinning out above the rhythmic
71: *Su, via, struggete* chug-chug-chug of the chorus:*** a final great cres- 71
cendo and a crashing finish.

Act II

The brief prelude would have us think we arc in for a gentle hunting scene, but when the hunters give
2: *Qual silvestre metro intorno* tongue* they sing of their delight in 'the chamois's 2
dying scream' and similar horrors: the sort of thing today's MFHs would instantly suppress.

In an episode which is chiefly padding (no movement on the drama front) the decent douce shepherds
4: *Del raggiante lago* strike up a serene evening hymn.** 4

9: *Selva opaca* Matilde's solo of calm beauty.** 9

26: *Tutto apprendi, o sventurato* Matilde's duet*** with Arnoldo starts over a rest- 26
less accompaniment: they reveal their love (over a persistent pizzicato bass) and reach a fine florid climax asserting their love passionately and repeatedly in high operatic fashion.

A trio (Tell, Arnoldo, Gualtiero) which starts with
30: *Allor che scorre* a manly stanza from each contender* and leaps into 30
high drama as Arnoldo learns his father has been killed; he reacts, half demented with frenzy, with a
33: *Troncar suoi* splendid lyrical outburst.** Tell urges Arnoldo to 33
take revenge: he says the revolutionary forces are about to gather: the trio ends with an orgy of patriotism: Hearts aflame! Liberty or Death! Revenge! Etc.

The forces do gather with a great deal of hailing, exclaiming, responding, all loaded with intense patriotism. The three egg on the troops with gung-ho
41: *Confuso da quel bosco* words of encouragement,* on the lines of the night 41
before Agincourt, though Tell sounds more like an old-time Marxist agitator than King Henry. The final
56: *Giuriam', giuriam' per nostri danni* hymn* of hate is enormous, noisy and rather 56
frightening.

Act III Sc 1

A tremulous prelude anticipates the lovers' meeting:
3: *Pel nostro amore* they meet: a great solo from Matilde*** in transports 3
of distress at the prospect of parting: intensely lyrical with loads of coloratura: a switch to verismo as she hears Gessler approaching: she urges Arnoldo to fly.

An item of pure gold, all eight minutes of it.

Act III Sc 2

18: *La tua danza si leggera*
Chorus time again: many of them, one memorable** 18
over an accompaniment of mouth music (subsequently borrowed frequently and variously e.g. for a pipe band number played by Highland regiments under the title of The Green Hills!). Followed by several perky Tyrolean tunes lacking only the wheeze of the accordion and the slap of bare hands on leather.

Tell arrested: Jemmy's fate debated (Gessler, Rodolfo, Tell, Jemmy and chorus). High drama:
35: *Quell' orgoglio insano*
much emotion.** The apple bit: Tell sombrely in- 35
structs Jemmy how to behave:* the pull on the 44
44: *Resta immobile*
bowstring against hushed woodwind chorus: Wham! Shouts of victory (the Swiss), rage (Gessler and Co.) and a lovely arioso passage from a much relieved
48: *Vittoria!*
Jemmy leading to the finale:*** will Matilde ensure 48
Tell and Jemmy's escape? Will Gessler get them? The soloists launch out above a chop-chop choral accompaniment (a hundred years and more ahead of the Swingle Singers): a choral contest between Gessler and the soldiers (evil) and Matilde, Jemmy, etc. and the Swiss people (virtuous and compassionate, and patriotic to boot). A great finale and a fine end to Act III.

Act IV Sc 1

4: *O muto asil' pianto*
A short but taxing aria for Arnoldo:* he deplores his 4
father's death: is really sad and quite miserable. Then a concerted piece in which he incites the Swiss to ac-
8: *Oh mia speran*
tion.** Big stuff and Arnoldo's finest hour. 8

Act IV Sc 2

15: *Sottratto a orribil' nembo*
Matilde returns Jemmy to his mama in a trio** start- 15
ing tentatively (Matilde solo) then the duet (Edwige and Jemmy) and finally a perky cabaletta to a steam organ accompaniment.

Edwige prays for Tell's deliverance: slow to start
22: *Tu che l'appoggio*
but with truly affecting closing cadences*** with 22
chorus.

The finale: first one of Rossini's better storms (no thunder): the dramatic death of Gessler: then the
31: *Tutto cangia, il ciel' s'abbell*
serene final chorus of heartfelt thanksgiving** by one 31
and all as the sun comes out over the Swiss countryside once again.

NOTES

William Tell	Rossini's thirty-ninth and last opera
First night	The Opéra, Paris, 3 August 1829
Reception	Satisfactory in every way
Libretto	Joug and Bis (amongst others) [And who are they anyway? Ed.]
Source	Play by Schiller (1804)

NEWS AND GOSSIP

Rossini approached the business of writing a French opera gingerly through three apprentice works based on Neapolitan models. *Tell* was his first completely French opera, and a monster. He took immense pains over its composition: the stories about *Tell* are not about how quickly he wrote it, but how long it took. During the innumerable rehearsals many cuts and changes were made, some of them unrecorded. So we cannot be certain of what the 'final' version actually did or did not contain. Rossini had taken aboard the conventions of Paris opera, including massive and spectacular scenery, a compulsory ballet, a different style of singing, etc., nevertheless the rehearsal period was clearly a life and death struggle. Which he won: *Tell* was a huge success both musically and politically for its nationalist sentiments chimed perfectly with the current political mood. It was also a success in Italy and today the Italian version tends to hold the stage. But although hailed as Rossini's masterpiece (wrongly: see below), it has not been performed much since, owing to the monumental forces required and its interminable length. 'Bleeding chunks' have sometimes been performed on their own and there is the story of the director of the Paris Opéra meeting Rossini in the street and telling him that his company would perform the second act of *Tell* that night. 'What?' said Rossini 'The *whole* of it?' *Tell* was Rossini's first wholly French opera: it was also his last. For several reasons, some of them mysterious, although he lived in Paris for a further 40 years, he never wrote again for the stage.

COMMENT

It is the custom to hail *Tell* as Rossini's masterpiece, but this must be a mistake. First because the patriotic sentiment that runs throughout the main plot is just too gung-ho for our taste today. No doubt in its day the audience caught fire at the cries of Liberty! Freedom! etc., but today we have seen a lot of not-so-virtuous small countries at the same game and thus the fervour of the gallant Swiss becomes a bit of a bore. So one great agitprop has gone. There is also a whiff of toy soldiers in the air (and often on the stage). Second, the forward thrust of the drama, both political and personal, is stopped dead in its tracks by an outbreak of the dreaded opera ballet, here several, together lasting for some half-an-hour. Nor does the inordinate number of choruses (some fourteen in all) speed the flow. Few producers have the guts to challenge the deplorable French convention of the opera ballet which always must halt the plot, disperse the mood and which is usually amateurishly choreographed and performed by a scratch group of out-of-work dancers. In *Tell*, the cavorting of the Tyrolean peasants not only stops the show but extends an already overlong evening. There is a lot of praise for the masterly musical and dramatic construction of *Tell* and indeed this is understandable, but this is only true if you eliminate the ballets (and the loss of ten or fifteen choral minutes could be a blessing too). Rossini had always been keen on structure: many of the musical numbers in his earlier operas were based on formal patterns (e.g. repeats of certain stanzas, slow–fast–faster progression and a self-contained key structure), but in *Tell* he goes further. Several of the Tyrolean tunes (Ranz des Vaches, Tyrolean hillbillies) we hear in Act I reappear in varied forms later in the opera though the ordinary opera buff might be forgiven for failing to notice this clever Dick stuff.

Despite all its drawbacks, *Tell* is on the verge of being a masterwork and without the ballets it could just become one. It retains its majesty and dramatic power and by far the best numbers lie in the personal dilemmas – Arnoldo's fraught love affair with Matilde; the news of his father's death; Matilde's farewell to Arnoldo; Tell's instructions to his son about how to behave when shot at with an apple on his head (an early example of verismo or operatic actuality): in addition there are at least four great choruses: and a ringing climax in the finale to Act I. Here Rossini was at the peak of his achievement and at the same time he was moving serious opera into new fields. So do not ever miss the comparatively rare chance of seeing *Tell*: it makes an evening full of good things and if from time to time it goes off the boil you won't have to wait long for it to bubble again. Alas, because of its slow pace, not in the top class. A beta.

Wozzeck

Psychiatric tragedy

Berg

The one where a simple soldier, bullied and battered by life, is driven to murder his woman after she has been seduced by his Drum Major. He subsequently drowns.

CAST

Wozzeck, a soldier	Baritone
Marie, his common-law wife and mother of his son	Soprano
A Captain	Tenor
A Doctor	Bass
The Drum Major	Tenor
Andres, another soldier	Tenor
Margret, Marie's neighbour	Contralto
Two apprentices, a madman	

3 acts: running time 1 hr 30 mins

STORY

Act I Sc 1 The Captain's room

We are in the midst of the army life of any army in the 1820s and Wozzeck is shaving his Captain who talks very freely for a man who has a cut-throat razor hovering near his mouth. The Captain philosophizes about the nature of time and manages to bully Wozzeck as he does so. He taunts him about his illegitimate child. Wozzeck replies that the poor can't afford to be as virtuous as the rich. He does his best.

Act I Sc 2 The countryside

Wozzeck and Andres are collecting firewood. Wozzeck sees visions. Andres sings a hunting song. Wozzeck interrupts with further visions, a severed head rolling about amongst toadstools, a chasm opening up in the earth beneath their feet, the last trump etc. He also seems to be dead scared of the Freemasons. The sun sets and they return to barracks. Not much firewood gathered.

Act I Sc 3 Marie's room

Marie holds up her child to see the military band go by. Margret from next door shouts through the window, Isn't that Drum Major a wonderful hunk of beef? Yeah, says Marie, he's lovely. The Drum Major salutes Marie and she waves back. I see you've got hot pants for that one says Margret: I saw what you were looking at and it wasn't his face. Bitch! says Marie and slams the window shut. She sings a lullaby to the child. Wozzeck comes in talking crazy. Some UFO has been following him around. Look at your little son says Marie. Ah yes says Wozzeck and dashes back to barracks. He's going right round the bend says Marie and such a decent chap too.

Act I Sc 4 The Doctor's study

The Doctor is pushing and poking at Wozzeck who is paid to be a human guinea-pig. I saw you pissing against a wall Wozzeck says the Doctor, that's bad and have you been sticking to your bean diet? Wozzeck indicates yes. Then we will soon get you onto the oxytetracyclamen and peroxedimentumin diet says the Doctor who is as crazy as Wozzeck and maybe more so. You bastard says the Doctor, pissing again, I'll murder you. But he restrains himself just. Wozzeck tries to explain his current crop of mad fantasies. You are now such a wonderful specimen of schizo peripetalis intimatestinalis dementia says the Doctor that I will give you a pay rise. Keep eating your beans, Wozzeck, shaving the Captain and don't ever piss again and you will prove my theory and I will get the Nobel Peace Prize. Show me your tongue.

Act I Sc 5 The street in front of Marie's door

The Drum Major is making a pass at Marie. Ain't I fine? Ain't I sexy? says he just feel me down here and I'm going to fuck you. He tries to. Get off says Marie. Come inside. They go inside.

Act II Sc 1 Marie's room. Morning sunshine

Marie looks at the earrings the Drum Major gave her. She sings to her child. Wozzeck comes in. Where did you get those earrings? he asks. Found them in the street says Marie. Two of a kind in the same place? says Wozzeck: never happened to me. He gives her money and goes. I feel terrible says Marie guiltily.

Act II Sc 2 A street in the town

The Captain and the Doctor meet and chatter obsessionally. The Captain tells the Doctor he is racing through life at a madcap pace. Too fast. The Doctor tells the Captain about some gruesome recent cases and looking him carefully up and down tells him he has all the symptoms of an almost immediate death from apoplexy. He forecasts a well-attended funeral. Wozzeck comes by. The Captain says how about the Drum Major, Wozzeck? Did you catch a whiff of him on your Marie? [Only it's all done by hinting about hairs, very complex: Ed.] Your woman is a good one isn't she Wozzeck? asks the Doctor. What is this you are telling me says Wozzeck. I think I'll go and hang myself. A strange man say the Doctor and the Captain.

Act II Sc 3 The street in front of Marie's door. Overcast

Marie is standing in the doorway. Wozzeck comes on. I can't see it says Wozzeck. What? says Marie. Sin says Wozzeck: it must be enormous. I can't smell it either. Did the Drum Major come here? asks he. He did: I know it. Bitch. Don't lay a finger on me says Marie, ever since childhood I have had a curious antipathy to being manhandled. I'd rather be knifed any day. She goes into the house. Knifed says Wozzeck to himself. Knifed. Uhu. . . .

Act II Sc 4 The garden of an inn

A rave-up in progress. Singing polytonal but cheerful. Dancing. Including the Drum Major with Marie. Wozzeck comes tearing in. God look at the way he's goosing her he says to himself all the world's a stewpot of lust. More singing. Wozzeck sits by the door. Let's go home says friend Andres who has sneaked out of the ruck. No says Wozzeck. Some people may go out through this door feet first. A convenient village idiot appears. I smell blood he intones in a piercing falsetto. I smell blood. The show goes on. Wozzeck sees everyone dancing in blood.

Act II Sc 5 Guardroom in the barracks

Sleeping soldiers sing with their snores. There is a cry from Wozzeck. He wakes Andres. Can't you hear them Andres? he asks. Can't you hear their voices coming through the wall? Go to sleep says Andres. Can't you see the blade of the big flashing knife? says Wozzeck. For Chrissake go to sleep says Andres. Enter the Drum Major, drunk. What a wonderful performer I am says he and what a good lay she is. Hey Wozzeck have a drink. (Wozzeck refuses.) Go on you bastard says the Drum Major. Drink. (Wozzeck whistles: dumb insolence.) The Drum Major beats up Wozzeck and leaves him prone. Staggers out. I'll get them one after the other says Wozzeck quietly to himself.

Act III Sc 1 Marie's room

Marie is guilty, guilty. She reads the Bible. She is rough with her child. She prays for mercy.

Act III Sc 2 A path through a wood by a pond. Dusk

Wozzeck and Marie come on together. I want to go home says Marie. No sit down here says Wozzeck. Are you afraid? Why are you trembling? It's the cold cold dew says Marie. Look the moon is rising it's blood-red. Why are you trembling Wozzeck? What do you want? she asks. Nothing Marie says he and plunges a knife into her. She dies. Dead! says Wozzeck.

Act III Sc 3 The bar-room of an inn

Girls and women including Margret are dancing to an atonal polka. Wozzeck tries a song but it's not a success. He calls to Margret to dance with him. They dance and sit down. Margret sings a song. She sees blood on his hands. Wozzeck says it's only a scratch. But no it's right up his sleeves. We smell human blood shout the crowd. Panic. Wozzeck runs for it.

Act III Sc 4 The path through the wood by the pond

Wozzeck stumbles on. He is frantically looking for the knife. He bumps into Marie's body. He finds the knife and throws it into the pond. He thinks it is too near the edge. He wades into the pond. I must wash off all this blood he says. The moon has gone blood-red. The water in the pond has turned into blood. He drowns.

The Doctor and the Captain walk by. They hear drowning noises from the pond. They wonder if someone might not be in there but think it best to hurry on.

Act III Sc 5 The street in front of Marie's door

Street children are playing. One runs in with the news that Marie is dead. They tell Marie's son his mother is dead. He goes on riding his hobby-horse. They run off to see the corpse. He waits a moment and then runs off after them.

MINUTES FROM START

LOOK OUT FOR

Act I Sc 1

The first scene* is in the form of a suite (although we would never have guessed this from the libretto or the score if Berg hadn't told us) which goes something as follows:

0 1. Prelude. The Captain torments Wozzeck as he 0
shaves him (the Captain's theme: on cor anglais). Music all over the place, scrappy, agitated. Wozzeck has a refrain – 'Jawohl, Herr Hauptman!' (Captain's motto again).

1 2. Pavane. The Captain goes dreamy and philo- 1
sophical. So does the music (brass) but soon agitates again.

2 3. A cadenza by a solo viola takes the lead over the 2
still-philosophizing Captain.

3 4. Gigue. The Captain torments Wozzeck. 3
Flighty accompaniment (three flutes), a hideous laugh.

4– 5. A second cadenza, by a double bassoon. 4–

4 6. Gavotte. Chunky brass behind the Captain's 4
nasty stuff about Wozzeck's bastard child.

5– 7. Double 1. Wozzeck fends off the Captain 5–
melodiously.

5– 8. Double 2. The Captain replies with a burst of 5–
cacophony.

5 9. Air.** Almost an aria. Wozzeck's testament. 5
The music is cogent and rather fetching. Poor Wozzeck. Fairly reprehensible solo violin. Ends in thunder (made by the strings banging the wood of their bows against their instruments).

7 10. Repeat of the prelude. But it isn't exactly what 7
we heard before (starts with the Captain's motto). Perhaps it's upside down or backwards, certainly the same mood.

8– Then a final short noisy symphony. 8–

Act I Sc 2

Spooky chords in the brass. The scene is 'a rhapsody on three chords' and the three chords are there but precious little rhapsody. Not much stick-picking either. Wozzeck is seeing terrible visions. Andres tries to sing a very difficult atonal hunting song but Wozzeck's panic (Freemasons!) breaks out in a sequence of huge eruptions from the trombones. Sud-
13: *Still, alles still* denly things go still* – soothing muted strings – the 13
world is dead and it is given a quiet little requiem by the orchestra – solo horn, trumpet, clarinet and then

violin over sustained string support.

Act I Sc 3

The military band approaches – rhythm as per real
bands, tunes impressionistic. Marie and Margret slag
each other off. Then, alone, Marie sings a tender lul-
17: *Mädel, was fangst* laby** to her child. Those who have been pretty well 17
Bergered by the music to date will find in this passage
an item that any ear can welcome. Marie's singing line
spins out clear and lovely over a gently supportive orchestra. She finishes and we drift into limbo with a
celeste and harp drip-dropping around timelessly.

Act I Sc 4

This madhouse scene between the crazed Doctor and
the loony Wozzeck is amazingly well caught by the
equally lunatic music. It doesn't really help to know
that the whole thing is written over a ground bass, in
this case a series of twelve notes heard on the cellos in
the first bit where the Doctor scolds Wozzeck for
pissing against a wall (coughing, in Bowdlerized versions). Berg lists twenty-one variations over this bass,
some of them very short, but there is no need to let
Berg's clever-cleverness distract you from the dramatic sound of the music. If you just take it as it
comes it works operatically and well. Look out espe-
26: *Wenn die Natur* cially for a nice bit* when both madmen drift into 26
waltz time and also for the Doctor's final burst of am-
29: *Er ist ein int'ressanter Fall* bition (variation 21).* The between-scenes sym- 29
phony is a nice one, opening with the woodwind
tearing off strips, then into a warm humid mass of
brassy stuff.

Act I Sc 5

A short but effective scene. First the swelling proud
music as both women admire the Drum Major's
31: *Geh einmal vor Dich hin!* chest, beard and bella figura generally,* then rape 31
music very loud and coarse as he assaults Marie, a
smidgin of romance as she gives way and then an orgiastic roar as they go through the door together. A
powerful brief encounter.

Act II Sc 1

Berg described the scene as a sonata-form movement, though it is of course nothing of the sort (see COMMENT). Berg clearly has something clever in mind but if he meant it for us it got lost in the post.

After a bit of gazing at the earrings from the Drum Major and shouting at the child Marie sings him a noisy song about gypsies which scares Wozzeck to death. Then some rather nice gloating over the
2: *'s ist gewiss Gold!* jewels.* Pedestrian exchanges with the simple Wozzeck – a climax as he hands her some money – a nice outburst of guilt from Marie (based on material from earlier in the scene). 2

Act II Sc 2

This time Berg's description of the scene, an 'invention and fugue on three themes', makes recognizable sense. The opening whimsical exchanges between the Doctor and the Captain are musically pretty free but with frolicky little phrases that give a backward glance to Bach and the baroque. We hear the first
10: *Ja richtig* fugue theme as the Captain speaks* (the Captain's 10
motto); it gives way to the second when the Doctor comes in (pizzicato cellos), then the third when Wozzeck enters (muted trombones), with all three subjects meshing in and out of the onward-moving mass
12: *Was wollen Sie damit sagen* of sound.** Woodwind and brass are favoured for 12
punching out the subjects. Finally all three sing together. This makes a really good ensemble although the determination of the Doctor to put over his jokes does take away from the impact of the terrible things that Wozzeck is hearing.

Act II Sc 3

15: *Guten Tag, Franz* This scene** is simply called Largo, which it un- 15
doubtedly is, in three parts:

1. Wozzeck accusatory, Marie frightened and soothing,
2. Wozzeck's attack and Marie's defence,
3. Wozzeck's final broody bit.

The orchestra is scaled down to chamber size (but the full orchestra returns to Marie's defence) and much of the material comes from earlier in the opera. Berg pulls off this scene brilliantly. Short, taut, bags of atmosphere and powerfully dramatic.

Act II Sc 4

This time Berg's description of the piece as a 'scherzo and trio' makes little sense. Suddenly a dive into the old diatonic with wrong notes, a style later to be greatly favoured by Shostakovich and Khachaturian

in their lighter moments. Musically everything is very jolly except for the final bit. Look out especially for the waltz sections and for Andres's short song
23: *O Tochter, liebe Tochter* (with a chorus).** Wozzeck's jealousy boils up omin- 23
ously (strings sliding about: woodwind alarmed and alarming) – and after a boring offering from the First Journeyman and a warning signal from the accordion
26: *Lustig, lustig . . .* the village idiot with his spooky falsetto** raises the 26
hairs on our necks and Wozzeck's mad vision of blood everywhere takes us into the final jangling waltz of death.

Act II Sc 5

Snores echo around from the sleeping soldiers. A
29: *Oh! Oh!* heart-stopping cry from Wozzeck.* He tells Andres 29
of his nightmare, noisily with deep brass grunts. He prays. More snores.

31: *Ich bin ein Mann!* Now what Berg calls a 'martial rondo'* begins with 31
the entry of the Drum Major. The refrain (well, something like that) returns each time the Drum Major takes a swig of brandy. He goes for Wozzeck. Look out for Wozzeck's whistle (piccolo) which the Drum Major takes over, mockingly, after he has floored Wozzeck (again noisily). This lively scene ends with Wozzeck saying – murderously and quietly – 'One after the other'.

Act III Sc 1

Marie, with the assistance of the Bible, broods on her bad behaviour. This scene is made up of a theme, variations and a fugue. The theme is there sure enough but the variations (seven in just over two minutes) are on such a microscale as to be almost invisible or rather uncatchable. But never mind that, the stern string theme and especially variations 5 and 6 (solo
2: *Es war einmal* horn),* Marie's guilt, sad and touching, and the 2
whole piece with its mini-fugues at the end, give us a powerful impression of the poor tortured lady's state of mind. She is musically pretty rough with her young son in variation 4 (14 seconds).

Act III Sc 2

So this one is an 'invention on a single note' which is not true in that there are lots of different notes but is true in that one note dominates (B), sometimes a plain pedal in the bass, sometimes a pedal with squirms,

sometimes cheeping and chiming in the treble. The
scene starts slow and dreamy until the blood-red
7: *Wie der Mond rot aufgeht!* moon rises to music of real menace.** The tension 7
builds over the pedal and bursts into thunder as Wozzeck plunges the knife into Marie's throat. As quick as lightning there is a very quick reprise of Marie-music from the past scenes and then the timps followed by the whole orchestra hammering out the one note as loud as they can play. Top that for an operatic murder.

Act III Sc 3

10 This time we have an 'invention on a rhythmic pat- 10
tern'. Fair enough. We start with a honky-tonk piano playing what is alleged to be a polka but sounds more like a fast passage from one of the Shostakovich piano concertos. Next we have an attempt at a song from Wozzeck (to the tune of the Lullaby in Act I) but he fails and passes the baton to Margret. She starts up boldly but he interrupts her and she notices the blood
12: *Aber was hast Du* on Wozzeck's hands. Now the music dramatizes* as 12
suspicion grows and the crowd in the bar join in. There is a noisy and rather frightening end to the scene. Screams and shouts. Wozzeck runs out to a roll on the side drums.

Act III Sc 4

'Invention on a six-note chord' is the technical description, and certainly that's how it begins. Wozzeck stumbles on to the chord. He is pretty far gone. Shouts, moans and has a sort of seizure as he finds the knife. Then things go quiet as he wades about and quieter still as the water closes over him (swirls in the strings, woodwind and brass). The water still speaks as the Doctor and the Captain go by talking casually over the water music (harp and celeste), but at last it is still. Now we have the most considerable orchestral
18 piece, a requiem for Wozzeck,** opening with a dig- 18
nified Mahlerian melody which sweeps along nobly until the brass butt in with an urgent call for a change of mood. The requiem ends in agony, perhaps Wozzeck's agony of poverty, jealousy and fear of insanity. The climax of the opera.

Act III Sc 5

After the requiem, a coda. Children's voices over a

21: *Ringel, ringel, Rosenkranz* lightly scored backing* tell Marie's child that his mother is dead. He rides on his hobby-horse regardless, singing like a cuckoo clock until, just before the curtain falls, he too runs out. 21

NOTES

Wozzeck	Berg's first opera
First night	Staatsoper, Berlin, 14 December 1925
Reception	Enthusiastic but a savage backlash from classics-loving oldies
Libretto and source	Büchner's play cut down by Berg

NEWS AND GOSSIP

Büchner's *Woyzeck* was a time bomb that took nearly a century to explode. There was a real-life Wozzeck (spelled Woyzeck) who was hanged for murdering his common-law wife in 1822. Büchner wrote the play in 1837, the last year of his life. The manuscript was found amongst Büchner's papers by one Franzos in the 1870s. Mice and mildew had made it almost unreadable (hence the misspelling Wozzeck). The play appeared in print but since the manuscript was in note form, Franzos got the scenes in the wrong order and it didn't make much sense. Some forty years later one Landau edited Franzos's version into a more dramatic shape and put it on in Berlin in 1913. It was a knockout. Berg was there on the first night and said to one of his mates 'Fantastic – it must be set to music.' He started making notes at once but was diverted by other commissions and by war service and didn't finish the old thing until 1922. He had cut Büchner's twenty-six scenes to fifteen but otherwise stuck pretty well to the Büchner/Franzos/Landau text. Being unknown and broke, he had to borrow the money to publish the score. He got three of the *Wozzeck* numbers performed at a concert. These set people talking and Erich Kleiber, the music director of the Berlin Opera, said he would stage *Wozzeck* 'even if it costs my job', which it very nearly did, owing to a press campaign against Kleiber during the run-up to the first night. The gossip was that there had been 137 rehearsals and that the general rehearsal had ended in a riot between the pros and antis. But the first night was a huge success, *Wozzeck* was hailed as a milestone in history, Berg became a hero, Kleiber was confirmed in his job and everyone lived happily ever after. But it took five years for *Wozzeck* to reach the German provincial houses, when there was a flush of seven performances in one year. *Wozzeck*'s spread across the world was sluggish: New York 1931 (under Stokowski), London 1952, Paris 1963. Today *Wozzeck* is only an occasional visitor. Everyone thinks it's a masterpiece, but it just doesn't draw the crowds. Berg is still less friendly to the ear than Monteverdi or Harrison Birtwistle.

COMMENT

Wozzeck is one of the great madmen of literature. He does not have the brute force of Caliban, the physical deformity of Quasimodo, nor is he loveable, like Lennie in *Of Mice and Men*, but he stirs our sense of pity as does none of them. Pity for the lunatic who is an object of fun, pity for the simple man bullied and bamboozled by clever dicks, pity for the visionary who is hagridden by visions as terrifying as any seen by William Blake or John Clare, pity for the simple peasant who loses his girl to the local macho man, pity for the man so poor as to have to sell his body like a living corpse to a quack doctor. Whatever the chemistry used by Büchner to make us feel for this crazy hulk of a man, it works. Wozzeck's madness becomes even more affecting because he lives in a world run by madmen, the Captain and his obsession with time and speed, the Doctor with his lunatic ambition for fame through a paper in the *Lancet*, and the Drum Major a macho man extraordinary. Only the women and children are sane, also perhaps the unimportant Andres. So in this nightmare world does Wozzeck's simple goodness draw us to his side.

Büchner's play and Berg's music together make *Wozzeck* into a classic. The music lives up to the expectations of the play. It has all the mad logic of Wozzeck's world, it carries us into his visions of terror, and it also underpins the shock-horror of the plot. What we hear in the opera house is only the tip of a musical iceberg. (And here a boredom warning: readers not interested in the inner workings of musical form should skip on to the next paragraph.) Beneath the surface lies a vast complex of musical forms, palindromes, parallels, acrostics and, no doubt, some elements of musical trigonometry as well. But you and I don't hear much of this at all and Berg himself wrote disarmingly about the opera as follows: 'There must not be anyone in the audience who . . . notices anything of these fugues, inventions, suites and sonata movements, variations and passacaglias. Nobody must be filled with anything except the idea of the opera.' This quote appeared in Berg's book *The Problem of Opera*, but it is more interesting for us to see it as the problem of Berg. Why did he strain and strive to underpin the opera with complex forms which are meaningless to the people for whom he was writing it, namely the general opera audience? Did they really give him a structural plan that helped him to write the opera the way he did? Were they like an author's sketches of the ground-plan for a novel? Was it a mental exercise for private satisfaction? Was it to prove to himself and maybe his circle of friends, all learned musicos, that he could do it? Then we come to the real problem, which is that his claims to be using the forms of symphonic music don't make much sense anyway. Instrumental music, music that people tend to call by that awful word 'absolute', is in every way different to the kind of dramatic music needed for opera. A symphony may be a drama within the head, but an opera is a drama on the stage. They belong to different departments of the art, indeed they are pretty well different arts. To base a scene in an opera on sonata form makes about as much sense as an architect building a house based on the structure of a Shakespeare play, with a floor for each act and a room for each scene. Sonata form is based on tonality. It depends on the contrast of the home key of the piece with the dominant key. Berg's music has no tonality so any resemblance to sonata form can only lie in trotting out the material in roughly the same order as in a sonata, which is really of no importance at all. The overall pattern – three acts each of five brief scenes – makes sense. But the alleged form within the acts – Act I a sequence of baroque and classical forms, such as the Suite, the Passacaglia, and the Rondo, and Act II a five-movement classical symphony – sometimes seem to be no more than broadly descriptive labels and when the music does match the description, the form doesn't seem to be doing anything that seriously helps to make the music any better or any more meaningful. There is one exception – the 'invention on a single note' (Act III Scene 2), which means what it says. But by Act III the labels are getting much more vague. Perhaps Berg was by then tiring of the game.

(Readers opting out from this digression into musical form please rejoin here.) So let us intrude no longer into Berg's private world of musical acrostics and simply acknowledge that *Wozzeck* has a score that will bowl you over however resistant you may be in theory to atonal, twelve-tone or serial music. The vocal parts often use Sprechtstimme which can loosely be described as singing as if you were talking, or speaking with a musical note for each syllable. The orchestra is used powerfully and often percussively, rather as Shostakovich used the piano as a percussion, not as a singing, instrument. The brass is heavily and often noisily employed. The rhythmic patterns can change like quicksilver. There are leitmotifs for the major characters which you may not catch, there are bits that recall the music of earlier bits treating of the same subject matter, which you will not always recognize, there are grunts, explosions, surprise fortissimos and sometimes curiously offhand musical support for important points in the plot, often the music is fragmented into little barks and shouts when we would expect a continuous line, but when all is said and done, Berg's score can sweep you away in the mad, mad world of Wozzeck so that you come to share his hallucinations and are purged with pity and terror. And what more can you ask than that? Alpha.

Zauberflöte, Die *see* Magic Flute, The

OPERATICA

Applause

Applause in the opera house is of two kinds – Automatic and Meant. Glitzies and Corporates (see under AUDIENCES) respond to a drop of the curtain with the Auto-clap, a languid application of the palm of one hand against the other meeting about fifteen inches in front of the navel. The Auto-clap will occur in any house at the same level of decibels and for the same length of time, whether the item applauded has been good or bad, a piece of pure magic or an imperial disaster. The Auto-clap forms the sound-base on which the meaningful or Meant applause stands. Meant applause can take several forms, very rapid clap-strokes close to the chest, resounding blows struck almost at arm's length, slow rhythmic clapping to force a seemingly reluctant artist to take yet another call. In certain cases a high degree of Meant approval is registered by cries of BRA*VO* in the UK and the USA and *BRA*VO in continental Europe. (*BRA*VA in the case of female artists is a form adopted only by Snobs and native Italians.) Booing is another matter. See under BOO.

Aria

An aria is a set-piece song and in the early days of opera it was a main event which would occur from ten to fourteen times in an opera. We pick up the aria in the earliest operas in this book (*Dido*, *Giulio Cesare*, Mozart) and we begin to lose it in late Verdi and early Wagner. There are no arias in *Wozzeck*.

Once an aria starts all action stops dead. The function of an aria is to provide a vocal gymnasium for the singer. What he or she sings about is no more or less than their state of mind at the time which may be jolly, dismal, suicidal (often), amorous (very often), etc. In opera seria arias are usually desperately serious and modelled in a style much used by Metastasio who was the daddy of all libretto writers for half a century.

The standard Metastasian text for an aria usually had two verses and then if it were a da capo aria, which most of the big fellows were, the first verse would be repeated (da capo: literally 'from the top') something as follows:

Stanza 1 My husband is dead
This is terrible news
My God this is a frightful thing
I am thoroughly upset by this news
Stanza 2 Without my husband
I am a ship without a rudder
Beaten by the winds
I drift aimlessly about

Stanza 3 (da capo)
My husband is dead
This is terrible news
My God this is a frightful thing
I am thoroughly upset by this news

[The Secretary of the Dead Poets Society tells me that this is a monstrous caricature of Metastasio's work. I therefore print below one of this fine poet's actual texts from his libretto for *Il Sogno di Scipione*:

The ocean rock turns white
And trembles beneath the foam
As if the towering sea
Would sink it beneath the waters
But no, though battered
The proud rock lives on
And as time goes by
The sea will quietly lap at its feet
(da capo)
The ocean rock turns white . . . etc.

Doesn't seem all that much better than mine: Ed.]

The da capo aria bestrode three centuries. The aria had many, many other forms but the da capo dominated all sung music, as sonata form ruled over instrumental music. Its basic structure was simple although its variants were multifarious. In its early form it is usually described using those capital letters A and B so beloved of musicos as follows:

A. (1) A short piece from the orchestra, a tutti or ritornello (because it keeps returning). Not usually more than 20 seconds.
(2) The first solo. Usually the main tune. Often copes with lines 1–4 of the text. Drifts into the dominant key.
(3) The ritornello again, in the dominant.
B. (1) The wild bit. Something like a fantasy, a development section or whatever in symphonic music. Always in the dominant, the relative major or the relative minor. But can range around and modulate into fairly, but not wildly, remote keys. With operators who can be fairly square (Handel) B can be a happy release from a prim and prissie A. B copes with lines 5–8 of the poem.
(2) Ends by preparing us for the tutti in the home key.
A. And so back to A again, da capo exactly as before. Same words and all.

In the days of orthodox opera seria each of the top singers had four arias. When they had sung their aria they disappeared. This must have given the scriptwriter quite a few problems in trying to keep the momentum of the story going along, but the truth is that there was no momentum and precious little interest in the story. The compulsory exits of the lead singers demonstrate that the whole elaborate apparatus of courtly opera was designed pretty well solely to show off the singers and everything else, libretto, recitatif, scenery etc., was incidental. Wagner was a long way off.

So it was that from the seventeenth century to the 1820s the aria was king. There was a different style for different operatic emotions: arias di sentimento, arias di strapito, arias agitata, infurienta and arias di rache. There were arias for every occasion – arias di lamento, arias del sonno (addressed to sleeping persons); arias for different singing styles – arias declamata, arias di bravura, arias di agilita – and types of character – arias di carattero – and so on until we reach the aria di baule (a suitcase aria, the one a singer carried round with him from house to house and inserted into whatever opera was on the bill) and the aria di sorbetto (a number sung by a small-part singer, a cue for the audience to go out to get ice-creams).

In the days of Handel an aria could have switched from an oratorio to an opera and it wouldn't have noticed. But came the bel canto operas and the aria grew into a florid, showy, theatrical item with curlicues all over, some of them written, some of them ad-libbed by the singer. It also changed its form into an A–B–A part one, fairly slowish and often labelled cantabile, followed by a fast to very fast part two called the cabaletta. The cabaletta was really only the tailpiece or coda to the main aria but it became the big event as excitement built up and the singer suddenly spurted into it, rather like a rider in the final sprint of a cycle race.

So the aria ran on as the staple form until Verdi in his later operas reduced the difference between accompagnato recitatif, arioso and aria almost to nothing. In *Otello* we have a few set pieces, in *Falstaff* almost none, but in *Aida* the aria returns, celestially. Even Wagner, an anti-aria man if ever there was one, found that the old thing, or at least a formal set-piece song (Senta's Ballad, Elisabeth's Greeting, the Prize Song) could be an enormous help even to a man who set out to compose seamless music dramas.

Atonality *See* TONALITY.

Audience

The opera audience is made up of several strata which can roughly be described as Snobs, Glitzies, Corporates, Casuals and Buffs.

The Snobs know a lot of facts about opera and tend to talk about them in public places, usually rather loudly. A Snob visits the opera for the purposes of getting some fresh input for his data bank. Unlike train spotters (whom in some ways they resemble) Snobs do not carry note-books but will punch up furiously on an opera's history before attending a first night (an event which no Snob can afford to miss) so that they may blind their fellow Snobs with irrelevant observations. Snobs are intensely competitive. A conversation between a couple of Snobs after a performance might go something as follows:

Snob 1 The way that Frutti ran up to the cavatina in Act II reminded me very much of Zbalione in the 1956 Scala production. He took the appoggiaturas in just the same old Italian style.

Snob 2 But much faster than Zbalione. Wouldn't you agree that the really definitive performance was by Mastitis in 1962 at the Unter den Linden?

Snob 1 Um. (He has to say Um because he wasn't there in the Unter Den Linden in 1962, being still at his prep school in Devon at that time and Snob 2 knows this.)

A few but by no means all critics are Snobs. To be fair, there are some Snobs who actually enjoy opera.

For Glitzies the opera house is a place of resort where they can make it quite clear that they are very rich, frightfully well-dressed and socially amongst the top dogs or at least striving to be so. Unlike Henley or Ascot opera is available for much of the year and so is invaluable in buoying up the social calendar which tends to sag after August. Rich Glitzies' wives sit on committees to raise funds for Opera Galas or Tributes to great stars who have passed over. An overheard conversation between Glitzies might go something as follows:

How lovely to see you – where's Tony?
Alas he had to fly out to Antigua to sort things out after the burglary.
Poor you.
Who on earth is that woman with Charles and Cynthia over there?
Didn't you know? That's the Brazilian Ambassador's ex who is now going around with Johnnie.
Of course it is.
Lovely music isn't it?
Quite lovely.
(They part).

Male Glitzies seldom talk unless they can pair off into a quiet corner and then the conversation is unlikely to be about opera.

Corporates can be identified as rows of grey-suited men sitting contiguously, sometimes Japanese and frequently wearing dark glasses. They are there because their corporation has public-spiritedly contributed a substantial sum to the house funds and the reward has come in the form of seats for executives. Corporates in town for a conference or seminar are almost all male and will sit in a solid wedge, resident Corporates may bring their wives and be scattered widely over the house. Corporates and their wives are generally silent since they don't know anyone but in the case of encountering other known Corporates the conversation of the males is likely to turn on such matters as the Dow Jones and Hang Seng and the females must needs deal in the smallest of small conversational change. Comments on the opera in performance are rare: the sets – if conventional – may be called 'very pretty' and if the music or the production be modern it will be said to be 'difficult to understand'. A conversation between an elderly Corporate American and his elderly Corporate wife alleged to have been overheard at the Munich opera went as follows:

The male (studying the back page of his programme)
Shirlene, pigeon, did you tell me this opera was Tan Hoser?
Shirlene That's right Harry, Tan Hawser.
Harry Is today Tuesday?
Shirlene That's right Harry, Tuesday.
Harry If it's Tuesday it must be Forced [Faust].

[I have been asked by my Chairman to say that this is terribly unfair, that lots of Corporates are highly cultivated people and that if we go on making fun of them like this they are likely to stop giving money to opera and where will we all be then? Ed.]

The Casuals form the great bulk of the opera audience and they are there because they like opera, because it is their wedding anniversary or because they are giving their aunt a birthday treat. Many of them would go more often if they could afford it and will happily sit in the Gods unless it is a special occasion when a decent but fairly remote seat in the lower part of the house is *de rigueur*. Many of them will have opera CDs at home. Some will have looked up the opera in Kobbé. They are the real audience and their response to any opera from performance Mozart to Strauss will be as fair as that of a jury. Some will find Monteverdi to Handel too dry for their tastes, nearly all will shy away from Berg and later. The Casuals will instantly recognize star quality and are susceptible to charm and good stage presence rather than the niceties of vocal technique. But they know good singing from bad and when a show really comes off they acclaim it. God bless the Casuals, every one.

The Buffs are hard-core opera addicts. They go to the opera as often as they can afford it. They may not know quite so much as some Snobs but what they do know is likely to be more relevant. Buffs may be general or may specialize in a type of opera – bel canto, Wagner, Mozart – or in some aspects – conductors, Italian trouser roles, stage machinery. The nearest thing outside opera to the upstairs Buffs are the Promenaders who have their own short season in the Albert Hall. Buffs will have CDs and tapes of operas, some will have books, all will save their programmes and keep them neatly filed. Buffs will argue about opera, think about opera, have lots of opera going round and round in their heads, in extreme cases will sing selections from opera in the bath and when verging on operamania will dream about opera in digital sound.

There can be Buffs amongst any class of opera-goer, even the Corporates and the Glitzies, but few of these can spare the time to qualify for true Buffdom. Downstairs Buffs will all be subscribers for regular seats throughout the season and members of the Opera Houses' Friends organizations. Upstairs Buffs will queue all night for Pavarotti.

The audiences for the permanent opera companies in the UK all have representatives of the above classes of opera-goer but in different proportions. The three regional companies – Scottish, Welsh and Opera North – are shorter on Snobs and they are not in the class of the Ascot and Henley lot but not one whit less socially aware. There is a civic element amongst Regional Snobs which is not relevant further south. Casuals make up an even greater percentage of the house and here there are many who can't truly be called Casuals in that they subscribe regularly for tickets for a whole season in advance. The Buffs are there in force, they are in any place in the world where the curtain goes up on Mozart, Verdi and Wagner.

Glyndebourne is strong on Snobs, Corporates and Glitzies and weak on Casuals. But the interesting thing about the Glyndebourne audience is the high incidence of Buffs amongst the unlikely classes. Thus at Glyndebourne you will find a higher proportion of Buffs amongst the Glitzies than you will in the Crush Bar at Covent Garden. This may be because for real Buffs every Glyndebourne production is a must, whereas for a non-musical Glitzie a single visit will count as a score (and the summer season is still on). Casuals have found it very hard and very expensive to get tickets for Glyndebourne. Perhaps the new house will make it easier.

The Coliseum has perhaps the warmest audience of the British companies. There is a low incidence of Glitzies and Corporates. The great majority of the house is made up of Casuals, many of whom are bordering on Buffdom. The Colly audience lacks the discrimination of the Covent Garden audience down the road perhaps because they desperately want the show to come off. They are quite easily pleased which is not a bad fault. There is no doubt that of the five companies English National Opera has the highest proportion of people in the audience who have come because they want to hear the opera and for no other reason. It is the biggest house in Britain and when full and enthusiastic it reacts like a football crowd made up entirely of supporters of the home team.

Covent Garden as the Royal opera house has all the disadvantages of status without wealth. This is due to the disgracefully unenlightened policy of successive governments towards the arts which has forced prices up to a level which is scandalously high and which has naturally led to the exclusion of thousands of Casuals and hundreds of Buffs, leaving the house with a dangerously high ratio of Glitzies and Corporates in relation to the rest. It is, of course, the main stronghold of the Snobs but they do little harm since their numbers are relatively small. On a Gala night when only the well-funded classes can afford to go Covent Garden has an audience that is probably about as musical as you would get by combining a world conference of bankers with the guest list of a top-class charity ball at St James's.

First nights suffer to a lesser extent, but as an opera gets into its run it is astonishing but true to say that the Covent Garden audience is as discriminating as any in the world. This is perhaps because the non-musicals amongst the well-funded classes are not demonstrative in their response, clapping quietly and in much the same muffled manner whether the show is good or bad and thus allowing the musically interested to make their feelings very clear, whether it be to the production itself or to the individual singers (see APPLAUSE).

By and large British audiences are every bit as musical as those on the continent and much fairer. At the Scala Milan for instance the audience is openly partisan. Sometimes the contest between rival cliques is as vicious as any at a match between Celtic and Rangers. This is because, although the Scala has every class of opera-goer, nearly every Italian is a Buff and so Buffdom (plus the Italian temperament) spreads widely amongst the Glitzies and the Corporates as well as through the rest of the house. The fate of a new production as of a lead singer is often known to the management (or at least feared) before the curtain goes up. If the Scala audience can be brutal the (very knowledgeable) Viennese audience can be mean minded. There is a political element amongst the great and powerful in the better seats that seeks to influence the opera house's affairs. This shows itself in the way that a production, a conductor, the singers (and especially the music director himself) are received. Except on rare occasions this tends to range from frigid to tepid. The Viennese audience accepts great orchestral playing as a matter of course and can be ungenerous towards great singing, although sometimes Viennese musicality and Viennese warmth will break through all barriers. The Viennese audience are again almost universally Buffs but Buffs without balls, tending to react to opera with their brains rather than their stomachs. The overlap between Snob and Buff in Vienna is considerable.

The *Bolshoi* has traditionally been the worst audience in the business, the great bulk of it being made up by Corporates of a different class, namely trades unionists, officials, etc. who had been shipped in from Murmansk or Vladivostok as a reward for having hewn a tremendous amount of coal in record time or the like. Their response was about as demonstrative as a card vote.

The *Paris* audience is strong on Snobs and Glitzies and generally less musical than in any other capital city. The French also talk more during the performance than any other race.

The *Berliners* are both warm and discriminating and enthusiastic Buffs abound in all classes. They tend to be loquacious, but only after the music has stopped.

The *Met* in New York has a huge audience with its full quota of Glitzies and enormous numbers of Casuals. They tend to react to fashion, effusive to a star who is riding high but slow to spot talent in lesser-knowns who have not yet made it to a feature article in the glossies. But the Met has a core of natural Buffs for Wagner and another for the bel cantos. The Met audience has little chance to show what it thinks of contemporary opera because the Met does not acknowledge that contemporary opera exists.

Audiences over the world are commonly unaware that they are part of the show. A warm audience can help a production to get into its stride, a cold audience can stop it in its tracks. It is only when the house and the stage come together in partnership that you get a great evening. Which means you should applaud whenever you feel you can (see APPLAUSE).

Authenticity

We live in times when authenticity is all the rage and the true blue Authenticks rule the roost. Fifty years ago nobody thought twice about playing Mozart with an orchestra of sixty. Stokowski arranged some of Bach's organ pieces, originally written for two hands and two feet, for a big band of a hundred (thus employing some 200 arms, to say nothing of perhaps forty mouths and four feet for the harps). We used to hear the B minor Mass sung by a choir of 120 accompanied by an orchestra of sixty. Today Mr Rifkin of Scott Joplin fame and a notable Authentick has arranged it for four solo voices, four choral voices and nine instruments. (This is out-authenticating authenticity. Surely Bach could have rustled up at least eight singers in the choir.)

But it's not only the size, it's the quality. Some twenty years ago the stampede back to original instruments began. The bows for stringed instruments became truly bowed and the horsehair became slacker. The valves and other clever devices to make the wind instruments versatile and more mellow were abandoned. A bassoon began to sound like a beast in a bottle, oboes like stagecoach trumpets, clarinets screamed and shrieked like seagulls. These nasty sounds were exacerbated by the fact that many of the instrumentalists who played them were doing so because they could not earn a living in any other way.

In two decades all of this has changed. The authentic instrument has been improved to a point where it is not only nearer the real thing but also usually in tune and agreeable to the ear. A cottage industry has sprung up all over Europe making instruments which in the furniture trade would be called repros. As the prestige of the Authenticks rose so did the standard of playing and today in the leading ensembles you have some of the finest instrumentalists in the country. So you will now find Authenticks in that holy of holies the pit at Glyndebourne for everything up to bel canto and maybe beyond.

This has not, however, settled the argument in principle, namely should you play a Mozart piano concerto, for instance, on a Steinway or on the nearest thing you can get to the instrument Mozart himself used. The Authenticks will say that a modern piano will distort the balance between orchestra and soloist and the clear ideal is to get as close as we can to Mozart's sound. The pragmatists will say a Steinway makes the work come off much better and if Mozart could have laid his hands on a Steinway he would have jumped at it. The Authentick view may prevail amongst academics and musicos but for you and me, the paying clients, the pragmatic argument must surely prevail. (See *The Ring – A General Hello*, page 555.) In the end it is a matter of forces for courses. Rossini overtures have never sounded better than when played by the New York Phil under Toscanini with a band maybe seventy strong. Purcell's *Dido and Aeneas* when performed by skilful Authenticks flowers in a delicate manner which no big band can match. We will happily listen to either style if it makes the piece come off.

The pioneering work of the Authenticks has also been a plus in beavering away at original sources and discovering things that make us perform a piece differently. But respect for the composer's wishes has now gone too far. When a new opera was put on from the time of Gluck right up to Birtwistle (Wagner excepted) the creative team and the management have always gone through roughly the same processes of cutting, patching, goosing up and adjusting to meet the needs of the singers etc., just as in the twenties and thirties – the extreme case – the American musical was often largely rewritten during its out-of-town pre-Broadway tour. But today what the composer wrote down for that one occasion – the first night – is regarded as holy writ. When the bel canto composers were alive they were quite happy to revise and rewrite a work to suit another theatre or another occasion – and often to allow other people to do it. Now they are dead no one dares to touch a single semiquaver. If you look at the old band parts in an opera house library, you will find many of them (including Wagner) peppered with alterations made by successive music directors. But the day came when the fiddling had to stop. No matter that pitch has changed in the last hundred years, that the fashion for four-hour operas is out, that no one wants to see a second-rate ballet in the middle of a first-rate opera, that a few touches to the prima donna's line will save Miss Smith from disaster – no matter what, the piece has to be done Authentick, exactly as it left the composer's pen, or rather as we think it did, for there are many many examples where we do not know exactly what happened on the first night and the work is only Authentick in terms of the composer's autograph (or the first printed score) which may be far adrift from the actuality.

Nobody wants a music director to rewrite a score. We want him to be true to the spirit of the work but not necessarily to the letter. In the case of the Earlies (Monteverdi up to Handel) personal judgement has to play a big part because the original score can sometimes be little more than the top and bottom line. But the music director is first and foremost an impresario whose job it is to make the piece come off. It is, of course, a help to have the world of scholarship at his back but we expect him to make use of the scholar's work so that he may give us *Dido and Aeneas* or *Giulio Cesare* in a form that he likes, we like and makes for a great performance on the night we are there and not a performance that aims only to get as close as possible, for better or worse, to the performance on the first night some two hundred and fifty years ago when we were not there.

Ballet

To discover why we have ballets in opera we have to go back to Paris some 150 years ago. The shows then put on by the Opéra pulled an audience which was more social than musical and the management found it helpful in keeping the elderly gents amused and in attracting the young bloods to put on what amounted to a twenty-minute soft porn floor show about halfway through the opera. The porn was artistic and very soft, just a large number of young women dancing around with very little on, and it must also be assumed that the choreography was pretty soft too and nearer to charity ball stuff than to Diaghilev. The ballet would also of course provide a field day for the designer with stunning scenic effects and pretty tableaux.

There are several good reasons why a set-piece ballet in an opera is a pain:

(1) It stops the plot of the opera dead in its tracks and by the time it starts again some people will have forgotten whether it was Filipo or Gaston who killed Aphrodisia, and why.

(2) It costs more to mount a ballet which today usually has to be stolen from the production budget and could better be spent on better middle-range singers or whatever.

(3) The standard of choreography and of dancing is usually abysmal. This partly relates to (2) above in that it is very costly to assemble a top-class team of dancers, and opera companies who have ballet companies attached find it impossible to schedule the ballet company to meet the needs of a twenty-minute opera ballet of little importance, whereas the opera company obviously can't job its dates around to catch the top dancers when they are free. There was a time when the great opera houses had their own ballet troupes on the payroll. But even then they were second rate. The most popular solution today is to get in six or eight really good session dancers who will put on a lively show even though it is out of scale with the sets, the music and the traditions of the work. Six acrobats, however ingenious, can't really look lavish amidst the splendours of *Aida*.

(4) Far the most important objection is that the ballet breaks the mood of an opera and generally lowers the emotional temperature. So in a great opera you get bits of Radio 3 music which suddenly drops to Radio 2 music as the ballet begins. Even the very best ballet music (*Aida*, *Faust*) is what used to be called 'light' and is a million miles away from the matter of being entombed alive or selling your soul to the prince of darkness.

Of course there is a place for dance in opera when it is a part of the story (*Salome*, *Carmen*) or of the background (*Ballo*, *Fledermaus*), but the artificial introduction of dance for its own sake belongs to another genre of show, the masque (*The Fairy Queen*) or the modern song-and-dance show (*Carousel*, *West Side Story*).

So I urge the bold men of opera to purge the operatic stage of ballet, to lead off the dancing girls and if the clients feel they have been short-changed to hand each one as they leave the opera house the complete ballets extracted from all ballet-carrying operas in a tastefully packaged cassette. It would cost the management less money and give the clients more pleasure.

Boo!

To an opera singer those three letters spell the most fearsome sound known to man. The Italian provincial opera houses are the heartland of the BOO, where it is used if not good-humouredly at least in the spirit of the football crowd who hoot in mock horror at a missed shot at goal. At the bigger houses, especially the Scala, it can be organized and vicious. In Northern Europe the BOO is heard less often though the further North you go the colder and more frightening it gets. There is no precise definition of the BOO-sound. The OO is audible but the B is silent as the P in Psmith. Continuous BOOing is often accompanied by cat-calls, again a sound with no clear definition but most frequently taking the form of whistles, usually atonal and in the high soprano register.

Chorus

The chorus in a major opera house may range in size from sixty to a hundred souls. Within the normal limits of human nature the chorus has a degree of togetherness which the orchestra lacks. In union matters their views are likely to be expressed with one voice or at most four (S.A.T.B.), whereas behind the scenes the orchestra will often fragment in factions sometimes as small as one clarinet. To an outside observer the chorus would seem to have a cushy life. The orchestra has to play every night for the full length of every opera whereas the chorus seldom has more than half-an-hour's work on stage, several operas have no chorus at all and many (all Mozart, except perhaps *Idomeneo*) only need a small one. Anyone who has anything to do with an opera chorus will deny this vehemently, pointing out that the chorus often has to change costume six times a night, that any slack week is packed full of rehearsals which are essential for the next upcoming big chorus opera and that a chorister's life is nothing but hard labour, in that nowadays choristers have to be able to sing in five languages, hang from trees, run through fog and worse. Even so one can only reflect how strange it is that choral singing must need roughly six times as much rehearsal as orchestral playing.

For the operas with really big stuff for the chorus (*Boris*, *Meistersinger*, *Tell*, many Verdis) the chorus is augmented by an intake of session singers from the outside world and here, of course, lengthy rehearsal is an absolute requirement. A big chorus can stun the ear in a most satisfactory fashion and there is no doubt that they bring to the opera the majesty and power that no solo star can match.

Different countries produce different choral sounds. The Russian chorus has the most telling filling in the bottom layer of the choral club sandwich. Their basses are dark, deep and as rich as chocolate spread. Quite sensational. Even the tenors sound like basses singing high. The top (soprano) layer is not so easy on the ear, being always shrillish and sometimes rising to the folk-song shriek. In the German chorus it is the powerful tenor sound that immediately penetrates the ear. The solo

German tenor has a light tone when compared with the likes of Caruso but when giving tongue en masse they make a bigger impact than an equal number of Italians, perhaps because of their slightly strangulated but penetrating tone. Whereas the Italian and the Welsh tenor section of a chorus can sound enthusiastic and jolly, the German tenors always seem to be suffering acute anguish. But German choral singing overall is mellow, musical and skilful.

No chorus can sing as badly as an Italian opera chorus on an off day, which may be caused by a tiff with the chorus master, a dislike for the conductor or a failure to secure better overtime rates. But on a good night, and in Italian opera, especially at the Scala, they can sing with such zest, such musicality and above all such feeling as to fill every bar with magic. No chorus can so surprise you with their range of sound, from a whispered *ppp* to a thunderous *fff*.

British opera choruses are a lot better than they used to be when they were hag-ridden by the long choral traditions of oratorio and especially *Messiah*. It often seemed that each voice was doggedly determined to sing its own part (horizontally, as in contrapuntal music) rather than sinking its identity into the quite different world of opera music where (after Handel) counterpoint is rare. But today the standard is high and a British opera chorus, although it can never sound like a German chorus (weaker tenors and different tenor tone), can be very fine, with a speed and accuracy of enunciation that can make the Italians sound as sluggish as a barber's shop quartet.

Ever since Tyrone Guthrie introduced widespread pockets of business into the Shakespearean crowd, members of the chorus have been permitted to have their own busy little dramas going on all over the place which can happen not only when chorusing but when standing silent as the diva expires. This can be tiresome, especially since most members of an opera chorus are frightfully bad actors. Fair scenes catch them at their worst, with all manner of mugging and gesturing accompanying the simplest transaction such as the purchase of a loaf of bread. Rustic scenes also give an opportunity for ghastly individual excesses.

The Germans, to do them justice, have always tended to treat the chorus as lumpen, whether to allow them to sing better or for lack of imagination, one does not know. In Russia, too, the chorus tends to march on and off in platoons and stand steady on stage. It is mainly in Britain that they suffer from hyperactivity, but there are signs that the younger British producer is calming down the chorus to act more as a chorus and less like animated figures in a Breughel painting.

The chorus master rehearses the chorus alone until late in the day, often as late as the penultimate stage rehearsal. Some conductors insist on taking the chorus rehearsals themselves, others expect the chorus to be delivered to them cooked to a turn. Age is the great enemy of the choral singer. Every chorister is regularly auditioned and it is a sad, sad day when the moment of truth comes and the chorister has to hang up his dinner pail, for the decline in their vocal powers is usually more evident to the management than to the singers themselves.

Conductors

There are those maestro-worshippers who see operas as nothing more than lumps of clay waiting to be fashioned into masterpieces by some great genius, there are others who will tell you that the maestro cult is a myth and that a good pit orchestra will take the singers and the conductor safely through any performance so long as the man or woman at the podium doesn't foul it up.

The second is, of course, rubbish, certainly once you get past the tyros and move in amongst the giants. A music director who is fully in control has as much power over a score as does a film director over a script, except that the music director can have his work sabotaged by what the stage director does, whereas the film man has command over all branches of the art. Both directors do their hardest brain-work before a note is played or the cameras turn, for the conductor must have his own view of a work as if he were the producer of a new edition of the operas in his repertoire and not just the man to steer the work through 'the way Strauss wrote it' or according to some vaguely remembered recording by Furtwängler. Nobody knows what Strauss heard in his head when he wrote it and to copy Furtwängler is like re-playing an old movie – great in its day, which was sixty years ago.

As well as a personal view of the score the conductor must have a will of iron to impose his wishes on maybe eighty sometimes uncooperative musicians within a fixed time limit: he must have an ear so he can spot which fiddle of sixteen played a wrong note: he must have an eye so that when he stops the orchestra and says 'From the top please' his gaze leaves Zerkin McTurkin who played the wrong note in absolutely no doubt that it was he who caused the stoppage: and he must be naturally speed-conscious so that he finds exactly the right tempo and pulse for each piece. This last is often what sorts out the conductor's range – Mozart, for instance, can be destroyed by being taken too fast (Karajan often, sometimes Solti), also the meaning of his music can be changed by taking it too slow (Böhm, much too slow but often worth it because it allows each phrase to bud, break and flower before your very ears in a way you will hear from no other conductor), whereas Davis and Haitink judge Mozartian tempi to perfection. This applies less critically to other composers, Wagner alone being a great survivor when played at any speed.

Most of the above is equally applicable to concert-hall conductors but the man in the pit has to cope with singers as well. It is a huge advantage if the conductor has been a singer himself, but there are very few who have known the sweating palms and dry throat on stage before the first entry, and the always present nightmare of a lapse of memory. The musical director has to try to persuade the singers to do it his way. Sometimes they won't. They have been singing it their way for seventeen years, only came in on Tuesday and have to sing it in Los Angeles again next week. The maestro has to lump it. He does what he can.

But the opera conductor's most important job is to keep the stage in kilter with the pit, to have the orchestra and singers come in on cue. Some do this in a sing-along fashion, mouthing the words as if they were in the prompt box. Some do it deadpan with little wheedling movements of the fingers. Most do it with the eyes, the conductor's most telling weapon.

It is rare for conductors to be equally good over the German and Italian repertory (e.g. Varviso mainly Latin, Haitink only Nordic). Some manage it (Karajan, Abbado), others excel in a narrow field (Davis – Mozart and Berlioz). Every one has his on day and his off day. Solti used sometimes to drive too hard. Klemperer would take a nap from time to time.

Orchestras can be as temperamental as singers. They are all sophisticates and most are cynics. Dark messages come up from the pit during rehearsal – 'It's not working out with Pitzmeister: they're not going to give him the overtime he wants.' Only the greatest gain their respect, and not always those.

Unlike the concert-hall conductor the opera conductor does not need to be concerned about his body movements. The audience can't see him, only the orchestra, and this considerably reduces the need for any balletics (Bernstein). Arm and stick movements are much the same but in many cases the face is different. In passages of great feeling you will not see that crucified Jesus Christ expression (Bernstein again) on the face of any pit conductor nor that soupy smile to welcome in a Mahler melody. He has no time for histrionics. He must be on the watch all the time. The deadpan men remain the same (Kleiber, Haitink), but the muggers still mug (Solti, Abbado – a little) and the nodders still nod (nearly everybody).

It's a tough job getting a good performance on the night, with similarities to steering a bill through parliament, coaching a top baseball team, winning a five-set game of tennis, or giving a three-hour one-man show. And he has to memorize the whole of *Paradise Lost* for a start. So when the maestro is coaxed reluctantly (or springs eagerly) from the wings to take his call, please remember folks that whoever he is he's had the hell of a hard time.

A digression. Over the last half century there has been quite a change in the conductor's attitude to his work. Beecham thought first of pleasing the audience. So did Stokowski in Philadelphia and Fiedler in Boston. Although Beecham treated the three Bs with a degree of respect, he would 'arrange' Handel, Grétry and their ilk and in the case of Delius would more or less tell him what to write. This resulted in a lot of good music which otherwise would never have been heard and Beecham's judgement was such that he never vulgarized or debased a composer like Handel any more than did Mozart when he rescored *Messiah*.

Today the rule is to put 'Authenticity' and the composer first and the audience second. Thus it is that dozens of serious-minded conducting men are rootling around with manuscripts 'restoring' passages to operas which earlier musical directors or managements have very sensibly cut out: see AUTHENTICITY.

Costume

The costume designer's contribution to an opera is variable. It can be decently conventional or it can steal the show. Some operas need costume more than others. The costume designer can't do (or shouldn't do) much about the attire of the bargees in *Tabarro* whereas *Turandot* offers a field day. The costume designer has to work within a brief agreed with the overall designer. Sometimes the designer will discuss only the general style and the colour plan and leave the costume designer to do his own thing. Sometimes he will take a close interest in the spacing of the buttons on the prima donna's chest. Sometimes they are the same person, and it is most often then that costume can take the starring role and bring all the colour, life and character to show by being heavily lit against neutral backgrounds.

At any early stage the costume designer produces sketches. Although the clothes usually have a strong resemblance to the finished article, the people inside them never do. The costume designer doesn't draw his costumes for Don José nor for Domingo who is going to sing the role, he draws for posterity and puts ghostly wraith-like figures inside his clothes. And this is sensible in a way because after Domingo there will, unless the show is such a dog that it is dumped, be many different shapes of tenor coming along to inhabit them. Within limits the same costume is jobbed about to suit each new incumbent but if there were a role first sung by Caballé (5 feet 3 inches and 45-inch waist) and subsequently to be filled by Sophie von Otter (5 feet 11½ inches and 29½-inch waist), then that would be pretty well the end of the road and there would have to be a remake.

Some singers accept their costumes without a murmur. Others create. It was most unwise to design a costume for Callas without consultation all along the road. Pavarotti, once into his rustic costume for Nemorino, didn't bother to take it off for supper after the show and was rumoured (falsely, of course) to have been shopping in Marks in it the next morning. The costume-consciousness of both male and female opera stars varies greatly.

So far we are of course talking about made costumes. It is a question with every show as to how far down you go before resorting to stock. A really grand new production may have new costumes for the whole cast including a chorus of a hundred. It depends on the budget and also the style. A mainly traditional *Boris* could have those hordes of dreary peasants mooching around in the gear used for the Muscovites in *Khovanshchina*. The soldiers in *Carmen* can look pretty well the same as the soldiers in *Vespri*. But if you have a sparky production of *Otello* set on an American battleship or *Butterfly* in a modern penthouse suite, then you may have to spend a bit on new costumes for everyone.

Opera houses have an enormous stock of costumes. Many racks of costumes will stand in warehouses for decades and the question, as with sets, is when to junk and when not to junk. It is, of course, unanswerable, the only certainty being that once the costumes for *Traviata* have been junked the next morning there will be this goddam designer on the line from Los Angeles enquiring if they are still available.

For several years perversity was common in costume design, as it was in productions more generally. No scene whose natural setting was in seventeenth-century Florence was complete without a chorus of city gents in trenchcoats with bowler hats and rolled umbrellas. Wellington boots and bomber jackets were commonly seen in the courts of kings. Royal servants would appear as waiters and waitresses. This tendency is happily on the wane and no costume designer has yet thought of dressing a twentieth-century opera in the clothes of ancient Rome. No doubt that will come.

Since World War II the costume designer has moved out of the shadows of the stockroom and the theatrical outfitters which were pretty well his habitat, in the UK at least, before today's opera companies were founded and proper wardrobe departments set up. Whereas the set designer can create the overall ambience for the opera the costume designer can do specific work in making costumes help to define character. In real life the costume designer's aim is to make beautiful people more beautiful, but in opera he has to make Sparafucile into the most villainous of villains whether he be a back-street assassin in mediaeval Venice or a member of the Mafia in the twentieth-century Bronx. When the costumes in an opera are striking we will notice them, discuss them, like them or hate them. When we don't notice them they may be doing just as influential a job, but on the subconscious.

Critics

Taken by and large opera critics are a pretty rum lot. Some of them are musicos who can write, others are journalists who are musical. There is much less consensus between them than with practitioners in other sections of the critical trade such as film, TV and theatre. Most of them have strong views which are in no way similar and whereas one would expect a scatter of opinions over almost any production, opera critics can and frequently do disagree on matters more nearly approaching fact:

> In the second act owing to Piozzi's [false name: Ed.] languid tempi the piece began to sag.
> Piozzi's brisk and businesslike approach to the score which kept things on the move throughout.

– or:

> She is beginning to have difficulty with her top notes and this is affecting her intonation.
> Although it is nineteen years since she first sang the part in this house her voice retains all its youthful quality and her Lucia [let's call her Lucia: Ed.] rings out as clear and as true as ever.

Yes: same artists, same performances. Ah well, it all adds to the variety of life.

The lowest form of critical life is to be found in the columns of the top end of the big circulation papers where the critic apparently thinks it is his job to tell you what he thinks you will think of the show and avoids telling you what he thinks of it himself. This is rather like doing Pick of the Day for TV and radio. Some people may find it useful, others do not want Arthur Earhole telling them in advance how they are meant to react to the new *Pearl Fishers* when they go to it next Tuesday.

Once we reach the broadsheets we find a very different kind of approach. There are those who will use any opera as a peg upon which to hang an ego trip. This can take many forms, a display of learning (and we can be well into Snob territory here), a biographical bit about how they first saw/heard the opera and how it struck their virgin mind, how their view of the piece was revolutionized by the Peratozsky production in Salzburg in 1968 and how they were forced to revise their attitude by what Pillini did with it at the Met five years ago, or it can be a dissertation on one of their current fads, like all operas written since 1900 are about the mother–son relationship. Any of the pieces will tell you probably more than you want to know about the critic himself but none will tell you anything much about the production.

As we move closer to critical high ground we pass through a band of perversity. In all branches of the critical trade there are the wild men, the anarchists who will wait until they see what everyone else is saying and then say the opposite. This is an attention-catching game and such critics can add greatly to the gaiety of life provided only one thing – they are brilliant writers. Even so, it is not easy to go on being an *enfant terrible* when you are fifty-five, and today even Tariq Ali is running a terribly well-mannered TV show.

Perversity can take many forms. It can run through the production saying everything that is generally thought to be good is bad and vice versa. It can say the piece should never have been put on (although people have been clamouring for it for years). It can say the piece should never have been written (although it is a central item in the repertory of all opera houses). It can say that the composer is no good and this is particularly effective if everyone else thinks he is, like Berlioz. Perversity can be an irritant, which is a good thing, and it is not to be despised, but when it becomes manufactured perversity it loses its undergraduate charm and can become as tiresome as the phoney outbursts of outrage we get so often from our politicians.

In contrast to the Perversies we have the Honest Jims. Honest Jim will give you all the facts about the production in a logical order. He will perhaps refer to the nature of the piece with, if required, *un peu d'histoire*. He will then tell you what the sets look like and who did them. His critique of the sets may be confined to a single adjective ('colourful', 'sombre', 'exotic') for he is not a visual arts man and has never entered the Tate. Jim will then give a brief general appraisal of the production – 'a sparkling revival with a cast every bit as strong as last year' – and roll up his sleeves to run down the roll call of the leading singers. He will seldom, if ever, be lavish in his praise – 'her well enunciated coloratura' – and never be more than mildly displeased. 'Disappointing' is a strong word for him (others would call the same performance lamentable, disastrous and her big aria a shambles). He will then, very deliberately, turn his gaze to the conductor and deal with him in measured tones, hand out one line to the orchestra, half a line for the chorus, a wind-up sentence and there's your 500 words ready to be faxed.

But do not despise Honest Jim. Although it may sometimes seem that he has a form in front of him with little squares on it –

		Good	Fair	Bad
Prima donna:	Intonation	☐	☐	☐
	High notes	☐	☐	☐
		Too fast	About right	Too slow
Conductor:	Speed	☐	☐	☐

– which he conscientiously fills in each night before doing his piece, do not despise him because he is giving a lot of information we want in a reliable, orderly way. Once again, it all depends on one thing – can Honest Jim write? If the answer is no I fear he will immediately plunge below the boredom threshold and must be found a job doing the law reports.

As we steadily approach the summit of our critical climb we pass through a region of rather good critics, many of whom write for weekly journals and the like and who are basically Honest Jims but Honest Jims with some fire in their bellies. They will warm to the performance of the new Russian bass and their enthusiasm will shine through on the page. They will feel contempt for the vulgarity of the scene by the swimming pool and we will think as we read them, how horrible it must be. There are many critics in this class and although they all may write good prose, not many of them, alas, have that magic power over the English language that makes the great critic, the man you must read before you have made the morning tea.

And so we arrive amongst the great and the good (and there are more good than great in our little country today). A good critic must first and foremost give it us straight from the shoulder. He must tell us without fear or favour what he really thought of it. However brilliant a writer he may be we do not want him to be clever-clever about the show. We do not want him to walk down Memory Lane, or if he must, let it be a very short stroll. We want him to discharge the essential duties of Honest Jim but in a much more entertaining fashion. But we want more from him than that – we want some fresh perception. We want him to see beyond the limits of our own vision. We want his judgements to reveal new things not only about the production but about the work, the composer, about the art of singing, about conducting, about music itself. He must have a passion for opera. He must rejoice in excellence. He must have a burning hatred of the pretentious, the phoney and the second-rate. If he can carry the brilliance of his attack beyond the aesthetics and into the politics of the opera world we will bless him. The ideal critic, in short, must do for opera what the late Ken Tynan did for theatre when he so rattled the bars of the drama establishment that English theatre took off into the new and golden age and has never really looked back. So that's a little job for someone, please, and let's get the state financing of opera sorted out while we are at it.

And now a footnote. It would be helpful to the operatic trade if critics would give up the habit of slaughtering young talent, particularly young singers and sometimes conductors too. The oldies who are famous and secure are fair game, although it can be distressing to see a critic dealing inelegantly with a great singer who has reached a certain age and is losing his/her voice. This is a sadness for us and a personal tragedy for them and there is no call to be ya-boo about it. But the young are a different matter and a dismissive or harsh notice can destroy confidence and maybe set back a promising career. Of course if the critic feels a singer has no talent he is entitled to say so. But is he sure there is no talent? Singing is a nervous business and you can't switch a young singer on to their best mode on any day at any time by pressing a button.

Libretto (literally 'a booklet')

In Mozart's time as soon as a composer got a commission for an opera he would hunt about for a suitable libretto. What he needed was a mail-order catalogue but of course there weren't any. So he would riffle through what they had in the opera house library, borrow from fellow operatics and send out messages on the grapevine. He would not think of commissioning a new libretto unless it was for a very grand occasion preferably paid for by the patron and he would no more think of writing it himself than of making his own piano.

There were many poets who had a pile of opera librettos (see ARIA), Metastasio being top of the pops with over thirty librettos on the shelf, one of which had been used by ninety different composers. These librettos were built around standard stories taken from Roman history and Greek myth and most of them were about as exciting as a Hillard and Botting Latin exercise. The passion and power of the Greek tragedies had gone, too much handling had rubbed the bloom off the myth and the Roman power game plots were stiff, rigid and nothing like as good as *The Godfather*. The same stories were written over and over by a dozen different scribes. Sometimes there was give-and-take between librettist and composer (Mozart gave Varesco a hard time when he was adapting the story of *Idomeneo* from an earlier version), but overall the traffic between the two didn't amount to much more than cutting ten lines here or popping in an extra stanza there. Looking at the texts of the Metastasian period today, one marvels at the care with which the poetry was constructed to meet the conventions of the day and most of it was surely wasted because once the singing started the importance of the text fell away into the background.

But with Mozart and da Ponte we get a good picture of a creative partnership between a writer and a composer. Da Ponte was professional, ingenious and a great wordsmith. Mozart had a clear idea of structure, a good dramatic sense and was decisive. There is no data that throws much light on their personal relationship but it is certain that they must have worked together as closely as Rodgers and Hammerstein, resulting in three of the world's great opera librettos, one of them (*Figaro*) with the spade work done by Beaumarchais, one of them (*Giovanni*) far from flawless in the way it tacks together two ancient plots – Don Juan and the Stone Guest – but nevertheless an outright winner, and the third (*Così*) an example of a perfectly engineered plot. In all three words and music come together in the finales to make the sort of unified music-drama that Wagner was to hammer on about so tediously in the next century, took so long to perfect and so many volumes of turgid prose to explain. Neither da Ponte nor Mozart wrote a single page about their philosophy for opera nor is it likely that they even formulated any theory about what they were doing. They just did it.

The bel canto composers inherited pretty well the old opera seria tradition. When in search of a libretto, they too hunted the opera libraries and sent faxes far and wide. But there was a change. The leading Italian composers began to look for bespoke librettos. Rossini found no close nor lasting partner in the course of writing his thirty-plus operas, but he did three times use texts by Romani, a name to be reckoned with and easily the most sought-after librettist of his day. Romani went on to become much more than a provider of texts for the next great bel canto, Bellini. He became his close friend and partner, writing the librettos for eight out of his ten operas. It would have been nine (all but Bellini's first) but alas they had a horrid row over the ninth (*Beatrice di Tenda*) and so Romani was off the picture for the tenth and last (*Puritani*). Romani also provided the libretto for eight of Donizetti's three score and more of operas (amongst them *Elisir* and *Anna Bolena*), but it was never a good relationship. Donizetti bitched that Romani never met his deadlines and he was constantly worried that Romani did not seem to like him (this was true). Romani did a great job for the Italian opera libretto by lifting it out of hackland and making it a task that real poets were happy to take on. Although today any most tragic bel canto libretto may seem better suited as a script for a comic strip than a real-life drama we have to give Romani his due for his ingenious poems, many of them quite beautiful in their fashion and every one of them expertly crafted.

Romani's successor was one Cammarano, who hit the headlines with Donizetti's *Lucia* and went on to write the librettos for a further six of his operas. Now the young Verdi came on the scene demanding quite a lot more from his librettists than the earlier bel cantos, including instant obedience. Romani did one opera for him but he disliked Verdi's style of composition because it went more for dramatic action and less for poetic expression and thereby diminished the importance of the poet. But Verdi did get two successful librettos from Cammarano, for *Luisa Miller* and *Trovatore*, the latter being completed by the poor man on his death bed. Verdi's most successful partnership was with Piave who wrote the librettos for almost half of Verdi's twenty-eight operas. He was a jobbing writer with no kind of literary reputation but he had two great virtues: he did what he was told (and quickly) and he had a spaniel-like devotion to his master (who nevertheless harried and bullied him unmercifully). For two of his last three operas (*Otello* and *Falstaff*) Verdi had the luck to work with the golden boy of the Italian theatre, Boito, a man of letters, a conductor and to become a composer of real merit. The two of them had already grappled with a revised version of *Boccanegra* and as a result Verdi spotted Boito's great potential as a librettist and so allowed him more freedom than he had ever given to anyone else.

With Boito the great period of the Italian librettist came to an end. There were plenty more good librettos written but now composers were looking for verismo, drama and action, not poetry of an elevated kind. It was as if television writers had had to switch from scripting the likes of *Barchester Towers* (*Traviata*) to something nearer *The Untouchables* (*Cav* and *Pag*).

Meanwhile, up in the north Wagner was thinking his thoughts and spinning his theories in a succession of prose works about how to write a really good opera. From an early age he was hooked on the idea of dramatic unity between words and music and for him it was an easy deduction that the only way to action this was for Richard Wagner to write the words to music composed by Richard Wagner. His first four operas were based on some existing written works, e.g. *Rienzi* was adapted from Bulwer Lytton's *Last of the Roman Tribunes*, but after *The Flying Dutchman* everything was pretty well his own invention. He dived into late mediaeval history and rootled out innumerable facts and myths about, for instance, Nüremberg (*Meistersinger*) and the song contests between fourteenth-century minstrels (*Tannhäuser*) and hung them on a strong story line and then shaped the whole thing with uncanny skill into operatic form. His great work, *The Ring*, was self-generated using the whole stockshop of northern myth to give it colour and incident (see *The Birth of The Ring*, page 632). But *Parsifal* was based more firmly on a legend already written up in poetry, and *Tristan* too was an interpretation of a pretty widely-reported mythological/historical happening.

Wagner produced his librettos with great sweat and toil in a mode that is just off poetry. They do not read well but they do their job. When the words are put together with the music the opera works, sometimes ponderously but always it does what he wanted it to do. Wagner took immense pains to reflect every nuance of the text in the music. The technique he used to do this beggars the imagination (see *The Ring – A General Hello*, page 553). With Wagner the libretto lost its independence. It was no longer a matter of setting words to music, it was a matter of fusing words and music together to make a music drama.

Opera was never quite the same after Wagner. Traditional operas with traditional librettos continued to be produced, sure enough, but the

Wagnerian ideal hung over the more serious fellows and Debussy, for instance, adapted Maeterlinck's lovely play *Pelléas et Mélisande* into something not far off a Wagnerian text (but much, much better). There was also a surge in the opposite direction, namely a move by composers to set the text of a great poem or prose work as nearly as possible in the words of the original piece. Tchaikovsky did this with *Onegin* in which some scenes are taken word for word from Pushkin's poem, thus outraging the literary snobs in St Petersburg who thought it a desecration of the nation's best-loved book. Berg cut Büchner's *Wozzeck* but otherwise remained faithful to the outline and in parts even to the text of the original play. Strauss stuck closely to Oscar Wilde's poem when he wrote *Salome*.

The last great writer/composer combination came when Richard Strauss and Hofmannsthal teamed up first on *Elektra* and then went on to produce *Rosenkavalier* and four other operas (six of Strauss's best). This was a partnership of equals. Both were sophisticated fellows who between them brought to opera a new and more worldly touch. They dealt with human emotions, sometimes cynically sometimes tenderly, in a style a million miles away from what Hofmannsthal called 'the intolerable erotic screamings' of *Tristan and Isolde*.

The opera libretto has taken many forms. The opera librettist has nearly always been number two to the composer. He has, on the whole, had an unhappy life. He has seen his work cut, vulgarized, distorted (as he would think) and he has been chivvied, bullied, abused and made to rewrite again and again to the point of despair. But interestingly enough not many walked off the picture and this may have been because no matter how intolerable the composer's behaviour, there is nothing in life quite like being a part of a great operatic success. The Olympic gold medallist may feel pretty good as he mounts the rostrum, but this is as nothing to the satisfaction given by the roar that goes up from the auditorium on the first night of an operatic smash hit. The composer of course will accept all of this as his due, but the librettist, usually a bookish man, will for once have a rare taste of glory too.

People will deride operatic librettos as some of the silliest things ever written. What do you expect of an opera anyway? they will say as they are told of heroines living as transvestite hermits (*Forza*), babies mixed up at birth (*Trovatore*), unlikely divine interventions (*Suor Angelica*) and of course they are right. A great composer can make something of an outrageously outré libretto (*Trovatore* again) but he can make much much more of a good one (*Traviata*). Indeed, before we can pass any opera as A1 we must look for a few simple qualities in the libretto, such as:

(1) The script should read like a good play – tragedy, drama, comedy, whatever – which would work on stage without music (*Figaro*, *Carmen*, *Elektra*).

(2) It should be credible within its own convention (*Meistersinger* yes, *Tannhäuser* no).

(3) It should make us like/love/hate/despise the characters just as if we knew them in real life (*Elisir* yes, *Tell* no).

These three qualities together plus great music put an opera amongst the alphas. Other operas may have wonderful music and may give you a splendid musical evening but if they have a lousy libretto they are only half an opera.

Lighting

It is lighting that dictates what an opera will look like just as much as the sets. Clever lighting can make a visually dreary opera sit up and shine, dull lighting can make a gorgeous set look ornery. Lighting is a tool to support the drama of a scene and indeed can take over the lead and make drama itself, lighting is there all the time, lighting is taken for granted, lighting works its will on the subconscious and not the conscious mind. Lighting is much, much more important than you think.

The lighting director should preferably be the Siamese twin of the set designer. Since this is unusual, the next best thing is for the two to have a harmonious view of what it is they are after. Colour of light and colour of paint, the texture of surfaces, how much light they reflect, the overall tone of the set, the nature of the costumes, the surface used on the floor – all of these items are as much the concern of one man as the other.

The lighting director looks at the drawings at an early stage, looks at the model (if there is one), and thinks. After thinking he will discuss his lighting strategy with the producer and the designer. He then will watch the stage rehearsals with a beady eye, and think again. He can do no more than plot and think until the first technical rehearsal, some three or four weeks before the first night. Now he can start fixing his hundreds of lamps and building his dozens of lighting cues. Some lamps can be on the gantry above the stage. Some can be in the wings. Some can be on the fringe of the proscenium arch, or on scaffolding fixed just outside it. Some light will come from the lighting ports sited at various levels at the back of the auditorium.

The lighting director does not have much time to do his work and never as much as he would like. By the end of the three technical rehearsals he will pretty well have his lamps fixed and his lighting cues built into the computer. He may have anything from 500 to 1000 ways, or separate lines to which a lamp can be attached. In the UK no house can yet swivel or focus a lamp by remote control. So every set-up has to have its own individual set of lamps.

During the stage and orchestra rehearsals he tests his lighting plot, often with the producer alongside him. Furtive figures steal about the environs of the stage, some with ladders, fixing a lamp here, adjusting one there. By the pre-general rehearsal he is fine-tuning. By the first night it is all over: he and his staff have nothing to do other than give the computer its go-ahead at each new lighting cue. But he will fiddle on right up to the end of the run.

There are several different kinds of lighting used on the stage. There is the ambient light covering the whole set, be it a ballroom or a sun-drenched piazza. There is key lighting which can orient the natural light source, most obviously the sun, although key lighting of this sort, once all the rage, is now out of fashion and in most exterior scenes the sun could be pretty well anywhere. There is spot lighting on an individual or group which again is much less used now than in the days of limelight. There is the use of light from the wings or backstage to mould the human form and make it stand out in 3D. Footlights, or floats, are now pretty well a thing of the past.

The mechanical part of the job is the least of it. It is the lighting director's aesthetic and dramatic sense that can make or break a show. Is the slow cold dawn at the start of Act III of *Bohème* a blue dawn of sheer iciness? Is it a grey dawn of hopelessness, under an aluminium pan lid pressing down on the affairs of the Bohemians? Is there a touch of pink in it, the promise of sunshine ahead for the street-sellers of Paris and, eventually, for Rodolfo and Mimi? This one man, the lighting director, has the power to evoke in your minds, or perhaps in the pits of your stomachs, without you knowing it, the mood, the expectation, that will best prepare you for the emotional adventures that are to come.

The lighting director can also shock you with a sudden blinding flash of light when the ghost of Charles V emerges from his tomb to offer his assistance to Don Carlos. He can put on a Brock's benefit night in the Wolf's Glen in *Freischütz* that will stun you. And he can bring real terror into the approach of the Commendatore in the last act of *Giovanni*.

So good on you, lighting director, say we, you who can be the unseen, unsung genius of the show, and never a curtain call. And if on some nights the lightning happens after the thunder or the stage lights come up before the last two prop men have got off, well, that can happen to anybody.

Opera – History and Form

Purcell's *Dido and Aeneas* was first performed at a girls' school in London in 1685, Gershwin's *Porgy* in a theatre in Boston in 1935. Thus the operas in this Guide stretch across 243 years and quite a lot happened along the road.

In the early days most of the action took place in the Po valley when

Monteverdi, who is generally thought to be the daddy of modern opera, started turning out stuff that we still love to hear today. Venice then became the opera metropolis from where it spread like Asian flu across all the courts of Europe which could afford it, and some that couldn't. This book picks up the baton with the opera seria of the mid eighteenth century (*Iphigenia*, *Orfeo*, *Idomeneo* and *Tito*), a form of opera which is hardly calculated to set the pulse racing. In those days, however, it was their idea of fun. After a huge meal they would troop over to the court theatre for three or four hours of opera seria plus a shorter opera with maybe an orchestral concert thrown in. Their musical appetites were enormous and if they consumed food and drink in matching quantities, it is a wonder that any of them were still awake at the first interval.

Opera seria were nearly always about Greek mythology or Roman history or the like. Often they were given on state occasions, by the host at a summit meeting, at a wedding or coronation, or some anniversary. The original story was usually pushed around a bit to identify the hero with the particular royal who was being honoured that day. The whole thing was done with a degree of adulation that even Mrs Thatcher would have found intolerable and there was often a personal message tagged on at the end – a licenza – of the most nauseating flattery that today would instantly earn its author *Private Eye*'s OBN first class. Since the number of fresh mythological stories was limited the same ones were permed over and over again and if a poet did a good job on a libretto (which was of course in verse) it would be used by more than one composer. Metastasio, who took all the Emmy awards in his day, wrote scripts for over fifty operas, half of which were performed in at least thirty different settings and one of which (*Artaxerxes*) was used as their chosen libretto by ninety (figures 90!) different composers.

An opera seria might start off with a chorus or a recitatif, something as follows:

Severus	How I wish Veriseverus would return from the Capitol.
Veriseverus	Here I am I have returned from the Capitol and I have news for you. Publius has informed Milo of Sextus's treachery.
Severus	Gods! And does Milo know that Servilia is planning to kill his brother's nephew Cinna?
Veriseverus	Indeed he fears that Amplex is now preparing to join with Cincinnatus to enlist great Caesar in the plot.

By this time every royal must have been pretty well rocked back on his heels unless he had done a good stint at Kobbé or had seen the other eighty-nine versions of the same piece. Maybe he had a royal racereader crouching by his ear helping him along the track like a private David Coleman. The story sped along in secco recitatif (see page 847) until it ran into the buffers on reaching an aria (see ARIA, page 803). Here it stopped dead while one of the characters sang about their state of mind for about three minutes. Now we come to the main purpose of the opera seria which was to give the singers a chance to show off their voices. There would be a powerful castrato at the top of the bill plus maybe two or three women, maybe a second or lesser castrato and at least one natural male voice. For the singers every aria was a show piece. They would bully the composer to adapt their numbers to suit their voices. This castrato might have a golden high D flat. So there must be at least four D flats in the piece with a long one at the end. The prima donna's voice began to turn into a train whistle above high C, so everything above that had to be transposed down one octave, and so on. When the singer had finished he withdrew from the stage and (usually) another character came on. So back into another bout of secco and another rush of narrative. At the end of an act there might be a very big solo, a duet or more occasionally a chorus full of bromides, maybe on the following lines:

Hail to our all-conquering and courageous monarch
A man who is universally known to be extraordinarily brave
And also outstandingly clement indeed even the gods
Are amazed at the clemency of this man which is only matched
By his bravery. Hail, Hail and Hail again to our monarch
Who is indeed both brave and clement. Hail.

Towards the end of the last act the plot speeds up to the denouement. The opera would end no doubt with polite upper-class applause and some conversation about how smart the morning's parade had been.

There were no laughs in an opera seria. The whole thing was taken very seriously indeed. The scenery might be a big deal with one or two spectacular effects contrived by the royal carpenters. The orchestra would consist of about thirty players many of whom would be cleaning shoes and polishing the silver by day. The opera would have been conducted by the music director from the keyboard or sometimes from the front desk of the violins.

And so did the seria ride along in the courts of Europe for more than fifty years. It was part of the royal calendar, like the military parades, the banquets and the fireworks that surrounded it. It didn't much matter if it were good or bad so long as it was there and done decently. A good chef was a plus so was a good music director. You could get a name for a good table or for good music. But so long as the table was laid properly, so long as the singers were at least adequate and the food edible, then you would hold your place in whichever division of the inter-state league table your potty little principality stood.

Gluck did his best to haul this cumbersome old form into something more dramatic and more musical. Mozart cast his magic over it (*Idomeneo*, *Tito*), but even he could not raise it to the level of the new-style operas he did with da Ponte.

In the second half of the eighteenth century a more lumpen form of opera ran alongside the aristos' opera seria. This was the Singspiel which came from the practice of adding a few songs to a stage play (but there's much more to it than that). The Singspiel, being a local product, was always in German, and this struck Joseph II as a frightfully good patriotic form of entertainment to counter the cultural threat of opera in Italian, French and opera in every tongue except that of God's musically most favoured race, the Germans. So in 1778 he set up a Singspiel company in Vienna and gave this odd form of musical theatre a subsidy. So Singspiel became a fashion. Hence we get Singspiels from people who probably really didn't want to write operas that way, including Mozart (*Seraglio*, the *Flute*). The Singspiel could be serious (*Fidelio*) but it was more often comic. It was, of course, a common form of music theatre in most countries (*The Beggar's Opera, Carmen*) but only got an official label in Germany.

While the Singspiel and the seria struggled on in their own patch in Northern Europe, the glorious age of bel canto dawned in Italy. It was Rossini who first broke surface above the raft of popular Italian composers who had been entertaining the common people for years (thanks to the royals who sponsored the theatres). With Rossini we are into a new world. Lots of good tunes, plenty of laughs and the show structured and presented pretty well as it is today. Tragedy too, but aimed at the tear ducts rather than the Greek ideal of purging the soul by pity and terror. The range of subject and style of treatment widened enormously, from *William Tell*, a big bombastic political piece, to *Italiana*, a zany comedy with a first-act finale fit for the Crazy Gang in their heyday.

The orchestra did not get much bigger but the players had to be able to play well. There were exposed solo parts for the woodwind. The lower strings rubbed away very much as in Germany but had to pick up the Rossinian often-changing rhythmic patterns instead of pounding out the steady all-on-the-beat stuff belonging to opera seria. The upper strings ranged more widely and moved faster. Dotted rhythms (tum ... ti-tum ... ti-tum) had gone, and the conductor had appeared.

The operas themselves still had secco recitatif to tell the story and set-piece arias (sometimes now called cavatinas) as a stopping-off point where the singers could flower. But now the plot sometimes unfolded in a more tuneful form of recitatif (arioso) and there were ensembles where people, if they did not yet actually do anything, at least wondered what they should do (confusion finales). The choruses were pretty well as dumb as ever but could be much grander (*Tell*). Even so they hammer away at one, or in extreme cases two, simple thoughts.

And there was a new invention – bel canto itself. This is a style of song with lots of ul-ul-uls on one syllable with the voice playing about in the most extravagant musical patterns – arabesques, arpeggios, runs, jumps, double axels, toe loops etc. – to show how well trained and also how beautiful the human voice can be. Some people find the vocal antics of bel canto as artificial as those contests where dogs jump through tyres, walk along see-saws, etc., but others delight in the sensational sounds that a bel canto soprano can emit.

As bel canto wended its way down the century it picked up two recruits in Bellini and Donizetti. Bellini hung towards the melancholic side of life. He was at his best writing long sweet tunes for young ladies who had lost their senses through sleep-walking or going crazy for love. Donizetti was a more robust figure who could be funny (*Elisir*), touching (*Elisir* again) or tragic (*Lucia*). He could write a tune that would stick in the ear, a tune to make your feet tap, a patter song or a sentimental ditty with equal ease and did so in more than sixty operas. Neither of the two radically changed the form of opera, but they introduced more arioso singing between numbers, set-piece recitatif got less, secco recitatif disappeared altogether. Characters began to become people and not symbols. The bel cantos set out to give you a good evening in the theatre and for a lot of people bel canto is still the heart and soul of the opera repertory. L.S. Lowry used to play *Norma*'s 'Casta Diva' all morning whilst he was painting. Each time the record wore out he bought another one.

Overlapping with the late bel canto we have the young Verdi, along with Mozart and Wagner one of the three great men of opera. Verdi barged his way into grand opera with some powerful but eccentric early work which brought the chorus up to be a prime mover in the opera game but otherwise ran pretty well along the bel canto track. But soon he gave opera gravitas and a higher status by tackling great subjects (*Macbeth*) with great music. He was not above producing a rattling good blood-and-thunder piece like *Trovatore* but he also began to make some of his opera persons into living and breathing people we could know and love (*Traviata*). He also composed operas of a truly grand style (*Carlos*, *Aida*) and he made it intellectually respectable (*Otello*, *Falstaff*).

In his later operas he changed the cheerful accompaniment (often cheerful even in the face of tragedy) of the little pit orchestra of the bel cantos into the great dark mass of sound that rolls around in the background to *Otello*, the mighty blasts of *Aida* and the quicksilver tone poem that is *Falstaff*. He did this not so much by enlarging the numbers (although his orchestra did grow progressively bigger), but by scoring the music as if the orchestra were an equal partner to the singer and not just their servant.

Both Rossini and later Verdi tangled with the Paris opera world which during the first half of the nineteenth century became the richest, most fashionable and most snobbish in Europe. In the 1850s the dominating figure was a man called Beer who for understandable reasons tacked his Christian name (Meyer) on in front of the beverage. Meyerbeer was an operatic adventurer who had ranged the opera houses of Europe touting his boring operas until he found his mark in Paris. Here he made it his job to make grand opera as grand as a lot of money, royal backing and giddy social scene could make it. To pass muster a Paris opera had to have five acts, a ballet (see page 812) plus a lot of hype and behind the scenes a queue of socialites pushing and shoving for some sort of association with it. The baneful influence of this kind of grand opera dragged on for years and it was this grand opera audience that booed *Tannhäuser* off the Paris stage (see page 702).

Wagner put an end to this tedious regime by his example as a composer and by his tireless lobbying for a better class of opera. He had two simple messages:

(1) Opera is a branch of great art. It is, if not exactly holy, one of man's noblest pursuits. So opera is a very serious business and please stop chattering at the back of the hall.

(2) Opera should be a music-drama in which text and music are wedded together in glorious unity (only he took 108 pages to make point one and three volumes for point two and hadn't quite finished even then).

So once Wagner got launched that was the end of curtain calls, giggling in the boxes, short little acts between lovely long intervals, dancing girls, jokes, tiaras and no doubt the ice-cream sales fell like a stone. How Wagner moved opera itself away from the old concept of a 'numbers' opera and developed his system of leitmotifs is discussed in section on *The Ring* (see page 556). Briefly, he more than doubled the size of Mozart's orchestra, wrote very long continuous acts of pretty heavy stuff, asked the scenery department to do impossibly grandiose things for him and eventually built his opera house in Bayreuth.

Of course there was other opera life continuing while the great Wagner was doing his reformation act in Germany and indeed in Paris it got even more frothy and Boulevardian with the lovely Offenbach and his successors turning out high quality French musical farce and fun.

Many people would say that with Verdi and Wagner opera reached its zenith. But it moved on. Puccini came in with an innings strong in sentiment and powerful melodies which pushed the characters in his operas pretty much as near to our own world as fictional characters get. Certainly Mimi (*Bohème*) is every bit as real as Little Nell and much less mawkish and Minnie (*Fanciulla*) is at least as real as Annie (*Get Your Gun*). Puccini wrote continuous music for his operas and even when a set piece is unleashed (Musetta's waltz, or 'Nessun dorma') it arises naturally out of the musical scene and subsides back into it without seams showing, as they do in early Wagner (Elisabeth's Greeting) or even late Verdi ('Celeste Aida'). So in his very different style Puccini did what Wagner wanted to do but in a much more agreeable way, with less toil, with fewer leitmotifs, no heavy breathing and in much smaller helpings (*Meistersinger* 4 hours, *Bohème* 1 hour 45 minutes).

After Wagner and Puccini the opera houses of the world settled down to play operas of the past in a steady rep which changed imperceptibly with fashion. At the turn of the century Mozart was still out and bel canto going into its slow decline, although Verdi was still pretty well in fashion. New Italian verismo operas such as *Cav* and *Pag* were in vogue, as was a lot of French light romantic stuff (*Werther*). Russian opera was being seen for the first time and needed a lot of bells and gongs. The world was waiting for a successor to Wagner and they got him in a less ponderous form in Richard Strauss. In his first two operas (*Salome* and *Elektra*) he seized on and developed Wagner's ideas. His orchestra was just as big, his ambition as high but the operas were not so long and didn't need so much scenery. What was going to happen next? He went on to produce a stream of more conventional operas and opera-goers found themselves back in the drawing room quite a lot and his music too became pretty well domesticated.

After Strauss, and with a few exceptions such as Britten, opera moved beyond the reach of the old opera community. There were few whistleable tunes, atonal music caused discomfort, there was no spectacle and the story was usually squalid and always gloomy. So it is that of all operas written in the musical language of the twentieth century only two (*Wozzeck* and *Bluebeard*) have proved popular enough to get into this book. But time will change that and it is interesting to note that twentieth-century operas with their generally more modest orchestras, less spectacular sets and concentration on words and music, are taking opera back to the scale of the opera seria. One of the future problems for opera may well be that whereas Wagner's operas were too big for comfort, some modern operas may be too small. The chamber opera (which is not written for the chamber at all but usually for something more like a warehouse) is nevertheless a difficult animal for the opera house to handle. With a few exceptions operas within the last twenty years have no glamour, make no money and nobody likes them except the composer and his friends. It is therefore hard at this moment to see what new works will refresh the pages of this book in fifty years' time.

Opera House

The words Opera House can mean anything from a custom-built laboratory-clean modern factory block with an auditorium like a posh cinema to a grotty old Victorian theatre probably built as a music hall a hundred years and more ago. In the middle lie the grand opera houses, the legacy of opera when she was the sport of royals, built as a public monument and given pride of place in the capital city, with a central site, well below the status of the palace itself but only just inferior to the Parliament building and well above the Mint, the Law Courts and the museums. The top international opera houses today are generally thought to be the Scala Milan, the Staatsoper Vienna, the Metropolitan Opera House New York and the Royal Opera House (Covent Garden) London, with Munich, Paris and Moscow all knocking at the door. This does not mean that other houses do not put on operas just as good but it does mean that the first-league houses have bigger choruses and orchestras on their books, have a higher budget for new productions, pay a higher top for stars and have a snob cachet that is not shared by the Grand Theatre Leeds or the Volksoper in Vienna.

The nineteenth-century ideal for the layout of an opera house was to have the building split into three equal areas, one third being the stage and backstage, one third auditorium and one third foyer. The Bolshoi in Moscow is the perfect example of this plan. The backstage is still just big enough to cope with its unhurried schedule, the auditorium (2,100) is laid out on the classical pattern of five loggia levels (or circles) a floor and a gallery, the foyer space is big enough for all those clients who wish to do so to sit down to a knife-and-fork supper at a roomy table.

But alas, things were not so good elsewhere. The value of real estate in Western capitals meant that the two outside ends of the Bolshoi layout were squashed in like a concertina. In the Royal Opera House Covent Garden, for instance, the backstage area is a half of what it should be and the foyer space for the circle and stalls is skimpy and there is none at all for the top half of the house. The Bolshoi vestibule where the customers take off their snowshoes and furry hats is only just smaller than the Covent Garden Crush Bar – its main foyer.

There are other problems. The great opera houses were built mainly in the 1850s when the production of opera was a leisurely affair and when the position of the arts in national life was much better understood. No-one fussed about spending on opera the amount of money it needed. Today the opera houses of the world are pummelled and chivvied towards maximum productivity and minimum cost. This means that each year the Intendant has to get out as many shows as he can, far more than the number for which the house was designed. Most major opera houses (Vienna excepted) work on the Stagione system. This means that you have two or three operas on show at the same time each with a limited run usually of between five and eight performances. Thus the singers have to sing only twice a week or at most three times, say on Monday, Thursday and Saturday. It also means that at least two operas are in rehearsal as well as the two or three that are running on the stage. This means heavy traffic backstage, indeed a scrum. Everything that can possibly be done outside the house is pushed out to warehouses and workshops, some of them perhaps twenty or thirty miles distant. The old houses just manage to cope with the near-impossible by working twenty-four hours a day for twelve months of the year, but it is touch and go both from the point of view of human endurance and physical wear and tear – and safety. All theatres are tinder-boxes and every opera house ends up by being burnt down (unless it is bombed to bits in a war) and many old houses run close to the fire regulations. You therefore have the paradox of the inside of the opera house – the grandest of all grand public venues – filled with rich people drinking champagne while less than a hundred yards away not-so-rich people are working in slum conditions which would have disgraced a Yorkshire mill-owner before Lord Shaftesbury got after him.

In sharp contrast to this the working areas of a new opera house such as Munich can comprise of broad acres of fully automated clear and cool factory space, including the construction shops and loads of room for storage. The stage is constructed of blocks that can be raised and lowered to give the floor any configuration the designer may want. Traps abound, lighting is automated, the scenery rolls silently on and off the stage into one of the several adjacent waiting rooms and the next set rolls equally silently in. The stage hands can play rummy during the intervals. Everything is wonderful except the auditorium. Here the acoustics are good, the seats better than on Concorde, everything is efficient and in the best of modern taste, but the magic has gone. The thrill and tingle that is given off like a mild electric shock by those cream and gold horseshoe tiers of the old houses is no longer there. The Scala gives any opera a flying start. In the modern house an opera has to generate its own warmth.

Each of the old opera houses has its own character. The Scala is the mother of all opera houses. It was built in 1778, holds 2,300 and stands as a monument to the place of opera in Italian life. Outside it is classical, statuesque, elegant but once you penetrate the maze of staircase and foyer to reach the auditorium, you feel the warm vibes of the tens of thousands of opera buffs who have applauded, catcalled and cheered opera on its way through history for the last two hundred years. The Royal Opera House Covent Garden (built in the same style in 1856 – holds 2,200) may not be so venerable as the Scala but it is prettier and every bit as glamorous. In contrast to the older houses the Met in New York is enormous (3,800) but ornery. It tries to catch the grandeur of the old horseshoe style but leaves you with the impression you are in a Hollywood movie house that has got a bit above itself with sparky lights in tinsel mountings, a drab colour scheme and tabs (main curtains) that are simply not *comme il faut* for Verdi and Wagner.

The Vienna house has been restored after bombing in World War II to something of its original state. The outside is exactly as it used to be (1860) and looks like a terribly important museum. The inside is quite unashamedly an updated repro of its old self (2,200) and has that cold, slightly phoney feel of English Edwardian classical, the sort of decor still found in the most expensive London hotels. Paris has its Opéra, a huge fussy affair which Debussy compared to a railway station, also its new Bastille. Berlin also has two houses – the main one which is Deutsche and the much more attractive Staatsoper (recently reclaimed from Karl Marx). Bayreuth has its Festspielhaus designed by Wagner with its seating all on one level. Germany has many statuesque provincial houses, Italy has over a dozen absolute beauties and in the UK we have a number of old theatres and music halls, some of them (as in Glasgow) reconstituted, or about to be at least slightly improved (Frank Matcham's London Coliseum). We also have the miracle of Glyndebourne, rebuilt and enlarged to cries of bravo from both the world of architecture and of music.

In the United States Washington has the efficient rather than glamorous Kennedy Centre Opera House (2,200) built on the old horseshoe pattern, Chicago's vast civic Opera House (3,600) is warm and welcoming but alas so big that only those with 100/100 hearing should sit near the back of the stalls, San Francisco has the War Memorial Opera House (3,000) agreeable if undistinguished and Los Angeles shares the L.A. Music Center (3,000) with the Oscar ceremonies to which it is better suited being modern with no operatic ambience whatsoever (but with good acoustics).

When you approach an opera house you don't normally spend a lot of time gazing at the bays separated by their Corinthian pilasters nor do you marvel for long at the balance of the columns as they divide up the area of the semi-rusticate facade. But ever so slightly you are being conditioned for the opera experience and as you enter the portals the influence of the house becomes important. It should welcome you in a dignified manner, it should be grand but not forbidding, it should lead you through foyers and up staircases that make your pulse beat a little faster, it should propel you into an auditorium that makes you gasp with pleasure, it should then place you in a seat of exquisite comfort from which you can see who's who and listen equably to the buzz and bustle of the pre-opera scene, and if after this you can hear the first notes of the overture perfectly balanced and as clear as a bell, then the house has done its stuff and now it's over to the opera.

There is one unanswered conundrum about the future of the opera house. At today's European standard size (2,200) it can't seat enough people to deliver enough revenue. If you make the house big enough to hold up to 4,000 (the Met) and take almost double the revenue a lot of people can't hear the music. All opera managements regard amplification as the sin against the holy ghost. There is something here that they have to work out.

Orchestras

It is fair to say (with acknowledgements to Tolstoy) that all pit orchestras are happy in the same way but every unhappy pit orchestra is unhappy for different reasons. Happiness comes from a good pay deal, a triumphant performance under the baton of a great maestro, a week with a moderate workload with time for some outside recording sessions, short operas with curtain down in time for the last train home and a temperature in the pit of under 85°. And lots of other things, like plenty of room for my left elbow, neighbours who don't count out loud and don't fidget or whisper, and intervals long enough to allow for a decent refresher.

A pit orchestra, unlike any other musical team, plays together almost nightly. But it never becomes a monolith because it is made up of from sixty to a hundred individuals each with their own temperament, their own ego, their own interests and their own views on how late Verdi should be played, how an opera house should be run, what's wrong with the educational system and should we give more aid to Russia. There is no topic upon which they will all think alike, except the incompetence of the management and the iniquity of paying concert orchestral players more than they deserve. They regard each new conductor warily and will only give him what he wants if they consider he deserves it. They conceal their love of music behind a mask of deep cynicism. They would rather die than admit they loved their job. Orchestral jokes are pungent, childish and usually malicious (e.g.: a famous middle-European maestro trying to convince the mutinous orchestra that he has an intimate knowledge of a new work – 'You think I know fuck nothing about the piece? I tell you I know fuck all.').

The orchestra manager is in charge of the orchestra's schedule of work, personal problems and pay negotiations. The leader is in charge in the pit and will decide on such matters as the bowing of new works in the string section, whether it is to be jackets on or jackets off, and whether representation should be made to the maestro about an extra rehearsal he has called. In the UK all members of pit orchestras are members of the Musicians' Union, one of the old-style unions, tough and forceful in looking after the short-term interests of its members, unimaginative and myopic on broader issues. It may come as a surprise to some that in at least one house the matter of the orchestra staying behind in the pit until the maestro had taken his curtain call and made his customary gesture to his colleagues in the pit was only brought about by union negotiation and only conceded in return for extra pay – otherwise players would have continued to bolt for the bus as the last note of the opera died away.

The disastrous old practice of allowing substitutes at rehearsals has almost (but not quite) disappeared. It is still possible for fourth horn A to play in a rehearsal but fourth horn X in performance. (In the bad old days it could have been half the orchestra, including nearly all of the principals.)

Mozart's pit orchestra varied in size between twenty-eight and forty players. After many years of playing Mozart with sixty plus, the fashion is now back to something nearer Mozart's size, perhaps 8 first violins, 8 seconds, 6 violas, 4 cellos and 2 basses (= 28), plus 2 woodwind and horns (8–10), percussion (1), say 38, plus trumpets and trombones as required. There is also a fashion now for period orchestras which are usually called Ensembles (Baroques, Enlightened, Gardiner's, Hogwood's, Norrington's, etc.) but these are a different animal and a pit orchestra would never be asked to play 'Authentic' because (a) it would scoff at the idea, (b) it couldn't do it, (c) it hasn't got ancient instruments (see AUTHENTIC). At the other end of the scale the orchestra manager may have to hire a score or more of freelance players to make up a Wagner orchestra of 105 with harps and percussion occupying the lowest tier of boxes, or with the first rows of stalls seats removed to allow room for a bevy of Wagner tubas deep underground at the back of the pit and maybe percussion and harps in the boxes at the side. The bel cantos need a few more than Mozart but many less than Wagner. Generally speaking, the more recent the opera the bigger the band up to about 1920 when the number began to shrink back again down to as little as 18 or 20 (Weill) but still could of course be enormous (late Strauss).

Pit orchestras are usually pretty stable communities. The departure of a first clarinet to a concert orchestra can be a shattering event. (Orchestral talent spotters are always thought to be on the prowl and the news or rumour that the manager of the Boston is in the house can cause a susurration of excitement in the pit.) There is plenty of time for friendships and enmities to develop and these can be long-lasting. As in most orchestras, generally there is a group of half-a-dozen or so players who form an official or unofficial committee and who 'speak for' the orchestra, but most of the rank-and-file can't be bothered, or don't have the guts, to tell them what to say. In public, orchestral behaviour is much better than it used to be. Chattering between players sharing a desk is still not unknown, though no one any longer dares to do the *Times* crossword in vision. The heavy brass and the extra percussion can be seen stealing out of the pit during a long break and stealing back again in the nick of time, sometimes wiping their lips on the back of their hands.

In the UK every pit orchestra thinks it is the finest in the land and it would be a bold person who tried to put them in order of merit. One thing is certain, and that is that on a good night the worst of them (whichever it may be) can play better than the best (be it nameless) on an off day. The Covent Garden orchestra in particular can rise to the heights when, for instance, performing *The Ring* under Haitink, but at a matinee of *Swan Lake* under a reach-me-down ballet conductor it can sound like a pre-war scratch orchestra on tour in Aberdeen. British orchestras have always been the quickest studies and the best sight-readers in the musical world but since the flowering of the music academies and colleges in the fifties and sixties standards have shot up to put them on a par with any Continental pit orchestra, except perhaps in Berlin and Vienna. Even these mighty folk have their drawbacks. The sweet soupy tone of Viennese strings are a bit too Mantovani for twentieth-century operas and tend to cherish the musical phrase for its own sake without too much regard to the dramatic sense of the scene. The Vienna Philharmonic under that great and wonderful musician Karl Böhm, for instance, would squeeze every ounce of music out of a score regardless of what was happening on the stage. Assassins would have to stand for minutes with dagger poised, heroines postpone a faint, heroes prolong a kiss well beyond the limits of credibility, whilst the orchestra dwelt lovingly on some musical morsel and decelerated almost to a standstill. No one can play the bel canto rep better than the Scala orchestra when in a good mood, the magnificent Berliners are unbeatable in the German rep, and on its day, and only on its day, the Met orchestra can be stunningly good over pretty well the whole range of opera.

It's hard work down there in the pit and hot, and it's nervous work for the soloists, particularly the wind soloists, and of these especially the first horn. So if they play well, applaud the orchestra as heartily as the maestro.

Producers

It is broadly the case that when you go to the opera the maestro is responsible for what you hear and the producer for what you see, but this is much too simple. Each one must have a clear idea of what the opera means to him and how it should be brought to life on the stage. The closer the two concepts, the more harmonious the relationship between the two principals will be. But harmony does not always generate a good show. It is quite possible to have a production that has been nothing but sweetness and light turn out to be a dead flop, and contrariwise some of the best shows have reached the stage with blood all over the floor. So long as the two principals can work within the limits of mutual tolerance there is no saying what may happen by the time of the general rehearsal. One or other may dominate, or (more common) there may be compromise. If things are going to go beyond the limits of tolerance the sooner this is known the better.

But most partnerships work out well enough. The two moments of most stress are usually when the maestro finds out exactly what it is that the producer is going to do as opposed to what he thought he was going to do, and when stage rehearsals start and the producer wants to do it this way but the maestro wants to do it that.

Over recent years opera production has followed successive fashions. Time was when all opera was produced with what one might call pantomime scenery, leaving a big hole in the middle of the stage where the principals could stand, heavily lit, and adopt a fixed stance (usually pugilistic for men and supplicatory for women) and belt out their piece untroubled by any requirement to move, to recognize any other character on stage or indeed to act at all. In the twenties and thirties, although most of the legitimate theatre remained faithful to Aunt Edna and provided her with the sort of sets she expected, the world of the experimental theatre was all agog (especially in France) with productions that were abstract, symbolist, expressionist, surrealist, dadaist, etc. Any romantic or realist setting for a play became intellectually disreputable.

This kind of revolutionary thinking crept into opera's holy of holies after World War II when Wieland Wagner and his brother Wolfgang revived the Bayreuth Festival. The romantic (pantomime) tradition of Wagnerian sets was swept away and stark modernism took over. *The Ring* was played on a stage filled with a huge tilted disc, *Tannhäuser* on a chessboard. From then on pretty well anything went. A new iconoclastic school of opera production sprang up (especially in Germany). By the fifties and sixties even the most traditional sets were well out of the pantomime age and we saw what were probably some of the most imaginative and elegant opera productions of the century. These came mainly from Italian producers (Visconti, Zeffirelli).

In the seventies and eighties the styles of opera production became absolutely various. Some producers came from the stage (Brook, Hall, Nunn) and worked wonders in making opera more dramatic. There was a set of international individualists who had nothing much in common except an abhorrence of reality (Frederick, Ponelle, Felsenstein, Kupfer,

Chéreau). At the same time the importance of star singers and especially of the diva declined and we moved into a period of 'producers' opera'. (But nothing could stop the rise of the Three Tenors.)

Some 'producer's opera' has been pretty dismal with a strong tendency to put all operas into a setting that reflects the producer's own gloom about our present world. Thus we have seen *Idomeneo* in a set that looks like Hiroshima after the bomb, and for all I know *The Flying Dutchman* sailing through atomic waste and Amfortas dying of AIDS.

But today the scene is changing again. There is now a band of young English producers (Pountney, Hytner, Vick) who seem to be much happier with themselves than were the tortured continentals of the last generation and who do find a setting and a style that actually sets the opera off to its best advantage. Their work has wit and loads of invention but they are serious fellows too and are doing a really great job for British opera (and for some Continental and American opera too). So more power to their elbows and may they get adequate budgets and brilliant music directors to support them. (See also PRODUCTION below.)

Production

The time it takes for a new opera to see the light of day is roughly double the period of gestation of an elephant, but unlike the elephant embryo which grows steadily and unseen, the opera goes forward towards its birth in fits and starts and its growth is fully exposed to public view. Every opera has a different case-history and every house has its own habits and customs. Nevertheless let us try to trace the prenatal growth of a hypothetical new production of *Carmen* in one of the major opera houses of the world, say the Royal Opera House London.

Prelude

In the international opera world top people meet other top people all the time. At any given moment up to half of the top intendants will not be at their desks. They will be in Santa Fe to hear how this amazing young Australian soprano copes as Elektra, or in Wexford to see the newly-exhumed opera by Bononcini, *The Three Testicles of Chiron*, which has never been seen by any living person before (and is unlikely ever to be seen by any living person again). On these trips and jaunts (and indeed also on their home ground) the intendants meet maestros, maestros meet intendants, both intendants and maestros meet producers. It is always the habit of such people on such occasions to say to each other 'When are you going to do something for us again?' or 'When are you going to let me do *Otello* in London?' (This is rather like saying to a casual acquaintance 'We must have lunch together sometime.') But just occasionally they mean it. Indeed the real reason for our Intendant's trip to Santa Fe is that he wanted a word with Maestro Bonponti to see whether it would interest him to do a *Carmen* in London in four years' time and if so whether he would be happy to work with Bakski as his producer.

Yes, Bonponti would be very happy to do *Carmen* but not with Bakski. Didn't the Intendant know that Bakski had just done a terrible *Ballo* in Vienna when he had run out of rehearsal time and that he was tone deaf anyway? He would, however, be happy to do a *Carmen* with Studd or Throgmorton.

The casting of Carmen herself is discussed. Bonponti points out that there are only two people in the world who can sing Carmen and neither is available. The Intendant says the brilliant young Icelandic mezzo Igla is available. She has made a terrific hit in Munich. Bonponti says he will listen to her tapes. The Intendant says he has got Primo to sing Don José. Everyone recognizes this as a coup. The rest of the cast is discussed in a more desultory fashion.

Bonponti has been signed. Studd will sign if Bonponti will agree Perimonde as the designer. Bonponti will not agree to Perimonde. He had just done a terrible *Forza* in Milan full of cubist stuff, and didn't everyone know that Perimonde was colour-blind anyway? Tintin is signed as the designer.

Act I Sc 1 Year minus four

After several hundreds of faxes and telephone calls the three principals manage to meet in Hong Kong where Bonponti is touring. They discuss their concept of *Carmen* and persuade Tintin not to site Act I outside an atomic power station. After a couple of meals together they become enthusiastic. They are going to make a great *Carmen*.

Months pass. Tintin has some drawings which he shows to Studd in Prague where he is working on a *Jenufa*. He has gone back to the atomic reactor, but Studd insists on tobacco. He likes the other designs. It's going to be a great *Carmen*.

Months pass. The three meet in San Francisco where Tintin is doing *Wozzeck*. At first sight Bonponti hated the designs. But, as improved by a couple of brilliant suggestions from him and a few strokes of the pencil, he has come to like them pretty well. Tintin, with the approval of the other two, takes on Wesley to do the costumes.

Months pass.

Act I Sc 2 Year minus three

All this time the Intendant has been tracking progress like a bloodhound. He urges all three to give him enough data to draw up a detailed budget. They all know that the show has got to come in at a budget of under a quarter of a million don't they? (Yes, yes, they do.) Tintin wants to make a model of all the sets. Drawing will not do them justice, especially Pastia's tavern which is going to be set inside a bull's mouth. The model room gets busy. Twenty-four faxes are sent to Bonponti asking him what rehearsal pattern he will require once the show gets on the stage. A man is despatched to Sydney to corner Bonponti and extract the data from him. The man comes back and says Bonponti can't be disturbed until after the first night of *Turandot*. The Intendant decides to send a second man. Studd turns in an eighty-page memorandum specifying his needs for a new world-beating *Carmen*.

Months pass.

Act II Year minus two

The first moment of truth. A draft budget has been produced. It amounts to £380,000. Everyone is told to cut it by 50% at once.

Weeks pass.

Serious discussions take place with Studd. He cannot have 140 smugglers on stage in Act II. Eighty is the maximum. There is no need to get new costumes for the twenty smugglers behind the hill because no one sees them in the dark. He cannot have twenty trained ballet dancers to mingle with the factory girls. Two will suffice. (And more cuts.)

Tintin is told that the bull's mouth is really off, especially the idea of having it moist. The tavern sets must come down to £3800 maximum.

It is suggested to Bonponti that his requirements for rehearsal time might be considered to be excessive. He says they are not excessive. No cuts are made to rehearsal time.

The Intendant says he has done a co-production deal with Los Angeles. All the sets must be adjusted to fit the Los Angeles stage.

Two weeks pass. The budget is down to £310,000.

Tintin is told that his idea of having two horses drag a dead bull across the stage just before the final curtain is off.

All production departments have details of the show. They are urgently requested to find economies.

Two weeks pass. The budget is down to £280,000. The chorus will wear stock costumes. The bull's mouth has gone. The mountain in Act II has been greatly simplified. It now has no caves and no funicular railway. By saving £15,000 on *Don Pasquale* the management decide they can go ahead.

Act II Sc 2 Year minus one

The chorus master slips in rehearsals of *Carmen* for the chorus when there is a slack week. Wardrobe starts work on the costumes. Studd insists on a Bauprobe (a mock-up of the sets on stage to see how they block out). The Bauprobe is a success. The construction department begins to make the sets.

Act II Sc 3 Minus six months
The chorus and available principals begin to be fitted for their costumes. Wesley (the costume designer) wants to change the materials because the colours haven't come out the way she expected. She is told she can't.

There are problems with the sets. The scene change between the tobacco factory and Pastia's tavern is going to take 47 minutes. This is sorted out by using part of the factory to double as the side of the tavern. Tintin says since they will save so much on the set budget, can he have the bull's mouth back if he gives up the moist idea? He is told that he can't.

Act III Sc 1 Minus 5–3 weeks
Bonponti arrives. Studd and Tintin are already there. Igla arrives with a sore throat. On Sunday there is the first technical rehearsal. Some of the more difficult sets are put up. The lighting director begins to plot his lighting patterns. During the week the principals are coached in studios by their repetiteurs. Bonponti roams the rehearsal rooms each day, especially Igla's, until he gets bored. The principals have piano rehearsals under Studd in the mornings and afternoons. There are orchestral rehearsals in the afternoons under Bonponti. Nearly all the costumes are now fitted, but Igla dislikes hers and demands changes to the bust. The wardrobe mistress has to do some brokerage between Wesley and Igla. Igla accepts the costume provided she can have a bigger fan to cover the bust. Primo arrives in week 4 and to everyone's surprise makes no fuss about anything except the quality of the reception on his hotel television set.

Act IV Sc 1 Days −14 to −5
Rehearsals move to the stage. The technical rehearsals (which take place on Sundays) run into a snag in that the mountain won't stand up properly now the caves have been removed. There is a Sitzprobe in which the principals sit on chairs in the centre of the stage. This probe is solely to get the musical texture right. No movement. No acting. There are four days of stage and orchestra rehearsals in the morning, one act on each day. Bonponti is now in charge of the schedule and the allocation of time. There is some tension between Bonponti and Tintin. Studd writes a fifteen-page memo to the management complaining that Bonponti will not give him enough time for stage work. Primo disappears one afternoon and is discovered to be singing in a charity concert in Rotterdam. His manager explains he can do this without missing any rehearsals and his absence is due solely to his great sense of compassion for Bosnian refugees. Next morning there is fog at Heathrow. Primo is late for the stage orchestra rehearsal. When he appears Bonponti addresses him as Mr Primo not as Carlos.

Act IV Day −4 to P (premiere) Day

Day −4. There is a piano dress rehearsal of all four acts. It goes well. The stage crew has solved the mountain problem. The lighting director thinks the sets are wonderful. Bonponti compliments Studd on the thorough way he has prepared the stage work. The Intendant comes to watch and is delighted. Everyone draws back to polish up their own thing in readiness for the pre-general the day after tomorrow.

Day −2. The pre-general is a disaster. There is a power cut at 9.30. Igla has not slept well and has to have an extended lunch break in order to see her astrologer. She comes back weeping. At 2.30 the leader informs the management that the orchestra may refuse to play on the first night unless the management gives some indication that they will consider favourably the orchestra's very reasonable wage demands. The management think this is a bluff and decide not to tell Bonponti. Bonponti hears about it from a trombone. He scribbles a note to the Intendant on the back of an envelope fully supporting the orchestra's stand. A 5K lamp falls off its mounting, narrowly missing a smuggler. There is a report of a small fire in Micaela's dressing room. The pre-general runs over its time, incurs premium payments, and curtain-up on the ballet that night is twenty minutes late.

Day −1. The general starts dead on time. The orchestra say they will play for the first night after all, but in mufti. Primo saves his voice so carefully that Bonponti asks him if he would prefer to go and lie down and allow his cover (understudy) to stand in for him. Primo sings louder. One of the chorus trips over a wire in a rush offstage and breaks a small bone behind his ear. Others fall over him and there are further minor casualties and a ten-minute hold-up. Otherwise the general goes well. Bonponti tries, unsuccessfully, to conceal his pleasure. Good luck tomorrow says everyone to everyone else.

P Day. People start drifting in after lunch. The pre-publicity has been quite good but everyone is sick with Tintin for giving a big interview attacking the management for not allowing him the bull's mouth. He says it embodied the apotheosis of his concept of *Carmen* and would have been the first onstage moist bull's mouth in opera history. The principals start to make up. Studd begins a tour of all dressing rooms with a good luck call but remembers he meant to warn the management about a defective trap and goes off to write them a memo. Bonponti lies prone in his dressing room with a handkerchief over his face. Tintin crouches in a corner lost in prayer. The audience arrives. The orchestra file in in evening dress. The curtain goes up. A new *Carmen* is born.

Note: Every opera house has its own habits but few realize how intensively an old-fashioned house with no side stages has to be worked.

During the last week of the hypothetical *Carmen* described above the daily schedule might have gone something like this:

2215	Curtain down on *Swan Lake*.
2300–0700	Night gang strike *Swan Lake* and set *Carmen* for next day's rehearsal. Put *Don Pasquale* sets at rear of stage for quick re-setting.
0800–1000	Day gang touch up *Carmen* set.
1030–1300	Rehearse *Carmen* on set.
1430–1830	Set *Pasquale*.
1930	Curtain up on *Pasquale*.

Recitatif

The function of recitatif is to tell the story. In the early days of opera it was either story-telling or singing. They didn't go on at the same time. Thus a pastoral opera would open with Amara telling us that she loves Bucon the next-door shepherd but alas her father is feuding with his father so they have to meet secretly. End of recitatif. Stop. Now she starts to sing her first aria. O the Joys and Fears of Furtive Love. Having finished she will exit and Bucon will come on telling us in recitatif again and at some length that he loves Amara. Stop. Now an aria from Bucon. The Sight of Her Fair Face Turns Me On. And so on. All of the recitatif would be secco (meaning 'dry'), that is accompanied by a harpsichord with possibly a cello doubling the bass line.

Sometimes when emotion wells up as a result of some dire event recounted in the secco (shock, fear, anger, etc., seldom pleasure or joy) the orchestra will creep in under the vocal line and give the recitatif much more meaningful support. This is called recitatif accompagnato and it was one of the eighteenth-century composer's main devices for jacking up the dramatic tension before a character dived into an aria of terror, fury, revenge or whatever. Mozart used accompagnato with great effect, perhaps the finest example being the big piece in Act I of *Giovanni* where the penny drops with Donna Anna and she recognizes the smooth-talking Don as the guy who murdered her father.

Recitatif moves in speech rhythms usually with a note for each syllable and at the speed of speech. This is often too fast for comprehension especially in plots with step-brothers, half-sisters and a large number of characters with Roman names. But in salons and princely private theatres of a small size it must have had a better chance of being heard, equal perhaps to the audibility of a caller at an American barn dance (hands-across-the-middle, feet-go-down-the-floor, left arm, right arm, ladies-go-before, etc.).

The bel cantos began to blur the clear distinction between recitatif and aria. They put in much more accompagnato and this began to have little snatches of melody in it (arioso). Then they started to tell the story in accompagnato and not use it just to reflect the character's mood. Secco got scarcer and by the time of Verdi it had gone altogether. An opera was orchestrated from beginning to end. But the function of recitatif has stayed with opera right up to the present day. There are passages even in *The Ring* where the tension drops, melody relapses into small fragments which do not make too much of a demand on the attention, the orchestra plays more quietly and the words come through in a quick succession. This is still a form of accompagnato although Wagner would not like to hear it described in such a manner. But you really can't tell the tale when the Valkyries are riding high or Siegfried is smashing anvils. So he had to do something.

Seats

The dress circle is best for combined sound and vision. If the orchestra is too noisy (Wagner, Strauss) a seat in the stalls will tone it down a bit and you will hear more of the stage. Higher in the house you may get better blended sound but if you get very high the stage can shrink to the size of an 8-inch TV screen. 16-inch is really as small as you will want to go, 24-inch is abundance. Assume you sit 8 feet away from your TV set and that the average proscenium opening is 40 feet. You can work out the equation quite easily if you are scholarly in trigonometry. It all depends how much you want to pay.

Boxes are sociable for conversation but unsociable in that at least one or perhaps two persons have to take bum seats. From boxes you can of course see only a part of the stage but from the stage box you have a bird's-eye view of the orchestra and with a pair of binoculars can read the band parts and see what cuts have been made, pick up bowing marks and comments scrawled on the margin and very occasionally grafitti. You can also see how much the conductor has memorized and how much he depends on the score by the way he turns the pages.

Every house has a different acoustic. In an unfamiliar hall Beecham would spend up to an hour pacing the full extent of the auditorium while his assistant took the rehearsal. He then adjusted the balance of the orchestra to suit the hall. Conductors in an opera house don't do this. (Except Solti.) Pick your seats carefully: you may be happy to sit behind a pillar but if the orchestra sounds like mushy pea soup you are in for a bad night. Every opera house has its quota of dud seats. In some houses they are in the majority.

Sets

Gone are the days when operas had backdrops at the back, cloths dropping in from above and flats ranged along the wings leaving a big open hole in the middle where the opera could happen. Today you may be faced with a purple dayglow mountain sticking right out into the auditorium, a pile of squashed cars in a junkyard reaching up to the flies, an empty stage with seventeen bicycles upside down in the corner or something that looks like a street in Hamburg after the bombers left. Pretty well anything goes and the only effective controls are the fire regulations and the budget.

The designer brews up his design concept in solitary confinement and then, often gingerly, approaches the producer.

'What are these things?' the producer will ask, turning the drawing round and round.

'Those are the perches,' the designer will reply.

'Perches?' asks the producer. 'Did you say perches?'

'Yes. You see, we are inside an aviary.'

'An aviary?'

'Yes, an aviary full of love birds.'

'And this pink thing?'

'That's the talisman which lies on the floor of the aviary.'

'Talisman? But there's no talisman in the libretto.'

'It's the talisman of love and it is absolutely central to my concept of *Tristan and Isolde*. You see, it represents love itself and after the Liebestod the Angel of Death rides in on a motorbike and takes it up to heaven. I can show you the place on the score.'

'But I thought we were going to set the whole piece in a Cornish tin mine?'

'I started with the idea of putting the aviary inside a tin mine. Double captivity, you see, a prison within a prison, just as Tristan is a prisoner of love within the context of being a prisoner of courtly chivalry. But then I came to see that the tin mine was not really necessary.'

'I see. I see. It's very striking. Let me think about it ....'

And so back to square one. (But the tin mine got lost too and the final concept is to set the first scene in a boat, the second in a summerhouse and the third outside a castle in Brittany with a birdcage motif in every scene and a picture of a tin mine in the programme.)

There is a more practical side to the setting of an opera. As the drawings get more and more detailed they go through the mangle, and this is for two reasons: compromises have to be made to meet the requirements of the maestro, the lighting director, the technical director, the chorus director, the construction shop, and secondly, the budget. There is no item on the opera direct expenditure list so susceptible to a cut (except possibly the costume and numbers of the chorus) as the set (see PRODUCTION). Some designers will lay off against this by putting in early drawings of such extravagance as to take the management's breath away (even the management of the Met). Then, after the bluster and cut session, they will still have a comfortable adequacy remaining (they hope). Others (God bless them) will accept the budget figures they are given and come back with a package right on the nail and will only create if they are asked to reduce their costs because the costume designer wants real rabbit fur on the fairies' shoulders.

Once through the eye of the budget needle, construction starts, in the majority of houses off the premises. Thus whatever the materials may be the sets have to be made in transportable units which are travelled up to the house for assembly at the first technical rehearsal (usually some three weeks before opening). Often at this stage it is not so much the sets themselves that cause problems as the time taken in the strike/re-set between scenes.

In the Rolls-Royce opera houses of continental Europe there are side stages (and sometimes a back stage as well) where all the sets for tonight's opera (and maybe tomorrow's opera too) can stand ready and alert to be swapped at a moment's notice for the set in use on stage. But in Britain's crummy, outdated labour-extravagant, decomposing old Victorian houses, the sets for the next scene and for tomorrow have to be stacked in every available nook and cranny adjacent to the stage. On a busy night the set storage area can look like the toast rack with eight slices of toast crammed into the spaces for four.

Sets can be the main worry in getting an opera through the house. Sets can be stunning yet kill the music in the opera stone-dead. Sets can become part of the opera's drama. Sets can be dull. Sets can be magic. Sets are a part of the opera's persona. Sets are terribly important.

Singers

Time was when the sole purpose of opera was to give singers a chance to show off their voices. The story and the accompaniment didn't matter much so long as the piece was composed as a sort of vocal obstacle course in the surmounting of which the singers could display the dexterity and power of their vocal chords. Even when ensemble opera became the fashion and later still when the swollen orchestras of Wagner and Strauss threatened to drown them, singers remained at least the principals among equals. And even today it is the name of the singer that is the main draw. Pavarotti will fill a house no matter who wrote the opera or who is conducting. Neither *Bohème* nor *Tosca* could do the same if the singers were the perfectly adequate Smith and Jones. Nor would Karajan's name alone have done so (but then he would never have allowed himself to be billed with Smith and Jones).

There are almost as many types of voice as there are of French cheeses. Here are a few of the main types:

Sopranos

The High Soprano Usually a clear bell-like voice that can pierce the air above all accompanying sounds, e.g. the Queen of Night in *The Magic Flute*, a part written by Mozart for his first love Aloysia Weber. He gave her quite a lot of coloratura, or fancy work, to do and high sopranos have to be prepared for this. Quite a rare bird, required by no more than half a dozen of the operas in this Guide. (Gruberova)

The Coloratura Only just lower than the High. Mainly required in bel canto operas, that is the Rossinis, the Bellinis, the Donizettis and the early Verdis. Must have a really flexible voice and be able to carry out all manner of gymnastics without drawing breath. Usually has a big chest. (Sutherland)

The General-Purpose Soprano This is a soprano voice that can take on most leading parts outside of bel canto and Wagner, that is to say Mozart, some late Verdi, Puccini, the Frenchies, Strauss, the moderns and even some of the Russians. (Te Kanawa)

The Wagner Soprano She used to be rotund and with the face of a prison wardress. Today she looks much prettier and sings nearly as well. She must have great powers of endurance and a very loud voice. (Behrens)

Mezzo Sopranos

There are not many leading roles for the mezzo, two of the best being Carmen and Rosina in the *Barber*. She can't get as high as the true soprano but is not generally required to deliver too many chest notes. So she sings a bit in the middle and a lot fairly high. Both the above roles are tremendously flashy parts, with loads of coloratura for Rosina. Most often the mezzo has a no. 2 role – the duenna, the sister, the housekeeper and sometimes can be of the older generation, mothers especially. (Berganza)

Contraltos

Contraltos are quite definitely lower than sopranos and generally evil – gypsies, wicked step-sisters, scheming mothers of rivals to the throne, poisoners, murderesses, etc. Their voices are nearly always powerful with booming chest notes that can frighten the horses. The late Dame Clara Butt of blessed memory could deliver a chest note that could have served to direct shipping in poor visibility. Some of the most beguiling voices of the last few decades have belonged to the lighter sort of contralto. (Baker)

Tenors

First and foremost we have the *Italian tenor*, common enough in the moderate to good reaches but rare and almost priceless when he moves into the world class of Caruso, Gigli, Lanza, Di Stefano, Pavarotti. Hispanic tenors can sound like Italian tenors and two of them, Domingo and Carreras, are of course in the world class. World-class tenors can fill any opera house ten times over, can attract an audience of thousands to open-air concerts in the rain, have groupies, fan clubs, tend to travel with a large posse of minders, have Swiss bank accounts and extremely complicated tax arrangements. The sound of a world-class Italian tenor in full cry has a streak of animal sensuality which cuts through all operatic politesse and leaves the listener, especially female listeners in middle life, gasping.

The Heldentenor The Heldentenor is a German invention and a phenomenon found only in Germany. He is really a pushed-up baritone and produces a pure tone which seems to come straight from the head whereas the voice of the Italian tenor seems to come from his whole body, including the lower stomach. The Heldentenor is therefore by comparison sexless but by no means homosexual. His voice is lighter but does not go so high as the Italian's and is shown off to its best in slow legato phrases. It is not suitable for jumpy stuff. Wagner's tenor roles can only be sung by Heldentenors and they also sound well in the Mozart tenor parts. Heldentenors are usually heroes and therefore usually good but although they are virtuous, pure, noble, etc., there are few characters in the Heldentenor repertory who would qualify for Mensa. (Kollo)

Northern Tenors Scandinavia has produced some great tenors with more manly voices than Heldentenors some of whom have managed Wagner and others the later Italian repertory. (Björling)

Welsh Tenors A reedy crew on the whole with some notable exceptions. The exceptions can hold their corner in the bel canto repertory against most Italians. (O'Neill)

Irish/Scottish Tenors These belong to the past rather than the present (except on CD) but when extant they had an extraordinary purity of tone, clarity of diction and precision of pitch. When they were pitched into opera the result was not unlike Benny Goodman playing the Mozart clarinet quintet – technique A1, understanding nil. (McCormack)

General-Service Tenors There are quite a number of these, of several nationalities, and none are quite good enough. Many have sweetness, intelligence and fine technique but lack the power to stun an audience in a big house. (Winbergh) This raises the most acute problem facing opera today – the tenor famine. After Domingo and Pavarotti – what? Or, rather, who?

Castratos, Countertenors, Male Altos and other Falsettos The first of this class of singer is extinct although there is still just available a recording of the last of the performing castratos which sounds like distant caterwauling and is therefore not helpful. There is a ghoulish interest in the study of the castrato who as late as in Mozart's day was the star name in the cast. Today it is impossible to imagine a male soprano 'with a voice like a bull', an expression used by the good Dr Burney during his musical travels in Europe in the 1770s.

Countertenors and male altos can be frightfully refined singers but they are milk-and-water stuff in comparison to a real tenor and however skilfully they pipe away in their head-voices or falsettos, it is generally much better to transpose the castrato part down one octave and give it to a tenor with balls and to hell with the purists. To give the part to a female is not a good option either, for who can believe in a female Roman emperor, general or brigand? Also the sexual chemistry of the piece is destroyed by having two women who are clearly not lesbians making love to each other. Or if it seems they are lesbians, then it's even more confusing.

Baritones

There are always more good baritones than opera has room for. There is even a sufficiency of world-class baritones. America produces baritones, the UK produces them, they abound in Germany, Italy and even France and in what used to be called the Balkans they are two-a-penny. Baritones can be dark-hued and pretty evil (Don Giovanni), comical (Don Pasquale), but are more often assigned to the rather boring no. 2 part than the no. 1. Baritones are enormously appreciated by the buffs and the musical but they do not have much glamour. They have no groupies trailing behind them, they do not have the same house-filling power as the star tenor nor do they get the same sort of fee. Also their sexual profile is lower, with certain exceptions (Don Giovanni). On the whole they are a rather ornery class of person, brothers, uncles, best friends, stewards, captains, with, of course, certain exceptions (Don Giovanni). (Allen)

Basses

If not so numerous as baritones, there is usually a good supply of world-class operatic basses. Indeed, the two overlap into what is called a bass–baritone. Both basses and baritones have the same kind of voice whereas baritones and tenors don't. A role like Hans Sachs can be sung by a low baritone or a high bass. Mozart's Sarastro can only be sung by a low bass. The operatic bass can come from several countries, America, Britain, Italy, Germany, even France. Further east the operatic bass takes on a different timbre (see below). Basses can be good – gods, priests, friendly fathers, wise kings – or, less frequently, evil – bad kings, plotters, schemers, etc. Basses tend to be older men, just as tenors are nearly always youthful. There are few examples in opera of a bass under twenty-five or of a tenor over thirty. Real life reflects this as a truth in the case of basses, whose voices do not really settle until their late twenties, but not in the case of tenors who will manfully struggle against anno domini by leaping onto tables or fighting flashy duels at the age of sixty, by which time they would really much prefer a bath-chair role. Alas opera has no place for bed-bound tenors, but most basses have it very easy indeed, especially kings who can, with luck, have no call to rise from their throne throughout a whole act. (Tomlinson)

Russian Basses This is a voice that is distinct from the general run of basses, just as much as the true Italian tenor in Tenorland. The Russian bass has sonority, volume, depth, darkness and a sort of subterranean reverberation which is the opposite of those high frequencies that dogs can hear and we can't, only we can hear these ones. He is best in Russian opera since if he is placed further west he tends to drag an Italian or a German opera towards the Volga. He is good in Debussy or Bartok. Next to the Russian bass the Balkan profundo can be even deeper and noisier although never quite with that special Russian magic that comes in other fields only from caviar and the films of Eisenstein. (Burchuladze)

Buffa Basses The Italians have a special breed of basses who are a sort of singing clown and ham up the buffa character parts in bel canto opera, often disastrously. Rarely buffas can be both good and funny (Panerai), but a successful buffa tends to linger on too long and cover up his loss of voice by singing falsetto, camping it up outrageously or adopting a sort of parlando, like Rex Harrison in *My Fair Lady*. However much the public love him, a buffa bass should never be granted tenure but retired at sixty-five or when he can no longer sing a patter song without stopping for breath, whichever occurs sooner.

Some things about singers

Nerves There is probably no profession more fraught with terror than that of the opera singer. He/she can have all the stage-fright of the actor or the ballet dancer (who at least know that barring some amazing accident they will be able to speak their lines or throw their limbs around as they did in rehearsal) plus the fear that their voice may not come out right, if at all. As they wait in the wings the mouth can dry out and the muscles round the larynx contract. So it is when the house manager comes in front of the curtain to say that Miss Della Bella has consented to sing in spite of a heavy cold, it may be that sometimes she really has a cold but it may also be that she is seeking some protection in case her voice doesn't come out right, and unless she is given it by the house manager she will not go on. No wonder there are stories about the tantrums of prima donnas (Callas), but it is often the lesser characters that suffer most. Keeping terror under control is called 'being professional', having a tantrum 'being a little difficult'. If audiences and critics knew what it is like to stand in the wings waiting for a cue they would encourage singers more than they do. Most singers are pretty tough eggs but a brutal notice can shatter the confidence of a young singer, as can a hostile reception.

Ensemble Like all performing artists, singers are interested in their own performance and not much else. If something helps them to shine they like it, if something gets in their way they don't. What gets in the way is usually another member of the cast who sings better, looks prettier or seems to be more favoured by the conductor or the audience. Add to this that opera casts in the big houses are ad hoc, that they are together for only a few weeks, often less, that they come from different countries, speak different languages and have different tastes in deodorants. So it is not surprising if the ensemble of an opera cast is not always all sweetness and light. Amongst the top singers there are some angels who will suppress their own egos to bring sunlight and joy into the rehearsal room, most are 'professional', which means they will do what they are asked sometimes with a good grace and sometimes not, and some are awkward bastards. The attitude of the bastard is usually 'I've done it my way for fifteen years and I'm not going to do it different for this young idiot'. This sentiment is, of course, unspoken and outwardly the bastard will be all smiles and compliance. 'Yes, yes, I see just what you mean,' he will say, 'let's try it again', whereupon he will do it just exactly as he did it before. 'Is that more what you wanted?' he will ask brightly.

Preparation A singer who is learning a new role in opera will probably already have studied the part with his own singing teacher. Once the opera moves into pre-production the singer will be taken on by a repetiteur, a member of the opera house's music staff who may be an aspiring conductor and who is certainly an accomplished accompanist. He will tutor the singer on the lines agreed with the maestro in charge of the production. This can be a rewarding partnership and many singers will tell you their interpretation of a part (now famous) is based on the days of study spent with a repetiteur backstage at this opera house or that. The singer then moves into rehearsal with the rest of the cast. Old hands may want to run it through to pick up the maestro's approach to the piece. Really grand singers will not enter the arena until the opera is well into rehearsal, and then as late as possible.

Stamina Did you notice that the tenor seemed to be singing much more softly in Act I and Act II than in Act III? You were right – he was holding back. There is a limit to what any voice, and particularly a tenor voice, can do in a week. This famous fellow has two *Toscas* (on Tuesday and Friday) and he is also appearing at a charity concert (naughty man) on Wednesday about which the opera house by whom he is engaged knew nothing until yesterday. Tonight he is nursing his voice very carefully. Not that anything is wrong with it, and he will belt out 'Stelle' in the last act at the pitch of his lungs. Except in Wagner, tenors generally have short bursts of activity with plenty of rest between and basses and baritones are thought to be able to sing for ever (Hans Sachs, Wotan). Sopranos are given enormously long and tiring parts (Brünnhilde, Elektra) with which only the marathon runners can cope. The female role with the most notes in all opera is Susannah in *Figaro*, but it is not high passion stuff and taxes the powers of memory and concentration more than the vocal apparatus.

Age All singers grow older but some do not care to recognize the fact. A soprano reaches her zenith in her forties and fifties and then in the normal course of events she begins a graceful retreat from opera (after several gala farewells) through Lieder to masterclasses. Aside from tenors the men last longer, often too long. In particular buffa basses who are popular idols (see above). Tenors are unpredictable. Di Stefano lost his voice overnight at the age of forty, Gigli was in full throat when he died at the age of sixty-seven. Russian basses are the most durable article and can continue to sing Musorgsky's *Song of a Flea* pretty well up to the last rites.

Surtitles

The arrival of surtitles in the opera house probably did more to enlarge the circle of opera-lovers than anything since the invention of the gramophone. Opera-goers who went simply to hear the music no longer have to grapple with the plot in glum perplexity. Opera-resistant spouses have become opera-tolerant, even opera fans. Conductors and singers find that the house is responding to subtleties and nuances in an opera as never before. People laugh at the jokes because they are funny not just to show that they understand Italian.

At first there was a mighty outcry amongst the opera elite against the invasion of their private world by the common opera-goer, as there was when the mediaeval church was outraged by the translation of the scriptures into the vernacular. But today in the face of the overwhelming success of the surtitle critical opinion has swung round and opposition is sustained only by a handful of pendants and snobs. Such people will say that the spell of an opera is broken by having to raise the eyes from the stage to the screen (to which the simple reply is if you know all about the opera you don't have to do it) and that the only way really to appreciate an opera properly is to study the score in advance. In fact their resentment probably stems from a sense that their privileged position is being invaded by the sweaty nightcaps and that opera is too precious to be thrown open to the plebs (an attitude illustrated by the legendary story of the duchess who after her first really satisfactory sexual experience turned to her partner and asked 'Is that what the common people call fucking?'

'Yes,' he replied. She thought for a moment. 'It's too good for them,' she said. 'It ought to be stopped.')

The form the surtitle takes can be a matter of debate. One school of thought would have us see the full text of the opera displayed. But this is impossible in patter songs and ensembles and tiresome when a number is repetitious. At the other end of the scale are those who would be content with signposts – no more than 'I love you' to describe a four-minute aria – but then the client feels cheated by not being told what the hell it is the singer is going on about, and also during a long pause the suspicion inevitably grows that the machine has broken down.

The creation of good surtitles is art just as is the translation of an opera text or the construction of an opera libretto. In the few years since they were first introduced the standard has improved enormously.

One benevolent result of the surtitle revolution will be to put an end to the need to translate operas into other languages, most particularly into English. This has always been a comparatively pointless exercise since it is often just as difficult to hear what they are singing in English as it is in a foreign language. Add to this that no libretto can be translated into another tongue without damage to the partnership between music and words (see *The Ring* page 553). Indeed operas that would benefit greatly from surtitles are the works of Benjamin Britten and it can only be a matter of time before English operas too get some much-needed help from the small screen (it's already done in Australia).

The story of the origin of the surtitle is bizarre. When European opera was first played in Hong Kong in Chinese it was found that the Western singing tones distorted the Chinese words out of all recognition. Thus when Tosca sang 'Vissi d'arte' it was generally thought that she was asking for a can of coke. To avoid this the clever Chinese put words down the side of the proscenium arch (in Chinese characters of course) and kept changing them to suit the sense of the scene. From Hong Kong the surtitle message spread to Canada and then on to Los Angeles where a system of manually operated slides was perfected (if that word can be applied to so Heath Robinson a process). Today the surtitle is operated by a computerized tape but it is still far from technically perfect.

Whereas it would be expecting too much to ask for a small VDU in front of every seat to be installed immediately (as in the poshest seats in aeroplanes), there should be a number of display points to give all of the clients an easy sight line. The surtitle gear is still too expensive to instal in outlying theatres where opera companies tour and where it is needed most. The degree of luminosity does not yet adjust to match the ambient light from the stage. And so on. But one day surtitles will be universally visible, beautifully written and as much a part of opera house life as the orchestra.

Tonality, Atonality

All of us have a bit of Pythagoras implanted in our ears, or rather the Pythagorean scale, alias the diatonic scale which we have heard in Western music from Purcell's *Dido and Aeneas* to *Sgt. Pepper's Lonely Hearts Club Band*. Pythagoras counted the number of vibrations made by a note (how *did* he do it?) whether it was the string of a harp or the column of air vibrating in the pipe of some shepherd he had hired to sit in his lab. He found that if he shortened the harp string until he got twice as many vibes he got the same note as before but higher. Similarly with the pipe. So he showed that the vibes of two notes an octave apart are in the ratio of 1:2. He found other simple ratios: 2:3 for instance – the fifth. In the key of C that is C to G. So on to the next one: 3:4 – the fourth – C to F. A little more remote was the whole tone: 8:9 – C to D. We won't go further than that in this lesson, particularly since if you were to add up the five whole tones and the two semitones in the octave of the well-known and well-loved diatonic scale the number of vibes would not come out quite right, that is not quite in the ratio of 1:2 on the dot as it should do, and this has kept learned musicos arguing for most of two of the twenty-five centuries since Pythagoras's discovery and pushed Bach into writing the 48 preludes and fugues to demonstrate (four times over) that an instrument could be tuned to spread the error evenly over the whole octave so that even Alfred Brendel would scarcely notice. So for God's sake let's leave that one alone.

All of this is just to show that the diatonic scale has a basis in science and isn't just a nice idea dreamed up by some prehistoric composer. But it did not come about at once. For about the first fifteen centuries after Pythagoras only the more important notes tended to be used, sometimes five, sometimes seven. These made up the Greek modes, of which there were several and the notes were permed around in different patterns right up to our mediaeval plainsong when (thank goodness) today's diatonic scale got the upper hand and pretty well ruled the roost until Arnold Schoenberg came along. Arnold, a modest man in many ways, thought fit to challenge the Pythagorean system with a new one of his own. To stick with the same old scale for five hundred years or so, he argued, tended to imply too great a degree of conservatism. So instead of sticking with the eight-note octave he switched to a scale of twelve equal tones that added up to nothing like an octave. To the ordinary ear this was pretty well musical bedlam. There was nowhere to come home to, no keynote, because there was no key. All the old landmarks, the trusty old dominant, the invaluable major third, the friendly fourth, had all disappeared. Suddenly you had been dropped into a featureless desert where all notes looked the same, there were no tunes, no keys, therefore no modulations, no major, no minor, no sense and absolutely no pleasure. But Arnold and his research assistants Berg and Webern persisted, gained a following, and today their work has changed the face of music. This is not to say that the theses of these three (often called the Second Viennese School) were adopted by all or even many of today's composers, but they showed that music could be written in new tonal systems and that the diatonic scale was not the only bus on the road.

Three of the operas in this book are written in musical language that is not all diatonic – *Pelléas*, in which Debussy writes freely in whole-tone modes which in some ways anticipate Schoenberg; *Bluebeard*, in which Bartok is even more atonal but still modalish though his modes are emphatically Hungarian; and *Wozzeck* which is the real McCoy, almost entirely atonal and just the sort of thing the Schoenberg team were out there to promote. There are short drifts of atonality in *Porgy* but nothing to notice too much and all composers, but especially the Russians, will trot out a folk tune with a few non-diatonic notes in it at the drop of a hat, maybe just to show (modishly) how much they admire folk music. This was an attitude Sir Thomas Beecham did not share as he made clear when he once said that he would try anything in life once except incest and folk music. [And knowing his tastes he could just as well have said atonal music: Ed.]

THE COMPOSERS

Note: In this section, the operas that are included in the *Opera* section are marked with a dagger.

Bartok, Bela 1881–1945

HABITAT Budapest until driven to the USA in 1940 by the threat of Hitler.
OPERAS *Bluebeard's Castle*†, his one and only.
LIFE AND TIMES A compulsive folk-song collector: musically very Hungarian. Wrote his best stuff for orchestra and string quartet. Taught at the Budapest Academy. Left for America regretfully.
COMMENT Bartok had a taste for folk music and also for the bizarre so long as it was Hungarian. *Bluebeard* has a rich helping of both. Bartok's music is not all that easy on the ear for trad opera lovers but once the listener gets over the Bartok hump it construes more easily than the music of the more austere atonalists. Very soon it grips the attention and astounds the ear with its wispy imaginative phrases, its sonority and its classical good sense. You know at once that you are listening to a master, although to begin with it is a little hard to catch what he is saying. But the listener to Bartok must be folk-song tolerant because he pulls in a lot of model stuff from the plains and the mountains. This gives his music its own very strong flavour. You can often almost smell the dung.

Beethoven, Ludwig van 1770–1827

HABITAT Bonn and Vienna.
OPERAS *Fidelio*†, his one and only.
LIFE AND TIMES Far too famous a figure to be encumbered by snippets in an opera guide, even a Good one.
COMMENT It would be an impertinence to try to size up Beethoven's general output but one must say that his power and glory came mainly from his instrumental music. In choral music he often writes too high for the sopranos (and sometimes the men's voices too) and when he gets over-excited (which he does quite often) the big volume of choral sound can seem a bit jumbled. Not as bad as the pea-soup of a Schumann symphony but definitely lacking the clarity of his writing for the orchestra. He also wrote well over 100 songs, some of which are really nice – the song-cycle *An die ferne Geliebte* is a little marvel – but he never seemed to drive full throttle when composing for the solo human voice, maybe because it could not supply him with the sudden bursts of tremendously loud sound he so delighted in when writing for the piano or the orchestra. But when all of that is said we have to remember that *Fidelio* has supplied

us with two of the most magical moments in all opera – the quartet and the prisoners' chorus, both in Act I, also the two truly operatic big arias in Act II plus the sequence of duet–trio–quartet that builds up so wonderfully to the trumpet call. Despite a patchy first act, *Fidelio* is a great opera. Had he composed 27 operas like Verdi, Beethoven would of course have become one of opera's giants.

Bellini, Vincenzo 1801–35 (died a couple of years younger than Mozart)

HABITAT From Sicily to Naples at seventeen, later to Milan and Paris. Operatic sorties to London and Venice.

OPERAS Ten altogether. Two now-forgotten early operas in Naples: his third opera, *Il Pirata*, a hit, later operas all sooner or later smash hits, except one (*Zaira*). *Sonnambula*†, *Norma*†, *Puritani*†.

LIFE AND TIMES Bellini's operatic success gave him the chance to break into Milanese society, which he did with relish, becoming a bit of a dandy and a famous ladies' man. He was a friend of Rossini who was born nine years before him and lived on for 33 years after his death. His great good fortune was to find the excellent Romani as his partner and librettist (see LIBRETTO page 823) for all but two of his ten operas. Unlike Donizetti and Verdi, he rationed his output to an opera a year. He was inevitably drawn to Paris as the centre of fashion both in music and in society. He died there unromantically of an acute inflammation of the large intestine.

COMMENT Bellissimo Bellini is the composer of the purest and most beautiful melodies in all opera. These can be long; an early strain will often be capped by another and yet another, climbing onwards and upwards to a climactic outburst of song which delights and surprises the ear in a way no other composer can match (e.g. 'Casta Diva' in *Norma*). He is ingenious in writing for two voices, first alternately, then overlapping and finally in full simultaneous accord. Similarly for an ensemble of five or more voices and chorus. He is not much interested in the orchestra, often the accompaniment is bland, sometimes no more than rhythmical breathing below the vocal parts (but sometimes he took great pains, e.g. Amina's second sleepwalking aria in *Sonnambula*). When the orchestra plays alone it tends to deal in stock gestures and his preludes, interludes and introductions are often fairly humdrum. There are passages of stock-pot recitatif but rarely for too long. Dramatic recitatifs can flower into arioso (but not often as in Donizetti). Arias illuminate the words of the text but do not reflect character: the same arias could be equally well sung by goodies or by baddies. He can use the chorus as an accompaniment where again he often employs them baying gently in the background beneath the voices of the principals. His big set pieces come off at strength nine. But Bellini's greatest glory lies in his arias, especially when tinged with romantic melancholy: he is strong with sorrow; excellent at despair; when jolly he can sound a little too near to operetta for comfort. Dramatically sound: all the big scenes are theatrically effective – the last fifteen minutes of *Norma* a knockout. If you like Bellini at all you will sooner or later come to love him.

Berg, Alban 1885–1935

HABITAT Vienna.
OPERAS Two: *Wozzeck*† and *Lulu* which he left unfinished.
LIFE AND TIMES A student with Schoenberg who was rattling the bars of the musical world by inventing a new basis for writing music, namely doing away with the old diatonic scale and writing free-floating atonal stuff. Along with Webern these two made up what came to be called the Second Viennese School. He spent his life studying, composing and publicizing the new music.
COMMENT For many people the music of Berg and the atonalists and twelve-toners is written in a foreign language which is hard to understand. Elderly ears in particular have become tuned to that old trusty, the diatonic scale, since they were kids. They have heard 'God save our diatonic Queen', they have grown up with diatonic Beethoven, the diatonic Beatles, the Top of the Pops, and Hymns Ancient and, although Modern, still absolutely diatonic. Once they lose the old diatonic many clients don't know what the hell is going on. (See TONALITY page 858.) But a great composer with true musicality can break through this sound barrier, and in his two operas Berg does it. By the time the curtain comes down on *Wozzeck* and *Lulu* the audience has forgotten they have been listening to a new form of music, they have been swept along by the intensity and power of Berg the great musician. (Although ten minutes after curtain up they would be thinking 'I can't understand/stand this stuff.') Technically Berg was something of a wizard, a wonderful orchestrator, sometimes percussive, brassy and noisy beyond belief, sometimes moving towards the frontiers of Viennese sweetness with little restless fragments of what one might call non-melody which stick in the ear. His methods of composition were complex, formal and geometrical. The twelve-toners used to write their at-the-time incomprehensible pieces allegedly in baroque forms such as fugues, suites, inventions, etc. But it is often hard to see any kind of relationship between the old and the new (see COMMENT, *Wozzeck*, page 799). The amazing thing is that Berg with his austere mathematical approach to composition can move us so profoundly and can make us share his deep sense of compassion for the lower depths of humanity.

Bizet, Georges 1838–75

HABITAT Paris, with three student years spent in Rome.
OPERAS *Pêcheurs de Perles*†, *Fair Maid of Perth, Carmen*†.
LIFE AND TIMES Bizet's short life is the story of many beginnings and few endings. He started on fourteen operas that he never finished. He finished four that were unperformed. Nine operas reached the stage. To the lasting shame of the French nation, all but six of his opera scores have been lost along with those of nearly all the operettas and incidental music for the theatre. This miserable legacy obscures the fact that Bizet was a tremendously active composer and in addition to the above tally there are records of literally dozens of other projects which ended in nothing.
COMMENT Bizet was blessed with the ability to write alpha-plus tunes in such abundance as is rare and found only in other great melodists like Schubert, Offenbach, Verdi and Kern. Some of these tunes he could graft into the fabric of an opera (the triangle tune in *Pêcheurs*, the motto of the premonition of death in *Carmen*). But he was not in any way a Wagnerian and his few tunes used in this way are more like the tutti holding together a concerto or an aria rather than a reference library of meaningful mottos. His orchestration is masterly, clear, effective, noisy when necessary, imaginative and with a great affection for the woodwind, especially when used as soloists. The flute solo in the entr'acte before Act III of *Carmen* could almost as well have been sung offstage by Micaela, so gentle and so human is its voice. He brought fresh touches of colour into his harmonies and a new zest and vigour to the vocal writing. There is none of the bel canto habit of vocal loitering in *Carmen*. The attempts at exotica in *Pêcheurs* do not really come off but the Spanishness of *Carmen* is a marvel. It sounds as authentically Spanish as rioja, yet Bizet had never been near Spain in his life. It was his one truly influential opera (which was nevertheless booed on its first night) and broke with the social/spectacular tradition of Meyerbeer and the suburban sentimentality of Gounod. It took opera forward on a new road, a road that ran in a different direction from Wagner's fourteen-lane highway and Verdi's Via Nazionale. But it was the way ahead, it was the road that led to verismo and to Puccini. Bizet was 36 when he died, one year older than Mozart. Although Mozart's operatic achievements were prodigious, we should remember that at 36 Verdi had only got as far as *Stiffelio* with all his mature operas to come, whereas Wagner was just launching *Lohengrin*. So what would Bizet have done with another thirty years or so of operatic life?

Cilea, Francesco 1866–1950

HABITAT Naples during his student days then Florence and Palermo.
OPERAS Five, none of which caught on except *Adriana*†.
LIFE AND TIMES Cilea was one of the Giovane Scuola or young lions that roamed around in the Italian operatic no-man's-land after Verdi. He was a scholarly musician and taught at the conservatories of Naples and Florence until he was getting on a little.
COMMENT His music is a delight: frothy, delicate, witty and when required pathetic too. A marvellous orchestrator with the lightest of touches. It is true that he did use mottos (although in *Adriana* they don't bother you in the least), but in every other way he was independent of operatic fashions and quite unaffected by the big noise made by Puccini and the alleged verismo of *Cav* and *Pag*. He was the Saki of Italian opera and the pity is he didn't stick to the opera house instead of disappearing into academia, where everyone says he was just a great teacher. But we would rather have had one or two more *Adrianas*.

Debussy, Claude 1862–1918

HABITAT Paris.
OPERAS Only one completed opera, *Pelléas et Mélisande*†.
LIFE AND TIMES The first of the true modernists. He broke with old-style diatonic music and experimented with modal music. He became a revered cult figure in French musical life. His influence over all music was enormous and especially affected scores of bad composers who thought (sometimes correctly) that by writing music that sounded like Debussy they wouldn't be found out.
COMMENT Debussy's only opera *Pelléas* is a true original. It has no recitatif and no arias but instead tells its operatic story by means of the characters talking to each other in a declamatory fashion. But the orchestra too is a main player and is just as important as the vocal line in conveying the mood, the feeling and the drama of the story as Debussy leads us along in a sort of operatic trance. Thanks to his orchestral style things happen as if in slow motion, people move as if in a dream. This Debussy brought about by what he called the orchestral decor. He matched Maeterlinck's power with musical poetry. Together they cast a magic spell. Symbols abound in the text, there are the mottos around in the music, but they are the mottos of *Parsifal* and not of *The Ring* and we don't have to spend time punching them up before the performance. Debussy's orchestration has its own sound, mellow, sensual and enormously adroit. He makes the woodwind work miracles for him and can cause an uproar when an uproar is called for. But the pace is generally that

of a sailing boat in a gentle breeze. You can see and hear everything as you glide through his score. But it is not all plain sailing. Debussy's score is at times profoundly disturbing and the sweetness and light of the early scenes give way to the impending tragedy of the last act. People who think, on a description like the one above, that *Pelléas* is the last thing they would want to see are generally wrong. *Pelléas* with its subtle attraction will seduce the most unlikely clients. Aberdeen undertakers succumb to its charms.

Delibes, Léo 1836–91

HABITAT The salons and theatres of Paris.
OPERAS Many ballets, operettas, much theatre music and four operas, now all lying in well-deserved obscurity except for *Lakmé*† (which some may feel deserves it too).
LIFE AND TIMES Delibes started young, having his first operetta produced when he was only nineteen. He lived his life amongst the foothills of grand opera – and in the shadow of the dreaded Meyerbeer – and perhaps served it best in his job as chorus master of the Opéra itself.
COMMENT A song-and-dance composer with ambitions above his station. Delibes could write a good short catchy tune but his inspiration often seemed to flag after four bars. His soufflé music is better suited to ballet, operetta and the Palm Court trio than to opera. A skilful orchestrator. Tchaikovsky admired him greatly, which perhaps says more about Tchaikovsky than Delibes.

Donizetti, Gaetano 1797–1848

HABITAT Mainly Naples and later Paris, but he was constantly shuttling about between the opera houses of Europe including Palermo, Milan, Parma, Rome, Genoa, Venice and Vienna.
OPERAS Sixty-five! Including *Elisir*†, *Maria Stuarda*†, *Lucia*† and *Don Pasquale*†.
LIFE AND TIMES It is a relief to report that unlike most figures in the gallery of famous operatics, Donizetti was a terribly decent fellow. He had a charming relationship with his old teacher, one Mayr, whom he cherished until his death, he was generous to his rival composers (more than they were to him), he was really fond of his wife, heartbroken when she died, was universally agreeable and widely liked. At the age of 25 Donizetti left his native Po valley for Naples which was to become his operatic base for the next sixteen years until he had a row with the King who stopped the production of *Maria Stuarda* on the grounds that it would subvert the authority of royals generally and who from then on

regarded Donizetti as something of a Commie. But by now he was famous and turning out operas at a speed of knots for houses all over Italy and later for Vienna and for the ultimate goal of all opera composers, the Paris Opéra itself. In the years between the death of Bellini (1836) and Verdi's first hit (*Nabucco*, 1842) Donizetti was No. 1 in the charts of European opera composers. Once in Paris his productivity slowed down. He died there of syphilis in 1848.

COMMENT Of the three bel canto composers Donizetti was the all-rounder. Rossini was at his best in comedy and melodrama, Bellini was happiest when melancholy, but Donizetti could box the compass of operatic moods and no bother at all. Of his four operas mentioned above he calls *Elisir* a light-hearted (giocoso) melodrama, *Maria Stuarda* a lyrical tragedy, *Lucia* a dramatic tragedy and *Don Pasquale* a buffa comedy, and who would be bold enough to claim that any one of these styles suits Donizetti better or worse than any of the other three? His ability to write a tune of any kind to meet any contingency at the drop of a hat was stunning. He could range effortlessly from Dr Dulcamara's sales-talk patter to the menacing power of the finale of *Maria Stuarda*, from the tender observation of Adina's furtive tear to the mad scenes in *Lucia*. Musically he took up the baton from Rossini and ran alongside Bellini, each one picking up some useful tips from the other on the way along the track. As Donizetti got into his stride he formed a more personal style: secco recitatif disappeared, the accompanied recitatif began to flower into mini-melodies (arioso) and the structure of a scene, of an act, of a whole opera, began to take on much stronger dramatic contours. No longer was it one thing after another – recitatif, aria, chorus, recitatif, romanza and finale, each one to some degree detachable, even interchangeable – Donizetti pushed the action forward in a strategic music-plan that gave shape to the whole piece. The last act of *Maria Stuarda* is masterly music drama, not so much in the Wagnerian sense of words and music being fused together as in the more common-sense approach of placing each step carefully to relate it to what went before and what comes next so that the scene reaches its final climax by a carefully engineered route to the top.

Donizetti had a great sense of theatre and a thorough understanding of what it takes to make a good plot. He also had two star librettists, Romani, the acknowledged No. 1 poet of his day, and after his death Cammarano, a real pro who later worked with a much harder taskmaster – Verdi. For singers Donizetti wrote in the way that would suit them best. He provided lots of fioriture for the females and bold declamatory strokes for the males but seldom stopped the show in its tracks just to allow a fireworks display. His scoring for the orchestra followed Rossini's lead, a firm line or backing from the strings with lots of colour and incident from the woodwind. Although perhaps his orchestration does not have quite all the magic of the old wizard, it is less brittle, more human than Rossini's and much, much better than dear Bellini's.

Donizetti had one trick (common to all three bel cantos) of introducing a terribly serious aria maybe about death with a cheery oom-pah accompaniment (see *Maria Stuarda* page 423) of the sort used as a backing for an old-style music-hall song. This can upset today's listener. But in Donizetti's time the galumphing oom-pah bass had no such connotation. Oom-pah could be read to be just as serious as 'Death and the Maiden'. It is what we have done to oom-pah since then that is the trouble. Offenbach, Sullivan, Sousa and the vaudeville theatre have turned it into a standby signal for a pop tune.

Donizetti was no great trail-blazer. He wrote pretty well within the traditions of opera as she then was. There are ornery patches even in his best operas (but hell, he turned them out at a rate of more than two a year). He did not generally find such meaningful employment for the chorus as did Mozart in *Idomeneo* or Verdi in *Nabucco*. But for all of this Donizetti could write music to make you cry, music to touch your heart, music to make you laugh and always music to set your feet a-tap. He had zest, ingenuity, wit and a great, great sense of theatre. He was the most human of the bel cantos, the most versatile, the most tuneful and the best.

Gershwin, George 1898–1937

HABITAT New York and Hollywood.

OPERAS Over a score of musicals, one full-length opera, *Porgy and Bess*†.

LIFE AND TIMES Gershwin lived in the songwriter's whirling world of Tin Pan Alley, Broadway musicals and Hollywood musicals. He fancied more serious stuff too, and made a big thing of studying jazz and blues and also classical music. His lifelong ambition was to unite jazz and symphonic music into a new American art form and he almost pulled this off with his piano concerto and *Rhapsody in Blue* and at last pretty well succeeded with *Porgy*.

COMMENT George Gershwin was a wonderful tune writer and his brother Ira a great lyricist. Between them and with a little help from their friends Hart, Rodgers, Hammerstein and Kern, they lifted the American musical to a level of sophistication and tunefulness (*Funny Face*) way above the lumpen Viennese operettas that were still being sobbed out by Richard Tauber in Volkstheaters all over Germany (*Frederica*). Gershwin set himself a great task – to write a full opera that would do for the American negro in the South what *Carmen* did for Spain and *Meistersinger* for Nuremberg and in which jazz and blues would mingle with modern classical music. (Well, fairly modern, because although Gershwin had rubbed shoulders with Prokofiev, Poulenc, Milhaud, Walton and Berg and had played tennis with Schoenberg – with twelve-tone balls – the classical bits in *Porgy* would seem to be more Puccini than Second Viennese School.) So he did it and mighty fine it is. But although it owes a lot to gospel and blues and New Orleans, it is really a one-off marvel created by a very musical man who could write tunes like 'Summertime', comic songs about the Bible, spiritual choruses and who was fortunate in having a metrical brother.

Giordano, Umberto 1867–1948

HABITAT Mainly Italy.
OPERAS Eleven completed operas including *Andrea Chénier*†.
LIFE AND TIMES One of the Giovane Scuola or group of young lions who roamed the Italian opera houses at the turn of last century. He roared early in life and then only a little, having three big successes before he was 30 and after that, although he shrewdly married into the family who owned the hotel in which Verdi resided – thus gaining access to some of the best operatic advice available – he was on the slide all the way.
COMMENT Giordano would have passed any exam in opera composition. He was a real pro and could write fluently, in the style of the day. His only problem was that he was a little dim. P.G. Wodehouse tells the story of an after-dinner speaker who was stopped in his tracks by a guest who yelled out at him 'Louder – and funnier!' Maybe this is the sort of advice Giordano got from Verdi, for he was a dogged trier and some of his more dramatic scenes come off really well (see the last scene of *Chénier* page 20). He was clever at weaving outside music into his scores (Russian folk music into his opera *Siberia* and French revolutionary songs into *Chénier*). His orchestration was unmistakably ornery and his tunes tended to be short-breathed and constantly hopping about from key to key. But let's not knock him into the scenery. If he had been a novelist his three best books would be called 'a good read'.

Gluck, Christoph Willibald 1714–87

HABITAT Workplace, the opera capitals of Europe, finally Paris; heart and home, Vienna.
OPERAS 44 including *Iphigenia*† and *Orpheus*†.
LIFE AND TIMES Air travel would have been a real help to Gluck. For the first thirteen years of his operatic life he flitted around all the great opera houses in Italy plus visits to London, Prague, Copenhagen, etc. It is a wonder he didn't charge for travelling time. By the time he was 40 he

settled in Vienna, married a rich wife, got a house job with a friendly neighbourhood prince and started to supply the lucky Viennese with a stream of operas and ballets. Ten years later he met Calzabigi. This was a bit like Rodgers meeting Hammerstein or Gilbert meeting Sullivan, except that Calzabigi was not content just to motor along in a steady partnership however successful it might be. He was a reformer who wanted to reform pretty well everything in the arts, but especially ballet and opera. So did Gluck. They started away reforming together like anything, starting with *Orpheus* (Vienna 1762). *Orpheus* was meant to shock and it did. Gluck carried on reforming (two more operas with Calzabigi) but he was a practical man and in order to keep his finances in good shape he had to slip in quite a lot of traditional work as well. During the last phase of his life he lived in Vienna and worked mainly in Paris. Here he put on his last five operas, all pretty well in the reformed mode. He also tried to reform the old Spanish customs and bad singing traditions of the Paris Opéra but being very short-tempered, rather ill and inclined to slip off to Vienna at the drop of a hat, it is doubtful how much reformation he brought about. In 1779 he had a stroke during rehearsals, left Paris, and composed no more.

COMMENT Gluck shared the common aim of all opera reformers, including Wagner, namely to bring opera nearer to the ideal of a continuous music drama. Away with the stiff old conventions of opera seria. Away with the idea of opera being a show place for singers. Away with transformation scenes and extravagant spectacle. Sing Something Simple was Gluck's motto, and the something should have words and music fitting together in such a way as to affect the human emotions as powerfully as could be. By these means Gluck changed the face of opera. He replaced secco recitatif with accompagnato. He structured each act dramatically. He moved the action forward in a series of tableaux. He cut the singer's role down to size. He assaulted the emotions with music carrying a message more powerful and more poignant than was possible in older forms.

Compared with the showbusiness flair of the bel cantos and the mighty forces of Wagner, Gluck's operas have the restraint and the refinement of chamber music. But although the resources are small and the means are simple, Gluck can make the earth move and we are much in his debt for taking his great leap forward into a new and richer operatic world.

Gounod, Charles-François 1818–93

HABITAT Paris.

OPERAS Twelve including *Faust*†.

LIFE AND TIMES Gounod lived his life in and around the opera houses of Paris when French opera was still under the spell of the dreaded Meyerbeer and Wagner and Verdi were the two top world-class players. Gounod was lucky in that his kind of romantic music struck a chord with the Parisian public of the day. He had his flops but he also had an early *succès fou* with *Faust* (1859) and he hit the jackpot once again with *Romeo and Juliet* (1867). It tells us something about French taste to learn that Verdi's *Don Carlos*, which was premiered in the same year as *Romeo*, was not given anything like so good a reception. During the Franco-Prussian war Gounod slipped across the Channel with his family. But he produced nothing in London, by now his reputation was on the slide and his last three operas all bombed out.

COMMENT Gounod could write a rousing tune, Gounod was a crafty man of the theatre, Gounod could orchestrate, Gounod could wring the sentimental tear. On this level Gounod is just fine. What Gounod cannot do is to treat the human condition in any depth. His characters give off the vibes of operetta as they sing the music of grand opera. His plots are built around scenes which come off OK but which together don't add up. If you don't ask too much of Gounod and have a taste for musical milk chocolate he will give you a good evening.

For some reason Gounod was (surprisingly) friendly with Wagner who saw him as something of a missionary figure trying to restore beauty, truth and artistic integrity to the French stage. This can only be a comment on Wagner's judgement or on the very low level of truth, beauty, etc. in Parisian musical life, for Gounod was the opposite of a reformer. He presented pleasantly packaged songs and scenes from operatic life which have given a lot of pleasure to a lot of people, and what is wrong with that?

Handel, George Frederick 1685–1759

HABITAT Halle, Hamburg, Florence and Hanover in early life, but then London for the last 46 years.

OPERAS 46 including *Giulio Cesare*†.

LIFE AND TIMES Opera in Handel's time was still pretty well always funded by royals. The court composer had to be something of a household politico and Handel wasn't very good at that, being fired from Hanover for taking the wrong line on EU policy. But his true value was known and he got a safe job in London where he was soon made Director of the Royal Academy of Music. In what was a rather more commercial climate Handel's job was to put on the operas, many of them his own, mainly at the King's Theatre, Haymarket. This he did for over 20 years under various sponsors. He had his flops, he had his sell-outs and he got into an operatic contest with a rival opera-monger, one Bononcini. For lack of an alternative interest such as football pools, the citizens became supporters of one or other of the rival operatic teams, leading to a high degree of disorder and operatic hooliganism including an on-stage no-holds-barred fight between two rival sopranos. This led to Handel's house being closed down.

All the operas Handel presented were within the fixed conventions of opera seria as practised in Italy where it was no more and no less than a platform for great singers. Handel would scour the Continent for talent like a big-game hunter, looking for the finest and rarest specimens. In the opera house itself the singers sang in front of scenery that was changed in full view of the audience and the composer led the small orchestra from a keyboard in the pit – nearer to the scale of the Wigmore Hall than the Scala. But fashion swung from opera to oratorio, support dwindled, and Handel composed his last opera, *Deidamia*, in 1741, eighteen years before his death.

COMMENT It is not possible to make an assessment of the great Handel as an opera composer alone, for the musical units in opera seria were written in a currency common to most of his music, particularly in oratorio. In both opera and oratorio arias were the big thing, nearly all of them da capo (see ARIA page 803) and the choruses, orchestral overtures and intermezzos could almost as well have appeared in *Messiah* as in one of his operas. There were no laughs in an opera seria. A serious item was followed by an even more serious item. What drama there was lay inside the head and did not show itself on the stage. The range of emotions was limited and each one pigeonholed under its own label (rage, despair, jubilation, etc.). The secco recitatif carried the story along between bouts of singing, the choruses were generally simple and not on the grand scale of *Messiah.* And yet the music itself is often quite splendid. Handel could write a tune, and he was a master of contrapuntal or horizontal writing when one voice (or instrument) gives out a tuneful musical pattern followed a few paces behind by a second and maybe a third and a fourth. We do not know what the orchestra sounded like, for the forces used tended to depend on who was available to play. There were always some upper strings, a string bass, a harpsichord, maybe half-a-dozen oboes, a few bassoons, trumpets and drums as required, and often much more. Handel is at his greatest perhaps in the slow dignified air ('Ombra mai fu' – 'Handel's Largo', 'Every Valley') but he can muster up great bursts of rage, cheerful whistleable ditties and tender soprano pieces. As a composer he was always tidy, always neat, never said in twelve bars what he could in eight and although he often asked the human voice to do extraordinary things, he offered it many of its most glorious opportunities.

Humperdinck, Engelbert I 1854–1921 (Not to be confused with Humperdinck, Engelbert II)

HABITAT Cologne, Munich and Bayreuth.
OPERAS Nine, all forgotten except *Hansel and Gretel*†.
LIFE AND TIMES Humperdinck became Wagner's copyist, dogsbody and fan. He worked with him on the first production of *Parsifal*. Later became a music teacher in Cologne.
COMMENT Wagner without the heavy breathing. Remembered as a one-work man, in *Hansel and Gretel* he dished up a gorgeously rich and sonorous score. Humperdinck could write a tune and made great play by weaving them together and reintroducing them in a new context. *Hansel and Gretel* is a gem. Don't be put off by the title 'Dream Pantomime' nor by the nursery tunes everyone knows. This is a real opera and a winner.

Leoncavallo, Ruggero 1857–1919

HABITAT Naples and Milan.
OPERAS Some eighteen operas, operettas and farces including the one and only *Pagliacci*†.
LIFE AND TIMES Leoncavallo's operatic life started with a bang. He saw Mascagni win an opera contest with *Cav* and immediately set to work to do some market research to analyse the elements that had made it so successful. This caused him to come up with *Pag* which was an immediate smash hit in Milan, then as now the HQ of Italian opera. A great career was predicted but alas Leoncavallo's talents seem to have run into the sand. After a number of grand opera flops he descended to operetta and then, after several operetta flops, to farces with titles like *The First Kiss*. But *Pag* will live for ever.
COMMENT It is raw emotion hung on a simple story that makes *Pag* a winner. Its success caused the scribes to make a cult of what they called verismo, but *Pag* is not really very vero. It is in fact melodrama, just as Maria Marten's murder in *The Red Barn* is melodrama. The verismo (or neo-realist) Italian film directors of 60 years later (de Sica, Visconti) make *Pag* look like high camp. But *Pag* was to make verismo the buzzword for operatics for some long time. What is sure is that *Pag* became top of the operatic pops at once, and coupled with *Cav* still draws the biggest crowds. Musically it is full of good simple tunes, melodramatically effective and with a mighty high emotional charge. The score has the essence of Italian opera running through it, it allows the singers (especially the tenor) to project the animal appeal of the Italian operatic voice directly at the audience's heart, stomach, viscera, or whichever organ it may be that leads a human being to laugh, shout and cry as a

result of hearing Leoncavallo's one-act barn-stormer (later extended to two acts).

Mascagni, Pietro 1863–1945

HABITAT Rome and the opera houses of Italy.
OPERAS Eighteen, all forgotten except *Amico Fritz* and *Cavalleria Rusticana*† (*Cav*).
LIFE AND TIMES Mascagni started brilliantly by wiping the eye of Italy's two most venerated names in opera. He showed the score of *Cav* to Puccini and also to the great publisher and musical mandarin Ricordi before submitting it for the Sonzogno prize (the equivalent of an Emmy for the best newcomer). No good, said one. Quite hopeless, said the other. Mascagni not only took the prize but registered a smash hit with *Cav* when it first opened in Milan. It would be nice to say he never looked back, but the truth is he never moved forward. Apart from *Amico Fritz* the rest of his work, including some orchestral scores for silent movies, lies in well-deserved obscurity.
COMMENT *Cav* is neither refined nor subtle. Its numbers need to be punched out with the zest of a New Orleans jazz singer. Musically it is conventional and its melodrama is highly melo. The singers must be able to sing very loud and make that direct assault on the senses that only the great Italian voice can make. But if you get all the pieces right – pow! – *Cav* will hit you fairly and squarely in the solar plexus and you will be on your feet yelling Bravo! with the rest of them. What the clever Mascagni realized was that big tunes (he could write a tune), strong situations and a plot with no hanging around plus a killing at the end, will deliver you an irresistible article – all the highlights of Italian opera squashed together into a very short period of time. *Cav*'s claims to verismo are stronger than those of *Pag*, but it is the verismo of passion if at all, not the verismo of everyday life. But there is no call to theorize over *Cav* any more than there is over *Coronation Street*. *Cav* is equally in touch with its public and both are bulletproof.

Massenet, Jules 1842–1912

HABITAT The theatres and opera houses of Paris.
OPERAS 26 completed operas and operettas including *Manon* and *Werther*†.
LIFE AND TIMES Massenet was the leading opera composer in France after the death of Bizet, which is rather like saying that John Major has been the outstanding figure in the Conservative Party after the departure of Thatcher. Anyone who has picked up any casual information about

Massenet will probably believe him to have been a lion of the Paris salons, successful, rich and with popular operas pouring out one after the other – and indeed they could not be faulted for thinking so, since this is exactly how Massenet describes himself in his autobiography. Alas, it is not quite true. Except for *Manon*, *Le Cid* and *Thaïs*, all his operas were flops, near-misses or mildly acceptable. Even *Werther* was turned down by the Paris Opéra and only made its mark when it played in Vienna. Nevertheless, he was the leading French composer of his day.

COMMENT Massenet was a really professional man of the theatre, an adroit orchestrator and could write a tune, a very long-breathed tune, what was called the 'phrase Massenétique'. Debussy kindly said that it was his 'ability to please' that his rivals found hard to forgive. But the operas as a whole are a slushy lot when serious and embarrassingly banal when light, as a recent production of *Chérubin*, perversely mounted at enormous expense by a great opera house, proved. *Werther* has its wimpish high spots, but they are pretty few. Massenet is summed up pretty well by the soubriquet 'La fille de Gounod'.

Mozart, Wolfgang Amadeus 1756–91

HABITAT Salzburg and Vienna. Many tours.

OPERAS Seventeen finished operas counting shorts and allsorts, including *Idomeneo*†, *Seraglio*†, *Figaro*†, *Giovanni*†, *Cosi*†, the *Flute*† and *Tito*†.

LIFE AND TIMES It was not by choice that Mozart wrote 46 symphonies, 26 piano concertos and only just over a dozen full-length operas. He would have written many more but in those days no composer would have dreamt of starting on any big work without a commission, and commissions for opera were in short supply.

In his childhood tours of Europe the question of opera did not arise. As a teenager in Salzburg he did get some local commissions but the tiny state was run by a penny-pinching holy Prince/Archbishop, who did not believe in subsidizing the arts. There was no state theatre, few good musicians and little enthusiasm for stage works. So Mozart's operatic work in Salzburg was put on by semi-amâteurs and the results must have looked more like an end-of-term college show than an up-market Viennese production.

His first great chance came when still as a teenager his father was touting him around the cities of northern Italy as an elderly child prodigy. He got three opera commissions in Milan. The first was a big success but one can only deduce that the second and third got lower ratings for he was not asked to come back again.

Maybe as a result of Milan Mozart got a commission from Munich for a buffa opera with the inscrutable title of *The Young Lady who Posed as a Gardener*. This was his first grown-up comedy, a good piece, full of fun, and something of a dry run for *Figaro*. Alas it had an impossible plot. Mozart got his big chance to show what he could do with the old seria form when he got a second commission from Munich, this time for *Idomeneo*. He went to work at white heat, injected passion into the arias, grandeur into the many choruses and almost (but not quite) luminosity into the characters. *Idomeneo* is a huge step forward in the history of opera but no one seemed to notice this at the time.

In the 1780s there were only three known types of opera. The first was the old opera seria form (a string of arias set to some classical plot and designed to show off the singers' voices (see OPERA – HISTORY AND FORM, pages 829–30). Then there was buffa, with a cheery farce-like plot usually based on a successful stage play, much looser in construction and much nearer to our idea of opera today. Both these forms were sung in Italian. Chauvinistic old Emperor Joseph II didn't like to see the world of opera dominated by Frogs (namely Gluck) or Wops (dozens of them including his own staff man Salieri), so in 1778 he stamped his imperial German foot and set up a National Singspielhaus in Vienna so that OIG (Opera In German) could take its place in the top European league (which it never did). The Singspiel form was really not much more than a play with musical numbers popped in, and shortly after he arrived in Vienna Mozart got the chance to try his hand at it. We do not know which type of opera Mozart preferred. But he had no choice. Composers were servants, so they had to be subservient. If an eighteenth-century opera commission were to be given in the present day, you might well hear a telephone conversation on the following lines:

'Could I please speak to Sir Harrison?'

'Birtwistle here.'

'Sir Harrison Birtwistle?'

'The same. Who is that?'

'Buckingham Palace. Her Majesty's Chamberlain of the Arts. Sir Harrison, I am honoured to inform you that Her Majesty the Queen has instructed me to invite you to produce an opera to commemorate the anniversary of the triumph of her horse Spindle in the Cheltenham Gold Cup this year.'

'An opera for Her Majesty? For Spindle? I am deeply honoured.'

'She would like the opera to be written in the style of Gilbert & Sullivan, Sir Harrison – not too long.'

'A short G & S style of thing? Certainly, yes. Of course. Of course.'

'Her guest on this occasion will be the Sultan of Oman and if it were possible to set the opera in the vicinity of the Gulf States Her Majesty would be obliged.'

'Gulf States? No problem.'

'I shall be sending you particulars of the Sultan and if you could see your way to reflecting his personality in one of the leading characters in the opera Her Majesty would be appreciative.'

'Certainly. Certainly. A tenor or a baritone?'

'The pitch of the voice is immaterial. Sir Harrison, may I remind you of one final point?'

'Yes please.'

'There will be the usual final aria – the licenza – addressed directly to Her Majesty in terms of gross flattery. Not too short.'

'Indeed I will make sure the final aria is appropriate.'

'Thank you Sir Harrison.'

'Thank you, Sir.'

(Sir Harrison Birtwistle's responses are of course couched in hypothetical eighteenth-century terms and do not reflect in any way his twentieth-century persona.)

This is the sort of message Mozart would receive without telephones but with every bit as much detail and probably a good deal of looking over the shoulder by royal spies as the work progressed. But a Singspiel was different, a freer form less geared to royal requirements and more to popular taste. *Seraglio* is the coarsest opera Mozart wrote but it showed he could be a popular entertainer, with its whistleable tunes, funny Turks and farcical Act I finale, and it paved the way for the glories of his second and last Singspiel, the *Flute*.

If Mozart had died in 1785 he would not have been remembered as an opera composer any more than Haydn. His piano concertos would have been what people valued most, plus some of his other instrumental music. But now something of a miracle was about to happen –he met da Ponte and together they created the three greatest buffa operas of their day, perhaps of any day. *Figaro* and *Così* were put on in Vienna to a goodish reception amongst the musicos of that city and *Giovanni* in Prague where it was a smash hit. But these three towering masterpieces did not run.

Mozart's next two commissions came at nearly the same time, one for a royal coronation in Prague (*Tito*) and the other, as part of a commercial venture by a mountebank impresario, for a Singspiel (the *Flute*). Both were an enormous success and both had a far greater number of performances in their day than the da Pontes. Aside from one or two short revival runs, the da Ponte trio sat on the shelf. Yet, believe it or not, the boring operas of Mozart's rival Salieri ran and ran. The adult Mozart managed to get seven operas on to the stage: Salieri nearly forty. And Vienna in those days thought of itself as the centre of musical taste. The shouts of Bravo Mozart! that have been heard over the past decade have been deafening, but alas they come just 200 years too late.

COMMENT Mozart hauled opera out of history and placed it firmly in the present day. We listen to Monteverdi, Gluck, Handel as we listen to concert-hall music. Dido's Lament may reach across the centuries to strike at our emotions, but this is rare. Most of their arias, duets and choruses are head-music rather than heart-music. In this way Mozart stands at the watershed between museum opera and living opera. And yet he never set out to be an innovator. Unlike Wagner, he did not have any great theories about what opera should be. He worked from job to job within traditional form whether he was composing a concerto, a symphony or an opera and as his natural genius grew, he enlarged that form. So we have a progression from the early piano concertos, some of which might have been written by Christian Bach, to the mighty C minor of 1786, from the toytown symphonies of his nursery years to the 'Jupiter', and from the simple recitatif and aria of *Apollo and Hyacinthus* to the glories of *Figaro* and the *Flute*. To Singspiel he gave in *Seraglio* good tunes, good humour and with its concerted finales he moved the old thing a shade nearer true opera. With the *Flute* he used the old Singspiel form to make something much greater, a magic pantomime with a mixture of fantasy and farce that lights up our imagination and touches our hearts. To the masonic bits he gave music of such serene beauty as to make us forget the quasi-religious hokum of the plot. To seria he brought nobility and drama. *Idomeneo* is no longer a stop–start procession of arias. Its mighty choruses and dramatic music push the story along and its deeply-felt solos give the characters a chance to become almost human. *Tito* in its different way is as fine a piece as *Idomeneo* but it comes as a bit of a shock to those who come to it fresh from hearing the three da Pontes. Could the man who wrote *Figaro* and *Così* write this antiquated stuff? they ask. The answer is yes, he could and did. Although he was fulfilling an order, and hard-pressed for time he clearly relished working in the old style and in doing so he brought the old seria form nearer to living opera than it had ever been before.

But it was the buffa operas that Mozart made especially his own. Beaumarchais gave the Mozart/da Ponte team a head start. *Figaro* was a brilliantly constructed play. It was also hilariously disrespectful of the above-stairs classes. Mozart and da Ponte made of this an even more brilliant opera, toning down the social satire and playing up the human comedy, as needs they had to to get it past the censors. The work they did together on *Figaro* led to one of the best librettist/composer combos of all time, for in *Giovanni* and *Così* they produced two more miracles. They brought wit and humanity into buffa, their plots worked brilliantly and their characters – thanks to the music as much as the words – live in our imagination as people just as real as Madam Bovary or Tom Jones.

All his life Mozart pined for a chance to write more opera. If we suppose he had got what he wanted and had become a purely opera composer turning out as many operas as Donizetti (65) it is impossible to know how this would have affected the course of European music (although the thought of three score mature Mozart operas instead of seven makes the mouth water). What is certain is that since his creative energy was directed mainly to concert music when the great day came and he landed a commission he could bring to opera a huge range of expertise he had gained in writing quantities of piano concertos, symphonies, masses and chamber music. So unlike the Bellinis of later years, he brought the orchestra into opera not as an accompanist but as a principal and he used his mastery of orchestration to point the plot, to describe the opera's characters in music, to set the mood, control the tempo and to make the orchestra a front runner along with the stage drama. He was the first composer to write music that is 'theatrical', that is music that has the smell of grease paint and the subterranean throb of excitement that can only come from the pit.

So it was that Mozart – in the best sense of the word – vulgarized opera. His buffas and Singspiels moved opera away from the cold climate of the court – away from the private chambers where a clutch of royals plus their retinues would be diverted for an hour or two by the work of their musical servants, he moved it into the theatre where the client who wanted to see opera could pay for it and get it. There were others doing it at the same time true enough but from amongst the many composers of the day only Mozart's operas live on to remind us of this sea-change in the history of opera.

The world in general sees Mozart, Wagner and Verdi as three equal greats in the history of opera, but for some of us, of the three, Mozart is the most equal.

Musorgsky, Modest 1839–81

HABITAT St Petersburg and Moscow.
OPERAS Only two completed and publicly performed, *Boris*† and *Khovanshchina*†.
LIFE AND TIMES Most famous Russian composers of the nineteenth century began as amateurs. Musorgsky was a rich young man with a family estate, a commission in the Guards, a foppish manner and a way with the ladies. He took lessons from fellow composer Balakirev but the collapse of the family fortunes forced him to join the civil service where he earned a poor salary no doubt for doing very little work. Some of his music was performed publicly and with four other musical mates (called The Mighty Handful) he messed about with many theories and ideas for many operas including the notion of setting one of Pushkin's novels to music pretty well verbatim. He finished the first version of *Boris* in 1869 but it was not publicly performed for five years which gave Musorgsky

the opportunity to keep picking over and revising it (see page 80). *Boris* was well liked but lay around unperformed because there was then little organized action on the opera front in St Petersburg. *Khovanshchina* followed twelve years later and was widely admired although there were dissidents.

COMMENT Musorgsky's two operas are sprawling masses of Russian music with no strong narrative line, no organized structure, very long and with lots of Russians wandering the stage, usually in a state of confusion. Having said that, stand by for the good news: Musorgsky's music, although unlike any Western music, is wonderful. The scoring has a sonority and a depth you will not hear elsewhere, the choruses take you into the heart of Russia, the drama of some scenes (some) is intense and the power of the whole mighty edifice gradually takes you over. By the time the curtain comes down you feel you have been on a long and absorbing trip through some of the most private parts of Mother Russia's history.

But the Musorgsky experience is one that no opera lover should be without. The music is western enough for us to take aboard and no sweat, but eastern enough to give a different colour and tone of voice from other opera music. And although very, very Russian, it is music that can speak to all nations.

Ponchielli, Amilcare 1834–86

HABITAT Mainly Milan.

OPERAS Eight including *Gioconda*†.

LIFE AND TIMES The all-powerful Giulio Ricordi, publisher and impresario, decided he would groom Ponchielli as Verdi's successor. Some hope. In 1872 Ponchielli had his first success with an opera called *I Promessi Sposi* and four years later went on to have a smash hit with *Gioconda* at the Scala. Although some of his later operas were modest hits, he never wrote anything in the same league as Verdi's majestic output either in quality or quantity (Ponchielli 8, Verdi 28). Perhaps his main claim to fame is that he was Puccini's professor at the Milan Conservatory and got him the libretto for his first opera. We know that Puccini was grateful for this help but fortunately he took a different path from Ponchielli the composer.

COMMENT Ponchielli was a good musician who never seemed able to organize his life or his operas in such a way as to make either of them come off. He could write a tune, he could orchestrate, he could call up a mood (the lagoon music in *Gioconda*), he could do everything an opera composer is called upon to do except write a successful opera. *Gioconda* most nearly comes off because with Boito adapting the libretto from a

Victor Hugo story, it would be hard to get a dud script, but even that has its longueurs, its incredulities and from time to time musically it limps. But it has its very good moments too and the best of all is perhaps to be found in the 'Dance of the Hours' which no amount of sending up can put down.

Puccini, Giacomo 1858–1924

HABITAT Lucca, Torre de Lago (Viareggio), Milan.
OPERAS Twelve counting the *Trittico* as three and including *Manon Lescaut*†, *Bohème*†, *Butterfly*†, *Fanciulla*†, *Rondine*†, *Tabarro*†, *Suor Angelica*†, *Gianni Schicchi*†, *Turandot*.†
LIFE AND TIMES Puccini grew up in an Italy which was feverishly searching for a successor to Verdi. As a student he entered his first opera for the famous Sonzogno prize (something like a Booker for first-timers) but lost out. It's not him then, said the Italian operatics – all except one, Giulio Ricordi, head of the great Ricordi publishing firm, who liked Puccini's piece. It is him, he said, he will be the next Verdi, and promptly took him on the payroll. For ten years Puccini produced nothing that showed he was going to succeed Verdi or indeed succeed at all. The shareholders objected to spending money on such a bum, but Ricordi stuck it out until – wham! – *Manon Lescaut* hit the stage in Turin and was an instant success. Ricordi acted as agent, manager, minder, Dutch uncle and procurer of librettos for Puccini until he (Ricordi) died (1912). He persuaded the script team of Illica and Giacosa to work with Puccini, which they did over the next ten years and produced his three greatest hits (although *Butterfly* was almost booed off the stage on its premiere, the wicked Sonzogno trying to get his own back). But it was soon seen as a winner and Ricordi could say to the world – So there: I told you so, it's the second coming sure enough. Puccini was now set up for life. Always a slow worker, he got even slower, hunting in the marshes round his home, travelling the world, eating too much and having car crashes (he was a demon driver) when he should have been at his desk. He was also, rightly, very fussy about his librettos and chucked out large numbers of projects. His trips to America to launch productions of his operas gave him a taste for the smartness of New York and also the folksiness of apple-pie America. As a one-time provincial lad from Lucca, he relished 'Le Hilife' but he was no prima donna. Beecham remembered him pacing the auditorium during a rehearsal of *Bohème* at Covent Garden: 'He seemed a nice little man,' said Tommy, 'and he never said a thing.' He was politically unsound during World War I because he lacked any sort of enthusiasm for the Italian cause. But Italy being an enlightened country and one which rates achievement in the arts far above patriotism, in due

course made him a Senator of the Realm. By the time he died it was clear, even to the Sonzogno gang of now aging young lions, that Puccini had indeed taken on Verdi's mantle. But alas, none of them, nor anyone else, was destined to take it over from him.

COMMENT Puccini gave Italian opera its last great ride. From the time of Rossini opera had been Italy's second most popular indoor sport. After the onslaught of the twelve-toners and other operatic antibodies, the movies, radio and the telly took over and all opera spiralled upwards and outwards to serve an international circle of buffs, aficionados, musicos and snobs. But in Italy's provincial houses where the bel cantos and Verdi still stalk the stage and meet the common people, the top of the pops is still Puccini.

Puccini did not move steadily forward through his operatic life getting better and better as did Mozart, Wagner and Verdi. He started uncertainly, as they all did, then did get better and better for a while, then in his last phase he lost his certainty of judgement and seemed to get worse and worse. *Manon* was his first big success and showed what he could do. It was a patchy work but some of the patches were glorious, especially where the music seized on a dramatic situation and swept off onto Cloud 9. Curiously enough, the weakness in *Manon* is not so much in the music as in the libretto, which is not well adapted from the novel, although half of Puccini's winning team Illica and Giacosa worked on it. The next three were the great hits – *Bohème*, *Tosca* and *Butterfly*. Now Puccini was writing in his natural style and at the top of his powers and he never did anything so good again. But the musical world around him was changing. The shadow of Wagner had become substance in lots of contemporary operas. Where people used to argue over his theories, now they would genuflect. Then Debussy too was a disturbing fellow, tampering with the diatonic scale in rather an effective way. As early as *Bohème* we find leitmotifs or mottos around (but they are harmless) and in *Tosca* the mottos are used with serious purpose. In *Butterfly* there is a definite drift away from the conventional tonality and harmonic system that had served opera since the early bel cantos. There are discords, wrong notes, strange key relationships – but these are only pushing out the frontiers of the land we know and love by a few inches, and not radical enough to transport the old-fashioned ear into a strange country.

But now for something entirely different – in *Fanciulla* it is clear that Puccini had taken thought and was writing in a new and more fashionable way. He is, one suspects, trying to keep up with the twelve-toners. Not that there is much modernity in the notation of *Fanciulla*, but one feels that Puccini's natural and glorious gift for simple melody is being stifled in favour of his desire to write clever. This is not to say that *Fanciulla* is inaccessible – it is not, and the second act especially is splendid stuff. But the first fine careless rapture has gone.

Out of regard for Puccini we will look the other way as we pass by *Rondine* and hurry on to the *Trittico*, a trio of opera allsorts, if ever there was one. *Suor Angelica* is the weakest sister in this family, written in the old style it is true, but without the old passion and with the addition of half a ton of sugar and a ludicrous libretto. There are flashes of the old Puccini but there are not many nor very bright. *Tabarro* finds us once again with Puccini the modernist. We are now several miles nearer to Debussy and Rossini is drifting away down the Seine almost out of sight. But this is the most successful of Puccini's modernist scores, it is all of a piece (with some pastiche grafted on), finds its own idiom and gives the little horror story just the right setting. *Gianni Schicchi*, the third leg of the *Trittico*, is a work of genius in the old style. It is the perfect operatic farce, fast, funny and short. Here is the old Puccini composing in the old Italian style but a new Puccini in that he shows a sense of humour that comes as a bit of a surprise after the laboured horseplay of the Bohemians.

Finally we have the unfinished *Turandot* with quasi-oriental overtones, not a really happy choice, and a quite definite departure from operatic tune writing, particularly in the scenes devoted to the tiresome Ping, Pang and Pong. One has a sneaking suspicion that in its phoney orientalism Puccini saw an escape route from the hard decision as to what style he should develop. The winning items in *Turandot* are the great choruses and of course 'Nessun dorma', a good old Neapolitan tenor aria written in the good old Neapolitan style.

But even in his modernist style Puccini is always dramatically effective. He was a composer who as he wrote the music saw the opera taking place before his very eyes in every detail. Indeed one can see him sketching the stage movement for each bar in a storyboard, as Hitchcock later drew a picture for each shot in a film he was going to make. In this way he was to some degree the director as well as the composer of his operas, and producers today mess around with his stage directions at their peril. His sense of theatre was impeccable (Act II of *Bohème*).

He had other great strengths. He wrote some of the most memorable tunes in Italian opera. If a client gets one of them on the brain (Musetta's waltz) he will be plagued with it for days and the long winding melody of the jealousy duet in Act I of *Tosca*, for instance, sticks in the ear like a leech. He could draw fresh sounds from the orchestra. The first phrase of *Tosca* is enough to frighten the horses. The prelude to Act III of *Bohème* is as well orchestrated as if it had been done by Richard Strauss (high praise). For an Italian he was unusually supple in rhythmic matters. No pounding on at four in a bar for page after page. Change of pace, change of time signature, change of rhythm off and on most of the time (*Butterfly* Act I). He understood how to get the maximum voltage out of the human voice and no one ever managed to screw a love duet up to such a frenzy of passion as he did (but a pity about those parallel octave passages he so often chucked in at the climax: they don't seem to work so well for us as they evidently did for him). His music wastes no time. His construction is taut. The score is always pushing the drama on. No lounging about in reveries, reflectives, retrospectives, no orgies of self-pity. Whereas Wagner rolls his stuff out at the pace of a Russian silent movie, Puccini is as fast as a Hollywood comedy.

It is still a little bit fashionable in some quarters to patronize Puccini. He lacks spirituality. He is a sensationalist. He is a little common. *Tosca* is a shabby little shocker. This used to be the theme song of that succession of English composers – the English Wets – who wrote their dim little pieces in the time vacuum after Elgar and it was also sung by some notable men of music such as Tovey and Britten. One can only deduce that this miserable stance was due partly to fear of the unknown – the unknown being passion in the raw, and heterosexual passion at that – or to a genuine preference for music that reached the heart – if ever – by a very slow and orderly process through the brain. But no criticism can touch Puccini today. *Bohème*, *Tosca* and *Butterfly* ride the opera houses of the world and they have become the engines that drag behind them the lesser operas of yesterday and the unpopular operas of today.

Purcell, Henry 1658–95

HABITAT Westminster Abbey and London.
OPERAS One true opera, *Dido and Aeneas*†, plus four semi-operas.
LIFE AND TIMES At the time of the Restoration the royal establishment recognized and rewarded talent in the arts wherever they spotted it (and this is a matter that should be brought forcibly to the attention of our present royals). Purcell was made court composer to the King at the age of nineteen and was also appointed organist to Westminster Abbey two years later, so well done the clerics too. Only in the last five years of his too-short life did he start writing for the theatre where the current taste was for musicals with a lot of dance numbers. Purcell lost his favourite singers in the Actors' Rebellion when the musicians' union of the day staged a walk-out and all the best singers combined to set up a rival theatre to the one where Purcell was contracted. He died before he had finished his last semi (*The Indian Queen*) and his brother Daniel completed it for him.
COMMENT It is bad luck for us opera aficionados that Purcell lived before regular opera took root in London. He wrote literally hundreds of songs and a lot of music for the theatre but alas, alas, only one short opera, and for a girls' school at that. His four semis have great operatic moments

but their opera-power is watered down by dances, masques, spoken passages and music to go with stage spectacle. So we are lucky to have even his short tragic masterpiece. The music of *Dido* reaches across the centuries and speaks to us as directly and as movingly today as if it had been written last week. He was a brilliant word-setter and no one since Purcell has ever succeeded in putting our lovely but hard-to-sing English language to music with such adroitness and certainty of touch. He had exactly the measure of what the human voice could do and he could write a tune.

Rossini, Gioachino 1792–1868

HABITAT Pesaro, Naples, the theatres of Italy and then Paris, but with his permanent home in Bologna.
OPERAS 39 including *Italiana*†, *The Barber*†, *Cenerentola*†, *Tell*†.
LIFE AND TIMES Rossini invented Italian opera as we know it today. He became the Napoleon of the European opera scene and like Napoleon suffered early retirement, though for different reasons. For two decades he wrote two operas a year, most of them smash hits. He was fêted in the capital cities of opera. His tunes were whistled in every street from Moscow to Cadiz. The literati of France adored him. Beethoven was jealous of him. He was rich, famous and went a little potty in middle life.

When he was a student he produced one-act farces which seemed to serve as a model for the construction of his first acts right up to *Tell*. He broke through with *La Pietra del paragone*, a smash hit at the Scala, when he was 20. He produced operas in Venice, Milan, Naples and Rome before settling in Naples in 1816. By this time he had delivered almost half of his total output of operas including *Italiana* and *The Barber*. After six years in Naples (sixteen operas), Paris, that great magnet for all Italian opera composers, claimed him. Stendhal, a leading figure in the Rossini fan club, greeted him with some really colourful hype: 'The glory of the man is only limited by the limits of civilization itself; and he is not yet 32.' In Paris he wrote and produced his last five operas including the monster *Tell*. King Charles X was dethroned in the revolution of 1830 and the new government cancelled Rossini's five-year contract with the Opéra. So, with the Hurrahs and the Oo-la-las of the Paris public echoing round Europe, he hung up his dinner pail and retired to Bologna where he lived quietly for nearly 40 years. Until recently this was thought to be a great mystery, especially since Verdi did the same vanishing act some years later. Did all the Italian opera men in Paris run out of gas when they reached the male menopause? The true answer is that Rossini had become a sick man both mentally and physically. He tried to conceal this under his ever-genial exterior, but it seems certain that he lost his mental focus and his ability to tackle any major work after his return to Bologna.

COMMENT With one bound Rossini took opera into a new world. When he arrived on the scene Italian opera was running into the sand with genteel little composers like Paisiello and Cimarosa turning out stuff that was no more than mildly agreeable. When he retired his two slightly younger contemporaries Donizetti and Bellini took over and when all three had finished they had raised a mighty edifice of 112 operas, not every one a hit but over a third of them good enough to make the CD catalogues of 1994.

Rossini was not just the advance guard for a new shoal of operas. He arrived in full force, fully armed and with all guns blazing. There was something military about his mode of attack. The opening act of the opera was strategically paced in the series of tactical moves that would most quickly capture an audience already softened up by an opening cannonade. This was the overture, an entirely Rossinian invention and nothing to do with opera itself (it really doesn't matter which overture you play before any one of the middle-period operas) but certainly designed to make the audience sit to attention. The typical Rossini overture is in a standard form, slow introduction, a fast piece with a first and second subject, then one of his famous crescendos and at least two changes of rhythm – no development – repeat from the beginning of the fast piece and a bang bang ending. But this is like describing a Rembrandt portrait in terms of the dimensions of the frame. What makes a Rossini overture so irresistible is the piquancy of the tunes, the orchestral colouring, the way he piles on the pressure, quickens the pace, turns up the volume and breaks into an oom-pah rhythm at the height of the excitement. He was a supreme orchestrator, what with woodwind soloists sometimes leading the band, sometimes picking up snatches given out elsewhere like a sea-lion catching fish, what with the easy melodious string backing, the absolute clarity of texture and the many tuneful patterns worked into the knitting, he could get effects that had never been heard before and not too often since. When you hear a top-class pit orchestra playing Rossini you can't but reflect how nice of him it was to make it possible for them to have such a whale of a good time.

For the voice he wrote in the fashion of the day, elegantly and elaborately. It was the time of coloratura or fioritura, flowery decoration of the vocal line with all manner of leaps, runs and curlicues. Coloratura is to plain singing what double axels, salchows and toe loops are to plain skating. Sometimes they were written out in full by the composer, sometimes the singer ad-libbed them, especially in the repeat of a da capo aria. The main purpose of the coloratura in opera again was the same as the jumps in competition skating, it was to show off the skill of the performer, and today we may sometimes feel that a big coloratura aria is not much of a thing of beauty in itself and that it certainly slows up the action. But if after dicing with death the singer pulls the coloratura off really well, then there is great satisfaction and relief around the house and a huge round of applause. Then the opera can start off again. But it can be rather like putting a high-wire act into the middle of *Hamlet*. Rossini's wires could be very high, e.g. 'Una voce poco fa', Rosina's big aria in *The Barber*.

Out of all of Rossini's 39 operas it is mainly the comedies, the giocosas and buffas that have survived. He had musical wit to match Beaumarchais's text in *The Barber*, he could write the perfect backing for the glorious idiocies of the first act finale of *Italiana*, he could be nimble enough to match the speed that farce must have on the stage. When he moved into grander opera, and with *Tell* in particular, it seems that there was no place for many of the things he could do best and a demand for a grandeur and nobility which his music didn't have. Musically the choruses in *Tell* reach a level that opera had never attempted before but their sentiments seem to us to be as banal as those of a glorified national anthem. Verdi would have found a way of making them into a great cry for freedom. In short, once he gets into the heavy stuff Rossini is better with the love interest than the affairs of state, but who is going to grumble about that?

Rossini brought discipline to Italian opera. He gave an opera, an act, an aria, a definite structure. His plans worked, his operas came off punctually, precisely and in a manner just as the audience expected and liked. He brought to opera an abundance of tunes, many of them amongst the best in the operatic repertoire. He conjured new sounds out of the orchestra. He gave his singers the flashiest numbers that could be devised by man. But the most amazing thing about Rossini is that he began with a vision of what opera could be, that he realized that vision and set going a tradition that is still the heart and soul of the repertory more than a hundred and fifty years later.

Strauss, Johann II 1825–99 (Not to be confused with Strauss Johann I, his father, and certainly not with Strauss Richard, a much more serious composer, nor yet Straus Oscar, not serious at all, operettas and film music)

HABITAT Vienna.
OPERAS Nineteen operas and operettas including *Fledermaus*†.
LIFE AND TIMES Strauss's father Johann I, Vienna's Waltz King, forbad his sons to follow him into the music trade. Whether this was because he wanted the family to diversify for fear of hard times in the dance-band world or whether it was for fear of competition, we do not know. Johann II disobeyed him and set up his own rival band and sure enough by the time his dad died (1849) he had become the Waltz King

himself. But the Vienna theatre owners who made their money out of musicals persuaded him to leave the family dance-band business to his brothers and to turn his hand to operetta because an undesirable Frenchie named Offenbach was having it all his own way in the theatres and music halls of Vienna. Strauss responded with a couple of moderately successful operettas, but then he hit the jackpot with *Fledermaus* and lived happily ever after. Well – not completely happily because he applied himself to grand opera and this proved to be beyond his powers.

COMMENT Although Johann II lacked the polka-power of his father, he was his equal and perhaps his superior in waltz-power. But there is a world of difference between writing waltzes for the ballroom and writing a score for an operetta in 3/4 time. There must have been dozens of competent musicians in Vienna who could have managed the musical mechanics of *Fledermaus* better than Strauss but nary a one who could have produced the great *Fledermaus* waltz. *Fledermaus* is a farce blessed with some wonderful tunes. The tunes nearly always come off, the farce sometimes. Strauss's technique for handling dramatic scenes was not sophisticated, his orchestration is as standard (and in its way as effective) as Glenn Miller, his tempi for most of the time are strictly ballroom and three-in-a-bar for forty minutes can get on your nerves – but he has the power to sweep away piddling reservations with a tune that whirls you into that pink-tinted wonderful waltzland where all good Viennese go in their happy but rather bourgeois dreams.

Strauss, Richard 1864–1949 (Not to be confused with Johann I or II or Oscar with only one S)

HABITAT Munich, Weimar, Bayreuth, Berlin, Vienna.

OPERAS Thirteen including *Salome*†, *Elektra*†, *Rosenkavalier*†, *Ariadne*†.

LIFE AND TIMES By taking the sensible step of marrying a brewer's daughter, Strauss's father could well afford to give his son a pretty classy musical education. Early in life young Richard showed that (a) he was an immensely talented composer and (b) that he was no slouch at self-promotion. At the age of nineteen he was working as a repetiteur at Bayreuth at the shrine of You-Know-Who (recently deceased). At twenty he persuaded the New York Phil to play his first symphony. He went on to write a large number of lieder and also the most successful and best promoted orchestral music of any living European composer. His concert pieces usually had a form with some catchy programme or story attached to them (*Don Juan*, *The Alpine Symphony*). He conducted opera and he conducted orchestral concerts and although the professional posts he held in the opera houses of Weimar and Munich sound pretty dim, they gave him a firm base from which to organize a stunningly successful career. He met his wife Pauline in 1887 which turned out to be a pretty big event. Not only was she a fairly starry opera singer but she was to feature very prominently both in his private life and in his operatic work, which he found it hard to keep apart. She even featured in one of his symphonies, which is a rare if not a unique event. They went to Bayreuth together. She sang, he conducted.

By the turn of the century Strauss had written most of his orchestral works. You could hear his stuff being played everywhere, as often as Beethoven and far ahead of Mozart (Mahler and Bruckner not yet having made it). After a couple of early duds Strauss's successful opera career began in 1905 with *Salome*. He had already got the reputation for being orchestrally controversial because he went well beyond Wagner in matters of dissonance and because his wild romantic noisiness upset the well ordered souls of the central European musicos. But with *Salome* it was sex, and not even straight sex but necrophilia. Also grand guignol. Respectable German burghers found it terribly hard to explain to their respectable hausfrau wives why a young lady should want to kiss the bearded mouth of the newly-severed head of a dead person. Also the mere name of Oscar Wilde sent a frisson of Sodom and Gomorrah through any decent society. *Salome* was censored and forbidden the stage in London and New York. Nothing could have suited Strauss better and *Salome* raised his profile immediately. He was decadent and wicked as well as being frightfully good, and the music was of an extraordinary new kind. (*Elektra* was not so shocking but still an amazing piece.)

Strauss had met Hofmannsthal through *Elektra* and now the two of them set about boxing the operatic compass. A romantic waltzy piece about Old Vienna was about as far away as you could get from the two demoniac girls Salome and Elektra, so they tried that, not without mixing some mild pornographic stuff in amongst scenes otherwise smelling as sweet as an attar of roses. The result: immense success, probably the greatest operatic hit of the century (see *Rosenkavalier*, pages 652–4). But this was the peak. Later operas were nearly all successes but they no longer made the front page of the tabloids. Musicos might find them as good as or better than the early shockers, but Strauss became respectable and lost his status as an *enfant terrible*. But he remained the unchallenged musical lion of his day, not only as a composer but as one of the very best conductors of any German music from Mozart up to his own. He was also the star of café society, and if a hostess got Strauss to come to one of her parties, she had made it.

And so his long long life rolled on towards World War II. In the 1930s a large number of German musicians left the country. Toscanini withdrew from Bayreuth on anti-fascist grounds. But the people at the top who were not Jews did not leave (Furtwängler, Karajan) and amongst these was Strauss, who had always claimed to be apolitical. He picked up the baton from Toscanini at Bayreuth. He cut off his relationship with his Jewish librettist Zweig. He accepted from Goebbels the presidency of the Reichsmusikkammer. But it didn't help him much. The regime didn't like his stuff. Not enough strength through joy and quite a lot of clever-clever talk of a kind unacceptable to a good Nazi. One opera was banned and others were officially discredited. After the war Strauss and his wife went into political quarantine in Switzerland where he wrote the calm and lovely music of his old age.

COMMENT Strauss was the last colossus of European opera. However you rate his works, his status over half a century as the leading opera composer is beyond question. And no wonder. A marvellously resourceful composer, he could pull things off that were enormously arresting, dramatic and sensational. But he also had the power to write quietly, to compose music of penetrating beauty, as gentle and sweet as any music has ever been. *Salome*, by its power and audacity, shook the world of opera to its foundations. In style, although it owes a lot to Wagner, it is not just 'post-Wagnerian'. Its huge orchestra is rougher, shouts louder and plays a different tune. Not yet the atonal or twelve-tone tune of the Schoenberg school who were still to come, but Strauss's own tonal tune which from time to time defects from the old Sol-Fa diatonic world. Yet such is the power of his musicianship that he carried his audience into this new world with their ears flapping and their pulses racing and they came out of it purged, as he meant them to be, with pity and terror. And his choice of subject was brilliant. Wilde's play, written in French verse, still has the power to shock. Imagine its effect on the just-out-of-the-Victorian-age opera-going middle classes of Europe. Even before the musicos had fully digested *Salome*, out came *Elektra* in the same idiom, but more so. And now he had started to work with Hofmannsthal, which was to be one of the greatest of operatic partnerships. Many will say *Elektra* is his finest work. *Rosenkavalier* was by far his most popular. These three, together with the madcap *Ariadne*, the first four of his mature operas, are the only ones to qualify for this Guide, which shows that his later drawing-room operas appeal more to the chattering classes and less to the great opera public.

Everyone wonders why Strauss gave up his 'modernist' style of writing after *Elektra*. Was it to show that he could do just about anything, like compose the sort of schmaltzy waltzy stuff and the coarse comedy we get in *Rosenkavalier*? Did Hofmannsthal persuade him to give over? Perhaps. Whatever the reason it may well strike us as a pity that a young composer who seemed to be going on a really exciting journey to new places should suddenly change direction and saunter back to the drawing rooms of Vienna where exquisite people were holding sophisticated conversations about life and art. But we should not underestimate Hofmannsthal. Whatever his influence on Strauss's style, his actual libretti were works of near genius and amongst the very few that might succeed on the stage as straight plays.

Strauss's power as a composer lay in his amazing power of invention. He surprises us at every bar. His tunes assault the ear and his music, even his orchestral music is intensely dramatic. Sometimes he tries too hard. The tone poems can sound overblown, especially all those horns in *Heldenleben*. Sometimes the mixture is just too rich for too long (*Don Juan, Till Eulenspiegel*). The listener craves for a lemon sorbet to cool the palate between course after course of rich meat. Occasionally Strauss slips into the coy and the pretty-pretty (the little black boy in *Rosenkavalier*). His music for comedy/farce (*Rosenkavalier* again, Act III) can be ornery. But he is a very accomplished composer and the only qualities lacking in his music which prevent him from being ranked amongst the really greats is that it has no nobility of spirit (Beethoven), nothing of Plato's ideal of goodness plus beauty (Mozart) – only beauty of a sweet soft-centred kind – none of Verdi's warmth of heart. Against this must be set his extraordinary power to make the orchestra obey his slightest whim. He ranks along with opera's greatest orchestrators, Mozart, Berlioz, Wagner, Rimsky-Korsakov, a technician extraordinary and one (in the early operas) commanding the biggest forces ever to be crammed into an opera house pit. The Strauss sound follows the Wagner sound in history and it is the last of its kind with its mountainous crescendos, huge rolling periods, and with its clarity of filigree detail too. Later composers were to break up this great sweep of sound into barks, bites, fragmentary snatches of melody and short repeated phrases. Strauss could do that too, but he was at his most majestic with *Elektra*'s long spun-out arias and the great trio for three sopranos that is the climax of *Rosenkavalier*.

Strauss was born before Verdi had written *Aida*. He died four years after the first production of Britten's *Peter Grimes*. During his lifetime the world of music changed out of all recognition. It was part of Strauss's genius that he could change with it. He brought the era of Wagnerian opera to a close and he more than anyone else in the new century kept German opera alive, lively, popular. We were lucky to have him, really.

Tchaikovsky, Peter Ilyich 1840–93

HABITAT Moscow.
OPERAS Ten completed operas including *Eugene Onegin*†.
LIFE AND TIMES Western music came late to Russia and not much that you would notice today was composed before the middle of last century.

When they did get going Russian composers wrote stuff that was frightfully Russian almost as if they were trying to prove that Russian culture could hold its own against the rest of the world. The leaders in this musico-nationalist campaign were five composers (Borodin, Musorgsky, Balakirev, Rimsky-Korsakov and Cui) called the Kuchka or Mighty Handful. Tchaikovsky was outside their circle, in many ways a loner, a homosexual, a melancholy man, but he had a head start over the Handful in that he had been professionally trained in the St Petersburg Conservatoire and they were all amateurs. Shortly after he left the Conservatoire he found a patroness in a musical railway queen who saw him all right for the next fifteen years. So he became Russia's first fully operational, fully trained professional composer.

His music was much better liked than the Strength Through Gloom stuff that the Handful were turning out. His ballets and the opera *The Maid of Orleans* were hits. The court took him up and he became the semi-official composer for the establishment. He was the only travelling Russian composer, going all over Europe, conducting a concert in New York and receiving an honorary degree from Cambridge. He was jeered at quite a lot by the Handful and their friends, both for writing romantic Westernized music and for being gay. His charmingly named brother Modest was a great comfort to him.

COMMENT Although not one of the Handful, Tchaikovsky's music still sounds frightfully Russian. Maybe not so Russian in actual sound as all those bells and tocsins in Musorgsky's *Boris*, but Russian in spirit, Russian in thought and very Russian in its many deep depressions and its rare bursts of demonic energy. For all its bustle and push, it is the pathetic bits of the Symphony Pathétique that we remember, not the noisy ones, and this is also true of his operas. The overtly Russian stuff in *Onegin* (folk songs, dances) he kept outside the main stream of the plot but no other country could have produced:

(a) Pushkin's verse novel
(b) such an aimless but moving story
(c) music so tender and so sad for the humiliated Tatyana.

For all his big stuff that is so successful in the concert hall, the concertos, the symphonies and the shorter show pieces, it is in his songs and his operas that you will find the essence of Tchaikovsky. He could write big tunes to catch the public ear, he could orchestrate brilliantly, he could write for ballet as could no one else, but the true spirit of this sensitive and melancholy man is to be found in the music of that long troubled night that led to Tatyana's doom.

It is time that Tchaikovsky's other operas were dusted down and brought out of the closet. Only *Onegin* and *The Queen of Spades* are in the repertory. He was a great opera composer and there are at least three other operas that we should be allowed to see. Just suppose all of Dickens was out of print except *David Copperfield* and *Little Dorritt*.

Verdi, Giuseppe 1813–1901 (born the same year as Wagner)

HABITAT His farm at Busseto, Milan, Genoa, Paris, but much of his life spent travelling between opera houses mainly in Italy but also including Moscow, London and Madrid.
OPERAS 28 including *Lombardi*†, *Ernani*†, *Attila*†, *Macbeth*†, *Luisa Miller*†, *Rigoletto*†, *Trovatore*†, *Traviata*†, *Vespri*†, *Boccanegra*†, *Ballo*†, *Forza*†, *Carlos*†, *Aida*†, *Otello*†, *Falstaff*† (and including *Aroldo*, though it is a rewrite of *Stiffelio*).
LIFE AND TIMES Both Harold Wilson and Verdi would have us believe that they started life as barefoot lads, but the evidence is against them. Verdi's father was no peasant but a pub-keeper in a village near Busseto which in turn is not far from Parma. Although Verdi was refused entry to the Milan Conservatory [to their eternal shame: Ed.], his father managed to give him a reasonable musical education. Verdi started adult life in a small job in a small town (still Busseto) running some of the local musical events. He wrote an opera in his spare time, submitted it to the holy of operatic holies, the Scala, and (Dio mio!) they put it on and it was a success. Verdi was 26 and full of yeast. He got a three-opera contract from the Scala but his next one, true to show business form, was a flop. As if this was not enough his wife and two tiny children died, leaving him pretty forlorn and unable to compose anything for over a year. But his next opera was the mighty *Nabucco* which we still can hear today with its huge choruses and foot-tapping tunes. It was a smash hit.

Now Verdi spent his 'years in the galleys'. From 1842 (aged 29) to 1853 (aged 40) he wrote sixteen operas in eleven years, thus giving birth to a new opera approximately every nine months. The operas were put on in Milan, Rome, Naples, Venice, Florence, Trieste, Paris and London, for which last city he reserved one of his few resounding flops. It was his practice to be present at each birth, cutting, adapting, coaching, worrying and finally, in nearly every case, rejoicing. By now he was the wonder man of the operatic world – what Andrew Lloyd Webber is to musical theatre today, only Verdi was more serious, and musical. The poor man cannot have had much time for extramural activities, but he did manage to team up with a soprano, one Giuseppina Strepponi, and the two of them moved to a farm he had bought near his home town of Busseto.

At this point in his life Verdi changed gear. In the next eighteen years he produced only six operas, that is at the rate of one every three years. But when you consider that some of the operas were much longer and all of them more complex, even this lower level of productivity could hardly be called slacking. His business methods became deliberate and precise. First came the negotiation with the theatre management for a commission. Verdi employed no agent or manager. He did every deal himself with Ricordi, his publisher and consultant, standing by his side. Having got this matter sewn up (including an agreed cast of star singers), he would start looking for a subject and the librettist who would best go with it. And so to work.

By now Verdi was much more than just the great man of opera. He was a national hero. Unlike today when it is thought to be quite the fashion to bust up big countries into their ethnic units (Russia, Yugoslavia), in Verdi's lifetime everyone was frightfully keen to do the opposite, to unite a lot of potty little kingdoms (in his case Italy) into one great mother state. The lobbyists for Unosis hunted through every one of Verdi's operas and managed to find all manner of hidden references to the idea of One Country. Most of them are pretty far-fetched and even Verdi's name was used as a political slogan VIVA EMANUELE RE D'ITALIA (Victor Emanuele was to be the first king of a united Italy). Verdi was courted by the top Unosist Cavour, and for a short time sat as a member of the first all-Italian parliament (and no doubt sat making sketches for *Rigoletto* on the back of the order papers).

After *Aida*'s premiere in Cairo (1871) Verdi wrote no more opera for sixteen years. He still travelled Europe watching over his productions. He looked after his farm. Like the good man he was, he gave time to good works. Strepponi, whom he had eventually married, had died and he had found a new and younger companion in Teresa Stolz. Perhaps it was her youth and her meeting with the young Boito that gave him the zest to write his last two operas, *Otello* and *Falstaff*, both so very different from what had gone before and both received with reverence. He died in 1901 and a month after his death the streets of Milan filled with tens of thousands of mourners led by the orchestra and chorus of the Scala singing the great choral number 'Va pensiero' from *Nabucco*. How unlike, how very unlike, the funeral of that other great genius of opera, Wolfgang Amadeus Mozart. For him it was five men, a cart and a snowstorm.

COMMENT Verdi was the great man of Italian opera for over half a century. In the game of operatic snakes and ladders no one had ever climbed so high a ladder (of 28 rungs) and no one so successfully avoided practically every snake except some very small ones. His learning curve raced upwards from the coarse but powerful earlies, *Nabucco* and *Ernani*, to the two immensely clever and elaborate end pieces, *Otello* and *Falstaff*.

Verdi's work is usually divided into three periods, but there is no great consensus as to where each period starts and stops. A sensible division might go as follows:

PERIOD I	From his first flop *Oberto* (1839) to *Attila*† (1836). Nine operas including *Lombardi*† and *Ernani*†	Early Verdi. Wonderful choruses, dreadful librettos, obviously a genius but not yet fully opera-trained.
PERIOD II	From *Macbeth*† (1847) to *Traviata*† (1853). Ten operas including *Luisa Miller*†, *Rigoletto*†, *Trovatore*†	Middle-period Verdi. Includes his threc most popular operas *Rig*, *Trav* and *Trov*.
PERIOD III	From *Vespri*† to *Aida*†. Six operas including *Boccanegra*†, *Ballo*†, *Forza*† and *Carlos*†	Mature Verdi. All great music. *Vespri* and *Carlos* are extra long, being Parisiens.
POSTSCRIPT	*Otello*† and *Falstaff*†	Late Verdi. Clever and complex.

Early Verdi is thrilling, in patches. Some three-star arias, many two- and three-star choruses, some of them a shade bombastic, some ornery bits, many situations which seem ridiculous to us (*Lombardi*, *Ernani*, *Attila*) but which he thought were 'strong'. Quite a lot of stop-one-thing, start-another. Certainly not seamless robes. But already he has proved roughly thirty-six times that he can write a world-beating tune.

Middle-period Verdi has most of his best-known tunes. Some of the plots are more credible, often because they are based on works by pretty good writers like Victor Hugo (*Rigoletto*), Schiller (*Luisa Miller*), Dumas (*Traviata*) and Shakespeare (*Macbeth*). A few of the numbers are organ-grinderly ('La donna e mobile') and there is still a lot of oom-pah about, but these operas are the ones that *are* Verdi to the great opera public.

The mature Verdis are great music but now he's having trouble with his plots again. *Vespri* is too outré, *Boccanegra* is impenetrable except to *Boccanegra* scholars, *Ballo* is bizarre, *Forza* is a farrago and although *Carlos* has a noble story, Verdi never managed to get it quite right. But mature Verdians will all tell you that here lies the master's finest work, especially perhaps in *Boccanegra* and *Carlos*, and they are right. The mature Verdi has left behind the formal structures of opera – arioso–aria–duet–ensemble–finale – with its own rules and conventions which had served the bel cantos so well. He has moved into a world where the drama and not the rule book dictates the form of the music (the Grand Inquisitor scene in *Carlos*). Each act has its own place. The arias and duets are often longer and more intense than in the middle period (*Forza*). The ensembles have a new magic (*Ballo*), the huge choral and orchestral effects are now part of the action (*Carlos*) and can pretty well blow the roof off (*Aida*).

Late Verdi is quite another thing. Wagner had been around for quite some time now. The world of bel canto was disappearing over the horizon. It was sixteen years since he had written an opera and he had reached the age when most people are content to mow the lawn and watch the telly. He was having a sort of late-life love affair with a young woman, and was in a new creative partnership with a young man, Boito. In *Otello* he wrote a piece in an entirely new idiom which carries all the passion and power of Shakespeare's play and uses a continuous flow of music to support the drama. There are no Celeste Aidas around. [Although there is the Willow Song: Ed.] In *Falstaff* he produced a work of enormous ingenuity and subtle musicianship. This is as far away from *Trovatore* as *Tristan* is from *Rienzi*. It is something of a miracle, but a miracle that is taking place on the other side of the hill from *Rig*, *Trov* and *Trav*.

Verdi's problem was not with the music but with the story. When a deal with a management had been signed then, and only then, he began casting about for a subject. He liked 'strong situations', stories that 'set him alight', he looked for novelty. His operas must be different. All of this would have been fine if Verdi had been any sort of a judge of a story. He could certainly pick out the strong situations, but often they were stuck in a plot that was so silly/incredible as to undermine the strength of the 'strong' scenes (the burning of the wrong baby in *Trovatore*, the transvestite hermit in *Forza*). Yet the adrenalin let loose by the strong but ludicrous moments in *Forza* clearly gave Verdi the sort of kick-start he craved to get him up to speed in 60 yards from standstill. Piave and Cammarano, his two most trusted librettists (seventeen operas out of twenty-seven), although immensely skilled at adapting the story into dramatic verse once it was selected, did not have much say in choosing it. They might propose but it was the maestro himself who decided. He was in truth a one-man opera factory and one can imagine the relief in the scriptwriting camp when the news got around that it was going to be a Shakespeare. Piave might make a phone call to his sidekick Mafei something as follows:

'Hi Antonio. Heard the news?'
'No. Tell me.'
'He's gone off Don Quixote set in Lapland.'
'Thank God. What is it now?'
'Macbeth.'
'Macbeth?'
'Shakespeare's Macbeth.'
'My God, with all those thanes?'
'That's it.'
'Dunsinane wood? Witches?'

'The whole lot.'

'Thank God. At least it works on the stage.'

'He wants it cut to two hours. Main cast cut to five. Non-singing ghosts. 'Storyline by Tuesday. OK?'

'By Tuesday? Mamma mia. Let's hope he sticks with Macbeth and doesn't go back to Moses and the Red Sea again.'

'More likely El Cid. He was on about him at lunch.'

'Oh well. Cheerio.'

'Cheerio.'

Once the storyline was in Verdi would work with his librettist in parcelling out the scenes and acts into arias, duets, ensembles, etc. He would then move on to sketch out the music for the opera. This he did on two staves. After a lot of hard work he would transfer these on to a skeleton score with only the most important instruments marked in, pack his bags, go to the city where the opera was to be produced and listen to the singers. Next he would adjust the score and complete the orchestration in a helter-skelter rush for the first orchestral rehearsal. He would then rule over the processes of production with a will of iron until the curtain went up on the first night. This may explain why Verdi never made a special pet of the orchestra until his mature and late periods. He didn't have time. During the middle period his orchestration is perfectly OK, but he doesn't make the orchestra into an important player in the game as did Wagner, and as Debussy was to do. But by the end of the day Verdi's orchestration was masterly (*Otello*, *Falstaff*). He could do it all right, given time.

But when it came to the chorus, this was a different matter. As early as *Nabucco* he showed what he could do (the first opera to give the chorus a star role since Mozart's *Idomeneo*). He also had an uncanny skill in the handling of an offstage chorus (last scene of *Trovatore* and many others).

He could write for the solo voice in a way that was in character. With Verdi you could no longer swap the same number from a baddie to a goodie without it noticing, as you could in earlier times. He wrote meaningfully for expiring sopranos (*Traviata*), distressed tenors ('Celeste Aida'), baritones imperious (Boccanegra quells the mob), baritones Machiavellian (Iago schemes and plots), wicked basses (Lord Eliot, the nasty of *Luisa Miller*), formidable basses (the Grand Inquisitor again), and arias for every occasion each one suited to its person, their plight and the occasion. He could also write wonderful ensembles but these were more general in their nature and (except for *Otello*) did not much advance the plot.

Aside from ballet music, there is not much work for the orchestra in the way of overtures, preludes and entr'actes. Maybe he felt they held up the action, maybe he felt it was a waste of time.

Verdi was one of the few composers included in this Guide who had a long, successful, mainly happy life. He started as a talented musical peasant and finished up as the great maestro, the polymath and sage of Italian opera. Also a national hero. Along with Mozart and Wagner he is one of opera's three greats, and today he still has twice as many operas in the repertory as either of them.

Wagner, Richard 1813–83 (born the same year as Verdi)

HABITAT Riga, Paris, Dresden, Weimar, Switzerland, Munich, Bayreuth.
OPERAS Fourteen including the *Dutchman*†, *Tannhäuser*†, *The Ring* (4)†, *Tristan*†, *Meistersinger*† and *Parsifal*†.
LIFE AND TIMES During his lifetime Wagner sent seismic tremors through the world of opera. He was to change it from being a nice evening's entertainment into a solemn celebration of High Art. Yet he started life if not quite as the ragged-arsed lad he would have us believe, at least as a poverty-stricken, ill-trained unsuccessful musician bumming his way around the theatres and opera houses of north Germany until at last he landed a decent but pretty dim job as musical director of a theatre in remotest Riga. Here he shared a very small apartment with one Minna Planer whom he had just married, her sister and a wolf cub. He was soon seriously in hock. He avoided paying his debts by means of a secret midnight exodus to Paris, where he started to get into debt again. All this time he was working on grandiose plans for several operas though only one (*Die Feen*) was to see the light of day. In Paris he was met by Meyerbeer who was frightfully decent to him, though why he should have taken pains over a bankrupt musician from the Baltic it is hard to know. Meyerbeer tried to help Wagner get his opera *Rienzi* on at the Opéra but failed. So Wagner wrote music criticism for the public prints including several pieces telling the Opéra management why they were doing everything wrong, which must have done wonders for his chances of getting a commission. Nevertheless, he sold them the idea of the *Dutchman* for a few bucks but they wouldn't let him develop it.

Just as it seemed he would be jailed for debt (for the second time) Meyerbeer helped to get *Rienzi* accepted by the Dresden Opera (which kindness Wagner repaid in later life by writing vitriolic anti-Semitic attacks on poor Meyerbeer). *Rienzi* turned out to be a wow, and the *Dutchman* followed a year later. Dresdeners were not so wild about this one but now Wagner (1843, aged 30) got the job of number two to the Dresden Intendant.

During his Dresden years Wagner began to brood on the subjects of the operas that were going to occupy him for the rest of his life. In politics he was a leftie and incautiously let this be known pretty widely. As a result, when the 1848 Revolution broke out he had to skip out pretty fast, being a marked man (one of the Dresden Ten). Wagner escaped to Switzerland where he lived on money he had managed to mesmerize out of two rich women. Minna was giving him a hard time and he had chronic constipation (a fact not sufficiently taken into account when discussing his music), but despite this he managed to force out *Lohengrin* which his pen-pal Liszt put on in Weimar. It went down well. Wagner was now working himself into a frenzy over *The Ring* and also his huge debts (third time) when he persuaded an admirer, one Wesendonck, to pay off his debts in exchange for all future income from his works. Wesendonck also gave him a home next to his own and Wagner promptly fell in love with his wife which stopped him dead in his tracks in the matter of working on *The Ring* and switched him on to *Tristan* instead. Meanwhile, he managed to engineer a production of *Tannhäuser* at the Opéra in Paris, but it ended in disaster (see page 702).

Wagner was allowed back into Germany in 1860 but within a few years he was under threat of being jailed for debt once again, this time in Vienna (fourth time). In the nick of time an angel appeared. Rich, royal and mad, this teenage (eighteen) fan bailed Wagner out. Ludwig II, the newly crowned king of Bavaria, paid his debts and gave him a luxury mansion in Munich and then set about building a jumbo-sized opera house fit for the production of the Master's masterpieces. But this was too much for the taxpayers to stomach. The Treasury put a stop to the opera house and now both Wagner and Ludwig became really unpopular. Wagner was sent off to compose in Switzerland while things cooled down.

Ludwig mounted *Meistersinger* (a success) in the run-of-the-mill royal theatre in Munich (1868) and *Rhinegold* (1869) and *Valkyrie* (1870). Wagner grumbled about the standards of the production but the first two helpings of the mighty *Ring* set all operatic Europe agog. Now people could see the stature of Wagner's work and the process of deification began (not that there weren't plenty of antis too). Wagner had by now taken up with Cosima, the wife of his friend the conductor Von Bülow, and he tried with a smokescreen of mendacity to conceal this scandalous matter from Ludwig. He needn't have bothered. When it did come out Ludwig just went on listening to bits of *The Ring* and didn't turn a hair.

Wagner's big idea was to set up a Festival Theatre in his own honour, built by him, at a place of his choosing and dedicated to the performance of his works and not the works of anyone else. This megalomaniac scheme actually came about in the chosen town of Bayreuth (1872). It took four years to get the theatre built and to get the first *Ring* cycle going and by then, of course, Wagner had naturally run out of money. In a pathetic attempt to raise funds he gave some concerts in the Royal Albert Hall

London, but the net profit was £700, about enough to pay for the costume of one Valkyrie. Once again Ludwig saw him right and from then on it should have been all gas and gaiters chez the Wagners (he had married Cosima by now), what with worldwide fame and the success of the whole range of his later operas but it wasn't. In Bayreuth Wagner did not produce nor conduct himself but he couldn't leave a production alone. He therefore made the lives of the producers and the music directors and everyone else on the picture pretty well unbearable. Also his megalomania led him to think that he could do for the human race in general what he had done for opera – namely reform it root and branch. So he set to work writing out his plans for the salvation of mankind, which included quite a lot of Nietzsche's notions plus vegetarianism, anti-Semitism and a good deal about Christ's blood. He died in the grand manner at Bayreuth at the age of 70.

As a composer Wagner was a genius. As a man he was distinctly unpleasant, being an egomaniac who believed that as a great artist he had a divine right to do anything, say anything, follow any whim regardless. He took no thought for anyone unless they could further his concerns or were women he wanted to go to bed with. He was anti-Semitic. He was a con-man. His philosophizing was a load of bunk. He was a liar. He was a congenital debtor. But here, strangely enough, his musical genius saved him from prison at least four times, for on each occasion he was bailed out by one or other of his admirers. Some people find it hard to separate the Dr Jekyll Wagner from Wagner the Mr Hyde, and rubbish his music because the man was such a horror. This is a mistake because his music is very very good, and was Byron such an angel anyway?

COMMENT Wagner's story really begins with the *Dutchman* and ends with *Parsifal*, ten huge steps in taking opera from where she used to be to where he wanted to put her. His aim was music drama, a seamless robe of music and words woven together to make a work of high art which was the noblest aim in life. High art should be produced not just for the rich and clever, but for all mankind to whom if it were good enough, it would have an instant appeal. (So those persons fidgetting at the back of the hall whilst Wotan is doing his stuff must either be suffering from original sin or else they are Jews.)

None of this pretentious stuff (Wagner must be the only composer who during his lifetime wrote almost as many words as notes) prevented him from getting on with his work on the operas. Here the theories he practised were revolutionary but practical. He did change the face of opera. He did make his vision come alive. The way he did it – the whole business of Wagner's methods of composing, leitmotifs (mottos), word setting, orchestration and all is fully discussed in the *General Hello* to *The Ring* (page 549).

If one takes an overall view of the Wagnerian saga one can see that the *Dutchman* was still pretty well a numbers opera (Senta's Ballad, the Sailors' Chorus). Some of the bits between numbers were a kind of souped-up recitatif but others were moving towards the vintage Wagner (the Dutchman's long solos in partnership with an active orchestra). This is what the later bel cantos would call arioso, but it is high-powered arioso with a continuous drive. There are mottos, not many, all unmistakable and often used like the bell on an ice-cream cart to let you know what vehicle is coming down the road. Wagner took great pains to make the overture into a concert piece and it turned out to be the best tone poem of its day, catching both the smell of the sea and the spookiness of the phantom ship wonderfully well.

There is no huge advance in the techniques for *Tannhäuser* and *Lohengrin*. Still there are numbers ('O Star of Eve' and Elsa's dream). The chorus does stalwart work, especially in *Tannhäuser*. There are a lot of good tunes and the mottos are used more widely than in the *Dutchman*.

Meistersinger is the most friendly of the later operas. It meets us on our own ground. Everyone is a human being, everything is real life, no Nibelungers, no sprouting staves. It has its set numbers but now they come only when there is a song required by the plot (the Trial Song, the Schusterlied, the Prize Song). There are mottos, but limited in number and very precise in what they mean (Apprentices, Masters, Cobbling). It is a huge work and for the last time the chorus plays a big part.

So to the mighty *Ring*. Now all Wagner's theories were put into practice with results that have amazed the world. The motto-work in itself is immensely complex, both from the musical and the psychological point of view. There is practically nothing in the field of human industry, including the building of the Great Wall of China, that so stuns the imagination as the amount of toil that went into the creation of *The Ring*. But at last there it was, the new thing, over a dozen hours of music drama, something quite different from what we used to call opera.

With *Tristan* Wagner moves into a new and dreamy world also into a new harmonic field which is a million miles away from the four-square diatonic *Dutchman* of twenty years before. Mottos stand for feelings, not things, and they are used with greater subtlety. The climaxes are emotional, not physical. No Ride of the Valkyries here and no terminal flames shooting up from Valhalla, but a lovers' duet and a lovers' death.

With *Parsifal* there was some retreat from the system of mickey-mouse mottos. Now mottos are even more general, they stand for concepts and ideas rather than specific things or feelings, e.g. the idea of the holiness of the Grail rather than for the jug itself, the idea of a holy wound rather than the hole in Amfortas's side. The secular bits of *Parsifal* have as much zest and zing as anything in *The Ring* but the music of the holy parts drifts upwards onto Cloud 9 where it is sometimes very beautiful and sometimes just a little nauseating when you consider the nature and characteristics of its creator.

It is impossible to imagine a world in which Wagner never happened. If we had lost either of the other two greats they would have left a devastating gap in the repertoire, but opera would have gone on. Mozart, at the time, was seen as one of many. Verdi carried Italian opera to glorious heights, but had there been no Verdi Puccini would no doubt have picked up the baton just the same. But without Wagner we would be missing the second act of all opera. In no other art did one man make such an impact. It is as if in the world of the visual arts the post-Impressionists had all been one man. He was at the same time a horror, a phenomenon and a genius. But he was Wagner, and he has left us some of the greatest work ever created by the human imagination.

Weber, Carl Maria 1786–1826

HABITAT A travelling man: roamed Germany and Austria with stops at Salzburg, Breslau, Stuttgart, Prague and Dresden.
OPERAS Eight including *Freischütz*†.
LIFE AND TIMES Until late in life Weber was an unlucky man. Once successful, he was a sick one. Starting off as a member of his father's travelling theatre company, he stopped off at Salzburg long enough to have some coaching in composition from Michael Haydn, Josef's brother and Mozart's friend. When still a teenager, he got the job of music director in Breslau. Here he tried to do something to raise standards which were no doubt dreadful, but the old hands in the orchestra saw him off and he was on the hoof again within a couple of years. After scraping a living in a number of minor jobs his first grown-up opera *Silvana* was put on in Berlin. It was a success, and maybe as a result he was appointed director of the Prague opera, which sounds great but actually it was pretty well amateur night again and he had to struggle and strive to get things shipshape. He had a preference for German opera and gave *Fidelio* its first Bohemian airing. After a row with the management Weber left Prague, by now a sick man (and remained pretty ill for the rest of his life), and took on the Dresden opera house. Here he once again started on the new-broom act and kept on sweeping for five years during which time he hit the jackpot. He had been working on *Freischütz* for five years. At last it was put on in Berlin. It was a triumph. Now he had no trouble in getting *Euryanthe* on in Vienna and after that *Oberon* in London. But by now his health had given out and he lived just long enough to see *Oberon*'s rapturous reception by the Londoners.
COMMENT Weber is one of the most underrated composers of the nine-

teenth century. His concert music is a lot better than Mendelssohn's later stuff and his operas are easily the best that were produced in Germany between *Fidelio* and the *Dutchman*. Alas, *Euryanthe* and *Oberon* are out of the repertory, so we have to make do with *Freischütz*, which is pure delight. It is a fact that children who have been brought up in an acting troupe never lose their sense of theatre and Weber is a theatre man to the fingertips. There is no opera of the period that is so full of cues for the linesman and the lighting director nor one that smells so strongly of greasepaint.

Weber is usually called a romantic opera composer and this in a sense is true. But he is not soppy-romantic like Walter Scott, he is more spooky-romantic like Mary Shelley. Boris Karlov could easily be lurking in the Wolf's Glen. Weber was such a good tune-writer, such a master of orchestration and in general such a perfect opera composer that it is a matter for amazement that *Euryanthe* and *Oberon* are not given a place in the sun.

Weill, Kurt 1900–50

HABITAT Berlin, Paris and New York.
OPERAS None. Some 30 musical works for the stage including *The Threepenny Opera*† and *Street Scene* (his best American work).
LIFE AND TIMES Weill was a son of the synagogue, his father being a Kantor, and a pupil of Busoni. He grew up as a synagogue organist, a musical odd-job man and passionate anti-Wagnerian. Following in the wake of Busoni he evolved a succession of very German theories about what opera was, could be and should be. His early attempts at opera are lost but some of his instrumental music written during his twenties is not. It got him known then and still sounds good today. He had no great success on the stage until his great *Threepenny* smash hit. His relationship with Brecht is not easy to read. Brecht was a whistle-train Marxist, Weill was not. Brecht says he dictated the tunes: Weill says he didn't. Lotte Lenya (whom Weill married a couple of times and divorced once) says their relationship was cordial: others say it was coldly professional. Both had the same ambition – to write a great opera, but this didn't happen, the only other really successful piece they produced being *The Rise and Fall of the City of Mahagonny*. It was while working together on this piece that they realized that they were incompatible and typically wrote a joint testament explaining in great psychological and ideological detail why this was so. [If Rossini fell out with a librettist he was more likely to have kicked him downstairs. Changed times: Ed.] When he went to Paris Weill was lionized but produced no great work. He escaped from Hitler's Europe in 1937 and went to America where he was humiliated in Hollywood but had some mild success on Broadway.

COMMENT If Weill had grown up in the Vienna of the Hapsburgs rather than in post-war Berlin he might have buckled down to some settled scheme of work and produced a string of masterpieces, for he was bursting out with talent and very clever. But the total uncertainty about any sort of values in art in the world he inhabited seemed to make it impossible for him to do much that was worthwhile except to write theses, a few brilliant café songs and one great Singspiel. His stock-in-trade was sentimental cynicism and his musical style was volatile. He took aboard jazz as was the fashion with all intellectual musicos between the wars, he admired Schoenberg and wrote in an idiom that was sometimes New Orleans, sometimes atonal, sometimes a bit of both, but most often a sort of spiky jazzed-up kind of Stravinsky. But he could write a tune. He had musical wit and he had a great sense of theatre, and these qualities gave us *The Threepenny Opera* – and in it we hear the authentic voice of the Berlin of the twenties.

ARTISTS

Conductors

Abbado, Claudio Milan 1933

LIFE AND TIMES Started operatic life by conducting Prokofiev's *The Love of Three Oranges* in Trieste in 1958. Debut at the Scala 1960, Covent Garden 1968. Instantly recognized as a conductor extraordinary. Resident conductor at the Scala 1969, Music Director 1971, Artistic Director 1977, by which time he was pretty well maestro of all he surveyed in that venerable company (but fed up with the corrupt and incompetent administration). Took on a lot of orchestral work including the LSO in 1972. Did a *Boccanegra* in Vienna in 1984 that really made the customers sit up. Was asked to take on the Vienna State Opera which he did in 1986. Gave it up on health grounds in 1991 but was still strong enough to carry on as Chief Conductor of the Berlin Phil and to continue with an opera production here there and most places but not much at the Scala, where his rival Muti held sway, nor at the Met, where he had had a row with the management in 1968 and never returned.
COMMENT Abbado is most opera buffs' first choice for the Italian repertory. You do not need to be a very advanced pupil to cope with Bellini and Donizetti but Verdi, and especially late Verdi, quickly sorts out the men from the boys, and here Abbado is supreme. Not much of a Wagnerian, he is friendly disposed to new operas (Nono, Berg) and likes making new discoveries amongst old ones (Rossini's *Viaggio a Reims*). An adventurous Intendant both at the Scala and in Vienna, so far as the latter city permits.

Abbado was already determined to be a conductor when he was ten years old. He attended a rehearsal taken by Toscanini as a result of which he decided that the Maestro's imperious methods were wrong and throughout his conducting life has stuck to a gentle non-dictatorial approach which seems to get him precisely the results he wants.

He is a scholarly musician who approaches the text of each opera afresh but the weight of his learning does not detract one whit from the élan of his performances.

Böhm, Karl Graz 1894 d. Salzburg 1981

LIFE AND TIMES Did quite a lot of wandering, being Music Director at Munich, Darmstadt, Hamburg, Dresden (some say his golden period 1934–43) and Vienna towards the end of the war, Buenos Aires after the war and a final innings in Vienna after that. An admirer and friend of Richard Strauss who dedicated one of his operas to him. Enormously respected in every corner of the musical world. Died in Salzburg. Conducted operas of his choice in every major opera house.

COMMENT Böhm's range of interest was confined pretty well to German opera and mainly to Wagner, Strauss and, above all, Mozart. He is the only conductor to have *three* versions of a Mozart opera (*Così*) in the CD catalogues today. An extraordinary musician and conductor who could coax each phrase in an aria or each part in an ensemble into its most beautiful shape. You can't do this at speed, so Böhm often conducted very slow; sometimes the pulse is so slow that you feel the patient may die. But he never does, owing to Böhm's firm beat giving a steady underlying impetus. A great conductor from a more leisured age.

Bonynge, Richard Sydney 1930

LIFE AND TIMES Started pretty humble as a specialist in vocal technique. Coached Sutherland. Married Sutherland (1954). Conducted Sutherland pretty well from then on. Made a lot of records with Sutherland. Music Director of Sydney Opera 1974–86.

COMMENT When he started conducting Bonynge suffered a good deal of derision. He had had no professional training and was only there, said the cynics, because he was Mr Sutherland. As the years went on the sniggering stopped. He proved himself to be an efficient and competent conductor and became a great authority on the history and nature of coloratura singing. And of all conductors, he knew best how to provide the right orchestral support for Joany, an important matter for all of us.

Davis, Sir Colin Weybridge 1927

LIFE AND TIMES Started as a clarinettist and because of bureaucratic college rules couldn't get into the conductors' class because he wasn't studying piano. So he got his experience outside. One day when the by-now tottering Klemperer fell ill Davis took up the baton and stood in for him, giving a smashing concert performance of *Don Giovanni*. Another ailing elderly maestro gave him a second chance when Beecham keeled over and couldn't do the *Flute* at Glyndebourne. This made Davis famous. Succeeded Solti at Covent Garden as Music Director 1971–86. Conducted first performance of *Peter Grimes* at the Met. First English conductor to work at Bayreuth (*Tannhäuser*). Subsequently became mainly orchestral.

COMMENT Few conductors have a narrower range of favoured composers and few can handle their chosen favourites better. Davis's list is Mozart and Berlioz of the past masters and Berg, Britten and Tippett of those who came later. He is one of the great Mozartians of our day, always getting the tempi exactly right, which is far and away the biggest thing a conductor can do for Mozart. There is only one correct tempo for a Mozart piece. If you play it too fast it cannot flower. If you play it too slow it wilts. Along with Beecham and Haitink, Davis is the only conductor of this century who can be trusted to get it right every time. His Berlioz is legendary. So are his moderns. But he has not had much traffic with the Italians.

Giulini, Carlo Maria Barletta 1914

LIFE AND TIMES Studied the viola in Rome, then conducting. Music Director of Italian Radio in 1944 (in charge of the final playout for Mussolini). Joined the Scala 1949 under Victor De Sabata. Debut 1952. Many international debuts and engagements, often at Covent Garden. In 1968 could no longer stand the incompetence and crookery of the Italian opera world and withdrew into an orchestral Mount Sinai for fourteen years. Music Director of Los Angeles Opera 1978–84. Then, rather like Glenn Gould with his piano, moved out of the public arena to make operas in the recording studio.
COMMENT Meticulous, scrupulous, fastidious, Giulini was a sort of musical saint. He could find the soul in any music that had any but was not so much at home with the rough-and-tumble of the early bel canto buffas. He was thought to be the greatest interpreter of Italian opera in the 1950s and 60s and indeed, listening to his recordings now, it must be said that they are the clearest, straightest and most truly musical records of the period, and make the illustrious combo of Karajan–Walter Legge (the maestro of EMI's recording studio) sound a bit flashy.

Haitink, Bernard Amsterdam 1929

LIFE AND TIMES Started out as a violinist: followed van Beinum to become the youngest-ever conductor of the Amsterdam Concertgebouw orchestra, subsequently associated with LPO (1967–), Glyndebourne (debut 1972, Music Director 1977–87) and Covent Garden (debut 1977, Music Director 1987–). Many, many international engagements.
COMMENT A musician's musician. Orchestras love him. They certainly get a chance to know him pretty well – thirty years with the Concertgebouw, ten at Glyndebourne and let's hope for yet another decade at Covent Garden. Grounded in Bruckner, Mahler. Excellent with Mozart (perfectly judged tempi, elegant phrasing), Wagner (entered into a life-and-death struggle with *The Ring* and won a resounding victory), Strauss (but perhaps not quite Viennese enough), also other north European composers. Italian opera outside his range and nor is he eager

to conduct atonal and other uncongenial contemporary works. But within his own territory a master. A scrupulously careful musician who takes his time to think things through. He does not try to do more than he can do really well (in this he is almost unique). Never miss a chance to hear him live in the opera house.

Karajan, Herbert von Salzburg 1908 d. Salzburg 1989

LIFE AND TIMES Became Music Director (also a Nazi) at Aachen in 1934 at the age of 26. Subsequently a legendary rise to operatic and orchestral fame; young lion of Berlin in 1930s until end of war, then Vienna Symphony Orchestra; Scala 1948/9: teamed up with Walter Legge of EMI: innumerable recordings in London with the Philharmonia 1950–4. *Ring* at Bayreuth 1951; Principal Conductor Berlin Phil (following Furtwängler) 1955; Artistic Director Salzburg Festival 1956; Vienna Staatsoper 1957, resigned after a row 1964; moved into films and TV in 1970s; continued as world's most highly-paid conductor until the Berlin Phil finally mutinied in 1987 and chucked him out.
COMMENT 'The music director of Europe', businessman, impresario, skier, yachtsman, film producer, conductor and musician. Some revered him, some did not. At the time when Beecham was struggling to overcome the shortcomings of his assistant Malcolm Sargent, someone asked him what he thought of Karajan. 'Karajan? Karajan?' he said, 'I believe he is a sort of musical Malcolm Sargent.' But there was no doubt that like Toscanini Karajan could hold an orchestra in his thrall and exact instant obedience. The standard of ensemble when he conducted was amazing, the precision absolute. But he was a prey to his own weaknesses, indulging in flashy effects, overblown emotion and often showing a streak of vulgarity. His performances of the great masters (Bach, Mozart) lack humility: he was best with those composers whose temperament was nearest to his own, both the old and the new Viennese school, Wagner, Strauss. A formidable man, a giant who demanded adulation and instant obedience from the whole world of music as if by divine right.

Levine, James Cincinnati 1943

LIFE AND TIMES Child prodigy pianist, public concerts at ten. Turned to studying conducting at the Juilliard school. Debut San Francisco (*Tosca*) 1970 and *Tosca* again for his debut at the Met 1971. The Met liked him, made him first Principal Conductor and then Music Director in 1976 and finally in 1986 Artistic Director as well. And so he became the commander-in-chief of all forces in the biggest and best-funded opera house in the world where he has already himself conducted over 1,000

performances. His Bayreuth debut was in 1982 with *Parsifal*.
COMMENT Levine is a phenomenon in many ways but especially in the matter of energy. He carries a huge managerial load and carries it lightly. He conducts more operas himself than any other Intendant and after a *Ballo* on Monday, on Tuesday he will be rehearing *Tosca* for Thursday when some conductors would be studying next month's score quietly at home. He is ebullient, jolly and has the opposite of what most people would identify as the artistic temperament. But make no mistake, he is a very great artist indeed, with an encyclopedic knowledge of music, with the ability to make other people play up to his own high standards and to get through an immense amount of work in a very short time. His repertory covers pretty well any opera written before 1925, but not much modern stuff because the Met just doesn't do that sort of thing.

Maazel, Lorin Neuilly, near Paris 1930

LIFE AND TIMES Trained in Chicago and Pittsburgh. Conducted at the age of nine at the New York World Fair, after which Toscanini patted him on the head. Conducting debut in Catania 1953. Debut at the Met (*Don Giovanni*) 1962. Then variously in Europe. First American conductor at Bayreuth (*Lohengrin*) 1963. 1965–71 Music Director of Deutsche Oper Berlin. Back to Bayreuth for *The Ring* 1968. Debut Covent Garden 1978 (late, as usual). The big moment came when he took the joint post of Intendant and Music Director at the Vienna Opera in 1984, but opera-house politics got the better of him and after a lot of pain and grief he had to withdraw. Since then active mainly in the Scala and in making films (Losey's *Giovanni*, Rosi's excellent *Carmen* and Zeffirelli's *Otello*).
COMMENT Maazel is vivid. He has a strong hold over his productions and things have to be done his way and just so. Always vigorous and adventurous, he sometimes pulls off a really great performance, but this is not invariably the case. Can go a little over the top in seeking bold strokes and strong emotion. Exceptionally wide range of repertory from Mozart through the Italians to Wagner and *Porgy and Bess*.

Mehta, Zubin Bombay 1936

LIFE AND TIMES His father founded the Bombay Symphony Orchestra. Studied in Vienna. Won competitions as a young conductor and got assistant's job with the Montreal and Los Angeles orchestras. Opera debut Montreal (*Tosca*) 1964, the Met (*Aida*) 1965, Covent Garden (*Otello*) 1977 (rather late in the day). Music Director of the New York Phil and lifelong association with the Israel Phil. Plenty of major opera engagements but no permanent post. Artistic Director of Florence's

Maggio Musicale in 1986. Conducted the Three Tenors event.
COMMENT Mehta is sometimes said to be a conductor who lacks profundity. This may be so, but he can make a show come off. Profound conductors may send the audience home pondering the greater truth of opera, but Mehta can bring the house to its feet and that's what most operas ask for. He attacks any score with abundant confidence. His rhythms are vigorous. His beat is firm. He is a bit of a romantic and best with the operas of Verdi's middle period and with Puccini.

Muti, Riccardo Naples 1941

LIFE AND TIMES Started life studying the piano and philosophy. Then conducting in Milan. Won competitions. Principal Conductor Maggio Musicale 1969 where he revived early Verdis and produced an uncut *William Tell.* [Was that wise? Ed.] Debut Salzburg 1971 and pretty well every year since. Opera performances in all the best houses. Long association with the New Philharmonia in London and the Philadelphia. Took over the Scala from Abbado in 1986 and has been there ever since.
COMMENT Along with his rival Abbado one of the two outstanding Italian conductors of our time. Unlike Abbado, he follows the disciplinarian tradition of Toscanini, but unlike Toscanini he can combine ferocity with wit. He is known for his ear, or rather his ears, for he has two, which can detect the perpetrator of a fuzzy note played by one violin out of 32. A formidable man with a veneration for musical scholarship. He will dig and delve to make sure that his version of Gluck's *Orfeo* is as near as possible to the original and where Beecham would have been scribbling in a bar here and there to make the thing sound better, Muti will be knocking them out to make it sound authentic. Muti's repertory centres on Mozart and Italian opera, but he can do anything. He can also put an electric charge into any piece he is conducting. He can cast a spell. He is a great conductor.

Sinopoli, Giuseppe Venice 1946

LIFE AND TIMES Became the boffin of electronic music at the Vienna Conservatoire in 1972. Opera debut Venice (*Aida*) 1978. Debut Covent Garden (*Manon Lescaut*) 1983 (first, for once), the Met (*Tosca*) 1985 and Bayreuth (*Tannhäuser*) also 1985. Many international bookings including *Butterfly* in Japan. Almost became Music Director of the Berlin Deutsche Oper in 1990 but a last-minute row with the management prevented it.
COMMENT You will not find two operatic buffs with the same views about Sinopoli. Can't keep a steady beat, no clarity of texture, will say one. Great rhythmic subtlety, allows his singers just the right amount of

freedom, will say another. Sinopoli is a searcher after the inner logic of a piece. If *Lulu* were a Rubik cube, he would solve it. The trouble is that simple souls who wrote the bel cantos do not require this degree of ratiocination. He is also a great believer in making the players and singers his partners in the challenge of reaching the finest possible performance. Sometimes his methods work brilliantly. Not always. He is at his best with late Verdi, Puccini and Wagner.

Solti, Sir Georg Budapest 1912

LIFE AND TIMES Studied under Dohnanyi, Kodaly and Bartok and then, as a pianist, became repetiteur to the Budapest Opera. Worked for Toscanini at Salzburg 1936–7. Opera debut Budapest (*Figaro*) 1938. Since Jews were debarred from official opera posts went back to the piano and won an international contest in 1942. Conducted *Fidelio* at Munich 1946. Music Director of the Bayerische Staatsoper 1946–52. Put on Strauss operas and was offered some fatherly advice from Richard. Then Frankfurt, Salzburg, Edinburgh 1952, Glyndebourne 1954, debut at Covent Garden (*Rosenkavalier*) 1959, the Met (*Tannhäuser*) 1960. Music Director Covent Garden 1961–71, Peter Hall's *Ring*, Bayreuth 1983, top engagements everywhere. Very active in the recording studio. Director of the Salzburg Festival 1992. Still going strong (very) at 82.

COMMENT Solti is a dynamo. Every working moment (and he doesn't sleep long) he is scheming, studying, plotting and planning in meticulous detail his next production. No one gives a work more thorough preparation. When he mounts the rostrum he knows what he wants precisely. It's never a matter of waiting to see how things turn out: he makes them turn out the way he wants them too. This high charge of energy comes through in performance. In the early days it was the fashion to say his operatic work was 'hard-driven'. There is a grain of truth here: in his early Mozarts, for instance, the pulse can be a little feverish. But once he reached maturity (let's say at the age of 60), it became possible for him to relax, to contemplate and to savour each phrase rather than to use it as a stepping-stone to the next one. He is a brilliant musician and brilliant too at casting an opera, also organizing anything from his next production to his life, which is surely completely scheduled in minutes and probably seconds well up to and beyond the year 2000. The great thing about Solti is that the show always comes off. Other conductors have their good nights and their off nights. With Solti there are only good nights and very good nights. He has recorded practically every opera you can think of and usually recorded them better than anyone else. Thank God for that say we, for when he dies (if ever) we shall have a rich legacy to remind us of one of the greatest opera conductors of the century.

Singers

Allen, Thomas Seaham 1944 Baritone

LIFE AND TIMES Trained in London. Debut with Welsh National Opera 1969. Glyndebourne chorus then returned to WNO in a wide range of roles. Debut Covent Garden (Donald in *Billy Budd*) 1971. Joined Royal Opera company 1972 (over a dozen leading roles). Debut the Met (Papageno) 1981, Salzburg (Ulysses) 1985. Many international engagements, also Glyndebourne.
COMMENT Most performers in opera are singers who can act (sometimes only a little), a few are actors who can sing, Allen is equally a singer and an actor. He can play a character so vividly as to make his version live on in the memory to the exclusion of all others. For those who saw his Giovanni he *is* the Don in person. Stand up the real Figaro, and Tom Allen rises to his feet. His Beckmesser is not only the best Beckmesser ever, he manages to turn one of the weakest links in *Meistersinger* into a strength. His voice is strong, even, agreeable. It is flexible too and he can cope with coloratura. His intonation is nearly always spot on. He is a gifted comedian. He is handsome. You can hear his words. He is, in short, a star and one of British opera's greatest assets.

Baker, Dame Janet Hatfield Yorks 1933 Mezzo

LIFE AND TIMES Studied in London and sang in semi-professional productions until her debut at Glyndebourne (Dido) 1966. Debut at Covent Garden (Hermia) 1966. Many subsequent appearances for both companies also ENO. Retired from opera 1982.
COMMENT Baker was an English singer. She sang in England and was at her best in English music. She was famous for her Dido, her Handel and for her parts in the Britten operas, although her repertory did of course extend to Monteverdi, Gluck and occasionally into the more standard rep (Dorabella, Octavian, Maria Stuarda). She had a deep-toned and vibrant mezzo voice which she projected with great dignity and authority. But she could be warm too and no one has sung Purcell's Dido more movingly than she did. A dab hand at coloratura. Everyone who worked with her liked and admired her.

Baltsa, Agnes Lefkas 1944 Mezzo

LIFE AND TIMES Studied in Athens, Munich and Frankfurt. Debut Frankfurt (Cherubino) 1968. Major German houses Salzburg and

Vienna 1969–70, Covent Garden (Cherubino again) 1976, the Met (Octavian) 1979. Then internationally and frequently.
COMMENT Baltsa's voice has changed almost out of recognition since she first sang Cherubino in a clear middle soprano register. It went both lower and higher but left an uncomfortable hole in the middle. Each part has its own beauty and her chest voice is particularly strong but the change of gear from the nether to the upper register is not always in synchromesh. But she is such a great artist and so clever an actress that she can overcome this problem in performance and have the house eating out of her hand regardless. She throws herself passionately into the more dramatic roles and her Carmen will not be forgotten by anyone who saw it.

Behrens, Hildegard Oldenburg 1937 Soprano

LIFE AND TIMES Started surprisingly enough as a Mozart singer. Then debut Covent Garden (Leonore) 1976, the Met (Giorgetta) in the same year. An unforgettable Salome at Salzburg 1977. A majestic Brünnhilde at Bayreuth 1983. And then from strength to strength.
COMMENT One of the few great Wagnerian sopranos still some distance away from drawing her OAP. Her voice is rich, has depth and enormous power. She cuts a fine figure on the stage and can act. She can cope with almost anything (not bel canto) but in the lighter Mozarts her metal would now be too heavy for the rest of the household to match. Best roles: Elektra, Salome, Brünnhilde. Never miss a chance to see her in one of these.

Berganza, Teresa Madrid 1935 Mezzo

LIFE AND TIMES First made her mark at the Aix-en-Provence Festival 1957. Debut Glyndebourne (Cherubino) 1958, Covent Garden (Rosina) 1960, the Met 1967 and then all over Europe. One of the most in-demand mezzos of her day.
COMMENT Berganza's voice is something special. It has a dusky overtone which can send a tremor down the spine. This she can draw across her usually clear and very nimble mezzo at will. Her voice is a beautifully trained, precise instrument and she can race through any item in Rossini's coloratura mezzo roles at a dazzling speed. When she takes on heavier stuff she becomes a dramatic actress too and her Carmen in the Peter Diamond production at the Edinburgh Festival in 1972 was thought by many to be the best ever. In the 1980s, mainly a concert artist.

Bergonzi, Carlo Parma 1924 Tenor

LIFE AND TIMES Started life as a baritone in Italian provincial houses (1948). Moved up a gear to tenor (1951). Debut at the Scala 1953, the Met 1956, Covent Garden (Don Alvaro) 1962. Sang regularly at the Met for over thirty years where he was a great favourite. Also in demand everywhere a first-class Verdi tenor was needed. Retired 1988.
COMMENT A beautiful cultured voice. He used it elegantly with great care and discretion. Lacked the power and the visceral appeal of the big-time Italian tenor. More of an Alfredo than a Turiddu. A real musician and never off pitch. Could sing the whole Italian rep but not much outside it.

Bumbry, Grace St Louis 1937 Soprano/Mezzo

LIFE AND TIMES Studied in the USA with Lotte Lehmann. Debut Paris (Amneris) 1960, Bayreuth (Venus) 1961 – the first black artist to be permitted inside those hallowed halls – Covent Garden 1963, the Met 1965, both as Eboli. Has appeared in all major houses.
COMMENT Bumbry has the most amazing ability to sing almost any role in the repertory. She has done Verdi and Wagner, both high and low, Carmen, Delilah, Gluck's Orpheus, Santuzza, Salome, Norma, Tosca, Gioconda, Leonore, Jenufa and Bess, to mention but a few. The Queen of Night is about the only thing left for her. She has a huge, warm, life-enhancing bottom and middle to her voice but she is just a little bit thinner on top. A fine figure on the stage, a little more stately than on her first appearance as Amneris.

Caballé, Montserrat Barcelona 1933 Soprano

LIFE AND TIMES Trained in Barcelona. Joined Basle Opera 1956. Minor international opera engagements until one night in 1965 she replaced Marilyn Horne in a concert performance of *Lucrezia Borgia*. Wow! A star overnight. Debut at Glyndebourne (Countess) and the Met (Marguerite) shortly after (1965). Debut Covent Garden (Violetta) 1972 (laggardly as ever). Frequently at the Scala and all top houses since then.
COMMENT For many years Caballé was regarded as a Donizetti specialist and such was her fame that many unknown early Donizettis were dug out to give her a new role. She was equally good in Verdi. Her secret weapon was her ability to spin out a long legato line and make it vibrate with emotion although the voice itself kept clear and steady. Her high pianissimos were magic. At one time she was hailed as Callas's successor but this was quite wrong. She had none of Callas's animal intensity and

although a dignified and in later days a stately figure on the stage, she had none of Callas's dramatic power as an actress. She sang Mozart well but those who admired her were apt to keep waiting for the coloratura passages that never came. At her best in the 1960s and early 70s.

Callas, Maria New York 1923 d. Paris 1977 Soprano

LIFE AND TIMES Left the USA for Greece at the age of fourteen. Trained in Athens. Local debut (Tosca) 1942 followed by other Athens performances. Returned to New York in 1945. Appeared in many Italian provincial houses 1947 onwards singing heavy stuff (even Wagner). Encountered Serafin in Verona who became her admirer, coach and latterly house conductor. He put her onto the bel canto track and very wise he was. Debut the Scala (1950), Covent Garden (1952), the Met (1956), all as Norma. Became a world and media star and continued to be one until long after her voice declined.

COMMENT When Callas was fat she sang much better than when she was thin. But then she looked and acted so brilliantly after she had lost weight (in the mid 1940s) that the balance was perhaps about even. Her voice was a wonderfully flexible and proficient instrument and she played upon it as a virtuoso violinist plays the fiddle. It had great dramatic power but after the early days the actual sound was not all that pleasant. Her tone was sharp and cutting when she was acting ferocious and outraged, and when she was passionate or intense it sounded strained. But quite lovely when she sang softly. But funnily enough this didn't matter too much because she was such a star that she swept you along into the drama in a way that no girl with a golden voice could have done. She was highly intelligent, a musical scholar and had completely mastered the classical Italian style. She was a great actress and could well have been a star in the legitimate theatre. From the early 1950s on she had problems with her voice which finally became too much for her in the mid 60s for latterly her intonation became a bit wobbly. This was one reason why she had the reputation of being so temperamental, the other reason being that she was just born that way. She was unique and we shall never see her like again.

Carreras, José Barcelona 1946 Tenor

LIFE AND TIMES Made his debut in his home town. Toured Italy. Debut at the Met (Cavaradossi) 1974, Covent Garden also 1974 (his big year). In 1987 when in top form contracted leukaemia. Made a rather miraculous recovery. Returned to Covent Garden 1991. One of the Three Tenors.

COMMENT A sweet lyric tenor without the wooden thickness of some

Spanish voices. Perfect intonation with occasional off-days. A real musician. Can phrase an aria quite beautifully. An elegant figure on stage. Better suited by light roles (Nemorino); big stuff (Wagner) beyond him. Best in bel canto. Always a joy to listen to him.

Christoff, Boris Plovdiv, Bulgaria 1914 Bass

LIFE AND TIMES The musical King Boris of Bulgaria spotted our Boris and sent him to Italy to be coached (to sing, amongst other things, Boris). Debut Reggio (Colline) 1946, the Scala (Pimen) 1947, Covent Garden (Boris) 1949 (many subsequent visits).
COMMENT Christoff's awesome appearance and uncanny acting ability made him the greatest Boris since Chaliapin. He could brood in the Russian manner as no other bass could brood, he could act regal, act mad and frighten us to death in the great clock scene. His voice was dark, firm and beautifully controlled, but not enormous. He could also sing the whole range of Verdi's baddies in a slightly central European manner. But he was always convincing no matter what the part.

De Los Angeles, Victoria Barcelona 1923 Soprano

LIFE AND TIMES Studied guitar and piano in Barcelona as well as singing. Debut Barcelona (Mimi) in 1941. Rocketed to fame as a concert singer. Debut Covent Garden 1950, the Met 1951. Bayreuth (Elisabeth) 1961. Travelled the world to sing opera and also in the concert hall.
COMMENT Los Angeles had great charm. There was something fresh and girlish about her voice right up to the time she gave up singing in opera. She had a sweet bell-like tone and was best in intimate friendly roles (Mimi, Butterfly, Manon). She could manage the lighter Wagners nicely, but she was no Turandot, Elektra and certainly no Brünnhilde. Amazing flexibility (trills and runs) and perfect intonation.

Dernesch, Helga Vienna 1939 Soprano/Mezzo

LIFE AND TIMES Studied in Vienna and moved into Division II of the German opera houses in 1961. Debut Bayreuth (Freia) 1965, Covent Garden (Sieglinde) 1970, the Met (Marfa) 1985. And in every major house.
COMMENT Dernesch started life as a dramatic soprano then in 1972 switched to take on the great mezzo roles of Klytemnestra, Herodias, Erda, Fricka, etc. Her voice is truly Wagnerian, powerful, rich and the ear welcomes it warmly (unlike many mezzos of yesteryear who bawled their way through those parts giving off huge waves of sound but not much

pleasure). Dernesch is a fine figure of a woman on stage but is inclined to follow the old adage that she who stands stillest sings best.

Di Stefano, Giuseppe Catania 1921 Tenor

LIFE AND TIMES Captured as a wild young Sicilian tenor and trained in Milan. First appearance in Reggio 1946. Debut at the Scala 1947. Instant sensation. The Met (the Duke in *Rigoletto*) 1948, Covent Garden (Cavaradossi) 1961 [shamefully late: Ed.]. Sang with Callas for many years as her preferred partner. In peak form in the 1950s. In the early 60s lost his voice suddenly and almost completely. Subsequent concert tours with Callas, also waning, were sad affairs.
COMMENT One of the great voices of the century. His high pure tenor had all the animal magnetism that makes the Italian tenor a voice apart. A natural not a hot-house-trained musician. Took a long time to learn roles (mainly bel canto) but when he had got them pat and let rip, O Boy! Sang with a streak of wild intensity in his voice which made Caruso, Gigli and Co. sound like show-business show-offs. Best in Puccini, good in bel canto.

Domingo, Placido Madrid 1941 Tenor

LIFE AND TIMES Taken by his parents to Mexico when nine years old. Studied piano and conducting. First role in Mexico as a baritone (1961). Member of the Israeli National Opera 1962–5. Sang a lot in Hebrew. Debut at the Met (Maurizio) 1968, the Scala (Ernani) 1969, Covent Garden (Cavaradossi) 1971. By now a world star. In demand everywhere and sang nearly everywhere. One of the Three Tenors (and one of the two greatest living tenors in the world).
COMMENT Smooth, rich lyrical tenor. Has a sweetness combined with power which is rare. Tremendous range. Can, and still does occasionally, sing baritone parts (prologue to *Pagliacci*). Perfect intonation, has never been known to be off the note. Timbre lacking the wild animal streak of the Italian tenor but has a Spanish intensity which compensates. An all-round musician with ambitions to conduct which is a pity. Plenty of people can conduct better than he. Only one other person can sing equally well. Plenty of time to conduct when the voice gets a little shaggy, so please Placido – sing now, conduct later. Best roles – can do pretty well anything but is perhaps best as Otello as seen in Zeffirelli's film.

Ewing, Maria Detroit 1950 Soprano/Mezzo

LIFE AND TIMES Protegée of James Levine. After training in the USA she had her debut at Rovinia in 1973 then appeared in several Division II houses in Europe and America. Debut Salzburg (Cherubino) 1976 also the Met same year same role. Debut Covent Garden (Salome) 1988. Many appearances at Glyndebourne in Peter Hall's (her husband's) productions as Carmen, Dorabella and Salome. And, of course, elsewhere.
COMMENT Ewing is both a star actress and a star singer, and this makes her a superstar. She can put on a bewitching performance whether doing a habanera as Carmen, singing a hymn to love as the moon-struck Cherubino or stripping to the buff as Salome (a rare event, and in the case of most Salomes this is fortunate). Her voice is charming, warm and nimble but light and it is only her acting ability (which is stunning) that allows her to triumph in the heavy stuff. But triumph she does, and although there must be evenings when she is dissatisfied with herself, the house has never been known to be dissatisfied with her.

Fassbaënder, Brigitte Berlin 1939 Mezzo

LIFE AND TIMES Very old Glyndebourne hands will remember Willi Domgraf-Fassbaënder who sang Figaro in the opening performance of the first Glyndebourne season of 1934. It was he who trained his daughter Brigitte at the Nuremberg Conservatory where he was on the staff. Debut in Munich 1961. Debut Covent Garden (Octavian) 1971, Fricka at Salzburg 1973, the Met (Octavian again) 1974. Then many roles in many houses, including parts in the moderns like Berg and Von Einem [who he? Ed.]. Now also works as a producer.
COMMENT Fassbaënder has a dark-hued rather sexy voice which suits Octavian down to the ground. Indeed he is lucky to have her for she makes a dashing and handsome character of him on stage. He could hardly do better. She is also very fine in ex-castrato parts such as Sextus in *Tito* but can be equally good out of trousers in softer roles such as Freia or Dorabella. Her intonation is absolutely rock-solid and she is a singer who always gives everything she has got.

Fischer-Dieskau, Dietrich Berlin 1925 Baritone

LIFE AND TIMES Trained in Berlin and made his debut there at the Städtische Oper (Posa) 1948. Sang many roles for this company. Then Munich, Vienna and in 1952 Salzburg, Bayreuth (Wolfram, Amfortas) 1954–6. Debut Covent Garden (Mandryka in *Arabella*) 1965. Many European engagements mostly in Germany.

COMMENT Fischer-Dieskau is a singer who thinks. Not only about the notes but about the motivation, the history and the place in music of the piece he is going to sing. He is a fastidious artist with a voice which is warm and full but not enormously powerful. He has sung all the Wagner roles that suit his range and some that test it (Hans Sachs). He can and does sing some of the Italian repertory but is at his best further north. A singer who is always a joy to hear and one who sings from his head and his heart rather than from his viscera. If you want the animal attack of the wilder Italian baritones, look elsewhere.

Freni, Mirella Modena 1935 Soprano

LIFE AND TIMES Local debut Modena 1955. Debut Glyndebourne (Zerlina) 1955, Covent Garden (Nanetta), Scala (Mimi) followed. Debut the Met (Mimi) 1965. Since then in enormous demand all over the opera world.
COMMENT Freni's voice is fresh, affecting and absolutely obedient to the demands she makes on it. She made her name with the lighter and straighter parts (Micaela, Mimi, Zerlina, Violetta, etc.) then moved into bel canto and in the 1970s took on heavier stuff (Desdemona, Aida). Her appeal is greatest when she is one of the simpler and sweeter heroines. Her prettiness and the young sound of her voice make her a moving Mimi or Tatyana. She is a natural Liu. Her voice is always clear, steady and easy on the ear.

Ghiaurov, Nicolai Velingrad, Bulgaria 1929 Bass

LIFE AND TIMES Trained in Moscow and St Petersburg. Debut Sofia (Don Basilio) 1955, Bologna 1958, the Scala 1959, Covent Garden 1962, the Met (Gounod's Mephistopheles) 1965, Salzburg (Boris) 1965. Many international engagements.
COMMENT Ghiarov's voice has a quality of instant magnetism. He has a slight huskiness that he can draw over his voice as an owl can draw a film over its eyes, and this is part of his secret. Anyone who has heard him as Prince Gremin giving Onegin his lecture on love and marriage will know how he can set the vibes a-jangle as he moves into this sweet and simple number. His voice can also be dark and (until recently) thunderous. He can make his voice change colour like a Bulgarian chameleon. He has perfect pitch. He is musical and he is clever. And, alas, he is reaching the end of his singing career.

Gobbi, Tito Bassano 1913 d. Rome 1984 Baritone

LIFE AND TIMES Studied in Rome. Debut Gubbio (Rodolfo) 1935. Sang for Rome Opera 1938–43. Debut the Scala (Belcore) 1942, Covent Garden (Belcore again) 1951, the Met (Scarpia) 1956. In demand everywhere. Sang frequently at the Met and even more frequently at Covent Garden.

COMMENT One of opera's all-time greats. A brilliant actor with a good voice, a balance of talent he shared with Callas, and when the two met in Act II of *Tosca* – O Boy! His voice was absolutely Italian, pure, flexible, in every way a lovely instrument, but it was not immensely powerful and it was part of his great acting ability that he made you think he was singing louder than he was. He was versatile, having over 100 roles in his repertoire, he was intelligent and he was popular. A bella figura on stage and a fascinating companion off it. In later years he tried his hand (successfully) as an opera producer (*Boccanegra*).

Gruberova, Edita Bratislava 1946 Soprano

LIFE AND TIMES Studied in Prague and Vienna as well as her native Bratislava where she had her debut (Rosina) 1968. Debut Vienna (Queen of Night) 1968. Joined the Venice company and has made it her base ever since. Debut Glyndebourne 1974, the Met 1977, both as Queen of Night. Covent Garden (Giulietta) 1984 (late again). By this time was in demand everywhere for coloratura roles.

COMMENT Gruberova's Bratislavian coloratura has no problems with the Italian repertory. Her technique is flawless, her voice clear, nimble and expressive. It has that special quality of being listener-friendly and brings with it every time a thrill of pleasure. She has an engaging stage presence. No matter how much of a stereotype the heroine of the evening may be, she will humanize her to the best of her ability. When on firmer dramatic ground she can be really moving, especially as Violetta. The most reliable Queen of Night in the business. Impeccable intonation. A truly great singer.

Horne, Marilyn Bradford USA 1934 Mezzo

LIFE AND TIMES Trained in the USA under Lotte Lehmann. Sang the dubbed voice of Dorothy Dandridge in *Carmen Jones* (1954). Sang for three seasons at Gelsenkirchen (1956–9). Debut San Francisco (Marie in *Wozzeck*) 1960. Debut Covent Garden (Marie again) 1964, the Met (Adalgisa) 1970.

COMMENT Like Bumbry, Horne can sing both high and low and this gives her access to a huge number of roles, including most of bel canto, Berg, Handel, late Verdi, Delilah, Gluck, etc. Her high is very bright and clear. Her chest notes can be heard a long way off and her middle is OK too. So she can be a real soprano or boom away as Azucena with equal facility. The timbre of her voice is rich and strong and has a touch of Lea & Perrins sauce in it which gives it a special zest. An amazing singer.

Hotter, Hans Offenbach (yes, there is such a place, am Main) 1909 Bass–baritone

LIFE AND TIMES Opera debut 1930 Munich (his first Wotan 1937) where he stayed on as a member of the company until 1972. Debut Covent Garden (Count Almaviva) 1949, the Met (Dutchman) 1950, Bayreuth 1952 where he became a regular performer over the next twelve years. Produced *The Ring* at Covent Garden 1962. Sang Wagner all over the place wherever and whenever a management could get him.
COMMENT One of opera's great names and funnily enough he couldn't always sing in tune. This disability was overcome (but only for some) by the majestic tone of his huge bass voice, by his great ability as an actor and by his intense commitment to the task in hand. He was a very serious artist. His most famous role was Hans Sachs but he stumped the stage as Wotan with good effect too. His wonderful rich God-given voice made him the top Wagnerian bass for over two decades.

Janowitz, Gundula Berlin 1937 Soprano

LIFE AND TIMES Studied at Graz. Debut with the Vienna Staatsoper (Barbarina) 1960. Joined the Vienna company and sang with it for thirty years. Debut Glyndebourne (Ilea) 1964, the Met (Sieglinde) 1967. Covent Garden (Donna Anna) 1974. Sang in all major opera houses. Went into opera management in 1990.
COMMENT To hear Janowitz sing is sheer delight. For pure beauty of tone there is no voice to match her. Strong men swoon when she sings, music directors forget to direct, stage crews creep into the wings as if summoned by Orpheus. The allure of her lyric soprano is too purely beautiful to be called voluptuous but it is at the same time seductive and cool. She has a range from Mozart through Wagner to Strauss. She holds a very special place in the memory of anyone who saw her in *Così* or indeed in any of the Mozarts.

Jerusalem, Siegfried Oberhausen 1940 Tenor

LIFE AND TIMES Started as a bassoonist. Became a singing bassoonist and then just a singer. Debut in Stuttgart 1975. Debut at Bayreuth (Froh) 1977. Sang pretty well the whole Wagner rep at Bayreuth from 1979 on. Debut at the Met (Lohengrin) 1980 and Covent Garden (Erik) 1986. Also sings lighter roles.
COMMENT One of the few, the very few Heldentenors who can cope with the Wagner rep. He has a true and expressive voice but can also belt it out when required, which in Wagner is pretty often. He does not have the enormous power of a Melchior but he has enough to make Siegfried or whoever audible above the orchestra, which in these days is a rare quality.

Jones, Dame Gwyneth Pontnewynydd 1936 Soprano

LIFE AND TIMES Made her breakthrough singing Lady Macbeth for the Welsh National Opera in 1963. Debut at Covent Garden (Leonore) 1964. Her Beethoven's Leonore was followed by Verdi's Leonora and she won great acclaim for both. Debut the Met (Sieglinde) 1972. Then top jobs all around – Vienna; Bayreuth, a great deal (1976 *Ring*); and often at Covent Garden.
COMMENT Welsh soprano, international star: much identified today with Wagnerian roles. She has an immensely powerful top range, can penetrate the orchestra even when Wagner is at his noisiest. Though loud, her tone at the top is always under control and quite beautiful, also a splendid range of chest notes. Midrange (and sometimes all over) Gwyneth is plagued by a wibble-wobble that can be quite off-putting. She projects herself into her parts with great emotional involvement. On her night a great singer. On a wobbly night wait for the high notes and the low ones, and as for the middle, pray for her.

Kollo, René Berlin 1937 Tenor

LIFE AND TIMES Member of the Düsseldorf opera company 1967–71. Began with light roles. Tamino at Salzburg 1974. Gradually moved on to the heavy stuff. Debut at the Met (Lohengrin) 1976, Covent Garden (Siegmund) also 1976. Sang Siegfried in the centenary *Ring* cycle at Bayreuth.
COMMENT For the last twenty years one of the few Heldentenors able to navigate safely through a big Wagner part. No Lauritz Melchior, but a good operational high tenor. His voice can have nobility but is scarcely heroic. Proficient and courageous. Intonation sometimes a bit dicey when tiring. At his best in the late 1970s/early 80s. Probably still best in lighter

roles but any tenor who can sing Wagner as effectively as he can is pretty well doomed to sing nothing else.

Ludwig, Christa Berlin 1928 Mezzo

LIFE AND TIMES Debut at Frankfurt 1946. Sang with the Frankfurt opera company until 1952 with little *réclame*. Joined the Vienna Staatsoper in 1955 and sang for them off and on for thirty years. Debut the Met (Cherubino) 1959, Bayreuth (Brangane) 1966, Covent Garden (Amneris) 1968 (late again). Between 1960 and 1980 she sang in all major opera houses.

COMMENT Ludwig was an all-rounder. She had no specialist roles but within the German repertory she could do pretty well anything from Mozart to Wagner and Strauss. Her voice was wonderfully expressive and it could change colour like a chameleon. So it is that Ludwig singing Dorabella sounds a different person from Ludwig singing Kundry, but equally satisfactory. Her acting helped her for she could lounge around looking like Venus one day and give a good impression of the busy Mistress Quickly the next. For two decades she was a joy to hear and a delight to see on the stage. Flashier stars may sell the tickets, but it is the great pros like Ludwig that keep the wheels of opera turning.

Marton, Eva Budapest 1943 Soprano

LIFE AND TIMES Marton broke out of Hungarian musical life in 1972 when she went to work for Frankfurt Opera for five years. Debut at the Met (Eva) 1976, Bayreuth (Elisabeth) 1977, Covent Garden (Turandot) 1977 (eleven years after the Met debut). Has appeared in all major opera houses.

COMMENT Marton has a voice of great power from the chest upwards and when it gets towards the top it has beauty and brilliance as well. She is fully equipped to sing the big roles (Wagner, Elektra, Salome) but unlike many of the old foghorn Wagnerians, she can sing lighter stuff too – e.g. Gioconda. Sings/speaks German and Italian equally well. A terrifying Turandot and a noble Brünnhilde.

Milnes, Sherrill Hinsdale, Illinois 1935 Baritone

LIFE AND TIMES Trained in the USA. Local debut Boston Opera (Masetto) 1960. Many USA appearances. Debut the Met (Valentin) 1965 and remained with the company for 25 years. Debut Covent Garden (Renato) 1971. Many subsequent engagements, mainly in the USA.

COMMENT A big handsome man with a big handsome voice. Milnes is a

Verdian, first second and third. His best roles come from middle and late Verdi (pretty well all of them, but especially Carlos, Rigoletto, Iago), although he can of course also do the Frenchies very nicely and make a convincing Don Giovanni. There is something in his nature that chimes with the plight of the Verdian baritone who is nearly always for one reason or another having a hard time. He has a brilliant top (almost a tenor) and sings with absolute commitment. He can also do the long legato line really well.

Murray, Ann Dublin 1949 Mezzo

LIFE AND TIMES Trained at the Royal Manchester College and in London. Debut at Snape with Scottish Opera (Alcestis) 1974. Debut Covent Garden (Cherubino) 1976, Salzburg (Nicklausse) 1981, the Met (Sextus) 1984. Many engagements in Europe.
COMMENT Murray seems destined to sing for a lot of the time in trousers. Certainly she is splendid in ex-castrato parts such as Sextus (in *Tito*), Cecilius (*Lucio Silla*), also as Cherubino and Octavian. But she can make an attractive Handelian female too, and also does a lovely Dorabella and a good Mélisande. But once you are into trousers in opera it is hard to shake them off, particularly if you look as young and as boyish as she does. She has a firm sharply focussed voice but seems able to round it off to be softer and more expressive when required. Good intonation, some acting ability and great natural musicality.

Nilsson, Birgit Vastra Karups 1918 Soprano

LIFE AND TIMES Studied in Stockholm. Debut the Royal Opera Stockholm (Agate) 1946. Five years later she broke out of Scandinavia and sang Elektra (Mozart not Strauss) at Glyndebourne. Now the news got around that here was a world-class voice. Debut in *The Ring* Munich 1954, also Bayreuth (Elsa) where she became a regular. Debut Covent Garden (*The Ring*) 1957, the Met (Isolda) 1959.
COMMENT To hear Nilsson moving into the Liebestod or Brünnhilde's final farewell to everything at the end of *Götterdämmerung* gives the listener a thrill that is pretty well unequalled in operatic life. She has a voice of clear beauty and as it climbs upwards and onwards into one of Wagner's great climaxes it gains in power and stature but never loses one whit of its purity of tone. There is no sign of strain or stress, she sings on effortlessly, like a bird, but of course much louder. Luckily her performances of these roles were recorded when she was in her prime and are there for all posterity to hear and recognize in her the greatest Wagnerian soprano of our time. She was also supreme as Turandot and Elektra.

Nilsson's intonation was perfect, she was a great dramatic actress, moved like a queen and was beautiful with it. If this sounds too good to be true, just ask some old opera hands, who will tell you it isn't.

Norman, Jessye Augusta 1945 Soprano

LIFE AND TIMES Trained in the USA she won an international contest in Berlin in 1968. Debut Deutsche Oper Berlin (Elisabeth) 1969, Covent Garden (Cassandra) 1972, the Met (Cassandra again) 1983. Then many international opera and concert performances.
COMMENT Norman has the rich vibrant voice of the black singer and a very special one, for it is a voice that has extraordinary power to reach the emotions. Her chest notes and her middle register are sensational. She is a natural musician and the days are gone when her voice sometimes seemed to take over and do its own thing. She now turns in highly disciplined performances and has a huge repertoire, from early seria (Handel) to Wagner and the moderns (Bartok). On stage she moves like a queen. Jessye Norman is a great lady in every sense. Once at the Edinburgh Festival it is alleged that when she was having problems with a swing door the porter suggested that she should try it sideways. 'Honey, I ain't got no sideways' she replied. She has wit as well as warmth in her singing and her voice is different from all others in opera, and three cheers for that.

Von Otter, Anne-Sophie Stockholm 1955 Mezzo

LIFE AND TIMES Trained in Stockholm and London. Debut at Basle (Alcina) 1983, Covent Garden (Cherubino) 1985, the Met (Cherubino again) 1988. Many appearances in major European houses.
COMMENT In her early days in opera von Otter was condemned to trousers (Cherubino, Hänsel, Orpheus, Sextus [toga role, not a trouser role: Ed.], Ramiro, Octavian, etc.). This was partly because she is a tall girl and makes a fine figure of a man and partly because most of the trouser roles exactly suit the range of her voice. But now that the opera world has recognized her very special quality (and has heard some great performances in the concert hall), doors are opening to a wider range of parts. Her special quality, which she shares with a very few other singers, is hard to describe. It is some kind of vocal magnetism that sends a message from the singer to the recipient saying Listen To Me. When this happens in the opera house the stage goes into limbo and the orchestra becomes disembodied and you have eyes and ears for the singer alone. If the message is received in the home from a CD, the milk will boil over, the phone go unanswered until the victim returns to consciousness. Von Otter has this quality Strength 9 and many others such as a beautiful and

well-trained mezzo voice and great musicality. She is one of the best things that has happened to opera in recent years.

Pavarotti, Luciano Modena 1935 Tenor

LIFE AND TIMES Surfaced in Reggio in 1961 where he won an international competition and made his debut as Rodolfo in *Bohème*. Stood in for that other great Italian tenor Di Stefano at Covent Garden (Rodolfo) in 1963, sang at Glyndebourne in 1964, teamed up with Sutherland in 1965 in a bel canto tour of Australia. After that he conquered the world including the USA. It is now at his feet. Crazy about racehorses. One of the Three Tenors.

COMMENT Nobody sleeps when Luciano takes the stage. The greatest tenor of our generation following directly in the line of Caruso, Gigli, Lanza, Di Stefano. He has purity of tone, smooth and sweet delivery, perfect intonation and an easy upward reach to high C. Above all his voice has that animal magnetism that sets the great Italian tenor apart from all other singers. No longer mobile on stage and never a great actor, his placid and agreeable personality attracts immediate sympathy. Thus he is perfectly suited by the part of the simple bumpkin Nemorino in *Elisir* but not perhaps so convincing as starving student Rodolfo in *Bohème*. To hear him live in the opera house in top form is a life-enhancing event.

Ramey, Samuel Colby, Kansas 1942 Bass

LIFE AND TIMES Started with the New York City Opera (Zuniga) 1973. Debut Glyndebourne (Figaro) 1976, the Scala (Figaro again) 1981, Covent Garden (yet again Figaro) 1982, the Met (Argante) 1984, Salzburg (Giovanni) 1987. Has sung nearly everywhere and is much in demand.

COMMENT A fine figure of a man who is both a splendid actor and a great singer. God's gift to the management when the rest of the cast is a bit thin. He can bring almost any production alive and while he is on the stage he dominates it. He has a rich vibrant bass voice which, whilst not profundo nor in any way Russian, can sound tremendously important (King Philip) and which can also be lightened to make Giovanni sound the carefree scoundrel that he is. A musical man and a great artist.

Ricciarelli, Katia Rovigo 1946 Soprano

LIFE AND TIMES Studied in Venice. Local debut Mantua (Mimi) 1969, then Italian opera houses until Scala debut (Angelica). Debut Covent Garden (Mimi) 1974, then Met (Mimi again) 1975. Then in all top houses.

COMMENT Ricciarelli has a vivid stage presence and acts a part with commitment. Some singers' heroines are all the same person, her heroines are different people. She has a voice that reaches out to you and begs you to consider favourably the plight of whichever unfortunate young lady she may be portraying at the time. It is a flexible voice and agreeable with a noticeable gear change at the lower end. She now sings mainly bel canto.

Schreier, Peter Meissen 1935 Tenor

LIFE AND TIMES Joined the Düsseldorf Opera 1959. To the Berlin Staatsoper as their leading lyric tenor 1961. Debut at the Met (Tamino) 1967, the Scala 1968. Then in great demand as a Mozart tenor. In 1970 took up conducting and had a hit with his *Idomeneo* in Berlin 1981.
COMMENT One of the best, perhaps the best Mozart tenor of our time. Sings with a seamless legato line. Voice beautifully produced and his material always meticulously prepared. His tone is peculiarly German, slightly nasal, penetrating and dense but never strident or coarse. Not quite enough power to fill a big house, therefore better at Salzburg or on a CD than in the Met. A fastidious and immensely knowledgeable musician. Will have a notable career as a conductor. Best role: Don Ottavio.

Sutherland, Joan Sydney 1926 Soprano

LIFE AND TIMES Trained in Sydney and in London. Joined the Royal Opera company 1952 and first appeared as one of the Three Ladies 1952. Many minor roles for Covent Garden and a few leading roles but she wasn't really known as a star until her Lucia in 1959 (produced by Zeffirelli). Even then international recognition came slowly. Debut the Scala (Lucia) 1961 and the Met (Lucia again) also 1961. But now the world had a measure of her metal and she was universally hailed as La Stupenda. Latterly she was a huge success everywhere she went, singing the bel canto repertory. She took her own company to Australia in 1965 with her husband, coach and musical director Richard Bonynge and latterly spent a lot of time over there.
COMMENT Sutherland had a phenomenal, almost superhuman, ability to sing bel canto. She could deliver all those runs, trills and whirligigs perfectly phrased, with absolute clarity and at immense speed. The notes flew as fast as in a famous fiddler's party piece and sounded much prettier. But Sutherland had other assets, firstly herself. She was no great actress and lacked the figure of a ballet dancer, but when she got into a part that suited her (La Fille du Régiment) the warmth and buoyancy of her nature

made her irresistible. She could make Norma into a moving character, but Mary Stuart was tougher going. Sutherland could sing very high and her range was enormous. Her voice was quite beautiful, all the way from top to bottom. The only problem she had as a singer was that she hardly enunciated her words at all and it was difficult to know just what the hell she was singing. But with a voice like that, and surtitles, this was a small consideration.

Te Kanawa, Dame Kiri Auckland 1944 Soprano

LIFE AND TIMES Swept the board of all singing prizes in New Zealand and Australia and came to train in London. Sang in the Camden Festival in 1969 and was talent-spotted and gave her Covent Garden debut (the Countess) in 1971. Repeated appearances at Covent Garden and on the Continent. Debut the Met (Desdemona) at three hours' notice 1974. Since then very famous with every operatic door open to her.
COMMENT In the opera world today Kiri is a star of stars; the only female to come anywhere near to the Three Tenors in pulling power. She has a glorious, mellow and generous lyric soprano voice, she is glamorous, sexy and with it all retains the flavour of the simple girl from the outback. Her voice is lovely whatever she sings, from the lightest of light to the heaviest end of her range, which is maybe the Marschallin. Tosca, which she tried, is dramatically beyond her. She has a natural musicality and gets along very well without being encumbered by scholarship. She is therefore a great natural singer but not an inspired interpretive artist. She always looks lovely on stage.

Tebaldi, Renata Pesaro 1922 Soprano

LIFE AND TIMES Local debut at Rovigo 1944. Sang in the concert to reopen the Scala in 1946 under Toscanini. La Scala company 1946–54. Debut Covent Garden (Desdemona) 1950, the Met 1955 where she became a member of the company and sang with them for nearly 20 years. Many international engagements.
COMMENT Tebaldi had a beautiful and absolutely Italian voice. She was completely at home with the whole Italian rep up to the big Verdis. As a singer she had great style but belonged to the old school who believed it was the job of the singer not to let things like acting get in the way of projecting their voice in the best possible manner. Later in her career she was won over to act quite nicely so long as it did not force her to crouch whilst going for a high E flat. The Met audience made quite a pet of her. Within her own range, a wonderful singer.

Tomlinson, John Oswaldtwistle (it's true) 1946 Bass

LIFE AND TIMES Studied at the Royal Manchester College. Debut with Glyndebourne Touring (Colline) 1972. Joined ENO in 1975 and sang a wide range of roles. Debut Covent Garden (Colline) 1979, Bayreuth (Wotan) 1988.
COMMENT A glorious bass voice, strong over the whole of its register and always true. Tomlinson is also a fine actor and can give a fresh interpretation to a role which has long been stereotyped. His Hans Sachs upset the romantics because Tomlinson presented us with a brusque, practical cobbler who wanted his man (Walter) to win. Not the usual dreamy old softie at all. He has lots of attack, lots of vigour and can cope equally well with the Italian and German repertory.

Vickers, John Prince Albert, Canada 1926 Tenor

LIFE AND TIMES Studied in Toronto. Joined the Covent Garden company in 1957 (debut as Gustavus III). Debut at the Met (Canio) 1960. Joined the Met company and sang there for 25 years, also Bayreuth, Salzburg, Vienna, Paris, etc. Much in demand for Wagner and other big roles. Now retired.
COMMENT One of the great heroic tenors of our time. Not exactly a Heldentenor (he didn't quite make the German heavy tenor noise), but every bit as satisfactory. A clear and agreeable Canadian voice, very powerful, pretty well always perfectly on pitch and enormously expressive. A big man who could throw his bulk into romantic roles in an astonishingly convincing fashion, and who wants a midget Siegfried anyway? Best role Peter Grimes, in which he was unforgettable.

Windgassen, Wolfgang Annemasse, Switzerland 1914
d. Stuttgart 1974 Tenor

LIFE AND TIMES Son of a Stuttgart tenor. Trained in Stuttgart. Member of the Stuttgart opera company 1945–72. Debut Bayreuth (Parsifal) 1951, Covent Garden 1955, the Met (Siegmund) 1957. Thereafter to be heard mainly in Wagner.
COMMENT Probably the leading post-war Wagnerian Heldentenor, although his voice was not all that helden. By nature nearer to a lyric tenor. Forced into heavy roles owing to the post-war lack of heavy metal. But very cleverly deployed his resources to make a really good job of Siegfried, Siegmund, Tristan et al. He had beauty of tone, good intonation, looked handsome, could move well. Was a solid asset to a Wagner production but never a star. Best role perhaps Florestan.

WORDS WORDS WORDS

Accelerando Means accelerating, of course. *Accel.* written on the score tells you to play the music faster, but gradually.

Accompagnato See RECITATIF.

Adagio At a slow pace. Not funereal (Largo), not up to cruising speed (Andante). Gliding along at about the rate of an unhurried swan.

Agitato Agitated.

Allegro At a brisk pace. Faster than Andante (cruising), not so fast as Presto (racing). Perhaps about the speed of an American trotter.

Andante Easy-paced. Going along nicely. Cruising speed.

Antiphon A form of early Christian chant in Latin.

Appoggiatura An extra note put in front of one of the main notes of a tune just to make things more interesting. Usually just higher than the main note. It shares the time value of the main note so the two together take up the same amount of time as the main note would have done if it had been left alone and unmolested. Appoggiaturas were sometimes written in by the composer, sometimes added by a singer who liked doing his own thing.

Arabesque As applied to music, a flourish. A fancy pattern. A short bout of vocal gymnastics.

Aria A solo song in opera. Not just any old song but one structured in a formal pattern. (See **Aria** in the OPERATICA section.)

Arietta A shortened form of aria.

Arioso A bit of a tune usually in the midst of recitatif accompagnato (see RECITATIF). The singer patters on in the usual agreeable but pretty tuneless way till they burst out with a lyrical phrase which is just long enough for you to register 'Ah! I liked that' before they go pattering on again, or maybe get fired up for an aria.

Arpeggio A harmonious broken chord that makes a big sweep upwards or downwards. Or to get a little technical, the notes of a chord, often the common chord (in C major the common chord is C–E–G–C), played upwards or downwards in quick succession for at least an octave or maybe two, three or four octaves, in extreme cases for as many octaves as your instrument has got.

Atonal Music which has no keynote and does not use the diatonic scale. Atonal music floats about as it pleases making patterns out of a series of notes which are not anchored to any fixed point. For a fuller explanation see **Tonality** in the OPERATICA section.

Ballad A popular song about a simple situation. *Barbara Allen* is a ballad. Schubert's *The Trout* is not, it is a Lied (plural Lieder), partly because it is by an up-market composer but mainly because it is a 'thinks' song and not a report of some event like a girl dying for love.

Bar A vertical line across the stave to divide the music up into units. There can be any number of beats in a bar but most commonly there are four, which is called common time. *Measure* is the American word for a bar.

Barcarolle A boating song associated with Venice and gondoliers. It has a lilting swing to it and glides along at an easy pace.

Baroque A period in music before Mozart and Haydn and covering the lifetime of Bach. The word Baroque applied to architecture and furniture too. The style was at the same time four-square and solid but had its own heavy kind of florid decoration. For a better definition, listen to Handel.

Basset horn A woodwind instrument closely related to the clarinet. Not a horn at all. A more pungent sound than the clarinet and a great favourite with Mozart. (Vitellia's rondo aria in *Clemenza di Tito* Act II.)

Basso profundo A layman's description of a deep bass voice. Musicos would shrink from using such an ornery phrase.

Bel canto Literally 'fine singing'. A style used mainly for solo arias in Italian operas from about 1750 to the 1840s. Bel canto has a clear melodic line but this is decorated by a lot of frills and curlicues, some written out by the composer, some ad-libbed by the singer, especially when a passage is repeated. Fioritura and coloratura are words used to describe this sort of thing. Rosina's aria 'Una voce poco fa' from *Barber* is a good example of bel canto. The words bel canto are used in this Guide to describe the operas of Rossini, Bellini, Donizetti and early Verdi. These are collectively called 'the bel cantos'. (See **Opera – History and Form** in the OPERATICA section.)

Bella figura There is no translation that will do justice to this admirable phrase. A peacock strutting about amongst barnyard fowls is a bella figura. Princess Di is a bella figura. A bella figura is handsome, elegant, beautifully dressed, cultured and full of social graces. Harold Macmillan was a bella figura, Harold Wilson was not.

Buffa Comic. In bel canto times a buffa opera meant a comic opera in a pretty well-defined kind. A buffa character had fixed buffa characteristics. The most common buffas were bass buffas, silly old men who wanted to marry their young wards, who were misers, or who wanted to marry off their daughters to rich aristos. Buffa singing includes patter songs. For a better acquaintance with buffa turn to Dr Dulcamara in *Elisir*.

Cabaletta The fast brilliant last section of (typically) a bel canto aria. Does much the same job as a brisk coda in symphonic music. It creates a climax, gives the singer a chance to show their metal and is more likely to get a round of applause than just ending the piece could.

Cadence A short bit of music in a longer piece of music that is complete in itself. In an aria (or a symphony) there may come a moment when the main drive forward stops and the composer writes a few bars to punctuate, or to beautify the piece, or to let some air into the system. A cadence can be like a musical backwater, but not one that holds you up for long.

Cadential A piece of music which is like a cadence or almost a cadence. See CADENCE.

Cadenza When the main action of an aria (or a concerto movement) is over, the soloist is given a chance to show off in a cadenza. The cadenza can be written out by the composer or it can be left to the artist. It can be in free time and doesn't need to refer to any of the material in the main piece, although it can if it wants to. There can be short cadenzas in the middle of a piece.

Canon Two or more voices (which can mean instrumental voices as well as human) in counterpoint. Voice one starts off with a tune (well, let's call it a tune though it is often no more than a musical pattern) and voice two chimes in a few paces behind singing/playing the same tune while voice one continues with other matters above it. Voice three follows voice two, etc. (See COUNTERPOINT.)

Cantata Literally 'a sung piece of music', as sonata is 'a piece of music that is played'. Today cantatas and sonatas are highly organized musical forms, cantatas being in the main churchy choral pieces and sonatas being solo instrumental pieces.

Canzone A real-life song not a part of the opera. A song which would still have been a song if the piece had been a straight play. Cherubino's song to the Countess in *Figaro* is a canzone. The Don's serenade to Donna Elvira in Act II of *Giovanni* is a canzone. The Prize Song in *Meistersinger* would have been a canzone if Wagner had been Italian and the opera had been some simple little piece.

Castrato A gentleman who had been arranged in such a fashion as to allow him to keep his voice unbroken throughout his life. Boys who were the best singing trebles would be selected for castration and as they grew up so their treble voices grew up with them. (See **Singers** in the OPERATICA section.)

Cavatina A short aria without the da capo, or repeat. (See **Aria** in the OPERATICA section.)

Celesta (Celeste) A row of bars each one giving out a different note when struck by its own kind of hammer. Has a keyboard. Makes a fairyland, toytown sort of noise (Sugar Plum Fairy).

Chaconne Originally a slow Spanish dance. It came to mean a set of variations written over a repeated pattern of notes in the bass, sometimes called a ground bass or just a ground. The ground was often eight bars long and so would be repeated twenty times in a chaconne that was 160 bars long. This sounds boring but it needn't be.

Chamber orchestra A small orchestra, usually of the size used in the days of Haydn and Mozart. Flutes, oboes, clarinets, bassoons, horns, strings, timps maybe, and trumpets to taste. Rarely trombones, seldom tubas and no gallery of percussive machinery.

Chorale A short hymn-like piece for singing in church, structured pretty formally. Solid chunky stuff mostly. Bach wrote a lot.

Coda A tailpiece. After the main events in a piece of music have reached their natural conclusion composers often stick on a little trailer as an envoi or a noisy bit of bustle to make an emphatic ending. These are codas and the coda can take many forms.

Coloratura Literally 'coloured', but it's not as simple as that. See BEL CANTO. A coloratura soprano is one who can sing bel canto.

Concertante As used in this Guide, means 'like a concerto'.

Concerto A piece written for a soloist and orchestra. A double concerto means two soloists.

Continuo The harpsichord accompaniment that runs along under the music. In the eighteenth century it continued from beginning to end, under orchestra, chorus and all. But it came into its own under the secco recitatif (see RECITATIF) where you can actually hear it. Originally for cello alone. Now always harpsichord with or without cello.

Cor anglais English horn. Not a horn at all but a deeper-toned member of the oboe family. If the oboe itself were a soprano the cor anglais would be a tenor. A lovely instrument. Wagner was a cor anglais fan.

Counterpoint Two or more tunes played at the same time. Usually one will start first and the second will follow a pace or two behind, then the third (if there is one) and so on. A tune which has a simple chord to support each important note is vertical writing. Tunes that run along together in counterpoint (sideways of course on the score) are a form of horizontal writing. The most highly organized form of counterpoint is a fugue, where anything up to six or eight 'voices' wend their way across the page each one doing its own variant of a single basic theme but fitting in, of course, to the master plan.

Crescendo Getting louder. The opposite, getting softer, is diminuendo. Rossini's overtures always had a crescendo in the middle which became one of his trademarks.

Cross rhythm Two rhythms going at the same time. In the finale to Act I of *Don Giovanni* there are three orchestras playing at the same time. Two of them are playing with a different number of beats in the bar. These are cross rhythms.

Czardas A Hungarian gypsy dance. Starts slow and speeds up into a whirlwind. Associated with gypsy fiddlers. Taken over and refined by gentlemen composers like Liszt.

Da capo Literally 'from the top'. Repeat marks at the end of a stretch of music mean 'Play It Again From The Start'. Da Capo or DC written at the end of an aria means 'Sing The First Bit Again'.

Descant A high soprano line soaring above the other parts and doing its own thing, that is to say not singing the main tune but putting some decoration of its own on top of it.

Desk Actually means a music stand. 'The front desk' of the violins means the first two violinists, the leader and the deputy leader, who sit in some glory in front of the rank-and-file violinists at the desk or music stand just by the conductor's left hand. 'Six desks' means twelve violins.

Diatonic The Sol–Fa scale, the system of music we all know best. All popular music, and until 1900 nearly all classical music, was diatonic. Before diatonic there were modes and plainsong and things like that. After diatonic there was Schoenberg. For a proper definition see **Tonality** in the OPERATICA section.

Diminuendo Getting softer. The opposite of crescendo.

Discord Two or more notes played at the same time that do not harmonize. The old diatonic system used by Haydn, Mozart and their friends was quite clear about what harmonized and what did not. Today the idea of a discord is pretty well out of date. All atonal music and plenty of other music besides is full of what used to be called discords and no one even notices.

Divertissement A diversion, a bit of fun. In opera it often means the dreaded ballet.

Dominant The note that is five notes up the scale counting the keynote as one. G is the dominant of C. The key of G is the dominant key of C major. Nearly all classical music has a sort of routine of going from the home key to the dominant key in an organized way, but let's not go into that too deeply now.

Dotted A dotted note is 50% longer than the same note without the dot. Thus a note that normally lasts for two beats if given a dot lasts for all of three. Dotted notes often tend to make the rhythm jerky.

Double bar A thick black double line across the stave of music. If it has two dots in front of it it means 'Go Back to the Last Double Bar'. If the two dots are behind it it means 'When you Come Back – This is Where you Start Again.'

Double stopping Playing a chord on a stringed instrument by drawing the bow across two or more strings at the same time, or as near as possible the same time. All virtuoso show-off pieces are full of double stopping because it sounds flashy and looks (and indeed usually is) very difficult.

Double time When the beat goes twice as fast as it did e.g. in a Rossini overture when the rhythm in the bass changes from: TUM–TUM–TUM to: TUMTI TUMTI–TUM TUM. Not a musicologist's term but one used by this Guide in the hope of being helpful.

Ecossaise A Scottish dance. In the classical rep there is no ecossaise that bears the slightest resemblance to the strathspey or reel as played by the Great Highland bagpipe nor to the great tradition of fiddle music founded by Neil and Nathaniel Gow. The ecossaise as it appears in ballet usually has a very bouncy rhythm and sometimes a ghastly imitation of the bagpipe's drone in the bass.

Entr'acte A piece of music – surprise, surprise – played between two acts. An interlude, an intermezzo.

ENO The English National Opera company, inhabitants of the London Coliseum or Colly.

Ensemble More than four people singing (or playing) at the same time but not so many as to make it a chorus (5–10 maybe). A quartet and less is definitely not an ensemble but a quintet and a sextet qualify.

Falsetto The sort of noise a man makes if he tries to sing as if his voice had never broken. It most often comes out as a weak piping treble. Widely used in speech by female impersonators and ventriloquists. Some tenors who can't reach a high note resort to a sort of high falsetto, but this is rather disgraceful.

Fifth The fifth note upwards in the diatonic – that is the ordinary schoolroom – scale. You count the note you start on. C to G is a fifth (C–D–E–F–G). For further and better particulars see **Tonality** in the OPERATICA section.

Figure A scrap of music with a definite shape. The first bar of the Sailor's Hornpipe is a figure (deedle-um-tum-tum).

Finale The end piece. In symphonic music, the last movement. In opera the ensemble or chorus that ends an act.

Funniest finale – Act I of *Italiana*, most famous – Act II of *Figaro*, noisiest – the finale to the prologue of *Boris*, and the quickest death in a finale – *Attila*.

Fioritura See BEL CANTO.

Forte, Fortissimo Literally, strong – but in music this means loud. Mezzo forte is fairly loud, forte just loud and fortissimo pretty well as loud as you can get. These degrees of loudness are marked on the score as *mf*, *f* and *ff*. Excitable composers (Beethoven) occasionally go up to *fff*, or fortissississimo.

Fugato A patch of fugal writing that sneaks in and out of a bigger symphonic piece, thus proving that the composer can write fugues, which is difficult. See COUNTERPOINT.

Fugue, Fugal See COUNTERPOINT.

Gavotte A stately and boring dance to slowish music which happily passed out of favour about a hundred and fifty years ago.

Gemütlich A coy Austrian word for that peculiarly Austrian sense of happiness in being together in a nice, jolly, cheery, pleasing, cosy and heart-warming atmosphere.

Gigue French for a jig.

Giocoso Jokey, amusing, light-hearted. Not such a heavy word as buffa which means broader, more knockabout stuff.

Glissando A sweep up and down a range of notes. It is executed on the piano with the thumbnail (impossible, of course, to catch the black notes) and on the harp with the front of the fingers in the normal fashion.

Grand Opera Difficult to say exactly where opera becomes grand. *Peter Grimes* is not Grand Opera, *Aida* is. Meyerbeer made opera as grand as possible with five acts, ballets and forest fires and shipwrecks on stage. But he didn't make it any better. Berg and Weill made opera as ungrand as possible so that their operas could speak to the people simply and directly. Today it's a little off to refer to any opera as Grand.

Ground, ground bass See CHACONNE.

Incipit A beginning bit. Mozart started a lot of pieces he didn't go on with and left us with just a few bars of each. These are incipits. In the LOOK OUT FOR bits of the opera section of this Guide the first few words of the relevant number are quoted. These are incipits too.

Interlude See ENTR'ACTE.

Intermezzo Music in the middle, e.g. between two acts. See ENTR'ACTE.

Interval The distance between two notes, or alternatively between two acts.

Inversion Upside down. A tune inverted can make a different tune that is quite acceptable. Bach used inversions as a tool of the trade when he was writing fugues. An interval inverted simply means it goes the other way. G to C inverted is C to G.

Intonation In tune. On the note. 'She had a little trouble with her intonation tonight' is a polite way of saying 'She was singing flat' (or, less frequently, sharp). Some singers have perfect intonation all of the time, others sing sharp or flat when in a state of stage fright or have a cold, others again are just all over the place and however magnificent their voice may be this can cause acute discomfort to their friends and ruin an evening for the audience.

Key, Keynote, Key structure See **Tonality** in the OPERATICA section.

Key signature The sharps or flats put into the stave at the beginning of each line of music to show in what key the piece has been written. No sharps or flats – C major.

Heckelphone A baritone oboe. Wagner grumbled to Herr Heckel that there was not enough heavy metal in the woodwind family and Herr Heckel obliged, but rather slowly, producing the first heckelphone after Wagner was dead.

Intendant The Director General, the Chief Executive of an opera house. He is responsible for everything. The buck stops with him, and in the opera world there is a buck a minute. He is equally a manager and an impresario and usually answerable to a board.

Largo/Larghetto Very slow. At the pace of a military slow march or a motorized hearse as it nears the cemetery. Larghetto a little faster.

Legato Smooth. Making one note in a phrase glide into the next. No hiccups, no breaks. Bellini wrote long legato melodies.

Leitmotif A musical tag attached to some person, thing, feeling or idea. When the composer wants you to think of any particular item he plays you its leitmotif, then you know to adjust your mind. For further and better particulars turn to the section on Wagner's *Ring* (page 556).

Libretto The text of an opera. See **Libretto** in OPERATICA section.

Light opera Operas that are light are of course comedies but not buffa. Buffa is an older and funnier form. Light operas tend to be romantic (*Frederica*) or jolly (*The Merry Wives of Windsor*) or both (*The Merry Widow*). *Fledermaus* is about the heaviest light opera and so just scrapes in as a proper opera. Light operas are more properly called operettas.

Maestro Used generally, a term of respect for a great musician. 'The Maestro' is the Music Director or the conductor in charge of whatever musical activity is afoot. Often used socially to flatter some minor figure into believing they are more important than they are.

Major/Minor (minore)

The major mode is bright and cheerful
The minor mode's a tearful earful

Much too simple, of course, but roughly true. The minor scale has many of the same notes as the major but some are moved a semitone downwards to give it a melancholy cast.

Mazurka A Polish dance. There's one in the Polish act of *Boris* and a much better one in Tchaikovsky's *Onegin*.

Melodrame Words spoken over music. There is some melodrame in Gluck, snatches of it in *Fidelio*, but it had mostly faded out of fashion before the operas in this Guide were written.

Metastasio/Metastasian form See **Libretto** in the OPERATICA section.

Mezzo In the middle. Mezzo forte – not too loud, not too unloud. Middling loud. For mezzo sopranos, see **Singers** in the OPERATICA section.

Mickey-mousing When the music points up the action on the stage exactly in synch and in great detail. A man sits down (downward slide in the basses), he drops a cup (clash of cymbals), his wife laughs at him (tittering flutes), he hits her (bark of surprise from the brass). And so on. It's usually rather distasteful.

Minuet A stately old-time dance written to music with three beats in a bar. After the dance happily fell into disuse the musical form took over the title. Nearly every classical symphony had a minuet as its third movement. There are a number of minuets in operas unfortunate enough to have a ballet.

Modal, Modes Before the system of music we know and love was invented there were many arrangements of notes to make a little system of their own. They might be five-note scales, six-or-more-note scales and each one had its own flavour. These modes lived on in folk music until radio etc. made all of the rural Western world diatonic. But many classical composers and later composers like Debussy and Bartok returned to the modes of their national folk music to give their music a fresh sound. (See **Tonality** in the OPERATICA section.)

Modulation A change of key. Modulation was one of the tools the composer used to change the foundations of his music. You can go plugging along in the home key for several minutes and everything feels safe and dandy then suddenly the man modulates into B flat minor and your stomach turns over. The earth has moved a little and now you are into strange territory. But never fear. He will modulate you back to the home key again safe and sound.

Motif A short unit of music. Can be a motto, i.e. standing for something like the king of the dwarfs or the true love of A for B. Can be just itself. The first four notes of Beethoven's Fifth Symphony used to be, and maybe still are, called a motif.

Molto Very. Agitato = agitated. Molto agitato = doing your nut.

Mouth music In the Highlands of Scotland when they lacked bagpipes and a fiddle at a dance some expert would supply mouth music – Humdara, Hodara, Heedara, Humpit, and so on, sometimes for hours.

Music Director Every opera company has a Music Director who is second in importance only to the Intendant (the boss of the whole show). He is a party to deciding the repertory, to the selection of visiting conductors and to major casting. He is responsible for the training and administration of the orchestra and of the music staff. He will also conduct a number of operas himself, some a lot (Levine) and some not so many, carefully selected (Haitink). When he does this he changes his persona and title from Music Director to Conductor, but he is usually known as Maestro, or by some less flattering name, whatever he does.

Music Theatre When the acting out of the drama is more important than the musical side of a show it is called Music Theatre. Stravinsky's *Soldier's Tale* and Brecht and Weill's *Mahagonny* are music theatre. *Midsummer Night's Dream* with Mendelssohn's music is a play with incidental music. Purcell's *The Fairy Queen* (singing, dancing and stretches of spoken poetry) is a semi-opera. *The Seraglio* (songs, recitatif, ensembles and choruses with spoken bits between) is a Singspiel.

Mute, Muted A mute is an object designed to stop an instrument from making its full natural sound. The mutes for stringed instruments are like very short combs made of wood or plastic which clamp onto the strings. A trumpet mute is a circular object about the size of a Kirriemuir scone and is stuffed inside the bell. Horns use their hands to do the same office. When muted, instruments sound as if they were being played in a fog, the tone no longer bites and there is a slightly ghostly feeling in the air.

Obbligato A light accompaniment. Often there is one instrument favoured in the obbligato, e.g. the basset horn obbligato for Vitellia's big rondo in Act II of *La Clemenza di Tito*, the flute obbligato for Lucia's mad scene etc.

Octave The same note, but eight notes higher or lower on the ordinary diatonic or schoolroom scale. C and C^1 as it is neatly expressed by the musicos. Actually the octave above our chosen note has twice the number of vibrations as the base note, the octave below half as many. For a further explanation see **Tonality** in the OPERATICA section.

Oom-pah (Oom-pah-pah) Usually a heavy note in the bass (OOM) followed by one chord above it (PAH) or just as often two (PAH). The PAHs lighter than the OOM. The kind of accompaniment that is common in Gilbert & Sullivan operas. (See Joseph Porter's big numbers in *HMS Pinafore*.)

Open note The note to which the four strings of a stringed instrument are tuned. (On the violin G–D–A–E, going upwards.) An open note gives off more sound than a note made when the string is pinned against the finger board.

Opera seria, buffa See **Opera – History and Form** in the OPERATICA section.

Operetta See LIGHT OPERA.

Oratorio A major work for chorus and soloists usually with a holy theme. *Messiah* is top of the pops in the oratorio league. Some of the opera serias could be performed as if they were oratorios and would hardly lose a thing.

Orchestration The art of translating a piano score (or a skeleton score) into a full orchestral score. Some composers (Mozart) would fill in the top line and the bottom line first plus any important parts for instruments in the middle and put in the filling later. Others were bar-by-bar men. Best orchestrators amongst composers featured in this Guide: Mozart, Rossini, Bizet, Tchaikovsky, Wagner and Strauss R. Weakest: Bellini and Strauss J.

Ornery A little more derogatory than Ordinary, which is just ordinary. Ornery is very very ordinary, perhaps just a little common.

Pantomime Mime. Whilst others are singing a character can tell us he is furious, overjoyed or whatever just by mugging. Or a herald can come on and give his message which is well or badly received in pantomime. Important things, such as death, are seldom consigned to pantomime but attempted assassination is frequent.

Parlando Singing that is almost speaking over music. Usually a few words of frightfully important prose (Rocco to Leonore in Act II of *Fidelio*). Sometimes just a name ('Carmen'). Parlando differs from MELODRAME in that its message is short, sharp and practical with minimum orchestral backing, whereas melodrame can be a poem spoken over a fancy accompaniment.

Passacaglia A set of variations written over a ground bass. See CHACONNE.

Patter song, aria etc. A song with very quickly spoken words. Starts with Rossini (how to start a rumour, *The Barber* Act II) and runs through Donizetti (Dr Dulcamara, *Elisir*) onwards to Gilbert & Sullivan (the model Major General, *Pirates*).

Parallel octaves Two voices or instruments singing/playing the same notes an octave apart. See OCTAVE.

Pavane A slow stately Italian dance imported into concert hall music quite a lot (Ravel's *Pavane for a Dead Infanta*) but rarely into opera.

Pedal A pedal is a sustained note in the bass over which the composer works his will. A pedal often helps the music to build to a climax. It gives a feeling of anticipation. Something is going to happen – what?

Pendant A cadence (a piece of music complete in itself) hooked onto the tail of a longer piece of music. The Dresden Amen (AA–A-A-A-AA-MEN) as featured in *Parsifal* is by nature a pendant.

Pentatonic A five-note scale (as made up of the black notes on the piano) known as long ago as in classical Greece and used off and on in folk music and more recently by modal-prone composers.

Perpetuum mobile Perpetual motion. Music which it would seem could go on for ever. A round is an example of perpetual motion. Once a round is started ('London's Burning') there is no reason ever to stop. There are some near perpetuum mobiles in *Fledermaus* and the vaudeville at the end of *Seraglio* comes close.

Piano As well as meaning the instrument (piano-forte, soft-loud, because of the pedals), also to play softly. 'Piano piano' is one of the constant cries heard from the conductor during orchestral rehearsals. He is trying to make sure we will hear the singers.

Pizzicato Plucked. Instead of stroking the string with the bow you tweak it with the tip of the finger.

Plainsong A type of modal singing once popular with monks and now with ancient music freaks.

Polonaise A Polish dance. Very popular in the nineteenth century with posh composers who wrote polonaises for the orchestra (and most notably Chopin for the piano) and also occasionally found its way into opera (*Boris*, the Polish act, *Onegin*, Act III).

Polytonal Using several schemes of tonality at the same time (see **Tonality** in the OPERATICA section).

Prelude A prelude can come before the whole opera or before an act or a scene. An overture can only come before the whole opera. Preludes differ from entr'actes (1) because they are not in-filling between two acts or scenes but are a build-up for the act/scene to come, (2) the word implies a full-blown orchestral piece like the prelude to Act III of *Lohengrin*, the noisiest prelude on record.

Presto, Prestissimo Very fast. As fast as a horse can gallop but the movement is more vigorous. The 80-metres dash is presto (the 400 metres is allegro and the 2,000 andante). Prestissimo is the speed that cars go in chase movies.

Prima donna The female star of an opera. Unfairly given the reputation of being tetchy and temperamental ('a bit of a prima donna'). Many prima donnas are as mild as milk (well, some are) and the lesser characters can be just as tiresome anyway.

Producer The producer is responsible for everything involved in putting on an opera except the music. Top producers are mainly freelance and move from house to house. There are likely to be one or two staff producers usually to mount revivals who, if they are very good, get a new production of their own once in a blue moon.

Prologue A piece not spoken but sung before the curtain goes up on the opera proper. Most famous prologue – *Pagliacci*.

Quaver One of the few poetically named notes. Half a crotchet. An eighth of a semibreve. A sixteenth of a breve. And a breve originally got its name because it was short. O Lord, how things do slow down.

Rataplan Rub-a-dub-dub in French. A drumming. A tattoo. And pronounced Rataplong.

Recitatif Tells the story. It's like reading aloud, but narrative only and sung to music. Roughly one note to each syllable and going pretty well at the speed of speech. There are two kinds of recitatif, secco which is accompanied by a harpsichord alone (sometimes with a cello touching in the bass notes) and accompagnato which is accompanied by the orchestra. (See **Recitatif/Aria** in the OPERATICA section.)

Refrain A piece of music, usually a chorus, which comes back time after time between intervening verses or whatever.

Relative major/minor Every key is shadowed by a close relative. Major keys can teeter on the brink of falling into the arms of their (rather more serious) relative minors, minor keys can hopefully anticipate a visit to their relative major, who is a much happier person. The relatives here are a minor third apart. The relative minor of C major is A minor. The relative major of C minor is E flat major. Relative keys have the same key signature.

Repetiteur A person on the staff of an opera house whose main job it is to coach the singers in their roles. Senior repetiteurs get to take orchestral rehearsals. This is a way up the ladder to becoming a conductor.

Reprehensible solo violin (R.S.V.) Reprehensible when it carries a message of mawkish sentimentality. Always close to the borderline of good taste, the violin solo has been debased over the years by its association with expiring heroines in silent movies, especially the Gish sisters, by a million Palm Court trios squeezing the last tear out of Tosti's 'Goodbye' and by Fritz Kreisler playing 'Träumerei'.

Reprise French for 'repeat'. Used by

musicos not because it is a prettier word than repeat, but because it is just that much more difficult to understand.

Requiem A solemn piece of music, originally a musical setting of the Latin mass for the soul of a dead person. (Grant them eternal rest.)

Rhapsody Music written in free style with no fixed form. Rhapsodies can be serious or sad. When applied to music the word has nothing to do with rapture, orgasms or anything like that at all.

Ritornello A short bit of music for orchestra alone which returns from time to time in the space between bouts of singing/playing by a soloist. Usually the same piece over and over. See also TUTTI.

Romanza A solo song, usually a bit sentimental. Not so long nor so complex as an aria. Always dealing with the more agreeable side of life such as love, joy, the beauties of nature, etc. Never rage, terror or anger.

Rondo A piece of music that has a tune which happens several times, with other stuff between. A rondo is not a theme and variations, it is the same theme coming round and round and round again.

R.S.V. See under REPREHENSIBLE SOLO VIOLIN.

Scale A series of notes moving in steps up or down and covering an octave. For example, the white notes on the piano from C to C. That is the simple diatonic scale. There are scales in the major, in the minor, the pentatonic mode and all sorts. See **Tonality** in the OPERATICA section.

Scena A scena is not a scene in the sense that the scenery is changed before and after it. It is a technical term meaning the music (usually recitatif) that goes before a bigger event like an aria or a duet. The build-up. On a score you will often see 'Scena ed aria' or 'Scena e duetto'.

Scherzo Literally a joke. Beethoven introduced it to replace the poncey old-fashioned minuet as the third movement of a symphony. Now means a light, cheerful or bizarre piece of music, still habitually clinging on to the old minuet measure of three in a bar.

Score The score is the music for an opera written out or printed on paper. It is laid out in a form that is universal – woodwind get the top lines, beneath them the brass, then percussion, voices next and strings at the bottom. The conductor usually has the score open in front of him, mainly for reference. You will notice he often turns several pages at a time (because he knows it by heart). Some conductors dispense with the score altogether in performance, though they need it during rehearsals, if only to say 'Go back to the double bar at the top of page 17.'

Secco See RECITATIF.

Semiquaver Half a quaver. (See QUAVER.)

Semitone The smallest distance between two notes on the piano. In the diatonic major scale (the ordinary schoolroom scale) there is a semitone between notes three and four (going up) and between notes seven and eight. In the key of C major they are from E to F and from B to C. The further East you go, the smaller the tones get, quarter tones, micro tones, etc.

Serenade Originally a piece of music sung by a guy to a lady on a balcony, always at night. It came to mean music played to pretty well anyone who need not be anywhere near a balcony, but still usually something to do with night. A morning serenade is strictly for the birds.

Serial music See **Tonality** (Atonality) in the OPERATICA section.

Sforzando Suddenly loud. Played with force. If a part in the music is marked sforzando (*sf*) it must stick out from the texture of what is going on and give you a bit of a shock. If you are dreaming and fail to start when the lights go green the effect on your nervous system when the driver behind hoots you is like what a sforzando should be.

Siciliana A sad melody with its own special rhythm. Often to do with nature, shepherds and the like. Can be a song or an instrumental piece.

Sinfonia Not just the Italian word for symphony. It meant many different things at different times in its career, such as an overture to an opera in the Italian style and a piece of orchestral music shoved in somewhere during the course of the opera itself.

Singspiel An opera with spoken dialogue between songs. (See **Opera – History and Form** in the OPERATICA section.)

Sonata form A way of writing a piece of (usually instrumental) music that became a standard model for pretty well all composers over two hundred years and is still found to be quite handy by some. There is a first bit with a succession of tunes that move from the home key into the dominant key. Then there is a pretty wild bit in the middle (the development) where the composer can do pretty well what he likes so long as he prepares the ground for the return of the first bit which is played again, this time all in the home key.

Sonority Depth and thickness of sound. Three trombones plus a tuba have sonority. Thirty fiddles playing fortissimo have volume.

Sotto voce Not quite under your breath but sung softly in something between a whisper and a quiet conversational tone.

Soubrette A maid, usually a lady's maid (Despina in *Così*). A soubrette part was common in many comic operas. Soubrettes were generally perky, worldly, down-to-earth young women. The part was often played for laughs and usually by an upcoming young soprano with a light, tinkling voice.

Staccato A sharp percussive way of playing a note. If you strike a note sharply on the piano and let your finger bounce off at once it makes a staccato sound. If you caress the note and let your finger linger it will sound legato. It is beyond the capacity of the human voice to sing in a truly staccato manner, but by putting in a lot of stops and going Ah-Ah-Ah-Ah very quickly one can get somewhere near it.

Stanza Several lines of poetry which together form a unit. What used to be called a verse when poetry was more disciplined. You can tell when a stanza has ended because there is more air on the page between its last line and the first line of the next stanza than there is between intra-stanza lines.

Stave The five lines drawn across a page upon which to write musical notes. Every stave has a squiggly thing (a clef) in front of it to show the pitch of the five lines. Thus the treble clef squiggle gives you a top line of F, the bass one a top line of A. Laboriously explained in this way it sounds complicated, but a professional musician can read music off the staves as easily as he can read the headlines in the *Sun*.

Stretto A pulling-together, a tightening-up, a speeding-up, in fact a musical climax of a special sort. The word has a technical meaning as applied to a fugue in which all the above hyphenated expressions play a part.

Strings In the opera orchestra these are violins split between firsts and seconds in roughly equal numbers, violas a few fewer than half the number of violins, cellos ditto, and from four to six double basses. 10–10–8–6–4 would be quite usual for a bel canto opera. 'Upper strings' usually means violins, 'middle strings' violas, sometimes with low violins and high cellos, 'lower strings' cellos and basses.

Strophe Music which is repeated for each verse in an aria. If it is different each time then the piece is through-composed.

Sturm und Drang Storm and stress. There was a period in classical music when composers (Haydn) went through a phase of thinking that Sturm und Drang (originally a literary notion) was a frightfully interesting idea and imported a bit of S & D into their music.

Subject (first, second, etc.) A theme, motif or pattern of notes that can be clearly identified. In a classical symphony the first subject is the one you hear first (surprise, surprise) then after a change of key in comes the second. In the old days the nature of the first subject was described as 'usually masculine in type' and the second subject as 'feminine'. Today it would be politically incorrect to use such terms without a disclaimer, such as this one.

Suite A group of dances which together make a complete musical bundle. Used to be formalized with a set progression from one kind of dance to another (Bach). Now looser and more general. Can be for any instrument and is also commonly orchestral.

Surtitles Captions displayed above the proscenium arch in an opera house to tell the clients just what is going on on stage. See **Surtitles** in the OPERATICA section.

Syncopation Shifting the beat forward or back from its usual place in the bar. As applied to the National Anthem, as follows:

STRAIGHT

GOD SAVE OUR GRA-A-CIOUS QUEEN

SYNCOPATED

GODSAVE OUR – GRACIOUS QUEEN

Symphony/Symphonic There is a world of difference between writing a symphony and an opera. All the drama of symphonic music takes place within the head. Operatic music supports the drama that is taking place on the stage. Some opera composers are more symphonic than others – Beethoven perhaps the most and Bellini perhaps the least.

Tarantella An Italian dance that starts fast and gets faster. And faster.

Te Deum An item in the repertory of church music.

Tempo Time. Fast tempo = quick time.

Tessitura The range of a piece of music in relation to the voice for which it was written. Sarastro's numbers in the *Flute* have a low tessitura for a bass. Some of Zerbinetta's stuff in *Ariadne* has a high tessitura for a soprano. Football songs on the terraces usually have a higher tessitura than the fans can manage.

'Thinks' When a singer is not singing to anyone else but is just thinking aloud. Very frequent in arias also common in ensembles. (See BEYOND THE CURTAIN, page IX.)

Third The third note up the scale. E is the major third above C (the first note is counted in: C–D–E). In the 'Cookhouse Door' bugle call the syllable 'house' is a major third above the 'cook' and the 'door'.

Timp Timpani.

Tocsin A large Russian bell which when struck gives off a huge wallop of sound.

Tone/Tonality See **Tonality** in the OPERATICA section.

Tone poem An orchestral piece with a programme, that is a secret script of which the listener usually only knows the title. Sometimes an event is clear from the nature of the music (death) but most often each listener writes his own script as the orchestra plays. Richard Strauss was the tone poem king (*Till Eulenspiegel*, *Don Juan* and many others).

Tone rows A series of notes picked out to make a pattern in atonal music. The atonalist's equivalent to a tune but it doesn't sound one bit like a tune. For a fuller explanation see **Tonality** in the OPERATICA section.

Tonic The keynote of the key in which a piece is written. C is the tonic of C major. Can apply to the whole key – 'this passage moves away from the tonic towards the dominant' etc.

Trill Two adjacent notes sung alternately rather quickly. A trill can get faster towards the end. A trill is an ornament, never essential. A trill is difficult to sing well.

Triple time Three in a bar. Waltz time. *ONE*-two-three, *ONE*-two-three. Listen to the Blue Triple Time Danube for an hour or two and triple time will be implanted on your mind for ever.

Triplet Three notes played in the time of two. Can sound like a slight speech impediment. It's like 'Cottontail' in 'Flopsy, Mopsy, Cottontail and Peter.'

Tutti All together. In a concerto or an aria when the soloist has done his stuff for some time he will reach a stopping point and the orchestra alone will come in with a contrasting tune. This is a tutti. In a long solo tutti crop up from time to time like punctuation.

Twelve tone See under **Tonality** in the OPERATICA section.

Unison All voices singing or playing the same musical line. No chords. Plainsong is in unison. Football songs on the terraces are in unison, or as nearly so as the fans can manage.

Vamp An oom-pah oom-pah played indefinitely until the singer or soloist is ready to come in to do their thing.

Vaudeville As applied to opera, a special form of solo-cum-choral singing and occurs only once in this Guide, namely in the finale to *Seraglio*, where it is fully described.

Verismo True to life. Grierson defined the word documentary as 'the creative interpretation of actuality' and that's not bad, but asking too much of opera. All verismo is relative. *Cav* is not so verismo as *Schindler's List*. But it is a lot more verismatic than *Ernani*.

Vibrato A vibration in the voice cultivated by singers (1) to express great emotion – love, hatred etc., (2) to help them to be heard above the orchestra and (3) because it is thought to sound nice anyway. If vibrato is not cultivated but natural it is called a wobble and can be a pain.

Voluntary A piece played on the organ before and after a church service as a *cordon sanitaire* between the holiness of worship and the wicked world outside.

Walking bass A bass line that stalks about steadily below whatever else is going on above it in the orchestra.

Whole tone (scale) The whole tone scale is a series of notes with two semitones between each one. It is quite different from the diatonic scale which is the one we all know and love. Debussy was sometimes a whole-toner. For a fuller explanation see **Tonality** in the OPERATICA section.

Woodwind The instruments in the orchestra that are blown and are not brass. The standard complement for opera up to Wagner is flutes, oboes, clarinets and bassoons. But there are lots of specials, such as piccolos, basset horns, cor anglais, bass clarinets, heckelphones, and plenty more too.

You-know-who Wagner.

Friends, Supporters, Colleagues and Minders

I would like to thank:

BAMBER GASCOIGNE for giving me the idea in the first place (and let it be noted that this handsome acknowledgement in no way affects the author's title to 100% of the copyright).

PAUL FINLAY for allowing me to share his immense knowledge of the backstage workings of an opera house.

ANNA HODSON for her dedicated editorial support and for supplying that meticulous attention to detail which is conspicuously lacking in some authors.

GAYNOR JOHNSON for being probably the best typist in the world and for her quite outstanding flair in deciphering what is probably the worst handwriting in the world.

MADELEINE LADELL for bringing her great musical scholarship to bear on the work of a wayward amateur and for her stalwart partnership in a life-and-death struggle with *The Ring*.

STANLEY SADIE for everything from lending me his scores to answering, as the great Cham of music, questions to which no one else had an answer.

CAROLINE SPEED for her help and enthusiasm until she was taken away from me to produce the 'Young Musician of the Year'.

And finally my personal assistant Beryl Milnes for organizing over the past three years that small part of my life which lay outside the writing of this book in such a way as to make the writing of it possible.